THE
PULPIT COMMENTARY

EDITED BY THE

VERY REV. H. D. M. SPENCE, D.D.

DEAN OF GLOUCESTER

AND BY THE

REV. JOSEPH S. EXELL, M.A.

REVELATION

Introduction

By REV. T. RANDELL, B.D.

PRINCIPAL OF BEDE COLLEGE, DURHAM

Exposition

By REV. A. PLUMMER, M.A., D.D.

PRINCIPAL OF UNIVERSITY COLLEGE, DURHAM

ASSISTED BY

REV. T. RANDELL, B.D.

PRINCIPAL OF BEDE COLLEGE, DURHAM; AND

A. T. BOTT, M.A.

LECTURER OF BEDE COLLEGE, DURHAM

Homiletics

By REV. C. CLEMANCE, B.A., D.D.

Homilies by Various Authors

REV. S. CONWAY, B.A.   REV. R. GREEN

REV. D. THOMAS, D.D.

NEW EDITION

FUNK & WAGNALLS COMPANY
LONDON AND NEW YORK

THE
REVELATION OF ST. JOHN THE DIVINE.

INTRODUCTION.

§ 1. THE TITLE.

1. *The Revelation.*—The name given to this book in our Bibles is the English form of the Latin equivalent of the Greek title 'Αποκάλυψις.[1] This Greek title is as old as the book itself, and forms the first word of the original text, where it constitutes an essential member of the opening sentence and paragraph. It was consistent with the Hebrew cast of the whole document that the Hebrew fashion of naming books by their initial words should be followed in this instance; but the classical and modern method of designating a literary work by the name of its principal theme happened here to lead to the same result: ἀποκάλυψις is not only the initial word of the book, but also a subject-title, descriptive of the largest portion of the contents.

In the Vulgate version the Greek word is retained, both in the title and at the commencement of the text. Its proper Latin equivalent, however, is not found by merely writing it in Latin letters, *apocalypsis*, but by combining the Latin renderings of its two component parts, taking *re* to represent ἀπό, and *velatio* as synonymous with κάλυψις. According to the etymological genius of the respective languages, just as the simple substantive *velatio*, or κάλυψις, signified the act of covering with a veil, so the compound

---

[1] The word ἀποκάλυψις is rare in profane Greek literature, Plutarch (a contemporary of the apostles) being apparently the earliest author in whose extant works it can be found; he uses it in its primary literal sense, and also in its secondary figurative meaning. The canonical books of the Septuagint only furnish a single (and literal) example of it, though the corresponding verb occurs many times. In the New Testament the substantive is found seventeen or eighteen times, and always with a figurative signification.

re-velatio,[1] or ἀπο-κάλυψις, meant the act of removing, turning back, or taking off the veil, in such a manner as to *dis-cover* what previously was hidden from view.

The Latin compound, unaltered except by the Anglicizing of its termination, has become thoroughly naturalized in our English language; and on that account it is, for biblical and ministerial use, preferable to the original title, which, even in its Anglicized form, "Apocalypse," has never ceased to be " Greek " to ordinary English ears.

2. *Of*. In the English title the preposition "of " must be taken in the sense of "to " or "by." The revelation was made by Jesus Christ *to* his servant John, and then the record of it was penned *by* John for the information of other servants of God. The things previously hidden were shown *to* John in visions, and were then described *by* John in writing, so that his fellow-servants might see them in his book. The true author of the primary act of revelation was Jesus Christ; Saint John wrote an account of what had been by Christ revealed to him, and that written account then became a revelation to all others who should read it or hear it. The things that were shown to John in a vision were shown to the rest of the world in John's book. This book was not a revelation to John himself, who merely recorded therein what had been shown to him in vision; but to us it is " *The* Revelation " *of* that new knowledge which Christ disclosed to John in another and a more mysterious way.

3. *Saint John the Divine*. The Greek epithet properly signifies " the one who discoursed about God "—one who not only spake God's messages, but described God's nature; one who did not confine himself to proclaiming the works of God, but was emboldened to declare the deep mysteries of the Divine existence.

§ 2. Author.

Both internal and external evidence lead us to accept the theory of the authorship of this book which ascribes it to the Evangelist Saint John. Four times the author designates himself by the name of John (ch. i. 1, 4, 9; xxii. 8), and on the first occasion adds that he was the same John " who bare witness of the Word of God," thus identifying himself with the writer of the Fourth Gospel and the first of the Johannine Epistles.[2] Clear external testimony begins with Justin Martyr about the middle of the second century; he refers to " John, one of the apostles of Christ, who prophesied in a Revelation made to him that the believers in our Christ should

---

[1] The word *revelatio* is unknown to classical Latinity, but is not infrequent in ecclesiastical literature. It is used in the Vulgate (1 Cor. i. 7), and in the African writers—Tertullian, Arnobius, and Augustine. It may therefore be added to the list of Africanisms in the Vulgate, which was first drawn up by Wiseman, and has been so largely increased by Westcott.

[2] If, as seems not improbable, the first three verses of ch. i. are (not an integral part of the original book, but) an attestation by some influential members of the primitive Church —perhaps the elders of Ephesus—this part of the evidence is in no way weakened.

spend a thousand years in Jerusalem " ('Dial. cum Trypho,' c. lxxxi. p. 308). Irenæus, in the latter half of the second century, knew the book well, quoted it largely, and plainly attributed it to the John who leaned on Jesus' breast ('Adv. Hær.,' iv. 20. 11, etc.); he also appeals to genuine and ancient copies, as well as to others in which the text had already become corrupt (ibid., v. 30. 1). Explicit statements that the Apostle John wrote the Apocalypse are also found in Tertullian, Hippolytus, Origen, and many later Fathers.

§ 3. DATE.

There are two principal theories regarding the date of the Apocalypse— the one ascribing it to about the year 69, or even earlier; and the other to about the year 96, or later. The reversed figures are easy to remember. The advocates of the earlier date refer St. John's banishment to the Neronian persecution, and believe the Apocalypse to have preceded the Fourth Gospel by a period of nearly or quite thirty years. Those who support the later date hold that the author was banished under Domitian, and that the Gospel was written before the Apocalypse, or, at latest, very soon after it. We believe that the earlier date is the right one, for the following reasons.

1. The internal evidence in support of it is very strong. The linguistic phenomena, the doctrinal expressions, and the methods of conveying Christian truth, in the two books are such as irresistibly lead the student to the conviction that the Apocalypse is much earlier than the Gospel. This argument has been ably drawn out by Canon Westcott (Introduction to St. John's Gospel in the 'Speaker's Commentary,' pp. lxxxiv.—lxxxvii.).

(1) Regarding the linguistic phenomena, he says, " Nor is it difficult to see that, in any case, intercourse with a Greek-speaking people would in a short time naturally reduce the style of the author of the Apocalypse to that of the author of the Gospel. It is, however, very difficult to suppose that the language of the writer of the Gospel could pass at a later time, in a Greek-speaking country, into the language of the Apocalypse."

(2) Regarding the doctrinal expressions: " The Apocalypse is doctrinally the uniting link between the synoptists and the Fourth Gospel. It offers the characteristic thoughts of the Fourth Gospel in that form of development which belongs to the earliest apostolic age. It belongs to different historical circumstances, to a different phase of intellectual progress, to a different theological stage, from that of St. John's Gospel; and yet it is not only harmonious with it in teaching, but in the order of thought it is the necessary germ out of which the Gospel proceeded by a process of life."

(3) Regarding the methods of conveying Christian truth: " Of the two books the Apocalypse is the earlier. It is less developed, both in thought and style. The material imagery in which it is composed includes the idea of progress in interpretation. The symbols are living. On the other hand, to go back from the teaching of the Gospel to that of the Apocalypse, to

clothe clear thought in figures, to reduce the full expression of truth to its rudimentary beginnings, seems to involve a moral miracle, which would introduce confusion into life."

2. The clear and positive external testimony against it is not strong, being reducible (as it seems to us) to the solitary statement of Irenæus, near the end of the second century, that the Apocalypse was seen towards the close of Domitian's reign. Domitian was emperor from A.D. 81 to 96. Irenæus, writing a century after the fact, may easily have made the mistake of putting the name of one famous persecuting emperor instead of the other, and it is remarkable that his statement is supported by no other writer earlier than Victorinus of Pettau, after a second interval of a century. Eusebius and Jerome, in the fourth century, do not strengthen what they merely repeat.

3. The remaining early evidence as to the time when the Apocalypse was written is certainly reconcilable with, and seems rather in favour of, the earlier date. We refer particularly to the oft-quoted passages of Clement of Alexandria, Tertullian, and Origen.

(1) Clement ('Quis Salvus Dives?' § 42, quoted in Eusebius, 'Hist. Eccl.,' iii. 23) says that St. John went from the island of Patmos to Ephesus "after the tyrant was dead (τοῦ τυράννου τελευτήσαντος); " that from Ephesus, as his head-quarters, he used to go when required to the neighbouring Gentile districts to appoint bishops in one place, to regulate whole Churches in another, to ordain clergy in a third; that in one of these journeys he entrusted a youth to the bishop's care, with a special charge; that the youth was nurtured and brought up by the ecclesiastic, and at last (τὸ τελευταῖον) baptized; that afterwards (μετὰ τοῦτο) the guardian's care relaxed, and the youth fell into bad company, who at first (πρῶτον μεν) enticed him to love their society, then led him on step by step (εἶτα . . ., εἶτα . . ., κατ' ὀλίγον προσειθίζετο), until at length (τελέως) he renounced his religion, and became a daring criminal and a chieftain of banditti; that after a lapse of time (χρόνος ἐν μέσῳ καὶ) an occasion arose when the apostle's presence was again needed at the same place, the people sent for him, and he came; that after settling the matter for which they had requested his visit, St. John inquired of the bishop respecting that which he had entrusted to his care; that the bishop did not at first understand what was meant, but, when St. John explained himself, told the youth's sad history; that the apostle, exhibiting most poignant grief, demanded a horse and guide, and rode off at once (ὥσπερ εἶχεν) to seek the lost youth, and that he succeeded in reclaiming him.

Clement's language leaves no doubt that he believed the whole of these events of St. John's stay in Asia, with Ephesus as his centre of operations, to have been posterior to "the tyrant's " death; and so Eusebius understood him. Clement does not give the name of "the tyrant" to whom he refers: but Eusebius, influenced (as we may reasonably suppose) by the express statement of Irenæus, with whose writings he was very familiar, takes it for granted that Domitian is meant; and many modern writers agree with him. Archdeacon Lee, for instance, in the 'Speaker's Commentary,' p. 415, goes so far as to say that "the tyrant" *could be no other than Domitian*. But when we reflect that Domitian's death did not take place till September, 96, and that it is highly improbable that St. John outlived the first century, we feel that it is impossible to compress the events of the foregoing narrative into the short intervening space of three or at the most four years—to say nothing of the difficulty of believing that St. John, in such extreme old age as he must have attained at the time of Domitian's death, could have commenced and carried on the active life which we have abundant reason for supposing he spent at Ephesus, even if we set aside the story of his riding on horseback into the mountains after the guerilla captain. If, therefore, Eusebius was right (as he probably was) in placing the long stay of St. John at Ephesus *after his exile in Patmos*, we hold that he must have been mistaken in supposing that "the tyrant" mentioned by Clement was Domitian. We differ so completely from Archdeacon Lee on this point, that we avow our conviction that "the tyrant" *must be some other than Domitian*.

And any schoolboy would perceive the fitness of the designation as applied to Nero, so proverbial for cruel tyranny, and so terrible a persecutor of the Christians. He died in the year 68, and we quite believe that he was the tyrant referred to by Clement. This would allow a period of about thirty years for the apostle's subsequent life and work in and around Ephesus, and some such period seems required by evidence derived from other sources and by the probabilities of the case.

(2) Tertullian is constantly associated with Irenæus and Clement of Alexandria—he completes the trio of eminent contemporaries whose works have in considerable bulk been preserved to us from the latter years of the second century. In a famous passage ('De Præscr. Hær.,' 36) he speaks of Rome as the place "ubi Petrus passioni Dominicæ adæquatur; ubi Paulus Joannis exitu coronatur; ubi Apostolus Joannes, postea quam in oleum igneum demersus nihil passus est, in insulam relegatur"—"where Peter suffered a death like our Lord's; where Paul was beheaded like John the Baptist; and where the Apostle John, after being plunged into burning-hot oil without being hurt, was banished to an island." We are quite willing to concede that this passage proves nothing as to the date of the Apocalypse, but we claim that it lends more support to the earlier than to the later of the alternative dates proposed. For, in the first place, it closely associates the banishment of St. John with the deaths of St. Peter and St. Paul, who are generally believed to have suffered martyrdom under Nero. And secondly, it expressly states that the banishment of St. John took place *at Rome*, which answers one objection made against the earlier date, viz. that the Neronian persecution was confined to Rome. Tertullian's view, whether right or wrong, seems to have been that St. John was once at Rome; that there he was accused, tried, and sentenced to exile; and that his place of exile was an island.

Another passage of his writings ('Apol.,' 5), sometimes brought forward as indirectly bearing upon the present question, says that Domitian was a milder persecutor than Nero, and implies that he himself restored those whom he had banished; but makes no mention of St. John. And indeed, upon the supposition that the case of St. John was in Tertullian's mind when he wrote this passage, it would not agree with the theory most in favour with the advocates of the later date for the Apocalypse, namely, that St. John was one of the exiles set free by Nerva after Domitian's death; neither would the general tenor of it agree with the notion that Domitian rather than Nero was styled emphatically "the tyrant."

(3) Origen, about the middle of the second century, having occasion in his commentary on St. Matthew ('Huet.,' i. 417 B) to mention that, "as tradition teaches, the Emperor of the Romans condemned John to the island of Patmos," goes apparently out of his way to remark that, in the Apocalypse, John himself does not say who condemned him. But Origen's language does not imply that there was any doubt as to *which emperor* had banished the apostle; much less does it assert that the name of the emperor was not given *because* St. John himself had not given it. It simply points out that it was from an external tradition and not from internal evidence (in St. John's own work, the Apocalypse) that people in the third century learnt the fact that St. John was banished by "*the* (not *an*) Emperor of the Romans." We cannot tell whether Origen had or had not any definite knowledge or theory as to *which* emperor the tradition blamed for condemning St. John; he certainly does not repeat Irenæus's assertion that it was Domitian; and there is nothing to show that he did not think it was Nero.

§ 4. PLACE.

It has always been the general opinion that the Book of Revelation was written in the same place where the revelation was seen, that is, in the island of Patmos, situated in the south-east of the Ægæan Sea. Patmos is about the same distance east-south-east of Miletus, as Miletus is to the south of Ephesus. It is situated in about 37° 20' north latitude, and 26° 35' east longitude; in that subdivision of the great Ægæan which classical geographers designate the Icarian Sea; and in that group of its innumerable islands which the ancients well named the "Sporades," *i.e.* the "scattered" ones. It is quite a small island, mountainous and almost barren. In the side of one of its eminences is the cave which tradition asserts to have been the very place where the apostle was favoured with the visions recorded in his book. And in the book itself St. John tells us (ch. i. 9) that he "was in the isle that is called Patmos." Then he immediately (vers. 10 and 11) relates that he heard a voice, saying, "What thou seest, write in a book;" from which it is fairly inferred that it was in the island of Patmos that the voice was heard, that the visions were seen, and that the book was written.

A few commentators have, however, held the opinion that the book was not written until after the apostle had left the island. They have supported their view by alleging the improbability of a banished man in St. John's circumstances possessing the time and materials and opportunity for writing; but such an allegation is not, after all, of very much weight. And one passage of the book itself (ch. x. 4) seems to imply that what the saint saw and heard he wrote down at once, on the spot; for he says, " When the seven thunders uttered their voices, I was about to write : and I heard a voice from heaven saying, Seal up the things which the seven thunders uttered, and write them not." The frequent reiteration of the command to write, which occurs at the beginning of each of the seven Epistles to the Churches, and five times besides (ch. i. 11, 19; xiv. 13; xix. 9; xxi. 5), is perhaps best understood on the supposition that the book was written piecemeal, each vision seen and utterance heard being at once recorded by him who beheld and listened.

Therefore, while we readily admit the *possibility* of the theory that the Book of Revelation was written after the author had left Patmos—a theory as ancient as the time of Victorinus of Pettau, and supported by Arethas, who assigns the Ionian district about Ephesus as the place of writing—we hold that internal evidence concurs with the mass of external opinion in supporting the *probability* that the book was committed to writing on that same island of Patmos, where the visions and voices were vouchsafed to "the disciple whom Jesus loved."

§ 5. Manuscripts.

Of the original Greek text of the Apocalypse there are about a hundred and twenty manscripts known to scholars ; and probably there are also in existence others whose existence is not at present known to any one beyond the owners and a small circle of friends, if even to the very owners themselves. It is also possible that some of the manuscripts which are now reckoned among the hundred and twenty containing the Apocalypse, may hereafter be found not really to contain that book at all. The list of Greek Apocalyptic manuscripts has had to be seriously modified during recent years from each of these causes.

The known manuscripts of the Greek text of the Apocalypse are thus only few in number compared with those of other parts of the New Testament. Of the Acts and Catholic Epistles there are more than twice as many, and of the Pauline Epistles thrice as many, to say nothing of the hundred and twenty-seven copies of the 'Praxapostolos' or 'Lectionary containing the Church Lessons taken from the Acts and Epistles.' Of the holy Gospels there are about eight hundred Greek manuscripts known, besides about four hundred copies of the 'Evangelistarium,' or 'Lectionary containing the Church Lessons taken from the Gospels.' So that we may fairly say there is ten times more material, in the form of Greek manuscripts, for settling the text of the Gospels than there is for that of the

Apocalypse.   No portion of the Apocalypse seems to occur in any Greek lectionary.

Moreover, we are obliged to confess that the manuscripts which have hitherto been fully used for the criticism of the text of the Apocalypse form only a small portion of those which are paraded in our lists.   Tischendorf, in his latest edition, does indeed refer to seventy-seven different manuscripts in the critical apparatus for this book; but to many of them his references are very rare, and it is certain that he had only an imperfect knowledge of more than half of those which he cites.   Tregelles, in 1872, only used thirteen, but all of them had been carefully collated throughout.   Scrivener, writing after the publication of the Revised Version, states that only thirty-one manuscripts of the Apocalypse had at that time been satisfactorily collated ; and we shall therefore be approximately right in supposing that to be the number upon which the Greek text of the Revisers, as well as the special edition of Westcott and Hort, is based.   At the present time, there are at least fifty Greek manuscripts of the Apocalypse, the texts of which are practically unknown.   The Greek text which is represented by our Authorized Version was probably based upon no more than *four* manuscripts, two of which—employed by the Complutensian editors and by Lorenzo Valla respectively—are now unknown, or at least unidentified.

As a partial justification of this strange neglect of the materials which have been spared to our times, it ought to be remarked that in all likelihood those manuscripts that have been most carefully examined include those which are intrinsically of the highest value, and that most probably a thorough investigation of all the rest would not seriously affect the form of the Greek text with which critics and Revisers have now made us familiar. But we hold that it is neither dutiful to God nor satisfactory to devout men to rest content with probabilities in such a matter, and that we ought to be ashamed of apathetic idleness, when by industry and effort *something* more might assuredly be done to restore the true words of God and to purify them from human error and corruption.

All the hundred and twenty known manuscripts are now preserved in European libraries, and are distributed as follows : Italy possesses forty-seven—thirty-five in Rome, five in Florence, four in Venice, one in Turin, one in Ferrara, and one in Messina.   France has twenty-three—twenty-two in Paris, and one in Poictiers.   England comes next, with twenty-two— ten in London, six in Oxford, two at Cheltenham, two at Parham Park in Surrey, one at Cambridge, and one at Leicester.   There are seventeen in Germany—Vienna, Munich, and Dresden have four each; Hamburg, Frankfort-on-the-Oder, Wolfenbüttel, Mayhingen, and Zittau have one each. Russia claims seven, of which five are at Moscow and two at Petersburg. Ireland, Spain, Sweden, and Switzerland have one apiece, located in Dublin, the Escurial, Upsal, and Basle respectively.

Those which have been satisfactorily examined are thus distributed : nine in London; four each at Oxford and Moscow; two each at Rome, Paris,

Petersburg, and Parham Park; one each at Vienna, Dresden, Frankfort-on-the-Oder, Mayhingen, Leicester, and Cheltenham. It is thus seen that the bulk of those not yet fully known are situated in Rome (thirty-three) and Paris (twenty).

The manuscripts vary in age very widely, the earliest belonging to the fourth century, and the latest having been written as recently as the seventeenth century. The average age is less than in the case of manuscripts of any other portion of the New Testament, and a surprisingly large number were written after the invention of printing. It is not always easy to fix the date of a Greek manuscript, even within a century; and different scholars have expressed different opinions regarding the dates of several of these hundred and twenty manuscripts of the Apocalypse; but they may be approximately classified in date as follows : One belongs to the fourth century, two to the fifth, one to the eighth, one to the ninth, perhaps two to the tenth, sixteen to the eleventh, fifteen to the twelfth, eighteen to the thirteenth, twenty-one to the fourteenth, eighteen to the fifteenth, seventeen to the sixteenth, and one to the seventeenth; of the remaining seven the age is not known.

The five most ancient of these manuscripts are written in uncial characters; all the others in cursive. In critical apparatus the uncials are designated by capital letters (A, B, C, P, and the Hebrew letter א [called "Aleph"]); the cursives are indicated by Arabic numerals (1, 2, 3, etc.). All the five uncials have been well collated.

The usual material of Greek manuscripts is vellum or parchment, and the majority of the manuscripts of the Apocalypse are made of this substance. But it is a natural consequence of the late date at which so many of them were written that no less than forty out of the hundred and twenty are made of paper. Three others are made partly of parchment and partly of paper; the Leicester manuscript is of this kind.

The contents of the Apocalyptic manuscripts are very various, only a few codices (about a dozen) containing the Apocalypse alone of the books of the New Testament. At least four combine St. Paul's Epistles with the Revelation, and at least another four combine the Revelation with one or more of the Gospels. But far larger groups, including more than thirty in each case, contain either the whole New Testament or all except the Gospels. At least ten include some part of the Greek version of the Old Testament. And a large number include much matter which is extraneous to Holy Scripture, such as patristic treatises and lives of the saints.

Often the text of the Apocalypse is accompanied by a Greek commentary, either in full, or epitomized, or in fragmentary parts. Thus, in some form or other, the commentary of Andreas is known to exist in twenty-one of these manuscripts, that of Arethas in seven, and that of Œcumenius in three; while six others are known to contain some Greek commentary, and probably these are not all that are similarly enriched.

Until the manuscripts have been properly examined, it cannot be known how many of them contain the whole of the Book of Revelation, but probably it is only in rare exceptions that this book is mutilated. As may be expected, when a mutilated copy is found, the lost portions are either the beginning or the end of the book. The Basle manuscript is a mere fragment, containing only twenty-seven verses; the Barberini codex at Rome has but seventy-one verses; the one belonging to Moscow University contains about one-third, and "Vaticanus, 1904" at Rome only about one-fifth of the Apocalypse; and eighteen other manuscripts have less considerable mutilations, which in several instances affect only a few verses. But the great majority of the copies are believed to contain the whole of the 405 verses of the Book of Revelation.

The primary authority for the Greek text of our book is the fourth-century uncial, ℵ (Aleph), the famous Sinaitic manuscript discovered by Tischendorf in 1844, brought to Europe in 1859, and first published at Petersburg in 1862.

Each of the two fifth-century uncials must also be placed in the front rank of documentary witnesses. They are A, the Alexandrian manuscript in the British Museum, first used for New Testament criticism in Walton's Polyglot; and C, the Ephræmi codex at Paris, first used in Kuster's reprint of Mill's Greek Testament in 1710.

Then, separated by the broad gap of three or four centuries, we have a second rank of authorities, consisting of the two remaining uncials, B and P. B is the manuscript numbered 2066 in the Vatican Library at Rome, first mentioned by Bianchini in 1748, but very imperfectly known until a century later: it must be specially borne in mind that *this is a totally distinct manuscript from the one called B in other parts of the New Testament.* P is Bishop Porphyry's manuscript at Petersburg, published by Tischendorf in 1865-9.

The cursives have been so imperfectly investigated that it is premature as yet to attempt to classify them as to their relative value. Some of those which are still uncollated may be among the best. If, however, we were asked to select the cursives which seem to us the best among such as are well known, and whose readings have been made accessible to all scholars, we should choose those numbered 1, 7, 38, 93, 94, and 95.

The following tables may be useful for reference :—

I. TABLE OF THE GREEK MANUSCRIPTS OF THE BOOK OF REVELATION WHICH HAVE BEEN SATISFACTORILY COLLATED.

Symb. or Numb.	Locality.	Library designation.	Century [and year] in which written.	Name of collator.	Year when good collation was published.	Book in which good collation was published.
א	Petersburg	Sinaiticus	IV.	Tischendorf	1862	Special
A	London	Alexandrinus	V.	Woide	1786	"
C	Paris	Ephræmi	V.	Tischendorf	1843	"
B	Rome	Vaticanus, 2066	VIII.	"	1869	Appendix N. T. Vaticani
P	Petersburg	Porphyrianus	IX.	"	1869	Mon. Sacra Inedit., vol. vi.
1	Mayhingen	Reuchlini	XII.	Delitzsch and Tregelles	1861-2	Handschriftl. Funde, i. and ii
7	London	B. M. Harleian, 5537	XI., 1087	Scrivener	1859	Codex Augiensis, etc.
8	"	B. M. Harleian, 5778	XII.	"	"	" "
13	Frankfort-on-Oder	Seidelii	XI.	N. Westermann	1710	Kuster's Mill's Gk. T.
14	Leicester	Hayne's Gift	XIV.	Scrivener	1859	Codex Augiensis, etc.
26	Oxford	Ch. Ch. Wake, 12	XI.	"	[Collated 1864]	In the press (1888)
27	"	Ch. Ch. Wake, 34	XI. or XII.	"	[Collated 1863]	In the press (1888)
28	"	Bodl. Baroc., 48	XV.	"	1859	Codex Augiensis, etc.
29	London	B. M. Harleian, 5613	XV., 1407	"	"	" "
31	"	B. M. Harleian, 5678	XV.	"	"	" "
33	Vienna	Lambec., 1	XIII.	Alter	1787	Alter's Gk. T.
38	Rome	Vaticanus, 579	XIII.	B. H. Alford	1872	Alford's Gk. T. / Tregelles' Gk. T
47	Dresden	A., 172	XI.	Matthæi	1785	Matthæi's Gk. T
48	Moscow	S. Syn., 380	XII.	"	"	" "
49	"	S. Syn., 67	XV.	"	"	" "
50	"	S. Syn., 206	XII.	"	"	" "
51	Paris	Reg., 47	XIV., 1364	J. G. Reiche	1847	Codicum aliquot, etc.; published at Göttingen
87	Cheltenham	Meermann., 118	XI. or XII.	Scrivener	1859	Codex Augiensis, etc.
89	London	Burdett-Coutts, II. 4	X. or XI.	"	(?)	In the press (1888)
90	Moscow	(?)	(?)	Matthæi	1785	Matthæi's Gk. T.
93	London	Lambeth, 1186	XI.	Scrivener	1859	Codex Augiensis, etc.
94	"	B. M. Addit., 11837	XIV., 1357	"	"	" "
95	Parham Park	82.17	XII. or XIII.	"	"	" "
96	"	67.2	XIV.	"	"	" "
97	London	B. M. Addit., 17469	XIV.	"	"	" "
98	Oxford	Bodl. Canonici, 34	XVI., 1515-16	"	"	" "

II. TABLE OF THE GREEK MANUSCRIPTS OF THE BOOK OF REVELATION WHICH ARE SOMETIMES CITED OR REFERRED TO, BUT WHICH ARE AS YET KNOWN ONLY IMPERFECTLY.

Symb. or Numb.	Locality.	Library designation.	Century [and year] in which written.	[1] Editor of New Testament by whom cited.	Remarks.
2	Paris	Regius, 237	x.	Stephen, 1550	Stephen numbered it ιε'
3	(?)	(?)	(?)		„ „ it ις'
4	Paris	Regius, 219	xi.	Wetstein, 1752	
5	(?)	(?)	(?)	L. Valla, 15th century	Known to Erasmus
6	Oxford	Bodl. Baroc., 3	xi.	Mill, 1707	
9	„	„ Misc., 74	xi. or xiii.	„ „	
10	Cambridge	Univ., 553	xiv.	„ „	
11	(?)	(?)	(?)	Fell, 1675	Described as "Petavii 2"
12	Rome	Alexandrino-Vat., 179	Later than xi.	„ „	Described as "Petavii 3"
15	Basle	A.N., III. 12	(?)	Wetstein, 1752	A fragment: iii. 3 to iv. 8
16	Hamburg	Uffenbach, 1 or 2	xv.	Bengel, 1734	
17	Paris	Coislin, 199	xi.	Wetstein, 1752	
18	„	„ 202, 2	xiii.	„ „	
19	„	„ 205	xi., 1079	„ „	
20	Rome	Vaticanus, 2080	xii.	Bianchini, 1749	
21	„	Vallicell., D. 20	xiv.	Scholz, 1836	
22	„	„ B. 86	xiii.	„ „	
23	Paris	Coislin, 200	xiii.	„ „	
24	Rome	Vatican, 2062	xi.	Bianchini, 1749	
25	„	Palatino-Vat., 171	xiv.	Amelotte	Used by Wetstein
30	Wolfenbüttel	XVI. 7	xiv.	Knittel	Used by Griesbach
32	Dresden	A. 95	x. or xv.	Matthæi	Not used by M. for Apocalypse
34	Vienna	Lambec., 34	xii.	Alter, 1787	
35	„	„ 248	xiv.	„ „	
36	„	Forlos, 29	xiv.	„ „	
37	Rome	Vatican, 366	xiii.	Birch, 1800	
39	„	„ 1136	xii. or xiii.	„ „	
40	„	„ 1160	xiii.	„ „	
41	„	Alexandrino-Vat., 68	xiv.	„ „	
42	„	Pio-Vat., 50	xii.	„ „	
43	„	Barberini, 23	xiv.	„ „	
44	„	Propagandæ, 250	xiii., 1274	„ „	
45	Florence	Laurent., IV. 32	xi., 1093	„ „	
46	Venice	S. Marc., 10 (86: 1)	xiv. or xv.	„ „	
55	Paris	Regius, 101	xiii.	Scholz, 1836	
56	„	„ 102, A.	x. or xiii.	„ „	
64	„	„ 224	xi.	„ „	
68	Rome	Vatican, 1904	xi.	„ „	Only 76 verses
69	„	Vat.-Ottob., 258	xiii. or xiv.	„ „	Last chapters are lost
79	Munich	No. 248	xvi.	Peltanus, 1547	First used as the basis of a Latin version of Andreas's Commentary
80	„	„ 544	xiv.	„ „	
81	„	„ 23	xvi.	„ „	

[1] We have given, wherever we could, the name of the *earliest* editor who cited each manuscript; all, or nearly all, in this list are cited by Tischendorf (8th edit.) and by Alford.

Symb. or Numb.	Locality.	Library designation.	Century [and year] in which written.	Editor of New Testament by whom cited.	Remarks.
82	Munich	No. 211	XI. or XIII.	Scholz, 1836	
88	Venice	S. Marc., 5 (86 : 4)	XV.	„	
91	Rome	Vaticanus, 1209	XV.	Mico, 1799	Supplement to B of the Gospels, the Acts, and the Epistles
92	Dublin	Montfortianus	XVI., 1580?	Barrett, 1801	
99	Rome	Vaticanus, 656	XIII.	Delitzsch, 1862	
100	Paris	Coislin, 224	X. or XI.	Montfaucon, 1715	
119	Rome	Palatino-Vat., 346	XV.	Sylburg, 1596	Basis of printed edition of Andreas, in Greek

III. TABLE OF THE GREEK MANUSCRIPTS OF THE BOOK OF REVELATION, THE READINGS OF WHICH ARE AS YET UTTERLY UNKNOWN, AND WHICH HAVE THEREFORE NEVER BEEN CITED IN THE CRITICISM OF THE BOOK.

Symb. or Numb.	Locality.	Library designation.	Century [and year] in which written.	By whom mentioned.	Remarks.
52	Paris	Regius, 56	XII.	Scholz	
53	„	„ 59	XV. or XVI.	„	
54	„	„ 61	XIII.	„	
57	„	„ 124	XVI.	„	
5ε	„	„ 19	XVI.	„	
59	„	„ 99ᵃ	XVI.	„	
60	„	„ 136ᵃ	XVI.	„	
61	„	„ 491	XIII.	„	
62	„	„ 239–40	XVI.	„	
63	„	„ 241	XVI.	„	
65	Moscow	Univ., 25	XII.	„	Contains one-third of Apocalypse
66	Rome	Vat., 360	XI.	„	Birch says this does not contain the Apocalypse
67	„	Vat., 1743	XIV., 1320	„	
70	„	Vat.-Ottob., 66	XV.	„	
71	„	„ 381	XIII., 1252	„	
72	„	Ghigi. R., IV. 8	XVI.	„	
73	„	Corsini, 838	XVI.	„	
74	Venice	S. Marc., 546	XIII. ?	„	
75	Florence	Laurent., IV. 20	XI. or XII.	„	} Probably these two are identical
76	„	„ IV. 30	„	„	
77	„	„ VII. 9	XV.	„	
78	Rome	Vat.-Ottob., 176	XV.	„	
83	Turin	No. 302	XIII.	„	
84	Florence	Riccardian, 84	XV.	„	
85	Escurial	ψ III. 17	XII.	Montana	
86	Florence	Laurent., 53	XIV., 1332	Scholz	Not numbered for the Apocalypse by Scholz
101	Venice	S. Marc., 6 (86 : 4)	XV. or XVI.	Holmes	A duplicate of 88
102	Ferrara	187, N.A. 7	XIV.	Burgon	
103	Poictiers	(?)	XVI.	Haenel	

Symb. or Numb.	Locality.	Library designation.	Century [and year] in which written.	By whom mentioned.	Remarks.
104	Cheltenham	Phillipps, 7682	(?)	Burgon	
105	Rome	Vallicell., F. 17	xiv., 1330	Scholz	
106	Zittau, in Saxony	(?)	xiv., xv., or xvi.	Matthæi	
107	London	B. M. Addit., 28816	xii., 1111	Scrivener	
108	Upsal	No. 11 Björnsthal, 1	xii.	Belsheim	
109	Paris	Regius, 2247 Arménien, 9	(?)	Burgon, in Scrivener	
110	Rome	Crypt-Ferr., A. α. 1	xiii. or xiv.	„	
111	Dresden	A. 124	xv.	„	
112	„	A. 187	xvi.	„	
113	Messina	PA	(?)	„	
114	Rome	Vatican, 542	xiv., 1331	„	
115	„	„ 1882	xvi.	„	
116	„	„ 1976	xvii.	„	
117	„	Alexandrino-Vat., 6	xvi.	„	
118	„	Vat.-Ottob., 283	xvi., 1572	„	
120	„	Angelic., A. 4. 1	xv., 1447	„	
121	„	Angelic., B. 5. 15	xv.	„	
122	„	Ghig., R. V. 33	xiv.	„	
123	„	Vat., 370	xiii.	Delitzsch	

Attempts have been made at various times to classify the manuscripts of the Greek text of the Apocalypse into groups, families, or recensions, according to the character of the text which they exhibit. Thus Bengel believed in an African recension, represented by such manuscripts as A and 80; and an Asiatic recension, to which 119 and the bulk of the cursives belonged. Hort would group most of the cursives together as exhibiting the Syrian form of text; and cannot find any manuscript, even among the five uncials, that has preserved in its purity any one of the pre-Syrian forms of text—neutral, Western, Alexandrian. Delitzsch thinks that the most real and useful division is into three groups, viz.—

(1) Andreas-texts, such as A, 1, 7, 28, 80, 81, 96, 119.

(2) Arethas-texts, such as B, 29, 33, 35, 82, 87, 93, 94, 95.

(3) Mixed-texts, such as 8 and 31.

It is strange that manuscripts which Bengel considered typical of different groups should be placed by Delitzsch in the same group; and it is also a significant fact that Delitzsch confesses that the Leicester codex is so peculiar as to defy classification under his system.

Probably one of the most important results of a thorough examination of all the manuscripts would be the discovery of the genealogical relations by which many of them are connected together. When Delitzsch paid special attention to these documents, a quarter of a century ago, he made it appear tolerably certain that the number of independent witnesses for the text could very easily be reduced by such discoveries. For example, he showed that the manuscripts numbered 28, 79, and 80 were probably all copied from the one numbered 99; if so, clearly we ought to strike 28, 79, and 80 out of the list of independent authorities—the four together possess no more weight than any one of them taken separately. Similarly, it seems probable that 35 is a transcript of 100, that 92 was copied from 14, that 101 is a duplicate of 88, and that 82 and B are very closely connected—perhaps copied from the same exemplar.

§ 6. Versions.

As with Greek manuscripts, so with versions or translations made from the Greek, those available for the Book of Revelation are both few in number and late in date, compared with those of other New Testament books.

1. *Syriac.* The great Syriac version of the Bible, known as the Peshito, did not contain the Apocalypse. The Curetonian Syriac version, which many critics suppose to be older than the Peshito, does not seem to have extended beyond the four Gospels; and the known range of the much later Jerusalem Syriac is similarly limited. But there are two other versions in Syriac, the Philoxenian (A.D. 508) and the Harklensian (A.D. 616), which have recently been proved to be much more distinct from each other than was once supposed; and each of these includes the Apocalypse. There are eight Syriac manuscripts mentioned in literature as containing this book, but the present locality of three of them is unknown, and one other is a mere fragment. They may be enumerated as follows :—

(1) De Dieu's, in the University Library, at Leyden, designated "Scaliger, 18," of the sixteenth century, first published in 1627. Harklensian.
(2) Ussher's, in the Library of Trinity College, Dublin, marked "B. 5. 16," written in the year 1625. Harklensian.
(3) Gabriel Sionita's, now unknown, used for the Paris Polyglot in 1633; probably the same that was written by Andreas de Leon for Pope Paul V. Harklensian.
(4) Moses of Mardin's, now unknown, but mentioned by De Dieu. Uncertain.
(5) One mentioned by Adler, formerly in the Library of St. Mark's, at Florence, but now missing. Harklensian.
(6) Earl of Crawford's, of the eleventh or twelfth century; the only known Syriac manuscript which contains the *whole* New Testament. The Apocalypse is Philoxenian.
(7) B. M. Addit., 17127, with a commentary; eleventh century (dated 1088).
(8) B. M. Addit., 17193 (f. 14 b), containing eight verses only. ? Philoxenian.

For a fuller account of these documents, see the articles on "Polycarpus Chorepiscopus" and "Thomas Harklensis" in Smith and Wace's 'Dictionary of Christian Biography,' written by Dr. Gwynn, Regius Professor of Divinity in Trinity College, Dublin, who informs us that he is preparing for publication the Syriac version of the Apocalypse in Lord Crawford's manuscript, with a Greek re-version. The Syriac Lectionaries do not contain any lessons from the Apocalypse, and with this agrees a phenomenon of Lord Crawford's manuscript of which we are assured by Dr. Gwynn, viz. that the Apocalypse "is not included in the lectionary-divisions with which, as regards the

Gospels and Acts, the codex is marked." Yet the Apocalypse stands between the Gospels and Acts in this manuscript.

All the printed editions of the Syriac version of the Book of Revelation have been, up to the present time, based upon very modern manuscripts of the Harklensian type; and that version was not made until the seventh century (A.D. 616). It evidently follows that the testimony of the Syriac version, as at present published, possesses no great value; the case may be quite different when the older exemplars of the earlier and closely literal Philoxenian translation become better known.

2. *Latin.* The Latin version, in its various forms, is by far the most valuable of all that are yet published, for the text of this book: perhaps it is also intrinsically and absolutely the best. In its latest form it is known as the Vulgate, and dates from the end of the fourth century. But we fortunately possess continuous texts of the Apocalypse in two earlier (ante-Hieronymian or Old-Latin) forms, known respectively as the African Old-Latin and the European Old-Latin.

The African form of this version is chiefly to be derived from the writings of *Primasius* (fl. 550), Bishop of Adrumetum, or Justinianopolis, in North Africa, whose commentary on the Apocalypse (in which the text of the book is given piecemeal) is printed in the sixty-eighth volume of Migne's ' Patrologia Latina.' A purely African text is also found in the Paris manuscript numbered " Lat., 6400 G," a palimpsest fragment, of which only parts of three pages of the Apocalypse are legible; it dates from the fifth or sixth century, was transcribed by Mr. Vansittart, and published in the ' Journal of Philology,' vol. ii. It is usually designated by the italic letter *h.*

The European Old-Latin exists in two manuscripts—one continuous, and the other giving detached passages. The whole book is found in *g, i.e.* Codex Gigas Holmiensis, at Stockholm, of the thirteenth century, published by Belsheim in 1879. Bishop John Wordsworth intends indicating this copy by the Greek letter γ. The extracts are given in *m,* which is at Rome, " Bibl. Sessor. 58," published by Mai, in 1852, and often spoken of as Mai's Speculum; it was formerly, wrongly, ascribed to St. Augustine; it was written in the sixth or seventh century.

Of St. Jerome's Vulgate Latin version the manuscripts are innumerable, and even the printed editions (especially the Clementine of 1592) are often referred to in critical matters. The manuscripts which have been selected by Bishop John Wordsworth for use in his forthcoming critical edition of the Vulgate, and which contain the Book of Revelation, are the following :—

    (1) F, or *fu.* = Codex Fuldensis, at Fulda, in Hesse Cassel; written for Victor, Bishop of Capua, and corrected by him, A.D. 541-6; published by Ranke in 1868.

    (2) A, or *am.* = Codex Amiatinus, in the Laurentian Library at Florence; written in the county of Durham, at either Jarrow or Wearmouth, by order of the Abbot Ceolfrid, between A.D. 690 and 716; published by Tischendorf in 1850, and again 1854, and also by Tregelles in his Greek Testament; generally considered the best copy of the Vulgate.

(3) Z₂, or *harl.* = Harleian., 1772, in the British Museum; eighth century; Bentley's M; from Rev. xiv. 16 to the end is lost. The Vulgate text of this copy is so much mixed with Old-Latin readings that it ought, perhaps, to be called an Old-Latin manuscript.

(4) D₂, or *arm.* = The Book of Armagh, at Trinity College, Dublin; of the eighth or ninth century; the Apocalypse stands between the Catholic Epistles and the Acts; represents the *British* recension of the Vulgate.

(5) G, or *germ.* = " Germanum Latum," or " Lat., 11553," at Paris; ninth century; called μ by Walker, who collated it for Bentley; exhibits a mixed text, sometimes cited as Old-Latin under the notation *g*; considered by Wordsworth to represent the Gallican recension of the Vulgate.

(6) C, or *cav.* = Cavensis, at the Abbey of the Holy Trinity, close to Corpo di Cava, near Salerno; probably ninth century; collated by Wordsworth, who classes this and the next in our list together as representatives of the Spanish recension.

(7) T, or *tol.* = Toletanus, now in the National Library at Madrid; tenth century; collated in 1588 by Palomares, whose papers were published by Bianchini, in 1740; re-collated by Wordsworth in 1882.

(8) K, or *kar.* = Karolinus, the noble volume called "Charlemagne's Bible," in the British Museum, Addit., 10548; ninth century; exhibiting the Alcuinian revision executed by order of Charlemagne in 797.

(9) V, or *vall.* = Vallicellianus, in the Library of Sta. Maria in Vallicella at Rome; ninth century; also Alcuinian.

(10) Θ, or *theod.* (N.B. This is quite distinct from Tischendorf's *theo.* or *theotisc.*, which signifies some fragments of a bilingual manuscript, in Latin and Old-German, of St. Matthew) = Theodulfianus, Lat. 9380 in the National Library at Paris; ninth century; of great value, as a text thoroughly revised by Theodulfus, Bishop of Orleans from A.D. 788 to 821.

3. *Egyptian.* The Apocalypse was comprised, as an appendix rather than an integral part of the canonical New Testament, in each of the two great Egyptian versions. These versions were made at so early a date that they would be of first-rate importance if they were well known and carefully published, but unfortunately they are not; and the Latin translations of them, from which alone critical editors have usually drawn their material, are very untrustworthy. The Egyptian text of the Apocalypse has never yet been critically edited, so far as we are aware; it is printed in the S.P.C.K. edition (Tattam's) of the New Testament in Coptic (Memphitic) and Arabic.

The best-known Egyptian version, sometimes loosely designated the Coptic, is now generally called the Memphitic; it is in the dialect formerly spoken by the inhabitants of Lower Egypt, of which the Arabic name was Bahirah, and the ancient capital Memphis. Bishop Lightfoot has devoted much attention to this version, and states that there is not a single authenticated case of a manuscript of it in which the Apocalypse is treated as of equal authority with the other canonical books. In the majority of cases the Apocalypse is contained in a separate manuscript; and in the two known exceptions, where it is bound up with other books, it is distinguished from them in some marked way. Lightfoot enumerates twelve Memphitic copies of the Apocalypse, but they are all of very late date, the earliest being dated A.D. 1321; all but one, if not that one also, are written on paper; and all but one are bilingual, giving the book in Arabic as well as in Memphitic.

Four of them are in Great Britain, four in Rome, and two in Paris. No critical collation of any of them has yet been published,[1] and consequently we cannot attach much importance to the testimony of this version as hitherto cited in textual criticism. The first use of it is found in Bishop Fell's Greek Testament, 1675, and Mill, in 1707, quite recognized its importance.

The second great Egyptian version is the Thebaic, in the dialect of Upper Egypt round about ancient Thebes, the district known to the Arabs as Sahid. The extant materials for a good edition of this version of the Apocalypse are much less abundant, or at all events are not so well known to ordinary scholars. We have been assured in conversation by Mons. Amélineau, who has made extensive literary researches in Egypt, that he knows of manuscripts which would enable him to publish a continuous and complete edition of the Thebaic version of this book; but from printed sources we have only been able to obtain information respecting four manuscripts that contain any of it: three are in the Library of the Propaganda at Rome, and one is at Paris; and all four together do not contain one-fourth of the book. Add to these some detached quotations in Tuki's 'Coptic Rudiments,' and parts of four verses (not one in full) printed in Ford's Appendix to Woide, and you have all the available material for a knowledge of the Thebaic version of the Book of Revelation. The book seems to have been excluded from the Thebaic canon of the New Testament, as it was from the Memphitic. Since we at present know nothing of the date of the Thebaic manuscripts, nor even at what time the version of this book was made, we cannot attach any importance whatever to its testimony as regards the Apocalypse. Portions of it were published, for the first time, in 1778, by Tuki; and others in 1810, in Zoega's 'Catalogue.'

4. *Armenian.* The Apocalypse is included in the Armenian version of the New Testament, which was probably executed in the fifth century, and made directly from the Greek original. The best printed edition is that edited by Zohrab at Venice, in 1789, and many manuscripts of it are in existence. But they are all recent in date, and the original form of the version has certainly been tampered with and corrupted (partly under the influence of the Latin Vulgate) in the intervening centuries. The value of the Armenian version is therefore not great.

5. *Æthiopic.* The Æthiopic was the earliest printed of all the Oriental versions, our book having been published by some natives of Abyssinia at Rome in 1548. It was reprinted in Walton's Polyglot with many errors of the press, and with "an unusually bad Latin translation." The best critical edition is said to be Bode's (Brunswick, 1753). The Æthiopic is a feeble version, and the extant manuscripts of it are even later in date than those of the Memphitic or Armenian.

No other version of the Apocalypse is worth mentioning. The Arabic,

---

[1] Although it is known that Paul Boetticher (who in 1854 took the name of Lagarde) has collated one, and that Tattam possessed another.

as best edited by Erpenius at Leyden, in 1616, seems to have been derived from the Memphitic. The Slavonic, in its present form, cannot be earlier than the sixteenth century.

§ 7. QUOTATIONS.

It is well known that all the available aids for the restoration of the true form of the original text of the New Testament are usually grouped under three divisions, viz. Greek manuscripts, versions, and patristic quotations. Having briefly treated of the first and second, we now come to the consideration of the third of these groups.

The Apocalypse is only seldom quoted by the Greek or Latin Fathers, with the exception of such as have written special commentaries upon this peculiar book. It happens, however, that the commentators are somewhat numerous, and for this reason we have a much greater abundance of Apocalyptic quotations than would otherwise have been the case.

Moreover, the extant manuscript copies of some of the commentaries give the text of the book itself in a complete, or almost complete, form. We have already mentioned the groups of cursives which Delitzsch terms the Andreas-texts and the Arethas-texts; and in the Old-Latin version (African form) we have alluded to the continuous text that is furnished in the commentary of Primasius.

Among writers of the second century, Irenæus is remarkable for citing the Apocalypse by name, although he does not specifically mention any other book of the New Testament; and Tertullian makes quotations from, or allusions to, almost every chapter in this book.

The following list includes all the most famous Fathers whose writings give important testimony to the language of the Book of Revelation. The Roman numerals indicate the century to which their evidence may most fairly be reckoned to belong; and the names marked with an asterisk are those of Fathers who have written commentaries on this book:—

LIST OF FATHERS.

Greek.	Latin.
Clement of Alexandria, II. and III.	Cyprian, III.
*Hippolytus, III.	*Tichonius, IV.
Origen, III.	*Victorinus of Pettau, IV.
Methodius, IV.	Ambrose, IV.
Eusebius, IV.	Jerome, V.
Gregory of Nazianzum, IV.	Augustine, V.
Gregory of Nyssa, IV.	*Primasius, VI.
Cyril of Alexandria, V.	*Cassiodorus, VI.
*Andreas of Cæsarea in Cappadocia, VI.	*Bæda, VIII.
*Arethas of the same, X.	*Ansbertus (Ambrose), VIII.
*Œcumenius, X.	*Berengaudus, IX.
	*Haymo, IX.

Important quotations of the Apocalypse also occur in a Latin work of unknown authorship, entitled 'De Promissionibus' or 'Dimidium Temporis,' often appended to the writings of Prosper of Aquitaine, and sometimes printed with the works of St. Augustine. It is generally believed to belong to the fourth century.

The earliest Apocalyptic commentaries are almost completely lost. That of Hippolytus is only known from an obscure Arabic summary, in which it is mixed up with later views; and that of Tichonius principally from notices in Augustine and Bæda. The work of Victorinus of Pettau is extant in two forms, a longer and a shorter, but both have been undeniably interpolated, and it is impossible to pronounce to what extent. Our next interpretations belong to the sixth century, and there are grave difficulties in ascertaining the true form of the original commentary of Andreas. Nevertheless, there are very many instances where we can feel quite certain as to the text of the Apocalypse used by a commentator, although we may be uncertain about his comment upon it; and the sacred text is, after all, the chief thing we wish to ascertain.

§ 8. HISTORY OF THE PRINTED TEXT.

The Greek text of the Book of Revelation was first printed, together with the other books of the New Testament, in the fifth volume of the Complutensian Polyglot Bible, at Alcala or Complutum, in Spain, in the year 1514. The promoter of the undertaking was Cardinal Ximenes, Archbishop of Toledo; the chief editor was James Lopez de Stunica; and the master printer was Arnald William de Brocario. Wetstein, Matthæi, and other scholars consider it certain that the Complutensian editors only used one Greek manuscript for the Apocalypse; this manuscript has not yet been identified with any in the foregoing lists, but it was decidedly superior in many respects to the one used by Erasmus two years later.[1] Erasmus, in 1516, edited the earliest-published Greek Testament, printed by Frobenius of Basle. He had but one manuscript of the Revelation, that now numbered 1; it was not quite perfect at the end of the book, and contained Andreas's commentary written in such a way as not to be always clearly distinguishable from the sacred text. Moreover, Erasmus prepared his edition with great rapidity, and hurried it through the press without due revision and correction. Hence his text, although *substantially* correct, is full of errors and imperfections in detail. While writers on textual criticism are justified in denouncing this edition as extremely bad, based on one mutilated manuscript, and that one not represented with the scrupulous accuracy required by modern scholarship, it must yet be borne in mind, and cannot be too often repeated, that as regards *doctrine* and *general drift* and *practical value*, there is no serious difference between the earliest and latest editions, the worst and the best.

---

[1] *Internal* evidence is very strongly in support of the theory that number 37 was the manuscript from which the Complutensian editors derived their text of this book; but there is no *external* evidence whatever in its favour.

It is quite true that Erasmus supplied the deficiencies (real or supposed) of his single copy by Greek of his own composition, taking the Vulgate Latin version as his guide; and that words and phrases which originated in this way, unsupported by any known Greek manuscript, cling to the received text at the present day. But the importance of these errors of judgment has been greatly exaggerated, and unmerited censure has been heaped upon an editor whose achievements, fairly considered, rather deserve our grateful praise.

Three editions of Erasmus's Greek Testament were published before he saw a copy of the Complutensian. He soon recognized the superiority of the text of the Apocalypse in the Spanish Bible, and in his fourth (and fifth) edition he amended from it at least ninety readings in this one book. Thus the later editions of Erasmus may be said to have been based upon two Greek manuscripts, besides a few readings which he found in the Annotations of Lorenzo Valla upon forty-three scattered verses of the book.

The famous French printer, Robert Stephen of Paris, used two other manuscripts, now called 2 and 3, of the Apocalypse, but still his text is in the main a mere reprint of the later Erasmian text. Matters stood thus when the English Authorized Version was made in 1611, and when the famous *Textus Receptus* of the Greek was published at Leyden in 1633, by the brothers Elzevir.

Indeed, it was not until a hundred and forty-three years after the first printing of the Apocalypse that the readings of a fifth manuscript were made available for the improvement of the text. In 1657 Walton's monumental Polyglot Bible was published, and therein were given all the variants of the Alexandrian manuscript, the excellent uncial in our British Museum.

Exactly half a century afterwards, in 1707, Mill's Greek Testament came from the Oxford press, and astonished the learned world. Besides some readings of foreign manuscripts at present unknown, it contains full collations of six English cursives of the Apocalypse. Kuster, in 1710, added the readings of the uncial C at Paris, and of one other cursive.

To the great Cambridge scholar, Bentley, belongs the credit of making the first attempt to apply all the then available materials to the formation of a more accurate Greek text. In 1720 he made public his *Proposals for Printing*, which contained the twenty-second chapter of the Book of Revelation in Greek and Latin, by way of specimen; but no further portion of his proposed edition was ever printed.

In 1734 John Albert Bengel published a new Greek text of the whole New Testament, which was very greatly in advance of anything of the kind that had previously appeared. He paid special attention to the Apocalypse, and wrote a valuable essay on the textual criticism relating thereto; he was also a very laborious commentator on the same. He reckons the number of Greek manuscripts of the book, known directly or indirectly to himself, as twenty.

Wetstein, in 1752, increased the number to thirty-one, and among the additions was the Vatican uncial B of the Apocalypse.

Matthæi's edition of the Apocalypse, published at Riga in 1785, was the first that was prepared (since the Complutensian) from Greek manuscripts only, without reference to previous printed editions. But, unfortunately, Matthæi's apparatus for this book was limited to five cursives (47, 48, 49, 50, and 90), and he ignored the collations published by previous scholars. In an appendix he gave collations of two other cursives (30 and 32), and in this way increased the stock of materials for future editors. Similarly, F. K. Alter, a German Jesuit, by his independent work, provided additional material, but cannot be said to have used it himself; he collated four copies of the Apocalypse (33, 34, 35, 36), all at Vienna. Also the Lutheran Bishop, Birch, a Dane, published, in 1800, collations, more or less complete, of ten other cursives (37—46), all in Italian libraries.

Griesbach, in 1806, took account of all these materials, besides adding a fresh collation (29) of his own.

Scholz, in 1836, made known *the existence* of about forty previously unknown manuscripts, but he only gave a thorough collation of one (51).

Lachmann's celebrated edition of the Greek Testament was weakest in the Apocalypse, which was published in 1850. He so restricted himself in the use of authorities that for a hundred and sixty-five verses of this book his sole Greek witness is the uncial manuscript A.

Tregelles, in many respects an imitator of Lachmann, used only thirteen manuscripts in preparing his edition, published in 1872. But most other recent editors, *e.g.* Tischendorf, Alford, and Wordsworth, have made use of all the material previously published. Probably the most carefully prepared texts of our own day are those edited (1) by Westcott and Hort, and (2) by the company of Revisers, both of which were published in 1881; as may be expected, they are very much alike.

Westcott and Hort say (ii. 262), "We are by no means sure that we have done all for the text of the Apocalypse that might be done with existing materials. But we are convinced that the only way to remove such relative insecurity as belongs to it would be by a more minute and complete examination of the genealogical relations of the documents than we have been able to accomplish, nor have we reason to suspect that the result would make any considerable change."

We ought to mention that the Greek text of the Apocalypse has been several times published apart from the rest of the New Testament. The best known of these special editions are those by Tregelles (1844), Wordsworth (1849), and Kelly (1860).

§ 9. Character of the Greek.

The Greek of the Apocalypse presents wider and more frequent deviations from the ordinary style of classical Greek than that of any other book of the New Testament. It may be generally described as Hellenistic Greek, but it has so many distinctive features that Winer considered it to need special treatment at the hands of any writer on the grammar of the New Testament. Most, if not all, of its peculiarities may be due to the Hebrew training of the author of the book; and, on the other hand, many of them have parallels in profane Greek literature; but their frequency in this book, and (in some cases) their extreme form, give it a unique character. The writer gives ample proof that he was acquainted with the rules and even the subtleties of Greek grammar; yet he departs from those rules and neglects those subtleties with such apparent carelessness that he has been accused of the grossest ignorance of the Greek language. But to students acquainted with Hebrew, the style of the Apocalyptic Greek presents very little difficulty, and its so-called roughnesses occasion little surprise. Bengel's explanation of the character of the Greek of this Book is as satisfactory as it is simple: " Johannem tibi, lector Apocalypseos, propone Hebraice cogitantem, Græce scribentem; et tute, quæ Græce legis, Hebraice recogita: omnia senties expedita."

Without discussing the equally remarkable though less obvious peculiarities in the use of the tenses, the order of the words, and the concatenation of clauses, we will enumerate some of the most easily recognized deviations from ordinary Greek that are found in this book; and for the purpose of this examination we will use the text which has been adopted and published by the recent Revisers.

For the sake of convenience we will arrange these deviations in two divisions, which we will term respectively "solœcisms" and "Hebraisms." But we must not be understood to use these terms in any rigidly scientific or etymologically accurate sense. We acknowledge that many of our so-called solœcisms are capable of being brought under well-known usages, whereby even the best classical authors are held to be justified in departing from ordinary grammatical laws. And we freely allow that Greek writers who never felt any direct Semitic influences are occasionally found to use the particular forms of expression which we are here denominating Hebraisms. We further admit that our classification is not logically defensible, and that our divisions are not mutually exclusive. But we hope that our nomenclature is convenient, and our arrangement practically useful, and therefore we make no further apology for it. The following are the chief superficial peculiarities of the Greek of the Apocalypse:—

I. *Solœcisms:* deviations from the ordinary rules of Greek grammar.

1. Discords of gender: instances where pronouns, adjectives, and participles, possessing distinction of gender, have not been made to agree with the substantives to which they severally refer; *e.g.—*

> Ch. ii. 27, αὐτοὺς, referring to ἔθνα.
> Ch. iii. 4, ἄξιοι . . . ὀνόματα.
> Ch. iv. 1, λέγων . . . φωνή. So ch. ix. 14; xi. 15.
>   8, λέγοντες . . . ζῶα.
> Ch. v. 6, ἀπεσταλμένοι . . πνεύματα.

Ch. vi. 10, λέγοντες . . . ψυχαί (in ψυχάς).
Ch. xii. 5, ἄρσεν . . . υἱον.
Ch. xiv. 3, οἱ ἠγορασμένοι . . . χιλιάδες (contrast ver. 1).
Ch. xvii. 3, γέμοντα . . . γυναῖκα.
16, οὗτοι . . . κέρατα and θηρίον.
Ch. xix. 14, ἐνδεδυμένοι . . . στρατεύματα.
Ch. xxi. 14, ἔχων . . . τεῖχος (comp. ch. iv. 8).

2. Discords of number : instances where declinable words have not been adapted in number to the other words with which they are connected ; e.g.—

Ch. vi. 11, ἑκάστῳ . . . αὐτοῖς.
Ch. viii. 9, διεφθάρησαν . . . τὸ τρίτον.
Ch. xix. 1, λεγόντων . . . ὄχλου.
Ch. xx. 13, ἐκρίθησαν . . . ἕκαστος . . . αὐτῶν.

3. Discords of case : examples in which words employed in apposition, or with reference to the same person or thing, are not put in the same case ; e.g.—

Ch. i. 5, ἀπὸ Ἰησοῦ Χριστοῦ, ὁ μάρτυς, etc.
Ch. ii. 20, τὴν γυναῖκα Ἰεζεβελ, ἡ λέγουσα.
Ch. iii. 12, τῆς καινῆς Ἰερουσαλήμ, ἡ καταβαίνουσα.
Ch. vi. 1, φωνή instead of φωνήν or φωνῆς.
Ch. vii. 9, ἑστῶτες . . . περιβεβλημένους.
Ch. viii. 9, τῶν κτισμάτων τῶν . . . τὰ ἔχοντα.
Ch. ix. 14, τῷ ἕκτῳ ἀγγέλῳ ὁ ἔχων.
Ch. x. 1, 2, ἄγγελον . . . ἔχων.
Ch. xi. 18, τοῖς φοβουμένοις . . . τοὺς μικροὺς, etc.
Ch. xiv. 6, 7, ἄγγελον . . . λέγων.
12, τῶν ἁγίων . . . οἱ τηροῦντες.
Ch. xvii. 4, βδελυγμάτων . . . τὰ ἀκάθαρτα.
8, κατοικοῦντες . . . βλεπόντων (attr. to ὧν).
Ch. xxi. 10, 12, τὴν πόλιν . . . ἔχουσα.

4. Ellipse of the transitive verb which is necessary to explain an accusative case ; e.g.—

Ch. iv. 4, [εἶδον] before εἰκοσιτέσσαρας πρεσβυτέρους, etc.
Ch. x. 8, [ἤκουσα] repeated before λαλοῦσαν and λέγουσαν.
Ch. xiii. 3, [εἶδον] before μίαν.

5. Participle used as finite verb ; e.g.—

Ch. i. 16, ἔχων.

6. Finite verb used as participle ; e.g.—

Ch. i. 4, ὁ ἦν.

7. Preposition not followed by its usual case ; e.g.—

Ch. i. 4, ἀπὸ ὁ ὤν.

The designation of the Deity in this verse is, when grammatically considered, very remarkable. It may be literally rendered : The " Being " and the " Was " and the " Coming."

II. *Hebraisms :* deviations from classical Greek style, produced by the influence of a greater familiarity with Hebrew style.

1. Redundancy of personal pronouns—

(1) After a noun or its equivalent (with definite article) which is, by the use of the extra pronoun, left " pendent."

(a) *Nominativus pendens; e.g.—*

Ch. ii. 26, ὁ νικῶν καὶ ὁ τερῶν . . . δώσω αὐτῷ.
Ch. iii. 21, similarly, ὁ νικῶν . . . δώσω αὐτῷ.
Ch. iii. 12, ὁ νικῶν, ποιήσω αὐτόν.

(b) *Dativus pendens; e.g.—*

Ch. ii. 7, τῷ νικῶντι, δώσω αὐτῷ. So ver. 17.
Ch. vi. 4, τῷ καθημένῳ . . . ἐδόθη αὐτῷ.

(2) After a relative.

(a) After a relative pronoun; e.g.—

Ch. iii. 8, ἥν . . . αὐτήν.
Ch. vii. 3, οἷς . . . αὐτοῖς.
9, ὃν . . . αὐτόν.

(b) After a relative adverb; e.g.—

Ch. xvii. 9, ὅπου . . . ἐπ᾽ αὐτῶν, with which we may compare ch. xii. 14, ὅπου . . ἐκεῖ.

2. The nominative (with definite article) used for the vocative; *e.g.—*

Ch. vi. 10,[1] ὁ δεσπότης ὁ ἅγιος καὶ ἀληθινός.
Ch. xi. 17, ὁ Θεός, ὁ παντοκράτωρ ὁ ὢν καὶ ὁ ἦν.
Ch. xv. 3, ὁ Θεός, ὁ παντοκράτωρ . . . ὁ βασιλεὺς τῶν αἰώνων.
Ch. xvi. 5, ὁ ὢν καὶ ὁ ἦν, ὁ ὅσιος.
7, ὁ Θεός, ὁ παντοκράτωρ.
Ch. xviii. 4, ὁ λαός μου.
10, ἡ πόλις ἡ μεγάλη, Βαβυλών, ἡ πόλις ἡ ἰσχυρά.
20, οἱ ἅγιοι καὶ οἱ ἀπόστολοι καὶ οἱ προφῆται.

3. Free usage of the preposition ἐν, as if it were completely the equivalent of the Hebrew בְּ, and proper wherever that would be employed; *e.g.—*

Ch. ii. 27, ἐν ῥάβδῳ σιδηρᾷ. So ch. xii. 5 and xix. 15.
Ch. v. 9, ἐν τῷ αἵματί μου.
Ch. ix. 19 (end), ἐν αὐταῖς (= "by means of their tails") ἀδικοῦσι.
Ch. x. 6, ὤμοσεν ἐν.
Ch. xiii. 10 (*bis*), ἐν μαχαίρᾳ.
Ch. xiv. 2, ἐν ταῖς κιθάραις αὐτῶν.
Ch. xix. 21, ἐν τῇ ῥομφαίᾳ (comp. ver. 15).

4. The employment of εἰς after γίγνομαι, like the Hebrew לְ after הָיָה; *e.g.—*

Ch. viii. 11, ἐγένετο τὸ τρίτον τῶν ὑδάτων εἰς ἄψινθον.

5. The Hebrew method of expressing a universal negative; *e.g.—*

Ch. xxii. 3, πᾶν κατάθεμα οὐκ ἔσται ἔτι.

The text is in a few passages so difficult to explain grammatically that we are almost obliged to suspect that the Revisers' text cannot be a faithful representation of what the apostle wrote. We would particularly instance the two following cases :—

(1) Ch. ii. 1, τῷ ἐν Ἐφέσῳ ἐκκλησίας. Similarly in ver. 8, but not in the superscriptions of the epistles to the other five Churches.

(2) Ch. ii. 13, ἐν ταῖς ἡμέραις Ἀντίπας ὁ μάρτυς μου.

[1] In ch. iv. 8, the *Ter-Sanctus* is perhaps not to be taken as vocative.

Perhaps we should group with these the very difficult genitive infinitive in ch. xii. 7, ὁ Μιχαὴλ καὶ οἱ ἄγγελοι αὐτοῦ τοῦ πολεμῆσαι μετὰ τοῦ δράκοντος.

In conformity with the Hebraizing character of the Greek, we find a somewhat frequent use of pure Hebrew words : ἀμήν, ch. i. 6, 7, and often; ἀλληλούϊα, ch. xix. 1, and thrice afterwards; ἀβαδδών, ch. ix. 11; and Ἀρμαγεδών, ch. xvi. 16.

The character of the Greek of the Apocalypse has been generally discussed in connection with the question of the authorship of the book. Most frequently it has been compared with the language of the Fourth Gospel. But the evidence of grammar, vocabulary, and style is not conclusive either for or against the identity of authorship between the two books. In 1851 Davidson wrote that from evidence of this kind "men of learning and acuteness have entertained contrary sentiments respecting the authorship of the Apocalypse. Schulze, Donker-Curtius, Seyfarth, Kolthoff, and Dannemann attribute the book to the apostle on the ground of its remarkable agreement with his authentic writings, in ideas, expression, and manner; while Ewald, Lücke, Credner, and De Wette believe the diversity to be so great as to justify a denial of John's authorship."

We are ourselves much impressed by the many and weighty coincidences, and think that (on the theory of the early date of the Apocalypse) there is sufficient reason to be found in the differences of date, subject-matter, and circumstances, to account for the numerous diversities in the language of the two books.

§ 10. AUTHENTICITY.

It is often difficult to see what is intended by writers when they use the term "authenticity," and perhaps a distinction should be drawn between the authenticity of a document and the authenticity of a statement. In the former case the term is almost synonymous with "genuineness;" in the latter, with "credibility" or "trustworthiness."

By the authenticity of the book entitled, 'The Revelation of St. John the Divine,' therefore, we mean the identity of the present book so called with the manuscript original work so called, of which St. John the Divine was the αὐθέντης. Taking it for granted that St. John wrote with his own hand a revelation, when we say that the last book of our New Testament canon is authentic, we aver that it is the same revelation which St. John wrote. If we adhered to the etymological and strictly literal signification of the epithet, no form of a book could be properly styled "authentic" except the original autograph and such copies as may have been transcribed by the author himself. But for all practical purposes we are justified in calling a book "authentic" when we merely mean that it is substantially and virtually the same as the author originally wrote it; and in this looser sense the epithet is applied to all faithful transcripts and printed copies, and even to translations.

Textual criticism proves that our Authorized Version of the Revelation repentance, obedience, steadfastness, and prayer that must be kept by both reader and hearers in order to bring a blessing. And if the words are to be kept, they can be understood. We have no right to set aside the Revelation as an insoluble puzzle (comp. Luke xi. 28, where, however, we have φυλάσσειν, not τηρεῖν). The time is at hand. The appointed time, the season foreordained of God (καιρός, not χρόνος), is near. We may ask, with F. D. Maurice, "Did not the original writer use words in their simple, natural sense? If he told the hearers and readers of his day that *the time* was *at hand*, did he not mean them to understand that it *was* at hand?" No doubt. But that does not preclude us from interpreting the inspired words as referring, not only to events near St. John's time, but also to other events of which they were the foretastes and figures. To us the meaning is that the type of the end has been foretold and has come, and the end itself, which has been equally foretold, must be watched for in all seriousness.

Vers. 4—8.—*The address and greeting.* Of this section only vers. 4—6 are, strictly speaking, the salutation; vers. 7, 8 constitute a kind of summary, or prelude—ver. 7 being more closely connected with what precedes, ver. 8 with what follows. The salutation proper (vers. 4—6) should be compared with the salutations in St. Paul's Epistles.

Ver. 4.—John. Evidently some wellknown John, otherwise some designation would be necessary. Would any but the apostle have thus written to the Churches of Asia? St. Paul had some need to insist upon his being an apostle; St. John had none. **To the seven Churches.** From the earliest times it has been pointed out that the number seven here is not exact, but symbolical; it does exclude other Churches, but symbolizes all. Thus the Muratorian Fragment: "John in the Apocalypse, though he wrote to the seven Churches, yet speaks to all." Augustine: "By the seven is signified the perfection of the universal Church, and by writing to seven he shows the fulness of the one." So also Bede: "Through these seven Churches he writes to every Church; for by the number seven is denoted universality, as the whole period of the world revolves on seven days;" and he points out that St. Paul also wrote to seven Churches. Compare the seven pillars of the house of wisdom (Prov. ix. 1), the seven deacons (Acts vi. 3), the seven gifts of the Spirit. The number seven appears repeatedly in the Apocalypse; and that it is arbitrary and symbolical is shown by the fact that there were other Churches besides these seven—

Colossæ, Hierapolis, Tralles, Magnesia, Miletus. The repeated formula, "He that hath an ear, let him hear what the Spirit saith to the Churches," proves that the praise and blame distributed among the seven are of universal application. **Asia** means the Roman proconsular province of Asia, *i.e.* the western part of Asia Minor (comp. 1 Cor. xvi. 19). **Grace** be unto you, and peace. This combination occurs in the salutations of St. Peter and St. Paul. It unites Greek and Hebrew elements, and gives both a Christian fulness of meaning. **From him which is.** Why should not we be as bold as St. John, and disregard grammar for the sake of keeping the Divine Name intact? St. John writes, ἀπὸ ὁ ὢν, κ.τ.λ., not ἀπὸ τοῦ ὄντος, κ.τ.λ. "If in Exod. iii. 14 the words may run, 'I AM hath sent me unto you,' may we not also be allowed to read here, 'from HE THAT IS, AND THAT WAS, AND THAT IS TO COME'?" (Lightfoot, 'On Revision,' p. 133). Note the ὁ ἦν to represent the nominative of the past participle of εἶναι, which does not exist, and with the whole expression compare "The same yesterday, and to-day, and for ever" (Heb. xiii. 8). Here every clause applies to the Father, not one to each Person; the three Persons are marked by the three prepositions, "from . . . and from . . . and from." It is a mistake to interpret ὁ ἐρχόμενος either of the mission of the Comforter or of the second advent. **The seven Spirits.** The Holy Spirit, sevenfold in his operations (ch. v. 6). They are before his throne, ever ready for a mission from him (comp. ch. vii. 15). The number seven once more symbolizes universality, plenitude, and perfection; that unity amidst variety which marks the work of the Spirit and the sphere of it, the Church.

Ver. 5.—**The faithful Witness.** This was his function—"to bear witness unto the truth" (John xviii. 37). The rainbow is called "the faithful witness" (Ps. lxxxix. 37). **The Firstborn of the dead.** Christ was the first who was born to eternal life after the death which ends this life (see Lightfoot on Col. i. 15, 18; and comp. Ps. lxxxix. 27). "The ruler of this world" offered Jesus the glory of the kingdoms of the world, if he would worship him. He won a higher glory by dying to conquer him, and thus the crucified Peasant became the Lord of Roman emperors, "the Ruler of the kings of the earth." The grammar of this verse is irregular; "the faithful Witness," etc., in the nominative being in apposition with "Jesus Christ" in the genitive (comp. ch. ii. 20; iii. 12; ix. 14; xiv. 12). **Unto** him that loved us. The true reading gives "that *loveth* us" unceasingly. The supreme act of dying for us did not exhaust his love. In what follows it is difficult to decide between "washed" (λούσαντι) and "loosed" (λύσαντι), both readings being very well supported; but we should certainly omit "own" before "blood." The blood of Jesus Christ cleansing us from all sin is a frequent thought with the apostle who witnessed the piercing of the side (ch. vii. 13, 14; 1 John 7; v. 6—8).

Ver. 6.—And hath made us kings and priests; rather, as in the Revised Version, *and he made us* (to be) *a kingdom*, (to be) *priests*. "Made us" is not co-ordinate with "loosed us;" the sentence makes a fresh start. "Kingdom," not "kings," is the right reading. Christians are nowhere said to be kings. Collectively they are a kingdom—"a kingdom of priests" (Exod. xix. 6), or, as St. Peter, following the LXX., gives it, "a royal priesthood" (1 Pet. ii. 9). Each member of Christ shares in his eternal priesthood. Unto God and his Father; more probably we should render, with the Revised Version, *unto his God and Father* (comp. John xx. 17; Rom. xv. 6; 2 Cor. i. 3; Eph. i. 3). Alford objects that when St. John wishes a possessive genitive to apply to more than one substantive, he commonly repeats the genitive; and he quotes John ii. 12; vi. 11; ix. 21. But in these passages he repeats not only the genitive, but the article. Here the article is not repeated, and τῷ Θεῷ καὶ Πατρὶ αὐτοῦ must be taken as one phrase. To him be the glory. The construction returns to that of the opening clause, "Unto him that loveth us." St. John's doxologies increase in volume as he progresses—twofold here, threefold in ch. iv. 11, fourfold in ch. v. 13, sevenfold in ch. vii. 12. In each case all the substantives have the article—"*the* glory," "*the* honour," "*the* power," etc. For ever and ever; literally, *unto the ages of the ages* (εἰς τοὺς αἰῶνας τῶν αἰώνων, *in sæcula sæculorum*). It occurs twelve times in the Apocalypse, besides once without the articles (ch. xiv. 12). In his Gospel and Epistles St. John uses the simpler formula, "for ever," literally, "unto the age" (εἰς τὸν αἰῶνα). (See Appendix E. to St. John, in the 'Cambridge Greek Testament.') An indefinite period of immense duration is meant (comp. Gal. i. 5 and Eph. ii. 2, 7, where the countless ages of the world to come seem to be contrasted with the transitory age of this world; see also Heb. xiii. 21 and 1 Pet. iv. 11).

Vers. 7, 8.—It is difficult to determine the exact connexion of these verses with one another, and with what precedes and follows. It seems best to make ver. 7 a kind of appendix to the salutation, and ver. 8 a kind of prelude to the whole book. They each give us one of the fundamental thoughts of the Apocalypse: ver. 7, Christ's certain return to judgment; ver. 8, his perfect Divinity.

Ver. 7.—He cometh. He who loveth us and cleansed us and made us to be a kingdom will assuredly come. While interpreting the verse of the second advent, we need not exclude the coming to "those who pierced him" in the destruction of Jerusalem, and to "the tribes of the earth" in the break-up of the Roman empire. With the clouds. This probably refers to Mark xiv. 62, "Ye shall see the Son of man . . . coming with the clouds of heaven" (comp. Dan. vii. 13, "Behold, one like the Son of man came with the clouds of heaven"). Aquinas and other writers make the clouds symbolize the saints, "who rain by preaching, glisten by working miracles, are lifted up by refusing earthly things, fly by lofty contemplation." And they also; better, *and all they who* (οἵτινες) *pierced him*. This is strong evidence of common authorship between the Fourth Gospel and the Apocalypse. (1) St. John alone mentions the piercing. (2) Here and in John xix. 37 the writer, in quoting Zech. xii. 10, deserts the LXX. and follows the Masoretic Hebrew text. The LXX. softens down "pierced" into "insulted" (κατωρχήσατο), "piercing" appearing a violent expression to use respecting men's treatment of Jehovah. (3) Here and in John xix. 37 the writer, in translating from the Hebrew, uses the uncommon Greek word ἐκκεντᾷν. The reference here is to all those who "crucify the Son of God afresh," not merely to the Jews. In what follows the Revised Version is to be preferred: "and all the tribes of the earth shall *mourn over* him." The wording is similar to Matt. xxiv. 30 and the LXX. of Zech. xii. 10. The mourning is that of beating the breast, not wailing, and it is "*over* him" (ἐπ' αὐτόν). Even so, Amen. Ναί, Ἀμήν, like "Abba, Father" (Mark iv. 36; Rom. viii. 15; Gal. iv. 6), combines a Hebrew word with its Greek equivalent (comp. 2 Cor. i. 20).

Ver. 8.—A prelude to the book. In the simple majesty of its solemn language it reminds us of the opening of St John's Gospel and of his First Epistle. 'I am *the* Alpha and *the* Omega" is here not followed by "the Beginning and the End," which the Vulgate and some other authorities insert from ch. xxi. 6 and xxii. 13. Who is "the Lord," that utters these words? Surely the Christ, as seems clear from ver. 17; ch. ii. 8; xxii. 13. To attribute them to the Father robs the words of their special appropriateness in this context, where they form a prelude to "the Revelation *of Jesus Christ*" as God and as the Almighty "Ruler of the kings of the earth." Yet the fact that similar language is also used of the Father (ch. vi. 6; xxi. 6) shows how clearly St.

John teaches that Jesus Christ is "equal to the Father as touching his Godhead." These sublime attributes are applicable to each. Like the doxology (see on ver. 6), the statement of these Divine attributes increases in fulness as the writing proceeds. Here "the Alpha and the Omega;" ver. 17 and ch. ii. 8, "the First and the Last;" in ch. xxi. 6, "the Alpha and the Omega, the Beginning and the End;" in ch. xxii. 13, "the Alpha and the Omega, the First and the Last, the Beginning and the End." Of these four, the second and fourth certainly apply to the Son, and the third certainly to the Father, the first probably to the Son. The Almighty. With the exception of 2 Cor. vi. 18, where it occurs in a quotation, this expression (ὁ Παντοκράτωρ) is in the New Testament peculiar to the Apocalypse, where it occurs nine times. In the LXX. it represents more than one Hebrew expression; *e.g.* Jer. iii. 19; Job v. 17.

Vers. 9—20.—*The introductory vision.* This section is introductory, not merely to the epistles to the Churches, but to the whole book. In it the seer narrates how he received his commission; and with it should be compared Isa. vi.; Jer. i. 1—10; Ezek i. 1—3; Dan. x., especially vers. 2, 7, where "I Daniel" is exactly parallel to "I John" here. The Revised Version is again much to be preferred to the Authorized Version.

Ver. 9.—In the tribulation and kingdom and patience. The order of the words is surprising; we should have expected "kingdom" to have come first or last. But "and patience" seems to be added epexegetically, to show *how* the tribulation leads to the kingdom (comp. ch. ii. 2, 3, 19; iii. 10; xiii. 10; xiv. 12). "In your patience ye shall win your souls" (Luke xxi. 19). "Tribulation worketh patience" (Rom. v. 3); and "through many tribulations, we must enter into the kingdom of God" (Acts xiv. 22). Bengel notes that it is in tribulation that believers specially love this book. The Church of Asia, particularly after the prosperous time of Constantine, had a low opinion of the Apocalypse; while the African Church, which was more subject to persecution, highly esteemed it. "Everything tends to show that the Apocalypse was acknowledged in Africa from the earliest times as canonical Scripture" (Westcott, 'On the Canon of the New Testament,' p. 238). Was in the isle. Here and in ver. 10 "was" is literally "came to be" (ἐγενόμην), implying that such was not his ordinary condition; comp. γενόμενος ἐν ῾Ρώμῃ (2 Tim. i. 17). That is called Patmos. St. John does not assume that his readers know so insignificant a

place. He does not say simply "in Patmos," as St. Luke says "to Rhodes" or "to Cyprus," but "in *the isle* t at is *called* Patmos." Now *Patmo* or *Patino*, but in the Middle Ages *Palmosa.* Its small size and rugged character made it a suitable place for penal transportation. Banishment to a small island (*deportatio in insulam* or *insulæ vinculum*) was common. "Aude aliquid brevibus Gyaris et carcere dignum" (Juv., i. 73). Compare the cases of Agrippa Postumus (Tac., 'Ann.,' i. 3) and of Julia (iv. 71). For a full account of the island, see Guérin's 'Description de l'Ile de Patmos,' Paris: 1856. For the circumstances of St. John's banishment, see Introduction. It was in exile that Jacob saw God at Bethel; in exile that Moses saw God at the burning bush; in exile that Elijah heard the "still small voice;" in exile that Ezekiel saw "the likeness of the glory of the Lord" by the river Chebar; in exile that Daniel saw "the Ancient of days." For the Word of God, and the testimony of Jesus. No doubt the Greek (διὰ τὸν λόγον) *might* mean that he was in Patmos for the sake of *receiving* the word; but ch. vi. 9 and xx. 4 are decisive against this (comp. διὰ τὸ ὄνομά μου in John xvi. 21). These passages and "partaker in the tribulation" here prove that St. John's "coming to be in Patmos" was caused by *suffering* for the Word of God. *The testimony of Jesus.* This, as in ver. 2, probably means the testimony that he bore, rather than the testimony about him. "Christ" is a corrupt addition to the text in both places in this verse.

Ver. 10.—I was in the Spirit. I came to be (see on ver. 9) in a state of ecstasy capable of receiving revelations; like γενέσθαι με ἐν ἐκστάσει (Acts xxii. 17; comp. x. 10; 2 Cor. xii. 2—4). On the Lord's day. The expression occurs here only in the New Testament, and beyond all reasonable doubt it means "on Sunday." This is, therefore, the earliest use of the phrase in this sense. That it means Easter Day or Pentecost is baseless conjecture. The phrase had not yet become common in A.D. 57, as is shown from St. Paul writing, "on the first of the week" (1 Cor. xvi. 2), the usual expression in the Gospels and Acts (Matt. xxviii. 1; Mark xvi. 2; Luke xxiv. 1; John xxi. 19; Acts xx. 7; comp Mark. xvi. 9). But from Ignatius onwards, we have a complete chain of evidence that ἡ Κυριακή became the regular Christian name for the first day of the week; and Κυριακή is still the name of Sunday in the Levant. "No longer observing sabbaths, but fashioning their lives after the Lord's day" (Ign., 'Magn.,' ix.). Melito, Bishop of Sardis (A.D. 170), wrote a treatise περὶ Κυριακῆς (Eusebius, 'Hist. Eccl.,' IV. xxvi. 2). Dionysius of Corinth (A.D. 175), in an epistle to the Romans, mentions that the Church of Corinth is that day keeping the Lord's holy day (Eusebius, 'Hist. Eccl.,' IV. xxiii. 11). Comp. also Clem. Alex., 'Strom.,' VII. xii 98 (p. 377. Potter); Tertull., 'De Cor.,' iii. and ' De Idol.,' xiv., where *Dominicus dies* is obviously a translation of Κυριακὴ ἡμέρα; and fragment vii. of the lost works of Irenæus. That "the Lord's day" (ἡ Κυριακὴ ἡμέρα) in this place is the same as 'the day of the Lord " (ἡ ἡμέρα τοῦ Κυίου) is not at all probable. The context is quite against any such meaning as that St. John is spiritually transported to the day of judgment. Contrast ch. vi. 17; xvi. 14; 1 John iv. 17; John vi. 39, 40, 44, 54; xi. 24; xii. 48. Whereas. seeing that the visions which follow are grouped in sevens (the seven candlesticks, seven seals, seven trumpets, seven vials), the fact that they begin on the first day of the seven is eminently appropriate. **Great voice.** The voice is evidently Christ's; but throughout the Apocalypse the speaker is frequently not named. By a construction common in Hebrew, "saying" agrees with "trumpet," the nearest substantive, instead of with "voice" (comp. Ezek iii. 12 Matt. xxiv. 31). "Therefore it is from *behind*, for all the symbols and references are to be sought for in the Old Testament " (I. Williams); comp. Isa. xxx. 21.

Ver. 11.—On ample evidence (א, A, C, and all versions), "I am Alpha . . . the Last; and " must be omitted; also "which are in Asia." **Write in a book;** literally, *into a book* (εἰς βιβλίον). Over and over again, twelve times in all, St. John reminds us that he writes this book by Divine command (ver. 19; ch. ii. 1, 8, 12, 18; iii. 1, 7, 14; xiv. 13; xix. 9; xxi. 5; comp. ch. x. 4). **The seven Churches.** The order is not haphazard. It is precisely that which would be natural to a person writing in Patmos or travelling from Ephesus. Ephesus comes first as metropolis; then the city on the coast, Smyrna; then the inland cities in order, working round towards Ephesus again. In short, it is just the order in which St. John would visit the Churches in making an apostolic circuit as metropolitan. With the exception of what is told us in these chapters, the history of the Churches of Pergamum, Thyatira, and Sardis in the apostolic or sub-apostolic age is quite unknown. It was an ancient objection to the Apocalypse that in Thyatira there was no Church (see on ch. ii. 18).

Ver. 12.—**To see the voice.** As in Gen. iii. 8, "the voice" is put for the speaker. This is the right method in studying the Revelation; we must, like St. John, "turn to see the voice." We must look, not to the events about which it seems to us to

speak, but to him who utters it. **The book** is " the Revelation," not of the secrets of history, but " of Jesus Christ." **Seven golden candlesticks.** The word λυχνία occurs in Matt. v. 15; Mark iv. 21; Luke viii. 16; xi. 33; Heb. ix. 2; and seven times in this book. In Exod. xxv. 37 we have seven λύχνοι on one λυχνία, seven lamps on one lampstand. So also in Zech. iv. 2. It is by no means certain that a similar figure is not meant here; the seven-branched candlestick familiar to all who know the Arch of Titus. If the Christ stood " in the midst of the candlesticks," his form would appear as that which united the seven branches. But it is perhaps more natural to understand seven separate lamp-stands, each with its own lamp; and these, in contrast with the seven-branched stand of the temple, may represent the elastic multiplicity of the Christian Churches throughout the world in contrast with the rigid unity of the Jewish Church of Jerusalem.

Ver. 13.—**In the midst of the candlesticks.** " For where two or three are gathered together in my Name, there am I in the midst of them " (Matt. xviii. 20; comp. 2 Cor. vi. 16). **Like unto the Son of man.** Here and in ch. xiv. 14 we have simply υἱὸς ἀνθωώπου, as also in John v. 27 and Dan. vii. 13; not ὁ υἱὸς τοῦ ἀνθρώπου, as in Acts vii. 56 and everywhere else in all four Gospels. It is not certain that the absence of the articles forbids us to render the phrase, " the Son of man; " but it is safer to render, "a son of man." The glorified Messiah still wears that human form by which the beloved disciple had known him before the Ascension (John xxi. 7). With the exception of Acts vii. 56, the full form, " the Son of man," is used only by the Christ of himself. **A garment down to the feet.** The word ποδηρής, *sc.* χιτών (*vestis talaris*), though frequent in the LXX. (Ezek. ix. 2, 3, 11; Zech. iii. 4, etc.), occurs nowhere else in the New Testament. The robe is an official one. The Rhemish renders it " **a** *priestly* garment down to the foote." Compare Joseph's " coat of many colours," which literally means a " coat reaching to the extremities." And in Exod. xxviii. 31 " the robe of the ephod " of the high priest is ὑποδύτης ποδήρης. The angel in Dan. x. 5, 6 is described in similar language: " whose loins were girded with fine gold of Uphaz " (comp. Isa. xxii. 21, " I will clothe him with thy robe, and strengthen him with thy girdle, and I will commit thy government into his hand", " Enough is said to indicate that the Son of man claims and fulfils the office which was assigned to the children of Aaron; that he blesses the people in God's Name; that he stands as their Representative before his Father " (F. D. Maurice).

Ver. 14.—**His head. From the garments of the great High Priest,** St. John passes on to himself. What he had seen as a momentary foretaste of glory at the Transfiguration, he sees now as the abiding condition of the Christ. In Dan. vii. 9 "the Ancient of days" has "the hair of his head like pure wool." This snowy whiteness is partly the brightness of heavenly glory, partly the majesty of the hoary head. The Christ appears to St. John as a son of man, but also as a "Divine Person invested with the attributes of eternity." **As a flame of fire.** "The Lord thy God is a consuming fire" (Deut. iv. 24). "I the Lord search the heart, I try the reins" (Jer. xvii. 10). The flame purifies the conscience and kindles the affections.

Ver. 15.—**Fine brass.** This may stand as a translation of χαλκολίβανος, a word which occurs here and in ch. ii. 18 only, and the second half of which has never been satisfactorily explained. It may have been a local technical term in use among the metalworkers of Ephesus (Acts xix. 24; 2 Tim. iv. 14). The Rhemish Version renders it "latten." In what follows, the Revised Version is to be preferred: "as if it had been refined in a furnace; and his voice as the *voice* of many waters." It is tempting to think that "the roar of the sea is in the ears of the lonely man in Patmos;" but the image seems rather to be that of the sound of many cataracts (comp. Ezek. i. 24; xliii. 2; Dan. x. 6). There is singularly little of the scenery of Patmos in the Apocalypse.

Ver. 16.—**He holds the Churches in his hand** as a precious possession, which he sustains as a glory to himself. These Churches are as planets, which shine, not with their own light, but that of the sun; which shine most brightly in the night of "tribulation," which (like him who holds them in his right hand) are a guide to the wanderer, and are ever moving, yet ever at rest. **Out of his mouth a sharp two-edged sword.** This metaphor runs through both Old and New Testaments. It is frequent in this book (ch. ii. 12, 16; xix. 15, 21; comp. Luke ii. 35; Eph. vi. 17; Heb. iv. 12; Ps. xlv. 3; lvii. 4; lix. 7; lxiv. 3; cxlix. 6; Prov. xii. 18; Isa. xi. 4; xlix. 2, etc.). The sharp words of men and the searching words of God are both spoken of under this figure of the sword. Tertullian and Richard of St. Victor explain the two edges as the Law and the Gospel. Other still more fanciful explanations have been given. "Two-edged" (δίστομος) is literally "two-mouthed," and perhaps expresses no more than the thorough efficiency of the sword. It occurs in ch. ii. 12 and Heb. iv. 12; also in classical Greek as equivalent to the more common ἀμφήκης. If a double meaning be insisted on, it may

be found in the double character of God's Word, which not only smites the wicked, but searches the good ; which cuts sometimes to punish, sometimes to heal. Thus in these very epistles to the Churches, penetrating words both of blessing and condemnation are uttered. The word for "sword" (ῥομφαία) occurs six times in Revelation ; elsewhere in the New Testament only Luke ii. 35. In classical Greek it is the heavy Thracian broadsword. In the LXX. it is used of the "flaming sword" of the cherubim which kept the way of the tree of life (Gen. iii. 24) ; also of the sword of Goliath (1 Kings xvii. 25). **His countenance was as the sun shineth.** It is the "Sun of Righteousness" and "the Light of the world." The exceptional glory of the Transfiguration has become constant now.

Ver. 17.—**I fell at his feet as dead ;** literally, *as one dead—as a dead man.* St. Peter had fallen at Jesus' feet when he became conscious of the ineffable difference between sinlessness and sinfulness (Luke v 8). How much more, therefore, would consciousness of the glorified Christ overwhelm St. John! Long years of contemplation of the incarnate Son would not prevent that. In like manner, Joshua (v. 14), Daniel (viii. 17, 27), and St. Paul (Acts ix. 4) are affected by the Divine presence. Fear not. Thus Christ encouraged the terrified apostles on the lake (John vi. 20) and at the Transfiguration. So also the angel cheered Daniel (x. 12), Zacharias (Luke i. 13), Mary (Luke i. 30), the shepherds (Luke ii. 10), and the women at the sepulchre (Matt. xxviii. 5).

Ver. 18.—**I am he that liveth.** This should be joined with what precedes. "I am the First and the Last, and *the Living One;* and I *became* dead, and behold I am alive for evermore, and I have the keys of *death and of Hades.*" "Became" or "came to be" (ἐγενόμην), as in vers. 9 and 10, indicates an exceptional condition. The "Amen" has been improperly inserted after "for evermore" (see on "for ever and ever," in ver 6) from liturgical usage. Most English versions omit it. The keys, as so often, are the sign of authority (ch. iii. 7; ix. 1; xx. 1; Matt. xvi. 19). Christ, as the absolutely Living One, who "has life in himself" and is the Source of life in others, has control, not merely over the passage from this world to the other, but over the other world itself. He can recall departed souls from their resting-place. The error of rendering Ἅιδης "hell" has often been pointed out; it is not a place of punishment, but the temporary home of the departed, who are awaiting the day of judgment. "Death," in all the best manuscripts and versions precedes "Hades ;" and this is the logical order.

Ver. 19.—**Write the things.** The true reading and most English Versions give, "write *therefore* the things;" *i.e.* because thou hast seen me and received thy commission from me. The omission of "therefore" comes from the Genevan Version. The threefold division of things probably refers to past, present, and future *visions*, not to the past, present, and future in history. But it is possible that "the things which thou sawest" refers to the visions, and "the things which are," etc., to the realities symbolized in the visions.

Ver. 20.—**The mystery.** In construction this is the accusative after "write." A mystery is the opposite of a revealed truth; it is a sacred truth kept secret, the inner meaning of something which is perceived, but not generally understood. **The angels of the seven Churches.** The meaning of these "angels" has been very much disputed. The common explanation that they are the bishops of the Churches is attractive on account of its simplicity. But it has very grave difficulties, especially for those who assign the Apocalypse to the earlier date of A.D. 68. It is highly improbable that at that very early time the seven Churches were already so fully organized as each to possess its own bishop. And granting that they were, and that the bishops might fitly be called "angels" or "messengers," would they not be called messengers of God or of Christ, rather than messengers of the Churches"? And would not the primitive Church have preserved this title as a synonym for "bishop"? "St. John's own language gives the true key to the symbolism. 'The seven stars are the angels of the seven Churches, and the seven candle-sticks are the seven Churches.' This contrast between the heavenly and the earthly fires—the star shining steadily by its own inherent eternal light, and the lamp flickering and uncertain, requiring to be fed with fuel and tended with care—cannot be devoid of meaning. The star is the suprasensual counterpart, the heavenly representative; the lamp, the earthly realization, the outward embodiment. Whether the angel is here conceived as an actual person, the celestial guardian, or only as a personification, the idea or spirit of the Church, it is unnecessary for my present purpose to consider. But whatever may be the exact conception, he is identified with and made responsible for the Church to a degree wholly unsuited to any human officer. Nothing is predicated of him which may not be predicated of it. To him are imputed all its hopes, its fears, its graces, its shortcomings. He is punished with it, and he is rewarded with it. . . . Nor is this mode of representation new. The 'princes' in Daniel (x. 13, 20, 21) present a very near if not an exact parallel to the angels of the Revelation" (Bishop Lightfoot, 'Philippians,' p. 198). The identification of the angel of each Church with the Church itself is shown in a marked way by the fact that, although each epistle is addressed to the angel, yet the constantly recurring refrain is, "Hear what the Spirit saith *to the Churches*," not "to the *angels* of the Churches." The angel and the Church are the same under different aspects: the one is its spiritual character personified; the other is the congregation of believers who collectively possess this character.

HOMILETICS.

Vers. 1—3.—*Introduction: the purport of the book.* In commencing a series of sketches which shall furnish in outline a homiletic exposition of such a book as this, the writer may well feel borne down with a sense of the responsibility of the task he has undertaken. And yet such responsibility, great as it is, is prevented from being overwhelming through the infinite joy and comfort he has himself derived from a repeated study of it—a study extending over some fifteen or twenty years, and now renewed for the special purpose of giving utterance to convictions of its value and glory, which deepen with each succeeding examination of its contents. Into the detailed opinions of the varied expositors as to whether the preterist, futurist, or historical interpretations are the most correct, it will neither be in his province nor to his taste to enter. There is another order of exposition—the spiritual—which, accepting whatever can be verified in the other three, sees rather throughout the Apocalypse an unfolding of the principles on which the great Head of the Church will carry forward his own work, and a parabolic setting of the fortunes of his Church as she moves forward to the final consummation of all things. As Dr. Lee remarks,[1] "the historical system assumes that single events, as they come to pass in succession, exhibit the full accomplishment of the different predictions of the Apocalypse," while "the 'spiritual'

[1] Introduction to the Revelation, 'Speaker's Commentary,' New Testament, vol. IV. p. 492.

application is never exhausted, but merely receives additional illustrations as time rolls on." Hengstenberg's remarks are worthy of being remembered:[1] "That the Christian may remain steadfast and fearless where he is, even though it should be in the midst of a falling world, this book is fitted to render for such a purpose a most important service. It has thus proved a blessing even to many who have very imperfectly understood it. For it is wonderful how the edifying power that resides in the book forces its way even through the most imperfect understanding of its contents, if only the soul that applies to it is hungry and thirsty, weary and heavy-laden, if it only stands in living faith on the Divinity of Scripture and the glorious consummation of the kingdom of Christ." In full accord with the convictions of the value of the Apocalypse, thus admirably expressed by the great evangelical German divine, do we now commence for homiletic purposes to unfold its plan. Our first sketch must needs be like the first three verses—introductory. Introductory, however, though the verses are, they are amazingly full of holy and blessed teaching. We have here—

I. THE NAME GIVEN TO THE BOOK. "The Revelation ($\dot{\alpha}\pi o\kappa\dot{\alpha}\lambda v\psi\iota s$[2])" (ver. 1). At the forefront of the book this is its avowal. It declares itself to be nothing less than the disclosure of what was behind a veil, and so invisible to mortal sight, until the veil was drawn aside and unseen things were thereby disclosed. That there are other realms than our globe, peopled with moral and spiritual beings, is again and again declared in Scripture; that there are mysterious forces of good and of evil in the distant places of creation is also told us. That there is many a contest over man in these far-off realms; that there is a Divine Being who watches over the conflict, and who will "bring forth judgment unto victory;" that the theatre on which the issue is to be fought out is this globe; and that at the consummation the direst enemies of the world and of man will be put to an utter shame;—all this could no *philosophy* forecast, nor any science teach; all this lies behind an impenetrable veil. If we are to know these things, they must be revealed to us, and this can be done only by our God! Note: As this is declared at the outset concerning this book, as such it must be regarded; until its claims be disproved, they should be reverently accepted.

II. THE METHOD OF THE REVELATION. The several steps are shown us—the *terminus a quo* and the *terminus ad quem*. We have: 1. *Its origin.* "God"—God the Father. If God be the Father of all men, that he should let them know something about himself is most reasonable. To suppose that he cannot, is to suppose that a father would build a house for his children, of such a kind that they could never find out where their father was! 2. *Its channel.* "Jesus Christ." God gave it to him. He is the Medium, the Mediator between God and man; and the clearest disclosures of God and his purposes come to us through the everlasting Son. 3. *Its agents.* (1) "He sent . . . by his angel." Angelic ministry is one of the steps by which the revelation is brought to us. The existence and ministry of angels are very clearly shown to us. (2) "To his servant John." The beloved apostle, in his old age and exile, received the revelation from angelic hands. 4. *Its mode.* "He signified it." The word means "to signify by symbols." 5. *For whom ?* "To show unto his servants," etc. The Word of God is committed as a trust to those who love and serve him. The faith was "once [for all] delivered to the saints." Why to these? (cf. Matt. xiii. 10, 11). Note: Here in outline is a wondrous sketch of *how* God reveals his truth.

III. THE CONTENTS OF THE REVELATION.[3] 1. *Events.* "Things which must shortly

---

[1] Hengstenberg on 'The Revelation,' vol. ii. p. 285.

[2] See Grimm's 'New Testament Lexicon' on this word (Dr. Thayer's edit., 1888).

[3] The student will find the following writers and works on the Apocalypse worthy of his attention: Alford, Bengel, Barnes, Doddridge, Godwin, Tregelles, Porter, Maurice, Lowman, Stuart, Fairbairn, Trench, Robinson, Stier; Dr. Lee's Commentary; article on 'Revelation,' in Schaff's 'Herzog;' Elliott's 'Horæ Apocalypticæ;' Grattan Guinness on 'The Approaching End of the Age;' also his 'Light for the Last Days;' and 'Romanism and the Reformation;' Dean Vaughan on the 'Revelation;' Commentary by Rev. Samuel Garratt; Auberlen on 'Daniel and the Revelation;' Gerhardt's 'Doctrine of the Apocalypse;' Archdeacon Farrar's 'Early Days of Christianity;' and Rev. E. Storrow's work, 'The Millennium: a Spiritual Reign of Christ,' 1886; also Dr. Boyd Carpenter's 'Exposition of the Revelation;' an article on the Apocalyptic "beast," by Rev. F. B. Proctor, in the *Clergyman's Magazine*, October, 1887; 'The Revelation of St. John,' by Dr. Milligan, 2nd edit., 1887;

come to pass." 2. *Such events as are necessarily involved in the bringing about of the Divine purposes.* "Must" (ver. 1). 3. *Events which*, in the prophetic forecast, *are near at hand.* "Shortly," *i.e.* in the reckoning of Heaven (cf. 2 Pet. iii. 8). The next great crisis of the world is the second coming of the Son of God. He is on the way. But at what point of time the Son of man will be revealed it is not given to man to know. The series of events that prepare the way for the second coming began immediately after the first and *are going on now.* Not a moment is lost. Heaven's great harvest-day is coming on.

IV. THE USE TO BE MADE OF THIS REVELATION. (Ver. 3.) Reading, hearing, doing. 1. *It was to be read in the Churches.* "He that readeth," equivalent to "he that reads it in the assemblies of the saints." The Word of God is not to be hid in a corner, but publicly read. It is not the preserve of the few, but the charter for the many. 2. *The people are to hear.* God's truth was to be set before men through the ear. The doctrine that it is more effective when set before the eye, finds in such a passage as this no support. 3. The hearers must *keep the things written therein.* Note: If the book is so obscure that no one can understand it, it is hard to say how men can keep the things that are herein written. The blessing pronounced on those who do keep them implies that they are sufficiently plain for that purpose. How, then, are we to "keep" these things? (1) Seize the principles of the book, and abide in them. (2) Study its prophecies, and wait for them. (3) Learn its promises, and lean on them. (4) Ponder its precepts, and obey them. "If ye know these things, happy are ye if ye do them."

V. THE BLESSEDNESS OF THOSE WHO RIGHTLY USE THIS REVELATION. "Blessed is he," etc. (ver. 3). It is not difficult to see in what this blessedness consists. 1. Such will have a good understanding; for they will know the meaning and plan of the world's course and destiny. 2. They will have a sure resting-place in the absolute certainty of the final triumph of truth and righteousness. 3. They will have a good hope. "Looking for the mercy of the Lord Jesus Christ unto eternal life."

Vers. 4—6.—*Salutation and song.* The writer of the book again gives us his name: "John." It is extremely unlikely, as the name John was by no means uncommon, that any other John than the apostle would have given his name thus briefly and without a word of explanation.[1] Those to whom the book was addressed are "the seven Churches which are in Asia." It does not lie within our province here to inquire whether these seven Churches are selected from others, "to symbolize the whole Church of God." We rather regard them as indicating the circle over which the influence of the Apostle John was chiefly felt, from his home at Ephesus. They range over about one-third of the district of Asia, called Asia Minor, not far from its western sea-board.[2] There is a separate letter for each of the Churches, which are distinct in their formation, responsibility, danger, duty, and fault. But what precedes these letters, and also what follows them, is for the whole of them, that they may read, hear, keep, and transmit to those that should follow after. We have in these three verses—

I. A SALUTATION. Here is evidently an outbreathing of holy love. But in what light are we to regard it? Is it the aged apostle himself expressing his own fervent desires that grace and peace may rest upon the seven Churches? or does he pen these words by commission of the Holy Ghost, as Heaven's own benediction? Exegetically, either view is tenable. Doctrinally, both would undoubtedly be included, since the actual difference between the two resolves itself into this: if the words were suggested

---

'The Parousia,' by Rev. J. Stuart Russell, D.D., 2nd edit., 1887. In the 'Popular Commentary on the New Testament,' edited by Dr. Schaff, the 'Commentary on the Revelation,' by Dr. Milligan, will be found worthy of careful study, especially his introduction, his interpretation of the mysterious number 666, and of the thousand years' reign; though we cannot think Dr. Milligan as successful in building up his own views as he is in demolishing those of others. A recent work entitled 'The Book of Revelation,' by Dr. Israel P. Warren, of Portland, Me., U.S. (1886), has an admirable introduction on the aim of the Apocalypse. That venerable and wise expositor, the Rev. Principal David Brown, D.D., has commenced (Oct. 1889) a series of papers on the Apocalypse, in the *Expositor.*

[1] Cf. Dr. Lee's 'Introduction to the Revelation,' § 1.
[2] Cf. 'The Seven Golden Candlesticks,' by Dr. Tristram.

to him, it would be the Holy Ghost that commissioned him thus to write; if they were prompted by his own apostolic fervour, it would be the Holy Ghost who stirred in him thus to feel; either way, therefore, the outbreathing is the result of a Divine inbreathing. This greeting to believers resolves itself into two parts. 1. *Here are great blessings specified.* They are two. (1) Grace. It is one of the most interesting historical features of early Christianity, and one of the most striking evidences that with it a new life dawned in the world, that from the very beginning of the Christian era there are both new epitaphs over the pious dead, and new benedictions for those who are living. This is an illustration. The word "grace," though a translation of a word that was common enough in the Greek language (χάρις), yet puts on a vastly grander meaning as soon as ever it is applied in distinctively Christian thought. The writings of the Apostle Paul had given it a sublimity before unknown. The word is used a hundred times in his Epistles, but only six times by John. Yet, in his use of it, it conveys a world of meaning (John i. 14, 16, 17; 2 John 3; ch. i. 4; xxii. 21). (2) Peace. Another word which, as light from Christ and his cross shines upon it, has a beauty not its own (John xiv. 27; xvi. 33; xx. 19, 21, 26; cf. also Eph. ii. 14; Col. i. 20; Phil. iv. 7). There is a peace (*a*) possessed, (*b*) made, (*c*) imparted and sustained —peace with God; peace in God; peace of conscience; peace in hope. 2. *The Divine origin of these blessings is here named.* They come from the Trinity in Unity. The doctrine of the Trinity is never taught in Scripture as an ontological abstraction, but a glorious reality for faith to accept and life to receive.[1] (1) From the Father. "From him which is, and which was, and who is coming." The great I AM—eternally self-existent, and yet who is, as it were, ever moving forward, unrolling on the page of history his unfinished and unfinishable Name. (2) From the Holy Ghost: represented here in his sevenfold majesty, as the Source of the manifold energy which streams from the eternal throne. (3) From the Lord Jesus, as (*a*) a Testifier of the truth from heaven, (*b*) the Beginner of the new realm of life, (*c*) the King of kings. Here are truth, life, power. The sovereignty of the world is Christ's. In him only are the temporal and spiritual authority rightly and effectively joined. How rich and full is this salutation! If such blessings come from such a Source, then they are (1) sure, (2) constant, (3) eternal, (4) personal, (5) beyond the reach of alien forces. Thus we are brought within sight of another theme for meditation, though it is not possible for us here to enlarge thereon; viz. the real endowment and large wealth of the Church of God.

II. A SONG OF PRAISE. The apostle, ere he launches forth on the disclosures which have been made to him, seems to give relief to his overburdened soul in the rapturous words of the fifth verse. He would have all believers join with him in one united chorus of gladsome thanksgiving. In expounding this song, let us first examine the basis of it, and then its contents. 1. *The basis of the song.* Again and again do prophet and psalmist invite us to "sing unto the Lord." Apostles oft bid us "rejoice in the Lord." But people will not, cannot sing joyously, unless there be something to make them glad, and thus to inspire the song. The basis of this song is twofold: (1) *There has been a great work effected.* A double work. (*a*) Evil removed. "Loosed us from our sins" (so Revised Version). The burden of sin and guilt once rested heavily. The guilt is cancelled by a forgiving word, the sin cleansed by purifying grace. And this has been done at no less a cost than the sacrifice of himself—"by his blood." Blood. Not the material fluid. Even the Levitical Law should raise our thoughts above that. "The blood thereof, which is the life thereof" (Lev. xvii. 11, 14). The blood of Christ is so precious because of *the life* in laying down which it was shed. He came and stood in our place, and, by bearing our burdens and atoning for our guilt, acquired a perfect right to loose the penitent for ever from his load. (*b*) Privilege bestowed. "He made us *to be* a kingdom." The pardoned and renewed souls form a new creation of redeeming grace—the kingdom of heaven upon earth. "Priests." Every believer is a priest unto God. He stands, as it were, between a world that knows not God, and him whom to know is life; that so he may point the way, yea, lead the wanderer home; that he may plead with him for God, and plead with God for him;—thus fulfilling the truly priestly function of helping man Godward. (2) *There is a love constantly vouchsafed.* "Unto him that loveth us (τῷ ἀγαπῶντι)" (Revised Version).

[1] See a great sermon on this theme in Huntington's 'Christian Believing and Living.'

The work effected is complete. The love which resteth on believers abideth evermore. To be perpetually an object of redeeming love may well move the heart to joy, and sune the lips to song! But what will the song be? Let us notice: 2. *The contents of the song.* We see at once that it is a song of praise to the Lord Jesus Christ. As the blessings descend from him and through him, so shall the praises of believers rise to him. (1) *The honour of achieving all this good is attributed to him.* "To him be the glory"—all the glory.

> "Nothing brought him from above,
> Nothing but redeeming love."

He could, as Creator, have blotted man out of being for his transgressions, and have brought nobler souls into life. But no; he rushed to our rescue, and gave up his life to ensure our own. He did all the work, and of it he shall bear the glory. (2) *The everlasting royalty is ascribed to him.* "And the dominion (τὸ κράτος)." The word means one or more of three things—strength, sway, victory. Here all three are included. Infinite might is his, who spoiled principalities and powers, and triumphed over them in himself. The sway of souls is his. He who died for them—and he alone —is worthy to rule them. To this end Christ both died, and rose, and revived, that *he* might be Lord. And the ultimate victory shall be his. "He must reign, till he hath put all enemies under his feet." It seems as if this song were the gladsome echo of the words, "the Ruler of the kings of the earth." For to this royalty of the Son of God the believer responds in triumphant jubilation. The will of the saved one is not only in entire acquiescence therewith, but he could not endure the thought of the world's sovereignty being anywhere else than in the hands of the Son of God. Yea, more, it is the thought of this sovereignty of Christ that makes his heart swell with noblest joy. For only those pierced hands can be trusted to guide earth's chariot-wheels. Only he who died for man shall by man be owned as Lord. Only this will be his fitting recompense for Calvary's woes, that the royal diadem encircling his brow shall be there amid the hallelujahs and praise of those whom he has redeemed, pardoned, sanctified, and glorified! How vast will the "gathering of the people be"! How ecstatic their cry, "Crown him, crown him, King of kings and Lord of lords"!

Ver. 7.—*The outlook: the second coming of our Lord.*[1] There are one or two more introductory themes presented to us, before we are fairly launched on the exposition of the visions and scenery of this book. In this verse we have a summing up of its specific outlook. The apostolic seer beholds the Son of man enthroned in heaven, and unfolds, in symbol, the movements on earth till the Lord returns again. Hence the view which bounds the scene is this—"he cometh." We propose in this homily to set forth the place which the New Testament assigns to the second coming of Christ, in its relation to the Divine dispensations, to the faith and life of the Church, and to the outlook of the world. We hope, in doing so, to avoid some evils which have given us much concern, and which seriously impede the preparation of the Church for her Lord's return. We must not, in thinking of our Saviour's coming again, be led to think of him as now absent from his Church in such sense as to leave her lonely, helpless, and forlorn. He is not only near his Church, but in it—the Holy Ghost is her Comforter. She is not desolate—the *real presence* is in the heart of every believer, in the assemblies of the saints, and at the feast of the Holy Communion. Nor must we let our attention be taken off from the responsibilities our Lord has entrusted to us, by any of the interminable and profitless disputes as to the day or the hour of his appearing. It may be questioned whether the evil one ever used a more powerful engine for perplexing and injuring the Church, than by dragging her into disputes of days and years, and so far taking off her attention from the words, "Be ye ready." Nor will it accord with the demands of our Lord on our fidelity if we allow ourselves to drift into the notion that the world is getting worse and worse, that the gospel is meant to be a failure, that the great work of winning the globe for Christ will never be done by any missionary effort, but will be brought about by the reappearing of our Lord. We have no scriptural warrant for any such conclusion, and we regard it as a most lamentably

[1] A valuable collation and arrangement of passages on the second coming of our Lord will be found in 'The Parousia,' by Rev. J. S. Russell, D.D., 2nd edit. (Fisher Unwin).

successful temptation of the devil to lure the Church of God away from throwing all her energy to the task of preaching the gospel to every creature. We may not think of the coming of Christ as if it were to effect the new creation of God's grace, or to build the temple of the Lord. That is being done now. Christ will come because the harvest of earth is ripe, and *when* it is ripe. His work will be that of judgment. He will come, not to assume his sovereignty, but to reveal it to an unbelieving world and to an exultant and victorious Church. There are nine views which we may take of the reappearing of our Lord.

I. THE SECOND COMING IS THE NEXT GREAT EVENT IN THE DEVELOPMENT OF THE DIVINE DISPENSATIONS. There are three points on which Old and New Testament prophecy bids us fix our gaze, all gathering round the word "coming:" the Redeemer is "the Coming One"—"coming in weakness to suffer;" "coming in the energy of his Spirit to create and build up and consummate the Church;" "coming in sublime manifestation to judge the world." All is, however, in the scriptural view, an unbroken unity—the working out of a Divine plan, not an evolution of blind force. Our Lord, in the discourse to his disciples recorded in the twenty-fourth chapter of Matthew, speaks of two events then in view—one, the destruction of Jerusalem; another, the end of the world. Of the former he says, "This generation shall not pass till all *these* things be fulfilled." Of the latter, "Of *that* day and hour knoweth no man," etc. And the latter is "the end of the age." When Peter spake on the Day of Pentecost, he declared that the outpouring of the Holy Ghost began on that day, as spoken of by Joel, ushering in, as it were, a period which was bounded in the far distance by "the day of the Lord." And so throughout the Epistles, "the day of Christ," "that day," "the day of the Lord," is uniformly the far point beyond which none can peer, and for which all things are waiting (cf. Acts i. 11; Phil. i. 10; 2 Tim. i. 12)—"looking for," "hasting unto," "waiting for the manifestation of the sons of God."

II. IT IS AN EVENT WHICH IS EVEN NOW ON THE WAY. He is coming (ἔρχεται). He is, as it were, moving towards us every moment. Not as if nothing were being done now, nor as if there were even a pause for a while. Not as if it were indifferent to us until certain signs meet our eye which tell that the end is close upon us. Not so—not so is the meaning of the text. *He is coming.* He is actually on the way. The train of events which will bring him to us has long ago begun to move; and only, only as we recognize this do we understand the meaning of the dispensation under which we live. Of old, whether men knew it or not, every event was made subservient to the first appearing; and now every event is being so guided and controlled as to prepare the way for the second. Not a moment is being lost.

III. THOUGH CERTAIN AS TO FACT, IT IS UNKNOWN AS TO TIME—AND UNKNOWABLE. "Of that day and hour knoweth no man;" "It is not for you to know the times and the seasons, which the Father hath put in his own power." Ever since the beginning of the Christian age there have been ever and anon men who have professed, by calculations of prophetic time, to assign dates for this or that; but again and again have their systems failed. When even such a one as Dr. Cumming[1] was obliged to own that if he could tell when the twelve hundred and sixty years began, he could tell when they would end, but that he must confess that the former was a mere conjecture, who does not see the futility of thus wasting time in the attempt to reveal what our Lord meant to conceal? There are manifestly high and holy ends to be served in this concealment. Did we know the precise moment when all things are to come to a stand, such knowledge would bring them to confusion. Besides, the texts in Mark xiii. 35 and Matt. xxiv. 36—44 are decisive on this point.

IV. THERE WILL BE SIGNS WHICH WILL PRECEDE THE COMING OF THE LORD. From those convulsions of nations, etc., of which many make so much, we gather no light, since they are to mark the entire duration of this dispensation, and hence neither of them can be taken as a sign of its immediate close. Nor will there be any change in the daily movements of men, any more than there was in the days of Noah, "until the flood came, and took them all away." True, "the heavens and the earth which are now, are reserved unto fire," etc.; but that fire will be one of the accompaniments of the second coming, not a sign to precede it. *The sign which will indicate* the approaching end will be the ripening alike of tares and wheat—bad and good. The bad will get

[1] In 'The Great Tribulation.'

worse, and the good will get better. Both will ripen. Then the end. The angel will thrust in the sickle because the harvest is ripe.

V. WHEN THE LORD COMES, HE WILL APPEAR IN HIS GLORY. (Matt. xxv. 31; 1 John iii. 1—3; Col. iii. 4, "As he is;" cf. also Heb. ix. 28, "Without sin.") Not as a "weary man and full of woes," but in majesty and might, "with great power and glory."

VI. THE SECOND COMING WILL CLOSE THE PROBATION OF THE RACE.[1] This present time is "the day of salvation" (Isa. xlix. 8; 2 Cor. vi. 2), during which "whosoever shall call on the Name of the Lord shall be saved" (Acts ii. 21). Ere it closes, we cannot doubt that, in some state of being or other, *every soul* will have been brought into direct contact with the Saviour for acceptance or rejection, so that when the Saviour comes men will give account to One who has all things in readiness for judging the living and the dead (1 Pet. iv. 5, 6). And as has been the soul's attitude towards Christ, according thereto will be the sentence from him. How can it be otherwise (cf. Matt. vii.)?

VII. THE SECOND COMING WILL BE FOR JUDGMENT. This word "judgment" means very much: and the judgment-period may be as long as "the day of salvation;" and we have long thought that in these two positions is the clue to the solution of the difficulties of the millenarian controversy. For the righteous it will mean manifestation, vindication, glorification. For the wicked it will mean manifestation, condemnation, shame. Both are included in Paul's description in 2 Thess. i. 7—10. Hence the earth will "wail because of him."

VIII. THE SECOND COMING IS CONSEQUENTLY THE "BLESSED HOPE" OF THE CHURCH, AND THE DREAD OF THE GUILTY. (Titus ii. 13.) This is emphatically "the hope" which is so repeatedly referred to in the New Testament; it is the distinctive feature of the Christian's faith (1 Thess. iv. 14—18). But guilt dreads it.

IX. THE SECOND COMING OF OUR LORD FOR AWARD OR PUNISHMENT casts a hue all its own on the *meaning* and *outlook* of our daily life (Matt. xxv. 1—30; 1 John ii. 28; 2 Pet. iii. 14; 2 Cor. v. 10; Rom. xiv. 9—12; Matt. vii. 21—27; 1 Cor. iii. 13—15). This—this is the intensely practical end which the disclosures of our Lord's reappearing are intended to serve. Not that we may dispute with one another who has the most exact calculation as to the day, the hour, the how; but that our only rivalry may be, who shall be most faithful in doing the work of the day in the day, and thereby best prove himself to be ready, ever ready, let the Lord come whenever he may! Of little worth will it be to any to know the moment, unless at the moment they are ready to go in unto the King. Only as we are ready can we say from the heart, " Even so, come, Lord Jesus!"

Ver. 8.—*The august Speaker declaring his Name from the throne.* One theme alone remains before we enter on the visions of this book. Ere we are told what is said, we have once more to be assured—Who says it? An all-important question, on the answer to which the value of what follows entirely depends, inasmuch as the Speaker declares himself, as if it were from him that the revelation proceeds, and as if it were from his lips that the words went forth. This being the case, since, according to the first verse, the Lord Jesus Christ is he who receives the revelation, and who, as the Mediator between God and man, is the channel through which it reaches us, we seem shut up to the conclusion that the words in the eighth verse are those of the Almighty Father himself (see Alford, *in loc.*). As such we now propose to study them. They set him before us in four aspects.

1. IN HIS SUBLIME SELF-EXISTENCE. "I am the Alpha and the Omega, saith the Lord God." The A and the Ω. These letters, being the first and last of the Greek alphabet, enclose, as it were, all the rest. These words should be compared with Isa. xli. 4; xliii. 10; xliv. 6. Note also the ἐγώ εἰμι, the pronoun declaring the personality of the Speaker; and the verb being that which indicates being, not becoming. The precision of the Apostle John in the distinctive use of these two verbs is remarkable (see John i. 1—14). There is no "coming to be" in the Divine nature. He only "is." The I AM THAT I AM. Note: In these words is the standing and sufficient

[1] Cf. ch. vi. in the present writer's work on 'Theories of Future Punishment' (Snow and Co.).

answer to the charge of anthropomorphism in Bible representations of God. But it will not be adequately profitable for us merely to admire the sublimity of the words; we must also set forth their vastness of meaning. What, then, do they import? The Most High is the A and the Ω, enclosing all. Then: 1. *All space is enclosed in his infinite presence.* (Ps. cxxxix.) 2. *All time is included in his endless age.* With him is no passing away. He but *is.* Events, as they move on, pass beneath his eye.

> " All thou dost make lies like a lake
> Beneath thine infinite eye.
> Years on years, and all appears
> Save God, to die."

3. *All events are encompassed by his changeless, boundless Being.* The (1) origin, the (2) progress, the (3) issue of each one, are perfectly known to him. 4. *All created beings are supported in the holdings of his power.* The "hollow of his hand" contains them. 5. *All history, from the beginning of creation to the consummation of all things, is encircled by his Spirit.* Scripture speaks of a beginning (Gen. i. 1). It also speaks of an end (1 Cor. xv. 24). With God is neither beginning nor end. The beginning and the ending which are enclosed within the limits of Divine revelation do but occupy, as it were, one instant of Jehovah's being! At a glance he surveys the whole.

II. IN HIS SUBLIME SELF-MANIFESTATION. "Which is to come." Here, it must be noted, is a verb, not of becoming, but of movement (cf. margin, ὁ ἐρχόμενος). Who is the Coming One? The Lord Jesus is, in both the Old and New Testaments, "he that cometh," and in the entire scope of Revelation his coming is regarded as a unity—a five-fold one: by the angel of his presence, to the patriarchs; by his Spirit, to the prophets; by his incarnation, to suffer; by Pentecostal gifts, to inaugurate his kingdom; and by his indwelling with the Church, to complete it; and hereafter by his reappearing, to consummate it. Yet in the text the Almighty Father speaks of himself as "the Coming One." It is even so. The Father is perpetually carrying on the process of a self-revelation to the world; and it is by the Lord Jesus Christ and his work that the Father is revealed. There is a ceaseless outgoing of the infinite energy. "My Father worketh hitherto, and I work." In this the Father is: 1. Always moving and energizing. 2. Always advancing. 3. Always controlling events so as to ensure determined issues. 4. Always revealing himself more and more. 5. Always bringing things out to light; judging, administering, all in equity. This—this is the sublime outlook for this and every age. Each as it rolls on will open up some new phase of the mysteries of Providence, and in so doing will disclose some new letter in the unfinished and unfinishable Name!

III. AS HE WHO IS NOW SPEAKING TO MAN. "Saith the Lord God (λέγει)." This is one of those utterances which compel us to form some theory of the origin and authority of this Book of Revelation. An utterance of some well-known and self-evident truth, which is known to be true, whoever may say it, will allow of almost any theory of authorship without *vitally* affecting the value of the words themselves. But it is not so here. The words of this verse are distinctly declared to be Divine. *And as such they must be regarded, until adequate reason to the contrary is shown.* The claim they make cannot be too reverently treated, if it be valid; nor too sternly rejected, if it be otherwise. We are not left in uncertainty. The high and holy elevation of the words is utterly inconsistent with invalidity of claim. Their grandeur is like that of the words of the Lord Jesus, which create the faith they require, and sustain the faith they create. The words are of God. Then they are *authoritative.* The question of authority in religion is much disputed nowadays. But there are three kinds of authority which will be admitted—*must* be—as long as the world stands. 1. The authority of intrinsic and self-evident truth. 2. The authority of superior knowledge. 3. The authority of rightful supremacy. It is the third kind which exists here.[1] The *Lord God* speaks: then the words must be authoritative, beyond dispute.

IV. AS HE WHO, BY ANNOUNCING HIMSELF AS THE SPEAKER, CALLS FOR OUR ATTENTION. This attention and reverent regard should be shown in: 1. Listening. 2.

[1] See a pamphlet on ' Is the Authority of the Church Divine?' by the present writer (Hodder and Stoughton).

Studying. 3. Obeying precept. 4. Trusting promise, finding in the attribute of almightiness a Divine and infinite pledge that not one thing will fail of all that the Lord hath spoken. With a sense of holy awe, let us now await the visions which are to be opened up to us, and hearken to the words which the heavenly Speaker will address to the Churches.

Vers. 9—19.—*The Saviour's revelation of himself.* We may divide our Saviour's teaching about himself into three parts, in chronological order. There are (1) the words which he uttered in the days of his flesh, before his Passion; (2) those which he spake during the forty days after his resurrection, and (3) those which came from heaven to the aged apostle when in exile at Patmos. As stage succeeded stage, the words became richer in glory. During the forty days after the Resurrection, the teachings concerning himself were in advance of those which preceded it (cf. Luke xxiv. 46, 47). And those on "the Lord's day" to the exile were greater than all the rest. What a Lord's day that was for the prisoner! Many would gladly share John's banishment if then heaven were brought so near. Let us reverently study the paragraph before us. In it we have a vision, a touch, a word.

I. A VISION. "I saw . . . one like unto the Son of man." *Where?* "In the midst of the seven candlesticks." In accordance with Old Testament symbolism, and the use of the figure here, the meaning is "that the Saviour was beheld in the midst of the Churches." His countenance was familiar, although it gleamed with a splendour which was concealed on earth, save when to the favoured three he was transfigured on the mount. His face did shine as the sun (ver. 16). He had about the breasts a golden girdle—the mark of royal state, and the emblem of dignified repose. His head and his hairs were white as white wool, signifying his prerogatives of majesty and glory. His eyes were as a flame of fire, piercing men through and through, burning up all hypocritical pretence. His feet like unto burnished brass, symbolizing firmness, might, and splendour. His voice was of unutterable majesty, as the sound of many waters. In his right hand seven stars, holding those who have the place of responsibility in his Church, in the place of security, honour, and renown. The overseers of the Churches are Christ's special care. Out of his mouth went a sharp sword. The sword of the living Word, which, with its diacritic power, is two-edged. It would not accord with the reverence due to our glorified Lord to attempt to transfer to canvas the symbols here employed. Rather is it for us to apprehend, spiritually, the meaning of each, and transfer that to our heart and conscience. And if this be done wisely and reverently, our eyes will see "the King in his beauty."

II. A TOUCH. Although there is no reason to suppose that the Lord appeared in the fulness of his glory to John, yet the vision was more than he could bear. "I fell at his feet as one dead." It is in mercy to us that so much of the glory of the Saviour is concealed from us. We could no more bear to see it in its fulness than our eyes could bear to gaze on the splendours of the noonday sun. Hence it is a necessity for us that as yet we should see only as through a glass, darkly. But in the case of the apostle, the fact of his being so overpowered by the disclosure was the occasion for a fresh display of Divine tenderness in a touch of love. "He laid his right hand upon me," etc. There was in this touch an assurance of Divine regard, in spite of the apostle's sense of his own unworthiness. There was an expression of love. There was an impartation of power, which revived and recruited the drooping and exhausted frame. If Jesus is apart from us, we are soon overpowered. But if he comes with a vivifying touch, making us feel how truly we belong to him, and how closely we are bound up with the dearest interests of his heart,—this revives us. We live again. We can look up anew, and wait joyfully for the sound of his voice.

III. A WORD. This is twofold. 1. *Of commission.* (Vers. 11, 19.) For remarks on the seven Churches, see homilies on ch. ii. and iii. 2. *Of revelation.* This is a marvellously comprehensive revealing of the glory of our Lord. It includes five disclosures. (1) What he was from eternity. "I am the First." Here the Lord Jesus identifies himself with the living God who spake by the prophets. There cannot be two firsts! He who is the First is Jehovah, Lord of hosts. Jesus is the First. Therefore Jesus is the one living and true God. Ere suns or stars were made, ere the angel-bands were created, ever, ever had the Son of God existed in the eternal recesses of the infinite age! We are here taught: (2) What he became in time. "I was dead;" Greek, "I became dead." Into this new experience he entered by means of his incarnation in human form. As man, he died. The infinitely strange experience of dying became his, by reason of the humiliation to which he stooped and of the sorrows beneath which he groaned. (3) What he was when John saw him. "The Living One." He was no more in the hold of death. He had come out victoriously on the other side, and had left death behind him for ever and for ever. The life of the Lord Jesus cannot be derived, or he would not be "the First." He lives and gives life. "He is the same yesterday, and to-day, and for ever." "I am alive for evermore." (4) What office he holds. "I have the keys of Hades and of death."[1] The word "Hades" means the realm of departed spirits. "Death" is the passage thereto. Over both Christ has supreme control. He has the "keys." "The spacious world unseen is his." All the departed dead are under the sway of the Lord Jesus. His mediatorial kingdom is far more *there* than *here*. At his own time Hades and death will both cease to be. And, note: (5) The Saviour discloses what he will be at "the end." "I am the Last." "He shall give up the kingdom to God, even the Father," and thus close his mediatorial work; yet then, then, he still will be the everlasting Son of the Father! 3. *Of cheer.* "Fear not." Christ demands reverence; but he would not have us dread him. He would not terrify us. But that sublime and transcendent greatness which would crush us if wielded by power alone, becomes, in the sway of his tender love, a refuge and pavilion in which we can hide! What can we not entrust to such a Redeemer? We can run no risk when we are in his keeping. We know whom we have believed, and we are persuaded that he is able to keep that which we have committed to him against that day.

Ver. 18.—*The extent of the Saviour's mediatorial dominion.*[2] As we pursue our studies of the Divine messages to the seven Churches, we shall find that our Lord addresses himself in some one distinctive aspect of his character and work to each Church, in accordance with the main burden of the letter which is to follow. But ere the letters to the separate Churches begin, our Lord makes an announcement respecting his mediatorial glory, which is of equal application to all the Churches, wherever they may be, and whatever may be their spiritual condition. It is this, "*I have the keys of Hades and of death.*" We will inquire—

I. WHAT IS THE PREROGATIVE WHICH OUR LORD HERE DECLARES TO BE HIS? It is evident that there is some office of authority indicated by the word "keys." Keys are the symbol of authority, the token of office (cf. ch. iii. 7). The authority of our Saviour is here said to be over "Hades;" not over "hell," the region of the bad; but over Hades, the realm of the departed, good *or* bad. Both. The word "Hades" carries with it no moral significance at all, except as the connection in which it is used gives it a moral aspect (Luke xvi. 23). The authority of our Saviour is over "death" also. This is, as it were, the gate opening to the invisible realm. The meaning of the words is that our Saviour has entire control over human destiny. Death is the last step, the one out of this life. Hades is the realm in which the departed are. All mankind, at death, pass into "the spacious world unseen." They go over "to the majority." To this realm death is the entrance-gate. Over the realm itself, and the entrance to it, Christ has the supreme control—the "keys" hang at his girdle. Let us indicate a few of the details of this doctrine. 1. *The time of the departure* of every individual from this world is under Christ's control. Christ gives us our moments, and withdraws them. And when our time has come, ready or not ready, through the strange avenue **if** death we must go. 2. *The entrance of a spirit* into the invisible realm is under Christ's control. In this unknown[3] region there are two great moral divisions, even as here. There is no confusion of souls. The believer departs to be "with Christ" (Phil.

---

[1] See a great sermon by John Howe, 'On the Redeemer's Dominion over the Invisible World;' and Rev. George Steward's 'Mediatorial Sovereignty.'

[2] See a sermon by the present writer on Matt. xvi. 18, in 'To the Light through the Cross' (Dickinson).

[3] So the etymology of the word "Hades" indicates. See an able article thereon by Dr Craven, in Lange's 'Commentary.'

i. 23); the unbelieving and ungodly, to "torments."[1] Their spirit carries with it its own sin and unrest. All are under Christ's sway. He is Lord of the dead and of the living. The state of any spirit in the invisible world will be according to its attitude with reference to the Lord Jesus Christ. 3. *Every believer will be, in Hades, as much in the guardianship of Christ as when on earth.* "Christ died for us, that whether we wake or sleep, we should live together with him." 4. *During the entire period until the completion of the mediatorial kingdom, the Redeemer will have sole authority in Hades.* To this end he died, and rose, and re-lived. 5. *At the time appointed by the Lord Jesus, the gates of both death and Hades shall be reopened.* Bodies shall rise, spirits shall put on the new and mysterious vesture. All must stand before the tribunal of Christ, to receive *through the body* the things done (2 Cor. v. 10). All this the Lord Jesus will direct and control. Death and Hades will no longer exist (ch. xx. 14). The great separation-day shall have come; and as men hear the "Come!" or "Depart!" will heaven or hell be theirs! But at every stage in the advance of souls Christ is Lord of all!

II. THE LORD JESUS CHRIST FITTINGLY HOLDS AN OFFICE SO SUBLIME.[2] 1. *The right to do so is his.* (1) As the eternal Son of God, all creation is his dominion. And by virtue of his supreme and eternal sovereignty over all, he must be the Head of the human race, as well as of every other order of created beings. But if he be the Head of our race, by eternal, native right, he must sustain such relationship to it in every stage of its existence. Be it so that this mysterious invisible realm of departed spirits would not have existed except as the result of the Fall; be it so that it is a part of the mischief which has smitten our race; yet, that such a state does exist is the clear teaching of Scripture, and that Christ is Lord of it is in accord with what we know of his position in the universe; for in all things he has become the Pre-eminent One. (2) He has also an acquired right as the Son of man, owing to his death-struggle on behalf of humanity, in which he spoiled principalities and powers. Who else should sway man in the unseen realms, but he who died for men? How long will it be ere believers apprehend the vastness of the mediatorial dominion of the Lord Jesus? He is Lord both of the dead and of the living! (3) It is an appointment of God the Father, that in all stages of man's being the Lord Jesus should have dominion over him. Who can read John vi. 37—40 without seeing that there is a great entrustment made over to our Lord as Mediator? This entrustment, according to John xvii. 2, is twofold. (*a*) He has power over all flesh. (*b*) He gives eternal life to those who are made over to him. We know not, indeed, Christ's method of governing souls between death and the resurrection. What we know not now we shall know hereafter. It is enough for us that Christ rules all, and will do, till the end. 2. *Those attributes are his that fit him for such sway.* (1) Omniscience. He knows (*a*) the Father's plans, (*b*) what is in man, (*c*) the appointed time for the consummation, (*d*) how to bring it about with unfailing certainty. (2) Omnipotence is his. He is able to keep us from falling, and to present us faultless before the presence of his glory with exceeding joy. He is all-sufficient. (3) Faithfulness. The great trust which he so perfectly comprehends, and is so able to fulfil, will find his faithfulness equal to his knowledge and power. His own self-sacrifice for the Church is guarantee of this. (4) He is the Living One. He is "the same yesterday, and to-day, and for ever." He has an unchangeable priesthood, and is able to save to the uttermost because he ever liveth.

III. THE DOCTRINE OF THE TEXT IS OF INFINITE VALUE TO US. 1. *Let us in faith and love adore him who makes the majestic claim of ruling life and death.* 2. *We have here a clue to the wondrous mystery of human existence.* In a lecture reported to have been delivered in the Senate House, Cambridge, on Wednesday, May 26, 1880, by Dr. Humphry, Professor of Anatomy, on the topic, 'Man, Pre-historic, Present, and Future,' the lecturer closed with the following words: "After all, to the burning

---

[1] Luke xvi. 23. See Grimm's 'New Testament Lexicon,' under the words ᾅδης and κλείς (Dr. Thayer's edit., 1888).

[2] John Howe has an incomparable sermon on this theme, entitled, 'The Redeemer's Dominion over the Invisible World.' Dr. Warren remarks, "At his resurrection, Jesus had come from that world, and had carried away its keys; in other words, had abolished it." But the *abolition* of Hades does not take place till we reach the scenes described in ch. xx. 11—14.

questions, whence? and where? whence comest thou, O man, and whither dost thou go? to which it might have been expected, by those who do not fully know their difficulties, that I should make, as regards the body at least, some answer, I am compelled to reply that we find ourselves simply floating on the streams of time. Sufficient for the day must be the knowledge thereof. Whether we peer fore or aft, it is obscurity. We are still—

> " ' Children crying in the night,
> Children crying for the light,
> And with no language but a cry.' "

But where science is compelled to leave off, the Saviour begins. And our faith, weaned from those who confess they know nothing, is transferred to him who is the Light of the world. 3. In regard to *questions which still remain unanswered*, we have perfect rest in Jesus. 4. *We have abounding comfort concerning the death of believers, and entire peace as concerns our own.* The writer was preaching from this text in the north of London, thirty years ago. A Christian lady was present who had been all her lifetime subject to bondage, through fear of death. The theme led the preacher to dilate on the guardianship of Christ over departed souls. The fearful one heard, was soothed, and on going home said, "Oh! my dread of death is gone. I have no fear now. Whenever my Father calls me, I am ready!" That night she was seized with a fit, and passed away. "Absent from the body, at home with the Lord." Finally, it is in this direction that the great difficulties which confront us as to the ultimate destiny of the great human family receive the only approximate solution. The great Redeemer's sway is over the whole race. But only a minute fraction of the race is on earth at any one moment! Where, where are the countless millions on millions who have gone hence? We can only answer—*They are all under Christ's sway.* He is guarding all his own with infinite love, and governing all others with absolute equity, getting all things in readiness to judge the living and the dead. This is all we know. It is enough. For fuller disclosures we can wait. As yet we could not bear to know more. Christ is Lord of all.

> "Hail to the Prince of life and death,
> Who holds the keys of death and hell!
> The spacious world unseen is his,
> And sovereign power becomes him well."

Ver. 20.—*The seven Churches.* It does not fall to our province to inquire into the reason why seven Churches only are here specified; nor do we enter into the symbolism of the number seven, nor burden ourselves with the inquiry whether these seven Churches are supposed to represent the whole of Christendom. These and other *vexatæ questiones* we leave for the student to ponder in his study. Hints for earnest pulpit teaching are alone our care. Historically, the seven Churches here specified did exist at the time of the Apostle John; they were not very far from each other, nor any of them at any great distance from the extreme western sea-board of Asia Minor. When studying the several letters to each Church, we shall endeavour to take note of what was peculiar to each. Here we note only some features that were common to them all.

1. THE SEVEN CHURCHES ARE SO MANY CENTRES OF LIGHT. "Seven golden candlesticks." Each Church is a light-bearer. The change from the Hebrew symbol of a seven-branched candlestick to the Christian one of seven candlesticks is noteworthy. In the Mosaic dispensation the Jewish Church was but one, with a priesthood at its head. Now there is not merely a Church; there are Churches. As the late Dean Alford remarks, "Their mutual independence is complete. Their only union is in him who stands in the midst of them." [1] Each of them, moreover, is a candlestick, or lamp-stand. Churches exist as light-bearers. Apart from this they have no *raison d'être.* They receive their light from Christ: the light of truth, that they may teach,

[1] *Contemporary Review*, vol. xv. p. 7. See also Archbishop Trench's 'Commentary on the Epistles to the Seven Churches;' Dr. Tristram's 'Seven Golden Candlesticks;' and Canon Tait's 'Messages to the Seven Churches.'

guard, and extend it; the light of purity, that they may keep themselves unspotted from the world; the light of love, that they may gladden others therewith. Churches are the only institution in the world that exist solely for this purpose. Hence they are composed of those who are the highest part of God's creation on earth—of those who are " born again," who are " being saved." Note further that they are likened to *golden* candlesticks. We see by this figure how high a value God sets on the several Churches, which are to be the light-bearers in their several localities.

II. THE SEVEN CHURCHES FIND THEIR CENTRE OF UNITY IN HIM WHO IS IN THE MIDST OF THEM. " In the midst of the seven candlesticks, one like unto the Son of man." In him they find their oneness. To him alone are they distinctly and severally responsible. It is quite possible to boast of a counterfeit independence. The independence of isolation, the independence of self-will, and so on, have no warrant in the Word of God. There is no Church independence sanctioned by Scripture which means anything less, or anything else, than absolute loyalty to the Son of God, and responsibility to him alone. At the girdle of our great High Priest alone hang the seals of authority and power. On earth he has entrusted the keys of the kingdom to the entire body of believers as a Christian priesthood; and woe be to any Church which allows any earthly ruler to wrest them from its hands! The events of the day are forcing this principle to the front after it has been obscured for ages.

III. EACH CHURCH HAS ITS OWN EXCELLENCE, DEFECT, DANGER, AND DUTY. So we find it with Ephesus, Pergamos, Thyatira, Sardis, and Laodicea. Two only are unrebuked—Smyrna and Philadelphia. Thus the state of things in the entire Church of Christ may be compared to that in a vessel built in water-tight compartments, where, though there may be a leakage in one part, the others may be sound. We see this in several Churches even now. One may be loyal to its Lord, and another not so. One may be losing its first love, and another may be all on fire. One may have a great reputation, and yet be dead. Another may be in poverty, and yet be rich in faith. One Church may be fast asleep, another may be abounding in every good work.

IV. THE SAVIOUR, IN THE MIDST OF THE CHURCHES, MANIFESTS HIMSELF TO EACH CHURCH ACCORDING TO ITS OWN SPIRITUAL STATE. To Ephesus, as " he that walketh in the midst "—to survey, to mark, to correct. To Smyrna, as " the Living One "—to give the crown of life. To Pergamos, as " he that hath the sharp sword "—to sever and to smite. To Thyatira, as " he whose eyes are like a flame of fire "—to see through and through, and to burn up evil. To Sardis, as " he that hath the seven Spirits of God "—to quicken the Church from death. To Philadelphia, as " he that hath the key of David "—to open to the faithful the temple of God. To Laodicea, as " the Faithful and True Witness "—to undeceive them in their sluggish conceit. Thus our Lord will be to his Churches according to what they are. And if there be a nominal Church which is not doing its Lord's work, it will certainly not have its existence prolonged for the sake of its own.

V. WHATEVER MAY BE A CHURCH'S DIFFICULTIES, OUR LORD EXPECTS IT TO OVERCOME. Not one of the letters to the seven Churches gives us the slightest reason to suppose that the adverse force might be so strong that any Church whatever would be justified in succumbing to it. There is abundance of power, of love, and of faithfulness in Christ to sustain any Church under any trial whatsoever.

VI. ACCORDING TO A CHURCH'S FIDELITY OR OTHERWISE, SO WILL BE ITS DESTINY. If unfaithful, the Church will be judged, chastised, and possibly swept away. If faithful, her Lord will set before her an open door, and no one can shut it. Note: 1. Churches have nothing to fear except from their own sluggishness and inaptness to meet the demands of their age. No artificial help can, in the long-run, perpetuate a dead Church; no artificial aid is needed for a living and faithful one. 2. There must not only be an overcoming on the part of a Church if it is to be continued, but also a personal overcoming on the part of each individual, if he is ultimately to share his Lord's victory. Let us not forget that just as a Church may be dead though a few in it are alive, so individual souls may be dead even where, as a whole, the Church is alive. The Lord is coming. Every one of us shall give account of himself. Every man shall bear his own burden.

HOMILIES BY VARIOUS AUTHORS.

Ver. 1.—*Revelation.* "The Revelation of Jesus Christ, which God gave unto him." The very word belongs to the Holy Scriptures, and is peculiar to them. None of the Greek writers use it in the sacred sense which we always associate with it. And this is not to be wondered at, for they had naught to tell with any authority on those profound questions with which it is the province of revelation to deal, and upon which the mind of man yearns for light. But when that light first flashed upon men, no wonder that they spoke of its manifestation as an unveiling, as an apocalypse, as a revelation. And the record of that revelation is our Bible. The word has become so familiar to us that we are apt to forget that the unveiling implies a previous veiling, and that both the one and the other fact suggest questions, not merely of great interest, but of much and practical importance to every one of us. Therefore let us consider—

I. THE VEILING IN THE PAST. The writer of the Book of Proverbs affirms that " It is the glory of God to conceal a thing; " and undoubtedly God did see fit for long ages to hide from the knowledge of men not a little of that which he afterwards was pleased to reveal. So that those dark days of old St. Paul called " the times of ignorance," and adds the too much forgotten and most blessed fact that "God winked at " those times; *i.e.* he did not hold men accountable for them, and would not bring men into judgment because of them. 1. *This ignorance hung like a pall over vast regions of human thought.* (1) *God.* Some denied his existence altogether. Yet more, forced to believe that the universe and themselves could not have come into being by chance, multiplied gods many and lords many, and invested them, not with the noblest, but the basest characteristics of humanity, so that they worshipped devils rather than gods—monsters of might and malignity, of lust and lies. So was it with the mass of men. (2) *Man.* They knew not themselves more than the true God. They knew that they were miserable, but how or why, or how to remedy their condition, they knew not. Of sin as the virulent venom that poisoned all the veins and arteries of their life they were ignorant, and of holiness as the alone road to happiness they knew still less ; the very idea of holiness had not dawned upon them. (3) And of *immortality*, the life eternal, they *knew* nothing. Nothing could be more dim or vague, more uncertain or unsatisfying, than their views as to what awaited them when this life was done. They beheld the sun and stars set and rise, but they bitterly complained that for man there was the setting, but no rising again. Over all these topics and those related to them the veil of ignorance hung down, and no light penetrated through its thick folds. 2. *But why was all this?* is the question that irresistibly rises in our minds as we contemplate this most mournful fact. A complete answer no man can give ; we can only suggest some considerations supplied to us from the Word of God, and from our observation of God's methods of dealing with men. (1) *Man's own sin* was, doubtless, one chief force that drew down this veil. This is St. Paul's contention in the opening chapters of the Epistle to the Romans. And the universal experience, so terrible but so true, that let a man *will* to be ignorant of God's truth, ere long it will come to pass that he is so, whether he will or no. Furthermore (2) such times of limited knowledge serve as *tests of character.* The faith of the good is tried, and thereby exercised and developed. Such faith shines out radiant on the dark background of the ignorance and sin that stretch all around. Hence Abraham became the father of the faithful and the friend of God. But the evil of evil, working in surroundings congenial to it, mounts to such a height, and becomes so glaring and abominable, that the justice of God in judging it is seen and confessed by all. And yet again (3) such times cannot be done away *until the instruments and conditions requisite for the bringing in of better times have been prepared.* Hence the advent of Christ was so long delayed. A people cosmopolitan—the Jews ; a language universal—the Greek ; an arena large, compact, organized, with free intercommunication—the Roman empire ; a period when the strife and din of war were hushed, and the different nations of the world had become welded into one—the period of the Roman peace ;—not till these all and yet others were had the fulness of time arrived. Till then the veil must yet hang down, and darkness cover the land. (4) *The futility of all other means* of uplifting and raising mankind needed to be made manifest. Hence one after another, military force, state-craft, commerce, philosophy, art, religion, had successively or simultaneously striven to show what they could do in this great enterprise. Scope of space and time had to be given them, and not till each had been compelled to confess, "It is not in me," was the way clear for "the bringing in of the better hope." Man had to be "shut up" to God's way, or nothing could keep him from believing that he could find, or from attempting to find, some better way of his own. It has always been so; it is so still. We will not turn to God until we are made to see that it is the best and the only thing to be done. And man takes a long time to see that. Some light is surely shed on this protracted ignorance, this long-continued veiling, by such considerations as these, and we may well wait, therefore, for the larger light in which we shall rejoice hereafter.

II. THE UNVEILING—the revelation that has been given to us. Note: 1. *Its nature.* It has shown to us God. In Christ he is made known to us. Atonement, how to obtain acceptance with him; regeneration, how to be made like unto him; immor-tality, our destined dwelling with him;—all this has been unveiled for us on whom the true light has now shined. 2. *Its necessity.* The darkness of which we have told above on all these great questions so momentous to our present and eternal well-being. 3. *Its probability.* God having constituted us as he has, with religious capacities and yearnings, and being himself what he is, it was likely that he would interpose for our good, and not let the whole race of man die in darkness and despair. Granted that God is, and that he is what the nature he has given us leads us to believe he is, so far from there being any antecedent objection to the idea that he should have interposed to save us out of our sin and misery, the great probability is that he would do just that which we believe he has done, and give us such revelation of himself and his wi as we possess in his Word. He who has planted in us the instincts of mercy and com-passion, who has given us yearnings after a purer and nobler life, who prompts us to rescue and to save whenever we have opportunity,—is it likely that in him there would be nothing akin to all this? The probability is all the other way, so that a revelation from him, whereby our evil condition may be remedied and man may be saved, comes to us with this claim on our acceptance, that it is in keeping with his nature and what that nature leads us to expect. 4. And when we examine *the revelation itself,* it is commended to us by the fact that we find in it the full setting forth of those truths which men had been for long ages feeling after, but had never yet found. Take these three amongst the chief of them. (1) *The Incarnation.* Man has never been content that the gulf between him and God should remain unbridged and impassable, and hence, in all manner of ways, he has striven to link together his own nature and the Divine (cf. on this subject Archbishop Trench's Hulsean Lectures, 'The Unconscious Prophecies of Heathendom'). Reason cannot discover the doctrine of the Incarnation, but the history of man's efforts after a religion give ample proof that this is a felt necessity of the human spirit; "For where is the religion of human device, where mythology, that has not sought to bridge over the awful chasm between the finite and the Infinite, between man and God, by the supposition of a union of some sort between the human and Divine? Sometimes by supposing God to be a Spirit dwelling in men as in the material universe; some-times by filling heaven with deities possessed of bodies, and having passions little differing from our own; sometimes by supposing actual descents of the Deity in human form upon the earth; and sometimes by celebrating the rise of great heroes and eminent men by an apotheosis unto gods, the heathen have sought to alleviate the difficulty which men must ever feel in seeking to have intercourse and relations with the Infinite and Eternal. How can the weak and sinful come nigh to the All-Perfect? How can the finite enter into relations with the Infinite? He cries out for a living, a personal, an incarnate God;" and this his great need is met by the revelation of God in Christ, and because so met the revelation is thereby commended powerfully both to our hearts and minds. (2) *The atonement.* This, too, has been a felt necessity of the human spirit. To answer the question—How can man be just with God? what have not men done? what do they not do even now? Scoffers think to make an easy conquest over the gospel by calling its doctrine of atonement "the religion of the shambles;" and by that sneer to dismiss the whole question of the truth of revelation to the region of ridicule and contempt. But at once there confronts them the whole force of human conviction as to the necessity and craving for atonement, which has found and yet finds expression in ten thousand forms, some of them, without doubt, horrible enough. No religion has ever found acceptance amongst any people in any age that ventured to ignore, much more to scoff at, this ineradicable demand of the human heart. "Be the origin of sacrifice what it may, its universal prevalence amongst men, and its perpetuation amongst peoples the most widely separated from each other, and in spite of changes of manners and customs and usages, in other respects of the most radical kinds, incontestably show that it has a firm root in man's deepest convictions, and lies embedded in his religious consciousness, to be parted with only as he ceases" to care for religion at all. Our revelation, therefore, coming to us as it does with blessed light on this great theme, and showing us how God in Christ has provided the perfect Sacrifice, of which all others were but vain attempts or dim types, commends itself thereby to every man's conscience in the sight of God. (3) And so, too, with the doctrine of *immortality.* "Let us eat and drink; for to-morrow we die," has been the practical outcome for the mass of mankind of the darkness in which they dwelt in regard to this great truth. "Without God, and without hope:" what blessedness above that of the mere sensual life was possible to them? What can keep men, taken as a whole, from living like the brutes if you tell them that they are to perish like the brutes? Down to that dread level they have gravitated more and more, and must. But a revelation which "brings life and immortality to light" cannot but be welcome to the hearts of men, uplifting, strengthening, regenerating them, so that if any man embrace it he shall, he must, become "a new creature." Thus does the revelation given us of God draw us to itself and to him; and our duty and delight should be to receive, believe, and commend it to all men everywhere, that they, too, may become partakers of the like precious faith. If in virtue of this revelation we can any of us say, and do say of the Lord, "He is my Refuge and my Fortress; my God, in whom I will trust," our next duty surely is to turn to our brother, who as yet knows not what we know, and say to him, "Surely he will deliver *thee.*"—S. C.

Ver. 3.—*The benediction on ministers and people who observe the sayings of this book.* "Blessed is he that readeth," etc. By the readers are meant those who, in the congregation, should read this book; and by the hearers, the congregations themselves; but neither readers nor hearers, ministers nor people, win this benediction unless, in addition to the reading and the hearing, they *keep* its sayings. But, notwithstanding the solemn commendation of this book, it is known to all students of God's Word that for a while it was not regarded as a constituent portion of the sacred Scriptures. Doubts were entertained concerning it by many writers of the fourth century, and some of them of much eminence in the Greek Church especially; but it has outlived all their objections and others of more modern days, and it was never more accepted as a genuine part of Holy Scripture than it is at this day. As one says, "We have seen its rise, as of a pure fountain, from the sacred rock of the apostolical Church. We have traced it through the first century of its passage, flowing from one fair field to another, identified through them all, and everywhere the same. As it proceeded lower, we have seen attempts to obscure its sacred origin, to arrest or divert its course, to lose it in the sands of antiquity, or bury it in the rubbish of the dark ages. We have seen these attempts repeated in our own times. But it has at length arrived to us such as it flowed forth from the beginning." The book is, therefore, all the more worthy of our reverent regard because of the ordeal through which it has had to pass, and its benediction on those who hear and obey it may be all the more confidently expected. Nor is that blessing barred by the unquestionable fact that very much in this book is difficult, obscure, and hard to be understood. No doubt it is so. But "even in the darkest parts there is already a glimmering light. Already we can see a clear testimony running through it to the holiness of God, to the power of Christ, to the providence which is working in or overruling all things, to the Divine purpose which all things and all men are willingly or unwillingly subserving, and to that final triumph of good over evil, of Christ over antichrist, of God over Satan, which will be the last and most decisive justification of the ways of God to men. All this lies on the surface of the book. And I know not that a more profitable occupation could be found for men of the world—men of business, men of activity, men of intelligence and influence—than the repeated perusal of a part of God's Word which says to them, even in its most obscure and mysterious disclosures, 'God is at work, God has a purpose, God will at length manifest his reign, in this world which you treat too much for the present as if it were all your own.' Take heed that you be not disregarding, that you be not 'even fighting against God,' and destined, therefore, to be overthrown when he triumphs. I know not that there is one chapter of the Bible which does not enforce upon us this great lesson " (Vaughan). But if it be asked, as it will and should be asked—wherein does the blessedness consist of which this text tells? we reply, in the beautiful words of the Litany, that they who read, hear, and keep the sayings of this book will find that these sayings do, by God's grace, " strengthen such as do stand, comfort and help the weak-hearted, raise up them that fall, and finally beat down Satan under our feet."

I. They "strengthen such as do stand." 1. Those to whom St. John wrote—for he it was, we feel persuaded, who wrote this book; he, the " son of thunder," who was so prompt to desire that fire might fall from heaven on the Samaritans who received not his Master, he would find in the denunciations of the dread judgments of which this book tells, a theme not altogether uncongenial; but those to whom he wrote—sorely *needed to be strengthened.* Whether the fiery trial which was to try them—" the great tribulation " as it is called in the seventh chapter—was the persecution under Nero or that under Domitian we cannot certainly say, but only that it was very terrible. The fear of it, falling on them with its frightful force, might well bear them off their feet and down into the depths of apostasy and denial of their Lord; and doubtless, but for the strength imparted through the sayings of the prophecy of this book, it would have done so. 2. *But these sayings gave them strength* still to stand, and to stand firm. (1) For these sayings showed them *Christ in the midst of his Church.* St. John saw him, not now as the despised and rejected of men, but in might and majesty; and saw him, too, walking amidst the seven lamps of gold, and holding in his hand the circlet of the seven stars, symbol of the angels of the Churches, as the lamps of gold were of the Churches themselves. So then they were not left forlorn and helpless; not left like a tempest-tossed ship bereft of her skilful helmsman, and for whom, therefore, no other fate than to be driven on the rocks or otherwise completely shipwrecked was possible. No; it was not so with them; for there in the midst of his suffering Church, walking amid the several congregations of the faithful, with eyes like a flame of fire, and feet like brass, there was their Lord; and what, then, need they fear the worst that their enemies could do? Yes; they were shown this by these sayings. And we of to-day are shown the like amid " all our troubles and adversities, whensoever they oppress us." " Lo, *I* am with you alway," was said, and this glorious vision of the Lord in the midst of the seven lamps of gold was given, not for believers of the primitive Church alone, but for us also on whom the ends of the world are come. Shall we not, must we not, therefore, be blamed if we read and hear, and keep not these sayings? (2) Further-more, they showed *the Lord actually using these very trials to accomplish his own gracious purposes* towards his Church. For by them he was *drawing the faithful closer to himself;* compelling them, by the very stress of the storm that was beating on them, to come, as he would have them do, yet more closely within the sure shelter of his love. And was he not also by these terrible trials fulfilling the word spoken by his fore-runner and herald, who said of him, " his fan is in his hand, and he will throughly purge his floor, and will gather the wheat into his garner, but the chaff he will burn with unquenchable fire"? Yes; he was in this terrible way *winnowing out the chaff,* sifting the wheat, ridding the Churches of those elements which were false and hurtful, and making it undefiled and pure. The army of the Lord would thus be delivered from those who would only bring defeat and disgrace upon it, and those only would be left in it who could be depended upon to fight manfully the good fight of faith. And this testing would be also *a revealing time,* as all such times are, to every individual amongst them. It would find out their weak places, and make every one of them, who was really Christ's servant, take to himself afresh the whole armour of God. And was he not *establishing a testimony* through their fidelity, by which future ages should be enabled more manfully to confess, and more steadfastly to endure, for his sake, as they, by like testimony of those who had gone before them, had themselves been enabled? The blood of the martyrs has ever been the seed of the Church, and even if they did " go forth weeping, bearing this precious seed," doubtless they should " come again with rejoicing, bringing their sheaves with them." " The noble army of martyrs praise thee." So we delight to sing; but how more mightily do they or could they praise him than by bearing testimony, as they have done and do, that the grace of Christ can sustain, and the love of Christ inspire, and the approval of Christ compensate, for all that here on earth man may inflict or our weak flesh endure? (3) And these sayings showed them also *the end of all that was then befalling them.* For the vision of St. John pierced the gloomy clouds of this lower world, and penetrated into the very presence-chamber of God. And there—what was it that was shown to them? What but the sure triumph of Christ, the utter downfall and doom of all his foes; and the glorious recompense of reward which awaited his faithful ones when they shall have come out of the great tribulation, and God shall have wiped away all tears from their eyes? If, then, these sayings were not only read and heard, but also kept, how could they do otherwise than impart strength of spirit, of heart, and mind?

II. And so also would they "COMFORT AND HELP THE WEAK-HEARTED." No doubt there were many such, as how could there but be, amongst those to whom St. John wrote? What fear and misgiving would throng many hearts in those dreadful days! What an agony of inward conflict would they have to go through ere ever they could take their stand firmly for their Lord! How would dear life, and ease, and the entreaties of beloved friends, and the many ties which bound them to life,—how would they all plead against the martyr-spirit and endeavour to overcome it, and to persuade the soul threatened with persecution for Christ's sake to some easy compliance, some plausible compromise, whereby the awful fate of those who refused obedience to the persecuting power might be escaped! What wavering of the will there must have been in instances not a few! what making and unmaking of resolution! How would timidity and weakness clamour and weep and break the heart of the terrified one! And whence was their help to come? Whence but *in the promised presence of their Lord,* that presence which the sayings of this book showed to them, realized in their hearts? Then, as troops dismayed and ready to retreat are rallied and recalled to resolute action by their leader coming to them and placing himself at their head, and encouraging them by word and look and deed, so would the weak-hearted to whom St. John wrote find comfort and help as they saw their Lord with them, at their head, beckoning and encouraging them on, and holding out to them the glorious promise of his reward. "To him that overcometh;" seven times over are these heart-stirring words addressed to the Churches; and at the hearing of them, as the soldier at the hearing of the trumpet-call, so would the faint and faltering follower of Christ recognize and respond to the summons to follow on, though his heart had been faint enough heretofore.

III. Blessed, too, would he be who rightly received the sayings of this book; for they would do not a little to LIFT UP THE FALLEN. 1. And *there were fallen ones amongst them.* Those who like the recreant Church at Laodicea, had gone utterly astray from Christ, and to whom no solitary word of praise could be addressed, but only loud call to repentance and solemn warning against their sin. 2. But these sayings of this book, how they would reveal their Lord whom they had so forsaken *coming to them both in anger and in love!* He could say to them, "I know thy works;" and to the hardened and impenitent his eyes flashed as a flame of fire, but to those who confessed and would forsake their sins these same sayings would show him as standing at the door and knocking for admittance, and promising that all should be forgotten and forgiven as in the fellowship of love they sat together at the same board, he with them and they with him. These sayings would be like the firm strengthening grasp of the Lord's hand to his sinking apostle, who but for that had perished amid the waves upon which he had ventured to walk. So would many a one who had stumbled and fallen find their feet again uplifted and upborne by the exceeding great and precious promises made to the repentant in these same sayings of this book.

IV. And so will the other great necessity of the Christian man—THAT HE SHOULD BEAT DOWN SATAN UNDER HIS FEET—be greatly aided if he hear and keep these sayings. For that vanquishment of Satan is no sudden act, no victory gained all in a moment, but is the result of long-continued Christian habit against which the assaults of our great adversary rage in vain. No rush of holy emotion, no mere giving up of ourselves to devout meditation, will ensure our victory. But it is the daily practice of Christian obedience in avoiding evil and following after that which is good, which makes it more and more hopeless for the tempter; he is compelled to give up the attack, and by his withdrawal from the contest confesses his defeat. So is he beaten down under our feet. The experience of every faithful Christian man confirms all this. He is not tempted as other men are, for it would be of no avail to try and seduce such as he. The habits of his life, the principles of his conduct, are far too settled in the opposite direction to that in which the tempter would lead him; he has so long resisted the devil that the promise has been fulfilled for him, "Resist the devil, and he will flee from you." But the great service which the sayings of this book, when they are heard and kept, render to such is that they foster and cherish those habits the result of which is the victory desired. The realization of Christ's presence, the dread of his displeasure, the longing for his approval, the love which he has enkindled,—how do all these, how must they, steady the wavering will, holding it back from what would displease Christ, and urging it on to that which he would approve? Fear, love, hope, —these mighty motives are ever at work, and all in the same direction of holy habit and obedience, until that which was painful and difficult at first has by long practice become easy, and that from which at first he shrank back he now goes forward to with cheerful alacrity and undaunted courage. It is the love of Christ, that love of which the sayings of this book so frequently tell, that love which carries along with it both hope and fear, it is this which constrains him, and by means of it he comes off more than conqueror in this holy war.

CONCLUSION. And for them and for us in all like circumstances of trial the force of these sayings of this book is greatly increased by the recollection that "the time is at hand." If a man deem that he may procrastinate and delay, if repentance and obedience be resolved on only for some future time, he will miss the benediction promised here. But if, on the other hand, he live day by day in view of his Lord's coming—and the coming of the Lord is for us practically the day of our death—if he feel that the time when all that the Lord has said shall be fulfilled is indeed at hand, then will all that this holy book has urged on him be listened to with yet greater attention, and the obedience rendered will be yet more prompt and eager. When he realizes, as God grant we all may, that the opportunity for winning the blessing promised is but short-lived, and that lost now it is lost for ever, how will, how must this spur us on, and make us diligent indeed to make our calling and election sure? We shall "give the more earnest heed to the things that we have heard, lest at any time we should let them slip," or "drift away from them," as the truer rendering is. The shortness of time, the nearness of Christ's judgment, will lend fresh force to the assurance, "Blessed is he that readeth," etc.—S. C.

Vers. 5, 6.—*Doxology; or, the upspringing of praise.* "Unto him that loved us," etc. It has been remarked that the writer of the Revelation had hardly set himself down to his work ere he felt that he must lift up his heart in joyful doxology. The very mention of the name of the Lord Jesus, by whose Spirit he was writing, starts him off in this heart-song of praise. He could not go on until he had given utterance to the irrepressible love for his Lord with which his soul was filled to overflowing. And this is his way. How many are the outbreaks of praise which we find in this book! It is a land full of fountains and springs and wells, out of which flow this river which makes glad the city of God. And St. John does not stand alone in this respect. All those holy men of old who were so privileged as to come into blessed contact with the Lord caught the contagion of praise. St. Paul is continually breaking forth into doxologies. "Now unto him that is able to do exceeding," etc. (Eph. iii. 20; and cf. Rom. xvi. 25; xi. 36; 1 Tim. i. 17; Heb. xiii. 20). And so St. Peter (1 Epist. iv. 11; v. 11). And so St. Jude (ver. 24), etc. Thus is it with all the sacred writers. Truly might it have been said concerning them all, "They *will* be still praising thee." And blessed are they whose hearts are thus attuned, ever ready to give forth praise, sweet, clear, strong, full, whenever the spirit of Christ's love touches them. Like as in those great concerts where royalty is expected to be present, the whole vast orchestra stand ready the moment the royal personages enter to begin the National Anthem; so should "praise wait" for God in all our hearts. And it has been pointed out how these doxologies grow in volume and emphasis as this book goes on. Here in these verses we read, "To him be glory and dominion for ever and ever." But in the fourth chapter (ver. 9) we read of there being rendered "glory and honour and thanks to him that sat on the throne;" and in ver. 11 we read the same, "Thou art worthy, O Lord, to receive glory and honour and power." The doxology has grown from two to three notes of praise in each of these verses. But in ch. v. 13 we read, "And every creature . . . heard I saying, Blessing, and honour, and glory, and power, be unto him," etc. Here we have four of these notes. But by the time we get to ch. vii. 12 we have reached the number of perfection, and may not ask for more : "Blessing, and glory, and wisdom, and thanksgiving, and honour, and power, and might, be unto our God for ever and ever. Amen." If you begin praising God, you are bound to go on ; like a river which at its outset is but a tiny rill, yet increases more and more as it flows along. *But what waked up this heart-song of praise which we have here?* There had been various and most blessed thoughts of Christ in St. John's mind. In this very verse he tells how Christ is "the Faithful Witness," *i.e.* the Witness which told to men the perfect truth as to God and the life eternal. And here he is "the First Begotten from the dead," *i.e.* the pledge and guarantee of the resurrection of all the dead, as were the firstfruits of the harvest of the rest of the harvest (1 Cor. xv. 21). Oh, blessed revelation this! Then was he not "Prince of the kings of the earth," *i.e.* supreme Lord and Master of them and of all that they do? In his hands they all are, and it is by his permission alone they rule. It was blessed and heart-inspiring to know all this, but *the* fount of St. John's praise was opened when his thought turned to those truths of which our text tells. When he thought of the Lord Jesus and of his great love, then he could contain himself no longer, but burst forth in this beautiful song of praise, "Unto him that loved us . . . Amen." Let us look a little at these words of praise, and try and discover the springs from which such praise flows forth. And they seem to me to be mainly three.

1. THE VIVID REALIZATION OF CHRIST HIMSELF. "Unto *him,* unto *him,*" the apostle repeats, and it is evident that before the eyes of his soul the Lord Jesus Christ was evidently set forth. He seems to see him—his looks, his movements, his Person ; to hear his words, and to catch the accents of his voice. Christ is to him as real as any of his fellow-men. And this is *most important* to the enkindling of love within our own souls. For the mere contemplation of love in the abstract will not stir them. You may tell me ever so much about maternal love, for example, but whilst it is contemplated in a merely general way, as that which belongs to many, it will not move me much. But tell me something about my own mother, and of her love to me, and that will be quite another matter. The most hardened and depraved have often been broken down and subdued to better things by memories of their mothers' love. But it was because it *was* their mothers' that it moved them so. And it is the same in regard to the love told of in our text. Had it been apart from a living person, apart from the Lord Jesus Christ, only a vague quality moving in the midst of men, however much it may have benefited them, it would never have aroused their gratitude or stirred their hearts. For that you must have such love centred in a person whom you can know and understand ; and better still if you have already known him and he you. And if we have not known Christ, if his Name be to us a mere word, if he be to us shadowy and unreal, scarce a person at all, we cannot enter into or sympathize with such enthusiasm as his disciple here expresses. Is it not a constant and just reproach against our poor laws that their administration of relief elicits no gratitude on the part of those relieved ? It benefits neither giver nor receiver. But let a benevolent person go himself or herself to those who need relief, and come into living personal contact with them, so that they may feel the good will for them that beats in their benefactor's heart, and how different the result will be then ! Conduct like that will wake up a response in almost the most insensate hearts, and the relief itself will be more prized for the sake of him or her who gives it than for itself. And so, did even Christ's love come to us apart from him ; did we not know and see him in it all; were we forgiven and saved we knew not how, or why, or by whom ;—we should feel no more gratitude on account of it than we do to the air we breathe or the water we drink. But when we see that it is Christ who loves us, Christ who washed us from our sins in his own blood, Christ who made us kings and priests unto God and his Father, then all is changed, and gratitude wakes up and praise bursts forth, and with Christ's apostle we also say, "Unto him that," etc. Oh, my brethren, try to get this personal realization of Christ. It was the sense of its

importance that first led to the use of pictures, crosses, crucifixes, and the like aids to such realization of Christ. They have been so much abused that many fear to use them at all ; and they are by no means the only or the best way to attain to the result which is so much to be desired. But by the devout reading of the Gospels and the Word of God generally, by much meditation thereupon, by frequent and fervent prayer, the image of Christ, now so faint and dim in many hearts, will come out clear and vivid, distinct and permanent, to your great joy and abiding good. You know how the picture on the photographer's plate is at first almost undiscernible, but he plunges it into the bath he has prepared for it, and then every line and form and feature become visible, and the picture is complete. Plunge your souls, my brethren, into the blessed bath of God's Word and thought and prayer, and then to you, as to St. John, Christ will become visible, and he will be realized by you as he has never been before. And the result will be that prayer will become to you delightful, as is converse with a dear friend ; and faith will keep her foothold firmly as ofttimes now she fails to do ; and love will come and stay and grow towards Christ in our hearts ; and heaven will have begun below. Such realization of Christ was one mainspring of this outburst of praise.

II. ANOTHER WAS ST. JOHN'S DEEP SENSE OF THE GREATNESS OF CHRIST'S LOVE. He tells of four great facts. 1. *Its compassion.* "Unto him that loved us." Before the apostle's mind there seems to rise up the vision of what he and his fellow-believers had once been—so foul and unclean, not with mere outward defilement, but with that inward foulness of the heart which to the Holy and Undefiled One could not but have been repulsive in the highest degree. And yet the Lord loved him. We can understand his pitying men so miserable, even whilst he condemned their sin ; and we can understand how, on their repentance, he might pardon them. But to take them into his favour, to make them the objects of his love, that is wonderful indeed. And thus has he dealt with all of us. And his love is not a fitful passing thing—a love that has been, but is not. The real reading of our text is in the present, the abiding sense : " Unto him that loveth us." Christ always loves his people. " Having loved his own, he loved them to the end." And it is so wonderful and unique a thing, that to mention it is description enough whereby it may be known that Christ is meant. For John does not mention our Lord's name, but just as the expression, " the disciple whom Jesus loved," was sufficient to identify John, so " him that loved us " is sufficient to identify our Lord. For none such as he was ever loved such as we were, or loved us in such a way. But for such love, when realized and felt as St. John felt it, how could he do other than render praise ? 2. *The costly cleansing.* " Hath washed us from our sins in his own blood." There is many a distressful condition into which a man may fall, and grateful will he be to him who saves him therefrom, as from sickness, poverty, affliction, disgrace, death ; but there is no condition so truly terrible as that of *sin.* That is the root-evil, the *fons et origo* of all else. Let that not be, and the rest change their nature directly, and can easily be borne ; but where sin is there they all become charged with a sting and venom which but for this they could not have. Therefore to be delivered from all other evil and not from sin would be no deliverance worthy of the name ; but to be delivered from sin is deliverance, salvation indeed, bringing along with it deliverance from all other evil whatsoever. And St. John felt this. He had heard how the Lord had said to the poor palsied one who had been let down through the roof into his presence, that he might be healed, "Son, be of good cheer ; thy *sins* be forgiven thee." That word told the man himself, and all mankind beside, that our sins are our greatest enemies. There is no evil that can befall a man comparable with that. But it is from this sum of all evils that Christ cleanses. *And at what cost ?* Nothing less than " his own blood." All manner of questions may be asked as to the relationship between the blood of Christ and our cleansing, and all manner of answers have been given, some more, some less satisfactory. But that is not now our concern. Only the fact that " without shedding of blood there is no remission," and that it *is* " the blood of Jesus Christ which cleanseth from all sin." And he was content to suffer death that so we might be saved. St. John had stood beneath the cross of his Lord, had been with him in Gethsemane, and he knew what this " washing us from our sins in his own blood " meant, what infinite love alone could have submitted to such a death. What wonder that his heart should overflow with praise ? 3. And then there was also *the coronation*

He "hath made us kings." Surely none could look less like kings than the shivering crowd of persecuted people to whom St. John addressed his book. In what sense, then, could it be that Christ had made them kings? Only, for the present, in the lordship he had given them over themselves, and over all the power of their adversaries. They could compel, by the force of the regal will with which their Lord had invested them their trembling flesh, their wavering purpose, their crowd of earthly affections, to a steadfastness and courage which of themselves they had never known. And when thus equipped, strengthened with all might, crowned as kings, by God's Spirit in the inner man, they could meet and defy, endure and vanquish, all their persecutors' power. It gave way to them, not they to it. Thus had the Lord made them kings. 4. And finally, *the consecration.* He "hath made us priests." True, no mitre decked their brow, no sacerdotal vestments hung from their shoulders; they belonged to no separate order, they claimed no ecclesiastical rank. But yet Christ had consecrated them. They were by him dedicated to God, they were holy unto the Lord, and in their prayers and supplications and manifold charities they offered, as priests should, "gifts and sacrifices for men." To hearts inflamed with the love of Christ this power of blessing and helping men, appertaining as it ever does to the priestly office, could not but be a further cause of gratitude and praise. Yes; the compassionate love, the costly cleansing, the coronation as kings, and the consecration as priests unto God,—these did, as they well might, call forth this fervent praise. But there was yet a third cause, and it was—

III. His CERTAINTY THAT THESE BLESSINGS WERE REALLY HIS. If he had doubted, he would have been dumb. Zacharias became so because he doubted, but his glorious song of praise burst forth when doubt and dumbness were together gone. And so will it be with ourselves. If we only hope and trust that we are Christ's, and Christ is ours; if we have not "the full assurance of the hope" which God's Word is ever urging us to strive after; but are often saying and singing—

> "'Tis a point I long to know,
> Oft it causes anxious thought:
> Do I love the Lord or no?
> Am I his or am I not?"

until a better and brighter condition of mind be ours,—we cannot praise Christ as St. John did. He was *certain* that Christ loved him, that Christ had washed him from his sins, that Christ had made him king and priest unto God; he had no doubt of it whatsoever. Oh for like precious faith!

CONCLUSION. If we do truly desire such faith, it is proof that some measure of it is in us already. If, then, we do know what Christ has done for us, let us join in this "unto him," and render to him : *Glory*—the glory which our renewed trust, our faithful witnessing for him, may bring to him. *Dominion*—over our own hearts chief of all, keeping back no faculty or power, no feeling or desire, no purpose or will, but surrendering all to him. And this "for ever and ever." Not a surrender made to-day and recalled to-morrow, but one to which, by his grace, we will for ever stand. Oh that we may! Give, then, your heartfelt "Amen" to all this. As we read this verse, let us join in the "Amen," let it be our praise also. Amen and Amen.—S. C.

Ver. 7.—*The mourning at the coming of the Lord.* "Behold, he cometh with clouds," etc. For the parallels and explanations of this mourning, we must turn to Zech. xii. 10, and to our Lord's words in Matt. xxiv. 30. These show that the mourning will be of very varied kind. There will be that contrasted sorrow of which St. Paul tells when he speaks of the "godly sorrow" and "the sorrow of the world." The former, that which will be the result of the outpouring of "the Spirit of grace and supplication" of which Zechariah tells; and the latter, that which has no element of hope or goodness in it, but tendeth only to death. Let each one of us ask—Which shall mine be? Consider—

I. THE COMING OF THE LORD. "Behold, he cometh with clouds." This tells: 1. *Of the manner of his coming.* In *majesty* (cf. the cloud of glory at Transfiguration). See the frequent gorgeous magnificence of the clouds; fit and apt symbol are they of the august majesty of the Lord. *Mystery.* "Clouds and darkness are round about him."

"Who by searching can find out God?" How incomprehensible by us are his movements and ways! *Might.* How the clouds rush along! with what speed, volume, force! They blot out the radiance of sun, moon, and stars; they darken the face of the earth. So will *he* come with great power. *Mercy.* The clouds herald "the times of refreshing" (cf. Acts ii.). So will he come to all them that love his appearing. Hence the Church's cry, "Amen. Even so, come, Lord Jesus: come quickly." 2. This coming *is to be understood literally.* If the words of Scripture have any meaning, they affirm this. Why should it not be? So was it at Sinai; so, in forecast, at the Transfiguration. Announcing it a short time previously (Matt. xvi. 28), our Lord spoke of it as "the Son of man coming in his kingdom." It is evident that the apostles and first followers of Christ understood his coming in a literal sense, and it is difficult to see how they could have understood it otherwise. True, their wish was father to their thought when they spoke of it, as they so often did, as close at hand, as likely to happen in their own lifetime. But they were not taught by Christ to affirm this; rather the reverse. For he said, "It is not for you to know the times," etc. (Acts i.). But they were right in believing the nearness of Christ's spiritual advents. For: 3. Christ's coming is *to be understood in a spiritual sense* as well as literally. All advents of Christ, though he be personally unseen, to judgment are real comings of the Lord. What else were the destruction of Jerusalem, the downfall of pagan Rome, the Reformation, the French Revolution, and yet other such events? And to every man at death (cf. Heb. ix. 27). "After death, judgment." Therefore it is ever true that he comes quickly. The Lord is at hand. He shall suddenly come; in an hour when ye look not for him; as a thief in the night. And in the sudden and marked manifestations of the Lord's displeasure which come now and again upon ungodly men; and as the direct consequences of their sin;—in these also should be seen the coming of the Lord. This truth, therefore, of Christ's coming should not be relegated to the region of speculative, mysterious, and unpractical truths, but should be, as God grant it may be by us all, held fast as of most momentous present and practical import to bear upon and influence all our daily life and thought and conduct. But St. John, in our text, has undoubtedly in view the literal coming of the Lord, and he tells of—

II. THE MOURNING THAT SHALL ATTEND IT. "All . . . shall mourn because of him." So then: 1. *None will be indifferent.* Many are so now. Try we ever so much to arouse them to religious thought and action, we cannot do so. The world and its concerns baffle all our efforts. But at the Lord's coming, the one thought of all will be concerning their relation to him. In the parable of the ten virgins (Matt. xxv.) we are told that "*all* those virgins arose and trimmed their lamps." The foolish had been careless about this hitherto, but now all were aroused and eager, though for them it was all too late. And so at our Lord's coming, "every eye shall see him," and all "shall mourn because of him." But: 2. *The mourning will be of different kinds.* (1) There will be that which belongs to *hatred*—the mourning of vexation, rage, terror. Thus will it be with those who shall be found impenitent at the last—the hardened, the reprobate, who persist in saying, "We will not have this Man to reign over us." Such is the deceitfulness of sin, that no truth, though none be more sure, is more commonly disbelieved. Ministers of Christ know too well, by experience gained at many death-beds, that "there shall be mourning at the last." What frantic efforts to hurry up the work of salvation that has been neglected all the life long! what vain looking to outside help there is when none such can avail! The writer has scenes of this sad kind vividly in remembrance, when the dying ones, do what he would, would in their fear persist in looking to him to help them. Such facts force one to believe that there will be mourning of this hopeless sort at the coming of the Lord. Yes, it is "a fearful thing" for an unforgiven man "to fall into the hands of the living God. (2) But there will be other mourning than this—the mourning *of love.* Love that grieves for good left undone or but imperfectly done, and for evil done. Of such mourning not a little will be found in those spoken of or suggested in our text, as: (*a*) *Mankind generally.* "Every eye shall see him," etc. And this looking upon Christ shall be the look of faith and love. Zechariah, in the parallel passage, teaches this—even of those who have "pierced him." James, the unbelieving brother of the Lord, seems to have been converted by the Lord's appearing to him. Saul the persecutor became Paul the apostle by the same means. And so, doubtless, not a few amidst the masses of mankind, who have known and felt how little their heathenism and varied misbeliefs could do for them, will, when they behold the Lord, exclaim, " Lo, this is our God; we have waited for him." And they will mourn their long estrangement, and the darkening of their hearts that their own sin has caused. (*b*) *Israel.* Special mention is made of them here and in Zech. xii. It was they " who pierced him." But it is told how they shall bitterly mourn when they see him, as if they mourned "for an only son." And it shall be a godly sorrow, though, as it should be, it will be heartfelt and deep. How could it be otherwise when they remembered how they *ought* to have received Jesus as the Christ! " He came to *his own* "—and they were " his own "—" and," etc. They rejected him, rejected him cruelly, persistently, generation after generation, age after age, and yet the Lord bore with them all this time; and now they see him—*him*, coming to help and save *them.* Yes; though they pierced him, hung him up and crucified him, yet, behold, he cometh, and not to destroy, but to save; and the sight of that breaks them down, as well it may. Ah! what tears of penitence will flow then! Yes; Israel shall mourn. (*c*) *The spiritual Israel*—the Church. The ancient prophet plainly has them in view as well as the literal Israel. And will not the Church of God mourn at her Lord's coming when she thinks what she might have done, and should have done, but did not do? It is the one sorrow that we shall take into the presence of the Lord, that we so ill served him who did all for us. Then the Church will see, as now oftentimes she is slow to see, that she is but an unprofitable servant, even when she has done her all. How will the Church think then of her apathy and indifference in regard to the masses of the ungodly outside her borders; of the half-hearted service she too commonly renders, her members spending more on their own luxury and ease than they surrender for Christ during a whole lifetime; of the strange things that have been done in the name of Christianity, and of the dishonour many so-called Christians have brought upon the holy name they bear? The Church, when she beholds her Lord, will mourn for these things. Would it not be well if she mourned more *now*, and so set herself to alter and amend her ways? (*d*) *Families* are spoken of as sharing in this mourning—those whom St. John speaks of as " all the tribes of the earth," and Zechariah tells of as " all the families of the land." And he specially dwells on this family, household, mourning, naming a number of these families as representative of all the rest. How suggestive this is to us all! For whatever else we may not be, we are all members of some family or other. And this divinely appointed institution of the family, how immensely powerful it ever has been and must always be for good or ill. What the families are the nation will be. And amid the families there will be mourning when the Lord comes. Godly parents, cannot you understand this? Do you not now, or would it not be much better if you did, mourn over your many failures in duty as regards the position God has placed you in? How intent you are on your children's secular good! and so you ought to be; but how little solicitude you display that their young hearts may be yielded up to the Lord! And how much more was thought of what the world and society would say, than of what would please Christ, in regard to the business, social, or marriage relationships into which you allowed or caused your children to enter! And if they have lost their love for Christ and his blessed service, whose fault is it? Oh, how will these things look in the presence of your Lord? Then let them be so to you now, and so is there less likelihood of your being " ashamed before him " at his coming. (*e*) *Individuals* are not omitted in this enumeration. " Every eye " means every individual person. There will be matter for the mourning of each one, one by one, separate and apart. Yes; that we were so late and laggard in coming to him; that when we did come, too often, for all the service we rendered him, we might almost as well have stayed away; that our conversion is so imperfect; that sin lurks and lingers in us, and often breaks out and overpowers us even now. The language of many a heart will be then—

> "Oh, how I fear thee, living God,
> With deepest, tenderest fears.
> And worship thee with humble hope,
> And penitential tears!"

Well will it be for us often to review our own personal lives in the light of the coming of the Lord. For it will send us swiftly to that "fountain opened for all sin and uncleanness," which Zechariah tells of in connection with this mourning—that most precious fountain of the Saviour's blood. And it will lead us to pray with greater fervour and frequency, " Search me, O Lord, and know my heart; prove me," etc. (Ps. cxxxix. 23).—S. C.

Vers. 9—20.—*The vision of the Lord.* That St. John should have been favoured with this glorious vision is but in keeping with what was often granted to the prophets of the Lord—to Moses, at the burning bush; to Isaiah, in the temple; to Jeremiah, at his consecration to his prophetic office, and likewise to Ezekiel; and to the three chief apostles, SS. Peter, James, and John, at the Transfiguration; St. John, at Patmos; and St. Paul, at Damascus and when caught up to heaven. All these visions were designed the better to fit and qualify them to speak for Christ to his people, and they teach us that those who are successfully to speak for Christ must have exalted ideas concerning him. In some form or other they must see his glory, or they will have but little to say, and that little they will not say as they should. " I beseech thee show me thy glory" may well be the prayer of all those who are to speak in the Lord's name. Such was—

I. THE PURPOSE OF THIS VISION as regarded St. John himself. But it had a far more general one—*to bless the Church of God.* They were dark days for the Church, days of fierce persecution, whether by command of Nero, or Domitian, who followed him twenty-five years after, we cannot say. But in those days, whichever they were, Christianity had not become a *religio licita*, and, therefore, was not as other religions, under the protection of the laws. It was looked upon as a branch of Judaism, which of all religions was the most hateful to the paganism of the day. And Christianity, in the popular estimation, was the most hateful form of Judaism. It would be certain, therefore, that if the chief authorities at Rome set the example of persecuting the Christians, the pagans of the provinces would not be long in copying it. Hence we can well understand what a fiery trial was now afflicting the Church of Christ. They were suffering, and needed consolation; fearful and fainting, and needed courage; in some cases, sad and shameful heresies had sprung up, and they needed to be rooted out; and in others, so-called Christians were leading careless, impure, and ungodly lives, and they needed solemn warning of Christ's displeasure. Now, this vision, the letters that follow, and this entire book, were all designed to meet their great necessities. What need have the people of God ever known but what he has made provision to meet it, and has met it abundantly? And this, let us be well assured, he ever will do.

II. THE CIRCUMSTANCES OF THE VISION. We are told : 1. *Of the beholder.* John. There may be doubt as to what John, and it does not much matter, for we know that we have here the Word of God, and that it was written by one of the most honoured servants of God. See how humble his tone. He does not "lord it over God's heritage," but speaks of himself as " your brother and companion in tribulation." He was so at that very hour. And "in the kingdom of Jesus Christ." For that he and they were to look forward with eager hope and confident expectation. And " in patience." This was the posture of the believer at such a time, the mind he needed to possess. We can bear tribulation if, as St. John was, we are cheered by the hope of the kingdom of our Lord, and are enabled to be patient unto the coming of the Lord. 2. *Where he was.* In Patmos; a dismal rock, lonely, barren, almost uninhabited save by the miserable exiles that were doomed to wear out their lives there. But there John had this glorious vision, and it teaches us that dreary places may become as heaven to us if we are given to see the glory of Christ. 3. *When he saw this.* "On the Lord's day." There can be little doubt but that "the first day of the week," the Christian Sunday, is meant, and what we are told of here as having taken place on this Sunday is but an early instance of what in substance and reality has taken place for many faithful worshippers in all parts of Christ's Church on every Sunday since. What wonder that the Sunday is precious to Christian hearts, and that all attempts to secularize it or in any ways lessen its sanctity are both resented and resisted by those who know what a priceless boon for heart, for home, for health, for heaven, the Lord's day is? 4. He tells us *the frame of mind in which he was.* " I was in the Spirit." His heart was much uplifted towards God; there had been a rush of holy feeling amounting to religious rapture and ecstasy, and then it was that this glorious vision burst upon him. Neither holy days nor holy places will avail us unless our hearts be in harmony with both day and place. But if they be, then the Lord often "brings all heaven before our eyes." What might not our Sundays be to us if our hearts, instead of being so earth-bound, as they too often are, were in the mood for drawing near unto God? 5. Next he tells *how his attention was called to the vision*. "I heard a great voice as of a trumpet" (ver. 10). The trumpet was an especially sacred instrument. It was associated with the giving of the Law (Exod. xix. 6), with the inauguration of festivals (Numb. x. 10), with the ascension of the Lord: "God is gone up with a noise, the Lord with the sound of a trumpet" (Ps. xlvii. 5). And so shall it be at the coming of the Lord and the resurrection of the dead (1 Thess. iv. 16; 1 Cor. xv. 52). The voice he heard was, therefore, not alone loud, clear, startling, like a trumpet, but also admonitory of the sacredness and importance of what he was about to hear and see. 6. *What the voice said*. "I am Alpha," etc. (ver. 11). Many manuscripts omit this sublime statement, but it seems in keeping with the trumpet-voice, and with what comes both before and after. The "great voice," simply commanding the apostle to write in a book what he saw, appears incongruous, but not with the august announcement, "I am Alpha," etc. The Church had believed this of "the Almighty" (ver. 8), but now it was to be thrilled with the assurance that this was true of their Lord. He, too, was Alpha, etc. (cf. for meaning, homily on ver. 11). Then, as Moses (Exod. iii. 3), turning to see whence the voice came, he beheld—

III. THE VISION ITSELF. He saw: 1. *The whole Church of Christ* represented by the seven lamps of gold. Seven, the specially sacred number, the number of complete-ness. These seven are mentioned because their names were familiar to those to whom he was writing. 2. *He beheld the Lord Jesus Christ*. These verses tell: (1) The form of his appearance. "I saw One like unto the Son of man." He of whom Ezekiel and Daniel had told in those prophecies of theirs, which this so often and so much resembles. But it was a vision of awe and terror to any mortal eye. Like so many Hebrew symbols, it is unrepresentable in art. The form is one which is almost incon-ceivable, and were any to seek, as some have done, to make a pictorial representation of it, the result would be grotesque, monstrous, and impossible. But the Hebrew mind cared nothing for art, only for spiritual truth; the external form was nothing, the inward truth everything. Art is careful to portray only the external, and it has attained to wondrous perfection in this respect; but the Hebrew desired to represent the inner nature—the mind, the heart, the soul. Hence it fastened upon whatsoever would best serve this purpose, and joined them together, utterly regardless of congruity, symmetry, or any other mere artistic law. Therefore we must look beneath the often strange symbols which we have in this vision would we know what it meant and said to the beholder. The golden-girdled garment told of royal majesty and authority; the hoary hair, of venerable age and profound wisdom; the eyes like fire-flame, of searching intelligence and of fierce wrath; the feet like molten brass, of resistless strength, which should trample down and crush all that stood in its way; the voice like the sound of the sonorous sea-waves, which are heard over all other tumults and noises whatsoever, subduing and stilling them, tell of that word of "all-commanding might" which once was heard hushing into silence the noise of many waters on the tempest-tossed lake of Galilee, and which, wherever heard, every tumult subsides and all at once obey. The seven stars grasped in the right hand told of power and purpose to defend them or dispose of them as he willed; the two-edged sword proceeding out of his mouth, of that awful soul-penetrating Word by which the secrets of all hearts should be made known, and by which all adversaries of the Lord should be slain; the countenance radiant like the sun, of the Divine majesty, so dazzling, so confounding, so intolerable, to all unhallowed and unpermitted gaze of man. (2) And this awful form was seen surrounded by the seven lamps of gold, as the dwellings of the vassals of a chieftain are clustered round his castle and stronghold, which rises proudly in their midst as if proclaiming its lordship and its protection over them. (3) And that this vision was designed to meet the manifold needs of those varied characters and conditions in the several Churches is evident from the fact that allusion to one or other part of it is made at the beginning of each of the letters which St. John was commanded to write and send; and that part is chosen which would most minister to the need of the Church to whom the letter was written. But it was as the invincible Champion of his Church that Christ came forth, and to persuade their fainting hearts of this he appeared in this wondrous form. And the vision is for all time, and every anxious heart should steadily look upon it, and strive to learn the comforting truths which it was designed to teach. (4) But the effect of the vision was at first overpowering. "I fell at his feet as dead." Well might it have been so.

"O God of mercy, God of might,
How should weak sinners bear the sight,
If, as thy power is surely here,
Thine open glory should appear?"

St. Peter cried out, "Depart from me, for I am a sinful man, O Lord!" though there was nothing in the appearance of Jesus to alarm and terrify. How much more when such a vision as this was seen, and such a voice was heard! "Fear was far more in the ascendant than holy joy. I will not say that John was unhappy, but certainly it was not delight which prostrated him at the Saviour's feet. And I gather from this that if we, in our present embodied state, were favoured with an unveiled vision of Christ, it would not make a heaven for us; we may think it would, but we know not what spirit we are of. Such new wine, if put into these old bottles, would cause them to burst." But (5) we are told how the Lord restored his prostrate disciple. By his touch of sympathy: he laid his hand upon him. He was wont to do this for the many that he healed when here on earth. And there was the touch of power. It was his *right* hand. Then came the Lord's "Fear not;" and when we hear *him* say that to us, our fears, as—

"The cares that infest the day,
Shall fold their tents like the Arabs,
And silently steal away."

And this was not all. He gave him most comforting instruction. He told him who he was—the incarnate Jehovah; the Saviour "who became dead," not who merely died, but, as the word denotes, "voluntarily underwent death." Surely John knew him, and would not be afraid of him. But now he was alive for evermore—he, the same in heart and will, though not in form. And possessed of universal authority. He had the keys, the insignia of authority, over the unseen world. Therefore, should any of them be hurried thither by their persecutors' rage, he would be there, and Lord there, so they need not fear. But he had the keys of death also. Hence none could open its gates unless he pleased; and none could be put to death whom he chose to keep alive. He "openeth, and no man shutteth, and shutteth, and no man openeth." Entrance there was governed, not by the will of man, but by *his* will. And finally, he explains part of the vision, and directs it to be written and sent to the seven Churches. The stars, they are, such as St. John himself was, the angels, the chief pastors of the Churches; and see, Christ has hold of them, grasped in his right hand, and who shall be able to pluck them thence, or separate them from his love? What comfort this for the fearful but faithful heart of the minister of Christ! And see again, *he* is in the midst of the seven lamps which represent the seven Churches. He is there as their sure Defence. Christ is in the midst of his Churches chiefly to protect, but also to rule and to inspect, and if needs be to judge and to punish. Even now he is walking amid his Churches. Let us remember this, and consider "what manner of persons we ought to be in all holy conversation and godliness." The voice of this vision says to us all, "Be of good comfort, but watch and pray."—S. C.

Ver. 11.—*The eternity and unchangeableness of Christ.* "I am Alpha and . . . Last." The vision St. John had just seen showed him indisputably that all the low and inadequate ideas which, during his Lord's life on earth, and during the times of trial, he and others had cherished concerning his Person were altogether wrong. And, though we cannot but believe that in the apostles' mind there must have been a great advance in their thoughts concerning their Lord, even yet it was needful, and now and in the terrible times before them it was more than ever needful, that they should rightly regard him. They would lose much, as we ever do, by wrong thoughts about Christ, and all thoughts that fell short of his true dignity and nature were wrong thoughts. Now, to bring the Church generally to true knowledge and understanding on this great matter, not only was the vision vouchsafed which St. John had then before him, but also the trumpet-like voice of the Lord himself was heard declaring who and what he was. And the importance of this declaration is seen by the prominence that is given to it, and its frequent repetition in more or less full form. We meet with it again and again. Its meaning and teaching are similar to that word in Heb. xiii. 8, "Jesus Christ, the same yesterday," etc. It asserts—

I. THE ETERNITY OF THE SON OF GOD. In the eighth verse it is spoken of the Almighty God himself. Here, and continually in other places, it is asserted of the Lord Jesus Christ. In the face of Scriptures like these, and they are very many, how can the honest believer in their authority assent to the popular modern hypothesis which would place and keep our Lord on the level of humanity, even though it be humanity at its highest level? If he were no more than man, how could words such as these be spoken and written concerning him? Now, if it had been desired to show that he was God incarnate, could language more clearly asserting it have been devised? Reject the Scriptures, the testimony of the Church from the beginning, the experience of believers, and the confirmation of the truth which we find in religions outside our own, and then we may reject the Church's faith; but assuredly it cannot else be done. But the text teaches also—

II. THE UNCHANGEABLENESS OF THE LORD JESUS CHRIST. It was needful that the former truth should be deeply impressed on the minds of the persecuted Church. It was the remembrance of the Eternal One that had steadied the minds and encouraged the hearts of their fathers in the days of old. On the plains of Dura, in the courts of Nebuchadnezzar and of Darius, that blest memory and faith had given invincible courage in the face of the fiery furnace and the fangs of fiercest beasts. And therefore it was reasserted here when like perils would have to be met and endured and overcome. But this further truth of the unchangeableness of Christ was no less needed to abide in memory and heart if they were to be found faithful even unto death. For: 1. *There would be great temptation to tamper with his commands.* Might not their stringency be relaxed? would not many of them admit of compromise, or of delay, or of some other departure from their literal and strict import? Under the pressure of fear, or worldly conformity, or the lurking love of sin, would there not be, is there not now, this temptation perpetually assailing? And therefore was it and is it ever well to remember that such setting aside of the Lord's commands cannot be suffered. They change not any more than himself. They were not lowered or relaxed for the tried and troubled ones of former ages, even when they had far less of sustaining truth to cheer them than had the apostolic Church, and still less than we have now. The Lord has cancelled no command, nor does he claim from us any less than he demanded at the first. He accepts half-hearted service no more now than when he said, "Thou shalt love the Lord thy God with *all* thy heart." But there were not a few to whom St. John wrote, and there are as many and more now, who from various motives would try to explain away this command and that which the Lord had laid upon them. For them the reminder of his unchangeableness, which is given in this his Name, was indeed necessary. 2. And their fidelity would be helped by the remembrance that *he was the same in his love.* What had he done for the most faithful of his servants that he had not done for them? Did he die for the martyrs more than for them? Were they not included when it was said, "He loved us, and gave himself for us"? Were not the unsearchable riches of Christ as open to them as to any believers? Did they owe less to Christ? or were they under less obligation to him than others? He had come from heaven to earth; he had lived, and suffered, and died, and risen again for them as for those whose hearts had most truly responded to all this love. Yes; as unchanged in his love toward them as in what he asked for from them, in what he deserved as in what he demanded. How well for them to remember this! 3. *And in the grace he would bestow.* They were not and could not be straitened in him. The treasury of his grace was not exhausted. He would supply all their need, as he had supplied that of all his servants. No good thing would he withhold from them more than from the saints and martyrs who by his grace had obtained so good report. "I am the Lord, I change not;" such was one chief meaning of his word, "I am Alpha," etc. And that immutability concerned his nature and his character, and there was no class amongst them in these days of trial but would find help in this sure truth. **And let us remember it likewise.** —B. C.

Vers. 17, 18.—*The Living One: an Easter Sunday sermon.* "Fear not," etc. 1. It is good to *say* words of good cheer. The cheerful word, the pleasant smile, the encouraging shake of the hand,—all these are good and helpful. As when with ringing cheers we send our troops off to battle. 2. But it is better still to be able, along with such words of good cheer, to show reason for them, and the solid ground you have for bidding your brother be of good cheer, and that he has for being so. If we can do this, how much more helpful our words are! Now, this is what our Saviour does here for St. John, and through him for all Christians always and everywhere. And if, as is possible, from the use of the expression, "the Lord's day," and St. John's naming it in close connection with our Lord's death, the day was not merely the first day of the week, but an Easter Sunday, and so especially "the Lord's day," then all the more may we well consider those reasons wherefore our Lord bade his apostle and all of us " Fear not." Now, our Lord declares in these verses four great facts, every one of which says, " Fear not " to him who believes it.

I. His ETERNAL EXISTENCE. He says: 1. "*I am the First*"—the First Begotten (cf. Ps. xl.; John the Baptist's, " He was before me;" also our Lord's words, " Before Abraham was, I am;" and John i. 1, "In the beginning was the Word "). 2. "*The Last.*" (Cf. " He must reign till he hath put all enemies under his feet;" " Then cometh the end," 1 Cor. xv.) 3. "*The Living One;*" equivalent to "I am he that liveth"—Jehovah. The claim is no less than this. Great, august, but intolerable if not true. But because true, it justifies our adoration and worship, and that to him every knee should bow. But it also says to us, " Fear not;" for it assures us that what he has been to his people he will be to them always (cf. homily on ver. 11). He had been everything to his disciples. "Lord, to whom shall we go?" said Peter in the name of them all: "thou hast the words of eternal life." Hence to lose him was to lose all. But this Divine title which he claims assured them that they should not lack any good thing. What he had been to them, he would be. And so to us.

II. His PERFECT BROTHERHOOD. He shares in all our sorrows, even the greatest of them. "I became dead;" this is a better rendering of ver. 18, than " I was dead." It does not say merely, "I died," or " I was dead;" that might be said of any saint in heaven, and will be said of all of us one day; but " I became dead "—it was his own voluntary act (cf. St. Paul: "He humbled himself, and became obedient unto death, even the death of the cross "). Now, our Lord's declaring this fact tells no doubt: 1. *Of his sacrifice and atonement.* That he was "the Lamb of God, which taketh away," etc. But I think the chief reason for its declaration here is to assert: 2. *His perfect brotherhood and sympathy with us.* That he was our very Brother-Man, who has been in all points tried as we are. Hence, however low any of us may have to go, he has been lower still. As Baxter sings—

> "Christ leads us through no darker room
> Than he went through before."

It was as if he would say to all to whom this book should come, "I know, my brethren, you have to bear trouble, perhaps to endure cruel death, but I know all about it; *I* became dead, I have been through it all, I have sounded the lowest depths of sorrow; and go, my beloved ones, where you will, underneath you shall find my everlasting arms. So fear not." And on Easter Day the joy of it is that the Lord comes to us, not merely as triumphant, but as One who has suffered, and to us who are suffering. And the message of the day is—

> " As surely as I overcame,
> And triumphed once for you,
> So surely you who know my Name
> Shall through me triumph too."

III. His VICTORY. "Behold, I am alive for evermore." Note that word "behold." It means that, in spite of all that death and hell could do, he is nevertheless alive for evermore. They sought to destroy him, but in vain. And the message of all this to those to whom it was sent was, " Fear not them which kill the body, but after that have no more that they can do." Your enemies can do you no real harm. And this is his word to us to-day. He points to himself, and says, "Behold" me; "I am alive for evermore." Therefore "Fear not."

IV. HIS LORDSHIP OVER THE UNSEEN. "I have the keys of death and of hell." The "key" means authority, power, possession; "death," him who had the power of death, or the state of death; "hell," the unseen world, the place of departed spirits; also the forces and strength of Satan (cf. "The gates of hell"). Now, Christ declares that he has authority over all this. Therefore, he having the keys: 1. *The door of death and the grave can only be opened by him.* Therefore their lives were unassailable, invulnerable, unless he gave permission. "Men of the world," their persecutors, were but his "hand." 2. *He can enter there when he pleases.* If, then, any of them should be put to death, he would not be debarred from them nor they from him (cf. "Though I walk through the valley of the shadow of death, I will fear no evil: for *thou* art with me; thy rod," etc., Ps. xxiii.). Death and the unseen world are his absolute possession. 3. *He can shut their gates when he pleases.* Therefore death and hell have power only so long as he pleases. If he lets them loose for a season, he can restrain them again. And he will finally shut the door upon them for ever. "The last enemy that shall be destroyed is death;" "He came to destroy the works of the devil." He shall shut the gates of hell, and when he shuts, no man openeth. Therefore "Fear not." Such is the message of Easter Day.—S. C.

Ver. 17.—*The "Fear nots" of Christ.* "Fear not." This is a characteristic word of the Bible, but especially of the Gospel, and chief of all, of our blessed Lord. For he not only, as in our text, spoke the word many times, but his whole message and mission to mankind was to banish the bondslave fear which had haunted them so long from their minds. "'Fear not' is a plant that grows very plentifully in God's garden. If you look through the flower-beds of Scripture, you will continually find by the side of other flowers the sweet 'Fear nots' peering out from among doctrines and precepts, even as violets look up from their hiding-places of green leaves." Take any concordance, and count the number of times and note the occasions where the heart-cheering word or its equivalent occurs, and it will be seen that it is indeed a characteristic word of God to man. From Genesis to Revelation, from earliest patriarch to latest apostle, the sweet echo and reverberation of this word is clearly audible. Dr. Watts's Catechism says, in its answer to the question, "Who was Isaiah?" "He was the prophet that spoke more of Jesus Christ than all the rest." And this is so, and for this very reason he is richest in comfort to the people of God, and you will see more of these "Fear nots" in his writings than anywhere else. "They grow like the kingcups and the daisies, and other sweet flowers of the meadows, among which the little children in the spring-time delight themselves, and the bank that is the fullest of these beautiful flowers is that which Isaiah has cast up." But let us listen now to those blessed words spoken by Christ himself, rather than by his Spirit through his prophets.

I. And first this one in our text which DRIVES AWAY DREAD AND DISMAY IN PRESENCE OF THE DIVINE GLORY. Not but what there is good reason for such dread at the thought of God. For how stands the case as between our souls and God? We have sinned—there is no doubt about that. And then there rises up before the soul the awful vision of God's majesty and might and of his wrath against sin. And the dread which this vision causes is deepened as we hear the accusations of conscience, as we listen to the reasonings founded on the necessity of penalty following sin. "Plato, Plato," said Socrates, "I cannot see how God can forgive sin." As we observe the reign of law, and note how therein every "transgression receives its just recompense of reward" (Heb. ii. 2), all this fills the awakened soul with dread, as indeed it cannot but do. But to such soul Christ comes and says, "Fear not." In many ways he says this; but chief of all by his cross and sacrifice, whereby he shows to us how without dishonour done to the Divine law, but rather with all honour rendered to it, God can "be just and yet the Justifier," etc. To him, our Redeemer and Saviour, let the soul convinced of sin and in dread on account thereof, at once turn, and soon shall be heard, in spite of all accusing, condemning voices, the blessed word of Christ that silences them all, and says to the soul that trusts in him, "Fear not." This same word—

II. MEETS THE RENEWED CONSCIOUSNESS OF SIN WHICH THE SENSE OF GOD'S GOODNESS

OFTEN PRODUCES. "Fear not," said our Lord to Peter; "from henceforth thou shalt catch men" (Luke v. 10). Peter was overwhelmed at the magnitude of the blessing bestowed on him. "He was astonished at the draught of fishes which they had taken." Had the number been but small, he would not have been astonished, but being what it was, he could only cast himself down before the Lord and cry, "Depart from me; for I am a sinful man, O Lord!" He had known and seen much of Christ before this; he had heard John say of him, "Behold the Lamb of God, which taketh," etc.; and he had believed and followed him. But never before, that we know of, had there been wakened up in him such sense of his own unworthiness as he gives utterance to now. What led to it? Not the quickened belief that Jesus was the Christ; not the sight of a miracle only, for he had seen other miracles before this—that at Cana, for example; but it was the sense of the Lord's goodness to him, not in this great haul of fish merely or chiefly, but in his condescension that he should make such as he was his friend, companion, and apostle. And such sense of the Lord's great goodness does have this humbling effect.

> "The more thy glories strike mine eye,
> The humbler I shall lie."

Where there is borne in upon our minds the great love of God to usward, the light of that love makes us see more clearly our own unworthiness of it. It will not puff any man up with pride, or make him thank God that he is not as other men are, but will work in him such humility and lowliness of heart as, whilst it qualifies him the better to do Christ's work, will need, and will have, Christ's "Fear not" to prevent it becoming over diffident and doubtful as to whether he can serve Christ at all. They who have been most honoured, as Peter was, "to catch men for life," as the Lord promised him he should, know how the sense of such unmerited goodness prostrates them before God in deepest self-abasement and in "penitential tears." And it is to this mood of mind —so blessed every way—that the Lord speaks his "Fear not." Let each one of us, would we know more of the Lord's goodness, especially in regard to success in all spiritual work, ask ourselves—What effect does that goodness have upon me? If it makes us proud and self-sufficient, that will be the signal for its coming to an end; but if, as it should, it humble us and make us feel more than ever how unworthy, because how sinful we are, then that will be the token that there is for us more blessing yet in store.

III. FORBIDS THE GIVING UP OF HOPE EVEN IN SEEMINGLY HOPELESS CASES. This is the lesson of the "Fear not" of our Lord's which is given in Luke viii. 50. If ever there was a seemingly hopeless case, it was that of the recovery of the little daughter of Jairus, after the messengers had come and told him, "Thy daughter is dead." No doubt he had fretted and fumed inwardly at the, as he would think it, deplorable interruption and delay which had occurred owing to the poor woman's coming and touching the hem of the Lord's garment, and so being healed, all which led to her discovery and confession, but likewise to much loss of time. But when the word came to Jairus that his dear child was dead, his distress and anguish must have been terrible, and were clearly visible to the Lord, who at once meets it with this "Fear not: believe only, and she shall be made whole." Now, this is a typical instance and a never-to-be-forgotten lesson for us all. Where Christ is concerned, or rather concerns himself for us, we need never, we may never, despair. 1. We may apply this lesson largely *to temporal events*, though not universally, because oftentimes his will plainly is not to deliver us from the temporal trouble which we fear. But even then we should not fear, for though not in form, yet in substance, he will give deliverance and help. He will always do what is best, though that best be in some other form than that which we have desired. 2. But the lesson is of universal application in regard *to spiritual blessings* which we seek at his hands. Many a dear one lies spiritually at the point of death, and if we have gone to Christ with the entreaty that he will come and heal, we are not to despair of our prayer being answered. We may not see the answer in this world—God's providence may have rendered that impossible, but still we are never to give up hope. "It is told of a woman who prayed long for her husband, how she used to attend a certain meeting-house in the north of England; but her husband never went with her. He was a drinking, swearing man, and she had much anguish of heart about him. She never ceased to pray, and yet she never saw any result. She went to the meeting-house quite alone, with this exception, that a dog always went with her, and this faithful animal would curl himself up under the seat, and lie quiet during the service. When she was dead, her husband was still unsaved, but doggie went to the meeting-house. His master wondered whatever the faithful animal did at the service. Curiosity made him follow the good creature. The dog led him down the aisle to his dear old mistress's seat. The man sat on the seat, and the dog curled himself up as usual. God guided the minister that day; the Word came with power, and that man wept till he found the Saviour" (Spurgeon). That instance is but one out of many more, all of which go to confirm the blessed lesson of this "Fear not." Let ministers and teachers, parents, and all who have those dear to them as yet unsaved, be encouraged to persevere in fervent prayer and believing endeavour on their behalf. "Fear not: believe only, and" thy beloved one "*shall* be made whole." And we may each one substitute our own selves for the daughter of Jairus, and read, "thy own soul" shall be made whole. For not seldom we are prone to despair about ourselves and to give up the contest. Old sins break out again, old habits reassert themselves, and we seem delivered over to them, and all our prayer and effort to be of no avail. "Fear not," says the Lord to all such. Another of these "Fear nots"—

IV. DEFIES PERSECUTION. Matt. x. 28, "Fear not them which kill the body." That entire chapter is an armoury of weapons wherewith the war with the world may be successfully waged. Not much of open and violent persecution exists in our day. The serpent has had its fangs drawn, and the mouths of the lions have been shut; but still the enemies of Christ know well enough how to inflict much of pain on those who will not take their side, but are faithful to the Lord. Many a working man and working woman who have to mingle in their daily employ with large numbers of others in warehouses, workshops, factories, and the like, can bear witness to the truth of this; and many a boy at school likewise. To all such this "Fear not" of Christ's specially comes. To be despised by men may be hard, but will it not be worse to be rejected of the Lord if you give in to the fear of man? And is not the glad welcome and "Well done" of Christ worth winning, even at the cost of a sharp, though short-lived persecution now? Surely it is. And think how little they can do. They cannot touch *you*. They may mangle and murder your poor body, though they are not likely to go so far as that; but that is not *you*. And when they have done that, they have no more that they can do. And how utter has been their failure in the past! One would have thought that the Church of Christ must have been exterminated long ago, considering what a ceaseless storm of hell's artillery has been beating upon her devoted head. But lo! here the Church of Christ is, invincible in him who himself is invincible. Satan, the prompter of all persecution, soon tires when he finds that failure follows all he does. "Fear not," therefore; be bold for Christ. Confess him, and he will confess you. This word –

V. DISPELS ANXIETY ABOUT THE SUPPLY OF EARTHLY WANTS. In Luke xii. 32 Christ says, "Fear not, little flock; for it is your Father's good pleasure to give you the kingdom." He had been warning them against troubled, distracting thoughts about temporal provision, bidding them seek first the kingdom of God, and all needful things should be added. And, to uplift them far above such anxiety, he bids them fear not, for the kingdom is to be theirs. And in confirmation of this word, does not observation attest that, as a rule—there are, no doubt, exceptions—the wants of the servants of Christ are, somehow or other, supplied? A good man has written against that verse in the psalms which says, "I have been young, and now am old; yet . . . *nor his seed begging bread* "—against this he has written, "Then, David, I have." Well, once and again he may have; but the rule is, "all these things" *are* added unto them. How it is done, whence it comes, or how much, is often a great puzzle. The cupboard may be very bare sometimes, and the cruse very dry; but supply comes as mysteriously but as surely as the ravens brought to the prophet his daily food. Yes; Christ makes good his word, and he will, brother, to *thee*. "Fear not," therefore. And let this blessed word serve us as it served St. Paul; for it—

VI. SUSTAINS UNDER APPARENT FAILURE. "Fear not," said the Lord to St. Paul; "lo. God hath given thee all them that sail with thee" (Acts xxvii. 24). It was the time of Paul's shipwreck. There seemed but a step betwixt him and death The ship was going to pieces; there seemed no hope nor help. And this was to be the end, apparently, of his apostolic career—Rome not seen, his work incomplete. But then, by his angel, the Lord sent to him this " Fear not." Let us be assured all things—all events, circumstances—must work; they do; they can never be quiet. And they must work together. They seem at times to pull different ways and to lead far apart from one another. But no; they are interlinked and connected one with the other by all manner of associations, so that they must work together, whether they will or no. And they must work together for good, and not evil, to them that love God. When the warp and the woof of the fabric are complete, good shall be seen to be the outcome of it all. So was it with all Paul's life and, not least, with this very ship-wreck. And this " Fear not " was sent to tell him that it would be so. Oh, how constantly God is better to us than all our fears! Our worst troubles are those that never come at all, but which we are afraid will come. We often think we are brought to a dead halt, but, lo! as in many a lake and fiord you come up to a promontory or what seems like a wall of rock, and lo! there is an opening through which you glide, and there you are with more room than ever. Then " Fear not;" but cast thy care on God, and he will sustain thee. Apparent failure is not real, and out of the darkest perplexity he can bring forth light.—S. C.

Ver. 20.—*The seven Churches: their common characteristics.* Seven times is heard the solemn charge, given at the close of each of the letters addressed to these Churches, " He that hath an ear," etc. And we would obey this word so far as we may, and, ere considering these letters one by one, would glance at their common characteristics. To the most superficial reader it is evident that in *arrangement and plan* they are all alike. The "angel of the Church" is addressed in each; then comes the title of the Lord, setting forth that aspect of his character which it was especially well for the Church addressed to take heed to. Then follows the Lord's solemn, " I know thy works," meaning that he had perfectly seen and so perfectly knew all they had done and suffered, all that they were or might be. Then, where, as in most cases, there was aught of good to commemorate, it is named first, before accusation of failure or faith-lessness is made. Then follows the earnest warning, and finally comes the promise to all that overcome, and the exhortation to hear and heed what has been said. This is the order of thought in them all, and the aim and purpose of all are one. But, looking at these letters as a whole, the teachings that they convey may be summed up under these three heads.

I. Ecclesiastical. For we may gain from these epistles some clear outlines and learn some of the fundamental principles of the primitive Churches. The picture may not be complete, the portraiture only a sketch; but what it does tell is distinct as well as important. We learn concerning the Churches: 1. *Their spread and increase.* (1) We are not told why these seven are mentioned and not others. It was not (*a*) because they were all, or for the most part, chief cities. Outside these there were, of course, many far more important—Antioch, Jerusalem, Alexandria, Rome, etc. And even near to these seven there were others greater than they, as Miletus, Colossæ, Hierapolis, and probably others. Some that are mentioned are quite insignificant. But perhaps, (*b*) being near one to the other, and all not far from Ephesus, St. John knew more of them. They all lay within the area of two ordinary English counties, and, following the order of their names, they formed a complete circle, starting from and returning to Ephesus. And (*c*) yet more, because in them the character and conduct told of were conspicuous. (2) Nor are we told why these seven only are named. Why not less or more? But the reason probably was to show, by the use of the symbolic number, seven, that what was said concerning these Churches was of world-wide and world-enduring importance. For " seven " is the sacred number, and indicates Divine selection, and so enforces the charge that those who hear what the Spirit saith should give all heed thereto. (3) But these being mentioned, the spread of the Church of Christ is shown. For if in places so obscure as some of these were the faith of Christ was found, how much more in larger places? We know that the tide has come in when we see that the little inland creeks are filled. We have no doubt then that the whole stretch of the sea-shore which, when the tide was out, was left uncovered, is now bright an ¹ sparkling with waves. So if to Thyatira and such places the gospel had spread, much more might we be assured that in more populous places it would also be found. 2. *Their fundamental principle.* That the Church should consist of true believers in Christ, whose faith worked by love and produced holiness of life. For when and wherever praise is given,—and large and blessed promises are held out—it is ever to those, who are faithful followers of the Lord. On the other hand, censure and threatening, warning and expostulation, are addressed only to those who are found unfaithful, or are in peril of becoming so. It is, therefore, evident that the place of any in the Church was due to their being regarded as sincere and true believers. If it was not expected of them to be this, wherefore such terrible blame and threats pronounced against them for not being so? It is plain that purity and holiness are regarded as their proper character; that as holy they were called into and continued in the Church, and that on no other ground had they a right there. No nationality and no religious rite could make men living members of the Church; only they were so who so believed in Christ that they became renewed in heart and life. And it is so still; God help us to remember it! 3. *Their form.* From the mention of these several Churches it is surely evident that at the first there was no idea that the Church of Christ was to be one visible organized body coextensive with the whole world. We believe in "one holy Catholic Church," but we dispute the right of any one organization to claim so august a title. Christ's prayer, "That they all may be one," *is* heard, and its answer is seen in the fact of the identity in love, faith, and character of all who are really his. And it is these in their totality, visible and known only to him, found in all sections of the Church, but confined to none, who make up the "holy Catholic Church." But, so far as visible form is concerned, we read not of "the Church," but of "Churches." Nor were these Churches national or provincial—one Church for a nation or province. All these seven Churches were in one province. Nor was their form presbyterian, for they were not welded together into one, but remained distinct and apart. Nor were they congregational—the Church consisting only of those worshipping in one building. For so there might have been, as there were not, many such Churches in any one of these seven cities. But their form seems to have been municipal rather than aught beside. The believers in one town or city might meet in several congregations, and probably in large cities did so; but we read of only one Church at such places; as the Church at Philippi, Corinth, Antioch, Rome, etc.; not "the Churches," but "the Church." But for the several congregations there were bishops and deacons, as many as might be needed. Hence we read of "the Church, with its bishops and deacons" (Phil. i. 1). Each congregation seems to have had its presiding officer and assistants, but such congregation, with these, did not form a separate Church; the Church consisted of all the believers in the city or town to which they belonged. And, surely, it was an "excellent way." But what matter the form in which the Church or Churches may be organized? It is the life within, the Divine life, begotten of the Spirit of God, that is the all-important thing. Without that the best form is no better than the worst; and with that the worst form serves almost as well as the best. 4. *Their ministry.* (1) The Churches were presided over by pastors. For by "the angel of the Church" we seem obliged to understand its chief pastor. No doubt it looks more simple and reasonable to regard the word "angel" as meaning an angel in the ordinary sense of the word. And those who say we should so understand it refer us to the fourth chapter of this book, where we read of "the angel of the waters;" and also to the words of our Lord, who speaks of the "angels" of little children ("Their angels do always behold," etc.); and it is urged that, as we must understand these passages as telling of angels who presided over, had charge of, "the waters" (as in ch. iv.) and of "children" (as in the Gospels), so here we must understand, by "the angel of the Church," the angel who had the charge of the Church, and was, therefore, its representative before God. And it is also urged that Michael is in Daniel represented as the guardian of Israel. And the Jews believed in such angels. "It is his angel"—so said those gathered at Mary's house when Peter, whom they thought to be in prison, knocked at the door. But in reply to all this there is one conclusive answer—How could John write a letter to an angel and send it to him? He could write and send to the Churches and their pastors; but to an angel! Hence we regard the chief pastor as meant by the angel. In Haggai and Malachi, prophets are called "messengers," or angels, and such, we believe, are meant here. But what a view of the pastoral office and its solemn responsibility we get when we thus understand this word! They are addressed as representing and responsible for the Churches over whom they preside. Well might St. Paul cry—and well may we— " Brethren, pray for us." (2) And there seems to have been a modified episcopate ; for the chief pastor had others with him (cf. Acts xx., " Elders of the Church "). Evidently there were several. But the angel seems to have been chief over the rest, as he is held responsible for the faith and practice of the Church. But this need not hurt any one's conscience. Means are not ends. We cannot follow *exactly* the scriptural pattern in all details. Were we to do so, it would hinder, probably, rather than help forward the end the Church seeks. And our divergences of practice should teach mutual charity and striving after oneness of heart even where there is not oneness of form.

II. Doctrinal. Note the sublime titles given to our Lord. They are all drawn from the vision told of in this chapter. But how plainly they teach *the Divine glory that belongs to our Lord!* As we read them over one by one, can we doubt, whilst we regard this book as inspired, as to who and what our Lord was? Here are titles that no creature, of however high an order of intelligence, or sanctity, or power, could dare to assume to himself or permit others to ascribe to him. There is but one conclusion, that he to whom these titles are given, and by whom they are claimed, is in truth *one* with the Almighty, the uncreated, the supreme God. Therefore let all the angels of God, and every creature of God, and, above all, every soul of man, worship him.

III. Religious. For they show, concerning the Christian life : 1. *Its solemnity.* We are under the eye of him who says as none other can, " I know thy works." Thus he speaks to us all. Others do not, cannot, know us as he does. Who, then, will dare to disobey ?

> " Arm me with jealous care,
> As in thy sight to live ;
> And oh, thy servant, Lord, prepare
> A strict account to give."

2. *Its nature.* (1) It is a battle. All have to wage a warfare. None are exempt. Not poor Sardis and Laodicea alone, the weakest and worst of the Churches, have this warfare to wage, but Smyrna and Philadelphia also, the strongest and best. Every one is spoken to and of as engaged in a conflict in which, if he do not overcome, he will be overcome. We cannot " sit and sing ourselves away to everlasting bliss." But a battle has to be fought, and only to those who overcome will the prize be given. (2) This battle has tremendous issues. Which excel in intensity, the promises to the faithful or the threatenings to the unfaithful, it is hard to say. But they are thus vividly contrasted in each letter, that we may the more readily see and deeply feel that this is no holiday pastime, no child's play, to which we are all inexorably called, but a serious, stern, and awful war. True, to-day, our foes are spiritual rather than tangible and visible ; not cruel and bloody men who hunt our lives to destroy them, but the unseen forces of hell which are within and all around us, and are the more mighty for that they are unseen. We have need to watch and we have need to pray. But there are (3) vast encouragements ; for (*a*) it is assured that all *may* overcome. We are not mocked. Even to Laodicea this was said, thereby implying that even for them, poor fallen miserable ones that they were, victory was possible, even they might overcome. And so now ; they who most of all are " tied and bound by the chain of their sins " (and some are dreadfully so), yet even they, " through the might of Christ their Lord," may conquer in the fight. (*b*) And we are told how. For the titles of the Lord in these several letters show him to be *an all-sufficient Saviour.* However many and varied are the wants of his Church, he meets them and ministers to their needs. Are they in peril ? He is their Guardian, holding them fast in his right hand. Are they beset by the powers of hell ? He is their eternal, their glorified Saviour, possessed of all power. Are they troubled by fierce persecutors or by false friends ? He who hath the sharp two-edged sword will avenge them. Are they wandering in heart and life, gone and yet going astray ? He whose eyes are as a flame of fire sees them and will follow them, and will surely and, if needs be, sternly correct them. Are they almost worn out with toil and trial ? He will uphold them, for has he not the seven Spirits of God ? Does he bid them set out in arduous service, telling them that there

is an open door before them? He encourages and cheers them, in that he hath the key of David, and that when he opens no man shuts. Does he tear off the false coverings by which their true and evil state is hidden? As he does so he reminds them that he is their faithful Friend and Counsellor. Surely here, then, is the general lesson to be learnt from these varied letters of the Lord—that there can be no stress or strait in which his servants may be, whether by their own folly and fault or by the malice and might of others, but what he has grace sufficient for all, and his grace *shall* supply all their need. Finally (c) observe the heart-cheering promise with which these letters all end. Imagery of the most sublime and exalted description is employed to set forth the glorious reward which now to some extent is given, but in the future far more fully shall be given to the faithful Christian. He is to eat of the tree of life, which is in the midst of the Paradise of God; the second death is to have no power over him; he is to be invested with kingly authority over the nations, like to that which Christ possesses; he is to be arrayed in triumphant and beautiful vestments, with white raiment is he to be clothed, and his name is to be confessed by the glorified Redeemer before all heaven; he is to become a pillar in the temple of God, and on him is to be written the Name of God, and the name of the city of God, from which he is to go no more out, he is to sit with Christ on his throne, as Christ is set down with the Father on his throne; he is to eat of the hidden manna, and to receive the white stone on which a new name is written, a name which no man knoweth, saving he who receiveth it. How great then are the encouragements held out to us all to cheer us on in our warfare; so that, if the battle be stern and the issues tremendous, we are not left to wage it at our own charges, but are daily helped by the grace of our Lord now, and animated by the sure prospect of that prize which shall be given hereafter to all who truly strive for it.

Such are some of the teachings common to all these letters. Others of a more special and particular kind they doubtless have, but these alone justify and enforce the sevenfold word, "He that hath an ear, let him hear," etc.—S. C.

Vers. 1—3.—*The revelation.* The interpretation of the Book of Revelation confessedly difficult, some portions in particular; hence many differing views. But the book designed for practical purposes; throughout it a rich vein of practical instruction. The homily seizes upon the practical truth—that truth which can be worked up into the practice of daily life.

I. THE ORIGIN OF THE REVELATION—GOD. It is the revelation "which God gave." Fountain of all truth; stamps its high character; to be received with becoming reverence, thankfulness, and obedience.

II. THE PROCESS OF THE REVELATION. Gradation of thought. "*God* gave" the revelation to "his servants" by *Jesus Christ*, "the Word of God," who "sent and signified it by *his angel*," who made it known unto the "*servant John*," who bare witness of "all things that he saw" unto all the "*servants*" of Jesus Christ. It is a word for the faithful bondservants, the true disciples of the Lord Jesus in all lands and in all ages.

III. THE SUBSTANCE OF THE REVELATION. It is "*the Word of God*," the outbreathing of the Divine thought, the Divine will and purpose. Of this Word of God, Jesus is the Medium of testimony. This "Word," testified by Jesus Christ, was made to appear to John; all things that he saw. It was a holy vision.

IV. THE BLESSING PRONOUNCED UPON THE FAITHFUL RECEPTION OF THE REVELATION. 1. To "him that readeth." 2. To "them that hear." 3. To "them that keep the things that are written." 4. For its fulfilment is near; "The time is at hand." It brings the blessing: (1) Of present comfort, light, and peace. (2) Of confidence in the Divine government of the world. (3) Of daily advancing preparation for the future kingdom of heaven to which it leads. (4) It is impossible to receive, hear, and keep any Divine word without therein receiving blessing.—R. G.

Vers. 4—7.—*The apostolic salutation.* The servant John, by no other name known, in fulfilment of his duty as the one by whom the great revelation was "sent and signified," hurries to pronounce his salutation to "the seven Churches which are in Asia"—typical examples of the one Church in its sevenfold, universal experience.

I. The salutation INVOKES BLESSINGS: 1. Of the highest character: "grace and peace." The entire revelation is, for the Church, a revelation of "grace and peace." It begins in grace; it terminates in peace. These the alpha and omega of gospel blessings, the origin and end. All is of God's grace; all tends to peace in man—to peace universal. 2. From the Source of all good, the Triune Source of all blessing. From the *Eternal*—" him which is, and which was, and which is to come "—the I AM—*Jehovah*; from the sevenfold Spirit; and from Jesus Christ, " the faithful Witness, the Firstborn of the dead, the Ruler of the kings of the earth." These ascriptions have special reference to the condition and necessities of the Church, whose living Head is " all in all." Christ, the Revelation of the Father, becomes prominent.

II. The salutation, therefore, ASCRIBES GLORY AND UNENDING DOMINION unto him; declaring (1) his love; (2) his redeeming work, fruit of that love; and (3) his constitution of his Church as a priestly kingdom—a kingdom of which he is the supreme Sovereign; a kingdom of priests, to offer up spiritual sacrifice continually, acceptable unto God.

III. The salutation further PROCLAIMS THE SECOND COMING of that Lord Jesus Christ who is the central theme of all the following revelation. 1. The fact of it. 2. Accompanying circumstances of it: " with the clouds." 3. In view of all: " Every eye shall see him." 4. Special reference to offenders : " And they which pierced him." 5. Consequence—universal mourning : " All the tribes of the earth shall mourn over him." Our hearts echo the cry, " Even so, come, Lord Jesus. Amen."—R. G.

Vers. 9—20.— *The vision of the Son of man.* The vision granted for the comfort of the suffering Church was made: 1. To a " brother and partaker " in all " the tribulation and kingdom and patience," sharing at the very hour, " in the isle that is called Patmos," the consequences of faithfully proclaiming the Word of God and bearing his testimony to Jesus. 2. He was in an exalted spiritual state: " in the Spirit "—under the control of the Spirit ; sensitively alive to the teachings of the Spirit ; filled with the Spirit. 3. On the Lord's day. 4. A great voice arrests his attention, and commands him to write and proclaim to the seven named Churches the vision which should be granted to him. The vision embraced—

I. A SYMBOLICAL VIEW OF THE CHURCH. " Seven golden candlesticks." A single seven-branched lamp-stand, representing the Church in its essential unity and sevenfold diversity. " And the seven candlesticks are seven Churches." The purity and glory of the Church may be symbolized in its being " golden."

II. A VIEW OF THE LORD DWELLING IN AND RULING OVER THE CHURCHES. 1. The presence of the Lord in the midst of the Churches is the one essential and abiding source of consolation to all believers, especially in the times of danger, persecution, and sorrow. The attention of the seer now confined to the vision of him who, though like a Son of man, is " the First and the Last, and the Living One." 2. Testimony to the Divine nature of our Lord. " I am the Alpha and the Omega, saith the Lord God ; " " I am the First and the Last," saith the " one like unto a son of man." Truly God was manifested in the flesh ! The descriptive view of the Lord is not to be imagined or delineated as a picture. It is grotesque ; its symbolical meaning only to be regarded. 3. The dress indicates his high-priestly office ; the head, hair, eyes, feet, and voice are symbolical representations. 4. The Lord's care and control over the messengers of the Churches symbolized by, " And he had in his right hand seven stars ; " " The seven stars are the angels of the seven Churches." 5. The Lord the Source of truth, and the truth the one weapon of the Lord's might : " Out of his mouth proceeded a sharp two-edged sword." 6. The human humble awe in presence of the Divine Lord : " And when I saw him, I fell at his feet as one dead." 7. The consolation of the Divine Lord to his affrighted, humble servant : " Fear not ; " confirmed by the glorious assurance, " I am the First and the Last, and the Living One ; and I was dead, and behold, I am alive for evermore, and have the keys of death and of Hades." From this, the manifested Lord, the sacred seer receives command to "write the things which thou sawest, and the things which are, and the things which shall come to pass hereafter."—R. G.

Vers. 1—3.—*Aspects of human history.* " The Revelation of Jesus Christ," etc. Human history seems to be presented here as (1) *a revelation,* (2) *a record,* and (3) *a study.*

I. AS A REVELATION. "The Revelation of Jesus Christ" (ver. 1). Ἀποκάλυψις Ἰησοῦ Χριστοῦ. To "reveal" means to uncover, to disclose. A revelation is an unveiling of the hidden. Whatever has not appeared, whether things or persons, is hidden or concealed from view. There are universes hidden from us as yet, that in the future may appear. There is only One Being in immensity that can reveal such things because he sees them, and that is God. Hence all that is known of "things which must shortly come to pass," or, indeed, things that will ever come to pass, is "the revelation of Jesus Christ, which God gave unto him." Observe that the revelation is *Divine*. Who can reveal the unseen and unknown but God? Christ was once unknown. He revealed him. His advent to earth was a revelation of himself to mankind. No one can reveal God but Christ, and no one can reveal Christ but God. But the *object* to which the revelation here refers is not any particular person, Divine or human, but the *future history of mankind*. This is hidden. "We know not what shall be on the morrow." "It is not for you to know the times or the seasons, which the Father hath put in his own power." He reveals the future history of mankind in two ways. 1. *By disclosing its essential principles*. All the events of human conduct are caused and controlled by two principles—good and evil. All human actions are traceable to one of these, and they are in constant conflict. The colossal image and the little stone, grace and truth, are ever here on this planet battling in human souls throughout the race. These principles Christ hath revealed, not merely in his teachings, but in his agony and bloody sweat. They shone out in lightning, and broke out in thunder on the ghastly heights of Golgotha. He who understands these opposing principles can foretell all human history. He who thoroughly knows the laws of *material* nature can tell to the hour when a comet will sweep the heavens, when the tide will overstep its boundaries, when celestial eclipses will occur; even so he who duly appreciates the force and tendency of these opposing *moral principles* will not greatly mistake in his auguries of the future of the race. "That which hath been is now, and that which is will be." 2. *By the dispensations of Providence*. Christ is the Maker and Manager of all human events. He is in all events; they are his *comings* to men, his advents. And present events are types and prophecies of the future. In this age the future can be seen, as in the buds and blossoms of this Spring you may see the buds and blossoms of all the springs that are to be.

II. AS A RECORD. 1. Here is *a commission from heaven to record certain things*. "He sent and signified it by his angel unto his servant John: who bare record of the Word of God" (ver. 2). "'Messenger' is the literal translation of ἄγγελον, and makes sense everywhere, which 'angel' does not, for the 'thorn in the flesh' was not an angel." No one can tell who the angel or messenger was; probably Christ himself. A "revelation" is one thing, a "record" another. What we call the Bible is not a "revelation," but the "record" of a "revelation." The things to be revealed are "things which must shortly come to pass." What we call providence is never at rest; its wheels are ever in motion. In the case of every man, family, community, nation, there are things that "must shortly come to pass." Those things continue from period to period and from æon to æon, and however differing in *form*, are identical in *spirit*. These all deserve "record." They are all streams from an inexhaustible fountain of life, branches from an eternal root of being. Things of the future grow out of the present by the eternal law of evolution. Countless generations will come and go; new revelations will have to be recorded. And thus the Bibles of the race will multiply through all time. 2. Here is a commission from heaven to reveal certain things, *addressed to a man*. "His servant John." He is a man. Men, not angels, are to be the chroniclers of the Divine for man. John is here the commissioned chronicler. He was in all likelihood the same disciple whom Jesus loved, the author of the Gospel bearing his name, and he to whom the Saviour, on the cross, entrusted his beloved mother. 3. Here is a commission from heaven to record certain things, addressed to a man *of the highest moral class*. He is here called his "servant," the servant of God—his willing, loving, loyal servant. In his Gospel he had borne "record of the Word of God, and of the testimony of Jesus Christ, and of all things that he saw." Heaven commissions men to record the things that are "coming to pass," and the men to do it are men in thorough sympathy with the true, the beautiful, and the good. *Moral goodness is an essential qualification of a true historian.*

III. As A STUDY. The "revelation" is given, the "record" is made, and now comes study. "Blessed is he that readeth, and they that hear the words of this prophecy, and keep those things which are written therein" (ver. 3). Observe: 1. *That historic events are of moral significance.* There is a Divine meaning in everything that is either produced or permitted by the All-wise and the All-good. There is not a circumstance that transpires in our individual life that does not say to us, "Thus saith the Lord." 2. *That the moral significance involves a Divine law.* Apart from its element to excite feeling, rouse the imagination, and stimulate speculative thought, it contains law. Hence it is not only said here, "Blessed is he that readeth, and they that hear the words," but they that "*keep those things that are written therein.*" The moral lessons which historic events teach are Divine laws, and come on the subject of them with binding force. 3. *That in practical obedience to this Divine law there is true happiness.* "Blessed is he." "We then," says an able expositor, "as living actors in the world, have not only to read and hear, but to *keep*—keep in mind and action those principles which preside over the development of all human history." "Be ye doers of the Word, and not hearers only." "Blessed are they that hear the Word of God, and keep it." He, and he only, who incarnates the great moral principles of history brings sunshine and music into his soul.—D. T.

Vers. 4, 5 (first part).—*Man divinely dignified.* "John to the seven Churches which are in Asia: Grace be unto you," etc. These words lead us to look on man as *divinely dignified.* Morally, men are degraded creatures; they have degraded themselves and they degrade one another. Man may and should honour his brother, but he cannot dignify him; if he is to be dignified at all he must dignify himself, and this he can only do as God wills and helps him. In these words he appears as *divinely dignified* in two respects.

I. MAN IS DIVINELY DIGNIFIED AS A REPRESENTATIVE OF THE DIVINE. John is here employed to represent Divine things "to the seven Churches which are in Asia" (ver. 4). The men who are employed by worldly kings—though they may be in a moral sense contemptible beings—esteem it a great honour to be their representatives in foreign courts. But how infinite the honour of him who is employed by the King "eternal, immortal, invisible"! 1. *He represents Divine good.* "Grace be unto you, and peace." Divine favour and Divine bliss, the sum total these of the highest good in all worlds and times. 2. *He represents the Divine Being.* He represents him: (1) In his absolute existence. "From him which is, and which was, and which is to come" (ver. 4). This is a periphrasis for the incommunicable name of Jehovah, the "I AM," the Unnamable and the Nameless, who is without beginning, without change, without succession, without end. Such a Being exists, and all men instinctively feel after him and forge for him names of great variety, but none appropriate—the Unknown and the Unknowable. (2) In his spiritual influence. "From the seven Spirits which are before his throne" (ver. 4). Does the seven mean the totality, or variety in unity, the one essence multiform in influence? The One Eternal wields endless influences through every part of his universe—material, intellectual, and moral. The well has many streams, the sun unnumbered beams. (3) In his transcendent Messiah. "And from Jesus Christ"—Christ the Anointed, the Messiah of God. This divinely anointed One is here set forth in three aspects. (*a*) In relation to truth. "Who is the Faithful Witness." What is truth? *Reality.* Christ came to bear witness of the reality of realities. As a Witness of God, Christ was a *competent* Witness. He was *intellectually* competent. He knew God. "No man hath seen God at any time; the Only Begotten of the Father," he alone knew the Absolute. He was *morally* competent. He had no motive to misrepresent him. He alone had the moral qualifications fully to represent him. You must be pure to represent purity, just to represent justice, loving to represent love. (*b*) In relation to immortality. The "First Begotten of the dead" (ver. 5). How was he the First Begotten of the dead; for did not Lazarus rise from the grave? Not in time, but in *importance.* He arose by his own power. No one else ever did. He arose as the Representative of risen saints. "Our vile body shall be fashioned and made like unto his glorious body." (*c*) In relation to empire. "The Prince of the kings of the earth." All power is given unto him. "He is exalted far above all heavens." Thrones, principalities, dominions, all are subject to him.

II. MAN IS DIVINELY DIGNIFIED AS A REPRESENTATIVE OF THE DIVINE TO MAN. "John to the seven Churches which are in Asia" (ver. 4). "The enumeration which presently follows," says Dr. Vaughan, "of the Churches designed, shows that Asia is here used in its narrowest sense: not of the quarter of the globe so denominated, not even of Asia Minor, but of one province on the western side of that country, expressly distinguished in two well-known passages of the Acts of the Apostles, from Cappadocia and Pontus, from Phrygia and Pamphylia, from Galatia, Mysia, and Bithynia." Not only is he divinely dignified who is employed as the Messenger of the Divine, but he to whom the Divine is sent. The seven congregations in Asia Minor were highly honoured of God as the objects of his redemptive message. How dignified of God is the man who is made at once the *Recipient* and the *Messenger* of Divine thoughts! —D. T.

Vers. 5—7.—*Christ and the soul.* "Unto him that loved us, and washed us from our sins in his own blood, and hath made us kings and priests unto God and his Father; to him be glory," etc. These words suggest a few thoughts concerning Christ and the soul.

I. CHRIST IS THE LOVER OF THE SOUL. "Unto him that loved us" (ver. 5). Other beings may love the human soul—angels may, saints may—but no one *has loved it as Christ has.* 1. He loved it with an *absolutely disinterested* love. Alas! we know but little of disinterested affection. With all our love for each other, there is generally a mixture of selfishness. But Christ had nothing to gain from the human spirit; its damnation would not diminish his blessedness; its salvation would not add to his ineffable bliss. He loved the soul for its own sake, as the offspring of God, endowed with wonderful capabilities, possessing in itself a fountain of influence that would spread indefinitely through all time and space. 2. He loved it with a *practically self-sacrificing* love. It was not a love that existed merely as an emotion, or that even wrought occasional services; it was a love that led to the sacrifice of himself. "He loved us, and gave himself for us." "Greater love hath no man than this, that a man lay down his life." 3. He loved it with an *earnestly forgiving* love. "When we were enemies Christ died for the ungodly." He loved those who were not only out of sympathy with him, but who were in malignant hostility to him; and his love was not only such as to incline him to listen to petitions for pardon, but as inspired him with an intense longing to forgive his enemies. "Herein is love." Who ever loved like this? Here is a love whose height, depth, length, breadth, passeth all knowledge.

II. CHRIST IS THE CLEANSER OF THE SOUL. "And washed ['loosed'] us from our sins in his own blood" (ver. 5). The moral restoration of the soul to the knowledge, image, and enjoyment of God is represented in a variety of figures in the Bible, which is a highly figurative book. When the lost state of the soul is represented as a state of *condemnation*, then its restoration is represented as *forgiveness* or *justification*; when its lost state is represented as *enmity to God*, then its restoration is set forth under the metaphor of *reconciliation*; when its lost state is represented as a state of *death* or *sleep*, then its restoration is set forth as a *quickening* and *awakening*; when its lost state is represented as a *bondage*, then its restoration is set forth as an *enfranchisement*; when its lost state is represented as a state of *pollution* or *uncleanness*, then its restoration is represented as a *washing* or a *cleansing*. All these figurative expressions represent one thing—the *moral restoration* of the soul; and this is spoken of in the text as wrought by Christ. "Washed us from our sins in his own blood." To be washed in blood is an expression that sounds incongruous and somewhat offensive; but it does not mean *material* blood, as the vulgar and the sensuous understand, but the *spiritual* blood, which is his *moral life*, his *self-sacrificing love*. The cleansing influence which is here applied to the blood is elsewhere applied to the "Name of Christ." Now "ye are clean through the word I have spoken;" again, "Sanctified through thy truth." Then to the "water of the Word," "That he might sanctify and cleanse it with the washing of water by the Word." The "Name," the "Word," the "Spirit," the "Truth," which are represented in such passages as cleansing the soul, must of course be regarded as meaning essentially the same thing as "blood" here, which stands for the *moral spirit* of Christ, which is the same thing as Christ himself. He it is who cleanseth the soul—cleanseth it by his life. The figurative language here is purely Judaic, taken 'rom the old temple ceremonies; for "almost all things were purified by the Law through blood." The grand mission and work of Christ are to put away sin from the soul. Sin is the guilt, sin is the curse, sin is the ruin of human nature. Sin is not so engrained, so wrought into the texture of the human soul that it cannot be removed; it can be washed out, it is separable from it, it can be detached.

III. CHRIST IS THE ENNOBLER OF THE SOUL. "Hath made us kings and priests unto God" (ver. 6). 1. *Christ makes souls "kings."* "I appoint unto you a kingdom, as my Father hath appointed unto me." Souls in their unregenerate state are paupers, prisoners, slaves; they are the mere creatures of internal passions and external circumstances. Christ enthrones the soul, gives it the sceptre of self-control, and enables it to make all things subservient to its own moral advancement. 2. *Christ makes souls "priests."* True priests are in some respects greater than kings. Kings have to do with creatures, priests with God. Christ, then, is the Ennobler of souls. Worldly sovereigns may and do bestow titles of greatness on men. The wonder is that they should have the audacity to attempt to ennoble by bestowing titles. They cannot bestow *greatness itself*. Christ bestows true greatness—greatness of thought, heart, sympathy, aim, nature. He alone is great whom Christ makes great; all others are in the bonds of corruption.

IV. CHRIST IS THE DEITY OF THE SOUL. "To him be glory and dominion for ever and ever." The souls whom Christ has loved, cleansed, and ennobled feel that he is their God, and render to him the willing and everlasting homage of their nature. "Unto him that loved us, and washed [loosed] us from our sins in [by] his own blood." God in Christ is the grand object of human worship, and those whom Christ has thus restored cannot but worship him. Worship with them is not a *service*, but a *spirit*; is not obedience to a *law*, but the irrepressible instinct of a *life*.

V. CHRIST IS THE HOPE OF THE SOUL. "Behold, he cometh with clouds, and every eye shall see him" (ver. 7). The high probability is that this is a prophetic description of Christ as he came in his providence to the destruction of Jerusalem. Between his final advent and this there are so many striking resemblances that the description of the one is remarkably applicable to the other. Applying the words to the final advent, we have four facts concerning it. 1. *Christ will come.* Reason and conscience, as well as the Bible, teach this. Enoch, the seventh from Adam, prophesied of it; Job knew that he would stand again upon the earth. Christ and his apostles frequently and unequivocally taught it (Luke ix. 26). 2. *His coming will be terribly grand.* "On the clouds of heaven." The grandest objects to mortal eyes are the heavens that encircle us. Their vast expanse and immeasurable height, all radiant with rolling orbs in boundless variety, seem to bear us into the awful depths of infinitude. Anything strange on the face of those heavens has always a power to strike terror on human souls. Christ is represented as coming on the clouds. Daniel, in a vision, beheld him thus (Dan. vii. 13). Christ himself declared that thus he would come (Mark xxiv. 30; xxvi. 64). Angels have declared the same (Acts i. 11). John beheld him on a "great white throne," so effulgent that the material universe melted away before it. How unlike the despised Galilæan! 3. *His coming will be universally observed.* "Every eye shall see him" (ver. 7). It is an event in which all are interested. Men *in all ages and lands*, from Adam "to the last of woman born." Men *of all social grades* and *mental types* are all vitally concerned in this stupendous event. Hence all shall see him. (1) All shall see him *immediately*. Now we see him representatively by his words, ordinances, and ministers. But then we shall see *him*. (2) All shall see him *fully*. Not one shall have a partial view, a mere passing aspect, but a full, complete vision. His full Person will fall complete on every eyeball. (3) All shall see him *impressively*. The universe had never had such an impressive sight of him before. 4. *His coming will be differently regarded.* (1) To some it will be a scene of poignant distress. "They also which pierced him: and all kindreds [the tribes] of the earth shall wail because of him [mourn over him]" (ver. 7). What inexpressible and inconceivable anguish will the rejecters of Christ experience then! (2) To others it will be welcomed with delight. "Even so, Amen." The good, in all ages, have said, "Come, Lord Jesus." To his true disciples it will be a period in which all difficulties will be explained, all imperfections removed, all evils ended for ever. But it is not in an outward or objective sense that this appearance of Christ is to be practically regarded.[1] It is a subjective appearance. The heaven on which he is to appear is the individual soul, and the "clouds of heaven" are the clouds of thought and feeling that roll within us.—D. T.

Ver. 5.—*The work of works.* "Unto him that loved us, and washed us from our sins in his own blood!" Washing in blood is an incongruity. The word translated "washed" should be "loosened," and the general idea undoubtedly is, "Unto him that loosed us from our sins by his own life [or, 'by himself'] be glory." The words refer to the *work of works.*

I. This is the most important of all works. Loosing a soul from sin. Sin is a chain of darkness, a chain that enslaves, not the mere body, but all the faculties of the soul, and confines it in the cell of moral ignorance and corruption. Fallen angels are represented as manacled in this chain of darkness. What a chain is this! It is (1) heavy, (2) galling, (3) strong, and (4) becomes stronger with the commission of every sin.

II. This, the most important of all works, is effected by Christ, and by him only. He is here represented as doing it by his own "blood." Sometimes the work is ascribed to " water," to the " Word," to " truth," to " grace," and to the " Spirit." The word is here used as a symbol of his self-sacrificing ministry. This is the work to which Christ gives his life. There is no other being in the universe that can break this chain save Christ. He came into the world to open the prison doors, and to set the captives free. " Ye shall know the truth, and the truth shall set you free."

III. That for this, the most important of all works, Christ receives the praises of eternity. "Unto him that loved us." True gratitude implies a belief in three things. 1. *A belief in the value of the service rendered.* Where the service is trivial, and of no importance, gratitude will not be very stirring or strong. 2. *A belief in the kindness of the motive which inspired the service.* If a man renders us a service, and we feel that his motive was sordid and selfish, we could scarcely feel gratitude, however greatly he benefited us. 3. *A belief in the undeservedness of the service on our part.* If we feel that the service rendered was merited by us, and that the author was bound in justice to render it, we could feel but little if any gratitude. Now, for these three reasons gratitude to Christ must rise to the highest point—a greater service could not be rendered; a kinder motive could not be imagined; a more undeserved benediction could not be conferred. " Unto him that loved us," etc. !—D. T.

Vers. 8, 9.—*A transcendent Being, and a remarkable character.* " I am Alpha and Omega, the Beginning and the Ending," etc. Here we have two objects arresting our attention and demanding thought.

I. A Being whose existence is transcendent. " I am Alpha and Omega, the Beginning and the Ending, saith the Lord, which is, and which was, and which is to come." Although these words are considered of doubtful authority, and probably an interpolation, they are a representation of the Infinite One. They not only agree with other declarations of him in sacred Writ, but they are repeated elsewhere. Here is : 1. *Eternity.* " I am Alpha and Omega." (1) Eternity in relation to all the past. " I am Alpha" that is, the First, the Beginning. There is not a creature throughout immensity that had not a " beginning;" but there is no point in the past in which he was not. Go back through all the million ages and through all the million millenniums, and you reach no point in which he did not exist. He occupied the boundlessness of immensity alone. No one thought or felt or moved but he. It as with him to determine as to whether there should be any other existence besides his own. The universes that have been, that are, and that are yet to be, were all in his eternal mind, in archetype and possibility. (2) Eternity also in relation to the future. " The Beginning and the Ending." All that have had a beginning will peradventure have an end; yea, certainly so, unless he determines otherwise. Both the commencement and continuance of all things hang on his will; but he will never have an end. All life may be extinguished, the whole universe go back to chaos and be lost in the abysses of nonentity; but he will be.

[1] See homily ' Voices and Visions from Eternity,' on vers. 10—17

> " Even as darkness, self-impregned, brings forth
> Creative light and silence, speech; so beams,
> Known through all ages, hope and help of man,
> One God omnific, sole, original,
> Wise, wonder-working wielder of the whole,
> Infinite, inconceivable, immense,
> The Midst without beginning, and the First
> From the beginning, and of all being Last."
>
> ('Festus.')

2. *Omnipotence.* "The Almighty." There is nothing impossible for him to do but wrong. " It is impossible for God to lie," to deceive, or defraud. This moral weakness is his glory. " God is truth, and light is shadow," says Plato. " The Lord is great in power : . . . he hath his way in the whirlwind and in the storm, and the clouds are the dust of his feet. He rebuketh the sea, and maketh it dry, and drieth up all the rivers : Bashan languisheth, and Carmel, and the flower of Lebanon languisheth. The mountains quake at him, and the hills melt, and the earth is burned at his presence, yea, the world, and all that dwell therein."

II. A MAN WHOSE CHARACTER IS REMARKABLE. Here is: 1. *A character of distinguished excellence described.* "I John, who also am your brother, and companion [partaker] in tribulation." John describes himself: (1) As a "*brother.*" His heart glows with a Christly fraternity for the good of all the Churches throughout all the world. (2) As a *sufferer.* He is " in *tribulation.*" The best men on earth are subject to suffering. He was a member of the kingdom of Christ, a loving, faithful, loyal subject of his spiritual empire. "The kingdom and patience of [which are in] Jesus Christ." In that kingdom he was a companion with all who suffered, a fellow-partaker of their tribulations. There has always been suffering in connection with the kingdom of Christ, and all the sufferers feel a blessed companionship. During the first hundred years, persecutions in this kingdom were very sanguinary and severe. 2. *A character of distinguished excellence banished by bloody persecutors.* " In the isle that is called Patmos." This was the scene of his banishment: a rocky island in the Mediterranean, about fifteen miles in circumference—a most wild, barren spot; a convict settlement, whither the Romans banished all criminal wretches they deemed unfit for liberty. On this desolate island, amidst the greatest villains of the age, this great character was banished. Strange that the providence of Heaven should have allowed one of the most Christly men on the earth at that time to live for an hour in such a scene. But Patmos to John and Patmos to the other residents was a different place. To John it was a theatre of sublimest revelations, the very gate of heaven. He was not alone there; he felt himself surrounded by a great " multitude which no man could number," with countless thousands of angels; and there he wrote a book to bless humanity through every coming age. 3. *A character of distinguished excellence banished by bloody persecutors for the cause of Christ.* " For the Word of God, and for the testimony of Jesus Christ." He was there, not because he had perpetrated any crime, but because he had rendered the highest sevice to his age. He bore " testimony of Jesus," and preached the " Word of God." "John had now," says Dr. Vaughan, " reached a late point in his long pilgrimage. The storm of persecution had broken upon him in his gentle and steadfast ministry at Ephesus, and had driven him to the little island of Patmos for the testimony of the truth. In that solitude, however, he was not alone. Shut out as he was now from all Christian converse, he was only the more fitted for converse with Christ. Debarred by no fault of his own from all Christian ordinances, expelled from that congregation in which for so long, day after day, he had uttered the message of truth and the call of love, he was admitted now to worship in the very sanctuary above, and to receive, if he might no longer give, instruction from the lips of the Divine Master himself."—D. T.

Vers. 10—17.— *Voices and visions from eternity.* "I was in the Spirit on the Lord's day," etc. Concerning this vision, and, indeed, nearly all the visions recorded in this Apocalypse, there are three facts to be predicated at the outset. 1. *It is mental.* What is here reported as heard and seen by John was not seen by his bodily eye or heard by his bodily ear. It was, I consider, *a purely mental vision.* It is one of the characteristic attributes and distinctions of man that he can see and hear objects that come not within the range of his senses. Though the eagle is reported to have a keen and far-reaching eye, and has borne its pinions into the region of sunny azure, it has no glimpse of the spirit-domain; whereas a man who may be even sightless and deaf has the power of seeing wonderful things and hearing wonderful things. The sightless bard of England lived in a bright world; his genius bore him aloft into regions where there was no cloud. These mental visions are of two classes—the *voluntary* and the *involuntary*. The former are the productions of creative genius, the latter are those dreams of the night when deep sleep falls on man. Mental visions are not *necessarily illusions.* They are often more *real* than those of the physical; they come further into the depths of our being. and convey to us impressions of things of which material phenomena are but the effects and expressions. 2. *It is credible.* Had it been reported that John saw with the *outward* eye, and heard with the *outward* ear, the things here reported, the report could not have been believed. The objects are so unique, so incongruous with all that is natural, so grotesque, and, we may say, so monstrous and unæsthetic, that we could not believe a man who said he saw them with his outward eye or heard them with his outward ear. A Being "clothed with a garment down to the foot, and girt about the paps with a golden girdle. His head and his hairs were white like wool, as white as snow; and his eyes were as a flame of fire; and his feet like unto fine brass, as if they burned in a furnace; and his voice as the sound of many waters. And he had in his right hand seven stars: and out of his mouth went a sharp two-edged sword: and his countenance was as the sun shineth in his strength." Who could believe a man who said he beheld these with his *bodily* eye? But as a *mental vision it is credible enough.* What grotesque shapes appear to us in dreams! what strange monstrosities rise to our *mental* eye! The deities that arose out of the imagination of Nineveh, Greece, and India, and throughout the whole domain of heathendom, were as unnatural and incoherent in their forms as the aspects of the *Son of man* before us. The reports of *mental* visions, however extraordinary, are credible; men believe in them. 3. *It is symbolic.* It has a deep spiritual meaning, it adumbrates mighty lessons, it is a picture of eternal realities. What are the great truths here symbolized? That a wonderful *voice* from eternity comes to man; a wonderful *personage* from eternity appears to man; and wonderful *impressions* from eternity are made upon man. Notice—

I. THAT A WONDERFUL VOICE FROM ETERNITY COMES TO MAN. "I was in the Spirit on the Lord's day, and heard behind me a great voice, as of a trumpet." We are told also that the voice that came to John was "as the sound of many waters." The *spiritual* condition of John when the voice came is worthy of note. He was "in the Spirit." This means, I trow, something more than being in the spirit in a *moral* sense—in the spirit of heavenly loyalty and devotion. In this condition all true men are; they are led by the Spirit; they walk by the Spirit. It is being in an elevated state of mind, a kind of *ecstasy* in which a man is lifted out of himself, in which, like Paul, he is taken up to heaven, and sees and hears things unutterable. He was in such a condition as this at a certain period here called "the Lord's day." All men who are in the Spirit in the *moral* sense—in the sense of vital godliness—feel and regard all days as "the Lord's day." But the days of spiritual ecstasies and transports are ever special. Perhaps the first day of the week is here referred to—the day of our Saviour's resurrection from the dead. Probably the association of that wonderful day served to raise his soul into this ecstatic state. Concerning the voice that came to him when in this state, it was marked by two things. 1. *The voice was marked by clearness.* "A great voice, as of a trumpet." The voice was clear, loud, strong, as a trumpet. It was a voice to which he could not close his ears if he wished to; its clarion-notes rang into him. 2. *The voice was marked by fulness.* "As the sound of many waters." "Daniel described the voice of the Ancient of Days as the voice of a multitude (Dan. x. 6); but the voice of the multitude was in earlier Hebrew writings compared to the sound of the waves of the sea, which the voice of the Lord could alone subdue (Ps. lxv. 7; xciii. 4). This image the evangelist adopts to describe the voice of Christ, strong and majestic amid the Babel-sounds of earth. That voice whose word stilled the sea sounds as the waves of the sea which St. John heard him rebuke." Is there any voice in nature equal to the voice of the old ocean—majestic, full, continuous, drowning all other sounds? The clamour and the din of a thousand armies on the shore are lost amidst the roar of the incoming waves. Such was the *voice* that came to John from *eternity*, and such a voice comes to all men in every condition and in every age, clear and full, bearing messages to the soul from the great Father of spirits. True, clear, full, and continuous though that voice be, it is only heard by those who, like John, are "in the Spirit"—whose spirits are alive and elevated with the real and the Divine.

11 THAT A WONDERFUL PERSONAGE FROM ETERNITY APPEARS TO MAN. "Like unto the Son of man." Christ was indeed the Son of man, not the son of a tribe or of a class, but the Son of humanity, free from all national peculiarities, tribal idiosyncrasies, or ecclesiastical predilections. Observe here two things. 1. *The scene of the appearance.* "In the midst of the seven candlesticks." The seven Churches, viz. those of "Ephesus, Smyrna, Pergamos, Thyatira, Sardis, Philadelphia, and Laodicea," are here represented as "golden candlesticks;" they are precious lights, they bear and diffuse the light of God. Why these seven Churches are here selected and addressed rather than other Churches, of which there were several, some more important than these, such as the Church at Corinth, Thessalonica, etc., I know not. It might have been because they had in their combination all those excellences and defects, needs and duties, which together represent the universal Church, the Church of all times and lands. It was in these Churches, these "candlesticks," that the "Son of man" now appeared to John. He who would see Christ must look for him in *true* Churches, the communions of holy men. 2. *The characteristics of the appearance.* Mark the description. He was "clothed with a garment down to the foot, and girt about the paps with a golden girdle"—a long, ample robe of regal authority. "His head and his hairs were white like wool, as white as snow." Does the white hair indicate decay? It frequently does so with us. Snowy locks are at once the sign and consequence of declining strength. Not so with him. He is "the same yesterday, and to-day, and for ever." "Fire," says Trench, "at its highest intensity is white; the red in fire is of the earth, earthy; it implies something which the fire has not yet thoroughly subdued, while the pure flame is absolutely white. This must be kept in mind whenever we read of white as the colour and livery of heaven." "His eyes were as a flame of fire" —eyes that penetrate into the deepest depth of the soul, discern moral distinctions, and burn with a holy indignation at the wrong. "His feet like unto fine brass, as if they burned in a furnace." This indicates strength at once enduring and resistless. "He had in his right hand seven stars." These seven stars represent, it is supposed, the chief pastors of the seven Churches. An ideal pastor is a moral star, catching and reflecting the light of the Sun of Righteousness. "Out of his mouth went [proceeded] a sharp two-edged sword." This is the Word of the truth, elsewhere called the "sword of the Spirit," quick and powerful, etc. The sword by which Christ fights his moral battles and wins his moral conquests is not the sword of steel, but the sword of truth. "His countenance was as the sun shineth in his strength." "Of the angel by the vacant tomb it is said his countenance was like lightning (Matt. xxviii. 3); here the countenance of the Lord is compared to the sun at its brightest and clearest, in the splendour of the highest noon, no veil, no mist, no cloud obscuring its brightness." Here, then, is the wonderful Personage which has appeared to us, the children of men, from eternity. Though he is "the Son of man," thoroughly human, he has an attitude and aspect that are superhuman. His voice clear as a "trumpet" and full as an ocean, his regal robes girt with a "golden girdle," his "hair white as snow," radiating effulgent purity, his feet strong as "brass," his hand clasping "seven stars," his mouth flashing out a "two-edged sword," and his countenance luminous as the "sun in his strength." What manner of man is this? The symbolical representation here indicates: (1) *Royalty.* He is robed as a king—"clothed with a garment down to the foot." Christ was a royal Man in the truest and highest sense—royal in thought, sympathy, aim, character. (2) *Purity.* His brow encircled with locks white as snow. "His head and his hairs were white like wool." The only morally spotless man the race has ever known. (3) *Penetration.* His eyes pierced into the deepest depths of human thought; they were "as a flame of fire." (4) *Firmness.* There was no vacillation of purpose, but inflexible and invincible. "His feet like unto fine brass." (5) *Dominion.* Having the brightest and purest intelligences in his possession and at his command. "He had in his right hand seven stars." (6) *Victory.* His victories are bloodless.

He conquers mind; he slays not existence, but its curses and its wrongs. " Out of his mouth went a sharp two-edged sword." (7) *Brightness.* No dark thoughts clouding his brow, indicating anger or sadness, but bright looks withal. " His countenance was as the sun shineth in his strength." This Man was the greatest gift of Heaven to the race. In him dwelleth not only all the fulness of what is purest and grandest in human nature, but all " the fulness of the Godhead bodily."

III. THAT A WONDERFUL IMPRESSION FROM ETERNITY IS MADE UPON MAN. "And when I saw him, I fell at his feet as [one] dead." It is a physiological fact that a sudden rush of strong emotions will stop the heart and arrest the current of life in its flow. What were John's emotions? Was there *amazement?* Was he amazed at seeing One whom he loved above all others, and with whom he had parted, some few years before, on the Mount of Olives, when a cloud received him out of sight, now in form sublimely unique and overwhelmingly majestic? Was it *dread?* Was he terror-struck at the marvellous apparition? Was it *remorse?* Did the effulgence of its purity quicken within him such a sense of guilt as filled him with self-loathing and horror? I know not. Perhaps all these emotions blended in a tidal rush that physically paralyzed him for a while. When Isaiah, in the temple, saw the Lord on high and lifted up, he exclaimed, " Woe is me! for I am undone." When Job heard the voice speaking out of the whirlwind, he exclaimed, " I abhor myself in dust and ashes." When Christ appeared to Peter, he cried out, " Depart from me; for I am a sinful man, O Lord." When the Roman ruffians, in the garden of Gethsemane, saw the moral majesty on his brow, and heard his words, such emotions rushed up within them as stopped their hearts, and they " went backward and fell to the ground." Eternity is constantly making solemn impressions upon man. In most cases, perhaps, the impressions are superficial and fugitive, but frequently in certain seasons and conditions of life they are terrible beyond description. There are but few men who have not felt at times something of the moral terrors of Eiphaz : " In thoughts from the visions of the night, when deep sleep falleth on men, fear came upon me, and trembling, which made all my bones to shake." No impressions, however, from eternity are so deep and salutary as those conveyed to the heart by profound meditations on the doctrines, the history, and the character of Christ. Such impressions are the means by which the all-loving Father renews the moral character of his children and makes them meet for his everlasting fellowship and service.—D. T.

Vers. 17, 18.—*Christ's ministry on earth, and his existence in heaven.* " And he laid his right hand upon me, saying unto me, Fear not; I am the First and the Last : I am he that liveth, and was dead; and, behold, I am alive for evermore, Amen ; and have the keys of hell and of death." These verses lead us to consider two subjects— the ministry of Christ on earth, and his existence in heaven.

I. CHRIST'S MINISTRY ON EARTH. " And he laid his right hand upon me, saying unto me, Fear not." John's vision of Christ struck him to the ground with fear. The remarks of Trench on these words cannot be overlooked: " The unholy, and all flesh is such that it cannot endure immediate contact with the holy, the human with the Divine. Heathen legend, so far as its testimony may be accepted, consents here with Christian truth. Semele must perish if Jupiter reveals himself to her in his gly, being consumed in the brightness of that glory. ' Thou canst not see my face for there shall no man see me, and live' (Exod. xxxiii. 20). For every man it is a dreadful thing to stand face to face with God. The beloved disciple who had handled the Word of life, lain in his Lord's bosom in the days of his flesh, can as little as any other endure the revelation of his majesty, or do without that ' Fear not ' with which the Lord reassures him here. This same ' Fear not ' is uttered on similar occasions to Isaiah (vi. 7), to Daniel (x. 12), to Peter (Luke v. 1), to the three at the Transfigura-tion, of whom John himself was one (Matt. xvii. 7). Nor is this reassurance confined to words only ; the Lord at the same time lays his hand upon him—something parallel to which goes along with the ' Fear not ' of three among the instances just referred to ; and from the touch of that hand the seer receives strength again, and is set, no doubt, upon his feet once more (Ezek. i. 28; ii. 1, 2). The ' right hand ' being ever contemplated in Scripture as the hand of power alike for God (Deut. xxxiii. 2; Isa. xlviii. 13; Acts vii. 55) and for man (Gen. xlviii. 14; Zech. iii. 1; Matt. v. 30), it is only fit that with the right hand of the Lord he should be thus strengthened and revived." The point here to be observed is that *Christ's ministry on earth is to remove fear.* Of all the passions that take possession of the soul there are **none more** unvirtuous in nature and pernicious in influence than fear. It implies a lack of trust in the personal, loving care of the great Father. It is hostile to all heroism and moral nobility of soul. Now, Christ's ministry is to remove this. He says to man, "It is I: be not afraid." (1) He removes fear of *poverty.* By unfolding the Fatherly providence of God. (2) He removes fear of *punishment.* By proclaiming the forgiveness of sins. (3) He removes fear of *death.* By unveiling a heaven beyond the grave. "In my Father's house are many mansions."

II. CHRIST'S EXISTENCE IN HEAVEN. "I am the First and the Last: I am he that liveth [the Living One], and was dead [and I was dead]; and, behold, I am alive for evermore, Amen; and have the keys of hell [death] and of death [Hades]." One might have thought that, after Christ had received such malignant treatment on this earth, his departure from it would be an everlasting termination of all his communications with it; that his last word on earth to men would be his last word to them until the day of doom ; that on his ascension to heaven he would withdraw himself with a righteous indignation from this corrupt planet, turn away from it, and speak only to intelligences who would devoutly hail his every utterance. Not so, however. Here, after a few years of personal absence from this earth, with unabated love for our fallen race, he breaks the silence of eternity, and makes such communications to John, on the isle of Patmos, as would be for the good of all coming generations. The words lead us to consider now his existence in heaven. Notice : 1. His life in heaven is *a life that succeeds an extraordinary death.* "I am he that liveth, and was dead." Life after death is a life in itself truly wonderful. Such a life we have never seen. But the life of Christ in heaven is a life succeeding a death that has no parallel in the history of the universe. There are at least three circumstances that mark off his death at an infinite distance from that of any other being that ever died. (1) *Absolute spontaneity.* No being ever died but Christ who had the feeling that he need never die—that death could be for ever escaped. Christ had it. "He had power to lay down his life." (2) *Entire relativeness.* Every other man that ever died, died for himself, died because he was a sinner and the seed of death was sown in his nature. Not so with Christ; he died for *others.* (3) *Universal influence.* The death of the most important man that ever lived has an influence of a comparatively limited degree. It extends but over a contracted circle. Only a few of the age feel it; future ages feel it not ; it is nothing to the universe. But Christ's death had an influence that admits of no measurement. It extended over all the past of humanity. It was the great event anticipated by the ages that preceded it. This is the great event that will be looked back to by all coming men. It thrills the heavens of God. "Worthy is the Lamb that was slain," is the song of eternity. Christ's death fell on the universe as the pebble on the centre of a lake, widening in circles of influence on to its utmost boundary. 2. His life in heaven is *a life of endless duration.* "I am alive for evermore." (1) His endless duration is a necessity of his nature. "I am he that liveth." There are moral intelligences, we amongst them, that may live for ever ; but not by *necessity* of nature. We live because the Infinite supports us; let him withdraw his sustaining agency, and we cease to breathe. Not so with Christ. His life is absolutely independent of the universe. He is the "I AM." (2) His endless duration is the glory of the good. "Amen." When Christ says, "I am alive for evermore," the unfallen and redeemed universe may well exclaim, "Amen." Whatever other friends die, the great Friend lives on. 3. His life in heaven is *a life of absolute dominion over the destinies of men.* "I have the keys of hell [death] and of death [Hades]." He has dominion over the bodies and souls of men as well when they are separated from each other as previous to their dissolution. "He is the Lord of the dead and of the living." From his absolute dominion over the destinies of men four things may be inferred. (1) There is nothing accidental in human history. He has the key of death. No grave is opened but by his hand. (2) Departed men are still in existence. He has the key of Hades (the world of separate souls) as well as of the grave. They live therefore. (3) Death is not the introduction to a new moral kingdom. The same Lord is here as there. What is right here, therefore, is right there, and the reverse. (4) We may anticipate the day when death shall be swallowed up in victory.—D. T.

Vers. 19, 20.—*Christ enjoining the record of his revelation to man and explaining its meaning.* "Write the things which thou hast seen, and the things which are, and the things which shall be hereafter," etc. These words suggest two general remarks concerning Christ.

I. THAT HE REQUIRES MEN TO RECORD THE REVELATIONS HE MAKES TO THEM. He is the great Revealer of God to humanity, and his revelations are ever-recurring and constant. And here we are taught that they are not only to be taught and studied, but to be *recorded.* The revelations here referred to are of three classes. 1. *Those which had been experienced.* "The things which thou hast seen." What things John had already seen! How manifold, wonderful, significant! What man of any reflection or conscience has not seen things from God? 2. *Those things which were now present.* "The things which are." Things that were at hand, that came within his observation and consciousness. There are eternal principles that underlie and shape all human history. These principles are as present as the air we breathe, although the majority of the race are unconscious of them. There are some which reveal themselves in vivid consciousness—these shall be recorded, their images shall be photographed on the heart. 3. *Those which were approaching.* "The things which shall be hereafter." With that inspiration of him who sees the end from the beginning, the human soul may catch a glimpse of all future times. The divinely inspired genius becomes to some extent independent of all space and time, overleaps all boundaries, geographic and chronologic. It seems to have been so with John on this occasion. In his visions the future ages of the world appeared down to the final trump of doom. John seems to have

> " Dipt into the future, far as human eye could see ;
> Saw the vision of the world, and all the wonders that would be."

Now, these three classes of things John had to write down—those that *had* unfolded themselves, those that *were* unfolding themselves, and those that *would* be to the end of time. Whatever man has seen or will see of the Divine, he is bound to record. " Write." Literature, though sadly corrupted and the source of enormous mischief, is a Divine institution. Rightly employed, it is one of the grandest forces in human life. Truth *orally* communicated is inexpressibly important and immeasurably influential. He who speaks truth rationally, faithfully, earnestly, devoutly, touches the deepest springs in the great world of mind. What bloodless and brilliant victories the truth has won in all ages! Albeit truth *written* has some advantages over truth spoken, for man seems to multiply himself by the book he has written. His book is a kind of *second incarnation,* in which he may live and work ages after the fingers that held his pen are mouldered into dust. Thank God for books, our best companions, always ready with their counsel and their comfort. They are arks that have borne down to us, over the floods of centuries, the vital germs of departed ages. Let men write them, but let their subjects be not the trashy things of time and sensual pleasure, the visions of a wild fancy or the speculations of a reckless intellect, but the *revelations* that Christ has made.

II. THAT HE EXPLAINS TO MEN THE MEANING OF THE REVELATION HE MAKES TO THEM. " The mystery of the seven stars which thou sawest in my right hand, and the seven golden candlesticks." There are two kinds of mystery, the *knowable* and *unknowable.* (1) *The unknown of the knowable.* It is conceivable that the whole created universe is knowable, even to the intellect of finite man. Yet what the most enlightened man knows is but a fraction of what to him is still unknown—a mystery. Hence every step in the advance of an earnest inquirer is turning the mystery of to-day into an intelligible fact of to-morrow. What is mystery to one man is not so to another; and what is mystery to a man to-day is no mystery to-morrow. The other kind of mystery is (2) the *unknown of the Unknowable.* He whom we call God is the great Mystery, the absolutely Unknowable—whom no man " hath seen or can see." Now, in the former sense the meaning of the word " mystery " is here employed.' In Christ's explanation here we have two things worth note. 1. *The ideal Christian pastor.* "The seven stars are the angels of the seven Churches." Who the angels were is a matter of speculation. Every settled Christian community, whether religious or not, has some leading person or persons amongst them. In these Christian congregations in Asia Minor there seems to have been some leading man. He was, no doubt, like Timothy in Ephesus—the pastor. Every true Christian minister or angel is a "star." His light is borrowed, but borrowed from the primal source—the "Sun of Righteousness." His orbit is Divine. Faithful teachers are stars that shall shine for ever (Dan. xii. 3); false teachers are wandering stars (Jude 13), or stars which fall from heaven (ch. viii. 10; vi. 13; xii. 4). 2. *The ideal Christian Church.* "The seven candlesticks which thou sawest are the seven Churches." Observe . (1) Christian congregations are lights. "Candlesticks." (2) They are precious lights. They are "golden." They throw the best kind of information upon an ignorant world. (3) They are imperfect lights. A lamp is a composite and requires constant care. No finite power can make the sun brighter or larger. Not so with the lamp. The lamp may grow dim and go out—the "golden candlestick" may be there, but no light issues therefrom. "It was thought by the ancients that if ever the fires which burned on the altar of Vesta became extinct, they could not be rekindled unless by being brought in contact with the sun."—D. T.

EXPOSITION.

CHAPTER II.

Ver. 1—ch. iii. 22.—*The epistles to the seven Churches.* Once more we have to consider rival interpretations. Of these we may safely set aside all those which make the seven letters to be pictures of *successive periods* in the history of the Church. On the other hand, we may safely deny that the letters are *purely typical,* and relate to nothing definite in history. Rather they are *both historical and typical.* They refer primarily to the actual condition of the several Churches in St. John's own day, and then are intended for the instruction, encouragement, and warning of the Church and the Churches throughout all time. The Catholic Church, or any one of its branches, will at any period find itself reflected in one or other of the seven Churches. For two Churches, Smyrna and Philadelphia, there is nothing but praise; for two, Sardis and Laodicea, nothing but blame; for the majority, and among them the chief Church of all, Ephesus, with Pergamum and Thyatira, praise and blame in different degrees intermingled.

The student will find it instructive to place the epistles side by side in seven parallel columns, and note the elements common to each and the order in which these elements appear. These common elements are: (1) *Christ's command* to the seer to write; (2) *his title,* which in most cases is taken from the descriptions in ch. i.; (3) the *praise,* or *blame,* or both, addressed to the angel, based in all cases on intimate personal knowledge—"I know thy works;" (4) the *charge* or warning, generally in connexion with Christ's coming; (5) the *promise to the victor;* (6) the *call to each individual* to give ear.

Vers. 1—7.—*The epistle to the Church at Ephesus.*

Ver. 1.—Unto the angel (see on ch. i. 20). "The angel" seems to be the spirit of the Church personified as its responsible guardian. The Church of Ephesus. "*In* Ephesus" is certainly the right reading; in all seven cases it is the angel of the Church *in* the place that is addressed. In St. Paul's Epistles we have "*in* Rome," "*in* Corinth," "*in* Colossæ," "*in* Ephesus," "*of* Galatia," "*of* the Thessalonians." Among all the cities of the Roman province of Asia, Ephesus ranked as "first of all and greatest." It was called "the metropolis of Asia." Romans visiting Asia commonly landed first at Ephesus. Its position as a centre of commerce was magnificent. Three rivers, the Mæander, the Cayster, and the Hermes, drain Western Asia Minor, and Ephesus stood on high ground near the mouth of the central river, the Cayster, which is connected by passes with the valleys of the other two. Strabo, writing of Ephesus about the time when St. John was born, says, "Owing to

---

¹ See an exposition on the first three chapters of this book by Andrew Tait, LL.D., F.R.S.E., 'Messages to the Seven Churches.'

its favourable situation, the city is in all other respects increasing daily, for it is the greatest place of trade of all the cities of Asia west of the Taurus.' Patmos was only a day's sail from Ephesus; and it is by no means improbable that the gorgeous description of the merchandise of "Babylon" (ch. xviii. 12, 13) is derived from St. John's own recollections of Ephesus. The Church of Ephesus was founded by St. Paul, about A.D. 55, and his Epistle to that and other Churches, now called simply "to the Ephesians," was written about A.D. 63. When St. Paul went to Macedonia, Timothy was left at Ephesus (1 Tim. i. 3) to check the wild speculations in which some Ephesian Christians had begun to indulge. Timothy probably followed St. Paul to Rome (2 Tim. iv. 9, 21), and, after his master's death, returned to Ephesus, where he is said to have suffered martyrdom at a festival in honour of "the great goddess Artemis." He may have been still at Ephesus at the time when this epistle was written; and Plumptre has traced coincidences between this epistle and those of St. Paul to Timothy. According to Dorotheus of Tyre (circ. A.D. 300), he was succeeded by Gaius (Rom. xvi. 23). In the Ignatian epistles we have Onesimus (probably not the servant of Philemon), Bishop of Ephesus. Ignatius speaks of the Ephesian Church in terms of high praise, showing that it had profited by the exhortations in this epistle. It was free from heresy, though heresy hovered around it. It was spiritually minded, and took God as its rule of life (Ignatius, 'Ephes.,' vi.—viii.). **Write** (see on ch. i. 11; and comp. Isa. viii. 1; xxx. 8; Jer. xxx. 2; xxxvi. 2; Hab. ii. 2). **Holdeth** (κρατῶν). Stronger than "had" (ἔχων) in ch. i. 16. This word implies holding fast and having full control over. In ver. 25 we have both verbs, and again in ch. iii. 11. A Church that had fallen from its first love (vers. 4, 5) had need to be reminded of him who "holds fast" his own; and one whose candlestick was in danger of removal had need to turn to him who is ever active (not merely is, but "walketh") "in the midst of the candlesticks," to supply them with oil when they flicker, and rekindle them when they go out. It is he, and not the apostle, who addresses them.

Ver. 2. — Owing to the inaccurate use of a corrupt text, the Authorized Version is here very faulty. The Revised Version is to be preferred throughout. **I know thy works.** This introductory "I know" appears in all seven letters. He whose eyes are "as a flame of fire" (ch. i. 14) has perfect knowledge of his servants, and this knowledge is the basis of the praise and blame. "Works," a favourite word with St. John, and very frequent in both Gospel

and Apocalypse, is used in a wide sense, including the whole of conduct (comp. John iii. 19, 20; v. 36; vii. 3, 7; viii. 39, 41, etc.; 1 John iii. 8, 12; 2 John 11; 3 John 10). **Thy toil and patience.** Explanatory of "thy works;" the Ephesians know how to toil and how to suffer patiently. They have "learned to labour and to wait." St. Ignatius says that he must be trained "in patience and long-suffering" by the Ephesians ('Ephes.,' iii.). And that thou canst not bear evil men. Again St. Ignatius supplies a commentary: "Now, Onesimus of his own accord highly praiseth your orderly conduct in God, for that ye all live according to truth, and that *no heresy hath a home among you;* nay, ye *do not so much as listen to any one,* if he speak of aught else save concerning Jesus Christ in truth" ('Ephes.,' vi.). The word for "evil" (κακός), though one of the commonest in the Greek language, is rare in St. John; it occurs only here and in ch. xvi. 2 (see note); John xviii. 23; 3 John 11. **Didst try them which call themselves apostles, and they are not.** It is incredible that this can mean St. Paul. Even allowing the prodigious assumption that the "Jewish Christianity" of St. John was opposed to the "Gentile Christianity" of St. Paul, what chance would an opponent of St. Paul have had in a Church which St. Paul founded and fostered? And had such opposition existed, could St. Polycarp, St. John's own disciple, have spoken of "the wisdom of the blessed and glorious Paul" ('Phil.,' iii.)? This mention of false apostles is doubly interesting: (1) as a fulfilment of warnings given by St. Paul himself to the Ephesian Church (Acts xx. 28—30; comp. 2 Timothy, *passim*); (2) as a strong incidental mark of the date of the book. In A.D. 68, when contemporaries of the apostles were abundant, the claim to be an apostle might with some show of reason be made; in A.D. 95 such a claim would be ridiculous. This Trench admits, and hence tells us that the meaning of "apostles" must not be pressed, "as though it implied a claim to have seen and been sent by the Lord Jesus." But this is just what "apostle" does imply (Acts i. 21, 22; 1 Cor. ix. 1).

Ver. 3.—The text followed in the Authorized Version is here very corrupt; we must read with the Revised Version, And thou hast patience (as in ver. 2), and didst bear for my Name's sake, and hast not grown weary. The last verb (κεκοπίακες) is closely akin to toil (κόπος) in ver 2. The seeming contradiction between "I know thy toil" and "thou hast not toiled" has caused confusion in the text. Yet οὐ κεκοπίακες does not mean "thou hast not toiled," but "thou hast not wearied of toil." It is all the more probable that this play of words is inten-

tional, because "bear" ($\beta\alpha\sigma\tau\acute\alpha\zeta\epsilon\iota\nu$) is used in
two different senses in ver 2 and ver. 3:
"canst not *tolerate* evil men," and "didst *endure* suffering" (comp. John xvi. 12). "So is
patience set over the things of God that one
can obey no precept, fulfil no work well-
pleasing to the Lord, if estranged from it.
The good of it even they who live outside
it honour with the name of highest virtue.
. . . Grand testimony this is to it, in that it
incites even the vain schools of the world
unto praise and glory ! Or is it rather an
injury, in that a thing Divine is bandied
about among worldly sciences" (Tertullian,
' De Pat.,' i.).

Ver. 4.—But I have (this) against thee, that
thou didst leave thy first love. The Authorized Version unwarrantably softens the censure by inserting "somewhat;" the Greek
means rather, "I have (this grave thing)
against thee." In "hath aught against
thee" (Matt. v. 23) and "have aught against
any" (Mark xi. 25), the "aught" ($\tau\iota$) is
expressed in the Greek; here nothing is
expressed. "Thy first love" is expressed
very emphatically with the article repeated;
"thy love, thy first one." The meaning of
it is much disputed. It cannot mean "thy
former gentleness towards evil men and
false apostles." It may mean "thy love of
the brethren," so much insisted upon in St.
John's First Epistle. More probably it means
"thy first love for me." Christ is here
speaking as the Bridegroom, and addresses
the Church of Ephesus as his bride (comp.
Jer. ii. 2—13). This thought would be
familiar to the Ephesians from St. Paul's
teaching (Eph. v. 23—33). It shows strange
ignorance of human frailty and of history
to argue that "a generation at least must
have passed away, and the thirty years from
Nero to Domitian must have elapsed, ere the
change here noted could come to pass."
Does this writer forget the Epistle to the
Galatians? In a very few years the Churches
of Galatia had left their first love. The
frequent and rapid lapses of Israel into
idolatry show the same thing from the time
when Aaron made the calf down to the
Captivity. This verse is certainly no obstacle
to the theory that the Apocalypse was
written about A.D. 68.

Ver. 5.—The exhortation and threat are
clear as trumpet-notes : "Remember, repent,
and return, or I will return and remove
thee." A modern heathen philosophy
teaches us that in this world to be happy
is to forget. That is not the teaching of
Christ The past is both an encouragement
and a warning to us; therefore "remember."
Some have to remember heights from which
they have fallen ; others, depths from which
they have been raised; others again, both.
Cicero ('Ad. Att.,' iv. 16) would remember

the one and forget the other. *Non recordor
unde ceciderim, sed unde resurrexerim.* The
present imperative here shows that the
remembering is to continue; on the other
hand, the repentance (aor. imp.) is a thing
to be done immediately, once for all. "The
first works" means "the fruits of thy first
love." Christ will have *works*, not feelings.
I come to thee. There is no "quickly" in
the true text; and the verb is present, not
future (comp. John xiv. 18). The coming,
of course, refers to a special visitation, not
to the second advent. The removing of the
candlestick is not the deposition of the
bishop, but the dethroning of the Church,
cancelling its claim to the kingdom, sever-
ing its union with Christ. Compare "The
kingdom of God shall be taken away from
you, and shall be given to a nation bringing
forth the fruits thereof" (Matt. xxii. 43).
The warning would seem to have been
heeded at first, judging from the account of
Ephesus in the Ignatian Epistles. But the
Church has long since. ceased to exist.
Ephesus itself is a heap of ruins. Except
thou repent. This repetition drives home
the charge given above; repentance is the
thing absolutely necessary, and at once.
This shows that what Christ has against
them cannot be a mere "somewhat"
(Authorized Version in ver. 4). It is nothing less than this—that with all their discernment of evil, and zeal against it, they
lacked reality. Their light still burned,
but in a dull, lifeless way; their service had
become mechanical.

Ver. 6.—They are again commended for
their good points. But it is possible to hate
what Christ hates without loving what he
loves. It is possible to hate false doctrine
and lawlessness, and yet be formal and dead
one's self. Who the Nicolaitans were we
cannot now determine with certainty. The
name Nicolaus may be intended as a Greek
equivalent of Balaam, but this is by no
means certain. Irenæus and Clement of
Alexandria write as if the sect of Nicolaitans existed in their day. A common belief
was that their founder was Nicolaus of
Antioch, one of the seven deacons. Irenæus
(i. 26), followed by Hippolytus ('Refut.,'
vii. 24), supports this view; Ignatius ('Trall.,'
9) and the Apostolic Constitutions (vi. 8),
are against it. The Nicolaitans may have
claimed him as their founder, or similarity
of name may have caused confusion with
a different person. The doctrine of the
Nicolaitans, and that of Balaam (ver. 14),
and that of the woman Jezebel (ver. 20),
seem to have this much in common—a contention that the freedom of the Christian
placed him above the moral Law. Neither
idolatry nor sensuality could harm those
who had been made free by Christ. The

moral enactments of the Law had been abrogated by the gospel, no less than the ceremonial. The special mention of "the pollutions of idols" and "fornication," in the decrees of the Council of Jerusalem (Acts xv. 20, 29), seems to show that this pernicious doctrine was already in existence in A.D. 50. In 2 Pet. ii. and Jude 7—13 a similar evil is denounced. It appears in other heretical sects, especially those of Gnostic origin, *e.g.* Cerinthians, Cainites, Carpocratians. In this way we may explain the statement of Eusebius ('Hist. Eccl.,' iii. 29), that the Nicolaitan heresy lasted only for a short time; *i.e.* its religious libertinism did not die out, but passed over into other sects. Note that it is "the *works* of the Nicolaitans," not the men themselves, that Christ hates. He loves the sinner, while he hates the sin. "It would have been well with the Church had this always been remembered" (Alford).

Ver. 7.—**He that hath an ear, let him hear.** These solemn conclusions of these epistles remind us of the conclusion of many of Christ's parables (Matt. xi. 15; xiii. 9, 43; Mark iv. 9, 23, [vii. 16]; Luke viii. 8; xiv. 35; not in St. John's Gospel, in which there are no parables). It is very noteworthy that, although the epistle is addressed in each case to a Church in the person of its angel, yet the concluding exhortation and promise are always addressed to the individual Christian. Each must hear for himself. His Church may perish, yet, if he overcomes, he shall live. His Church may be crowned with eternal life, yet, if he is overcome, he will lose the reward. What the Spirit saith to the Churches; not "what he saith to *this* Church." The contents of each epistle are for all; for each individual Christian and for the Church at large, as well as for the particular Church addressed in the epistle. The epistle in each case is not from John, who is only the instrument, but from the Son of God and from the Spirit of God (ch. i. 4). In the first three epistles the exhortation to hearken *precedes* the promise to the victor; in the four last it *follows* the promise, and closes the epistle. Is this change of arrangement accidental or deliberate? There should be a full stop at "Churches." In the Authorized Version it looks as if "what the Spirit saith" were confined to the promise in the second half of the verse. This error was avoided by Tyndale and Cranmer. It comes from the Genevan and the Rhemish Versions. The verb to "overcome" or "conquer" (νικᾷν) is strongly characteristic of St. John. It occurs seven times in the Gospel and the First Epistle, and sixteen times in the Revelation; elsewhere only in Luke xi. 22; Rom. iii. 4 (quotation from

Ps. li. 6) and xii. 21; comp. especially xxi. 7, where, as in these epistles, it is not stated *what* is to be overcome. We might render, "to the victor," or "to the conqueror." The expression, "tree of life," of course comes from Genesis; we have it again in ch. xxii. 2, 14. It means the tree which gives life. So also "the water of life" (ch. xxi. 6) and "the bread of life" (John vi. 35). In all these cases "life" is ζωή, the vital principle which man shares with God, not βίος, the life which he shares with his fellowmen. The latter word occurs less than a dozen times in the New Testament; the former, which sums up the New Testament, occurs more than a hundred times. The **Paradise of God.** The word "Paradise" occurs only thrice in the New Testament (Luke xxiii. 43; 2 Cor. xii. 4). It is of Persian origin, and signified a park or pleasure-ground. In the New Testament it seems to mean the resting-place of departed saints. There is strong evidence (B, versions, Cyprian, Origen) in favour of reading, "the Paradise of *my* God" (see notes on ch. iii. 2, 12). In considering this passage, Gen. iii. 22 should be carefully compared with John vi. 51. "For him who conquers" the curse which barred Adam from the tree of life will be revoked by Christ.

Vers. 8—11.—*The epistle to the Church at Smyrna.*

Ver. 8.—The metropolitan, setting out from Ephesus to visit the Churches of Asia, would naturally go first to Smyrna. It ranked as one of the most beautiful cities in Asia; but its magnificence must at times have seemed poor compensation for the neglect of the architect, who, in planning the city for Antigonus and Lysimachus, omitted the drains. In time of floods the streets became open sewers. For its fidelity to Rome against Mithridates, it received exceptional privileges, but suffered heavily when Dolabella laid siege to Trebonius, one of Cæsar's assassins, who had taken refuge there. When eleven cities of Asia competed for the honour of erecting a temple to Tiberius, the senate decided in favour of Smyrna. This temple was no doubt standing in St. John's time. But just as Artemis was the great goddess of the Ephesians, so Dionysus was the great god of Smyrna. Dionysus represented the mysteriously productive and intoxicating powers of nature—powers which are exhibited most abundantly in the vine, which in the neighbourhood of Smyrna is said to have borne fruit twice in a year. He was regarded as the dispenser of joy and fertility, the disperser of sorrow and care. Hence the myth of his death and resurrection, which was frequently re-

hearsed and acted at Smyrna—a fact which
gives special point to the greeting in this
epistle—"From him who became dead, and
lived" The priests who presided at this
celebration were presented with a crown; to
which there may be allusion in the promise,
"I will give thee the crown of life." Not
long after the martyrdom of its first bishop,
St. Polycarp, Smyrna was destroyed by an
earthquake, in A.D. 178, and was rebuilt by
Marcus Aurelius. Earthquakes, fires, and
pestilences have always been common there.
But in spite of such calamities, it continues
to flourish. From the large proportion of
Christians there, it is known among Mohammedans as "the infidel city." Christianity seems never to have been extinguished
in Smyrna, which shares, with Philadelphia,
the honour of receiving unmixed praise in
these epistles. "Down from the apostolic
times a Church has existed here, and she
has repeated, with more or less boldness
and distinctness, the testimony of her martyr-
bishop, 'I am a Christian'" (R. Vaughan).
The stadium in which he suffered may still
be seen there. We have already (see on ch.
i. 20) decided that "the angel" of each
Church is probably not its bishop. But,
even if this were the meaning, this epistle
could not be addressed to St. Polycarp, if
he was martyred A.D. 155, in the eighty-
sixth year after his conversion, and the
Apocalypse was written in A.D. 68. The
First and the Last, who became (ἐγένετο)
dead, and lived (see notes on ch. i. 17, 18).
As in the epistle to Ephesus, the words of
the address are taken from the titles of
the Christ given in the opening. It is no
mythical deity, with his mock death and
resurrection, but the absolutely Living One,
who indeed died, and is indeed alive for
evermore, that sends this message to the
suffering Church of Smyrna. In the epistle
to the Church in Thyatira we have what
seems to be an allusion to the worship of
Apollo, similar to that to the worship of
Dionysus here.

Ver. 9.—I know thy tribulation, and thy
poverty. "Thy works" has been inserted
here and in ver. 13 in order to make the
opening of all seven epistles alike. The
uncials A, C, P, and the Vulgate, Coptic,
and Æthiopic Versions omit the words in
each place. The Sinaiticus inserts them here
and omits them in ver. 13, where they are
plainly awkward in construction. Like all
wealthy cities, Smyrna showed the extremes
of wealth and poverty side by side. It would
be among the poor that Christians would in
the first instance be found, and their Christianity would lead to their spoliation; in
this much of their "tribulation" would consist. But thou art rich (compare the close
parallel, 2 Cor. vi. 10; viii. 2; Matt. vi. 20).

And the blasphemy from them which say
they are Jews, and they are not. We have
here strong evidence of the early date of the
Apocalypse. Throughout this book "Jew"
is an honourable name for the worshippers
of the Christ; "Gentiles," a name of reproach for those who oppose the Christ (ch.
ii. 9; i i. 9; xi. 2, 18; xii. 5; xvi. 19; xviii.
3, 23; xix. 15, etc.). These persecutors of
the Church of Smyrna are Jews in name,
but in reality are rather Gentiles—opponents,
and not worshippers of the Messiah. The
view taken in the Fourth Gospel is utterly
different. There "the Jews" are almost invariably the opponents of Christ; the word
occurs about seventy times, and nearly
always with this shade of meaning. Assume
that the Gospel was written a quarter of a
century later than the Apocalypse, and there
is nothing strange in this. Long experience
of Jewish malignity in opposing the gospel
has changed the apostle's views respecting
his countrymen. He has become fully convinced of the inveterate and widespread
character of the national apostasy. To him
"the Jews" have become synonymous with
the enemies of the cross of Christ. Assume
that the Apocalypse was written about the
same time as the Gospel, and how shall we
account for this utter difference of view in
the two books? Assume that the Gospel
was written long before the Apocalypse,
and how shall we explain the fact that experience of Jewish hostility has turned the
apostle's abhorrence of "the Jews" into such
admiration that to him a Jew has become
synonymous with a believer in Jesus Christ?
It is remarkable that, in the ' Martyrdom of
St. Polycarp,' the Jews are said to have
been present in great numbers, and to have
been foremost (μάλιστα 'Ιουδαίους προθύμως)
in collecting wood with which to burn him
alive. A synagogue of Satan (comp. cn. iii.
9; John viii. 44). This is in marked contrast to "the synagogue of the Lord"
(Numb. xvi. 3; xx. 4; xxxi. 16). With the
exception of Jas. ii. 2, συναγωγή is, in the
New Testament, always used of Jewish
assemblies, never of Christian. This usage
soon became habitual in the Church (see
Trench, 'Synonyms of the New Testament,'
p. 4).

Ver. 10.—Fear not the things which thou
art about to suffer. We must bring out the
difference between "to be about to" (μέλλειν)
in the first two clauses, and the simple future
(ἕξετε) in the third; compare "I will show
him how many things he must suffer for m
Name's sake" (Acts ix. 16). The devil, w
inspires the "synagogue of Satan," is to
allowed to afflict them, as he afflicted J
(For "behold," see note on ver. 22.) 1
expression, "some of you" (ἐξ ὑμῶν), i
interesting link of style between this b

and the Fourth Gospel and the Second Epistle; we have a similar construction in John i. 24; vii. 40; xvi. 17; 2 John 4. (For a warning of like import, but to the persecutors, not the persecuted, comp. Matt. xxiii. 34.) That ye may be tried. The common meaning of πειράζειν, as distinct from δοκιμάζειν, is here conspicuous; it is "to try" with the sinister intent of causing to fall. But what is temptation on the devil's side is probation on God's side (comp. 1 Pet. iv. 12—14). Ten days. It is unwise to make anything either mystical or rigidly literal out of the number ten, which here is probably a round number. The question is whether the round number denotes a small (Gen. xxiv. 55; Numb. xi. 19) or a large number (Numb. xiv. 22; 1 Sam. i. 8; Job xix. 3). The former seems probable. It is not impossible that some analogy between their case and that of the "four children" (Dan. i. 12, 15) is suggested by the ten days' probation. Be thou faithful unto death; literally, become thou faithful; show thyself to be such (γίνου πιστός). Note how completely the angel of the Church is identified with the Church. In this one verse we have complete mixture of the two modes of address: "Thou art about to suffer . . . some of you . . . ye shall have . . . I will give thee." "Unto death" does not merely mean "to thy life's end," but "even if fidelity involves death;" compare "becoming obedient even unto death, yea, the death of the cross" (Phil. ii. 8). The crown of life. The Authorized Version, by ignoring the article ("a crown of life"), sadly detracts from the meaning. It is the well-known crown, the crown which is truly such, in contrast to earthly crowns, and perhaps with a special reference to the crowns given at Smyrna to the priests of Dionysus at the expiration of their year of office. The word στεφανηφόρος has been found in inscriptions at Smyrna in this connexion (comp. Jas. i. 12, where the same phrase occurs; also 1 Cor. ix. 25; 1 Pet. v. 4). Excepting ch. xii. 3; xiii. 1; xix. 12 (where we have διάδημα), στέφανος is the regular word for "crown" in the New Testament. "Of life" is the genitive of apposition; the life is the crown, just as in "the Word of life" (1 John i. 1) the life is the Word. It is impossible to determine whether St. John has in his mind the crown of a king, of a victorious athlete, or of a triumphant warrior. The XII. Tables provided that he who had won a crown might have it placed on his head when his dead body was carried in the funeral procession. St. John, both at Rome and in the East, would have seen this ceremony, possibly in the case of a crowned priest at Smyrna. "The crown of life" would be the exact opposite of that. The narrative of the

martyrdom of St. Polycarp draws to a close with these words: "Having by his patience vanquished the unjust ruler, and having thus received the crown of immortality," etc. The writer seems to have had ch. ii. 10 in his mind.

Ver. 11.—He that hath an ear (see on ver 7). Shall not be hurt of the second death; more literally, shall in no wise be injured at the hands of the second death. The negative is the strongest form; the injury seems to be of the nature of a wrong, and the second death is regarded as the source of the wrong (οὐ μὴ ἀδικηθῇ ἐκ). In ch. xx. 6 "the second death" is almost personified, as here: "Over these the second death has no authority." The phrase is peculiar to this book (see ch. xx. 14 and xxi. 8, where it is defined to be "the lake of fire"). The corresponding phrase, "the first death," does not occur. The one is the death of the body, to which the faithful Smyrnæans must submit; the other is the death of the soul, from which the crown of life secures them: though they die, yet shall they live, and shall in no wise die, for ever (John xi. 25, 26). This second death, or death of the soul, is absolute exclusion from God, who is the Source of eternal life. The expression, "the second death," seems to be borrowed from Jewish theological phraseology. (On the repetition of the article, "the death, the second (death)," see note on ver. 13.)

Vers. 12—17.—*The epistle to the Church at Pergamum.*

Ver. 12.—Pergamum is the usual form both in Greek and Latin writers; "Pergamus" is very rare. And if Πέργαμος were right here, why "Pergamos" any more than "Ephesos"? The city lies north of Smyrna, in Mysia Major, or the right bank of the Caïcus. Pergamum is first mentioned by Xenophon, and becomes important and magnificent under Attalus, the friend of the Romans (B.C. 241—197), and his son Eumenes (B.C. 196—159). Its library was second only to that of Alexandria; but Mark Antony took it to Egypt, and gave it to Cleopatra. Parchment gets its name from Pergamum, and Galen the physician was born there. Pliny writes of "longe clarissimum Asiæ Pergamum"—a description which probably has reference to its buildings. It still exists under the slightly changed name of Bergamah, or Bergma; and its ruins still tell of the magnificent public edifices which have caused it to be described as a "city of temples," and again as "a sort of union of a pagan cathedral city, a university town, and a royal residence." Its idolatrous rites were frequent and various, and the contamination which they spread is manifest from this epistle. The sharp two-edged sword (see notes on ch. i. 16 and ii. 13). How much this weapon is needed is shown by the evils protested against.

Ver. 13.—I know where thou dwellest. The words, "thy works and," are certainly an insertion here—both external and internal evidence are against them. Even where Satan's throne is. We must translate θρόνος "throne" here. as in ch. i. 4; iii. 21; iv. 2, 3, 5, 6, 9. 10, etc. Throughout the Apocalypse heaven and hell are set over against one another; and as God has his throne, so also has Satan. The Authorized Version inconsistently alternates between "seat" (ch. xi. 16; xiii. 2; xvi. 10; Luke i. 52) and "throne," even in the same verse (ch. iv. 4). "The throne of Satan" has perplexed commentators. It probably refers to the infamous idolatry practised at Pergamum, which had a cluster of temples to Zeus, Apollo, Athene, Dionysus, Aphrodite, and Æsculapius. These all lay together in a beautiful grove called the Nicephorium, the pride of Pergamum, as the temple of Artemis was the pride of Ephesus. Some have thought that the mention of Satan points to the serpent, which is so prominent in the cultus of Æsculapius. But the context leads us rather to understand the abominations connected with the worship of Dionysus and Aphrodite. Others, again, think that "the *throne* of Satan" indicates the persecuting judgments pronounced against Christians; for Pergamum was a great judicial centre. We must be content to leave the question open. Thou holdest fast my Name. We have the same expression (κρατεῖν with the accusative) three times in this epistle and again in ver. 25 and ch. iii. 11. Just as in the literal sense κρατεῖν with the accusative means "to seize" a man, *i.e.* his whole person (Matt. xiv. 3; xviii. 29; ch. vii. 1; xx. 2), as distinct from laying hold of a part (Matt. ix. 25; Mark v. 41), so in the figurative sense κρατεῖν with the accusative is "to hold fast" the whole of (Mark vii. 3, 4, 8; 2 Thess. ii. 15), as distinct from keeping a share in a possession common to many (Heb. iv. 14; vi. 18). On the emphatic repetition obtained by denying the opposite, "holdest fast and didst not deny," see notes on ch. iii. 8. The Greek text in what follows is a good deal confused, and cannot be determined with certainty; but the general sense is clear. In any case, "my witness, my faithful one" (Revised Version), is more accurate than "my faithful martyr" (Authorized Version). The reduplication of the article is frequent in St. John's writings, but in some cases it produces clumsiness to reproduce it in English: ὁ μάρτυς ὁ πιστός occurs here of Antipas, and in ch. i. 5 of Christ;

compare ἡ ἀγάπη ἡ πρώτη (ch. ii. 4), ὁ θάνατος ὁ δεύτερος (ch. ii. 11; xx. 14; xxi. 8), ἡ ῥομφαία ἡ δίστομος (ch. ii. 12), τὸ μάννα τὸ κεκρυμμένον (ch. ii. 17), ὁ δεσπότης ὁ ἅγιος (ch. vi. 10), with John iv. 9, 11; v. 30; vi. 38, 42, 44, 50, 51, 58; vi. 38; vii. 68; viii. 16; xii. 26; xiv. 15, 27; xv. 9, 11; xvii. 13, 24; xviii. 36; 1 John ii. 7; 2 John 13. Of Antipas nothing is known. The name is a shortened form of Antipater, as Nicomas of Nicomedes, Artemas of Artemidorus, Hermas of Hermodorus, Zenas of Zenodorus, Menas of Menodorus, Lucas of Lucanus, Demas of Demetrius; and therefore is not derived from ἀντί and πᾶς. Much mystical trifling has been expended over the name Antipas, which no doubt is the actual name of a once well-known sufferer for the truth. Probably of the Pergamene confessors, Antipas was the only one who was called upon to suffer death. The silence of Church history respecting a martyr thus honoured in Scripture is strange. Attalus, one of the chief martyrs of Lyons, was of Pergamum (Eusebius, 'Hist. Eccl.,' V. i. 17; comp. IV. xv. 48). The repetition of "where Satan dwelleth" emphasizes this point, like the repetition of "repent" in ver. 5. It rather confirms the view that by "Satan's throne" is meant the judgment-throne where the martyrs were condemned.

Ver. 14.—But I have a few things against thee. They are few in comparison with the things commended; but they are very serious; and there must be a sad want of care in the Church at Pergamum to allow such things. These corrupt teachers are alluded to in 2 Pet. ii. 15 and Jude 11. Like Balaam, they debased spiritual gifts to the vilest purposes, and thus became a σκάνδαλον, a snare or stumbling-block, to others. Like the Nicolaitans, they held that the freedom of the gospel placed them above the moral Law, and conferred licence to commit the foulest sins. The liberty to eat meats which might have been offered to idols was made a plea for liberty to take part in idolatrous rites (1 Cor. viii. 10; Justin Martyr, 'Trypho,' xxxv.; Irenæus, I. vi. 3), and for introducing heathen orgies into Christian ceremonies. The doctrine of these antinomian teachers was "the doctrine of Balaam," because, like him (Numb. xxxi. 16; Josephus, 'Ant.,' iv. 6. 6; Philo, 'Vita Mosis,' i. p. 647), they prostituted their influence to the seducing of God's people into idolatry and impurity. The similarity of this doctrine with that of the Nicolaitans is obvious; but that Nicolaus (which is equivalent to "conquering the people") is intended as a translation of Balaam (which is *possibly* equivalent to "lord of the people") is mere conjecture. That there were two sects side by side at Pergamum is the natural meaning of this passage; and though their doctrines were alike in being antinomian in principle and licentious in result, yet there is no need to identify them. Among countless small improvements made by the Revisers, note that the remarkable word εἰδωλόθυτον, which in the Authorized Version is rendered in six different ways, is by them rendered consistently (Acts xv. 29; xxi. 25; 1 Cor. viii. 4, 10; x. 19; ch. ii. 14, 20).

Ver. 15.—So hast thou also some that hold. As in vers. 13 and 14 "hold" is κρατεῖν with the accusative (see notes on ver. 13). What does "also" mean? Probably, "As Israel had Balak to seduce them, and Balak had Balaam, so hast thou," etc.). Others take it, "As the Church at Ephesus has Nicolaitans, so hast thou." The reading of the Authorized Version, "which thing I hate," must certainly yield to that of the Revised Version, "in like manner," which is supported by all the best manuscripts and versions. In the Greek there is much similarity between the two readings, OMIΣΩ and OMOIΩΣ. "In like manner" refers to the similarity between those who hold the doctrine of the Nicolaitans, and those who hold the doctrine of Balaam. It confirms the view that two sects are meant.

Ver. 16.—Repent therefore; or else I come to thee quickly (see on ver. 5). Some take "in like manner" with this verse: "In like manner (as Ephesus) repent therefore;" but this is not probable. Repent of having allowed some members to follow the examples of Balaam and of the Nicolaitans. With the sword of my mouth (comp. ch. i. 16 and ii. 12). It is possible that there is here another allusion to Balaam. It was with a drawn sword that the angel of the Lord withstood him (Numb. xxii. 23), and with the sword that he was slain (Numb. xxxi. 8; Josh. xiii. 22). Those who follow Balaam in his sin shall follow him in his punishment; and the Church which allows such things will have to suffer along with those who commit them (comp. 2 Thess. ii. 8).

Ver. 17.—He that hath an ear (see notes on ver. 7). To him that overcometh. Again it is made clear that the individual can free himself from the corruption and condemnation of his Church. He may live in the very abode of Satan, and within hearing of damnable doctrines; yet if he overcomes the wiles of Satan, and listens to the Spirit rather than to the seducers, "he shall eat of the hidden manna which restores the spirit that the flesh-pots of Egypt have weakened. He shall have the white stone of absolution, the true spiritual emancipation, which the Balaamite and Nicolaitan emancipation has counterfeited" (F. D. Maurice). "The manna, the hidden manna" (see notes on

ver. 13), is differently explained : by the repetition of the article, the epithet "hidden" is made very distinct. There is probably some allusion to the manna stored up in the ark in the holy of holies (Exod. xvi. 33), and also to the true Bread from heaven, whose presence is now hidden from us; or the reference may be to the loss of the ark, with its contents, when Nebuchadnezzar took Jerusalem (2 Esdr. x. 22). There was a tradition that Jeremiah had hidden the manna, and that it would be brought to light again in the Messianic kingdom. A share in those things which eye saw not, and ear heard not, and to the heart of man never occurred (1 Cor. ii. 9), will be granted to the conqueror—a foretaste of them here, and a full participation hereafter (comp. ch. xxii. 4 and 1 John iii. 2). "To eat" (φαγεῖν) is an insertion into the true text borrowed from ver. 7. I will give him a white stone, and upon the stone (ἐπὶ τὴν ψῆφον) a new name written. "White" and "new," as Trench points out, are keywords in the Apocalypse; and it is natural that they should be so. White is "the livery of heaven," where white robes, white clouds, white horses, and white thrones abound (ch. i. 14; iii. 4, 5, 18; iv. 4; vi. 2, 11; vii. 9, 13; xiv. 14; xix. 11, 14; xx. 11). And "new" is almost as frequent as "white" in the book which tells of a new heaven and a new earth, in which is the new Jerusalem; where the inhabitants have a new name, and sing a new song, and where all things are made new (ch. iii. 12; v. 9; xiv. 3; xxi. 1, 2, 5). But in spite of the familiarity and appropriateness of the two epithets, "white" and "new," a sure interpretation of the white stone with the new name upon it cannot be found. Trench's dictum, that "this book moves exclusively within the circle of sacred, that is, of Jewish imagery and symbols," and that an allusion to heathen or profane customs is inadmissible, is arbitrary and cannot be proved. As already shown, there may be references to the rites of Dionysus, to the games, and to the crown placed on the corpse of a victor. Here there may be an allusion to the white pebble of acquittal used in courts of justice, or to the lot used in elections; and the word ψῆφος favours these views. Or again, the reference may be to the tessera, or ticket, which the victor in the games received to admit him to the tables where he was fed at the public expense. Among Jewish symbols a reference to the "stone with seven eyes" (Zech. iii. 9) seems to be quite out of place. Nevertheless, Trench's explanation of the "white stone" as an allusion to the Urim and Thummim, which the high priest wore behind the square breastplate of judgment has much that is very attractive. This precious thing may well have been a diamond, for there was no diamond among the twelve stones of the breastplate. On each of these stones was written the name of a tribe; but what was written on the Urim none but the high priest knew. The usual supposition is that it was the sacred Tetragrammaton—the ineffable name of God. All this seems to fit in singularly well with the present passage. But if this explanation is to hold, "he that receiveth it" must mean he that receiveth the white stone, rather than he that receiveth the new name. The "new name" is not a fresh name for himself (Isa. lxii. 2; lxv. 15), but a fresh revelation of God's Name and nature, which only those who have received it can comprehend (comp. ch. xiv. 1; xix. 12). A variety of other explanations will be found in the 'Speaker's Commentary,' Smith's 'Dictionary of the Bible,' art. "Stones," in Alford, and elsewhere. Whatever the allusion may be, the general sense is clear. He that overcometh shall be admitted to the heavenly holy of holies, and to a glory and knowledge incomprehensible to those who have not experienced it (1 Cor. ii. 9). He shall be made a priest unto God.

Vers. 18—29.—*The epistle to the Church at Thyatira.* The circuit now turns southwards. From Ephesus to Smyrna, and from Smyrna to Pergamum, was movement almost due north. Thyatira is on the Lycus, close to the Roman road between Pergamum and Sardis. It was refounded and named Thyatira by Seleucus Nicator, after the conquest of Persia by Alexander. It was strongly Macedonian in population; and it is worth noting that it is in Philippi, a city of Macedonia, that Lydia of Thyatira is found (Acts xvi. 14). An inscription in Greek and Latin shows that Vespasian restored the roads thereabouts. Three other inscriptions mention the dyers (οἱ βαφεῖς), for which Thyatira and the neighbourhood ('Iliad,' iv. 141) were so famous, to which guild Lydia belonged (Acts xvi. 14). There is no allusion to the trade here; and modern authorities differ as to whether it survives or not at the present day. But the statement that "large quantities of scarlet cloth are sent weekly to Smyrna" (Macdonald's 'Life and Writings of St. John,' p. 187) seems to be decisive. Apollo, the sun-god, was the chief deity at Thyatira, where he was worshipped under the Macedonian name of Tyrimnas. There is, perhaps, a reference

by contrast to him in the epistle, in the opening description of the Son of God, and in "the morning star" to be given to "him that overcometh." A similar allusion to the worship of Dionysus was traced in the epistle to Smyrna. The modern name of the town is *Ak-Hissar,* "the white castle," so called from the rocky hill overhanging it, on which a fortress formerly stood. Of the nine thousand inhabitants, about three thousand are Christians, who have the trade of the place in their hands. The ancient Church of St. John the Divine has been turned into a mosque.

This fourth and therefore central epistle is the longest of the seven. In some respects it is the most solemn of all. Here only is the majestic title, "the Son of God," introduced. In the introductory vision the expression used is "Son of man" (ch. i. 13). "The Son of God," frequent in the Gospel and Epistles of St. John, occurs nowhere else in the Apocalypse. It may be suggested by Ps. ii. 7, "Thou art my Son; this day have I begotten thee;" for Ps. ii. 9 is quoted in ver. 27 (comp. also ver. 26 with Ps. ii. 8).

Ver. 18.—Who hath his eyes like a flame (see notes on ch. i. 14, 15).

Ver. 19.—I know thy works . . . and thy works. This glaring tautology is a mistranslation. The Revised Version is correct both in the order of the words and in the rendering. We have first the general statement, found in most of these epistles, asserting intimate personal knowledge: "I know thy works." Then we have, in two pairs, these works particularized, "thy love and faith," and "thy ministry and patience." Finally, we have the knowledge "that thy last works are more than the first." "Thy," in the central clause, belongs to all four substantives. Whatever may be thought of 1 Cor. xiii., ἀγάπη in St. John's writings must certainly be translated "love," and not "charity." *Love* and *faith* produce as their natural fruit *ministry* to the sick and needy and *patience* in enduring tribulation. Διακονία, excepting here and Heb. i. 14, occurs only in the writings of St. Luke and of St. Paul; it is specially frequent in the Acts (i. 17, 25; vi. 1, 4; xi. 29, etc.) and in 2 Cor. (iii. 7, 8, 9; iv. 1; v. 18, etc.). That thy last works are more than the first. With the momentous change of πλείονα for χείρονα, this looks like a reminiscence of Matt. xii. 45 (comp. 2 Pet. ii. 20). Πλείονα probably means more in value rather than more in number; compare πλείονα σημεῖα τούτων (John vii. 31); πλείονα καρπόν (John xv. 2); πλείονα θυσίαν (Heb. xi. 4). But both excellence and number may be included. In any case, the Church at Thyatira exhibits *growth* in good works, which is the surest sign of life. Like Ephesus, Thyatira is both praised and blamed; but whereas Ephesus has gone back (ver. 5), Thyatira is going forwards. The two Churches are in some respects the exact opposite one of the other. In Ephesus there is much zeal for orthodoxy, but little love; in Thyatira there is much love, but a carelessness about false doctrine.

Ver. 20.—But I have against thee that thou sufferest. This is certainly right. "A few things" (ὀλίγα) is an insertion in some inferior authorities. Others insert "many things" (πόλλα); the Sinaitic inserts "much" (πόλυ); while the best authorities have nothing between κατὰ σοῦ and ὅτι; and then ὅτι must be rendered "that" rather than "because." The construction is the same as in ver. 4. There is a right and a wrong suffering; and the Church in Thyatira exhibits both. The enduring of tribulation (ὑπομονή) is commended; the toleration of evil (ἀφεῖς) is rebuked. It is not said that Jezebel receives sympathy or encouragement, but merely that she is let alone; her wickedness is left unchecked, and that is sinful. For this use of ἀφίεναι, comp. John xi. 48; xii. 7. It is difficult to decide between "the woman" (τὴν γυναῖκα) and "thy wife" (τὴν γυναῖκα σοῦ), authorities being much divided; the balance seems in favour of the former. But even if "thy wife" be preferred, there is no need to understand Jezebel as indicating a distinct person. We are in the region of figures and metaphors. Perhaps all that is indicated is that the angel of the Church at Thyatira is suffering from the tolerated presence of a baneful influence, as did Ahab, "whom *Jezebel his wife* stirred up" (1 Kings xxi. 25). And if it is not certain that any individual false prophetess is signified, it is scarcely worth while to speculate as to who this individual is. Jezebel may be a person, or she may be a form of false doctrine personified. If the former, Jezebel is doubtless not her real name, but a symbolical name of reproach, and what her name and status were we have no means of knowing. In any case the error represented by the name is closely akin to that of the Nicolaitans and to "the doctrine of Balaam." Whatever differences of detail there may have been, all three made Christian liberty a plea for an antichristian licence which claimed to be above the moral Law. And she **teacheth and seduceth.** This is an independent statement, and must not, as in the

Authorized Version, be made to depend upon "thou sufferest." For the construction τὴν γυναῖκα Ἰεζαβήλ ἡ λέγουσα, compare τῆς καινῆς Ἱερουσαλήμ, ἡ καταβαίνουσα (ch. iii. 12). The word for "seduce," or "lead astray" (πλανᾶν), in the active is frequent in St. John, especially in Revelation (xii. 9; xiii. 14; xix. 20; xx. 3, 8, 10; John vii. 12; 1 John i. 8; ii. 26; iii. 7). A comparison of these passages will lead to the conclusion that the word implies seduction into error of a very grave kind. It is not clear whether "fornication" is to be understood literally, or, as often in the Old Testament, in the spiritual sense of idolatry. The former seems more probable. "My servants" means all Christians, as is clear from ch. vii. 3 and xxii. 3; it must not be limited to those in authority in the Church. (For "things sacrificed to idols," see notes on ver. 14.)

Ver. 21.—Here again the Revised Version must be preferred; the Authorized Version follows a corrupt Greek text. With the construction, "I *gave* her time *that* (ἵνα) she should repent," comp. ch. viii. 3; ix. 5; xii. 14; xix. 8; John xvii. 4; 1 John iii. 1; v. 20. With "willeth not to repent," comp. John vi. 21, 67; vii. 17; viii. 44. Jezebel "despised the riches of Christ's forbearance and long-suffering, not believing that his goodness led her to repentance" (Rom. ii. 4). The whole passage should be compared with this (see also Eccles. viii. 11—13; Ps. x. 6; 2 Pet. iii. 3, 4, 9).

Ver. 22.—Behold! The exclamation "arrests attention, and prepares the way for something unexpected and terrible." It is one of the many differences between the Fourth Gospel and the Apocalypse, that in the former ἴδε is the dominant form, while in the latter ἰδού is the invariable form (καὶ ἴδε in ch. vi. 1, 5, 7 is a spurious addition); ἰδού is very rare in the Gospel; ἴδε is found nowhere in the Apocalypse. In the Epistles neither form occurs. **I do cast her into a bed.** Βάλλω, not βαλῶ, is the true reading; the future has been substituted for the present to match the futures in ver. 23. Forbearance having failed, God tries severity; and, as so often in his dealings with man, the instrument of wrong-doing is made the instrument of punishment. The bed of sin becomes a bed of suffering. Compare "In the place where dogs licked the blood of Naboth shall dogs lick thy blood, even thine;" and "I will requite thee in this plat, saith the Lord" (1 Kings xxi. 19; 2 Kings ix. 26). Βάλλω is one of many words which has become weakened in meaning in late Greek: it often means no more than "place" or "put" (John v. 7; xii. 6; xiii. 2; xviii. 11; xx. 25). In the passive it is rather common of being *laid up* in sickness (Matt. viii. 6, 14; ix. 2; Mark vii. 30). But perhaps we should rather compare such expressions as "cast into prison, into the sea, into the fire, into Gehenna" (Matt. xviii. 30; xxi. 21; xviii. 8, 9). It may be doubted whether there is any significance in the fact that her sin is spoken of as πορνεία (ver. 21), whereas those who sin with her are said μοιχεύειν. Idolatry is spoken of both as whoredom and as adultery. In the one case it is a *contrast* to the marriage tie between God and his faithful worshippers; in the other it is a *violation* of it. Jezebel anticipates the harlot of ch. xvii., as Balaam anticipates the false prophet of ch. xiii. The remarkable construction, "repent *out of*" (μετανοῆσαι ἐκ), is peculiar to this book (vers. 21, 22; ix. 20, 21; xvi. 11; but in Acts viii. 22 we have μετανόησον ἀπό, and in Heb. vi. 1 we have μετανοία ἀπό (compare the converse, μετανοία εἰς, Acts xx. 21). "*Her* works" is to be preferred to "*their* works." Αὐτῆς might easily be changed to αὐτῶν, either accidentally, owing to the preceding ἔργων, or deliberately, because it seems strange to talk of repenting from the works of another person. But the point is that those who have become partakers in her sins have abandoned their own works for hers; and it is therefore from her works that they are bidden to repent (compare "my works" in ver. 26).

Ver. 23.—And her children (placed first, in emphatic distinction from those who have been seduced into temporary connexion with her) I will kill with death. With ἀποκτενῶ ἐν θανάτῳ, comp. LXX. in Ezek. xxxiii. 27 and Lev. xx. 10; and θανάτῳ τελευτάτω, Matt. xv. 4 and Mark vii. 10; the phrase recurs in ch. vi. 8. Those who have not merely been beguiled into sin by her, but are united to her in a permanent moral relationship (John viii. 44), shall perish in some signal manner by the visitation of God. Thus we have three parties marked off: (1) Jezebel herself, the source of all the mischief; (2) her children, who are even such as herself; (3) her victims, who have been led astray by her. She and her children are to be visited with sickness and death, because they will not repent, and the others with tribulation, if they do not repent. Her doom and that of her children is certain; that of her victims may yet be averted. Moreover, the one seems to be final, the other remedial. And all the Churches shall know; literally, *shall come to know, shall learn by experience.* This statement seems conclusive with regard to the purpose of these epistles. Although addressed to local Churches at a particular crisis, they are for the instruction of "all the Churches" throughout the world, and throughout all time. He which searcheth

the reins and the heart (comp. Rom. viii. 27; Ps. vii. 9; Jer. xi. 20; xx. 12). But ἐρευνᾷν in this connexion is a New Testament word; the LXX. do not use it, but ἐτάζειν, a word which is not found in the New Testament, or δοκιμάζειν, etc. Ἐρευνᾷν occurs thrice in St. John's writings (John v. 39; vii. 52), and thrice elsewhere (Rom. viii. 27; 1 Cor. ii. 10; 1 Pet. i. 11). We need not attempt to make any sharp distinction between the *reins*, which were believed to be the seat of the desires, and the *heart*, which sometimes represents the affections and sometimes the conscience. Put together they are equivalent to "the devices and desires of our own hearts." And I will give to each of you. From the angel of the Church the Lord turns abruptly to the individuals in the Church (comp. Matt. xvi. 27; Rom. ii. 6).

Ver. 24.—But to you I say, to the rest in Thyatira. The "and" after "I say" in the Authorized Version is a false reading, which it shares with the Vulgate and Luther: "to you" and "to the rest" are in apposition. Which know not the deep things of Satan, as they say. Two questions confront us here, and it is not possible to answer either with certainty: (1) Who is it who say something? (2) What is it that they say? (1) Note that "say" (Revised Version), not "speak" (Authorized Version), is right; the Greek is λέγουσιν, not λαλοῦσιν. The nominative to "say" may be either the faithful in Thyatira, "who have not this doctrine," and who show their detestation of it by calling it "the deep things of Satan;" or the holders of this doctrine, who profess to be in the possession of profound knowledge of a mysterious kind. Of these two the former is rather tame in meaning. Moreover, we should have expected "as ye say" to harmonize with "to you I say." Therefore we may suppose that it is those who *have* this doctrine who are indicated in "as they say." (2) What, then, did they say? Did they call their doctrine "deep things," which the Lord here enlarges into "deep things of Satan," in order to declare its true character? Or did they themselves call their knowledge "the deep things of Satan," which they fathomed in order to prove their mastery over them? The former seems better. It is improbable that any sect, nominally Christian, would in so many words claim special knowledge of "the deep things of Satan." Rather, he who condemns the "synagogue of Satan" (ver. 9) at Smyrna, and the "throne of Satan" (ver. 13) at Pergamum, here condemns the "deep things of Satan" at Thyatira. In any case, "deep things" is the prominent thought. It is some early form of Gnosticism that is indicated, and we know from various sources that " deep " was a favourite expression of theirs with regard to the knowledge which they professed. "The Valentinians have formed Eleusinian orgies, consecrated by a mighty silence, having nothing heavenly in them but their mystery. If, in good faith, you ask questions with contracted forehead and frowning brow, they say, ' *It is profound* ' " (Tert., ' Adv. Valent.,' i.). Similarly, Irenæus states that they claimed to have found out the " deep things of Bythos "—" *profunda Bythi adinvenisse se dicunt*" (II. xxii. 1). Βυθός (equivalent to " depth ") is the primary being or god of the Valentinian system, another name for which is Ἄρρητος (equivalent to " unspeakable "). Hence elsewhere, for *profunda Bythi*, Irenæus uses the expression *profunda Dei* in speaking of these Gnostic claims (II. xxii. 3). Similarly, Hippolytus ('Refut.,' V. vi. 1) states that the Naassenes called themselves Gnostics, saying that they alone knew the depths—τὰ βάθη γινώσκειν, which is singularly close to what we have here. Note, however, that here the true reading is τὰ βαθέα, neuter plural of the adjective βαθύς, not (as in 1 Cor. ii. 10) τὰ βάθη, plural of the substantive βάθος. See also the fragment of a letter of Valentinus, preserved in Epiphanius (' Contra Hær. adv. Valent.,' i. 31). **I cast upon you none other burden.** An obvious echo of the decision of the Council of Jerusalem respecting these very sins, fornication and idolatry, in reference to Christian liberty (Acts xv. 28, 29), where the very same word (βάρος) is used for " burden." In Matt. xi. 30; xxiii. 4; Luke xi. 46; Gal. vi. 5, the word for " burden" is φορτίον, whereas βάρος is used in Matt. xx. 12; 2 Cor. iv. 17; Gal. vi. 2; 1 Thess. ii. 6. Here, as in ver. 22, the true text gives βάλλω, not βαλῶ; and obviously the word should be rendered in the same way in both verses, not " cast " in one place and " put " in another. " None other " means none other than a more determined opposition to these specious abominations. Hold fast your own doctrine, and denounce the false. Others, much less probably, interpret " none other burden " than the sufferings in which they exhibit the " patience" for which they are praised (ver. 19). This gives a very poor meaning, and, moreover, breaks the connexion with what follows: they are certainly not told to hold fast their sufferings, but Christ's precepts as to faith and conduct.

Ver. 25.—**Howbeit. Not simply** ἀλλά or δέ, but πλήν, which occurs nowhere else in St. John's writings. Although no other burden than this is imposed, yet remember what it implies. Hold fast the love, and faith, and service, and patience, and the *growth* in these virtues, for which thou hast

been commended (ver. 19). Comp. ch. iii. 11, where a similar charge is given to the Church at Philadelphia. The Greek for " till I come " is remarkable—ἄχρις οὗ ἂν ἥξω; where the ἂν conveys a touch of indefiniteness as to the date specified—*until the time whensoever I shall come*. We have a similar construction in 1 Cor. xv. 25.

Ver. 26.—**And he that overcometh.** The usual promise (vers. 7, 11, 17; ch. iii. 5, 12, 21) is here closely connected with the charge which immediately precedes. In this and in the remaining three epistles the proclamation, " He that hath an ear," etc., follows instead of preceding the promise. **Keepeth my works.** This is a phrase thoroughly characteristic of St. John's style; compare for this use of " keep," ch. i. 3; iii. 3, 8, 10, etc.; John viii. 51, 52, 55; ix. 16; xiv. 15, 21, 23, 24, etc.; 1 John ii. 3, 4, 5; iii. 22, 24, etc.; and for " works," in the sense of works which Christ does or approves, comp. ch. xv. 3; John vi. 28, 29; vii. 3, 21; xi. 3, 4, etc. " My works" here are in marked contrast to " her works" in ver. 22. " He that overcometh, and he that keepeth " is a *nominativus pendens*; and such constructions are specially frequent in St. John (comp. ch. iii. 12, 21; John vi. 39; vii. 38; xv. 2; xvii. 2; 1 John ii. 24, 27). Links of connexion between the Revelation and the Gospel or Epistles of St. John should be carefully noted. The phrase for " unto the end " (ἄχρι τέλους) occurs only here and Heb. vi. 11; but comp. Heb. iii. 6, 14; 1 Cor. i. 8. "Unto the end " (εἰς τέλος) in John xiii. 1 probably means " to the uttermost," not " to the end of life." **Authority over the nations.** " Authority" is better than " power" for ἐξουσία, not merely as implying that the power is rightly held and exercised, but also to mark the parallel with " Have thou *authority* over ten cities" (Luke xix. 17; comp. Matt. xxi. 23, 24, 27; Acts ix. 14; xxvi. 10).

Ver. 27.—The verse is not a parenthesis. **He shall rule them.** Here; ch. xii. 5; and in xix. 15, the LXX. rendering of Ps. ii. 9 is adopted; ποιμανεῖς αὐτούς, "Thou shalt *rule* them," or more literally, " shalt *shepherd* them," instead of " shalt *break* them," which almost certainly is the meaning of the Hebrew. The Hebrew original, *trhm* without vowel-points, may represent either *tirhem* or *terohem;* but the latter is required by what follows; " shalt dash them in pieces." Nevertheless, the gentler rendering better suits the requirements of these passages in the Apocalypse. The rule over the nations is to be strong, but it is to be loving also. To those who obey it, it will be a shepherding; only those who resist it will be dashed in pieces. Precisely the same expression is used in ch. vii. 17 of the

Lamb shepherding his saints, and in John xxi. 16 in the charge to St. Peter to shepherd Christ's sheep. It is not easy to determine whether the "rod" ($\dot{\rho}\alpha\beta\delta os$) is a king's sceptre, as in Heb. i. 8, or a shepherd's staff, as in 1 Sam. xvii. 43; Micah vii. 14; and Zech. xi. 7. As the vessels of pottery are broken to shivers. The future tense is a false reading: the insertion of "they"— "shall *they* be broken"—is a false rendering. $\Sigma\upsilon\nu\tau\rho\dot{\iota}\beta\epsilon\iota\nu$, "to shatter," occurs in a literal sense in Mark v. 4 and John xix. 36; and in a figurative sense in Luke ix. 39 and Rom. xvi. 20. As I also have received from my Father. The Greek is $\dot{\omega}s$ $\kappa\dot{\alpha}\gamma\dot{\omega}$ $\epsilon\dot{\iota}\lambda\eta\phi\alpha$, not $\kappa\alpha\theta\dot{\omega}s$ $\dot{\epsilon}\gamma\dot{\omega}$ $\dot{\epsilon}\lambda\alpha\beta o\nu$. He shall receive authority from me, as I also have received from my Father (comp. John xvii. 18; xx. 21; Luke xxii. 29; Acts ii. 33).

Ver. 28.—I will give him the morning star. In ch. 16 Christ himself is "the Bright and Morning Star." Therefore here he promises to give himself to him that overcometh. The morning star has ever been proverbial for brightness and beauty, and, as the harbinger of the day, is the bringer of light, life, and joy. Moreover, a star is often a sign of royalty: "There shall come a star out of Jacob, and a sceptre shall rise out of Israel" (Numb. xxiv. 17); and as such it appeared to the Wise Men (Matt. ii. 2).

HOMILETICS.

Vers. 1—7.—*Ephesus: the declining Church.* This letter to the Church at Ephesus, as well as all the others, is sent to the Church through its "angel." It is not very easy for an English reader to understand to what office in the Church such an expression can refer. The various meanings of "bishop" or "overseer," "pastor," "messenger," have been assigned. We do not accept either to the exclusion of any other. We will, however, indicate some historic matters concerning Church officers, and then leave the student to draw his own conclusions. It is well known that some of the offices of the earliest Christian Churches were named after those of the later Jewish synagogue.[1] The word "presbyter" is one of these. Among the synagogue officers we find one to which, by reason of our different form of organization and worship, we have no exact parallel. This officer was appointed to be the leader of Divine worship, going up before the ark, to conduct the service. He was not one ordained to a permanent office; but exercised it only as he was occasionally appointed thereto. Any lay member of the congregation might thus serve, provided he possessed the necessary qualifications. He was required to be in sympathy with the people, pure in life, ordering well his family, with a good voice, able to read and expound, and to conduct with a devotional spirit the worship of the people, to whom he must be acceptable, as their representative therein. He was regarded as their legate; the mouthpiece of those who were present, and the deputy of those who were absent through illness or otherwise. There should not be any fierce disputation about this, for evidently we have no *such* officer in any of the main forms of Church government. There are those whose duties correspond in some respects, but none whose position is precisely the same. What name should we give him? Not bishop, and not pastor; for his was not a permanent office. Not a president; for he did not belong to the rulers of the synagogue—he acted only for the time as leader of the worship, as expounder of truth; as the people's mouthpiece in prayer. The Jews had a name for such a one. He was called the "angel of the Church." Now, it is far more likely that, at the outset of Christian Church-life, it would be easy to find men who could occasionally than such as could permanently discharge such duties. In the transition period between the passing away of the synagogue-forms and the settlement of new ones, it would be natural to use the old and familiar phrase, "the angel of the Church," although the office indicated by the name in former days was merging into the more sacred one of a permanent overseer of the Church. Although, therefore, there is now no office in the Church precisely corresponding to this old Hebraistic phrase, yet it is intensely interesting to find it retained as one of the last dying echoes in Scripture of the ancient forms; as a connecting link between the old and the new. At that time, if any message were sent to a Church, it would be sent to them through the "angel," who had to conduct their worship, at any rate *pro tem.* But whether Ephesus or any one of the seven Churches had, at

[1] See articles by Rev. J. E. Yonge, M.A., in the *Clergyman's Magazine*, vol. i., new series, 1887.

the time of receiving these letters, substituted a temporary by a permanent officer, there are no data to enable us to affirm. Can we not well imagine the interest and excitement of the people, when the leader of their worship opened a roll—prefacing, perchance, the reading thereof by saying, "Our loved Apostle John, who used to teach among us, but who is now in banishment at Patmos, has been caught up in the Spirit on the Lord's day, and has been moved to send, in the Name of the Lord Jesus, the following letter"? With what deep emotion would its words be heard! In it there are six lines of thought suggested.

I. THE ASPECT IN WHICH THE SAVIOUR PRESENTS HIMSELF TO THEM. It is two-fold. 1. As holding the stars in his right hand. 2. As walking in the midst of the seven golden candlesticks (see homiletics on ch. i. 9—19, sect. I.; 20, sect. II.). The first indicates the special care of Christ over the ministers of his Church. It is not for a minister to "lord it over God's heritage," or to attempt dominion over their faith; but he is guilty of a sinful and a mock humility if he does not "magnify his office," and if he does not regard it as a trust from the Lord Jesus. He will also wrong his Saviour if he does not take comfort in the thought that, as a minister of the Church, he is the object of his Lord's especial care. The second indicates the active energy of Jesus in watching over his Churches, to administer strength, help, comfort, commendation, cheer, rebuke, or warning, as the case may require. There is also a reminder that the Lord has an omniscient eye, to discern the state of things in every one of his Churches. "I know thy works." This attribute of the Lord Jesus is one which should awake the utmost solicitude in any Church, that it may be approved of him.

II. THE SAVIOUR'S ESTIMATE OF THE CHURCH. 1. There had been much good, which, indeed, had by no means died out. They had laboured, even unto toiling (ver. 2). They had endured, when work had to be done under trying circumstances, in the midst of a great city, the inhabitants of which were carried away by the worship of the great goddess Diana. There was still an abhorrence of evil, and a keen and faithful detection of error in doctrine (ver. 3). They had applied to some false apostles a test so severe and so successful, that they were exposed and put to shame. And towards the close of the epistle the commendation is again renewed, as if to show how lovingly our Lord notices every virtue. 2. But still there is a grave charge against the Church. A charge not modified by the word "somewhat," which the Authorized Version thrusts into the translation. "I have it against thee—thou hast left thy first love.[1] Note: It is quite possible for all the machinery of a Church to be in full working order, while at the same time the spirit of love and zeal which first set it ageing is on the decline. This is a great evil; for (1) it is no part of the structure of the spiritual constitution that any decline should befall it; (2) there is no difficulty against which Christ has not warned us; (3) there is no emergency for which his grace is not all-sufficient; (4) there is no other object to which our love can be legitimately trans-ferred; (5) Christ is very jealous of our love; (6) it is a grief and dishonour to him, whose love is a constant flame, to let our love flicker as it does; (7) outside work and energy will not continue long where love is on the decline. No engine will continue to run long after the fire has gone out.

III. THE SAVIOUR'S REBUKE. "I have it against thee." "As many as I love, I rebuke and chasten." Although it be the case that we must all stand before the tribunal of Christ, it is also the case that we are under his all-searching eye even now. "I the Lord search the heart."

IV. THE SAVIOUR'S DIRECTION. "Repent," etc. There is a way back to the cross. It is the same as that by which the sinner came at first. Repent. There must be direct, personal confession to the Lord Jesus. It is indeed a great wrong done to a Church when its members bring a current of cold air with them, and leave it behind them everywhere; but the greatest wrong is towards that Saviour whose cause has been so solemnly espoused, and for whom the professor has sworn to live and die. Cold-hearted professor! thy Saviour calls to thee to renew thy broken vow, and to return to him.

V. THE SAVIOUR'S WARNING. It is twofold. 1. The declining Church will sooner

[1] Uhlhorn, in his 'Christian Charity in the Early Church,' has some instructive historic illustrations of the decay of motive power in the early Churches.

or later receive from Christ some stern reminder of its sin. "I will come unto thee." "The time is come that judgment must begin at the house of God." 2. If the warning be unheeded, the Church will in time disappear. "I will remove thy candlestick out of its place." Our Lord Jesus does not desire the prolonged continuance of a Church whose love is on the decline. A cold Church does not and cannot represent Jesus in the world; it is no longer accomplishing the object for which Churches are formed, and therefore there is no reason why it should continue. Where our Saviour would be most gracious he will, in such a case, be most severe. Churches, as such, are judged in this life.

VI. The Saviour's promise. It is made to individuals. "To him that over-cometh." It pertains to another realm, even to "the Paradise of God." The word "paradise" means an enclosed, park-like place, with all arrangements for refreshment, comfort, luxury. It is first used in Scripture for the garden of Eden, in which was a tree of life. At the Fall, man was barred both from Paradise and from the tree of immortality. We read no more of it till Christ says to the dying thief, "To-day shalt thou be with me in Paradise"—the word being used to denote the realm of the blessed in the invisible world. Still the tree of life appears no more till we get it mentioned here, as in the higher realm of everlasting life, in the Paradise of God. There it is in Christ's own keeping. The fruit of it HE will give to the victor! That is, to drop the figure, whosoever overcomes, to him, in the nobler and the deathless realm, Christ will be the Giver and Sustainer of a life that shall never, never die. There there will be no temptation to decline, for within the gates of that Paradise no tempter can ever come; and the supply of vital power shall be so rich and constant that all inward tendency to decline shall cease for ever. What a motive power is this! Earthly cities, with their witchery and glare, may be before us and around us to-day. But beyond, beyond is the Paradise of God, with its halcyon rest, its genial clime, its steadfast life. And oh! let us not lose sight of the words, "I will give." The communion with Christ will be close and intimate; we shall see face to face. Here the provisions of God's love and grace are often marred through coming to us by such imperfect channels. But there the Lamb who is in the midst of the throne shall feed them, and shall lead them to the fountains of the water of life! How large the promise! how attractive the vision! how glorious the reward! Surely it is worth while to struggle for a little here, that we may pass for ever to a realm where we shall struggle no more. "Wherefore take unto you the whole armour of God, that ye may be able to withstand in the evil day, and having done all, to stand."

Vers. 8—11.—*Smyrna: words of cheer from a reigning Saviour to a suffering Church.* In some respects this letter awakens more interest in the Church to which it was addressed than any other of the seven. Out of the seven Churches, two only are unrebuked. Of these two, Smyrna is one. It is a poor Church, but Jesus calls it rich. It is beset with opposition, but it has the Lord for its Advocate, and is addressed by him in words of cheer and of hope. Not only, however, is this Church interesting to us on account of its high moral and spiritual standing, but also on account of the historical details which are preserved to us concerning it. The Book of Revelation was in all probability written about the year A.D. 96. Under Marcus Aurelius, in the year 168, there was martyred that venerable teacher of the gospel—Polycarp. When he was urged to deny Christ, he said, "Eighty-six years have I served Jesus Christ; he has been a good Master to me all these years, and shall I forsake him now?" Deduct-ing eighty-six years from 168, we come back to the year 82 as the time of Polycarp's conversion. This being so, Polycarp would have been a Christian for fourteen years at the time when this letter was addressed to the Church at Smyrna. Ignatius tells us that in the year 108 he found Polycarp the overseer of the Church there, and Tertullian says that he had been placed in that office by the Apostle John. This being the case, there can be but little doubt that this letter was sent when Polycarp was in office in the Church to which it was addressed; while there can be no reasonable question that he was a prominent sharer in the sufferings which afterwards came upon the believers there.[1] We leave to the student the task of showing the striking illustra-tion this letter receives from the history referred to in the footnote, as all the space

[1] See Eusebius's 'Ecclesiastical History,' bk. iv. ch. xiv. and xv.

at our command is required for the strictly homiletic exposition of it. There are no fewer than seven lines of meditation here suggested. We have—

I. A LIVING SAVIOUR OVER ALL. (Ver. 8.) To the members of this poor and struggling Church the Lord Jesus presents the fact of his mediatorial dominion to them for their comfort and support. For a struggling Church to see enthroned on high the Son of God as Head and Lord, is "better than life." "The First." Then he was before these changeful scenes began. "The Last." Then he will be after they shall have closed. "Who was dead." Then he understands what it is "to resist unto blood." "And lived." *Re-vixit!* Then he has conquered death. He reigns. And as a reigning Saviour he addresses the suffering Church.

II. A LIVING SAVIOUR KNOWING ALL. Other epistles begin, "I know thy works." This and the next begin, "I know thy tribulation." It is possible for a Church so to be placed that activity is out of the question. Endurance may be the only possible form of service. It may be a duty to give up any attempt at sowing or reaping for a while, in order to secure the field on which the harvest must be won. In the old times of persecution, with the Jews, religion was regulated by priestcraft, and among the pagans, by statecraft. Christians knew no priest but Jesus, and no law for the conscience but the law of the truth and the Spirit of God. If for a while the storm would beat about this Church, it would be an unspeakable comfort to hear the voice of Jesus saying, "I know it all." Note: There are some professors now who delight to make a show, and never dream of pleading poverty except when they are asked to give to the cause of God! But here the plea of poverty comes not from the Church; the recognition of that came from the Lord Jesus. *This makes all the difference!*

III. A LIVING SAVIOUR ESTIMATING ALL. "Thou art rich." These words, as a testimony from the Lord Jesus, speak volumes for the genuineness of the life and for the power of faith and love which were in the Church. "Hath not God chosen the poor of this world rich in faith, and heirs of the kingdom which he hath promised to them, that love him?" It is all-important that we should learn to see light in God's light—to reckon silver and gold as corruptible things, and to regard faith, love, and the good hope through grace as the only durable riches. Note: Christ values his Churches according to what they *are*, as well as according to what they *do*. If their trials are such that all they can do is to bear them, and to wait God's own time—well. So, if in old age Christians find their powers of active service fail them, though they may *do* less, they may *be* more. It is not only needful for us to quicken sluggish Christians to activity, it is also needful (and perhaps, in this age of feverish heat and restlessness, even more so) to show to believers that it is by being as well as by doing that they can please, serve, and glorify their Lord. There may be much activity with a very defective inner life. But if the "being" is right, the right "doing" is sure to follow.

IV. A LIVING SAVIOUR FORESEEING ALL. "Ye shall have *tribulation*"—θλῖψις, *tribulatio*. In this the devil would have a hand. The persecution of Christians is here regarded as the work of the evil one. Paul's thorn in the flesh was a "messenger of Satan." He wanted to do this or that, but Satan hindered. Satan goes about as a roaring lion. The object was, "that ye may be tried." Satan tries for a bad purpose; God, for a good one. Satan, to destroy the faith; God, to prove and strengthen it. Satan, to put out the fire; God, to make it blaze the more! Note: All this is foreseen by Christ. Not one trial shall befall that is unforeseen and unprovided for by him. He is planning to outwit the evil one, by making his grace so conspicuous in the evil day, that men shall glorify God the more when they see what his grace enables believers to bear.

V. A LIVING SAVIOUR LIMITING ALL. "Ten days." We take the force of this expression to be equivalent to "A little while, and it will be over!"

> "Griefs of God's sending all have an ending;
> Sunshine will come when the tempest is past."

It is not always that the Churches of God shall be harassed by the enemy. Hostile power shall rage not a moment longer than our heavenly Father shall please.

VI. A LIVING SAVIOUR CHEERING THEM AMID ALL. "Fear not." "In the world ye shall have tribulation; but in me ye shall have peace." "Fear not them which

.ll the body, and after that have no more that they can do." "Lo, I am with you alway, even unto the end of the age."

VII. A LIVING SAVIOUR PROMISING LIFE AT THE END OF ALL. "Be . . . and I will give thee a crown of life. . . . He that overcometh shall not be hurt of the second death." There is underlying the word "hurt" the notion of injustice, and the phrase is equivalent to "The hand of injustice may strike once," but that is all. It shall be powerless then. "Neither can they die any more." The promise is, however, not merely negative; it is positive. "Life." And surely it must be, as Canon Tristram suggests,[1] something more than an accidental circumstance, that out of the seven cities whose Churches are addressed, only those two in which the Churches are unrebuked, viz. Smyrna and Philadelphia, "have retained their importance, their population, and even their Churches in comparative freedom through the trials and vicissitudes of centuries, to the present day;" not, however, without much tribulation. And as it is in the sphere of discipline, so in that of reward. Churches in this life; individuals also in the next; and those believers who have, like the Master, "endured the cross, despising the shame," shall in another state realize the promise, "Where I am there shall also my servant be." They shall have a crown—a crown of life, of glory, of righteousness. These shall be the crown, not merely its characteristics. Life, that lives on and is evermore to be. Glory, that shall be fadeless in its splendour. Righteousness, that shall be spotless in its perfection. The evolution of the spiritual man has infinite ages before it. This age cannot limit its being. This earth has no scope for its growth. As there is a life beyond the present life, so there is a death beyond the present death. He who is born twice can die only once, but he who is born only once will die twice. But if the first death were extinction, a second would be impossible; and if the first death had no notion of extinction in it, so neither may the second. Better, far better, a life of suffering in, with, and for Christ, than to have all possible luxury and no life in Christ! And, by the help of God, we may be "faithful;" and this is all that is required of us. We are but imperfect servants at the best, but we need not be unfaithful. Our position may not be one of ease, but we can be *faithful*. It is not said, "Well done, good and rich servant;" nor "Well done, good and successful servant;" but "Well done, good and faithful servant." "Ah!" say some, "in such stirring times, methinks it was easy to be faithful. Give me a chance of immortalizing myself by martyrdom, and then——" Ah! how easy it is for distance to throw a romantic glamour over even the sufferings of the past. If they who speak like this had to *lie upon a bed of spikes*, it would be a severer test than they now deem it. But this is not likely to be required of us. "He that is faithful in that which is least, is faithful also in much." A daily fidelity in cross-bearing, in small vexations, in little trials, amid the glare and glitter of a deceptive world, and the incessant temptations to desert the standard,—this is what the Master asks for from us. "Be faithful unto death."

Vers. 12—17.—*Pergamos: the impure Church.* In studying this letter to the Church at Pergamos, we will arrange our thoughts in two divisions.

I. LET US STUDY THE CHURCH ITSELF. We gather four things concerning it. 1. *It is directly under the eye of Christ, and responsible to him.* This is a feature common to all the Churches. But it is imperative on us ever to keep this fact in the foreground of our thinking about Church-life. 2. *It was in a very peculiar situation.* Some three days' journey north of Smyrna, on the banks of the Caïcus, in the province of Mysia, was Pergamos situated.[2] The ruins of it even now attest its greatness in ancient times, when it stood high on the roll of famous cities. It was the abode of royalty; it was the metropolis of heathen divinity. Our Lord looks at it as the place "where Satan's throne is." Not all its palaces, temples, and towers, not all the prestige of its worship, could hide its iniquity from our Saviour's eye. When we are taught to look at the world's great cities in the light in which Jesus views them, while many are saying, "What a noble city!" we shall say, "Satan's throne is there." Not that the beautiful in art, and the costly in material, and the strong in structure, are not reckoned by Christ at their real value; but that where men worship these things for their own sake,

[1] See Tristram's 'Golden Candlesticks,' p. 45; Canon Tait's chapter on the Epistle to the Church at Smyrna is specially suggestive and valuable

[2] See Trench, Tristram, Tait, *et al.*

where they are used to hide corruption, and where impurity of motive and of life poison all, material beauty is forgotten in the moral badness. "Man looketh on the outward appearance; the Lord looketh on the heart." We have, however, a further clue to the reason why Pergamos was called "Satan's throne." There paganism reigned supreme; impure, sensuous, licentious worship was observed. Its tutelary deity was Æsculapius. His grave was a place of refuge. His emblem was the serpent. His name was "Saviour." His priests performed charms and incantations; crowds resorted to his temple, where lying miracles of healing were alleged to be performed. The eating of things offered to idols would make it impossible for Christians to enter into the social life of the Pergamenes without a compromise with idolatry; and so fierce was the opposition of the citizens to the Christian faith, that in the early days of the Church, Antipas had to seal his testimony with his blood. Are there not many of our cities of which our Lord would say, "Satan's throne is there"? 3. *This Church was weakening its power of resistance by tolerating mischief within its pale.* (Vers. 14, 15.) Some held the teaching of Balaam, leading to a compromise with idolatrous rites. Others held the teaching of the Nicolaitans; *i.e.* there were those *in the Church* who held false doctrine, turning the grace of God into lasciviousness, and who, by a time-serving policy, ingratiated themselves into the tolerance, if not into the good will, of the idolaters, while they did not keep themselves from the lusts of the flesh. In a word, instead of the Church being and giving a protest against the world, the world was creeping into the Church, and corrupting it. The Church grievously lowers its position when it endures sin within its pale, and when it retains within it those who, while nominally holding the Christian faith, do not live the Christian life. How can a Church give a bold, unflinching, and powerful testimony for Christ against the world if its own hands are not clean, if it is seen catering for the smiles and pandering to the tastes of those who are " of the earth, earthy "? 4. *This looseness in discipline and life was the more disappointing because of its contrast with the past.* Time had been when the Church was known for its staunch adhesion to Christ, and for fidelity even unto death (ver. 13). Of Antipas we know nothing more than is named here. No historic roll, save this, refers to him. But Christ never forgets. To be remembered by him is fame enough. But at that time when Antipas was martyred, the Church itself held fast Christ's Name, and did not deny the faith. So that it is the more saddening to see such a declension. The fact cries aloud to Churches as well as to individuals, " Let him that thinketh he standeth take heed lest he fall." No prestige of the past can serve for the future or even for the present. It is comparatively useless for Churches to proclaim a past fidelity unless they can show a present one. Nor is it enough to remain nominally true to Christ's Name and doctrine, if looseness of morality, or if conformity to the world, finds a place within. If so much of the wooden and earthy is built up into the fabric of the Church, it will have a sore trial by fire. "The time is come that judgment must begin at the house of God."

II. LET US SEE HOW THE SAVIOUR APPEARS TO THIS CHURCH, AND WHAT HE SAYS TO IT. We have observed before that our Lord shows himself to the Churches according to what they are. It is remarkably so here. 1. *How does our Lord here represent himself?* (Ver. 12.) As having a sharp, two-edged sword. This indicates: (1) That our Lord has the supreme right of critically judging, not only the state of the whole Church, but of every member in it. No one else has any such right. It belongs to Christ alone. We all stand, even now, before his tribunal. (2) That there is infinite power of discrimination. There is no confusion. Worthy and unworthy members may, perchance, be mixed up in a common fellowship. Christ never confounds one with another. At every moment the two-bladed sword discriminates between the precious and the vile. (3) The action is as precise as the discrimination is severe. The sword is " sharp." Even of earthly judges it is true that " they bear not the sword in vain." Much more is it true of the Supreme Judge. Let careless ones tremble. " Woe unto them that are at ease in Zion!" No one can be lost in a crowd. No one can poison a Church of Christ with impunity. Hearts awake to righteousness will thank God for this; but it is enough to make careless and inconsistent professors tremble; for if ever the hypocrite attempts to pass with the true Israel of God, down will fall the lightning-gleaming sword, and divide infallibly between them! 2. *What does our Lord say?* (1) He calls on the Church to repent. (a) On the whole Church. Supposing a Church to have evil men within its pale, how can it "repent" of that? There is but one way. If it be wrong to have them, repentance cannot consist in retaining them. They must be "put away" (1 Cor. v.). Discipline is an imperative feature in a Church's life. Without it, any Church imperils its very existence. (b) On the false ones to repent. The guilt of a hypocrite within the Church is, cæteris paribus, greater than that of the worldly without the Church, because committed under the cloak of religion. (2) He warns (ver. 16). "I will fight against them with the sword of my mouth." "Begin at my sanctuary" (cf. Ezek. ix. 6; 1 Pet. iv. 17). (3) In spite of difficulty, our Lord expects men to conquer. "To him that overcometh." Difficult, indeed, it would be. To resist evil anywhere in the world is hard enough. To resist it where Satan's throne is, is harder still. To conquer it when it is poisoning the Church is the very hardest of all. Yet Christ expects this. The conquest of difficulty is the world's glory; and shall the Church do otherwise than delight therein?[1] For no forms of evil can be so strong as to overmatch the power with which he will supply us. (4) For the victor there is a glorious promise (ver. 17). (a) The "hidden manna." If the believer will shun the idol-feasts, and renounce the luxurious banquets in which the ungodly revel, he shall hereafter feed on richer food, even the "hidden manna." What is this? Surely the Lord Jesus Christ himself. But does not the Christian feed on him here? Yea, indeed. But so much interferes with the enjoyment. Who can enjoy a feast, however rich, with unalloyed delight, when the songs of revelry and lewdness, and the cries of woe and sin, are sounding in the ears, or while earth's impurity and corruption are ever before our eyes? Here our enjoyment of spiritual food is mixed with alloy. But there is a feast provided for us out of sight. Whoever reserves himself wholly for Christ's service here is one of those for whom the hidden feast is reserved. (b) The "white stone." Among some, white stones were symbolic of happy days; with others, signs of acquittal; in the Olympic games, white stones with the victor's name were given to the victor. A white stone was thus often a mark of honour among the heathen. But from none of these heathen customs do we get our conceptions of our Lord's meaning here. The passage will interpret itself. This white stone is (a) a token between the victor and Christ; (β) a token between him and Christ alone; (γ) a token which it was a privilege and honour to possess; (δ) a token the privilege and honour of which were read in the name inscribed upon it. Surely with these data we can, by comparing Scripture with Scripture, easily see what that secret token may be in heaven, between Christ and the believer, which shall certify to him his special privilege and honour. "I will give to him ... upon the stone ... a new name written, which no one knoweth but he that receiveth it" (cf. ch. iii. 12). The new name is Christ's own new name—Jesus. No one knows the meaning of this Name but the victor. None but saved ones can possibly read it. They can read it fully when they have overcome. And even then it will require an eternity to understand it; for as the salvation grows from more to more, so will it ever expound the meaning of the great, the infinite Name. Thus as his life as a Christian on earth was a secret between him and his Lord, when in the midst of the struggle; so shall it still be a secret between him and his Lord when, having overcome, he is perfected in heaven. Note: In the presence of this letter, so solemn and yet so gracious, let us remember: (1) That each member in each Church is distinctly and personally responsible to the Lord Jesus Christ. With him alone our account stands. (2) Each one stands as it were between these two alternatives—between the two-edged sword of judgment, and the white stone of honour. The one discovers, divides, judges, avenges, pierces; the other is an eternal love-token between the Saviour and the saved. (3) If there has been hitherto any unreality in our confession, or any impurity in heart and life, or any compromise with the world, let us heed the words, "Repent: or else I will fight against thee." In one hand Christ holds the sword, the sharp edge of which we must feel except we repent. In the other he holds the gem, flashing and gleaming with the brightness and whiteness of the star, and says, "If thou wilt leave thy sins and cleave to me, that sparkling diamond of purest lustre is thine, a love-token for ever between thee and me."

Vers. 18—29.—*Thyatira: victors for Christ reigning with him.* In some respects

[1] Cf. Green's 'High Alps of New Zealand,' pp. 2, 3.

this letter is very similar to the last. In one respect it is unique. Its similarity arises from the fact that in Thyatira, as in Pergamos, there was much that was excellent clogged with much that was impure; that the Saviour stood before the Church as a heart-searching Saviour; that unless the evil were put away the Church would be severely judged, as a lesson and warning to the Churches round about; that the evil ones themselves would be visited with tribulation and with death; that the only burden which the Lord would put on the Church was that it should put away the evil and hold fast the good "until he come." The feature in this epistle which is absolutely unique is the remarkable promise which is given to "him that overcometh"—a promise, verbally at least, unlike any other in the New Testament, and one which has given rise to some interpretations which are totally repulsive to Christian feeling, and alien from the spirit of the Word. And we confess that it would not surprise us if some Christian should say, "Either I do not understand this promise, or else its fulfilment would be little joy to me; to promise me that I should 'rule the nations with a rod of iron,' is to promise me something from which I altogether shrink. I have no wish to break people into shivers." We are the more anxious, therefore, to clear up this part of the epistle (the only intricate one), since some, of coarser mould than others, have gathered therefrom that it would be the work of the righteous, in the millennium, to go about, sword in hand, *slaying the wicked* ! One hopes it is not irreverent to say, we trust other work will be ours. We should lose the spirit of the promise in the letter if we were to put any such interpretation thereon; we should be guilty of neglecting to compare Scripture with Scripture. Undoubtedly, Christ promises to the victor power over the nations. Whether or no it would be a blessing for us to have it must depend on what the power, or authority, is. There is the power of the sword as wielded by the warrior; the power of the sceptre in the hands of a king; the power of the staff as borne by a shepherd; and the power of the truth in the mouth of a faithful witness. To ascertain which kind of power is here intended, we must advance slowly and thoughtfully, and in harmony with the whole Word of God. For to attempt to interpret the words as if they stood absolutely alone, and out of appropriate relation to the entire revealed plan of God, would be foolish and even reckless.

I. THE LORD JESUS CHRIST HAS RECEIVED FROM HIS FATHER POWER (ἐξουσία) OVER THE NATIONS. Since the promise is "to him will I give . . . as I also have received of my Father," it is all-important, for the elucidation of the promise, that we should see what this authority is which Christ has received. We are told in the following passages: John xvii. 2; Ps. ii. 7—10; cxxxii. 11; 2 Sam. vii. 11, 12; Isa. ix. 6, 7; Jer. xxiii. 5; Acts ii. 29—36; v. 31; 2 Pet. iii. 22; 1 Cor. xv. 25, etc. We must allow no such falsification of Scripture as is involved in the affirmation that the kingdom of Christ is not yet in being. For the word εἴληφα (ver. 27) is decisive against that. The kingdom of Christ has, indeed, varied stages of development. There is the present state of things, during which our Lord is subduing evil by the Word of his grace and the Spirit of his power. The next stage of it will be reached when "he hath put all enemies under his feet." The final development of it (so far as revealed to us) will be in the heavenly state. There is, however, one special method of Christ's ruling which is here specified. In ver. 27, ποιμανεῖ αὐτοὺς ἐν ῥάβδῳ σιδηρᾷ ; but in Ps. ii. 9 the same verb is used (LXX.), and is translated "break"—ποιμανεῖς αὐτοὺς ἐν ῥάβδῳ σιδηρᾷ. Again, in Micah vii. 14 it is also used, and is there translated "feed,"—ποίμαινε λαόν σου ἐν ῥάβδῳ σου. So Micah v. 4, καὶ ποιμανεῖ τὸ ποίμνιον αὐτοῦ ἐν ἰσχύϊ Κυρίος. Thus the same word is rendered "break," "tend" "feed," "rule." The fact is that the Lord is regarded as a Shepherd of the flock. The shepherd's care is to "tend" the flock; in doing this he feeds and leads the sheep, and breaks the power that would ravage among them. This is precisely the case with the Lord Jesus as the Shepherd and Bishop of souls. He feeds, leads, and rules his own, and breaks the opposers' power. He will rule in judgment; "he will not fail nor be discouraged till he hath brought forth judgment unto victory." His Word is the "rod of his strength;" his Spirit is the breath of his power.

II. THE LORD JESUS AND HIS PEOPLE ARE UNITED IN A CLOSE FELLOWSHIP OF WAR AND OF VICTORY. Even now they are planted together, crucified together, dead, buried, risen, sitting, living together; and they are destined hereafter to be glorified together. They are one with him in heart, life, and suffering; they will be united with him in triumph **and in glory. From this point of view, is not the puzzling and repelling** aspect disappearing **from this promise? and does it not begin to gleam with glory? Out** of this present oneness with Christ, the fulfilment of the promise in the text must certainly come. Several steps of thought will show this. 1. *Those who are contending with sin without and within are fighting for Christ.* To them life's great conflict is all for Christ. And to them the world and life seem to have naught in them that is worth all the responsibility and care of a battle, save as Christ is coming thereby to be enthroned in, and the evil one dethroned from, the hearts of men. The life of the individual Christian, and the collective life of Churches, are of value only as they help on this end. 2. *Wherever souls are won for Christ believers share the joy of their Saviour's victory.* It is, in fact, a triumph for them when their Lord wins any trophies of honour. For them to live is Christ. Their joys are indissolubly bound up with that of their Saviour. 3. *Believers are constituted by Christ as a great commonwealth of kings and priests unto God.* Priests, to lead men to God; kings, to sway them for him. With the sceptre of a right royal dominion they are to sway the world for Jesus, and we hesitate not to say they are doing it. (1) By the power of clear and strong argument they are breaking the false philosophies of the day to shivers. (2) By the power of holy living the people of Christ are shaming the world. Men like Paul and John are not found save in the Christian camp. (3) There is a growing yearning in believers to draw closer together, and to combine their forces against the foe. *And they will do it!* For: 4. *Christians are an army of warriors as well as a powerful commonwealth.* (Eph. vi.) Their weapons are not carnal; but they are mighty through God. Their watchwords are, "The Word of God *only!*" "The cross of Christ *only!*" "The might of the Spirit *only!*" 5. *Christians will win the day;* and *the day of Christ's triumph will be the day of theirs.* They will lift up their heads when the enemy has fled. 6. *Their ultimate triumph will involve the "breaking to shivers" of all opposition.* "If we suffer, we shall also reign with him." Having been co-workers with him, we shall have taken part in crushing his enemies and ours. And we must not lose sight of the promise, "And I will give him the morning star." Christ says elsewhere, "I am . . . the Morning Star." So that the promise is equivalent to, "I will give him myself." Yes. But *as* a morning star. When the long and weary struggle is over, and the dark night of sin has passed away, then will be seen, distinct and clear, ere break of day, the star heralding the approach of morn. From the obscurity of the conflict Christ shall shine forth in clear and cloudless splendour, blest presage of a heavenly day which no dimness shall obscure, no sin shall mar, no night shall close. And then—then, where will they be who have raged against our Lord and against his Christ? "As the vessels of the potter they shall be broken to shivers!" Then the dominion shall belong to the saints of the Most High. They "which have followed" him, "in the regeneration, when the Son of man shall sit upon the throne of his glory, they also shall sit upon twelve thrones, judging the twelve tribes of Israel." What may be the detail of all this none may venture to say. But the principles on which that share in Christ's sway will be based, and the methods by which it is even now being wrought out, are perfectly clear, and are intended to have an inspiring influence upon Christian workers and warriors. For note: (1) What an encouragement this is to cleave to Christ through evil and through good report!

> "For right is right, since God is God,
>   And right the day must win;
> To doubt would be disloyalty,
>   To falter would be sin."

(2) What an argument for those who are halting, to cleave forthwith to their Lord, and to take part with him in breaking evil to shivers! By stern loyalty to Christ in the struggles of this sinful world, we may prove our fitness for larger trusts in the world where the struggle shall be over. (3) Let each one remember the dread alternative between which he stands—either that of "reigning with Christ," or of being "broken to shivers."

HOMILIES BY VARIOUS AUTHORS.

Vers. 1—7.—*The epistle to the Church at Ephesus.* Ephesus was a notable place in the days of St. John. It and Corinth, on either side of the Ægean, and between which there was a regular traffic, have been likened to the Liverpool and New York of our day, on either side of the Atlantic. Ephesus was large, populous, wealthy, the capital of the province and the centre of the religious worship of the great Diana, whose magnificent temple was accounted one of the wonders of the world. Nor is the place less notable in sacred history than in secular. The great names of SS. John and Paul, of Timothy and Apollos, are intimately associated with it; and the history of the planting of the Church there, given in Acts xviii. 19 and xix., is full of interest. It was the chief of the seven Churches to which St. John was bidden to write. We have previously spoken of the title which in this letter the Lord takes to himself, and will therefore come at once to the contents of the letter itself. Noting—

I. THE COMMENDATION SO GREAT AND HIGH THAT IS GIVEN TO THIS CHURCH. It is indeed a great thing to have such commendation bestowed on any Church or individual Christian. Happy they or he who deserves it. The Church at Ephesus is commended for: 1. *Their works.* " I know thy works." No idle, listless people were they, but active, alert, open-eyed to note and enter where the kingdom of Christ might gain new subjects. The Lord looked down upon them with approval, and here tells them, " I know thy works." 2. *Their labour.* Twice is this mentioned (vers. 2, 3), and it denotes the Divine delight in the quality as well as the quantity of their works. It was strenuous, whole-hearted, earnest. Too many who work for the Lord do so as if with but one hand, or even with one finger. It is the merest shred of their activity that they give to the Lord's work. But here it was as "with both hands earnestly." And they did this though it involved: 3. *Their suffering.* Thou "hast borne" (ver. 3). It means that they were not allowed to labour as they did unmolested. There would be plenty, as we know there were, from all manner of motives, to raise opposition and to resent what they so little liked, indeed hated. Cruel, fierce, relentless, unjust, the sufferings might be and were that their enemies inflicted, and which they had borne; but these did not daunt, dismay, or deter them from going right on. For next: 4. *Their patience is commended.* Generals in the armies of earth value highly what is called *élan* in their troops—the dash and rush and enthusiasm with which the brave fellows spring to the attack; but they value yet more " staying power"—that which depends more on dogged pertinacity and enduring courage than on aught beside. And there is the like of this in the spiritual warfare. High, eager courage at the outset, hearts filled with enthusiasm,—yes, these are good; but better still is what will ever be needed, and that is the grace of patience, the power to endure and not to faint. Thrice is this great and indispensable grace commended in this epistle, as if the Lord would show in how high esteem he held it. Oh for this power to labour on and not weary in well-doing, to be patient and faint not! For one who has this there are many who will set out and set out well, but they soon get hindered and turn aside or stop altogether, and some even turn back to the world they had professed to leave. Blessed, then, is this grace of patience. 5. *Their holy intolerance.* There is an intolerance, and there is far too much of it, which is the fruit of conceit, of spiritual pride, of abject narrowness, of gross ignorance, and blind bigotry. They in whom it is found are perhaps amongst the very chiefest enemies of the Church of God, although they loudly boast to belong to its very elect. The intolerance of such is never holy. But, on the other hand, there is a tolerance which is a mere giving in to wickedness because we have not enough zeal for God and righteousness to withstand it. Such people boast of their broadness, but it is far too much of what Carlyle once called it when indignantly repudiating some of its teachings, " None of your heaven-and-hell amalgamation societies for me!" Of such people it could never have been said, as is here said of the Ephesian Church, " Thou canst not bear them which are evil." They would have palliated and explained and found some plausible pretext for even the most evil deeds. Now, in righteous contrast to these, the Ephesian Church would have no compromise with evil. That which is told in Acts xix. indicates this admirable quality in them. They brought their costly books of magic and burnt them—not selling them, or giving them away, or shutting them up, but getting right rid of them altogether, though so much might have been urged for milder measures. But these books, contaminated as they were with the foulness of idolatry, burning, they believed, was best for them, and burnt they were. It was a prelude to that after-excellence of character which is here commended of the Lord. Under the ban of this righteous wrath two sets of persons deservedly came, both being generally described as "them that are evil." (1) Pretended apostles. Renan and those who with him accentuate so strongly the undoubted differences that there were between Christians of the Pauline and the Petrine types, affirm that by "those who say they are apostles, and are not," John meant Paul. But they seem to forget that it is added that the Ephesian Church had "found these pretended apostles false." If, then, Paul was one, it is strange that, instead of finding him out as false, the Ephesian Church and its bishops—in the scene at Miletus—should have cherished the most tender affection and reverence for him; and that Polycarp, one of St. John's most distinguished disciples, should speak of Paul, as he does, as "the blessed and glorious Paul." No; it was not such as Paul that St. John meant, but wolves in sheep's clothing, base, bad men, lured by the bait of the influence and power which they saw the true apostles had, and pretended to be such in order that they might make gain for themselves. But it could not have been very difficult to detect such as these, and, being put to the test, they were cast out for what they were. Woe to the Church that tolerates, knowingly, impostors in her midst! that lets them remain amongst the true, though they be false! (2) The Nicolaitans (see Exposition). They were practically antinomians. The sect flourishes still. Nicolaitans are everywhere, because everywhere there are men who will profess, believe, and do almost anything by which they think they may escape the hard necessity of obeying the moral laws of Christ. Well is it for the Church, well is it for every one of us, to allow no pretence whatsoever to palliate evil deeds. Even the grace of God may be turned into lasciviousness, and it seems impossible to keep men back from presumptuous sins—sins, that is, for which they find, or think they find, encouragement in the doctrines of God's great mercy, and the all-atoning efficacy of our Saviour's death. But the Lord hates the deeds of such men, and may he help us to hate them too. The Church at Ephesus hated them, and are especially commended of the Lord for that they did so. But now the Lord says to them, "One thing thou lackest." Surely if ever there was a Church that seemed able to ask, without fear of an unfavourable reply, "What lack we yet?" this Church was such a one; but now, behold, the Lord turns from commendation to—

II. THE CENSURE. "I have . . . because thou hast left thy first love" (ver. 4). And this censure is very grave. It speaks of the conduct it condemns as: 1. *A grievous fall.* "Remember . . . whence thou art fallen." That which they had left and lost had lifted them high in the Divine love, had made them exceeding precious in his sight. But now all was changed. The Lord looked not on them now as he once did; they had "with shame to take a lower place." 2. *A calling for prompt and practical repentance.* They were to "repent" and "do" their "first works." 3. *Terrible in its consequences* if there were not this repentance (ver. 5). Let Gibbon tell how, after more than a thousand years had passed—such was the Lord's long-suffering—the dreadful threat was fulfilled, and the light of the lamp of gold that represented Ephesus was, with all the rest, faithful Smyrna and Philadelphia alone excepted, finally quenched. Then "the captivity or ruin of the seven Churches of Asia was consummated; and the barbarous lords of Ionia and Lydia still trample on the monuments of classic and Christian antiquity. In the loss of Ephesus, the Christians deplored the fall of the first angel, the extinction of the first candlestick of the Revelation; the desolation is complete; and the temple of Diana or the church of Mary will equally elude the search of the curious traveller. The circus and three stately theatres of Laodicea are now peopled with wolves and foxes; Sardis is reduced to a miserable village; the god of Mahomet, without a rival or a son, is invoked in the mosques of Thyatira and Pergamos; and the populousness of Smyrna is supported by a foreign trade of the Franks and Armenians. Philadelphia alone has been saved by prophecy or courage. At a distance from the sea, forgotten by the emperors, encompassed on all sides by the Turks, her valiant citizens defended their religion and freedom above four score years; and at length capitulated with the proudest of the Ottomans. Among the Greek colonies and Churches of Asia, Philadelphia is still erect, a column in a scene of ruins;

a pleasing example that the paths of honour and safety may sometimes be the same" (ch. lxiv.). But this grave censure, and the awful consequences that ultimately ensued, lend urgency to the inquiry as to—

III. THE SAD CHURCH-CONDITION THE CENSURE INDICATES. Probably it pointed: 1. *To a slackening in those qualities for which they had been commended.* And the moral atmosphere of a place like Ephesus could not but try them very severely. Even Timothy had to be warned against yielding to the sensuality of the place, and also against that rigorous asceticism to which tempted ones often resort as a sure defence against such sin. But the needs-be that there must have been for such exhortation shows how strong the stream of evil tendency was in the place, and how difficult to continuously maintain that firm stand which in the first ardours of the Christian life they had taken and for a long while been faithful to. And undoubtedly this is how, in our own day, this leaving of our first love shows itself. What sincere Christian heart is there that has not once and again been pierced as he has remembered how true this censure is for himself? That sad but well-known hymn of the saintly Cowper, "Oh for a closer walk with God!" is but one continued comment on this all too common sin. And so common has it become that we now almost expect that there will be this slackening of zeal when the first novelty of discipleship has passed away. The "goodness" of such will be, we all but assume, "as a morning cloud and as the early dew that goeth away." And the present all but impossible practice of personal and private pastoral dealing with individual souls lets this condition of things go on with all too much facility. But he who is faithful with himself will mark with sorrow the decline of his own spiritual life. When he has to drag himself to duty; when prayer and worship and work for Christ are turned from, in heart if not in act; when there is no longer any glow or fervour of feeling Christwards; when temptation, once resisted and spurned, now approaches and solicits, and is suffered so to do;—all these, and others like them, are symptoms, sure and sad enough, that the Lord has this against him, that he has left his first love. And this fact shows itself also: 2. *In the altered spirit in which work is done.* And this, we expect, was the gravamen of the charge as it referred to the Ephesian Church. We are not told that they had left off their works. But it was possible for them to continue and even to increase them, and yet this censure to be deserved. For it is the motive at which the Lord looks. Ere ever he would restore the recreant Peter to his apostleship, thrice over was the question asked, "*Lovest* thou me?" as if the Lord would teach him and all of us that love to himself is the one indispensable qualification of all acceptable service. And if from any one out of a multitude of other motives—mixed, and maybe mean, manifold certainly, as they are sure to be—the works we do are done, for all acceptance with Christ they might as well, and sometimes better, have been left undone. You may work and labour, suffer and be patient under it, hate many evil things and persons, and yet there be scarce one shred of love to Christ in it all (cf. 1 Cor. xiii.). It is well, indeed, for us to ask ourselves not merely what we do, but why? The answer to that might lead to some strange self-revelations, but they would be salutary too. Without doubt they would be if they led us to listen to—

IV. CHRIST'S ENCOURAGING CALL TO COME BACK TO HIMSELF. For he does not close this letter without such call, which may "he who hath ears to hear" hear indeed. In what was said on the common characteristics of these letters, it was noted how they all taught that all might overcome. Victory was possible to all; none need despair. And this lies in these last words of the letter. It said to the Church at Ephesus, "You need no longer yield to that which draws you away from me; you can resist, you can overcome, and so return to me whom you have left." Such is the force of the words, "to him that overcometh." And then, that the possible may become the actual, Christ holds out the prize of victory, the recompense of their return to their first love (ver. 7). The promise seems to point back and on. Back to the primeval Paradise from which our first parents and all their descendants were shut out, lest they should eat of the tree of life. Now it is promised that that prohibition shall be withdrawn, the flaming sword of the cherubim "which turned every way, to keep the way of the tree of life," shall be sheathed, and access granted once more. But the Paradise shall not be the primeval one, but the heavenly, "the Paradise of my God"—so the Lord speaks of it. Far more, then, than all that has been lost shall be theirs if they repent and return.

and so win the victory and overcome. **The temptations to which they were** exposed were for ever clamouring that they should seize upon the sensual pleasures of this short life, and fill it up with them, such as they were. But the Lord's promise holds out to them the prize of a pure and perfect and perpetual life in the presence of God, and amid the pleasures for evermore which are in the Paradise of God. And that prize is held out to us as to them, and if it work in us our Lord's will and purpose, it will lead to that diligent culture of the soul, by constant and fervent prayer, and by the cherishing of all spiritual affections, and by yielding to all the Christward drawings of which once and again we are conscious ; and so the soul's first love left and lost shall be found again ; though it was as dead, yet shall it be alive once more.—S. C.

Ver. 1.—*The stars, the lamps, and the Lord.* "He that holdeth . . . golden candle-sticks." We may well pause on the threshold of the first of these letters to the Churches to consider, as we have not done before, the truths that underlie the sublime symbols of the stars and the lamps of gold and the holding of the stars in the Lord's right hand, and his walking in the midst of the lamps of gold. Here, as well as through-out these letters, "He that hath an ear, let him hear."

I. THE STARS. The Lord himself has told us whom these represent—the angels of the Churches ; and in a previous homily we have given reasons for understanding these angels as the chief pastors of the several Churches. "If each Church had its angel, who had a letter addressed to him, who is spoken to in words of rebuke and exhortation, who could sin and repent, who could be persecuted and die, who could fall into heresies and be perfected by suffering, it seems to me a violent and unnecessary hypothesis that a superhuman being is in question." Furthermore, the name "angel," when applied to these august beings who dwell in the immediate presence of God, does by no means set forth their nature, but only their office and function of "messenger," which is what the word means. And is it not a most appropriate name for a Christian pastor ? Not alone does he represent the Church over which he presides, and is largely responsible for its character and condition ; but also he is, or should be, strictly speaking, their messenger, their angel. For is it not his bounden duty to go from them to God, and from God to them ? Woe betide him if he fail herein ! "God forbid," said the venerable Samuel, "that I should sin against the Lord in ceasing to pray for you" (1 Sam. xii. 23). And God forbid that any pastor now should sin against the Lord and his own soul and the souls committed to his charge by ceasing to pray for them. The path to the throne of grace should be a beaten track by him, and he should carry to their Lord their sins and sorrows, their cares and wants, and plead them as his people's messengers and representative before the Lord. And he should come from God to them. It is ill when he goes into his pulpit or pastoral work if he has not first been with God, and come from him to his people and his work. Yes, pastors are, or should be, "angels," in that their office is to go to and fro between their people and God as his messengers and theirs. But wherefore are they called "stars"? We are not distinctly told ; we can only conjecture and suggest. Stars : 1. *Are symbols of honour, dignity, authority, rule.* "A star," it is said, "shall come out of Jacob;" and this is explained by the added parallel sentence, "and a sceptre shall arise out of Israel" (Numb. xxiv. 17). And wherever stars are symbolically spoken of, this idea of dignity and authority is seldom wanting. The Lord lovingly appoints this symbol that he might let all men know, however much his faithful pastors might be despised by the world for their poverty and manifold meanness, as the world counts meanness, nevertheless in his esteem they rank high, they are as stars. Now, if any pastor, on the strength of this august symbol, should demand all manner of deference and submission, and find that instead thereof he gets only contempt and disregard, let him not blame anybody but himself. If he demand deference, he will not get it ; but if he deserve it, he will be likely to get too much of it. The honour and authority of the ministry must be such as is spontaneously given ; it can be had in no other way. But this symbol tells also : 2. *Of the pastor's duty.* (1) He is to lighten the darkness of men, as the stars were to give light by night ; the darkness of ignorance, of sorrow, of sin. (2) He is to reflect the light of the Sun of Righteousness. Not by his own light, but by light reflected, is he to enlighten others. (3) He is to keep his appointed course, in obedient, reverent service rendered unto God. "Wandering stars" are outcast from God. Men should ever know where to find the minister of God; his orbit—the holy ways of God—he should never quit. (4) He should be above the world—his conversation in heaven, his citizenship there. (5) He should be a sure guide for men's souls, as are the stars to the benighted, the traveller, the mariner; and, like the star of Bethlehem, he should ever guide men to Christ. (6) And passing from the symbols to that which is meant, we find that pastors and Churches will very much resemble each other. "Like priest, like people," is true, but so is "Like people, like priest." A minister who, though he should be, is yet not as an angel, nor as a star, may, by his faithlessness, dim and darken, if not destroy, the light of the lamp he was appointed to tend. A congregation, a Church, a parish,—to what depths may it not fall under the influence of a prayerless pastor! And, on the other hand, one who comes to the sacred office in all the ardour of his "first love" may, by the chill freezing atmosphere in regard to God and his cause which he finds around him, be gradually dragged down to their level, and become even as they. Ah! what would any do were it not that the Lord holds the stars in his right hand, and walketh amidst the lamps of gold?

II. THE LAMPS. We regard this word as every way more congruous than "candlestick." Candlesticks are not only a modern and mean article of furniture, but they were never used in the temple or tabernacle at all, and they suggest anything but the sacred and elevated idea that is here intended. We know that by these golden lamps the Churches are meant. But why are they thus called? Not without reason, we may be sure. 1. *The lamps are to give light.* That is their function. They are "lit not for themselves, but for their uses." Continually is this emblem made use of to tell of the character and conduct of Christ's people, what it is or should be. Radiant, cheering, silent, penetrating, beneficent, revealing, manifesting its source, but not itself. We see the sun, but not the rays which stream from it. So men are to see our light, but to glorify not us, but God. Such should the Churches be. 2. *Their light is not their own.* The lamp must be lit and fed. In vision Zechariah saw this truth set forth when he beheld the great temple lamp, and by the side of it the two olive trees, from which, through golden pipes, the sustaining oil was continually supplied. Christ lights every one of these lamps, and if, like John the Baptist, we are a burning and shining lamp—lamp, not light; Christ is the Light-giver—and if, as he was, we are light, it is because "we are light in the Lord." And the Holy Spirit nurtures the light. That was the meaning of Zechariah's vision. "Not by might, nor by power, but by my Spirit, saith the Lord of hosts"—such is the added explanation of the vision. Thus the light of these lamps of gold is not their own; they neither impart it at the first nor sustain it afterwards. Christ and the Spirit of God are the sources of the Church's light. 3. *Their light is combined light.* Each lamp has one burning light, but that one is made up of the combined illumination of every member of the Church. Just as the character of any given Church is the resultant of the varied spiritual forces that each member supplies, so the light of its lamp is the combined effect of the light in each individual. "A Church is not to be merely a multitude of separate points of brilliancy, but the separate points are to coalesce into one great-orbed brightness." 4. *It is to be consecrated light.* All in the ancient tabernacle and temple that was used in the immediate service of God was to be of gold. The gold showed that the service of the vessel, or instrument, or whatever it was, was for God, dedicated and due to him. And this truth the gold of which the lamps are formed sets forth. Churches are for God, for his service and glory. May all Churches heed this!

III. THE LORD. What is the relation between the stars, the lamps, and the Lord? Is it not that of: 1. *Owner?* He holds the stars in his strong right hand. They are his. He walks amid the lamps of gold as amid the possessions of his own house. 2. *Protector?* Who shall pluck the stars from his hand, or loosen his blessed hold? Who shall touch one of those lamps to hurt or harm it whilst he walks continually in their midst? 3. *Searcher?* The stars and the lamps are ever beneath his eye. He says to each one, "I know thy works." 4. *Disposer?* We are in his hand and power, to be dealt with as he wills. Though none other but he, yet he can unloose the grasp in which the stars are held, and can remove the lamp out of its place. May he forbid that this awful necessity should ever arise, for then the light of stars and lamps alike are quenched, and the blackness of darkness for ever is their portion! And: 5. All this (vers. 1—4) *he is evermore.* "Lo, I am with you alway, even unto the end of the world." Not for the primitive Church alone, but for the Church of all ages, is this most surely true. To-day may every faithful pastor say to himself, "I am my Lord's; he holds me in his right hand." And every Church of Christ may by faith behold him walking to-day—to cheer, to bless, to restore, to uplift, to chide, to strengthen, to quicken, to console, to save—amid the lamps of gold.—S. C.

Ver. 4.—*Going back in the ways of God.* "Nevertheless I have . . . first love." There is no stage of our heavenward journey that is so hard as that which we go over for the third time. When in the ardour of our first love we first traversed that part of the road, we went along vigorously, with a strong elastic step. And when we went back, though we went slowly enough at first, like as when the boy's ball, which he has flung high into the air, when ceasing its upward ascent, begins to descend, that beginning is slow, but quickens every second. And so on the backward road we quicken speed in a mournful way. But when we have finished this retrogression, and with a startled shock discover what we have lost, but, by God's exceeding grace, resolve to recover it— *hic labor hoc opus est*—this is toil indeed. Our text brings before us the case of those who have thus gone back, and whom the Lord is lovingly rousing to the resolve that they will regain what they have lost. Note—

I. WHAT THEY LEFT AND LOST. It was that blessed early condition of peace and joy Godward which the beginning of the religious life so often witnesses. "All things were new—Christ was new, the Word a new light, worship a new gift, the world a new realm of beauty, shining in the brightness of its Author; even the man himself was new to himself. Sin was gone, and fear also was gone with it. To love was his all, and he loved everything. The day dawned in joy, and the thoughts of the night were songs in his heart. Then how tender, how teachable! in his conscience how true! in his works how dutiful! It was the Divine childhood, as it were, of his faith, and the beauty of childhood was in it. This was his first love; and if all do not remember any precise experience of the kind, they do at least remember what so far resembled this as to leave no important distinction." There was fervour of feeling: a great outgoing of the soul towards Christ; much prayer, and that very real; hearty service; delight in worship—the sabbath, the sanctuary, the sacred service; the avoiding, not sin only, but its occasions, the "hating of the garment spotted by the flesh;" in short, there was a close walk with God. Blessed, blessed time, the primeval Paradise of the soul, the golden age, the leaving of which one might mourn, even as our first parents mourned when they were driven forth from Eden to the thorns and briars of the wilderness!

II. HOW IT CAME TO BE LEFT. Many are the explanations that might be given. In some, absorption overmuch in business; in others, the influence of unspiritual and worldly companions; in others, intellectual doubts, insinuated into the mind by unbelieving or sceptical books; in others, the chill moral atmosphere of the Church itself; in others, some lingering, lurking lust reasserting itself; and so on in ever-increasing variety; but each one knows for himself how the going back was brought about. But that we may not make sorry those whom God has not made sorry, we would add the caution not to regard every fluctuation of feeling as proof of this going back. Some are for ever tormenting themselves in this way, and so kill the very love they are looking for, and in looking for it. "The complications of the heart are infinite, and we may become confused in our attempts to untwist them." Men dig at the roots of their motives to see that they are the right ones, and the roots of tender plants cannot stand such rough handling. But whilst there are some who distress themselves when they have no need, there are more who have great need, and yet are not distressed as they should be. Let such consider—

III. WHAT COMES OF LEAVING OUR FIRST LOVE. 1. *The Spirit of God is grieved.* Can a father see his child turn cold and sullen towards him, and not be grieved? And in view of such turnings back from him, must not our Lord be in a very real sense "the Man of sorrows" still? 2. *Sinful men are hardened in their sin.* Their boast is that there is no reality in religion; that it is all a spasmodic passing thing; that the fervour of it in the beginning will soon cool down, and here is another proof that there is nothing in it. 3. *The Church of God is distressed.* Its members had relied upon those who have gone back, had hoped for much good from them, had looked to see them carrying on and extending the work of God around them, and now they are disappointed and made ashamed. The enemies of God blaspheme, and those who have gone back are the cause. 4. *And they themselves suffer most of all.* (1) They are miserable; they have enough of religion left to give them disrelish for the ways of the world, but not near enough to give them the joy which belongs only to those who are whole-hearted in the service of God. (2) And they are on the verge of great and awful judgment. If they still go back, it will be "unto perdition;" and if, in God's mercy, they be made to stop ere they have gone to that last length, it will most likely have to be by some sharp scourging process, with many tears, and amid terrible trouble both without and within. What a pitiful journey that must have been when the wretched prodigal resolved at length that he would "arise, and go to his Father"! In what humiliation, fear, shame, distress, he had to urge his weary way along the return road! Only one thing could have been worse—that he should not have come back. Oh, you who are forsaking Christ, if you be really his, you will have to come back; but no joyous journey will that be for you. No, indeed! It never has been, and never can be. Still blessed be the Lord, who forces you to make it, difficult and hard though it be. It is the hand which was nailed to the cross, and the heart which there was pierced for you, that now wields the scourge which compels you, in sorrow and in shame, to come back to him whom you left. But—

IV. WHAT FOLLY IT IS TO LEAVE HIM AT ALL. Ministers of Christ are so fond, as well they may be, of proclaiming God's pardoning love, that they too much pass over his preserving love. We take it too much for granted that men will go off into "the far country," as that foolish younger son did; and we forget that much-maligned elder son who stayed at home with his father, and who was therefore far more blessed than the other could ever be. He could not understand his father's gentleness to that ne'er-do-well brother of his—as many still, and ever since the gospel has been preached, have failed to understand God's gentleness to returning sinners; and so he complained. But how did his father answer him? It is too little noted. "Son, thou art ever with me, and all that I have is thine;" the meaning of all which was, "What, my son! *you* complain at my forgiving and welcoming your poor wretched brother! you *who are so much better off, you* complain!" Yes, he was better off; his lot, as is the lot of all those who never leave their first love, is far the preferable one, and there is no need that we should choose the other. Never let it be forgotten that he who brought you to himself will *keep* you near to and in himself, as willingly as, surely more willingly than, he will receive you after you have gone astray. To be pardoned, ah! well may we thank God for that; but to have been preserved, to have been "kept from the evil so that it should not hurt us," to have been "kept in the love of God,"—for that more thanksgiving still is due; and may God grant that we may be able for ever and ever in his blessed presence to render it unto him.—S. C.

Vers. 8—11.—*The epistle to the Church at Smyrna.* This city was situated in the same district of Asia Minor, some forty miles to the north of Ephesus, in which all these seven Churches were, at the mouth of a considerable river, in a most beautiful bay. The lands lying round were very fertile, bearing grapes in abundance, as befitted the city where the god Bacchus was the deity most honoured by the people. The city itself was large, beautiful, populous, wealthy. It was called, "The lovely one;" "The crown of Ionia;" "The ornament of Asia." It still exists and retains much of its old prosperity. Many Jews were there then as now and as is ever the case in busy trading seaports, and they would easily supply that contingent of Jewish persecutors by which the Church there was afflicted. We will speak—

I. OF THE SAINTLINESS OF THE CHURCH AT SMYRNA. This is attested in this letter. 1. *Negatively.* No blame is given; there is not one word of censure, as there certainly would have been had there been occasion for it. He who could say with the authority of omniscience, "I know," and whose eyes were as "a flame of fire," would have at once discerned fault if fault there had been. No; this Church seems to have come nearest of all to that ideal Church which is "without blemish, having neither spot, nor wrinkle, nor any such thing." But this is attested also: 2. *Positively.* Direct affirmation of their high and holy character is given by the Lord's declaration, "Thou art rich" (ver. 9). Yes; rich in the favour and love of God; rich in the gifts of the Holy Ghost; rich in the blessed prospect of the crown of life, which assuredly should be theirs; rich in present knowledge, consolation, and hope; rich in the help and blessing they should impart to others. Poverty there might be and was in regard to this world's wealth, but over against it was to be set, and doubtless they did so set it, the wealth of the kingdom of God which they knew was theirs. Let us ask ourselves—Would we have sided with them in their estimate of the relative value of the two riches? Would we have counted the spiritual wealth they chose greater riches than all the glittering, present, and tangible treasures of the world? They made such choice. Pray for grace to do the same.

II. THEIR SORROWS. "Many sorrows shall be to the wicked," saith God; but once and again, and maybe yet again it will be so, many sorrows have befallen God's saints, even the most loving and faithful of them. It was so with the suffering Church at Smyrna. Their sorrows are described as: 1. *Tribulation.* Already the storm of persecution had burst and was beating fiercely on the despised community that dared defy the pagan population, and the worship that was established in the city. Judging from what we know actually took place there and elsewhere at this period, there would be no lack of persecutors of all sorts in whom the deep hatred of the Christians, which had become all but universal, would urge them on to the infliction of all manner of suffering which might well be, and could only be, described as "tribulation." 2. *Poverty.* In wealthy cities such as Smyrna, where buying, selling, and getting gain was the all-absorbing occupation, and where success, which meant wealth, was, as elsewhere and as in our own day, all but worshipped, poverty was not merely odious, but even infamous. And in all probability the poverty of not a few of the Christians at Smyrna was directly traceable to the fact of their being Christians. They would be shunned and disliked, and it is easy to see how soon, under such circumstances, men who had been prosperous hitherto would fall into poverty. And the temptation to abandon a faith which involved such results must have been very strong, especially when they could not but know that they would abandon their miserable poverty at the same time, and return to the prosperity which they had lost. Ah! if now Christ could only be served at the cost which the Christians at Smyrna had to bear, how many would come to his service? how many would continue in it? But Christianity has long ago found out a way to make the best of both worlds, though whether to the enhancement of her power and glory may be gravely doubted. 3. *Slander.* The strong word "blasphemy" is employed, for the revilings of their enemies would, as such ever do, glance off from the Lord's servants to the Lord himself, and would become blasphemies—revilings against the Lord. What form these took, or on what they were based, we do not certainly know; but with the records of the New Testament and of Church history in our hands, we may reasonably infer that they had to do with the relations of the Christians: (1) To the government of the day; accusing them of sedition and disloyalty, for which their persistent refusal to offer sacrifice to the emperor would afford plausible pretext. (2) To society. Not a few of the popular games and festivals, as well as more social gatherings, involved sacrifices to idols, and from these the Christians would stand rigidly aloof. Thus they would be regarded as morose, misanthropical, and in other ways odious. They would be, as they were, denounced as haters of the human race. (3) To morality. It was charged against them that their assemblies, which they were commonly obliged to hold at night, were for the vilest of purposes. There was no vice or crime which was counted too bad to charge them with. (4) To God. The Jews would say of them, as Christ forewarned his disciples that they would, even as they had said it of him, that they were servants of Beelzebub (cf. Matt. x.). Hence any who slew them thought they did God service. Such probably were some of the blasphemies which were spoken against them, and which they had to bear as best they might. Foul-mouthed Jews, "synagogues of Satan," and no true children of Abraham, as they said they were, but were not, together with those of "the baser sort" amongst the heathen, would be quick to invent and spread these slanders, and to wound with worse than words if but they had the power. And they were to have it (ver. 10); for: 4. *Their prospects were ever darkening.* Very interesting in the light of this letter is it to read what is told us of Polycarp, St. John's own disciple, and who was, if not the very angel, yet an angel of the Church at Smyrna to whom this letter was sent. We possess a letter of his writing, a description of his character, and a detailed record of his martyrdom. And this last so beautifully illustrates the prophecy, the charge, and the promise of this letter, that it is well worthy of our notice in connection with what is here said of the Church of which he was the beloved, the honoured, and faithful pastor, when he won the martyr's crown. In the year of our Lord 167 a cruel persecution broke out against the Christians of Asia Minor. Polycarp would have awaited at his post the fate which threatened him, but his people compelled him to shelter himself in a quiet retreat, where he might, it was thought, safely hide. And for a while he remained undiscovered, and busied himself, so we are told, in prayers and intercessions for the persecuted Church. At last his enemies seized on a child, and, by torture, compelled him to make known where he was. Satisfied now that his hour was come, he refused further flight, saying, "The will of God be done." He came from the upper story of the house to meet his captors, ordered them as much refreshment as they might desire, and only asked of them this favour, that they would grant him yet one hour of undisturbed prayer. The fulness of his heart carried him on for two hours, and even the heathen, we are told, were touched by the sight of the old man's devotion. He was then conveyed back to the city, to Smyrna. The officer before whom he was brought tried to persuade him to yield to the small demand made upon him. "What harm," he asked, "can it do you to offer sacrifice to the emperor?" This was the test which was commonly applied to those accused of Christianity. But not for one moment would the venerable Polycarp consent. Rougher measures were then tried, and he was flung from the carriage in which he was being conveyed. When he appeared in the amphitheatre, the magistrate said to him, "Swear, curse Christ, and I will set thee free." But the old man answered, "Eighty and six years have I served Christ, and he has never done me wrong: how, then, can I curse him, my King and my Saviour?" In vain was he threatened with being thrown to the wild beasts or burned alive; and at last the fatal proclamation was made, that "Polycarp confessed himself a Christian." This was the death-warrant. He was condemned to be burnt alive. Jews and Gentiles, the whole "synagogue of Satan," here described, alike, hastened in rage and fury to collect wood from the baths and workshops for the funeral pile. The old man laid aside his garments, and took his place in the midst of the fuel. When they would have nailed him to the stake, he said to them, "Leave me thus, I pray, unfastened; he who has enabled me to brave the fire will give me strength also to endure its fierceness." He then uttered this brief prayer: "O Lord, Almighty God, the Father of thy beloved Son Jesus Christ, through whom we have received a knowledge of thee, God of the angels and of the whole creation, of the whole race of man, and of the saints who live before thy presence; I thank thee that thou hast thought me worthy, this day and this hour, to share the cup of thy Christ among the number of thy witnesses!" The fire was kindled; but a high wind drove the flame to one side, and prolonged his sufferings; at last the executioner despatched him with a sword." So did one of Christ's poor saints at Smyrna die, "faithful unto death," and winner of "the crown of life," and never to "be hurt of the second death." But if these were, and they were, the sorrows and sufferings that they had to endure, what sustained them? Note, therefore—

III. THEIR SUPPORTS. For it is evident such would be needed. The very word of the Lord to them, "Fear not," indicates how great the peril was of their being crushed and heart-broken under the tribulations through which they were called to pass. Despondency and despair threatened them. To meet this their Lord was ready with his aid. It was given in manifold ways. He did not merely say to them, "Fear not," but showed them abundant reason wherefore they should not fear. 1. And first and chief: *His own Name.* "I am the First and the Last . . . alive" (ver. 8). Here, as throughout these letters, that aspect of our Lord's character is turned to the Church addressed which it most needed to consider and lay to heart. It was so with the Church at Ephesus. They were reminded of the Lord's nearness to and knowledge of them and of his power and purpose to dispose of them according as their work should be. And now here, when he would comfort and strengthen the fearful, he tells them that about himself which could not but lift up their hearts, as doubtless it did. "*I am the First;*" i.e. "I am at the head and beginning of all things; all were ordered and arranged according to the counsel of my will; nothing comes by chance; nothing has been left unprovided for. "*And the Last;*" i.e. "When men and Satan have done their all, and nothing is left more that they can do, and they shall have gone to their own place, I shall remain, and of my kingdom there shall be no end. Therefore, remember, the eternal God is thy Refuge, and underneath thee are the everlasting arms." " *Which was dead;* " i.e. " I have entered into all that can by any possibility be before you. I, of my own will, went down into the pain and darkness of death; I know all about it, O my people, and know how you feel, for I was in all points tried like as you are. And I entered into death that I might be the better able to help you. And see, I live! Sin and hell did their worst against me, but, behold, I am 'alive for evermore.'" When the apostle saw the vision of his Lord, and fell at his feet as dead, it was this same word, this same august Name of the Lord, that lifted him up again. And it was to do the same for the depressed and desponding Church at Smyrna. And next: 2. *His knowledge,* so perfect and complete, of them and all that concerned them. "I know thy works," he tells them, and then he goes on to give them details which showed the fulness of his knowledge. And that which they could not but believe, for the proof of it was before their eyes, would help them to believe in his knowledge when it affirmed what as yet was very far from being evident to them. He said to them, "Thou art rich." He, then, knew of treasure-store of good which they did not; of recompense of reward so vast that their present poverty should be all forgotten. And he knew that all the accusations of their enemies were not true, as, perhaps, sometimes, in their more misgiving moods, they had half feared some of them might be, and were in consequence staggered beneath them. But now he came and declared them to be not true, but " blasphemies." They need trouble themselves, therefore, no more about them. And he knew the future as well as the present; what the devil, through his willing workmen, would do to them. He knew it all; knew why he would do it—" that they might be tempted," not tried, but seduced, and made to deny their Lord. He saw through it all, and now told them of it to brace them more firmly for the struggle before them. And he knew that the struggle, though sharp, should as certainly be short. "Ten days," he says, as we say, " A mere nine days' wonder; " by which we mean a merely passing, temporary, brief thing. So their trial should be so short that it should hardly have begun before it was ended. And should some of them be condemned to die, as they would be, let them be faithful right up to that point, and death should prove to them the goal of the race, where they should find their Lord, the Judge, waiting with the crown of victory in his hand, reaching forth to bestow it upon them. And this is how further the Lord cheers them, by— 3. *The glorious prize* he promises them. That prize was life; the crown was the life; the life eternal, blessed, holy, for ever with the Lord. So that the moment the headsman's axe, or the flame of fire, or the fangs of fierce beasts, put an end to the poor troubled life they now had, that moment the Lord should give them, in place of it, this crown of the eternal life. So that even death could only do them good, and as to the second death, most assuredly—such is the force of the Greek—that should do them so harm; that which should be the overwhelming horror of Christ's enemies should not even come nigh unto them, the overcoming ones, but life, eternal life, life with their Lord for ever, that should be theirs. Oh, is not all this a " sursum corda " indeed? And it is but the type of what the same ever-blessed Lord will ever do. Hence he says, " He that hath an ear, let him hear." Well, then, my tried and tempted brother, mind that you hear. And you, godly working man in shop or factory, with a multitude of mocking mates, who well-nigh wear your life out with their ungodly ways; and you, dear boys or girls at school, who have to run the gauntlet of sneers that stab, and taunts that torment your very soul; and whosoever you may be, child of God, that has to bear tribulation for Christ;—you have ears to hear; then do hear, for Christ meant this word for you.—S. C.

Ver. 10.—*The severe law of Christ.* " Be thou faithful," etc. Beneath the city of Rome there is a long succession of subterranean streets and galleries, quarried from the rocky strata of the soil. These are now opened, and strangers may visit them. They are remarkable; they are even wonderful; they are the most astonishing cemeteries in the world. They are called the Catacombs; they are the burial-places of the martyrs of the young Christian faith. The inscriptions over innumerable tombs are to be read even yet; they seem fresh, almost as if painted yesterday, and they are fragrant with the flowers of immortality. Many of the inscriptions are passionately, touchingly affectionate. They speak tenderly of the star of hope which had just risen on the confines of the grave; they stand in wonderful contrast to the despair of paganism and the poetry of Horace. Thither, from torturing racks and burning coals, the early Christians conveyed revered and beloved forms, precious dust. They deposited them there with tears, but in the full assurance of the life beyond the death, beyond the flame and dungeon. It is remarkable that in these low Catacombs Christian art had its birth—art, which is always the struggle of mind with death; and in this palpable carving in the stone, and the floral delineations of the pencil, the chisel and palette were first consecrated there. When John wrote, the martyrs were crowding into the Catacombs; and, not only so, the profession of the Christian faith everywhere had an outlook to martyrdom. It is said these words were addressed to Polycarp, and were the prophecy of his death beneath the persecution of the mild Aurelian; for, however mild and merciful an emperor could be to others, he could only be merciless to Christians. But there is a deeper lesson than the merely pleasant revival of an historical story, however venerable and affecting that story may be; it is that which underlies all such stories and all such texts as that before us now—the lesson that every crown is won only as we bear the cross. Such are the conditions under which we live. This is the everlasting lesson

> " On whose still-recurring page
> Naught grows obsolete with age."

Let us trace it for a little while. It is true—

I. In PHYSICAL LIFE. The body that is to become agile, healthy, strong, must not be pampered or allowed to lie at home in indolence. Athletes are not made so. But by discipline, toil, severe exercise.

II. In MENTAL LIFE. What drudgery and grind at tasks arid as sand, and demanding severe effort of mind in proportion to their dryness, have to be submitted to! Scholarship is not to be attained by mere wishing for it. Look at the men who have won prizes in this department of life, and the traces of their toil will be seen furrowed in their countenances, and, too often, in worn and wasted frames.

III. In MORAL LIFE. Innocence is pleasing enough, but if it is to be uplifted into virtue, it must be tried and disciplined. Temptation is the athletic of the soul, the indispensable training for its attainment of high moral excellence. A cloistered virtue is rarely a robust one; it is in the arena of the world, where the stress and strain of fierce temptation will have to be endured, that we gain real strength. And so—

IV. In THE SPIRITUAL LIFE. Excellence in any of those regions of life of which we have already spoken is not easily attainable; one obstacle and another stand in the way, and must be overcome. But most of all must we expect to meet opposition when we strive for excellence in the spiritual life. The school is so hard a one that we should never go to it of our own accord, and therefore God sooner or later sends us all there. And some he sends early and keeps them late. And in it are heard strong cries and tears, agonized prayers, and often the moan of pain and the wail of the bereaved. There are broken hearts not a few, and souls overwhelmed with woe. What is the meaning of it all—the disappointment, the weariness and distress, the whole creation groaning and travailing together in pain even until now—what means it, but that our spirits are thus being taught and trained and educated for the higher life of God? Verily for this crown there is no other way than the way of the cross. And that we may the less shrink from it, our Lord himself came down from heaven to earth, and lived here our life, and, above all, bore our cross, only that his was much heavier and sharper than ours. " I love to lie here and look at that," said a poor dying girl to the writer, who was visiting her one day, and noticed a porcelain cast representing our Saviour bearing his cross, which was hanging at the side of her bed; " it helps me," she said, " to bear my pain better." Ah! yes; that Christ has borne his cross does help all who trust in him the better to bear theirs, and so the better and sooner and surer to attain to that spiritual excellence for which all the often stern disciplines of life here are preparing us.—S. C.

Vers. 12—17.—*The epistle to the Church at Pergamos.* It would be altogether fitting to take the title of this letter from that which our Lord takes as his own, and term it, " *The sharp two-edged sword.*" For this letter is largely illustrative of its work. In ch. i. we saw it in St. John's vision; here we see it in the experience of the Church. But whilst the main reference is to that vision, there is further appropriateness from the allusions to the wilderness-life of Israel, with which this letter abounds. Balaam's vile work against them—the sin into which they fell, the sword which Balaam saw in the hands of the angel of the Lord seeking to stay him in his evil way, and the sword with which at last he was slain, seem all to be suggested. Then the mention of the manna belongs also to that same wilderness-life. It was well that the ungodly at Pergamos should be reminded of that sword, and the faithful of that manna. But it is from the vision told of in ch. i. that the name our Lord here assumes is mainly taken. Note—

I. WHAT IS MEANT BY THIS SWORD. With the Bible in our hands, we cannot long be in doubt on this question; for at once there occurs to the memory the familiar text in the Epistle to the Hebrews, which tells how the Word of God is "quick and powerful, and sharper than any two-edged sword." And there is that other which is like unto it in the Epistle to the Ephesians, "The sword of the Spirit, which is the Word of God." And in Isaiah we have a similar expression, " He hath made my mouth like a sharp sword." And even human and evil words are thus symbolized, as in the Psalms: "Their words are swords and arrows, even bitter words;" and again, "Their tongue is a sharp sword." And the comparison is a frequent one. The Word of God, therefore, is evidently what is meant by this sword with two edges.

II. THE MANNER OF ITS OPERATION. In this letter this power of the sword is seen at work. In the vision, St. John had observed that the breath proceeding from the mouth of him who was "like unto the Son of man" took the form and shape of a sharp two-edged sword, such as was in common use in the armies of the day. Hence St. Paul, speaking of this sword, says, "The Lord shall destroy the wicked one with the breath of his mouth " (2 Thess. ii. 8). And in the brightness of the glory with which the entire vision was surrounded, the sword-like form seemed to flash and glitter as if it were a veritable sword proceeding out of the mouth of the Son of man. And in this letter we see that sword which the vision symbolized exercising its mighty power. We see: 1. *Its point,* piercing even to the dividing asunder of that which had been so blended together as scarce to be distinguished or separated. For the character of the Church at Pergamos was like that of well-nigh all other Churches, a mixture of evil and good. There was that which could be urged in its favour, and that also which could be charged against it to its shame. And this sword is here seen dividing them. (1) It separates the good, and there were such. (*a*) They had been faithful to Christ's Name. They had loyally stood by it even when to do so had involved awful peril—peril in which one Antipas, who had been eminent for his fidelity, had been slain by the infuriated foe. Yet in those fearful days—days like those of the persecution which arose about Stephen in Jerusalem—the faithful at Pergamos had not flinched. (*b*) And the Church had been fruitful. It was no small honour to have nurtured in her midst such a soul as that of Antipas. It is a sign of the marked grace of God when a Church becomes the home, chosen and beloved, of holy souls; when they find in it an atmosphere helpful and stimulating to all that is good within them. (*c*) And all this under great disadvantages. " I know," the Lord says, " thy works, and where thou dwellest, where Satan's seat is; " and this is told of again lower down in the same verse; thus implying the Lord's recognition of the fact that to serve him there was indeed difficult, and so all the more honourable and meritorious. Now, why Pergamos came to be regarded as the devil's head-quarters, his seat and throne, it is not easy to say. The place was one of great beauty, adorned with magnificent temples, possessed of a superb library containing hundreds of thousands of volumes. Our word " parchment " is derived from the dressed skins which were so largely used at Pergamos, and on which the books were written. Hence these skins came to be called by the name of Pergamos, or parchment. The place was not, as Ephesus or Smyrna, famous for trade, but for its culture and refinement. It was a sort of union of a pagan cathedral city and university; and a royal residence, gorgeous in its magnificence, further adorned it. Jupiter was said to have been born there, and temples to him and to innumerable gods were on every hand. The whole tone of the place must, therefore, have been utterly opposed to the faith of Christ.

It had no liking for the purity, the self-denial, and the unworldliness of the Church, but revelled in the very reverse of all these things. All that could sap and undermine the faith and the faithful was there in full force. It was Satan's throne indeed. Now, for that even there they held fast Christ's name, they deserved, and here receive, high commendation from the Lord. But the sword (2) separates the evil; for there were amongst them (a) men who held the truth in unrighteousness. This was what Balaam did. No man ever knew, no man ever professed, a purer faith, a holier doctrine, than did he; and yet, blinded by his greed of gain, he held it so imprisoned in unrighteousness that it had no power over him, and left him unchecked to all the wickedness of his heart. Now, there were such men at Pergamos; and where have they not been and are they not still ? And (b) there were those who perverted the gospel to licentiousness. There were the Nicolaitans. And they, too, have had, and have still, their successors: God keep us from being of their number! But then the good and the evil were so blended together that to separate them was beyond mere human power. In the brightness of the good some might not perceive the evil; in the darkness of the evil others might not perceive the good. But the sword of the Spirit severs them. For Churches, for individuals, Christ by his Word does this still. Pray him to do so for ourselves. 2. *Its double edge.* For it had this as well as its piercing point. And this, probably, that as with the literal sword the soldier in the thick of the fight might strike on the right hand and the left, with the back as well as the front, so with this sword of the Spirit foes on either hand might be smitten down. Thus is it in this letter. (1) It smites presumption and all high-handed sin. Read the awful threatenings here. How they hew down those who set themselves against the Lord! (2) Despondency and despair. This is a peril on the other side, a foe to faith as formidable as the other; and by this sword the Lord smites this adversary also. Read the sweet, soothing, soul-assuring promises (ver. 17). (a) "The hidden manna." It means that support and sustentation of the soul as it presses on through the wilderness of life, heavenward, which the Lord will give, and does give, to his faithful ones, as the manna sustained Israel on their march Canaanwards. "I am the true Bread from heaven," said Christ (cf. John vi.). It is real, substantial, effectually supporting the soul, as ten thousand facts testify. But hidden, because unseen and unknown by the world. "Your life is hid with Christ in God." What, then, though weary leagues of barren, burning sand lie between God's Israel and their home? here is promise of all need supplied, every want met. (b) The white stone with the new name; *i.e.* Christ's faithful shall have given them personal assurance of their membership in the family of God (cf. "The Spirit beareth witness with our spirit that we are the children of God"). Now, the white stone is that on which a communication is written (cf. Luke i. 63). Hence it tells of a communication, real, in writing as it were, to the soul of the believer. And this communication consists of "a name." When a child is born into a family, a name is given it. So in God's family. To the children of the world it will be said, "I never knew *you*;" but for his own children there is a name given. And a *new* name, indicating admission to higher privilege and favour, as did the names of Abraham, Sarah, Israel, Hephzibah, Beulah, Peter. They were all new names, and all told of new grace and favour from God. And a name unknown to all but the receiver. The proofs of the believer's sonship are known only to himself and God. The Spirit's witness: who can put that into words, and tell it out to others? Many a one cannot tell you why he knows he is God's child, but he does know it. The white stone has been given to him, and blessed is he. And is not this a stay against all despair, despondency, and everything of the kind? As the well-known verse sings—

> "When I can read my title clear
> To mansions in the skies,
> I bid farewell to every fear,
> And wipe my weeping eyes."

CONCLUSION. All this supposes that you are of the *overcoming* ones. This word is "to him that overcometh." Not to them that are overcome. But you may overcome. By fervent prayer, by unreserved consecration, by constant "looking unto Jesus," by use of all means of grace, so abide in Christ, and he shall make you "more than conqueror."—S. C

Vers. 18—29.—*Epistle to the Church at Thyatira.* Careful readers of these letters will observe how in this and the foregoing ones St. John seems to be contemplating great historical events recorded in the Old Testament. In the first, the allusion to " the tree of life " and the " Paradise of God " carries us back to the story of the Fall and the expulsion from Eden. In the second, Noah and the Flood are apparently referred to in the promise of life as the reward of fidelity, and the not being " hurt of the second death ; " for the Flood was the second death of humanity, and the waters of the Flood may point us to that awful lake by which the ungodly at the last shall be overwhelmed, and which St. John calls the second death. In the third, the wilderness-life of Israel, the ruin wrought on them by Balaam, and " the manna " which was their food,— these form the groundwork of the letter to Pergamos. Then in the fourth, that before us now, we come on to the times of the monarchy, and that dark period when Ahab ruled over the northern kingdom, and Jezebel led him and his people into all the vileness of idolatry. A thorough Jew as St. John was, and having complete knowledge of the ancient Scriptures, they being his one book, would be quick to find analogies and illustrations of the spiritual condition of the Churches in the checkered history of mankind, and especially of Israel, as recorded in those Scriptures. And the tragedy—for it was no less—associated with Jezebel (cf. ' Macbeth,' and see whence Shakespeare got his inspiration) ; and the flashing fire in the eyes of the fierce Jehu, and the burnished brass of his swift-revolving chariot-wheels as he furiously drove along on his journey of vengeance to slay the proud, idolatrous queen who had led all Israel astray,—this avenger might well come into the mind of St. John as he thought of the spiritual tragedy at Thyatira, and of an avenger more awful still, " the Son of God," whose eyes were " as a flame of fire and his feet like molten brass," and who was swiftly hastening to take vengeance on the guilty leader of whom Jezebel was the prototype, and that guilty Church. A fit name for this letter would be " *The wrath of the Lamb,*" for much concerning that wrath is shown in it.

I. ITS REALITY. The letter is full of fearfulness to those whom it concerns, and was without doubt intended so to be. There is scarce a soft, gentle word in it, but all is stern from first to last. The inscription, the contents, the very promises at the end, are all marked by the same character. The Church had connived at, or at least had offered no strenuous opposition to, most awful and flagrant wrong, which had been taught and practised in her very midst ; and in the wrath that this aroused all their righteousness—and they had much—is little more than named, and seems scarcely mentioned. The letter is hardly anything else than one vehement outpouring of the Lord's wrath and threatenings of his sore displeasure. *The symbols* show this. The eyes like as a flame of fire, and the feet of incandescent, glowing, molten brass, suggest strongly the twin ideas of rage and ruthless resolve to execute it upon those against whom it is directed. They bring before us a truly terrible aspect of the character of our Lord, but one which is real and actual, though far too much ignored both in thought and teaching. We say and sing far too exclusively, " Gentle Jesus, meek and mild ; " and this, notwithstanding the very Gospels themselves give not a few indications of a power of holy and awful anger which he who so graciously took up little children in his arms yet evidently had within him. Hearken how he speaks to the scribes and Pharisees ; listen to his reiterated " woes " denounced upon hypocrites ; and observe as a momentous fact that the most fearful utterances of the whole Bible fell from our Saviour's lips. And this Book of the Revelation, is it not like the prophet's scroll, written both within and without, and full of scarce anything but " lamentation and mourning and woe " ? And all of it is the Lord's doing, either directly or through his agents. The Bible, therefore, gives but little countenance to that far too general idea that the character of Christ is only gentleness and love. And there is, and there ought to be, no such character anywhere. That love which is said to go out to everybody generally goes to nobody in particular, except the man's own self above all. It is a mere easiness and softness, utterly unreliable, and of little moral worth. But when there is real love, the obverse side will be a corresponding wrath against all that injures what is so much loved. What is tenderer, and at the same time fiercer, than a mother's love ? Even amid the beasts of the field it is so. A bear robbed of her whelps, woe betide the despoiler if the mother overtake him ! And all that wrath which is told of in the Bible, and especially in this book, those eyes which, against the Jezebels that seduce his people, are " as a flame of fire," once wept over Jerusalem and by the grave of Lazarus. If he could not hate, he could not love; and because he does so love, therefore is the wrath of the Lamb so real and terrible a thing.

II. ITS SEVERITY. (Vers. 22, 23.) God does do even now what is meant by these expressions. Out of men's own wickedness he makes whips to scourge them. How dreadful and irreparable is the ruin which even here and now often overtakes the ungodly! There is no need for laboured argument to prove that there is a hell hereafter: many men spend their lives in hell now. Their intense realization of their shame, their fall; the horror which good men have of them; the ruin they have brought upon themselves, and yet more upon those who trusted and loved and depended upon them;—all this is hell, and is a fearful corroboration of the sure teaching of God as to the judgment he forewarns us of hereafter.

III. ITS FORBEARANCE. "I gave her space to repent." Sentence upon an evil work is not executed speedily, and hence men too often, therefore, all the more set their hearts steadfastly to do evil.

IV. ITS JUSTICE. The Lord denounces here, we think, not a person, but a party some evil knot of persons in the Church, who were to the rest what the woman Jezebel, Ahab's wife, was to Israel—their seducer and leader in all abominable ways. Vers. 22 and 23 seem to imply that there was not one person merely, but a dominant party in the Church, who were guilty of the sins which had so roused the wrath of the Lord. True, we have the phrase, "thy wife Jezebel," and this has led some to suppose that the pastor of the Church was afflicted with a detestable woman as a wife—such things do happen; but when we remember how "the harlot" is the continual name with which corrupt Churches are branded, we are permitted to regard the whole as symbolical. The phrase may therefore be regarded as telling of a pestilent and powerful set belonging to the Church, and therefore it could be said, "*thy* wife," who were as Jezebel. And we must regard the sins spoken of as being literally what they are said to be. And who that knows the power of these sins to waste the conscience, pollute the mind, ruin the body, paralyze the will, and every way turn man into worse than the very brutes, and so to make the Church in which they were practised a byword, a hissing, and a rebuke, can wonder that, as has ever been the case, the wrath of God arose against them until there was no remedy? Because of them the Flood came, the cities of the plain were overwhelmed with fire, the nations of Canaan were exterminated; and to-day, given the sin, there, not far off, is the judgment of God. Beware of them, for they "war against the soul," and against all the well-being of mankind, so that, in mercy to the human race, God has branded them with his severe displeasure.

V. ITS DISCRIMINATION. "The Lord knoweth them that are his," and his eye was upon them even in that corrupt Church. They had refused to be beguiled by the specious pretences of these ungodly teachers that their doctrines were profound, not for the uninitiated; that they were "deep" things—deep things of the devil, the Lord in indignation adds—though they pretended that they came from above. But this "rest of you in Thyatira" would have none of the doctrine; they spurned it as they should. And now the Lord tells them that no other burden should be put upon them. To have to endure such people amongst them, and to have the Name of Christ so dishonoured, this was burden enough. Therefore only let them abide in all those good and blessed qualities which characterized them, and which he commemorates in ver. 19, and then in that coming glory foretold in Ps. ii. they shall share, and from being despised and borne down with the burden of the wicked, they shall with Christ rule over them, and restrain them effectually as with " a rod of iron," and as now they were powerless to do; and best of all, he who is " the Root and the Offspring of David, and the Bright and the Morning Star " (ch. xxii. 16), he will give himself to them; the lay-star should arise in their hearts, the joy of the Lord should be theirs for evermore.

> "Grant, Lord, that I may come
> To thy saints' happy home,
> Where a thousand years one day appears;
>   Nor go
> Where a day appears
> As a thousand years,
>   For woe!"

S. C.

Vers. 1—7.—*The epistles to the Churches:* (1) *The epistle to the Church in Ephesus: the decay of early love.* The Ephesian Church highly commended for many things—for "toil" in service and for "patience" in tribulation; unwearied endurance in suffering; repudiation of "evil men," and fidelity in trying them "which call themselves apostles, and they are not;" and even "hating the works" which the Lord says, "I also hate." But the works of the Church are all known to him who "walketh in the midst of the seven golden candlesticks;" and he has an accusation to bring against the otherwise faithful Church: "I have this against thee, that thou didst leave thy first love." Love is the very core of the Church's life; it is the central, hidden spring of all good service; it is the truest evidence of the purity and reality of the Church's health. The departure from the first love is—

I. THE SIGNAL OF THE LOSS OF THE VITAL SPRING OF THE CHURCH'S RELIGIOUS LIFE. The outward forms may be perfect, zeal may be maintained, patience unwearied, orthodoxy untarnished; but if love—the soul's secret energy—be impaired, time only is needed to bring the Church to utter decay.

II. IT IS AT ONCE THE CAUSE AND INDICATION OF A FALLEN CONDITION OF THE CHURCH. "Remember therefore from whence thou art fallen."

III. IT EXPOSES TO THE JUDICIAL LOSS OF ALL. "Or else I come to thee, and will move thy candlestick out of its place." The means of recovery are: 1. *Recollection.* The thoughtful recall of the Church to its earlier condition. The very watchword of the epistle is "remember"—compare, contrast thy present with thy past state. 2. *Repentance*—ever to follow the recollection, which is the needful after-thought, the first step in the process of true repentance. How would a faithful review bring the keen sense of loss, and lead the Church to rue its loss and fall and danger! 3. *Renewal.* "Do thy first works." A true repentance will declare itself in works answerable to amendment. To every one that truly heareth and "overcometh," the words of promise hold out the cheering assurance of life "in the Paradise of God."—R. G.

Vers. 8—11.—(2) *The epistle to the Church in Smyrna: the Church exposed to suffering.* The dark shades of coming sorrow gather about a Church already distinguished by tribulation and poverty and rude reviling. "The devil is about to cast some of you into prison;" so saith he "which was dead, and lived again." Even death in bitterness of persecuting violence will fall upon some. The All-seeing One discerns the coming storm, and cheers his faithful people to stand firm in the day of their suffering, and to be "faithful even unto death." Great is that fidelity which can remain unimpaired, even though life be forfeited in the struggle. The Lord of life promises life to them who fall in the great cause; and though they be hurt severely in the present or the coming afflictions, yet shall not "the second death" "hurt" him that overcometh. The watchword of this epistle is "*Fear not.*" This rallying word of the great Captain is strengthened, and the heart of the Church is assured—

I. BY THE CHARACTER OF HIM WHO UTTERS IT. "*The* First and the Last, which was dead, and lived again." The assurance from the revived Lord, who had conquered death and proved himself superior to it, would be the most cheering to them who were threatened with death. If they suffer with him, they shall also reign with him.

II. BY THE ASSERTION THAT ALL IS ENDURED IN VIEW OF THE LORD OF THE CHURCH. "I know thy tribulation." The eye of the sympathizing Lord is upon them. They are not forgotten—forsaken. Jesus is near.

III. BY THE TEMPORARY DURATION OF THE AFFLICTION. "Ye shall have tribulation ten days." It is a measured time, and a brief one. It is not for ever. The Lord, who placed bounds to the sea, has put a limit to the sufferings of his Church. It shall pass away. "Weeping may endure for a night, but joy cometh in the morning."

IV. BY PROMISE OF THE FINAL REWARDS OF ETERNAL LIFE, and by assurance of exemption from the "hurt of the second death." The first death may conquer them and lay them low, but they shall ultimately triumph. If fidelity be maintained even unto and in spite of death, the highest rewards shall be given. "Be thou faithful unto death, and I will give thee a crown of life."—R. G.

Vers. 12—17.—(3) *The epistle to the Church in Pergamum: the faithful Church waning from internal decay.* He "that hath the sharp two-edged sword" bears it not in vain. It is a keen weapon of judgment against all adversaries, and may be a true and effectual warning to faithless ones within the Church and threatening ones without. The adversary has his seat in the city where this Church finds its centre. With persecuting violence assailing it, this Church has maintained its faithfulness to its Lord. External opposition was met by a noble fidelity : " Thou holdest last my Name, and didst not deny my faith." Yet did evil lurk—errors in " teaching," corruption in worship and in manners. Heretical departures within the sacred enclosure were more to be feared, because more truly a source of danger, than outward foes. The call of the Lord to the Church is clear as a clarion-cry. It is in the one watchword of the epistle, " *Repent.*" This is the one immediate and imperative duty, and it is urged by the following motives.

I. IT IS THE IMPERATIVE DEMAND OF THE RIGHTEOUS LORD. That he should utter the word of warning and admonition is sufficient. No one ought to wait to find other motive for obedience; every motive is folded up within this one. It is the Lord's cry to repentance. His word only has authority within his Church.

II. IT IS THE JUST AND NECESSARY STEP IN THE PROCESS OF RECOVERY. Repentance alone can save them. Without it judgment must come. The " therefore " throws the Church back upon the consideration *why* it should repent. The error, the wrong, the departure, demand the lowly penitence, the humble confession, the renewed devotion.

III. BY THE TERRIBLE ALTERNATIVE OF THE DIVINE INVITATION. " Or I come to thee quickly." The Lord comes to his needy Church to supply its wants; to his Church in sorrow to comfort it ; but in judgment if it be unfaithful.

IV. BY THE HEAVY JUDGMENTS WHICH ARE THREATENED IF REPENTANCE BE WITH-HELD. " I will make war against them with the sword of my mouth." That sword pierces to the depths of the sensitive soul. Of all judgments the Lord's sword is the heaviest. It is the sword of his mouth, his word of condemnation, in which, as in a kernel, all judgment lies hidden.

V. Repentance is further urged BY THE GRACIOUS WORD OF PROMISE, which also is a word of encouragement to the faithful and incorrupt. 1. To him that overcometh will I "—the righteous Judge—" give of the hidden manna "—the secret nourishment of his spiritual life. " Instead of feasting on things offered to idols, I will satisfy him with the true Bread—that which cometh down from heaven. I am that Bread. I will myself be his daily satisfying Portion. He shall feed on that which was sacrificed to God." Christ is the soul's Bread, the soul's Portion, and in him the soul has everything. 2. To him also shall be given "a white stone "—if of acquittal, how precious ! To be acquitted at his bar is not merely to be acquitted, but to be received into favour and to be enriched in the highest degree. 3. "And in the stone a new name." Is this a revelation of his own ineffable Name ? The greatest bliss of heaven will be in knowing the Divine Name. Truly to know him is life eternal. But it shall be special to each, each having his own position and his own special vision, " which no one knoweth but he that receiveth it."—R. G.

Vers. 18—29.—(4) *The epistle to the Church in Thyatira : the growing Church exposed to corruption of doctrine.* With the highest title, " the Son of God," the Lord of the Church speaks—the Lord who searches as with eyes of flame and with burning, consuming fire, and treads down his enemies beneath his feet. The vision is unusually impressive, as the state of the Church is unusually momentous. The letter is extended, and describes the commendable condition of the Church, the subtle danger that threatens its life, the terrible judgments pronounced upon the corrupters of the Church's purity, the one word of demand, the watchword of the epistle—" *Hold fast* " —" Hold fast that which ye have till I come; " with the abundant promise to him who, doing so, triumphantly "overcometh." Leaving ampler exposition, our eye rests upon the one word, " *Hold fast.*"

I. This call to fidelity is BASED ON THE COMMENDABLE STATE OF THE CHURCH. Happy they to whom the Lord can say, " Hold fast," keep that thou hast, persevere. Of this Church the Lord knows—and knows to commend—its " works, and love, and faith, and ministry, and patience," and growing usefulness.

II. IT IS SIGNIFICANT OF THE LORD'S APPROBATION OF THE CHURCH'S STATE. Here is no word of exhortation to repent. The keen, searching glance of the flaming eyes does not detect any fault in the body of the Church. In the absence of condemnation is the Divine justification and approval. His smile is upon his faithful ones, against whom no accusation can be raised. If a few are faulty in one particular, the bulk of the Church is pure. A difference is drawn between her children and the rest that are in Thyatira: "as many as have not this teaching." The Lord delights in his Church characterized by zeal, by love, by triumphant faith, by unwearied patience, by abundant works.

III. The call to fidelity is MADE NECESSARY BY THE PRESENCE OF GRIEVOUS AND SUBTLE DANGERS. False teachers are abroad—or, at least, a false teacher—against whom, as would seem, some one in power had not been sufficiently guarded. "Thou sufferest," etc. The holiest and most active Church has its dangers from the subtle breath of error—even zeal and love may be drawn aside. The very fervour of spirit which is commended lays itself open, by its own honesty of purpose, to the deceits of the designing. "Hold fast" warns of danger near as truly as it approves of the possession held.

IV. The exhortation is further enforced by A VIEW OF THE TERRIBLE JUDGMENT THREATENED AGAINST THE SEDUCTRESS. (Vers. 21—23.)

V. BY THE EVER-PRESENT THOUGH GRACIOUSLY VARIED PROMISE TO THE FAITHFUL. (Vers. 26—28.)—R. G.

Ver. 1—ch. iii. 22.—*The seven epistles compared: homiletic prologue.* In order to avoid repetition when we come to deal specially with each epistle, it seems desirable to notice some circumstances common to all and some peculiar to a portion.

I. THE CIRCUMSTANCES OF THESE LETTERS COMMON TO ALL. What are these? what are the points on which they all seem to agree? 1. *In all Christ assumes different aspects.* He does not appear to all alike. He approaches each in some special character. Thus: (1) To Ephesus he appears as one "who holdeth the seven stars in his right hand, and who walketh in the midst of the seven golden candlesticks." (2) To Smyrna he appears as "the First and the Last, who was dead, and is alive." (3) To Pergamos as he of "the sharp sword with two edges." (4) To Thyatira as "the Son of God, who hath his eyes as a flame of fire." (5) To Sardis he appears as "he who hath the seven Spirits of God, and the seven stars." (6) To Philadelphia as "he that is holy and true, and hath the key of David." (7) To Laodicea as "The Amen, the faithful and true Witness." 2. *In all Christ addresses himself through a special officer.* "Unto the angel."[1] Who is the "angel" is a matter of controversy, and, to me, of little interest. Some seem very anxious to make him a bishop. If by "bishop" is meant a man who lives in a palace, fares sumptuously every day, rolls in chariots of wealth, and is invested with high-sounding titles, I do not think he could have been a bishop. No doubt he was the appointed messenger of the little community—one who had to receive and convey communications of general interest. 3. *In all Christ declares his thorough knowledge of their moral history.* Not merely the muscular, but the mental; not merely the works done *by* the body, but the works done *in* the body. 4. *In all Christ promises great blessings to the morally victorious.* "To him that overcometh." It is not said that every conqueror can have the same reward. To one is promised the "tree of life." To another, "to eat of the hidden manna," to receive a "white stone, with a new name written on it." To another, "power over the nations." To another, to be "clothed in white raiment." To another, to be made a "pillar in the temple of my God." And to another, "to sit with me in my throne," etc. To every moral conqueror there is a promised reward. 5. *In all Christ commands attention to the voice of the Spirit.* "He that hath ears to hear, let him hear." "The Spirit"—the Spirit of truth and right, of love and God. 6. *In all Christ's grand aim is spiritual culture.* His admonitions, promises, and threats in each case tend in this direction. 7. *In all Christ observes a threefold division.* (1) "There is a reference to some of the attributes of him who addresses the Church. (2) A disclosure of characteristics of the Church, with appropriate admonition, encouragement, or reproof. (3) Promises of reward to all who persevere in their Christian course and overcome the spiritual enemies who assault them" (Moses Stuart).

II. CIRCUMSTANCES IN WHICH SOME OF THEM DIFFER. 1. We find two, namely,

[1] See Excursus at end of ch. xxii.

Smyrna and Philadelphia, who *received commendation.* They do not seem to be blamed for anything in doctrine, discipline, or manner of life. Of Smyrna it says, "Thou art rich," that is, "rich" in the elements of moral goodness. Of the Church of Philadelphia it is said, "Thou hast kept the word of my patience." 2. Two of them, namely, Sardis and Laodicea, are *censured.* Of the Church of Sardis it is said, "Thou hast a name that thou livest, and thou art dead." Of the Church of Laodicea, "I know thy works, that thou art neither cold nor hot: I would thou wert cold or hot." 3. Three others are both *praised and blamed.* Those written to Ephesus, Pergamos, and Thyatira contain mingled censure and commendation. In some respects they deserve the one, and in some the other. In three cases, however, the approbation precedes the blame, thus showing, as Moses Stuart says, and as Paul in his Epistles shows, that it was more grateful to commend than to reprove.—D. T.

Vers. 1—7.—*The words of Christ from eternity to the congregation at Ephesus.* "Unto the angel of the Church of Ephesus," etc. The quality of words, whether weak or potent, pure or unvirtuous, useful or otherwise, depends evermore upon the *character of the author.* Hence the words of truly great men, intellectually and morally great, are the most blessed of all the blessed things we have; they are the organs of the highest light and choicest life. Hence the words of Christ have a value unsurpassed and unsurpassable. They are spirit and they are life. No words have ever sounded on our atmosphere or appeared on the pages of universal literature approaching his in intrinsic value or spiritual usefulness. Here are his words after he had tabernacled on this earth for thirty long years, endured the agonies of crucifixion, slept in the darkness of the grave, and been in eternity for nearly three score years. Such words assuredly claim our supreme attention. They are addressed to the Church at Ephesus.[1] For homiletic convenience the words of Christ in this epistle may be divided into four classes: (1) Those which concern himself; (2) those which concern the congregation; (3) those which concern the Divine Spirit; and (4) those which concern moral conquerors.

I. THOSE WHICH CONCERN HIMSELF. These refer to two things. 1. *To his relation to the Church.* "These things saith he that holdeth the seven stars in his right hand, who walketh in the midst of the seven golden candlesticks." The "seven stars" are the leading ministers of the seven Churches. These he holds in his own hand. He holds the universe in his hands; he holds all men in his hand, good or bad. But the *true ministers of his Word* he holds in a *special* sense. He holds them with all the care and tenderness with which a loving father holds by the hand his weak and timid child on a dreary and dangerous path. Not only does he *hold* the ministers of these Churches

---

[1] "Ephesus, the chief city of Ionia, *Asiæ Annen* (πρώτη τῆς Ἀσίας), as the Ephesians themselves styled it, asserting in this style for Ephesus that primacy which Smyrna and Pergamum disputed with it, had now so outstripped both its competitors that it was at once the civil and ecclesiastical centre of that 'Asia' with which we have to do. Wealthy, prosperous, and magnificent, a meeting-place of Oriental religions and Greek culture, and famous on many grounds in heathen antiquity, it was chiefly famous for the celebrated temple of Diana, one of the seven wonders of the world, about which we read so much (Acts xix.). But Ephesus had better titles of honour than all this. It was a city greatly favoured of God. St. Paul laboured there during three years (Acts xx. 31); he ordained Timothy to be bishop there (1 Tim. i. 3; Acts xviii. 19, 24, 26); and Tychicus (Eph. vi. 21);—all contributed to build up the Church in that city. And, if we may judge from St. Paul's Epistle to the Ephesians, and from his parting address to the elders of the Church (Acts xx. 17—38), nowhere does the word of the gospel seem to have found a kindlier soil, to have struck root more deeply, or to have borne fairer fruits of faith and love. St. John, too, had made it the chief seat of his ministry, his metropolis, during the closing years of his protracted life; from whence he exercised a wide, though not wholly unquestioned, jurisdiction (Eph. iii. 9, 10) over the whole of 'Asia.' How early that ministry there began it is impossible to say, the date of his withdrawal from Jerusalem being itself uncertain, and uncertain also whether he at once chose Ephesus for the middle point of his spiritual activity. From a Church to which so much was given, much would be required. How far it had profited as it ought by these signal advantages, how far it had maintained itself at those spiritual heights to which it had once attained, will presently be seen" (Archbishop Trench).

in his hand, but he *moves* amongst them. "He walketh in the midst of the seven golden candlesticks.' "Christ," says Dr. Vaughan, "walks himself among his candlesticks, and each separate lamp, of all the thousands which make up the branches of one candlestick, is as much trimmed and tended and fostered by Christ himself as if there were no other but that one, and as if there were no human agency at all constituted for its oversight." 2. *To his knowledge of the Church.* "I know thy works." He knows human works as no one else knows them. He knows not merely the *overt* acts, but inner motives ; not merely the deeds done *by* the body, but *in* the body. His eye peers into those deep and vast regions of soul into which no other eye can pierce. "I know thy works." He knows what is in man. In the works which he knows are comprehended the trials endured. "Thy labour, and thy patience." The painful discovery of falsehood in those who called themselves apostles or ministers of Christ, and also all declension in what is good. "I have somewhat against thee, because thou hast left thy first love." The fact that Christ so thoroughly knows us should make us *real, solemn, circumspect, earnest.*

II. THOSE WHICH CONCERN THE CONGREGATION. 1. *He credits them with the good they possess.* "Thou hast patience, and for my Name's sake hast laboured, and hast not fainted." There are four things which he sees in them to commend. (1) Their repugnance to wrong. "Thou canst not bear them which are evil [or, 'evil men ']." To loathe the wrong for its own sake is one of the finest features of character. It is common, perhaps, to hate evil men when they are in *poverty*, suffering, and disgrace ; but in such hatred there is no virtue. To hate evil in men of *great possessions* and high offices, millionnaires, premiers, princes, kings, is in truth somewhat uncommon ; albeit evil in such is more heinous, more loathsome and damnable, than evil anywhere else. It is sublimely grand to see men loathing the wrong as seen in the principalities and powers of this world. (2) Their patience in toil. Work is the duty of all, and the work of a genuine Christian in this life is most self-sacrificing, laborious, and trying. Hence patience is required—required on account of the opposition it has to encounter and the tardiness of the results. "Wherefore, beloved brethren, be ye steadfast, unmovable," etc. (3) Their insight into character. "Thou hast tried them which say they are apostles, and are not, and hast found them liars." It is a rare thing for men to discern the real character of their fellow-men, especially of that of their religious teachers—those who have set themselves up as "apostles." Hence the popularity of pulpit charlatans. All honour to the men at Ephesus ; their eye was keen enough and heart brave enough to try the character of their teachers, which on scrutiny they found to be "liars." (4) Their hostility to error. "But this thou hast, that thou hatest the doctrine of the Nicolaitanes, which thing I hate." "We may suppose," says one of our most learned modern expositors, "that the Nicolaitanes were the antinomians of the Asiatic Church—persons who taught that the conduct is immaterial if the faith be right ; that a *man* may *say he hath faith*, and, if so, may be indifferent altogether to his works ; or who at least, if they did not teach this, yet encouraged the deceitful heart in drawing this inference, by failing to set strongly and even sharply before men the utter ruin of an inconsistent and unholy life, and then not least, but most of all, when that sinful life is combined with the loud profession of a saving faith." Error is an evil in whatever character it appears and region it operates. Error in chemistry, surgery, medicine, mechanics, navigation, etc., is often fraught with terrible results. To oppose error, therefore, is a virtue. 2. *He reproves them for the declension they manifest.* "Nevertheless, . . . thou hast left thy first love." Christly love is the life and sun of the soul ; it is the beginning and end of genuine religion. Without charity—love—we are nothing. There is a danger of this waning. Some of the angels have lost it. Many good men have experienced its decay. This is a great evil ; it is the sap leaving the tree, and the foliage withers, and death descends from branch to root. Christ implies that men are responsible for this loss. Where this love exists it can not only be maintained but increased—the spark may be fanned into a flame. 3. *He urges them to reform.* In order to increase this waning love, he exhorts them to do four things. (1) *To remember.* "Remember . . . whence thou art fallen." Review the past, and call to mind the sweet, delicate, blooming affection of thy first love, with all the fresh joys and hopes it awakened. This memory will help resuscitation. (2) *To "repent."* Repentance does not mean crying, confessing, and throwing yourself into ecstasies, but a *change* in the *spirit* and *purpose* of life. (3) *To reproduce.* "Do the first works." Go over thy past life, reproduce thy old feeling, and reattempt old effort. This can be done; we can relive our lives, the best as well as the worst portion of them. (4) *To tremble.* "Or else I will come unto thee quickly, and will remove thy candlestick out of its place." "Terrible warning this! Let declension go on, and ruin is inevitable. This is true with individuals as well as with communities. In losing the candlestick, what a loss! The loss is midnight" (Caleb Morris).

III. THOSE WHICH CONCERN THE DIVINE SPIRIT. "He that hath an ear, let him hear what the Spirit saith unto the Churches; To him that overcometh will I give to eat of the tree of life, which is in the midst of the Paradise of God." Two things are here implied. 1. *That the Divine Spirit makes communication to all the Churches.* He speaks through material nature, through our spiritual constitution, through human history, through Jesus Christ. "God, who at sundry times and in divers manners spake in time past unto the fathers by the prophets, hath in these last days spoken unto us by his Son." Blessed thought! The Divine is in communication with the human, and has constant and special communication with the Churches. Christ, the Incarnation and the Minister of the Spirit, hath said, "Lo, I am with you alway, even unto the end of the world." The Spirit's words, as of old, bring life, order, light, and beauty out of chaos. 2. *That proper attention to these communications requires a certain ear.* "He that hath an ear." What is the ear? Not the mere ear of sense, nor the mere ear of intellect; it is the ear of the *heart*, the ear of *sympathetic love.* It is said that Christ opened the "ears of his disciples, that they might understand the Scriptures." The moral ear and eye of man are closed against the manifestation and voice of God. "The natural man discerneth not the things of the Spirit." Unless a man has the sentiment of melody in him, you may peal into his ear the most magnificent strains of music, and he feels no inspiration. Nothing comes to him but sound. As he who lacks an inward sympathy with the loftiest class of thoughts can listen unmoved to the grandest utterances of Plato, Milton, or Shakespeare; so he who lacks the ear of spiritual sympathy will be utterly unaffected by the communications which the *Spirit* makes to the Churches. "He that hath ears to hear"—it does not matter who he is, rich or poor, rude or cultured—"let him hear."

IV. THOSE WHICH CONCERN MORAL CONQUERORS. "To him that overcometh will I give [to him will I give] to eat of the tree of life, which is in the midst of the Paradise of God [in the Paradise of God]." Observe: 1. *Life is a battle.* Enemies abound within and without. Spiritual excellence can only be reached by struggling, strenuous and unremitting. 2. *Life is a battle that might be won.* "Him that overcometh." Thousands upon thousands have won the battle and shouted, "Victory!" at the close. 3. *The winning of the battle is glorious.* "I will give to eat of the tree of life, which is in the midst of the Paradise of God." "The reference to conquering is a prominent feature of St. John's other writings. The word, used but once in the other three Gospels (Luke xi. 22), and but once by St. Paul (Rom. xii. 21), is found in John xvi. 33; 1 John ii. 13, 14; v. 4, 5; and occurs in all these epistles to the Churches. The promise of the tree of life is appropriate : (1) To the virtue commended. Those who had not indulged in the licence of Nicolaitanes shall eat of the tree of life. (2) To the special weakness of the Ephesians. To those who had fallen, and lost the Paradise of first loving communion and fellowship with God (comp. Gen. iii. 8; 1 John i. 3), is held out the promise of a restored Paradise and participation in the tree of life (comp. ch. xxii. 2—14; Gen. iii. 22). This boon of immortality is the gift of Christ: 'I will *give.*' It is tasted in knowledge of God and of his Son (John xvii. 3); it is enjoyed in their presence (ch. xxii. 3, 4)" (Bishop Boyd Carpenter).—D. T.

Vers. 8—11.—*The words of Christ to the congregation at Smyrna.* "And unto the angel of the Church in Smyrna," etc. This letter is addressed to the Church at Smyrna. "Smyrna is not mentioned elsewhere in Scripture, so that we have no means of ascertaining when, and by whom, the Christian faith was first planted there. We may, however, conjecture that that great commercial city did not escape attention either by St. Paul or his associates in missionary effort during his three years' stay at Ephesus. Smyrna stands at the head of one of the finest bays in the world, and from its central position, its easy access, and excellent harbour, it commands the commerce of the Levant.

It is the chief city of Ionia, and is situate about forty miles north of Ephesus. It was a very ancient city, and was one of the seven that claimed to be the birthplace of Homer; and it is considered that its claim in this respect was better founded than that of any of the other cities which contended for the honour. It was subject to various vicissitudes both physically and politically. It was overthrown by earthquakes, damaged by conflagrations, laid waste by invasion, and held in turn by Æolians, Ionians, Lydians, and Macedonians. In A.D. 177 it was destroyed by an earthquake, but rebuilt by Marcus Aurelius, with more than its former splendour. It is now one of the most flourishing of the cities of Asia Minor, and, indeed, the most important. Its population amounts to 140,000, of whom there are 20,000 Greeks, 8000 Armenians, about 2000 Europeans, and 7000 Jews. There are more Christians in Smyrna than in any other Turkish city in the world; and it is therefore peculiarly unclean in the eyes of the strict Moslems, who call it Giaour Izmir, or Infidel Smyrna. Religious toleration has always been more fully permitted in Smyrna than in any other cities under Mohammedan control, and rarely has Turkish fanaticism been directed against Europeans. It is a great centre of missionary effort; and in Smyrna the light of Christianity has never been extinct from apostolic times" (Dr. Tait). In this epistle there are five points that arrest our attention. (1) *Wealth in poverty;* (2) *fiends in religion;* (3) *saints in persecution;* (4) *duty in trial;* and (5) *victory in death.*

I. WEALTH IN POVERTY. "I know thy works, and tribulation, and poverty, but thou art rich." "I know thy tribulation, and thy poverty." The poverty here is secular, not spiritual; the wealth spiritual, not secular. These two conditions of being are separable, and are, in the vast majority of cases in human life, detached. Sometimes you find, as in the case of the Laodiceans, secular wealth associated with spiritual poverty; and modern society here in England abounds with examples of this condition. Secular princes, moral paupers; but in Smyrna the case is different. It does not seem morally proper that, according to the order of administrative righteousness, these two conditions should be separate. The sight of secular abundance, where there is moral destitution—the destitution of true virtue—is repugnant at once to our conscience and our reason. Nor is the sight of virtuous affluence in connection with secular indigence and want a less incongruous sight. Antecedently, we should have concluded that, under the government of righteousness, in proportion to a man's *moral excellence* will be his *temporal prosperity;* and the converse. Looking at these conditions, separate as they seem to have been in the case of Smyrnæan Christians, which is the better? Decidedly the condition of spiritual wealth with secular poverty, and for the following reasons: 1. *Secular wealth is of contingent value; spiritual is of absolute worth.* All earthly property is but life-leased, and all life-leased property decreases in value every day. Not so spiritual; in all worlds and in all times it is of equal worth. 2. *Spiritual wealth is essentially virtuous; not so secular.* There is no virtue in the possession of material wealth. It comes to a man sometimes independently of his efforts, and often by efforts that involve the sacrifice of all the great principles of religion and fair dealing. Wealth may, indeed, often stand as the effect and sign of great tact, keen-sightedness, and resolute perseverance, but not always, alas! of righteous dealing. The history of fortune-making is too often the history of low cunning, moral falsehood, and legal fraud. *Moral* wealth, however, is virtue itself; all must feel it is praiseworthy; it secures the "well done" of conscience, the approval of all pure intelligences, and of the great God himself. It is intrinsically meritorious and praiseworthy. 3. *Spiritual wealth is essentially a blessing; secular often a bane.* Virtue is its own reward; it is the paradise of the soul. But secular wealth often undermines the health, enfeebles the intellect, and carnalizes the heart. 4. *Spiritual wealth is inalienable; secular is not.* How often temporal wealth takes to itself wings, and flies away! At death all goes; not a fraction is carried into eternity. Not so spiritual. Character we carry with us wherever we go. 5. *Spiritual wealth commands moral respect; not so secular.* A wretched flunkeyism shouts "Hosannah!" to a man in lordly mansions, or wrapt in purple robes, however corrupt in heart he may be. But strip the hero of his grandeur, and reduce him to pauperism and beggary, and the miserable devotee will recoil with disgust. But *spiritual wealth* commands *moral reverence* everywhere.

II. FIENDS IN RELIGION. "I know the blasphemy of them which say they are Jews, and [they] are not, but are the [a] synagogue of Satan." Though the "Jews" here described are fiendishly bad, they had their synagogue, their place of worship. They perhaps attended to the forms of religion, read and expounded the Scriptures in their own way, but their religion was fiendish. "Are the synagogue of Satan." Satan has ever had much to do with religion. Religion, not godliness, is at once his shrine and his instrument. Religion has been and still is the greatest curse of the world; it is the nursery and the arena of every fiendish sentiment. It was religion that put to death the Son of God himself. There are churches and conventicles that are rather the "synagogues of Satan" than the temples of Christ; in their assemblies there are fiends in human form, service, and voice. They breathe the spirit of intolerant sectarianism and bigotry, and disseminate degrading and blasphemous views of the all-loving Maker and Manager of the universe. The difference between what is called religion and Christliness is the difference between light and darkness—life and death. Satan has ever had his synagogues.

III. SAINTS IN PERSECUTION. "Fear none of these things which thou shalt suffer: behold, the devil shall cast some of you into prison, that ye may be tried; and ye shall have tribulation ten days." Christ, when on earth, assured his disciples that they should have "tribulation." In the world they shall have "tribulation." And now from the heights of eternity he sounds the same warning. The words suggest four things concerning their persecution. 1. *It was religious.* It came from those who belonged to the synagogue, and those who prided themselves on being Jews—descendants of Abraham, who was the father of the faithful. A spurious religion has ever been the chiefest and the bitterest fountain of persecution. Inquisitions have been constructed, chains have been forged, tortures have been inflicted, and martyr-fires been kindled by the men of the synagogue. 2. *The persecution was severe.* "I know thy tribulation." It consists of impoverishment, "blasphemy," and reviling, and imprisonment. "Cast some of you into prison." Corrupt religion dries up the fountains of social sympathy in the human breast, dehumanizes human nature—turns man into a devil.[1] 3. *The persecution was testing.* "That ye may be tried." As if Christ

[1] Referring to this subject, the following remarks from a modern expositor will repay perusal: "It would not be for your good, and it would not be for the good of God's cause on earth, that your false parts should be covered up and disguised to the end, or that your life on earth should be one of smooth, easy, tranquil routine, making no demand upon your principles, upon your courage, or upon your Divine strength: you are to be cast even into prison that you may be tried" (Dr. Vaughan).

"Vast numbers of Jews had congregated in Smyrna for the sake of commerce, and whenever they had the opportunity of resisting Christianity, they were not less zealous than Alexander the coppersmith, and his companions at Ephesus, in waging war against its supporters; and the missionaries of the cross had as much to fear from them as from the Bacchus-worshippers with whom they were surrounded. It is thought, not without some probability, that the martyrdom of Germanicus and others of Smyrna, who suffered under Marcus Aurelius, is alluded to in a passage where it is said, 'The devil shall cast some of you into prison;' and we know from the manner in which the Jews joined with Satanic rage in carrying out the martyrdom of Polycarp, how virulent they were in their persecution of the Christians, and how powerful was a body they were in Smyrna. Smyrna, in ecclesiastical history, is celebrated as the Church over which Polycarp presided as bishop. Polycarp was the disciple of St. John, and there is a strong probability that he was the 'angel' of the Church here addressed. He was contemporary with St. Ignatius, who was also a disciple of St. John, and who suffered martyrdom in A.D. 107, eleven years after the messages to the Churches were delivered. Now, there are two letters of Ignatius extant—one addressed to the Church at Smyrna, written by him from Troas; and the other addressed directly to Polycarp, who was then Bishop of Smyrna. Archbishop Usher is at considerable pains to show that Polycarp was the Angel of the Church at Smyrna, over which Church he must have presided seventy-four years. That he was an extremely old man when, in A.D. 167, he suffered martyrdom, we learn from the interrogation of the proconsul, who, after asking him if he was Polycarp, added, 'Have pity on thy own great age.' When further urged to reproach Christ, and his life would be spared, he said, 'Eighty and six years have I served him, and he hath never wronged me; and how can I blaspheme my King who hath saved me?' These eighty and six years cannot be the entire age of Polycarp, but the period which elapsed from his conversion, which must have taken place, according to this calculation, in A.D. 81, so that fifteen years must have passed from the time he first knew Christ until the epistle to the Church at Smyrna was written. This,'

had said, "You are to be subject to a trying, a sifting, a testing process. It must be shown, to yourselves and to those who look on, what there is in you of empty, hollow, cowardly profession. I cannot excuse you from this necessity." 4. *The persecution was short.* "Ten days." It is idle, puerile, to inquire what exact period of time is involved in these words. I take the idea to mean brevity. It is a short period. All the afflictions of the good are brief. "Our light affliction," etc. The storm may be sharp, but it will be short. Great trials seldom last long. The sufferings of the good here are not penal, but disciplinary; not judicial, but paternal. "What son is he that the father chasteneth not?" etc.

IV. DUTY IN TRIAL. How are the trials to be endured? 1. *With courage.* Servile fear is at once an unvirtuous and pernicious element in the mind; it is inimical to the healthy growth of our faculties, and to the maturing of our moral manhood. Hence Christ everywhere proscribes it. He enjoins courage: "Fear not," be intrepid, be brave, endure with magnanimity, struggle with invincibility. "None of these things move me." said Paul; and: 2. *He enjoins faithfulness.* "Be faithful." Do not let the fiercest storms cause you to swerve one iota from rectitude. "Quit you like men;" "Be strong in the Lord." Be faithful to your God and your conscience. 3. *He enjoins perseverance.* "Unto death." If you can be faithful up to death you will be faithful afterwards, for your obligations will remain, your temptations will be gone. 4. *He enjoins reflectiveness.* "He that hath an ear, let him hear what the Spirit saith unto the Churches." Let the mind ever rest in deep and devout thought on the Divine which is speaking everywhere on all things.

V. VICTORY IN DEATH. "He that overcometh shall not be hurt of the second death." The "second death" is the death of the soul, the death of that which makes all life valuable. From such a death the truly loyal and faithful shall be delivered,

says Archbishop Trench, 'will afford quite sufficient time for his promotion to the highest seat of honour in the Church.' But positive testimony is borne to this fact by Irenæus, who affirms that he had in his youth often talked with Polycarp, who had been consecrated Bishop of the Church at Smyrna by St. John; and like testimony is given by Tertullian. If, then, we are to regard Polycarp as the Angel of the Church of Smyrna, there will be considerable light thrown upon the particular references mentioned in the message to that Church, especially those relating to them 'who say they are Jews, but are not;' and the exhortation and promise at the end of the epistle will have their apposite force and application.

"Τάδε λέγει ὁ πρῶτος καὶ ὁ ἔσχατος, ὃς ἐγένετο νεκρὸς, καὶ ἔζησεν—'These things saith the First and the Last, which was dead and lived again.' The Head of the Church here reveals himself as One who had triumphed over death, and by that victory was able to sustain those who were about to undergo cruel torments and meet death in its most terrible form. Wild beasts and fire were the dread alternatives which the heathen persecutors presented before the suffering Christians. When the proconsul said to Polycarp, 'I have wild beasts; I will expose you to them unless you repent.' 'Call them,' replied the martyr; 'our minds are not to be changed from the better to the worse, but it is a good thing to be changed from evil to good.' 'I will tame your spirit by fire,' said the proconsul, 'since you despise the wild beasts.' 'You threaten me with fire,' answered Polycarp, 'which burns for a moment and will soon be extinct; but you are ignorant of the future judgment and of that fire that is reserved for the ungodly.' What could have given martyrs such courage—what but the conscious presence of him who walked with the three children in the fiery furnace of Babylon? It is recorded that the multitude of Jews and Gentiles, who clamoured loudly against Polycarp, called on the asiarch, Philip, that he would loose a lion upon him; and the popular cry of the heathen in times of persecution was '*Christianos ad Leonem!*' Now, under such circumstances nothing could bear them up but the assurance that they were in the hands of him who is 'the same yesterday, to-day, and for ever;' who passed through the bitter pangs of death, and is now alive for evermore. Death in its most appalling forms might be near at hand, the most cruel persecution that ever was invented by the malignity of the servants of the prince of darkness might be imminent; but whence those fears? 'When thou passest through the fire thou shalt not be burned, neither shall the flame kindle upon thee.' Like the bush at Horeb, the Church may burn, but it will not be consumed, for Christ is in the midst of it. They may kill the poor body, but they cannot kill the soul, which, when the earthly pitcher is broken, shall shine like Gideon's lamps. Like the chariot of fire in which the prophet ascended, so the flame of persecution, how fiercely soever it may burn, will only bear the soul of the martyr to the bosom of his God" (Andrew Tait, LL.D., F.R.S.E.).

and, more than this, he shall have a "crown" and a "wreath of life." A crown stands for the most elevated distinction, the highest honour. This distinction James calls "a crown of life;" Paul, "a crown of glory;" Peter, "a crown of righteousness." What is the crown of life? *Perfect moral manhood.*—D. T.

Vers. 12—17.—*The words of Christ to the congregation at Pergamos.* "And to the angel of the Church in Pergamos," etc. "Few, if any, parts of the world present greater attractions than Pergamos to the student of nature, history, or art. It is associated with memorable names and wonderful exploits. It is the native land of Homer, the oldest of the world's poets, and of Herodotus, the father of history, and "three of the seven wise men here began their life. Among the wonders of the world it boasted its Temple at Ephesus, its Mausoleum in Caria, and its Colossus at Rhodes. The finest work of art, the celebrated Venus, is attributed to this people." Pergamos is not the least attractive spot in this important district of the globe. It is about three days' journey from Smyrna, on the banks of Caïcus, in the province of Mysia, a little river famed in classic story. It stands under the modern name of *Bergama*. Though it has fallen from its original grandeur, it has not become a desolation, or an abode for wild beasts. In the passage before us we have the record of the language which Christ, from the deep silence of eternity, addressed to a congregation of his professed disciples there. In looking into this language we discover (1) *a tone of authority;* (2) *a discrimination of character;* (3) *a reformative demand;* and (4) *a promise of blessedness.* Here we have—

I. A TONE OF AUTHORITY. "These things saith he which hath the sharp sword with two edges." A sword is an emblem of authority; a "two-edged one" may express authority as well as terrible force. In ver. 16 of ch. i. it is said, "Out of his mouth went a sharp two-edged sword." It is a *moral,* not a material sword—the sword of *truth;* a sword that inflicts no wounds upon existence, but upon the *errors* and *wrongs* of existence. Two remarks are suggested. 1. *Christ's truth is authoritative.* The sword is an emblem of authority. In every utterance of his we have it. "Thus saith the Lord." It comes, not for mere study or speculation, but with a binding force. It is not merely to be studied, but obeyed. 2. *Christ's truth is mighty.* It is a "two-edged sword." It cuts in all directions, cuts to the central roots of error. What battles it has fought! what victories it has won! It destroys all wrong thoughts, all corrupt passions, all wicked resolves. "It brings into captivity every thought to the obedience of Christ."

II. A DISCRIMINATION OF CHARACTER. "I know thy works." The passage suggests: 1. That *Christ is fully acquainted with circumstances under which all moral character is formed.* Christ describes exactly the moral position in which the Church lived. "And where thou dwellest, even where Satan's seat is." "Satan's seat" was there. It was the metropolis of a heathen divinity—Æsculapius, the god of healing. "In his honour a living serpent was kept and fed in the temple, while the serpent-worship was so marked a characteristic of the place, that we find this reptile engraved on many of its coins. Again, the practice of the priests of Æsculapius consisted much in charms and incantations, and crowds resorted to his temple, where lying miracles of healing were vaunted to be performed, which were doubtless used by Satan to obstruct and counterfeit the work of the apostles and the gospel" (Rev. H. B. Tristram, LL.D., F.R.S.). Here, too, we are told that in this city was held the "doctrine of Balaam, who taught Balac to cast a stumbling-block before the children of Israel, to eat things sacrified unto idols, and to commit fornication." Also the "doctrine of the Nicolaitanes." The people holding these doctrines taught the people to eat things sacrificed to idols, and to commit fornication. "The eating of idol meats would, in such a city as Pergamos, be as great a stumbling-block as caste at the present day in India. To refuse to partake of things offered to idols was not only to renounce idolatry, it was more; it was to abstain from almost every public and private festivity, to withdraw, in great measure, from the social life of the place." Here, too, we are informed, Antipas, Christ's faithful martyr, was slain. Such was the Satanic scene in which the disciples of Christ lived and wrought in Pergamos. Here they formed their character and accomplished whatever good they did. Here is one of the million proofs that *man's moral character is not necessarily formed by external circumstances,* however antagonistic those circumstances may be. Our benevolent Maker has invested all moral minds with the power not only to rise above external circumstances, but to subordinate the most hostile to their advantage. 2. *That the eye of Christ recognizes every part of a man's character, whether good or bad.* In all characters, even the best, there is a mingling of the good and bad, and the elements of each are recognized. Mark what is here said concerning the good of the Church at Ephesus. "Thou holdest fast my Name, and hast not denied my faith." Mark also what is said concerning the evil in them. It would seem that they did not sufficiently resist the wrong. "I have a few things against thee, because thou hast there them that hold the doctrine of Balaam, who taught Balac to cast a stumbling-block before the children of Israel, to eat things sacrificed unto idols, and to commit fornication." It would seem from this that they might have done more than they did in expelling by moral force such base and pernicious characters from their midst. So far as they failed they were defective in faith, zeal, and courage. Thus Christ marks the evil and the good in the character of his disciples, approving the one and reproving the other.

III. A REFORMATIVE DEMAND. "Repent; or else I will come unto thee." 1. Repentance is *moral reformation.* It is not a mere change in theological belief, in outward conduct, or in ecclesiastical relations and rituals, but in the heart, in the master disposition of the soul. It is the turning of the whole from the selfish to the benevolent, from the wrong to the right. It is, moreover, a law binding on all men. His word commands man everywhere to "repent." It is the necessity of all men. "Unless ye repent ye shall all likewise perish." 2. Repentance is an *urgent necessity.* "Repent; or else I will come unto thee quickly." I will come in retributive justice, and that quickly—quick as the lightning. "I will fight against them with the sword of my mouth." Not a material sword, but a *moral.* His word has a power to destroy as well as to save. A word of his can annihilate the universe. He has only to will, and it is done. His word carries fatal pestilences, devastating storms, and blighting famines. What an argument of terror is this urging the duty of moral reformation!

IV. A PROMISE OF BLESSEDNESS. "He that hath an ear, let him hear what the Spirit saith unto the Churches; To him that overcometh will I give to eat of the hidden manna, and will give him a white stone, and in the stone a new name written, which no man knoweth saving he that receiveth it." The promises here made by the Spirit are to a certain class—those who have conquered. Who are the conquerors in life's battle? Not those who by sword or bayonet or any deadly instruments have destroyed the mortal lives of men. Such are not the victors, but *victims* to their own vanity, ambition, greed, and brutal passions. The real conquerors in life's battle are those who conquer *all the evils in their own nature*, and get the mastery over all their impulses and passions. He is the sublimest conqueror who has crushed most of the *wrongs and evils* of life. Two blessings are here promised to such. 1. *The choicest nourishment.* The "hidden manna." "I will give to eat of the hidden manna." Though they absent themselves from the sumptuous feasts of idolatry, referred to in the previous verses, they shall have food far better—the "hidden manna." Food fulfils two functions—it satisfies and it strengthens. The best food is that which supplies the most happiness and the most vigour. This "hidden manna," which is Christ, does this. (1) His *doctrines* are bread to the *intellect.* They are full of nourishment for the mental powers. (2) It is *fellowship*—is bread to the *heart.* Loving intercourse with him will develop, strengthen, and gladden all the sympathies of the heart. (3) His *spirit* is bread to the whole *life.* To partake of his spirit, the spirit of supreme love to God, consecration to the true and the right, and universal sympathy with man, is to get that which will invigorate every faculty and fibre of our being. His spirit is indeed the strength of humanity. It is the moral wine that gives at once the highest elevation to soul, and the strongest character. "He that eateth me"—my moral spirit—"even he shall live by me." It promises: 2. *The highest distinction.* (1) The *sign* of distinction. "A white stone." "Perhaps," says Dr. Tristram, "the white stone, the pure and sparkling diamond, may be placed in contrast with the charms supplied to the votaries of Æsculapius, with the cabalistic characters inscribed on them, and which were worn as amulets to protect them from disease. This spiritual stone, inscribed like the Urim, with a name which no man knew, may set forth the revelation which the Lord will make to his faithful people, of mysteries hidden before from kings and prophets, like the hidden manna and the Urim, seen by the high priest alone, but which revelation of the glory of God can only be known by those who have received nim." (a) This may be a sign of *acquittal*. In the ancient Greek courts of justice it was customary to signify the judgment pronounced upon the accused by throwing a stone into an urn; the *black* stone expressed condemnation, the *white* acquittal. Thus Socrates was convicted and condemned. There will be a public expression at the last day of the acquittal of those who have won the battle. (b) This may be a sign of *qualification*. It seems that before the Levites and the priests under the Law were allowed to minister at the altar, they were examined, in order to ascertain whether they were ceremonially clean or not. Ritualistic purity was regarded as the necessary qualification for office. Those who were found to have this qualification had a "white" stone presented to them. He who came forth from the examination bore this sign of fitness for his sacerdotal vocation. Thus the "white stone" here may mean that he who wins the moral battle of life will be regarded as fit for the high services of the celestial world. (c) This may be a sign of *public honour*. It was customary in the Grecian games to give a "white stone" to him who had won the victory. He who held this stone was entitled to be supported at the public expense, had free access to all the festivities of the nation, and was regarded as illustrious in all great gatherings. Thus he who wins the moral battle of life shall be publicly honoured. "A crown of glory is prepared for him, which the Lord, the righteous Judge, shall give unto him at that day." He will have free admission into all the honours of eternity. (2) The *character* of the distinction. What is the character? It is something *new*—it is a new name. "In the stone a new name written, which no man knoweth saving he that receiveth it." What is this new name, the knowledge of which is entirely a matter of individual consciousness with him who has it? This is it, "sons of God." No one knows anything of this sonship but he who is the subject of it.—D. T.

Vers. 18—29.—*The words of Christ from eternity to the congregation at Thyatira.*
"And unto the angel of the Church in Thyatira," etc. Thyatira was situated between Pergamos and Sardis, a little off the main road which connected these two cities. It was a Macedonian colony, founded by Alexander the Great (or whom I should rather designate "Alexander the *Contemptible*") after the overthrow of the Persian empire. The Macedonian colonists appear to have introduced the worship of Apollo, honoured as the sun-god, under the name of Tyrumnas. It has been thought by some that the description here given of Christ—"the eyes of flame"—was selected in allusion to this worship of the sun-god, under the form of some dazzlingly ornamented image. Certainly close commercial intercourse connected the daughter colony with its mother city. There seem to have been various mercantile guilds in the colony—bakers, potters, tanners, weavers, and dyers. The dye-trade was, perhaps, the most important. Lydia, the seller of purple, was in all likelihood connected with the guild of dyers; and her appearance in Philippi is an illustration of the trade relations of Macedonia and Thyatira. To her the Christian community of Thyatira may have owed its beginning. "She who had gone forth for a while to buy and sell and get again, when she returned home may have brought home with her richer merchandise than any she had looked to obtain" (Trench). The population was of a mixed character, and included besides Asiatics, Macedonians, Italians, and Chaldæans. Of all the homiletic sketches on this epistle, I know of no sketch so clear and comprehensive, so philosophic and suggestive, as that of the late Caleb Morris—one of the greatest, if not *the* greatest preacher that has appeared in London during the century. Those whom the popular sentiment designates "princes of preachers" seem to me to shrink into contempt in his presence. "There are," he says, "four things in this epistle to which we shall call attention—*the commendable in character, the reprehensible in doctrine, the indispensable in duty, and the blessed in destiny.*" How forcibly every item in this epistle is brought out by these four general divisions![1] To attempt a plan equal to this in all points of excellence would be presumption. Albeit, as it would be supererogatory and useless to repeat what others have said, I shall endeavour to bring all the important elements of the chapter under one general heading—*the moral character of mankind;* and here we have it in three aspects.

[1] See *Homilist*, vol. **xxiv.** p. 276.

I. As THAT IN WHICH CHRIST FEELS THE PROFOUNDEST INTEREST. He who is here called the "Son of God," no doubt feels an interest in every part of the great universe. But material worlds and systems, methinks, concern him not so much as the *moral* character of God's spiritual offspring. In souls his interest is profound, practical, and permanent. Two remarks are suggested. 1. *His interest springs from an absolute knowledge of the primary elements of character.* "I know thy works;" and again he says, "I am he which searcheth the reins and hearts." He peers into those spheres of mind into which the vulture's eye cannot pierce, no, nor the keenest eye of angelic intelligence; the sphere where character is generated, where its elements float in invisible germs; the arena where the moral battles are fought, where victories are won and defeats endured. Our interest in objects is often blind, and so it often happens that we are entranced with admiration for objects which we learn from sad experience to be worthless, base, and abhorrent. Not so with Christ. He knows what *character* really is, its elements whether good or bad. 2. *His interest fills him with the deepest concern for the progress of the good.* "I know thy works, and charity [thy love], and service, and faith [and ministry], and thy patience." "Charity" and "service"—love and its administrations; "faith" and "patience"—faith in its practical endurance; and all these in their progressive development, and "the last to be more than the first." Moral goodness wherever it exists is *progressive.* Unlike all other life, the more it grows the more the craving and the more the capability for growth. "From glory to glory," etc.

II. As THAT WHICH IS TRANSMITTED FROM GENERATION TO GENERATION. In the long black roll of human infamy there is not a blacker name than that of Jezebel, the wife of Ahab. She was "the great seducer to idolatry in the later history of Israel, and as the worship of the Phœnician Astarte, or Venus, was accompanied with the grossest impurity, her name became the synonym of all that was debasing and profligate." Some suppose that this Jezebel in Thyatira, who embodied the character of the old Israelitish, fiendish idolatress, was the wife of the bishop of the congregation at Thyatira. It might be so, for many a worthy bishop has been matrimonially linked to a Jezebelitish woman. Ay, what is worse, many a Jezebelitish woman, married, has entrapped young unmarried bishops to their disgrace and ruin. But I am disposed to regard the name here as symbolical of some proud, persecuting, self-constituted authority on religion, haughtily vaunting claims of superior religious piety and theological intelligence. Now, centuries had passed away since Jezebel, the wife of Ahab, ended her execrable history and passed into the retributive future; yet her *character* appears in Thyatira, breathing the same passions and repeating the same conduct as of yore. Thus moral character is transmitted. I inquire not into the philosophy of this patent and awful fact in human history, nor into its moral propriety; certain it is that in the present generation the same characters appear as in the generation that lived before the Flood. We offer three remarks on the transmission of moral character, as suggested by the letter before us. 1. *The transmitted character does not free the possessor from its responsibility.* The party here addressed, whether an individual, a faction, or a community, is spoken of as responsible; ay, and it would seem that even the bishop of the Church had not a little responsibility for the existence of this Jezebelitish character—a character that used its influence on the side of ungodliness, licentiousness, and adultery. The grand mission of Christly men is to expel evil from the community, to crush the wrong, not by force and persecution, but by Divine moral suasion and high Christian example. The work of a Christly man is to slay with the sword of the Spirit all the moral Jezebels within his reach. But whilst the disciples of Christ are held to some extent responsible for the existence of bad characters in their midst, the characters themselves are conscious of their responsibility. The fact that they inherit the bad temper and principles of their ancestors, however near or distant, does not relieve them from the remorseful consciousness that they are the authors of their own character. Every pang of remorse, every tear of compunction, every sigh of moral regret, demonstrate to the greatest sinner that he is the author of his own vile character, and no other. 2. *The transmitted character might be got rid of by its possessor.* "I gave her space [time that she should] to repent of her fornication; and she repented not [willeth not to repent of her fornication]." Even the wickedest person, man or woman, has time given him for repentance. God hates nothing that he has made. He wills not the death of any sinner, but rather that he should turn and be saved—should repent and live. It was so even with the immoral person here spoken of; time was given her; but she would not use it. There was no will to repent. Therefore, for the sake of others, the time must now be shortened, and after one more trial judgment must follow. Repentance is the method of ridding one's self of a bad character, and this repentance every man can and ought to accomplish. Men are not machines or automatons, but free agents. The will is the rudder of the soul; it either steers the ship into the wished-for haven, or drives it on to shoals and quicksands. 3. *The transmitted character might entail enormous evils on others.* In truth all evil characters must do so. " And I will kill her children with death." All have their moral offspring, children like unto themselves. The evil propagates the evil, as the good the good. "No man liveth unto himself." Our moral children do our work, and that work is like that of Jezebel. Who knows the injury that the moral children of Jezebel did to the bishop and the Christian community of Thyatira? They encouraged licentiousness and idolatry, and committed fornication, and ate things " sacrificed unto idols."

III. AS THAT WHICH DETERMINES THE DESTINY OF MANKIND. Here mark two things. 1. *The outcome of the bad.* " Behold, I will [do] cast her into a bed, and them that commit adultery with her into great tribulation, except they repent of their deeds [her works]." The chamber of voluptuousness shall become the chamber of torture. " And I will kill her children with death." Those in whom she has propagated her foul character, under the cover of higher piety and deeper intelligence, shall meet with destruction. Death shall be their fate—the death of all that makes life worth having. " The wages of sin is death." " Be not deceived; God is not mocked: for whatsoever a man soweth, that shall he also reap." " I will give unto every one of you according to your works;" your works shall determine your doom. 2. *The outcome of the good.* Three great blessings are here stated as coming to such. (1) Freedom from future suffering. "But unto [to] you I say, and unto [to] the rest in [that are in] Thyatira, as many as have not this doctrine [teaching], and which have not known [know not] the depths [deep things] of Satan, as they speak [say]; I will put [cast] upon you none other burden." Whilst those whose impious Gnosticism, intolerant spirit and gross sensuality would meet with anguish and death, all who were free from these abominations would be secure from future evil. " I will put [cast] upon you none other burden." You need not apprehend any future evil. Elsewhere we are told that " he will keep him in perfect peace whose mind is stayed on him." Another blessing is: (2) Elevation to true royalty. " But [howbeit] that which ye have already hold fast till I come." Those who hold fast with an unrelaxing grasp all the good they had, triumphed over evil, and held on loyally to the end, shall have " power over the nations." What power? Moral power—power over the minds and hearts of nations. He only is the true sovereign who governs *minds and hearts.* All other sovereignties are shams. The morally right has in it the highest elements of might. Right is might, and there is none other. " He shall rule them with a rod of iron." Right is a rod of iron unbreakable and all-crushing, dashing to pieces, shivering into atoms all the kingdoms of error and wrong. He is the greatest king of his age who has the most truth and goodness in his soul; hence the " saints one day shall judge the world." Hail the period! merciful Heaven, hasten it! Another blessing is: (3) Inheritance of the highest possession. " I will give him the morning star." " Morning star"—bright harbinger of a day whose skies shall have no cloud, whose atmosphere no storm, whose sun shall rise and set no more. Christ himself is the " Morning Star." This is the title he gives himself: " I Jesus am the Root and Offspring of David, and the Bright and Morning Star " The good man shall have Christ, and, possessing him, shall have more than the universe itself " All things are yours," etc. So that out of the *moral character* of mankind will bloom their Paradise or flame their hell. Therefore what we have good in us let us not only " hold fast," but nourish into higher developments. Let us so cultivate the " Divine tree " that its roots shall deepen, its fibres strengthen, its branches multiply, its foliage become more magnificent, and its fruits more abundant every day.—D. T.

Ver. 25.—*Christian excellence.* " But that which ye have already hold fast till I come." These few words give us three ideas concerning Christian excellence.

I. CHRISTIAN EXCELLENCE IS AN ATTAINMENT. The words are addressed to Christians at Thyatira, and they are represented as having "charity," or love to Christ, and "patience," or holy fortitude and magnanimity under all the trials of life. These are all elements of Christian excellence, and these they are represented as having *attained*. They had reached the goodness they possessed by holy efforts in the use of means. 1. *Christian excellence is an attainment in contradistinction to a native growth.* It does not spring up in the soul as an indigenous germ. It is a seed that has been taken in and cultivated. 2. *Christian excellence in contradistinction to an impartation.* In a sense it is a gift of God; not in the sense in which life, and light, and air, and the seasons of the year, are the gifts of God,—blessings that come upon us irrespective of our own efforts; but rather in the sense in which the crops of the husbandman, the learning of the scholar, the triumphs of the artist, are the gifts of God,—blessings that come as the result of appropriate labour. We shall neither *grow* good nor be *made* good. We must *become* good; we must struggle after it.

II. CHRISTIAN EXCELLENCE IS AN ATTAINMENT THAT REQUIRES FAST HOLDING. "Hold fast" whatever is attained. Little or much should be retained: 1. *Because it is worth retaining.* Its value will appear by considering three things. (1) The priceless instrumentality employed to put man in possession of it. The mission of Christ. (2) Its essential connection with man's spiritual well-being. There is no true happiness apart from it. (3) Its capability of unlimited progress. It may be as a grain of mustard, but it can grow. What glorious harvests are enfolded in one grain of true goodness! It should be held fast. 2. *Because there is a danger of losing it.* (1) Men who have had it have lost it before now. (2) Agencies are in constant operation here that threaten its destruction. Hold it fast, therefore.

III. CHRISTIAN EXCELLENCE IS AN ATTAINMENT THAT WILL BE PLACED BEYOND DANGER AT THE ADVENT OF CHRIST. "Hold fast till I come." An expression this implying that it will be secure enough afterwards. He comes to every Christian at death. "I will come again, and receive you unto myself." When he thus comes: 1. *He crushes for ever our enemies.* He bruises the head of Satan under our feet. 2. *He removes from us everything inimical to the growth of goodness.* 3. *He introduces us into those heavenly scenes* where there will be nothing but what ministers to the advancement of goodness. Take heart, Christian; the struggle is not for long!—D. T.

EXPOSITION.

CHAPTER III.

Vers. 1—6.—*The epistle to the Church at Sardis.* This Church is one of the two which receives unmixed reproof. Smyrna and Philadelphia receive no blame; Sardis and Laodicea receive no praise. Sardis lies almost due south of Thyatira, on the road to Philadelphia, between the river Hermus and Mount Tmolus. It had been in turn Lydian, Persian, Greek, and Roman, and, like its last Lydian king, Crœsus, had been celebrated for its wealth. The auriferous stream Pactolus, in summer almost dry, flowed through its market-place ; but its chief source of wealth was its trade. In A.D. 17 "twelve famous cities of Asia fell by an earthquake in the night. . . . The calamity fell most heavily on the people of Sardis, and it attracted to them the largest share of sympathy. The emperor [Tiberius] promised

ten million sesterces (£85,000), and remitted for five years all they paid to the exchequer" (Tac., 'Ann.,' ii. 47). A little later Sardis was one of the cities of Asia which claimed the honour of erecting a temple in honour of Tiberius, but the preference was given to Smyrna (' Ann.,' iv. 55, 56). Of the inscriptions which have been discovered at Sardis, nearly all are of the Roman period Cybele, or Cybebe, was the chief divinity of Sardis; but no reference to this nor to any of the special features of the city can be traced in the epistle. In the second century, Melito, Bishop of Sardis, held a very prominent place among Asiatic Christians, both in personal influence and in literary work. Among his numerous writings was one on the Apocalypse of St. John. The prosperous and luxurious capital of Lydia is now represented by a few huts and a collection of ruins buried deep in rubbish. It still retains its ancient name in the form *Sart*.

The Church in Sardis has no Nicolaitans, no Balaam, no Jezebel. But there is worse evil than the presence of what is morally and doctrinally corrupt. The numbness of spiritual torpor and death is more hopeless than unwise toleration. The Church in Sardis, scarcely out of its infancy, has already the signs of an effete and moribund faith ; and it is possible that this deadness was a result of the absence of internal enemies.

Ver. 1.—He that hath the seven Spirits of God (see notes on ch. i. 4, 16, 20 ; but observe that this designation of Christ does not occur in the opening vision). In ch. v. 6 the Lamb is seen "*having* seven horns and seven eyes, *which are the seven Spirits of God*." The seven Spirits being the Holy Spirit in his sevenfold activity, it is manifest (as Trench observes) that this passage is of importance in reference to the doctrine of the double procession. The Son hath the Spirit, not as One who receives it from the Father, but as One who can impart it to men. As man he received it ; as God he gives it. And a Church sunk in spiritual deadness specially needs such a gift. Hence the repetition about having the seven stars, which appears also in the address to the Church in Ephesus (ch. ii. 1). Note, however, that here we have ἔχων for κρατῶν, which would not have been appropriate to express the Son's possession of the Spirit. It is he who holds in his hand the angels of the Church that also has the Spirit wherewith to quicken them. Those that are alive owe their life and growth to him. Those that are dying or dead may be restored to life by him. Thou hast a name that thou livest, and thou art dead. This, again, is thoroughly in the style of the Fourth Gospel. St. John frequently states some gracious fact, and in immediate sequence gives the very opposite of what might have been expected to result from it. "Thou hast a reputation for life, and (instead of being full of vigour and growth) thou art a corpse." This has been called "the tragic tone" in St. John (comp. John i. 5, 10, 11 ; iii. 11, 19, 32 ; v. 39, 40 ; vi. 36, 43, etc.). In all these cases the contrast is introduced by a simple καί, which may be rendered "and yet ;" but the simple "and" is more forcible. Beware of the unworthy literalism which suggests that the Bishop of Sardis bore a name which implied life, *e.g.* Zosimus, or Vitalis. As already stated (notes on ch. i. 20), it is improbable that "the

angel" means the bishop. And in any case "name" is here used in the common sense of character or reputation. Comp. Herod., vii. 138, where the historian says that Xerxes' expedition *had the name* (οὔνομα εἶχε) of being directed against Athens, but was really a menace to the whole of Greece. We have very similar uses of ὄνομα in Mark ix. 41 and 1 Pet. iv. 16. The Church in Sardis had a name for Christianity, but there was no Christianity in it.

Ver. 2.—Be watchful ; literally, *become watching*. The use of γίγνομαι implies that the watchful state is not the normal one—a change is needed before the watching can come about (comp. ch. i. 9, 10, 18 ; ii. 8 ; iv. 2 ; vi. 12, etc.). The use of the present participle instead of an adjective (" watching" for "watchful") makes the charge more definite ; not merely "be of a watchful character," but "become a watcher" (comp. ch. xvi. 10 ; Mark i. 4 ; ix. 3, 7 ; Heb. v. 12). Stablish the things that remain, which were ready to die. The reading, "*were* ready to die," is the best attested, and as being less smooth than "are ready to die," was more likely to be altered. It anticipates the time when the command will be obeyed : "which were ready to die when thou didst begin to stablish them." No doubt τὰ λοιπά may be masculine in signification, and mean those members of the Church who have still some life in them. But this interpretation anticipates ver. 4, which apparently introduces a new fact. It seems better, therefore, to retain the neuter, and interpret "the things that remain" as meaning the few good elements of faith and practice which still survived. The externals of the Christian life were there ; otherwise it could not have been even nominally Christian. And these externals might be made realities to support the revived life of the Church. For I have found no works of thine. The difference between the Authorized Version and the Revised Version here depends upon the presence or absence of the article before ἔργα. The balance of probability is against τά, and its absence makes the reproach stronger. Fulfilled before my God. The substitution of "fulfilled" (Revised Version) for "perfect" (Authorized Version) is important. The Greek is πεπληρωμένα (John xvi. 24 ; xvii. 13, etc.), not τέλεια (1 John iv. 18). And "fulfilled" is better than "complete" (Alford, Tregelles), in order to bring out the connexion with the numerous places in which the same verb occurs, especially in the writings of St. John (ch. v. 11 ; John iii. 29 ; vii. 8 ; xii. 38 ; xiii. 18 ; xv. 11, 25, etc. ; 1 John i. 4 ; 2 John 12) ; in many of which passages "complete" would not stand as a rendering. "Fulfilled," or "made

full," means made up to the right standard
of excellence. The works of the Sardian
Church have been weighed, and found wanting before God. "A minister of Christ is
very often in highest honour with men for
the performance of one-half of his work,
while God is regarding him with displeasure
for the neglect of the other half." "Before
my God" is undoubtedly the true reading,
whatever may be the case in ch. ii. 7.
Only in the writings of St. John does Jesus
Christ speak of the Father as "my God;"
and this fact is one more link between the
Fourth Gospel and the Apocalypse. In
this chapter we have five instances—here
and ver. 12 (comp. ch. ii. 7 [possibly] and
John xx. 17). In Matt. xxvii. 46 Christ
adopts the language of Ps. xxii. 1, and
addresses the Father as "my God;" and St.
Paul uses similar language (Eph. i. 17).
The expression, "before God" (ἐνώπιον τοῦ
Θεοῦ), is specially common in the Apoca-
lypse and in the writings of St. Luke and
of St. Paul; it does not occur in either St.
Matthew or St. Mark.

Ver. 3.—Remember therefore how thou
hast received and didst hear (comp. ch. ii. 5).
Like the Ephesians, the Sardians are reminded of the better condition from which
they have receded. They are of those
"who, when they have heard the Word,
straightway receive it with joy; and they
have no root in themselves, but endure for
a while" (Mark iv. 16, 17). The "how,"
as is shown by the verbs "receive" and
"hear," refers to the readiness with which
they accepted the gospel, rather than to the
power with which it was preached to them.
The tenses are instructive: the aorist applies to the hearing at some definite period
in their history; the perfect implies the
permanent result of the act of reception.
Keep and repent. Keep what thou didst
hear. "Keep" is better than "hold fast,"
to mark the difference between τηρεῖν (ch. i.
3; ii. 26; iii. 3, 8, 10, etc.), and κρατεῖν
(ch. ii. 1, 13, 14, 15, 25; iii. 11, etc.).
Here again the tenses should be noted: the present imperative indicates that they are to
continue to keep; the aorist, that they are
to repent once for all. We have a similar
combination of tenses in "Take these things
hence at once; continue to refrain from
making my Father's house a house of
merchandise" (John ii. 16; comp. John v.
8, 11; Acts xii. 8; 1 Cor. xv. 34). "Remember" here and in ch. ii. 5 is with equal
fitness the present imperative: "continue to
remember." I will come as a thief. The
"on thee" after "come," though well supported, is probably not genuine. Wherever
this figure is used in the New Testament
of the coming of Christ, the word used is
κλέπτης, "a thief," and not λῃστής, a "rob-

ber" or "bandit." This shows, what is also
plain from the context, that secrecy, not
violence, is the point of the similitude
(comp. ch. xvi. 15; Matt. xxiv. 43; Luke
xii. 39; 1 Thess. v. 2; 2 Pet. iii. 10). Thou
shalt not know what hour; literally, thou
shalt in no wise come to know during what
kind of an hour. The negative is the
strongest form, οὐ μή (ch. iii. 11; iii. 5, 12).
The verb is γινώσκειν, which implies ac-
quisition of knowledge (ch. ii. 23, 24; iii. 9).
The pronoun is ποῖος (John x. 32; xii. 33;
xviii. 32; xxi. 19; and especially Matt.
xxiv. 42; Luke xii. 39); and "hour" is in
the accusative (John iv. 52).

Ver. 4.—But thou hast a few names in
Sardis. The "but" (Revised Version)
must be added, and the "even" (Authorized Version) omitted, on conclusive evidence. "Names" is here used in the sense
of persons (Acts i. 15 and ch. xi. 13, where
the Revised Version has "persons"); there
is no reference to the totally different use of
"to have a name" in ver. 1. Bede remarks,
"He knoweth his own sheep by name, as he
knew Moses by name, and writeth the names
of his own in heaven." These few are like
the few righteous in Sodom. Though they
consent to abide in the Church, they do not
leaven it, nor does their presence save it:
"They shall deliver but their own souls by
their righteousness" (Ezek. xiv. 14, 16, 18,
20). The word for "defile" (μολύνειν)
occurs only here, ch. xiv. 4, and 1 Cor. viii. 7.
Its radical meaning is "to besmear," and so
"to befoul." That of μιαίνειν (John xviii. 28;
Titus i. 15; Heb. xii. 15; Jude 8) is rather
"to stain," which is not necessarily "to
befoul." That of κοινοῦν (Matt. xv. 11—20;
Mark vii. 15—23; Acts x. 15; xi. 9; xxi.
28; Heb. ix. 13) is "to make common or
profane." In most cases all these three are
rendered "defile" in our version. These
few in Sardis have kept themselves "unspotted from the world" in which they live.
Neither the corruption of heathendom nor
the torpor of a moribund Church has infected them. Their contact with a dead
body has imparted no life to the body and
no defilement to them. There is no need to
press the metaphor and give a special meaning to "garments"—whether their souls, or
their bodies, or their consciences, or their
baptismal robes. The metaphor is implied
in "putting on the new man" (Eph. iv. 24;
Col. iii. 10), "putting on Christ" (Rom. xiii.
14; Gal. iii. 27), where the word for "put
on" is ἐνδύεσθαι, "to be clothed with."
They shall walk with me. In accordance
with Christ's high-priestly prayer (John
xvii. 24; comp. Rev. xxi. 24). In white.
This elliptical expression (ἐν λευκοῖς) for "in
white robes" occurs in the New Testament
only here and John xx. 12, and is another

small link between the two books. The word "white" (λευκός), excepting in Matt. v. 36 and John iv. 35, is in the New Testament always used of *heavenly* purity and brightness. Thus also Plato, Χρώματα δὲ λευκὰ πρέπουτ' ἂν θεοῖς εἴη ('Laws,' 956); and Virgil of the souls in the other world, "Omnibus his nivea cinguntur tempora vittâ" ('Æneid,' vi. 665). (See notes on ch. i. 14.) As we might expect, the word is specially frequent in Revelation. Of course, the white garments referred to here, vers. 5, 18, and ch. iv. 4, are quite different from the undefiled garments just mentioned. The one is the imperfect purity of struggling saints on earth, the other the perfect purity of glorified saints in heaven. The promise, therefore, is threefold. (1) They shall walk, *i.e.* they shall have life and liberty. (2) They shall have Christ as their constant Companion. (3) They shall be in unsullied glory. And why? Because they are worthy. The merit is not theirs, but Christ's, in whose blood they have washed their robes (ch. vii. 14; 1 John ii. 2), and by whose grace they are preserved in holiness (1 John i. 7). It is because they have by God's help fulfilled the conditions which he has promised to accept, that they are worthy. The nearest approach to this declaration of worthiness on the part of God's saints seems to be Luke xx. 35 (not xxi. 36) and 2 Thess. i. 5, 11. But in all these passages they are "*accounted* worthy" (καταξιωθέντες) rather than "worthy" (ἄξιοι). In ch. xvi. 6 we have the opposite worthiness of those who have earned the "wages of sin" instead of the "gift of God" (Rom. vi. 23). Such persons are literally worthy, and not merely accounted worthy.

Ver. 5.—**He that overcometh shall thus be arrayed in white garments.** It is difficult to see on what principles of criticism Alford retains the reading of the Textus Receptus, οὗτος, instead of that rightly accepted by the Revisers, οὗτως. The latter has a very decided balance of external evidence in its favour; the former is a corruption very likely to occur either accidentally or in order to introduce a construction very frequent in St. John (John iii. 26; vi. 46; vii. 18; xv. 5; 2 John 9). The change from "clothed" (Authorized Version) to "arrayed" (Revised Version) here and elsewhere is no doubt made in order to mark the difference between περιβεβλημένος and ἐνδεδυμένος. But neither the Authorized Version (xvii. 4; xix. 8) nor the Revised Version (xi. 3; xv. 6) is consistent. The Authorized Version generally renders both words "clothed." The Revised Version generally has "arrayed" for περιβεβλημένος, and "clothed" for ἐνδεδυμένος. The Authorized Version is singularly capricious in

having "garments" for ἱμάτια in ver. 4, and "raiment" for the same word in ver. 5. The construction, περιβάλλεσθαι ἔν τινι, occurs again in ch. iv. 4, and once or twice in the LXX. (Deut. xxii. 12); the usual construction is with the accusative. The promise in this verse is again threefold, the last of the three promises in ver. 4 being repeated here as the first in this triplet. Repetitions of a similar kind are very frequent in the Fourth Gospel (i. 1, 5; x. 11; xiii. 20; xv. 19; xvii. 9, 16, etc.). I will in no wise blot out his name. The negative, as in vers. 3 and 12, is in the strongest form. Here we seem to have a figure borrowed from the custom of striking the names of the dead out of the list of citizens. But the figure is a very ancient one, as is seen from parallels in the Old Testament. The present passage, Ἐξαλείψω . . . ἐκ τῆς βίβλου τῆς ζωῆς, is singularly close to the LXX. of Ps. lxix. 29, Ἐξαλειφθήτωσαν ἐκ βιβλίου ζώντων; and to Exod. xxxii. 33, Ἐξαλείψω αὐτὸν ἐκ τῆς βίβλου μου; comp. Ps. cix. 13; Dan. xii. 1; and for the exact expression, "the book of life," see ch. xiii. 8; xvii. 8; xx. 15; xxi. 27; and (without articles) Phil. iv. 3, where Bishop Lightfoot comments as follows: "The 'book of life' in the figurative language of the Old Testament is the register of the covenant people (comp. Isa. iv. 3; Ezek. xiii. 9). Hence 'to be blotted out of the book of the living' means 'to forfeit the privileges of the theocracy, to be shut out from God's favour.' But the expression, though perhaps confined originally to temporal blessings, was in itself a witness to higher hopes; and in the Book of Daniel first it distinctly refers to a blessed immortality (comp. Hermas, 'Vis.,' i. 3; see also Luke x. 20; Heb. xii. 23)." And I will confess his name. Without the smallest manuscript authority or any encouragement from previous versions, Latin, German, or English, the Genevan and Authorized Versions here render καί "but"! The simple connexion with "and" is thoroughly in St. John's style: "He shall be . . . *and* I will . . . *and* I will" (comp. vers. 12, 17; ch. ii. 26—28, etc.; John i, 4, 5, 10, 11, 14, etc.). This is the third of the promises: (1) he shall be in unsullied glory; (2) he shall never lose his heavenly citizenship; (3) he shall be publicly acknowledged as a citizen by the Judge. This third point is a combination of Matt. x. 32 ("before my Father") with Luke xii. 8 ("before the angels of God"). "We may observe of this epistle that in great part it is woven together of sayings which the Lord had already uttered in the days during which he pitched his tent among men; he is now setting his seal from heaven upon his words uttered on earth" (Trench).

Ver. 6.—**He that hath an ear.** As in the

others of the last four epistles, and unlike the first three, this exhortation follows the promise to the victor. No satisfactory explanation of the change of arrangement seems to have been given by any commentator. The order in the four last epistles seems best. The exhortation forms a fitting conclusion to each, as in the synoptic Gospels to parables (see notes on ch. ii. 7, and comp. ch. xiii. 9).

Vers. 7—13.—*The epistle to the Church at Philadelphia.* The circuit continues in the same direction. Philadelphia lies about thirty miles south-east of Sardis, on the road to Laodicea. It is said to owe its name to *Attalus* Philadelphus, King of Pergamum, B.C. 159—138. But it is by no means certain that he was the founder. A trustworthy tradition as to its *Egyptian* origin points to *Ptolemy* Philadelphus, who had estates in Asia Minor (Theocr., xvii. 88). Lying at the western edge of a district whose highly volcanic character earned it the name of Phrygia Catacecaumene, Philadelphia was constantly suffering from earthquakes (cf. ver. 12). It was destroyed along with Sardis in the catastrophe of A.D. 17 (Tac., 'Ann.,' ii. 47). But the advantages of its position, commanding the way to the pass between the Hermus valley and the Mæander valley, and the richness of its vine-produce (Virgil, 'Georg.,' ii. 98), seem to have induced the inhabitants to cling to the site. The coins of Philadelphia often have the head either of Bacchus or a Bacchante on one side; and it is a known fact that volcanic soil is specially favourable to vine-growing. Yet in Roman times it was not equal to Ephesus or even Laodicea; and for law-courts its citizens had to go to Sardis. Nevertheless, it has outlived all these three, and still continues on the same site, and perhaps within the same walls, as of old. At the close of the fourteenth century it was the last Byzantine city to surrender to the Turks, and, when it did succumb, made better terms than any of the others. To this day it retains the privilege of free Christian worship, with the use of bells for service, and processions in public—a thing allowed by the Turks in no other inland city of Asia Minor. It has a bishop and a dozen churches, and it is said that about a third of its fifteen thousand inhabitants are Christian. Its modern Turkish

name is *Allah Shehr,* " the city of God," or, as others write and render it, *Ala Shehr,* " the striped city." In any case the coincidence with " the name of the city of my God " (ver. 12) is purely accidental. (For an eloquent account of Philadelphia, see Gibbon, ' Decline and Fall,' ch. lxiv.)

It is doubtful whether there are any local allusions in the epistle; but some have fancied that " thou hast a little power" (ver. 8) and " a pillar in the temple " (ver. 12) are such (see notes in each place). The name of " Little Athens," which Philadelphia sometimes bore, on account of its numerous temples and festivals (Acts xvii. 16, 22), shows that the little Christian community would have to contend with a specially vigorous form of heathenism. It had also to contend with a colony of hostile Jews, which was no doubt largely augmented after the destruction of Jerusalem, when fugitive Jews came to " worship before the feet " of the Philadelphian Church (ver. 9). Hence the epistle of Ignatius to the Philadelphians treats of Judaism as one of their chief dangers (c. vi., viii., ix.). There were men among them who questioned the authority of Gospels and Epistles, and admitted only the Old Testament Scriptures (τὰ ἀρχεῖα) as binding. Some had tried to lead even Ignatius himself astray (vii.). Altogether his epistle gives a less happy picture of the Philadelphians than that which we have here, where (as in the epistle to the Church at Smyrna) the Philadelphian Church receives unmixed praise. Whether the large proportion of Old Testament language and imagery which is found in this epistle has any connexion with the Jewish colony in Philadelphia is uncertain. Perhaps most of the Christians had been originally Jews.

Ver. 7.—**He that is holy, he that is true** It is doubtful which of these two clauses should precede: authorities are somewhat evenly balanced. Christ, the Speaker, here claims to be " the Holy One " (ὁ ἅγιος), and therefore God (ch. vi. 10; comp. ch. iv. 8; John xvii. 11). In the Old Testament " the Holy One " is a frequent name of God, especially in Isa. i. 4; v. 19, 24; x. 7, 20; xii. 6, etc.; Job vi. 10; Jer. l. 29; li. 5; Ezek. xxxix. 7; Hos. xi. 9; Hab. iii. 3. etc. The word does not occur in Homer or Hesiod, nor in the Greek tragedians. but is very frequent in the LXX. and the New Testament. Its radical meaning is separation. The two epithets "holy" and "true" must not be merged in one as "the truly holy." The "True One" has a very distinct meaning of its own. Note that the adjective used is ἀληθινός, not ἀληθής. Ἀληθής, *verax*, is "true" as opposed to "lying;" ἀληθινός, *verus*, is "true" as opposed to "spurious," "unreal," "imperfect." Christ is "the True One" as opposed to the false gods of the heathen; they are spurious gods. Both adjectives, and especially ἀληθινός, are characteristic of St. John. The latter serves to bind together Gospel, Epistle, and Apocalypse. It occurs nine times in the Gospel, four times in the First Epistle, and ten times in the Apocalypse; twenty-three times in all; in the rest of the New Testament only five times. It is the word used of "the true Light" (John i. 9; 1 John ii. 8); "the true Bread" (John vi. 32), and "the true Vine" (John xv. 1). Applied to God, we find it in John vii. 29; xvii. 3; 1 John v. 20. He that hath the key of David. Observe that none of these titles come from the opening vision in ch. i., although by no means all the material there found (ch. i. 13—16) has been already used. The source of the present appellation is obviously Isa. xxii. 20—22; but it is worth noting that Isa. xxii. 20 has much that is parallel to the unused material in ch. i. 13; so that the opening vision would seem to direct us, as this passage certainly does, to Eliakim as a type of Christ. As Trench observes, Isaiah foretells the promotion of Eliakim "with an emphasis and fulness" which would surprise us if we did not see in it not merely the description of "a revolution in the royal palace" of Judah, but "the type of something immeasurably greater." Shebna, whose name shows him to have been a foreigner, had misused his dignity and power as steward or controller of the royal house—an office analogous to that held by Joseph under Pharaoh and by our prime minister. For this he was degraded to the inferior office of royal scribe or secretary (Isa. xxxvi. 3; xxxvii. 2), while Eliakim was made "mayor of the palace" in his room. The παστοφόριον of the LXX. and *præpositus templi* of the Vulgate would lead us to suppose that Eliakim's office was sacerdotal; but this is certainly a mistake. Luther's *Hofmeister* is much nearer the mark. A key would not be an appropriate symbol of a priestly office. In possessing "the key of the house of David," Eliakim had control over the house of David. Therefore in this passage Christ claims the control of that of which the house of David was a type. He is Regent in the kingdom of God. He that openeth, and none shall shut, and

shutteth, and none openeth. The various readings here are numerous, but not of much moment: "shall shut" is much better attested than "shutteth" in the first half. "The keys of the kingdom of heaven" (Matt. xvi. 19) are not to be confounded with "the key of knowledge" (Luke xi. 52). They belong to Christ, but have been committed to his Church, but not unreservedly. "He still retains the highest administration in his own hands" (Trench): and if the Church errs in binding or loosing, he cancels the judgment. The Church may open where Christ will shut, and shut where Christ will open. He alone openeth so that none shall shut, and shutteth so that none can open.

Ver. 8.—I know thy works. Once more Christ's judgment is based upon intimate personal knowledge. A question arises whether the next sentence, introduced by "behold," should be parenthetical or not. It is possible, as in the Authorized Version and previous English versions, and also in the Vulgate, to avoid what is certainly an awkward parenthesis. On the other hand, it seems clear that in ver. 1 and ver. 15 ὅτι depends upon οἶδα, "I know thy works, *that* thou," and does not introduce a fresh sentence; "I know thy works: *for* thou." Then must not ὅτι depend upon οἶδα here? But either arrangement makes good sense, and perhaps the omission of the parenthesis makes the best sense: "*Because* thou hast little power, and hast made a good use of that little, I have given thee an opportunity of which none shall deprive thee." This seems to be the obvious meaning of the "opened door," in accordance with 1 Cor. xvi. 9; 2 Cor. ii. 12; Acts xiv. 27; Col. iv. 3. The Philadelphian Church, in spite of its small advantages, whether in numbers or prosperity, kept Christ's word when called upon to deny him; and for this it shall ever have the privilege of giving others an entrance into Christ's fold. The aorists, ἐτήρησας and ἠρνήσω, appear to point to some definite occasion. On "keep my word," see notes on ch. i. 3 and ii. 26. The antithetic parallelism, "didst keep and didst not deny," is thoroughly in St. John's style, and is one of many instances of the Hebrew cast of his language (comp. ch. ii. 13; John i. 3, 20; iii. 16; x. 5, 18, etc.; 1 John i. 5, 6; ii. 4, 10, 11, 27, 28). The ungrammatical repetition involved in ἣν οὐδεὶς δύναται κλεῖσαι αὐτήν recurs in ch. vii. 2; xiii. 12; xx. 8. Such frequent solecisms argue imperfect grasp of the language (comp. Mark vii. 25; Acts xv. 17).

Ver. 9.—Behold I give of the synagogue of Satan. The true reading seems to be neither δίδωμι nor δέδωκα, but διδῶ, from the form διδόω, which is fairly common in classical Greek. The construction, ἐκ τῆς συναγωγῆs, the partitive genitive used as subject or object of a verb, is frequent in St. John's writings (John i. 24; vii. 40; xvi. 17; 2 John 4; comp. John vi. 39; xxi. 10). The Church of Smyrna was encouraged with a promise that their Jewish opponents should not be victorious over them. The Philadelphian Christians are told that they shall be victorious over their Jewish opponents. As before (ch. ii. 9), those who "say they are Jews, and they are not." are Jews who refuse to believe in the Messiah and reject the Gospel. The only true Jews are those who accept the Christ. They are not, but do lie. Antithetic parallelism, as in ver. 8 and ch. ii. 13. I will make them to come and worship at thy feet. This would be fulfilled when the destruction of Jerusalem drove large numbers of Jews into Asia Minor. Every city which had previously had a Jewish colony would then receive a great influx of refugees. This augmented Jewish settlement at Philadelphia was to furnish some converts to the Christian Church; but, as we learn from the epistles of Ignatius, these converts tainted the Church with a stubborn form of Judaistic error. Hence the need of the warning in ver. 11. Compare "The sons also of them that afflicted thee shall come bending unto thee; and all they that despised thee shall bow themselves down at the soles of thy feet" (Isa. lx. 14; xlix. 23). Know that I have loved thee. The "I" is emphatic: "I will cause them to recognize that in this you received a blessing manifestly Divine."

Ver. 10.—Because thou didst keep (see notes on ch. i. 3 and ii. 26) the word of my patience, I also will keep thee. This is the Divine *lex talionis.* "Forgive, and ye shall be forgiven; give, and it shall be given unto you" (Luke vi. 37, 38); keep, and ye shall be kept. Compare "I know mine own, and mine own know me" (John x. 14). "The word of my patience" may mean either the gospel, which everywhere teaches patience, or those sayings of Christ in which he specially inculcates this duty (Luke viii. 15; xxi. 19; Matt. x. 22; xxiv. 13). In "I also will keep thee" the two pronouns are in emphatic contrast. From the hour of temptation. The phrase, τηρεῖν ἐκ, occurs elsewhere in the New Testament only in John xvii. 15 (comp. Jas. i. 27, where we have τηρεῖν ἀπό, and 2 Thess. iii. 3, φυλάσσειν ἀπό). It is not certain that the common explanation, that ἀπό implies exemption from trial, while ἐκ implies preservation under trial, holds good. "Temptation" (πειρασμός) generally has no article in the New Testament (Matt. vi. 13; xxvi. 41; Mark xiv. 38, etc.; comp. especially Luke viii. 13). Here it has the article, as if "the temptation" were to be of no ordinary kind.

The word does not occur elsewhere in St. John's writings. In order to bring substantive and verb into harmony, the Revised Version renders πειρασμός "trial," the word for "to try" being πειράσαι. "World" here is not the κόσμος, "the ordered universe" (ch. xi. 15; xiii. 8; xvii. 8), but the οἰκουμένη, "the inhabited earth" (ch. xii. 9; xvi. 14). The phrase, "to dwell upon the earth," κατοικεῖν ἐπὶ τῆς γῆς, is peculiar to the Apocalypse (ch. vi. 10; viii. 13; xi. 10; xiii. 8, 14). "The hour of trial" seems to be that which Christ had foretold should precede his coming, especially the triumph of antichrist. Hence the declaration in the next verse.

Ver. 11.—I come quickly. Contrast ἔρχομαι σοι (ch. ii. 5. 16), which is a *threat,* with ἔρχομαι πρὸς ὑμᾶς (John xiv. 28; comp. ch. xvi. 7; xvii. 11, 13) and ἔρχομαι used absolutely (ch. iii. 11; xxii. 7, 11, 20), which is a *promise.* Here the declaration is one of encouragement to the Church—her trial will be short; her reward is near at hand (see notes on ch. i. 1). Hold fast. The same verb (κρατεῖν with the accusative) as in ch. ii. 1, 13, 14, 15, 25. The epistle of Ignatius shows that this warning was needed. Owing to the stubborn Judaism of some in the Philadelphian Church, the central truths of the gospel were in danger. Take thy crown. Not merely "take away" (ἄρῃ) from thee (1 John iii. 5), but "receive" (λάβῃ) for himself (Matt. v. 40). Such seems the natural, though perhaps not the necessary, meaning of the word, and so Jerome renders it *accipiat,* not *auferat.* Thus Jacob received Esau's crown, and Matthias Judas's, and the Gentiles that of the Jews. But the matter is not of much moment; the prominent thought is the loss to the loser, not the gain to any one else.

Ver. 12.—Him that overcometh will I make a pillar. (For construction, ὁ νικῶν, ποιήσω αὐτὸν, see on ch. ii. 26.) The "overcoming" is a present continuous process, but will have a termination, and then he who has faithfully fought the daily battle will be made *a pillar,* steadfast, immovable. St. John may be alluding to (1) the two pillars of Solomon's temple set up in the porch, and called *Jachin* (יָכִין, he will establish) and *Boaz* (בֹּעַז, in him is strength); see 1 Kings vii. 15, 21 and 2 Chron. iii. 17. Both names signify steadfastness and permanence, and would serve to render emphatic the superiority in these respects of the reward to come when compared with the evanescent nature of present suffering. *A pillar* is constantly used as a figure of strength and durability (see Jer. i. 18; Gal. ii. 9). (2) A contrast may be intended between the immovableness of the Christian's future position and the liability of pillars in the Philadelphian temples to succumb to the effects of the frequent earthquakes which took place there (see on ver. 7). Such pillars, moreover, were frequently sculptured in human shape. (3) Matthew Henry suggests that a reference may be intended to monumental pillars bearing inscriptions; the signification being "a monumental pillar of the free and powerful grace of God, never to be defaced or removed; not a support—heaven needing no such props." But it seems much more likely that St. John is alluding to the Hebrew temple. In the temple. The *temple* is ναὸς, the shrine, the dwelling-place of God, not ἱερὸν, the whole extent of the sacred buildings. The latter word occurs often in St. John's Gospel, but never in the Apocalypse. The *temple* in the Revelation is the abode of God, the sacred shrine into which all may be privileged to enter, both in this world and in the world to come. Of my God (see note on ch. iii. 2; ii. 7). And he shall go no more out. "And out of it he shall in no wise go out more:" such is the full force of the Greek. The conqueror's period of probation will be over, and he shall be for ever free from the possibility of falling away. Trench quotes St. Augustine: "Quis non desideret illam civitatem, unde amicus non exit, quo inimicus non intrat?" And I will write upon him the name of my God (cf. ch. xxii. 4, "His name shall be in their foreheads;" and ch. ix. 4, "Those which have not the seal of God in their foreheads;" the former passage referring to the elect in heaven, the latter distinguishing Christians on earth from their heathen oppressors). In the passage under consideration the action is future; it does not refer to holy baptism, but to the sealing of the faithful upon their entrance into glory—a sealing which shall settle for ever, and make all things sure. "To write the name upon" anything is a common figurative expression in Hebrew to denote taking absolute possession of, and making completely one's own. Thus Joab fears that Rabbah may be called after his name, *i.e.* looked upon as his, if David should be absent at the capture of it (2 Sam. xii. 28; cf. also Numb. vi. 27). The struggling Christian is encouraged by hearing that a time will come when he will without any doubt become God's own, incapable of being removed or claimed by other. In the rabbinical book, 'Bava Bathra,' 75. 2, it is noted that there are three applications of the name of God: (1) to the just (Isa. xliii. 7); (2) to the Messiah (Jer. xxiii. 6); (3) to Jerusalem (Ezek. xlviii. 35). A reference may be intended to the frontlet of the high priest, upon which was inscribed, "Holiness to the Lord" (Exod. xxviii. 36). The inscription

is threefold: (1) the name of God; (2) the name of the new Jerusalem; (3) the name of Christ. For God was the Christian maintaining his warfare; to the Church, the new Jerusalem, was he rendering this service; under Christ, as Captain, was the fight being accomplished. Again, the victorious Christian was (1) to belong completely to God; (2) to possess the citizenship of the new Jerusalem; (3) to enter into the glory of Christ, which was the *new* name, that which he knew not yet. We can here trace an analogy to the baptismal formula. (1) The name of God the Father, whose we are made; (2) God the Holy Ghost, whose indwelling guides and sustains his Church, the new Jerusalem; (3) God the Son, by whose Name we shall enter glory. And the name of the city of my God, which is new Jerusalem; rather, *the city . . . new Jerusalem* (see Revised Version). In Ezek. xlviii. 35 the name given to the city Jerusalem is Jehovah Shammah, "the Lord is there;" and in Jer. xxxiii. 16 Jehovah Tsidkenu, "the Lord our Righteousness." Either of these *may* be meant; but, as Alford points out, the holy name itself has already been inscribed. In any case, the victorious one is to be openly acknowledged a citizen of the new Jerusalem. The old Jerusalem was destroyed, and her citizens scattered; but a new Jerusalem, of which the true Israelites are the citizens, should reunite the faithful. It is noticeable that without exception, throughout the Revelation, St. John uses the Hebraic form of the name Ἱερουσαλήμ, while in the Gospel Ἱεροσόλυμα always occurs. He almost seems to distinguish thus between the earthly Jerusalem and the heavenly—the home of the true Israel. Which cometh down out of heaven from my God. "Which cometh down" (ἡ καταβαίνουσα), a grammatical anomaly (cf. ver. 11; ch. ii. 20 and iii. 12). The name "new Jerusalem" is always coupled in the Revelation with the phrase, "coming down from heaven" (see ch. xxi. 2, 10). The spirituality and holiness of the Church is thus set forth, since its being is wholly due to God, in its creation and sustenance. And I will write upon him my new name; *and mine own new name* (Revised Version). This is not any of the names given in the Revelation, but that referred to in ch. xix. 12, ὃ οὐδεὶς οἶδεν εἰ μὴ αὐτός, which no one knew except himself. The passage is a promise that when Christ makes us completely his own by writing his own new name on us, he will admit us into his full glory, which is at present incomprehensible to us. Such comprehension is one of the things "which shall be hereafter" (ch. i. 19), and which cannot now be known to us, "for now we see through a glass, darkly; but then face to face: now I know in part; but then shall I know even as also I am known" (1 Cor. xiii. 12).

Ver. 13.—He that hath an ear, let him hear what the Spirit saith unto the Churches (see on ch. ii. 7). Of the condition of the Church in Philadelphia we know nothing from Holy Writ, except what is contained in the passage before us. But its comparative immunity from trouble and destruction, and its continued existence to the present day (see on vers. 7—13, "Philadelphia"), render it probable that the message of the apostle was not without some effect. Thus Gibbon writes: "In the loss of Ephesus the Christians deplored the fall of the first angel, the extinction of the first candlestick, of the Revelation; the desolation is complete; and the Temple of Diana or the Church of Mary will equally elude the search of the curious traveller. The circus and three stately theatres of Laodicea are now peopled with wolves and foxes; Sardis is reduced to a miserable village; the God of Mahomet, without a rival or a Son, is invoked in the mosques of Thyatira and Pergamos, and the populousness of Smyrna is supported by the foreign trade of the Franks and Armenians. Philadelphia alone has been saved by prophecy or courage" ('Decline and Fall,' c). 64.

Vers. 14—22.—*The epistle to the Church in Laodicea.* Laodicea, on the Lycus, a tributary of the Mæander, lay some fifty miles to the south-east of Philadelphia. The modern Turkish name, *Eskihissar*, signifies "the old castle." It is situated on the western side of the valley of the Lycus, on the opposite slopes of which, some six or eight miles distant, were Hierapolis and Colossæ, with which it is associated by St. Paul (Col. iv. 13, 16). Named at first Diospolis, after its tutelary deity, Zeus, it subsequently became Rhoas, and finally received its name from Antiochus II., in honour of his wife, Laodice. There were several other cities of the same name, from which it was distinguished by the addition of the words, "on the Lycus." It was a wealthy city, its trade consisting chiefly in the preparation of woollen materials. It was advantageously situated, too, on the high road leading from Ephesus into the interior. Though, in common with the other cities of Asia Minor, visited by earthquakes, it quickly recovered; and it was the proud boast of the Laodiceans that, unlike Ephesus

and Sardis, they required no extraneous assistance to enable them to regain their former prosperity. This fact undoubtedly explains the temptations to which the Laodiceans were liable, and the reference in ver. 16 to those who were neither cold nor hot, and that in ver. 17 to those who said they were rich and had need of nothing (see on vers. 16, 17). The Christian Church there may have been founded by Epaphras, through whom St. Paul probably learned of the existence of false doctrine there (Col. ii. 4, 8 and i. 8), for the Epistle to the Colossians seems to be equally addressed to the Laodiceans (Col. iv. 16). The importance of this Church continued for some time, the celebrated Council of Laodicea being held there in A.D. 361, and a century later its bishop held a prominent position (Labbe, iv. p. 82, etc.). But its influence gradually waned, and the Turks pressed hardly upon it; so that at the present time it is little more than a heap of ruins. The warnings of the Apostles SS. Paul and John, if heeded at all for a time, were forgotten, and her candlestick was removed.

Ver. 14.—And unto the angel. Those expositors who understand "the angel" of a Church to signify its chief officer, may with some plausibility argue that at Laodicea it seems almost certain that this was Archippus. In his Epistle to Philemon, a wealthy convert of Colossæ, St. Paul sends greeting to Archippus (Philem. 2). If Archippus were the son of Philemon, he might very well have been Bishop of Laodicea at the time of St. John's message. Moreover, the son of a wealthy and influential Christian, though likely to have been selected as bishop in the neighbouring Church, may have lacked the zeal necessary for the thorough performance of his work; and would thus incur the marked rebuke of St. Paul, "Say to Archippus, Take heed to the ministry which thou hast received in the Lord, that thou fulfil it" (Col. iv. 17), which appears immediately after the mention of the Laodicean Church. The Apostolical Constitutions also assert that Archippus was first Bishop of Laodicea. Of the Church of the Laodiceans write; or, *of the Church in Laodicea* (τῆς ἐν Λαοδικείᾳ ἐκκλησίας) These things saith the Amen. The word "Amen" is here used as a proper name of our Lord; and this is the only instance of such an application. It signifies the "True One." It is a word much used in St. John's Gospel, where it appears repeated at the commencement of many discourses, "Verily, verily." In Isa. lxv. 16 "the God of Amen" (אמן) is rendered in the LXX. by ἀληθινός; in the Authorized Version by "truth" (cf. the use of the English "very" as an adjective—"the *very* one," *i.e.* the *real* or *true* one). The term is peculiarly well adapted to our Lord (who is the *Truth*, John xiv. 6), not only as a general name or title, but especially in connexion with this solemn announcement to the Laodiceans. There was great need of the truth being openly proclaimed by him who is the Truth to those who, though nominally Christians, were ensnared by the *deceitfulness of riches* (Matt. xiii. 22), and were deceiving themselves in the attempt to make the best of both worlds by their lukewarm Christianity. It was the purpose of this epistle to draw aside the veil which was hiding the truth from their eyes, and to bring them to a realization of that most difficult of all knowledge—a knowledge of self. The faithful and true Witness—an amplification of "the Amen." The epithet "faithful" asserts the truthfulness of Christ's work as a Witness; "true" (ἀληθινός) signifies "real and complete." He is a *faithful* Witness because his witness is true; and he is a *true* Witness because in him is the complete realization of all the qualifications which constitute any one really and truly a witness. "Faithful" (πιστός) has the passive meaning of "that which is worthy of faith," not the active meaning of "he who believes something." Trench well points out that God can only be *faithful* in the former sense; man may be *faithful* in both senses. Christ was a Witness worthy of faith, since he possessed all the attributes of such a witness. He (1) had seen what he attested; (2) was competent to relate and reproduce this information; (3) was willing to do this faithfully and truly. The Beginning of the creation of God. There are two ways in which these words might be understood: (1) that in which "beginning" is taken in a passive sense, and which would therefore make Christ the first created thing of all the things which God created; (2) the active sense, by which Christ is described as the Beginner, the Author, Moving Principle or Source of all the things which God created. That the latter meaning is the true one is plain from the whole tenor of Holy Scripture. The Arians, attempting to disprove the Divinity of our Lord, quoted this passage, attributing to it the former sense. But ἀρχή is often used actively, and may well be so used here—a view which is confirmed by the abundant evidence of our Lord's Divinity found elsewhere in the Bible, and nowhere more plainly asserted than in the writings of St. John. The self-

reliant Laodiceans are thus directed to place their trust in him who is the Source of all things, rather than in those created things of which he is the Creator.

Ver. 15.—I know thy works; and because they are not what they should be (vers. 16, 17), I give thee this admonition, which is nevertheless a warning and a token of my love (ver. 19). That thou art neither cold nor hot: I would thou wert cold or hot. The lukewarmness of which the Epistle complains was produced by a fallacious sense of security, begotten of ease and prosperity. In truth those "secure," without care, had become the careless ones. Active opposition may well be a less deadly evil than careless ease. The persecution of a St. Paul may be diverted into the zeal of an apostle; but how can any active good be got from that which is utterly stagnant and without motive power? The man who, by wilful action, increases a disease, may repent of his deed, and try to recover from the danger to which he has exposed himself; but he who lives on in careless ignorance of the existence of the malady can never improve himself until he has awoke to a full knowledge of his own state. Some understand "cold" to mean "untouched by the power of grace," and "lukewarm" to denote those who, having received the grace of God, had not allowed it full scope in bringing forth works meet for repentance (Matt. iii. 8) And just as there was more hope of the real conversion of the "cold" publicans and harlots, who "went into heaven" (Matt. xxi. 31) before the self-satisfied, "lukewarm" Pharisees, so there is more hope of an unconverted sinner than of him who, having once been roused to a sense of God's will, has relapsed into a state of self-satisfied indolence and carelessness. The sentence is *not* a wish that the Laodiceans should become hot or cold; it is a regret that they had not been one or the other. Our Lord is not wishing that any of them may become cold, but regretting that, when he comes to review their conduct and to pronounce judgment, many of them cannot even plead that they "knew not the way of righteousness," but belong to that worse class, "which after they had known it, turned from the holy commandment delivered unto them (2 Pet. ii. 21; see also John ix. 41).

Ver. 16.—So then because thou art lukewarm, and neither cold nor hot, I will spue thee out of my mouth. The distaste and nausea produced by lukewarm food, which the stomach naturally rejects with loathing, are used as a figure in which to express the abhorrence of Christ for those who lacked zeal in his service (cf. Lev. xviii. 28 and xx. 22, "That the land spue not you out also")

But the sentence is not irrevocable; there
is still hope of averting it: Μέλλω σε ἐμέσαι,
" I am about to spue thee," *i.e.* if a timely
repentance does not avert the impending
doom. (Contrast the absoluteness of the
future in ch. ii. 5, etc., ἔρχομαί σοι ταχὺ καὶ
κινήσω.)

Ver. 17.—Because thou sayest, I am rich,
and increased with goods, and have need of
nothing. The Epistle is still addressed
indirectly to the Laodicean Church, directly
to the angel. No doubt spiritual riches are
immediately referred to; but spiritual pride
and lukewarmness are frequently produced
by worldly prosperity, such as that which
Archippus (if he be the angel addressed;
see on ver. 14) and the Church over which
he presided enjoyed. It is not enough for
the wealthy Christian to contribute a portion
of his wealth, and then to consider his task
done and his reward sure. Greater zeal
than this is requisite before he can deem
his duty discharged. Moreover, the greater
the zeal that exists, the less will be the
inclination to rely upon what has been
accomplished, or to think it sufficient; for
when all has been done we are still to call
ourselves unprofitable servants (Luke xvii.
10; cf. Hos. xii. 8, " I am become rich, I have
found me out substance: in all my labours
they shall find none iniquity in me that
were sin "). And knowest not that thou art
wretched, and miserable, and poor, and
blind, and naked; *and knowest not that thou,
even thou thyself, art the wretched one*. The
self-satisfied spiritual pride of the Pharisee
caused him to regard with complacent pity
the condition of the publican. But he was
mistaken; he himself was *the wretched one*,
who was to be pitied. So with the Laodicean
Church. How different the conduct of St.
Paul, who recognized his own wretchedness
(Rom. vii. 24, where the same word ταλαίπωρος is used)! The following words are
adjectives. These Christians, in their
spiritual pride, were *miserable*—deserving
of pity; *poor* in the wealth accumulated by
zeal in God's service; *blind* as to their real
condition and their fancied spiritual safety;
and *naked* of the cloak with which charity—
fervent love of God—would have covered
them.

Ver. 18.—I counsel thee to buy of me
gold tried in the fire, that thou mayest be
rich; *gold refined by the fire* (Revised Version). It is doubtful whether ver. 17
should be connected with ver. 18 or with
ver. 16—whether the self-satisfied condition
of the Church is given as the reason why
"I will spue thee out of my mouth," or as
the reason why "I counsel thee to buy of
me." The Revised Version follows the
Authorized Version in connecting vers. 17
and 18; and this view is supported by

Alford, Bengel, Düsterdieck, Ebrard. But
Trench prefers the other view. The Authorized Version seems correct, for the reason
why "I will spue thee" is given in ver. 16,
and another separate reason would probably
(though not certainly) not be added. Though
St. Paul (Col. ii. 3) had pointed out to the
Laodiceans (see on the epistle generally,
vers. 14—22; and cf. Col. iv. 16) where "are
hid all the treasures of wisdom and knowledge," they had not heeded the lesson, and
now Christ once more counsels them to
obtain true riches from the proper source.
They are to buy *from me;* the emphasis
being laid on *me*, in contradistinction to
their trust in themselves. They are *poor*
(ver. 17), and must therefore obtain *gold
refined by the fire*—gold superior to that on
the possession of which they so prided
themselves, that they may indeed *be rich*.
To buy this gold by giving something of
equal value in exchange, they were truly
unable. Yet it was to be bought, and would
entail the sacrifice of something which,
though perhaps dear to them, would be
nothing in comparison with the return they
would obtain. Note the Revised Version
rendering *may become rich*, repeating and
enforcing the fact of their present destitution. And white raiment, that thou mayest
be clothed. Laodicea is said to have been
famous for the raven blackness of the wool
which was prepared and dyed there. This,
perhaps, explains the point of the reproof
contained in these words. " Notwithstanding thy trust in the excellence of the apparel
for which thou art famous, thou art yet
naked (ver. 17), and needest clothing; that
clothing can be obtained only from me, and
is far superior to that of which thou boastest,
since it is *white*, the emblem of all that is
purest and best; not black, like your own,
which is a type of darkness, the darkness
of ignorance and sin. Mine is indeed the
garment of righteousness, the marriage-
garment with which thou mayest enter the
presence of thy King." And that the shame
of thy nakedness do not appear. The
nakedness will certainly be made apparent
at some time. If it be persistently overlooked or ignored now, it will be made more
glaring in the future, when God turns upon
it the brightness of his presence. In the
Revised Version "appear" is even more
emphatically rendered "be made manifest"
(φανερωθῇ). "Stripping," in the Bible, is
commonly used to denote putting to shame:
Hanun cut off the garments of David's
servants (2 Sam. x. 4); the King of Assyria
was to lead away the Egyptians naked and
barefoot (Isa. xx. 4; see also ch. xvi. 15);
while supplying with clothes, or an additional quantity of clothes, was intended
to show honour: thus Pharaoh arrayed

Joseph in vestures of fine linen (Gen. xli. 42); Joseph gave Benjamin five changes of raiment (Gen. xlv. 22; see also Esth. vi. 9; Ezek. xvi. 10; Dan. v. 29; Zech. iii. 4; Luke xv. 22). And anoint thine eyes with eyesalve, that thou mayest see. This is, of course, a reference to the "blindness" of ver. 17, of which the Laodiceans were ignorant. "Eyesalve" is κολλούριον—colly-rium, perhaps so called because made up in the shape of a cake of bread—collyra. We cannot but think, in connexion with this passage, of the miracle of the healing of the blind man by the anointing of his eyes by our Lord—a miracle witnessed and related by St. John (John ix.). The subsequent incidents and discourse, too, forcibly illustrate the state of the Laodiceans, so much like that of the Pharisees, to whom were addressed the words, "If ye were blind, ye should have no sin; but now ye say, We see; therefore your sin remaineth" (see on ver. 15).

Ver. 19.—As many as I love, I rebuke and chasten: be zealous therefore, and repent. As many as. Not one whom God loves escapes chastening; if he be not chastened, he is not a son (Heb. xii. 8), for "all have sinned, and come short." "I love" is φιλῶ, I love dearly; not merely ἀγαπῶ. I rebuke (ἐλέγχω), to reprove, so as to convict of sin and turn to repentance; the work of the Holy Ghost, who should "convict the world of sin" (John xvi. 8). This verse is a solace and encouragement for the Laodiceans. They were required to make the sacrifices demanded of them, not so much that they might be punished for their transgressions, but to prove themselves the number of God's elect. The stern reproof administered was a pruning, which was an evidence of God's loving care for them; the final sentence, "Cut it down," had not yet gone forth. But though thus intended for encouragement rather than condemnation, yet it could not but contain implied reproach, however tender. No one can be exhorted to change his path and to seek that which is holy without being reminded that he is unholy and has wandered from the right way. Those in Laodicea who took this message to heart must needs think of their unchastened life—the life full of prosperity and self-satisfied security, into which so little zeal had been infused, in which so little need for repentance had been felt. The Church, indeed, needed some of that chastening, that persecution, and hardship, which should arouse her from the perilous slumber of ease into which she had fallen, and call forth some zeal and self-sacrifice, the frequent and natural result of opposition.

Ver. 20.—Behold, I stand at the door, and knock; behold, I have stood (ἔστηκα) at the door, and am knocking (κρούω). "These gracious words declare the long-suffering of Christ, as he waits for the conversion of sinners (1 Pet. iii. 20); and not alone the long-suffering which waits, but the love which seeks to bring that conversion about, which 'knocks.' He at whose door we ought to stand, for he is the Door (John x. 7), who, as such, has bidden us to knock (Matt. vii. 7; Luke xi. 9), is content that the whole relation between him and us should be reversed, and instead of our standing at his door, condescends himself to stand at ours" (Trench). The view, that stand at the door signifies "to come quickly" (Düsterdieck), as in ch. ii. 5, 16; iii. 3, 11, is scarcely in accordance with the context, since the whole passage has changed from rebuke and menace to patient beseeching and loving exhortation. These words recall the frequent use by our Lord of this figure of knocking, and especially Luke xii. 35, 36, "Let your loins be girded about, and your lights burning; and ye yourselves like unto men that wait for their lord, when he will return from the wedding; that when he cometh and knocketh, they may open unto him immediately." If any man hear my voice, and open the door, I will come in to him, and will sup with him, and he with me (see the parallel passage in Cant. v.). Christ knocks and speaks. A distinction has been drawn in the work of conversion, corresponding to these two actions. The knocking is likened to the more outward calls of sickness, trouble, etc., by which he makes his presence known; while the voice, which interprets the knock and informs us of the Personality of him who knocks, is the voice of the Holy Spirit, speaking to us, and explaining the meaning of our trials. Man's free will is here well and plainly set forth. Though the opening, to be effective, needs the help and presence of Christ, yet he does not forcibly effect an entrance; it is still within the power of man to disregard the knock, to refuse to hear the voice, to keep the door fast shut. To take food with any one is an outward sign of brotherly love and reconciliation. Christ will sup with those who do not drive him away, and they will sup with him. The whole figure is an image of the perfect nature of the sinner's reconciliation with God, and of the wonderful goodness and condescension of Christ. But we may well see an allusion to the Holy Communion, by which we are reconciled to God through Christ, and by which we may even now have a foretaste of the final supper of the Lamb, which shall eventually last for ever.

Ver. 21.—To him that overcometh will I grant to sit with me in my throne, even as I also overcame, and am set down with my Father in his throne. The climax of the promises made to the seven Churches (cf. ch. ii. 7, 11, 17, 26—28; iii. 5, 12). There are two points to be noticed in this promise: (1) the position promised to the conqueror, "in my throne;" (2) the two thrones mentioned. (1) Note the expression, "*in* my throne" (not ἐπὶ, but ἐν τῷ θρόνῳ), which occurs nowhere else. The mother of St. James and St. John had requested for them a place on the right hand and the left of our Lord—the highest dignity which she could conceive. The twelve apostles are promised to sit on twelve thrones, to judge the tribes of Israel. But Christ offers a yet higher honour, viz. to sit in his throne; placing us in the closest relationship with himself, and exalting us to his own glory. (2) The throne promised is not that which Christ now occupies with his Father, but his own. Christ is now sitting on his Father's throne, mediating for his Church on earth, and waiting till his enemies be made his footstool (Ps. cx. 1). To that throne there is no admission for humanity, though Christ shares it in virtue of his Godhead. But when his enemies have been made his footstool, and death, the last enemy, is destroyed (1 Cor. xv. 26), and the necessity for his mediation exists no longer, since the Church militant will have become the Church triumphant, then will be erected Christ's own throne, which glorified man may share in common with him who was man, and who has so exalted humanity as to render such a condition and such a position possible.

Ver. 22.—He that hath an ear, let him hear what the Spirit saith unto the Churches. The seven messages were not merely separate admonitions addressed only to each particular Church, but all the epistles were meant for all the seven Churches, and, after them, for the universal Church. Each Church had an especial failing brought more emphatically before it; but still the seven warnings are one whole, for the edification of all. As it behoves the individual Christian to avoid and repent of all sin, and yet to fix his attention on the cure of some besetting sin to which he is peculiarly liable, so these messages, though intended to be read by all, and heeded by all, place vividly before each Church its besetting sin, which more particularly requires attention. And as the sins to be avoided are to be avoided by all, so the separate rewards are promised to all who overcome. They are, therefore, not really distinct rewards, but rather different phases and views of one great whole, which shall be enjoyed in its entirety by those who have struggled victoriously with the trials and temptations of the world.

HOMILETICS.

Vers. 1—6.—*Sardis; or, the dead Church.* This epistle presents no exception to the general rule which we have pointed out regarding all the seven, viz. that our Lord Jesus Christ presents himself to each Church in that special aspect in which it was most appropriate for that Church to regard him. Here he is spoken of as " he that hath the seven Spirits of God "—a phrase used only in the Apocalypse, and yet, in its meaning, harmonious with all the rest of God's Word. This leads us at once to observe—

I. HERE IS A VERY REMARKABLE EXPRESSION TO DENOTE THE DIVINE ENERGY. It is one which shows the infinitude thereof in the Third Person in the Trinity. The number seven is repeatedly used here. It is the symbol of perfection and completeness. We have seven Churches, seven seals, seven thunders, seven vials, seven plagues, seven trumpets. The expression, "the seven Spirits of God," is found in ch. i. 4 and v. 6, as well as in this passage. There is an invariable sequence in the coming of life or power from the Persons in the Trinity, and a corresponding one in the upgoing of devotion from us to the Father, the Son, and the Holy Ghost. Blessings are *from* the Father, *through* the Son, *by* the Spirit. Our access is *by* the Spirit, *through* the Son, *to* the Father. The Energizer in each case is the Holy Ghost. His energy is infinite, both in variety and measure. It is absolutely full, complete, and boundless. If, however, this energy is infinite, it can reveal itself. It has done so. For observe—

II. HERE IS AN EQUALLY REMARKABLE EXPRESSION CONCERNING OUR LORD JESUS CHRIST. We are here bidden to think of him as *having* the seven Spirits of God. Having risen to heaven, "he received gifts for men, that the Lord God might dwell among them." As Mediator, he has received of the Father the promise of the Holy Ghost. He is, in his own glorious Person, the channel of all grace from God to the spirit of man. He has, *i.e. holds*, the seven Spirits of God. He is not only the Lamb of God, which taketh away the sin of the world, but he also baptizeth with the Holy Ghost.

The two are of equal importance. Without the one the other would be impossible. The atoning work was completed on earth; the baptizing work is ever being carried on in heaven. The Gospels record the one; the Acts and the Epistles recount and expound the other. His work of humiliation on earth laid the basis of pardon. His baptizing work as our exalted Redeemer is the secret of power. He has "the seven Spirits of God" ("for the Father giveth not the Spirit by measure unto him "), that he may ever give life and power to those who with open hearts long for "all the fulness of God." Note: The coming together of the Spirit of God and the spirit of man is the secret of inspiration, revelation, religion, regeneration, consecration.[1] When the Spirit of God unveils a truth, there is revelation; when he inbreathes into a man, there is inspiration; when he renews, quickens, and inspires, there is religion, even regeneration and consecration. The Holy Ghost may either illume the mind with truth, or set it on fire with love. And when his power is exerted in all its sevenfold might, any one so charged with Divine energy may receive it in any form whatever, for the purpose of fulfilling any kind of life-work which God may have for him to do. There is no limit to our possible equipment for service.

III. THIS IS THE SPECIAL ASPECT OF OUR LORD'S WORK AT WHICH A DEAD CHURCH NEEDS TO LOOK. The Church at Sardis was "dead." It had not always been so. At one time it had so much vitality that it had acquired a "name" for being full of quick and quickening force. And, among men, its name still stood. But he whose eyes are as a flame of fire, and who walks among the golden candlesticks, observed a decline in piety. There was as yet the same outside appearance, and yet it was already injured even unto death. We do not read of any opposition or tribulation of any kind that the Church at Sardis had to meet;—it was *dead*. And neither Satan nor any of his hosts will care to disturb either a dead Church or a dead pastor. Nothing would better please the powers of evil than to see such a Church falling to pieces because there was no spirit to keep the bodily framework together! It is no wonder to find such a Church's works defective. "I have not found thy works filled up before God." Either there were spheres of duty which were altogether neglected, or else those duties were discharged in a spirit grievously lacking in fervour. It is sad indeed when the Lord Jesus sees any Church to be dead! For observe: 1. *It is incongruous.* For what is the Church? It is, in theory at least, a company of men "alive unto God," bound together for his worship and work. In the world, indeed, death is what we expect to see; but in the Church—— Death here is fearfully out of place. Nor let us think of Sardis as the only city where a dead Church was to be found. There is very much even now that makes many a pastor sigh and cry, "Oh the death!" Such lethargy, inertness, and slumber steal over this Church and that, so that it is far easier even to move the world than such a Church as this. Surely this is fearfully incongruous for a Church to be so untrue to its name. 2. *This death is needless.* For he who hath the seven Spirits of God is Lord of his Church. He loves to enrich her with the fulness of life. He is ever ready to hear the prayers of his own. The gift of the Spirit is the one promise of his Word, and its bestowment the one purpose of his life. It has but to be received from him by faith. Then why should any Church be lagging and flagging? There is no occasion for it whatever. 3. *This death is unnatural.* For it shows that, in spite of the profession of the Church, many in it are holding on to the world. They put on a Christian uniform, and then fight on the world's side. One of the terrible punishments of olden time was for living men to be chained to a corpse. Not less terribly unnatural is it for the name and honour of a living Saviour to be in any way tied to a dead Church! 4. *This death is dishonouring to the Lord Jesus.* By dead professors Christ is wounded in the house of his friends. For many a young convert, coming to the Church as the home of a spiritual brotherhood, gets there his first chill of disappointment. And if we were asked—Who are most responsible for the scepticism of the age? we should reply—Dead professors! 5. *This death is offensive to the eye.* Spiritual death anywhere is offensive. But, in the Church, which professes to be the very enclosure of life, it is unutterably so. How odious must it be to the Lord and Giver of life to see his own Name and ordinances yoked with spiritual death, especially when he lives and reigns on purpose to give life! 6. *A dead Church is in a state in which Christ calls aloud for a review of its condition.* There is a fourfold call. (1) Ɓ

[1] Cf. homily by the present writer on Deut. xxxiv. in the 'Pulpit Commentary.'

watchful. Become so. (2) Strengthen what is left. All is not lost. (3) Remember the past—those happy days of receiving the truth. (4) Repent. It is high time, when death has seized on a Church, that its position should be seriously reviewed with the purpose of amendment unto life. Note: (a) The life in Christ is not so at the command of the Church as to warrant its dispensing with all possible care for the maintenance of a continual inflow thereof. (b) The death of a Church is not such a death is that of a corpse. Its responsibilities are not lessened by the fact of its death. 7. *This death is most perilous.* "If therefore," etc. (ver. 3). Thus again we meet with the thought that, if a Church is not doing its Lord's work, it certainly will not be spared for the sake of its own. It will matter nothing in the great gathering-day of eternity whether any particular Church survives or no. Some Churches make much of their freedom. Some make much of their scriptural order. But life is of more importance than either one or the other. And if any Churches cease to be alive, others with really hearty, earnest life will survive them, though they may be less exact in their form and order. Dead Churches will shrink and sink out of sight; and the Lord Jesus will write a branding epitaph on their tomb: "A dead Church, that once had a name to live."

IV. IN A DEAD CHURCH THERE MAY YET BE SOME LIVING SOULS. A Church, as such, may expire in its own shame, yet there may be in it a few living ones. We can see the reason why the living ones are spoken of here as those "who have not defiled their garments;" for in the old Hebrew Law death was defilement. A man who touched a dead body was defiled. In Sardis, though the Church was dead, yet not every member was so. So that it seems there may be, thank God, even in a dead Church, some who, though surrounded with death, never touch it, but live always and everywhere in contact with the Living One, and so "keep themselves unspotted from the world." Note: A man must be in connection with a living Saviour if he would maintain his life. He must not depend on the Church for it!

V. TO LIVING SOULS IN A DEAD CHURCH THE SAVIOUR HAS WORDS OF CHEER. Here is a promise which is, in itself, a cluster of promises; but the promises are not to the Church as a Church, only to individuals—to those who avoid the touch of the dead now, who are daily overcoming, and will finally overcome. 1. Living on Christ now, hereafter they shall walk with him. 2. They shall be clothed in white raiment (see ch. xix. 8). 3. They shall be had in remembrance before God. "I will not blot his name out of the book of life" (cf. Mal. iii. 17; Phil. iv. 3; Luke x. 20; Heb. xii. 23). 4. They shall be avowed as Christ's at last. "I will confess his name" (cf. Luke xii. 8; Matt. xxv. 34—40). How strictly the Lord Jesus individualizes in the treatment of souls! If there are living souls in a dead Church, or dead souls in a living Church, they will be dealt with by him, not according to the state of the Church, but according to their own. "Every one of us must give account of himself to God." As the inner life here was one between Christ and him, so the public acknowledgment of him will be by Christ of him. He will not be confessed "as a member of the Church at Sardis" or anywhere else. In the great decisive day we shall be saved, not as adherents of any name or cause on earth, but only as those who lived on Christ, and drew their life from him, keeping themselves unspotted from the world. Note how solemn the alternative—Alive? or, dead?

Vers. 7—13.—*Philadelphia: the sovereignty of the Lord Jesus over the house of God.* Although we know less of the Church at Philadelphia than of that at Smyrna, yet we think of it with almost equal feelings of affectionate regard. It is one of the two out of seven for which our Lord has no rebuke. He has for it only words of spur and cheer. It is weak, with "little strength." It is trusty. It has kept the faith. It has boldness, for it has "not denied Christ's Name." Demands had been made on its powers of endurance; but it had still kept the word of God's patience. It was vexed by some who boasted that they were Jews, and yet were not. *True* Judaism involved an acceptance of the claims of Jesus. The Church at Philadelphia understood this, and swerved not from its loyalty to the Saviour. Hence there is for it a series of inspiring exhortations and promises, crowned by one of the noblest pledges to the victor over ill. The main stress of our present homily will lie in an answer to the inquiry—In what aspect is such a Church invited to look at and think of the Lord Jesus Christ? The reply to this, with all that is involved thereby, will "open up" that part of this letter which seems chiefly to require elucidation (cf. ver. 7). Our topic is—*The sovereignty of the Lord Jesus over the house of God.* We will inquire—

I. WHAT IS THE HOUSE OF DAVID? Our Lord declares himself as "he that hath the keys of David" (cf. 2 Kings xviii. 18, 26, 37; Isa. xxii. 15—22). Shebna had held the high office of being over the house of David, *i.e.* prefect of the palace (for a similar expression and its meaning, see Gen. xli. 40). Shebna, for his pride, luxury, and tyranny, was deposed, and Eliakim was appointed in his place. Isaiah speaks (xxii. 22) of the authority which would be entrusted to him. The words uttered respecting Eliakim are here quoted and applied to our Lord Jesus Christ, as being over the house of David, and being entrusted with authority there. So that, as that which was said of Eliakim is true in its highest sense of the Lord Jesus, we can see in Eliakim a type of Christ. Eliakim was over the house of David in the earthly sphere; Christ is over the house of David in the spiritual sphere. Still, all is not yet quite clear. For if Eliakim is a type of Christ, as being over the house of David, so also was David himself, over whose house Eliakim was set, a much more striking type of Christ. Are we not hereby involved in some confusion of thought? By no means. The words in Heb. iii. 6 make the whole matter clear : "Christ, as a Son over his own house." So that the Lord Jesus combines in his own Person the antitype of both Eliakim and David. He is the Eliakim who is over the house. He is the David whose is the house. Let us now compare Isa. ix. 6; Matt. xxviii. 18; ch. xxii. 16. We may now go a step further, and say—By as much as Christ is greater than David, by so much is his house greater than the house of David. The administration of the entire kingdom of God is put into his hands—the kingdom of nature, the kingdom of grace, and the kingdom of glory. The first is his as the everlasting Son of the Father; the second is his as the Priest upon his throne; the third will be his till he shall have delivered up the kingdom to God, even the Father, that God may be all in all. Now, the house of David is *that part of Christ's kingdom over which, as Son and Lord of David, he now rules as the Head.* This is Christ's own house. He died that he might acquire it; he lives that he may rule it. It is composed of those on earth who are Israelites indeed, in whom is no guile, and of those gone from earth, who have washed their robes and made them white in the blood of the Lamb. Let us now inquire—

II. WHAT IS THE AUTHORITY OF CHRIST OVER THIS HOUSE? "He that hath the key of David," etc. The "key" is the symbol of authority, the token of possession. The authority of the Lord Jesus is absolute; he "openeth, and no man shutteth; and shutteth, and no man openeth." Regarding the "house" as "the Church of the Lord Jesus Christ," observe: 1. *It is only by Christ that any one is admitted to the house,* i.e. *to the Church.* There is, indeed, an external, visible organization; there is also an inner and invisible realm of saved souls. The latter alone is the Church properly so called; in the former, "They are not all Israel that are of Israel." We cannot expect absolute purity in the most saintly group. There may be some Jonah in every ship, some Achan in every camp, some Judas in every Church. Church rules and regulations as to purity of fellowship are laid down clearly in the Word of God; yet, even at the best, it is but an approximation thereto that we are able to attain. Men may be received into a visible Church by human agency, but into the invisible by Christ alone. The law is not, "In such and such a Church, in Christ;" but, "Whosoever is in Christ is in the Church by a right which none may deny, and which none ought to dispute." 2. *Christ furnishes his members with such gifts and graces as are needed for service in the Church.* (Cf. Eph. iv. 7—13; Rom. xii. 6—8; 1 Cor. xii. 4—11; 1 Pet. iv. 10, 11.) He provides workers for the Church (1 Cor. iii. 10, 22). 3. *Christ opens up the spheres in which his people may do service.* "I have set before thee an open door" (see 2 Cor. ii. 12; 1 Cor. xvi. 9; Acts xvi. 9, 10; xviii. 9—11; xxiii. 11). 4. *Christ regards his servants as responsible to him alone.* (Matt. xxv. 14—30; Rom. xiv. 10—12; 1 Cor. iv. 1—5.) He expects them to be absolutely at his bidding (Luke xiv. 33). He requires fidelity (Luke xvi. 10; 1 Cor. iv. 2; ch. ii. 10). 5. *He appoints the discipline which is to be administered in the Church on earth to its unworthy members.* He has given to the Christian priesthood the power of binding and loosing in his name, and no Church can trifle with this power except at its peril (see 1 Cor. v.; Matt. xvi. 19; xviii. 17—20; 1 Tim. iv. 20; i. 19, 20).[1] 6. *He appoints their reward here and here-*

---

[1] See Canon Tait's admirable work, 'The Messages to the Seven Churches of Asia Minor,'

after. There are four principles on which he will bestow them : they will be proportionate; there will be both grace and equity in their bestowal; they will be granted to every one; and will be love's own recompense of love's acts even in its slightest services (cf. Matt. v. 19; xxv.; xix. 27—xx. 16). 7. *When his servants depart hence he still has the sole charge of them.* He never lets them slip out of his hands (ch. i. 18; Matt. xvi. 18 (Revised Version); Rom. xiv. 8; 1 Thess. v. 10). After death the believer is still "*in Christo.*" 8. *At his manifestation in glory he will manifest his saints too.* (Col. iii. 4.) Then the supreme concern of each will be to be well pleasing to him (2 Cor. v. 9). Thus from beginning to end the authority and control of the Lord Jesus over the house of God is entire and complete.

III. WHAT ARE THE MORAL ATTRIBUTES HERE NAMED, THE POSSESSION OF WHICH FITS OUR LORD FOR AN OFFICE SO SUBLIME. 1. *He that is holy.* The Holy One, separate from evil, with perfect hatred of it. Then he is One who will be very jealous of the honour of his house. Holiness is the law of the house; if it be lacking, judgment will begin at the house of God (cf. Isæ. iv. 3). 2. *He that is true* (ὁ ἀληθινὸς, not ὁ ἀληθής). Not "true" in distinction from being untrue; but (1) the True One, in distinction from false assertors of supremacy; (2) the true, in distinction from the wrong ideal; (3) the true, as perfectly answering to the perfect ideal, as contrasted with all partial and imperfect realizations of it. The perfect embodiment of the True and Living One is he. Where else could the key of David be so well entrusted? Only his hand can safely hold it. Well may we adopt the words of Doddridge—

> " Worthy thy hand to hold the keys,
> Guided by wisdom and by love;
> Worthy to rule o'er mortal life,
> In worlds below and worlds above."

If the key of the house of David had been in less worthy hands, that house would long ago have fallen to pieces. Therefore—

Note : 1. How should we glory in the sway over the house of God being in Christ's hands, and nowhere but there! 2. Let every Church recognize this Headship of Christ alone, and wherever he "opens a door" of usefulness, go in at once. 3. Let every individual submit himself humbly to Christ's disposal, to be in everything and at every step directed and controlled by him. Ever should our prayer be, " Lord, what wouldst thou have me to do?" It is only thus that our life can have before it an intelligible and right end, in which we are sure to succeed. When "for us to live is Christ," then only may we be sure that "in nothing we shall be ashamed." Finally, let us ever remember the responsibility which attaches to us for observing when Christ sets before us an open door. It is quite true that no man can shut it, but it is also true that, if we fail to go in, the door may be closed again, and then no man can open it; but our opportunity, once missed, will have been missed for ever. Churches and men alike that fail to embrace opportunities of greater power and usefulness, have sunk back to a lower position than before; they do, they w they must. Either to grow or to shrink is the alternative before us all. The law applies everywhere : "To him that hath shall more be given; to him that hath not, from him shall be taken away even that which he hath." He that is faithful in the few things is the one whom his Lord will make ruler over the many things, and who will enter into the joy of his Lord.

Vers. 14—29.—*Laodicea : self-conceit and self-deceit.* Here is a Church which has an utterly mistaken view of itself. It thinks itself as well off as need be. Our Lord declares it to be in a desperately bad condition. It is addressed by Christ as by the "faithful and true Witness," as the "Beginning of the creation of God;" not as the beginning in the sense of "the first part of," but in the sense of the Beginner, in whom the creation had its beginning, and still has its continuance, meaning, plan, and end. He, to whom all created being stands open, deigns to give his clear, searching testimony to a self-deceived Church as to its state before him. There are three matters at which we must glance—the Witness, the testimony, the counsels.

pp. 332—385, not only for his remarks on the matter of discipline, but also for his comment on the entire epistle. There is so much that is of great value, that we are disinclined to criticize, even where we do not entirely concur.

I. THE WITNESS. "Faithful," *i.e.* trusty and trustworthy. "True," answering to the ideal, being all that a witness can be. Whatever can make a witness valuable belongs to Christ. *We* speak because we believe; *he* speaks because he knows. He is the "Amen." He alone can speak with absolute positiveness that there can be no inaccuracy in his words. In bearing testimony to the occurrence of an external fact, a very moderate amount of ability, combined with fidelity, might suffice. But when testimony is borne concerning the inward and spiritual state of a Church, infinitely more is needed than such commonplace requirements. He only can be a competent witness of the spiritual state of any man, and *a fortiori* of the spiritual state of any body of men, who can discern the thoughts and intents of the heart; who knows in the case of each the relation between privilege, capacity, and attainment; who understands perfectly the difference between what is and what ought to be, and the entire bearings of the spiritual state of to-day on eternal interests. Evidently, therefore, no one is a competent witness in such matters but he who says, "I the Lord search the heart, and try the reins of the children of men." But he is. And he who is thus perfectly competent is also absolutely true. Nor was it only of this particular Church, at this particular time, that Christ was a faithful and true Witness; he is this to every Church at every time. A Divinely rigid inspection of every Church is ever going on. It is not only true that we *must* all stand before the judgment-seat of Christ, it is also true that we *do* all stand before it *now*. There is a royal judgment of professors and of Churches going on at every moment, and the value of each Church is not what it is in the eyes of man, but what it is in the eye of the heart-searching Lord. The most solemn inquiry we can put is, "What does Christ think of us?" We may stand well before other Churches, but, oh, if Christ thinks ill of us, that spoils all! Let us therefore consider—

II. THE TESTIMONY BORNE BY THIS WITNESS. In the judgment here pronounced as to the state of the Church at Laodicea, there is a principle expressed which may be detached from the special details of Laodicean Church life, because it holds good whatever those details may be; it may be looked at quite independently of time or place, because it bears equally on all Churches at every time and in every place. That principle is indicated by the words, "I would thou wert cold or hot." Evidently, to be fervent in religion is so blessed that it is perfectly easy to understand why our Lord should say he would rather we were *hot* than lukewarm; but it is not, at first sight, so clear why he would rather we were *cold* than lukewarm. Yet our Lord declares *that lukewarmness is more offensive to him than entire coldness would be.* Let us inquire: 1. *What this lukewarmness is.* In answering this question, our safest course will be to follow the evidence given in this letter as to what Christ saw, from which, perhaps, we may gather what he means. Four features. (1) There was *profession.* Here was a company of avowed disciples gathered together in Laodicea to form a fellowship, to maintain Christian worship, and to advance the honour of the Saviour's name. (2) The Church was *exceedingly well pleased with itself.* "Thou sayest, I am rich," etc. Laodicea was a great commercial city, rolling in wealth; and the Church may have been satisfied either with its worldly status, or (which, perhaps, is the more probable) with its spiritual progress. (3) Yet it was a Church *unique in its emptiness.* "Thou knowest not that *thou* art the wretched, and miserable, and poor, and blind, and naked one."[1] Laodicea was the poorest of all the seven. In two Churches there was good with no specified ill; in four, good and ill were mixed together; in one there was ill with no good—that was the Church at Laodicea. There is in it nothing to be commended. The true gold of spiritual wealth was *not there*; the white raiment of personal purity, *not there*; the anointing of the Holy One, *not there*. A poor Church indeed! But the worst has yet to be told. (4) *Christ himself was outside it!* He is outside the door, has been standing there for some time, and was still knocking and asking for admission. The question at once starts itself— *When is Christ outside a nominal Church?* We reply: (*a*) When in its fellowship respectability is thought more of than fervour; (*b*) when in the pulpit eloquence is extolled more than the truth is appreciated; (*c*) when talent is more craved than spiritual power; (*d*) when wealth and status are recognized, and growth in grace is not. We know a Church which makes its boast of the number of mayors of the borough who have been members with it; and another that boasted that it had not a single tradesman on its Church-roll! Oh this worldliness! it is killing

[1] Note the definite article here: σὺ εἶ ὁ ταλαίπωρος

Churches. Christ is not in them, and will not be, till they repent. It is no uncommon thing to name the name of Christ with the tongue, even when the Spirit of Christ is not in the heart. It is clear enough, then, what Christ means by lukewarmness. There was care enough and interest enough to hold together an external fellowship, and to maintain all outward Church proprieties; but the soul was lacking—the living Christ was not there. Let us now inquire: 2. *What entire coldness would have been.* A few words will suffice here. If the Laodiceans had either never heard the gospel at all, or if, having heard it, it had never convinced their understanding, or if, although mentally persuaded of its work and of its Divine origin, they had never had sufficient glow of soul to unite in a Christian fellowship, and had never made any avowal whatever of any attachment to the Lord Jesus,—in such a case there surely would have been coldness. Let us now ask: 3. *Why lukewarmness is more offensive to Christ than coldness.* Why is a man who has just warmth enough to lead him to take some interest in religious services, and to keep his place in a Christian congregation, and no more, more displeasing to Christ than one without any warmth at all? For many reasons. (1) There is a wider discrepancy between profession and practice. For the Church-member may fairly be supposed to have convictions clear enough to make a fervid man of him, if he would but let them have scope and play. But, as it is, there is an inward schism in the man. (2) The lukewarm professor is more difficult to reach. Of all men whose consciences are hard to touch, those are the most so who have "made a profession," and then settle down in it in a state of self-complacency. (3) Hence their position is peculiarly perilous; for, owing to their satisfaction with themselves, there is far less chance of the arrow of conviction piercing their souls. Hence the peril of their self-deceit being undisturbed until too late. (4) Such a one is more guilty than others, for he has made a vow which he does not pay. He confesses his responsibilities, and yet takes no pains to discharge them. (5) He effects more mischief than others. Many an ardent convert gets his first chill from lukewarm members of the Church. In fact, this lukewarmness threatens to pull down a Church; yea, it will do it if a check be not put upon it. (6) Our Saviour will reject it, consequently, with special displeasure. Nothing is so offensive to him as a corpse in religion's cloak. When great pretensions are nothing more than pretension, then the greater the pretence the greater the offence. The more true any one's nature is, the more odious is untruth to him. What, then, must it be to the Lord Jesus Christ?

III. THE COUNSELS OF THIS FAITHFUL AND TRUE WITNESS. Although the heavenly Witness is severely faithful, there is in his words a ground-tone of the deepest tenderness. In them, and indeed in each one of them, there is enough for a separate homily; but space can only be found for a few words. Note: (1) There is an assurance that his love is not withdrawn. He is grieved, he is dishonoured, still he loves. (2) His love finds a twofold expression: (*a*) he convicts; (*b*) he chastens. Hence his gracious counsels. 1. They are called on to be zealous. There are ways and means of reviving a flagging zeal. "He that would be warm must keep near the fire;" and he that would become spiritually warmer must get near the cross, and keep there. 2. Repent. A lukewarm Christian has need to repent as much as though he had never repented at all; for he has "lost his roll," and cannot then indeed tell whether he ever had one. 3. They are urged to get all their need supplied. Laodicea was a thriving commercial town. Christ speaks to the people there in their own familiar dialect. "Buy"—where? what? (1) Of Christ; without money and without price. (2) Gold. Raiment. Eyesalve. 4. They are reminded that the door must be opened to Christ. It is terrible beyond all power of expression when Church-doors are closed against Christ, and when he is kept outside the very community whose only *raison d'être* is that it may entertain and honour its Lord. 5. They are entreated to open the door and to admit the living Lord. What can this mean? Surely nothing less than to let his Spirit rather than the world-spirit have the supreme control. In a word, the Church is exhorted to become true to its profession, and to let him, whose sacred Name it avows, be once again its sovereign Lord. But we must not forget the next point. 6. The Church is to open its doors to Christ, by individual members opening their own hearts to him. "If *any man* hear my voice, and open the door, I will come in to him, and will sup with him, and he with me." Finally, if, listening to the counsels of Infinite Wisdom and Love, they, receiving a living Christ again, become once more a living Church, and overcome this downward tendency, then Christ will cause them to share with him his own honour at last. The Master conquered, and he expects the disciple to do the same. The Lord overcame for us; we may overcome in him and by him. Note: Victory is possible *only when Christ is within us.* If we keep him outside, not all the sanctuary teaching, nor the services, nor songs, nor ordinances, nor forms of godliness, nor parental virtue, can ever prevent us from falling miserably back to perdition. If we keep Christ out of our hearts, he will spue us out of his mouth.

HOMILIES BY VARIOUS AUTHORS.

Vers. 1—6.—*The epistle to the Church at Sardis.* Were any one visiting the actual sites where the several Churches spoken of in these letters once stood, he would, ere he came to Sardis, have gone a long way round the circle on the circumference of which they all were. Beginning with Ephesus at the southern end, and proceeding northwards along the sea-shore, he next would come to Smyrna, then to Pergamos, then to Thyatira, and then, coming down the inland side of the rude circle we have imagined, he would reach Sardis, and proceeding on would come first to Philadelphia and then to Laodicea, the last of the seven. But now we have come to Sardis—a notable city in the ancient world, because associated with the great names of Cyrus, Crœsus, and Alexander. With this historic fame, however, we have nought to do, but with the religious condition of the Church there as shown in this letter. And, as in all the previous letters, so here, the title assumed by the Lord Jesus has special reference to the condition and need of the Church addressed. Ephesus needed encouragement and warning alike. The Lord, therefore, speaks of himself as "he who holdeth the seven stars in his right hand." Smyrna needed strong support under her heavy trial. The Lord therefore speaks to them as "The First and the Last, who," etc. Pergamos needed that the Word of God should be sharply and severely brought to bear upon her. The Lord therefore tells of himself as "he who hath the sharp sword with the two edges," etc. Thyatira needed to be reminded of the holy and awful wrath of the Lord against such as she was harbouring in her midst. The Lord therefore declares himself to be "he whose eyes are as a flame of fire," etc. And now this Church of Sardis needed to be won back again to true godliness, for though she had a name that she lived, she was dead. The Lord therefore speaks of himself to her as "he who hath the seven Spirits of God, and the seven stars." Now note how this name of the Lord bears—

I. ON THE SIN WITH WHICH THE CHURCH WAS CHARGEABLE. Observe concerning this sin: 1. *It was not that of others.* Nought is said of Nicolaitans and followers of Balaam, or of such as Jezebel was. Nothing of false doctrines or of vicious life. These things which are denounced so terribly in other letters are not charged against this Church, and we may therefore assume that they could, perhaps they did, thank God that they were not as those other Churches were. 2. *Nor was it that they did nothing.* On the contrary, their works are mentioned repeatedly. No doubt there were all wonted ministries, religious observances, charities, and missions. There must have been, for: 3. *They were no scandal to others.* On the contrary, they had a name, a reputation, an honourable character, as a living Church. Laodicea deceived herself, thinking she was rich; but it is not said she deceived others. This Church, Sardis, did deceive others; she was reckoned by them to be really living, though in fact she was dead; and very probably she had deceived herself also. But: 4. *Their works were not perfect before God.* Well enough before men, but before *him* quite otherwise. They were of such sort that he said of those who did them, that they were "dead." They were done, as were the prayers, alms, and fastings of the hypocrites, "to be seen of men." Assuredly not with single eye or with pure motive. They had their reward: people talked of them, and gave them credit as having life. But before God they were dead. Let us remember that it is as "*before God*" everything is to be estimated. Let all who engage in any form of Christian service remember this. It is terribly apt to be forgotten. Remember how St. Paul said, "It is a small thing to me to be judged of you or of any human judgment: he that judgeth me is the Lord;" "I labour to be accepted of *him*." The one question for us all is, how will our work appear before God? For: 5. *Their condition was one most displeasing to him.* The severe tone of the letter proves this.   True, we have had such severity before, and shall have it again; for rebuke, and often stern rebuke, was what was needed then and still is by the majority of Churches, always and everywhere.   Nevertheless, there is no one of these letters in which the tone is more severe, or the smiting of the sword of the Spirit sharper, or the solemnity of the appeals addressed to them more arousing or impressive.   The epistle to Laodicea is the only one which can be compared with it, and it is to be noticed that the wrong in that Church, whilst very great, is like this in Sardis, that it is free from the foul stains either of vice or heresy.   In the sight of the Lord of the Church there is, it is evident, something more hateful to him than even these.   Love to the Lord may linger in hearts even where these are; but if love, the true life of every Church and every individual soul, be gone, then are they to be described as none others are, for they are "dead."   Hence in this letter there is no softening, mitigating utterance at all, no mention of good works, but the key-note of the epistle is struck at once, and a startling one it is.   But: 6 *What was the cause of it all?*   Now the name our Lord takes to himself in this letter reveals this cause.   He by that name declares that in him and from him is all-sufficient grace.   Treasure store inexhaustible, riches unsearchable, both for pastor and people.   For his were "the seven Spirits of God," and his "the seven stars."   And yet, in spite of all this, they were as they were.   Oh, was it not shameful, is it not shameful, utterly inexcusable, when the like exists now, that, though abundance of grace is in Christ for us all, we should yet be what he terms "dead"?   It was plain, therefore, they had not sought that grace; the fulness of the Spirit's help neither pastor nor people had implored; and so, as we find, they had given in to the world's ways.   It is evident from the honourable mention of the "few" who had "not defiled their garments," that the rest had.   That is to say, they had given in to the world's ways.   Hence St. James speaks of pure religion as being in part this, "Keeping your garments unspotted from the world."   And in proof of this there seems to have been a good understanding between the Church and the world at Sardis.   They seem to have got along together very well.   In every other Church, save this and Laodicea, mention is made of some "burden" which the enmity of the surrounding world laid upon the Church.   But not here.   As it has been well said (Archbishop Trench), "The world could endure it because it, too, was a world."   This Church had nothing of the spirit of the "two witnesses" (ch. xi. 10) who "tormented them that dwelt in the earth" by their faithful testimony; or of the Lord Jesus either, who "resisted unto blood, striving against sin," and because he would not yield was crucified (cf. also Wisd. ii. 12, etc.).   But there was nothing of all this at Sardis.   It might have been said of them, as was cynically said the other day of a certain section of ministers of religion amongst us, that "you would find them very well-bred, and you might be quite certain they would say nothing to you about your soul."   It is an ill sign when the Church and the world are so happy together.   There has been compromise somewhere, and it is rarely the world which makes it.   It is bad to have no life at all in God's love; it is worse to have had it and to have lost it; but it is worst of all—and may God in his mercy deliver us therefrom—to have the name and reputation of possessing this life, and yet to be, in fact, as it was with Sardis, dead in regard thereto.   For all around us conduces to deepen such fatal slumber of the soul, and there is an everlasting soothing of them by themselves, the Church and the world alike, saying continually, "Peace, peace," when there is no peace.

II.   ON THE PUNISHMENT WITH WHICH THE CHURCH IS THREATENED.   (Ver. 3.)   This solemn warning of danger speaks of the Lord's advent to judgment.   But: 1. *What is that judgment?*   The name the Lord has assumed in this letter reveals it.   Now, that name was meant partly to show that they were without excuse, but also to remind that, as the Spirit is his to give, so also is it his to withdraw and to withhold.   As he can open the doors of grace, and then no man can shut; so also can he shut them, and then none can open.   This, then, was what they were to fear, lest he should leave them alone, lest he should take his Holy Spirit from them.   David dreaded this, and implored that the Lord would not deal so with him.   Better any punishment, any suffering, any pain, any amount of distress, than that the soul should be thus left alone of the Lord.   2. *And this judgment would come "as a thief;"* they should not know when or how.   There was an ancient proverb that the feet of the avenging gods are shod with wool.   *Dii laneos habent pedes.*   The meaning is simply what is here said, that the Divine judgment comes silently, stealthily, secretly, invisibly, unexpectedly, " as a thief." Who can mark the hour when God's Spirit leaves a man? Who sees the master of the house rise up and shut the door? It is not always true, as the much misleading verse tells—

> " While the lamp holds out to burn,
> The vilest sinner may return."

Before that lamp is quenched, the Holy Spirit's blessed flame may have been quenched, and he, resisted, grieved, done despite to, may have for ever gone away. And it is equally untrue to affirm that the point of death bars all return. It is not death, but the determined character of the soul, that decides that matter. Death cannot shut the Spirit out nor life ensure that he remain, but the fixed bias and character into which we have settled down. And then: 3. *There follows the blotting out of the name*, etc. (Ver. 5.) Of him who overcomes Christ says, " I will by no means blot out his name." Hence it is implied that the rest he will blot out. Yes, the name may be in that book ; through the blessed atonement and sacrifice of our Lord Jesus Christ our names are there; but the question is—Will they be allowed to stay there? The branch may be in the Vine; it is so; but " if it bear not fruit, then," etc. Christ has put us all in, but we can force him, all unwilling, to blot us out again. And to be as Sardis was will do this. Have mercy upon us, O Lord !

III. On their restoration. Their sin had not altered the fact that he still had " the seven Spirits," etc. And should the Lord's earnest word have the effect designed, it would, and we may well believe it did, awake many that slept, and arouse them from the dead, that Christ might give them life. And how would they be encouraged by this revelation of the Lord's grace! " How sweet the name of Jesus " would sound in their ears ! Did it not enable them to say to their adversary, " Rejoice not against me, O mine enemy : when I fall I shall arise ; when I sit in darkness, the Lord shall be a light unto me." The effort they would have to make would be severe, but here in this name was abundance of grace for all their need. And to encourage them the Lord points them : 1. *To the "few" who had overcome*. There was, then, no irresistible might in the thraldom in which they were held. These had overcome, so might they. The grace that enabled these was waiting for them likewise. Not only would these " few " be greatly strengthened by the Lord's remembrance of and special promise to them, but the rest also would learn that victory was possible for them through him who had the " seven Spirits," etc. 2. *To means that, if faithfully used, would be effectual*. (1) Let them become wakeful—such is the meaning. This was a primary and imperative need. And when thus awake, let them (2) remember how they had received and heard. With what earnestness and joy and devotedness of spirit they had begun their Christian career! Let them look back on that. And let them (3) hold fast, *i.e.* keep, what remained, for all was not lost yet. The door of hope was not shut. And let them (4) repent, *i.e.* have done with all habits, practices, and conduct, with all ways of thinking and speaking, which had lured them into and all but lost them in their deceitfulness. Let them confess it all before the Lord, and come away from it at once and for ever. And (5) let them strengthen the things which remained. As the traveller crossing the Alps in snow-storm, all but benumbed, striking his foot against the body of one who had just before passed that way and had sunk down in the snow, overcome by the deadly torpor of the cold—as he, roused by the blow and proceeding to use all efforts to awaken the fallen one, happily succeeds, he is made at the same time altogether wakeful and alive himself : so let any whose own spiritual condition is feeble try to make others strong, and they, too, in the endeavour will win strength. Let them thus act. And next he points them to : 3. *The reward of these who overcome*. (1) The white robe, symbol of victory, purity, joy. (2) The fellowship with Christ. " They shall walk *with me* in white." What enhancement of their blessedness this! (3) The retention of their names in the book of life. " I will by no means blot out," etc. All the loving purposes which he cherished for them when he entered their names there, they shall realize and enjoy. (4) The confession of their names before his Father and his angels. What a compensation for the contempt of the world ! how insignificant and despicable is that contempt when placed over against this honour which Christ here promises ! Ah ! who would stay in the sad state of

Sardis when a way like this is opened out of it for them? All grace is his, and his for us, if we will avail ourselves of it ; for he " hath the seven," etc.—S. C.

Ver. 4.—*The present blessedness of the consecrated life: a Whit Sunday sermon.* " They shall walk with me in white: for they are worthy." This is Whit Sunday, and its very name carries us back in thought to the literal and impressive manner in which the Christian Church of the early centuries was wont to interpret our text when she celebrated the Feast of Pentecost. For it was at this feast—so the Book of the Acts tells us—that there were reaped for Christ and his Church those famous firstfruits of the harvest of converted men, which in the ages to come Christ's ministers should gather in. On that day there were added to the Church some three thousand souls, who were all straightway baptized according to St. Peter's word, " Repent, and be baptized every one of you in the name of Jesus Christ for the remission of sins, and ye shall receive the gift of the Holy Ghost." The Day of Pentecost, therefore, became a chosen day in the early Church for the reception by baptism of converts to the Christian faith. On that day they who had lived heretofore in Judaism or in heathenism were clothed in white robes, and gathered in numerous throngs at the baptisteries of the churches; there, with music and holy psalms, and with many elaborate symbolic ceremonies, they received the initiatory rite of the Christian Church. But the most striking feature of the day was the procession of white-robed candidates, and that so fastened itself on the mind of the Church, that the day which commemorated the Feast of Pentecost came to be called, as it is amongst us still, Whit or White Sunday, Alba Dominica, or the white Lord's day. Those who were on that day baptized had been counted worthy—for they had renounced heathenism or Judaism, and had confessed Christ—to be numbered amongst the Christian fellowship. And hence they were arrayed in white garments; for was it not written, " They shall walk . . . worthy "? And it is told how not seldom these baptized ones would ever afterwards carefully preserve their white robe as a perpetual reminder of their vow of consecration to Christ, and at the last, when they lay down to die, they would have it put on once more, and in it they would be buried. But whilst it is interesting to note how the mind of the ancient Church expressed by such symbolism its understanding of this word before us, it is more important to us to get beneath the metaphor, and to ascertain its meaning for ourselves to-day. And that meaning is surely this—that the consecrated Christian life is a blessed life. The white robe of the baptized told them, no doubt, of the character and responsibilities of that life; that its character was to be holy, and that their responsibility and obligation were to strive after holiness, and to be content with nothing less. But in our text it is not so much responsibility and obligation that are meant, but the blessedness of the Christian life. Let us speak, therefore—

I. Of the worthiness which wins the white robe. The few in Sardis who are to be counted worthy are they who, unlike the rest, " have not defiled their garments; " that is, the character, which is the vestment of the soul, and which they had received, they had kept undefiled. For a new character is given to him who truly comes to Christ; he is a new creature, and the blood of Jesus Christ cleanseth him from all sin. This is no mere doctrine of theology, but a fact in Christian experience. For the mind in which we come to Christ is in nature, though not in degree, Christ's own mind—that mind of which his atoning death was the expression; the mind that condemns sin, that trusts in the forgiving love of God, and desires above all else the love of God. Such was the mind in which Christ died, and which was the real atonement. For the mangled flesh of the Lord and the bleeding body had no atoning power save as they declared the mind which was in him. And it was a mind that could not but be infinitely acceptable to the Father, could not but have been a full, true, sufficient atonement, oblation, and satisfaction to his heart, the Father-heart of God. And because, whenever we come really to God in Christ, the movements of our minds are in this same direction, and we come clothed in this mind, though it may be but imperfectly, yet because our mind is like in nature, though not in degree, to the perfect mind of Christ when he died for us, therefore are we accepted in him, and for his sake pardoned, and made possessors of a new character—his mind—which is the garment we are to keep undefiled, and which those who are counted worthy do keep undefiled.

II. Of the white robe itself. It tells: 1. *Of purity.* "Blessed are the pure in heart." Oh, the joy of this ! It is good, when temptation comes, to be able to grip and grapple with it, and to gain victory over it, though after a hard struggle. Oh, how far better this than to miserably yield, and to be "led captive by Satan at his will"! But even this falls far below the blessedness which the white robe signifies. For it tells of an inward purity, like to his who said, "The prince of this world cometh, and hath nothing in me." There was nothing in him on which the tempter's power could fasten, and to rise up to this heart-purity is the glory and joy promised by the white robe. 2. *Of victory.* White was the symbol of this also, as well as of purity. He who went forth "conquering and to conquer" rode upon a white horse—so the vision declared. They who had come out of the great tribulation were clothed in "white robes," and elsewhere we are told they had "overcome by the blood of the Lamb." And this blessedness of victory the consecrated soul enjoys. "Sin shall not have dominion over" him. "In all things" he is "more than conqueror." One of the very chiefest blessings of the Christian faith is that it makes the weak strong, and to them that have no might the faith of Christ increaseth strength. Facts of everyday Christian experience prove that it is so. 3. *Of joy.* White garments are the symbol of this also. And the truly consecrated heart shall know "the joy of the Lord." The saints of God in all ages have found that "he giveth songs in the night." Who should have joy if not the true-hearted Christian man?

III. How WE MAY WIN AND WEAR THESE WHITE ROBES. Through entire surrender to Christ. There is no other way. If we retain our own will and keep urging its claims, these white robes are not for us. The consecrated life is clothed thus, and that life alone.—S. C.

Vers. 7—13.—*Letter to the Church at Philadelphia.* If asked to sum up in a word the main lesson of this letter, I would quote the saying of our Lord recorded by St. Luke, "Fear not, little flock." Such is the effect of a right reading of this most precious epistle. It is a heart-cheering word to all such Churches, and to every one of like character. For Philadelphia was—

I. LITTLE. "Thou hast a little strength" (ver. 8), or rather, "Thou hast small power." It refers not to her spiritual strength, for that was not small, but perfected in her weakness. She was mighty through God who upheld and sustained her. Hence the expression is to be regarded as referring, probably, to her membership as but few in number, to her wealth as but very small, to her knowledge and gifts as being but slender, to great and distinguished men amongst her as being very rare, to her social position as being quite humble. Hence she was small in human esteem, one of those "weak things," which, however, God often chooses wherewith to accomplish his own purposes. And many a Church, beloved of the Lord, is like Philadelphia, having only "a little strength." But also she was—

II. MUCH TRIED. Looking at this letter, we can gather what some of these trials were. It seems that: 1. *Their place amongst the people of God was denied.* We gather this from what is said as to the assertion of the Jews, who, as at Galatia and everywhere else, affirmed that they only, the descendants of Abraham, were the Israel of God: none else had part or lot therein. In ver. 9 emphasis is to be laid on the word "they" in the sentence, "which say they are Jews." St. Paul was perpetually fighting against this exclusiveness, and was for ever teaching that in Christ Jesus there was "neither Jew nor Greek." But all the same, it caused considerable uneasiness amongst the early Gentile believers. There was much to be urged out of the Scriptures in favour of the real descendants of Abraham, especially if they were also "as touching the Law blameless." They seemed to many as a privileged order, a spiritual aristocracy, admission into whose circle was indeed to be desired. Hence so many Gentiles submitted to the rite of circumcision (cf. Epistle to the Galatians, *passim*). And the taunts of the Jews at Philadelphia against the Christians, as being not really God's people at all, was one form of the trials they were called upon to bear. And still there is many a believer, excommunicated by man, but not at all so by God; denied his place in earthly Churches, though it be abundantly his in the Church of the Firstborn. Catholics have denounced Protestants, and Protestants one another, and both have retorted, and all have been wrong, and sinful in being wrong, whenever those whom they have denounced have shown that they did unfeignedly trust and love and obey

Christ the Lord. The cry, "The Church of the Lord, the Church of the Lord are we!" is often raised by those who have no right to it, and against those who have. Thus was it at Sardis. 2. *They had to encounter active opposition.* Endeavours seem to have been made to shut the door of usefulness which the Lord had opened for them. His emphatic declaration that none should shut that door implies that there had been those who had tried to do so. And how often since then have dominant and cruel Churches made the same attempt in regard to communities they did not like! Witness the persecutions of Vaudois and Waldenses in Switzerland, of Hussites and others in Bohemia, of Lollards, Protestants, and Puritans in England, of Covenanters in Scotland, and of Catholics in Ireland,—all has been, with more or less of difference, the repetition of what was done at Philadelphia in the days of St. John. And there appears to have been : 3. *Attempts to make them apostatize.* The meaning of the latter part of ver. 8 is, " Because though thou hast but little strength, nevertheless thou hast kept my word, and hast not denied my Name." Hence we gather—and the tenses of the verbs used imply it also—that there had been some definite attempt of the kind we have said. Like as Saul in his persecuting days forced the unhappy Christians who fell into his power "to blaspheme," so similar force had apparently been used, but, by virtue of Christ's sustaining grace, with no effect. For, notwithstanding all, they were—

III. FAITHFUL. They kept Christ's word, and did not deny his Name; and the first was the cause of the last. Their history illustrates the value of the word of Christ. They clung to it, they would not let it go, they had nothing but this, but this they had and clave to. Twice is it named : "Thou hast kept my word;" "Thou hast kept the word of my patience." And this latter and fuller form reveals a further aid to their faith which they found in Christ's word. "For the word of Christ, as the Philadelphians knew it, was not a word calling them to easy and luxurious and applauded entrance into the kingdom, but to much tribulation first, and the kingdom with the glory of it afterwards." And not only as a word which told them at the beginning that patience would be needed, did it help them; but yet more as the word which revealed Christ their Lord as the great Example and Source and Rewarder of patience; so that, however hard to bear their trials might be, they could turn in thought to their Lord, and behold him meekly bearing *his* cross—so much heavier than theirs; and they had seen him also sustaining his tried servants again and again, and they knew that he would do the same for them, and they believed that he would assuredly reward their patience. Yes, it was the word of his patience to which they clung, and in the strength of which, though tempted and tried sorely, they would not deny his Name. And their way must be our way, their strength ours, when we are tried. And they were—

IV. GREATLY BLEST. The Lord gave them large reward. To this day the suffering Smyrna and the much-tried Philadelphia alone remain of these seven Churches. Through all manner of vicissitudes the Christian faith has been upheld by them to this day. But see the recompenses spoken of here. 1. *Christ confesses them, and denies their slanderers.* He pronounces for them and against their foes. Such is the significance of the august and sublime title which the Lord here assumes. It tells of the names of the Lord God of Israel. He was the Holy, the True, the King of Israel, of whom David, with his great authority opening and shutting according to his will, was the Old Testament type and representative. "The key of David" means the power and authority of David, and Christ claims to be as he was, and far more, the Representative of God, and the Possessor of his authority and power. Now, it was by this great and glorious Jehovah that the Jews at Philadelphia affirmed that the Church there was disowned and denied. They said, "You have no part in this God, but we only." But in utter contradiction of this falsehood, he, the Holy One himself, comes forward, and declares that the persecuted Church had part in him, but that they, her slanderers, had not. "Ye Jews say ye are Jews, but in any real sense ye are not; ye do lie; but this my despised, yet faithful Church, *I* have loved her, and I, the Holy, the True, the King of Israel, do now confess her as she has confessed me." And often and often has the Lord done the like of this. "When wrong has been done to any of his servants here on earth, he will redress it in heaven, disallowing and reversing there the unrighteous decrees of earth. It was in faith of this that Huss, when the greatest council which Christendom had seen for one thousand years delivered his soul to Satan, did himself confidently commend it to the Lord Jesus Christ; and many a faithful confessor that at Rome or Madrid has walked to the stake, his yellow *san benito* all painted over with devils, in token of those with whom his portion should be, has never doubted that his lot should be with him who retains in his own hands the key of David, who thus could open for him, though all who visibly represented here the Church had shut him out, with extreme malediction, at once from the Church militant here and the Church triumphant in heaven." And the grim cells of Newgate, and the bare bleak hedgerows of our own land, have often been the scenes of similar revelations to God's persecuted ones. God has taken their side, and pronounced for them as he did for the Church at Philadelphia. 2. *Their Lord makes them abundantly useful.* "Behold, I have set before thee an open door, and no man can shut it." His Name declared his power to do this, and here he affirms that he has exercised that power on their behalf. By the "open door," usefulness, opportunity of service and of doing much good, is meant (cf. 1 Cor. xvi. 9; 2 Cor. ii. 12; Acts xiv. 27; Col. iv. 3). Now, this Christ declared he had done for them. Perhaps it was by giving them favour in the sight of the people, or by breaking the hold of heathenism, arousing a spirit of inquiry, raising up able teachers, giving them entrance into fresh circles. Fidelity to Christ has given to it a key that will turn the most difficult lock, and open the most closely shut door. 3. *Their enemies should submit themselves.* As Saul the persecutor became Paul the apostle. And again and again out of the ranks of the Church's fiercest foes have come those who have first surrendered their hearts to her cause and then their lives to her service (cf. the conversion of Constantine and of Rome generally). In that this word was literally fulfilled. 4. *They should be delivered from the hour of temptation*—that dread hour which was drawing near so swiftly (cf. Ps. xci.). Perhaps they would be taken home first, delivered so "from the evil to come." And if not that, raised in heart, as the martyrs perpetually were, above all fear; or some wondrous deliverance should be found for them. They knew that hour was coming, and no doubt they had often shuddered at the prospect. But oh, what joy to be told by their Lord that he would deliver them! 5. *The eternal recompense—the crown.* Their Lord was quickly coming; let them hold on but a little longer, and then this crown should be theirs. In ver. 12 this crown of recompense is more fully described: (1) As being made "a pillar in the temple of my God," *i.e.* they should perpetually abide there, dwelling in the house of the Lord for ever. Now we come and go, in fact and in spirit. Not so there. "He shall go no more out." It is a curious coincidence that amongst the ruins at Philadelphia there stands to this day a solitary tall pillar; it strikes the eye of the traveller, and suggests irresistibly this glorious promise made to the believers who lived there long ago. An ancient geographer says of the place, "It is full of earthquakes, and is daily shaken, now one part, and now another suffering, so that one wonders any should have been found to build or inhabit it." Now, to the Christians, who saw daily in their city the image of their own precarious position, Christ says, "I will make him who overcomes a pillar in the temple of my God," and he shall go no more out"—shall not totter and fall as these stone pillars do, but shall abide stable and sure for ever. (2) As being identified with: (*a*) God. "The Name of my God" Christ will write upon him. It shall be evident that he belongs to God. "Surely this was the Son of God"—so spake they who had crucified the Lord: they could not help seeing the Name of God written upon him. (*b*) "The city of my God." Jews had cast them out, but the God of the true "holy city" had declared it theirs, and that their true home was his own city. There are many of whom we say, "We hope they are going to heaven;" there are some of whom we say, "We are sure they are," for their identification with heaven is so complete. (*c*) Christ's own Name—that aspect of Christ's love by which the believer realizes that he is Christ's and Christ is his.

> "So, gracious Saviour, on my breast,
> May thy dear Name be worn,
> A sacred ornament and guard
> To endless ages borne."

S. C.

Vers. 14—21.—*The epistle to the Church at Laodicea.* It was a wealthy city in which this Church had her home, and it was large and beautiful also. It stood on one of the great Roman roads which led away to Damascus and Arabia. Hence there was a large stream of traffic continually flowing through it, and its inhabitants became very rich. At the time when this letter was sent them they were building for themselves one of those huge amphitheatres which the Greeks and Romans of the day were wont to build in all their chief cities, and where those too often barbarous and degrading sports, in which they so much delighted, might be carried on. As a further evidence of their wealth, it is recorded how, when their city was almost destroyed by one of those earthquakes by which the whole region was so often disturbed, they rebuilt it entirely at their own cost. A Church was early formed there, and was one of considerable importance. It was probably founded by one or other of those earnest-minded brethren, who, like Epaphras, whom Paul names in his letter to the neighbouring Church at Colossæ, and who were commissioned by St. Paul for such work, probably during his sojourn at Ephesus. We know that Epaphras was a near neighbour, Colossæ being only some six or eight miles distant from Laodicea ; and hence it is likely that he—" faithful minister of Christ, and beloved fellow-servant," as St. Paul calls him (Col. i. 7; iv. 12)—had something to do with the planting of the Church there. And we can have no doubt but that the Church was once in a very flourishing condition. The Epistle of St. Paul to the Ephesians was intended, it is all but certain, as much for the Laodiceans as the Ephesians, if not more so. The high praise which we find in that letter is therefore to be regarded as given to Laodicea, which now, when St. John writes to it, is so sadly fallen. And in Col. ii. 1, 5, St. Paul speaks of them and of the " steadfastness " of their " faith in Christ " (cf. also Col. iv. 13—16). But a sad change had come over them, and the result is this letter before us now. Note—

I. THEIR CHARACTER AND CONDITION. They are charged with being " neither cold nor hot,". but lukewarm. That is to say, that whilst there was not absolute denial of the faith and disregard of all Christ's claims, there yet was neither the fervent zeal, the devout spirit, nor the all-sacrificing love, springing from a vigorous faith, which would make a Church glow with holy fervour and sacred heat. And this half-and-half, neither one thing nor the other, condition *is all too common* amongst not a few who profess and call themselves Christians. How many Churches, and how many church-going people, may, and probably have, seen their portraitures in this sad letter to the Church at Laodicea! They cannot be said to be cold and so utterly disregardful of religion, or of Christian faith and custom; but as certainly they are not " hot," not filled with love and zeal and desire towards Christ, willing to do all, bear all, be all or anything or nothing, so only as the honour of his Name may be increased, and the boundaries of his kingdom enlarged. Christians are to be known by their ardour, and so tongues of fire came and rested upon their heads on the great Pentecostal day. But Laodicea and the like of her show nothing of this kind, nor will nor can they whilst they remain as they are. And the common run of men *like to have it thus*. Cold makes them shiver; heat scorches them,—they like neither; but to be moderately warm, tepid, or but little more; that is pleasant, is safe, is best every way, so men think. The cynic statesman's parting charge to one of his agents, " Surtout, point de zèle," is, in fact, what the ordinary Christian vastly prefers for himself and for others. They confound zeal with eccentricity, fervour with wild and ill-considered schemes, earnestness with rant, enthusiasm with mere delirium and extravagance; and, under pretence of discountenancing these undesirable things, they desire neither for themselves nor for others that glow of Divine love in their souls which is desirable above all things else. *They congratulate themselves* upon being moderate, sober-minded people, and they pity the poor deluded enthusiasts, to whom it is a dreadful thing that sin and sorrow should prevail as they do, and who, therefore, are in the very forefront of the battle against them. Laodiceans think well and speak well of themselves, and other people credit them with what they say, and hence they are self-complacent and well satisfied, and wonder why anybody should doubt or differ from them. They do not hear the world's sneer or see its mocking look when their names are mentioned; still less do they hear the sighing of the sorrowful heart which yearns to see the Church of Christ rise up to her Lord's ideal and intent. But they go on saying and thinking that they are well to do, and have need of nothing. But their condition *is abhorrent to the Lord ; he* cannot abide it. nauseates it, would rather far that they were either cold or hot; either extreme would be better than the sickening lukewarmness which now characterizes them. To such it was that the Lord said, " The publicans and harlots go into the kingdom of God before you." Whilst of the irreligious multitudes he only said, as he looked on them with compassion, " They are as sheep having no shepherd." Elijah said, " If Baal be God, serve him; " " better be hearty in *his* service than serving neither God nor Baal, as you now are." And experience confirms this seemingly strange preference which the Lord declares. We could understand that he would men were " hot" rather than "lukewarm; " but that he would rather that they were " cold "— without religion altogether—than as they are, that seems a strange preference. But, as St. Paul says, " If a man think himself to be wise, let him become a fool that he may be wise; " by which he meant that a man who thinks himself wise when he is not, there is more hope of a fool becoming wise than he, for his self-conceit stands in his way. And so in the matter of a man's real conversion to God, he who knows he has no religion is more likely to be won than he who thinks he is religious and has " need of nothing." There is more hope, therefore, for the cold than for the " luke-warm," and hence our Lord's preference. And this condition is one *which drives the Lord away*, chases him forth from his Church. Christ is represented, not as in the Church, but as outside, standing at the door, and knocking for admission. He has been driven out. He cannot stay either in that Church or in that heart which loves him with but half or less than half a love. *We* do not care to stay where we are not really welcome: we get away as soon as we can. And our Lord will not stay where the love which should welcome and cherish his presence is no longer there.

II. How CHRIST DEALS WITH THEM. 1. *He reveals to them their true condition.* And to make them more readily receive his revelation, he declares himself by a name which ensured that his testimony was and must be infallibly true. He tells of himself as "the Amen, the faithful and true Witness." Therefore they may be sure that he could not err and would not misstate what he, as the Son of God, "the Beginning of the creation of God," saw and knew, and now declared to them to be true. And so he tells them how it is with them, though they knew it not and kept saying the very reverse. Hence he tells the Church, "Thou art the wretched one and the pitiable one, and beggarly and blind and naked." Ah! what a revelation this! how it would startle and shock them! No doubt the Lord intended that it should. Their condition justified these words. They thought that they were certain of their Lord's approval. He tells them that no shivering criminal waiting in terror the judge's sentence was ever more really wretched than they. And that they thought as they did proved them " blind." And as those whom it was designed to degrade were stripped " naked," so as " shameful " were they in the sight of the Lord and of his angels. 2. And by thus revealing their true state, *he rebukes and chastens them*. What humiliation and distress and alarm must this revelation have caused! But next: 3. *He counsels them what to do.* He will not leave them thus, but points out the way of amendment. He bids them " buy of me." But if they were so poor, how could they buy ? " The sacrifices of God are a broken spirit : a broken and a contrite heart, O God, thou wilt not despise." This is the money wherewith they must buy. And when they have laid out this money, and have become possessors of what it will surely purchase, they will tell you, if you ask them, that even this money he gave them from whom they went to buy. And what is it they will get in exchange ? (1) " Gold tried in," etc. This is faith (cf. 1 Pet. i. 7). " The trial of your faith, being much more precious than gold and silver." Oh, to be " rich in faith " ! They are rich who have it. (2) " White raiment that," etc. True righteousness of character, the holiness which becometh saints (3) " Eyesalve that," etc. The illuminating grace of the Holy Spirit. Such is the way of amendment : coming thus poor to the Lord, gaining faith, holiness, wisdom— so shall we rise up from the condition which the Lord cannot abide to that which he loves and will ever bless. Shall we not follow this counsel ? He does not compel, but counsels. Let us also thus buy of him. 4. *He waits for their repentance.* " Behold, I stand at the door," etc. How true it is he desireth not the death of a sinner, but rather that he turn from his wickedness and live! What a picture this well-known and ever-to-be-loved verse presents ! Our Lord, who died for us, standing there outside, seeking to enter in. 5. *He encourages them to repent.* See his promises. (1) " I will sup with him, and he with me." Communion with himself. A piece of clay gave forth a sweet fragrance. It was asked whence it had such fragrance. It replied that it had long lain by the side of a sweet-smelling rose, and so it had become filled with its sweetness. So our claylike souls, if we be in communion with Christ, shall come to be as he. Ah, then, "open the door," and let your Lord in. (2) He holds out to those who "overcome" the same reward as he had when he overcame—"to sit with me in my throne, even as I," etc. (ver. 21). It tells of the highest, holiest joys, of the everlasting kingdom of God. So would he lure them to himself. Shall he not succeed? "Behold, he stands at the door and knocks."—S. C.

Ver. 20.—*The Saviour, the soul, and salvation.* "Behold, I stand at the door," etc. These words, so well known and much loved, however their primary intention may have had regard to a sinful community like the Church at Laodicea, nevertheless lend themselves so aptly to the setting forth of Christ's dealing with individual sinful souls, and have been so often used in this way, that once more we employ them for the like purpose. They supply three vivid pictures.

I. OF OUR SAVIOUR. "Behold, I stand," etc.; and they reveal him to us in all his grace. He is represented: 1. *As in constant nearness to the soul.* He *stands* at the door. He does not come for once and then depart, but there he continues. 2. *And he knocks* at the door: not merely stands there. The soul is like a great palace that has many doors. And Christ knocks sometimes at the one door and sometimes at another. There is: (1) The door of the *intellect.* To this he comes with the evidence of the reasonableness of his faith and claims. (2) Of the *conscience.* To this he shows the goodness and righteousness of that which he asks; how he *ought* to be obeyed. (3) Of *love.* He wakes up, or seeks to wake up, the spirit of gratitude in response to all he is and has done for the soul. (4) Of *fear.* The alarm of the awakened conscience, the fearful looking for of judgment, are the means he uses. (5) Of *hope.* The blessed prospect of eternal peace and purity and joy. 3. *And he knocks in many ways.* (1) Sometimes by *his Word.* As it is quietly read in the sacred Scriptures, some text will arrest and arouse the soul. Or, as it is faithfully, lovingly, and earnestly preached: how often he knocks in this way! And (2) sometimes by *his providence.* Sickness; bereavement; loss of wealth, or friends, or other earthly good; disaster; the approach of pestilence; nearness of death; trouble of mind, body, or estate;—all are the Lord's knockings. And (3) sometimes by his Spirit. These more often than any. "The Spirit . . . says, Come." 4. *And we know that he does this.* Have we not been conscious of his appeals again and again? 5. *See what all this reveals of him.* (1) His infinite patience. How long he has waited for some of us, year after year, and is not wearied yet! (2) His gracious condescension. That he, our Lord and Saviour, should thus deal with us. (3) And, above all, what infinite love! Behold, then, this portrait of our all-gracious Saviour and Lord, and let it draw your hearts to him as it should.

II. OF THE SOUL—the soul of each one of us. Our text shows the soul: 1. *As the object of Christ's anxious concern.* He would not else be thus standing and knocking at the door of our hearts. And the reason is that he knows: (1) The soul's infinite value and preciousness. He knows its high capacities—that it can love and worship, resemble, and rejoice in God. (2) Its terrible peril. Were it not so, there would not be need for such anxious concern. It is in peril of losing eternal life and of incurring eternal death. It is nigh unto perishing—a lost sheep, a lost piece of silver, a lost child. 2. *As exercising its fearful power.* Refusing Christ, keeping him outside the soul. Many other guests are admitted freely, but not Christ. (1) The soul has this power of refusal. None other has. Not the stars of heaven, not the mighty sea, not the raging winds, not the devouring fire. All these obey. But the soul can refuse. (2) And here it is exercising this power. That Christ is kept outside the soul is the testimony of: (*a*) Scripture. Texts innumerable tell of the estrangement of the human heart from God. (*b*) Conscience. Does not the ungodly man know that Christ does not dwell within him, that he has no room for him—however it may be with other guests—in his soul? And the strange, sad reluctancy to speak for Christ to others shows how partial is his possession of even Christian souls. (*c*) Facts. See what men are and say and do; mark their conduct, their conversation, their character; examine the maxims, principles, and motives which regulate them, and see if Christ be in all or any of them. And this, not only in men brought up in ungodliness, but often in those trained in pious homes, and from whom you would have expected better things. (3) And this is the soul's own doing. It voluntarily excludes Christ. When his appeal is heard, and very often it is, men *divert* their thoughts, distract them with other themes; or *deaden* their convictions, by plunging into pleasure, business, sin; or *delay* obedience, procrastinating and putting off that which they ought promptly to perform. Ah, what guilt! Ah, what folly! (4) And this is the sin "against the Holy Ghost, which hath never forgiveness." Not any one definite act, but this persistent exclusion of Christ. The knocking of the Lord is heard more and more faintly, until at length, although it goes on, it is not heard at all. The sin has been committed, and the punishment has begun. But the text contemplates also the happier alternative. 3. *The soul claiming its greatest privilege*—opening the door to Christ. He says, "If any man will open," thereby plainly teaching us that men may and should, and—blessed be his Name—some will, open that door. (1) The soul can do this. It is part of its great prerogative. It could not say, "Yes," if it could not say, "No;" but because it can say, "No," it can also say, "Yes." (2) And the opening of the door depends upon its saying, "Yes." This is no contradiction to the truth that the Holy Spirit must open the heart. Both are essential; neither can be done without. It is a co-operative work, as consciousness and Scripture alike teach. But the Spirit ever does his part of the work; it is we only who fail in ours. May we be kept herefrom!

III. SALVATION. The result of such opening the door is this, and the picture that is given of it is full of interest. 1. *Christ becomes our Guest.* "I will sup with him." Now, if we invite any one to our table, we have to provide the feast. But what have we to set before Christ that he will care for? Ah, what? "All our righteousnesses" —will they do? Not at all. In this spiritual banquet that which he will most joyfully accept is ourselves, coming in contrition and trust to rest upon his love. "The sacrifices of God," etc. (Ps. li.). Let us bring them; *they*, but naught else, will be well-pleasing to him. But the scene changes. 2. *Christ becomes our Host.* "He with me." Ah! now what a difference!

> "Blest Jesus, what delicious fare!
> How sweet thine entertainments are!"

This we shall soon realize. (1) There is full, free pardon for every sin. (2) Next, the assurance of his love, that he has accepted us. (3) Power to become like him— renewing, regenerating grace. (4) His peace, so that in all trial and sorrow we may "rest in the Lord." (5) Power to bless others, so that they shall be the better for having to do with us. (6) Bright hope, blessed outlook to the eternal inheritance. (7) And at last, in due time, that inheritance itself. Such are some of the chief elements of that banquet at which Christ is the Host; and all the while there is sweet, blessed intercourse, hallowed communion, with himself. He is "known to us in the breaking of bread."

CONCLUSION. How, then, shall it be? Shall we still keep the door of our hearts barred against him? May he forbid! We can do this; alas! some will. But we can open the door. Do that.

> "In the silent midnight watches,
>   List! thy bosom door!
> How it knocketh—knocketh—knocketh—
>   Knocketh evermore!
> Say not 'tis thy pulse is beating:
>   'Tis thy heart of sin;
> 'Tis thy Saviour knocks and crieth,
>   'Rise, and let me in.'
>
> "Death comes on with reckless footsteps,
>   To the hall and hut;
> Think you, Death will tarry knocking
>   Where the door is shut?
> Jesus waiteth—waiteth—waiteth,
>   But the door is fast;
> Grieved, away thy Saviour goeth:
>   Death breaks in at last.

"Then 'tis time to stand entreating
    Christ to let thee in;
At the gate of heaven beating,
    Waiting for thy sin.
Nay—alas! thou guilty creature;
    Hast thou then forgot?
Jesus waited long to know thee,
    Now he knows thee not."

S. C.

Vers. 1—6.—(5) *The epistle to the Church in Sardis: the decaying Church on the brink of ruin.* The sad spectacle is presented here of a Church dying out. To the angel it is said, "Thou hast a name that thou livest, and thou art dead." This is the judgment of him who hath "the seven Spirits of God, and the seven stars." He holds the stars in his hand, for safety in danger, for punishment in unfaithfulness. They cannot escape from him. The Lord of life is the Lord also of death and judgment. The watchword is significant of the slumbering, exposed state of the Church; it is the sharp word of the ever-wakeful Lord—*Watch.* "Be thou watchful, and stablish the things that remain, which are ready to die."

I. THIS CALL IS RENDERED NECESSARY BY THE CONDITION OF THE CHURCH. 1. The deceitful semblance of life though death lurks within. How strikingly opposed is the appearance to the reality! If all were not actually overcome by death—as the word "repent" would imply—yet were they on the brink of death; nay, death reigned. A remnant may remain, but of the body as a whole it must be said, "Thou art dead." Or, in more accurate language, spiritual death, which is as a sleep, has palsied the strength and virtue of the Church. "Thou hast a name that thou livest, and thou art dead." 2. The good that remains is on the verge of ruin. "The things that remain" were "ready to die." Sad, indeed, is the condition of any Church when its last remnant of good is tainted; when a deadly disease seizes upon the last living hope. 3. The imperfectness of all their works in the sight of God. Whatever may have been their appearance to the eye of man, "before God" every work is judged to be unfulfilled, imperfect, incomplete. The strength of the life, the vital force, is abating; all the activities of life, therefore, are faulty. As is the life, so is the work of life.

II. THE CALL IS RENDERED NECESSARY BY THE CRITICAL CONDITION TO WHICH THE CHURCH IS REDUCED.

III. BY THE THREAT OF SPEEDY JUDGMENT IF THE SIGNS OF REPENTANCE ARE NOT FORTHCOMING. "If therefore thou shalt not watch, I will come as a thief, and thou shalt not know what hour I will come upon thee."

IV. THE CALL IS FURTHER URGED BY THE GRACIOUS PROMISE TO THE FEW REMAINING FAITHFUL ONES.

V. AND IT IS RENDERED THE MORE IMPRESSIVE BY THE WORDS WHICH FORM THE BACKGROUND OF HOPE TO EVERY ONE THAT OVERCOMETH. These include: 1. Purity. 2. Perpetuity of blessed life. 3. Honourable recognition: "before my Father and before his angels."—R. G.

Vers. 7—13.—(6) *The epistle to the Church in Philadelphia: the Church in her fidelity rewarded.* The "holy" and "true" One—the Holy One who is Truth, who has supreme power, opening and shutting at his will, and whose work none can withstand, he speaks his word of commendation and blessing and promise to his steadfast Church. The symbolical word is *fidelity.* The reward comprises—

I. THE LORD'S DISTINCT RECOGNITION OF THE CHURCH'S FIDELITY. "I know thy works." To fight in view of the sovereign, and of the observing nation—a stimulus to bravery, patience, and endurance. The eye of the multitude the stimulus to many great and worthy enterprises. But the watchful eye of the Lord—"he that is holy, he that is true"—is the true encouragement and sustaining stimulus to the suffering and toilsome Church in all ages. This recognition descends to the details and particulars of service. 1. "Thou hast a little power." A true estimate of the Church's ability. 2. Faithfulness to the truth. Thou "didst keep my word." 3. Steadfastness in the hour of trial. Thou "didst not deny my Name." The reward further comprises—

II. THE OPENING OF ENLARGED SPHERES OF USEFULNESS. "I have set before thee an open door." Useful employment in the Lord's service is the highest honour. The token of approbation of past service found in the call to greater works.

III. THE SUBJUGATION OF THE ENEMIES OF THE CHURCH. "I will make them to come and worship at thy feet." The true reward to the Church is not found in her elevation, but in the conversion of the enemies of the truth.

IV. THE TESTIMONY BEFORE THE ENEMIES OF THE DIVINE LOVE FOR THE CHURCH. Weary may be the days of the Church's endurance, but all will be forgotten in the Lord's gracious recognition "in the last day," when he shall "confess" them before his Father and before the holy angels—confess them as his; own and acknowledge them.

V. DEFENCE IN THE HOUR OF SPECIAL TRIAL. They who according to their strength serve the Lord will, in the hour of their weakness, find him to be their strong Rock of defence. "I also will keep thee from the hour of trial."

VI. BEYOND LIES THE EVER-ABIDING FULNESS OF BLESSING TO HIM WHO IN FAITH-FULNESS CONQUERS. Here specified. 1. The permanent abode in the eternal temple of the Lord—the everlasting fellowships of heaven. 2. Recognition as the Lord's; his Name written upon him. This distinction the highest. 3. Special personal recognition as holding the closest relation to the Redeemer. "Mine own new Name."—R. G.

Vers. 14—22.—(7) *The Epistle to the Church in Laodicea.* The "Amen, the faithful and true Witness," speaks to the untrue and unfaithful Church, whose outward appearance contrasts so with her internal state. Deceptive pretentiousness receives its rebuke. The lukewarm—neither hot and fervent in devotion nor lowlily acknowledging itself to be cold; neither fervid in holy affection nor consciously lacking holy fervour and confessing it—lacking the true warm fervour of love, and either not knowing the lack, or, knowing it, yet acknowledging it not, but pretending to have it,—this deceitful state receives the severest rebuke from the Lord, the ever "true" One, who despises all untruth and all deceptiveness.

I. THE CHURCH'S STATE DESCRIBED. "Thou sayest, I am rich; . . . thou knowest not thou art poor and blind and naked, thou miserable one." 1. Actually spiritually poor; beggared. 2. Ignorant. 3. Presumptuous self-deception.

II. THE LORD'S COUNSEL TO HIS DECEIVED CHURCH. 1. Seek ye the true riches; buy of me gold; buy without money and without price the true spiritual things. 2. Buy of me "white garments"—the true spiritual virtues; the things thou lackest. Thy debased and faulty form, thy shame, is uncovered. Only of me canst thou buy the robes of righteousness. 3. Buy also "eyesalve," the true spiritual illumination, "that thou mayest see"—the Holy Spirit, Teacher, Illuminator, Light, who is eyes to the blind, life to the dead.

III. THE APPENDED THREAT, WITH ITS EXHORTATION AND GRACIOUS ENTREATY. 1. The Lord's threatenings are gracious promises in disguise. "I reprove and chasten as many as I love." The Lord's love lingers long after human goodness has waned. The blind, the naked, the poor, the miserable, are still loved, and therefore reproved by word of mouth and by judgment and chastening correction and discipline. 2. Because I love, because I reprove, therefore "repent"—acknowledge, deplore, depart from thy sins. "Be zealous;" seek to rekindle the dying fire of holy love. 3. The Lord's entreaty thrown into a pictorial representation of (1) patient, long-suffering love: "I stand at the door;" (2) of repeated appeal: "and knock;" (3) of ready response to the first yieldings of the hearkening and opening heart: "If any man," etc.; (4) even happy and unbroken fellowship is promised: "I will come in and sup," etc.

IV. The whole is supplemented by A FINAL ENCOURAGING PROMISE. "He that overcometh, I will give to him to sit down with me in my throne." So the Lord who condescendingly sits at the board of the house, the door of which is opened to him, calls the humble dweller therein to sit with him in high glory on his throne. Happy they who, having ears, hear; and who hearing, obey.—R. G.

Vers. 1—6.—*The words of Christ to the congregation at Sardis.* "Sardis," says Dr. Eadie, "was a city of ancient Lydia. Its modern name is *Sert Kalesi,* and it lies about thirty miles south-east of Thyatira, and two miles south of the river Hermus.

It is, however, but a miserable village, inhabited chiefly by shepherds, though it is one of the stopping-places of the Persian caravans. The original city was plundered by Cyrus, and afterwards desolated by an earthquake, the ruins of it being still visible a little distance to the south of the present town. Nothing is now to be seen but a few mud huts, inhabited by ignorant, stupid, filthy Turks, and the only men who bear the Christian name are at work all day in their mill. Everything seems as if God had cursed the place, and left it to the dominion of Satan." A modern traveller says, " I sat beneath the sky of Asia to gaze upon the ruins of Sardis from the banks of the golden-sanded Pactolus. Beside me were the cliffs of that Acropolis which centuries before the hardy Median scaled while leading on the conquering Persians whose tents had covered the very spot on which I was reclining. Before me were the vestiges of what had been the palace of the gorgeous Crœsus; within its walls were once congregated the wisest of mankind, Thales, Cleotolus, and Solon. Far in the distance were the gigantic tumuli of the Lydian monarch, and around them spread those very plains once trodden by the countless hosts of Xerxes when hurrying on to find a sepulchre at Marathon. But all had passed away! There before me were the fanes of a dead religion, and the tombs of forgotten monarchs, and the palm tree that waved in the banquet-halls of kings." Who founded the Christian community at Sardis, or the exact period when the gospel was first preached there, are questions that have not been, and perhaps cannot be, settled. The address of Christ to this community, as recorded in these verses, forcibly calls our attention to the consideration of three things—*the general character of the many; the exceptional character of the few;* and *the absolute Judge of all.* Notice—

I. THE GENERAL CHARACTER OF THE MANY. They were in a very lamentable condition. 1. *They had a reputation for being what they were not.* "Thou hast a name that thou livest, and [thou] art dead." It was bad enough for them to be " dead," that is, all but destitute of that supreme sympathy with spiritual goodness which is the essence of moral life. It was worse still for them to have the reputation of life, and for them to believe in that reputation. The sight of death is bad enough, but death garbed and decorated with the semblances of life makes it more ghastly to behold. How this community obtained this name for living, this high reputation in the neighbourhood, does not appear, albeit it is not difficult to guess. Perhaps it made loud professions, appeared very zealous and active, and paraded its affected virtues. Then, as now, perhaps, men were taken by their contemporaries to be rather what they appeared than what they were. In these days, and in our England, there are Churches that have the reputation of wonderful usefulness. All their doings, their prayers, their sprinklings and dippings, their pulpit deliverances and their psalmodies, their architectural expansions and numerical additions, are emblazoned in the so-called " Christian" journals, so that they have a great name to live, whereas spiritually they may be all but dead. Reputation is one thing, character is another. Everywhere in a corrupt world like this the basest characters have the brightest reputation, and the reverse. The barren fig tree was covered with luxuriant leafage. " Thou hast a name that thou livest, and art dead." 2. *They were in a state of spiritual consumption.* "That are ready to die." It would seem that, whilst they were not *all* spiritually dead, there was a spiritual consumption amongst some. "Things ready to die." What things are these? The greatest things in the universe, eternal principles of virtue and truth. What things are comparable to these? To them literatures, markets, governments, are puerilities. There is a spiritual consumption, and the symptoms are manifest. *Weakness, morbid appetites, false views of life,* etc. 3. *They were in a state requiring prompt and urgent attention.* "Be [thou] watchful, and strengthen [stablish] the things which remain, that are [which were] ready to die." What is to be done? (1) They were to be vigilant. "Watchful," wakeful, to shake off slothfulness, open their eyes to eternal realities, fan the dying sparks into a flame. (2) They were to be curative. "Strengthen the things which remain." How strengthen? Appropriate the true remedial element, fruit from the tree of life; use wholesome food, the " sincere milk of the Word;" take proper exercise —inaction leads to disease; "exercise thyself unto godliness;" inbreathe the pure atmosphere of holiness. (3) They were to be recollective. " Remember therefore how thou hast received." Call up all the good of the past. (4) They were to be repentant.

"Hold fast, and repent." They were to renounce all that was pernicious to spiritual health, and pursue a right course. "Hold fast." Grasp with all the tenacity of their being the good that comes up to memory, as the drowning man lays hold of the rope thrown out on the surging waves. 4. *They were in a state of alarming danger.* "If therefore thou shalt not watch, I will come on thee as a thief, and thou shalt not know what hour I will come upon thee." Such words as these Christ uttered while a tenant of this earth (Matt. xxiv. 32). Retribution generally moves stealthily as a thief. "The feet of the gods are shod with wool," says the old Greek proverb.

II. THE EXCEPTIONAL CHARACTER OF THE FEW. "Thou hast a few names even in Sardis which have not defiled [did not defile] their garments." "These few names," says Dr. Tait, "are here to the credit and honour of the Church, the few 'things' in connection with the Church in Pergamos were against it and to its condemnation He who was the angel of the Church does not seem to have known the few names, just as the prophet did not know the seven thousand in Israel who had not bowed their knees to Baal." Here, then, is goodness amidst social depravity. Three remarks are suggested. 1. *That true goodness can exist under external circumstances the most corrupt.* Sardis was one of the most dissolute cities of ancient times, but here were Christians. Man is not the creature of circumstances. 2. *That true goodness, wherever it exists, engages the specific attention of Christ.* Christ noticed the goodness in Sardis; and why? (1) Because it is the highest manifestation of God upon earth. (2) Because it is the result of his mediatorial mission. (3) Because on it depends the progress of humanity. 3. *That true goodness will ultimately be distinguished by a glorious reward.* The words, "walk with me," etc., imply three ideas. (1) Triumph. (2) Fellowship. (3) Progress.

III. THE ABSOLUTE JUDGE OF ALL. Who is the absolute Judge both of the *many* and the *few?* He is thus described: "These things saith he that hath the seven Spirits of God, and the seven stars." The absolute Judge of character is here presented in three connections. 1. *In connection with the highest influence.* "He that hath the seven Spirits of God." Elsewhere we read, "He whom God hath sent speaketh the words of God: for God giveth not the Spirit by measure unto him" (John iii. 34). The Divine Spirit is everywhere. The *amount* of its possession by any moral being is conditioned by that being's receptive capacity. No man ever appeared on earth who had the receptive capacity in such measure as Christ had it. He was *filled* with it. He opened his ministry by saying, "The Spirit of the Lord is upon me," etc. The more a man has of this Spirit, the more he can communicate of life and power and blessedness. 2. *In connection with the highest ministry.* "The seven stars." These were, as we have seen, the angels of the seven Churches. What is the highest human ministry? The ministry of the gospel. Those engaged in this work are here called "stars," and these stars are in the hands of Christ. He moulds them with his influence, he burnishes them with his holiness, he fixes them in their orbits, he guides and sustains them in their spheres. He is, in truth, their Centre and Sun. From him they derive their order, their vitality, and their power. 3. *In connection with the highest Being.* "I will confess his name before my Father." The Father is the greatest Being in the universe. The relationship of Son implies: (1) *Resemblance.* (2) *Reciprocal love.* The Son identifies himself with all his true disciples. "I will confess his name before my Father, and before his angels."—D. T.

Vers. 7—13.—*The words of Christ to the Church at Philadelphia.* "And to the angel of the Church in Philadelphia," etc. On a slope of Mount Tmolus stood Philadelphia, a city of Lydia, lying between Sardis and Laodicea. Attalus Philadelphus, after whose name it was called Philadelphia, founded it B.C. 140. It was a commercial city of commanding position and considerable importance, and well fortified withal. Through its adjoining valley the celebrated Xerxes led his forces on his way to Greece. On account of the volcanic nature of its soil it became celebrated for the cultivation and the excellence of its vines. It had been visited by numerous earthquakes, and in the reign of Tiberius most of its population forsook it and fled to the fields, apprehending destruction. It survives to the present day, and is called by the Turks, *Allah Shehr,* "the city of God." The ruins of a church wall are still visible, and about five thousand members of the Greek Church, with a bishop and about fifteen clergymen, reside in its midst. Nowhere else is it mentioned in sacred Scripture. This wonderful letter brings under our notice *a character to be adored, an energy to be coveted,* and *a destiny to be sought.*

I. A CHARACTER TO BE ADORED. This character is here exhibited as : 1. *Holy.* " He that is holy." No man ever appeared on this earth so entirely and unquestionably pure as Christ was. He was " separate from sinners." None of his most malignant contemporaries could convince him of sin. Judas, after the betrayal, cried out, " I have sinned, in that I have betrayed the innocent blood." He was, indeed, " the holy, the harmless, the undefiled " Son of God. His spotless and undoubted holiness is a most incontrovertible argument for the Divinity of his gospel. 2. *True.* " He that is true." He is true in the highest sense. (1) True in *sentiment.* All his sympathies were in accord with eternal reality. (2) True in *speech.* All his language was in exact agreement with his sentiments. (3) True in *character.* No shifting from eternal right. " To this end was I born, to this end came I into the world, to bear witness to the truth." He stands in the world's history, amidst the world's shams, like the sun amidst the ever-shifting clouds. 3. *Supreme.* " He that hath the key of David." What this means I know not. It cannot mean, however, that Christ in any moral sense resembled the moral character of David. One thing, however, is clear, that David obtained terrible authority over all the resources of Israel. He had a " key " to the resources of the kingdom, and Christ has a key to the moral empire of heaven. He has supremacy of the highest kind. " He that openeth, and no man shutteth ; and shutteth, and no man openeth." " He dispenses and he withholds God's treasures ; he gives or he denies this or that talent, this or that blessing. In a yet more solemn meaning of the words, it is his to admit into and his to exclude from the eternal kingdom of glory. In spiritual and eternal things, wherever there is a door, Christ has the key of it " (Dr. Vaughan). All the doors to human usefulness, dignity, and happiness are at his disposal.

II. AN ENERGY TO BE COVETED. " Thou hast a little strength [power]." This Church had a little power. What was it? Not physical force, not intellectual capacity, not regal rule, but *moral.* Force to resist the wrong and pursue the right, force to serve the Almighty and to bless mankind. In relation to this moral strength notice : 1. *It is the energy of true usefulness.* " Behold, I have set before thee an open door [a door opened], and no man can [which none can] shut it: for thou hast a little strength." It is implied that a little moral strength fits a man for usefulness to some extent. Hence the door of opportunity is thrown open to him. Every man has a mission in life, but he only is qualified to enter on it who has moral strength. Alas! the millions are morally impotent, and they live and die without entering on the prosecution of their great duty in life. 2. *It is the energy of loyal obedience.* " And hast kept [didst keep] my word." This moral strength enables a man to hold on to duty, to hold on to the right with all the tenacity of life, to feel with Job, " Though he slay me, yet will I trust in him ; " like Paul to say, " I count not my life dear unto me," etc. 3. *It is the energy of true courage.* " And hast not denied [didst not deny] my Name." " The tenses used," says Bishop Carpenter, " point back to some epoch in the history of this Church when some heavy trial or persecution arose which tested the sincerity, fidelity, or Christian love of the faithful." Who can estimate the temptation which every good man has in a world of infidels, often malignant, to deny his Lord and Master? Peter yielded to it. What invincible courage is required! Courage like that which Paul had when he said, " God forbid that I should glory," etc. ; and again, " Who shall separate me from the love of Christ? Shall tribulation ? " etc. 4. *It is the energy of moral sovereignty.* " Behold, I will make them of [I give of] the synagogue of Satan, [of them] which say they are Jews, and are not, but do lie ; behold, I will make them to come and worship before thy feet, and to know that I have loved thee." Who are those spoken of as " of the synagogue of Satan " ? Were they the Judaizing Christians, or persecuting Jews? Why spend time with Trench, or other critics, to start such an inquiry ? No one can determine, nor does it matter ; they were moral antagonists to the congregation at Philadelphia. Concerning them we are here told that the men of moral strength will bring them to their feet ; they will not only subdue them, but inspire them with love. High moral power is the highest sovereignty that one man can wield over another ; it subdues the heart.

Political rule is but a mere worthless shadow and pretence compared with moral. **5.** *It is the energy of Divine approval and protection.* " Because thou hast kept [didst keep] the word of my patience, I also will keep thee from the hour of temptation." III. A DESTINY TO BE SOUGHT. What a distinction awaits those who possess and rightly employ this true moral strength! **1.** *A crown lies within their reach.* " Behold, I come quickly: hold that fast which thou hast, that no man [one] take thy crown." Christ is coming to every man, and coming with speed, coming in the events of man's history and in his exit by death. When he comes there is a " crown " for him, if he holds faithfully on to the true and the right. The allusion here is to the public games of Greece, in which the winner obtained a garland of laurels. But what is that garland to the crown here referred to? The eternal weight of glory, a "crown" which shall outshine yon permanent sun. " Be faithful unto death, and I will give thee a crown of life." **2.** *Divine security is assured.* " Him [he] that overcometh will I make [I will make him] a pillar in the temple of my God, and he shall go [out thence] no more out." " The promise," says an eminent critic, " is that of a secure and permanent position in God's heavenly temple. Philadelphia is said to have been singularly liable to earthquakes; not a building, common or sacred, but it might suddenly fall in ruins. The promise here made is that no such risks shall await the heavenly temple or those who have been built into it." **3.** *Sublime distinction is promised.* " I will write upon him the name of my God, and the name of the city of my God, which is new Jerusalem, which cometh down out of heaven from my God: and I will write upon him my [mine own] new name." " On the sides of the four marble pillars which survive as ruins of Philadelphia, inscriptions are to be found. The writing would be the name of God, the name of the heavenly Jerusalem, the new, unknown name of Christ himself. The allusion is to the golden frontlet inscribed with the name of Jehovah. He will reflect the likeness of God; and not only so, he will bear the tokens—now seen in all clearness—of his heavenly citizenship. And a further promise implies that in the day of the last triumph, as there will be new revealings of Christ's power, there will be unfolded to the faithful and victorious new and higher possibilities of purity. Thus does Scripture refuse to recognize any finality which is not a beginning as well as an end—a landing-stage in the great law of continuity."

CONCLUSION. " I cannot," says Trench, " leave this epistle, so full of precious promises to a Church which, having little strength, had yet held fast the word of Christ's patience, without citing a remarkable passage about it from Gibbon, in which he writes like one who almost believed that the threatening promises of God did fulfil themselves in history. ' In the loss of Ephesus the Christians deplored the fall of the first angel, the extinction of the first candlestick, of the Revelation ; the desolation is complete ; and the Temple of Diana or the Church of Mary will equally elude the search of the curious traveller. The circus and three stately theatres of Laodicea are now peopled with wolves and foxes ; Sardis is reduced to a miserable village ; the God of Mahomet, without a rival or a Son, is invoked in the mosques of Thyatira and Pergamos ; and the populousness of Smyrna is supported by the foreign trade of the Franks and Armenians. Philadelphia alone has been saved by prophecy or courage. At a distance from the sea, forgotten by the emperors, encompassed on all sides by the Turk, her valiant citizens defended their religion and freedom above four score years, and at length capitulated with the proudest of the Ottomans. Among the Greek colonies and Churches of Asia, Philadelphia is still erect—a column in a scene of ruins —a pleasing example that the paths of honour and safety may sometimes be the same.' "—D. T.

Vers. 14—22.—*The words of Christ to the Church at Laodicea.* " And unto the angel of the Church of the Laodiceans," etc. " Laodicea is in the south-west of Phrygia, on the river Lycus, not far from Colossæ, lying between it and Philadelphia, destroyed by an earthquake A.D. 62, rebuilt by its wealthy citizens without the help of the state. This wealth (arising from the excellence of its wools) led to a self-satisfied, lukewarm state in spiritual things. In Col. iv. 16 it is mentioned. The Church in later times was flourishing, for one of the councils at which the canon of Scripture was determined was held in Laodicea in A.D. 361. Hardly a Christian is now to be found near its site" (Fausset). We have here certain solemn and significant facts concerning *a corrupt Church,* such a Church as that which was existing at this time in Laodicea.

I. ITS REAL CHARACTER WAS THOROUGHLY KNOWN. There was an eye that peered into its deepest depths, knew well its moral elements and temperature. He who thus looked into and through it is thus described. 1. He is "the Amen." This is the Hebrew word for "verily," or "truly"—a word of energetic assertion and familiar use. In Christ, we are told, "is Yea and Amen." He is positive and declarative Truth. What he predicates is true to reality; what he predicts will be realized, whether lamentable or otherwise. 2. He is "the faithful and true Witness." What is a true witness? (1) One who has an absolute knowledge of the subject of which he affirms. And (2) one who is absolutely above all temptation to misrepresent. Christ has no motive to deceive, no evil to dread, no good to gain. 3. He is "the Beginning of the creation of God." He seems not only to have been the First of the creation, but in some sense the Originator. He is the *Beginning,* the *Continuance,* and *Purpose* of all. This is a mystery unfathomed, perhaps fathomless. This is the transcendent Being who knew thoroughly this Laodicean Church, and who knows all Churches. "I know thy works"—know them in their hidden germs and ever-multiplying branches.

> "Oh may these thoughts possess my breast,
> Where'er I roam, where'er I rest;
> Nor let my weaker passions dare
> Consent to sin, for God is near."

II. ITS SPIRITUAL INDIFFERENTISM IS DIVINELY ABHORRENT. "I would thou wert cold or hot." Cold water is refreshing, hot water is sometimes pleasant, the tepid is always more or less sickening. Well does an old writer say, "Lukewarmness or indifference in religion is the worst temper in the world. If religion is a real thing, it is the most excellent thing, and therefore we should be in good earnest in it; if it is not a real thing, it is the vilest imposture, and we should be earnest against it. If religion is worth anything, it is worth everything; an indifference here is inexcusable." 1. *Spiritual indifferentism is a most incongruous condition.* All nature seems in earnest: seas and stars are on the gallop; plants and animals rush onward on the lines of decay or growth; the minds of all moral beings are flowing with more or less speed in one direction or another. 2. *Spiritual indifferentism is a most incorrigible condition.* Theoretical infidelity we may break down by argument, but moral indifferentism cannot be touched by logic. The spiritually indifferent man shouts out his Creed every Sunday, damns the atheist, and yet himself is "without God in the world." Truly such a state of mind must be abhorrent to him who demands that all should love him with their whole heart, soul, and strength. What an awful supposition that man can sicken and disgust the Infinite! "I will spue thee out of my mouth." Moral depravity nauseates the holy universe.

III. ITS SELF-DECEPTION IS TERRIBLY ALARMING. "Thou sayest, I am rich, and increased with goods [have gotten riches], and have need of nothing; and knowest not that thou art wretched [the wretched one], and miserable, and poor, and blind, and naked." 1. *Look at the condition in which they fancied themselves.* "I am rich, and increased with goods." They fancied themselves rich and independent. "Have need of nothing." They wished to be all this, and the wish is evermore the father to the thought. Ah me! it is by no means uncommon for men to fancy themselves to be what they are not. If you go into lunatic spheres there you may see dwarfs fancying themselves giants and illustrious heroes, paupers thinking they are millionnaires, and poor beggars kings of the first order. But elsewhere I find in all the departments of human life that are considered to be sane, scenes scarcely less absurd. 2. *Look at the condition in which they really are.* "And knowest not that thou art wretched [the wretched one], and miserable, and poor, and blind, and naked." "Wretched," though they may dance and sing; pitiable, though lauded by princes, premiers, and peers; "blind," though the physical optics are sound; and "naked," though robed in splendour. Wretched, pitiable, blind, naked in soul: what a condition is this! what terrible self-deception! "The first and worst of all frauds," says Festus, "is to cheat one's self. All sin is easy after that."

IV. ITS MISERABLE CONDITION NEED NOT BE HOPELESS. 1. *Recovery is freely offered.* "I counsel thee to buy of me gold tried [refined] in the fire, that thou mayest be rich; and white raiment [garments]," etc. Is there irony here? How can the poor buy gold, become rich, procure white garments, and salve for the diseased eyes? No; there is no irony here. The blessings here offered require no outlay of material wealth. All is to be won by true faith, and all can believe. "Ho, every one that thirsteth, come," etc. 2. *Recovery is divinely urged.* "Behold, I stand at the door, and knock." Here observe: (1) Christ's *attitude towards* the soul. He does not come occasionally and depart. He "stands," implying his deep concern, his infinite condescension, and his wonderful patience. He waits to be gracious. (2) Christ's *action upon* the soul. He stands not as a statue, but knocks—knocks at the door of *intellect* with truths, at the door of *conscience* with principles, at the door of *love* with transcendent charms. (3) Christ's *purpose with* the soul. His mission is not to destroy, but to save it. "I will come in to him." The language implies: (*a*) Inhabitation. "I will come in to him." (*b*) Identification. "Sup with him, and he with me." Thus sinners are urged to deliver themselves from their miserable condition. 3. *Recovery is divinely rewarded.* "To him [he] that overcometh will I grant [I will give to him] to sit with me in my throne, even as I also overcame, and am set [sat] down with my Father in his throne." What are the thrones here? Are they some material seats in some radiant and remote part of the universe—the one provided for the Father and the other for the Son? The question is childish, sensuous, and unspiritual. What is the true throne of a human soul? (1) It is the throne of an *approving conscience.* That mind alone can rest whose conscience applauds him, and that soul alone can feel exalted and dignified whose conscience chimes to him, "Well done." (2) It is the throne of *moral rule.* He who subordinates the material to the spiritual, the animal to the intellectual, the intellectual to the moral, and the moral to God, occupies the true throne. He is king, and none other.—D. T.

EXPOSITION.

CHAPTER IV.

This is the commencement of the second great division, which embraces ch. iv.—xxii. 5, that in which the revelation, properly so called, takes place. Ch. iv. and v. contain the first of the seven visions, which is itself a prelude to the rest.

Ver. 1.—**After** this; or, *after these things* (μετὰ ταῦτα). There is no good ground for supposing, as some do, that, after the events narrated in ch. iii., an interval occurred in the visions, during which St. John possibly wrote down the matter contained in the first three chapters. Nor is there any justification for assigning what follows to a time after this world. It would be pressing ταῦτα very far to make it apply to these present things of the world; and μετὰ ταῦτα certainly need not mean "the things after this world." The expression is used here in its ordinary, natural sense: "After having seen this, I saw," etc.; introducing some new phase or variety of spectacle. I looked; or, *I saw* (εἶδον). No fresh act of *looking* is signified. *I saw* in the Spirit, as formerly (ch. i. 10, 12). And, behold, a door; or, *and, behold, a door, and the first voice.* Such is the construction of the Greek. Was

opened in heaven; or, *an open door, in heaven.* St. John did not see the action of opening the door, but he saw a door which had been set open, through which he might gaze, and observe what passed within. Alford contrasts Ezek. i. 1; Matt. iii. 16; Acts vii. 56; x. 11, where "the heaven was opened;" and supposes that the seer is transported through the open door into heaven, from which position he sees heaven, and views all that happens on the earth. Victorinus aptly compares the *open door* to the gospel. And the first voice which I heard, as it were, of a trumpet talking with me. Omit the "was" which follows, as well as the colon which precedes, and repeat "a voice," as in the Revised Version: *And, behold, an open door in heaven, and the first voice which I heard, the voice which was, as it were, of a trumpet.* The voice signified is not the *first,* but the *former* voice; viz. that already heard and described in ch. i. 10. The possessor of the voice is not indicated. Stier ('Reden Jesu') attributes the voice to Christ; but it seems rather that of an angel, or at any rate not that of Christ, whose voice in ch. i. 15 is described as "of many waters," not as "of a trumpet." Which said. The voice (φωνή) becomes masculine (λέγων). Though *whose* voice is not stated, yet the vividness and reality of the vision causes the writer to speak of the *voice* as the personal being whom it signifies. **Come up hither.** That is in the Spirit—for the apostle "immediately was in the Spirit" (ver. 2). He was to receive a yet higher insight into spiritual things (cf. 2 Cor. xii. 2, where St. Paul was "caught up into the third heaven"). **And I will show thee.** It is not necessary, with Stier (see above on ver. 1), to infer that these words are Christ's. Though from him all the revelation comes, he may well use the ministry of angels through whom to signify his will. **Things which must be hereafter;** or, *the things which must happen hereafter.* The things which it is right should happen, and which, therefore, must needs happen (δεῖ). "Hereafter" (μετὰ ταῦτα); as before in ver. 1, but in a somewhat more general and less definite sense—*at some time after this;* but when precisely is not stated. The full stop may possibly be better placed before "hereafter;" in which case "hereafter" would introduce the following phrase, exactly as before in this verse. There is no "and;" καί, though in the Textus Receptus, is omitted in the best manuscripts.

Ver. 2.—**And immediately I was in the Spirit.** Omit "and" (see above), so that the passage may be rendered, *After these things, immediately, I was in the Spirit;* a new scene was opened out, as before (in ver. 1). St. John was already *in the Spirit;* but now receives a fresh outpouring of grace, enabling him to see yet more deeply into the mysteries of the kingdom of God. **And, behold, a throne was set in heaven;** or, *a throne was situated* (ἔκειτο). There is no action of placing or setting up. Compare the vision of Ezekiel, "In the firmament that was above the head of the cherubims there appeared over them as it were a sapphire stone, as the appearance of the likeness of a throne" (Ezek. x. 1), where the throne appears above the cherubim, in the position of the cloud of glory (cf. also Isa. vi. 1, 2, where the seraphim are above). **And one sat on the throne.** Probably the Triune God, to whom the Trisagion in ver. 8 is addressed. Some have thought that the Father is indicated, in contradistinction to the other Persons of the Holy Trinity, and that it is from him that the Son takes the book in ch. v. 8. But as Cornelius à Lapide remarks, "The Son as Man may well be said, especially in a sublime vision like this, to come to God." The Person is not named, because (1) the Name of God is incommunicable; it is the "new Name" (see on ch. iii. 12); or (2) because the seer describes only what is seen; or (3) it is suppressed from a sense of reverence.

Ver. 3.—**And he that sat was to look upon**

like, etc.; or, *he that sat like in appearance* (ὁράσει). The word ὅρασις is found in this verse and in two other places only in the New Testament, viz. in Acts ii. 17 (where it is part of a quotation from Joel) and in ch. ix. 17. In the latter place the expression is ἐν τῇ ὁράσει, and the presence of the preposition, together with the article, seems to justify the rendering "in the vision." In the Septuagint ὅρασις is frequently used to signify either "vision" or "appearance" (see 1 Sam. iii. 1; Isa. i. 1; Lam. ii. 9; Ezek. vii. 13; Dan. i. 17 and viii. 1; Obad. 1; Nah. i. 1; Hab. ii. 2; and many others, where it is "vision." Also Judg. xiii. 6; Ezek. i. 5, 13, 26—28; Dan. viii. 15; Nah. ii. 4; 1 Sam. xvi. 12; and many others, where it is "appearance"). In the classics, ὅραμα signifies a "vision;" ὅρασις, "sight," the power of seeing. **A jasper and a sardine stone.** The *jasper* was the last, and the *sardius* the first stone of the high priest's breastplate (Exod. xxviii. 17). The jasper was the first, and the sardius the sixth of the foundations of the heavenly Jerusalem (ch. xxi. 19, 20). Much doubt is attached to the whole subject of the precious stones of the Bible. The modern jasper is opaque, while it is evident that the jasper of the Revelation is remarkable for its translucent character (see ch. xxi. 11, "jasper stone, clear as crystal;" xxi. 18, "The building of the wall of it was of jasper; and the city was pure gold, like unto clear glass"). It is evident that the stone was characterized by purity and brilliancy—features which seem to point it out as the modern diamond. The varying colour, which, according to some authorities, the jasper possessed, is not inconsistent with this view. It is curious, too, that in Exod. xxviii. 18, the Hebrew יַהֲלֹם, which in the Authorized Version is rendered "diamond," is represented in the LXX. by ἴασπις; while in ver. 20, יָשְׁפֵה the English "jasper," is ὀνύχιον. The *sardius* was the carnelian, always red, though somewhat varying in shade. The name has been variously derived from (1) the Persian *sered*, yellowish red; (2) Sardis, as the first place of its discovery; (3) while carnelian is connected with *carneus*, as being of the colour of raw flesh. But (4) Skeat derives the word from *cornu*, a horn; the term being thus an allusion to the semitransparent nature of the stone. The pure jasper, together with the red sardius, may fitly typify God's purity and mercy together with his justice and judgment. **And there was a rainbow round about the throne.** The Greek ἶρις, which is used here, is not found in the LXX., where τόξον is invariably found, probably to avoid reference to a term which was so pre-eminently heathen. The rainbow is here, as always (see Gen. ix. 12,

13), a token of God's faithfulness in keeping his promises. It is, therefore, a fit sign of comfort to those persecuted Christians to whom, and for whose edification, this message was sent. In sight like unto an emerald. The σμάραγδος is our modern green emerald. It was highly valued in Roman times. It was one of the stones of the high priest's breastplate, and the fourth foundation of the heavenly Jerusalem (ch. xxi. 19). The description in this verse recalls Ezek. i. 28, "As the appearance of the bow that is in the cloud in the day of rain, so was the appearance of the brightness round about." Some have found a difficulty in the association of a rainbow with its varied colours, and the single green hue of the emerald. But of course it is the form only of the rainbow which is alluded to, not every quality which a rainbow may possess. A circular green appearance was seen round the throne, which perhaps may be described as a green halo. If the purity of the jasper (see above) be allowed to symbolize God's purity and spirituality, and the sardine, man clothed with flesh, the green emerald may fitly represent God's goodness displayed in nature.

Ver. 4.—And round about the throne were four and twenty seats. Throughout the vision no past tense is used. The vision represents the worship of heaven (so far as it can be presented to human understanding) as it continues eternally. *Thrones . . . seats.* Render both by the same English word, as in the Revised Version. Some doubt is attached to the case of the first θρόνοι. Θρόνοι is found in B, P; and this makes the construction nominative after ἰδού (cf. ver. 2); but א, A, 34, 35, read θρόνους, which causes εἶδον to be understood. The point is immaterial, as the meaning is the same. And upon the seats I saw four and twenty elders sitting. Omit "I saw" (see above). The number twenty-four, the double of twelve, represents the Churches of both the old and the new covenants. The elders are the heads or representatives of the body to which they belong (see Exod. xix. 7; xxiv. 1, and many others; see also the list of *elders* in Heb. xi.). In the Christian Church the same distinction exists (see Acts xiv. 23, "ordained them *elders;*" Acts xx. 17, St. Paul sent for *the elders* of Ephesus; Acts. xxi. 18, "The elders were present"). So here the *elders* represent the saints of both the Old and New Testaments. Thus they offer "the prayers of the saints" (ch. v. 8). Christ, moreover, promised twelve thrones to his disciples (Luke xxii. 30) though not to the exclusion of the saints of old, for both are conjoined in ch. xxi. 12, 14. In ch. xv. 2, 3, the victorious ones sing "the song of *Moses* and of the *Lamb.*" Other interpreta-

tions which have been advanced are (1) that the twenty-four elders represent the great and minor prophets (St. Hippolytus); (2) higher angels—the celestial priesthood, as denoted by their white garments and the number twenty-four, the number of courses of the Levitical priesthood (Reuss); (3) simply angels (Hoffmann); (4) the elders of the Church at Jerusalem (Grotius); (5) the doubled twelve signifies the accession of the Gentiles (Bleek, De Wette); (6) the books of the Old Testament, then the Jewish Church, while the four living creatures denote the Gospels, that is, the Christian Church (Wordsworth). (For this last view, for which there is much to be said, see Wordsworth, *in loc.*) Clothed in white raiment; the natural garb of heaven, symbolical of purity. And they had on their heads crowns of gold (στεφάνους, not διαδήματα). The crown of victory, not necessarily the kingly crown. Possibly a reference to the priestly crown (see on ch. ii. 10). Trench and Vaughan, however, are of opinion that the crowns here denote the kingly condition of the saints. But Christians are nowhere in the New Testament described as "kings."

Ver. 5.—And out of the throne proceeded lightnings and thunderings and voices. The *present* tense (see on ver. 4). The whole symbolical of the power and majesty of God, as of old he manifested his presence on Sinai. "There were thunders and lightnings and . . . the voice of the trumpet" (Exod. xix. 16). And there were seven lamps of fire burning before the throne, which are the seven Spirits of God. The Holy Spirit, represented in his sevenfold operation, by lamps, which illumine. The same idea is expressed under another figure in ch. v. 6, where the searching, enlightening power of the Holy Spirit is typified by *seven eyes.*

Ver. 6.—And before the throne there was a sea of glass like unto crystal. *Sea of glass,* or *a glassy sea.* The quality of "glassiness" may refer to the pure *appearance* of the sea; or it may mean that the sea was in consistency like unto glass; that is, solid and unyielding, so that there was nothing strange in the fact that it supported weights. In either case, the notion is repeated by parallelism in the next clause, "like unto crystal." But the glassy sea may mean "a glass laver," and bear no reference to what is usually called a sea. The brazen laver is described (1 Kings vii. 23) as a "molten sea." St. John may therefore mean that before the throne of God was a laver of the purest material, just as the brazen laver was before the temple. One difficulty here presents itself, viz. that there would be no use for a laver in heaven, where all is pure, and the figure therefore appears a little incongruous. But as it stood *before* the throne, where all who came would have to pass by, it may fitly typify the waters of Baptism, passed by all Christians; and the figure would be aptly suggested to St. John by the furniture of the temple to which he has such constant allusions. And in the midst of the throne, and round about the throne. This may mean either (1) that, the throne being rectangular, the four living beings were in the middle of each side of the parallelogram; or (2) while one was in front of the throne, the other three formed a semicircle round it, one being directly behind, and two towards the ends. Were four beasts; or, *four living creatures* (Revised Version); or, better still, *four living beings* (ζῶα). The "beast" (θηρίον) of ch. vi. 7; xi. 7, etc., must not be confounded with the "living ones" of this passage. The one quality connoted by the term here used is the possession of life. The question of the precise meaning and interpretation of the vision of "the living beings" is a difficult one, and much has been written concerning it. The vision is evidently connected with the appearances described in Isa. vi. and Ezek. i. and x., and which are called in Isaiah "seraphim," in Ezekiel "cherubim." We are led, therefore, to inquire what mental ideas were pictured to the Jews under the symbolical forms of cherubim and seraphim. Cheyne shows ('Prophecies of Isaiah,' vol. ii. p. 272) that the name *cherub* is probably connected with *kirubu*, the winged ox-god of the Assyrians, and with *kurubu*, the vulture or eagle (cf. the γρύπες, the guardians of the treasures of the gods); and he infers that among heathen nations the mythic cherubim denote the cloud-masses which appear to guard the portals of the sky, and on which the sun-god issues at break of day. With regard to the seraphim, he compares the name of the fiery serpents (*s'rāfīm*) of Numb. xxi. 6, and concludes that the term was symbolical of the lightning, the weapon of the gods. Now, in Old Testament passages the cherubim and seraphim are always pictured as the attendants of God, and the workers of his purposes and judgments—an idea which may readily have been assimilated by the Jews from the conceptions of their heathen neighbours. Thus cherubim with the flaming sword are placed at the entrance of the garden of Eden (Gen. iii. 24); Jehovah rode upon a cherub, and did fly (2 Sam. xxii. 11; Ps. xviii. 10); he communes with his people from between the cherubim (Exod. xxv. 22); he is the Shepherd of Israel, who dwells between the cherubim (Ps. lxxx. 1); the temple in Ezek. xli. 18 is adorned with cherubim, as being the dwelling-place of God; they are the attendants of the glory of God in Ezek. i. 22—28; and the seraphim fill an analogous position (Isa. vi. 2). We

may therefore infer that the appearance of the "living beings" implied the presence of some order of beings in attendance upon God, the workers of his will, and the manifestation of his glory. Again, the term used (ζῶα) and the characteristics of the appearance naturally and almost irresistibly lead us to interpret the form as one symbolical of *life*. The human face, the ox as the representative of domestic, and the lion of wild animals, and the eagle among birds, appear to be typical of the four most conspicuous orders of animal life. The ceaseless movements described in ver. 8 portray the same idea. The four living beings draw attention to the woes heaped upon created life (ch. vi. 8). The *eyes* denote never-resting activity. We may therefore believe that the living beings are symbolical of all creation fulfilling its proper office—waiting upon God, fulfilling his will, and setting forth his glory. It is noteworthy that the human face, as distinct from the Church, which is represented by the four and twenty elders, appears to indicate the power of God to use, for his purposes and his glory, that part of mankind which has not been received into the Church—the part which constitutes the "other sheep, not of this fold" (John x. 16). These representatives of created life worship God, and give (ver. 11), as a reason for ascribing glory and honour to him, the circumstance that "thou didst create all things, and because of thy will they were, and were created." The following are other interpretations: (1. The living beings represent the four Gospels. This view is held by many ancient writers, though there are many variations in assigning to each Gospel its own representative. Victorinus considers the *man* to be a type of St. Matthew, who sets forth prominently the human nature of our Lord; the kingly *lion* is referred to St. Mark; the sacrificial *ox* to St. Luke; the aspiring *eagle* to St. John. Amongst the supporters of this interpretation (though varying in the precise applicability) are St. Augustine, St. Jerome, St. Athanasius, St. Irenæus, St. Gregory, St. Ambrose, Andreas, Primasius, Bede, I. Williams, Wordsworth (for a full exposition of this view, see Wordsworth, *in loc.*). (2) The four great apostles: St. Peter, the lion; James the brother of the Lord, the ox; St. Matthew, the man; St. Paul, the eagle (Grotius). (3) The Church of the New Testament; as the Church of the Old Testament was represented by the standards of four tribes (see Numb. ii.), on which these devices were emblazoned according to tradition (Mede). (4) The four patriarchal Churches: the *man*, Alexandria, famed for learning; *the lion*, Jerusalem, "propter constantiam" (Acts v. 29);

the *ox*, Antioch, as "*parata obedire mandatis apostolorum*;" the *eagle*, Constantinople, remarkable for men "*per contemplationem elevati. ut* Greg. Naz." (De Lyra and à Lapide). (5) The four cardinal virtues (Arethas). (6) The four elements (the 'Catena,' p. 246)—a view not materially differing from that first set forth above, bearing in mind the idea of the ancients that all creation was formed from the four elements. (7) The four motive powers of the human soul : reason, anger, desire, conscience (à Lapide, quoting Greg. Naz.). (8) The doctors of the Church (Vitringa). (9) Four attributes of our Lord : his humanity, sacrificial life, his kingly nature, his perfect and spiritual nature soaring beyond all other men (Arethas-Cramer, p. 245). (10) The four orders : pastoral, diaconal, doctoral, contemplative, (Joachim). (11) The four principal angels (à Lapide). (12) Four apostolic virtues (Alcasar). (13) The attributes of divinity : wisdom, power, omniscience, creation (Renan). **Full of eyes before and behind.** From Isa. **vi.** 2, 3 the idea of *six* wings is borrowed, and also the "Holy, holy, holy" from Ezek. **i.** 5, 6; the *four figures and four faces* (which are united in Ezekiel, but made separate in the Revelation) ; and from Ezek. **x.** 12 the body *full of eyes.* The *eyes* denote unceasing activity. If the four living beings all faced towards the throne while standing on each side of it, St. John would see them in various positions, and observe the back as well as the front.

Ver. 7.—And the first beast was like a lion, and the second beast like a calf, and the third beast had a face as a man, and the fourth beast was like a flying eagle. (Upon "beast" (ζῶον), see on ver. 6. For the signification, see also above on ver. 6.) Whether there was any difference in the forms as a whole, or whether the difference consisted chiefly or solely in the face, cannot be certainly known. Each being is symbolical of some class or some quality of which it is representative. (For the application, see on ver. 6.)

Ver. 8.—And the four beasts had each of them six wings about him; and they were full of eyes within. The stop should probably be after "wings:" *are full of eyes about and within.* In Isa. **vi.** 2 we have "six wings; with twain he covered his face, and with twain he covered his feet, and with twain he did fly." These actions appear to indicate reverence, humility, obedience. The eyes denote ceaseless activity. **And they rest not day and night, saying.** In the Authorized Version "day and night" is attached to "rest not," but probably should be taken with "saying," for, if connected with the negative phrase, "nor" would be more likely to occur than "and."

But the point is practically immaterial, since the sense of the passage is the same in both readings. These representatives of *life* display the characteristics of life in its fullest energy. They have no part in anything which savours of death—no stillness, rest, or sleep. **Holy, holy, holy.** The thrice-repeated "holy" has very generally been held to indicate the Trinity of the Godhead. Such is evidently the intention of the English Church in ordering this passage to be read in the Epistle for Trinity Sunday. This ascription of praise is often, though wrongly, spoken of as the "Trisagion."[1] **Lord God Almighty.** "Almighty" is παντο-κράτωρ, the "All-Ruler," not παντοδύναμος, the "All-Powerful." The former, as Bishop Pearson says, embraces the latter. **Which was, and is, and is to come.** This phrase is no doubt intended to attribute to God the quality of eternal existence. But it may also symbolize three aspects or departments of God's dealings with mankind : the *creation*, which has been effected by the Father ; the *redemption*, which is now occurring by the intercession of the Son ; and the final perfect *sanctification* by the Holy Ghost.

Ver. 9.—And when those beasts give; or, *and as often as the living beings shall give.* The expression has a frequentative force, and also points to a continued repetition of the act in the future ; perhaps a contrast to the past, since before the redemption the Church, as being of the whole world, could not join in the adoration. **Glory and honour and thanks.** The Eucharistic hymn recognizes the glory and honour which are the inseparable attributes of God, and renders the thanks due to him from his creation. **To him that sat on the throne, who liveth for ever and ever;** or, *to him sitting on the throne.* The Triune God (see on ver. 2). "Who liveth for ever and ever" declares that attribute which was ascribed to God, in the song of the living beings, by the words, "which was, and is, and is to come" (see on ver. 8).

Ver. 10.—The four and twenty elders fall down before him that sat on the throne, and worship him that liveth for ever and ever. *Shall fall*, etc. The tenses are all future except the present "sitteth" and "liveth." The four and twenty elders are the representatives of the universal Church (see on

---

[1] The "Trisagion" is "the hymn Ἅγιος ὁ Θεός, ἅγιος ἰσχυρός, ἅγιος ἀθάνατος, ἐλέησον ἡμᾶς, which is sung, according to the rite of Constantinople, in connexion with the Little Entrance. . . . In the Roman Liturgy it is sung only on one day of the year, viz. Good Friday, in the special office called the Reproaches" ('Liturgies, Eastern and Western,' Hammond, p. 380).

ver. 4). And cast their crowns before the throne, saying. Their *crowns* of victory, στεφάνους (see on ch. ii. 10 and iv. 4).

Ver. 11.—Thou art worthy, O Lord; or, *thou art worthy, our Lord and our God.* In B, the Syriac, Andreas, Arethas, Theodore-Stud., Arm., and many others, ἅγιος, "the holy one," is added. To receive glory and honour and power (τὴν δόξαν, etc.). The presence of the article either (1) denotes universality, and the expression is thus equivalent to "all glory," "all honour," "all power;" or (2) refers to the glory and honour mentioned in ver. 9. The former view seems more probable (cf. ch. i. 6). The Church is represented as ascribing to God all power (δύναμιν); that power which he exercises in its fulness in heaven, and which, though partially abrogated on earth, he will nevertheless again take up, as foretold in ch. xi. 17. For thou hast created all things; or, *for thou didst create all things* (τὸ πάντα)—*the universe.* The representatives of creation thank God for their existence; the Church sees in his creation reason to ascribe power to him. Thus the reason for the doxo-logy is given—"because thou didst create." And for thy pleasure; much better, as in the Revised Version, *and because of thy will* (διὰ τὸ θέλημα). When God willed it, the universe had no existence; again, when he willed it, the universe came into being. They are, and were created; or, *they were, and were created* (Revised Version). There are three variations in the reading of this passage: (1) ἦσαν is read in ℵ, A, al[40] [fere Vulgate, Coptic, Syriac, Arethas, Primasius (in another version), anon Augustine, Haymo; (2) εἰσί is read in S, P, 1, 7, 35, 49, 79, 87, 91, *et al.* et Andreas; (3) οὐκ ἦσαν is read in B, 14, 38, 51. "They were" signifies "they existed," whereas before they were not in existence; "and were created" points to the manner of coming into existence and the Person to whom this existence was due. If εἰσί be read, the meaning is the same. Οὐκ ἦσαν would simplify the sentence very much. It would then run: *For thy pleasure,* or, *At thy will they were not existent, and again, at thy will they were created.* But the weight of authority is against this reading.

HOMILETICS.

Ver. 1.—*Things which must be hereafter.* However nearly expositors may approximate in their interpretation of the Book of Revelation up to the close of the third chapter, yet, when the "things which must be hereafter" begin to be unfolded, they part company, and diverge into so many different paths and by-paths, that it will not be possible for us to trace out all of them. Nor is it desirable. Our purpose is a purely homiletic one, viz. to unfold the principles of the Divine method and government, so as to help those who minister to the instruction and building up of the people of God. In this section of the Commentary we do not intend to turn aside to discourse on individual texts, however attractive and beautiful they may be, but *to open up the plan of God* as it is laid down in the Apocalypse ; yet not so as to minister to an idle and peering curiosity, but so as to inform the understanding, establish the faith, and animate the hope of believers. It has been our conviction now for twenty years (a conviction deepened by each successive study of this wondrous book) that if men will but note its silence as well as its speech—what it withholds as well as what it unfolds —if they will refrain from filling in chasms that the book leaves, and will aim at seizing the principles involved, rather than at fixing details and dates of events, there is no book in the Word of God that will be found richer in spiritual food, or clearer in its heavenly light ! There are several leading schemes of interpretation of the book. There is : 1. The *preteritist ;* which regards the book as indicating events which have passed long ago; which closed with the destruction of the Jewish city, temple, and polity, and with the setting up of the Christian Church—*it* being "the holy city, new Jerusalem." 2. The *extreme futurist.* Whereas according to the first everything has happened which is here recorded, according to the second nothing has yet occurred. Even the seven Churches are seven Churches of Jews to be formed after the first resurrection, and all that is in the rest of the book is to follow on from thence. Between these two extremes there are, however, three others; the greater number of inter-preters belonging, in fact, to one or other of these three. 3. Some regard the book as virtually a progressive history, dating from the imprisonment of St. John in Patmos under the Emperor Domitian. In their view the seven seals, vials, and trumpets indicate a triple series of events which may be either consecutive or simultaneous. In both cases, however, the interpretation is adopted of " a day for a year." 4. Others, again, regard the book as including a symbolic representation of things occurring on earth at the time of the apostle; and in addition thereto, a symbolic representation of events extending over twelve hundred and sixty days, which will usher in the coming of our Lord. 5. A fifth and rapidly increasing school of expositors adopt what is called (and rightly) the spiritual interpretation of the book; *i.e.* instead of fixing this or that earthquake, pestilence, or famine as the one specially referred to, they hold [1] "that this book of sublimity contains a pictorial representation of events which commenced at the Christian era, and will run on to the end of the world." So also Godet remarks, concerning the six seals, that they represent, each of them, not a particular event, but "the categories of the principal judgments by which God supports, throughout all time, the preaching of the gospel." [2] The spiritual interpretation is that to which for many years past we have felt ourselves shut up, and we are glad to find it adopted by Dr. Lee in his exposition. He says, "The imagery of the book describes, in accordance with the whole spirit of prophecy, the various conditions of the kingdom of God on earth, during its successive struggles with the prince of this world;" and again, "The 'spiritual' application is never exhausted, but merely receives additional illustrations as time rolls on, while the 'historical' system assumes that single events, as they come to pass in succession, exhibit the full accomplishment of the different predictions of the Apocalypse." [3] Hence, at this stage of our unfolding of the plan of the book, we would lay it down as the basis of our exposition that, without attempting (for reasons yet to be given) to indicate anything like an estimate of the time over which our dispensation has to run, *we shall find in this book, from beginning to end, such a disclosure of the principles and methods of God's working, in bringing about the second coming of the Lord, as may well fill us with holy awe, while we are contemplating the character of the scenes through which God's Church must pass on her way to her destined glory!* It will spare us much useless labour if we note what God has *not* said in this book, as well as what he *has* said; *e.g.* (1) We have few definite marks of time. We have, of course, the point of commencement, viz. the exile of John in Patmos in the reign of Domitian, and we have also at the end the new Jerusalem in its glory; but for estimating the duration of the whole period, and for its division into periods of years, we have, practically, no data at all. [4] (2) We have few marks of place. We are not told whether the opening of this seal or that is to find its sphere of fulfilment over the Roman empire, or within the Jewish state, or over the wide world, or, if over a portion of it, what that portion is. (3) Nor have we any marks to show us whether the seven seals, vials, and trumpets represent seven distinct series of events, or, if so, whether they are synchronous or consecutive, nor, in either case, over what time each one lasts, nor whether there is any space between one and the other; nor, if there be, how much it is. For aught we know, they may even lap over, one on to another. Now, when all these points are left open in the sacred Word, it seems to us to be going far beyond the limits of a proper reverence for God's Word, to assign definitely this or that figure to this or that special event, time, and place, when the figure *alone* is employed, and neither time nor place indicated at all. If, *e.g.*, there is a series of symbols indicative of famine, if this book says nothing as to where or when the famine is to be; and if, moreover, in this the Apocalypse agrees exactly with our Lord's words, that there should be "famines . . . in divers places" ere the end shall come, we cannot venture to say that it refers to this or that famine, but simply that on this globe, which is the Lord's, and which is being prepared for his second coming, famine is one among the many incidents which our God foresees and controls, and which he will make subservient to the bringing-in of the great and dreadful day of the Lord. It may be urged

[1] Robinson, p. 11.

[2] 'Essai sur l'Apocalypse:' Étude Biblique, deuxième série, pp. 349, 350. The whole paragraph is worthy of careful study, but is too long for the space at our disposal.

[3] 'Speaker's Commentary,' p. 491b, 492a.

[4] Dr. Cumming wrote, long ago, the significant words, "If I could tell you when the twelve hundred and sixty years begin, I could tell you when they would end." The latest and perhaps the most elaborate effort to fix days and years is the work of Mr. Grattan Guinness, on 'The Approaching End of the Age,' in which great ingenuity is wasted on a hopeless attempt to know the times and the seasons which the Father hath put in his own power.

by way of *objection* : " *If so much is unsaid, and therefore uncertain, all is uncertain, and the book is useless.*" Not so; there is very much that is fixed and clear; very much more, indeed, on the principle of interpretation for which we contend, than on any other ; and not only so, but the value of the book is, to us, immeasurably greater. Let us, then, now lay down some definite propositions, which may prepare our way for the further unfolding of this book.

I. THERE IS IN THE BOOK A CLEAR GENERAL PLAN. Its key-note is, " Behold, I come quickly." Its disclosures end with the in-bringing of the new heavens and the new earth. Its historic starting-point is the exile of the beloved apostle. Its conception is that all forces in nature, incidents in history, and movements of providence, are preparing the way of the Lord. The standpoint of the apostle is not earth, nor is it heaven. He is caught up in the Spirit. Looking down, he sees earth in trouble and storm ; looking up, he sees heaven in glory and rest. And if we look behind the symbolic drapery of the book, we shall find in each paragraph or section some principle indicated which will give us a clue to the higher spiritual meaning of the whole. Historic incident is among things " seen and temporal ; " principles are among things " unseen and eternal." If we can seize hold of these, and thereby get some clearer view of the methods of God's working, we shall look with a far more intelligent gaze on " the ways of God towards man."

II. THE UNFOLDINGS OF THE BOOK AS TO THE CONFLICTS OF EARTH ARE A GREAT STAY TO OUR FAITH. Suppose we were without the Apocalypse : when we look over all the desolations of earth, and think of the slow progress Christianity makes, should we not be often ready to despair? But when the conflict in all its fierceness and wildness is set forth here, we can refer to our chart, and say, " We were told of it beforehand." We understand the Master's words, " Now I have told you before it come to pass, that, when it is come to pass, ye might believe." Without this book " the events of Christian history would be to us shortsighted creatures a very serious and painful obstacle to faith ; but by the help of this book these very events confirm our faith." [1]

III. THE ISSUE OF THE WHOLE IN THE GLORY OF THE NEW JERUSALEM IS A STIMULUS TO OUR HOPE. However dark the passage, the end of it is light and glory. The King shall yet reveal himself as King of kings and Lord of lords. This is emphatically " the blessed hope." It revives our courage by the way.

IV. CERTAINTY AS TO ISSUE, BUT UNCERTAINTY AS TO TIME, IS THE ONLY CONDITION OF OUR LIFE WHICH IS CONSISTENT WITH THE DUE PERFORMANCE OF EVERYDAY DUTY. To know the moment when the stop should be put on all things would paralyze human exertion. Not to know that " all is working for good " would be the death-blow to our joy in the Lord. The blended certainty and uncertainty are the very best conditions for us, the most calculated to lead us to watch and pray that we may " be ready," and may not be ashamed before Christ at his coming.

Ver. 1—ch. v. 14.—*The opening vision : heaven ; its throne ; its inhabitants ; its songs.* The fourth and fifth chapters of this book should be read together. They form a fitting introduction to the disclosures which follow. Before we have presented to us the series of visions which unfold to us the struggles of earth through which the Church must pass on her way to the end of the age, we have a glimpse of the heavenly world, its occupants, its songs, together with a sight of " him who is in the midst of the throne." Ere the last great inspired prophecy is to be unrolled, the Apostle John has a glimpse of the seat of power in heaven. Ere he sees those scenes of mingled awe and terror which his pen will have to record, he is permitted to peer within the sacred courts above. He sees their glory, learns their thoughts, and hears their songs, as, from heights far, far above us, they survey the majesty of the great Three in One, and send up their songs of praise to their God, for what he is in the glory of his nature, and for the grandeur of his works in creation and redemption. Among the many noble sculptures of Thorwaldsen at Copenhagen, there is one of the Apostle John. His countenance is suffused with heavenly serenity. He is looking up to heaven. His tablet is before him. His pen is in his hand, but it is not touching the tablet, nor will

[1] Cf. ' Exposition of the Book of Revelation,' by Rev. W. Robinson, of Cambridge, pp. 11—13 ; Bishop Boyd Carpenter's ' Commentary on the Revelation,' introduction to ch. vi.; Dr. Milligan's ' Baird Lecture,' 2nd edit., pp. 146—160.

the apostle venture on a word till it is given him from above. Exquisitely indeed has the sculptor caught the spirit of the beloved apostle as he awaits the revelation from on high. Let us, in arranging our homiletic exposition, follow the leadings of the narrative. We have—

I. A GLIMPSE INTO THE UPPER WORLD. "A door was opened [1] in heaven." We need not look on this as if it were bare literalism. Yet, beyond all question, there are objective realities far greater than those which John beheld. From beginning to end of these visions we see heavenly objects set forth in earthly language, that we may be "raised from our dead selves to higher things," and yet may not be bewildered and overwhelmed at the representation of a glory so far above us. Nor should we forget that, although this is the only book of the New Testament in which the heavenly world is set forth with anything of detail, yet the existence of that world is assumed by our Lord and his apostles throughout their teaching. This earth is not the only realm in which holy souls dwell, nor is the continuity of blessed life broken off as, one by one, they "go home." There are, moreover, "angels, principalities, and powers;" and over the two spheres of being, angels and men, our Lord is the Pre-eminent One. Thus, though the Apostle John gives us some fresh detail, he by no means takes us into an unknown land. It is "the Father's home." A voice is heard. Read, not "the first voice which I heard," but "I heard the first voice" (cf. Dean Alford, in loc.; ch. i. 10); i.e. the voice of him who is the Alpha and the Omega. From him the word comes, "Come up hither, and I will show thee things which must be hereafter." (From this we gather with certainty that, whatever the events may be which were to be indicated, the commencement of them cannot possibly date from an earlier period than the imprisonment of John in Patmos.) To this call the apostle responded. He rose in the Spirit's might, and, with piercing spiritual gaze, looked into heaven.[2] In order for a vision to be intelligible, it is necessary that there should be one spot on which the eye can fasten, as a point of repose. Without this its glances would wander in painful unrest. There is a law corresponding to this in the mental constitution. In the study of any science whatever, minor matters have to be set in relation to some leading truth. It is so in theology. If religious truth is looked at as all detail, without anything like a centre, or like a vertebral column from which and to which the varied branchlets of truth diverge and converge, nothing will be rightly understood. So with the spiritual life. It requires its centre-point, which is Christ. If, moreover, in the vision before us, there were only a series of unconnected items, it would distract us. But it is not so. There is a centre. *There is a throne,* the seat of power and authority, from which all orders proceed, before which all creatures bow. A throne is set in heaven. Under this familiar symbol our God vouchsafes to set before us the truth that there is a point around which the universe revolves. A throne. Isaiah saw it; Ezekiel saw it; John sees it; and, with what is grouped around it, it gives us a glimpse of the glories of the heavenly world and of the dwellers there, and forms the background of the scenes of mingled mercy and judgment which are to be witnessed on earth. 1. *There is One upon the throne*—the eternal Father, glorious in his majesty. 2. *Encircling the throne there is a rainbow*—the symbol and sign of a covenant of peace. Majesty and mercy are met together. While in this low region of cloud things often look so dark and lowering that we are tempted to think earth's chariot-wheels are running wildly, could we but see things from that higher standpoint that saints and angels take above, we should see that the everlasting throne remained firm and true, and that the rainbow of peace was encircling it around! 3. *Round about the throne* there are four and twenty minor thrones. On these are four and twenty crowned elders; and from what is said of them in the ninth verse of the fifth chapter, we gather that they are representatives of God's redeemed Church. Why twenty-four? No suggestion so much approves itself to us as the one that they represent the twelve patriarchs of the Old Testament and the twelve apostles of the New. The two Churches of the two economies are one in Christ. "They without us could not be made perfect." These elders are seen clothed in white, in token of their purity; crowned with gold, to

---

[1] "Not 'opening,' but 'open,' so that there may be the freest intercourse between heaven and earth" (Milligan, *in loc.*).

[2] "In this chapter we pass from the sufferings and temptations of the Churches below to the unsullied glory above" (Bishop Boyd Carpenter).

indicate their triumph. **4.** *Out of the throne* proceeded lightnings and thunderings and voices. What can these symbolize but the outgoings of Jehovah's power, whereby from his throne forces go forth which cause the earth to tremble; that while before the throne there was the symbol of perpetual calm, yet from thence should come mighty powers that should shake terribly a sinful world. Here we have also seven lamps of fire. These are interpreted for us. "The seven Spirits of God" sent forth into all the earth. Here is the Holy Ghost set forth in all the sublime majesty of his sevenfold energy. **5.** *Before the throne.* What is there? "A sea of glass like unto crystal." All calmness there. "No mighty waves of turbulent roar." "Jehovah sitteth above the waterfloods;" the tossing, angry waves of earthly revolutions affect not the perfect calm of the heavenly world! All is "ethereal purity and majestic repose."

II. THE INHABITANTS OF HEAVEN ARE SEEN. 1. *Angels* are there (ch. v. 2, 11). 2. The four and twenty *elders* are there (ch. iv. 4; v. 8, 11). 3. Four *living ones* are there, in the midst of the scene, between the throne and the crystal sea: one like a lion; the second like a calf; the third having the face of a man; the fourth like a flying eagle. In Ezekiel's vision each one had four faces; here, each has one face, each one has six wings about him. So in Isaiah's vision, with twain they covered their face, in holy awe; with twain they covered their feet, in token of humility; and with twain they flew, in token of obedience. Each one, moreover, is full of eyes before and behind—the symbol of the keen penetration of perfected intelligence. Surely we have, in these unusual forms, representations of the highest advance of creaturely existence; in which the several features of knowledge, excellence, and strength, which here are severed, are there joined in one. They worship before the throne. Worship and work mark the highest orders of created being as well as the lower. 4. Nor are these all. There is an innumerable *host*: "myriads of myriads, and thousands of thousands," representing the vast company in the realm of life, where "they cannot die any more." 5. We have yet to behold *One* around whom all the heavenly hosts gather in worship; but he comes in view as the Object of adoring song. He is "the Lamb as it had been slain." His glory we shall view as we proceed to study—

III. THE FIVE SONGS. Too seldom is the grand progression of song noticed, as recorded for us by the apostle. 1. First, *the Trisagion*, or song of praise to the thrice-holy God (ver. 8). This song is sung by the four living ones. The higher orders of created existence, with their vast powers of spiritual discernment—"full of eyes"—see infinitely more glory in the great eternal God than we can with our feeble powers and in this land of shadow and of care. They adore him for what he is; the perfection of his holiness is the delight of their souls. A diseased eye dreads the light in which a healthy one rejoices. Sinful men dread God's holiness; perfect beings find in it the inspiration of their praise. 2. Secondly, *the song of creation.* (Vers. 10, 11.) It is not only what God *is* that fills holy beings with rapture, but also what God *does*. The work of his hands in creation fills them with delight. And the higher beings rise in the scale, the more delight will they have in aught that reveals God. An angel could see more of God in a blade of grass than an uncultured soul could do in a blazing star. "*Thou* createdst all things." Whether they know what were the Divine methods of creation, we cannot say. The fact that *God did all* is that in which they glory; and also the fact that he did all by his own will, and for his own good pleasure. But the grand unfolding of heaven's song is far from complete as yet. The theme is continued in the fifth chapter.

HOMILIES BY VARIOUS AUTHORS.

Vers. 1—11.—*The high court of heaven.* If the portions of this book hitherto considered have had their difficulties, those on which we now enter are far more beset therewith. But the solemn sanctions given to the reading and study of this book send us, in spite of its difficulties, to the earnest examination of its sayings, certain that in them, even in the most mysterious of them, there lies a message from God to our souls. May he be pleased to make that message clear to us. This fourth chapter gives us the first part of the vision of what we have ventured to call "the high court of heaven." The next chapter reveals more. But in this part note—

I. THE VISION ITSELF. St. John begins his account of it with a "Behold." And well may he do so. He repeats this when he sees the "throne" and him that sat upon it. Again in ch. **v.** 5, when he sees Jesus, the "Lamb as it had been slain." And if in like manner this vision come to us, we shall be filled, as he was, with wonder, with adoration, and awe. St. John saw: 1. *A door set open in heaven.* The sky was parted asunder, and in the space between, as through a door, he witnessed what follows. 2. *The throne and its Occupant.* He could see no form or similitude, any more than Israel could when God came down on Mount Sinai (cf. this vision and that, Exod. xix.). All that St. John saw was one "like unto a jasper stone and a sardius." The pure, perfect, flashing whiteness, as of a diamond, but with the carnelian redness, **the** fiery gleams of the sardius (cf. the "sea of glass mingled with fire," ch. xv. 2). Such was the Being who sat upon the throne—that throne, probably, as that which Isaiah saw (Isa. vi.), being "high and lifted up," some stately structure befitting so august a court. 3. *The rainbow,* overarching the throne, the mild and beautiful green, emerald-like rays predominating amid its seven-hued splendour. Then: 4. *The assessors* of him that sat upon the throne. On either hand of the throne were twelve lesser thrones—twenty-four in all; and upon them were seated twenty-four elders, clad in white robes, and with crowns of gold on their heads. 5. Then in the space before the throne were seen *seven burning torches.* Not lamps, like those that symbolized the seven Churches, and which were after the manner of the seven-branched lamp which stood in the holy place in the ancient temple; but these were torches rather than lamps, destined to stand the rude blasts of the outer air rather than to gleam in the sheltered seclusion of some sacred edifice. 6. Then further off, beyond that central space, was the "sea of glass," like crystal. Clear, bright, reflecting the lights that shone upon it, but not tempest-tossed and agitated, unstable and ever restless, like that sea which day by day the exile in Patmos beheld barring his intercourse with those he loved, but calm and strong, firm and restful,—such was this sea. Then, also in the central space, or probably hovering, one in front, one on either side, and another at the rear of the throne, were: 7. *The four living ones.* The "four beasts," as, by the most melancholy of all mistranslations, the Authorized Version renders St. John's words, appear here to occupy the same relation to the throne as did the cherubim which were upon the ark of God in the Jewish temple. Strange, mysterious, unrepresentable, and indescribable forms. As were the cherubim, so are these; their faces, their eyes—with which it is said they "teem," so full of them are they—and their six wings, are all that we are told of; for the lion and ox-like aspect, the human and the eagle, tell of their faces rather than their forms, and do but little to enable us to gain any true conception of what they were. Such were the mysterious beings whom St. John saw in immediate attendance on him who sat upon the throne; and as such, standing or moving around or hovering over the throne, we cannot certainly say which. And all the while there were heard, as "in Sinai in the holy place," voices, thunderings, and lightnings, proceeding from the throne. Such was that part of the vision with which this chapter is occupied. As we proceed we find the scene is enlarged, and more Divine transactions take place thereon. But now note—

II. THE MEANING OF THIS VISION. And: 1. *The door set open in heaven.* This tells, as did the vision of the ladder Jacob saw, of a way of communication opened up between earth and heaven. 2. *The throne and its occupant.* "The whole description is that of a council in the very act of being held. It is not to be taken as a description of the ordinary heavenly state, but of a special assembly gathered for a definite purpose" (cf. 1 Kings xxii. 19). And this symbol, which mingles reservation with revelation, and conceals as much as it declares, bids us think of God in his majesty, glory, supremacy, and as incomprehensible. "Who by searching can find out God?" It is a vision of the great God—we know that; but of his nature, substance, form, and image it tells us nothing, nor was it intended that it should. But many precious and important truths concerning him it does tell. Of his awful glory, of his unsullied purity and spotless holiness, of the terror of his vengeance, of his interest in our concerns, of the worship and adoration of which he is worthy, and which he ever receives; of the character, condition, and service of those who dwell in his presence; of the ministers he employs; and much more. 3. *The rainbow overarching the throne.* This is the emblem (cf. Gen. ix. 12—16) of God's gracious covenant which he hath established for evermore. And it told to St. John and to Christ's Church everywhere that, awful, glorious, and terrible as our God is, all that he does, of whatsoever kind, is embraced within the mighty span of his all-o'erarching grace. The Church of Christ was to pass through some dreadful experiences, to endure fearful trials, and they are not ceased yet; but she was to look up and see that all God's ways, works, and will were within not without, beneath not beyond, because and not in spite of, his all-embracing love. All were to find shelter, expanse, and explanation there. It was a blessed vision, and, unlike the ordinary rainbow, may it ever be seen by us, and its teaching believed. 4. *The four and twenty elders.* These represent the whole Church of the Firstborn, the blessed and holy ones whom God hath made kings and priests unto himself. Their white robes tell of their purity, their victory, their joy, as white robes ever do; and their golden crowns (cf. Exod. xxxix. 30), the peculiar possession of the priest of God, tell of their high and holy functions in the presence of God. The priest's office was to intercede with God for man and with man for God, to be—as was he, the great High Priest, the Lord Jesus Christ—in sympathy alike with man and God, seeking to unite man to God, even as God was willing to unite himself with man. But seeing them there, associated with God, does it not tell that the holiest and most blessed of the saints know and approve of all he does? This is why the saints are so blessed, because they do so know God. They understand what he does, and why; and hence those dark facts of human life which so bewilder and distress us cause no distress to them; for they, whilst in deep love and sympathy with us who are left sorrowing here below, have come to know, as here they could not, and as we cannot, the loving and holy wisdom and the omnipotent grace which are working in and through all these things. If, then, those who know are of one mind with God in regard to them, surely we may learn therefrom to "trust and not be afraid." 5. *The torches of fire.* These are said to be "the seven Spirits of God"—the holy and perfect Spirit of God in the varied diversity of his operations (1 Cor. xii. 4). The witness of the Spirit as well as of the Church to the ways of God is shown. He too, as well as they, testify that God is holy in all his ways and righteous in all his works. 6. *The sea of glass.* If it were merely the sea that was seen here, we should regard it, as many do, as the symbol of the depth and extent of the judgments of God (cf. Ps. lxxvii. 19). But it is a sea of glass, like crystal, and its clear calmness, its firm strength, its perfect stillness—for we are told (ch. xv. 2) that the redeemed "stand upon" it—all this reminds us of the results of God's holy rule. "Thou rulest the raging of the sea, the noise of their waves, and the tumults of the people" (Ps. lxxxix. 9; lxv. 7). Here, then, is another witness for God and his ways—the progress of peace on earth, concord amongst men; the orderly, quiet, and undisturbed life; the security and peace which are amongst the marked results of the progress of the kingdom of God in the world. Let the results of missionary enterprise amid savage peoples now civilized and at peace attest this. 7. *The four living ones.* The meaning of this part of the vision is not clear or certain. All manner of opinions have been held. We regard them as answering to the cherubim of the Old Testament, and they are apparently the representatives of those who stand nearest to God, and by whom he mainly carries on his work. Hence the chief ministers of the Church of God—prophets, priests, evangelists, and apostles. The ancient Church very generally regarded these "four living ones" as the representatives of the four evangelists, and in many a picture, poem, and sculpture this idea is portrayed. But we prefer to regard them as part of the symbol, and not the whole. And the different creatures which are selected for these four are the chiefs of their several kinds: the lion amongst beasts, the ox amongst cattle, the eagle amongst birds, and man amongst all. And these several creatures tell of the main qualifications for the ministry of God: courage and strength, as of the lion; patient perseverance in toil, as of the ox; soaring aspiration, "to mount up on wings as eagles," heavenly mindedness; and intelligence and sympathy, as of the man. Ministers so qualified God chiefly uses in his great work. Their wings tell of incessant activity; their being "full of eyes," of their continual vigilance and eager outlook on all sides, their careful watch and ward in the Divine service. Such are his ministers. It is said they represent the whole sentient creation of God. But we find them told of here as leaders of worship, as singing the song of the redeemed (ch. **v.** 9), with harps and golden censers "full of odours, which are the prayers of saints." They say, "Thou hast made us kings and priests," etc. Surely all this belongs more to human, redeemed ministries than to vague abstractions, such as "representatives of creation." And if so, then such being the ministers of God is a further reason for the trust, the confidence, and the assured hope of the Church of God in all ages. And then all are heard as well as seen, and that which we have is the Trisagion, the Ter-Sanctus, the "Holy, holy, holy," which Isaiah heard when in the temple. He also saw the vision of the Lord of hosts. And the uplifting of this holy song serves as the signal for the yet fuller outburst of praise which the twenty-four elders, rising from their seats and reverently placing their crowns of gold at the Lord Jehovah's feet, and prostrating themselves before his throne, render unto him that sitteth upon the throne, saying, "Worthy art thou," etc. (ver. 11). The vision is all of a piece. It strikes terror into the hearts of God's adversaries, as—to compare great things with small—do the pomp and paraphernalia of an earthly tribunal strike terror into the heart of the criminal who is brought up to be tried, and probably condemned, at its bar; but fills with holy confidence the hearts of all God's faithful people by the assurance of the holiness, the wisdom, the love, and might of him that ruleth over all, and in whose hands they and all things are.

III. Iᴛs ɢᴇɴᴇʀᴀʟ ɪɴᴛᴇɴᴛ ᴀɴᴅ ᴘᴜʀᴘᴏsᴇ. Beyond the immediate needs of the Church of St. John's day, surely it is designed to teach us all: 1. *The reality of the heavenly world.* The seen and the temporal do not a little dim and often shut out altogether the sight of the unseen and eternal. It is difficult to realize. Hence whatever tends to bring to bear upon us "the powers of the world to come" cannot but be good. And this is one purpose of this vision. 2. Another is *to awaken inquiry as to our own relation to the judgment of God.* How shall *we* stand there, abashed and ashamed, or bold through the atoning sacrifice of Christ which we have believed and relied upon? How shall it be? 3. *To excite desire and aspiration after participation in its blessedness.* Hence the door is set open in heaven, that we may long to enter there, and resolve through Christ that we will. "What must it be to be there?"—that is the aspiration which such a vision as this is intended to awaken, as God grant it may.—S. C.

Ver. 6.—*The cherubim.* "In the midst . . . . were four living ones full of eyes before and behind." There can scarce be a doubt that these mysterious beings are the same as in the Old Testament are called "cherubim." Who and what they were, and what they have to teach us, is an inquiry not without difficulty, but assuredly of much interest and profit. Let us, therefore—

I. Rᴇᴠɪᴇᴡ ᴛʜᴇ Sᴄʀɪᴘᴛᴜʀᴇ ɴᴏᴛɪᴄᴇs ᴏғ ᴛʜᴇ ᴄʜᴇʀᴜʙɪᴍ. They are mentioned in connection : 1. *With the expulsion of Adam and Eve from Eden.* We read, "So he drove out the man, and he placed at the east end of the garden of Eden cherubim, and a flaming sword, which turned ev ry way to keep the way of the tree of life" (Gen. iii. 24). Now, from this passage we learn but little as to the nature of these exalted beings—only that they were deemed worthy to occupy the place where alone perfect righteousness could dwell. But from the word rendered "to place," which signifies rather "to place in a tabernacle," and from expressions which we find in ch. xiv. 14—16, it seems as if this "place" wherein God had appointed the cherubim had become a sort of local tabernacle, and was called "the presence of the Lord," from which Cain mourned that he was driven out; and so for a long time it remained, probably until the Deluge. For how else could the idea of the cherubim, so connected with that place, and apparently so familiar to the Jews, have continued in their minds? That it did so is shown by the fact that Bezaleel (Exod. xxxi.), when he was bidden make cherubim of gold for the ark of God, knew exactly what he was to do. Here, as at Eden, they were where sinful man could not approach. Then the next mention of them is: 2. In connection with *the ark of the covenant* in the tabernacle (Exod. xxv. 18—20). Such were the commands of him who, but a little while before, amid all the majesty and awe of Sinai, had commanded, "Thou shalt not make unto thee any graven image, nor any likeness of anything," etc. (Exod. xx.). This command was engraven upon stone, and placed within that very ark of the covenant upon which the golden cherubim stood. And Solomon, too, with apparently the full concurrence of David and of the priests of the Lord, substituted for these cherubim, or else added to them, two others of colossal size, whose wings, stretching overhead, filled the most holy place in his new and gorgeous temple (1 Kings vi. 23). Besides this, the figures of cherubim were multiplied in the varied forms of gold work and tapestry which were about the temple. Woven into curtains, placed as supports of the priests' laver at the entrance of the sanctuary, they were found on all sides, although they certainly seemed like plain contradiction and disobedience to the law which forbade the making of all such images. But we have no clear idea what they were like. We are told only of their wings, their faces, and their posture—not anything more. And the command against graven images helps us, I think, to understand partly what they were not. For that command contemplates only objects, regarded as sacred, which might be used as idols and for worship. And these cherubim fulfilled the very letter as well as the spirit of the Law. They were unlike "anything in heaven above," etc. If you seek to put together the various descriptions given of them in the Bible, you get an impossible combination, an unnatural union of bodily parts and organs, such as no known creature of God ever possessed. And still less were they designed to represent the supreme God. They were simply symbols divinely appointed, the meaning of which it is ours to discover. Then : 3. *Isaiah's and Ezekiel's visions.* (Isa. vi.; Ezek. i. 10.) Ezekiel describes certain "living ones" that he saw in vision. In ch. x. he sees again, but now in Jerusalem, these "living ones; " and he says, " This is the living one that I saw under the God of Israel by the river of Chebar, and I knew that they were the cherubim." And then he proceeds (ch. x.) to describe them. And : 4. *In the vision of St. John.* (Cf. ch. iv. 6—9.) With slight modifications, it is evident that we have the same mysterious beings referred to. Therefore inquire—

II. WHOM DO THEY REPRESENT ? They are called "living ones," and therefore not the mere elemental forces of nature. This has been argued from Ps. xviii. 10, where it is written, " He rode upon a cherub, and did fly : yea, he did fly upon the wings of the wind." But the swiftness of movement attributed to these beings, their many wings, so that Ezekiel compares their going to "a flash of lightning," is sufficient to account for what we read in the psalm. But now, gathering together the scattered notices of them which we have reviewed, we learn : 1. *They represent servants of God.* Every passage that speaks of them shows this. In Eden ; in the tabernacle and temple ; in Isaiah's vision in the temple, and in Ezekiel's ; so, too, in St. John's. 2. *Chief ministers of God.* See how near they are to him, standing to represent him or in closest attendance upon him. 3. *But human,* not merely creatural and sentient. From the creature forms, or rather countenances, ascribed to these "living ones," they have been regarded as representations of God's sentient creation (cf. homily on vers. 1—11). But they worship God ; they join in the song, " Worthy is the Lamb; " they are in sympathy with God's servants here on earth, bearing golden censers "full of odours, which are the prayers of saints." So, then, as they are chosen and chief amongst the servants of God, so also are they human. But : 4. *Holy also.* These " living ones " represent, not humanity as we see it, but as it shall be in the presence of God by-and-by. Their position in Eden, where no sin might be, and in the most holy place, and in closest attendance upon the throne and upon him that sat upon it,—all prove how holy, how sinless, they must be. And : 5. *Redeemed.* They could only be where they are in consequence of redemption. We know that sinful man was not allowed to enter Eden, whence he had been driven out, nor the most holy place, nor the presence of God. Therefore something must have been done, in and upon and for them. Moreover, their song, " Worthy is the Lamb " (ch. v. 12), and their standing on the mercy-seat over the ark of the covenant—that mercy-seat which was sprinkled with the blood of atonement—show that it is to redemption they, as we and all the saved, owe their all. And : 6. *Perfected.* See the creatural symbols, the lion, ox, etc. (cf. former homily), which tell of those qualities which go to make up the perfected character of the saints of God—courage and submission, aspiration and thought. Of such service and servants do the cherubim, these " living ones," tell.

III. THEIR MINISTRY TO MAN NOW. It is full of interest to observe the seasons when the visions of the cherubim were given. These occasions have all one common characteristic—they were when the way man had to take was very dark and drear.

As when our first parents went forth from the blessed Eden to the thorns and thistles of the wilderness which was to be their future home.   So, too, when "that great and terrible wilderness," amid which the Israel of God had to wearily wander for so many years.   And when Isaiah was called to his ministry of sorrow because of his people's sin (Isa. vi. 9, 10).   And Ezekiel, when in the sore captivity at Babylon he strove to comfort and cheer the hearts of his countrymen.   And St. John saw them in the midst of the tribulations and persecutions which befell the Church of his day.   So that the ministry of the cherubim seems to have been, besides all else that it was, a ministry of consolation to troubled and sorrowful men.   To tell them what and where one day they should surely be, whatever their hard lot may be now; that they should be redeemed, holy, in the presence of God, serving him day and night in his temple— serving him, too, with perfect service, and he who "dwelt between the cherubim" should dwell among them for evermore.   It was as a "Sursum corda" to the dejected, downcast children of God, bidding them be of good cheer and "hope in the Lord."   And this is the purpose of this revelation still.—S. C.

Vers. 1—6.—*The Divine government symbolized.*   In the forms of earth the formless heavenly things are represented—the Divine government which in our thoughts is so often restricted to the conditions of human government.   It is needful to remind ourselves that when we have conceived the most lofty notions of the Divine rule, we are infinitely below the real and actual.   "As the heavens are higher than the earth, so are my ways higher than your ways, and my thoughts than your thoughts."

I. THE THRONE SYMBOLICAL OF THE DIVINE GOVERNMENT.   A government by law and authority.

II. THE OCCUPANT OF THE THRONE, whom no man hath seen nor can see, represented as "like a jasper stone and a sardius," symbolical of essential holiness and punitive justice.   Symbols have but their limited teaching.   Here the two aspects of the Divine Name represented which the circumstances of the Church needed—persecuted, suffering.   The defence of the holy ones by the holy God; the punishment of the enemies of truth, who are enemies of all who love the truth.   "I will repay, saith the Lord."

III. THE DIVINE THRONE ENCOMPASSED BY SYMBOLS OF COVENANTED MERCY.   "The rainbow"—"the symbol of grace returning after wrath."

IV. THE DIVINE THRONE ENCIRCLED BY THE REPRESENTATIVES OF THE CHURCH. 1. The high honour to the Church.   2. Divine recognition of.   3. Utmost glory of: they sit on thrones—fulfilment of many promises.   4. Their character—purity, indicated by "white robes."   5. Their kingly honour : "on their heads crowns of gold."   6. The universality and unity of the Church represented in the "four and twenty elders"—"the twelve tribes of Israel," "the twelve apostles of the Lamb."

V. THE SYMBOLS OF THREATENED JUDGMENTS PROCEEDING FROM THE THRONE are "lightnings, and voices, and thunders," all effected by the manifold operations of the Holy Spirit of God—"seven lamps of fire."

VI. THE DEPTH AND PURITY OF THE DIVINE ADMINISTRATION SYMBOLIZED in "a glassy sea like unto crystal."   "Thy judgments are a great deep."

VII. TO THE RIGHTEOUSNESS, JUSTICE, WISDOM, BENIGNITY, OF THE DIVINE GOVERNMENT ALL CREATURE-LIFE BEARS WITNESS.   Thus the four living creatures.—R. G.

Vers. 6—8.—*The song of the living creatures.*   Here is represented the praise of the Divine Name by the universal creature-life.   The highest, the cherubic forms, speak for all.   It is a representative song.   "All thy works praise thee, O God;" "Let everything that hath breath praise the Lord."

I. THE SONG OF THE UNIVERSAL CREATURE-LIFE IS A CEASELESS SONG.   "They have no rest day and night."   That which is represented is that which should and which shall be.   It is the ideal.   Wicked man puts himself outside of the otherwise universal chorus; but he shall also be brought to sing.   "Thou wilt make the wrath of man to praise thee."   Throughout the widespread universal life a never-ending song of praise ascends ; angel and archangel, cherubim and seraphim, continually do cry.   All creatures in their vast variety, their marvellous structure, their mutual service, praise him who gave them birth.

II. The creature's song called for by the holiness of God. This the first, the chiefest attribute of the Divine Name. "His Name is holy." In the creature's elevation the essential holiness of God shall become the central light into the depths of which, with eager if with veiled eye, shall the holy ones seek to inquire. This the essential "beauty of the Lord."

III. The creature's song called for by the eternity of God. The Everliving One is praised by every living one. Each, receiving his life from the Life, shall render back that life in ceaseless songs of praise. The unfathomable depth, the infinite beyond, the eternal past, true matter of praise to the creature: "which was, and is, and is to come."

IV. The creature's song demanded by the omnipotence, the all-mightiness, of God. The Lord God is the Almighty. To this high subject the limited, feeble creature rises as more and more he searches into the vast works of the Almighty hand which none can let or hinder.

V. The song of the creature, as is most meet, is a song of praise, the true praise being, not the attempted estimate of the Divine Name by the creature-mind, but the simple assertion of the Divine excellence: "Holy, holy, holy," etc.—R. G.

Vers. 9—11.—*The Church's song of praise.* The elders speak for all and appear for all. In them all are present. As is promised again and again, the Church surrounds the throne. It is the sign of the Church's recognition and highest honour.

I. The subject of the song. That of "the living creatures" is "the Lord God," the Almighty, the Ever-living. The subject of the Church's song is the creative power of God, in recognition of which "glory, honour, and power" are ascribed. It is the ground of hope for the final triumph of the Divine kingdom over the opposing kingdom of evil which is so soon to be brought into view.

II. The song is offered by the Church's representatives; it symbolizes the entire Church rejoicing in the universal song of praise. "When the living creatures shall give glory." The Church's song of praise for redemption will presently be heard; but it is preceded, as is most meet, by praise to God "for his excellent greatness and for his mighty acts."

III. The song is presented by the Church in lowly prostration. Never do the songs of praise from the earth rise higher than when presented in the lowliest humility. Not only do the elders "fall down before him that sitteth on the throne," but in recognition of his absolute supreme authority, they "cast their crowns before the throne." In presence of the one Lord, all authority, all honour, all might, must be ignored.

IV. The matter of the song recognizes the exalted worthiness of the Most High, to whom pertains the highest "glory, honour, and power," illustrated in the creation of all things.

V. The song terminates in an adoring acknowledgment of the final end of creation. "Because of thy will." "He spake, and they were created: he commanded, and they stood fast." The "will" expresses the pleasure of God, and for his pleasure they are, and were created. The end of their being is not to be found in themselves, but in the Divine will. It is worthy. And as by the Divine will all things are, so all things will be made to serve that will, yea, even the rebellious elements in human life, for he will make the wrath of man to praise him.—R. G.

Ver. 1.—*Man's higher sphere of being:* (1) *Humanly accessible.* "After this I looked, and, behold, a door was opened in heaven: and the first voice which I heard was as it were of a trumpet talking with me; which said, Come up hither, and I will show thee things which must be hereafter." Disrobe this chapter of its strange metaphorical costume, brush away all the symbols, and there appears a supermundane world, here called heaven—man's higher sphere of being; a world this, unseen by the outward eye, unheard by the outward ear, untouched by the tactile nerve, lying away altogether from our five senses. That such a world exists is, to say the least, highly probable, if not morally certain. Universal reason conducts to the belief in, and the universal heart yearns for, such a scene. He who is so thoroughly acquainted with the universe as to be incapable of a mistake, so inflexibly sincere as to be incapable of deception, has said, "In my Father's house are many mansions: if it were not so,

I would have told you." I may observe, in passing, that from the first verse of this chapter to the first verse of the eighth chapter inclusive forms an interesting paragraph of thought for suggestion. Now, this supermundane world, or man's higher sphere of being, we have here presented in two aspects—*humanly accessible* and *spiritually entered.* Each of these we shall employ as the germ of a separate homily. In the text it appears as *humanly accessible.* Notice—

I. THERE IS A DOOR TO ADMIT. " A door was opened in heaven." What is the "door"? Christ says, " I am the Door: by me if any man enter in, he shall be saved, and shall go in and out, and find pasture " (John x. 9). He shall enter into this supermundane world with absolute safety and abundant provision. He is "the Way." Christ's absolute moral excellence makes him the Door of admission to all that is pure, beautiful, and joyous in the universe. " Beholding as in a glass the face of the Lord, we are changed into the same image from glory to glory," etc. Two things may be predicated about this door. 1. *It is transparent.* He who looks into Christ's character looks into heaven. In his spirit we see the light that animates all heaven, and the principles that set all heaven to music. He who knows Christ experimentally knows heaven, and no other. 2. *It is ample.* Millions have passed through it, and millions more will to the end of time; thousands are passing through it, and all the men of coming generations will find it wide enough.

II. THERE IS A VOICE TO WELCOME. " And the first voice which I heard was as it were of a trumpet talking [speaking] with me; which said [one saying], Come up hither, and I will show thee things which must be [come to pass] hereafter." Whither? Up the heights of the supersensuous universe, lying even beyond the stars. Thither in imagination we may ascend. Who, indeed, in the stillness of the night, has not heard as it were a " trumpet " coming down into his soul from those bright orbs which in teeming legions traverse the infinite fields above?

> "Whoever gazed upon their shining,
> Nor turned to earth without repining,
> Nor longed for wings to fly away,
> And meet with them eternal day?"

" Come up hither," they seem to say. Let not your minds be confined to your little, cloudy, stormy, perishing planet. Earth was only intended as the temporary home of your bodies, not the dwelling-place of your souls. The great universe is the domain of mind. We roll and shine in our mighty spheres around you to win you away to the serene, the height, and the boundless. "Come up hither," immortal man, wing your flight from orb to orb, system to system; count our multitudes, mark our movements, gauge our dimensions, breathe in our brightness, rise beyond us, scale the wondrous heavens still far away, revel in the Infinite, be lost in God. But the elevation to which we are called is not local, but *moral.* "Seek those things which are above." What are they? Truth, rectitude, holiness, fellowship with the Infinite. Herein is true soul-elevation. To this the "trumpet" bids us. Hear this trumpet from the infinite silences around you, from departing saints above you, from the depths of conscience within you, " come up hither."

CONCLUSION. Are we morally ascending? Then we shall experience three things. 1. Increasing dominion over the world. 2. Constant growth in moral force. 3. Augmented interest in the spiritual domain.—D. T.

Vers. 2—11.—*Man's higher sphere of being:* (2) *Spiritually entered.* "And immediately I was in the Spirit: and, behold, a throne was set in heaven, and One sat on the throne," etc. We need not suppose that the supermundane world appeared to John's bodily eye in the forms in which it is here presented. It was a mental vision and nothing more, and a *mental* vision is often more real, more significant, more impressive, than a *material.* Commentators of this book have treated these objects as those which were addressed to the senses of the apostle, and have thus turned it into a wilderness of confusion; and preachers have used it to excite the imagination, stir the sensibilities, and stimulate the wildest and idlest speculations concerning a man's higher sphere of being. The whole is a mental vision. We shall take the vision not as a symbolic puzzle, or even a metaphorical representation, but merely as an *illustration* of two things.

I. THE EXTRAORDINARY CHARACTER of man's higher sphere of being. All thing
here seem to be of a unique nature and order. An air of the wonderful spreads ove
all. 1. *The general appearances are extraordinary.* Observe the *social appearance*
are extraordinary. Royalties abound. "A throne was set in heaven," with one
Occupant supreme, as brilliant in aspect as a precious stone. "He that sat was to look
upon like a jasper [stone] and a sardine stone [sardius] : and there was a rainbow round
about the throne, in sight like unto an emerald [to look upon]." Then there were
other royalties and dignities seated round the central throne. "And round about the
throne were four and twenty seats [thrones]: and upon the seats [thrones] I saw four
and twenty elders sitting, clothed [arrayed] in white raiment [garments]; and they
had on their heads crowns of gold." Now, the social appearances of this world are
nothing like this. Everywhere there is degradation, not dignity; heads encircled with
poverty, sorrow, and care, not "crowns of gold." Indeed, the great bulk of our social
world do not even see the throne of the *Supreme One* in the heavens. They see the
motion of the mere material machinery, or a scheme of what they call laws and forces,
but not the One central and universal Ruler of all. Man's higher sphere of being,
socially, is widely different to this. In the higher one free moral agents are the ruling
power, not blind forces. And then over all there is One, and but One over all, on the
central throne. Again, the *physical phenomena* are extraordinary. "And out of the
throne proceeded [proceed] lightnings and thunderings [thunders] and voices : and
there were seven lamps of fire burning before the throne, which are the seven Spirits of
God." True, we have lightnings and thunders here occasionally, but articulate voices
in the heavens we hear not, nor do we see torches of fire blazing before the throne.
The firmament that spreads over the higher sphere of being will no doubt, in many
respects, be very different to the heavens that encircle us. So, also, with the waters.
"Before the throne there was [as it were] a sea of glass [a glassy sea] like unto crystal."
We have a sea here rolling in majesty round three parts of the globe, but it is not like
glass or crystal, ever calm, sparkling, and clear; it is never at rest, often lashed into
fury, and black with rage. How calm and clear will be our higher sphere, "a sea of
glass," mirroring the peacefulness and the glory of the Infinite! The *living creatures*
also are extraordinary. "Round about the throne were four beasts [living creatures]
full of eyes before and behind. And the first beast [creature] was like a lion, and the
second beast [creature] like a calf, and the third beast [creature] had a face as [as of]
a man, and the fourth beast [creature] was like a flying eagle. And the four beasts
[living creatures] had each of them [having each one of them] six wings about him;
and they were full [are full] of eyes within [and round about]." Although we have
on this earth such beasts and birds and faces of man as here represented, a striking
difference is indicated. They had " six wings" and were "full of eyes." Whilst some
have the courage of the lion, the patience of the ox, the towering tendency of the
eagle, and the sympathy of the man, they are all endowed with transcendent organs of
vision and powers of speed—they teem with eyes and wings. It is here suggested, then
—I do not say that it is intended to be taught, for I am not gifted with the power to
interpret such passages—*that man's life in the higher sphere of being differs widely
from the present.* " Eye hath not seen," etc. 2. *The supreme service is extraordinary.*
What is the supreme service in that higher sphere? Worship. "And they rest not
[have no rest] day and night, saying, Holy, holy, holy. Lord God [the] Almighty,
which was, and [which] is, and [which] is to come. And when those beasts [the
living creatures] give [shall give] glory and honour and thanks to him that sat [sitteth]
on the throne, [to him] who liveth for ever and ever, the four and twenty elders fall
[shall fall] down before him that sat [sitteth] on the throne, and worship [shall wor-
ship] him that liveth for ever and ever, and cast [shall cast] their crowns before the
throne," etc. The worship there is the one ruling, intense, unremitting service. It is
anything but that here; business, pleasure, aggrandizement,—these are the great and
constant services of life. Real worship is indeed rare.

II. THE REAL ENTRANCE into man's higher sphere of being. " Immediately [straight-
way] I was in the Spirit." It is suggested that this higher life, this supermundane
world, is entered by the Spirit. " Flesh and blood cannot enter the kingdom of
heaven." There are two ways by which man can enter the invisible. 1. *By the efforts
of the imagination.* The whole scene before us is evidently the product of the imagina-

tion. Extraordinary visions men often have in the stilly watches of the night, in the season of dreams. But imagination can act more accurately, if not more vividly, in the hour of consciousness and intellectual activity. Thus Milton beheld his heavens and his hells, his angels and his devils. We can all, by the force of imagination, penetrate the visible, the material, the tangible, withdraw the sublunary curtain and step into the world of spiritual wonders. 2. *By the influx of a new spirit.* It is not uncommon for men to come into possession of a new *ruling* spirit, and with a new spirit comes a new world. When the *philosophic* spirit enters a man (and it does so in the case of a few in every age and land), the man is ushered into a new world—a world of high thoughts, invisible forms, and remedial forces. When the *commercial* spirit enters the rustic lout, he soon finds himself in a new world—a world of speculations and struggles, of losses and gains. When the *parental* spirit enters the soul, it is borne into a world before unseen—a world of solicitude, absorbing interests, pains and pleasures, sorrows and joys. When the *genuinely religious* spirit enters the soul, it enters this higher sphere of human life—the world of brightness and beauty, the world of an "innumerable company of angels, the spirits of just men made perfect," etc. "And immediately [straightway] I was in the Spirit." "Heaven lies about us in our infancy," and we have only to be in this spirit to realize it. The great Teacher taught that no man can see the kingdom of God, unless he comes into the possession of this spirit. "That which is born of the flesh is flesh, and that which is born of the Spirit is spirit."

CONCLUSION. Search not for an *outward* heaven, but rather search for that new spirit, that *spirit of Christliness,* that will let you into the heaven that lies about you and within you. Were the twelve hundred million men that tenant this earth to-day to come into possession of this spirit, they would arise on the morrow and exclaim, "Behold, a new heaven and a new earth!" Evermore the state of a man's soul determines his universe. The ruling life within him measures out, builds up, and moulds the external.—D. T.

Ver. 10.—*Man in heaven.* "They cast their crowns before the throne." Far am I from pretending to the power of explaining this book. There is ample scope here for the play of imagination. Here is a field which, under the culture of a vivid fancy, is capable of producing theories and speculations suited to every variety of taste, every grade of intellect, and every degree of culture. In this chapter John has a *mental,* *Divine,* and *symbolical* vision of heaven : the "door is opened," and a voice commands him to ascend and enter. By "heaven," of course, I do not mean heaven as a place, but *as a state of the Christly soul—the heaven within, a subjective paradise.* The text leads us to infer—

I. THAT MAN IN THIS HEAVEN HAS REACHED THE HIGHEST DIGNITY. He has "crowns." We are not to suppose, of course, that there are *material* crowns in heaven; these, whether formed of gold, or diamonds, or both, are the mere toys of earth; but crowns are used here as the emblem of the highest dignity. The earth has nothing higher to offer man than a crown; men have hazarded their lives and waded through seas of blood to get a crown. Because of the importance which universal man attaches to a crown, it is employed to represent the *dignity* of men in heaven. This crown is called in the New Testament "a crown of righteousness." Earthly crowns are often associated with iniquity; their history is one of violence and wrong. But the dignity reached by men in heaven will be "righteous"—it will be in harmony with universal rectitude. There is no being in the universe that can charge them with having reached their position by unjust means. It is called "a crown of life." The crown which the visitors in the Grecian games obtained soon withered and died; the weaved garlands soon became dust. The crowns which sovereigns wear in more modern times are corruptible, the diamonds will grow dim, and the gold will wear out; but the crown of man in heaven is "a crown of life." It is not something put on; it is the expression of his being. The crown is to the man what the blossom is to the tree, what the halo is to the sun—something rising out of the being—the fruit of his life. It is called "a crown of glory." What is glory? Paul says, "There is one glory of the sun and another of the stars;" and we may say there is one glory of the earth and one of the heavens. The things to which men attach the idea of glory are puerilities in the estimation of Heaven. Take the most magnificently attired sovereign of the world, surpassing all other monarchs of the earth in the pomp and pageantry of his movements, what is the glory of that poor mortal, on which the empty crowd stares with wonder? It is only the glory of a gaudy actor on the stage, garbed in the tawdry and tinselled robe, put on for the hour for popular effect. But this is a glory altogether different. It is the glory of an intellect in harmony with the truth, the glory of conscience in sympathy with the right, the glory of the soul centred in God. What is there so glorious as a noble soul? If this be the state of man in heaven : 1. *Let us have faith in the improvability of our nature.* When we look round upon society, and see the gross sensuality, the dishonesty, the profanity of men, we feel disposed to loathe our very species; but when we look to heaven, we feel that the worst are capable of improvement—that "dry bones can live." "Such were some of you," etc. 2. *Let us be consoled under the departure by death of the good.* "I heard a voice from heaven, saying unto me, Blessed are the dead which die in the Lord ; " "These are they which came out of great tribulation ; " "Sorrow not as those that are without hope." 3. *Let us not judge of providence without taking into account the future as well as the present.* "I reckon," says the apostle, "that the sufferings of this present time are not worthy to be compared with the glory which shall be revealed in us."

II. That man in this heaven ascribes the dignity he has reached to Jesus Christ. "They cast their crowns before the throne." This implies: 1. *A conviction that they owed all their honours to Christ.* Whence did they obtain their crowns? 2. *A readiness to acknowledge their obligation.* The greater our natures the more ready to acknowledge our obligation. 2. *The surpassing glories of Christ.* He is in the midst of the throne, and all ascribe their all to him. Napoleon I., after he had conquered empires, and planted his foot upon the neck of kingdoms, determined to be crowned emperor. To give pageantry and lustre to the occasion, he compelled the Pope of Rome to be present. In the act of coronation, the emperor refused to receive the crown from the pope; his proud spirit told him he had won it himself : he placed it upon his own brow, thus declaring to the spectators and the civilized world the fact that he was indebted to himself only for imperial power. How different this to our Cromwell, who in spirit towered high above all the Napoleons of history! After the crown of England had been offered to him by successive Parliaments, he refused it! Great souls are above crowns. All in this subjective heaven of goodness cast their "crowns " at the feet of Christ, and say, "Thine is the kingdom, the power, and the glory."—D. T.

EXPOSITION.

CHAPTER V.

Ver. 1.—**And I saw.** As in ch. **iv. 1,** this phrase introduces a new incident in the vision. That which had been witnessed remained, but a further development now takes place. Ch. iv. relates the revelation of the glory of the Triune God (see on ch. iv. 2) surrounded by his Church and creation. The glory of Jesus Christ, the Lamb, is now set forth, since he is the only One worthy to receive and declare to his Church the mystery contained in the sealed book. In the right hand ; *upon the right hand* (ἐπί). That is, lying upon the hand, as it was extended in the act of offering the book to any one who should be able to open and read it. Of him that sat on the throne. The Triune God (see on ch. iv. 2). A book written within and on the back side. In Ezek. ii. 9, 10 the "roll of a book " is "written within and without;" another of the numerous traces in the Revelation of the

influence of the writings of this prophet upon the writer of the Apocalypse, though the picture of the Lamb, which follows in this chapter, imparts a new feature peculiar to St. John's vision. The roll was inscribed on both sides. Mention is made of such a roll by Pliny, Juvenal, Lucian, Martial, though Grotius connects ὄπισθεν, "on the back," with κατεσφραγισμένον, "sealed," thus rendering, "written within and sealed on the back." The fulness of the book, and the guard of *seven* seals which are opened in succession, denote completeness of revelation (on the number *seven* as denoting full completion, see on ch. i. 4). This book contained the whole of "the mysteries of the kingdom of heaven" (Matt. xiii. 11). It is noteworthy that—so far as we can gather from the Revelation—the book is never read. The breaking of each seal is accompanied by its own peculiar phenomena, which appear to indicate the nature of the contents. And the opening of the seventh seal especially is attended by a compound series of events; but nowhere are we explicitly informed of the contents of the book. Alford well remarks, "Not its contents, but the gradual steps of access to it, are represented by these visions." This view seems to be held also by Schleiermacher. Düsterdieck considers that the roll is never read, though the incidents attending the opening of each seal portray a portion of the contents. Wordsworth and Elliott understand that, as each seal is broken, a part of the roll is unrolled and its contents rendered visible; and these contents are symbolically set forth by the events which then take place. According to this view, the whole is a prophecy extending to the end of the world. The popular idea is that the roll was sealed along the edge with seven seals, all visible at the same time. If, as each seal was broken, a portion of the roll could be unfolded, of course only *one* seal—the outermost—could be visible. This is not, however, inconsistent with St. John's assertion that there were *seven* seals—a fact which he might state from his knowledge gained by witnessing the opening of the seven in succession. The truth seems to lie midway between these views. We must remember that the Revelation was vouchsafed to the Church as an encouragement to her members to persevere under much suffering and tribulation, and as a support to their faith, lest they should succumb to the temptation of despair, and, unable to fathom the eternal purposes of God, should doubt his truth or his ability to aid them. But we are nowhere led to believe that it was the intention of God to reveal *all* things to man, even under the cloak of symbolism or allegory. There is much which must necessarily be withheld until after the end of all earthly things; and, just as no mortal can possibly know the "new name" (ch. iii. 12), so no one on earth can receive perfect knowledge of the "mysteries of the kingdom of heaven," which were symbolically contained in the book, and which, through the intervention of the Lamb, may one day be published; though a portion—sufficient for the time—was shadowed forth, at the opening of the seals; which portion, indeed, could never have been given to us except through the Lamb. We understand, therefore, that the book is symbolical of the *whole* of the mysteries of God; that, as a whole, the contents of the book are not, nor indeed can be, revealed to us while on earth; but that some small but sufficient portion of these mysteries are made known to us by the power of Christ, who will eventually make all things clear hereafter, when we shall know even as we are known (1 Cor. xiii. 12). The events attending the

opening of the seals are therefore a prophecy of the relations of the Church and the world to the end of time. Many opinions have been held as to the antitype of the book. Victorinus thinks it to be the Old Testament, the meaning of which Christ was the first to unlock. And Bede and others consider that the writing within signified the New Testament, and that on the back, the Old. Todd and De Burgh think the roll denotes the office of our Lord, by virtue of which he will judge the world. Sealed with seven seals; *sealed down with seven seals; close sealed* (Revised Version). Grotius connects ὄπισθεν, "behind," with κατεσφραγισμένον, "sealed down," thus reading, "written within and sealed down on the back."

Ver. 2.—And I saw (see on ver. 1). A strong angel; ἰσχυρόν, rendered "mighty" in ch. x. 1. Possibly, as De Wette and others think, so called because of higher rank—De Lyra says Gabriel; but probably on account of the *great voice*, which sounded "as a lion roareth" (ch. x. 3). Proclaiming with a loud voice, Who is worthy to open the book, and to loose the seals thereof? *with a great voice.* "Worthy" is ἄξιος, fit morally, as in John i. 27.

Ver. 3.—And no man in heaven, nor in earth, neither under the earth, was able to open the book, neither to look thereon; *no one in the heaven, or on the earth* (Revised Version). That is, no one in all creation—in heaven, or on earth, or in the place of departed spirits. No one was able "to look thereon" (that is, "to read therein") as a consequence of no one being fit to open the book.

Ver. 4.—And I wept much (ἔκλαιον); *I burst into tears, and continued weeping.* A strong expression in the imperfect tense. Because no man was found worthy to open and to read the book, neither to look thereon. The words, "and to read," should be omitted. They are found in few manuscripts. The equivalent phrase follows, "neither to look thereon."

Ver. 5.—And one of the elders saith unto me, Weep not. One of the elders, as representing the Church (see on ch. iv. 4), bids St. John to take heed to him who was about to disclose to some extent the future of that Church. There is, of course, no indication that any particular individual is signified, though some have striven to identify the elder. Thus De Lyra mentions St. Peter, who was already martyred; others referred to by De Lyra, say St. Matthew, who, in his Gospel, declares Christ's power (Matt. xxviii. 18). Behold, the Lion of the tribe of Juda. The title is accorded to Christ, in illustration of the following act. The Representative of the royal and w torious tribe of Judah was he who had prevailed to open the book, where others had failed (cf. Gen. xl. 9, "Judah is a lion's whelp;" Heb. vii. 14, "For it is evident that our Lord sprang out of Judah"). The Root of David. The *Root* of David is a synonym for *Stem* or *Branch* (cf. Isa. xi. 1, "There shall come forth a Rod out of the stem of Jesse, and a Branch shall grow out of his roots;" and Rom. xv. 12, "Esaias saith, There shall be a Root of Jesse"). Further, Christ may be said to Lave been the Root of David, by virtue of his pre-existence and his creative power. It is one of the paradoxes of the Incarnation, that he who is the Root of David should also be a Branch. Hath prevailed to open the book; *hath conquered* (ἐνίκησεν). Not, as the Authorized Version appears to read, that the act of victory consisted in the opening of the book, but the ability to open was a consequence of a former act of victory, viz. the redemption. So in ver. 9 the ascription of praise runs, "Thou art worthy *because* thou wast slain" (on the infinitive epexegetic, see Winer). Some see a reference here to ch. iii. 7, "He that openeth, and no man shutteth." And to loose the seven seals thereof; *and the seven seals thereof* (Revised Version). Omit "to loose."

Ver. 6.—And I beheld. Again a new feature of the vision is indicated (see on ver. 1). And, lo, in the midst of the throne and of the four beasts, and in the midst of the elders. For a description of the position of the throne and the living beings and the elders, see ch. iv. 6. The passage would, perhaps, be more plainly rendered, "Between the throne and the four living creatures on the one hand, and the elders on the other, stood," etc. The repetition of "in the midst" is a Hebraism (cf. Gen. i. 4, 6, 7, LXX.). The Lamb would thus occupy a central position, where he would be visible to all. Stood a Lamb. The Greek word ἀρνίον, which is here employed, and which is constantly used throughout the Apocalypse, occurs elsewhere in the New Testament only in John xxi. 15. The *Lamb* of John i. 29 is ἀμνός. This word has therefore been brought forward as an evidence that the writer of the Gospel was not also the writer of the Apocalypse, since, when the word is applied as a title of our Lord, the term differs. But the passage John i. 29 is a quotation from Isaiah, and the writer naturally adheres to the form found in the LXX. version in that place. But on other occasions, when he is free to employ his own diction, as in John xxi. 15 and in the Apocalypse, he invariably employs the term ἀρνίον. Some have found in the fact that ἀρνίον (*arnion*) is originally a diminu-

tive form of ἀμνός (*amnos*), a reference to the lowliness and meekness of our Lord; and they see a contrast in the *power* indicated by the seven horns. But such interpretations, however helpful and suggestive, are not warranted by anything in the grammar of the word; since, although no doubt originally a diminutive, the word had lost all such force in St. John's time; so much so, that the varying cases were formed from both words. As it had been slain. We are here confronted with what Stuart calls an "æsthetical difficulty." How could the Lamb, which was alive, standing, and active, exhibit any appearance which would give St. John the idea that it had been slain? Similarly, in the following verses, how could the Lamb *take* the book, or the four living beings handle harps and bowls, or the elders play on harps while also holding bowls? In the first place, it is perfectly immaterial to inquire. St. John is not giving a circumstantial narrative of certain historical facts which occurred in the material, sensible world; but he is reproducing ideas conveyed to him in some way (certainly not through the senses), which ideas are symbolical of events occurring in the natural and spiritual worlds, and of the condition of men or bodies of men. Therefore, if we can ascertain what these mental pictures are intended to portray to us, it matters not in what way the ideas were conveyed to the mind of the seer. In the second place, it must be remembered that the whole is a vision; and that although St. John says, "I saw," in point of fact none of the mental impressions which he obtained were conveyed through the senses. Just as a person relating a dream says, "I saw," when in reality his eyes had been shut and his senses asleep, so the writer here says, "I saw;" and just as in a dream we receive distinct ideas concerning an object without knowing how or why we know the particular fact, and that, too, when such qualities seem contradictory to others with which the object is invested, and yet no incongruity is apparent to us, so St. John realized that these objects possessed qualities which, in the sensible world, would have been impossible. Having seven horns. Throughout the Bible an emblem of power. Moses blessed the tribe of Joseph in the words, "His horns are like the horns of unicorns: with them he shall push the people together to the ends of the earth" (Deut. xxxiii. 17). Hannah sang, "Mine horn is exalted" (1 Sam. ii. 1). The *seven* denotes perfection (see on ch. i. 4; v. 1, etc.). The symbol, therefore, attributes to the Lamb complete power (cf. the words of Christ in Matt. xxviii. 18, "All power is given unto me in heaven and in earth"). **And seven eyes.** The *seven eyes* symbolize perfect knowledge—omniscience (cf. Zech. iv. 10, "They shall rejoice, and shall see the plummet in the hand of Zerubbabel with those seven; they are the eyes of the Lord, which run to and fro through the whole earth; " and 2 Chron. xvi. 9, "For the eyes of the Lord run to and fro throughout the whole earth, to show himself strong in behalf of them whose heart is perfect towards him"). **Which are the seven Spirits of God.** "Which" refers to the *seven eyes* (cf. ch. i. 4, "The seven Spirits which are before his throne;" and ch. iii. 1, "He that hath the seven Spirits of God, and the seven stars;" and ch. iv. 5, "Seven lamps of fire burning before the throne, which are the seven Spirits of God"). The Holy Ghost, proceeding from the Father and the Son, with his sevenfold gifts, is indicated by these symbols of illumination. For he illuminates and makes brighter those in whom he dwells, and renders clearer to them those things outside themselves, and enables them more fully to appreciate the manifold wisdom of God. **Sent forth into all the earth.** That is, the seven Spirits are sent forth (ἀπεσταλμένα; though, as πνεύματα, "the spirits," are also ὀφθαλμοί, "the eyes," A reads ἀπεσταλμένοι).

Ver. 7.—**And he came and took the book; or, and he came and he hath taken it.** "Hath taken" is perfect (εἴληφε), while "came" is the aorist (ἦλθε). If the difference is intentionally significant, it renders the description somewhat more vivid. (For the consideration of the question *how* the Lamb could do this, see on ver. 6.) Wordsworth contrasts the spontaneous act of the Lamb in taking the book of his own accord as his right, with the call to St. John to take the little book (ch. x. 8). **Out of the right hand.** The position of power and honour. He to whom all power was given in heaven and in earth (Matt. xxviii.) is the only One who can penetrate the mysteries and dispense the power of God's right hand. **Of him that sat upon the throne;** *of him that sitteth.* That is, the Triune God (see on ch. iv. 2). The Son in his human capacity, as indicated by his sacrificial form of the Lamb, can take and reveal the mysteries of the eternal Godhead in which he, as God, has part.

Ver. 8.—**And when he had taken the book.** "Had taken" (ἔλαβε) is here aorist, not perfect, as in ver. 7. The text should probably read, *when he took the book;* that is to say, the adoration offered coincides in point of time with the act of taking the book. The four beasts and four and twenty elders fell down before the Lamb. *The four oeasts* as representing animated creation;

the *four and twenty elders* as representative of the Church (see on ch. iv. 4, 6) **Having every one of them harps.** (On the difficulty of *how* each one could hold harps and bowls, see on ver. 6.) It is possible that the phrase refers only to the elders; for these seem more suitably employed in offering *the prayers of the saints* than the representatives of all creation. If, however, as Wordsworth considers, the four living beings and the twenty-four elders together symbolize the Church, the phrase would apply to both. The κινύρα of 1 Sam. xvi. 16, 23 (the κιθάρα of this passage) was played with the hand, and the instrument indicated was probably more of the nature of a guitar than the modern harp. **And golden vials full of odours.** The Revised Version "bowls" is better than "vials." The idea is, no doubt, taken from the shallow bowls which were placed upon the golden altar (Exod. xxx. 1—10), and in which incense was burned. The *odours* are the *incense.* In the same chapter of Exodus directions are given concerning the preparation and use of the incense, which was always a symbol of prayer, and always offered to God alone (cf. Ps. cxli. 2, "Let my prayer be set forth before thee as incense;" also Luke i. 9, 10; Isa. vi. 3, 4) **Which are the prayers of saints.** *The saints;* that is, the members of the Church of God. Some authorities consider "vials" the antecedent of "which;" but it seems best to refer "which" to "odours," though the sense is not materially different, since the former includes the latter.

Ver. 9.—**And they sung a new song, saying.** *They sing;* the worship is unceasing. The song is *new* because it is only now, subsequent to the accomplishment of Christ's work of redemption, that the song can be sung. It is not "Thou art worthy, for thou *wilt redeem*," but "thou *didst redeem.*" Victorinus says, "It is the preaching of the Old Testament together with that of the New which enables the world to sing a new song." **Thou art worthy to take the book, and to open the seals thereof.** (For a consideration of *the book*, and the opening of it, see on ver. 1.) **For thou wast slain, and hast redeemed us to God by thy blood.** The reason why Christ is worthy. *And didst redeem unto God by thy blood out of every kindred*, etc. Though the reading "us" is supported by various manuscripts, and similarly the first person is used in ver. 10, yet, on the whole, it seems better to omit it, the phrase being taken in a partitive sense—"Thou didst redeem unto God by thy blood *some* out of every kindred, etc., and hast made *them*, etc., and *they* shall reign." Again, "Thou didst purchase us *at the price of* thy blood" would, perhaps, give the sense more correctly; for such is the force of the words, "in thy blood" (ἐν τῷ αἵματι). The words point to a particular act performed at a definite time, viz. the death of Christ, by which he repurchased men from sin and Satan for the service of God; the price of the purchase being the shedding of his own blood. The words show, too, that the fruits of the redemption are intended for the whole world; not limited to any chosen nation, though some are excluded by their own act. Out of every kindred, and tongue, and people, and nation. This fourfold classification continually recurs in the Revelation. It includes all the bases of classification of mankind, all the circumstances which separate men, the barriers which were overthrown by the redeeming work of Christ.

Ver. 10.—And hast made us unto our God kings and priests; *and didst make them to be unto our God a kingdom and priests.* Of those whom thou didst redeem from every nation, thou didst make a kingdom and priests. Wordsworth remarks that these honours conferred upon the redeemed imply duties as well as privileges. They receive the princely honours conferred upon them only on condition that they also become priests, presenting themselves, their souls and bodies, a living sacrifice to God (Rom. xii. 1, 2), and, being a *holy* priesthood, offering up spiritual sacrifices acceptable to God by Jesus Christ (1 Pet. ii. 5). (On the person of "us," see on previous verse.) And we shall reign on the earth; or, *and they reign on the earth* (see on ver. 9). The interpretation of this passage will necessarily be influenced to some extent by the view adopted of the millennium (see on ch. xx.). Those who expect a personal reign of Christ on the earth for a thousand years naturally consider that in this **verse** reference is made to that period. And if the thousand years be understood to denote the time which elapses between the first and second comings of Christ, that is to say, the present time, the two passages—that in ch. xx. 4 and the one before us—may be connected, and intended to refer to the same time. We have, therefore, to inquire in what sense the word "reign" is used, and how the redeemed can be said to reign on the earth at the present time. In the first place, nothing is more plainly taught us than that Christ's **reigning**, his power, and his kingdom on earth are a spiritual reign, a spiritual power, a spiritual kingdom; though the Jews and our Lord's disciples themselves frequently erred by supposing that his kingdom would be a visible, worldly power. It seems natural, therefore, that if such is the meaning of Christ's reigning, that of his servants should be of the same nature: and we ought not

to err in the same way as the Jews did, by expecting to see the redeemed exercise at any time visible authority over their fellowmen. The redeemed reign, then, spiritually. But it will be well to inquire more fully and exactly what we intend to signify by this expression. The word "reign" is not often used of Christians in the New Testament. In Rom. v. 17 we read, "Much more they which receive abundance of grace and of the gift of righteousness shall reign in life by one, Jesus Christ." And in 1 Cor. iv. 8, "And I would to God ye did reign." In both these places St. Paul seems to intend a reigning over self—an ability to subdue personal passions; a power which comes from the "abundance of grace and of the gift of righteousness" which are mentioned, and which are possessed only by the redeemed, through Jesus Christ. This ability to subdue personal passions and ambitions is what the apostle wishes for the Corinthians, and of which many of them had shown themselves to be destitute, or only possessing in an inadequate degree. It is the truth which is expressed by Solomon in the words, "Better is he that ruleth his spirit than he that taketh a city" (Prov. xvi. 32); and in the words of the Collect for Peace in the Morning Prayer of the Church of England, "Whose service is perfect freedom;" or, as it should be rendered, "Whom to serve is to reign." The representatives of the Church and of creation, then, adore the Lamb, through whose redeeming act grace may be given to men of every kindred and tongue, to enable them to overcome sin and Satan, and in the freedom of God's service to reign on earth as kings and conquerors over all unworthy passions. In this way, too, we account for the present tense of the verb, which is most probably the correct reading.

Ver. 11.—And I beheld marks a new feature of the vision, viz. the introduction of the angelic host as taking part in the adoration of the Lamb (see on ch. iv. 1). And I heard the voice of many angels; *a voice.* The angels who have "desired to look into" the mystery of the redemption of the world (1 Pet. i. 12) have now had declared to them "by the Church the manifold wisdom of God, according to the eternal purpose which he purposed in Christ Jesus our Lord" (Eph. iii. 10, 11); and are thus enabled to join in the song of the redeemed. Round about the throne and the beasts and the elders. The innumerable company of angels encircle the throne and the beasts and the elders. Thus the throne is in the vision seen as occupying the centre, the four living creatures are placed round it in different directions; the elders form the next circle, and the angels enclose the whole.

The Lamb is in the midst before the throne (see on ch. iv. 6). " Thus," says Bisping, " the redeemed creation stands nearer to the throne of God than even the angels (see Heb. ii. 5)." And the number of them was ten thousand times ten thousand, and thousands of thousands. The readings vary here, though the sense of the passage is not affected. After πρεσβυτέρων, " elders," (1) the Authorized and Revised Versions, following א, A, B, P, etc., render as above; (2) 1, Erasmus, Stephens edit. 1550 (though the last probably *per errorem*), omit " and the number of them was ten thousand times ten thousand;" (3) Vulgate, both manuscripts and Clementine edition, simply omit " ten thousand times ten thousand;" (4) 38, Andreas (one manuscript) omit only the last words, "and thousands of thousands." The number is, of course, not to be taken literally, but as expressive of an exceeding great multitude.

Ver. 12.—Saying with a loud voice; *a great voice* (Revised Version) ; λέγοντες, "saying," is irregular construction, and to be referred to *angels* as being a nominative understood. Worthy is the Lamb that was slain; *that hath been slain* (Revised Version). Again, as in ver. 9, the worshippers give the reason for considering Christ worthy to receive ' their adoration. It is because he had been slain and thus redeemed the world. To receive power, and riches, and wisdom, and strength, and honour, and glory, and blessing. The sevenfold nature of the adoration attributed to the Lamb is probably indicative of its complete and perfect nature. (On the meaning of λαβεῖν, "to receive," to take as a right what is offered, see Thayer-Grimm.) *Power* (δύναμις) is the ability to perform which is inherent in one's nature. *Strength* (ἰσχύς) is the attribute by which that power is put into operation; it frequently denotes physical strength. *Riches* (cf. John i. 16, " And of his fulness have all we received;" also Eph. iii. 8, "The unsearchable riches of Christ;" also Jas. i. 17, "Every good gift and every perfect gift is from above, and cometh down from the Father of lights;" also Acts xvii. 25, " He giveth to all life, and breath, and all things "). The whole sevenfold ascription is spoken as one, only one article being prefixed. In this respect it differs from ch. iv. 11 and ch. vii. 12, where we have " *the* glory" and " *the* honour," etc. (see on ch. iv. 11).

Ver. 13.—And every creature which is in heaven, and on the earth, and under the earth, and such as are in the sea, and all that are in them; *and every created thing which is in the heaven, and on the earth and under the earth, and on the sea, and all things that are in them* (Revised Version).

All animated creation now joins in the ascription of praise. Those *under the earth* are probably the "spirits in prison " of 1 Pet. iii. 19, though Vitringa understands the expression to be used of the devils " who unwillingly obey Christ," and even declare his glory, as in Mark i. 24, " I know thee who thou art, the Holy One of God." *The sea* is meant literally ; the apostle's object being to include all animated beings wheresoever existing. It has been remarked that St. John's exile at Patmos would render him familiar with the appearance of the sea, and account for its frequent use in the Apocalypse, both literally and symbolically. The things *on the sea* would signify, not merely ships with their inhabitants, but also those animals in the sea which are known to men by dwelling near the surface. " All things that are in them " serves to render emphatic the universality of the description, as in Exod. xx. 11 and Ps. cxlvi. 6, " The Lord made heaven and earth, the sea, and all that in them is." Heard I saying. "Saying " is masculine, λέγοντας in א, B, P, Vulgate, Andr. *a, c*, Arethas, Primasius. But the neuter, λέγοντα, is read in A, 1, 12, Andr. *p, bav*. Blessing, and honour, and glory, and power; *the blessing, and the honour, and the glory, and the dominion* (Revised Version). The Revisers have wisely rendered κράτος, "the dominion," by a different word from δύναμις, "power," of ver. 12, both of which in the Authorized Version are rendered "power." The article, too, serves to give greater emphasis, making the expression tantamount to "all blessing," etc. (see on ch. iv. 11). Nothing is signified by the omission of three attributes. The number four is symbolical of the complete creation, and may be used on that account; but probably the omission is to avoid repetition, the four attributes given being typical of the seven just previously uttered. Be unto him that sitteth upon the throne, and unto the Lamb for ever and ever. That is, unto the Triune God (see on ch. iv. 2). Christ, as having part with the Father and the Holy Ghost in the Godhead, sits upon the throne, and is worthy with them to receive adoration. But in his special character as the Redeemer, he is also singled out to receive the praises of the redeemed.

Ver. 14.—And the four beasts said, Amen. And the four and twenty elders fell down and worshipped him that liveth for ever and ever. (On the signification of the four beasts as representative of creation, and the four-and-twenty elders as typical of the Church, see on ch. iv. 4 and 6.) Three stages are marked in the hymn of adoration before this concluding verse : (1) the four living beings and the four and twenty elders worship the Lamb, and commemorate their redemption by him; they are able to sing "a new song"—the song of the redeemed; (2) the angels join in the worship of the Lamb, ascribing to him the consummation of all perfection ; (3) then all created things praise God and the Lamb. In conclusion, the representatives of redeemed creation once more join in the eucharistic hymn, and prostrate themselves in worship before the Triune God.

This forms the end of one act of the heavenly drama. The opening of the seals now follows, and a description of the attendant circumstances is given.

HOMILETICS.

Vers. 1—14.—*Continuation of vision.* In the preceding homily we noted that the apostle records five songs. We have already referred to two of them. We now have the three remaining ones before us. 1. The third song is *the new song—of redemption.* Creation being effected, what is to be done with it? Of what events is earth to be the scene and the witness? and what are the developments which Providence has in store? See. In the right hand of him who sits upon the throne there is a book—a roll, written within and without (a rare thing, except through pressure of matter, to write on the back of a roll). Written—by whom? Surely we are left to infer that the writing was that of Jehovah; that the book was his; that in the writing were indicated the things which were to come hereafter, yea, what was to take place on this globe! But this book, with the writing of Jehovah in it as to what shall come to pass, is fast sealed. Seven seals. They must be opened ere the mystery of the future can be told. As yet it is fast wrapped and folded up. Who shall open that book and interpret what is there? The apostle (ch. v. 2) saw a mighty angel, and heard him proclaim "with a loud voice, Who is worthy," etc.? And no one was worthy—for no one was able, either in heaven or on the earth, neither under the earth—to open it or to look into it. *No one in all creation!* The task is too great for man or angel. Must the roll be ever closed? Is the secret will of God expressed therein to be for ever an insoluble riddle? No one responds. There is awful silence; till later on it is broken, but only by the sobs of the weeping John! At length, one of the elders comes. The tears of an apostle are a magnet to him. He can tell more of trials and triumphs than even he who had leaned on Jesus' breast. "Weep not! The Lion . . . hath prevailed." Hath *conquered?* Has there, then, been a conflict ere the book could be opened? At this point a new form, before unnamed, appears. "And . . . a Lamb, standing, *as it had been slain*" (ver. 6). This John had long before heard another point him out, saying, "Behold the Lamb of God!" Since then, *that* Lamb of God had been made an offering for sin; and now the traces of that self-offering are seen in heaven. He, the offered Lamb, comes, full of strength ; with an authority all his own he approaches right up to the throne, nearer than all created ones, and *takes* the book, etc. (ver. 7). When he in majesty and might takes the book into his own hands, then the apostle's tears are dried, and heaven's silence gives place to song. In the hands of Jesus the seals will give way, and under his mediatorial reign will the will of God be disclosed; *i.e. in the hands of Jesus the developments of providence become disclosures of redemption.* And lo! at this stage new music is heard. "They are singing a new song" (ver. 9). New, for it celebrates a new revelation of God, a new work of God, and a new unfolding of the plans of God. New—ever new. It can never become old. It is a song of praise from the living creatures and the redeemed ones [1] to him who was slain for them. [2] Such a song is this as creation could not inspire. Still there is more to follow. 2. The fourth is *the "assenting chorus of the host of angels"* [3] *to the Lamb that was slain* (vers. 11, 12). We are taught clearly enough, in the fifteenth chapter of Luke, that angels sympathize in the redeeming work of our Lord, and witness his joy when one sinner is saved. How fully in accord with this it

---

[1] "The twenty-four elders, representing as they do the whole Church of God, are represented as offering the praises and prayers of the whole Church—the harps representing the former, the censers the latter" (Alford, *in loc.*)

[2] Tregelles retains "us" in ver. 9.

[3] The phrase used by Dean Alford.

is to find them joining with the ransomed and taking up the song, "Worthy is the Lamb that was slain"—although from angel-voices we miss the most tender, the most touching feature of the heavenly song! Their praise may be more sublime; their love cannot be like ours. Still, the song swells in grandeur. **3.** The fifth is *the song of all creation to God and the Lamb.* (Ver. 13.) "*Every* creature . . . heard I saying, . . . unto him that sitteth upon the throne, and unto the Lamb." All intelligent and holy beings, everywhere, join in a grand concert of praise, alike to the Father and the Son. The love of the Father devised all. The love of the Son undertook, effected, and administered all; and to him, with the Father, shall endless honour be given by an admiring and adoring universe. One burst of harmony fills the courts of heaven. We cannot but feel that we are in the presence of the sublimest scenes that can ever in this state be unfolded to mortal view. In fact, *we could not bear more.* A fuller disclosure would overwhelm us. As it is, there is enough concealed to quicken our eager expectations; enough revealed to give us several practical principles to work with in the light thereof.[1]

WHAT MAY WE LEARN FROM THIS SUBLIME VISION? Or rather, What are the truths concerning the Divine Being and his plans which lie couched therein? They are many. **1.** We see that gathering round the throne, hymning like songs, interested in like themes, are the inhabitants of heaven and the redeemed on and from the earth. There is a oneness of sympathy between them, and all are in full sympathy with God. This is the thought of the fifteenth chapter of Luke. **2.** We see that the first and foremost Object of their adoring song is the Triune Jehovah; the Thrice-Holy One. He who sitteth upon the throne is the adorable Centre in whom all holy beings find their everlasting home. God is adored for what he is, as well as praised for what he does. He himself is infinitely greater than all his works. **3.** By the highest orders of beings there is seen in creation matter for adoring praise. It is a revelation of God. It is a witness for him. His perfections are written there.

> "He formed the seas, he formed the hills,
> Made every drop and every dust,
> Nature and time with all their wheels,
> And pushed them into motion first."

And whether, in our theories of how things came to be as they are, we are evolutionists or non-evolutionists, whether we side with convulsionists or anti-convulsionists, either way we see matter for jubilation and song. "*Thou* hast," etc. There is no atheism in beings higher than we are. The best men on earth are not to be found in the atheists' camp. "Blessed are the pure in heart: for they will see God" everywhere. **4.** Creation expresses only in part the Divine mind. There is a book written, in which are recorded both purpose and plan; and where the earth is looked on as the dwelling-place of man, where man is known to have sinned against God, it cannot but be a question of absorbing interest—How will God deal with man? What will be the Divine treatment of sin? **5.** It is in our Lord Jesus Christ alone that we are furnished with a key to the workings of providence. He alone can take the book and open its seals. He has accomplished a vast redemptive work. He has undertaken a trust. He has all power in heaven and on earth. In the administration of his work, he unfolds and carries out the plan of God. "The Father loveth the Son, and hath put all things into his hand." **6.** Through Christ's prevailing to open the seals, the history of this globe comes to be the history of redemption. Our Lord Jesus Christ presides over all governments, empires, kingdoms, and thrones. He is "Head over all things to his Church," and subordinates all to the inbringing of his everlasting kingdom to the regeneration of earth, to "making all things new." Thus creation is but the platform on which redemption stands, and it is destined to witness its crowning glory in the re-creation of *men* in the image of their God! "We, according to his promise, look for new heavens and a new earth, wherein dwelleth righteousness." Finally, owing to redemption's work, a new song of praise is heard in heaven, in which angels and men and "every creature" join. Redemption is the new song for them all.

[1] There are many valuable remarks as to the bearing of the grand contents of this and other Apocalyptic chapters upon the question of the *date* of the book, by Principal Dr. David Brown, in the *Expositor*, October, 1889, p. 281.

> "The highest angel never saw
> So much of God before."

In creation there is seen the work of his hands. In providential government, the wisdom that controls. In redemption, the grace that saves and the out-gushing fulness of a mighty heart that loves! "That was not first which was spiritual, but that which was natural, and after that which was spiritual." The first creation vivified earth; the second vivified man. And not only so, but the song will be ever new. Its theme will never tire. Its strains will never weary the ear. So long as saved men love to recall how much they owe unto their Lord, so long as they love to contrast what they receive with what they deserve, the song will be ever new to them. And as long as holy beings in all worlds delight to celebrate the noblest disclosures of the heart of God, so long will redemption's song be new to them all! Note: We need not, we ought not to wait till we get to heaven ere we begin that song. Nay, we cannot. We cannot help singing it now.

> "E'er since by faith I saw the stream
> Thy flowing wounds supply,
> Redeeming love has been my theme,
> And shall be till I die!"

HOMILIES BY VARIOUS AUTHORS.

Vers. 1—14.—*The adoration of the Lamb.* The theophany of ch. iv. is continued in this. We are permitted to see more of the high court of heaven, and to witness the purpose of its session, the centre of its adoration, and the transactions in which its members share. We have surveyed the throne and him that sat thereon, the rainbow above the throne, the crystal sea, the burning torches, the elders and the cherubim, and their worship of God. But now the vision is enlarged, and we behold the seven-sealed book, or scroll, held in the right hand of him that sat on the throne; then the coming forth of a mighty angel, who challenges all in that august assembly, and all everywhere, be they who they may, to open the book. Then follows the hush of awful silence, which is the only response the angel's challenge receives; whereat St. John weeps much. Then is heard the voice of one of the elders, bidding him "Weep not," and at once the chief portion and purpose of the whole vision is disclosed. St. John sees, fronting the throne and attended, as was he who sat thereon, by the living ones and the elders, the "Lamb as it had been slain." Strange, incongruous, and almost inconceivable is that figure, with its seven horns and seven eyes. Great painters, as Van Eyck, have tried to portray it, but they have rather lessened than enlarged our conceptions of the truths which the symbol as it stands here in this vision so vividly sets forth. Here, as everywhere in this book, it is the ideas, and not the forms which symbolize them, which are of consequence. And, then, the Lamb is represented as coming and taking the book out of the hand of him that sat upon the throne; whereupon the first adoration of the Lamb takes place. The "living ones" and the elders, each now seen with harp and censer of gold full of odours—they, together, sing the "new song." And, lo, on the outskirts of this heavenly scene, gathering round and enclosing the whole, appear now myriads of angels, and they lift up their voices in like holy adoration of the Lamb. And now a third burst of praise, and from a yet more varied and multitudinous choir, is heard by the enraptured seer. From the heavens above, from the earth beneath, and from the regions of the departed—from those whom the earth covered over in the quiet grave, and those whom the sea had swallowed up,—there arose their anthem of praise to God and to the Lamb. And with the united "Amen" of the four living ones and the elders, as they prostrate themselves in worship, this vision of the adoration of the Lamb ends. Observe Christ as—

I. The Centre of all revelation. We behold him: 1. *In his premundane glory.* We cannot know, and yet less comprehend, much of this. Only that he came forth from God, was in the beginning with God; that he dwelt in the bosom of the Father, in glory which he had with the Father before the world was. But what words could make this clear to our minds ? We wait to understand. 2. *In his Incarnation.* We trace him from the manger at Bethlehem, all through his earthly life and ministry, to Gethsemane, Calvary, and the tomb. And we see him rising from the dead and afterwards ascending to the right hand of God. But we are permitted also to see him as—

II. THE CENTRE OF HEAVENLY ADORATION. See where he is—"in the midst of the throne," standing on that central space immediately in front of the throne, the Centre of all that holy throng, on whom all eyes rest, to whom every knee bows, and every tongue confesses. And what a circle that is ! See its members. But he is the Centre; to him their adoring worship is given. Are we in sympathy with this ? Is he the Centre of our heart's worship and love?

III. THE REVEALER AND ADMINISTRATOR OF THE PURPOSES OF GOD. 1. *God has such purposes.* The book held in his right hand is the symbol thereof. It contains his mind, his will, his decrees. Nothing is left to chance. All is ordered and settled. 2. *But that book is sealed.* Completely, absolutely ; this is the meaning of the seven seals. If one seal were removed, which by man it can never be, but a portion of those purposes would be disclosed. "His ways are past finding out." 3. *But it is essential that that book should be taken and opened.* Hence the angelic challenge, and St. John's tears when none was found to accept that challenge. What would the world be without the revelation of God ? We know ; for "the dark places of the earth are full of the habitations of cruelty." Would that we thought more of our own obligation to the revelation of God's will, that we might, as we ought to, be more eager that others should possess it who now have it not! 4. *The Lord Jesus Christ comes forward.* There can be no manner of doubt that he is meant. Though described as "the Lion of the tribe of Judah," yet he is seen as a Lamb—a little Lamb (ἀρνίον), and with the marks of its slaughter yet upon it, the scars and wounds of his sacrifice yet visible. He advances and takes the book. And so we learn that he is the Trustee, the Depositary, the alone Revealer of the Divine will. All truth is in his keeping. (1) Of prophecy. It was he who opened, and yet opens, the minds of his disciples, that they should understand what was foretold concerning him. (2) Of the gospel. It is he who shines in our hearts to give the light of the knowledge of God in the face of Jesus Christ. But especially is meant here: (3) Of providence—how God would deal with the Church, the world, with individual souls. This book discloses all this; he shows to us what God has done and will do. 5. *But he is not only the Revealer, but the Administrator of the Divine purposes.* As he opens each seal that which he discloses is at once accomplished. He is seen controlling and ruling all. What joy to think of this ! For he is—

IV. PERFECTLY QUALIFIED TO BE ALL THIS. Observe in the vision his seven horns. This means : 1. *He has fulness of power.* The horn is the symbol of strength. Hence "seven horns" mean fulness of strength. Christ is "mighty to save." The gates of hell shall not prevail against him. They will, they do try, as they have long tried, but in vain. For: 2. *He has also the fulness of the Spirit.* The Lamb was seen with "seven eyes," and these are explained as denoting the same as the seven torches (ch. iv. 5), the seven, that is, the perfect, full, complete power, though diverse in working, of the Spirit of God. For Christ's victory is to be achieved, not over human bodies, but over human spirits, and his power must and does correspond to the opposition he has to meet. And over all the earth his Spirit goes: has not that Spirit come to us, and when he comes the human spirit ceases to resist, and is blessed in yielding? 3. *And he has all right.* "Thou art worthy :" so sing all the heavenly choirs. (1) The Lamb is seen "as it had been slain." The sacrifice of the Lord Jesus is represented perpetually in Holy Scripture as the righteous ground of our redemption. The forgiveness of man's sin was to be by no mere gracious letting the guilty go free, let what will come of the Law which he has violated. Not so, but in and by the sacrifice of Christ, the Law was magnified and made honourable ; by no means "made void," but established. We linger not now to explain this—if, indeed, any one can fully explain it —but we simply assert what Scripture everywhere affirms. Moreover : (2) He is commissioned by God. He receives the book from him. God "sent forth his Son," "gave his only begotten Son." 4. *And his is fulness of love.* "For thou wast *slain*, and hast redeemed us by *thy blood* "—this is the overwhelming thought which prostrates the souls of all his redeemed ones in an agony of insolvent gratitude ; that he, Son of

God, who was with God and was God, that he should have been content to come
hither to this thorn-strewn earth of ours, and to live here the life of a poor, meek man,
and then to die upon the cross for us—"herein *is* love;" and herein is also his
supreme qualification to reveal and administer the will of God.

V. THEREFORE IS THE ADORATION OF THE LAMB. Let us join in it. We shall do
so if we remember what he has revealed, and that he is the Administrator of all our
affairs.—S. C.

Ver. 5.—*The mediatorial power of Christ.* "And one of the elders saith," etc. St.
John is first shown Christ as Head of his Church, ruling here on earth. This his first
vision. Then he is transported to heaven, and sees the throne set there, and its
attendants and their worship. Then the coming forth of the Son of God, and the
representation of his mediatorial sovereignty. But first there is the vision of the throne
of God, for he is the Source and End of all authority. God was and shall be "all in all."
But his power is seen in this vision as delegated to Christ as Mediator. For this vision—
    I. SYMBOLIZES THE MEDIATORIAL POWER OF CHRIST. It does this by representing:
1. *The Lamb in the act of taking the book out of the hand of him that sat on the
throne.* Note the book in God's hand; the challenge of the angel, unanswered; and
St. John's distress thereat. But now the Lamb prevails, etc. The meaning of the
book, or roll, is the plan or policy of a state, the will and purpose of a ruler. God
speaks of his book; of blotting out names therefrom. Scribes were important personages because of their agency in preparing such decrees. The taking of the book,
therefore, is as when a minister of state in our days receives his portfolio; it signifies
his commission to know, comprehend, and execute the counsels and decrees therein
contained. Thus, as receiving his commission, the vision represents our Lord. 2. *The
origin of his mediatorial power.* It was derived from the Father. Christ ever affirmed
that he "received of the Father," that he came "not to do his own will, but the will
of him that sent him;" Christ was "the Man whom he had ordained;" "God hath
spoken unto us by his Son;" "All things are committed unto me of my Father," etc.
The mystery of the Trinity is perhaps insoluble by us, but as to the truth of the
doctrine, it pervades, not this vision only, but the whole Bible. 3. *The nature of
it.* The vision represents Christ as One that was capable of, and had suffered, death.
He was, therefore, human as well as Divine. His human origin as well as his
Divine glory are both shown, and because he was the God-Man he became Mediator
between God and man. 4. *The exercise of his mediatorial power.* This by his taking
the book and loosing the seals thereof, whereupon, as each seal is opened, that which he
thus discloses is at once begun to be accomplished. The Apocalypse discloses the fate
and fortunes of the Church, and of the world as related to it. Information and reserve
characterize these disclosures. They tell of a great struggle, in which all creatures
engage; that it is for moral ends, and centres round man. Hell and its plans and
apparent triumphs are shown; also her overthrow, and at last the full redemption of
the Church and the establishment of the kingdom of God. Now, all this Christ not
only reveals, but executes. For this he has the seven horns of omnipotent might, and
the seven eyes of omniscient wisdom. But it is in their execution that the Divine
purposes are fully revealed. As yet we know but parts of them. The apostles
only knew the Scriptures when, not before, they were fulfilled. And how vast is: 5.
The extent of his power! It is over all physical and all moral natures; over the
present and the future; over the grave and death; over angels and devils; over every
soul in every land, age, and condition. All are subject unto him. God "left nothing
that is not put under him" (1 Cor. xv.). And: 6. *Its final end and completion.* It has
such an end. The very idea of a "book" is that of something which comes to an end,
which is for a definite and limited purpose. Christ must reign, not for ever, but "till
he hath put all things under his feet." Then cometh the end (cf. 1 Cor. xv. 24—28).
The book is a definite thing. The existing systems of grace and providence are not
everlasting; they subserve ends beyond and higher than themselves; they are but
preliminary and initiative; their completion is yet hidden, and will fill and brighten
eternity. Further, the vision—
    II. EXHIBITS THE BASIS ON WHICH HIS MEDIATORIAL POWER RESTS. He "prevailed,"
but by right, not by force; in virtue of his being: 1. *The Lion of the tribe of Judah.*

(Gen. xlix. 9.) Hence his right was from his office, the position it was predicted he should fill. And his life and his conquest over Satan, sin, man, death, all verified the truth of Jacob's dying prophecy. 2. *The Root of David.* Hence, by descent also, as Heir of him to whom God's promises of universal rule had been given. But chiefly because he was: 3. *The Lamb slain.* Thus the pre-eminent right secured by his atonement is set forth. The Lamb is the Centre of heaven. Hence his cross claims his crown; the sufferings of Christ, the glory that should follow. The term " worthy " is used in reference to this right thus obtained. The cross affirms every principle of moral law. As all creation is for moral ends, so supremely is the cross of Christ. He is worthy because he was slain.

III. REVEALS THE RESULTS CONTEMPLATED BY HIS MEDIATORIAL POWER. They are four. 1. *To set forth the glory of the Son of God.* See the adoration of the Lamb, how intense, how universal, how unceasing. All things are for him, as they are by him. All men are to " honour the Son, even as they honour the Father." And by his mediation this glory is secured. He had glory before the world was. But he has far more now, and yet more shall be his. He is seen amid all the confusions and calamities of life to be our one Hope and Stay. " Christ is all and in all," and *so* is he glorified. 2. *To secure the accomplishment of man's redemption.* " Thou hast redeemed us: " so the heavenly choirs sing over and over again. And Christ has his redeemed. See how the Church is described: as the bride; heir; joint-heir with Christ; kings; priests unto God; his body, etc. Yes, Christ *hath* redeemed us. 3. *To demonstrate the unity of the Divine counsels and the progressive character of the Divine works.* The mediatorial system is not external to, but part of the system of, the universe. It is essential to its moral order and bound up with all its history. Sin was an inroad upon, and an invasion, violation, and disruption of, the Divine rule. Inevitable if the gift of free-will was to be granted as it was; and hence some means for the reparation of this great disaster had to be found, and for the demonstration of the consistency of the wise, the holy, and the all-loving God. All human sin, protracted so awfully and so wearily age after age, is yet but an episode in the course of the Divine administration; like as a war is but an episode in the history of a nation. And the mediation of Christ is the method of God for undoing the evil man's sin has wrought. 4. *To issue in the glory of the Father and to show this as the end and aim of all things.* " That God may be all in all: " such is its chief end; as for each one of us, so for all human history, and all the Divine dealings with us in Christ our Lord. Let us by self-surrender to Christ fall in with that blessed purpose, and so one day rejoice in its perfect fulfilment. (Adapted from notes of sermon by late Rev. G. Steward, of Newcastle.)—S. C.

Ver. 6.—*The goings forth of the Holy Ghost.* " The seven Spirits of God which are sent forth," etc. In all possible ways the Church declares her faith in the Lord Jesus Christ and his redemption. By the name, Christian; by the sacrament of the Holy Supper; by symbols—the cross everywhere; by her literature, etc. And all this is right; the example of it is given in Scripture, for Christ is the Alpha and Omega of the Bible: " Him first, him last, him midst, and without end." *But this is not all the truth.* For it is equally true that the holy and perfect Spirit of God is sent forth into all the earth—working in, upon, for, and around us everywhere. The doctrine is most blessed, and an essential part of the gospel of Christ, though it has not the prominence in our thought or speech that " the truth as it is in Jesus " receives. We do not realize as we should that the Holy Spirit is the Christ within us, and whose coming made it "expedient" that the Christ who in our nature died for us upon the cross " should go away." Note—

I. THE EVIDENCE FOR THE GOING FORTH OF THE SPIRIT OF GOD. We see the Spirit striving with men in the days of Noah; as yet earlier and more successfully—because the striving was with matter, not with mind—we see him bringing order out of chaos at the Creation. " Whither shall I go from thy Spirit?" asks the psalmist; "or whither shall I flee from thy presence?" David piteously pleads, " Take not thy Holy Spirit from me! " His presence is recognized in every part of the sacred history, and in the New Testament Pentecost is told of, and the truths concerning him are dwelt upon still more at large. In this Book of Revelation we read once and again of his gracious work (cf. ch. i. 4: iii. 1: iv. 5: v. 6. Cf. also conclusion of all the letters to the seven Churches, ch. ii. and iii.). At ch. xix. 10 we are told that "the testimony of Jesus is the spirit of prophecy." The Holy Spirit confirms the "voice from heaven" (ch. xiv. 13), which declares, "Blessed are the dead which die in the Lord. Yea, saith the Spirit," etc. It was under the influence of the Spirit the book was written: "I was in the Spirit," St. John repeatedly affirms. And at the end of the book the Spirit is heard along with the bride and others, bidding all come and take the water of life freely. Scripture, therefore, does plainly tell of a Spirit—the Spirit of God, "sent forth into all the earth."

II. THE MANNER OF HIS GOING FORTH. This seen: 1. *In nature.* (1) Creation. He is called "the Spirit of life." "Thou sendest forth thy Spirit, they are created." (2) At each returning spring. 2. *Amongst men.* Here it is that the Divine Spirit's work may be most manifestly seen. (1) As a fact, there is much good amongst men who have not been and are not within the circle of the Church—much that is lovely and of good report and worthy of all praise. See the laws and literature of ancient nations; and the lives of their noblest men. Who that is acquainted with ancient history will for a moment deny this? And to-day there is much of good that yet is, formally, without the circle of the Church. No doubt a large part of this is owing to what Carlyle called "a great after-shine" of Christianity. The inspiration of many professedly non-Christian moralists is Christian after all. They have unconsciously absorbed it, and then reproduced it as from some other source. (2) Now, whence comes all this? Many say that "natural goodness" is sufficient to account for it. And that there is some good in every man, we can hardly deny. And we are unable to accept the Augustinian theory that such goodness, being unconnected with faith, "has the nature of sin." For is not this doctrine perilously near that of which our Lord speaks in Matt. xii. 24, where his enemies attributed his deeds to the prince of devils? We know of no such thing as natural goodness. How can it coexist with the universal corruption which we confess? But we do know of God as the Source of goodness, and of Satan as the inspirer of evil, and to him we cannot ascribe the goodness of which we are speaking. We therefore look for its source in that going forth of the Spirit of God of which the text tells. Does not all light come from the central sun? The flame that leaps forth from the coal, heated above a certain temperature, and with which we are so familiar, is but latent light liberated at length after having been imprisoned there since the days when it first was radiated from the one central sun. And has not science showed that life only can produce life? Dead matter cannot originate it; it must come from life. And this is true in the realm of moral and spiritual life also. And does not Scripture assert this? St. James says, "Do not err, my beloved brethren, Every good gift . . . cometh down from the Father of lights," etc. (Jas. i. 17). And St. John (i.) tells of "the light that lighteth every man that cometh into the world." We therefore claim *all* goodness as due to the going forth, etc. 3. *In the Church.* Here, of course, it is most of all to be seen. Let the waters of a lake be agitated by any cause, the greatest movements will be seen nearest the point where that which stirred the waters came into contact with them, although the movements will not stay until the whole body of the lake has been more or less affected thereby. And so, because the Church is the point of contact, amid the wide extent of humanity at large, with the blessed power of the Spirit of God, therefore in the Church will his power most of all be seen, though his power goes forth far beyond. In the Church it is seen in all *stages* of the spiritual life—in conviction, conversion, inward peace, bright hope, growing holiness. And in all the *manifestations* of that life—trust, fidelity, charity, zeal, self-denial, love, joy, peace, etc. It is more evidently seen in great spiritual movements like that at Pentecost, in which vast numbers of human hearts are touched, moved, and saved thereby. Then everybody notes it, and asks, "What strange thing is this?" But it may be seen, also, in equally real operation in the case of individuals who, one by one, the Holy Spirit draws to God. And this going forth shall be seen again: 4. *At the resurrection.* "The Spirit of him that raised up Jesus from the dead shall also quicken your mortal bodies," etc. (Rom. viii. 11). Each spring season is God's perpetual parable of the resurrection. The whence, the whither, and the cause are all portrayed when

"The spring-tide hour
Brings leaf and flower."

CONCLUSION. If we be asked—Why, if it be so that the Spirit of God thus goes forth, why is the world no better? we can only reply: 1. The higher the life the longer its development demands. What wonder, then, that "the end is not yet"? 2. The Spirit may be resisted; is so. The old fable of the sirens is of everyday fulfilment. The sweet, seductive song of the siren-like world lures souls in myriads to abandon the leading of the Spirit of God. Is it not so? The wonder is, not that so few escape, but that any do. No wonder, therefore, that his work is slow. 3. But it is sure. The Spirit is likened to fire—to torches of fire (see ch. iv.), which will stand the rough blasts of the world and the tempests of sin, and yet burn on. And as fire transforms and strives strenuously till it gains its ends, so we believe the Spirit will, for we "believe in the Holy Ghost." 4. What reception has he from us? Doubt him not, resist him not, but seek his aid for yourselves, for others, and, as you so do, you will increasingly believe in, see, and rejoice in, the goings forth of the Spirit of God.—S. C.

Vers. 9, 12—14.—*The triple doxology.* In these sublime chapters these doxologies stand out prominently. Note concerning them—

I. WHAT IS COMMON TO THEM ALL. They are all ascribed to the Lamb. Exclusively in the first two; united with "him that sitteth on the throne," in the third; but in all the Lamb is prominent. From this we learn: 1. *We cannot render too much honour to Christ.* He is seen "in the midst of the throne," and the Centre of all that heavenly circle, and the Object of their united adoration. We therefore cannot exceed in our worship of him. We scarce know how, we need not know how, to distinguish between him that sitteth on the throne and between him that is in the midst of the throne. The worship of one is the worship of the other, and of the other of the one. Christ is everything to us—"all in all," as St. Paul affirms, and as this vision shows. The fact is, we cannot worship God without worshipping Christ. No man cometh or can come to the Father but by him. The very thoughts and ideas that we have of God we gain through him. Those varied human expressions concerning God which we find in the Old Testament are but anticipations of the confirmation they were to receive through him who, coming from the Father, should take our nature and so reveal the Father to us. 2. *Nor can we think too much of the cross of Christ.* It is to him as to the Lamb, the Lamb slain and who hath redeemed us by his blood, that this adoration is given. It is the cross of Christ that speaks peace to the contrite heart, that assures of perfect sympathy the sad and distressed mind, that gives new strength and resolve to the tempted soul. Well does Watts sing—

> "Oh, the sweet wonders of that cross
> On which my Saviour groaned and died!
> Her noblest life my spirit draws
> From his dear wounds and bleeding side."

II. WHAT IS PECULIAR TO EACH. 1. *The first doxology.* (1) *Offered by:* (*a*) The four living ones. Representative (see previous homily) of perfectly redeemed humanity—the condition in which man shall be when Christ has drawn all men unto him; when he shall have put all enemies under his feet. They are represented as "four," to signify the world-wide scope of Christ's redemption: "They shall come from the north and from the south, from the east and from the west." (*b*) The twenty-four elders. These represent the Church of God. They are twenty-four because of the twenty-four courses of priests (1 Chron. xxiv. 3—19). They are the instruments by which mankind at large shall be won for God. The manifold wisdom of God is to be made known through the Church. (2) *By means of:* (*a*) The outward homage of the body: "they fell down." The attitude of the body not merely symbolizes, but often assists, the worship of the mind. The posture of reverence is helpful to the feeling of reverence, and therefore is not to be regarded as unimportant. (*b*) Music and song. They had "harps," and they "sung a new song." Music alone of all the arts is to be perpetuated in heaven. We read not of painting or sculpture, but music and song are there. For music is the utterance of thoughts too deep for words. Much is given to us besides language to express our thoughts—tones, looks, tears, cries, and music also. Moreover, music is symbolical of the life of heaven. As in music so there, there is no self-will. Music is only possible by absolute obedience to the laws of harmony. Obedience is its life. And how glorious is that music which is consecrated to God's praise! (c) Intercessions for those on earth. This seems to me the significance of the incense-laden censers, the "vials full of odours," which are spoken of. How can the Lord of love be more truly worshipped than by sympathies, thoughts, and deeds of love? Is it to be imagined that the blessed in heaven cease to care for their poor troubled brethren on earth?—that the love they had for them is all gone, evaporated? God forbid! And here it is shown that as here on earth they loved to pray for and with them, so in heaven they do the same (cf. ch. vi. 10; cf. also Luke i. 10; Exod. xxx. 36—38). In such intercession Christ sees the fruit of the Spirit he has given them. (3) *On the ground of:* (a) The worthiness of Christ. (b) The redemption he has wrought—so real, so universal, so costly. (c) The results of it: "made us kings," etc. (ver. 10). Such is the first doxology; it is the praise of the redeemed for their redemption. We do not now seem to value it so highly; many other things seem to us more precious—wealth, friends, success, pleasure. But when we see things as they really are, then this gift of gifts, all gifts in one, our redemption, will be prized and praised as now it too seldom is. 2. *The second doxology.* This, though joined in—as how could it be otherwise? —by those who sang the first, is more especially that of the angels. In myriads upon myriads they gather round and cry, "Worthy is the Lamb." Unto these "principalities and powers in the heavenlies" is made known, "by means of the Church," the manifold wisdom of God (Eph. iii. 10). These "things" they "desire to look into" (1 Pet. i. 12). How, then, can they, who rejoice over one sinner brought to repentance (Luke xv.), fail to be filled with rapture when they behold that which the Lamb slain has done? Therefore to him to whom all this is due they render praise, affirming the certain truth that all the power, the riches of grace, the wisdom, and might, which were conspicuous in man's redemption, and the honour and glory on account thereof, are to be ascribed to the Lamb. "By grace are ye saved, not of yourselves"—such is the reminder the angels give. We are slow to recognize this, and too ready to attribute overmuch to ourselves. 3. *The third doxology.* (Ver. 13.) The Church, the angels, have uttered theirs; and now creation, in all her forms—man living and dead not excluded, for "those under the earth" (cf. Job x. 21, 22; Isa. xiv. 9), those who have departed this life and are now in the realm of the shadow of death—are named, and they all unite in this praise (cf. Phil. ii. 10). St. Paul seems to teach (Rom. viii. 19—23, and especially ver. 21), that there shall be a redemption for it also—a deliverance "from the bondage of corruption." When we think of the sorrows and sufferings of those creatures of God who have no sins of their own to answer for, being incapable of sin, though not of suffering, it is a blessed revelation that in some form or other unknown to us they shall share in the blessings Christ hath brought. The psalms are full of invocations to creation in its various forms—the seas, the trees, "everything that hath breath," "all creatures"—to "praise the Name of the Lord." And here in this vision we behold creation, along with angels and redeemed men, uniting in this praise. Who that has heard the marvellous echo of shout or horn amid the Alps does not remember how the sound spreads and travels on further and further, till height and crag and soaring summit seem to hear, and at once give back the sound? So with the adoration of the Lamb, the doxologies of which this chapter tells. They begin, as they should, with the redeemed Church and saved man; they are caught up by the myriads of angels, they are heard and repeated by the whole creation of God. How is the reflection forced upon us of the relation in which *we* stand to this all-glorious redemption. In the face of this universal praise dare we reject or trifle with it? What madness! Shall we not embrace it with our whole heart, and seek to know the joy and every blessedness of it more and more, so that at the last, with all the saved, we may fall "down and worship him that liveth for ever and ever"? And if we are trusting in Christ, let there be in our lives and on our lips more of praise. Let us not be for ever wailing our litanies, but let us learn more of the language of praise. We have been too remiss in this. But whenever we have caught the blessed spirit of these doxologies, how good it has been for us! The devil is eager enough to dishonour Christ: all the more let us be eager to praise.—S. C.

Vers. 1—7.—*The sealed book.* The homily must be based upon the interpretation.

For our guidance we take the view which regards this sealed book as a title-deed, the background of the figure being found in Jer. xxxii. 6—16. It is the title-deed of the purchased possession—the redeemed inheritance—which no one has a right to touch or open but him to whom it belongs; concerning whom it may be said, " The right of redemption is thine to buy it." Concerning "the Lamb," this is recognized by the song of "the elders: " " Thou wast slain, and didst purchase unto God with thy blood men of every tribe, and tongue, and people, and nation." The redemption of men is therefore the ground of the worthiness, the ability, the right to open the book, to loose the seals, to look thereon. " The Lamb that was slain " alone may take the book "out of the right hand of him that sat on the throne."

I. THE BOOK. 1. Not the book of "the Revelation." 2. But the roll of the covenant—the title-deed. 3. A sealed document. Not representing the hidden nature of its contents. The breaking of the seals not a disclosure. The breaking of the seals coincident with stages in the process of taking possession of the purchased inheritance. 4. The book pertains to the Lamb. To him who is the Lamb—the Redeemer—belongs the possession. To him belongs the title-deed. He takes possession of his own.

II. THE REDEEMER. 1. The Lamb. "The Lion of the tribe of Judah " is also the Lamb. The latter symbolically representing his sacrificial character. He is the Lamb, as he is the Offering and a Sacrifice. 2. The Lamb appeared " as though it had been slain." " We have redemption in his blood." Whatever the Lamb of sacrifice represented he was in the utmost degree—a means and a pledge of salvation, an Offering, a Propitiation. 3. But the Lamb liveth again. Thus is presented to the eye of the seer the most cheering of all objects—the crucified and slain but risen Lord, the Conqueror of death, then of sin and of all that side with sin. 4. He has perfect power: " seven horns." 5. Perfect, sevenfold, spiritual grace : " seven eyes which are the seven Spirits of God." He is perfect as a Redeemer. The price of his own blood he has paid : " With thy blood ; " " A death having taken place for the redemption of the transgressions that were under the first " and second " covenants ; " " How much more shall the blood of Christ ! " " Having obtained eternal redemption."

III. THE REDEEMED INHERITANCE. 1. Men " of every tribe, and tongue, and people, and nation." 2. Redeemed from alienation, from sin and dispersion. 3. To be a kingdom. 4. Also a priesthood. 5. Exalted to honour : " they shall reign," even on the earth. This the one work of him who goeth forth conquering and to conquer. The true Redeemer by price of his blood, by power of his Spirit. Of this redeemed possession he holds the title-deed. He only is worthy. He is the rightful heir.—R. G.

Vers. 8—10.—*The song of the redeemed host.* The triumphant host, the redeemed possession, purchased unto God, give their glory. The whole Church in their representatives give ceaseless praise to him who in humility bare their sins in his own body on the tree.

I. THE SONG OF THE CHURCH IS EVER UNTO, AND IN PRAISE OF, THE LAMB. Never can those harps be unstrung ; never can the song of redemption cease to mingle with the song of the universe. Ever will he be " matter of all their praise."

II. THE SUBJECT OF THE SONG IS THE WORTHINESS OF THE LAMB. "Thou art worthy " to receive and hold the title-deed of the inheritance. The possession he has purchased. It is his. His be the title to it. He claims, and justly claims, a redeemed race as his. To this the sealed book is the title-deed. The taking possession by power of that which he had purchased by price is the work represented throughout the Revelation.

III. THE SONG IS THE TRIBUTE OF THE REDEEMED HOST TO HIM TO WHOM THEIR REDEMPTION IS DUE. The lowly song of the redeemed stands over against the humiliation of " the Lamb." His " worthiness " takes the place of the "curse" which he bore. The jeers of the multitude on earth are exchanged for the song of the thankful host in heaven. He who was slain now liveth for ever. Truly he sees the travail of his soul, and is satisfied.

IV. THE SONG REVERTS TO THE GRACIOUS PROCESS OF REDEMPTION. 1. The acknowledged need. He who confesses Jesus to be a Saviour thereby acknowledges his lost condition. 2. Sacrificial death of the Redeemer: " Thou wast slain." 3. The redemptive character of his work : " And didst purchase with thy blood." 4. The redeemed

REVELATION. **N**

a Divine possession. They are purchased " unto God ; " they are made a kingdom and priests " unto God."

V. THE SONG RISES INTO A JOYFUL RECOGNITION OF THE EXALTED STATE OF THE REDEEMED. Seen : 1. In their relation to God. 2. In their compact union as a kingdom under Divine rule. 3. In their universal priesthood holding its privileged and acknowledged approach unto God. 4. In their elevation to highest dignity in the dominion assigned to them on earth. This last a secret comfort to the persecuted and downtrodden Church. In the final triumph, honour, and glory, the suffering host of God to find its reward.—R. G.

Vers. 11—14.—*The angelic and universal chorus.* Now the song bursts out beyond the circles of the redeemed host. " The voice of many angels," even " ten thousand times ten thousand, and thousands of thousands," bears onwards the same burden of song, " Worthy is the Lamb," and the chorus is completed only when it is taken up by " every created thing which is in the heaven, and on the earth, and under the earth, and on the sea ; " and the song ascribes " the blessing, and the honour, and the glory, and the dominion " unto " him that sitteth on the throne, and unto the Lamb," and that " for ever and ever."

" The whole creation join in one
To bless the sacred Name
Of him that sits upon the throne,
And to adore the Lamb."

The vision is prophetic—it anticipates the final condition, the ultimate triumph of redemption, the ultimate acknowledgment of it. It is the song from the redeemed, and declares the widespread influence of redemption. It is creation's song. All creatures, " every created thing," praises the creating and redeeming Lord.

I. IT IS THE UNIVERSAL RECOGNITION OF THE BLESSINGS OF REDEMPTION. 1. The angelic host, forming a semi-chorus, exult in the gracious work of the Lamb—in which figure must be seen represented the total idea of redemption by " the Lamb of God." Angels, who desired to " look into " these things, have found in them matter for praise. High above the incidents of the human history rises the image of him to whom all is due. 2. The " great voice " of the many angels " and the living creatures and the elders " is exceeded by that of " every created thing " in heaven, earth, and sea, even " all things that are in them." This voice of the entire, the grand chorus, the holy seer heard. It was his to discern the beneficent effect of redemption, his to catch the re-echoing song of all things as they praised the holy Name. It stands as the counterpart to " God cursed the ground for man's sake." All is ordered and readjusted. The disturbance by sin gives place to the harmony of all creation " in him " in whom all things are " gathered together in one." 3. All is followed by the solemn " Amen," the reverent assent of the four living creatures—representatives of all creature-life, not excluding the Church.

II. IT IS CREATION'S TESTIMONY TO THE GLORY OF GOD IN THE REDEMPTION OF MEN.

III. IT IS DECLARATIVE OF THE UNIVERSAL INTEREST IN THE HISTORY OF THE REDEEMED RACE. The angels, who rejoiced over one sinner repenting, rejoice now in the completed work of the universal redemption. They who saw " first the blade," and sang over it, now behold " the full corn in the ear," and offer their loudest praise to the Lord of the harvest. Herein is signified the unity of the entire creation. Subtle links bind all in one. Each part is helpful to the other. There is mutual harmony, and there are mutual dependence and relationship. The whole finds its termination in a new act of adoring worship : " The four and twenty elders fell down and worshipped." As is most meet, the praise of all is paid to him " of whom and to whom and for whom are all things."

The Church below may learn : 1. The certainty of the final triumph of the Lamb in his own conquering work of redemption. 2. The identification of the work of redemption with the purposes of creation. 3. The duty of praise to God for this his unspeakable gift. 4. The sympathy of the angelic and universal life in the spiritual career of the redeemed.—R. G.

Vers. 1—5.—*The government of God.* "And I saw," etc. Concerning the government of God, observe—

I. THAT IT IS CONDUCTED ACCORDING TO A VAST PRECONCERTED PLAN. There was a book, seven pieces of parchment rolled together, and each one sealed, in the hand of him that "sat on the throne." The Almighty never acts from *impulse* or *caprice*, but ever from plan or law. And this plan is truly vast, wonderfully comprehensive. It is "written within" and on the "back side." This book contains the germs of all books—the archetypes of all existences, the outlines of all histories. "In thy book all my members were written, when as yet there were none of them." All that shall happen through the vast futures of individuals, families, nations, worlds, are mapped out on the pages of this wonderful book. The universe in all its parts and complicated movements is but the practical and palpable working out of its contents. The world is God's great will in action. Predestination is no special doctrine of the Bible; it is written on every part of nature. It includes as truly the motions of an atom as the revolutions of a world—the growth of a plant as the conversion of a soul. True philosophy, as well as Christianity, resolves everything but *sin* into the predestination of Infinite Love.

II. THIS VAST PRECONCERTED PLAN IS SEALED IN MYSTERY. Two thoughts are here suggested concerning its mystery. 1. *That it transcends all finite intelligence.* Some high spirit in the Divine empire is here represented as exclaiming, "Who is worthy to open the book, and too lose the seals thereof?" The question falls on the ear of universal mind, and produces no response; the challenge rings through the creation, and no one accepts it. "No man in heaven; nor in earth, nor under the earth, was able to open the book, neither to look thereon." I refer this mystery, not to the Creator's intention, but to the *creature's incapacity.* His glory is not in concealing only, but in manifesting. Concealment arises not from any effort on his part, but from the necessary limitations of finite intellect. The deep purposes of the Infinite can never be unsealed and deciphered by the finite. "His judgments are a great deep." 2. *That it is frequently the source of great mental distress.* "I wept much, because no man was found worthy to open and to read the book, neither to look thereon." The most earnest thinkers in all ages have shed many tears in wrestling with some of the dark problems of God's government. This mystery is, however, an inestimable means of spiritual discipline. It soberizes, humbles, stimulates.

III. THAT THE MYSTERY OF THE PLAN IS TO BE EXPOUNDED BY CHRIST. "And one of the elders saith unto me, Weep not: behold, the Lion of the tribe of Judah, the Root of David, hath prevailed to open the book, and to loose the seven seals thereof." Both the meaning and the figures employed, and the statements in succeeding verses, make it evident that the reference is here to Christ. He, indeed, is the Revealer of God's plans—the Logos. He discloses the eternal purposes in various ways. 1. *In his creative acts.* "All things were created by him." Creation is a bursting of one of the seals of that book, and a publication of some of its contents. Stars, suns, and systems are but the palpable forms or diagrams of infinite ideas. 2. *In his redemptive operations.* By his personal history on this earth eighteen centuries ago, and by his spiritual agency from Adam to that period, and from that period in a higher form to this hour, he burst other seals, and brought to light some deep things of the eternal mind. 3. *In his judicial conduct.* "The Father judgeth no man, but hath committed all judgment unto the Son." In the last day what new disclosures will be made!—D. T.

Vers. 6—10.—*Christ the Expounder of the mystery.* "And I beheld, and, lo," etc. This passage presents to us *Christ as the Expounder of the mystery of the Divine government.* Various orders of intelligence surround him as he takes the "book;" they prostrate themselves at his footstool with "harps" and "vials" and "song." Notice—

I. Christ, as the Expounder of the mystery of the Divine government, OCCUPIES A CENTRAL POSITION, AND ASSUMES THE MOST EXTRAORDINARY ASPECTS. 1. Look at the *position he occupies.* He is in the "midst of the throne;" he is in the very centre of the intelligent creation. He attracts all, he enlightens all, he governs all, he blesses all with new life and beauty. 2. Look at the *aspect he assumes.* In his Person are combined the marks of suffering humanity and the attributes of perfect Divinity.

" Stood a Lamb as it had been slain," the marks of Calvary on his Person, having " seven horns," perfect power, and " seven eyes," perfect knowledge. Blessed thought. *Our nature is associated with Divinity on the throne of the universe.* Its human scars preach, in mute but thrilling force, love and justice in the ear of all spirits; and its Godhead glories command the reverence and praise of all.

II. That Christ, as the Expounder of the mystery of the Divine government, AWAKENS IN ALL CLASSES OF HOLY MIND INEFFABLE DELIGHT. "And when he had taken the book, the four beasts and four and twenty elders fell down before the Lamb, having every one of them harps," etc. These numbers probably designate indefinite multitudes of representative classes. Their attributes and aspects are further developed in other places of this book. The language here employed may denote the characteristics of their delight. 1. Here is *humility.* They " fell down before the Lamb." The profoundest reverence mingled with their joy. 2. Here is *harmony.* Here are harps, emblems of music. I do not know that we are authorized to assume from such symbolical language that there is vocal or instrumental music in heaven. It is not the sound but the spirit of music that is there. 3. Here is *acceptableness.* " Golden vials full of odours." Its breathing ecstasies ascend as fragrant incense to God. 4. Here is *prayerfulness.* "The prayers of saints." Death terminates the saint's need of prayer for certain objects, such as forgiveness, deliverance from error, and victory over foes, but not the *spirit* of prayer—the spirit of felt dependence upon God. This humble, harmonious, acceptable, and prayerful delight Christ awakens in the universe as the Expounder of God's great plan.

III. That Christ, as the Expounder of the Divine government, is DEEMED WORTHY OF THE OFFICE BECAUSE OF HIS REDEMPTIVE ACHIEVEMENT. "Thou art worthy to take the book, and to open the seals." Why ? "For thou wast slain, and hast redeemed us to God." Observe : 1. He has *redeemed.* The redemption of God consists in a deliverance from the power of sin. 2. He has redeemed by *sacrifice.* What was the sacrifice ? A few self-denying efforts ? a world ? No; *his life.* By the sacrifice of his life itself. 3. He has redeemed, by sacrifice, *all classes.* " Out of every kindred, and tongue, and people, and nation." 4. He has redeemed all classes by sacrifice *to the highest honours.* "And hast made us unto our God kings and priests : and we shall reign on the earth." They are priests in relation to their Maker, offering up the sacrifice of a devout and grateful soul; they are kings in relation to their race, wielding a governing influence over their thoughts and hearts. A true Christian is a moral sovereign.

What a work is this redemptive work! Well may the universe deem Jesus worthy to "open the book," because of what he has done to save the world !—D. T.

Ver. 9.—*The worship of heaven.* "They sung a new song." These few words suggest two thoughts concerning the *worship of heaven.*
I. IT IS JUBILANT. "They sung." Singing is the natural language of joy. The worship is not mechanical, not irksome. It is the outbreaking of the soul into rapture —the rapture of gratitude, admiration, reverence, and love.
II. IT IS FRESH. "A new song." There is nothing monotonous. Souls have an instinctive craving for variety, and the Creator has amply provided for this instinct. In the life of souls there is something fresh every hour—fresh *sceneries,* fresh *occurrences,* fresh *engagements,* fresh *thoughts.*—D. T.

Ver. 9.—*The uniqueness of Christ's blood, or his sacrificed life.* "Redeemed us to God [Revised Version, 'purchased unto God'] by thy blood." The expression, "*blood of Christ*" is used by millions who have no accurate idea concerning its import. Blood is life, and the essential idea is *Christ's self-sacrificed life.* Notice—
I. THERE IS SOMETHING SUBLIMELY UNIQUE IN ITS NATURE. Things are said of it that could not possibly be said with propriety of the blood of any other man in any age or time who has sacrificed his life. Millions of men have been sacrificed; they have lost their life, but not in the way in which Christ was sacrificed. Some have been sacrificed by *assassination,* some by *war,* some by *capital punishment,* some by *accident ;* most against their will, although some voluntarily, either by suicide or superstitious fanaticism. But in the case of Christ's sacrificed life there was nothing like this. Two facts especially marked off his sacrificed life from that of any other sacrificed life.

1. *It was in accordance with the eternal plan of God.* "He was the Lamb slain from the foundation of the world." There was nothing accidental about it, nothing out of keeping with the eternal order of things. 2. *It was voluntary in the sense in which no other man's death was voluntary.* Amongst the millions of men who have died most freely, not one has felt that he need not die at all if he chose—that he could continue here for ever. But this Christ felt. There was no law in heaven or earth to force him to the fate. "I have power to lay down my life, and power to take it up." 3. *The life he sacrificed was absolutely free from all imperfections.* Not one of all the teeming myriads who departed this life has been entirely free from sin. All have had on them, to a greater or less extent, the common stain. But Christ was immaculate. His greatest enemies could not convict him of sin. Pilate and all his judges could find no fault in him. He was "holy," "harmless," and "separate from sinners." Another remark suggested concerning the blood of Christ is—

II. THAT IT IS SOMETHING SUBLIMELY UNIQUE IN ITS EFFECTS. In different passages in the New Testament results are ascribed to this blood, which could not, with any propriety or the slightest approach to truth, be ascribed to the blood of any other man. 1. *These effects are variously represented.* It is represented as *reconciliation.* His sacrificed life was the *atonement.* It is represented as *purifying.* "It cleanseth from all sin." Through it men are "made white." "Unto him that loved us, and washed us," etc. It is represented as an *essential element of soul-life.* "Whoso drinketh my blood hath eternal life"—something that has not only to be applied to the soul, but taken into it. It is represented as a *ransom.* "Redeemed us to God by his blood;" "purchased by his blood." It is the power to deliver from the guilt and dominion of sin. It is represented as a *conquering force.* "Overcame by the blood of the Lamb." Of whose blood have these results ever been predicated, or can ever be? 2. *These effects are universal in their influence.* It "cleanseth from all sin;" it makes the "great multitudes which no man can number," white. How extensive has been its beneficent influence on humanity already! But its present area of influence, as compared with its future, is less than a little lake to the ocean. 3. *These effects are eternal in their blessings.* "Whoso drinketh my blood hath eternal life."

CONCLUSION. The subject: 1. *Serves to explain both the essence of the gospel and the essence of personal holiness.* Christ's sacrificed life is the gospel, and hence the very effects that are here ascribed to his blood are elsewhere ascribed to the gospel, to the *truth* of the gospel, to the *grace* of the gospel, to the *word* of the gospel; all these are said to cleanse, to redeem, to conquer, to make white, etc. Not only does it serve to explain the essence of the gospel, but the essence of *personal holiness.* That principle of love which led Christ to sacrifice his life must be appropriated by us as a vital ruling element if we would be holy. His sacrifice upon the cross will be worthless to us unless we sacrifice ourselves in love; hence we must become conformable unto his death. 2. *Serves to correct the mischievous way in which the blood of Christ is popularly represented.* Men talk of Christ's blood as if it was the crimson fluid that coursed through his veins that saves, washes, cleanses, etc.; or at any rate, that it was his blood which qualified him to be a Saviour. It was not his blood; the blood was nothing only as it expressed his self-sacrificing love. Supposing that the criminal law of Rome at the time in which Christ lived had required that capital offenders should be put to death by hanging, or strangling, or suffocating, or by taking poison like Socrates. Had Christ been sacrificed in any of these ways, would the power of his self-sacrifice to save humanity be one whit the less? Not so. It was his self-sacrificing love, not the form of his mortal agonies, that made him the Saviour of the world.—D. T.

Vers. 11—14.—*The worthiness of Christ to receive man's riches.* "And I beheld," etc. We learn here that all heaven, with its "ten thousand times ten thousand, and thousands of thousands," agree in declaring that Christ, who is in the midst of the throne, is worthy to receive, not only power, wisdom, strength, honour, and glory, but *riches,* all riches mental and material. Who will gainsay the testimony of witnesses so enlightened, so honest, and so numerous? We shall regard the word as referring to *material* riches, gold. Gold is precious in more senses than one; it is a moral potentiality, and hence it is thought of in heaven and sung about there. Our subject is—*Christ is worthy to receive man's worldly wealth.* How can he receive it? He is far up the heights of the universe, beyond the vision and the reach of man. How do the monarchs receive the tributes of their people? Not *directly*, but through established agencies. Christ has established an agency on this earth for this purpose, and that agency is his Church. Whatever is done to further the evangelizing views and well-being of his Church, he regards as being done to him. "Inasmuch as ye have done it unto the least of these my brethren, ye have done it unto me." Why is Christ worthy to receive your wealth?

I. BECAUSE HE IS THE ORIGINAL PROPRIETOR OF IT. The gold that any man holds in his hand is his in a very secondary sense. His property a few years ago was in the possession of others, and a few years hence it will pass from him into other hands. All material wealth belongs to Christ. "The beasts of the forest are mine, and the cattle upon a thousand hills;" "The wild beasts of the field are mine," etc. (see also Job xli. 11; Deut. x. 14; 1 Chron. xx. 19). Man is but the *trustee* of his wealth; Christ is the Proprietor.

II. BECAUSE HE HAS ENABLED YOU TO PROCURE IT. Why have you wealth more than others? Has it come to you through *heirdom, legacy,* or your own *industry?* In either case you have it through Christ. Perhaps you ascribe it to your shrewdness, your industry, your management: but whence came these? All business aptitudes and opportunities are the gift of Christ. All the conditions by which your wealth has been attained are according to his arrangement.

III. BECAUSE HE GIVES YOU THE QUALIFICATIONS TO ENJOY IT. Do you enjoy your wealth?—enjoy all the conveniences, comforts, and powers which it imparts? If so, why? All do not. The miser does not, the invalid does not, the idiot does not. Who gave you the unmiserly spirit, the bodily health, the mental capacity, by which you enjoy your riches? All the qualifications that you have for enjoying your property are his gifts.

IV. BECAUSE HE WILL MAKE THE BEST USE OF IT. 1. *The best use of it for your-selves.* There is no better investment. In truth it is for your sake that Christ wishes you to give it to him. He could have planted churches on every hill, schools in every valley, written his Bible on the broad heavens; but he knew right well that you would be better blest by contributing of your property to the diffusion of his truth. Your contributions to him serve you in many ways. (1) Serve to *test your character.* Until you can give *freely* that which you value most, what evidence have you of your love to him? None. (2) Serve to *detach you from materialism.* Wealth tends to materialize the soul. Every contribution to spiritual objects counteracts the tendency. It is another step up the ladder whose foot is deep down in materialism, but whose top reaches to the holy heavens of spirit and love. (3) Serve to *ennoble your character.* It is a great thing to be trusted, to be thrown upon your honour. Christ trusts you. 2. *The best use of it for the world.* When you are gone, Christ's Church will be here working with the means you have entrusted to it, and working to spread *truth, virtue,* and *happiness* through the world. "Worthy is the Lamb to receive riches." Don't shirk collections, don't regard them as trials. Hail them as blessings, and remember that " it is more blessed to give than to receive."—D. T.

EXPOSITION.

CHAPTER VI.

Ver. 1.—And I saw. A new departure in the series of visions is marked (see on ch. iv. 1). We have here the commencement of the Revelation proper, to which the first five chapters have formed an introduction (cf. Tabular analysis). The vision of the *seals,* which, although related first, exhibits events concurrent with those symbolized by the *trumpets* and *vials,* is contained chiefly in ch. vi. Ch. vii. is occupied with an account of an episodal character, similar to that which occurs in ch. x. 1—xi. 14 after the sixth trumpet; and the vision is completed by the opening of the seventh seal, described in ch. viii. 1. The opening of the first seal pictures the triumph of Christ and his Church, for the comfort and hopeful assurance of those to whom St. John was writing, and for the edification of struggling Christians of all time. To this theme, touched upon here proleptically, the apostle returns at the conclusion of the *trumpets;* the first six of which bear a general likeness to the last six of the *seals.* When the Lamb opened

one of the seals; *one of the seven seals* (Revised Version). The insertion of "seven" (ἑπτά) is supported by A, B, C, ℵ, and others; Vulgate, De Dieu's Syriac, Andreas, Arethas, Primasius, Victorinus, Æthiopic. (On the *right* of the Lamb to open the *seals*, see on ch. v.) And I heard, as it were the noise of thunder, one of the four beasts; *the voice of thunder . . . four living creatures* (Revised Version). (For the *four living beings*, see on ch. iv. 6.) Here each living being invites attention to the revelation of the future of that creation of which they are all representative. The *thunder* is the usual accompaniment of a special revelation of the Divine will, and indicative of the majesty of him whose will is declared (see ch. **x.** 3 and xiv. 2; also Exod. xix. 16; Acts ii. 2). Nothing in the text warrants us in particularizing the four living creatures in these four invitations uttered by them, though many writers have endeavoured to do so. Thus, adopting the order in ch. iv. 7, they have supposed that the first voice was uttered by the lion, since the revelation of the first seal is distinguished by the prophecy of victory. The sacrificial nature of the second living being —the steer—is thought to be connected with the slaughter predicted under the second seal by the vision of war and persecution. The man is considered typical of the heresy which it is believed the third seal predicts, and especially of the false opinions concerning the Incarnation; while the eagle is regarded as a symbol of resurrection and the harbinger of the final victory of the just over the death and Hades of the fourth seal. **Saying, Come and see.** The Revised Version omits "and see." The Textus Receptus, without any apparent authority, reads Ἔρχου καὶ βλέπε, "Come and see." Ἔρχου, "Come," simply, is read in A, C, P, fourteen cursives, several versions, two manuscripts of Andreas, etc.; while Ἔρχου καὶ ἴδε, "Come and behold," is found in ℵ, B, thirty-four cursives, various versions (including the Coptic), two manuscripts of Andreas, etc.; and the Syriac omits Ἔρχου, "Come." The authorities are thus very evenly balanced; but the addition of καὶ ἴδε, even if not warranted, seems to indicate that the sentence was generally considered to be addressed to St. John; and was intended as an invitation to him to witness the appearances which accompanied the breaking of the seals. Alford contends that the cry, "Come," is addressed, on behalf of creation, to the Lord Jesus, and is a petition to him to speedily bring these things to pass, that his own advent may follow. In support of this, Alford remarks that there is no example of the use by St. John of Ἔρχου in the sense of "Come and see," "Come hither," without

ὧδε, or some qualifying particle; but, on the contrary, it is exactly the expression used of our Lord's advent in ch. xxii. 17, 20, "The Spirit and the bride say, Come," etc. Though there is much reason in this contention, yet, on the whole, the weight of evidence, as stated above, makes it probable that the sentence is addressed to St. John.

Ver. 2.—**And I saw.** The usual introduction to a new vision, or a special feature of a vision (see on ch. iv. 1). **And behold a white horse.** The whole vision appears to be founded on that of Zech. i. 8—12. *White* is always typical in the Revelation of heavenly things (cf. ch. i. 14, "His hairs were white;" ch. ii. 17, "a white stone;" ch. iii. 4, 5, 18; iv. 4; vi. 11, and vii. 9, 13, "white garments;" ch. xiv. 14, "white cloud;" ch. xix. 11, 14, "white horses;" ch. xx. 11, "white throne"), and indeed in the whole of the New Testament (cf. Matt. xvii. 2; xxviii. 3; John xx. 12; Acts i. 10), the only exceptions being Matt. v. 36 and John iv. 35. The *horse*, throughout the Old Testament, is emblematic of war. Among the Romans a *white horse* was the symbol of victory. **And he that sat on him.** On a consideration of the whole of the visions attending the opening of the seals, it seems best to interpret this vision as a symbolic representation of the abstract idea of the Church as a victorious body. In a similar way the following appearances are typical of war, famine, and death. Some interpret the rider to mean Christ himself— a sense not materially different from that given above, since by the victory of Christ the Church collectively and Christians individually are enabled to triumph; and in his body, the Church, Christ triumphs. This appearance is repeated, with additions, at ch. xix. 11. The revelation thus begins and closes with an assurance of victory. God's end is attained in a mysterious way. Many trials and afflictions are to trouble the earth, but through all God is working to bring his Church triumphantly through the struggle. And what is true of the Church as a whole is true of each individual soul. Those to whom St. John wrote could not understand, as many now do not understand, for what purpose God permitted them to suffer. For such St. John's message is intended to be a support; not, indeed, by removing present troubles, but by declaring the final victory of those who endure to the end. Thus, then, as a preparation for the woes to be revealed, and as an encouragement after disclosing the prospect of prolonged trial, the vision of the Church triumphant is vouchsafed, both at the beginning and the end of the Revelation. Bisping and others understand the vision as a personification of war; Bengel and Reuss consider that it means conquest, or a particul r conqueror (Vespasian and Trajan being denominated), just as in Jer. xxi. 7 and xxxii. 36 the King of Babylon is connected with war, famine, and pestilence. Elliott, with others, interpret the rider as meaning the Roman empire, just as the ram (Dan. viii. 3) signified the Persian, and the goat (Dan. viii. 5) the Grecian empires. Todd sees in this appearance a particular aspect of Christ's second coming. Victorinus, following Matt. xxiv. in his exposition of the *seals*, sees in the first *seal* the Word of the Lord, which is like an arrow (cf. Heb. iv. 12). Andreas sees in the first *seal* a vision of the Church's triumph over Satan in apostolic times; and similarly, in the second, the martyrdom of Christians in the age immediately following. Bede believes the *seals* to foreshadow the future history of the Church. Wordsworth, after St. Augustine, expounds the first *seal* as the advent of Christ and the Gospel, and the following ones as depicting subsequent troubles of the Church, which are specified. Had a bow. The *bow* and arrows are used as signs of power by Old Testament writers. In Zech. ix. 13 we have, " When I have bent Judah for me, filled the bow with Ephraim ; " in Hab. iii. 8, 9, " Thou didst ride upon thine horses and thy chariots of salvation ; thy bow was made quite naked ; " in Ps. xlv. 5, " Thine arrows are sharp in the heart of the king's enemies." The general idea of the vision is perhaps taken from Zech. i. 7—12 and vi. And a crown was given unto him. In Zech. vi. 11, quoted above, we have a parallel passage, " Make crowns, and set them upon the head of Joshua the son of Josedech, the high priest ; and speak unto him, saying, Thus speaketh the Lord of hosts, saying, Behold the Man whose name is The Branch." The *crown* is στέφανος, as in ch. ii. 10—the crown of life, the crown of victory. And he went forth conquering, and to conquer ; *came forth conquering, and that he may conquer.* This is the key to the whole vision. Only of Christ and his kingdom can it be said that it is to conquer. All earthly empires are more or less temporary in character ; only of Christ's kingdom shall there be no end. A strife there must be between the powers of earth and the powers of heaven ; the gospel did not inaugurate a reign of earthly peace, but the end is not doubtful ; Christ and his Church *came forth conquering, and that* they *may conquer* finally, whatever earthly trials may intervene.

Ver. 3.—And when he had opened the **second seal ;** *he opened* (Revised Version). The tense is aorist. The circumstances described accompanied the act of opening, as in the case of the other seals. I heard the **second beast say, Come and see ;** *I heard the second living being say, Come.* (On the four

living beings as representing creation, see on ch. iv. 6.) For the omission of " and see," and the discussion of the question to whom the words are addressed, see above, on ver. 1. As there stated, some believe the second living being here specified to be the ox, which, on ac ount of its sacrificial character, invites the prophet to behold the result of the war which is personified by this vision. Wordsworth, interpreting the living beings to mean the Gospels, here sees a reference to St. Luke's Gospel, which depicts the sufferings of Christ, and considers that the ox here summons St. John to witness the persecution of the martyrs.

Ver. 4.—And there went out another horse that was red. There is a very general agreement that the red horse signifies *war* —slaughter by the sword which was given to " him that sat thereon." Slight variations of the application occur. Wordsworth, following the more ancient expositors, thinks that only that aspect of war is intended which consists in the persecution of the saints ; while Alford and others would not restrict the meaning, but consider that war in general is meant, relying upon the following words, " that they should kill one another," and quoting our Lord's prophecy, " I came not to send peace, but a sword " (Matt. x. 34). Both views may be correct. Though there had never been persecution, war would be one of the great afflictions from which Christians in various ages suffer, and in which they need consolation : but we may well believe that St. John, in writing to Christians who were themselves being grievously persecuted, should refer especially to the slaughter of the saints, as one of the trials inflicted upon them with God's knowledge and permission. The Revelation, intended as a support to those to whom St. John wrote, and applying directly and specially to their situation, has yet a wider application, and foreshadows the fate of each individual Christian and the Church in general throughout all ages. And power was given to him that sat thereon to take peace from the earth ; *and to him that sat upon him it was given him to take peace out of the earth.* The pronoun is redundant ; it has no special signification (see ch. ii. 26 ; iii. 12, 21). " The peace " (τὴν εἰρήνην) ; that is, peace in general, not *the peace* left by the first appearance. " Power " (cf. ch. iv. 11 ; i. 6 ; vii. 12). A few authorities omit ἐκ, " out." " The earth " has been erroneously restricted to the Roman empire or to Judæa. The whole world is meant. Here is a repetition of our Lord's prophecy, " I came not to send peace, but a sword " (Matt. x. 34). The sword directed against the saints of God is, by God's providence, converted into an instrument for the refining and conversion of his kingdom. As in the death of Christ, Satan was foiled with his own weapon, and by death came life, so what is intended by the enemies of God to be the extermination of Christianity is the means of increasing and strengthening his Church. And that they should kill one another; that is, that among the inhabitants of the earth some should kill others. As explained above, this includes both the slaughter of the saints and war in general. The verb σφάττω, "to sacrifice," is peculiar to St. John, being found only in the Revelation and in 1 John iii. 12. The use of this verb seems to imply that the vision more immediately contemplates the death of the martyrs. And there was given unto him a great sword. Here, again, μάχαιρα, though used also in a wider sense, signifies strictly the sacrificial knife, the natural instrument of the slaughter mentioned. It is the LXX. word used in Gen. xxii. 6, 10, in the account of the sacrifice of Isaac, where it is also closely connected with σφάττω, "to sacrifice," the verb used in this passage.

Ver. 5.—And when he had opened the third seal; *when he opened*, as in the case of the other seals (see on ver. 3). I heard the third beast say; *the third living being saying*. (On the *living beings*, see ch. iv. 6.) Wordsworth takes the *third living being* to be that with the human face, and considers it to be typical of the whole vision of the third seal, by symbolizing the source of the next trial of the Church; namely, the rise of heresy, which he thinks is depicted by this appearance. But probably the four living beings represent all creation, and thus invite St. John to witness the troubles in store for mankind in general. (For a full consideration of this point, see on ch. iv. 6.) Come and see. The majority of authorities omit "and see" (see the corresponding passage in vers. 1 and 3, where also is discussed the question as to whom the sentence is addressed). And I beheld, and lo a black horse. The *black* is typical of woe and mourning—the result of the scarcity foretold in the following words. This vision is typical of famine; it is the second of the three trials foretold—war, famine, death (cf. Ezek. xiv., where the "four sore plagues" are wild beasts, the sword, famine, and pestilence). St. John seems to foretell the recurrence of three of these troubles to try mankind in general, and Christians in particular. Those who interpret the vision to mean scarcity of faith, or in other words the prevalence of heresy, do so on the supposition that the events denoted at the opening of the seals follow each other in historical order. They therefore assign these events to the period subsequent to A.D. 300, when persecution had ceased, and

the rise of heresies took place. Others, accepting the historical view, yet consider the vision to foretell famine; and Grotius and Wetstein point to the famine in the reign of Claudius as the fulfilment. But it is not probable that the meaning of the book is so limited in extent; but rather that its prophecies point to events which have happened, and are recurring, and will continue to recur until the end of the world. We therefore understand that this vision denotes famine in the ordinary sense, as one of the trials awaiting the members of the Church of God at various times during the existence of the Church on earth. This affliction may happen concurrently with, or antecedent to, or subsequent to, any of those trials denoted by the other visions, and even the victorious career of the Church as foretold under the first seal; for by suffering the Church conquers and is made perfect. And he that sat on him had a pair of balances in his hand. Ζυγός is rightly rendered "a balance," as in Ezek. xlv. 10; not (as it primarily meant) a "yoke." The idea intended to be conveyed is that of scarcity so great that food is weighed carefully as something very rare and precious, though there is not yet a complete absence of food.

Ver. 6.—And I heard a voice in the midst of the four beasts say; *I heard as it were a voice in the midst of the four living creatures*, *saying* (Revised Version). The speaker is not perceived by St. John; the words proceed from somewhere near the throne (but the exact situation is left doubtful), which is surrounded by the four living creatures (see on ch. iv. 6 for the consideration both of the position and of the nature of the four living creatures). Alford points out the appropriateness of the voice proceeding from the midst of the representatives of creation, when the intent of the words is to mitigate the woes denounced against creation. Those who consider the living creatures to be symbolical of the Gospels, and who interpret this vision as a prophecy of heresy (see on ver. 5), also see an appropriateness in the fact of the voice issuing from amidst the living creatures, since by the power and influence of the Gospels heresy is dispelled. Wordsworth recalls the custom of placing the Gospels in the midst of the Synod in the ancient Councils of the Church. A measure of wheat for a penny, and three measures of barley for a penny; *a chœnix of wheat for a denarius, and three chœnixes of barley for a denarius.* The *chœnix* appears to have been the food allotted to one man for a day; while the *denarius* was the pay of a soldier or of a common labourer for one day (Matt. xx. 2, "He agreed with the labourers for a penny a day;" and Tacitus, 'Ann.,' i. 17, 26, "Ut denarius diurnum stipendium foret." Cf. Tobit v. 14, where *drachma* is equivalent to *denarius*). The chœnix was the eighth part of the modius, and a denarius would usually purchase a modius of wheat. The price given, therefore, denotes great scarcity, though not an entire absence of food, since a man's wages would barely suffice to obtain him food. Barley, which was the coarser food, was obtainable at one-third of the price, which would allow a man to feed a family, though with difficulty. A season of great scarcity is therefore predicted, though in his wrath God remembers mercy (cf. the judgments threatened in Lev. xxvi. 23—26, viz. the sword, pestilence, and famine; also the expression, "They shall deliver you your bread again by weight"). **And see thou hurt not the oil and the wine.** The corollary to the preceding sentence, with the same signification. It expresses a limit set to the power of the rider on the black horse. These were typical articles of food (cf. Ps. civ. 14, 15, "That he may bring forth food out of the earth; and wine that maketh glad the heart of man, and oil to make his face to shine, and bread which strengtheneth man's heart;" and Joel i. 10, "The corn is wasted : the new wine is dried up, the oil languisheth"). Wordsworth interprets, "The prohibition to the rider, 'Hurt not the oil and the wine,' is a restraint on the evil design of the rider, who would injure the spiritual oil and wine, that is, the means of grace, which had been typified under those symbols in ancient prophecy (Ps. xxiii. 4, 5), and also by the words and acts of Christ, the good Samaritan. pouring in oil and wine into the wounds of the traveller, representing human nature, lying in the road." Ἀδικήσῃς: ἀδικεῖν in the Revelation invariably signifies "to injure," and, except in one case, takes the direct accusative after it (see ch. ii. 11; vii. 2, 3; ix. 4, 10, 19; xi. 5). Nevertheless, Heinrich and Elliott render, "Do not commit injustice in the matter of the oil and wine." Rinck renders, "waste not." The vision is a general prophecy of the future for all time (see on ver. 5); but many writers have striven to identify the fulfilment of the vision with some one particular famine. Grotius and Wetstein refer it to the scarcity in the days of Claudius; Renan, to that in the time of Nero; Bishop Newton, to the end of the second century. Those who interpret the vision as a forewarning of the spread of heresy, especially single out that of Arius.

Ver. 7.—**And when he had opened the fourth seal, I heard the voice of the fourth beast say; when he opened,** as in vers. 1, 3, and 5. The events narrated accompany the action of opening the seal. *Of the fourth living being* (see on ch. iv. 6). The individual is not specified (see on ver. 1); but Wordsworth specifies the living being like a flying eagle, by which he understands the Gospel of St. John (but see on ch. iv. 6). *Saying.* Though λέγουσαν, the feminine accusative, to agree with φωνήν, "voice," is adopted in the Textus Receptus, and supported by the sole authority of 1, yet א, A, B, C, P, and others read λέγοντος, the masculine genitive, agreeing with ζώου, "living being." **Come and see.** The Revised Version omits "and see" (see on ver. 1). "Come" is probably addressed to St. John (see on ver. I).

Ver. 8.—**And I looked;** *I saw.* The usual expression drawing attention to a new sight or fresh phase of the vision (see on ch. iv. 1; ver. 2, etc.). **And behold a pale horse.** *Pale* (χλωρός, "greenish-white, livid"); the colour of one stricken with disease or death, or moved with emotions of terror. The same word is used of the green grass in ch. viii. 7 and in Mark vi. 39, and of the vegetation in ch. ix. 4; but, applied to man, it is generally connected with terror, disease, or death. The Greek poets use it as an epithet of fear, and Thucydides thus describes the colour of persons affected by the plague. **And his name that sat on him was Death, and Hell followed with him.** The preposition differs from that used in the preceding verses: it is here ἐπάνω, "above," not ἐπί, "upon." *And he who was sitting above him, his name* [was] *Death.* Here we have it plainly stated that the vision is a personification of Death—death in general, death in any and every way, as indicated in the latter part of the verse. This supports the view taken of the first three visions of the seals (see on ver. 2). *Hades* follows with *Death,* not as a separate infliction, but as the necessary complement of Death in the completion of the vision, swallowing up and guarding, as it were, those seized by the latter. *Death* is personified in a similar way in Ps. xlix. 14, "Like sheep they are laid in the grave; death shall feed on them;" and *Hades* in Isa. xiv. 9, "Hell from beneath is moved for thee to meet thee at thy coming." The two are also conjoined in ch. i. 18, "The keys of hell and of death;" and in ch. xx. 13, 14, "Death and hell delivered up the dead." Hades cannot signify the place of torment, as Hengstenberg thinks, since these trials are to be inflicted on Christians, not on the wicked merely. Nor is it consonant with the context to suppose (as Ebrard) that *Hades* signifies "the dwellers in Hades." And power was given unto them. The reading "them" is supported by A, C, [P], א, n 17, 49 (1.40 e sil) Andreas; while B and the Vulgate read αὐτῷ, "him." The context shows that both are intended. **Over the fourth part of the earth.** There is a general consensus of opinion that this expression betokens a part of mankind. Why the *fourth* part is selected is difficult to say. Alford suggests that a reference is intended to the four first seals, each one of which embraces in its action a portion of mankind. But the first seal can hardly be interpreted in this way. Probably the intention is to denote that a part of mankind must be afflicted in this particular way, though no definite proportion is signified. In other words, the second, third, and fourth seals depict troubles which Christians and all mankind will have to undergo; some being afflicted more especially in one way, others in another. The troubles mentioned are not an exhaustive catalogue, but are typical of all sorrows; the selection being probably prompted by the Old Testament passages quoted below, viz. Lev. xxvi. 23—26; 2 Sam. xxiv. 13; and Ezek. xiv. 21. "The fourth part" is an expression found only in this passage. Züllig agrees with Alford in the explanation given above. Hengstenberg, and somewhat similarly Volkmar, think it denotes the partial character of this judgment. Elliott, with very little reason, follows the Vulgate reading, "over the four parts of the earth;" Isaac Williams also thinks the judgment is universal, since that is the idea that the number *four* signifies, which, however, is a different thing from a *fourth part*. **To kill with sword, and with hunger, and with death, and with the beasts of the earth.** The passage is another example of the influence of the prophecy of Ezekiel upon the composition of the Apocalypse. In Ezek. xiv. 21 the "four sore judgments" are "the sword, and the famine, and the noisome beast, and the pestilence." This indicates the signification of θανάτῳ in this place; viz. death by pestilence, not, as in the preceding passage, death in any form (comp. Lev. xxvi. 23—26, where the judgments threatened are the sword, pestilence, and famine. Cf. also the alternative punishments of David (2 Sam. xxiv. 13); also 4 Esdr. xv. 5, "the sword, and hunger, and death, and destruction"). The wild *beasts of the earth* (θηρίων) is very probably a reference to the death of many Christians in the pagan amphitheatres; though the meaning is not necessarily restricted to this form of death. Those to whom the Apocalypse was first addressed would irresistibly be reminded of our Lord's words in Matt. xxiv. 7, 13, "Nation shall rise against nation, and kingdom against kingdom; and there shall be famines, and pestilences, and earthquakes, in divers places. . . . But he that shall endure unto the end, the same shall be saved." It is as though St. John echoed the words of

our Lord, "These are the words which I spake unto you, while I was yet with you, that all things must be fulfilled which were written in the Law of Moses, and in the prophets, and in the psalms, concerning me" (Luke xxiv. 44); and would say, "I am commissioned to relate these visions of the present and future trials of all in the world, which, however, have been already foretold you by our blessed Lord himself." While, therefore, this passage may be understood literally, since doubtless the Church has suffered all these afflictions at different times, in different members of her body, yet we must understand these four typical judgments to be representative of trouble in all its forms; the fourfold character pointing to its universal nature (see on ch. v. 9). This has led many writers to see in these inflictions trials of a spiritual nature—a view which may well be included in the proper application, but must not be pressed to the exclusion of any other more literal interpretation. We may thus sum up the results of our investigation of these eight verses. They relate the circumstances attending the opening of the first four seals, and doubtless typify various phases of the trials which are permitted by God to afflict Christians on earth in common with all mankind. Each of the four visions is preceded by the invitation of one of the four living beings, which are representative of creation; and a second feature common to these four visions is the appearance of a rider as the personification of the idea set forth. (1) The visions open with a personification of *Christianity*, and an assurance of the ultimate victory which it will gain over the powers of the world. (2) Then appears a vision of *war*, as one of the typical troubles of mankind, which will ultimately be overcome by the triumph of Christianity. (3) Next follows *famine* with all its attendant evils, though it is not permitted to extend to the extremity of the extirpation of mankind. (4) Fourthly comes death in every form—a trial of which every one feels the weight at some time. These four do not picture consecutive events; they may be successive or concurrent; the first is certainly being fulfilled side by side with the others. We may, therefore, be able to point to a particular period or event as *a* fulfilment of any one of these, but we cannot assign definite times to each as *the* complete and ultimate fulfilment, since the trials which are signified must extend to the end of time. And, in conclusion, while the first application was doubtless intended for the support of the Christians of St. John's age in their temporal difficulties, we must consider the visions equally intended to console Christians of every age, and even to portray the spiritual conflict, destitution, and apostasy which must and will continually arise while the Church remains in part in the world.

Ver. 9.—And when he had opened the fifth seal; *and when he opened,* as in vers. 1, 3, 5, 7, which see. The second group of visions connected with the opening of the seals now commences. The first group deals with events more immediately attached to this life. By the visions of the first four seals St. John has shown that it is with God's knowledge and consent that afflictions and persecutions are allowed to try the faith of his servants on earth; while yet the ultimate triumph of those who endure is certain. In the last three appearances he goes a step further—he gives his readers a glimpse of events more immediately connected with the life in the world to come. He shows them (1) the faithful, resting from their labours, though longing, in sympathy with those left on earth, for the completion of Christ's triumph; (2) the circumstances attendant upon our Lord's final coming, which he describes in language which is almost a repetition of Christ's words on the same subject; (3) the inexplicable life with God in heaven, which is denoted by the silence following the opening of the last seal. I saw under the altar. This representation is doubtless suggested by the arrangements of the temple. Victims were sacrificed on the brazen altar which stood at the door of the tabernacle (Exod. xxxix. 39 and xl. 29), and the blood was poured out at the foot of this altar (Lev. iv. 7). The martyrs are therefore regarded as having offered themselves as sacrifices upon the altar of God by yielding up their lives for him. St. Paul uses a similar figure concerning himself. In 2 Tim. iv. 6 he says, " For I am now ready to be offered ['to pour out as a libation,' σπένδω], and the time of my departure is at hand; " and in Phil. ii. 17, " If I be offered upon the sacrifice and service of your faith." Bleek and De Wette understand the golden altar of incense (Exod. xxx. 1), and consider that the figure is representative of the hearing of the martyrs' prayers. Bossuet says the altar is Christ The souls of them that were slain; *them that had been slain.* An "æsthetical difficulty " (see on ch. iv. 6). How could St. John *see* the souls? Of course, he did not see them with his bodily vision, nor indeed did he thus see any part of the revelation. He "sees" them while "in the Spirit," *i.e.* he is somehow made conscious of the existence of the souls. *Slain;* σφάττω, "sacrificed;" the same word used of the Lamb in ch. v. 6. The word is in harmony with the use of the word "altar," with which it is naturally connected. It fixes the signification of the altar, which therefore cannot bear the meaning ascribed by Bleek and De Wette, as mentioned above. St. John sees

the *souls* only of the martyrs, since their bodies will not be reunited with their souls until the judgment-day. Meanwhile, the *souls rest* (see ver. 11) in peace, yet in expectation of the final accomplishment of their perfect bliss, which the words used in ver. 10 show them to desire. Wordsworth quotes (as illustrating this passage) Tertullian, " The souls of martyrs repose in peace under the altar, and cherish a spirit of patience until others are admitted to fill up their communion of glory;" and Irenæus, " The souls of the departed go to the place assigned them by God, and there abide until the resurrection, when they will be reunited to their bodies; and then the saints, both in soul and body, will come into the presence of God." For the Word of God, and for the testimony which they held. B, Syriac, add, " and of the Lamb." *On account of the word,* etc. Exactly the same expression which St. John uses in ch. i. 9 in describing the cause of his own exile at Patmos. The language is peculiarly St. John's (cf. ch. i. 2, " John : who bare record of the Word of God, and of the testimony of Jesus Christ, and of all things that he saw;" also ch. xii. 17, " The dragon . . . went to make war with . . . them which have the testimony of Jesus Christ;" also ch. xix. 10, " I am thy fellow-servant, and of thy brethren that have the testimony of Jesus: worship God: for the testimony of Jesus is the spirit of prophecy.' The " Word of God " is of course *the truth which God has declared,* not *the Word* as in John i. " The testimony which they held " may differ slightly in signification in different places. It may mean (1) the testimony or truth which Christ has imparted to Christians; or (2) the active showing forth of the Christian faith by word or deed. The latter is evidently the meaning here, since for this active manifestation of Christianity they whose souls St. John now sees in glory had been slain, which would not have occurred had they merely received the Word of God without showing it outwardly (cf. ch. i. 2).

Ver. 10.—And they cried with a loud voice, saying; *i.e. the souls cried.* Ebrard, Düsterdieck, Hengstenberg, make" the slain" nominative, in contradistinction to the " souls," which is both unnecessary and unnatural. Züllig compares Gen. iv. 10, " The voice of thy brother's blood crieth unto me from the ground." How long? (comp. Zech. i. 12, 13, " How long wilt thou not have mercy on Jerusalem? And the Lord answered with good words and comfortable words "). No doubt the souls waiting in Paradise are answered by " comfortable words," yet, not having lost their interest in earthly struggles, nor their longing for the triumphant vindication of God's glory, they cry, " How long? " not as needing the time to be shortened for their own sakes, for *they rest*, though not yet entered into the fulness of God's glory. O Lord, holy and true; *O Master, the holy and true* (Revised Version). "Master" (δεσπότης) is the correlative of "servant" (δοῦλος). This is the only instance of its occurrence in the Apocalypse. (On "true," see previous passages.) Dost thou not judge and avenge our blood. The cry is not a petition for personal revenge, but a request for the termination of those ills which for a time afflict man, and the termination of which must, by virtue of God's eternal justice, be accompanied by visible retribution on the wicked. (Cf. Bede, "Those souls which offered themselves a living sacrifice to God pray eternally for his coming to judgment, not from any vindictive feeling against their enemies, but in a spirit of zeal and love for God's glory and justice, and for the coming of that day when sin, which is rebellion against him, will be destroyed, and their own bodies will be raised. And so in that prayer wherein Christ teaches us to forgive our enemies, we are also taught to say, 'Thy kingdom come.'") The passage has given rise to varying interpretations, which are thought to be more consonant with the spirit of the gospel. Thus I. Williams would understand the souls to represent only the Old Testament saints, especially as it is not explicitly said that they died for the witness of Jesus, as in ch. **xx.** 4. On them that dwell on the earth. That is, on the worldly, those who have taken the side of the world in its conflict with Christianity.

Ver. 11.—And white robes were given unto every one of them; *and there was given to each one a white robe.* Στολὴ λευκή, "a white robe," is supported by A, C, [P], ℵ, B, etc. The white robe of righteousness, the wedding-garment of Matt. xxii. 11, 12, is the sign of the blessedness of the saints. *White* is the colour of heavenly victory in the Apocalypse (see on ver. 2). The vision has recalled the past sufferings of the martyrs and their present expectation of the final consummation of their hopes, which is to be not yet. The other side is now to be shown; though they have not yet reached their final bliss, they have received the *white robe*, they are free from possibility of defilement, the victory is won, and they have *rest.* Comfort and encouragement are thus afforded to those still struggling in the world, who have not as yet attained to the white robe of perfect righteousness. And it was said unto them, that they should rest yet for a little season. Ch. xiv. seems to determine the exact signification of ἀναπαύσωνται, viz. "rest in peace," "rest from their labours," rather than specifically "cease from uttering this cry" (ver. 10), as

explained by De Wette and others. *For a little time* (χρόνος); that is, till the second coming of Christ, for the time which is to intervene before that event is frequently spoken of as a *little time* (see on ch. i. 1; xx. 3; xii. 12; comp. Hag. ii. 6, 7, "Yet once a little time, and I will shake the heavens, and the earth, the sea and the dry land, and all nations, and the Desire of all nations shall come"). The time of the world is *little* in comparison with eternity. This *little time* is depicted and set forth under the six seals; it comes to an end at ch. vii. 17, and merges into eternity in ch. viii. 1. Some expositors (of the historical school) understand a χρόνος to be a definite, arbitrary number; *e.g.* Bengel considers it to be 1111⅑ years (see 'Speaker's Commentary,' p. 485). Until their fellow-servants also and their brethren, that should be killed as they were, should be fulfilled. ℵ, B, P, read πληρώσωσιν, "shall have fulfilled" [*i.e.* their course]; A, C, read πληρωθῶσιν, "should be completed." "Their fellow-servants also and their brethren" may not denote two separate bodies, notwithstanding that καί occurs twice, but, as Alford remarks, it may point out the same persons viewed in two aspects—first, the Christians needed to proceed with and finish Christ's work as his servants; second, the same ones needed to complete the number of his family. But it seems more likely that a reference is intended to two classes of Christians—first, *their fellow-servants,* that is, all Christians, who may, however, not suffer martyrdom; and, second, *their brethren,* the martyrs, who, like them, should yet be killed.

Ver. 12.—And I beheld when he had opened the sixth seal; *and I saw when he opened.* The events described accompany the opening as in the case of the preceding visions (see on vers. 1, 3, 5, etc.). The sixth seal describes the end of the world— the transition of the saints from earth to heaven, with the accompanying circumstances. It is important to remember that the whole is a vision, and we must therefore guard against expecting a literal interpretation of the language used. Following the manner of the prophets, and the description given by our Lord himself of the judgment-day, St. John portrays the wonder and awe and consternation which will then be prevalent under the figure of falling stars, etc. How much, if any, may, in the destruction of the world, literally come to pass, it is impossible to say; but we must be content to receive the general impression which is undoubtedly intended to be conveyed to us, without pressing the individual particulars too far. The symbolism, as usual, bears evidence of its Old Testament origin; and the influence of our Lord's description in Matt. xxiv. is noticeable. The special revelation of God's presence or of his judgments is usually depicted under the figure of terrestrial commotion (see on ch. vi. 1; also Isa. ii. 19; xiii. 13; xxxiv. 4: Ezek. xxxii. 7, 8; Hos. x. 8; Joel ii. 30; Hag. ii. 6). The last three seals seem connected more especially with life in the next world. The fifth seal displays to us the souls of the faithful in peace, but desiring the perfect consummation of their bliss; the sixth announces the certainty of future judgment, when all will be set right, when the righteous will be preserved and the wicked justly recompensed; the seventh typifies the indescribable joy and peace of heaven. It seems reasonable, therefore, to consider the passage ch. vi. 12—vii. 17 as all contained under the sixth seal; since, although set forth at rather greater length than the other seals, it all follows in natural sequence—the destruction of the earth, the fear of the wicked, the preservation and joy of the righteous; and then follows heaven, portrayed under the opening of the seventh seal. Some have tried to separate ch. vii. as "an episode," or rather two episodes, commencing at, and marked off by, the μετὰ τοῦτο of ver. 1 and μετὰ ταῦτα of ver. 9, "after these things." But this expression, though undoubtedly marking the beginning of a fresh phase of the subject, does not necessarily imply the opening of an entirely new and unconnected discourse. This view of the sixth seal is in harmony with what appears to be the general plan of the visions of the seals. It is important to bear in mind, in our interpretation of the Apocalypse, these two principles—first, **the book was addressed to certain Christians for a definite purpose**, and its object would be set forth so as to be comprehended by them; second, the truths thus contained must be such as to be applicable to the position of mankind in general in all ages. We have, therefore, to inquire to whom and for what purpose the book was primarily written, and then how the lessons contained can benefit mankind in general. It thus appears that the message was originally intended as an encouragement and a support to those Christians who were being persecuted, and were suffering in various ways, and whose patience might be inadequate to preserve them through trials so severe or so long. The visions of the seals would speak plainly to such as these. The first four would tell them that, though they must not doubt of Christ's final victory, it is yet with God's knowledge and permission that this life is afflicted with troubles of different kinds; it is not because God is weak, forgetful, or unjust. Then, lest any should be tempted

to ask, "Is it worth while? If Christianity involves all this suffering, would it not be better to be as the world is, and escape?" a picture of the future is given. The fifth seal shows that, immediately upon the completion of this life, the souls of the righteous are at peace; and the sixth seal shows that a day of reckoning will certainly come for the world; while the seventh seal is an assurance of heaven. It *is* worth while, therefore, to endure and to persevere, both on account of God's reward to the just, and his retribution upon the unjust. Thus would the signification of the visions be easily comprehended by those for whom they were originally intended; and the same lessons are equally valuable for the Church at all time. Grotius considers that this vision refers to the destruction of Jerusalem; Elliott, Faber, and Mede refer its accomplishment to the beginning of the fourth century; Wordsworth sees the "last age" of the Church represented; Stern thinks it indicates the general state of the Church; Wetstein, the commotions in Judæa previous to the destruction of Jerusalem; while Cunninghame and Frere see a reference to the French Revolution of 1789. But these interpretations do not fulfil the conditions mentioned above, since the Christians to whom this book is addressed were ignorant of those events yet in the future. **And, lo, there was a great earthquake.** Omit "lo." The earthquake is the usual manifestation of God's presence or special dealing with men (*vide supra*). This is the answer to the question of the saints in the fifth seal—the period of probation is finite. **And the sun became black as sackcloth of hair.** Thus Isa. l. 3, "I clothe the heavens with blackness, and I make sackcloth their covering" (cf. Matt. xxiv. 29). **And the moon became as blood;** *the whole moon* (cf. Joel ii. 31, quoted in Acts ii. 20).

Ver. 13.—**And the stars of heaven fell unto the earth** (cf. Matt. xxiv. 29, "The stars shall fall from heaven"). The figure of "stars" is sometimes used to typify "rulers," as in Numb. xxiv. 17, "There shall come a star out of Jacob;" Isa. xiv. 13, "I [Lucifer] will exalt my throne above the stars of God." Some have thus been led to find a particular application of this sentence. Stern considers that the falling away of Christian rulers is signified; while many refer it to the overthrow of pagan rulers. **Even as a fig tree casteth her untimely figs, when she is shaken of a mighty wind;** *her unripe figs.* Probably the unripe figs of the spring, many of which would be shaken down by a strong wind, or possibly the winter figs, which commonly fall off while unripe. The figure is doubtless suggested by Isa. xxxiv. 4, taken in conjunction with the parable of Matt. xxiv. 32.

Ver. 14.—And the heaven departed as a scroll when it is rolled together; *and the heaven was removed as a scroll when it is rolled up. The scroll*—the parchment book or roll, which is spread out to read, and, when read, rolled up and put away. The passage is apparently founded upon Isa. xxxiv. 4. "The host of heaven shall be dissolved, and the heavens shall be rolled together as a scroll," etc. And every mountain and island were moved out of their places (cf. Isa. xl. 4, "Every mountain and hill shall be made low;" also Jer. iii. 23, "Truly in vain is salvation hoped for from the hills, and from the multitude of mountains"). The enumeration of *seven* objects in vers. 12—14 seems to denote the all-extending nature of God's judgment.

Ver. 15.—And the kings of the earth. The first of the seven classes mentioned. The enumeration is again all-extensive, embracing all classes, and men of every degree of social distinction. Bishop Newton is probably not correct in seeing an allusion to particular kings. And the great men; *princes* (Revised Version). Μεγιστᾶνες are the grandees, the courtiers, as distinguished from those who are governors and hold military command, and who are subsequently mentioned as the "chief captains." And the rich men, and the chief captains. The Revised Version reverses the order, and places "chief captains" first. The chief captains (χιλίαρχοι) are those holding military rank (cf. Mark vi. 21, "Herod made a supper to his lords, high captains," etc.; John xviii., "The captain and officers took Jesus;" Acts xxi. 31, *et seq.*, "The chief captain of the band"). And the mighty men. Probably those possessing great bodily strength. And every bondman, and every free man, hid themselves in the dens and in the rocks of the mountains. "Every" is omitted before "free man" by A, B, C, Vulgate, Syriac, Andreas, and Arethas. The dens; in Revised Version *caves* (cf. Isa. ii. 19, "And they shall go into the holes of the rocks, and into the caves of the earth, for fear of the Lord, and for the glory of his majesty, when he ariseth to shake terribly the earth"). Again, as in vers. 12—14, the enumeration is sevenfold; thus denoting the universality and com-

pleteness of the extent of the judgment (see ch. i. 4; v. 1, etc.).

Ver. 16.—And said to the mountains and rocks. Fall on us, and hide us from the face (cf. Hos. x. 8, "They shall say to the mountains, Cover us; and to the hills, Fall on us;" also Luke xxiii. 30, "Then shall they begin to say to the mountains, Fall on us; and to the hills, Cover us") of him that sitteth on the throne. The Triune God (see on ch. iv. 2). And from the wrath of the Lamb. The result of the wrath of the Lamb is depicted in ch. xxi. 8. God's wrath with the wicked is the assurance of his mercy and love for the righteous. Thus in ch. xi. 18, we have, "The nations were angry, and thy wrath is come, and the time of the dead that they should be judged, and that thou shouldest give reward unto thy servants," etc. Similarly, in ch. xiv. 10—13, the *wrath* of God upon the wicked is associated with the peace of the faithful.

Ver. 17.—For the great day of his wrath is come. *Of their wrath*, which is read in the Revised Version, is found in ℵ, C, 38, Vulgate, Syriac; but αὐτοῦ, "his," is supported by A, B, P, Coptic, Andreas, Arethas, Primasius. The article is repeated, making the term almost a proper name—*the day, the great [day]*. Alford remarks that this of itself should be sufficient to keep commentators right in confining their interpretation of this seal to the last judgment (cf. Joel i. 15; ii. 1, 2; Acts ii. 20; Jude 6). And who shall be able to stand? *Who is able* (Revised Version). Thus Mal. iii. 2, "Who shall stand when he appeareth?" And Nah. i. 6. Thus, then, the question in ver. 10, "How long?" is answered; not by limiting the length of time, but by a renewed assurance of an awful termination of the course of the world, at the appearance of the Judge. The dread attending that end is vividly portrayed, and the fear of the wicked, with their conscience-stricken inquiry, "Who is able to stand?" an answer to which is required for the edification of the faithful. And, therefore, the seer immediately describes the preservation of the righteous from amidst the destruction of the wicked, and their raptured praises, a joyous contrast with the despairing fate of those whose doom has just been narrated.

HOMILETICS.

Vers. 1—17.—*Six seals opened.* The *ground-thought* of this book is "The Lord is coming." Concerning this Professor Godet remarks, " L'histoire du monde dans son essence se résume dans ces trois mots: Il vient; il est venu; il revient. C'est sur cette idée que repose le plan du drame apocalyptique."[1] Even the prophecies of the

[1] 'Essai sur l'Apocalypse : Études Bibliques,' deuxième série, p. 291.

Old Testament, which dealt so largely with the first coming, shot far ahead and reached even to the second, *e.g.* Joel. Our Lord himself is very clear on this topic (Matt. xxiv. and xxv.). So also are Paul, Peter, and John. Nor should we think of our Lord's second coming as if it were merely a far-distant something with which we are as yet unconcerned. We are told that star touches star by means of an ethereal invisible medium which joins them. Even so the first and second comings of our Lord *touch each other* by means of the events now going on, whose train began from the one and will reach to the other. Not a moment is lost in the interval. During these apparently slow lingering centuries, in which day follows day with unbroken regularity, one day so much like another that comparatively few leave any distinct impression on the mind, not a moment is there but some work is being done to prepare for our Lord's return. He is now on his way, and at the appointed time "he that shall come will come, and will not tarry." The *plan* of this book gives us (1) the point of departure, (2) the final consummation, (3) a symbolic setting of the events which will fill up the space between the two termini; in which we have "l'épopée de la lutte supréme entre Dieu et Satan, pour la possession de l'humanité comme prix du combat." In this chapter we have set before us in marvellous vividness six features by which the way is to be marked which leads to the consummation. These we will take in order, not omitting to press home their teachings for the conscience and the heart.

I. ALREADY OUR LORD HATH GONE FORTH CONQUERING AND TO CONQUER. (Vers. 1, 2.) One of the four living ones says, "Come." It is a call to the apostle, not a representation of the Church's cry to her Lord.[1] The apostle responds. He sees under the first seal emblems which point plainly and distinctly to the Lord Jesus. The white horse (cf. ch. xix. 11—13). The bow (cf. Ps. xlv. 3—5). The crown (ch. xiv. 14); symbol of conquest and might. The errand on which he goes forth, "conquering and to conquer;" conquering as he goes, as a matter of fact; speeding on, that he may conquer still. Certainly the mission of our Lord is the only one which can be thus described. He is to know nothing but success. His progress may *seem* to be retarded, as we judge of things, but it never is so according to the Divine conception. We may not be in a position to trace continuous advance. But we know who it is that has gone forth; we believe in his might, his wisdom, his love. He has never yet lost an hour, and never will.

II. MANIFOLD FORCES, INCIDENTS, AND AGENCIES ARE ALSO AT WORK UPON THE EARTH. The first seal certainly indicates *triumph*; the second, *war* (vers. 3, 4); the third, *famine* (vers. 5, 6); the fourth, *death*, whether by sword, famine, pestilence, or wild beasts (vers. 7, 8); the fifth, *martyrdom* (vers. 9—11); the sixth, *convulsions*, terrible and appalling, of various kinds. Now, what do these symbols—triumph, war, famine, pestilence, martyrdom, convulsion—mean? Some say, The changing phases of the Church itself; the progress of the Christian power going forth in triumph; then degeneracy, corruption, and controversy creeping in; then darkness, ignorance, and a famine of the Word; then the pestilential mystery of iniquity; then martyrdom; then great upheavings and mighty tribulation, preparing the way of the Lord. Others regard them as indicating a state of things which had occurred before John's exile—the triumph and peace of the Augustan era; war under Caligula; famine under Claudius; pestilence following on famine; martyrdom under Nero; the convulsive breaking up of the Jewish state and polity. Certain it is that *before* John's exile these six or seven features followed each other, and *exactly in this order*. Whence some may conclude that *that* must have been the intent of the symbols. But, singularly enough, if we *begin* with John's exile, it is the fact that in the Roman empire, hastening to its fall, these varied phases—triumph, war, famine, pestilence, martyrdom, convulsion—also succeeded each other *in this very order*, so much so that if any one had desired to write from the history of the changing fortunes of that empire an illustrative commentary on this chapter, he could scarcely have used more fitting phraseology than Gibbon has done in his history of its decline and fall. Yet we are sure that he, at any rate, had no intention of being a Scripture expositor. We learn from him that there was an era of great prosperity in the Roman empire from the year 96. This was followed by a long

---

[1] See on one side, Dean Alford; on the other, Archdeacon Lee; a third view is suggested n Bishop Carpenter's Commentary, *in loc.*

series of strife and civil war, as if to show on what a frail foundation the virtue of the Antonines had reared the felicity of the empire. That period of strife was succeeded by famine, and that again by pestilence; then followed the dreadful era of the Diocletian martyrdom, and the break-up of the Roman empire, the subjection of paganism, and the establishment of Christianity in its place. Be it remembered, then, that not once only can the student put his finger on the map of history, and say, these six—triumph, war, famine, pestilence, martyrdom, convulsion—succeeded each other, and *in this order*, but once and again. And let us not forget that our Saviour named these—just these—*in nearly the same order*, and said that they would occur "*in divers places.*" [1] War, famine, pestilence, martyrdom, convulsion, are to occur *repeatedly.* Hence we are driven to the conclusion that these symbolic representations of the six seals do indicate the varied features which should mark the progress of the age, ere the Church is brought in, in the fulness of her redemption. All the forces symbolized here have been at work for ages on different parts of the earth; each of them recurs again and again, and will do so through the whole stretch of this dispensation. Here our God seems to say to us, "You see these terrible forces—war, famine, pestilence, martyrdom, convulsion. I see them too. There is nothing but what is in the seven-sealed book. Fear not. All the seals will be opened by the Lamb that was slain. All these terrors are but preparatory agencies clearing the way for the 'day of the Lord'!"

III. THE PRESSURE ACCUMULATES AS THE END DRAWS NEARER. While we cannot pretend to draw a sharp line between one seal and another, it is manifest from the entire chapter that, as the end approaches, the pressure increases. The sixth seal is surely indicative of convulsions so great as to produce a consternation which will shake society to its foundations. One of these later phases will be the upheaving of nations, disorganization of visible Churches, and widespread unsettlement of faiths. "Every mountain and island were moved out of their places." Yet this is but the sixth seal, not the seventh; a preparation for the end, not the end itself, although many may think it so. It is "the great tribulation"—a tribulation so great that many will cry out in agony, "The great day of his wrath is come!" Yet it will not be that, but only a preliminary to it.[2] These words, "The great day of his wrath is come!" are not the sacred writer's own, but the cry of the terrified ones. God will yet shake, not earth only, but also heaven (cf. Luke xviii. 8; Hag. ii. 6, 7; Heb. xii. 26; Matt. xxiv. 29, 31). Let us beware of man's frequent and false alarms. Christ's word in Matt. xxiv. 4—6 should be a perpetual guard against them.

IV. THE ADVANCE OF THE DAY OF THE LORD WILL SEEM TO THE WORLD AS THE APPROACH OF A DAY OF WRATH. (Vers. 16, 17.) "The great day of their wrath is come." *Their* wrath—even that of him that sitteth on the throne, and of the Lamb. Wrath? Why? Should not any signs of the appearing of the Son of God to "judge in righteousness" be hailed with gladness? When our Lord himself actually described such terrors as being the "birth-pangs" (ἀρχὴ ὠδίνων, Matt. xxiv. 8) of a new creation, should not his approach be welcomed with song? Why this conception of wrath? Why connect "wrath" with *the Lamb of God?* It is only on account of the sin in which men have lived; only because, by fighting against the Lord and his anointed, they have treasured up for themselves "wrath against the day of wrath." When their armour in which they trusted is stripped off, and when the playthings with which they toyed are snatched away, and the delusions with which they were spell-bound shall be dispersed like the mists of morn, they will cower in terror before the God whom they defied. This "great tribulation" will be a wondrous leveller. They who sported with sin will be no longer in sportive mood. Let us note here the unnaturalness of sin. It is depicted as bringing about *five* perversions.

[1] Matt. xxiv. "The seals unfold the general aspects of the world's history after Christ's ascension. . . . The visions of the book may have preliminary applications, because the principles on which they are constructed are eternal ones" (Bishop Boyd Carpenter). See also W. P. Grant's 'Exposition of the Revelation' (Hodder and Stoughton: 1889), pp. 156, *et seq.*, for some valuable remarks on the manifold interpretations of this chapter.

[2] Again and again, in periods of great tribulation, people have declared the end of the world to be at hand. For some illustrations of this fact, see Elliott's 'Horæ Apocalypticæ,' vol. i. pp. 386, *et seq.*, 5th edit.

REVELATION.

8

1. The unfoldings of God's plan in the varied workings of his providence, which should be viewed with holy awe and peaceful serenity, do, to a guilty man, bring terror and dread, oft amounting to despair. Let a man be at peace with God, and he can look on to see how Jesus rules the world, with joy and hope; but unbelief and sin prevent all this, and make every new opening full of ominous foreboding. 2. In their anguish and despair they call to the mountains and hills to help them! They dare not address the God whom at their ease they despised! But "Nature," the god of the atheist, will be found to be a god that cannot save. 3. They think to find refuge in being hidden from God. As if that were possible! As if, were it possible, it could bring them ease! Oh, how frightful are the perversions effected by sin! The face of him who is the chief among ten thousand, and the altogether lovely, is to the bad a distressing sight, arousing abhorrence and deepening their woe. 4. The sinner who up to the last rejects the Son of God, sees at last in him only wrath. That Being who is only perfect Love, will seem to the wicked to be full of anger indignation, and avenging power. 5. The fifth and last perversion which we notice is that, instead of welcoming the perfect adjustments of a righteous Judge as that which should bring the long-wished-for rest to a weary world, they, knowing they are in the wrong, view them with an affrighted horror for which there is no solace, and with an immeasurable distress for which nature has no balm. He who neglects grace in the "day of salvation" must receive equity when the day of grace is over. And when equity has to deal with wrong, what course is open but entire and everlasting condemnation? The bulwark of righteousness is the doom of sin.

HOMILIES BY VARIOUS AUTHORS.

Vers. 1—17.—*The opening of the seals.* The Book of Revelation may be said to consist—with the exception of ch. ii. and iii.—of a vast picture-gallery. And this not so much because of the number of the pictures, as their sublimity and extent. Ch. i. is the portraiture of "the Son of man." Then there is a vast canvas, stretching from ch. iv. to xi., and representing the judgment and fall of Jerusalem. Then from ch. xii. to xix. another similar one, representing the judgment and fall of Rome. Then yet another, much smaller, representing the final conflict and overthrow of the enemies of Christ; and then, the last and most precious of all, in ch. xxi. and xxii., the glowing picture of the new Jerusalem, the saints' eternal home. Now, in looking at a great picture we need to study it carefully, closely, continuously, and portion by portion. We have tried to do so in regard to the first of these, and also in regard to two most important sections of the second one. In this vast second scene we have viewed the high court of heaven, and the inauguration of Christ's mediatorial reign, which was the subject of ch. v. And now we come to another most interesting but unquestionably difficult part of the same great subject—the opening of the seals. Indeed, the interpretation of this book, from the beginning of this chapter onwards, is one concerning which the only certain thing is that absolute certainty concerning any given interpretation is unattainable. It matters little, however, for the profitable reading of the book, that there is and must be this uncertainty as to the actual meaning of the many mysterious symbols with which it abounds; for whether we regard them as telling of the history of the Church in its relation to the world continuously to the end of time; or whether, as surely is the more reasonable way, we take them as telling of those tremendous events which, when St. John wrote, had begun, and were shortly to come to pass, the time being at hand, and by which the Church of Christ was so much affected, —whichever way we read these symbols, their main lessons for us and for the Church in all ages is one and the same; and these, by patient, prayerful study, we may hope to learn. As to this ch. vi., the sheet-anchor for its interpretation is our Lord's discourse in Matt. xxiv. and its parallel in Mark. No doubt that discourse, as this book, looks on to the times of the end; but as surely it contemplated, as does this book also, events which many of them—not all—were nigh at hand. God's judgment on Judaism and the Jews is its near subject, as the same is of the vision of which this chapter forms a part. And now let us look at—

I. THE SIX SEALS TOGETHER, or rather, at what is disclosed by the opening of them all. And, without doubt, *terror* is their one badge and mark. The four horses with their riders all tell of terrible things. The souls under the altar, whom we see at the opening of the fifth, cry for vengeance on their murderers, and all horrors seem accumulated in one at the opening of the sixth. The reading of the chapter makes one's heart tremble; our flesh shudders with fear at the visions of distress which, one after the other, are unfolded. There is a seventh and a very different vision at the seventh seal; but the opening of that will not be for a long while, and therefore we first consider these six which are near in time and in character also. And whether we read the pages of Josephus, or whether we regard Gibbon as furnishing the more accurate explanation of these symbols,—in either there will be found more than enough to warrant all that St. John has here portrayed. The dreadful days of the fall of Jerusalem were drawing on, and none who know the history of the horrors that preceded and accompanied that event can question that they were more than enough to fill up all that these vivid and terrible symbols import. Our Lord says of those days that "except they should be shortened, there should no flesh be saved." And yet—and here is the marvel—it is "the Lamb," he who is the Ideal of all grace and love, he it is who presides over, directs, and governs all these events, dreadful as they are. And then the highest, the holiest, and most beloved of his ministers, they who cluster closest round the throne of God and the Lamb, appeal to him and pray him to "Come." At the opening of each of the first four seals one of the four living ones thus appeals to Christ. It is evident, therefore, that they are in full sympathy with him in this matter, and would not have him do otherwise. And it is the same with the whole of that high court of heaven. There must be, then, in all these and in all such things —and this is their lesson for us—a force for the furtherance of God's blessed will amongst men such as less stern methods could not have. True, in one aspect it is all the result of man's wild wickedness and folly.

> "Man, proud man,
> Dressed in a little brief authority, . . .
> Plays such fantastic tricks before high heaven
> As makes the angels weep."
>
> ('Measure for Measure.')

And to many minds, when you have recited the different events that led on, one by one, to the final catastrophe, you have sufficiently explained the whole; there is no need to bring God, as St. John does, into the matter. But we are distinctly taught that all these things are the working of his will, the carrying out of his high plans and purposes. They are not by chance, nor by the will of man, but of God. And accepting this as true, we are led to the inquiry—Wherefore uses he such means? Various answers may be suggested: so only can the proud, unruly wills of sinful men be humbled; so only can the Church be roused and stimulated to do her proper work; so only can her faith be disciplined, tried, and developed; so only can men be made to know, "Verily there is a God that judgeth in the earth;" and so only can gigantic obstacles to men's good and the extension of Christ's kingdom be got out of the way. All history shows this. But whilst this and far more may be said, it yet remains for us to remember, and that with gratitude, that dark, drear, dreadful, desolating as such events are, and diabolical as are many of the men who are the chief actors in them they yet, all of them, are under the absolute control of him whose love and wisdom and power enable him to know unerringly when to let such events run riot in their rage, and when to restrain them or remove them altogether. And what is best he is sure to do; and always he will make them "work together for good."

II. THE OPENING OF THE FIRST SEAL. (Ver. 2.) The vision of the white horse and its rider bearing a bow, with its sharp arrows ready for conflict, and wearing a crown, the emblem of victory. In Zech. i. 7—11; vi. 1—8; Hab. iii. 8, 9; Isa. xli. 2; Ps. xlv. 4, 5; we have similar representations of the horseman told of here, and his identity seems settled by ch. xix. 11—16, where he is distinctly called "the Word of God." When the first seal was broken, then there passed across the stage, as it were, this vision. But of whom else can we think as corresponding to the rider of the white horse, than of him of whom we read in Ps. xlv., "In thy majesty ride prosperously because of truth and meekness and righteousness; and thy right hand shall teach thee terrible things. Thine **arrows** shall be sharp in the heart of the king's enemies; whereby the people fall under thee"? Of the Lord Jesus Christ going forth conquering and to conquer, in spite of, in the midst of, and by means of, all the dread events which are afterwards declared—of him we believe the vision tells. Not of any ordinary human warfare; still less of the prosperous condition of the Roman empire under the Antonines; but of Christ our Lord. And most cheering is it to be taught that, let come what will, however calamitous and distressful the events of life, nothing can stay his course. They cannot bar his way, but will be made by him to further that way. This first vision is, therefore, full of good cheer. And let it not be forgotten that the vision has an individual application as well as a world-wide one. It tells every believing soul, "Christ will overrule all that happens; thy trials and crosses, thy disappointments and disasters, shall not hinder his purposes of good for thee. He goeth forth 'conquering and to conquer,' and who can turn him aside?"

III. THE OPENING OF THE SECOND, THIRD, AND FOURTH SEALS. These give the visions of the red, the black, and the pale horses. Cruel war, black famine, and all-devouring death, by pestilence probably, are meant by these visions. And more summarily and distinctly they are foretold by our Lord. "Wars and rumours of wars," "famines and pestilences,"—these with other woes he plainly predicts; and his meaning is, we are sure, the meaning of St. John. Famine and pestilence were the common accompaniments of war. But they are not to have unrestrained power. For as in the discourse of our Lord, so here in the vision of St. John, there are plain suggestions that in wrath God remembered mercy. The voice that proclaimed the nearly twelve times enhanced cost of wheat and barley, tells—as does also the blackness of the horse which suggests the black lips, the sign of extreme hunger—of dreadful famine. But that same voice tells also of distress mitigated, not suffered to become utter destitution. This is the meaning of the added charge, "See that thou hurt not the oil and the wine." It is a difficult saying, but coupling it with the express words of our Lord that "for the elects' sake" these dreadful days should "be shortened," we take them as telling that, whilst owing to the ravages of war there should be, as there could not but be, great scarcity in those things which, as corn and barley, depended upon constant cultivation; yet the olive and the vine should still yield their increase, they not requiring to be replanted year by year, and being in various ways likely to be less affected than the level corn-lands which lay along the plains, and which therefore became the common camps and fighting-grounds of hostile armies, to the utter destruction of all things grown thereon. Moreover, that to death and Hades were given power, not over all the earth, but over only one-fourth part, this seems also to point to the same blessed truth that the instruments of God's judgment are held in and not allowed to do their work a hair-breadth beyond their appointed limit. "He does not willingly afflict nor grieve the children of men," though, as these visions do plainly tell, he will ruthlessly both afflict and grieve when man's sin and folly make it needful that he should. As a loving mother will hold down her own dearly loved child to the surgeon's dreadful knife, if only so it can be saved from death, so will the Lord, the Lamb of God, pour out upon us of his awful judgments, if by our sin we force him thereto. As we read of these visions, this should be our prayer that never may we thus force him to deal in such manner with us. May his love constrain us, never our sin constrain him.

IV. THE OPENING OF THE FIFTH SEAL. Here no living creature cries "Come," but the appeal comes from the martyred saints themselves. We have had no mention of an "altar" before, but now it is seen as part of the vision which unfolded itself before St. John. "They shall deliver you up to be afflicted, and shall kill you"—so had our Lord foretold, and here the actual fulfilment of that word is symbolized. Not to the martyrs under Diocletian, yet less to those under papal Rome, but to those who were, in St. John's own day, fast falling beneath the persecutor's sword, does this vision specially belong. Nevertheless, it is designed for the consolation and support of all Christ's persecuted people in every age and in every land. Hence Milton, with all possible appropriateness, sang concerning the martyrs of the Alpine mountains, whose sufferings righteously roused the rage of their fellow-believers here in England—

> "Avenge, O Lord, thy slaughtered saints, whose bones
> Lie scattered on the Alpine mountains cold;
> Even them who kept thy truth so pure of old.

> When all our fathers worshipped stocks and stones,
> Forget not: in thy book record their groans
> Who were thy sheep, and in their ancient fold
> Slain by the bloody Piedmontese that roll'd
> Mother with infant down the rocks. Their moans
> The vales redoubled to the hills, and they
> To heaven. Their martyred blood and ashes sow
> O'er all the Italian fields, where still doth sway
> The triple tyrant; that from these may grow
> A hundredfold, who having learned thy way,
> Early may fly the Babylonian woe."

But this **vision** tells not alone of martyrdoms, but of the righteousness of God in the avenging of their blood upon the earth. We see it is just and what ought to be. Yet more are we shown that "the Lord is mindful of his own." See the condition of these martyred ones. Not yet perfect or complete, but nevertheless, oh, how blessed! At rest, in victory, sanctity, joy—so their white robes tell, and expecting some even yet better thing in the triumph of Christ and his Church over all evil which in due time shall surely come to pass. What comfort there would be and is in all this, in regard to *those who had suffered* death! Those who mourned them would know now that blessed indeed are the dead which die in the Lord. And in regard to *the mystery of a persecuted Church*, would it not teach them that though

> " Careless seems the great Avenger; history's pages but record
> One death-grapple in the darkness 'twixt false systems and the **Word;**
> Truth for ever on the scaffold, wrong for ever on the throne.
> Yet that scaffold sways the future, and behind the dim unknown
> Standeth God within the shadow, keeping watch above his own"?

And when they came to face such death themselves, oh, how would this vision help them, as in fact it did, to be faithful unto death, and to face it unflinchingly, unfalteringly, as Christ would have them do.

V. THE OPENING OF THE SIXTH SEAL. (Vers. 12—17.) Nearly every detail of this dread event is given by our Lord (Matt. xxiv.). And St. John's language is modelled largely on that of the older prophets (Joel ii. 30, 31; Isa. l. 3; xxxiv. 3, 4; ii. 12, 19; Hos. x. 8; Jer. iv. 23—26). And in the great catastrophe by which Judaism was overthrown, and in the fall of Rome, and in the events which usher in the last great and terrible day of the Lord, have been and shall be seen the fulfilment of this awful vision. There is that which is called "the wrath of the Lamb"! Not Scripture alone, but historic fact alike declare this. And it will be poured out on the ungodly when the Lord shall come again. How will that day find us? Confident, or ashamed and dismayed? The answer may be known. How does Christ find us now? Trusting and obeying him, or disregarding and disobeying? As now, so then.

> " Lord, in this thy mercy's day,
> Ere it pass for e'er away,
> On our knees we'll fall and pray,
> Have mercy, Lord!"

S. C.

Vers. **1, 2.**—*The conquering Lord.* The Revelation has its parts. A division is to be made here. There are many revelations in the one. And the truth to be taught is set forth again and again in differing figures and series of representations. We look not for chronological continuity and sequence. The book has one theme, one truth, dividing into its several streams; that truth is, in the present section, the triumph of the Church's Lord. With this assurance the Lord gives comfort to his struggling, suffering, persecuted Church. With the breaking of the first seal a vision is revealed: "and I saw." The symbol is simple and comprehensive. It reaches to the end from the beginning. It is a vision of the Redeemer as the conquering Lord. But it is the Lord prepared for battle. Conquest is preceded by conflict. He goes forth to make war. This aspect prevails throughout the book. "The Lord is a Man of war."

I. We think of THE FOES AGAINST WHOM THE ANTAGONISM OF THE LORD IS RAISED.

Not here named, but implied. In one word *sin.* Sin lurking in the hearts of men; sin embodying itself in the lives of men. Hence sinners—all who ally themselves with evil, who are the agents of evil, "servants of sin," "children of the wicked one." Thought of as an army led forward by "the prince of the power of the air, the spirit that now worketh in the children of disobedience." In the conquest of this is the conquest of the persecuting foes of the first Churches, the form in which sin was then rampant.

II. We think of THE ONE CONQUEROR IN WHOM THE WHOLE IDEA OF THE ARMY IS REPRESENTED. He only is in view, for all victory is of him. He only slays and conquers. We see the Conqueror prepared to do battle, seated on the war-horse, carrying the war-weapon.

III. We think of THE NATURE OF THE CONFLICT. In the symbol this appears only in the person of the Conqueror, and in the colour of the horse—it is in righteousness. White is the consecrated colour; it is the symbol of purity.

IV. We think of THE INEVITABLE CONQUEST. The crown—the laurel crown is upon the Conqueror's brow. It is the symbol of anticipated victory: "He shall reign."

V. THE ASSURING WORD. "He came forth conquering, and to conquer." The whole revelation in this word. Again and again this is represented. Here the true comfort. He shall bring into subjection to himself whatever is not in harmony with his Name, and that in the individual heart and in the universal sphere.—R. G.

Vers. 3—11.—*Scenes of suffering.* No sooner has the vision of the Conqueror passed before the eye of the seer, than a darkening series in slow procession bring him from the contemplation of the source of the Church's comfort and hope to the scene of the Church's conflict, the earth. Herein is depicted the afflictions through which the Church should pass. Well was it that an assurance had been given of final triumph. Always from conditions of sorrow the Church could look back upon the great and comforting promises of redemption and triumph. The second, third, fourth, and fifth seal represent the sad truth that, in the great history of redemption, great and grievous sorrows would befall the faithful. It is a re-echo of the Lord's own words. "They shall deliver you up to councils; they shall scourge you," etc. Often has the little flock had to look back upon these words when torn by grievous wolves. Truly the kingdom of heaven is at times entered only through "much tribulation."

I. THE SUFFERING OF THE CHURCH ARISES FROM THE EXCITED ENMITY OF THE WORLD, THE SPIRIT OF WHICH IS CONDEMNED BY "THE WORD OF GOD AND THE TESTIMONY" HELD BY THE FAITHFUL.

II. THE SUFFERING OF THE CHURCH AT TIMES REACHES THE UTMOST DEGREE OF SEVERITY. "They were slain." Not only the earliest sufferers, but many also "their fellow-servants and their brethren." The Church in its conflict with the worldly power uses its own weapons of truth and righteousness; but the weapons in the hands of the enemies of the truth are carnal. It is the long story of bitter, painful, cruel, ungodly persecution.

III. THE SUFFERING OF THE CHURCH FROM THE EXCITED ENMITY OF THE WORLD MAKES ITS GREAT APPEAL TO THE LORD OF THE PATIENTLY ENDURING BELIEVERS. "How long, O Master?"

IV. BUT THE CHURCH'S SUFFERING HAS ITS LIMIT DEFINITELY MARKED. It is "yet for a little time." It is not for ever; but until their fellow-servants and their brethren had finished their course.

V. THE SUFFERING OF THE CHURCH IS FINALLY REWARDED IN THE SPIRITUAL ELEVATION AND PURIFYING OF THEM THAT ENDURE. "There was given to each one a white robe."

VI. THUS THE CHURCH IN ALL AGES IS ENCOURAGED PATIENTLY TO SUFFER IN FAITH AND HOPE THE CRUEL PERSECUTION OF A WICKED WORLDLY POWER.—R. G.

Vers. 12—17.—*The final judgment of the enemies of the Church.* The time of the suffering comes to an end. Evil cannot for ever triumph. The Lord reserves his rewards for his faithful ones. Nor can the enemies of truth and righteousness escape. Suffering as the Church was when St. John wrote these wonderful words, an assurance that their wrong should not go unjudged and unavenged was needful to uphold the sinking, fainting, feeble, suffering ones. "Vengeance belongeth unto me: I will recompense, saith the Lord." Now do the enemies prove "it is a fearful thing to fall into the hands of the living God." The breaking of the sixth seal is the signal for a just judgment of the cruel persecuting ones—the wolves that ravened the flock of God. It is the response to the cry, "How long, O Master, the holy and true, dost thou not judge and avenge our blood on them that dwell on the earth?" The "little while" is concluded; the cup of iniquity full. Terrific and awe-inspiring in the utmost degree is the picture of "the great and terrible day of the Lord."

I. THE REPRESENTATION OF THE DIVINE JUDGMENT ON THE UNGODLY ANTAGONISTS OF THE CHURCH TAKES THE FORM OF AN UPHEAVAL OF THE VISIBLE UNIVERSE. It is the destruction of the worldly sphere. All those things that seem to be fixed and permanent are moved out of their place. The earth is rent and quakes; the sun is darkened; the moon is as blood; the stars fall like unripe figs; the heaven is removed as a scroll; the mountains and islands are moved from their places. So is taught the instability of all earthly things—the earthly, which is the sphere of the Church's enemies.

II. THE DIVINE JUDGMENTS INSPIRE THE UTMOST TERROR INTO THE HEARTS OF THE UNGODLY WORLDLY POWERS. They fear—they fly—they seek death.

III. THE DREAD OF THE UNGODLY IS EXCITED BY THE VISION OF HIM WHO IS DEAR TO THE FAITHFUL. The ground of offence is antagonism to him that sitteth on the throne, and to the Lamb, to whom the Church gives glory. The judgment upon the adversaries is found in the revelation of the Divine government, and the power and authority of the despised Redeemer. As the obedient and faithful ones find their joy and rejoicing in the presence of God and the Lamb, so do the enemies of truth find therein their greatest punishment.—R. G.

Vers. 1—17.—*The seven seals; or, the development of good and evil in human history.* "And I saw when the Lamb opened one of the seals, and I heard, as it were the noise of thunder, one of the four beasts saying, Come and see," etc. In this chapter we have the breaking open of six of the seals of that mystic roll containing the Divine plan of the *government of the world*, and as held in the hands of Christ who is *the great Expounder.* The opening of these seals suggests to our notice and presses on our attention *the constant development of good and evil in human history.* Notice—

I. THE DEVELOPMENT OF GOOD IN HUMAN HISTORY. By the good, I mean the true, the beautiful, and the right. Good and evil are here working among the moral tenants of this planet; perhaps it is not so in other planets. In heaven there is good, and good only; in hell, evil, and perhaps evil only; but on the earth the two are at work simultaneously, constantly, and everywhere. Taking the conquering hero as going forth on the "white horse" as an illustration of the right and the good on this earth, it is suggested: 1. That the good is embodied in *a personal life.* "Behold a white horse, and he that sat on him [thereon]." The right in this world is not a mere abstraction, it is embodied in human life. In Christ this was so in perfect kind and degree. "Grace and truth came by Jesus Christ." He was the Right--incarnate, breathing, living, acting; and this, not only during his corporeal life here, but in all his disciples through all times. He is in them; he is the conquering Hero destroying the works of the devil. 2. That the good embodied in a personal life is *aggressive in its action.* "And he went [came] forth conquering, and to conquer." Right is an invading force; it is ever making aggressions on the wrong. This is according to its very essence. Wherever the sunbeams break, darkness departs; so with the right, it is always conquering. Wonderful are the conquests it has achieved in past ages, and its victories are still proceeding, and will proceed until it becomes the might of the world. This right is not something elsewhere, it is here; not something that has been, but something that is and shall be. The supreme King of righteousness is constantly proceeding on his triumphant march, and one day "every knee shall bow to him, and every tongue confess." In its aggressiveness it moves: (1) Righteously. "A white horse." The horse is the instrument which the right employs to bear it on to victory. The good is not only pure in its nature and aims, but pure in its methods. (2) Triumphantly "He that sat on him [thereon] had a bow." The bow carries the arrow, and the arrow penetrates the foe. Truth wins its victories by the arrows o conviction. (3) Royally. "There was given unto him a crown." Right is royal, the only royal thing in the universe, and the more perfectly it is embodied, the more brilliant the diadem. Hence Christ is crowned with glory and honour. He is "exalted above all principalities and powers," etc. Kind Heaven, quicken the speed of this "white horse;" and may the victories of its triumphant Rider multiply every hour; and soon may "the kingdoms of this world become the kingdoms of our God," etc.!

II. THE DEVELOPMENT OF EVIL IN HUMAN HISTORY. I take the passage as giving illustrations of five great evils at work in human life. 1. *War.* "And there went out another horse that was red ['and another horse came forth, a red horse']: and power was given to him that sat thereon [and it was given to him] to take peace from the earth, and that they should kill [slay] one another: and there was given unto him a great sword." Mutual murder, man destroying his brother. This evil refers to no particular period or place; it has been going on from the days of Cain and Abel through all times even unto this hour. The spirit of murder burns throughout the race. The "red horse" is ever on the gallop. His ruthless tramp echoes through all souls and communities. "Whence come wars? Come they not from your lusts?" etc. Alas! that there should be found in a country calling itself Christian governments that should be feeding and fattening this "red horse" of rapine and bloodshed. 2. *Indigence.* "I beheld, and lo [I saw, and behold] a black horse: and he that sat on him [thereon] had a pair of balances [a balance] in his hand. And I heard [as it were] a voice in the midst of the four beasts [living creatures] say, A measure of wheat for a penny, and three measures of barley for a penny." "Whilst making food scarce, do not make it so that a chœnix (a day's provision of wheat, variously estimated at two or three pints) shall not be got for a penny. Famine generally follows the sword. Ordinarily from sixteen to twenty measures were given for a denarius" (Fausset). The state of want here described means no more than that the whole of a man's labour is exhausted in the purchase of the bread required for one day; and this certainly does not amount to that indigence which prevails amongst thousands of our countrymen who are starving for bread where wealth and luxury abound. This evil, then, like the others, is not confined to any age or clime, but is here and everywhere. Let every man trace this national indigence to its true source. 3. *Mortality.* "Behold a pale horse: and his name that sat on him was Death, and Hell [Hades] followed with him. And power was given [there was given authority] unto them over the fourth part of the earth, to kill [slay] with sword, and with hunger [famine], and with death, and with the beasts [wild beasts] of the earth." "The colour pallid or livid," says Bishop Carpenter, "is that deadly greenish hue which is the unmistakable token of the approach of death. The rider is Death, not a particular form of death, but Death himself. Attending him, and ready to gather up the slain, is Hades. The fourth seal is the darkest and the most terrible. Single forms of death (war and famine) were revealed in the earlier seals; now that the great king of terrors himself appears, and in his hand are gathered all forms of death—war, plague, famine, pestilence. For the second time the word 'death' is used it must be taken in a subordinate sense, as a particular form of death, such as plague or pestilence." This mortality is, then, another evil confined to no period or place. Death reigned from Adam to Moses, and from Moses to Christ, and from Christ to this hour. Men are dying everywhere—all are dying. With every breath I draw, some one falls. 4. *Martyrdom.* "I saw under [underneath] the altar the souls of them that were [had been] slain for the Word of God, and for the testimony which they held: and they cried with a loud [great] voice, saying, How long, O Lord [Master, the], holy and true, dost thou not judge and avenge our blood?" Who is the martyr? The words suggest: (1) He is one who dies for the truth. "Slain for the Word of God." He is not one who has merely been murdered, or one who has been murdered on account of his own convictions, but one who has been put to death for holding *right* convictions—belief in the Word of God. Such a belief which they attested by ample testimony. (2) He is one who in heaven remembers the injustice of his persecutors. "How long, O Lord!" The Almighty is represented as saying to Cain, "The voice of thy brother's blood crieth unto me." As if the earth itself was craving for justice, and groaned for retribution of wrong. The cry of the martyr in heaven is not for vengeance, for all heaven is full of love; but the cry is rather for information when justice will be done: "How long?" As if they said, "We know that thou wilt judge and avenge our blood sooner or later: but how long?" The truly good in all ages have an unbounded confidence in the rectitude of the Divine procedure. "I know," said Job, "that my Vindicator liveth." Justice will come sooner or later. (3) He is one who in the heavenly world is more than compensated for all the wrongs received on earth. "And white robes were given unto every one of them [and there was given them to each one a white robe]." They have white raiment in heaven—the emblem of purity. They have repose in heaven: "rest for a little while." They have social hopes in heaven: "Until their fellow-servants also and their brethren, that should be killed as they were, should be fulfilled." 5. *Physical convulsion.* "And I beheld when he had opened the sixth seal, and, lo, there was a great earthquake; and the sun became black as sackcloth of hair, and the moon became as blood," etc. Observe: (1) Our earth is constantly subject to great physical convulsions. Geology reveals some of the tremendous revolutions that have been going on from the earliest dawns of its history; and such changes are constantly occurring. Volcanoes, earthquakes, deluges, tornadoes, seas overflowing their boundaries and engulfing whole continents, etc. Perhaps no generation of men have lived who have not witnessed some of the phenomena here described: "the great earthquake, the sun becoming black as sackcloth, the moon as blood, mountains and islands removed," etc. (2) Great physical convulsions are always terribly alarming to ungodly men. "The kings of the earth, and the great men [princes], and the rich men, and the chief captains, and the mighty men [the rich], and every bondman, and every free man, hid themselves in the dens [caves] and in the rocks of the mountains. And said [they say] to the mountains and rocks, Fall on us, and hide us from the face of him that sitteth on the throne, and from the wrath of the Lamb: for the great day of his [their] wrath is come; and who shall be [is] able to stand?" Fear is an instinct of wickedness; terror is the child of wrong. "The wicked flee when no man pursueth."

> "Oh, it is monstrous! monstrous!
> Methought the billows spoke, and told me of it;
> The winds did sing it to me; and the thunder,
> That deep and dreadful organ-pipe, pronounced
> The name of Prosper: it did pass my trespass."
>
> (Shakespeare.)

(3) The alarm of ungodly men is heightened by a dread of God. "For the great day of his [their] wrath is come; and who shall be [is] able to stand?" Dread of God is the soul of all fear. "I heard thy voice in the garden, and I was afraid." How unnatural is this dread of God—the dread of one who is at once the Essence and the Fountain of all good! "Hide us from the face of him that sitteth on the throne, and from the wrath of the Lamb." The "wrath of the Lamb"! This is a monstrous phenomenon. Who has ever seen a lamb in a rage, meekness aflame with indignation? A more terrific idea I cannot get. "The wrath of the Lamb."

CONCLUSION. In these "seals," then, we have human history. We need not puzzle ourselves about the meaning of the utterances in this chapter, or search for some mystic meaning. It is full of current events occurring in all times and lands, and we are here commanded to study them. At each event some living creature, some Divine messenger in the spiritual empire, says, "Come and see." "Come and see" the triumphant Hero of the good, going forth on the *white* horse conquering, and to conquer; mark the aspect, the movements, and the progress of good in the world in which you live; take heart and speed it on. "Come and see" the *red* horse, the spirit of murder and bloodshed, that is creating discords and fightings everywhere, rifling families and communities of all concord, filling the air with the cries of the dying, and the wails of the widow and the orphan. Come and study the demon of war; study it in order to destroy it. "Come and see" the *black* horse trampling in the dust the food which Heaven has provided, and which man requires, thus leaving millions to starve. Study this national poverty until you realize the true causes and apply the true cure. "Come and see" the *pale* horse hurrying through the world, visiting in his turn every individual, family, community, nation, trampling underfoot all men, regardless of character, age, position, nation. Study death, its moral causes, its final

issues. "Come and see" "the souls of those who were slain for the Word of God."
Study martyrdom, despise the persecutors, and honour their victims. "Come and see"
the great physical convulsions of nature. Study the physical phenomena of the world,
and cultivate that love for the God in all, who is over all, and that confidence in his
love, wisdom, and power which will enable you to be calm and triumphant in the
most terrible physical convulsions, enabling you to sing—

> "God is our Refuge and Strength,
> A very present Help in trouble;
> Therefore will not we fear,
> Though the earth be removed,
> And though the mountains be carried
> Into the midst of the sea ;
> Though the waters thereof roar and be troubled,
> Though the mountains shake with the swelling thereof."

Brothers, who shall tell the seals that will be broken open in our book of destiny
during the year? Ere we commenced our existence, all pertaining to our life through
all the ages we have to run was mapped out and registered, even in minutest detail,
in the Divine roll of destiny. All the events of our lives are but the breaking of the
seals of that book. With every fresh event, every new effort, some fresh seal is
broken. What seals are yet to be broken? what Divine archetypes are yet to be
embodied? what latent forces are yet to be developed? What these ears have yet to
hear, these eyes have yet to see, this mind yet to conceive, this heart yet to experience !
"Go thou thy way till the end be ; for thou shalt rest, and stand in thy lot at the
end of the days."—D. T.

Vers. 9, 10.—*Departed martyrs.* "And when he had opened," etc. By common
consent this is a sketch of departed martyrs, *i.e.* men "that were slain for the Word of
God, and for the testimony which they held." If they had been slain for anything else
they would not have been martyrs.

I. THEY LIVE IN SACRED SECURITY. "I saw under the altar the souls of them."
The "souls," not the bodies; the bodies had been destroyed, their ashes were left
behind. Souls can exist apart from the body—a wonderful fact this. These souls were
"under the altar." They were in a position of sacred security. No one could touch
them there, safe for ever from their persecutors.

II. THEY LIVE IN EARNEST CONSCIOUSNESS. They have an earnest consciousness of
the *past.* "How long, O Lord, most holy and true." They remember the earth,
remember the cruelties they received on the earth, and long, not maliciously, but
benevolently, for justice being done to their persecutors. No doubt their desire was
that God should strike such a moral conviction into their hearts on account of their
wickedness that would lead them to repentance.

III. THEY LIVE IN HOLY GRANDEUR. "White robes were given to them." Or
more probably, "a white robe," emblem of purity and conquest.

> "Their blood is shed
> In confirmation of the noblest claim—
> Our claim to feed upon immortal truth,
> To walk with God, to be divinely free
> To soar and to anticipate the skies.
> Yet few remember them. They lived unknown
> Till persecution dragged them into fame,
> And chased them up to heaven. Their ashes flew
> No marble tells us whither. With their names
> No bard embalms and sanctifies his song.
> And history, so warm on meaner themes,
> Is cold on this. She execrates, indeed,
> The tyranny that doomed them to the fire,
> But gives the glorious sufferers little praise."
>   (Cowper.)

                                                              D. T.

Vers. 15, 16,—*The wonders of the last day.* " And the kings of the earth," etc. The last day, the day of days, will be a day of wonders. The words indicate three of the wonders of that day.

I. MEN DREADING THE FACE OF CHRIST. "The face of him that sitteth on the throne." Here are men preferring annihilation to a sight of *that* face. What is the matter with that face? It was, indeed, the human face Divine, the serenest, the loveliest, the kindliest face ever seen on earth. It was a face whose expression towards men was, " Come unto me," etc. What change has come over it now? Why are men afraid of it now? Their guilty consciences have made that face terrific. The sight of that face will call up such memories of their ingratitude, their folly, their impiety, as will make existence intolerable.

II. THE LAMB WROUGHT INTO WRATH. "The wrath of the Lamb." How strange and unnatural is this! The wrath of *love* is the most terrible of wrath. 1. *It implies the greatest moral enormity in the object of it.* The wrath of malign natures is soon kindled, is capricious, often rages without reason. But when love is indignant, there must be fearful enormity in the object. 2. It exerts most *agonizing influence upon the conscience of its object.* The anger of malign natures seldom touches the conscience of its victim, but often awakens contempt and defiance. Not so when love is indignant; the indignation of love is crushing. What power on earth is so withering as the indignation of a parent who is essentially benevolent and loving? 3. It is *unquenchable until the reasons for its existence are removed.* The wrath of malign natures often burns itself out, but the wrath of love is a determined opposition to evil.

III. HUMANITY CRYING FOR ANNIHILATION. "And the kings of the earth, and the great men . . '. hid themselves in the dens and in the rocks of the mountains; and said to the mountains and the rocks, Fall on us, and hide us," etc. Love of life is the strongest instinct in human nature, and hence the dread of death. Here is the chief and first of all dreads. What will men not give away to avoid death? But what a change now! They earnestly cry for that which they dreaded! They cry for annihilation. 1. The cry is *earnest.* " Mountains and rocks." The language breathes earnestness. Existence has become intolerable. It is a curse that can no longer be borne. 2. The cry is *general.* " The kings of the earth, the great men, the rich men, and the chief captains, the mighty men, every bondman and every free," etc. The conquerors of the world, the iron masters of nations, men whose names struck terror through ages, now quail in agony and cry for extinction. 3. The cry is *fruitless.* They cry to the " mountains and rocks." What can they do for them? Can they hear them? Have they hearts to feel? No; insensitive, immovable, these remain amid the wildest shrieks. But were they to fall on them would they crush them? The material universe cannot crush a soul. It is an inextinguishable spark. God alone can quench a soul.—D. T.

Ver. 16.—" *The wrath of the Lamb.*" " Hide us from the wrath of the Lamb." Wrath is a terrible thing. But the most terrible of all wrath we have here—the *wrath of the Lamb.* " Hide us." Who says this? " The kings of the earth, the great men, and the rich men, and the chief captains, and the mighty men, and every bondman, and every free man." These men had, no doubt, braved terrible things during their existence, but they could not brave this. It struck an overwhelming horror into their souls. What makes this wrath so terrible?

I. ITS UNEXAMPLED STRANGENESS. Who ever saw a lamb in a rage? The wrath of a lion, a tiger, or a bear,—this is common, this is natural. But the lamb is essentially meek, tender, yielding. Of all creatures this is the last creature that could be excited to wrath. As a rule, whatever is strange is more or less alarming. A strange comet, a strange heaving of the sea, or a strange vibration in the earth. The wrath of a tender, loving, meek-minded man is a far more terrible thing than the wrath of an irascible nature. The more difficulty you have in exciting wrath the more terrible it is when it appears. When the Lamb is in wrath it implies some terrible provocation, and that provocation is sin. The wrath of the Lamb is an ocean of oil in flames. Well may it strike terror. Another reason why this wrath is so terrible is—

II. ITS INFINITE PURITY. The lamb is the emblem of innocence. The wrath of the Lamb is not a passion, but a principle. It is not malign, but benevolent. It is not against existence, but against its sins and its crimes. Anger in man is necessarily an evil. Hence we are commanded to be "angry and sin not." Learn from this that we turn our greatest blessing into the greatest curse. Our optic and auricular organs may be so diseased as to give to the most beautiful objects and most melodious sounds in nature a power to convey into us the most poignant anguish, and so our moral nature may become so corrupt as to turn love into wrath, and blessedness into misery.—D. T.

Ver. 17.—*The last judgment; or, the dawn of the retributive era.* "Who shall be able to stand?" There will assuredly come a day of judgment, or the dawn of the retributive era. The material universe symbolically prophesies some such moral crisis in the history of man. The flowing river, the growing plants, the breathing tribes, the planetary systems, all tend to a crisis. The unremitting increase from age to age in the human family, viewed in connection with the limited capacity of this planet to sustain animal existence, irresistibly indicates some such a turning-point in human history. The universal and concurrent references of the human conscience through all ages and lands give a high probability to the dawn of such a moral juncture. The sentence preceding our text calls it a *great day.* It will be great on account of the number and variety of the moral beings that will be assembled together; great on account of the results which will then be effected—redemptive providences ended, and the agencies of a righteous retribution brought into full play; great on account of the Divine glories which will then be displayed. Our point is, "Who shall be able to stand on that day?" In order to illustrate this solemn question with that simplicity that may make it spiritually serviceable to us now, I shall suppose a case. What under a *legal* charge could enable you to look calmly forward to the coming day of trial, feeling that you could stand? We can only conceive of six things which would answer that purpose.

I. A CONSCIOUSNESS OF INNOCENCE, AND THE POWER OF SHOWING THAT THE CHARGE HAS NO FOUNDATION. The feeling of innocence in itself would brace you with energy, and enable you to look onward with imperturbed heart to the day of trial. But if you felt that in connection with this you have the power of demonstrating your innocence to the full conviction of the court, would you not feel even the stronger and calmer still? Now, have you this in relation to the day of judgment? Are you conscious of your innocence? Still less are you conscious of the power to demonstrate it? No; your conscience condemns you, and "God is greater than your conscience, and knoweth all things." This, then, will not serve you, will not enable you to *stand* in the judgment.

II. AN ASSURANCE THAT THE EVIDENCE WILL BE FOUND INSUFFICIENT TO CONVICT. You may know that you are in reality guilty, you may be certain of the impotency of the evidence; there may be no witnesses, or, if there are, they may be shown by the able counsel you have engaged to be unworthy of belief. You may be sure that his genius is sufficient so to colour and torture the evidence as to destroy its worth. All this might make you feel, in the supposed case, that you can stand in the trial. But have you this in relation to the day of judgment? No, no. There will be: 1. The omniscient Judge. He knows everything about you. 2. The people to whom and through whom you have sinned. All your sins against God have had to do with men. The falsehoods you have spoken have fallen on some ear, and your dishonesties, cruelties, seductions, will have to do with those who then by thousands confront you eye to eye. Were you to dare to deny the charge, a million voices would confound you with their contradiction. 3. The conscience within you bearing the strongest testimony against you. This, then, will not serve you—will not enable you to stand in th judgment.

III. A FEELING THAT THE CRIME WITH WHICH YOU ARE CHARGED IS VERY INSIG-NIFICANT. "It is true," you may say, "I am guilty, and the evidence of my guilt is irresistible; but the deed is so very unimportant that the case, if entertained in court, will result in a mere nominal penalty." This would enable you to feel that you could stand the trial. But have you this for the day of judgment? No. Sin, believe me, is no trifling matter. 1. Think of it in relation to *God.* It is a violation of the most righteous laws; for he is your Proprietor, and you are his stewards. It is a violation of the most wonderful love. He is your loving Father. 2. Think of it in its bearing on *yourself* and on the *universe.* "One sinner destroyeth much good." What would you think of the man who, infected with a pestilential disease, ran malignantly from house to house in order to spread it ? Sin is a pestilence. Think of the judgments it has brought upon the world ; think of the crucifixion of Christ, and talk no more about the *insignificancy* of sin. This, then, will not enable you to stand in the judgment.

IV. A FELT CAPABILITY OF PROVING THAT THE CRIME WAS COMMITTED ACCIDENT-ALLY, NOT BY PURPOSE. If you were well assured that on the day of trial you could prove that you did not intend to commit the act, you might look forward without any agitation or misgivings. But have you this in relation to the day of judgment ? No. You know that your sin has not been *accidental*, but *intentional*—not an *exception* in your history, but the *law*; not an occasional *act*, but the *habit* of your existence.

V. FAITH IN THE SYMPATHY OF THE WHOLE COURT IN YOUR FAVOUR. If you felt assured that on the day of trial the whole jury would be composed of none but warm and attached friends, and that the judge himself would have the kindest and strongest sympathies in your favour, you would have strong hope in being able to stand. You know how love blinds the soul to faults, and turns even opposing evidence to its own account. In such a case mercy is almost sure to triumph over judgment. But have you any hope of anything like this, that will serve you at the day of judgment ? None. True, he who will be the Judge on that day is love, and is full of the tenderest mercy now. But whilst no change will have taken place in his nature, he will then, notwithstanding, appear and act as the inexorable Just One.

VI. AN ABILITY TO PROVE THAT YOU HAVE RENDERED SIGNAL SERVICE TO THE STATE. Suppose that you had, by some heroic campaign, hurled back from your country's shores the advancing tide of a terrible invasion; or by some scientific discovery given a new impulse to the industry of the population, and introduced a new and bright era into commerce ;—in such a case you might have hope of being able to stand in trial. Though loud guilty, your past services would be felt to be such a set-off as would obtain for you an acquittal, or at any rate reduce your punishment to a mere nominal thing. But have you anything like this to serve you on the day of judgment ? Have you any hope of being able to show that you have been of service to the universe ? No, no. You will feel then that the universe would have been better off had you never existed. Had you never thought, never acted, never been, there would have existed less crime and less misery in the creation.—D. T.

EXPOSITION.

CHAPTER VII.

Ver. 1.—And after these things. Μετὰ τοῦτο, or, as some cursives read, μετὰ ταῦτα, is generally regarded as denoting the close of the sixth seal and the commencement of a new subject, interjected by way of episode between the sixth and seventh seals. But, even if not looked upon as an integral part of the revelations made under the sixth seal, the connection is so close that the two must be regarded practically as one. The incidents of the seventh chapter are evidently the complement of those narrated in the closing verses of the sixth. They take up the question with which that chapter closes, " Who is able to stand ? " and afford comfort and help to those suffering Christians who were so sorely in need of a renewed assurance of the certainty of their final reward. It seems better, therefore, on the whole, to consider the sixth seal to extend to the end of ch. vii. Vitringa takes this view, which appears to be supported also by Wordsworth. Alford,

while separating ch. vii. from ch. vi., as "two episodes," remarks, " The great day of the Lord's judgment is not described; it is all but brought before us under the sixth seal, and is actually going on in the first of these episodes." I saw four angels. Of the nature of these angels we are told nothing. They are evidently ministers of God's will, and the mention of them following immediately upon the preceding description seems to connect the whole account more closely with Matt. xxiv. 29, 30, where the angels gather the elect from the four winds. It does not seem probable that " evil angels " are meant, as understood by some writers, since what they do is apparently done at the command of God. Standing on the four corners of the earth. That is, standing in the four opposite directions, and thus controlling all the earth (cf. Isa. xi. 12; ch. xx. 8). The number four is the symbol of universality and of creation (see on ch. v. 9). Holding the four winds of the earth (cf. Jer. xlix. 36; Dan. vii. 2; Matt. xxiv. 31). The angels may have been the " angels of the winds," just as in ch. xiv. 18 an angel has power over fire, and in ch. xvi. 5 we read of the "angel of the waters." The *winds* have been interpreted in two ways, neither of which seems strictly correct. The first is to give a literal meaning (as Düsterdieck) to the winds, and to understand literal wind-storms as part of the judgment upon the earth. The second method interprets the winds as symbols of the judgments of the first six seals, which are held in suspension, while the elect are sealed. The truth probably is that the *winds*, like the *earthquake*, the rolling-up of the heaven as a scroll, etc., are part of the figurative description of the destruction of the world at the judgment-day : which destruction, like that of Sodom, is delayed for the preservation of God's elect. That the wind should not blow on the earth, nor on the sea, nor on any tree. Πᾶν δένδρον, "every tree," is read in א, P, 1, 36, Andreas, etc. The earth, the sea, the trees, are mentioned as things likely to be affected by the action of the winds ; the two former, of course, embracing those things situated upon them, and the last being specially mentioned, perhaps, as a class of things which are peculiarly liable to destruction from wind. Wordsworth and others, interpreting symbolically, consider that the blasts of wind on the earth typify earthly powers, opposed to those of heaven, while the sea is emblematic of nations in a state of agitation against God, and the trees represent the great ones of this world. This interpretation, therefore, regards the objects mentioned as the enemies of God, which, by his command, are preserved from destruction and allowed to flourish in ease and apparent security, until the time of the sealing of God's servants has been accomplished. But it seems better to regard the winds as forming part of the general description by which God's judgment is foreshadowed. It is not unusual in the Bible for the wind to be mentioned in connection with destruction and judgment (cf. 1 Kings xix. 11 ; Job i. 19 ; xxi. 18 ; xxx. 15 ; Ps. i. 4 ; cxlvii. 18 ; Isa. xi. 15 ; xxvii. 8 ; xxxii. 2 ; xli. 16 ; Jer. xxii. 22 ; Dan. ii. 35 ; vii. 2).

Ver. 2.—And I saw another angel ascending from the east ; *from the rising of the sun*. Again no individual angel is particularized, though an archangel *may* be intended, as he has authority over the first four. He proceeds from that quarter whence comes light ; and, like the Sun of Righteousness, he rises with healing in his wings ; for his mission is to render secure the servants of God. Wordsworth thinks Christ, or a messenger from Christ, is meant—a view shared by Hengstenberg ; Vitringa says the Holy Ghost : Victorinus,

the Prophet Elijah. That this angel was of like nature with the first four appears probable from the words in ver. 3, "till we have sealed the servants of our God." Having the seal of the living God. The sealing instrument with which they seal God's servants. Of its nature we are told nothing beyond what is contained in ver. 3. He is specially referred to as "the *living God*," since, by this sealing, *life* is imparted. We have here the shorter expression, "the living God," not, as in all other places of the Apocalypse, "him that liveth for ever and ever" (see ch. iv. 9 ; v. 14 ; x. 6 ; xv. 7). And he cried with a loud voice to the four angels (cf. ch. i. 10 ; v. 2 ; vi. 10) to whom it was given to hurt the earth and the sea ; that is, by letting loose the winds, as shown by vers. 1 and 3. Bengel and Rinck, looking only at the immediate context, thought that the hurt was done by preventing the winds from blowing on the earth and cooling it in the scorching plagues which follow (ch. viii. 7). The *trees* are not mentioned, being included in *the earth* ; and this appears to indicate that the expression, "the earth, the sea, and the trees" (vers. 1 and 3), signifies the world in general, without being intended to represent individual parts, as the great men, etc. (see on ch. v. 1).

Ver. 3.—Saying, Hurt not the earth, neither the sea, nor the trees. *Hurt not*, by loosing the four winds, as stated on ver. 2. The destruction prepared for the guilty world is not allowed to fall until God's elect have been gathered in, and preserved free from danger (cf. Matt. xxiv. 31, where immediately after the appearance of the Son of man, his elect are gathered from the four winds). (For the signification of the *earth*, the *sea*, and the *trees*, see on vers. 1 and 2.) Till we have sealed the servants of our God in their foreheads. The angel associates himself with the first four, as being on an equality with them in this work, although he alone is stated to possess the seal (ver. 2). Of the nature of the sealing nothing more is indicated. The *forehead* is naturally mentioned as being the most conspicuous part of man, as well as that which we are accustomed to regard as the noblest and most vital part. The idea may be compared with that in Ezek. ix. 4, 6. It is remarkable, too, that the word in Ezekiel rendered "mark" is the name of the Hebrew letter *tau*, of which the ancient form was a cross (cf. the sign of the cross in baptism ; also ch. iii. 12, "I will write upon him the Name of my God . . . and my new Name ;" and ch. xiv. 1, "Having his Father's Name written in their foreheads"). "The servants of our God," says Bengel, is a title which especially belongs to holy men in Israel (cf. Gen. i. 17 ; Deut. xxxii. 36 ; Isa. lxi. 6). Those who hold the preterist view believe that the Christians who escaped the destruction of Jerusalem are indicated by this expression. The sealed are probably those referred to by our Lord in Matt. xxiv. 22, 24, 31, as "the elect."

Ver. 4.—And I heard the number of them which were sealed. The description of the actual operation of sealing is omitted (cf. Ezek. ix., where it is also omitted). And there were sealed an hundred and forty and four thousand. Omit "and there were." This number—the square of 12 multiplied by 1000—is typical of a large and perfect number. No one has ever said that the number should be taken literally; and there are evident reasons why it could not be so intended. We have, therefore, to inquire what is its symbolical signification. The number 12 is always typical, in the Apocalypse and elsewhere, of a complete and perfect number. It is formed of 4 multiplied by 3. Four is generally representative of the created universe, and 3 of the Godhead (see ch. v. 9). 4 plus 3, that is 7; and 4 multiplied by 3, that is 12, indicate a perfect number—a number which includes and embraces everything. And thus 12 multiplied by 12 denotes the most exhaustive and perfect completion. The number 1000 is generally used to denote a large and complete, but somewhat uncertain, number (cf. ch. xiv. 1; xx. 2; xxi. 16, etc.). Thus the square of 12 multiplied by 1000 has the signification of a large number not definitely fixed, but nevertheless perfect; that is to say, not omitting a single one of those who should be included in the number. We are therefore taught that at the judgment-day, before the destruction of the world is allowed to take place, a large number, consisting of those who have proved themselves to be God's servants, will be preserved and set apart; and that, although the number may be large, yet it will be perfect, not one of those who are worthy to be selected being overlooked or forgotten. This number subsequently is increased, being included in the "great multitude which no man could number" of ver. 9, and which is formed by the whole company of the redeemed. Of all the tribes of the children of Israel. The Authorized Version here appears to give the correct sense of πᾶς, "every." The number is made up not necessarily by an equal number from each tribe, but by a number from the twelve tribes viewed as a whole. As explained above, the number one thousand, though signifying "completeness," is not a definite number. Here, as elsewhere, it is the spiritual *Israel* which is signified. In support of this view, we may remark: (1) The constant use in the Apocalypse of the terms "Israel," "Jew," "Jerusalem," etc., in

the spiritual sense; and it seems scarcely credible that the writer of the book, who throughout insists on the fulfilment in the Christian religion of all things Jewish, should in this place, for no apparent reason, deliberately make a distinction between Jew and Gentile. The terms are constantly used to denote the *spiritual* Israel, the *spiritual* Jerusalem, etc., except where allusion is made to some historical fact, as in ch. ii. 14; v. 5: xxii. 16; xv. 3 (cf *Jews*, ch. ii. 9 and iii. 9; *Israel*, ch. xxi. 12; *Jerusalem*, ch. iii. 12 and xxi. 2, 10; *Babylon*, ch. xiv. 8; xvi. 19; xvii. 5; xviii. 2, 10, 21; *Sodom and Egypt*, ch. xi. 8; *Euphrates*, ch. ix. 14; xvi. 12; *Sion*, ch. xiv. 1; *Jezebel*, ch. ii. 20; *David*, ch. iii. 7; *Gentiles*, ch. xi 2). (2) The improbability of the omission of the tribe of Dan, if the literal Israel were meant. (3) The general testimony of ancient commentators, which is the view of those who appointed this passage for use in the Liturgy on All Saints' Day. Some, however, have considered that the hundred and forty-four thousand are distinct from, and not included in, the multitude of ver. 9. They believe the former indicates the converted from among the Jews, and the latter those saved from the Gentiles. Thus Bengel, Düsterdieck, Ebrard, Grotius, etc. But it may be remembered that in ch. xiv. 3, 4, the hundred and forty-four thousand redeemed from the earth and from among men is not confined to Jews. By other commentators the number has been thought to denote converts in the age of Constantine, etc.

Ver. 5.—Of the tribe of Juda were sealed twelve thousand. There are various lists of the tribes in the Old Testament, no two of which present the same names in the same order. It does not seem probable that any special design underlies the selection and arrangement here. First, with regard to the selection, we observe that Dan and Ephraim are omitted, the number being completed by inserting Levi, Joseph, and Manasseh. Although Ephraim and Manasseh are sometimes inserted instead of Joseph and Levi, and sometimes omitted, there seems only one example of a list in which any one of the others is omitted, viz. that in Deut. xxxiii., where no mention is made of Simeon. It has been thought that Simeon was purposely passed over by Moses on account of his ill conduct (see Gen. xxxiv.)—conduct for which, unlike Levi, he afterwards made no sufficient atonement. This has led many commentators (Hengstenberg, Wordsworth, etc.) to conclude that Dan finds no place here because of the idolatrous worship of the tribe (Judg. xviii.). Many ancient writers (Bede, Andreas, etc.) account, somewhat similarly, for the omis-

sion by supposing that, in accordance with a
very commonly received opinion, antichrist
would arise from this tribe—an opinion
probably originated by a comparison of the
" serpent" of Gen. xlix. 17 with ch. xii. 9 ;
xx. 2. A third group, amongst whom are
Ebrard, Düsterdieck, De Wette, Grotius,
referring to an ancient Jewish tradition that
the tribe of Dan had become extinct, and
relying on the omission of this tribe in
1 Chron. iv.—vii.—though Hushim (1 Chron.
vii 12) may be the sons of Dan (see Gen.
xlvi. 23)—believe that the children of Dan
no longer existed, and were therefore omitted.
In the insertion of the name Manasseh
(i.e. " Forgetting ") Bengel sees an intended
allusion to the omission of Dan, who is, he
thinks, omitted for some mysterious reason.
Ewald believes that St. John wrote ΔAN,
and that MAN., the abbreviated form of
" Manasses," was substituted by error; and
he appeals to manuscripts 9, 13, which,
however, have "Dan" in place of "Gad."
Moreover, Irenæus, Origen, Arethas, have
" Manasseh," and state plainly that Dan was
omitted. It is certainly curious in connection with this conjecture that, if it were true,
that is to say, if "Dan" should be read in
place of "Manasseh," we should have a more
intelligible order of arrangement. In that
case, speaking generally, the elder sons
would come first, the younger last; all the
pairs of brothers are kept together (only
that, in the case of the six brothers,
there is a division into two lots) ; Judah
naturally is placed first before Reuben,
owing to the prominent place held by him
in the Apocalypse in connection with our
Lord. The order would then be—

Juda, } sons of	Simeon,
Reuben, } Leah.	Levi, } sons of
Gad, } sons of	Issachar, } Leah.
Aser, } Zilpah.	Zabulon,
Nepthalim, } sons of	Joseph, } sons of
[Dan,] } Bilhah.	Benjamin, } Rachel.

Of the tribe of Reuben were sealed twelve
thousand. As remarked above, Judah probably precedes Reuben from the greater
importance he would possess in the mind
of the writer of the Apocalypse, who continually exalts Christ, "the Lion of the
tribe of Judah" (ch. v. 5). Of the tribe of
Gad were sealed twelve thousand.

Ver. 6.—Of the tribe of Aser were sealed
twelve thousand. Of the tribe of Nepthalim
were sealed twelve thousand. Of the tribe
of Manasses were sealed twelve thousand.
(For the insertion of Manasses and the
omission of Dan, as well as the order of
the names of the tribes, see on ver. 5.)

Ver. 7.—Of the tribe of Simeon were sealed
twelve thousand. Of the tribe of Levi were

sealed twelve thousand. Of the tribe of
Issachar were sealed twelve thousand.
Though Levi was excluded in the partition
of the earthly Canaan, he is included
among the partakers of the heavenly
Canaan.

Ver. 8.—Of the tribe of Zabulon were
sealed twelve thousand. Of the tribe of
Joseph were sealed twelve thousand. Of the
tribe of Benjamin were sealed twelve thousand. Ephraim is omitted, while Manasses
is inserted. Wordsworth considers that
this is on account of the rebellious character
of the tribe of Ephraim (see 1 Kings xii.
25 ; Isa. vii. 9, 17 ; Hos. v., etc.). But
Ephraim is sometimes identical with Joseph
(cf. Ps. lxxviii. 67 ; Ezek. xxxvii. 16), who
here finds a place among the twelve.

Ver. 9.—After this I beheld, and, lo, a
great multitude, which no man could
number ; after these things, I saw, and
behold a great multitude, etc. Here, as in
ver. 1, a fresh phase of the vision occurs,
indicated by μετὰ ταῦτα, " after these
things ; " but not, perhaps, commencing
(as so many writers think) an entirely new
and disconnected vision. It is the immediate prelude to the opening of the seventh
seal (see on ch. viii. 1). Ch. vi. recounts
the terrors of God's judgments on the
wicked, and especially those of the final
judgment; but lest the godly should be
dismayed and ask, "Who is able to stand"
(ch. vi. 17) on that great day? it is revealed
that the faithful are first selected and preserved. This occupies the first eight verses
of ch. vii. But all is not yet quite ready
for the opening of the seventh and last seal.
There is, besides those sealed on the last
day, an innumerable company with whom
the former are joined in one body ; and a
glimpse is afforded of their conjoint adoration and of that supreme bliss which is
entered upon, but not described, under the
seventh seal. The "great multitude which
no man could number" includes, therefore,
the hundred and forty-four thousand of ver.
4. They have escaped the terror of the
final judgment of the world (see ver. 3),
but have formerly experienced tribulation
(see ver. 14). Of all nations, and kindreds,
and people, and tongues ; out of every nation
and [all] tribes and peoples and tongues.
The classification, as in ch. v. 9, is fourfold,
symbolical of completeness in matters of
creation (see on ch. v. 9 ; iv. 6, etc.). Stood
before the throne, and before the Lamb;
standing before, etc. We are carried back
to the description given in ch. iv. 1—4 and
v. 6—11. Clothed with white robes ; arrayed
in (Revised Version). See on ch. iv. 4 and
vi. 2 for white—the emblem of victory
and righteousness. And palms in their
hands. Φοίνιξ, "palm," occurs in the New

Testament only in this place and in John xii. 13. Trench states that no symbol of heathen origin is used in the Apocalypse; and he connects the palm-bearing multitude with the celebration of the Jewish Feast of Tabernacles. Wordsworth and Hengstenberg take the same view; and there is much to be said in favour of it, though Alford and others connect the image rather with the Greek and Roman sign of victory. In the first place, the word is used by St. John in John xii. 13, where doubtless it is connected with the celebration of the Feast of Tabernacles. Secondly, the use of such an image would more naturally occur to one so familiar with Jewish customs and ritual as the writer of the Apocalypse; and, moreover, the idea commemorated by this feast—that of the enjoyment of rest and plenty, the possession of the promised Canaan after toil and delay—is peculiarly applicable to the condition of those here described. Thirdly, the idea seems carried on in the mind of the writer, and referred to in ver. 15 in the words, "shall spread his tabernacle over them" (see Revised Version).

Ver. 10.—And cried with a loud voice; *and they cry*, etc. The present tense expresses the unceasing nature of their occupation (Alford). Saying, Salvation to our God; that is, "The praise and honour due for our salvation belongs to God, since he is the Cause of our salvation." Note the similarity to the "Hosanna" of the palm-bearing multitude of the Feast of Tabernacles (see John xii. 13; 2 Macc. x. 6, 7; Ps. cxviii. 25). Which sitteth upon the throne, and unto the Lamb. To the Triune God, and to the Lamb (see on ch. iv. 2; cf. ch. v. 13; xii. 10).

Ver. 11.—And all the angels stood round about the throne, and about the elders and the four beasts; *were standing . . . the four living beings.* (For a consideration of the positions here indicated, see on ch. v. 11.) The throne in the centre with the four living beings was surrounded by the elders, having the Lamb in the midst, between the throne and the elders. Forming a circle round the whole were the angels. (On the *elders* as representing the Church, and the four *living creatures* as symbolical of creation, see on ch. iv. 4, 6.) And fell before the throne on their faces, and worshipped God. As in ch. v. 14 and xi. 16, 17, praise is accompanied by adoration and worship.

Ver. 12.—Saying, Amen. In ch. v. 14 the four living creatures respond "Amen" to the praises uttered by the angels; here, in response to the praise offered by the redeemed in ver. 10, the angels utter "Amen," preparatory to joining in the universal adoration. Blessing, and glory, and wisdom, and thanksgiving, and honour,

and power, and might, be unto our God for ever and ever. Amen. *The blessing*, etc.; that is, "all blessing," etc. (see on ch. iv. 11). The terms of the ascription are the same as those in ch. v. 12, except that we have here εὐχαριστία, "thanksgiving," substituted for πλοῦτος, "riches" (see on ch. v. 12). The sevenfold character of the ascription of praise denotes its universal and all-embracing character (see on ch. i. 4; v. 1).

Ver. 13.—And one of the elders answered. The *elder* speaks because he is typical of the Church, concerning which the exposition which he delivers is to be made (see on ch. iv. 4). Where an explanation is made of visions which refer to the Church, the active part is taken by the elders, while angels introduce visions of which the signification is unexplained (cf. ch. v. 2; vii. 1, 2; viii.; x. 1, 3, etc.; and v. 5). Saying unto me, What are these which are arrayed in white robes? and whence came they? The elder questions that he may teach (Bede).

Ver. 14.—And I said unto him, Sir, thou knowest; *and I say unto him, My lord* (Revised Version). The expression denotes the utmost respect and reverence, which afterwards induce the seer to worship the angel (see ch. xix. 10; xxii. 8). The structure of this part of the vision recalls Ezek. xxxvii. 3, "And he said unto me, Son of man, can these bones live? And I answered, O Lord God, thou knowest" (cf. Zech. iv. 2, 4, 5; John xiii. 21). And he said to me, These are they which came out of great tribulation; *which come out of the great tribulation* (Revised Version). The repeated article is especially emphatic. The question arises—What is "the great tribulation" referred to? Probably all the tribulation which has been passed through by the redeemed, all that which pertained to the life through which they have passed. This tribulation is now completed and past, and is therefore referred to as "the great tribulation." "These are they which have passed through the great tribulation of their life on earth." This is the view taken by Alford. Düsterdieck refers the expression to the last great trial of the saints before the coming of the Lord. Some point to particular persecutions as the reference intended, and others consider that "the last great trial to be expected under the seventh seal" is meant. And have washed their robes, and made them white in the blood of the Lamb; *and they washed*, etc. That is, during their past life, while they were experiencing the great tribulation, they washed their robes (cf. ch. iii. 4, 5, where those who have "not defiled their garments" and those "that overcome" are to be clothed in white). Those that over-

P

come and are undefiled, therefore, are those
who have washed themselves in the blood
of the Lamb, through which only their
victory is possible or effective. Arethas,
Bede, De Lyra, consider that the robes are
washed of those who have endured martyrdom, and that they are washed in the blood
of the Lamb, because it is the blood of his
members.

Ver. 15.—Therefore are **they before the
throne of God.** That is, because they have
been washed, and have their robes made
white, they are before the throne (cf.
Eph. v. 25—27, "Christ loved the Church,
and gave himself for it; that he might
sanctify and cleanse it, . . . that he might
present it to himself a glorious Church, not
having spot, or wrinkle," etc.). And serve
him day and night in his temple. As described in ch. iv. 8, 11; **v.** 8—14; vii. 12;
xi. 15, etc. *Temple* (ναός) is here, as in ch.
iii. 12, the "dwelling-place," the shrine, of
God, *i.e.* heaven. Thus are the redeemed
made "pillars" in his temple (ch. iii. 12).
**And he that sitteth on the throne shall
dwell among them;** *shall spread his tabernacle
over them* (Revised Version). The same
verb that occurs in John i. 14; ch. xii. 12;
xiii. 6; xxi. 3. The allusion (not an uncommon one with St. John) is to the
Shechinah which overshadowed the mercy-

seat. God's presence among them, co-
dwelling with them, is the happiness of his
people (cf. John xvii. 24, "Father, I will
that they also be with me," etc.; 1 John iii.
2, "We shall be like him; for we shall see
him as he is ").

Ver. 16.—They shall **hunger no more,**
neither thirst any more; neither shall the
sun light on them, nor any heat; *shall the
sun strike upon them* (Revised Version).
The passage is evidently founded upon Isa.
xlix. 10 (cf. the punishment of the fourth
vial, ch. xvi. 8).

Ver. 17.—For the **Lamb which is in the
midst of the throne shall feed them;** *shall
be their Shepherd.* Compare the description
of the position of the Lamb given in ch.
v. 6. The position here indicated is the
same as that there described. The Lamb
is between the throne and those surrounding
it, towards the middle of the throne. Christ
is set forth in the character of Shepherd, as
in John x. 11 and xxi. 16. And shall lead
them unto living fountains of waters; *and
shall guide them unto fountains of waters of
life* (Revised Version). "Of life" is an
addition to the passage as found in Isaiah
(cf. John vii. 37—39, where the expression
is used of the Holy Spirit). And God shall
wipe away all tears from their eyes. A
reference to the *tribulation* of ver. 14.

HOMILETICS.

Vers. 1—8.—*The Church on earth, sealed in the great tribulation.* The visions of
this chapter are set between the sixth and seventh seals. The great tribulation, to
which the opening of the sixth seal is the prelude, is not that of the final day of wrath,
for we are but at the sixth seal, and not the seventh. Nor can this great tribulation
be any merely local calamity, for according to vers. 9—14 those coming out of it are
of all nations, and kindreds, and people, and tongues. It is so widespread and terrible
as almost to force upon us the question, "Who shall live when God doeth this? What
will become of the Church?" To such an inquiry this chapter is our answer. It shows
us the Church in two divisions. The first division is on earth, sealed in the great tribulation; the second division is in heaven, caught up out of the great tribulation. In this
homily we deal with the first division. By the first three verses of the chapter we are
clearly taught that the work of destructive convulsion is held in suspense, until the work
of the sealing is done. Four angels are "holding the four winds of the earth;" another,
coming from the sunrising, has the seal of the living God. Until every one of the
servants of God are marked off from the rest, no judgment is to fall. This sealing is
impressed on the hundred and forty-four thousand of all the tribes of the children of Israel.
Here we have the figures of the old covenant brought forward to illustrate the blessedness of those under the new, yet surely the restrictions of the old covenant are not to
be retained. These sealed servants of God are not the natural, but the spiritual Israel,
even "the Israel of God." Hence our theme is—*The servants of God preserved in
great tribulation; or, good men kept in bad times.*[1]

I. THERE ARE, IN THE WORD OF GOD, INTIMATIONS OF DARK AND HEAVY STORMS
BURSTING OVER THE EARTH. The tribulation, during which these sealed ones are
guarded, is plainly the one referred to immediately before, indicated also in ver. 14 of this
chapter, as "the tribulation, the great one." That we must regard this as indicative of

[1] Dr. Boyd Carpenter's remarks on this passage are admirable.

manifold upheavings in different lands and ages is evident, not only from the considerations specified in preceding homilies, but also from the fact that those who are seen by the apostle as "coming" out of it are from all nations, and kindreds, and people, and tongues. Again and again wars, famine, pestilences, persecutions, revolutions, will desolate the earth, recurring again and again, ere the end shall come, at divers places and at divers times. There is, moreover, some great mystery of lawlessness which is yet to break forth. And again and again may the Church have to recall her Saviour's words, " Because iniquity shall abound, the love of many shall wax cold." No judgment from the hand of God is or can be so perilous for the world as these outbreaks of human sin. We know how they will end. The Lord will " consume them by the Spirit of his mouth, and destroy them with the brightness of his coming." But meanwhile, many will depart from the faith, but not all. For—

II. AMID THE SEVEREST TRIBULATIONS THERE WILL BE SOME WHO ARE THE SERVANTS OF GOD. It seems to us unquestionable that we are to regard the " Israel " here, not as the Jewish, but the Christian commonwealth, although here, as so often throughout the book, Jewish imagery is employed. But according to the text, it is not the *whole* of each tribe that are marked as the servants of God, only a number *out* of them. " They are not all Israel that are of Israel." " He is not a Jew which is one outwardly." "Not every one that saith unto me, Lord, Lord, shall enter the kingdom of heaven." They who are really with Christ are " called, and chosen, and faithful." They " follow the Lamb whithersoever he goeth." And when the sorest and severest trials come, there will certainly be many who are the true Israel of God.

III. ON EVERY SERVANT OF GOD THERE IS A GRACIOUS EYE. In the midst of a world's sin and unbelief they are recognized *individually* as bearing a distinct and separate character. Each one is known. No one is confounded with another. " The eye of the Lord is on them that fear him." Every one is known who sighs and cries over the abominations of Jerusalem. " They that feared the Lord spake often one to another, and the Lord hearkened and heard it." Every infant voice that prays is heard amid the roar of the elements and the crash of worlds. Every household altar, every family circle bending before the throne, every group of friends holding converse on the things of God,—all, all are known on high. Each one is the object of loving and of infinite regard. Not one is left outside the holy thought and care of our redeeming God. He watches over all. He singles out each.

IV. CONSEQUENTLY, ON EVERY SERVANT OF GOD THERE IS A SPECIAL SEAL. When the Israelites were to be marked off from the Egyptians, there was the sign on their doorposts—the blood of the slain lamb. When, in Ezekiel's vision, the angel of destruction goes forth, the cry is heard, " Go not near the men on whom is my mark." Again and again in the New Testament is there mention of a Divine " seal " on believers. The symbol is reproduced here. The seal is (1) a token of redemption ; (2) a mark of possession ; (3) an indication of resemblance ; (4) a badge of service ; (5) a pledge of security. The mark is, indeed, visible to no human eye. It is graven by no human hand. The writing is by the finger of God, and it cannot be obliterated. Whatever the trouble may be that sweeps over the world, the sealed one will never be lost in the crowd.

V. ON ALL WHO BEAR THIS SEAL, DIVINE PROTECTION SHALL REST. So runs the text. "Hurt not . . . until." Divine judgments are represented as actually being kept back for their sakes. We get the same thought in the Book of Genesis : " I cannot do anything till thou be come thither." We have its equivalent in the Lord's own words, " But there shall not a hair of your head perish." And if it were necessary for the safety of one servant of God, the lightning should be held in check, and the thunders forbear to roll, till that one had escaped out of danger. Nor must we lose sight of the Divine purpose in this. It is that there may be a living seed of virtue and piety left on earth whatever judgments may befall. *How* that may yet be secured we cannot say. We can but gather from what God has already done. We know : 1. That God has wondrously guarded the life of believers in times of peril : Daniel ; Shadrach, Meshach, and Abednego ; Ezra ; Rafaravavy ; Luther. 2. That they have been kept alive in famine : Elijah. Again and again is it proved here, " They that seek the Lord shall not want any good thing." Amid the darkest and the hardest times, when perils have abounded, when doctrine has been corrupted and even disowned, then has God kept for himself " a holy seed," and has enabled his witnesses to put on an " armour of light," from which foul error glanced off in the twinkling of an eye! This is the history of the past. This is the fact of the present. This is the forecast for the future. The same faithful care of which many can even now bear witness shall be continued till the last believer is safely gathered home.

VI. THE DOCTRINES TAUGHT IN THIS SECTION ARE FULL OF BLESSED TEACHING. 1. *The fact that there is a Divine recognition of every true and pure one, even in the worst of times, should inspire every struggler for the right with a holy courage.* Some may, in severe struggles, be so disheartened that they are ready to say, " It is of no use. I cannot breast the storm. I'll give up. The conflict is too severe." No, no. Let them pause ere coming to such a conclusion. "The eyes of the Lord run to and fro through the whole earth, to show himself strong in the behalf of those whose heart is perfect towards him." If they are clinging to the Lord, his seal is on them. He sees them. He cares for them, and he will bring them through. 2. *This fact should lead to the fresh exercise of holy trust.* The representation of our text is a revelation to faith. It would be valuable, even though it were but the reasonable tenet of a philosopher; but it is priceless as the revelation of our God. In the former light it would be attainable by the few; in the latter it is addressed to all. It is a Divine assurance in which faith may find infinite repose. " God is my Salvation : I will trust, and not be afraid." 3. *This fact is also of great service as an illustration of the Divine method of securing the triumph of righteousness and truth,* viz. by preserving in the world men who are right and true. There is no other way. But there is this. It is God's way, and it is one the carrying out of which he alone can ensure. God will shake the heavens and the earth, but only with the view of ensuring that "things which cannot be shaken may remain." God will let nothing be lost which is worth keeping. "Every plant which my heavenly Father hath not planted shall be rooted up." But all that is good and pure and God-like will live through every storm. 4. *This fact shows us what infinite joy and wisdom attach to the service of God.* " In peaceful times, when matters go well," says one, "and there is a fair wind, one is not so deeply sensible of this. . . . But when times of tribulation and chastisement arise, then does the Divine election form a blessed feature in the condition of those who are under the protection of the Almighty." Whatever the storm carries off, that which belongs to God must remain unharmed. Then it is no vain thing to serve the Lord. It is worth while to be faithful even in the most troublous times. 5. *This fact shows up most strikingly the old truth that " the Lord doth put a difference"* between those who are his and those who are not. Always the difference is infinite. But it is not always manifest. It will be some day. " Behold, the day cometh, that shall burn as an oven. . . . Then shall ye return, and discern between the righteous and the wicked, between him that serveth God and him that serveth him not." When "every mountain and island are moved out of their places," and every refuge of lies shames those who have hidden therein, all who are on the " Rock of ages " shall be eternally secure!

Vers. 9—17.— *The Church above, caught up out of the great tribulation.* We have before called attention to the fact that in this chapter we have, first, a part of the Church on earth, sealed in the tribulation ; second, a part of the Church in heaven caught up out of it.[1] The first and most natural inquiry concerning the second part of this chapter is, "At what point of time are we to fix the occurring of the glorious realities set forth in this vision ?" And from the structure of the chapter the reply which is necessitated thereby is as obvious as the question itself is natural. It is evidently while the tribulation, the great one, is raging below that the blessed ones are seen in perfect calm. For this part of the vision comes, like the former part, not at the close of all things, but between the sixth and the seventh seals. Nor is this the only clue we have. In ver. 14 we read, "These are they which are coming out of the tribulation, the great one ; " not, " These are they which *came,*" as if all were past; nor yet, " These are they which *will come,*" as if all were future ; but, " These are they which *are coming.*" There is a continuous pouring in of them from the world of care to the realm of peace ; and this will go on till all be gathered home. At the same time, it will be well for us

---

[1] " The sealing assured us that God's hidden ones would be safe in trouble; this tells us that they have come safe out of it " (Bishop Boyd Carpenter, *in loc.*).

to observe that this passage is not necessarily a picture of the glorified state, for that will not be ushered in until the second coming of the Son of God. However true it may be that there is as real a continuity between it and the state here described as there is between the latter and their earthly life, still we need not confound the two stages of the development of being. Very much harm has been done to the revealed doctrine of the blessedness of the righteous after death by so speaking of it as to leave no apparent room for the distinction between it and the state of glory which will begin at the reappearing. As yet, however, the unfoldings of this book have not brought us so far on. We are still only at the sixth seal. The new heavens and the new earth are not yet in view. The great tribulation is not yet over. The Church of God is still a divided one, part on earth, and part in heaven. The first part shielded while in the midst of evil; the second part raised above it, caught up, while the tribulation is yet raging here, to the perfect calm that abides there. Hence the title of our present theme may be made even more specific, viz.—*A look at our friends who are already in heaven.* The paragraph before us suggests seven questions.

I. WHERE ARE THEY SEEN? Ver. 9, "Before the throne, and before the Lamb." These words give us no clue to the locality of heaven. This we do not need. Any part of "the Father's house" is home to his children. But they give us what is of far greater interest and moment. They represent rather a state than a place. "Before the throne." More conscious than when clad in fleshly garments here of the immediate, all-surrounding, and all-pervading presence of God. "Before the Lamb." More directly in view of that Saviour whom having not seen they loved. The veil of sense and the limitations of earth no longer obstruct their sight or cripple their service. They are for ever with their God, where they have wished and longed to be.

II. WHAT IS THEIR APPEARANCE? They are seen "standing." This word is not redundant. It is no pleonasm. They *stand*, in token of subjection and of service to him that *sitteth* upon the throne. They have "white robes." "The fine linen is the righteousness of saints." They are "without fault" before the throne of God. They have "palms in their hands"—tokens these at once of honour and of victory. The struggle is over. The conflict ended. The victory won.

III. WHENCE CAME THEY? "Out of every nation;" they are "of all tribes and peoples and tongues." The separation brought about by the sin and confusion of earth is done away in Christ. In heaven its effects disappear. There the barrier caused by diversity of tongues will cease. And the final union of all tongues and tribes in the heavenly state will present the true solution of the long-vexed question of the unity of the human race. Every land will yield its tribute of souls to Jesus, and will thus prove, in the common destiny of men, that God made of one blood all nations of men. In the immediate presence of God and the Lamb, "life's poor distinctions" will disappear for ever. It will be seen that Jew and Greek, bond and free, are all one in Christ Jesus.

IV. HOW CAME THEY THERE? The answer to this question is twofold. 1. *They came through the pathway of a common experience.* "Out of the great tribulation." One and all have had tribulation in some form or other. But they have left it all behind. They are freed from it now. [Note: The fact indicated here, that "the great tribulation" was one which touched "all nations, and kindreds, and peoples, and tongues," is of itself subversive of any theory which would limit it to a merely partial or local sorrow. The terms of the verse require us to regard the tribulation as widely extended both as to space and time.] However great the differences which mark the lot of men on earth, all who reach heaven will do so through "many tribulations." 2. *They reach heaven on the ground of a common redemption.* The atoning sacrifice of the Lord Jesus availed for them all. The cleansing virtue of a Saviour's grace purified them all. "They washed their robes;" *i.e.* in their earthly life they experienced this sanctifying grace. [Note: Here is suggested a mighty theme for the preacher in connection with the death of Christ, viz.: (1) That the death of Christ has a world-wide meaning. (2) That it will have a world-wide efficacy as long as the race shall last. (3) That it not only saves out of condemnation, but ensures a purifying power. (4) That therefore it will be the theme of universal song.] In that glorious world no impurity is seen.

V. WHAT DO THEY MISS? (Ver. 16.) 1. "They shall hunger no more," etc. They have no more the incumbrance of a bodily frame like this, demanding incessant attention. How often, when in this state, is the activity of the spiritual life interrupted by the demands of the fleshly life! In this respect, as well as others, the flesh lusteth against the spirit. The spirit is willing, but the flesh is weak. But on high, such clogs burden the blessed ones no more. 2. They are free from unfavourable influences from without. Neither shall the sun smite them with its scorching blaze, nor any heat —the quotation is from Isa. xlix. 10, where the Greek word means the sirocco, or scorching blast, and the Hebrew word, the mirage. We may include both. They are subject to no influences to lower spiritual vitality; no illusion of a hollow and deceitful world will again appear to lure them away. 3. No tear shall be shed. God shall wipe every tear away. "Perhaps this," said a great preacher, "is the tenderest little sentence in the whole Bible (one of the greatest geniuses born in these islands said he could never read it without a tear in his eye), 'God shall wipe away all tears from their eyes.'"[1] No more shall the mingled scenes of life and death agitate the soul. All dying shall be over. All sorrow have passed away. Blessed state, even if known mainly by such negatives as these!

VI. WHAT DO THEY ENJOY? 1. *The real presence of God.* Ver. 15, "He . . . shall dwell among them." It is not possible to give the sense of these glorious words except by a paraphrase. They include (1) the thought of a tent *over* them, and (2) that of an abiding presence *with* them (cf. Exod. xl. 34; Numb. ix. 15; Lev. xxvi. 11; Isa. iv. 5, 6; Ezek. xxxvii. 27). 2. *The Lamb . . . shall be their Shepherd.* He who is in relation to God the sacrificial Lamb, will be in relation to his people their tender Shepherd. "He that hath mercy on them shall lead them." 3. *They shall be led by* "*fountains of the water of life.*" Here they had droppings from the stream; there they have the fulness of the fountain. Here the water of life reached them through earthen channels; there they shall be at the fountain-head! Entire satisfaction. Perfect security and repose.

VII. HOW ARE THEY OCCUPIED? But one aspect of their occupation is given here. "They serve him day and night in his temple." The details of this service we must die to understand. Here we have presented to us the service of praise. Their song is to God and the Lamb. Their theme, "the salvation." And all the glory of it is ascribed equally to the Father and to the Son! We gather, indeed, one feature of this service— it is *unwearied* : "day and night." Probably each believer has his favourite thoughts about the heavenly state. "My favourite conception of heaven," says one, "is rest." "Mine," says another, "is work." "Mine," says a third, "is love." "Mine," says a fourth, "is praise." What a mercy that they will all be realized; yea, all be infinitely surpassed!

We may gather up, in conclusion, several inferences from these glorious disclosures of the heavenly state. 1. For the doctrine of continuity in its grandest form and in its highest application we must come to the Word of God. The life in God, begun here, is destined to live on without a break, and to know nothing but eternal advance! The life above is the continuation of one which was redeemed and renovated below. 2. Here, too, the true law of human progress is seen. It is not that the race shall advance while individuals become extinct, but that there shall be advance of the race by reason of and in the fact of the salvation of the individual. 3. Let us be supremely thankful to our Lord Jesus Christ that we are permitted to believe, not only in the progress of humanity, but also in our own. 4. It surely should be a great comfort to us to think of the blessed ones who are gone before, being thus caught up to this glorious life. 5. Let us magnify the grace of God in putting such honour on this little globe of ours, as to make it his nursery-ground on which he rears his plants for heaven. Here, here, the great work is going on of training characters which are to thrive *for ever* in more genial climes. The state of blessedness which is to ripen in another world is one which is begun here; and the thought of attaining to such blessedness may well have elevating power.

[1] 'The Divine Order,' by Rev. T. Jones, p. 27.

HOMILIES BY VARIOUS AUTHORS.

Vers. 2, 3.—*The sealed of God.* This chapter tells of a time of suspended judgment. All things were ready. The awful calamities told of when the sixth seal was broken are on the point of descending upon the earth. "But a whole chapter intervenes. Might it not be apprehended that amidst convulsions so terrific the Church itself might founder? Who shall secure Christ's servants against being involved in that catastrophe? Such is the misgiving to which the particular revelation now before us would minister." A season of suspense is commanded; destruction is to be delayed until the servants of God be sealed. The command comes from that quarter whence Christ himself, the Day-spring from on high, the Morning Star, came on his mission of mercy and of hope. The four winds are the symbols of God's judgments (cf. Jer. xlix. 36, 37). The angels who are about to let them loose are bidden pause. Like as, ere the last judgment came upon Egypt, there was time given to enable the people of God to sprinkle the lintel and door-posts of their houses with the blood of the Paschal lamb, which was God's seal of preservation for them. And like, too, to that remarkable parallel, from which, indeed, the imagery of our text is derived, which we find in Ezek. ix. 2—6, 11. As was the object of the sealing there, so it is here. Now, whether we take the primary reference of the impending judgments, which for a while were delayed in their execution, to be those, as we think, which were then about to fall upon Jerusalem and the apostate Church of Israel; or those which at the time of Constantine, through the threatened overwhelming of the empire, were imminent on her frontiers; or those which corruption, venality, and hypocrisy, engendered by Constantine's having made Christianity the court religion, were about to bring upon the Church; or—which is probably the most correct way to understand St. John—we include all these, and all other similar ones, not omitting the last great judgment of all, which at any time may have hung or shall hang over nations, Churches, and communities—however we interpret this revelation, it is as true as the judgments themselves that the merciful Lord does grant seasons of suspense, his judgments are delayed until his servants are marked, proclaimed as his own, and secured from real evil by his own sovereign and sacred seal. For historical illustrations of this sealing we may wisely turn to the pages of Josephus and of Gibbon, the historians of the Jewish war and of the fall of Rome. And so exact are oftentimes the correspondences between authentic history and these visions of St. John, that we can hardly be surprised that not a few have declared that what is called the historical interpretation of the book is the only true, reasonable, and reliable one. It certainly is fascinating for its interest, but as for its reliableness, that may be admitted when its advocates can show anything like near agreement amongst themselves. It is better, therefore, to take the broader view, which admits all these correspondences, and the applicability thereto of these various visions, but which refuses to limit their meaning and application to anything less than all like correspondences which have occurred since St. John wrote, and which shall occur to the end of time. Now, to a thoughtful observer, it can hardly be a question but what our own days are days of suspended judgment, and days also in which the sealing of the servants of God is going on. For man's sin, as ever, clamours for judgment from God, and righteousness wronged and slain upon the earth cries, like the blood of Abel, unto God that he should avenge it. And the judgment will one day come. The history of nations and Churches is scattered over with the records of such judgments, and will be so again, until men learn wisdom and turn unto the Lord. But our security, whenever they come, is in the seal of God, told of here. Let us think, then, of this seal, the sealed, and the sealing. And—

I. THE SEAL. 1. *What is it?* With the Scriptures in our hand, we can have no doubt that the Holy Spirit of God is meant (cf. 2 Cor. i. 21, 22; Eph. iv. 30). The work that he does in and upon his people is the sure sign and seal that they are his. "The Holy Spirit is God's seal. Where he is there is safety. Where he is God sees his mark, his own possession, one who belongs to him, one over whom he watches, one whom he will keep in that ' hour of temptation which shall come upon all the world, to try them that dwell upon the earth.' " 2. And this seal is *the holy character* which the Spirit of God creates in and impresses upon a man. The Spirit does other and blessed work upon us besides this. **It is by him we are led to put our trust in Christ;** by him we are assured that we are Christ's, and that he is ours, that we are pardoned, accepted, saved; by him also we are comforted and sustained under trial, and made possessors of the peace of God which passeth all understanding; and by him, hope, the blessed hope of eternal life, the onlook to things eternal, which is so full of joy, is created and preserved and strengthened more and more. But all this is *within* the man; the seal is that which is impressed *on* him, is that which we call the man's character. And it is a holy character, such as the Holy Spirit would of necessity produce. 3. And it is *the seal of the living God.* It belongs to him, his sign and mark. There is none other like it, nor has been, nor can be. Holy character can come but from the grace of God alone, from the operation of the Holy Spirit given by God in response to earnest desire. We cannot produce it in ourselves by any mere act of will, by any moral discipline, by any rules or regulations we may devise or adopt. Except a man be born of the Spirit he cannot become a member of the kingdom of God. Holy character—that which shone pre-eminently in the Lord Jesus Christ, who, as none other, was "holy, harmless, and undefiled," who "knew no sin"—is the result of the grace of God, is the impress of the seal of the living God, which is the Holy Spirit of God. 4. And it is *a visible thing.* The seal being "on their foreheads" is meant to teach this fact. And holy character is a visible thing. If invisible it assuredly does not exist. Men may prate for ever about their experiences and their feelings, but if there be no manifest holy character, then the seal of the living God is not there. Have we this seal? Is it plain and conspicuous as would be the impress of a seal upon our forehead? It is fatal to be without it; for "if any man have not the Spirit of Christ, he is none of his." Therefore to quicken our own self-inquiry in this matter, let us consider—

II. THE SEALED. And we observe concerning them: 1. *They are not numerous.* But twelve thousand out of each tribe—a very few compared with those left unsealed. A mere handful, but a "remnant saved." 2. And *they are out of, not coextensive with, the professing Church of God.* Not all Israel are of Israel (Rom. ix. 6). They all professed loudly to be of the seed of Abraham, but their entire history shows how little they, as a people, possessed the Spirit. To be a professed member of the Church may be quite another thing from being one of the sealed of God. 3. And they are *from no one part of the Church.* Twelve tribes are told of, not any one or two. "Nulla salus extra Ecclesiam," by which Rome means her Church and none other, for other she would affirm there is none. And the like sectarian exclusiveness is chargeable against not Rome alone. But wherever it is found, the fact told of here, that the sealed come from all sections of the Church, plainly condemns it. We ought to rejoice that in all Churches the sealed ones are to be found, and are limited to none. Indeed, those tribes which loomed largest in the eyes of men, such as Ephraim and Judah, furnished no more of these sealed ones than did those who were least, such as "little Benjamin," and other like smaller tribes. Many who were first should be last, and the last first. And it often is so still. 4. *Portions of the Church may become so corrupt as to furnish none of the sealed.* The tribe of Dan is left out. It first fell into idolatry, and was for centuries one of the head-quarters of that calf-worship whereby "Jeroboam made Israel to sin." This may account for its omission in this list of the tribes, and if so suggests the reason wherefore none of the chosen of God were found amongst its people. And there may be Churches and congregations now without one earnest godly person amongst them. Let us ask how is it with the Church or congregation to which we belong. 5. *They do not suffer from not belonging to any specially privileged portion of the Church.* If any tribe was specially privileged it was that of Levi. They were regarded as the Lord's portion; the priesthood belonged to them. They were deemed too sacred to be classed with the other more secular tribes. But here they have no advantage; they are with the rest, and no more of God's chosen come from them than from any other tribe. We might have thought it would have been otherwise; but it is not so, and it suggests the truth that the working of God's Spirit in and upon men is independent of what we call privilege. It is good and blessed to have means of grace, aids to worship and faith; but, if the soul will yield itself up to God, he will not let it suffer loss for the lack of these things when, as is often the case, they may not be had. 6. *The Lord knoweth them all.* "The foundation of the Lord standeth sure, having this seal, The Lord knoweth them that are his." In keeping with this we find the number of the sealed that which denotes fixedness and completeness. They are all there, all delivered, not from earthly trials, but from Divine judgments; not one of them is lost. Blessed are they on whom this seal of the living God is found. For note—

III. THE SEALING. What was its purpose and intents? These were various according to those whom it was designed should be affected by it. 1. *The sealed ones themselves.* (1) The sealing should assure them that God would ever keep a people for his Name in the midst of the earth. As they saw the seal of God upon here one and there another, and as they remembered how it had ever been so, they would be saved from the despair which fell upon Elijah, who thought he alone was left to stand up for God. But God showed him the seven thousand sealed ones, and so comforted him. And as we behold them now we are assured that such shall never be wanting. (2) It would mutually encourage them. It would show them that they were not alone; the joy and strength which come from the communion of saints would be theirs. (3) It would be full of help to themselves; for as a seal attests validity and genuineness in that to which it is attached, so this seal would prove that their title to be called children of God and heirs of eternal life was valid and true. And as a seal is a mark of ownership—like our government broad arrow on all its property—so this seal was God's declaration they were his; and blessed is that soul that is assured of this. And as a seal secures and guards, as the tomb of our Lord was sealed, so this seal is the guarantee of deliverance and safety amid all possible ill. It was this seal which made Paul break forth into that pæan of exultant praise with which the eighth chapter of his Epistle to the Romans concludes. And similar gladness shall it give to all upon whom this seal is found. But: 2. *To the unsealed* this sealing has intent and purpose. To lead them to confess the beauty of holiness. This has ever been the mighty converting force. The holy character wrought by the Spirit of God has made such impression upon the minds of ungodly men that they have been constrained to gaze at it, to admire, to confess its excellence and goodness, and to feel the wretched contrast of their own lives, and to long after the like seal of God for themselves. And so it has won many to inquire, to repent, to believe, and to be saved. "Let your light so shine," etc (Matt. v. 16). 3. *To the ministers of his judgments.* That they might spare the sealed ones. They do. The retreat of the Christians to Pella ere Jerusalem fell, the protection granted to the Church at Rome—Augustine tells of it—in the midst of the havoc that Alaric and his Huns wrought upon the rest of Rome, are illustrations. The passing over of the houses of Israel has been repeated again and again in like circumstances, and will be repeated whensoever such circumstances recur. As the badge of the white cross secures immunity in the midst of war to those who wear it, for it is known that they are ministers of mercy, go where they will, so the seal of the living God, the holy, beautiful, Christ-like lives of his people, have often made men love and honour them, prize and preserve them amid horrors of battle, or of famine, or of pestilence, or aught beside. And at the last great judgment-day, when the angels of wrath see the seal of the living God, they will pass over those on whom it is found. What urgency, then, does all this lead to St. Paul's well-known words, " Grieve not the Holy Spirit of God, whereby ye are sealed unto the day of redemption!"—S. C.

Ver. 3.—*The wrath-restraining power of righteousness.* "Hurt not the ... till we have sealed," etc. These words send back our thoughts to like words addressed to Lot at Sodom, by the angel who was urging him to flee therefrom. "Haste thee," said he, "escape thither [to Zoar]; for I cannot do anything till thou be come thither" (Gen. xix.). Sodom's ruin was suspended till Lot was safe. The wrath of God was ready to burst forth on the wicked cities of the plain, but it was restrained until the one righteous man in them was removed out of danger. "Until then," so the destroying angel said, "I cannot do anything." That incident is one out of many more, and our text tells of one of the chiefest of them, by which it is shown that goodness has greater power than wickedness. And this is a very instructive fact, and has parallels innumerable. God's recognition of the wrath-restraining might of righteousness is clearly shown in the prayer which Abraham offered for those sinful cities (Gen. xviii.). Abraham believed in it to so great an extent that he pleaded that if there were fifty, or forty-five, or forty, or thirty, or twenty, or even ten righteous found in those cities, the Lord would spare them for their sake. And the Lord promised in each case, even were there only ten, that he would. And how often guilty Israel was spared the vengeance due to their sins for the sake of Moses who interceded for them! And the covenant made with their fathers—how often that is given as the reason why God's gracious dealing was continued to them! And once and again we read of forbearance and goodness shown to miserably guilty monarchs, such as Rehoboam, Manasseh, and others, because of the favour God bore towards David, their great and godly ancestor. In the prophecy of Ezekiel (ix.) there is given the vision of the man with the ink-horn by his side, who, ere Jerusalem could be given over to vengeance, was commanded to set a mark on those who sighed and cried for the abominations done in her. That mark was as the blood of the Paschal lamb on the lintel and door-posts of the houses of Israel, which secured that household on whose dwelling it was found; and so, until this marking had taken place, the guilty Jerusalem could not be touched. And so here St. John sees an angel, having "the seal of the living God," who cries with a loud voice to the four angels to whom it was given to hurt the earth and the sea, saying, "Hurt not the earth, neither the sea, nor the trees, till we have sealed the servants of our God in their foreheads." Terrible judgments were about to break forth on the earth, but not until the servants of God were sealed could these judgments begin. *And historic fact* wonderfully corresponds to inspired vision. Before the actual blockade of Jerusalem by Titus, the Christians at Jerusalem, warned, as one ancient Father says, "by a certain oracle given to their leaders by revelation," or, as another says, "by an angel," took refuge across the Jordan, in the Peræan town of Pella. Thus from the horrors of that final siege, and from the fearful slaughter that went on in Jerusalem when at last the city was taken, these servants of God were delivered. And so also, we are told in Matt. xxiv., that ere the last judgment of the world takes place, the elect shall be gathered together from the four winds, from one end of heaven to the other. They shall be taken to be with their Lord, where the vengeance coming on his foes cannot harm them. But what in all these instances we would chiefly note is, not so much the blessed security of the righteous themselves when the evil day comes on sinful men, as the restraining power their presence has on the coming of that evil day; how it delays it, holds it back, sometimes altogether turns it aside, or when it comes shortens it; as our Saviour said, "For the elects' sake those days shall be shortened." Verily his disciples are "the salt of the earth"—that preserving force which hinders the world from becoming one mass of corruption. Without such salt human life would become putrescent, and must at once be buried out of sight. Everywhere and always the tares are allowed to continue and increase, not for their own sake, but for the sake of the wheat amid which they have been planted by the enemy. Unskilful servants crave permission to go and pull them up forthwith, but are forbidden by the Lord, "lest," he says, "in pulling up the tares ye pull up the wheat also." Because of the "few names in Sardis" which had not defiled their garments, that Church which had nothing but the name of a living Church was nevertheless spared; had she been altogether dead, she would not have been. It is everywhere true that, like as it is with the body, whilst the principle of life lingers, the process of corruption cannot do anything against it; but when life departs, then soon it returns "dust to dust, ashes to ashes," and our loveliest and dearest ones have to be buried out of our sight. So, too, is it *in the moral relations of man to God*. Where there is some good thing in man towards God, this spiritual life, faint though it be, acts as a mighty conservative force in the individual and in society at large. It is this which keeps earth from being as hell. Sometimes, in some places and in some respects, we almost feel that it is like hell, for life then and there seems so horrible; but more commonly there are scattered amongst society those persons, principles, and habits which still make life worth living, which are its preserving salt, which stay moral corruption, and hold back the Divine judgments against man's evil, and give hope of there being one day a realm in which "the people shall be all righteous," a new heaven and a new earth, wherein dwelleth righteousness. And what is true in the broader aspects of human life is true also *in individual and in more limited senses*. Have we not read of that beloved queen who interceded for the doomed citizens of Calais, and won from her stern husband the pardon which, but for the love he bore her, would never have been granted? Have we not known, also, instances—do we not perpetually see them?—in which former good conduct, righteous deeds done in days gone by, have tempered the severity with which otherwise failures in present conduct would be visited? How we grieve when some soldier-hero has deserved punishment! how we all feel that his past heroism should tell, as it does tell, in mitigation of his sentence! And have we not known many an instance in which, for the sake of some beloved and honoured one, whose name is ever dear to us, we show kindness to those they loved, though such may be utterly unworthy of kindness, and, but for the name they bear or the relationship in which they stand to those so dear to us, they would have been dealt with in far other way? These are but common instances in common life of that great law which underlies Scripture facts, such as that told of in our text. But *the supreme example* of all others of the wrath-restraining power of righteousness is seen *in the effects of our Saviour's work*, which we every one are advantaged by. Death was threatened against our first parents if they ate of the forbidden fruit. But why did not that death, which had been so solemnly declared, and so fearfully apprehended and shrunk from by the guilty parents of our race—why was not that death inflicted? In the day that the forbidden fruit was eaten, the eaters thereof did *not* die, but were spared. Why? The answer is the same as that which must be given if it be asked why *we* are spared, notwithstanding our sin and manifold ill desert. It is because Christ was and is the Propitiation for the sins of the whole world. Beneath the broad shelter of God's love in him, man's Mediator and Redeemer, we are sheltered, protected, saved. We are underneath the shadow of the Almighty; and so, likewise, were the first transgressors. Therefore their threatened doom was not executed. And still it is he who comes between us and the eternal consequences of our sins. The burden of their guilt, the terror of their condemnation, the sting of their remorse, the doom they merit,—all these and yet other consequences of our sin are by Christ warded off from every believer. They can do nothing against us whilst Christ has place in our hearts. He is the great High Priest, with censer full of the fragrant incense of his all-availing intercessions, who stands between the living and the dead, and so the plague is stayed. He is our City of Refuge, within which the avenger of blood can do us no harm; the one Propitiation, by whom our transgressions are covered over and done away. Blessed for ever be his Name! And if we ask—*Why is it that righteousness has this wrath-restraining power,* which in so many instances, and in this supreme instance especially, we have seen it has? the answer will be that given in the well-known words, " The righteous Lord loveth righteousness." Yes; he loveth it, and hence wherever it is found he showeth favour towards it, and for the sake of it will do and forbear to do much. As David for Jonathan's sake was willing to show kindness to any of the rival house of Saul, notwithstanding their disloyalty, so, for the sake of righteousness, all that belong to it, even though the relation be remote, are blessed because of it. It is dear to the heart of God; he has embodied it in his own nature; he has made it the foundation of his throne; it is the household law of his eternal home; he has written it upon the conscience of man; he has made obedience to it fruitful of reward, and disobedience of sorrow; in Christ he has manifested it to the world, and for the sake of it Christ was content to die. In every way conceivable God has shown his love for it, and hence we can understand wherefore it is that he invests it with such power that its presence in a community or family lays its hand even on his own hand, and restrains the vengeance that sin deserves. Yes; it is dear to the heart of God; " the righteous Lord loveth " it; only those who possess it stand in his presence or can be permitted to come there. And he has endowed it with an overcoming power, so that not only shall light have no counsel with darkness, but wherever it comes it immediately gives the signal for the darkness to flee away. So does righteousness, wherever it is, begin to make war with sin, and ultimately the victory shall be seen to be altogether its own. Though often beaten back and down, buffeted and trampled upon, yet it rises again and renews the conflict, and will carry it on until the righteous cause is triumphant and the evil overthrown. No wonder, therefore, that the righteous Lord loveth it, and for its sake does so many, so wonderful, and so gracious things. But now let us ask— *What is this all-important truth to teach us?* Surely it should arouse in our minds some such questions as these—*Am I in the Righteous One?* We have seen how he is the supreme example of righteousness restraining wrath. Ah! what shelter have we, or can we have, when the storm of the

Divine displeasure shall fall and beat upon us? Who then will be our refuge and strength, if Christ be not? "Behold, O God our Shield, and look on the face of thine anointed!" When we pray this prayer, who can we think of but the Lord Jesus Christ? He is our Shield, our Champion, our Defender. Are we, then, in him? "How shall we escape if we neglect so great salvation?" *And are we like that Righteous One?* If we be truly in him, we shall be in some measure like him; and if so, shall belong to that blessed company of whom Christ said, "Ye are the salt of the earth." What are we? Of those on whose account favour and grace are shown to a land, and life is made peaceful and wholesome; or of those who help to swell that torrent of iniquity which not only degrades, but destroys? Oh, how we ought *to value the presence of righteous men* in our midst! They are the true safeguards of our national well-being. It is upon the character of a people, more than on anything else, the general good depends. No favourable outward circumstances, no wise organization, no well-ordered political constitution, can long uphold any community if the character of its members be godless and depraved. Sore calamity must come upon them, as it ever has, ere long time elapse. Of what amazing folly and sin, then, are they guilty who persecute the godly; who do their bad best to detach them from the faith, and to make them deny their Lord? It is an undermining of the very foundations of the house in which we live; a destruction of that upon which our all depends. Oh, let us be afraid, even if we be not servants of Christ ourselves, to do anything which would injure them or lessen their influence and power. Remember God hath said, "He that toucheth you toucheth the apple of mine eye." But, by *surrender of yourself* to Christ, come amongst them; be of their number; help forward their cause. Times of judgment are coming; the great judgment of all draws nigh. But "who shall stand in that day?" The reply is not, "No one shall be able to stand," for some, many, shall. All shall who have on them the mark of God, the sealing of the servants of God—that seal of the Holy Spirit "whereby we are sealed unto the day of redemption." Oh that that mark may be more and more manifest on us now! So shall our Lord be glorified; so shall our fellow-men be blessed through us, whether they confess it or no; and so at last, when the consequences of ill-doing have to be borne, and the harvest of sin is reaped, then shall judgment be restrained until we are gathered where harm can never come.—S. C.

Ver. 12.— *What "Amen" means.* "Saying, Amen." There is probably no more dishonoured word in the Bible than this. It has come to mean, in the minds of many, a mere signal for leaving off—the beneficent word that announces that the time of weariness and restraint is over, and that they may go back to what is of far more interest to them than God's Word or worship can ever be. They look upon it as meaning no more than the word "Finis" at the end of a book, which tells them that there is no more to come. But when we remember that the word was one which was perpetually on our Saviour's lips, and that it is one of the august names which he claims for himself, we can at once see that to regard it as a mere mechanical symbol, as a mere note of termination, like a period or full stop, is terribly to degrade it, and such as it could never have been intended for. And we are all of us in danger of forgetting, in our frequent use of the word, what it really means. But its mere interest demands more respectful and reverent usage of it. *It is almost a universal word.* It is told of two strangers meeting on board ship in Eastern seas, and ignorant of each other's language, that they at length discovered that they had two words in common. One was "Hallelujah," and the other "Amen." You will hear this sacred word in Mohammedan mosques from Calcutta to Morocco, in all the liturgies of Greek, Roman, and Anglican Christians, and there is no sect of Christians anywhere that does not use it. And *it is a most ancient word.* It has come down to us from the ancient Jewish people, and was heard amidst the rocks of Sinai in those far-off days of old. It has been likened to one of those granite boulders which we sometimes find in the midst of a flat plain, and which has been borne along by old-world glaciers and torrents, and carried far away from its native home. So this word has been borne down by the stream of time till it has reached our shores and this our day. But its importance lies in the great spiritual truths it teaches us. As—

I. GOD'S DESIRE FOR OUR RESPONSE. The word is associated perpetually with the utterance of prayer and the declaration of Divine truth. Now, God desires such response: 1. *In worship.* "Let all the people say, Amen." It is the people's word, was so not alone in the Jewish Church, but in the Christian as well. Hence St. Paul pleads for the use of plain language in worship, so that the unlearned may be able to say "Amen" at the giving of thanks. And in the early Church the acts of the presiding minister were not deemed complete without the assent of the people in their loudly expressed "Amen." Especially was this so in thanksgiving at the Lord's Supper. The whole congregation so said "Amen" that it was as a shout or cheer, and was heard far off, and like a peal of thunder reverberating through the spacious church. But it is the inward assent and response that is craved; the outward goes for very little if this be lacking. And how can it be present when we allow ourselves—as so many do—in listlessness and inattention and indifference? But if it be present, how precious, how uplifting, how full of help, that worship becomes to those who unite in it! Let us hold down our minds, and as Abraham drove away the birds which sought to devour his sacrifice, so let us drive away those flitting, wandering thoughts which are ever on the wing, and which destroy our sacrifice of prayer or praise. But in order to this inward assent and response, there must be like faith. If I do not believe in God as the heavenly Father, as my Father, how can I say "Amen" to prayer addressed to him? If I regard the Lord Jesus as no more than a noble-hearted and saintly Jew, how can I prostrate myself in worship at his feet? But the chief hindrances to this inward response are not those of the intellect, but of the heart. It is not because we come to the house of God with our minds cobwebbed and confused with doubt, but rather because we come with hearts absorbed with worldly things, that the "Amen" God desires is not forthcoming, though our lips may loudly say, "Amen." What a falsehood the word becomes when our hearts are not in it! 2. *In regard to the declaration of truth.* It is given when the word comes with power. As when Chrysostom preached, the multitudes who thronged the vast church could not restrain themselves from shouts and cries and tears, so greatly were they moved. And the preaching of even false doctrine, as in the mosque at Mecca—so it has been related—yet when the people heartily believe, they are greatly moved by it, and break forth into loud cries of "Amen, amen!" under the spell of the preacher's voice, and by the power over them of the doctrines he and they alike believe. But God desires this response in regard to his truth; and again and again it has been given. At Pentecost; at Philippi, where the Lord opened the heart of Lydia, and then of the jailor; at Corinth, where Paul tells how unbelieving men came into the assembly, and, under the prophetic word, were convinced, and fell down and confessed the presence of God in their midst. But oh for much more of such response! As worship is no good without it, so neither is preaching, and nothing can compensate for it or be put in its place.

II. SINCERITY IS ESSENTIAL IN ALL OUR APPROACHES TO GOD. The word "Amen" comes from one which signifies "that which is reliable, that which can be trusted," as the massive foundation-stone, the strong pillar, or other such sure support. Our Lord declares of himself, "I am the Truth;" and St. John tells of him as "the Amen," which means the same. And St. Paul tells how all God's promises are "Yea and Amen in Christ Jesus." And before his most weighty words our Lord was wont to utter his "Amen, amen," which in our versions is rendered "Verily, verily." At the end of the books of the Bible it is generally found, and everywhere it is the attestation of the truth of what has been or is to be said. And at the end of our prayers, it is as if we protested, "Lord God, I mean this." Formerly men headed their wills with the words, "In the name of God, Amen." But the meaning is ever the same—a declaration of truth and sincerity in regard to that which it precedes or follows. And hence our being commanded to say "Amen" shows God's demand for sincerity. They who worship him must worship him in truth. It is like signing our name—a thing we are very careful about in our secular affairs, knowing the responsibility it involves. Would that we were similarly thoughtful when we utter, as we often do, this solemn word "Amen"!

III. CHRIST IS THE ALONE GUARANTEE AND PLEDGE OF SUCCESS. For "Amen" is one of Christ's own names. The word was ever on his lips, and he is "the Amen." And his love and power lie underneath and behind it wherever it is sincerely uttered. It is a virtual calling upon him for his help—a call he will not disdain. If he be "the Amen" of our prayer and service, then he will make that real which we can only ask may be so. It is his endorsement of our petition. And when at length life's pilgrimage is done, and the shadows of our earthly days are deepening down into the night of death, if our hope and trust be in him who is "the Amen," then amidst the increasing gloom we shall see him coming to us, according to his word that so he would come; and our last word shall be, "Amen. Even so, come, Lord Jesus."—S. C.

Vers. 14, 15.—*The redeemed in heaven.* "These are they," etc. We long to know something of the life to come, the unseen world, the abode of those who die in the Lord. And here in this chapter a glimpse, which suggests much more than it reveals, is given to us. Especially is this desire for knowledge concerning the blessed dead intense when any of our own beloved ones are amongst their number. And of whom is not this true? Hence we search the Scriptures to gather up any the least hint that they may give; we study the records of the transfiguration of our Lord on the holy mount; we ponder the many sayings of his apostles on this most interesting theme; and this section of the Book of the Revelation, which tells of it more expressly, has made the whole book precious for its sake. We know not where heaven is, but here we have a vivid picture of the place and those who dwell there. It was doubtless given in order to cheer the hearts of the afflicted and depressed Church of St. John's day, and we may well believe that it ministered blessed help and hope to them, as it has done to myriads since. Note—

I. WHO ARE IN HEAVEN. St. John tells us that: 1. *They are a multitude.* Heaven is no unpeopled place. It is the answer given by the Lord to the question his disciples asked him when he was on earth, "Are there few that be saved?" Then he did not see fit to answer it plainly, but here there can be no question as to the reply. For: 2. *They are "a great multitude,"* one that "no man can number." How could it be otherwise? Would God have created and perpetuated the race of mankind knowing—for how could he not know the issue of his own work, "Known unto God are all his works?"—that sin and Satan would win the most of them? How, in such case, could our Lord be said to have "destroyed the works of the devil"? Without doubt sin doth abound, but grace doth much more abound. If, at the time St. John was made glad through this vision, as we are through him, already there were in heaven this mighty multitude, what must they be now? and what will they be when the end cometh, and our blessed Lord hath delivered up the kingdom to the Father? They had already "begun to be merry" (Luke xv.). What must the holy mirth be now? and what shall it not be? 3. *A miscellaneous multitude.* "Out of every kindred and nation," etc. How greatly, then, do they err who think and teach that only those nations who here on earth have heard the joyful sound of Christ's holy gospel can furnish contingents to that redeemed throng upon whom St. John delightedly gazed! What did our Lord go to "the spirits in prison" for, as St. Peter tells us he did, if not to bring them there the joyful tidings which here on earth they had not heard? How little we yet comprehend of "the breadth, and length, and depth, and height" of the love of Christ! Surely this vision should help us to a larger understanding of that infinite love. 4. *To them all life had been full of trouble.* They had all of them "come out of great tribulation." Whilst we may not omit the final tribulation of which our Lord tells in Matt. xxiv., and to which the opening of the sixth seal refers, we cannot limit it to that. "Man is born to trouble;" he is "of few days, and full of misery." "The whole creation groaneth and travaileth together in pain until now." To how few would life be worth living were it not for the hope of a better one! But we are placed here as at a school, and the trials of life are the appointed methods of instruction whereby we unlearn evil and learn good. The poor often envy the rich; but if all were known, the lot in life, or rather ere eternal life be gained, of us all is much alike. "The rich and the poor meet together," and share in their common inheritance of trouble. But from all this they have now "come out," and are "before the throne of God and the Lamb." 5. *They had all been lost but for Christ.* For they had all sinned. None of them had kept their garments undefiled. But he who came "to seek and to save them that were lost" found them; by his Spirit drew them to himself; by his blood washed their sin-stained robes, and made them white; and now, all of them, not one excepted, are in heaven full of adoring gratitude to him who redeemed and saved them by his own blood. None are there on any other ground, nor can any ever be. On what, then, are we relying for the hope we all cherish of one day being where they are?

II. WHAT THEY DO THERE. 1. *They celebrate the heavenly harvest-home.* They carry "palms in their hands," branches of the palm. No reference is here to heathen uses of the palm as symbol of victory and the like. But far sweeter and holier reminiscence is awakened. The scene before us is the antitype of the most joyous and inspiriting of all the observances of Israel—that of the Feast of Tabernacles. It was held at the close of the year's outdoor labours; with it the season of rest began. "All was safely gathered in." It commemorated God's care of them in the old wilderness-days, and afterwards his continual care of them by the gifts of his providence. The feast was a most joyous one. The Jews said that he did not know joy who knew not the Feast of Tabernacles. One chief feature of the feast was the universal carrying of palm branches (cf. Neh. viii. 14—17). Such is the scene from which the imagery of St. John here is drawn. It told of the troubles of the wilderness ended; the harvest-home of the Church come. It speaks of everlasting joy. 2. *They serve.* Day and night in God's temple is this service rendered. But in another place St. John says, "I saw no temple therein;" and hence we must understand by the temple all heaven and earth, for all, as was the ancient temple, are to be filled with his glory. And as to the service, who can describe, who can limit, who can sufficiently set forth, its beneficence, its joy, its glory? 3. *They show forth the praises of God and the Lamb.* (Ver. 10.) Festal joy, service, worship, the worship which consists in heartfelt praise, —such are the occupations of heaven.

III. THEIR EXCEEDING BLESSEDNESS. 1. *They want not.* They neither hunger nor thirst. 2. *They weary not,* as in the travel and toil of the wilderness they had done, when the fierce heat of the sun smote them; and as in the hard toil of life. 3. *They weep not.* The poet Burns used to say he could never read this without tears. And when we think of what life is now—a place of tears—and that there there shall be none, one's heart may well rejoice. But there are also the unspeakable joys that come from: 4. *The realized presence and love of the Lord Jesus Christ.* He shall be as a Tent to cover them, as a Shepherd to feed them, as a Guide to lead them to fountains of living water.

CONCLUSION. Have we those we love in heaven? Rejoice concerning them. Are we on the way there ourselves?—S. C.

Vers. 1—8.—*The Church's security assured.* Although the vision of judgment has been granted to the seer, an arrest is put upon its execution, and an entirely new series of representations is given. It is illustrative of the entire character of the book. It is one long illustration of the going forth conquering and to conquer by him that sitteth on the white horse. But there is no chronology. The truth here illustrated is ever repeated. Not only in the final acts of judgment will the faithful people be secure, but when God sends his judgments upon the ungodly the Church has always his comforting assurance of protection. By this vision the heart of the Church is comforted. "Only with thine eyes shalt thou behold and see the reward of the wicked." Whatever judgments befall the earth, the righteous people are secure in the guardian love of their Lord. This is declared to the tried ones by the vision of the sealing. A vision which is—

I. A TOKEN OF THE DIVINE RECOGNITION OF EVERY INDIVIDUAL BELIEVER. Each is sealed on his forehead. "The Lord knoweth them that are his."

II. IT IS A PLEDGE OF PERSONAL SECURITY. In the general judgments many even of the faithful suffer. This is inevitable. But the anomalous words of our Lord shall be fulfilled, "Ye shall be delivered up by parents . . . put to death, hated of all men; and not a hair of your head shall perish." In all judgments the lowly believer may rest in the assurance of personal safety. All shall be well in the end if the Lord's seal is upon the forehead.

III. THE VISION IS A GRACIOUS REVELATION OF GOD. It is of his goodness that he has thus shown beforehand his careful defence of his own in times of judgment and fear. "I have prayed for thee, that thy faith fail not."

IV. THE VISION AFFORDS GROUND FOR THE UTMOST ENCOURAGEMENT TO FAITH AND

HOPE. It is a spring of pure consolation. The Divine warrant of safety each believer may ever carry with him. The cruelties of men may bring him suffering, but not the judgments of God. Ever may the disciples know that when the Lord proceeds to judgment he will first seal his own.—R. G.

Vers. 9—13.—*The Church triumphant.* The comfort of the former vision is heightened by a subsequent one. The host of God is sealed. Safety amidst judgment is pledged. But greater things are reserved. The holy seer is permitted to witness the Church in its final triumph.

I. THE FINAL TRIUMPHANT HOST IS INNUMERABLE. The former vision was limited, definite. It prepared the way for a larger view. The " little flock " has grown into an innumerable company. This is the true answer to the question, hitherto unanswered, " Lord, are there few that be saved ?" To a Church in its incipient condition a small and feeble folk in the midst of ungodly thousands, the vision of a final host beyond count is of the utmost comfort. It has ever been so.

II. THE FINALLY TRIUMPHANT CHURCH IS REPRESENTED IN ITS WIDE COMPREHENSION. It is "out of every nation." This is the true vision to be held before the eyes of the Church in her missionary labours. All tribes and all peoples and all tongues shall be finally found amongst the faithful and elect children.

III. THE TRIUMPHANT CHURCH IS EXALTED TO THE UTMOST HONOUR. They stand " before the throne and before the Lamb." Thus is indicated their individual recognition ; thus is fulfilled the word of their Lord's promise.

IV. THE CHURCH IS REPRESENTED IN ITS FINAL SANCTITY—" arrayed in white robes "—AND INVESTED WITH THE SYMBOLS OF TRIUMPHANT EXALTATION—" palms in their hands."

V. THE VISION REVEALS THE REDEEMED HOST ASCRIBING ITS REDEMPTION TO GOD AND THE LAMB. It is the becoming burden of the eternal song. All is " of him."

VI. THE CHURCH OF EARTH IS FOUND IN ALLIANCE WITH THE ANGELIC HOST OF HEAVEN. " All the angels were standing round about the throne."

VII. THE UNITED CHOIRS OF EARTH AND HEAVEN ASCRIBE TOGETHER ALL GLORY, HONOUR, MIGHT, MAJESTY, AND DOMINION UNTO GOD FOR EVER AND EVER.

Nothing more likely to comfort and uphold the Church struggling in the waves of bitter cruel persecution than this gracious vision. To the Church in all ages this has been the lofty reach of joyful anticipation.—R. G.

Vers. 13—17.—*The eternal blessedness.* The vision is yet heightened. A further brightness overspreads the scene. The comfort of hope is yet expanded. Arrested by one of the elders, the seer lowlily refrains from declaring who constitute the triumphant host, and receives the consoling assurance that they are from the fields of earthly suffering, toil, and danger. They are now exalted far above all worldly power. The final blessedness of the righteous is—

I. BLESSEDNESS FOR WHICH THEY ARE PREPARED BY EARTHLY TRIBULATION. Even the rugged ways of earthly obedience lead to heaven's gates. But all toil and tribulation are o'er.

II. The final blessedness is BASED ON AN ATTAINED SANCTITY. " They have washed their robes, and made them white in the blood of the Lamb."

III. This blessedness INCLUDES : 1. Recognition They are " before the throne of God." 2. Perpetual service. They serve God " day and night in his temple." 3. They enjoy the perfect protection of the Divine presence. " He that sitteth on the throne shall spread his tabernacle over them."

IV. IT SECURES THEM EXEMPTION FROM THE SORROWS OF THE EARTHLY LIFE. " They hunger no more, neither thirst any more," nor shall the sun or any heat strike upon them.

V. THE FINAL BLESSEDNESS OF THE RIGHTEOUS HAS ITS FRUITION IN A GRACIOUS ALLIANCE WITH THE ETERNAL. The Lamb " shall be their Shepherd," and shall guide them to the perpetual fountains of life and felicity ; and God shall himself exempt them from all further sorrow or suffering. He " shall wipe away every tear from their eyes." Thus every trace of the tribulation of earth shall be removed ; and blessedness of the highest possible character shall be the final lot of them who now endure for truth's sake. Thus in the midst of the earthly raging power is the persecuted Church of God assured, in all ages, of a final, a certain, and an ample recompense.—R. G.

Vers. 1—3.—*A sketch of an impending judgment.* "And after these things," etc. The text points to a judgment that is overhanging the world, entrusted to angels for its execution, and who are restrained in their work by a special messenger from heaven on account of the godly tenants of the earth. This is a view of the passage which scarcely admits of any data for a different opinion. From the words we see—
I. THE WORLD EXPOSED TO JUDGMENT. It is represented as exposed to "the four winds of the earth." Winds are the symbols of judgment. Thus in Jer. xlix. 36, 37 we read, "And upon Elam will I bring the four winds from the four quarters of heaven, and will scatter them toward all those winds; and there shall be no nation whither the outcasts of Elam shall not come. For I will cause Elam to be dismayed before their enemies, and before them that seek their life : and I will bring evil upon them, even my fierce anger, saith the Lord ; and I will send the sword after them, till I have consumed them." And in the prophecy of Daniel (vii. 2) we have these words, "I saw in my vision by night, and, behold, the four winds of the heaven strove upon the great sea." The *four* winds indicate the *universality* of the judgment. They were to come from the four points of the compass—north, south, east, west. Whether this universal judgment refers to the destruction of Jerusalem, or some other judicial event that is passed, or points to some future period of retribution in the history of the world, I stay not to inquire. One thing is certain, that there is a universal judgment impending over this earth. It hangs over "every corner of the earth." Its winds will rush in fearful tornadoes from all the points of the compass. Conscience, providence, and the Bible all point to this universal judgment.
II. THE JUDGMENT ENTRUSTED TO ANGELS. The words speak of "four angels, to whom it was given to hurt the earth and the sea." Angels are the ministers of God. He employs them to execute his judgments. 1. *They appeared amidst the terrors of Mount Sinai.* Deut. xxxiii. 2, "The Lord came from Sinai, and rose up from Seir unto them ; he shined forth from Mount Paran, and he came with ten thousands of saints : from his right hand went a fiery Law for them." Again in Ps. lxviii. 17 we read, "The chariots of God are twenty thousand, even thousands of angels : the Lord is among them, as in Sinai, in the holy place." 2. *They appeared with our Saviour in the destruction of Jerusalem.* (Matt. xxiv. 30, 31.) 3. *Angels have been frequently engaged in executing Divine judgment on this earth.* They acted in connection with the destruction of Sodom, and an angel dealt out judgment to the Egyptians in the destruction of their firstborn (Exod. xii. 22). An angel wreaked vengeance on the people of Jerusalem on account of the sin of David (2 Sam. xxiv. 16, 17). An angel destroyed the mighty army of Sennacherib (2 Kings xix. 35). 4. *Angels are represented as active in the final day of retribution.* (Matt. xiii. 39—41 ; xxv. 31 ; 1 Thess. iv. 16 ; 2 Thess. i. 7—9.)
III. THE ANGELS RESTRAINED BY A MEDIATOR. "And I saw another angel ascending from the east, having the seal of the living God : and he cried with a loud voice to the four angels, to whom it was given to hurt the earth and the sea, saying, Hurt not the earth, neither the sea, nor the trees, till we have sealed the servants of our God in their foreheads." Observe : 1. The *glorious origin* of this angel. He ascended "from the east ; " from the fountain of glory—the east, whence the stars appear, and the glorious sun comes forth to flood the world with light. 2. The *Divine credentials* of this angel. "Having the seal of the living God." 3. The *great earnestness* of this angel. "Cried with a loud voice." Who is this angel? Who is represented in this particular case I know not. But I know that the great angel of the covenant answers well this description. He came from the orient depths of glory with Divine credentials and with great earnestness, in order to stay the angels of retribution from executing their terrible commission. Our great Redeemer holds back the hand of the destroying angel, and the burden of his intercession is, "Hurt not the earth, neither the sea." To Christ we owe the postponement of the judgment.
IV. THE MEDIATOR RESTRAINING BECAUSE HIS WORK IS UNFINISHED. Why does this intercessory angel, rising from the glorious east, interpose to prevent the judicial angels from discharging their dread commission? Because there was a work to be

done. The servants of God were to be "sealed in their foreheads." The image of the sealing is derived from the Book of the Prophet Ezekiel (ix. 2—6, 11). Its object was to mark out certain persons as belonging to God, and thus to save them from the miseries of the impending judgment. The effect of the seal visible in the forehead would be like that of the blood on the door-posts of the Israelites in the last terrible plague of the Egyptians. " When he seeth it he will pass over the door, and will not suffer the destroyer to come in unto your houses to smite you." Two thoughts are suggested. 1. *That there are men who are yet to receive the seal of God.* Thousands in ages gone by have had his likeness impressed upon them, and thousands are being impressed in this age, but there are millions more to be sealed in future times. There are men from unborn generations who are to be sealed. 2. *That the judgment is delayed until the number of the sealed ones is complete.* " Hurt not the earth, neither the sea, nor the trees, *till* we have sealed," etc. Thus our blessed Mediator is keeping up the world until all his disciples are gathered into his fold, and his purposes of mercy realized. In the majesty of infinite mercy he stands as it were in the midst of the universe. He sees the storm of judgment brooding in the heavens. He sees the angels of justice quartered in every part of the firmament, ready to execute their terrible commission. He waves his hand, and bids them halt. " Hurt not the earth, neither the sea, nor the trees, till we have sealed the servants of our God in their foreheads." Let not even such a breath of judgment pass from your hand as shall wake a ripple on the " sea," or stir a leaf on the " trees." Let mercy reign supreme until my work is finished. Then, when all my redeemed ones are sealed with the seal of God "on their foreheads " and made secure, then let loose your awful winds. Let them rush with their tornadoes of fire, and roar with their thunders of retribution, and destroy this earth; for the mystery of God will be finished.

> " Accuse not Heaven's delay ; if loth to strike,
> Its judgments, like the thunder-gather'd storm,
> Are but the greater."

(Webster.)

D. T.

Vers. 1—8.—*The Divine management of the world.* " And after these things I saw four angels standing on the four corners of the earth," etc. The subject of these verses is the *Divine management of the world,* and they suggest two facts concerning it.

I. THAT GOD EMPLOYS THE HIGHEST ORDER OF CELESTIAL INTELLIGENCES IN THE CONDUCT OF HIS GOVERNMENT. " After these things [after this] I saw four angels standing on [at] the four corners of the earth." The existence of intelligences in the universe, varying in capacity and degree, but all loyal to Heaven and transcending immeasurably man's attributes of wisdom, power, and speed, is suggested by analogy and abundantly taught in the Scriptures, both the Old and the New. Now, these creatures are here represented as occupying all parts of nature, " standing on the four corners of the earth," and thus controlling the winds of the world—the east, the west, the south, and the north. They are endowed with power to turn the winds to any point of the compass, and to regulate them to any degree of power or temperature, raising them to a fury that will shake the earth, and reducing them to a calmness hushing the world to sleep. Is there anything absurd in this ? Assuredly not. It is natural, rational, and consistent with every part of nature. Everywhere through the universe God acts by mediation. Nowhere throughout immensity does he appear to act directly, matter on matter, and mind on all. The principle is enunciated in the Old Testament. " It shall come to pass in that day, I will hear, saith the Lord, I will hear the heavens, and they shall hear the earth; and the earth shall hear the corn, and the wine, and the oil ; and they shall hear Jezreel " (Hos. ii. 21, 22). The mere scientist accounts for the various objects and phenomena of the material world by what he calls blind forces or natural laws; I prefer ascribing all under God to the " angels standing on the four corners of the earth, and holding the four winds." A wonderful view of the universe, truly, we have here. True, a telescope opens to my vision world upon world and system upon system, until imagination reels at the prospect, and my spirit seems crushed with a sense of its own insignificance ; but in these words I have a telescope by which I see the wide fields of the air, the rolling planets, the minute and the vast, the proximate and the remote, peopled and working, reaching in regular gradation from my little being up to the ineffable throne, and all under God.

II. THAT GOD, IN EMPLOYING THESE AGENCIES, ENJOINS ON THEM A SPECIAL REGARD FOR THE INTERESTS OF REDEEMED MEN IN THE WORLD. "And I saw another angel ascending from the east, having the seal of the living God," etc. Why not "hurt the earth"? Why not reduce all nature to a wreck? There is a grand, benevolent reason : "till we have sealed the servants of our God in their foreheads." "Of the tribe of Judah were sealed," etc. (vers. 5—8). The Jewish mind regarded Israel as especially the elect of God, and all the tribes in their esteem were specially Divine. This, of course, was a fiction of national vanity. But take them here as a symbolical representation of all the truly good men upon the earth, and we have the idea that God requires all his intelligent ministries to regard the interests of such. The seal must be regarded as implying security. Here is an angel rising as it were from "the door of the dawn," from the east, with a seal in order to effect the security of the good. Angels, we are taught, are "ministering spirits, sent forth to minister to those who shall be the heirs of salvation." Numerous are the instances recorded in the Bible in which we see them render assistance to man. They rescued Lot from Sodom, and guarded Daniel in the lion's den; they directed Joseph and Mary into Egypt, and liberated the apostles from prison; they directed Cornelius to Peter, and wafted the spirit of Lazarus to the skies. They rejoice over the conversion of sinners; they have a charge over the righteous, they encamp round about them, they bear them up in their hands. Their ministry implies : 1. *That there is some method by which they can aid man.* 2. *That man's salvation is of paramount importance.* 3. *That service to the lowest is consonant with the highest greatness.* 4. *That man's obligation is to seek the spiritual good of his fellows.*—D. T.

Vers. 9—12.—*The human population in heaven (No. 1).* "After this I beheld, and, lo, a great multitude, which no man could number, of all nations," etc. There is one book, and only one, that presents to us humanity in heaven, and that is the Bible. This passage gives us a vision of unnumbered multitudes of men who once traversed this earthly scene of sin and sorrow, now in the bright world of the good. Of this human population in heaven four things are suggested.

I. ITS NUMBERS ARE TOO GREAT FOR CALCULATION. "After this I beheld, and, lo, [those things I saw, and behold] a great multitude which no man could number." The vastness of the population may be looked upon in four aspects. Here is : 1. *A reproof to all sectarianism.* Religious sects, which, alas! abound, even in Christendom, and which are a calumny on the gospel, nourish in the minds of their votaries the idea that heaven will be peopled mainly, if not entirely, by those within their own pale. Genuine religion knows nothing of sects. Men went to heaven by millions before churches or chapels existed. 2. *An encouragement to all Christly work.* The best men on earth are the men employed in a Christly spirit to make men Christly. They find the opposition so strong, the wicked so numerous, and their efforts apparently so unsuccessful, that they often lose heart. But let them realize that the human population of heaven, even in the days of John, was so vast that no arithmetic could calculate; that population has been increasing from that date to this, and will increase in future ages so that it may be that no human being will be found in the universe without a Christly heart. Hell is only a little cloud upon the azure of immensity, and that cloud may one day be blotted out; it is only one discordant note in the harmonies of God's great empire, and that note will ultimately be hushed in eternal silence. 3. *A response to all philanthropic desires.* In every human soul, I presume, there is an instinctive desire for the well-being of the race. True, this Divine instinct, like all others, is not only universally perverted, but dormant and submerged in depraved passions ; but it is there, and awaits a resurrection. Here is the response to such an instinct. 4. *An attestation of benevolent Creatorship.* There is atheology popular, even in England in these days, which propounds the belief that the millions of mankind are doomed to bondage and blackness and darkness for ever. Such a damnable doctrine reveals the Creator as malevolent, and spreads a gloom of ghastly horror over all created things. No; love is the fontal source of all things.

II. ITS VARIETY INCLUDES ALL THE RACES OF MANKIND. "Of all nations [out of every nation], and kindreds [of all tribes], and people, and tongues." All the men of this earth have their own little theatres of life and action. They are divided by space, by time, by physical relationship, by culture, by national distinctions, and thus become barbarians one to another. Now, from all these scenes and departments of life the human population in heaven is made up. The human population in heaven is not known as Britons, or Frenchmen, or Germans, etc., nor as those of noble or ignoble blood, nor as those speaking this language or that, but as one grand confederation and brotherhood, in which all distinctions are lost. Learn here: **1.** *That our highest aim should be to become true men.* We should struggle out of social castes, religious denominationalism, and national distinctions, and become true men, for these men alone populate heaven. **2.** *That our highest love should be for men.* Not love for lords or ladies, or nobles, or even for sages and poets, nor even for country, but for *men ;* reverence man everywhere, in whatever land we find him, in whatever condition; respect him because *he is a man.* A true man is the grandest creature under the heavens. Let us all become such, and respect such, and such only.

III. Its gloriousness transcends all description. "Stood [standing] before the throne, and before the Lamb, clothed with [arrayed in] white robes, and palms in their hands." Mark: 1. *Their position.* "Stood [standing] before the throne." This is an emblematic description of the highest dignity. Moral goodness, and that alone, is Divine dignity. The Divine throne is not material, it is spiritual; it is perfect *moral excellence.* 2. *Their attire.* "Clothed with [arrayed in] white robes." Life everywhere has its robes, its forms; robes which it makes for itself, which grow out of itself as foliage out of the vital sap. Souls have their robes, and holy souls have robes white with purity. All their manifestations are pure. 3. *Their blessed rest.* "Palms in their hands." The palms, Archbishop Trench considers, represents here not emblems of victory, but are emblems of rest.[1]

IV. Its engagements are rapturous in devotion. "And cried [they cry] with a loud [great] voice, saying, Salvation to [unto] our God which sitteth upon the throne, and unto the Lamb," etc. No doubt the engagements of this vast human population in heaven are very varied, according to their personal idiosyncrasies, capacities, and proclivities. But in every department there is worship, the Supreme is adored—adored not formally or perfunctorily, but earnestly; they cry with a loud voice, "Salvation!" *Restoration* from their former earthly condition is the master theme. Ah! what is included in this salvation? It is restoration from *ignorance* to *true knowledge,* from *impurity* to *holiness,* from *bondage* to soul-*liberty,* from *selfishness* to *benevolence,* from *materialism* to genuine *spirituality,* from the reign of *wrong* to the reign of *right.* This is the supreme theme of the saved in all worlds and for ever, and ascribed to God and none other in heaven or earth.—D. T.

Vers. 13—17.—*The human population in heaven* (*No.* 2). "And one of the elders answered, saying unto me, What are these which are arrayed in white robes? and whence came they?" etc. Here is an illustration of three facts in connection with the human population in heaven.

I. Their earthly life was marked by great trial. "And one of the elders answered, saying unto me, What are these which are arrayed in white robes? [these which are arrayed in the white robes, who are they?] and whence came they? And I said [say] unto him, Sir [my lord], thou knowest. And he said to me, These are they which came [come] out of [the] great tribulation." An elder in those realms—struck, it may be, with certain peculiarities in their appearance and worship—puts to John the interrogatory what they were, and whence they came, and the reply he receives is that they had come out of "great tribulation." Tribulation is the common lot of humanity, and ever the discipline of the good. 1. This should teach us *contentment* under our trials. "No temptation hath happened," etc. 2. This should inspire us with *magnanimity* under our trials. The tribulations are useful. Like the gales of the mariner, they bear us away from scenes on which our heart is set. The darkest thunder-cloud terrifies but for an hour; it soon passes away, and leaves the air clearer and the heavens brighter than before.

II. Their celestial circumstances are pre-eminently glorious. "Have washed

[1] See volume of sermons by Archbishop Trench, published by Macmillan, p. 365.

their robes, **and** made them white in the blood of the Lamb." Look at : 1. *Their appearance.* In white robes emblems of purity and conquest. 2. *Their position.* " They are before the throne." A throne is the emblem of regal authority, and before this throne we are always appearing in this life, but we are not conscious of it. 3. *Their employment.* " Serve him day and night; " indicating the entire consecration of their time and powers. They serve him in every department of action. Serve him *lovingly, wholly,* and *constantly.* 4. *Their companionship.* " He that sitteth on the throne shall dwell among [spread his tabernacle over] them." They enjoy intimate communion with the Sovereign of all. 5. *Their blessedness.* " They shall hunger no more, neither thirst any more; ... and God shall wipe away all tears." They are freed from evil, and brought into the full enjoyment of all blessedness.

III. THE DIFFERENCE BETWEEN THE EARTHLY AND HEAVENLY CONDITION IS ATTRIBUTABLE TO CHRIST. " They have washed their robes, and made them white in the blood of the Lamb. Therefore are they before the throne." Three things are implied : 1. That they were originally polluted. 2. That the self-sacrificing love of Christ has a purifying influence. 3. That their cleansing by this influence had taken place when on earth.

CONCLUSION. Mark well the " therefore " of the text. Why are men so different in heaven to what they are on earth—in character, circumstances, spirit, different ? Not because of the priestly services of any sect, nor because of their own intellectual attainments, but because they have had their " robes washed in the blood of the Lamb ; " it is because of Christ they are in heaven.—D. T.

EXPOSITION.

CHAPTER VIII.

Ver. 1.—**And when.** Καὶ ὅταν, instead of καὶ ὅτε (as in the other seals), is read in A, C, and gives a certain indefiniteness which does not belong to any of the rest (Alford). Ὅτε is, however, found in א, B, P, Andreas. **He** had opened the seventh seal; *he opened.* As in the case of the other seals, the silence accompanies the opening (see on ch. vi. 1, 3, 5, etc.). This completes the number, and sets the roll free (ch. v. 1). The contents of the roll do not, however, become visible, nor are they portrayed otherwise than by the silence of half an hour (see on ch. v. 1). **There was silence in heaven;** *there followed a silence* (Revised Version); *a silence became;* i.e. where there had not been silence previously, owing to the praises set forth at the close of ch. vii. This image may have been suggested by the silence kept by the congregation without, while the priest offered incense within the temple (cf. Luke i. 10). This thought, too, may have led to the following vision, in which the angel offers incense (ver. 3), and in this sense the vision of the trumpets may be said to have grown out of the seventh seal, though a similar act precedes the visions of the seals (see ch. v. 8). But in no other way is there any connection between the two visions; the events narrated under the vision of the trumpets are not an exposition of the seventh seal, but a separate vision, supplementing what has been set forth by the seven seals. The silence is typical of the eternal peace of

heaven, the **ineffable bliss** of which it is impossible for mortals to comprehend, and which is, therefore, symbolized by silence. In the same way the *new name* is left unexplained, as something beyond the knowledge of man in this life, and reserved for the life in heaven (see on ch. iii. 12). It is the sabbath of the Church's history, into the full comprehension of which man cannot now enter. The interpretation of this seal varies with different writers, according to the view taken of the vision as a whole. Bede, Primasius, Victorinus, Wordsworth, agree in considering that it denotes the beginning of eternal peace. Those who take the preterist view variously assign the *silence* to (1) the destruction of Jerusalem (Maurice); (2) A.D. 312—337 (King); (3) the period following A.D. 395 (Elliott); (4) the millennium (Lange); (5) the decree of Julian imposing silence on the Christians (De Lyra), etc.; Vitringa thinks it relates to the time when the Church will be triumphant on earth; Hengstenberg, the astonishment of Christ's enemies; Ebrard, the silence of creation in awe at the catastrophes about to happen; and Düsterdieck, similarly, the silence of those in heaven, waiting for the same events. **About the space of half an hour.** Most writers are agreed that the *half-hour* represents a *short* time. But if (as we have indicated above) the silence is typical of the eternal rest of heaven, how can it be short? Possibly the answer is that the shortness refers to the time during which the seer was contemplating this aspect of the vision. **He had** now arrived at the end; the fate of the Church had been in some measure foreshadowed, and the final assurance is peace in heaven. That part of the fate in store for the Church cannot be expounded by the seer. He is permitted, as it were, to visit the threshold for an instant, and then he is called away. His message is not yet complete; he is summoned to receive yet further revelations. But may not the half-hour signify "a long time"? The seer, in his vision, after beholding a succession of events, experiences a pause—complete silence for the space of half an hour. This time would appear almost interminable in such circumstances; and the phrase may therefore be intended to express "an exceedingly lengthened period," such as a stillness of such a length in the midst of numbers would appear to St. John. Here, then, closes the vision of the seals. The first four, prefaced by the assurance of final victory, deal with events more immediately connected with this life, and explain to the suffering Christian of all ages that it is part of God's eternal purpose that he should be exposed to persecution, trial, and temptation while in the world, and that such suffering is not the result of God's forgetfulness or heedlessness. The last three seals refer to three sets of events connected with the life hereafter. The fifth shows the security of those who have departed this life; the sixth portrays the safe gathering of God's own and the fear and condemnation of the unjust at the judgment-day; the seventh affords a prospect rather than a sight of the eternal sabbath of heaven, undescribed because indescribable. The whole is thus completed; the seer is called away to review the ages once more—to behold new visions, which shall impress more fully, and supplement, the truths which the visions of the seals have, in a measure, revealed.

Vers. 2—6 form a preface to the vision of the trumpets, and serve both to connect this vision with what has gone before, and to indicate the cause of this further revelation. The series of mysteries embraced under the seals is completed, and has so far accomplished its purpose, which is to fortify the patience of the saints by the assurance of God's providence and their ultimate victory and reward. But this is only one part of the seer's mission; there is not only a message of encouragement to the faithful, but a warning for the worldly and apostate. No doubt the same ground is covered to some extent by both announcements; since what is encouragement and hope for the righteous is judgment for the wicked. But whereas, in the vision of the seals, the punishment of the wicked holds a subsidiary place, being only introduced for the purpose of demonstrating God's protection of the just, in the vision of the trumpets the destruction of the ungodly is the main theme, being intended, like the denunciations of the prophets of old, for a warning to those in sin, if haply any may yet be saved. It may, indeed, be said to be an answer to the cry in ch. vi. 10, "How long, O Lord, holy and true, dost thou not judge and avenge our blood on them that dwell on the earth?" The same longsuffering delay of vengeance tempts the "foolish body" to say in his heart, "There is no God." While by the vision of the seals God is careful not to break the bruised reed, in the vision of the trumpets he vouchsafes a call to those who are less deserving of his consideration and mercy.

(1) The trumpets then form a series of visions denouncing God's judgments against the wicked.

(2) They form an independent vision, and do not grow out of the seventh seal, in the sense of portraying what is intended to be disclosed under that seal. The number seven, alike in the case of the seals and in that of the trumpets, indicates the complete nature of each series, which is moreover demonstrated by their general character.

(3) The incidents depicted are synchronous with those of the seals; that is to say, they relate to the history of mankind from the beginning to the end of time and the commencement of eternity.

(4) As in the case of the seals, they are general indications of God's judgments; and though particular events may be partial fulfilments, the complete fulfilment is in all time.

(5) In their general features there are some points of resemblance and some of difference on a comparison with the seals.

(a) They may be divided into groups of four and three. In both visions the first group of four deals more immediately with the natural world, the last group of three has more connection with the spiritual life.

(b) They terminate in a similar way, in the victory of the redeemed, who sing the praises of God.

(c) In both, greater elaboration or episode occurs after the sixth revelation.

(d) The nature of the seventh seal is un-disclosed, and this is to a certain extent paralleled in the trumpets by the silence concerning the third and last woe.

(e) In consonance with the general pur-pose of the trumpets, there is no preliminary assurance of victory as with the first seal; this is reserved to the end.

(6) Several reasons may be suggested for the employment of the figure of *trumpets*, by which to announce each vision.

(a) It was the instrument in use among the Israelites for assembling people, either for warlike or peaceful purposes (cf. Numb. x. 1, 9, 10).

(b) It was thus intimately connected with solemn proclamations or the delivery of God's messages of judgment or warning, and is thus used in the New Testament in describ-ing the judgment-day (cf. Lev. xxv. 9; Amos iii. 6; 1 Cor. xv. 52; 1 Thess. iv. 16).

(c) The use of trumpets on seven days at the destruction of Jericho, the type of all that is worldly, may have suggested the form of the vision here, in the announcement of the judgment and destruction of the world.

Ver. 2.—**And I saw the seven angels which stood before God; and to them were given seven trumpets;** *which stand* (Revised Version). "And I saw" introduces the new vision, as in ch. v. 1; vi. 1, etc. Probably not during the *silence* (as Alford), but sub-sequent to it. "The seven angels" probably refers to a particular order of angels, or rather to those with a special mission; though, with our limited knowledge, it is impossible to determine exactly who they are or what their mission is. The passage in Tobit xii. 15 is so similar as to be at once suggested: "I am Raphael, one of the seven holy angels which present the prayers of the saints." But here *the seven* do not present the prayers of the saints, but *another angel* does so (ver. 3). De Wette and others think *the seven* are archangels (cf. 1 Thess. iv. 16, "With the voice of the archangel, and with the trump of God"). Arethas, Ewald, etc., identify them with "the seven Spirits of God" (ch. i. 4; iv. 5; v. 6). Others incline to the opinion that *the seven* are only dis-tinguished from the other angels by being the seven who sound the trumpets, just as four others are alluded to in ch. vii. 1. (On the use of the number *seven*, see above; also on ch. i. 4; v. 1, etc.)

Ver. 3.—**And another angel came.** No particular angel is specified. Some writers, unable to accept the passage as meaning

that the Church's prayers are offered by means of an angel, prefer to believe that Christ himself is indicated. (Thus Bede, Elliott, Primasius, Vitringa.) But, besides that the difficulty has no real existence, the same expression occurs in ch. vii. 2, where there is no doubt of its meaning. Moreover, in no passage of the book is our Lord repre-sented under the form of an angel. With regard to the office of the angels, Alford remarks (while supporting the view that the word here bears the ordinary significa-tion), "They are simply λειτουργικὰ πνεύ-ματα, and the action here described is a portion of that their ministry. *Through whom* the prayers are offered, we all know. He is our only Mediator and channel of grace." So also Wordsworth, "The angel is not here represented as giving *efficacy* to the prayers of all saints, but as taking part in them. There is a *communication* of prayer between *all* saints (namely, the saints de-parted, and the saints on earth), and the *holy angels* in heaven." And stood at the altar. The Revisers, accepting the reading of ℵ, B, C, Andreas, adopt *over the altar.* The Authorized reading follows A, P, 1, 17, 36. Alford remarks, "'Επί with genitive, not simply *juxta*, nor *ante*, but *super*; so that his form appeared above it." *The altar* has been already mentioned (ch. vi. 9). If the view there taken be correct, and the *brazen altar* of sacrifice intended, the two altars mentioned in this verse are not iden-tical; the second represents the golden altar of incense which stood before the veil (Exod. xxx. 6), but which now stands before the throne of God, the veil having disap-peared. This view seems to be the correct one. The second altar is distinguished from the first by the addition of the qualifi-cation, "which was before the throne," as well as by the epithet "golden"—facts which are not mentioned in connection with the throne alluded to in ch. vi. 9. The order of events followed here, though not given in minute detail, resembles the ceremony of the Jewish worship. In the temple, the priest took burning coals from off the brazen altar, and proceeded to the altar of incense, on which to burn incense (Lev. xvi. 12, 13). There appears to be a kind of progression in the insight which the seer affords us of the heavenly worship. In ch. iv. 1 a door is opened, and St. John sees into heaven; he is, as it were, without the sanctuary. In this place he is permitted to advance in his vision within the sanctuary, and to observe the golden altar. In ch. xi. 19 and xv. 5 the most holy place is disclosed, and the ark of the covenant is seen. Alford and Düsterdieck believe only one altar is here mentioned, and identify it with that of ch. vi. 9. De Wette, Hengstenberg, Words-

worth, think one altar only is intended, and
that it is the altar of incense. Bengel,
Ebrard, Vitringa, support the view given
above. Bossuet says the altar is Christ, to
whom the angel brings incense, that is, the
prayers of the saints. Having a golden
censer. The word λιβανωτός is found only
here and in 1 Chron. ix. 29 (LXX.). In
the latter place it is rightly rendered "frankincense;" but the meaning here evidently
requires "censer." It is described as of
gold, in the same way that all the furniture
of the heavenly realms is described in the
Apocalypse. And there was given unto
him much incense. Apparently following
the analogy of the temple service, the first
angel brings in his *golden censer* fire from
the brazen altar of sacrifice, and now there
is "given unto him," by another angel, incense to burn at the *golden altar* of incense.
(For *incense*, see on ch. v. 8.) That he should
offer it with the prayers of all saints; *add
it unto the prayers of all the saints* (Revised
Version). The prayers are to be incensed,
so as to (typically) render them pure and
acceptable to God. Upon the golden altar
which was before the throne. That is,
probably, the altar of incense, distinct from
the altar mentioned earlier in this verse
(see above).

Ver. 4.—And the smoke of the incense,
which came with the prayers of the saints,
ascended up before God out of the angel's
hand; *and the smoke of the incense with the
prayers of the saints went up*, etc. (Revised
Version). The prayers, accompanied by the
incense, and typically purified by it, are
received by God. He hears the prayers;
and the judgments against the wicked, which
follow in the trumpet-visions, constitute the
answer to them. This makes more probable
the view that the following visions are
judgments against the world, and not (like
the seals) trials to the Church.

Ver. 5.—And the angel took the censer,
and filled it with fire of the altar, and cast
it into the earth; *taketh the censer, and he
filled it with the fire of the altar, and cast
it upon the earth* (Revised Version). The
angel now returns to the altar of burnt
offering, whence he takes fire, which he
casts upon the earth. This action denotes
that God's judgments are about to descend
on the earth, and it therefore forms the
visible token of God's acceptance of the
prayers of the saints, and his answer to
them. And there were voices, and thunderings, and lightnings, and an earthquake;
and there followed thunders, and voices, etc.
(Revised Version). The manifestation of
God's presence or of his judgments is continually accompanied by awe-striking phenomena, such as are here described (see on ch.
vi. 12).

Ver. 6.—And the seven angels which had
the seven trumpets prepared themselves to
sound. This verse takes up and continues
the narrative of ver. 2; the intervening
passage serves to indicate the immediate
cause of the judgments now about to descend, viz. the "prayers of the saints" (ver
4). (On the number *seven*, as signifying a
complete number, see ch. i. 4; v. 1, etc.)
Cf. the sounding of the trumpets at Jericho,
and the other passages quoted in the comment on ver. 2.

Ver. 7.—The first angel sounded; *and
the first sounded* (Revised Version). The
word "angel" should be omitted here,
though found in the other trumpets. The
first four are marked off from the last three
(as in the case of the seals) by distinctive
features. The first four refer to the natural
life, while the last three are connected more
closely with the spiritual life of man. The
first four are connected and interdependent;
the last three are distinct and more detached. The last three are specially marked
off by the announcement of the angel in
ver. 13. And there followed hail and fire
mingled with blood; *mingled in blood*. The
English Version is ambiguous, but the Greek
makes it clear that it is the hail and the
fire that are mingled, and that both together
are sent in blood. There is an evident likeness between the judgments of the trumpets
and the plagues of Egypt. The resemblance
is only general, but it serves to corroborate
the belief that the trumpets declare God's
judgments on the world, not the trials of
the Church. The Church is the true Israel
which exists uninjured by these manifestations of God's wrath in the midst of the
world of Egyptian wickedness. The question next naturally arises—What are the
judgments referred to, which are thus to
afflict the ungodly while leaving the righteous
unhurt; and when and how they are to take
place? The answer evidently is — All
troubles of the wicked, which are the consequence of misdoing, whether these troubles
overtake them in this life or in the life to
come. In the words of Alford, "These
punishments are not merely direct inflictions of plagues, but consist in great part of
that judicial retribution on them that know
not God, which arises from their own depravity, and in which their own sins are
made to punish themselves." This seems
to follow from the view which we have
taken of the trumpet-visions. They depict
God's judgments on the wicked in all ages.
Just as the seal-visions were found to relate
to the trials of God's people in all time, and
the fulfilment is not completed by any one
event or series of events, so now the seer is
called upon to return, as it were, to his
former starting-point, and follow out a new

path, where he would find displayed the troubles which have afflicted or shall afflict the ungodly. It is very doubtful how much of the imagery used in this series of visions is to be interpreted as applying to some definite event, and how much is to be considered merely as the accessories of the picture, necessitated by the employment of the symbol, and not needing particular interpretation. It is possible that the seer intended first to set forth the judgments which were to descend on those powers which, at the time of the vision, were pressing so heavily upon Christians, and among which the Roman empire held the prominent place. But it also seems probable that the woes symbolized are general types of the judgments in store for the wicked of all ages, perhaps in this life, certainly at the last day. The *blood* is not found in Exodus. It is mentioned in close connection with hailstones and fire in Ezek. xxxviii. 22, and a similar thought occurs in Joel ii. 30. The passage may describe the ruin wrought by war; the consequences of fire and sword. Wordsworth sees the fulfilment in the Gothic invasion of Rome, which descended from the *north*, here typified by the *hailstorm* (but see on ch. xvi. 21). The vision would thus answer to that of the second seal, though with this difference, that under the seal war was permitted as a trial to the Church; here it is sent as God's vengeance against the persecutors. And they were cast upon the earth. "That is," says Wordsworth, "on the earthly power, opposed to Christ and his Church, which is the kingdom of heaven." But the words seem rather to describe the destruction of inanimate creation, as in the seventh plague of Egypt. The punishment would undoubtedly fall upon mankind eventually, though immediately upon the earth and its productions. Vitringa says the *earth* denotes the Roman empire; the *sea*, the barbarous races. And the third part of trees was burnt up, and all green grass was burnt up. Insert *and the third part of the earth was burnt up*, as in the Revised Version. "A third of all the trees, etc., on the earth," rather than "all the trees, etc., on a specified third part of the earth." The *third part* is almost unanimously considered to represent "a large part, but such that the greater part was still uninjured." We are reminded again of the seventh plague, where "the flax and the barley were smitten: but the wheat and the rie were not smitten" (Exod. ix. 31, 32). Wordsworth interprets the *trees* to mean the "princes" of the Roman empire; the *grass*, the common people. So also Hengstenberg. Elliott thinks "the third part of the earth" denotes the western part of the Roman empire, the

eastern and central parts at first escaping the visitation. Bengel sees here a type of the wars of Trajan and Hadrian. Vitringa considers that the famine under Gallus is signified. Renan points to the storms of A.D. 63—68 as the fulfilment.

Vers. 8, 9.—And the second angel sounded, and as it were a great mountain burning with fire was cast into the sea. Jer. li. 25 contains a somewhat similar description, with, however, a different meaning. There the mountain is the heathen power; here it is the instrument of the punishment of the ungodly world. Alford objects to calling the mountain a volcano, though that, or something of the same nature, seems obviously to be meant. The contiguity of such appearances to St. John in the Isle of Patmos may have suggested the idea. The judgments appear to increase in severity as we go on. The first affects vegetation, thus causing trouble, but not destruction to men; the second begins to affect animal life; the third causes many men to die; and the following ones affect men as direct punishments. The vision may be said generally to typify great trouble and commotion. The figure is used in other places to denote something remarkable and awe-inspiring (cf. Matt. xxi. 21; 1 Cor. xiii. 2; Job ix. 5; xxviii. 9; Judg. v. 5; 1 Kings xix. 11; Ps. xlvi. 2; Isa. xxxiv. 3; liv. 10; Ezek. xxxviii. 20; Micah i. 4; Nah. i. 5). It is also the symbol of a great power. In Isa. ii. 2 it signifies the Church; in Amos iv. 1 an earthly power; in Isa. xli. 15 the enemies of Israel. We may therefore conclude that a judgment of great magnitude and force is foretold; and though it is possible to point to particular events (such as the overthrow of Rome by the Gothic power) as a fulfilment of the prophecy, yet we must remember that the complete fulfilment will not be accomplished until "all enemies are put under his feet." And the third part of the sea became blood; and the third part of the creatures which were in the sea, and had life, died; and the third part of the ships were destroyed; *even they that had life* (Revised Version). (On the "third part," see on ver. 7.) Whether one third part of the sea, separated in some way from the rest, and all the creatures in that third part, or whether a third part diffused over the whole extent, is meant, it is impossible to say. The whole is a vision, and not subject to natural laws. The meaning is evident. As before, a large part, but not the largest, is signified :and this time the judgment is directed against another portion of creation. The sea, as well as the productions of the earth, can be used by God as his agent by which to punish and warn mankind. The attempt to press the vision into a particular application has led to a variety of interpretations. Wordsworth and Elliott both think that the destruction of Roman ships is foretold; the former pointing to the ships as the instruments of commerce and luxury, the latter referring to the destruction of the Roman navy. Bengel, Grotius, Vitringa, see here a vision of war. Hengstenberg believes the *sea* to typify this world; the *living creatures*, mankind; and the *ships*, villages and towns. Those who place the fulfilment of the vision in time subsequent to the sealing of ch. vii. fail to see that the trumpets do not follow the seals in chronological order, but that both are being fulfilled side by side in the same epoch; viz. that of the existence of man.

Ver. 10.—And the third angel sounded, and there fell a great star from heaven, burning as it were a lamp. In the Old Testament trouble is foretold under the symbol of darkened stars (cf. Ezek. xxxii. 7; Joel ii. 10). In Matt. xxiv. 29 the falling of stars is part of the general picture of the coming of the judgment-day. The description here may therefore symbolize an act of judgment—one more of the troubles inflicted by God upon the guilty world. The frequent use of the symbol, *star*, as a type of one in an exalted position, has led most commentators to interpret the star of individual rulers, especially of those who poisoned the waters of Divine truth by heresy. But it seems more likely that the event here portrayed carries one step further the description of God's vengeance on the wicked, which has been already partially set forth. At first vegetation, then the sea, now the land waters, are smitten. The star, as the means employed by God, is typical of the awe-striking nature of the punishment, and is indicative of the fact that the judgment is the act of God, and proceeds directly from heaven, and is not to be attributed to merely natural circumstances. And it fell upon the third part of the rivers, and upon the fountains of waters. Not upon a third part of the fountains, but upon all fountains, just as in ver. 7 "all green grass" is visited with the plague. As stated above, another part of creation (and therefore another portion of mankind) is afflicted. It is, of course, impossible to point out the complete fulfilment of this judgment, which is yet being fulfilled, but we may mention as illustrations the trouble caused to man by means of land waters, by floods, by drought, by pestilence. As before, only *part* suffers from this visitation; the greater part is spared.

Ver. 11.—And the name of the star is called Wormwood. The plant known to us under the name of *wormwood* is doubtless identical with the Ἄψινθος of this passage.

The present English word is a corruption of *wer-mód* (equivalent to *ware-mood*), which may be rendered "mind-preserver," a name given to the plant by the Saxons, on account of its fancied virtues; for it was believed to be a protection against madness. Such properties were formerly frequently ascribed to plants possessing bitter and nauseous tastes, such as that of the wormwood. Varieties of the plant are common in Palestine, and are widely distributed in the world. Among the ancients it was typical of bitter sorrow. Thus Lam. iii. 19, "Remembering my misery, the wormwood and the gall;" Jer. ix. 15, "I will feed them with wormwood." Here, therefore, the name indicates the effect of the star, viz. to cause intense trouble and sorrow. And the third part of the waters became wormwood; that is, became bitter as wormwood, that is, charged with sorrow and disaster. The general effect of the incident is described in the name given to the chief actor, as in the case of the fourth seal (see ch. vi. 8). And many men died of the waters, because they were made bitter; *many of the men.* Possibly (though not necessarily) of the men dwelling near the waters. For the first time mention is made of the death of *men*, though, doubtless, it is implied in the preceding judgments. We may notice the contrast in the miracles of Moses, who sweetened the waters of Marah (Exod. xv.), and of Elisha (2 Kings ii. 22).

Ver. 12.—And the fourth angel sounded, and the third part of the sun was smitten, and the third part of the moon, and the third part of the stars. Still the created universe is the direct object of these visitations. The planets were smitten, but we are not told with what instrument. As Alford points out, this may teach us not to lay too great stress upon that part of the visions which describes the means. Our attention is to be fixed upon the effect, the stroke, not upon the mountain or the star by whose means the result is attained. (For the signification of *the third part, vide supra.*) In the Bible, frequent use is made of this figure to express trouble and commotion (see Isa. xiii. 10; xxiv. 23; Jer. xv. 9; Ezek. xxxii. 7; Amos viii. 9; Matt. xxiv. 29). The sun, etc., are also looked upon as examples of stability. Thus Ps. lxxii. 5, "As long as the sun and moon endure" (see also Ps. lxxii. 17; lxxxix. 36). The vision may therefore be suggestive of God's power over things the most permanent and stable, and thus demonstrate to Christians his ability to punish "the ungodly who prosper in the world." Thus Job ix. 7 attributes omnipotence to God, "which commandeth the sun, and it riseth not; and sealeth up the stars" (see also Ps. cxxxvi.

8; Jer. xxxi. 35). Thus, then, God can turn even the benign influences of the sun and planets into means for the destruction of man. In the countless evils which have their origin in the excess or defect of the power of the sun, we may see an illustration of the fulfilment of this judgment. We may point out that the very existence of such visitations as are here portrayed preclude the possibility of the fulfilment of the trumpet-visions being subsequent in time to those of the seals. So as the third part of them was darkened, and the day shone not for a third part of it, and the night likewise; *that the third part of them should be darkened, and the day should not shine for the third part of it, and the night in like manner.* Probably, total darkness for a third part of the day and night is meant; not a third of the usual amount of light during the whole day and night (as Bengel and others). Renan, as a preterist, sees the fulfilment in the eclipses of A.D. 68. De Lyra, Wordsworth, and others see in this judgment a symbol of the infidelity, heresies, apostasies, and confusions in the world in the seventh century and at other times. Vitringa, adopting the historical view, refers the fulfilment to particular periods of the Roman empire.

Ver. 13—And I beheld, and heard an angel. "An eagle" (Revised Version) is read in ℵ, A, B, Vulgate, Syriac, Coptic, etc., while "angel" is found in P, 1, 16, 34, 47, etc. One manuscript (13) has ἀγγέλου ὡς ἀετοῦ. St. John sees *one eagle*, the symbol of what is swift and unerring in swooping upon its prey. Thus Job ix. 26, "The eagle that hasteth to the prey" (see also Hab. i. 8; 2 Sam. i. 23). This is the meaning of the appearance of *the eagle*, which announces the swiftness and certainty of the

coming woes. De Wette and others unnecessarily understand "an angel in the form of an eagle." De Lyra interprets it as St. John himself. Wordsworth, relying chiefly on the force of εἷς, believes that Christ is signified; but it is extremely doubtful whether the force of the numeral can be pressed so far. Others see a reference to the Roman legions, etc. The figure may have been suggested by Matt. xxiv. 28. Flying through the midst of heaven; *flying in mid heaven* (Revised Version). Not "midway between earth and heaven," but "in the direct line of the sun." The word is found only here and in ch. xiv. 6 and xix. 17. In the former it is rendered as in this place, in the latter it is translated "in the sun." The eagle is thus plainly visible to all. Saying with a loud voice, Woe, woe, woe, to the inhabiters of the earth! "Woe" is followed by "inhabiters" in the accusative case, according to ℵ, B; though the dative is read in A, P, and some cursives. "The inhabiters of the earth" are the ungodly, the worldly, those on whom God's wrath had been invoked by the saints at rest (ch. vi. 10), whose prayer is now answered The triple denunciation renders the threatened judgments more emphatic and terrible. By reason of the other voices of the trumpet of the three angels, which are yet to sound; Greek, *out of the other voices* (denoting from whence the woe proceeds) *who are yet to sound.* "Trumpet," in the singular, because taken distributively—"of each trumpet." The three woes are described in (1) ch. ix. 1—11; (2) ch. ix. 12—21; (3) ch. xi. 15—19. They perhaps refer to spiritual troubles, instead of being concerned (as in the case of the first four trumpets) with temporal judgments.

HOMILETICS.

Ver. 1.—*Silence in heaven.* "Silence in heaven"? and that for "about the space of half an hour"?[1] What *can* this mean, or how can it furnish an expositor with material for instructive teaching? The question is a natural one, and it is capable of being answered. This verse is neither to be dismissed as if unintelligible, nor slighted as if unimportant. It is full of most intense significance, and will be found to illustrate the truth that some of the most obscure and unpromising verses of the Word of God do yield to the devout and careful student the most stimulating and helpful teaching. It will be remembered that the sixth chapter closed amid representations of gloom and tribulation; in which the alarm was so great that many would think the great day of God's wrath was come. Yet in this supposition they would be wrong; for the seventh seal had yet to be opened. At the same time, so great was the trouble there depicted as to suggest the question—Who shall live when God doeth this? As a relief to the anxious one, the Apostle John bids us see the security of the Church of God—a part being on earth, sealed in the tribulation, and a part in heaven, caught up out of it.

[1] On this half-hour, and other Apocalyptic measurements of time, see Hooper's 'Apocalyptic Researches,' in the *Clergyman's Magazine*, January, 1888.

This cheering scene having been witnessed, the apostle beholds the opening of the seals resumed—an indication of the coming of severer woes than any which have been yet recorded.   At this stage, however, of the exposition it seems best to lay down the following principle: *Whatever judgments come down upon the region below, they are seen by the apostle to be the consequences of activities in the region above.*   No stroke falls on earth that is not directed from heaven.   The two worlds move in concert. The time-accomplishments of one world correspond to the time-appointments of another.   Hence, if there should be a pause in the activities of the higher realm, that would bring about a pause in the movements of the lower.   Such a pause in heaven John observes.   This would indicate some intervening period of comparative quietude on earth.   But what space of time in the revolution of earth's ages those thirty minutes indicated, or what specific epoch of tranquillity upon earth was thereby set forth, it is not possible for us to say.   We know only that, while the apostle notes silence above, there is a calm below; and that this calm is but the prelude to a more intense activity than ever.   And thus we have set before us, in unmistakable symbolism, this truth—*That in the developments of God's plans in providence, there are times of comparative quietude, during which it seems as if the progress of things was stayed awhile.*   Respecting this, we will ask three questions, which we will endeavour also to answer.

I. WHAT IS INTENDED WHEN WE SPEAK OF PROGRESS BEING APPARENTLY STAYED? There are in the Word of God great promises and prophecies which open up a glorious vision for the future days.   There have been also great events which have excited in the Church of God the strongest hopes, and which ever and anon form a restful background.   In the retrospect of mighty wonders in days gone by, God's people take heart and hope for the days to come (Isa. li. 9—11).   To such periods there succeed long years in which either no appreciable advance is made towards the inbringing of the new heavens and the new earth; or if in one direction some progress appears, in another the cause of righteousness seems checked afresh by new developments of error, folly, and sin.   Years on years roll by, our towns and cities grow with accelerating rapidity, and a larger area of dense population becomes an area, so much the larger, of religious indifference.   The prophets of God are crying, " Flee from the wrath to come."   They long for some manifestation of Divine power to startle man.   But no.   Man goes on sinning. And our God seems a God that " does nothing" (Carlyle).   The thunder is rolled up. The lightning is sheathed.   There is a prolonged lull.   There is " silence in heaven." The sceptic makes use of the quietude to ask, " Where is the promise of his coming?" The careless one settles down at his ease, and cries, " The vision that he seeth is for many days to come."   Hollow professors desert in crowds, and go over to the ranks of the enemy.   Some faint-hearted ones, if they do not hoist the white flag and capitulate, think perhaps their message is over-weighted, and cast some of it away.   Others, more loyal, continue to give out the message in its fulness, yet are beginning to tremble. Others, again, make the silence a plea for mightier prayer.   They cry, " It is time for thee, Lord, to work; " " Arise, O Lord, plead thine own cause."   And still—still there is "silence in heaven."   No voice is heard from the invisible realms to break in upon the steady course of this earth's affairs, or to arouse and convict a slumbering world!

II. WHAT DOES THIS SILENCE MEAN?   This "silence " is liable to be misinterpreted. Perhaps this is the one fact which is a sorer strain on the faith of believers than any other.   As Faber plaintively moans—

" He hides himself so wondrously
As if there were no God ;
He is least seen when all the powers
Of ill are most abroad."

What does it mean?   1. *Negatively.*   (1) It does not mean that this world of ours is cut adrift in space, or that the human family are left fatherless and lone.   Our Lord Jesus has given us too many assurances to the contrary for us to come to such a conclusion.   (2) Nor does it mean that time is being lost in the development of the plans of God.   Catastrophes are not the only means of progress.   There is as real an advance when the tiny blade is making its way noiselessly through the sod as when the reapers cry, " Harvest home! "   (3) Nor does it imply that God is indifferent to the sin which he is ever witnessing. "The Lord is not slack," etc. (4) Nor does it imply that God is working on any other plan than that which he has laid down in the book. The revealed purposes of God as indicated in Scripture, and the plans of God as unfolded in providence, run upon precisely the same lines (Ps. l. 21; lxxiv. 11). (5) Nor does the silence mean that God will ultimately let sinners escape with impunity (Rom. ii. 3, 4). 2. *Positively.* It is intended that we should learn positive lessons from "silence in heaven." (1) We are not to expect startling providences at every turn of life. Now and then they may come, and do. But they are not the common methods of Divine working. The lightning-flash which rends the oak comes occasionally as if to reveal the reserve forces in nature. But the light which falls so gently on the opening eyelids is new every morning. (2) We are to be guided more by what God says than by what we see before our eyes. The book gives principles which are eternal. This or that event may be but a tiny point of detail, which can only be judged of by the larger whole. God's Word is our only safe guide. (3) There are other sides to, and other forms of, God's working than those which startle and alarm. Over and above providential working among the nations, there is a living and life-giving Spirit, making "all things new." And it is this silent, secret working of God's Spirit by which he will build up "the new Jerusalem." The roar of the cataract startles the ear, but it is the gentler dew which renews the face of the earth. The thunder of the avalanche marks less advance than the silent ripening of the corn. (4) By the silence of heaven God would test his people's faith, and quicken them to more fervent prayer. There is "silence in heaven" that there may be less silence among the faithful on earth. (5) God would thus teach us to study principles rather than to gaze on incident. The moment of an earthquake is not the time for the calm and accurate study of science ; and times of intense upheaving are not those in which we can master principles; they are rather periods in which we need to put them out to use as the emergency requires. We can only study them when there is "silence in heaven." (6) Certainly, another reason is that the wicked may have space for repentance (cf. 2 Pet. iii. 9). The most marvellous of all the Divine attributes is his patience.

III. WHAT SHOULD THIS SILENCE TEACH US ? AND WHAT EFFECT UPON US SHOULD IT HAVE ? 1. Let us learn anew to exercise faith in the spiritual power which God wields by his Spirit, rather than in the material energy which shakes a globe. The greatest work of God is that which is the most still. Newspapers chronicle incident; but who could write an editorial on the growth of a spirit? "The kingdom of God cometh not with observation." 2. Let us use Heaven's time of keeping silence as a time for breaking ours (Isa. lxii. 1, 6, 7). 3. Let the ungodly make use of the space given for repentance, by turning to the Lord with full purpose of heart. Let them not wait for terrors to alarm. Ice may be shivered into fragments, but it is ice still. Better to let the warm beams of God's love melt the icy soul. 4. Let us lay to heart the certain fact, that, although judgment is delayed, come it will. We know not when. We know not how. But "we *must* all stand before the judgment-seat of Christ."

Vers. 1—5.—*Prayer and fire.* For some time there had been "silence in heaven." During this time there was a corresponding period of calm on earth. Then the prayers of the saints were rising to heaven, fragrant with the incense which mingled with them. As the sequel to these prayers, and as the answer to them, the angel takes fire in the censer and casts it on the earth. From that point a new series of activities unfolds. On these we shall touch in the next homily. Meanwhile we are detained by the thought of the connection between the prayers of the saints and the fire cast on the earth. As far back as the times of the Hebrew psalmist, the Church of God used such words as these : "By terrible things in righteousness wilt thou answer us, O God of our salvation" (Ps. lxv. 5). Our Lord himself declared, "I am come to send fire on the earth " (Luke xii. 49, 50). He yearned for the conflict to take place, which must inevitably come—albeit that, ere it should come, he would have to undergo a terrible baptism of suffering and of blood. So that we get revealed to us a wondrous unison of thought, as regards the Lord, and as regards his Church under the Old and New Testaments— *That " terrible things " on earth will mark the advance of God's kingdom upon it, as the result of a Saviour's sufferings and a Church's prayers.*[1]

[1] " We may send up prayers, and the answer may come down a judgment ; for often it is

I. THE AFFAIRS OF THE KINGDOM OF GOD TOUCH THIS EARTH AT EVERY POINT OF ITS CONCERNS. There are two common defects among Christian people in reflecting on the things of God. Some concern themselves almost exclusively with the outward development of God's kingdom in national life. Others, again, are almost equally absorbed with the aspect of God's work which concerns the salvation of the individual. Both should be included in one view. Each one may begin with himself in his religious concern, but no one may end there. We may, indeed, be thankful that, in the great affairs of worlds, God does not forget our small concerns; at the same time, we should often lose the thought of our own interests in our anxious care for the honour and glory of our Lord and for the growth of his kingdom. The pith of all the concentrated prayers of the saints is, "Thy kingdom come." Earthly thrones, political parties, Church politics, are only of service as they are helping to fulfil the will of God. And never will Christian people attain to the glory of their grand confession till they have public spirit enough to lead them to "seek *first* the kingdom of God and his righteousness."

II. IN THE DEVELOPMENTS OF GOD'S KINGDOM THE UNFOLDINGS OF EARTH ARE AFFECTED BY AGENCIES ABOVE AND BEYOND IT. The main theme of our text presents us with the glorious and inspiring truth of an angelic ministry. That there should be one bond of moral sympathy uniting holy men and angels is not surprising when both are creatures of God. God uses us. He uses them. They are all ministering spirits. Among them there is no discord. They move in perfect accord with the will of him who sitteth upon the throne, wondering oft, perchance, as they look down upon earth, that it should harbour any treasonable revolt against the throne of God!

III. UPON THIS EARTH A CLAIM HAS BEEN MADE BY ONE IN HUMAN FORM, TO SUPREME SOVEREIGNTY OVER IT—a claim that, as things are, produces violent disturbance. It is true he came "not to judge the world but to save the world;" yet, from the nature of the case, even that saving process involves "sending fire on the earth." Satan is wrought up to fury when his subjects leave his bondage to serve freely their rightful Lord. "When a strong man armed keepeth his palace, his goods are in peace, but when," etc. Kings have risen in revolt against the doctrine that there is another King, one Jesus. Priests are indignant when told that the priesthood of believers renders official priests a sham. Mammon's worshippers are wroth against the claims of Jesus. And, as the result of long, long ages of sin, huge ecclesiastical establishments, despotisms, international confederacies, vast hierarchies, great commercial concerns based on selfishness rather than righteousness, have taken usurped possession. *And they must all be overthrown* before perfect peace can be brought in. But how it is all to be done the great Lord alone can tell.

IV. THERE ARE TWO POTENT FORCES AT WORK WHICH ARE TO THE PEOPLE OF GOD THE PLEDGE THAT ALL THESE CONFEDERACIES OF EVIL WILL SOONER OR LATER BE BROKEN UP. One of these is the work of the Lord Jesus Christ, followed as it is by his reigning power. In thinking of all these forces which are set forth in the chapter before us, it would be strange indeed if we lost sight of "him who is in the midst of the throne" to direct and inspire the whole. Our Lord's baptism of blood was but the earnest of his after-administrative sway. At his death the prince of this world was (potentially) cast out. "He must reign till he hath put all enemies beneath his feet." And while there is this regal force working earthward from heaven, there is another force working heavenward from earth—even the prayers of the saints. Our Lord himself has revealed the law that prayer is one of the hinges on which the world's movements turn. "Ask, and it shall be given you." And, more than all, he has not only told us to pray, but he has set us a-praying by the energies of his Spirit. Pray we must; pray we will. We cannot help it. Nor will the prayer be lost. God has not vainly said to the seed of Jacob, "Seek ye me."

V. IT IS THE DIVINE APPOINTMENT THAT, AS THE OUTCOME OF THIS DOUBLE FORCE, THERE SHOULD BE A DOUBLE SET OF RESPONSIVE PHENOMENA. 1. There is a new-creating force of the Holy Spirit, slowly it may be, but surely, building up the new

only through judgment that true Loving-kindness can make her way" (Carpenter). "The prayers are that God will vindicate his own cause,.and they are answered by him who, when his people cry to him, will arise to judgment" (Milligan). For a very widely different conception of the meaning of this passage, see Carratt's 'Commentary.' 2nd edit., p. 88.

heavens and the new earth, which will emerge when all that must be shaken and over-thrown is put away. This work is essentially and exclusively *constructive*. 2. There is another kind of agency—the providential—which is largely *destructive*, which clears the ground for a new advance. It is this overturning force which we have yet to see in action. The Jewish temple and nation had to be overthrown to prepare the way for a new step in advance. Struggle and bloodshed in Italy prepared the way for the downfall of the pope's temporal power. The war in America proved the destruction of slavery. Thus, as we look back on them, we see how destructive action hastens the progress of the world. So it has been. So it will be.

VI. IT IS DISCLOSED TO US IN THIS BOOK THAT MANY OF THE MOST FIERCELY DESTRUCTIVE EVENTS BY WHICH THE ILL IS TO BE OVERTHROWN, are the Divine method of answering his people's prayers. It is in response to prayer that the angel casts fire on the earth. Prayers sent up in calm are answered in storm.

> " When we stand with Christ on high,
> Looking o'er life's history,"

then—then shall we see more clearly than it is possible to do now, that the most "terrible things" have but prepared the way of the Lord. *Difficulty:* A difficulty may here suggest itself to some. The question may be asked—But are we to under-stand that God's saints are expected to pray for, or even that it is right for them to pray for, terrible judgments? We reply—Not so do we understand the matter; but thus: believers pray, "Arise, O God, plead thine own cause;" and then they leave it in the hands of God to answer the prayer in the way which seems best to him. Note: Do not let us be alarmed if, when God rises up, some tremendous shaking occurs. Such shakings *must* come. Empires, monarchies, kings, tyrannies, priesthoods, visible Churches, hierarchies, creeds, *must* be shaken. But why? "That those things which cannot be shaken may remain." Let Christians hold fast, watch, pray, wait, in perfect calm. Finally, let all preachers and hearers summon each other out from the prayer-less crowd, and gather in among the praying ones. History gives us many an instructive parable. There was once a little company in an upper room—not more than a hundred and twenty—praying. At that very time there sat on his royal seat a Roman emperor, surrounded with all the pomp and power of the world. In the little company in the upper room there was a seed of life and progress that has been fruitful ever since, and is more so now than ever. In the court of Rome there was a worm of corruption silently and surely gnawing all the splendour, and bringing it to utter ruin. If we court the world's smiles and wealth and applause, we may make a show, but only for a time. If ours is the breath of prayer, we shall reign when the pomp of earth has vanished for ever away!

Ver. 7—ch. ix. 21.—*The first six trumpets.* The eighth and ninth chapters are confessedly the most intricate part of the book. Yet they are full of Divine teaching which we could ill afford to lose—teaching thrown into a form altogether peculiar to this Apocalyptic book, which will amply repay the closest attention which we can give to it. Here we have the sounding of the first six trumpets under the seventh seal. According to historical interpreters of the two main schools, their fulfilment was accom-plished, at least in part, in the events indicated in the following table :—

Trumpets.	Fulfilment according to Archdeacon Farrar.[1]	Fulfilment according to Rev. E. B. Elliott.[2]
First trumpet— Hail and fire mingled with blood are cast upon the earth, and one-third part of earth and trees and all green grass is burnt up.	Years of burning drought, rains of blood, disastrous con-flagrations and earthquake, as those in Lyons, Rome, Jeru-salem, Naples, etc. (A.D. 63 to A.D. 68).	The invasion of the Roman empire by Alaric, King of the Goths (A.D. 395 to A.D. 410).

[1] 'Early Days of Christianity,' vol. ii. 261—270. For a careful discussion of the main question here involved, see also Mr. P. W. Grant's 'Exposition,' pp. 217—228.

[2] 'Horæ Apocalypticæ,' 5th edit., vol. i. 346, *et seq.*

Trumpets.	Fulfilment according to Archdeacon Farrar.	Fulfilment according to Rev. E. B. Elliott.
Second trumpet— A great mountain is cast into the sea : one-third part of the sea, of the creatures therein, and of the ships, is smitten.	Great calamities connected with the sea and ships such as those of which the time of Nero furnished abundant instances.	The invasion of the Roman empire by Genseric, King of the Vandals (A.D. 423 to A.D. 468).
Third trumpet— A star falls from heaven : one-third part of the rivers and fountains is smitten, and the waters are made bitter.	The overthrow of Nero, the ominous failure of the Julian line, and the bitterness occasioned thereby.	The invasion of the Roman empire by Attila, King of the Huns (A.D. 433 to A.D. 453).
Fourth trumpet— A third part of the sun, moon, and stars is smitten.	Ruler after ruler, chieftain after chieftain, of the Roman empire, and of the Jewish nation, died by murder or suicide.	Final conquest of Rome and the Western empire by Odoacer, King of the Heruli (A.D. 476 to A.D. 490).
Fifth trumpet— A star falls from heaven : a great swarm of locusts from the abyss.	The star = Nero. The host of locusts = demons. Stier is quoted as saying, "In the period between the Resurrection and the fall of Jerusalem, the Jewish nation acted as if possessed by seven thousand demons."	The star = Satan. The locusts = the sudden rise of Mohammedanism. The five months = a hundred and fifty years. In 612 Mahomet commenced his prophetic mission. In 762 Christendom was delivered from the terror and persecution of the Saracens.
Sixth trumpet— The army of the horsemen is seen, numbering two hundred millions, with fire-breathing horses	"The swarms of Orientals who gathered to the destruction of Jerusalem in the train of Titus, and the overwhelming Parthian host which was expected to avenge the ruin of Nero."	The Turks from the Euphratean frontier, subverting the empire of Eastern Christendom, and taking Constantinople. The ensign of one, two, or three horse-tails marks distinctively the dignity and power of the Turkish pacha. From the loosing the four angels to the slaying the third part of men was an hour, a day, a month, and a year; *i.e.* 396 years 118 days, which is just the time from the loosing of the united Turco-Moslem power from the Euphrates to the fall of Constantinople (January 18, 1057, to May 29, 1453).

That there is, in both the earlier and later series of events given in the above table, a remarkable correspondence between the symbolic pictures in the text and the recorded facts of history, no one who has studied the whole matter can question. Nevertheless, we cannot but agree with a remark of Archdeacon Farrar himself, who, after pointing out the incidents given in the centre column as a fulfilment of the Apocalyptic visions, says, "These vaticinations do not belong in the least to the essence or heart of the Apocalypse. *They are but passing illustrations* of the great principles—

the hopes and warnings—which it was meant to inculcate.[1] So, also, it is remarked by another singularly able and luminous writer on this book,[2] " The predictions of these two chapters are manifold, not single, in their fulfilment. Wherever war has been employed, under God's overruling providence, to humble pride and to break up overgrown and overbearing powers, there have these chapters had an accomplishment again and again, and each separate accomplishment has been in its turn a prediction of the prognostication of the greatest accomplishment and of the last. Those hordes of invading barbarians which broke up the monster empire of Rome, and out of whose conquests modern Europe eventually grew, were one fulfilment—they were not the only fulfilment of these prophecies. Never were the figures of the locust-swarms, with their teeth as of lions and their hair as of women, more strikingly exemplified than in those irruptions. But they did not exhaust the prophecies before us. When the mighty power of the French empire at the beginning of this century was broken up by a coalition as of God's hosts mustering for the battle against human pride and human ambition, then was there a new fulfilment, itself prophetic of another and another, till the last of all. The words of God are manifold in their application, just because they deal, not with instances only, but with principles." It is also obvious that since there are given in the tabular form above at least two distinct series of events, illustrating and confirming the prophecy, *it is not possible, in the face of such well-known historic facts, to regard the prophecy as fulfilled completely in either.* We have deemed it needful, at least once, more fully than is our wont, to draw this out and set it before the eye, that the student may see that in the fact of several fulfilments being already accomplished, there is a distinct proof of the main thesis on which our homiletic exposition of the Apocalypse is based—that we have before us a series of pictures and parables designed to set forth the principles and methods of the Divine government, and the varied fortunes through which God's Church must pass on her way to the consummation of all things. These principles are indicated in the chapters before us, and we will now endeavour to set them forth.

I. THE WORLD IS HERE LOOKED AT AS BEARING A GREAT BURDEN OF SIN. (Ch. ix. 20, 21.) And to such a height is sin seen to rise that it is as if the Most High were practically excluded from his own world. Two classes of evils are specified here—one in which that which is no god is worshipped; another in which the commands of God for the regulation of life are entirely ignored. And these are precisely the two forms in which in every age the claims of God have been set at nought. That which we call idolatry is such whether man worships idols of wood and stone, or whether he regards matter and force as potentially adequate to all things. Yea, if there be a difference, the idolatry of the heathen is preferable to that of the materialist. For in pagan idolatries the worship is paid to that which is fashioned by the hand of man—or to that which is brought into being by a Supreme Power, as representing the Power which is at the back of all. But in materialism there is no Being of any kind, no Power to which worship is paid. The Maker of all is ignored. Paganism worships that which can neither see, nor hear, nor walk, as representing that which can. But materialism knows no object of worship at all, and is chargeable with the supreme absurdity of attributing the evolution of sight, hearing, thinking, loving, from that which can neither love, think, hear, nor see! It is not, however, the absurdity of this which is noted in the text, but its sin. It is a robbery of God. "If I be a Father, where is my fear? If I be a Master, where is mine honour?" The second form of evil is immorality—murders, sorceries, fornication, thefts—sufficiently suggestive of all the violations of the laws of morals under which this earth groans. And these two evils—irreligion or false religion, and immorality—are the sum of all ill in the world. Could we but see the whole mass of sin in its combination, it would be to us most amazing that the Most High God did not sweep away at once all these abominations. God's patience is the most wonderful of all his attributes. "I have nourished and brought up children, and they have rebelled against me."

II. THE PERIODS OF QUIETUDE WHICH EARTH MAY WITNESS WILL NOT ALWAYS CONTINUE. (Ch. viii. 5, 6.) We had occasion to observe in a previous homily that there

---

[1] 'Early Days of Christianity,' vol. ii. p. 270. (The italics are ours.)
[2] Dean Vaughan, 'Lectures on the Revelation of St. John,' *in loc.* To the same effect, Drs. Lee, Milligan, and Carpenter.

are apparent lulls in the Divine procedure. God "keeps silence." There may, for a while, be no "taste of thunder in the air," nor any threatening sign of gathering hosts. Men may be reckoning, as in 1851, that a time of unusual peace is near. And to this conclusion they may come hastily, through forgetting that universal peace never can be assured till there is universal righteousness. Following in rapid succession on the apparent auguries of peace in 1851 were the Crimean, the American, and the Franco-German wars. The time will come when war shall cease unto the ends of the earth. But it is not yet.

III. THERE ARE PENT-UP DESTRUCTIVE FORCES ONLY WAITING TO BE LET LOOSE. (Ch. ix. 1, 14.) The "abyss" was full of "locusts;" the "four angels" were bound in the great river Euphrates. In both cases these were tremendous destructive forces, "shut up" or "bound" for a while. But they could only exert their power under Divine permission. Not till the command is given to loose them can they show themselves. No seal can be opened nor any trumpet sounded save under the direction of him who is in the midst of the throne. "The Lord reigneth," and foresees all with exact precision, to the year, the month, the day, the hour.

IV. WHEN SUCH FORCES ARE LET LOOSE, THE EFFECT WILL BE STARTLING AS THE BLAST OF A TRUMPET. (Ch. viii. 2.) The imagery of the Apocalypse is gathered in the main from the Old Testament. Of old, trumpets were sounded, mainly, for one or other of two purposes—they marked an epoch for the Church; they proclaimed war upon the world. And we cannot but be struck with the variety of symbolism under which the effect of the trumpet-sounding is set. But however great the variety in each case, there is indicated the smiting, even to its overthrow, of some great world-power. By the first trumpet, destruction sweeping over the earth is shown. By the second, the downfall of some nation or empire. By the third, the overthrow of some sovereign. By the fourth, a widespread storm. By the fifth, a tremendous rush of evil, as if organized by the very devil himself. By the sixth, a succession of destructive plagues. And who can read history and not know that precisely such events are ever recurring again and again?

V. WHEN IN THE PROVIDENCE OF GOD SUCH DESTRUCTIVE FORCES ARE LET LOOSE, THEN THE MAIN FACTORS ON WHICH NATIONAL WEALTH DEPENDS INSTANTLY FAIL. (Ch. viii. 9.) How much is indicated in that symbolic expression, "a third part of the ships were destroyed"! If anything like this were to occur to British ships, a large portion of our material defences, and even of our supplies of food, would be in a moment withdrawn! Yes; we are absolutely in God's hands. We hold the common blessings of life most entirely at his disposal. The world is governed for God's purposes, and not for ours.

VI. HOWEVER ACTIVE THESE DESTRUCTIVE AGENCIES MAY BE, THEY HAVE THEIR LIMIT. (Ch. ix. 4, 5.) Neither nature nor man can be injured beyond God's permissive line. To the men who have not the seal of God on their foreheads, there should be distress and torment; but even *their* lives should not be at the mercy of others, but should be guarded by a higher Power. Albeit in some cases so great should be the distress that men should seek death and should not find it. But the text implies that to those men who *have* the seal of God on their foreheads no harm of any kind should come. In the worst of times there should be round them a special guard. Nothing will be lost or hurt that is God's. The mightiest agents of destruction, though apparently uncurbed, yet have their curb. God girds them, though they do not know him. We have seen in the appalling wildness and savage grandeur of a mountain pass, when the wild winds were howling as if they would rend the very rocks in pieces, a tiny flower sheltered in its little nook, safe in its little bed of earth, turfed as richly as though on it God had spent special care; and the same wind that rent in pieces the rocks before the Lord, blew to that little flower the tiny morsel of soil that was wanted to nourish its roots, and the little drop of spray from the roaring cascade beneath that was needed to refresh its petals. Wild winds were roaring, torrents were rolling, dashing, and foaming, yet the little flower bloomed up on high, safe, serene, and calm. So shall it be in "the great tribulation" with those who have the seal of God in their foreheads. As Paul Gerhardt sings, in respect of the Thirty Years' War, "As faithful mothers in severe storms on earth anxiously keep and guard their little ones, so also does God, when tribulation and distress arise, press his children to his bosom" (cf. Hengstenberg, *in loc.*).

VII. IT IS THE FUNCTION OF THESE WILD DESTRUCTIVE AGENCIES TO CLEAR THE WAY OF THE LORD. That is implied in the whole series of trumpets. In every case there is very much that is swept out of the way. As settlers in regions of forests have first to clear the ground, so is it with these overturning providences. "Our God shall come, and shall not keep silence . . . a fire shall devour before him." "I will overturn, and overturn, and overturn, till he shall come whose right it is." [1] This is the meaning of the whole.

VIII. THERE IS ONE EFFECT WHICH THEY WILL NOT ACCOMPLISH. (Ch. ix. 20, 21.) They will not bring men to repentance. It is not by such judgments of terror that men will be converted. A thunder-peal may alarm, but it does not cure disease. The earthquake may shake a house, but will not repair or cleanse. So the judgments of God may make the heart tremble, and yet not subdue it. Men who have resisted the gentler calls of God's grace will steel themselves against the smart of his rod. Pharaoh's plagues terrified him, but yet hardened him. We are often tempted even now to say, "Oh, if God would but break the awful stillness, or if he would show us in letters of flame that he is—men would hear!" No, they would not. They would begin to try to account for the sound and the flame by attributing them to some purely physical cause. "Lord, when thine hand is lifted up, they will not see." "If one went unto them from the dead, they will repent." "If they hear not Moses and the prophets, neither will they be persuaded, though one rose from the dead."

These truths, so clear amidst all the difficulty of detail, should lead us to ponder such thoughts as these: 1. If now, with us, it is a time of comparative calm, do not let us think God unobservant, nor reckon securely on a continuance of ease and quiet. Your home is peaceful just now, perhaps; you may be comparatively free from care. And because of this you may be at ease in Zion. But it will not always be a time of ease with you. The day of cloud and care will come. 2. Let us regard every common providential mercy as the voice of God. There is a sacredness surrounding us always. God is in the gentle light and dew, as well as in the lightning and the tornado. "Whoso is wise, and will observe these things, even they shall understand the loving-kindness of the Lord." 3. Let us bless God that he speaks to us ever in the mild and gentle voice of the gospel. This is his sweetest, clearest voice. 4. It is by the Word of his grace that he will do his constructive work, and by the energy of his Spirit. The throwing-down of obstructions may be effected by providential events. The building-up of the new heavens and the new earth will be secured by his conquering love. "The Lord will send forth the rod of his strength out of Zion." "The sword of the Spirit is the Word of God." 5. Then do not let us wait for God to thunder ere we listen to his voice. "One thing hath God spoken, yea, two things are there which I have heard : that power belongeth unto God ; and that unto thee, O Lord, belongeth mercy ; for thou renderest to every man according to his work" (Ps. lxii. 10, 11). If he repent, mercy will forgive. If he finally rebel, justice must condemn. 6. Seeing we know not when any of these trumpets may again be sounded, let us learn to hold everything we have at the Divine disposal, and to say, "If the Lord will, we shall live, and do this, or that."

HOMILIES BY VARIOUS AUTHORS.

Ver. 1.—*Blessed silence.* "There was silence . . . half an hour." *No one certainly knows what these words mean.* Every one can see that they tell of a pause, an interval between the opening of the seventh seal and the sounding of the first of those trumpets of which this eighth chapter mainly speaks. It may be—as one great expositor suggests— that during that Lord's day in which St. John was in the Spirit, and during which he saw in stately procession the series of magnificent visions, or heard, one following the other, the varied voices which spoke—it may have been that for about half an hour of that thrice-holy day no voice, whether from the throne, or from the living ones, or from the holy angels, or from the multitude of the redeemed, or from the distracted and despairing enemies of God, was heard. All was still, still as is often *the half-hour before the thunder-storm bursts.* As before the rattling peal, and the lightning flash,

[1] On the whole of this passage, see the Commentaries by Dr. Milligan and Bishop Boyd Carpenter; also Rev. P. W. Grant's 'Exposition,' pp 258—261.

and the tornado of rain and wind, there is a hush, the air all but motionless, no move-ment anywhere, not even the rustling of a leaf or the swaying of the corn, a solemn pause as if the elements were gathering up their strength preparatory to the rush and rage of the tempest that is so soon to break; so here, all that had preceded, the visions and voices of which the former chapters tell, so awful and soul-subduing as many of them were, seem to have said to all the inhabitants of heaven, "Be still, and know that I am God; I will be exalted among the heathen, I will be exalted in the earth." Angel and the four cherubim, martyred saint and redeemed multitude,—all are still. "There was silence in heaven." We venture not to affirm what exact events in the history of the Church, or of the world as it affected the Church, are pointed at by this silence; conjectures, several most ingenious and interesting, have been made by this interpreter and that, but who out of them all is right? or if any of them be so, who can say? The key to the complete unlocking of the symbols of this book seems either to have been lost, or at any rate put aside for the present. But we can readily see that *there was good reason for the silence spoken of.* As the judgments of God went on, blow after blow falling upon the cruel enemies of the Church; as the righteous wrath of God arose and overwhelmed the persecutors of his people;—must not they who beheld all this have felt that in the presence of such manifestations of God speech and all utterance were out of place? What could they do but "be silent before the Lord, for he was raised up out of his holy habitation"? And *besides this solemn awe, what wonder and amazement* there must have been at the overthrow of their seemingly invincible foes! Think of the power of Rome only at this period. Her laws were administered from Britain to the Euphrates, from the Baltic to the equator. She was the incarnation of earthly power. And there would be also the *silence of adoring, worshipful love.* That amid all that wild fury of bloodshed and destruction God had known how to deliver and preserve his own. And there would be *the silence of expectation,* of eager intent, gazing forward to see what next would be revealed. As men hold their breath, and their hearts almost stand still, and their lips utter no word, in presence of some near anticipated terror, so here—there was silence like to that. And though we cannot explain it, yet is this silence in heaven *very suggestive to us here on earth.* Once and again, when our Lord marked some glaring fault in those about him, he would rebuke it by holding up the contrast which was presented in heaven. When, for example, the scribes and Pharisees murmured at his receiving sinners, our Lord told them that in heaven there was joy over one sinner repenting. *And so amid the din and clatter of this noisy age,* and men loving to have it so, it is well to be reminded that in heaven there became silence for a while. For that which had place in heaven has much need to have place here. We sing—

> " In sacred silence of the mind,
>   My heaven, and there my God, I find.'

But it is to be questioned if many believe this. Therefore they seldom cease what Carlyle calls "that chaotic hubbub, in which their souls run to waste." "Out of silence," he adds, "comes thy strength. Speech is silvern, silence is golden; speech is human, silence is Divine." The absence of it causes much mischief. Therefore *we plead for the following of the heavenly example* here told of—for intervals of quiet, for times of silence, for seasons of meditation, reflection, thought. It is well there should be the "Selah"—the pause, which we so often are directed to in the psalms. Our Lord sets us the example. He was wont to secure such seasons by his retirement to moun-tains and groves, where all night he would commune with God. *For lack of such silences moral fibre is weakened.* If a locomotive is to do its work, it must cease its noisy letting off steam. Great talkers are rarely great doers. Words waste strength. How often our Lord strictly charged those whom he had healed not to go and talk about it! The temptation to do so would be great, but if yielded to all the spiritual blessing would be lost. Hence he so "straitly charged them." Little good—so the 'Pilgrim's Progress' tells us—was got out of the Mr. Talkative of whom the book tells. But silence stores up strength. *And the Spirit's work is hindered.* How often the birds, which our Saviour said snatched away the good seed which had been sown—how often they take the form of idle foolish talk, which, entered into at the very doors of the sanctuary render hopeless all prospect of holy impression being retained or good purpose fulfilled! The Lord was wont to take people aside when he would bless them. It is so now. *And when men would resist the Spirit they shun these silent seasons.* The accusers of the woman taken in adultery could not endure the Lord's silence, his answering them not a word, and hence they heap their questions upon him, and demand an answer; for any answer would be less terrible than that dread silence. *Would we grow in grace, such silences are essential.* The habit of retreat, of quiet before God, must be cultivated. All growth is silent. Who hears the springing of the corn, the unfolding of the flower, the increase of the body in stature? And so is it with the growth of the soul. Like the noiseless building of Solomon's temple, of which **Heber** sings—

> "No hammer fell, no ponderous axes rung;
> Like some tall palm the mystic fabric sprung."

And so in the building-up of spiritual character, in growth in grace, silence, stillness, must be secured. Spiritual worship is silent in its essence, though not in expression. Submission is silent. "I was dumb, I opened not my mouth; because thou didst it" (Ps. xxxix.). So was it with Aaron, "the saint of the Lord;" when in one awful judgment-stroke he saw his two ungodly sons smitten dead, it is told that he uttered not a word. Knowledge of God demands silence. "Mary kept all these things, and pondered them in her heart." We must be still would we know God to be God. He is not in the earthquake, nor the fire, but in the still small voice. O blessed silence, O grace and might of holy quietness, sweet stillness of the soul, in which the footfall of God is heard, and his voice speaks joy, and the angels of patience and hope visit us, and Faith renews her strength!

> "Silent Spirit, dwell with me;
> I myself would silent be."

And *to encourage us to seek these quiet hours,* how often does God take us apart from the noise and rush, the everlasting din and bustle, of our common life! *Seasons of sickness* are designed to be such times of silent retreat, when we may "commune with" our "own heart upon our bed, and be still," and so have leisure to attend to the life within. Sabbaths, these days of the Lord in which we should be, as St. John was, "in the Spirit," are they not God's messengers to us, saying, "Rest; be silent from thy common speech, thy common work; meditate on things eternal; let there be pause in the activities of thy daily life; imitate as best thou canst the season of silence of the saints in heaven"? *And the unseen world,* the place of the departed, that intermediate condition in which till the resurrection the souls of believers rest, this also is merely another divinely given retreat for the soul—a going down into silence, as the psalm calls it. White robes are theirs (see ch. v.), which tell of the love of God to them, and that they are cleansed in the blood of Christ, and rest, quiet, calm, in the presence of the Lord. Sleep for all the bodily powers, but not for the soul. That—now that the once busy hands and feet are at rest, and the heart throbs no more, and the tongue utters no word, none, though often we here long

> "For the touch of a vanished hand,
> For the sound of a voice that is still"

—that now lives unto God, where "he hath hid his beloved in his pavilion from the strife of tongues." There, the Martha-like activity over, we may, like Mary, sit at the Master's feet and share in that "good part," as here on earth was but rarely possible for us. So great is the value of these silences, of one of which our text tells, and to which it has turned our thoughts, and not unprofitably, we trust, but so that it has been good for us to muse on the "silence" there was "in heaven for half an hour." —S. C.

Ver. 2.—*The ministry of angels.* "And I saw the seven angels." These holy beings are continually spoken of in Scripture, and in no book of the Bible more frequently or emphatically than in this. From their first mention in connection with the touching story of Hagar and her child, which we read of in Genesis, down to their constant ministry, now of mercy, now of terror, which we read of in these closing pages of the Bible, we are continually meeting with references to them. It, therefore, cannot but be important to us to understand what we may on this most interesting but most mysterious subject. For we cannot think that their work and ministry are finished, and that now they have nothing to do with us, nor we with them. We feel sure that the reverse is the truth. True, there has been much of mere imagination in the representations that have been given of angels by poets and painters both. They have been the makers of men's common ideas concerning angels, and have caused not a little misunderstanding and misreading of the Scriptures on this theme. Jewish fables and legends of various kinds have been mingled with the plain teaching of God's Word, and hence the whole subject has come to be wrapped in a haze of difficulty and doubt, leading, in many cases, to complete denial of the existence of angels at all. But a careful study of the Scriptures will show that the truth as to the angels is one full of consolation and of sacred impulse; of solemn warning also; in short, that it is part of that truth which is "profitable for doctrine, for reproof," etc. Consider—

I. THE REALITY OF THE ANGELIC WORLD. And there can be no doubt but that 1. *The Scriptures plainly assert it.* They are spoken of there in clear and positive manner as to their high dignity, their sanctity, their power, their blessedness, their heavenly home, their employments, their vast numbers, and their immortality. All this is told of the *holy* angels. But there are *evil* angels likewise, who are represented as serving under their prince Satan, as the holy angels serve under God. They are evil and wretched, and full of all malignity and wickedness. 2. *And all this is not mere accommodation, on the part of the Scriptures, to popular ideas and beliefs.* This has been long and loudly asserted. No doubt there were all manner of strange beliefs on the subject of the spirit-world. The ancients peopled the universe around with all kinds of strange inhabitants, and the Jews were only less credulous on these matters than the heathen around. Hence it is said that our Lord and his apostles accommodated themselves to these ideas, and represented the various facts of nature and providence *as if* angels or demons were employed about them, but not teaching that such actually was the case. But this theory has only to be stated for its untenableness immediately to appear. And the plain teaching of Scripture would have been more readily received had not poets and painters—those mighty manufacturers of so much, and manifold, and often mischievous mistake—persisted in always representing angels in one way—beautiful youths with wings. Milton is very great upon their wings. But the result of this has been to relegate the whole doctrine of angels to the region of myth and imagination, and to rob the Church of the comfort and help the real truth as it is given in the Bible would afford. The fancies and fables of heathendom were but one more out of the many instances in which, as St. Paul describes them, they were feeling after the truth. 3. And *why should there be any doubt as to the reality of angels?* Is not all life, from the lowest zoophyte up to the most gifted of the sons of men, one continual ascent? But why should the progression halt with us? why should there not be an ascent beyond, as there is up to, ourselves? All analogy leads us to think there is, and to be on the look-out and expectation for orders of beings that may span the vast distance which must for ever separate us and God. The Bible and analogy confirm one another. But a more important and difficult inquiry relates to—

II. THEIR NATURE, ORIGIN, AND HISTORY. Who and what are they? 1. *Much has been assumed concerning them,* but resting on very slender foundations; as: (1) That they existed long before the creation of man, in vast throngs, sinless and blessed, in attendance upon God. (2) That they were altogether different in nature from man. (3) That some of them kept not their first estate, and hence are reserved in chains unto the judgment of the great day. (4) That Satan, their chief, dared to rival God, and with his confederates to "defy the Omnipotent to arms." Milton represents Satan as telling how God—

". . . to be avenged,
And to repair his numbers thus impaired,
Whether such virtue, spent of old, now failed
More angels to create (if they at least
Are his created) or to spite us more,
Determined to advance into our room
A creature formed of earth, and him endue
With heavenly spoils (our spoils)."

But may it not be that: 2. *Angels are perfected men*—"the spirits of the just made perfect"? Young, the author of the 'Night Thoughts,' thus sets forth this belief—

> "Why doubt we, then, the glorious truth to sing?
> Angels are men of a superior kind;
> Angels are men in lighter habit clad,
> High o'er celestial mountains winged in flignt,
> And men are angels loaded for an hour,
> Who wade this miry vale and climb with pain
> And slippery step, the bottom of the steep."

But on such a theme as this we want Scripture, and not poetry, to tell us what we are to believe; and from Scripture we gather: (1) That there is no being higher in nature than man except God himself. For man was created in the image and likeness of God. Now, is an angel more than this? Could he be more without being God? Hence, however blessed and glorious the condition of angels may be, in nature they are not and cannot be higher than man. (2) And if they be a different order of beings from men, beings of another nature and kind, why, then, were men created at all? If the motive of our heavenly Father in creating man was, as we believe it to have been, to gather round him a race of pure, holy, happy beings, his children, on whom he might lavish his love, and in whose blessed companionship he might for ever rejoice; if there were already such a race of beings in existence, why was man formed? Why was he made to pass through all the manifold miseries of this life, its unnumbered sins and sorrows, if already there were an infinite host who from the first were already what man can only become after so many and so great struggles and trials and cares? If all the sanctity and blessedness of the angelic character could exist without all man's preliminary sorrow, for what reason, then, was unhappy man created? But if, on the other hand, it be true that there is no other entrance to the angelic state than this weary life of ours, and if in order that we may be angels it is necessary that we first be men, then the mystery of life, often so mournful a mystery, has some light shed upon it, and we can bear it more patiently. But if all that man is to be could be attained without his trials, as on the common belief in regard to angels it could, then, may we not ask, "To what purpose is this waste?" (3) These angels are in Scripture called men. See the angel that wrestled with Jacob; that appeared to Joshua, to Manoah; the three angels that came to Abraham, are called "the three men;" the angel that appeared as a writer to Ezekiel and *passim* both in the Old Testament and in the New Testament. (4) And there is no proof that they were only men in appearance and not in reality. Why should they not be what in appearance and name they seem to be? (5) And our Lord said that in the resurrection we shall be "as the angels." And in the Epistle to the Hebrews we are said to have "come to . . . myriads of angels, to the general assembly and Church of the Firstborn, . . . and to the spirits of the just made perfect." But do not these three expressions tell of different facts in connection with, not different, but the same persons? Certainly "the spirits of just men made perfect" are the same as "the general assembly and Church of the Firstborn," and if so, they are the same as the "myriads of angels." 3. *And all this is not set aside by the statements in 2 Peter and in the Epistle of Jude.* In both these Epistles it is said that God "spared not the angels that sinned, but cast them down into hell." It is on these statements, amplified and enlarged by Milton and others, that the popular belief is based. But it is to be noted that the two statements in these Epistles are but copies one of another or of some common document. Place the passages side by side, and this will be evident, the writer of 2 Peter probably copying from Jude. And it is not to be forgotten that the canonical authority of these two Epistles is the least and lowest of all the Scriptures. But even were it not so, the source whence their statements on this question are taken is well known. They are a quotation from the apocryphal Book of Enoch—a book of no authority and little worth, but which was familiar to those to whom these Epistles were written; and, hence, illustrations drawn from it, whether true or not, would serve the writers' purpose, and are therefore made use of. It therefore cannot be allowed that these two isolated statements—though they are one rather than two, and of such doubtful authority—should set aside what Scripture and reason alike teach on this most interesting theme.

CONCLUSION. See some of the consequences of this understanding concerning the angels. 1. *The future life becomes far more real to us.* For now that we have identified the angels, as we think has been done, with "the spirits of just men made perfect," we are delivered from that vagueness of idea as to those who have gone away from us through their having died in the Lord. They are no longer formless, incorporeal, unimaginable beings, mist and cloud-like rather than human, but we know that it is as the disciples believed—the angel, the spirit of their Master resembled him. His resurrection-body did resemble his former material body so that he could be recognized as we know he was. 2. And we know some of *the occupations of that heavenly state.* So long as we regarded angels as a different order of beings from redeemed men, we could not regard their work as that which one day shall be ours. But looking upon them as ourselves as "we shall be," we can see what vast store of holy employ and sacred service awaits us. See their manifold service as shown in this chapter only. Heaven is not an everlasting sitting on "green and flowery mounts," an "eternity of the tabor," as one has described it, but a life of holy and blessed service for God and for man.—S. C.

Ver. 2.—*The trumpet-symbol.* "To them were given seven trumpets." Many instruments of music are mentioned in the Bible, but the trumpet is the one that stands out prominent amidst them all. There are stringed instruments, of which the chief is the harp; and there are those whose sound is produced by striking the stretched skin of which they are made, as the cymbals; but none are named so frequently as the trumpet. In Numb. x. 1—10 there are given express commands for their construction, and throughout the Bible, from the giving of the Law at Sinai down to the sounding of the last trump, and this vision of the seven trumpets, we continually meet with them. We are, therefore, justified in attaching significance to them and regarding them as symbolizing truths God would have us learn. For he commanded both their making and their use. They played a prominent part in connection with the divinely ordained worship both of the tabernacle and the temple, and the whole land of Israel echoed at divinely appointed seasons with their spirit-stirring notes. A glance at a concordance will show how constantly and on what occasions they were used. What, therefore, may we learn from them? They teach—

I. GOD HAS A MESSAGE FOR US. Had they been a merely man-devised instrument, we could not have said this; but when we find that they were adopted by God in his service, we cannot err in regarding their clear, loud notes as telling of his message and will. And, in fact, they were used to indicate to Israel the advent of seasons of worship—the new year, the new moon, the jubilee, and other occasions when God commanded his people to render special service. And these special messages remind us of God's great message to mankind, which he has given to us in his Word. He has not left us unthought of, uncared for, uninformed. It was not likely that he would. He has made known to us his will.

II. THE MANNER OF THAT MESSAGE. Such truths as these are suggested by this trumpet-symbol. 1. *How urgent!* The trumpet-blast was startling, arousing; its clear, loud note penetrated the dullest ear, and reached those afar off, and forced all to listen. And such message of urgency God's Word brings to us. "Awake thou that sleepest, and arise from the dead!"—so it speaks to us. "How shall we escape if we neglect," etc.? It is no mere matter of indifference, but life and death hang upon it. And: 2. *How warlike!* The trumpet-note was emphatically the music of war. Jeremiah (xlii. 14) represents as a blessed condition not then attainable, and a land all unlike his own, "where we shall hear no sound of trumpet." And in this vision of the seven trumpets war is their most prominent meaning. And thus we are reminded of our Lord's words, "I came not to send peace on earth, but a sword." God's Word is a battle summons, a call to "fight the good fight of faith." It is what we do not like, but which we must accept, would we share those rewards which are given "to him that overcometh." 3. *How terrible!* The hosts of Midian fled in dismay when the blast of Gideon's trumpet burst on their startled ears. Terror seized on them and made them an easy prey. And in this chapter it is the terribleness of the judgments of God upon his enemies which the seven trumpets tell of. And God's Word is terrible to those who know him not. The Bible is a dreadful book to the impenitent man when awakened, as one day he will be, to his real condition before God. It is like the prophet's scroll to him, written within and without, of sorrow, lamentation, and woe. To the froward it shows itself froward. But: 4. *How animating* to the hearts of the people of God! The trumpet, like the loud cheering of troops as they dash forward in the fight, heartens them; and the trumpet-sound was designed to do this. And God's Word is full of heart-cheering truth to all them that trust in him. And: 5. *How joyful* was the sound when it proclaimed, as so often the trumpet did, the advent of some glad festival, some "acceptable year of the Lord," the jubilee especially! And in the Feast of Tabernacles the general hilarity was heightened by the frequent sounding of the silver trumpets by the priests. "Blessed are the people that hear the joyful sound"—this is said of God's message of grace, and such joyful sound is the characteristic note of the gospel. And: 6. *How irresistible* is the trumpet-sound! The lofty massive walls of Jericho fell down flat before the trumpet-blast. The dead, so insensible to all else, shall hear that call; "for the trumpet shall sound, and the dead shall be raised." "All that are in the graves shall hear his voice, and shall come forth." And so to-day where God's Word comes in power, dead hearts are roused and sleepers awake. O blessed power of God's Word, that it will, it must, have obedience rendered to it! "He speaks, and it is done; he commands, and it stands fast." But if resisted now—as too often it is—the obedience that will have to be rendered at the last will be to the word, "Depart, ye cursed!" But now it bids us "come." Let us hear that.—S. C.

Vers. 3—6.—*Prayer.* The vision of the opening of the seven seals is completed. We are not told what took place when the seventh seal was opened, only that then there was a solemn pause—"silence in heaven for half an hour." After the opening of the sixth seal the progress of events was interrupted, that the mark and impress of God might be put upon the Israel of God—those out of the Jewish nation who were to be delivered out of the impending judgments. Then was shown, also, the beatific vision of the great multitude of the saved out of all nations. Then comes the opening of the seventh seal (ver. 1); but of its contents we have no record; perhaps in this world we never shall have. We are told only of the "silence" that ensued. That silence may point to the blessed calm of heaven, where God hides his people "in his pavilion from the strife of tongues." And also to the amazement and fear which had fallen on the foes of the Church, a little while before so loud and fierce, now so still in awful fear. And now begins a new series of visions, not succeeding the former in order of time, but parallel and simultaneous, and running up to the same issue. This new series is that of the seven trumpets. Seven angels are seen to whom the trumpets are given, but ere they sound there is seen that of which these verses (3—6) tell—the angel at the golden altar, the altar of incense which stood before the throne. To this angel is given much incense, which he mingles with that which is already on the altar. This vision is not alone mysterious, but full of interest and instruction. It teaches us much concerning *prayer.*

I. THAT IT IS CHARACTERISTIC OF ALL SAINTS. God's holy ones, his saints, all of them pray. Their prayers are represented as being on the altar before the throne. There are none of the holy ones whose prayers are not there. Prayer is common to them all. "Behold, he prayeth," was the Lord's unanswerable argument to Ananias, that Saul the persecutor was really converted. And it is ever a sign that a man belongs to the company of the "holy ones," the saints.

II. THEY ALL PRAY IN THE NAME OF THE LORD JESUS CHRIST. Their prayers are on the altar. The altar sacrifice ever tells of Christ and of his perfect sacrifice, the ground of all our hopes, the source of all our salvation, and the basis of all our prayers. And hence the prayers of all saints are represented as resting on the altar, as the incense, type of all such prayers (ver. 8), rests thereon. The name of Christ may not be uttered in word, but when any appeal to God as he is made known to us only in Christ, and especially in Christ on the cross, and when they pray in the spirit—the lowly, meek, trusting spirit—of Christ, then, though his blessed name may not be mentioned, their prayers are really in his name, and find acceptance thereby. The Lord's prayer does not name Christ, but assuredly it is a prayer in his name. And thus all true prayer is in him, and rests on the altar of his sacrifice.

III. THAT THE BLESSED ONES IN HEAVEN JOIN THEIR PRAYERS WITH OURS. There is a communion of saints. Great question has arisen as to who the angel was that is seen in this vision, standing at the altar with much incense. Some, as Hengstenberg, affirm that he represents no one; that he is to be regarded as having no symbolical significance, but as only belonging to the form, not the substance, of the vision. Others, the Church of Rome, that he is one of the angel-intercessors; and hence is deduced that Church's doctrine of the worship of angels and saints. Others again, Protestants, in order to avoid this doctrine, say the angel is none other than the Lord Jesus Christ; that he is here interceding for his people as he is wont to do. But in this book the Lord Jesus Christ is never called an angel, nor represented as taking the place or form of an angel. Further, the "much incense" is said to be "given to" the angel, just as the trumpets were given to the seven angels. But the Lord Jesus Christ intercedes for us, not on the ground of any excellence that is given to him, but on the ground of his own inherent worth, and what he himself has done and suffered on our behalf. He has redeemed us by "his own blood." Furthermore, it is to be noted that that which the angel brings to the altar is the same as that which is already there. Incense is "the prayers of saints," and their prayers are incense. That, therefore, which the angel brings is not something different from what is on the altar, but merely an addition of the same kind. But that which Christ gives to our prayers is a worthiness and acceptableness such as they have not of themselves, and cannot have until given by him. It is by no means the same, but far other as the angel's was not. And the angel brings his incense to the altar, as do the saints themselves; his prayers and theirs are accepted on the same ground. Hence, for these reasons, we cannot regard the angel spoken of here as being the Lord Jesus Christ. But we regard the angel as one of the blessed in the presence of God, one eminent in prayer, one to whom the spirit of grace and supplication had been given in large measure, and so he had "much incense." And he joins on his prayers, unites them with the prayers of all saints. No doubt he had often done so when on earth, and now he does so in heaven. There he had with them besought God to bless and keep his Church in sore peril and distress, and this prayer he continues. Why should this not be? We know the angels sympathize with the people of God on earth. There is joy amongst them over every sinner that repenteth. They, therefore, must know what transpires here, and how can they do otherwise than be in fullest sympathy with the "prayers of all saints"? Can we think that they cease to care for those they loved on earth now that they themselves are in heaven? The mother in heaven for her children left here? Do those who loved on earth lose that love yonder? God forbid! Hence we look on this "angel" as one of the blessed ones who is uniting his much prayer together with that of all saints, and together their prayers, as the streaming cloud of fragrant incense, a sweet odour of acceptableness, rise up before God.

> "The saints on earth and all the dead
> But one communion make,
> All join in Christ their living Head,
> And of his grace partake."

IV. Such prayers move the hand that rules all things. The answer of these prayers comes in the form of command—for we must assume such command—to sprinkle the enkindled incense on the earth. Hence the angel takes the golden censer and "fills it with the fire of the altar, and casts it upon the earth." And then at once are heard voices and thunders, and the lightning flash, and earthquakes are seen—signs similar to those with which God came down upon Mount Sinai. So now he is about to interpose in response to the prayers which have been presented to him. And the seven angels prepare themselves to sound, lift their trumpets to their lips, and are about to peal forth their terrible blasts. It is all a vivid picture of the prevalence of the prayers of the people of God. Mighty things are these prayers, weapons of resistless force, fearful for the ungodly when their answer involves the sinner's doom, but blessed always for those who pray. Why do we not avail ourselves far more than we do of this Divine force? This vision bids us pray, pray perseveringly and unitedly, pray in Christ's name; and it shows us the holy ones in heaven praying with us, and bow our prayers prevail. Who, then, would not pray?—S. C.

Vers. 6—13; ch. ix.; xi. 14—18.—*The war-trumpets.* I. ALL THESE TRUMPETS TELL OF WAR. The first six are proclamations of war, and the symbols that follow on their sounding set forth varied aspects of war. The last proclaims war ended and victory won.

II. BUT WHAT WAR? There can be little doubt that, as in all prophetical writings, facts within the immediate or near horizon of the writer form the basis of his predictions, and furnish the groundwork of the great moral and spiritual truths, and of the future historic facts to which, by way of resemblance, they direct our thought. Therefore: 1. *The wars of the period* in which the writer lived and wrote must be looked to—" the things which are and which are about to happen " (ch. i. 19) —for the primary explanation of the vivid, mysterious, and manifestly applicable symbols which the visions connected with these seven trumpets present to us. Let Josephus be consulted, and in his pages will be found more than enough to furnish material for all the awful images which we find here. The dread drama of the Jewish war was in full action. The massacres and desolation, the poisoning of the very springs of life, the torture, the inroads of locust-like hordes of Arab, Idumæan, and other armies,—all the appalling horrors which St. John speaks of, were all there; his imagery was ready to hand, and, as an intense Jew, the calamities that befell his people could not but have roused in him deepest sympathy, and made his words burn, and his thoughts glow, as they do in this wonderful book. That he was far removed from the immediate scene of these events would make no difference. And besides the Jewish war, there were the civil wars which were distracting the Roman empire: rebellions and revolts; this general and the other determined to mount the imperial throne, let the cost in bloodshed and the risk be what it might;—such were the surroundings of St. John's life, and to them we primarily look for the explanation of what he says. But we cannot doubt, either, that: 2. *The wars which led to the fall of the empire* find their foreshadowing here. The historic expositors affirm that these alone are what St. John meant, and that the successive invasions under Alaric, Genseric, Attila, and Odoacer, and, after them, of the Saracens and Turks, are what is here portrayed. They ask of those who doubt their interpretation, " Now, if it had been intended to predict these events, could they have been more clearly and accurately described?" Certainly the correspondences are close, and the examination of them is so interesting that more sober conclusions are apt to be abandoned. But remembering the purpose of this book, the comforting and strengthening of the persecuted Church of his own day; and the method of all prophetical writings, to lay hold on present and near facts;—we cannot think that, however much foreshadowed these then-distant facts might have been, they were in the mind of the apostle when he wrote. For not to these wars only do these symbols apply, but to: 3. *All war.* If a deterrent from war be needed, as it often is, then the study of these vast canvases on which the Divine artist has painted successive pictures of the horrors of war cannot but be advantageous. The first shows *the devastation it causes;* the trees and the growing grass and corn destroyed by the wild war-storm which is likened to hail and fire mingled with blood. The second, *the destruction of commerce.* A great mountain, symbol of some vast earthly power—burning, set on fire with rage and lust of conquest —is cast into the sea, the highway of commerce. The waves are dyed red with blood, the fish die, the ships perish. The third, *the overthrow of cities and civilization generally.* On the banks of rivers the chief cities of the world have for the most part been placed. The historic interpreters point out how as Genseric, with his Vandals, made the shores of the Mediterranean his chief battle-ground, so, as this third picture represents, Attila fell—swiftly like a stone, burning like a torch, with fury—upon the river-side cities and populations which lay at the bases of the mountains, the springs of the great rivers, and made their life bitter to them. Yes, it was so; and it is what all war does and has done. Cities and civilization suffer irreparably, must do so. The fourth, *political overthrow.* The sun, moon, and stars—symbols of government, of kings and the chief rulers of men—these cease to rule and fall from their high places when the fortune of war goes against them. It was so amongst Jews and Romans alike. The fifth—a more dreadful picture than any and more completely drawn (ch. ix.)—tells of *the intolerable tortures* which war—child of hell and the pit and the devil that it is—inflicts upon the miserable people amid and upon whom it is waged. They are not exterminated but tortured, as if with the stings of scorpions. They would fain die, but may not; they live on and suffer. The invading armies, like locusts for number, power, and destructiveness, waste and ruin and oppress them day by day. What a picture of war is here! And the sixth,—this tells of *the destruction of human life and the deterioration of human character* which war causes. One third part of the human race perishes, and the rest, instead of repenting themselves of their sins, become hardened. Whatever special war it was that St. John had in his mind when, with such seeming particularity of place and time and circumstance, he wrote concerning this sixth trumpet-blast, it is certain that the effects told of are the common accompaniments of war. If the career of the Turks and their conquests be, as is asserted, the wars here meant, and which extended from A.D. 1055 for nearly four hundred years, and which, according to the year-day theory, is just the period which the one year and month and day and hour spoken of would signify, then the resemblance is doubtless striking, even to the identification of the " brimstone, fire, and smoke " with the gunpowder which was first used in the siege of Constantinople. But there is no need to limit the reference of the vision to those circumstances, as it will apply to many similar ones. But all these visions are descriptions of war—those " wars and rumours of war " which our Saviour foretold should be ere the end come; and the comfort for God's troubled people is in that which the seventh trumpet declares, that through and by, amid and in spite of them, *the kingdoms of this world fall to Christ.* There is comfort in this—just that comfort which the Church in the apostolic age and many times since has sorely needed. Were it not for this final declaration, how wearyingly, how despairingly, should we look on all the turmoil and disasters which have resulted from the ever-recurring wars which men have waged! We could see no reason or end in them. But when the seventh angel sounds his trumpet the outcome of all is seen, and the result recompenses for all that has gone before. But yet more should we see in these visions the setting forth of: 4. *God's war with the ungodly.* This is what we most of all should learn from them. (1) And they show how, in order to subdue " the unruly wills of sinful men," God is wont, when milder means fail, to send judgments of a very awful kind. Every one of these visions sets forth such judgment of God. (2) And when one will not suffice, another is sent. The dread procession of them seems never done passing by. (3) And they become more and more terrible. There is a manifest enlargement in the scope and severity of these successive judgments. The ominous cry of the eagle which is heard after the first four trumpets have sounded declares this as does the consideration of the judgments themselves. Such is God's way : who can deny that it is so? (4) But in wrath he remembers mercy. The judgments are not universal, nor exterminating. The reiterated mention of the " one third part " as being the sufferers, not the whole, shows wherefore and with what hope in regard to men's repentance they were sent. (5) But, alas! they seemed to fail in their purpose. After so many and so terrible visitations men did not repent; they seemed only, like Amon, to sin " more and more." But it should seem as if, when God's judgments, as in the case of the plagues of Egypt, no longer merely fell on what was outside their life, no longer merely tormented them, but now smote that life itself, as did the judgment of the sixth trumpet, the last of these dread visitations, then some kind of repentance was produced. But we cannot certainly say. (6) Victory, however, is the outcome of all. How could it be otherwise? Can man for ever defy the Almighty? Blessed be God, he cannot, and sooner or later rebel man will have to lay down his weapons and own Christ Lord of all.

CONCLUSION. But wherefore will man wage this war at all? God desires it not, but has sent the message and the ministry of reconciliation. We, then, as " ambassadors for Christ, as though God did beseech you by us : we pray you in Christ's stead, be ye reconciled to God."—S. C.

Ver. 13.—*The body and the bird.* " And I saw, and I heard an eagle, flying in mid heaven, . . . Woe, woe, woe, for them that dwell on the earth!" The true reading of the text is given in the Revised Version. It was not " an angel flying," but a solitary eagle or vulture, that St. John saw. Hovering high overhead, a mere speck in the sky, and its harsh cry sounding as if it uttered over and over again the ominous words,

"Woe, woe, woe!" Now in vision, but often in reality, he had doubtless seen such hovering bird, and heard its bitter cry. And when we think of this vision, and remember who they were on whom the judgments of God were coming, we are reminded of our Lord's words, "Wheresoever the carcase is, there shall the eagles be gathered together" (Matt. xxiv. 28). For he and his apostle had the same scenes in view, the same sinful people, and the same dread judgments of God. Both beheld both the body and the bird—the eagle of judgment and the corruption that it would seize upon. When our Lord spoke, and yet more when his apostle wrote, the ill-omened bird was clearly visible, and its woeful cry could be distinctly heard. What the Lord said St. John saw. "For in the lands of the East, when a wild beast falls in the desert, or a horse or camel on the highway, there is for a time no stir in heaven. But far above human ken the vulture is floating poised on his wings and looking downward. His eye soon distinguishes the motionless thing, for he hunts by an eyesight unequalled in power among all living things, and like a stone he drops through miles of air. Others floating in the same upper region see their brother's descent, and know its meaning. One dark speck after another grows swiftly upon the horizon, and in a few moments fifty vultures are around the carrion. Now, thus inevitable, swift, unerring, as the vultures' descent on the carcase, is the judgment coming of the Son of man to corrupt communities and corrupt men" (Stopford Brooke). Given the body, the bird will not be far off; where the carcase, there the vulture. In God's government it has ever been so, is now, and will be in all ages, in all lands, and under all circumstances.

I. THIS EAGLE HAS OFTEN BEEN SEEN. It has long hovered over and at last descended upon: 1. *Corrupt communities.* As the inhabitants of the earth in Noah's day, on whom "the Flood came and swept them all away;" the cities of the plain ere the fire-storm fell; the Canaanitish nations whose judgment was long delayed "until the iniquity of the Amorites was full." It hung over Jerusalem in the days of Jeremiah, over Babylon in the old age of Daniel, and over the Jewish nation when St. John beheld it "in mid heaven." And over Rome the eagles of judgment were indeed gathering. For she had become so corrupt and hateful to God and man that there was nothing for it but to let the long-delayed sentence be executed, and in the pages of this Book of the Revelation, and in those of the secular historian, he who will may read of, perhaps, the most tremendous fulfilment the world has as yet ever seen of the inexorable law that "wheresoever the carcase is, there," etc.

> "Rome shall perish—write that word
> In the blood that she hath spilt;
> Perish hopeless and abhorred,
> Deep in ruin as in guilt."

Yet further illustrations. The Reformation, which was the judgment of the Catholic Church; the French Revolution, etc. 2. *Corrupt men.* "The mills of God," says the poet, "grind slowly, but they grind *exceeding small.*" Many imagine that the great laws of God will be, no doubt, fulfilled amid nations and Churches and other bodies of men, but they will not take note of individuals. That, however, is not true, though many think it is. Look over the lives of the many bad men and women of whom the Bible tells; but where amid them all can the sinner find any encouragement to go on in his sin? Are they not all of them illustrations of God's law of judgment? And so universally is this law recognized that no poorest novelist will write his wretchedest story, and no tawdry theatre dare represent on its stage a drama which ignores or fails to pay homage to this law. They all know and confess that over the vile and bad the vulture of judgment hovers, and will swoop down on them ere long. And to-day this law is at work. See that blear-eyed, ragged, shivering, and every way disreputable-looking wretch who is reeling out of the gin-shop, and, as he staggers along, poisoning the air with his foul breath and yet fouler words—what a wreck the man is! Health gone; and character, and home, and friends, and livelihood, and all that made life worth having, gone; and life itself going likewise. The vultures of judgment have plucked him bare of all, and they are at their awful work still. Go into the wards of our hospitals, and amid many whom misfortunes and not sin have brought there, you will yet see not a few dying a miserable death, horrible to look at, to listen to, to speak or even think of. Go to the cells of our prisons, to lunatic asylums, to convict yards, or where mounting the steps of the gallows on which they are to suffer the last penalty of the law,—in all such places, and amid all such scenes, and branded as it were on the brow of all such transgressors you may read the eternal law, " Wheresoever the carcase is, there," etc. That eagle St. John saw, and—

II. It is good that it should be seen. In the physical world, if there were no scavengers, no agents whereby what is corrupt and corrupting could be rendered harmless, life could not go on. And so in the moral world, floods and sulphur fires, and Joshua-led armies, hosts from Babylon or from Rome, French Revolutions and the like, —it is awful, terrible, but still beneficent and essential work that they do upon the moral and spiritual corruptions against whom they have been sent. But blessed is that sinful community and that sinful man who sees the eagle in mid heaven, and fears and turns from his wickedness and so lives.

III. Men sometimes think they see it when they do not. Poor Job—his friends, his comforters, would have it that his dreadful sufferings were judgments of God upon him. It was the common and cruel, though baseless, belief of their day. " Lord, who did sin, this man or his parents, that he was born blind ? " There we find the same notion yet living on, even in our Lord's day. And it is not dead vet. But, thank God, there are many sorrows and distresses which are not judgments at all, any more than the hard lesson which a master may set his pupil to learn is a sign of his displeasure. It is not so, but a means of discipline and improvement and honour to the pupil; therefore, and for no other reason, is it given. And so with not a few of the scrrows God sends to us, as he sent such to Job.

IV. And often fail to see it when they might and should. Job, and many another since, failed to see it. He asserts that there are villains—godless, cruel, all that is bad—and yet they prosper wonderfully. " They are not in trouble as other men, neither are they plagued like other men. There are no bands in their death, and their strength is firm : " so said another perplexed one. There seems to be the corrupt and corrupting carcase, but no vulture descends upon it. The body there, that is certain, but not the bird But let such perplexed ones remember : 1. *The bird may be invisible.* It may be so far up in the sky, so far away, that our limited eyesight cannot travel so far, it is out of our range. That may be. Or : 2. *It may be restrained.* God is " long-suffering, not willing that any should perish." Or : 3. *It may have already descended, and be doing its work, and you not know it.* Conscience may rend and tear like a vulture, and the man may carry a very hell within him—thousands do—that makes all outward prosperity a mockery, and powerless to relieve. There is not one drop of water in it all wherewith he can cool his tongue, so tormented in this fire is he. Read ' Macbeth.' And : 4. *If it come not now it will fasten on him the moment he reaches the next world's shore.* Ah, yes ; if a man have made his soul carrion-like, the eagle of judgment *will* find him sooner or later in trouble ; from without or within, here or yonder—there is *no* escape. Remember, then : (1) They are fools who make a mock at sin. (2) Turn from it, and pray for the heart to love and dread the Lord, and to diligently live after his commandments.—S. C.

Vers. 1—13.—*The purpose of revealing judgment.* The process of the conquest of evil is varied. It is now by severity of judgment, now by the gentleness of mild rebuke or moderated chastisement. Again the voice of the teacher arrests attention, and the appeals of truth stimulate to righteousness. Hidden behind all is the gracious operation of the Holy Spirit of the Lord, working all things according to the counsel of his holy will. His hand is unseen, and the revelation is needed to show and assure men that there is a Divine power at work, though it be hidden. The *revelation* of the Divine judgments against evil has thus its high purpose apart from the purposes answered by those judgments themselves. Throughout the whole the cry may well arise, " The Lord reigneth ; let the earth rejoice; let the multitude of isles be glad thereof." The purposes contemplated by the pictorial representations congregate mainly, if not exclusively, around the Church—the smitten, suffering, enduring Church. The earthly powers, waging their warfare under the leadership of the prince of evil, Apollyon the Destroyer, do not read the holy books. They are truly sealed books to them. And the imagery is only to be interpreted by the Church when she is driven by the persecuting oppressive power of the world to seek consolation. The purpose then concerns the Church mainly, if not exclusively; and we may conceive that purpose to be achieved—

I. IN THE ENCOURAGEMENT OF THE CHURCH TO PATIENT ENDURANCE. For the Name of the great Lord the believing people suffered much. They were weak in presence of their so great foes. Only the assurance of a final triumph could embolden them to endure patiently.

II. IN THE SUPPORT OF THE CHURCH IN ITS HOLY WARFARE AGAINST THE OPPOSING EARTHLY SPIRIT. Fierce indeed was the conflict, and again and again it is so; but throughout the whole shines the revelation of the righteous judgment of God. His eye is open upon the sufferers, and his aid is pledged for their defence.

III. IN WARNING THE FAITHFUL AGAINST THE EVILS OF APOSTASY. Great are the subtle powers which seek to undermine and sap the fidelity of the godly. Only by many means, of which this is one, can the obedient host be stimulated to faithfulness.

IV. The end is further reached IN THE DEEP AND ABIDING COMFORT OF THE SORROWFUL BELIEVERS in all their antagonism to evil and to the worldly power which is set against them.—R. G.

Vers. 2—5.—*The effectual prayer.* A new series—another—opens upon the view of the holy seer. These are scenes in which is symbolically represented the method by which the Divine providence will execute those sovereign purposes which are specially contemplated in the redemption of the persecuted Church in its struggle with the various developments of evil in the world. Not always does evil present itself as an antagonistic power. It is soft, subtle, and alluring, drawing the feet of the unwary believer into ruinous paths by "the baits of pleasing ill." This aspect comes into prominence in the course of the revelation. But, as the book is an unfolding of the methods of conquest in all the conditions of danger, so now those which relate to the progressive triumph of the truth of the providential chastisements, are set in order. The space over which the sounding of the trumpets reaches is great; the seventh in ch. xi. declaring, as in other places, the final triumph, and so completely rounding another setting forth of the one idea of the book—the triumph of Messiah, "conquering, and to conquer." Another series of "seven" is before us—"seven angels," having "seven trumpets;" but "another angel" is first and intermediately present, having a golden censer, with the incense of which mingles "the prayers of the saints." Afterwards, from the same censer, coals of fire are taken and cast on the earth, and "thunders, and voices, and lightnings, and an earthquake" follow. They are represented to us in vast cosmical changes, the disturbances of the affairs of men in answer to the cry for judgment. But the judgment of the Lord need not always be of severity—certainly the end of the Lord is to be very pitiful. Mercy, redemption, recovery, salvation, blessing, are the ultimate ends in view. Thus must all be interpreted. The lesson taught is *the certain Divine response to humble prayer.* Here the Church finds—

I. ENCOURAGEMENT TO PERSEVERING INTERCESSION on behalf of the ungodly and unsubdued world.

II. A MOTIVE TO PATIENT ENDURANCE of the antagonism which evilness always suggests. Evil is at enmity against righteousness, even though it be not violent in its methods.

III. A HELP TO FAITH. Faith has respect to the promise of God, and beholds its fulfilment. Here the setting forth of the Divine response to prayer becomes the cheering encouragement to perseverance.

IV. A STIMULUS TO UNWEARIED LABOUR. If the certainty of success is not the ground of faith, it is its appropriate stimulus. Thus is the Church in all ages to be cheered.—R. G.

Vers. 6—13.—*Restricted judgment.* In wrath the Lord ever remembers mercy. In the sounding of four of the seven angels this idea is most prominent. Afflictions of various kinds are seen to rest upon the earth, but they are confined in each case to one-third. It is not a final overthrow, nor is it a vision of destruction. In the disturbance of the material world is portrayed the upheaving in the spiritual, and the gentle threat of the Divine displeasure. The avenging his own elect is a call to men to forsake evil, while it is an encouragement to the faithful to endure. By the disturbance in all the world, or material sphere, men are warned against placing their confidence in these things which may be so shaken. The judgments are chastisements—a part suffers tor the good of the whole. The eye is plucked out to save the whole body. Here a portion—a third part—suffers that the whole perish not. These restricted judgments or chastisements of the Lord have their great use—

I. IN AWAKENING THE ATTENTION OF MEN TO THEIR SPIRITUAL CONDITION. Truly a voice as of a trumpet! In the carelessness of spiritual slumber great evils may silently lurk beneath the surface. The sharp probe of pain awakens the slumbering spirit, and leads to inquiry and self-examination.

II. IN STIMULATING TO REPENTANCE. He also finds the way of disobedience to bring pain to him; and will be urged thereby to turn from the evil path and to seek the ways of obedience, wherein are rest and peace.

III. IN THE PREVENTION OF FURTHER SINFULNESS. They are the hedge of fire, warning off from forbidden paths. No vindictiveness or harsh severity prompts him who with fatherly hand chastises his erring and mistaken children.

IV. These chastisements have their final use as disciplinary processes IN ADVANCING RIGHTEOUSNESS. The clear declarations of Scripture in the classical passages on chastisement declare the end to be "that we may be partakers of his holiness." Sharp is the piercing pain, keen the edge of suffering; but the good features of the character called into play in bearing up under sorrow are developed thereby: and the spirit, checked from walking in the wrong path, is stimulated to choose the right and the good. That which applies to the individual life applies also to the life of tribes and nations of men. To these the present passage relates. Judgments on "the third part" are designed to be corrective and admonitory to the whole.—R. G.

Ver. 13.—*The bitter consequences of iniquity.* Before the fifth angel sounds his trumpet, a vision is granted of a flying eagle, which, with "a great voice," declared "Woe for them that dwell upon the earth, by reason of the other voices of the trumpet of the three angels who are yet to sound!" Corrective judgments have already been manifested, but the full fruits of evil, in themselves judgments and designed for correction and restraint, have not been developed. The voice of the great eagle anticipates them, and prepares for their delineation. The general principle, therefore, claims thought at present—*woe follows from the working of evil.*

I. THE INEVITABLE CONSEQUENCE OF WRONG-DOING IS SUFFERING. 1. The laws of righteousness are absolutely and only good. 2. They describe the true path of the human life. 3. In the observance of the true laws of life—the laws of righteousness—conditions of blessedness are secured; for it cannot but be that life held according to the laws of life is only good. 4. Any departure from the laws of life—righteousness—must bring a proportionate disturbance, pain and sorrow.

II. THE DIVINE WISDOM AND BENIGNITY SHOWN IN MAKING THE CONSEQUENCES OF WRONG-DOING PAINFUL. By this means men are warned away from wrong. The sharp pain of burning is a merciful provision. The hand incautiously laid in the fire might be consumed for want of the sharp twinge of pain to apprise of danger. It is well that the way of transgressors is hard. The prickly hedge guards the path of life, lest men straying from it should fall into untold evils.

III. THE PAINFULNESS OF WRONG-DOING A JUST WARNING AGAINST TRANSGRESSION. Although virtue that is founded on a mere escape from the evils of disobedience is a low form of virtue, it is nevertheless a worthy motive for avoiding that its consequences are painful.

IV. THE NATURAL CONSEQUENCES OF WRONG-DOING AN ADMONITORY INDICATION OF THE DIVINE DISPLEASURE, and a worthy expression of it. It is a testimony on the level of the human heart. Higher testimonies to be given. But the cold and thoughtless arrested by these means.

V. IN PUNISHMENTS BY PAIN LIES THE PLEDGE AND FIRST ELEMENT OF MORAL CORRECTION. The punishment and bitterness of evil not a final end. High moral purposes are graciously contemplated. "Woe, woe, woe!" is the sad prediction of the ever-coming bitterness of all wrong-doing.—R. G.

Vers. 1—6.—*Soul-silence.* "And when he had opened the seventh seal, there was silence in heaven about the space of half an hour," etc. This portion of the dream of John, like other portions, has Jewish elements of thought brought into strange and grotesque combinations. In dreams there are no new objects or elements of thought or emotion, but old ones brought into unique forms by an ungoverned imagination. Whilst they are evermore difficult, if not impossible to interpret, they are at all times available for the illustrating and impressing of truth. The words may be fairly taken to illustrate *soul-silence.* "There was [followed] silence in heaven about the space of half an hour." That is, silence for a time. It is suggested—

I. THAT SOUL-SILENCE OFTEN FOLLOWS GREAT EXCITEMENT. The opening of the seals, the unfolding of the wonderful dispensations of the Divine government up to the close of the world's history, must have excited the feelings and strained the faculties of the spectators to an unusual intensity. The soul-lake was no longer without a ripple; it was heaved into swelling surges. It is ever so in *soul-life;* after great tumult there comes a calm. This is always and pre-eminently the case with the genuinely faithful and holy. From the storms of remorse, secular anxieties, and social bereavements, the soul of the genuinely Christly rises into a "peace that passeth all understanding." In truth, in the case of all regenerate souls, great excitement is often the condition of peace and tranquillity. It is not until the storms of *moral conviction* become so terrible that the spirit cries out, "Lord, save, or I perish!" that the omnific voice, "Peace, be still!" will take effect, and there comes a "great calm." Blessed silence this! How grand is such a silence! It is the highest gift of man, nay, Divinity itself.

> "How grand is Silence! In her tranquil deeps
> What mighty things are born! Thought, Beauty, Faith,
> All good;—bright Thought, which springeth forth at once,
> Like sudden sunrise; Faith, the angel-eyed,
> Who takes her rest beside the heart of man,
> Serene and still; eternal Beauty, crown'd
> With flowers, that with the changing seasons change;
> And good of all kinds. Whilst the babbling verse
> Of the vain poet frets its restless way,
> In stately strength the sage's mind flows on,
> Making no noise :—and so, when clamorous crowds
> Rush forth, or tedious wits waken the senate-house,
> Or some fierce actor stamps upon his stage,
> With what a gentle foot doth silent Time
> Steal on his everlasting journey!"
>
> (Barry Cornwall.)

II. THAT SOUL-SILENCE IS OFTEN FOUND ABSORBING WORSHIP. "And I saw the seven angels which stood before God; and to them were given seven trumpets," etc. Here begins a new series of visions. The seven trumpets follow the seven seals, and this series extends to the close of the eleventh chapter. The "seven trumpets" are given to the seven angels or ministers that stand in the presence of God. But it is not with these seven angels or messengers that we have now to do; they will engage our attention further on. Our concern at present is with the angel connected with the altar—"the angel that stood at the altar, having a golden censer; and there was given unto him much incense, that he should offer [add] it with the prayers of all saints upon the golden altar which was before the throne." This symbolical representation of worship is derived from the Jewish temple, and it may illustrate to us the fact : 1. That the prayers of saints on earth *are of great practical interest in the spiritual universe.* (1) They are offerings that are acceptable to its Supreme Ruler. "And the smoke of the incense, which came with the prayers of the saints, ascended up before God." True prayer is acceptable to the Infinite Father. (2) In rendering them acceptable to God, his highest spiritual ministers are deeply engaged. Here is an angel standing towards the altar with a golden censer, receiving incense that he might give it "with the prayers of all saints." Elsewhere, in numerous passages of Holy Writ, angels are represented as rendering spiritual assistance to good men. May they not be constantly doing so by inbreathing those heavenly thoughts that will inspire the soul with the

REVELATION.

10

holiest devotions? 2. That the prayers of saints on earth *exert an influence on the things of time.* We are told, "the angel took the censer, and filled it with fire of the altar, and cast it into the earth: and there were [followed] voices, and thunderings, and lightnings, and an earthquake." The prayers have gone up, and the sprinkling of the ashes earthward symbolize their effects on the earth. What convulsions, what revolutions, the prayers of the saints have effected on this earth ere now! and what they effect now they will continue to do. Now, in the midst of all this devotion there would seem to be a period of *silence.* The profoundest hush, the deepest silence of the soul, are found in *worship.* Here all its faculties work harmoniously, and all its sympathies flow as a deep river without a ripple on its surface. "The Lord is in his holy temple; let all the earth keep silence before him." The realization of the Divine Presence can never fail to hush the soul into profound tranquillity, and in this tranquillity its grandest possibilities germinate and grow. "Silence," says an illustrious thinker, "is the element in which great things fashion themselves together, that at length they may emerge full-formed and majestic into the daylight of life which they are thenceforward to rule."

III. THAT SOUL-SILENCE OFTEN SPRINGS FROM HIGH EXPECTANCY. "And the seven angels which had the seven trumpets prepared themselves to sound." And as the angels raised their trumpets to their mouths ready to blow, a breathless expectancy would be excited. In earnest waiting there is generally silence—waiting for the last breath of a friend, waiting for the verdict of a jury which decides the deliverance or the destruction of a human life. Holy souls that now witnessed the scene of the trumpets about to utter a blast felt that great things were coming, that stupendous events were rolling up on the wheels of Providence, and there was "silence in heaven about the space of half an hour." What wonderful things are before us all! Were we all earnestly waiting for these things, waiting for the "manifestation of the sons of God," waiting the advent of him who is to wind up the affairs of the world, how silent should we be!—D. T.

Vers. 7—13; ch. ix. and x.—*The "seven trumpets:" the revolutions of matter and mind.* "The first angel sounded, and there followed hail and fire mingled with blood, and they were cast upon the earth: and the third part of trees was burnt up, and all green grass was burnt up," etc. We take these verses, extending from the seventh verse of the eighth chapter to the end of the tenth chapter, together, because they all refer to the "trumpets," and are records of a portion of John's most wonderful dream. A dream can be recalled, narrated, but seldom, if ever, rightly interpreted. It is generally, perhaps, uninterpretable. Pietistic simpletons and speculative pedants have propounded their interpretations and are still doing so; and what literary rubbish is the result! But though a dream may be incapable of interpretation, it can generally and usefully be used as an *illustration of great truths.* Thus we endeavour to use all these mysterious and multifarious visions that John had in Patmos. This vision serves to illustrate—

I. SOME OF THE WONDERFUL REVOLUTIONS THROUGH WHICH OUR WORLD IS CONSTANTLY PASSING. After the sounding of each of the seven trumpets, what a series of marvels was evolved! There are two classes of marvel here. 1. *Those in the material sphere.* As the first four seals were introduced by the cry of "Come," it has been observed that the first four trumpets are followed by judgments on natural objects—the earth, the sea, the rivers, the lights of heaven. What followed the blast of the first trumpet? "There followed hail and fire mingled with blood, and they were cast upon the earth: and the third part of trees was burnt up, and all green grass was burnt up." "Trumpets," says Moses Stuart, "the usual emblems of war and bloodshed, are chosen as emblems of the series of judgments now to be inflicted." Does the language here *literally* refer to some physical events that will befall this earth? From the character of the whole book, which is metaphorical, this is not likely. But events of an astounding character are suggested as occurring on this earth. After this the second trumpet sounded, "and as it were a great mountain burning with fire was cast into the sea: and the third part of the sea became blood." The words suggest the idea of some volcanic mountain discolouring the ocean so that it appears as blood, destroying a great portion of the creatures that lived in its depth and that floated on its waves. Then, with the sounding of the third trumpet, another terrible event occurs: "And there fell a great star from heaven, burning as it were a lamp, and it fell upon the third part of the rivers, and upon the fountains of waters," etc. The greater part of the rivers that roll over the earth, and the wells that spring from beneath, were embittered and poisoned, and many of the human race expire. When the fourth trumpet sounded the heavens are terribly affected. "The third part of the sun was smitten, and the third part of the moon, and the third part of the stars; so as the third part of them was [should be] darkened," etc. But all the terrible events that followed the blasts of these four trumpets seem only preparatory for some more terrible judgments that were to follow. "And I beheld [saw], and heard an angel [eagle] flying through the midst of [in mid] heaven, saying with a loud [great] voice, Woe, woe, woe, to the inhabiters of [for them that dwell on] the earth by reason of the other voices of the trumpet of the three angels, which [who] are yet to sound!" Whatever particular revolutions the blasts of the four trumpets here refer to—if any—one thing is certain, that great changes are taking place constantly in those regions of matter mentioned here—the earth, the waters, the heavens. *Geology* shows this. What our earth is to-day, its mountains, its valleys, its rivers, and its oceans, as well as its animal and vegetable productions, is the outcome of changes that have been going on through countless ages. Nature is constantly building up and pulling down. "The mountains falling come to nought," etc. *Astronomy* shows this. The telescope discovers shattered planets, stars that, perhaps, shone brightly once in our heavens, also new orbs and comets. All things are in a state of flux and reflux. According to Peter, all the changes that have been only tend to a greater change. "The day of the Lord shall come as a thief in the night, in which the heavens shall pass away with a great noise, and the elements shall melt," etc.[1] What is the *practical lesson* to be drawn from all these tremendous revolutions? "Trust in him who liveth for ever."

> "There's nought on earth that does not change;
> All things are shifting on the stream;
> Whatever comes within our range
> Seems just as fleeting as a dream.
> There is no rest but in thy Word,
> No settled hope but in thy Name;
> Root thou our souls in thee, O Lord,
> For thou art evermore the same."

2. Those in the *spiritual* sphere. There are three more trumpets sounded which have been designated *woe-trumpets*, and their blasts seem to introduce wonderful things in the spiritual domain. That there is a spirit-world is too universally admitted to require proof. It comes to our credence, not merely as a matter of philosophic reasoning, but as a matter of consciousness. This spirit-world, of which each human being is a member, as well as the higher order of intelligences in the universe, though invisible and impalpable, is ever active and all-influential, the spring and sovereign even of all material forces and phenomena. What is matter but the creature and servant, the effect and evidence, of spirit? Great and mysterious changes in the *spirit*-world seem to follow the sounding of the *fifth* trumpet. *Moral evil* appears: (1) In forms alarming. "I saw a star fall from heaven [from heaven fallen] unto the earth: and to him was given [there was given to him] the key of the bottomless pit [the pit of the abyss]," etc. A messenger from heaven, like a bright star, descended and exposed the region of moral evil—he opened the "bottomless pit." Moral evil is indeed a pit. (*a*) It is fathomless. No one can explain its origin and its countless intricate ramifications; it is the "mystery of iniquity." (*b*) It is consuming. It is like a "great furnace." In whatever spirit moral evil exists, it burns, it gives pain, and works destruction. (*c*) It is obscuring. "The sun and the air were darkened by reason of the smoke of the pit." The passions and thoughts which sin generates in the spirit mantle the moral heavens in gloom. How often is this bottomless pit covered up in the soul, hid alike from self and society! Thank God, Heaven sends a messenger, like a star, from heaven to open it and to enlighten it. Do not let us look for this bottomless pit beneath us, or anywhere external; *it is within us*, if sin be in us. (2) In forces terrific. "And there came out of the smoke locusts upon the earth: and unto

[1] See 'Septem in Uno' on "Phases of Man's External Universe," p. 592.

them was given power," etc. Orientals dread an advent of locusts as one of the most terrible visitations ; grass, trees, plants of all description, fall before them. The locusts here sketched are of an order the most terrible. A modern writer describes the locusts here as "malicious as scorpions, ruling as kings, intelligent as men, wily as women, bold and fierce as lions, resistless as those clad in iron armour." These awful forces that go forth amongst men to inflict torture and ruin were: (a) All in connection with the "bottomless pit." They were, so to speak, bred in the depths of that moral pit, and became the servants of that pit. Whatever inflicts pain on humanity is forged in the depth of that bottomless pit. " Whence come wars ? " etc. (b) They tended to make life intolerable to man. " In those days shall men seek death, and shall not find it; and shall desire to die." Death is universally regarded as the greatest evil, but such is the state of misery here that it is sought as a relief. How often is the life of a man rendered intolerable because of his sins, and he has recourse to the razor, the rope, the river, or the poison ! From the "bottomless pit" of our own sins rise those tormenting fiends that render life intolerable. (c) They were under the direction of a controlling agent. " And they had a king over them [they have over them a king], which is the angel of the bottomless pit [the angel of the abyss]," etc. The meaning of the words "Abaddon " and " Apollyon," both in Hebrew and Greek, is "destruction." All these locusts—in other words, all the *forces that torment humanity*—are inspired and directed by one great spirit, the spirit of destruction, which goes to and fro through the earth like a lion, seeking whom it may devour. Greater and more terrible changes in the *spirit-world* seem to follow the sounding of the *sixth* trumpet. In this second " woe " the spirit of destruction takes a wider sweep. It goes forth from the four parts of the earth, it increases the number and the terror of its messengers. " Two hundred thousand thousand," a countless number, and they appeared as horses with heads of lions, panoplied with fire, and breathing smoke and flame. By this greater destruction is wrought amongst men—it strikes down a third part of the race. Thus ever the agencies of torture and ruin that visit man, working in connection with the " bottomless pit " of sin, multiplying in numbers and magnifying their malignant proportions. The trial that gives pain to the sinner to-day, may be only as an insect compared with the trial that, like a lion, may torture him to-morrow. So long as the " bottomless pit " remains within, torturing fiends will increase in number, and augment in malignant passion and strength. More strange changes in the *spirit-world* we find following the sounding of the *seventh* trumpet. Before the blast of this seventh trumpet, however, there is the advent of another wonderful messenger from heaven. This messenger is robed in a mystic cloud, a rainbow encircling his brow, his face bright as the sun, his feet like pillars of fire, having in his hand a " little book." He seems to take possession of the whole world, plants one foot on the sea and the other on the earth, breaks forth with the voice of a lion, and his utterances were followed by seven thunders, from which a voice out of heaven sounded, saying, " Seal up those things which the seven thunders uttered, and write them not." Again this wonderful angel or messenger from heaven, surrounded with all this mystic grandeur, whilst standing on the earth, lifts up his hand to the heavens, and swears " that there should be time no longer." After this the seventh trumpet sounds, proclaiming that the mystery of God was finished. In the tenth chapter three things are powerfully struck upon our attention. (1) *A proclamation of the end of time.* "Time shall be no longer." Time is but limited duration. What is time to man on earth becomes eternity to him when he quits it. It is but a *mode* of being. In truth, whenever a human spirit rises from the material to the spiritual, from the particular to the universal, time with him is no longer; he is free from all its limitations. He moves no longer on a little river or creek; he is afloat on the immeasurable ocean. (2) *The communication of a new revelation.* What was contained in this "little book " that had not appeared before ? Something vital to man's interest. Such Divine books or rolls are constantly coming to us. They come to man in every day's experience, in true thoughts, and in spiritual intuitions. (3) *The personal appropriation of truth.* The angel said, " Take it, and eat it up." Divine truth is not something for intellectual speculation ; it is not something for memory, but diet for the life. It must be transmuted into the moral blood and sent through the heart into every fibre of our being. These " seven trumpets," then, suggest and illustrate those revolutions which are everywhere going on, not only through the material, but through the spiritual states of being. In sooth, those that occur in the material are but the results and symbols of those which are transpiring in the great world of mind. In the inner world of soul what revolutions are constantly going on in every man's experience! Big schemes like mountains burning with fire cast into the sea, bright stars of hope and promise falling from the firmament of the soul, fire and smoke issuing from the "bottomless pit" of evil within, smoke that obscures all that is bright, terrible and tormenting forces, like armies of locusts, devouring every budding leaf, and, with a scorpion's sting whose virus rankles in all the nerves of the heart, so that men sometimes seek death and cannot find it. "Voices and thunders." Strange shapes with "thunderous voices" in the heavens. Ah me! these changes are no dreams, they are visions neither of the day nor the night; they are the great realities of the spirit-world.

II. THE SPIRITUAL PERSONALITIES BY WHICH, UNDER GOD, THESE REVOLUTIONS ARE EFFECTED. Here are "seven angels" with their "seven trumpets." That there are, in the great universe of God, countless spiritual existences, varying endlessly in faculty, position, force, and occupation, admits of no question by those who believe in the Divinity of the Scriptures. It is here suggested that to these may be ascribed all the changes that take place in the history of our world. Is it not more rational to trace all these changes to the agency of such *spiritual personalities* than to what scientists call the laws and forces of nature? The "force of motion" is in the *spirit*, not in *matter*. Matter is inert; it has no self-moving energy. Or, further, is there anything more unreasonable that a high order of spiritual existences should work all the changes we see in earth and sea and sky than the fact that all the products of civilization are the results of the *agency of man*? Is it not the *human spirit*, acting through its physical organization, that has covered the earth with architectural buildings, not only piled up the huge cathedrals, castles, palaces, and countless public edifices, but also innumerable residences of every size and shape? Was it not the *spirit* in man that constructed the bridges, that spanned broad rivers; tunnelled through huge mountains a way for mighty oceans to meet and mingle; covered every sea with the fleets of nations; transformed wildernesses and deserts into fertile meadows, vineyards, and gardens; constructed engines to bear men over sea and land almost with lightning velocity? If the human spirit has worked and is working such wonders as these, is there anything unreasonable in supposing that a *higher* class of spirits can direct the winds, kindle the lightnings, launch the thunders, roll the planets, and heave the ocean? Manifestly not. The universe teems with *spiritual personalities*, and matter everywhere is the *creature*, the *symbol*, and *servant* of spirit. The dream suggests two things concerning the work of these spirits. 1. *Their work is departmental.* Each had his own trumpet, and each produced his own results. The same trumpet was not used by all. This seems to be the Divine plan. Each living creature endowed with activity, from the tiniest to the greatest, has its own sphere and scope for action. One cannot do the work of another. It is so with men. In all temporal enterprises men themselves act upon this principle; the master mind in manufacture and commerce gives to each man his part; and this is the plan of God with us all. To each man he has given a mission, and that mission none can rightly discharge but himself. The higher spiritual existences, it would seem, act in this way. In the material department, it may be, one has to do with the management of the winds and stars and all the inorganic spheres. To another class is given the management of life, vegetable and animal. Thus, too, it may be in the moral realm. "He giveth his angels charge over us"—some to instruct the ignorant, some to console the sorrowful, some to strengthen the wavering, some to encourage the feeble and oppressed. 2. *Their work is gradual.* All the trumpets do not sound at the same time, and from the first to the last numberless ages might intervene. The great Maker and Manager of the universe works out his great plans by what appears to us slow degrees. He is in no haste; he has plenty of time at command. How gradually this earth progressed from chaos to its present condition! How gradually the human race advances in knowledge, in civilization, and in morality! How unlike our method! If we have a work on hand, the more important we deem it, the more impatient we are to realize its accomplishment. The sense of the brevity and uncertainty of life impels us to this haste. But "one day with him is as a thousand years, and a thousand years as one day." Does not this teach us to be *concerned more with the moral character of our work than with its results ?* Our question should be, " Is it right?" not, " What will be the issue?" The results will not appear in our time, not for ages on, it may be. A good act is like an acorn dropped into good soil; it will require countless ages fully to develop itself. In the motive is at once the virtue and the reward of all labour. Does it not also teach us *to be patient in well-doing, to be hoping ever ?* Our work, if right, is Divine, and if Divine, it cannot fail. " Be ye steadfast, immovable, always abounding in the work of the Lord."

III. THE GRAND PURPOSE TO WHICH ALL THE REVOLUTIONS ARE DIRECTED. All the revolutions here referred to have a bearing on the minds of men, breaking the monotony of their sinful condition, rousing their fears, so terrifying them as to make their existence so intolerable that they sought death as a relief. And then it is stated that a new revelation from heaven is given them—a " little book " that was to be appropriated. Moreover, it is stated that the grand purpose was the finishing of the " mystery of God." And what is that mystery but the *moral restoration of mankind ?* It is a glorious thought that all the changes that take place in the universe are for the benefit of souls—that all is moral discipline. Nature is a grand school in which the great Father makes his children " meet for the inheritance of the saints in light." " Lo, all these things worketh God oftentimes with man, to bring back his soul from the pit, to be enlightened with the light of the living." Evil is not an end. Good is the end, and evil is ever rushing to it like streams and rivers to the ocean-world. The evils of this world, like the furious storm that spreads devastation over sea and land, will one day die away in a clear sky and a pure atmosphere, and leave the world all beautiful and bright. (See also the three following homilies.)—D. T.

EXPOSITION.

CHAPTER IX.

Ver. 1.—And the fifth angel sounded, and I saw a star fall from heaven unto the earth; *a star from heaven fallen unto the earth* (Revised Version); not *saw a star fall.* (For the distinctive character of the last three judgments, see on ch. viii. 2.) " A star " sometimes signifies one high in position. Thus Numb. xxiv. 17, " There shall come a star out of Jacob; " Dan. viii. 10, " And it cast down some of the host and of the stars to the ground." In ch. i. 20 " the stars " are " the angels of the seven Churches; " in Job xxxviii. 7 the angels are called " stars; " in Isa. xiv. 12 we have Satan referred to thus : " How art thou fallen from heaven, O Lucifer, son of the morning!" It seems, therefore, that Satan himself is here referred to under this symbol. The trumpet-visions hitherto have portrayed troubles affecting the outer man ; now begin to be set forth those yet more terrible visitations which, affecting his spiritual nature, are seen more directly to emanate from the devil. He has fallen " from heaven unto the earth; " that is, whereas formerly heaven was his abode, the sphere of his work while yet obedient to God, he now has no office or power, or entrance there, but is permitted to exercise what influence he possesses on the earth (cf. Luke x. 18, " I beheld Satan as lightning fall from heaven "). This is the view of Tertullian. Arethas, Bede, Vitringa, Alford, believe an evil angel is meant: Wordsworth

thinks an apostate Christian teacher is signified ; Andreas, Bengel, and De Wette believe a good angel is intended ; others see particular emperors, etc.; while Hengstenberg thinks the figure represents not one, but a number of persons, including Napoleon. And to him was given the key of the bottomless pit ; *of the pit of the abyss* (Revised Version). That is, as Wordsworth explains, of the aperture by which there is no egress from or ingress into the abyss. Christ holds the key (ch. i. 18), but for a season Satan is permitted to exercise power. The *abyss* is the abode of the devil and his angels; the present abode, not the lake of fire, into which they are subsequently cast (ch. xx. 10).

Ver. 2.—And he opened the bottomless pit; *pit of the abyss,* as above. This phrase is omitted by ℵ, B, Coptic, Æthiopic, and others. It is inserted by A, B, many cursives, Vulgate, Syriac, Andreas. And there arose a smoke out of the pit, as the smoke of a great furnace. The smoke of the incense (ch. viii. 4) purified the prayers of the saints, making them acceptable before God ; the smoke which ascends from the abyss clouds men's minds and darkens their understandings. And the sun and the air were darkened by reason of the smoke of the pit. The air, becoming filled with the smoke, obscured the light of the sun, so that both appeared dark. This darkening of the atmosphere may have been suggested by the description of the locust-plague (Exod. x. 15), or by the account in Joel ii. But it is the smoke, not the locusts, which is here said to cause the obscurity; the locusts issue forth out of the smoke. It is doubtful whether we ought to seek any particular interpretation of *the smoke;* it is probably only accessory to the general picture. If we may press the meaning so far, it is perhaps best to regard the smoke as the evil influence of the devil, which darkens men's understandings, and from which issue the troubles which are the result of heresy and infidelity, portrayed by the locusts (cf. 2 Cor. iv. 4, "In whom the god of this world hath blinded the minds of the unbelieving," etc.).

Ver. 3.—And there came out of the smoke locusts upon the earth. The *locust* is constantly referred to in the Bible, and various illustrations are drawn from their character-istic features. In the East they appear in great numbers, and men are helpless against their devastating power. Sometimes an attempt is made to check their progress by lighting fires, and this practice may have suggested the above description of the locusts proceeding from the smoke. The irresistible destruction which they cause is alluded to in Deut. xxviii. 38; Joel ii. 25; 2 Chron. vii. 13; their number in Ps. cv. 34; Nah. iii. 15. The air is sometimes tainted with their dead bodies (Joel ii. 20). The natural features of the locust are fully dwelt upon in vers. 7—10. As an illustration, we may quote Niebuhr, who gives an Arab's description of the locust : "In head like the horse, in breast like the lion, in feet like the camel, in body like the ser-pent, in tail like the scorpion, in antennæ like a virgin's hair." Three out of these five points of resemblance are mentioned in vers. 7—10. The *locusts* here symbolize heretics and infidels. Some writers (*e.g.* Wordsworth) apply the symbol to the Mohammedans (see Wordsworth, *in loc.*, where the parallel is very fully worked out). But though this may be, and pro-bably is, a fulfilment of the vision, it would be wrong to thus restrict our interpretation. Scarcely any one cause has contributed more to the trouble and destruction of men than the violence which is the result of religious hatred. Whether it be the heathen idola-ter, the warlike Mohammedan, or the Chris-tian bigot, who is the agent, the effect is the same. It may be said, too, that if the minds of Christians also had not been darkened by the prejudicial influence of Satan, who is the cause of their unhappy divisions, heresies, and apostasies, these troubles could scarcely have fallen upon mankind. The innumerable occasions of such violence may be well illustrated by the countless number of the locusts; and the effect lives after the

death of the authors, tainting the moral atmosphere. It is true that the true Chris-tian sometimes suffers also; but that is an aspect which is set forth in the visions of the seals. Here another view is set forth, namely, that the ungodly are themselves punished, and punished severely, by means of this evil influence of the devil. Many other interpretations have been suggested : (1) evil spirits (Andreas); (2) Roman wars in Judæa (Grotius); (3) the Gothic inva-sion (Vitringa); (4) De Wette and Alford believe that the interpretation is unknown. And unto them was given power, as the scorpions of the earth have power. That is to say, just as the natural scorpions of the earth have power to cause suffering, so these allegorical locusts of the vision ap-peared to possess the means wherewith to plague mankind. The *scorpion* is "gene-rally found in dry and in dark places, under stones and in ruins, chiefly in warm climates. . . . The sting, which is situated at the ex-tremity of the tail, has at its base a gland that secretes a poisonous fluid, which is dis-charged into the wound. . . . In hot climates the sting often occasions much suffering, and sometimes alarming symptoms" (Smith's 'Dictionary of the Bible').

Ver. 4.—And it was commanded them that they should not hurt the grass of the earth, neither any green thing, neither any tree. The force of this plague is to fall directly upon mankind, not, as in the former judg-ments, upon the earth, and then indirectly upon men. This appears to be stated with the greater plainness, because it might readily be inferred, from the nature of locusts, that the immediate object of their destructiveness would be the vegetation of the world. But only those men which have not the seal of God in their foreheads; *but only such men as have not,* etc. (Revised Ver-sion; cf. ch. vii. 3, to which this is an allu-sion). Here, by proleipsis, the servants of God are described as "those that have the seal of God in their foreheads." It is not stated, nor is it necessarily implied, that the seal is visible to man at the time of the in-fliction of this judgment upon the ungodly. In a similar way our Lord speaks of the elect (Matt. xxiv. 22), not thereby implying that there is any visible manifestation by which the elect may be known to men though known to God (so also Titus i. 1 · Mark xiii. 22, etc.). Thus also it is said in 2 Tim. ii. 19, "The foundation of God standeth sure, having this seal, The Lord knoweth them that are his." The frequent use of the term to denote those who were sealed by baptism may have led to the em-ployment of the expression in this place, as being equivalent to "the servants of God" (cf. Eph. i. 13; iv. 30; 2 Cor. i. 22). The locusts may not hurt God's servants (see on ver. 3). Thus we are taught that God in reality preserves his own, though it may sometimes appear to man as though the innocent suffer with the guilty.

Ver. 5.—And to them it was given that **they** should not kill them, but that they **should** be tormented five months; *and it was given them* [i.e. the locusts] *that they* [the locusts] *should not kill them* [the unsealed], *but that they* [the unsealed] *should be tormented five months.* The devil and his agents have not unlimited power committed to them; they are restrained within limits by the will of God. The evils which follow in the train of heresy and infidelity are not as yet permitted to kill (cf. Job i. 12), for this judgment extends only to the natural life of man. God reserves the final killing to himself at the great judgment-day. This is shown in the limitation, "five months." This apparently meaningless period becomes explicable, when we remember that the usual duration of a locust-plague is *five months*, viz. from April to September. The visitation is for the natural period of such occurrences; the torment is to extend to the natural period of man's sojourn on the earth. It does not extend into the next life; other and special means are adopted for man's punishment then, as set forth under the seventh trumpet. Various other explanations have been given of the *five months.* (1) Five years of Gothic rule (Vitringa). (2) Five months = 5 × 30 days; each day represents one year; therefore 150 years are signified, viz. (*a*) of the Saracens, A.D. 830—A.D. 980 (Mede); (*b*) Mohammed's conquests, A.D. 612—A.D. 762 (Elliott). (3) Hengstenberg believes 5 to signify a part of the complete number 10, and thus to symbolize an incomplete period, as compared with the period of the seventh trumpet. (4) Bengel, following the principles assumed by him, makes the *five months* to equal 79½ natural years, and assigns the period to A.D. 510—A.D. 589. (5) Others take the expression to mean "a short time" merely. (6) Wordsworth interprets it as meaning a limited time permitted by God, and thinks the Mohammedan period is signified. And their torment was as the torment of a scorpion, when he striketh a man. "Their torment," that is, the torment of the unsealed, according to Alford; the torment of the locusts (viz. that which they inflict), according to others. In either case the meaning is the same. The last clause, "when he striketh a man," is perhaps added in contradistinction to the injury naturally inflicted by locusts, whose efforts are directed against the vegetation.

Ver. 6.—And in those days shall men seek death, and shall not find it; and shall desire

to die, and death shall flee from them; *shall in no wise find it . . . and death fleeth from them* (Revised Version); οἱ ἄνθρωποι, "the men;" that is, the unsealed, who suffer this judgment. This is a characteristic biblical method of expressing great anguish. Thus Job iii. 20, 21, "The bitter in soul; which long for death, but it cometh not" (cf. also Jer. viii. 3; Job vii. 15; Luke xxiii. 30; and ch. vi. 16). The description portrays great anguish of mind, and should not be pressed to a literal interpretation, though many have illustrated the passage by pointing to actual occurrences of the kind.

Ver. 7.—And the shapes of the locusts were like unto horses prepared unto battle; rather, *the likenesses of the locusts;* that is to say, the general appearance. This similarity is brought out in Joel ii., and is alluded to in Job xxxix. 20. The parallel is worked out at some length in Tristram's ' Natural History of the Bible,' p. 314. In what way they appeared "prepared unto battle," is shown in ver. 9. And on their heads were as it were crowns like gold; *crowns like unto gold.* The language is carefully guarded so as to make it understood that this feature is altogether supernatural. The *crowns* of *gold* probably denote the conquering nature of the locusts, and thus they add to the power with which the locusts have already been invested. They may also signify the exalted temporal position of those symbolized by the locusts. Some writers believe the helmets of soldiers are typified, and others the turbans of the Mohammedans. And their faces were as the faces of men. Notwithstanding the general resemblance of the locusts to horses, which resemblance is most clearly shadowed forth in the structure of the head, yet their faces gave the seer the idea of the human countenance. How this was brought about we are not told. Probably St. John himself in his vision received the impression without knowing by what means. The circumstance seems to point decidedly to the fact that human agents are denoted by the locusts.

Ver. 8.—And they had hair as the hair of women. This (like the succeeding clause) seems merely the enumeration of an additional feature, in which these creatures resembled locusts, and which helped to establish their claim to the name. The antennæ of the insect are probably referred to. Wordsworth sees here an allusion to the flowing hair of Mohammed and the Saracens. And their teeth were as the teeth of lions. The powerful nature of the teeth of the locust is a remarkable feature of the insect; and it is here more fully referred to in order to enhance the general terror of their aspect (cf. Joel i. 6).

Ver. 9.—And they had breastplates, as it

were breastplates of iron. Again, a natural feature of the locust is specifically alluded to, in order to portray the terrible nature of their appearance. The horny substance which appears behind the face of the locust is not unlike the plates of iron with which the breast and shoulders of war-horses were protected. And the sound of their wings was as the sound of chariots of many horses running to battle; *the sound of chariots, of many horses rushing to war* (Revised Version). The sound of the two things together, viz. that of rushing horses, and that of the chariots which they draw. The same simile is used in Joel ii. 5.

Ver. 10.—And they had tails like unto scorpions, and there were stings in their tails; *and they have tails like unto scorpions, and stings* (Revised Version). The next words are included in the following clause. Not that their tails possessed the appearance of scorpions (as Bengel, Hengstenberg, and others), but that their tails were like the tails of scorpions in respect of having stings in them. Cf. 2 Sam. xxii. 34; Ps. xviii. 33, "He maketh my feet like hinds" (omit "feet"); also ch. xiii. 11, "Two horns like a lamb" (see the description of the scorpion quoted above, under ver. 3). And their power was to hurt men five months; *and in their tails is their power to hurt*, etc. (Revised Version) (see the preceding clause). As no Greek manuscript gives the reading of the Textus Receptus followed by the Authorized Version, the probability is that this is an example of a passage in which the Greek of his edition was supplied by Erasmus, by the simple process of retranslating into Greek the Vulgate Version. By the possession of the noxious sting, the locusts here described are represented as being yet more terrible than the natural locusts. (See the description of the locusts given under ver. 3. For the signification of the "five months," see on ver. 5.) They limit the period of this judgment to the time of man's existence on this earth.

Ver. 11.—And they had a king over them, which is the angel of the bottomless pit; *they have over them as king the angel of the abyss* (Revised Version). Most commentators contrast with the condition of the natural locusts, who have no king (Prov. xxx. 27). "The angel" evidently points to the "star" of ver. 1, who is Satan himself. Some think a particular angel, not Satan, is intended. Alford unnecessarily hesitates to decide that Satan is meant, owing to ch. xii. 3, 9. Whose name in the Hebrew tongue is Abaddon, but in the Greek tongue hath his name Apollyon. *Abaddon* is the Hebrew אֲבַדּוֹן, a noun representing the abstract idea "destruction" (Job xxxi. 12), but more frequently employed to designate the nether-

world (Job xxvi. 6; xxviii. 22; Prov. xv. 11; Ps. lxxxviii. 12). Apollyon (ἀπολλύων, present participle) is the Greek ἀπόλεια (by which the LXX. renders אֲבַדּוֹן) personified. It is in conformity with St. John's usual practice to give the two forms of the name (cf. John i. 38, 42; iv. 25; ix. 7; xi. 16; xix. 13, 17). In the name we have summed up the character of him who bears it. He is the "destroyer," the one who causes "perdition" to mankind. Cf. the words of our Lord given by St. John (John iii. 44), "He was a murderer from the beginning." Bengel and others contrast with "Jesus" the "Saviour." Perhaps the height of absurdity is reached by those writers (Bleek, Volkmar) who see in the name Apollyon a reference to (N)apoleon.

Ver. 12.—One woe is past; *the one woe*, or *the first woe*. "Woe" (ἡ οὐαί) is feminine; perhaps because expressing the idea of tribulation, such words being generally feminine in the Greek. Some have thought that these words are a further announcement by the eagle of ch. viii. 13; but there is nothing to lead us to suppose that they are not the words of the writer. And, behold, there come two woes more hereafter. Omit "and:" *behold, there cometh yet two woes hereafter*. The verb is singular in אֲ, A, and others; the plural is found in אֲ, B, P, and others. Alford says, "singular, the verb applying simply to that which is future, without reference as yet to its plurality." But probably οὐαί, although written as a feminine in the preceding clause, being really indeclinable, is treated as a neuter; and thus the singular verb is made to agree with the neuter plural, in conformity with the rules of Greek grammar. The second woe extends from this place to ch. xi. 14, and the third woe is contained in ch. xi. 14—19, especially in ch. xi. 18.

Ver. 13.—And the sixth angel sounded, and I heard a voice; *I heard one voice*, perhaps in contradistinction to the *four* horns next mentioned. From the four horns of the golden altar which is before God; *the golden altar before God*. The balance of authority seems in favour of retaining τεσσάρων, "four," although the Revisers omit it. It is inserted in B, P, Andreas, Arethas, Primasius, etc., but omitted in אᶜ, A, Syriac, Coptic, Bede, etc. Many commentators (*e.g.* Vitringa, Hengstenberg) lay special stress upon it; and some represent the horns as the *four* Gospels, which speak with *one* voice. The voice issues from the altar, as in ch. vi. 10; xvi. 7. The voice, issuing from the resting-place of the souls of the martyrs, denounces the impending woe. The altar is the golden altar of incense (ch. viii. 3) which is *before* (the throne of) God, and which, in the earthly temple, stood before the veil (Exod. xl. 26). This altar had four "horns" projecting at the corners (Exod. xxx. 2; see also Smith's 'Dictionary of the Bible,' art. "Altar").

Ver. 14.—Saying to the sixth angel which had the trumpet. Tregelles reads, "Saying to the sixth angel, Thou hast that the trumpet," etc.; but the common rendering is much more probable. Here the angel is represented as directly causing the incidents which follow; in the other cases, we are only told that each angel "sounded." Loose the four angels which are bound in the great river Euphrates. This vision has led to a great variety of interpretations. Some are obviously absurd; in all these is considerable doubt and difficulty. The following is offered as a possible solution to some extent, though it is not pretended that every difficulty is satisfactorily disposed of. In making this suggestion, the following circumstances have been borne in mind: (1) The trumpet-visions seem constructed upon a systematic plan, and therefore it seems likely that this judgment, like the fifth and the seventh, is a spiritual one (vide supra). (2) The objects of this punishment are those who commit the sins described in vers. 20, 21. (3) The vision must have borne some meaning for those to whom it was first delivered. It seems unlikely, therefore, that events are here portrayed which could not possibly have been foreseen and understood by the early Christians. This seems to exclude (except possibly in a secondary sense) all reference to the papacy, etc. (as Wordsworth). (4) Whether the angels here described are good angels or bad angels makes no material difference to the main part of the vision, which is to set forth punishment for the ungodly, sanctioned or originated by God. (5) The object of the punishment is to bring men to repentance, but it largely fails to do so (ver. 21). We therefore conclude that the whole judgment portrays the spiritual evils which afflict the ungodly in this life, and which give them, as it were, a foretaste of their doom in the life to come. Sin frequently brings unrest and trouble immediately in its train; seldom, if ever, peace and satisfaction. The stings of sin are, perhaps, none the less potent because their effect is frequently unseen by the general public. The terror of the murderer, the shame of the thief, the abasement and physical suffering of the impure, the delirium tremens of the drunkard, are very real torments. The number of such inflictions is, indeed, great enough to be described as "two myriads of myriads" (ver. 16); they destroy a part, but not the greater part (ver. 15, "the third part") of men; and yet how largely they fail to bring men to repentance! Such

punishment is a foretaste of hell, as seems to be foreshadowed in the "fire and smoke and brimstone" of vers. 17, 18. Wordsworth and others contend that the "four angels" are good angels, who have been hitherto restrained. As remarked above, the point is not a material one, but it seems more probable that evil angels are intended. Their loosing does not necessarily mean that they are loosed at a time subsequent to this vision, but only that they are under the control of God, who allows them freedom to carry out this mission. Thus also, in the case of the other judgments, it has been pointed out that the period of their operation may extend throughout all ages, from the beginning to the end of the world. They arise from the Euphrates. Many writers point out that this river was looked upon by the Israelites as the natural source from which sprang their enemies (see Isa. vii. 20; viii. 7; Jer. xlvi. 10). Indeed, the Euphrates was looked upon as the boundary of the Jewish kingdom (Gen. xv. 18; Deut. i. 7; xi. 24; Josh. i. 4; 2 Sam. viii. 3; 1 Chron. v. 9); hence those coming from out of the Euphrates were frequently enemies. The expression may be merely accessory to the general filling up of the picture, or it may teach us that the punishments which follow flow from their natural source, viz. men's sins (cf. ch. xvi. 12, where the Euphrates is certainly alluded to as the source from whence arise hostile hosts).

Ver. 15.—And the four angels were loosed, which were prepared for an hour, and a day, and a month, and a year, for to slay the third part of men. The alterations in the Revised Version make the meaning much plainer: which had been prepared for the hour, and day, and month, and year, that they should kill, etc. That is to say those "which had" in God's foreknowledge "been prepared" in order to operate at the exact period required—the exact year, month, day, and even hour. Each knew his appointed time. Four is the number used to denote universality in things of this world (see on ch. iv. 6). The number, therefore, seems to imply that the power of the angels is of universal extent. The third part are destroyed; that is, a great part, though not the larger (cf. ch. viii. 7, et seq.).

Ver. 16.—And the number of the army of the horsemen; and the number of the armies of the cavalry. No horsemen have hitherto been alluded to; but they are apparently the destroying host under the direction of the four angels. The symbol is, no doubt, chosen to signify power, of which horsemen or cavalry are an emblem. Were two hundred thousand thousand; or, twice myriads of myriads (cf. Jude 14—16, which is a quotation from Enoch; also Dan.

vii. 10). **The number is, of course, not to be** taken literally, but as signifying an exceeding great multitude. And I heard the number of them. Omit "and." St. John "heard the number" possibly from one of the elders, who had before instructed him (cf. ch. vii. 13). He states this, since so vast a multitude would be innumerable.

Ver. 17.—And thus I saw the horses in the vision, and them that sat on them. That is, according to the description following, not "thus, in such numbers as I have described." Having breastplates of fire, and of jacinth, and brimstone. 'Εχοντας, "having," probably refers to both horses and riders, though it may refer to the riders only. The Revised Version renders *jacinth* more exactly as *hyacinth*. Alford translates, "*breastplates*, fiery-red, fuliginous, and sulphureous." It seems to be rightly concluded that the *hyacinthine* hue answers to the "smoke" further on in the verse. "The expression, 'of jacinth,' applied to the breastplate, is descriptive simply of a *hyacinthine*, i.e. dark-purple colour" (Smith's 'Dictionary of the Bible'). The description intensifies the terrible nature of the vision, and it is doubtful whether these details should be pressed to a particular interpretation. If they bear any meaning at all, they seem to point to the doom in wait for the wicked, whose portion is fire and brimstone (cf. Ps. xi. 6). And the heads of the horses were as the heads of lions; and out of their mouths issued fire and smoke and brimstone; *proceedeth fire*, etc. (Revised Version). Here, as in the preceding clause, the intention is evidently to enhance the terrible appearance of the vision. The "smoke" corresponds to the *hyacinth* hue, mentioned in the previous part of the verse (*vide supra*). The horses, in accordance with a well-known poetic figure, are said to breathe out "fire and smoke." Brimstone is mentioned in addition, in order to set forth plainly the fact that their acts are directed against the wicked (cf. Gen. xix. 24; Job xviii. 15; Ps. xi. 6; Ezek. xxxviii. 23; Isa. xxx. 33; Luke xvii. 29). Lions' teeth are mentioned in the description of the locusts, with the same purpose (ver. 9). It is difficult to see why Alford should imagine that the *fire, smoke,* and *brimstone* proceed separately from different divisions of the host: it was not so in the case of the breastplates.

Ver. 18.—By these three was the third part of men killed, by the fire, and by the smoke, and by the brimstone, which issued out of their mouths; *by these three plagues* (as in Revised Version) . . . *the brimstone, which proceeded.* Although the last clause technically is attached to "brimstone" only, yet the description applies to all three of the

things mentioned. "The third part"—again a large, but not the largest, part of mankind (see on ch. viii. 7). The locusts were forbidden to *kill* (ver. 5); these horsemen are permitted to do so. Each judgment of the trumpet-visions appears to increase in severity. We may here see portrayed the terrible and destructive character of the results of sin. Such results are experienced to the full by the *third* part of men, the large class who "repent not of their murders, nor of their sorceries," etc. (ver. 21).

Ver. 19.—For their power is in their mouth, and in their tails; *for the power of the horses is,* etc. Another example of disagreement between Erasmus and all the Greek manuscripts (see on ver. 10). For their tails were like unto serpents, and had heads, and with them they do hurt. "Are like," and "have heads," in the present tense. Here (unlike ver. 10) the tails are like serpents themselves. The image is not uncommon among the ancients. We may paraphrase the passage thus: "Their power is for the most part in their mouth; but also, to some extent, in their tails; for their tails are like serpents," etc. An endless variety of interpretations have been given to these details, which are probably not intended to bear any distinct signification. Bengel refers to a species of serpent in which the head and tail were so alike as to be with difficulty distinguished; which he thinks may have suggested the image. Many apply it (though in different ways) to the Turkish horse, who fight as they retreat, etc.

Ver. 20.—And the rest of the men which were not killed by these plagues; *the rest of mankind* (Revised Version). That is, the two-thirds (ver. 18). Some understand "these plagues" to refer to the first six trumpets. It may be so, but it seems more correct to limit it to the sixth, as the same phrase, which occurs in ver. 18, must be so limited. *Mankind* must be taken to mean the worldly only. Of the ungodly, some are killed (the third part), the rest yet do not repent. The vision is not concerned with the fate of the righteous. Yet repented not of the works of their hands, that they should not worship devils, and idols of gold, and silver, and brass, and stone, and of wood: which neither can see, nor hear, nor walk. "The works of their hands" refers to idolatry, as shown by the succeeding words. This verse begins to prepare us for the seventh judgment. Men will not repent; therefore the last final judgment becomes necessary. The absurdity of idolatrous worship is frequently thus set forth by Old Testament writers (cf. Ps. cxv. 4; cxxxv. 15; Isa. ii. 8; Ezek. xxii. 4; Hos. xiii. 2). See also the description in Dan. v.

23, which seems to- have suggested the wording of this part of the vision. It has been well remarked that in this verse mention is made of sins against God; in the following verse man's sins against his neighbours are detailed.

Ver. 21.—Neither repented they of their murders, nor of their sorceries, nor of their fornication, nor of their thefts. *Sorceries;*

magic, witchcraft, and enchantments; *e.g.* the magic of the Egyptian magicians (Exod. vii. 22). Sorcery is mentioned in Gal. v. 20 (where it is described as "witchcraft") in connection with idolatry. *Fornication* (cf. Bengel, "Other crimes are perpetrated by men at intervals; there is one continual fornication within those who are wanting in purity of heart").

HOMILETICS.

See homiletic section, ch. viii.

HOMILIES BY VARIOUS AUTHORS.

Ver. 20.—*Man's stubborn will.* "And the rest . . . yet repented not." The fatal obstinacy of wicked men, the dreadful hardness of the human heart, sin's searing of the susceptibilities of the soul,—such is the mournful fact that the text, repeated again in the next verse, as if to summon our special attention, vividly reveals. Implied or stated in it are such truths as these—

I. ALL MEN NEED REPENTANCE. The judgment fell only on some, but all deserved it; all had sinned, and all should have repented. When we see God's judgment falling on any one, our reflection should be not, "How evil he must have been!" but "How merciful of God to spare me!"

II. GOD PLEADS WITH MEN TO BRING THEM TO REPENTANCE. These judgments of which we read are not God's primary dealings with men. He does not *begin* in this manner. There has been much that has preceded this. God has pleaded with men by his Spirit in their *consciences.* By *his goodness,* giving them all manner of providential mercies. Then, more especially by *his Word,* delivered by revelation, through his messengers, etc. And in these last days he has spoken to us by *his Son,* in the message of the gospel. Men always knew that their deeds were evil; the sense of sin was everywhere; and they knew that God would have them repent. And there were some who did, and therefore held aloof from the abominations of the rest. And since Christ has come the Divine pleadings have been more than ever heard.

III. BUT THESE MILDER METHODS OFTEN FAIL. All history shows this, as well as the Bible, and our own experience confirms it. See our Saviour weeping over Jerusalem. That sorrow had been known before, and has been since.

IV. STERNER METHODS ARE THEN TRIED. In these Apocalyptic visions we have portrayed over and over again these more awful means which God employs to bring men to repentance. In Israel's history how often they were tried! and they often succeeded, as, blessed be God, they often succeed now. This is their purpose.

V. BUT EVEN THESE, AT TIMES, AND FOR LONG TIME, FAIL. This is the declaration of our text (cf. also Jer. v. 3; viii. 6; Rom. ii. 4, 5). So was it with Pharaoh, when the plagues one after another, which in many respects resembled these trumpet-plagues, came upon him. The invariable effects of the Divine law, which ordains that sin persisted in becomes fixed habit which cannot be shaken off, and of which, therefore, the writer of the Book of Exodus says, "The Lord hardened Pharaoh's heart;"— this Divine law was illustrated in him. So again and again in Israel's history, "until the wrath of the Lord arose against them, and there was no remedy." In men, too, like that wicked King Amon, of whom it is said, "But Amon sinned more and more." True, the psalmist says, "Before I was afflicted I went astray, but now have I kept thy Word." But though it might have been true of him, it is as often as not, if not more often, true that men go astray after affliction just as they did before. "Though thou bray a fool in a mortar, yet will not his folly depart from him." So, with equal, if not greater truth, does the proverb assert that opposite and most melancholy fact of which the Bible all life, and our text here say so much. "God's visitations pass lightly over souls asleep in sin. Which of us has not lived through a thousand of them, and never seen, never noticed, never given heed to, one? Death, sudden death, coming into our street, or into our home,—which of us has not hardened his heart again, after a very brief pause, against lessons which this ought to teach, and sinned on as before? Oh the desperate hardness of the human heart! What can melt it save omnipotent grace?"

VI. WHAT IS THE REASON OF THIS? The answer is manifold, as, for example: 1. *Those that are spared argue from that fact that they need not repent.* The Jews thought that those on whom the tower of Siloam fell must indeed have been sinners. Our Lord told them that was not the case, and, said he, " Except ye repent, ye shall all likewise perish." And no doubt "the rest of mankind" told of in our text congratulated themselves, not only that they were spared, but that they did not deserve what had befallen the others. There was, therefore, no need for them to repent—so would they argue, as do and have done their successors ever since. 2. *Sin deadens belief in God.* It makes men practical atheists. God, therefore, is not recognized in aught that occurs. 3. *God's judgments are put down to secondary causes.* Everything can be explained; they know how and why things fell out as they did. They look not beyond or above those causes which are close at hand and can be readily understood. Hence their own sin and God's displeasure thereat, being far too abstract and remote factors, are not even considered. 4. *" Perfect love casteth out fear."* This is true in a sense the apostle never meant. Let the heart love sin, as it is so prone to do, and that love will utterly cast out the fear of God. And some sins, especially, will do this; those that are named in these verses will. *Idolatry*, which lulls the conscience whilst it gives free licence to sin. *Gain gotten in ungodly ways*—"thefts," as they are here called. Who does not know how the petty pilferer develops into the practised thief, embezzler, robber, and forger, until he has graduated in all such villainy? *Lust*— "fornications," as it is here termed. Let those who have known its hell and have told its dark dread secrets be believed, when they affirm that, indulged, it becomes ungovernable. Against it the fear of God has no chance. *Cruelty*—"murders" is the name given it here; that, too, grows with deadly speed and force. The Herods, Neros, and Henry the Eighths, Duke Alvas, and the entire spawn of the Inquisition,— they were once tender, humane, gentle-hearted. But, like the tiger that has tasted blood, it will have blood whenever it can. And: 5. *The law of habit.* We spoke of this just now. Character ever tends to become permanent. "He that is holy" to be "holy still "—blessed be God for this!—but "he that is unrighteous, . . . he that is filthy," to be "unrighteous," to be "filthy *still.*" You may bend the sapling, but not the tree.

VII. HOW INTENSELY SERIOUS ARE THE TEACHINGS OF THIS FACT! Is it true that, though God sends judgment after judgment upon men, they will yet not repent? Then: 1. *More judgments and worse will come.* Assuredly it will be so. We cannot imagine God allowing himself to be for ever baffled by the unruly wills and affections of sinful men. " Our God is a consuming fire; " and until the dross be separated the fire will burn on. How awful, therefore, is the prospect for ungodly and impenitent men! 2. *How we need to watch and pray lest we be hardened through the deceitfulness of sin!* Ah, what fools they are, "who make a mock at sin; " who dally with it, count it a trifle! Better play with vipers and scorpions. 3. *What imperative need there is of the power of the Holy Spirit!* The disciples were in despair about their work. However should such as they persuade and convert men? The Lord promises to send the Holy Spirit, and " when he is come he shall convince the world of sin, of righteousness, and of judgment." The baptism of the Holy Ghost—that is the need of the Church if she is ever to win the world for Christ. 4. *Surrender to Christ*, prompt, complete, abiding, that he, according to his Name, may save us from our sins,—this assuredly is our bounden duty, our true wisdom, because our sure safeguard, and our only one. —S. C.

Vers. 1—6.—*The evil effect of degeneracy : the fallen star.* Homiletic expositions aim to avoid as far as possible the topics of controversy. Yet must they be definite in their view of the interpretation of the words of Holy Scripture. Their own sphere is the moral and practical. They speak with no authority in the department of exposition. The view taken of this figure does not confine its reference to any individual person; although some individuals have gained a special notoriety. Many who have occupied the place of "stars," which are "the angels of the Churches," have fallen from their place and ceased to be illuminating powers, and their degeneracy has been the occasion of a temporary triumph of evil in one form or other. These have let loose the spawn of hell. Here the sad picture is presented of the ill effects of such degeneracy. It may be moral or intellectual descent; although the alliance with evil would seem rather to confine it to a departure from goodness and righteousness. A mere mental aberration not equally destructive. The great power of evil is found in that unfaithfulness to truth which issues in degeneracy of manners and life. The evil of such degeneracy is—

I. WIDESPREAD. From the position and influence of him who has been as a leader and guide of others. His life known, his influence great, his example contagious. Men follow leaders; and the welfare of the world is now advanced, now retarded, by the fidelity or unfaithfulness of them who are charged with high trust and responsibility.

II. DESTRUCTIVELY INJURIOUS. In proportion to the influence which any one wields is his power for good or evil. If one falls from a high position, he drags down others. The angel of light, become an agent of evil, opens the bottomless pit. He brings the utmost evil upon men such "as have not the seal of God upon their foreheads."

III. BITTERLY AFFLICTIVE. The injury caused is great in the social degeneracy, in the weakening of moral principle. A pillar of the house trembles, all becomes less secure. But the painfulness is great: 1. To him who falls. 2. To them whom he drags down with him. 3. To them whose sympathies being only with goodness are afflicted by anything that tends to degeneracy of manners, to feebleness of faith, or to the lowering of the tone and felicity of human life. 4. To the widespread, outlying multitudes, amongst whom the spread of goodness is retarded by every act of unfaithfulness and every instance of degeneracy and defection.—R. G.

Vers. 7—11.—*The triumph of evil through unfaithfulness.* Satanic power is encouraged by human unfaithfulness. The utmost power of evil is let loose, and with destructive energy works only evil, and the direst evil, amongst the children of men. The evil character of the effects of unfaithfulness is represented by figures which suggest the greatest painfulness, and which are repulsive in the extreme. The sun and the air are darkened by "smoke" issuing from the opened "pit of the abyss"— the smoke "as of a great furnace." The power of "locusts" and "scorpions of the earth" reveals the most painful and repulsive effects, for "their torment was as the torment of a scorpion when it striketh a man." So great is this that men "seek death," though unavailingly. They are as "horses prepared for war," crowned with kingly power, having faces as of men, and hair as of women, and teeth "as the teeth of lions," covered are they with "breastplates of iron," and the sound of their wings as "the sound of chariots of many horses rushing to war;" they have "tails like unto scorpions, and stings," and in these is "their power to hurt men." The whole are leagued together under the leadership of "the angel of the abyss," whose name "in Hebrew is Abaddon, and in Greek Apollyon, *i.e.* Destroyer." Thus is set forth the evil, repulsive, and deadly power of those forces which are called into play by unfaithfulness and degeneracy. One falls, but he lets loose many forces of evil, which he, once having called into activity, cannot arrest. It is a bitter woe to the earth, such as it has suffered many, many times in the great history. The lesson is for all times; for in many times the sad scene has been enacted. This section of the "revelation" declares to us—

I. THAT IN THE DEPARTURE FROM TRUTH AND GOODNESS ERROR AND EVIL BECOME PREVALENT. Every false doctrine is a cloud of darkness upon the path of the human life.

II. IN THE DIMINUTION OF THE HEAVENLY THE HELLISH POWERS PREVAIL. Finally, darkness shall be held back as in chains. But here it is let loose, and in the loss of the heavenly power the earthly, rather the hellish, gains ascendancy.

III. IN A DEPARTURE FROM THE PEACEFUL OBEDIENCE OF RIGHTEOUSNESS THE DESTRUCTIVE AND PAINFUL EFFECTS OF SIN ARE PROVED. The ways of pleasantness and the paths of peace forsaken, there are only the hard ways of the transgressor to walk in.

IV. THE BROKEN ALLEGIANCE TO GOD ISSUES IN THE TRIUMPH OF THE DESTROYER. The authority of the Prince of peace being rejected, another king, even Apollyon, usurps his throne. So men carelessly exchange good for evil, and sell life for an empty world. —R. G.

Vers. 12—21.—*The inefficiency of judgments to lead all to repentance.* The voice of suffering innocence does not pass unheeded. The Lord of sabaoth is long-suffering and very merciful, even towards the disobedient and towards the enemies of the truth; but the angels of judgment and punishment, bound and restrained, must at length be loosed. Though the Lord suffereth long and is kind, yet he will avenge his own elect which cry to him day and night. We learn—

I. THAT THE END OF JUDGMENT IS REPENTANCE. This is the object always kept in view by him who judgeth right. All his judgments are therefore blessings in disguise. "He doth not willingly afflict." The cry from them who suffer wrongfully is not immediately answered in judgment upon their oppressors. He can requite his own in other ways. Yet, though judgment be stayed against an evil work, it is finally "loosed," lest the hearts of men be set in them wholly to do evil.

II. THAT THEY WHO PLACE THEMSELVES IN OPPOSITION TO THE SERVANTS OF TRUTH EXPOSE THEMSELVES TO THE JUST AND TERRIBLE JUDGMENTS OF GOD. Even the prayers of the righteous, which are accepted before the throne, cry for vengeance. The evil workers who place themselves in antagonism to the struggling Church are met, not only by the feeble arm of "the little flock," but by the might of him who, as a good Shepherd, defends even with his life them who are his own sheep.

III. THAT EVEN THE SEVERITIES OF JUDGMENT ARE INSUFFICIENT TO LEAD ALL TO REPENTANCE. That many are saved through the judgment is obvious to all observers. Yet is there a hardness of heart that seems to increase by the pressure of outward calamity. All do not see the Divine hand in the meted judgment; and many rise in greater rebellion by how much the strokes of that hand are severe. "The rest of mankind, which were not killed with these plagues, repented not of the works of their hands."

IV. We further learn that IT IS THROUGH DEVOTION TO EVIL THAT MEN ARE PREVENTED FROM REPENTANCE. Men harden their hearts even in the midst of Heaven's fiery judgments. Many happily learn righteousness, and repent of their evil ways, but of some—"the rest"—alas! always a remnant—it is to be said, "They repented not." They are devoted to evil. They are the willing slaves of lust and vice. They are greedy to do iniquity. The fiendish spirit finds its embodiment in them, and men are as though possessed with devils. If these are to be saved, other means must be devised. —R. G.

Vers. 1—3.—*Moral evil in the universe.* "And the fifth angel sounded," etc. We take these verses to illustrate *moral evil in the universe.* Moral evil is a "pit." A pit is a scene of *confinement* and *darkness.* Moral evil, or sin, wherever it exists in the spirit, imprisons the faculties and blinds the vision. Socrates has well said, "No man is a free man who has a vice for his master." All corrupt souls are reserved in chains of darkness. Sin is slavery, sin is midnight. In relation to moral evil as a "pit," four things are suggested.

I. IT IS EXPOSABLE. "The fifth angel sounded, and I saw a star fall from heaven unto the earth: and to him was given the key of the bottomless pit." Moral evil, in its incipient state, so stupefies the faculties and blinds the conscience that the subject only becomes aware of it by the advent of a messenger from heaven; an angel from heaven uncovers it, makes it bare to the soul. How do the savages, how do the millions whose souls are buried in sensuality, become conscious of sin? Only by a special message from heaven. What says Paul? "I was alive without the Law once, but when the commandment came, sin revived, and I died." That is, Paul fancied he was alive—that is, all right—until the Divine message came. Every genuine gospel minister may be said to be a star from heaven with the "key of the bottomless pit," that key with which he opens it and exposes it to the consciences of his hearers. Peter, on the Day of Pentecost, was such an angel; he uncovered the pit of moral evil within his hearers, and they exclaimed, "Men and brethren, what shall we do?"

II. IT IS FATHOMLESS. "Bottomless pit." It is an abyss without a bottom. Moral evil is fathomless. 1. Who can fathom its *origin?* We can account for sin in *this* world on two principles. (1) On the *principle of internal tendencies.* The human being, from the very commencement of its existence, seems to have a disposition to go wrong. (2) On the *ground of external influences.* He comes into a world where all human beings are more or less tainted with sin; the moral atmosphere which he breathes is more or less corrupt. But in the case of the first sinner neither of these conditions existed; all his propensities were toward the right, and all external influences tended toward the right. 2. Who can fathom its *issues?* What are its bearings, ramifications, ultimate results? Problems these which the highest created intellect could, perhaps, never solve. Moral evil is, indeed, a "bottomless pit."

III. IT IS BURNING. "A great furnace." Sin, or moral evil, is fire; like all fire it exists in two states, *latent* and *active.* Where it becomes active it is consuming and transmuting; it consumes the good and transmutes its embers into evil, and in all it inflicts agony on the soul—the agony of moral regrets for the past, and terrible forebodings for the future. Every sinner has a "furnace" within him, a furnace that must break forth into awful activity sooner or later.

IV. IT IS OBSCURING. "A smoke, . . . and the sun and the air were darkened by reason of the smoke of the pit." How great the obscuration of moral evil! It clouds all the moral stars of truth in the soul, and mantles the moral heavens in gloom. 1. *How benighted men are on the eternal question of right!* The foundations and laws of moral obligation are, in the daily course of human action, buried in darkness. 2. *How blinded men are to the eternal conditions of well-being!* Men look for happiness *without* instead of *within;* in the *senses,* not in the *soul;* in *matter,* not in *mind;* in the *creature,* not in the *Creator.* Thus, in truth, our moral heavens are starless and our path is a wilderness. We walk in darkness and have no light.

V. IT IS ALARMING. "And there came out of the smoke locusts upon the earth, and unto them was given power." It is here represented that from the fathomless abyss, burning and smoking, there issued a host of scorpion-locusts resembling war-horses, with crowns like gold, with the face of men, the hair of women, the teeth of lions, having breastplates as of iron, and the sound of their wings like the sound of chariots and of horses charging to battle. In Oriental lands and distant ages nothing was regarded with greater horror than an army of locusts; their numbers darkened the heavens, their wings rattled as thunder, and their mission was to devour What hellish squadrons, to terrify and destroy the soul, issue from the fathomless abyss of moral evil! Terrible armies come in the memories of the past and in the apprehensions of the mysterious future.

CONCLUSION. Do not ask—Where is hell? Place it not in some underground region, or in some burning planets far away; the fathomless, burning, and tormenting pit is in *the soul of every morally unrenewed man.* Thank God, there are remedial means on this earth for the quenching of its fires, and the annihilation of all the squadrons of tormentors it sends forth.—D. T.

Ver. 6.—*The extremity of anguish.* "And in those days shall men seek death, and shall not find it; and shall desire to die, and death shall flee from them." We take these words as a *picture of the extremest anguish.* Here we have—

I. A STATE OF MISERY IN WHICH DEATH IS SOUGHT. 1. *Death is universally regarded amongst men as the greatest evil.* It is the "king of terrors." It gives terror to every-thing terrible in the world. The ravenous beast, the furious storm, the destructive pestilence, the engulfing earthquake, are only terrible because death is terrible. 2. *The relief which men generally seek in this world in their sufferings is from death.* The mariner will forsake his ship with valuable cargo, the king will resign his kingdom, the wounded will suffer the amputation of every limb, if thought needful, to avoid death. Yet here we have a state of being where *death is sought as a relief.*

II. A STATE OF MISERY IN WHICH DEATH IS SOUGHT AS A RELIEF IN VAIN. "And death shall flee from them." It is miserable to seek relief in the most deeply felt evil, but to seek it in such an evil in vain adds wondrously to the misery of the case. Fatigue, disappointment, the consciousness of lost energy, add to the anguish. Earth runs from death, hell runs after it and runs in vain. In conclusion, I infer: 1. *That the fact that men are exposed to such a state of being implies that some sad catastrophe has befallen our nature.* Could Infinite Goodness have created beings designed and fitted by their nature for such a state? Nay; deep within us has the Great One planted the love of life, and to seek death is to go against our nature. Sin explains it. 2. *That there is something in the universe to be dreaded by man more than death, and this is sin.* Death, though an evil, is not to be compared to sin. Sin, though robed in beauty and adorned with a thousand attractions, is the evil of evils. 3. *That Christianity should be hailed as the only means to deliver us from this extremity of anguish.* It destroys sin, it "condemns sin in the flesh."—D. T.

EXPOSITION.

CHAPTER X.

Ver. 1.—And I saw. We have here the commencement of what many writers call an episode, or rather two episodes, which intervene between the sixth and seventh trumpets, just as ch. vii. occurs between the sixth and seventh seals. But as in the latter place we saw only a greater elaboration in the introduction to the seventh seal, and not a detached relation, so here ch. x. and xi. 1—14 form a gradual transition from the sixth to the seventh trumpet, and supplement what is set forth under those trumpets. The passage is so far a digression, as it is occupied chiefly in setting forth the fate of the Church rather than that of the ungodly; but it only does so to demonstrate the wickedness of the world, and the inevitable nature of the last great punishment. Ch. ix. ends (almost in a tone of surprise) with the words, "Neither repented they," etc.; therefore the angel now declares that, as all the warnings vouchsafed have brought men as a whole no nearer to God, the last final punishment must now fall. But, as if the measure of God's mercy were not yet fully filled up, it is shown how he has given to the world two witnesses, by which men might be induced to repent. But this, too, only serves to add to the condemnation of the world, which wrests this gift to its own destruction. We thus have the connection. God has sent punishments as warnings. But he not only has done this, he has also given direct instruction by the witness of his Word; man has despised both; therefore the end must come. Although the main object of the trumpet-visions is to set forth the woes inflicted upon the wicked, yet the seer, as it were, hesitates to indicate the last dread punishment until he has alluded to the opportunities which God has afforded mankind of escaping that end. Another mighty angel come down from heaven; *coming down out of heaven* (Revised Version). So in the vision of the seals, at this point the advent of *another angel* ushers in the following incidents (ch. vii. 2). He is probably *another angel* as distinguished from the *sixth angel* (ch. ix. 13). There is not sufficient reason for supposing that Christ is meant. Wherever our Lord is referred to in the Revelation, it is always in a mode which cannot possibly be mistaken (cf. ch. i. 13; v. 6, etc.). St. John's position is now upon the earth. In the vision he is either in heaven or on the earth, as required. He thus sees the angel apparently coming down from heaven. Clothed with a cloud. The symbol of majesty (cf. Exod. xvi. 10; Luke xxi. 27; ch. i. 7, etc.). And a rainbow was upon his head, and his face was as it were the sun, and his feet as pillars of fire. Omit "was." The description shows the celestial dignity of the messenger. Perhaps there is a reference in the *rainbow* to the merciful character of this angel's mission, and the faithfulness and patience of God. The two last clauses express the same idea, viz. the bright and glorious appearance of the angel. God's glory is reflected in his messenger, as formerly it was in Moses (Exod. xxxiv. 29, 30).

Ver. 2.—And he had in his hand a little book open. Ἔχων, "having," is read in א, A, B, C, P; εἴχεν, "he had," in a few cursives, the Vulgate, Andreas, Arethas, Primasius. The meaning is the same. The word βιβλαρίδιον, "little book," is a diminutive of βιβλίον (ch. v. 1), which is itself a diminutive of βίβλος. This form of the word is found nowhere else; the corresponding usual form is βιβλιδάριον. The book is probably *little* in comparison with that in ch. v. 1. The latter contained all God's purposes, and the seer was not permitted to read it—only part was indicated to him. This book contains only a small portion of God's methods of dealing with man, and St. John is commanded to receive the whole. The contents are indicated in ver. 11 and the following chapter. The book is *open*, as a sign that what is contained therein is to be revealed. Bede thinks the New Testament is signified by it; Wordsworth sees in it the spiritual power of Rome; Hengstenberg considers that it contains the judgment of the degenerate Church. And he set his right foot upon the sea, and his left foot on the earth. Thus it is indicated that the revelation which is to follow affects the whole world, and is not partial in its operation, as were the judgments set forth under the earlier trumpets. Wordsworth (following Hengstenberg) sees in the *earth* an emblem of worldly power, and in the *sea* a symbol of the agitation and turbulence of nations.

Ver. 3.—And cried with a loud voice, as when a lion roareth ; *and he cried with a great voice, as a lion roareth* (Revised Version). What the angel *cried* we are apparently not told. Probably the whole incident is intended merely to set forth the powerful and terrible nature of the messenger who is to deliver God's message. The figure is a very common one with the prophetical writers (cf. Isa. xlii. 13 ; Jer. xxv. 30 ; Hos. xi. 10 ; Joel iii. 16 ; Amos i. 2 ; iii. 8). And when he had cried, seven thunders uttered their voices ; *and when he cried, the seven*, etc. (Revised Version). This, again, is a repetition of the idea contained in the preceding clause. The Jews were accustomed to call thunder the seven voices, and to regard it as the voice of the Lord (cf. the repetition in Ps. xxix.), in the same way that they regarded lightning as the fire of God (Job i. 16). We have, therefore, most probably, a national idea of the Jews, made use of to express the simple fact of the loud and mighty character of the utterance of the angel (cf. the note on *Euphrates* in ch. ix. 14). If this be so, it is unnecessary to seek for any more subtle interpretation of *the seven thunders*, as that they represent the seven crusades (Vitringa), etc.

Ver. 4.—And when the seven thunders had uttered their voices, I was about to write ; *and when the seven thunders spoke, I was*, etc. It seems that St. John, in his vision, thought himself to be writing down the incidents as they were displayed before him. This he supposed himself to be doing in obedience to the command in ch. i. 11, 19. He accordingly is proceeding to do so here, when he is stopped by the angel. And I heard a voice from heaven saying unto me. Omit " unto me," with ℵ, A, B, C, P, all the versions, Andreas, Arethas, Primasius, etc. Throughout the Apocalypse we find frequent mention of *a voice*, without any definite statement as to the possessor. In ch. i. 11, 12, 13 ; iv. 1 ; xviii. 4 ; xxi. 5, 15, the *voice* appears to be that of Christ or God the Father. In ch. xiv. 13 it may be that of Christ or an angel ; in ch. xix. 9 it seems to be the angel's voice ; and in ch. vi. 6 it apparently proceeds from the four living beings ; while in ch. ix. 13, although the command appears to be the command of God, the locality from which the voice issues appears to bear reference to the souls of the saints, and their cry for vengeance. Here it seems best to identify the " voice from heaven " with that of ch. i., where it is probably Christ himself (see on ch. i. 10). Seal up those things which the seven thunders uttered, and write them not (cf. Dan. xii. 4, " But thou, O Daniel, shut up the words and seal the book, even to the time of the end ; " also Acts i. 7, " It is not for you to know the times or the seasons, which the Father hath put in his own power ; " also ch. xxii. 10, " And he saith unto me, Seal not the sayings of the prophecy of this book : for the time is at hand "). As stated in the note on ver. 2, not all God's purposes are revealed. Here we have a positive indication that some truths are withheld. It is useless to speculate on the nature of that which is purposely concealed from us. The probable conclusions which we may deduce are well put by Alford : " From the very character of thunder, that the utterances were of fearful import ; from the place which they hold, that they relate to the Church ; from the command to conceal them, first, encouragement, that God in his tender mercy to his own does not reveal all his terrors ; secondly, godly fear, seeing that the arrows of his quiver are not exhausted, but besides things expressly foretold, there are more behind not revealed to us."

Ver. 5.—And the angel which I saw stand upon the sea and upon the earth lifted up his hand to heaven ; *the right hand* (Revised Version) is supported by ℵ, B, C, P, Syriac, Coptic, Æthiopic, Armenian, Andreas, Arethas, Primasius. It is omitted in the Textus Receptus, which follows A, 1, 17, 36, Vulgate ; cf. Dan. xii. 7, a chapter also referred to in the preceding note (*vide supra*). In Daniel both hands are uplifted, here only one ; in the other is the book. The action was customary among the Jews in swearing (see Gen. xiv. 22 ; Deut. xxxii. 40). (Upon the signification of " standing upon the sea and upon the earth," see on ver. 2.)

Ver. 6.—And sware by him that liveth for ever and ever. The Triune God (cf. ch. i. 11 ; iv. 10, etc. ; also Deut. xxxii. 40 ; Ps. xlv. 6 ; Heb. i. 8, etc.). Who created heaven, and the things that therein are, and the earth, and the things that therein are, and the sea, and the things which are therein. Though the balance of authority is in favour of the last clause, yet it is omitted by ℵ*, A, and some cursives (cf. Exod. xx. 4). These two characteristics of God—his eternity and his omnipotence—are referred to in order to demonstrate the certainty of the fulfilment of the prophecy which follows. That there should be time no longer (ὅτι χρόνος οὐκέτι ἔσται) ; *that time no longer shall be.* This may be rendered : (1) Time (a finite terminable period, as opposed to eternity) shall no longer exist, but eternity shall be entered upon. (2) There shall be no more time, in the sense of " there shall be no longer any delay " in the infliction of the last judgment, set forth under the seventh trumpet. The solution seems to be that both meanings are implied. There seems to be a reference to the words of ch. vi. 11, to the ἔτι χρόνον μικρόν, during which the saints were to rest and await the infliction of God's wrath upon the ungodly. The visions of the first six trumpets have shown how, in the period of the world's existence, the ungodly do not escape judicial retribution. But that is not all ; the force of the six judgments not having served to reduce the worldly to repentance, there can be no more delay, the last final judgment follows. But the last judgment, which follows quickly upon the other six (ch. xi. 14), is for eternity (ch. xi. 18). The advent of this woe is, therefore, simultaneous with the end of χρόνος, or "time," by which we signify that definite period, cut out of eternity, as it were, which is coeval with the existence of the world, and ceases with its destruction. The expression, therefore, implies, " The measure of God's punishments, viewed as opportunities for repentance, is exhausted ; there is a limit to his endurance ; the allotted time having been run, and his mercy to a large extent having been spurned, there is no more delay ; " then falls the last final blow, which is at the end of " time," and at the beginning (for many) of eternity. Ebrard renders, " A space of time in which to repent "—a meaning compatible with the explanation given above. Others render, " The time of the fulfilment shall not be yet, but it shall be when the seventh trumpet sounds ; " but this interpretation makes χρόνος equal καιρός. Others, again, have made χρόνος, a chronus, equal a definite number of years, and have endeavoured to compute the exact equivalent of the period (see Bengel, in loc.).

Ver. 7.—But in the days of the voice of the seventh angel. The meaning naturally seems to be, " There shall be no longer time ; but, on the contrary, in the days of the seventh trumpet, the last judgment shall fall, the end will come, and all things will be made manifest ; the mystery of God will be finished." Wordsworth renders, " No delay, save only in the days," etc., and believes that the passage points to a brief respite, during which men may yet repent. When he shall begin to sound ; when he is about to sound [his trumpet]. Alford points out the propriety of the expression. " When the seventh angel does sound, the completed time of the fulfilment is simultaneous

with his blowing (cf. ch. xi. 18), so that it is properly said that the fulfilment comes in the days when he is about to blow." The mystery of God should be finished ; also (or then, as Revised Version) the mystery of God was fulfilled. " The prophetic past " (Wordsworth). " The mystery of God " is all that man does not now understand in connection with God's dealings with man, but of the existence of which he is cognizant, e.g. the existence of evil in the world, and God's modes of dealing with that and all mankind, which we only know in part. God's plans are being steadily and surely worked out, though we are not able to comprehend them. As he hath declared to his servants the prophets ; literally, as he evangelized his servants the prophets ; or, as in the Revised Version, according to the good tidings which he declared to his servants the prophets. Thus Amos iii. 7, " Surely the Lord God will do nothing, but he revealeth his secret unto his servants the prophets." The promise of the complete fulfilment of the mystery of God is good news indeed for the fainting Christian, for it tells of the end of his trials and the overthrow of his enemies.

Ver. 8.—And the voice which I heard from heaven spake unto me again, and said ; and the voice which I heard out of heaven, [I heard] again talking with me and saying. The construction is irregular. " The voice,' viz. that mentioned in ver. 4, which is probably that of Christ himself (see on ver. 4). Go and take the little book which is open in the hand of the angel which standeth upon the sea and upon the earth ; Go, take the book, etc., according to A, C, which is adopted in the Revised Version. Little book, βιβλαρίδιον, as in ver. 2, is found in ℵ, P, Andreas ; and βιβλιδαρίον in B, Andreas, Arethas. (On the signification of the " little book," see on ver. 2 ; and also for the meaning of the last clause, see the same place.)

Ver. 9.—And I went unto the angel, and said unto him, Give me the little book ; and I went away to the angel, telling him to give me the little book. Alford understands that the seer goes from his position in heaven to the angel on earth. But he is probably, in his vision, already on the earth (see on ver. 1). And he said unto me, Take it, and eat it up ; he saith. This part of the vision is founded on Ezek. ii. 9—iii. 3. The act is no doubt intended to convey the idea that the seer is to carefully receive, to digest thoroughly, as it were, his message in order to deliver it faithfully. Thus in Ezek. iii. 10 the prophet is told, " All my words that I shall speak unto thee receive in thine heart, and hear with thine ears. And go, get thee to them of the captivity, unto the children of thy people, and speak unto them," etc. And it shall make thy belly bitter, but it shall be in thy mouth sweet as honey; cf. the vision of Ezek. ii. 9—iii., where the sweetness only is immediately mentioned; but the bitterness is implied later on in Ezek. iii. 14. The sweetness expresses the pleasure and readiness with which St. John receives his commission; the bitterness symbolizes the grief which possesses him when he thoroughly takes in the nature of his message. The pleasure with which he receives the angel's commands may proceed from joy at the thought that the final overthrow of the wicked is the final deliverance of the saints; or it may be that he feels himself honoured at being chosen as the medium for conveying God's message. Compare the readiness of Isaiah (vi. 8) to fulfil a similar office, and his subsequent fear and hesitation (Isa. vii. 4). The bitterness of the seer follows when he realizes the terrible nature of the judgment he is to announce (cf. Jer. viii. 21, " For the hurt of the daughter of my people am I hurt "). Various other explanations, more or less allegorical, have been suggested. Thus Andreas explains that the first sweetness of sin is afterwards converted into bitterness. Origen, quoted in the ' Speaker's Commentary,' " Very sweet is this the book of Scripture when first perceived, but bitter to the conscience within." Maurice supposes that St. John's joy proceeds from the expectation that the book will announce the fall of the great Babel-empire of the world, and his disappointment follows when he discovers that it predicts the fall of Jerusalem. Bede explains that the bitterness in the belly indicates the reception by the seer, but the sweetness in the mouth is the declaration to others.

Ver. 10.—And I took the little book out of the angel's hand, and ate it up; and it was in my mouth sweet as honey: and as soon as I had eaten it, my belly was bitter (see above). The angel, foreseeing the

nature of the contents, alludes to the bitterness first; the writer narrates his experiences in the historical order.

Ver. 11.—And he said unto me. Λέγουσιν, " they say," is read in ℵ, A, B, and thirty cursives, and is adopted in the Revised Version. Λέγει, " he saith," is found in P and seventeen cursives. Λέγουσιν leaves the speakers quite indefinite, amounting, in fact, to no more than " it was said " (Alford); cf. τρέφωσιν in ch. xii. 6; also Dan. vii. 5, 13. Thou must prophesy again. *Thou must,* because it is laid upon thee by God's command. It is to be done *again,* because the seer has already to some extent set forth God's will in the earlier part of the book; and he is now required to proceed with the delivery of his message. " Prophesy " (as in ch. xi. 3) has rather its literal than its derived meaning. It is the telling forth of God's purposes, and may refer to past as well as present or future events. The sentence refers to the announcements made in the following part of the Apocalypse (*vide infra*). Bede and others take it to mean the Gospel of St. John, which was, perhaps, afterwards composed (see Introduction). Victorinus thinks it points to the period of St. John's return from Patmos to Ephesus, where the Apocalypse may have been published. Before many peoples, and nations, and tongues, and kings; *concerning many peoples,* etc. (ἐπί, with dative). These are the objects of the prophecy, not the audience. This serves to explain the reference in the preceding sentence. The message is not delivered *to,* but *about* peoples, etc. The fourfold enumeration seems to point to the breadth of the signification—it embraces the whole of mankind (cf. ch. v. 9). This is the end of what is called by many writers the first episode; the second follows. The incident is often alluded to as the " new commission " of St. John; but it seems less a new commission than a solemn re-enactment of the command delivered in ch. i.

HOMILETICS.

Vers. 1—7.—*The mystery of God—finished!* According to some historical interpreters, the close of the ninth chapter sets forth in symbol the inrush of the Turkish power and the downfall of Constantinople. Apparently necessitated by such a view, the angel of the first verse of the tenth chapter is the reality of which the dominant papal power was the mimicry—a messenger of heaven with new light piercing the gloom. His setting one foot on the sea and another on the earth indicates his taking possession of Continental Christendom and insular England. The seven thunders are the anathemas of papal Rome. They may not be uttered, because they are the roarings of man and not the sayings of God. We cannot accept this interpretation, nor anything like it. On the understanding that this book forecasts in symbolic outline the fortunes of the Church of God on her way to the final consummation, it would be somewhat strange if the lines of history and those of prophecy did not present some mutual correspondence. But it by no means follows that any one apparent correspondence is *the* fulfilment of the prophecy, although it may be partially so. Besides, our text tells us that the great proclamation of the angel who set his feet on sea and land was that in the days of the seventh angel the mystery of God should be finished. Now, nothing is more certain than that, at the time of the Reformation and by its agents, there was no such proclamation made as this. Besides, even now the mystery of God is not finished, nor anything like it; consequently, it is not possible for us to assign the proclamation of this angel to anything that happened three hundred years ago. Repeated studies of the entire Apocalypse do but confirm the conviction of twenty years' standing, that *we must give up date-fixing entirely*; that while the book forecasts the future, it so does it as to confirm the word that "it is not for us to know the times or the seasons, which the Father hath put in his own power;" that we may expect, at divers times and places, and in divers manners, oft-recurring fulfilments of the Apocalyptic word; and that the book contains, for our guidance and help, an indication of Divine principles and methods rather than incident in detail. We shall have a fresh illustration of this if we now study this paragraph, letting the seventh verse be the centre around which our thoughts may turn.

I. HERE IS A STRIKING NAME GIVEN TO THE SCHEME OF PROVIDENCE. "The mystery of God." A "mystery" is (1) that which is altogether and necessarily a secret in the mind of God; (2) that which, though revealed as a fact, is beyond our understanding as to mode; (3) that which, even when revealed, we know only in part, (4) that which, disclosed in symbol, will be interpreted by the explanation of the word or the event; (5) that which, though complete in the Divine mind, is only unrolled, piece by piece, before us; (6) that which, from its nature, can only be disclosed to those who are in a fit state of mind to receive it, and which, to others, must remain shrouded in concealment. In one or other of these senses Scripture speaks of the mystery of the seven stars (ch. i. 20), of the kingdom of heaven (Mark iv. 11), of the resurrection (1 Cor. xv. 51), of the gospel (1 Cor. ii. 7), of the proclamation of the gospel to the Gentiles (Eph. iii. 3), of the union of Christ and his people (Eph. v. 32), of the final completion of the Church (Eph. i. 9), of the Person of Christ (1 Tim. iii. 16), of the Christian faith (1 Tim. iii. 9), of the intricacies of sin (2 Thess. ii. 7; ch. xvii. 5), of the purposes of God (ch. x. 7). This last is the one referred to in the text. It is something of which there is a complete and perfect plan in the mind of God, but of which we see only a part before our eyes. The future depends on the will of God. And who can discern that? "What man knoweth the things of a man, save the spirit of man which is in him? Even so, the things of God knoweth no man, but the Spirit of God." And our finite minds could not take in the entire plans of an infinite mind. A large part must needs be concealed; not merely because the book does not disclose all, but because we could not apprehend all.

II. THE PHRASE WHICH AT FIRST SUGGESTS PAINFUL PERPLEXITY HAS A DESCRIPTIVE TERM ATTACHED TO IT, WHICH AT ONCE RELIEVES AND INSPIRES. Before us is "mystery." But it is *God's* mystery! To him it stands forth distinctly and clearly, without a fringe of haze. From him the entire providential plan emanates. With his full knowledge of consequences, sin was permitted to intrude. The entire control of all is ever in his hands. The diadems of royalty never fall from his brow, nor does the sceptre of dominion ever tremble in his hand. "The government is on his shoulder." And though the book speaks of it relatively to us, as his mystery, yet to him it is no mystery at all.

III. THE MAIN FEATURE OF THIS MYSTERY IS THAT IT IS ONE OF GOOD TIDINGS; *i.e.* it is the *gospel* mystery (ὡς εὐηγγέλισε). As we remarked before (homily on ch. v.), when the seven-sealed book is opened by the Lamb, it is clear that the unfoldings of providence become the unveilings of grace. Over and above the scheme of moral government, there is set this plan of redeeming love; and the wheels of time are rolling on and speeding forward to work out the great salvation, of which one sentence will sum up the outcome, "Where sin abounded, grace did much more abound!"

IV. THE MYSTERY WILL UNFOLD ITSELF ON THE LINES LAID DOWN BY THE PROPHETS OF THE OLD AND NEW TESTAMENTS. "According to the good tidings which he declared to his servants the prophets." It has been thus hitherto. History has thus far developed according to the sayings of Moses and the prophets. Moses, in his words to the children of Israel, foretold what would happen to the Jewish people in after ages if they were unfaithful to their God. The twenty-eighth chapter of Deuteronomy is being fulfilled to this day. So also, in the several prophets, there is sketched a ground-plan of " the sufferings of Christ and the glory that should follow; " *e.g.* in the well-known fifty-third of Isaiah there is not one single word which we are at a loss to verify, as we put side by side what Old Testament seers foretold and what New Testament evangelists and apostles declare. Further on, we read our Lord's predictions concerning the fall of Jerusalem. They have been fulfilled. History is thus the repeated fulfilment of prophecy. What has been will be again. And with no misgiving we declare that what is yet to be witnessed on earth will correspond with the prophetic words of the apostles and prophets of our Lord and Saviour. We are looking for " the blessed hope —the glorious appearing of the great God, even our Saviour Jesus Christ."

V. THE TIME OF THE END IS FORESEEN. When the seventh angel is about to sound then the mystery of God would be finished; *i.e.* as far as the plan of providence is indicated in the book of prophecy, it will be consummated. The "end" will be this: "The kingdoms of this world are become the kingdoms of our Lord and of his Christ, and he shall reign for ever and ever." But let us not forget the sense in which this word "finished" is, must be, intended. It cannot mean that from that point God will reduce all to a blank, or become inactive, or cause the glory of redemption to be no more. Ah no! We cannot doubt that the advance will be still from glory to glory. But the mystery will be finished, *as far as God hath seen fit to tell us in his Word.* " Finished, according to the good tidings," etc. These give at once the intent and the limitation of the mystery which is thus to be "finished." Revelation is bounded both ways, back and front. We know nothing prior to that beginning when God created the heavens and the earth. We know nothing later than " the end, when " Christ "shall have delivered up the kingdom to God, even the Father, that God may be all in all."

VI. THIS FORECAST RECEIVES VAST ADDITIONAL WEIGHT FROM THE GLORY OF THE BEING BY WHOM THIS DISCLOSURE IS MADE. He is " a mighty angel." He appears in the name of Heaven; and is invested with the insignia of majesty, pomp, and might. There is a sevenfold symbolism here. He is " arrayed with a cloud "—at once the sign of the Divine presence, and a symbol of the mystery which surrounds the throne. There is " a rainbow upon his head "—the token of the covenant of peace. His face is "as the sun "—pure and bright with the burning blazing light of holiness. His feet are " as pillars of fire; " by his tread he puts down sin; with fire, he burns it up. He has in his hand " a little book open." This is strikingly different from the sealed book which only the Lamb could open. The open book contains the message which the apostle is to declare. He set his right foot upon the sea, etc., standing sublimely in possession of both in the name of Heaven. He cried with a great voice, as a lion roareth. His voice is full of strength. He lifts up his right hand to heaven, and swears by him that liveth for ever and ever that there shall be no more delay.[1] Long as the time may seem to be during which the world rolls round wearily with its burden of sin, when a certain point of time is reached, " a short work will the Lord make upon the earth." The consummation will be delayed not a moment too long, and the honour, majesty, and might of Heaven are pledges of the fulfilment of the word.

VII. WHEN THE MYSTERY OF GOD IS FINISHED, WHERE SHALL WE BE? Finished it will be. "The mouth of the Lord hath spoken it." As surely as at the end of one cycle of events the Saviour cried, " It is finished! " so surely when another cycle has run its round will there come another, " It is done!" The Author of our faith is also its Finisher. The Redeemer's cross finished the mystery of the old covenant; his crown shall finish the mystery of the new covenant. And when the end cometh we shall be—where? We shall stand in " our lot " at the end of the days. But what will our lot be? With the righteous or with the wicked? For then the distinction will be manifest. No one will then be in doubt as to his own position before God. Surely it is of infinite moment to us that, when the mystery of God is finished, we should be on the right side. There is, indeed, a smaller "mystery of God" which is working out. " Every man's life is a plan of God" (Bushnell). " I girded thee though thou hast not known me." God is working it out according to his gospel. " He that believeth on

---

[1] Cf. Archdeacon Lee's ' Commentary,' *in loc.*, for the several interpretations of this phrase. See also Bengel and P. W. Grant on the passage.

the Son hath everlasting life," etc. And amid the "wreck of matter and the crash of worlds" we shall want a Friend in whom we can repose amid all the convulsions that shake this globe. There is One—and One only, of whom it is eternally true, "Thou art the same." That One is Jesus. He says to us, "Him that cometh I will in no wise cast out." Here, then, let us cling. He will not let us go, nor let us be harmed, though this earth be burned up. In him is everlasting rest.

> "Then let the earth's old pillars shake,
> And all the wheels of nature break;
> Our steady souls should fear no more
> Than solid rocks when billows roar!"

Vers. 8—11.— *The little book and its mission.* In one of the most interesting chapters in Mr. Elliott's 'Horæ Apocalypticæ,' the correspondence between this vision of "the little book open" and the bringing forth of the open Bible at the time of the Reformation is indicated at considerable length. According, however, to the plan of exposition which alone seems to us to accord with the aim of the Apocalypse, the production of an open Bible at the Reformation was but one illustration at a particular time of that which this chapter teaches for all time. We shall get far more light from the chapter if we regard it as indicating principles that are eternally true, than as forecasting what was a passing incident in the course of history. We have before seen how largely the imagery of the Apocalypse is based on that of the Old Testament. The precise analogue of this section will be found in the Book of the Prophet Ezekiel, the second and third chapters, which should be studied side by side with this. The paragraph now under review is literally laden with riches of Divine teaching.

I. THERE IS A WIDE CONTRAST BETWEEN THE BOOK "SEALED WITH SEVEN SEALS" AND "THE LITTLE BOOK OPEN." Obviously, the thought first suggested thereby is that in the one case we have enclosed that which is wrapped in impenetrable secrecy; in the other, that which is meant to be opened to all. This of itself sets us on a clear track of thought. The sealed book contains the secret plans of Providence; the open one, the revealed teachings of his will, and the disclosures of his grace. The former is only and wholly in the hands of him who is seen in the midst of the throne—"a Lamb as it had been slain." The latter is meant for the guidance of men on earth, and as such is put into human hands. In the one case "no one in heaven or on earth is found able or worthy to open and to read the book, or even to look thereon." In the other case the book is already open, and the apostle is bidden to take the book out of the angel's hand.

II. THE LITTLE BOOK, OPEN, IS COMMITTED TO THE APOSTLE'S CARE. The charm of this symbolism is that it is so luminous that he who readeth may run. The message of God's revealed will, and the counsels of his redeeming grace, are entrusted first to the "angel," and then by him to the exiled apostle. This is the same process of transmission as is given to us in ch. i. 1—3. Our Lord Jesus Christ is the Supreme Revealer. All the angelic hosts are commissioned by him. They are the immediate instruments by whom the word is handed down to the apostles and prophets of the New Testament. Under the new dispensation, as under the old, holy men of God spake as they were moved by the Holy Ghost.

III. THE APOSTLE, HAVING RECEIVED THE BOOK, HAS TO EAT IT UP. Eating a book? Yes; where is the difficulty? The phrase is familiar enough—"read, mark, learn, and *inwardly digest*," etc. What is eaten comes to be assimilated, and so to become a portion of one's own flesh and blood. Before the eating, it lies outside us. Until it is eaten, it is only that which would nourish if it were eaten, but by no other process than by our eating it, can it serve its purpose or ours. This is one of God's parables in nature. His words of truth and grace are meant to be the life of human souls, on which they grow and thrive. If the words of God are not so used, they so far miss *their* aim, and souls miss *their* support. So long as God's Word is something outside us, it will profit us little. It is to be received by faith as God's own message to us, and on it we may live day by day, esteeming the words of his mouth more than our necessary food. And specially is this spiritual digestion of God's words needed when a man's mission is to give out those words to others for their life. We cannot speak to others of the virtues of heavenly food when we have not fed on it ourselves. Nor can we tell to others the soul-thriving power it conveys when we ourselves are spiritually starving. The assimilation by reading, thinking, faith, and prayer is necessary if God's Word is to be the support of our souls.[1] None should aim at this more earnestly than those who have a Divine impulse to teach and preach Jesus Christ.

IV. THE LITTLE BOOK, WHEN EATEN, PRESENTED A STRANGE MIXTURE OF SWEET-NESS AND BITTERNESS. The words of the Bible, says a late eminent divine,[2] "nourish him by their bitter qualities as much as by their pleasant; he needs both and accepts both." "There must be a sweetness unspeakable in the actual living taste of a Divine communication; in the assurance . . . that the love which lies beneath all law . . . is showing itself forth in our very selves . . . But then the sense of this law defied in the world, defied in ourselves? . . . Is there no revulsion in that? Does not the book become the bitterer afterwards, in proportion as it was delicious at first?" Even so. Tonics are often bitter. The working out of God's grace in the salvation of those that believe are sweet enough. But the woes which must follow the rejection of grace are bitter indeed, and yet the prophet must be prepared to accept both, to feed on both, and to speak forth both.

V. WHEN THE BOOK IS EATEN, THE WORK OF PROPHESYING IS TO FOLLOW. "Thou must prophesy again over many peoples, and nations, and tongues, and kings"[3] (ver. 11). 1. The work of God under the New Testament is to be carried forward by the prophet, not by the priest. There are no official priests now. Those who call themselves such are shams. All believers, indeed, as such, are priests unto God; but there is no order of a priesthood under the Christian dispensation. Even under the old economy God set aside the priest, again and again, so that the prophet might come to the front. 2. Then, too, the prophet can only do his work rightly when God's message has been so digested that it is a part of himself. No one to whom God's Word is merely a some-thing outside of him can ever show the people the way of life. 3. See the breadth over which the Divine Word is to be promulgated. "Many nations and tongues." Every child of man is to hear the Word. 4. See the entire social scale included : "peoples" and "kings." From the lowest to the highest. The Word is as needed by, and as suited for, the palace as the hut. It is a common message for all. 5. There was to be a reissue of the prophetic Word under the Christian economy. Such we take to be the meaning of πάλιν. Of old the prophets had borne witness for God. But now the institution of prophecy is to recommence under Christ, and to be extended over a wider field than ever it had been before. 6. This open book entrusted to the prophet's care is never to be handed to any who would close it up again. Rome forbids the use of the Bible by the common people. Why? Because with her the priest smothers the prophet. Ever let us insist on keeping "the little book open;" and, in letting its contents, sweet or bitter, as they may be, be known to all the people.

The theme of this homily is a most appropriate one as a basis for opening up either the value of a Christian ministry or the essential principle of Protestantism, that "the little book" should ever be kept open, and its contents unfolded to the people. It suggest two queries. 1. *What has come out of the principles of this chapter, historically?*

---

[1] "Elliott regarded this little roll as the Bible opened anew to mankind at the period of the Reformation. The period affords many magnificent illustrations of the vision, but it does not exhaust its truth, since in every age the reverent study of the Word of God has given freshness and strength to forgotten truths, and has saved men from the bondage of tra-ditional notions. From among such students have arisen God's witnesses" (Bishop Boyd Carpenter).

[2] Rev. F. D. Maurice, 'The Apocalypse,' pp. 185, 186.

[3] On this clause Dr. Macdonald strangely remarks, "This is another of the proofs, found in the Apocalypse itself, that John's imprisonment could not have taken place under Domitian, for he would then be too old for the extreme work here carried out." Of course this assumes (1) the non-symbolic nature of the reply; (2) that John's prophesying must be *vivâ voce.* But (1) whatever John's age at the time of the Apocalypse being written, he never fulfilled this injunction by word of mouth; (2) by means of the writings he has left behind he is prophesying before many peoples, and nations, and tongues, and kings, in a way he certainly could not have done at any period of his earthly lifetime. So that Dr. Macdonald's "proof" totally falls to the ground.

(1) The demand for a free and open Bible, in the language of the people. (2) The institution of preaching as an ordinance of God. (3) The contention for liberty of prophesying according to God's order, apart from the restrictions imposed by man. (4) The incessant publication and republication of it as the will of God—That none should walk in darkness, but should know the Word of light and life. 2. *What should come out of them, practically?* (1) A perpetual protest against the closing, withholding, or neglect of "the little book." (2) The constant prayer that prophets may ever be raised up and qualified to go everywhere, preaching the Word. (3) Every teacher and preacher should take care to eat the book, and to digest its contents, in order that he may fulfil his function of prophesying. (4) That which the prophet must digest in order to prophesy, the people themselves must feed upon in order that they may live and grow and thrive. God's Word in the heart is the only certain nutriment of a noble life.

HOMILIES BY VARIOUS AUTHORS.

Ver. 2.—*The little book; or, characteristics of revelation.* "He had in his hand a little book open." Like as there was an interval between the opening of the sixth and seventh seals, so is there between the sounding of the sixth and seventh trumpets. The record of this latter interval, and of the events which took place in it, stretches through this tenth chapter down to ver. 13 of ch. xi. This chapter is occupied with the account of the little book which St. John saw in the hand of "another strong angel coming down out of heaven." The other "strong angel" is spoken of in ch. v. 2, in connection with the seven-sealed book held in the right hand of "him that sat on the throne, and which only the Lion of the tribe of Judah" was found worthy to take and open. This book told of here is described as "little" as compared with that, and, probably, in contrast with it. Now, although the historical interpreters affirm that this little book means the Bible, as we have it, yet the difficulties that beset this interpretation are so many and so great, that it has been abandoned by all the more reliable expositors of the Apocalypse as inconsistent with its avowed purpose to declare the "things that must shortly come to pass," and the time of which was "at hand;" still, what is here said of this "little book" does suggest to us not a few of the most interesting and important characteristics of the Word of God. For note—

I. THE AMBASSADOR WHO BRINGS IT. Much may be learnt concerning any message that is sent by an earthly monarch from the character and rank and insignia which belong to the messenger. If the business which he has to transact be of great importance, and it be desired to impress its significance upon the minds of those to whom he is sent, he himself will be of such dignity, and accompanied with such tokens of authority and power, as will prepare those to whom he comes rightly to receive the message he brings. So here, he who brings God's message to mankind is one of no mean order, and the tokens of his authority are of the most impressive kind. 1. *He comes from heaven.* The Bible is not a merely human production. It is inspired by God; it is a message from heaven. It contains what no human mind could have known or invented; it speaks with an authority that they who receive the message realize to be from God. Inspiration cannot be argued and so demonstrated to the intellect, but it speaks to the soul, and is felt to be present in the Scriptures, which therefore are declared to be the Word of God. It wakes up a response in the soul, quickening, informing, strengthening, consoling, uplifting, sanctifying it, as no mere human words have ever done or can do, save as they draw their inspiration from this source. 2. *It is mighty in its power.* It was "a strong angel" that St. John saw, suggesting to him and to us the strength of that message which he was commissioned to bring. What trophies of its power has not the Bible won? Where is the age, the country, the rank, the character, the intellectual condition, the circumstances of any kind, amid and over which it has not proved strong to subdue and bless and save? 3. *Its truths fill the soul with awe.* The angel was "clothed with a cloud"—symbol this of the majesty and mystery that surround and invest the foundation-teachings of the Word of God. The soul can only bow in reverence and awe before them, and confess its feebleness in their presence. 4. *But they are crowned with blessed promise and grace.* "The rainbow was upon his head." Though there be so much that we cannot penetrate or comprehend, nevertheless the predominant characteristic is that of "grace," that of which the rainbow was at the first and is ever the beautiful and blessed symbol. Even those awful judgments of God spoken in ver. 7 are there declared to be part of "the good tidings which he declared to his servants the prophets" (see Revised Version). And when we preach out of the Bible we are said to preach the gospel. This is its main character and intent. 5. *They irradiate and illumine all our earthly life.* "His face was as it were *the sun.*" "Truly the light is sweet, and a pleasant thing it is to behold the sun"—so says Eccles. xi. 7. And the confession of this radiant grace, this blessed light which streams forth from the Word of God, is a commonplace of all the sacred writers and of all who have rejoiced in that light. 6. *And they shall never be driven forth or removed.* "His feet as pillars of fire," and ver. 2, "He planted his right foot upon the sea, and his left foot upon the earth." His invincible power is signified by "the pillars of fire;" and his having set his feet upon the earth and sea tells of "the immovable steadfastness of the heavenly Conqueror against all the resistance of his enemies." He is come to stay, and he cannot be driven forth. When and where has not the attempt to dislodge the Word been made? But it has never succeeded. All Church history proves this. In many ages and places it has been death to keep a copy of the sacred writings. Wherever they were found, they were ruthlessly destroyed, and often they also with whom they were found. But every copy of the Bible that we possess to-day proves how partial and ineffective all such endeavours were. Glory be to God that they were so!

II. THE DESCRIPTION GIVEN OF IT. "A little book open." 1. *A book.* The Bible is not the revelation itself, but the record of it. But without the record the revelation would not have availed us. Great scorn has been poured on the idea of "a book revelation," and an immense deal of poor wit has been expended upon the idea that God should have used such mean materials as books are made of as the vehicle of his revelation of himself. But the Bible is *not* the revelation, only its record; and it is reason for eternal gratitude that his revelation has been so given that it can be thus recorded. In what other way could the knowledge of God have been so well preserved or spread abroad? (Cf. on this 'The Eclipse of Faith,' by H. Rogers.) 2. *Its seeming insignificance.* It is "a little book." In these days of gold and guns, when wealth and armies are thought to be the great means of accomplishing everything, the spiritual force that lies hidden in "a little book" counts but for little. But what hath not God wrought by it? And we may be grateful that it is little, and not a ponderous library which it would need a lifetime even to know part of, but one small volume which can be read and reread and carried everywhere as we will. No doubt the littleness of the book here spoken of is intended to be in contrast with that vast volume told of in ch. v., which was written within and without, so complete, so full, was it. This tells of but "part of his ways;" that seems to have been the declaration of all his will. But it suggests the seeming insignificance, both in form and force, of that which we call the book of God, but whose insignificance is, indeed, only seeming, not real. 3. *It is to be an open book.* St. John saw it "open" in the hand of the angel. There have been and there are those who would have the Word of God closed, if not entirely, yet to large extent. They affirm it is not a book for the common people, but for the priests of the Church; and for centuries it was kept closed, and is even now looked upon with more or less of dislike. But, blessed be God, it is open, not to the eyes alone, but to the mind. For though it contains the profoundest truths that the intellect of man has ever studied, still it contains also those truths—and they are the most numerous and important—which the humblest and least instructed are able to receive and rejoice in. God hath caused the vision to be written and made "plain," so that the unlearned may learn, and the most simple comprehend.

III. THE VOICES FOR AND AGAINST IT. We read that the angel cried with a loud voice, and that the seven thunders uttered their voices. Now: 1. *The angelic voice* suggests: (1) The *startling effect of the Word of God upon mankind.* The angel's voice was "as when a lion roareth." So did the Word of God affect men. See when at the Reformation it was first freely given to Europe. How it roused men's minds, awoke them from their lethargy, nation after nation heard the sound and broke away from the superstition and sins in which they had so long lived! And it is so still. "What must I do to be saved?" is the intense, the sometimes agonized cry, of men whom the lion-like, awful voice of the Word has aroused from their sin. The conviction of sin which the Holy Spirit produces through the Word is, often, to men "as when a lion roareth," arousing them indeed. (2) The assured *persuasion it gives concerning the mystery of this present life.* The solemn oath of the angel (vers. 5—7) did but represent what the Word of God accomplishes. As he gave, so it gives, solemn assurance that what now is—so much of it so mournful, so full of mystery—is not ever to be, but shall have an end. Life is a mystery now, even in these comparatively calm days of ours; but what must it have appeared to the persecuted outraged Church of St. John's day? And were not we assured that what we now see is but *part* of God's ways, one link in the chain of his purposes, only a portion of his one great, wise, holy, and loving plan, how could we believe in him as either wise, holy, just, or loving? The mind would rush to atheism, and the man to suicide; for what better could be done? But the Word of God, like the solemn oath of this strong angel, assures us of God that

> " His purposes are ripening fast,
> Unfolding every hour ;
> The bud may have a bitter taste,
> But sweet will be the flower."

2. *The thunder-voice.* (Ver. 4.) The *brutum fulmen*, the full-voiced anger of him who uttered it. The question comes—Whence this voice of the seven thunders? It has, we think, been too hastily assumed that St. John is referring to the sevenfold voice of the thunder mentioned in Ps. xxix. And, doubtless, in this book thunders are referred to as coming forth from the throne of God (cf. ch. iv. 5). But the true interpretation is given, we think, in the strikingly parallel passages in Dan. viii. 26 and xii. 4—9, where that which the prophet is commanded to "seal up" is not what God shall do, but what his people's enemies shall do against him and them. And so here, we believe, the thunders tell of the wrathful response, the angry mutterings, of God's enemies against his truth. And thus regarded, they tell of *the opposition the Word arouses in the world of the wicked.* It has ever been so. In St. John's day; at the era of the Reformation, witness the cursed cruelties which the Roman Catholic Church in those days perpetrated in the Netherlands, in our own land, and wherever also she had power. And still those "dark places of the earth, which are full of the habitations of cruelty," are filled with rage when any real invasion of them is made by the messengers of the Word. Still Christ's Name is as a "sign to be spoken against." And it was fitting that these voices should not be written. The purpose of this book was to console and strengthen the Church, not to distress and alarm. Hence the Divine forces on the side of the Church and against her foes are what this book mainly reveals. It tells us, "The Lord is on our side; we will not fear what man can do unto us."

IV. THE DIRECTIONS CONCERNING IT. As it was with the "little book" so must it be with the Word of God : 1. *It must be received as from God.* If we look upon the Bible as on "any other book," as on ordinary literature, we shall lack that reverential docile spirit which is necessary in order to receive its truths. The book was to be taken from the hand of the angel (ver. 8). 2. *It must be taken into the soul.* This is the meaning of the strange command, "Take it, and eat it up." It is as when Jeremiah said, "Thy words were found, and I did eat them ;" as when our Lord said, "Except ye eat the flesh of the Son of man," etc. (John vi.). We are to "read, mark, learn, and inwardly digest" its truths; make them part of our very self. So must it be with those who would know the power of God's Word. 3. *When so taken, it will produce both sorrow and joy.* The *first* taste will be pleasant. "In thy mouth sweet as honey." And it is so. Is it not a joy that we have a revelation from God at all; that we are not left in the dark as to our whence and whither; that we are assured God is "our Father which art in heaven;" that our salvation is "without money and without price," for that Christ died for us? Yes; "sweeter also than honey and the honey-comb" are these precious truths. But the *after-taste* will cause distress and pain. Witness the Saviour's tears wept over lost souls, and the like tears shed still by those who know "the fellowship of his sufferings." That men should resist and reject such a Saviour; that we should so long have done so, and do not yet wholly receive him ;—yes, this after-taste hath pain. 4. *When eaten, it qualifies for witness-bearing for God.* (Ver. 11.) This is the real qualification, this deep experimental knowledge of the power of God's Word. All else is as naught compared with this. Only such God ordains to be his prophets. Thus doth this "little book," though it meant not the Bible, tell of the Bible.—S. C.

Ver. 6.—*No more time.* "The angel . . . sware . . that there should be time no longer." This word of the angel is capable of being rendered, and has been rendered, in three different ways. Take it as meaning—

I. THE TIME IS NOT YET COME. It is easy to believe that the persecuted people of St. John's day, as often since, might have thought that the judgments which they witnessed and the distresses they endured could not but be the beginning of the end. Our Lord knew that they would think so, and hence (Matt. xxiv.) warned them that they should see and suffer much; but "the end" was "not yet." They had asked what should be the sign of his coming, and of "the end of the age." They were eagerly expecting it. At his ascension they asked the like question again. The apostolic Epistles are full of evidence that the second coming of our Lord was expected as near at hand. St. Paul wrote his Second Epistle to the Thessalonians to dispel this idea, or at any rate to moderate its effects. And when Jerusalem fell, and when the Roman empire fell, it was confidently believed that the end of all things was close at hand. And had we lived in those awful days, it is likely that we should have thought so too. And we know how calculations have been made as to the time of the end. The illustrious Bengel reckoned that it would be in 1836, and his mistake is on record as a warning to all who would make similar rash statements, though even yet the warning is neglected by some. But our Lord has told us that it is not for us "to know the times and the seasons" (Acts i.), and all human calculations are therefore foredoomed to error. And it is well for us that we cannot know. "Ignorance is bliss" in regard to such a subject. Could we fix the date, those far off from it would harden themselves in their sin; those near at hand would become as the Thessalonians did, unfitted for their daily duty, and would not, as St. Paul bade them do, "mind their own business." And so in regard to what is to each one of us as the end of all things, the date of our death, we are kept in merciful ignorance of it. And to keep us therein God has so ordered our lives that there is no hour of it in which men may not die, and in which many do not die, and no hour of it in which they certainly know that they must and shall. Hence little children die, and young men and maidens, boys and girls, as well as the old and grey-headed. Ruthless and cruel are seemingly not a few of the visitations of death, cutting down youth in the first freshness and bloom of life, often not sparing the bride and mother in the fulness of their joy, forcing the hot tears from the young husband and wife as they mourn hopelessly over the cradle that held the little one whose life was to them dearer than their own. Such things are. And to some they seem horrible and cruel. But it is in order that we all may be delivered from that paralysis of hope and energy which would come upon us, as it comes upon the convicted felon in the condemned cell, if we knew the actual moment when we must die, and could count off every hour that draws us on to the inevitable doom. Therefore is it well that we do not know the time or the season. And in regard to the end of the world, what mercy is there in the fact that the time is not yet, that "the master of the house" has not yet "risen up, and shut to the door"! For now many will enter who then will not be able. We are thankful that Christ has not yet "accomplished the number of his elect." And they who are his, how much they yet have to do to learn and to obtain before they are prepared to meet their Lord! "The bride has" not yet "made herself ready;" but she must and will, and that she may "the Bridegroom" tarries. Therefore, if this be the meaning of the angel's oath, that "the time is not yet," we rejoice in it both for ourselves and for myriads more.

II. THERE SHALL BE NO MORE TIME. And this we believe is the meaning here—that there shall be no longer delay, postponement, no more weary waiting, no longer any lingering of the accomplishment of God's purposes. So regarded, it was for the Church of St. John's day a blessed *sursum corda,* a cordial and good cheer, helping them to endure patiently and to hope on more and more. The "mystery of God" shall soon "be finished," so soon that, as we say "we are come" to any city when we see its towers and spires rising before us, although we may yet be some considerable distance from its gates; so, because the time is so short, we may say it is over, the waiting-time is past—it exists "no longer." And thus: 1. *The Christian may comfort himself.* True, the age drags out its weary length, but each individual life is short, and generally long before even that short life is done the recompenses of God, the earnest and pledge of the yet larger recompenses of eternity, are given. "The Lord is not slack concerning his promises"—how often we have gratefully to confess that! Yes; they are so given, even here and now, that the believer is constrained to own, "Goodness and mercy have followed me all the days of my life." Tares are undoubtedly amongst the wheat, to its sore detriment and harm, but they are not always to be there; it is a mystery that they are there at all; we would like to go and pull them up, but we cannot; but the harvest draws on, and then the trouble will all be over. But: 2. *The enemies of God should be afraid.* The avenging gods—so the old pagan world believed—have their feet shod with wool. Men hear not their silent approach, and they may be upon them, they often are, in a moment. The sinner never knows how near God's judgment upon his sin may be. Of many the angel hath sworn that there shall be time no longer; the judgment of God shall fall. In a moment, in bright noonday, when the sky is without a cloud, unseen and unheard, the last link that binds the mass of snow and ice to the mountain-side is severed, and the avalanche rushes down into the depths below. Do not the events of every day prove, now on this sinner against God's laws, and now on that, that God hath sworn concerning them, "there should be time no longer"?

III. ALL TIME SHALL CEASE. Thus also our text may be understood. "Time" and "duration" are not synonymous terms—the latter includes eternity as well as time; but time and eternity, notwithstanding their common quality of duration, are contrasted in Scripture as being of essentially different natures. Time means the present condition of things; eternity, that condition which belongs to the age to come. "The things that are seen are temporal, but the things which are unseen are eternal." Time is of the age that now is; eternity, of the age that is to come. Thus understood, it is not difficult to believe that time—this age—shall cease. The Bible speaks of "ages." The word is commonly rendered "world," but its true meaning is "age." Thus it speaks of "ages of ages," "this age," "the age to come." And every branch of science tells of different "ages." Geology speaks of them and marks them off one from another by different names. History, biology, philology, all speak in similar way. All tell of ages when the condition of things was altogether different from what we see now, and how one age has succeeded and prepared for another. Therefore that there should be a passing away of the present age to which time belongs, and that it should be followed by one in which time, as we understand it, should be no more, is affirmed, not only by the Bible, but by manifold other evidence beside. And not only shall there be succession, but advance. There have been ages in which we can trace no form of life. These have been succeeded by others which have had life, but only in its lower forms. These again by others possessing higher forms, and at length the highest of all, that of man. And in harmony with all this the Bible bids us look on to an infinitely better condition of things than now we know of, in the age or world to come, whereof the sacred writers speak. Here "the whole creation groaneth and travaileth together in pain even until now;" but there "the creation itself also shall be delivered from the bondage of corruption," etc. (Rom. viii.). The inscrutable problem of this present life, "the mystery of God," as it is termed in ver. 7, shall "be finished," and there shall be 'a new heavens and a new earth, wherein dwelleth righteousness." And the means whereby all this shall be brought about, not only the Bible, but scientific research also, reveal with startling clearness. The Bible says that the angels of God "shall gather out of his kingdom all things that do offend, and them that work iniquity." Science says that in the progress of the ages the fittest alone survive. All that are incapable of the higher life that is to be disappear and perish, and the fit and worthy alone remain. Such is the solemn "Amen" of science to the teachings of the Word of God. And are there not like facts visible even now amidst mankind? Growth and advancement in races, tribes, nations, families, and individuals, the records and observation of human life, are full of such happy facts; but, on the other hand, there are the mournful facts amid the same subjects, of degeneracy, decay, and death. Character determines these things, and the Bible says the same. Oh, how, then, does all this appeal to every soul! For what am I preparing myself? Must I be doomed to die because I am not fit for the better life that is to be when time shall be no longer? or—and God grant it may be so!—am I by virtue of my living union with the Lord Jesus Christ, who is himself "the Life," destined for glory, honour, and immortality with him in the Eternal? That this may be so is why our pulpits and sermons are for ever re-echoing with the appeal, "Come to Christ." The Bible and experience alike attest that it is through living faith, carrying along with it, as such faith ever does, the surrender of the will, the heart, to him, that we become vitally grafted into him, and so in his life—the eternal, the blessed, the glorious—do for ever share. For he said, "Because I live, ye shall live also."—S. C.

Vers. 1—7.—*The word of assurance and consolation.* The Book of the Revelation is written for the comfort of the Church in presence of her oppressing foes. It is designed to sustain the faithful people in well-doing, when the severities of cruel dealing make their lot hard and almost unendurable. Their patience is often severely tried; sometimes it has yielded under heavy pressure. Here is afforded another word of promise which is calculated to sustain the faint of heart. A vision is granted of "a strong angel" who brings assured promise of a certain and even speedy termination of the time of suffering and of struggle. "The mystery of God, according to the good tidings which he declared to his servants the prophets," shall be "finished." This is the encouragement to hope; and to the Church in the early times, under the pressure of her first destructive persecutions, this would be a word of the utmost comfort. It is the re-echo of "Behold, I come quickly." This word of consolation is of great preciousness and help to the suffering Church; for—

I. IT IS GIVEN BY THE LORD HIMSELF. The strong angel "coming down out of heaven, arrayed with a cloud," can be none other than the Lord himself. The surrounding symbols are his, and his alone. "The rainbow was upon his head;" "his face was as the sun, and his feet as pillars of fire." It is the reflection of the Divine glory in Christ. When he cries the seven thunders utter their voices, and his great voice was "as a lion roareth." From the word of such a one the Church may always gather the utmost comfort.

II. IT GIVES THE PROSPECT AND PLEDGE OF RELEASE. The suffering Church writhes in its anguish; but a definite limit is put to the days of sorrow. "In the days of the voice of the seventh angel, when he is about to sound." This is not indefinite and uncertain: "There shall be time no longer"—there shall be no more *delay.* Relief is certain and speedy. This is assured by oath, even by the voice of the angel who "sware by him that liveth for ever and ever, who created the heaven, and the things that are therein, and the earth, and the things that are therein, and the sea, and the things that are therein." This oath is for truest confirmation.

III. The word of consolation and promise IS GIVEN IN THE MOST SOLEMN AND ASSURING MANNER. This seen in the whole vision—the person, attitude, message, oath, and surrounding testimonies.

IV. IT IS THE TRUEST, THE UTMOST ENCOURAGEMENT TO HOPE. Upon this vision the Church should ever reflect in the time of suffering and fear. It is possible patiently to endure and hold out when a definite and assured prospect and pledge of relief is given. The words, "declared to his servants the prophets," shall have their fulfilment; "the mystery" shall be "finished."—R. G.

Vers. 8—11.—*The little book; or, the sweetness and bitterness of the prophetic office.* The consolation of an assured end having been given, the holy seer, and in him the Church in all ages, becomes prepared to receive tidings that shall prove "bitter" and painful. The final victory is assured. The word is "sweet as honey" in the mouth of him who receives it, which reception is represented by the figure of "eating the little book." It is sweet, for it is impossible to be an agent of God for any work without a certain pleasurableness. But the sweetness is temporary. So is it a pleasant thing to receive a message from the Lord, but it may be a very painful thing to communicate it to men. The reception of "the little book," whatever that book may mean, is a preparation to prophesying "again concerning many peoples, and nations, and tongues, and kings." The words which follow are mingled words of sadness and comfort—comfort for the Church in her obedience; sadness for the ungodly, rebellious, and opposing nations. In the symbol before us there seems to shine out from the midst of many teachings one respecting the prophetic office itself. For a moment attention is directed to the seer himself and his own states. Thus have we set forth *the prophetic office—the honourableness of its calling; the painfulness of its duties.* Nothing is said as to the twofold character of the message—" the little book "—but only the twofold effect upon the seer. Our thoughts, then, are upon him.

I. THE HOLY OFFICE OF PROPHET IS THE MOST HONOURABLE AND EXALTED AMONGST MEN. To speak for God, as his agent; to declare his message; to receive the Word from his lips, by his inspiration; to be entrusted with his Word to men—be it a word of condemnation, of warning, of promise, of mercy, or hope—is a most sacred, hallowed burden. To speak to men in God's Name is higher than to speak for kings. The "ambassador for Christ" stands at the head of diplomatic agents. How holy, how awful, how responsible, his office! The calling to such office cannot but have its sweetness to the faithful servant.

II. OF ALL OFFICES THIS, WHEN RIGHTLY COMPREHENDED, IS THE MOST PAINFUL. To deal with words of judgment and threatening; to speak of sin; to warn of punishment; to have close alliance with righteousness amongst men who reject it; to be burdened with spiritual care; to stand in antagonism to prevalent sentiment, and strive to raise men to altitudes of goodness;—cannot but be a burden too heavy to be borne were the prophet unaided. He is in error who views the calling to the prophetic office too lightly; he is also in error who thinks triflingly of the painfulness of its responsibilities.—R. G.

Vers. 8—11.—*God's Word.* "And the voice which I heard from heaven," etc. The "little book," or roll, here might be fairly taken to illustrate God's *redemptive truth,* or the gospel. The following thoughts are suggested.

I. THIS GOSPEL IS BROUGHT TO MAN FROM HEAVEN. "The voice which I heard from heaven spake unto me again, and said, Go, and take the little book." Redemptive truth is a special revelation to man sent by God from heaven. Men could never have reached the *redemptive idea* by the study of nature or by philosophic research; or, were the human mind to traverse through the whole world of natural science and to search into every part, it would never discover this "little book." The way in which alienated humanity can be brought into a loving sympathy with God transcends human discovery. "Ear hath not heard, eye hath not seen." Divine messengers brought this "little book" to man, and Christ embodied it.

II. THIS GOSPEL IS TO BE APPROPRIATED BY MAN. "And he said, Take it, and eat it up." The object of the gospel is not merely to enlighten the mind, to stimulate inquiry, or to excite emotions, but to be *appropriated as food,* to satisfy the hunger and to invigorate the faculties of the soul. "The Word must become flesh," it must course through every vein, beat in every pulse, and strengthen every fibre of our being. It is the bread of life that came down from heaven, the fruit of the tree of life. The spirit of this "little book" must become the inspiring and the regnant spirit of our being.

III. THIS GOSPEL HAS A TWOFOLD EFFECT ON MAN. "It shall make thy belly bitter, but it shall be in thy mouth sweet as honey." It is both sweet and bitter. In its disclosures of infinite love and promises of future blessedness it is indeed "sweet," but in its convictions of sin, reproofs, and denunciations it is indeed "bitter." It produces in the soul sorrow and joys, sighs and songs, and its bitterness will remain as long as one particle of depravity continues in the heart. The experience of a Christly man is a very mixed experience during his life on earth; yonder it is all sweetness.

IV. THIS GOSPEL, APPROPRIATED, QUALIFIES MAN FOR HIS MISSION. "And he said unto me, Thou must prophesy again before many peoples, and nations, and tongues, and kings." Prophesying, or indoctrinating men with Divine ideas, is the grand mission of every man; but this mission can only be realized after the teacher himself has appropriated the Divine Word. When he has it in him, not merely as an idea or a theory, but as a living power, then he will be able to "prophesy" with regard to "peoples, and nations, and tongues, and kings."—D. T.

EXPOSITION.

CHAPTER XI.

Ver. 1.—And there was given me a reed like unto a rod. We are not told by whom the *reed* is given, but in ch. xxi. the angel has the reed, and so also in Ezek. xl., upon which the incident seems founded (see Ezek. xl.; and cf. the reference to the outer court in ver. 17). The reed is "like a rod;" that is, like to a *staff*. It is for a measuring-line, as in Zech. ii. 1. And the angel stood, saying. Omit all except "saying," as in the Revised Version. Λέγων is used absolutely, not as qualifying κάλαμος, "reed," as Andreas (cf. ch. iv. 1; xiv. 7; xix. 6). Rise, and measure the temple of God; rather, *rouse and measure*, etc. The imperative verb does not imply anything as to the previous position of St. John. "The temple" is ναός, the shrine or dwelling-place of God (as in ver. 19; also ch. iii. 12; vii. 15), the inner temple, as distinguished from the *outer court* next mentioned. It scarcely seems possible to doubt that *the temple* is here figuratively used of the faithful portion of the Church of Christ. The word is plainly thus used in ch. iii. 12 and vii. 15; and is frequently found with this signification in St. Paul's writings, which were probably known to St. John. Düsterdieck and others think that St. John refers literally to the temple at Jerusalem, and to the earthly Jerusalem. But, if so, this portion of the Apocalypse stands self-condemned as a prediction which was falsified within a year or two of its enunciation; for in ver. 13 it is expressly stated that the tenth part of the city fell. And nowhere else in the book do Jerusalem and the temple signify the earthly places. The object of the measurement is generally thought to be to set apart or mark off that which is measured from that which is felt without; but opinions vary as to why the temple is thus set apart, some thinking that it is the literal temple which is given over to destruction, others believing that the measuring is a token of the preservation of the Church of God. But may not the command have been given to St. John in order to direct his attention to the size of the Church of God? This is the common meaning of the expression throughout the Bible; it is so in Zech. ii. 1—5, a passage upon which this is possibly founded; and it is so in ch. xxi. 15. Moreover, there seems a good explanation of the reason why such an incident, thus explained, should occur here. The six trumpets have spoken of the large portions of mankind against whom they were directed; the sixth has declared that

men did nevertheless **not repent.** The seventh trumpet is about to announce yet more terrible woe for the worldly; and, previous to this, a brief but vivid description is given of the oppression to be suffered by the Church—a description inserted here in order to lead up to, and demonstrate the absolute necessity for, the terrible final judgment. Among the ungodly are even some who are nominally members of the Church, who are typified by the *outer court.* No one could be more conscious that only a portion of the Church—"the elect"—was to be saved than the writer of the Epistles to the seven Churches (ch. i.—iii.). Might not the seer and his hearers be inclined to ask, "Who, then, can be saved? Are there any who escape when so much is said about the punishment in store for men?" In answer to such questions, the seer is bidden to remember, what is apt to be forgotten in the dejection caused by the contemplation of the huge amount of wickedness which undoubtedly exists in the world, viz. the large number of good men who form God's temple. It is to be noticed, also, that no mention is made of the command being actually carried out. It is as if the uttering of the command were sufficient to direct the attention of St. John to the fact which was to be conveyed to him, and that, therefore, the necessity for carrying out the injunction existed no longer. It therefore seems probable that "the temple" must be interpreted symbolically. It is the dwelling-place of God, the place in which he is worshipped; that is, the multitude of true believers, or the faithful Church. St. John is bidden to measure it, in order to sustain the faith and hope of himself and his hearers. It is placed in antithesis to the *outer court*, the faithless portion of the visible Church of God, which is given over to the Gentiles—the type of all that is worldly. And the altar, and them that worship therein. The altar of incense alone stood within the ναός; but this may be only an accessory detail in the general description, and not to be pressed to a particular interpretation. "Them that worship therein" directs our thoughts to the individual members of the one body which collectively is "the temple."

Ver. 2.—But the court which is without the temple leave out, and measure it not; for it is given unto the Gentiles; *it hath been given* (Revised Version). Not merely "leave out," but "cast out." The "court which is without the temple" was entered only by Jews. It seems, therefore, here to signify part of the Church, but that part which is separated from the inner circle of true believers, and given over to the world, which is here symbolized by "the Gentiles." The *Gentiles*, the *nations*, throughout the Apocalypse, signifies either (1) all mankind whatsoever; or (2) that portion of mankind which is left when the true Church of God is withdrawn, and therefore which embraces the unrighteous part of mankind in contrast to the godly (cf. ch. ii. 26; xiv. 8; xvi. 19; xviii. 23; xxii. 22). The latter is the signification here. And the holy city shall they tread underfoot. The holy city— Jerusalem—always in the Apocalypse the type of the Church. "They shall tread" need not necessarily refer to "the nations," though the context naturally leads to this signification; but it may be impersonal, amounting to no more than "the holy city shall be trodden underfoot." St. John seems to apply the words of our Lord concerning the literal Jerusalem to the description of the fate in store for the typical Jerusalem (cf. Luke xxi. 24). "The nations" are the instrument by which the Church is trodden underfoot, and the mention of the Gentiles in connection with the apostate portion of the Church leads to the description of the oppression of the faithful by the world. The seer is bidden to take courage by a contemplation of the numbers of those preserved by God, but is warned, nevertheless, not to expect from that fact immunity for the Church from the persecution of the world. Forty and two months. Καί, "and," is inserted contrary to the common practice when the larger number precedes (so also in John ii. 20; v. 5). This period of three years and a half is certainly symbolical. It is the half of seven years—a perfect number. It therefore denotes a broken, uncertain period; a space of time which is certainly finite, but the end of which is uncertain. This seems to point necessarily to the period of the world's existence during which the Church is to suffer oppression. This period is mentioned (1) in ver. 3 under the form of twelve hundred and sixty days, where it denotes the same period that is referred to here; (2) in ch. xii. 6 as twelve hundred and sixty days, and in ch. xii. 14 as "a time, and times, and half a time," in both of which passages the signification is the same as that given above; (3) in ch. xiii. 5 it is called, as here, forty-two months, and describes the same period. The expression is founded on Dan. vii. 25 and xii. 7. In the latter place the time signified is certainly the period of the world's existence. We therefore see (1) that its natural meaning, in connection with the number seven, (2) its signification in Daniel, and (3) its apparent use in all passages in the Apocalypse, tend to cause us to interpret the symbol as above.

Ver. 3.—And I will give power unto my two witnesses. Omit "power." What is given follows, viz. "they shall prophesy," etc. The voice, speaking in the name of Christ, says, "*My:*" "The two witnesses of me;" τοῖς, "the," as though they were well known. There is much diversity of interpretation in regard to "the two witnesses." It seems reasonable to understand the two witnesses as representative of the elect Church of God (embracing both Jewish and Christian) and of the witness which she bears concerning God, especially in the Old and New Testaments. The following considerations seem to support this interpretation. (1) The vision is evidently founded on that in Zech. iv., where it is emblematical of the restored temple, which only in the preceding verse (ch. xi. 2) is a type of the elect of God's Church (*vide supra*). (2) The Apocalypse continually represents the Church of God, after the pattern of the life of Christ, in three aspects—that of conflict and degradation; that of preservation; that of triumph (see Professor Milligan's Baird Lectures, 'The Revelation of St. John,' lect. ii. and v.). This is a summary of the vision here. (3) Much of the Apocalypse follows our Lord's description in Matt. xxiv. In that chapter (vers. 13, 14) we have, "He that shall endure unto the end, the same shall be saved. And this gospel of the kingdom shall be preached in all the world for a witness unto all nations; and then shall the end come." Again, a brief description of this vision. (4) It is not probable that two individuals are meant; for (*a*) as we have shown throughout the Apocalypse, the application is invariably to principles and societies, though this may include particular applications in certain cases; (*b*) it is inconceivable that Moses and Elias, or any other of the saints of God, should return from Paradise to suffer as these two witnesses; (*c*) our Lord expressly explained the reference to the coming of Elias, and declared that he had already come; and (*d*) there seems no more reason for interpreting these two witnesses literally of two men, than for interpreting Sodom and Egypt in their ordinary geographical signification in ver. 8. (5) The details of the fate of the two witnesses agree with the interpretation given—the whole vision being understood as symbolical. Thus (*a*) the picture of the two witnesses is evidently formed after the pattern of Moses and Elias, on account of the conspicuous witness they bore and the hardship they suffered, as well as their preservation and final vindication. Moreover, Moses and Elias are typical of the Law and the prophets, or the Scriptures

—the means (as stated above) by which the Church chiefly bears witness of God. (*b*) The time during which they prophesy; (*c*) the clothing in sackcloth; (*d*) the appellation of candlesticks and olive trees; (*e*) their power to hurt; (*f*) their apparent death; (*g*) the torment they cause; (*h*) their resuscitation; (*i*) their vindication; (*k*) the immediate advent of the final judgment;—all agree (as shown below) with the interpretation given. (6) Witness is constantly connected in the Apocalypse and elsewhere with the Church, and generally with suffering, sometimes with triumph (cf. ch. i. 2, 5, 9; vi. 9; xii. 11, 17; xx. 4). (7) In ch. xix. 10 we are told, "The testimony [witness] of Jesus is the spirit of prophecy," exactly the quality with which the two witnesses are credited (ver. 3), and which is the work of the Church. And they shall prophesy; that is, "prophesy" in its literal meaning of forthtelling God's will and his judgments on the wicked, and so of preaching repentance. This is emphatically the work of the Church, and is accomplished chiefly through the Scriptures. It is this prophesying that torments (see vers. 5, 10). A thousand two hundred and three score days. Or, forty and two months (ver. 2). During the period of the world's existence (see on ver. 2) the Church, although "trodden underfoot," will not cease to "prophesy." Clothed in sackcloth. Thus, symbolically, is expressed the same fact as in ver. 2. The Church there is "trodden underfoot" during the period of the world; here it is said that she is to perform her office during this time "clothed in sackcloth." The treatment by the world of both the Church of God and the Word of God is represented by the apparel of mourning and woe, which is the lot of the Church on earth.

Ver. 4.—These are the two olive trees, and the two candlesticks. The "two olive trees" and the "two candlesticks" are here identical. Thus, while St. John uses the figure of Zechariah, he does not apply it in every detail. In the prophet, but one candlestick is mentioned. "The two olive trees," which supply the material for the candlesticks, are fit emblems of the Old and New Testaments; the candlesticks typify the Jewish and Christian Churches. These are identical so far as being God's witnesses; the Church derives her stores from the Word of God, the light of the Word of God is manifested through the Church. Standing before the God of the earth; *the Lord of the earth* (Revised Version). The participle is masculine, though the preceding article and nouns are feminine, probably as being more in keeping with the masculine character under which the two witnesses are

depicted. Perhaps he is described as the "Lord of the earth," since the witnesses are to prophesy before all the earth (cf. ver. 9 and Matt. xxiv. 14).

Ver. 5.—And if any man will hurt them, fire proceedeth out of their mouth, and devoureth their enemies; *if any one willeth to hurt them*, etc. Most probably a reference to the act of Elijah (2 Kings i. 10). Perhaps there is a double reference in the *fire proceeding out of their mouth*; it is the *fire* of their witness, which refines and purifies and convinces some; it is also the fire of condemnation, which follows those who reject the testimony. The figure is found in Jer. v. 14, "I will make my words in thy mouth fire, and this people wood, and it shall devour them" (see also Hos. vi. 5; Ecclus. xlviii. 1). And if any man will hurt them, he must in this manner be killed; *any one shall will* (future) is read in the Revised Version, and is supported by א, A, 38; θέλει (present) is found in B, C, P, Andreas, Arethas. "In this manner;" that is, by *fire*. Such, throughout the Scriptures, is the form under which the final judgment of those who reject God's message is shadowed forth. The description is not more opposed to a general interpretation than it is to an individual interpretation of the two witnesses.

Ver. 6.—These have power to shut heaven, that it rain not in the days of their prophecy: and have power over waters to turn them to blood, and to smite the earth with all plagues, as often as they will; *the power . . . the heaven . . . the waters . . . every plague* (Revised Version). The whole verse is descriptive of the powers entrusted to Moses and Elijah, and is intended to convey the idea that the power which supported them would likewise support the two witnesses. It is doubtful whether the meaning should be pressed further than this. If we do so, it may, perhaps, be said that (in the words of Wordsworth) "if any one despises God's witnesses, they have the power, like Elias, to shut heaven, and exclude all who reject them. The dews of Divine grace are withheld from all who scorn them." It is thus a fulfilment of our Lord's words, "Whosoever hath, to him shall be given, and he shall have more abundance: but whosoever hath not, from him shall be taken away even that he hath" (Matt. xiii. 12). And again, besides the punishments which are finally to fall on the ungodly, it is the case that the rejection of God's will is followed on this earth by troubles which would be avoided were men to listen to the witness borne of him.

Ver. 7. And when they shall have finished their testimony. This is a difficult passage. How can the Church's testimony be said to be *finished* while the earth still exists? The explanation seems to lie in the words of our Lord, "When the Son of man cometh, shall he find faith on the earth?" (Luke xviii. 8). Christians are forewarned that, as the ages roll on, faith will wane. Though the Church be apparently destroyed, she is not really dead, but will rise again. As our Lord, after finishing his testimony, completed his work by his death and subsequent ascension, so the time will come when the Church shall have completed all that is necessary, by offering to the world her testimony, and shall then be so completely rejected as to appear dead. Her enemies will rejoice, but their time of rejoicing is cut short (see below). After three and a half days comes her vindication, and her enemies are struck with consternation; for it is the end, and they have no further opportunities for repentance. Thus Hengstenberg says, "They shall only be overcome when they have finished their testimony, when God has no further need for their service, when their death can produce more fruit than their life." The beast that ascendeth out of the bottomless pit shall make war against them, and shall overcome them, and kill them; *the beast that cometh up out of the abyss.* The article points to *the* beast which is described elsewhere in the Apocalypse (ch. xiii. 1; xvii. 8), and which is mentioned here by proleipsis. "The fourth beast," which is read in A, may have been suggested by Dan. vii. 7. ℵ[1] has "the beast which then cometh up." The *beast* is Satan, perhaps manifested in the form of the persecuting world-power (see on ch. xiii. 1). His nature is indicated by the use of the noun θηρίον, "a wild beast," the opposite, as Wordsworth says, of 'Αρνίον, "the Lamb." The beast ascends out of the abyss for a brief reign upon the earth, and is "drunken with the blood of the saints," as described in ch. xvii., but he ascends only to go into perdition (ch. xvii. 8). It is well to remember that the whole vision is symbolical. The intention is to convey the idea that the Church, in her witness for God, will experience opposition from the power of Satan, which will wax more and more formidable as time goes on, and result in the apparent triumph of the forces of evil. But the triumph will be brief; it will but usher in the end and the final subjugation of the devil.

Ver. 8.—And their dead bodies shall lie in the street of the great city, which spiritually is called Sodom and Egypt, where also our Lord was crucified; *their dead body* (in the singular), according to A, B, C, Arethas, and others. The plural is read in ℵ, P, Andreas, Primasius, and others. Omit

"lie upon the highway . . . their Lord." "The great city" is referred to in ch. xvi. 19; xvii. 18; xviii. 10—19. Its signification is always the same, *viz.* the type of what is ungodly and of the world, and it is always consigned to punishment. Jerusalem, the type of what is holy, is never thus designated. Here we are plainly told the *spiritual,* that is, the symbolical nature of the designation. *Sodom* and *Egypt* are chosen as the type of what is evil (cf. Deut. xxxii. 32; Isa. i. 10; Ezek. xvi. 46; xx. 7, etc.). It was in this city, that is, by the influence of this world-power, that the Lord was crucified. In describing the fate of the Church, St. John seems to have in mind the life of Christ. His witness, the opposition he encountered, his death for a brief time at the completion of his work, his resurrection and ascension, and triumph over the devil, are all here reproduced. "The bodies lie in the street" symbolizes, according to Jewish custom, the most intense scorn and hatred.

Ver. 9.—And they of the people and kindreds and tongues and nations shall see their dead bodies three days and a half, and shall not suffer their dead bodies to be put in graves; *and from among the peoples and tribes,* etc., *do* [men] *look upon,* etc., *and suffer not,* etc., *in a tomb* (Revised Version). The fourfold enumeration points to the wide distribution of the state of things symbolized (cf. ch. iv. 6; v. 9, etc.), and seems of itself almost sufficient to demonstrate that the two witnesses are not two individual persons who are hereafter to appear. The period is but three days and a half; again, as in vers. 2, 3, a broken, that is, a finite but uncertain period; but, as compared with the three years and a half—the period of the world's existence—very short. (On the signification of the last clause, see on ver. 8.) It is the usual Eastern mark of contempt and degradation. The whole verse, together with the preceding and succeeding verses, describes symbolically, but graphically, the scorn and contempt to which the Church and God's Word will be subjected by men.

Ver. 10.—And they that dwell upon the earth shall rejoice over them, and make merry, and shall send gifts one to another; because these two prophets tormented them that dwelt on the earth; *rejoice and make merry, that dwell* (present, though future in meaning; the present tense rendering the description more graphic). Those dwelling on the earth are the ungodly, the worldly. "They send gifts," in accordance with Oriental custom on joyful occasions (cf. ver. 9). "The prophets, the witnesses, tormented;" probably rather by the delivery of their message, which would affec[t] the conscience of men, than by the plagues referred to in ver. 6, though both may be meant. Alford, Bengel, and Düsterdieck favour the latter view of the two; Hengstenberg takes the former.

Ver. 11.—And after three days and a half the Spirit of life from God entered into them, and they stood upon their feet. "The three days and an half," viz. those mentioned in ver. 9, which see. Not merely "life from God," but the "Spirit from God" (cf. the vision in Ezek. xxxvii., especially vers. 9, 10). "The Spirit of life" has been in the Church of God previously, but she has become "dry bones;" "the Spirit" is now breathed anew into her, and she is restored and magnified before the world. And great fear fell upon them which saw them. "Beheld" (θεωρέω) occurs in the Apocalypse only here and in the next verse. *Fear*, on account of the vindication of those whom they had treated with contumely, and on account of the judgment to follow, which was even now shadowed forth.

Ver. 12.—And they heard a great voice from heaven saying unto them, Come up hither. The reading ἤκουσα, "I heard," for ἤκουσαν, "they heard," in a correction of א, and in B, Coptic, Armenian, Andreas, may have arisen from the similarity of the passage to ch. vi. 6; ix. 13. Düsterdieck, who reads, "I heard," points out that in ch. vi. 11; ix. 4, the phrase used in addressing others is, "It was said unto them." Thus the fate of the Church is that of her Lord, and it is the fate of each individual who may witness of God. Suffering, apparent extinction, perhaps, but ultimate triumph and ascension into the presence of God is their common inheritance. If so be that they suffer with him, they are also glorified with him (Rom. viii. 17). Alford remarks that "no attempt has been made to explain this ascension by those who interpret the witnesses figuratively of the Old and New Testaments, or the like." Is it not the resurrection of the just, of the witnesses of God, and their exaltation at the beginning of the last judgment? Thus St. Paul says, "But each in his own order: Christ the Firstfruits; then they that are Christ's, at his coming. Then cometh the end" (1 Cor. xv. 13). This "end" is immediately referred to by the seer. And they ascended up to heaven in a cloud; and their enemies beheld them; *in the cloud*. The parallelism with Elijah and Christ (see vers. 5, 6, 8) is carried still further. The Church is triumphantly vindicated and glorified as they were; the only difference is that now all men behold it. *The cloud* is not that which hides them from view, but rather, like that in ch. xiv. 14, something

which exalts and enhances the glory of the witnesses. The effect upon the worldly is told in vers. 11, 13.

Ver. 13.—And the same hour was there a great earthquake. In the visions of the seals it is set forth, under the sixth seal, how the destruction of the world is accompanied by earthquakes, etc.; the fear of the wicked is portrayed, and the preservation of the just takes place at the same time. Here, under the sixth trumpet, we have the same events shown forth, the triumph of the godly being mentioned first, though the rest happens "in that same hour." This is the conclusion of the sixth judgment, the consequence of the non-repentance mentioned in ch. ix. 21. The intervening narrative (ch. x. 1—xi. 12) serves to show that opportunities of knowing God's will are given to men, as well as warnings of judgment in case of disobedience. Vers. 13 of ch. xi. might follow ch. ix. 21, but for the desire of the seer to demonstrate the long-suffering goodness and mercy of God. And the tenth part of the city fell, and in the earthquake were slain of men seven thousand. Both the Authorized Version and the Revised Version have in the margin, "names of men, seven thousand," and some writers make much of the expression. Thus Alford says, "As if the name of each were recounted;" and Wordsworth, "Persons known and distinguished." But, in truth, the phrase is a Hebraism, to which we can attach no special significance (cf. Acts i. 15; ch. iii. 4). Whatever may be the system of interpretation adopted, this passage presents many difficulties. The whole account appears to relate to the judgment-day, and it is therefore more peculiarly prophetic than many parts of the Apocalypse, and for that reason its meaning must needs be more or less obscure. The account in this verse informs us that a part (a tenth) of the city (that is, of the wicked) suffers destruction; that the number so destroyed is described as seven thousand; that the rest (nine-tenths), in fear, recognize the power of God, to which they had hitherto refused attention. What is the final fate awarded to the nine-tenths we are not told. We have, therefore, to inquire the meaning of the numbers given. Now, it seems inherently impossible to interpret these numbers literally, and, moreover, as we have repeatedly seen, it is not the habit of the writer of the Apocalypse to indicate exact numbers. We must, therefore, try to discover the symbolical meaning which St. John attached to these expressions, the qualities rather than the quantities which he intended to signify. In the Bible *the tenth part* invariably signifies the tithe—the portion due from the community to God or to the ruler (cf. Gen. xxviii. 22; Lev. xxvii. 32; Numb. xviii. 21; 1 Sam. viii. 15, 17). It seems probable that this was the idea intended to be conveyed, viz. that God was now exacting his due, that men who had refused to recognize what was due from them to God were now forced to recognize his sovereignty by the exaction for punishment of a tithe, and as an evidence that all are under his sway. But, it may be objected, are not all the wicked punished at the judgment? This verse really seems to hint at a possibility of some course by which, even at the last moment, a chance of escape may be presented to men. But it does not distinctly state this; it seems, indeed, purposely to leave the fate of the rest of the ungodly untold. All it does assert is that God comes to the wicked as a Conqueror or a King, and exacts what is due to himself. But, further, why are *seven thousand* men slain? Again interpreting symbolically, *seven* involves the idea of completeness (see on ch. i. 4; v. 1, etc.). A thousand signifies a large number, though not an infinitely large number, for which we have "thousands of thousands," etc. This number, therefore, informs us that God's vengeance overtakes a large number, and that that number is complete, none escaping who deserve to be included. Perhaps this is mentioned as a precaution against any possibility of mistake in the interpretation of the "tenth part." It is as though St. John would say, "In that hour God exacted vengeance, demanding what was due to his justice; but do not imagine that that vengeance reached only a small part of mankind. It was far-extending and complete, though I do not attempt to define its exact limits, which cannot be known until the judgment-day itself shall reveal everything." And the remnant were affrighted, and gave glory to the God of heaven. *The rest gave glory*, being, perhaps (though not necessarily), repentant (cf. Josh. vii. 19; John ix. 24; ch. iv. 9; xiv. 7; xvi. 9). Possibly we have here a hint of God's uncovenanted mercies (*vide supra*), though there is nothing sufficiently definite to encourage men to postpone the day of repentance. No mention is made of the ultimate fate of "the remnant." "The God of heaven," in contrast to things of the world, upon which their affections had been hitherto set (cf. ch. xvi. 11). In these two places alone of the New Testament is this expression found; but it is not uncommon in the Old Testament (cf. Ezra i. 2; Neh. i. 4; Dan. ii. 18).

Ver. 14.—**The second woe is past.** The full description of this woe occupies ch. ix. 13—xi. 14. The account describes the natural spiritual punishment which is in-

flicted upon men in consequence of their sins (ch. ix. 13—21). This is insufficient to lead men to avert the final judgment by timely repentance. We have then a further description of God's long-suffering, and the rejection of his mercy, accompanied by an assurance of the safety of the faithful (ch. x. 1—xi. 10). This brings us to the end of the world (ch. xi. 11—14), just as the sixth seal led to the same termination (ch. vii. 12—17), and both are followed by the seventh, which gives a reference to the eternal peace of heaven. And, behold, the third woe cometh quickly. Omit "and." It is not said, in the case of the other "woes," that they come *quickly*. In his description of the preservation and glorification of the Church under the form of the "witnesses," the writer had been led to anticipate in some degree what follows under the seventh trumpet. Thus the seventh comes *quickly*. When events have progressed so far that the faithful Church is ascended to heaven with her Lord, then immediately follows the eternal rest set forth under the seventh trumpet. But this period is described as "the third woe," because it is the period of the final punishment of the wicked; and it is the judgment of the ungodly which is the theme of the trumpet-visions, although mention is incidentally made of the preservation and reward of the just. This is the time foretold in ch. x. 7. Just as in the case of the seals, the period of the seventh seal is recorded but not described, so here, in the case of the seventh trumpet, its advent is recorded, and its nature is indicated in ver. 18, but no further description is given of the *woe;* only a slight reference to the bliss of those who are secure in heaven. Thus St. John does not attempt a complete picture of either the blessings of heaven or the woes of hell.

Ver. 15.—And the seventh angel sounded; and there were great voices in heaven, saying. The participle "saying" is masculine, λέγοντες, in A, B; the feminine, λέγουσαι, is read in ℵ, C, P. Though the latter would be more correct, grammatically, yet irregular construction in such cases is not uncommon in the Apocalypse. The *voices* were possibly those of the angels rejoicing in the triumph of the kingdom of God. Or perhaps they proceeded from the four living beings, since the elders are next mentioned (ver. 17) as offering the praises of the redeemed Church which they represent. At the opening of the seventh seal there was silence in heaven; here, at the sound of the seventh angel's trumpet, *voices* are heard "in heaven," but there is silence as to the fate of the wicked, with whom the trumpet-visions have been chiefly concerned. In the revelation of the fate in store for the Church, as well as in that of the doom awarded to the ungodly, the visions stop short of describing circumstances connected with the life after the judgment-day. The kingdoms of this world are become the kingdoms of our Lord, and of his Christ; and he shall reign for ever and ever. Ἐγένετο ἡ βασιλεία, in the singular, is found in ℵ, A, B, C, P, and versions, and is adopted by the Revised Version. Ἐγένοντο αἱ βασιλεῖαι, the plural, is read in two cursives. We can understand the first part of this verse by referring to ch. xii. 10. God's power and authority is established by the final overthrow of Satan. It naturally follows the account, in vers. 12, 13, of the vindication of God's witnesses, and of the glory rendered by the rest of mankind. With God the Father is associated Christ, by whose means the overthrow of the devil is effected, and by whom his servants overcome (cf. ch. i. 6; v. 9; vii. 14; xii. 11). This is the final victory; henceforth "he shall reign for ever and ever."

Ver. 16.—And the four and twenty elders. "The elders" represent the Church (see on ch. iv. 4); they are those who were made "a kingdom" (ch. i. 6); they therefore fitly take up the burden of praise to him who has now established his universal and everlasting kingdom. Which sat before God on their seats; *which sit before God on their thrones* (Revised Version). Thus they are described in ch. iv. 4. Fell upon their faces, and worshipped God. (So also in ch. iv. 10; v. 14; xix. 4.)

Ver. 17.—Saying, We give thee thanks. The only instance in the Apocalypse of the use of this verb. It is found in John vi. 11, 23, and xi. 41, but in none of the other Gospels, though frequently in the Epistles. "The elders" are peculiarly indebted to God, since the establishment of his kingdom is the victory of the Church. O Lord God Almighty, which art, and wast, and art to come; *the Almighty.* Omit "and art to come" (Revised Version), with ℵ³ᵃ, A, B, C, P, Andreas, Arethas, Primasius, Syriac, Armenian, etc. (ch. i. 4; iv. 8). Perhaps the future is purposely omitted, since God's "coming" is now an accomplished fact (cf. also ch. xvi. 5). Because thou hast taken to thee thy great power, and hast reigned; *because thou hast taken thy great power, and didst reign* (Revised Version). God never ceased to reign, though for a time he abrogated his *power.* This *power* he has now reassumed, and the elders thank him for it, for it is the assurance of the end of the suffering of the Church of God. So in ch. iv. 11 the elders declare that he is worthy to receive the *power* which he now visibly exercises. It has, indeed, been exercised

before. The preservation of the Church set forth in the visions of the seals, and the punishment of the ungodly shown under the trumpet-visions, are effected by means of this power; but now that power is visibly exercised.

Ver. 18.—And the nations were angry (cf. Ps. ii. 1, which appears to be in the mind of the seer, for ver. 9 of the same psalm is referred to in ch. xii. 5). "The nations" raged in the period of their persecution of the Church, as set forth under the visions of the seals. They were angry, says Hengstenberg, at the progress of the kingdom of God, after the Word was made flesh. And thy wrath is come; *thy wrath came.* This verse points conclusively to the judgment-day, the events of which, however, as before remarked (see on ver. 15), are merely indicated, not fully described. This is the last final infliction upon the wicked, the seventh of the trumpet-plagues. And the time of the dead, that they should be judged; *to be judged.* Vitringa and others understand this judgment to refer to the dead martyrs who are now vindicated; but the meaning probably extends to all the dead, both classes of whom are referred to in the following part of the verse. And that thou shouldest give reward unto thy servants the prophets, and to the saints, and them that fear thy Name, small and great; and shouldest destroy them which destroy the earth; *and to give their reward . . . and to destroy,* etc. Though μικροὺς καὶ τοὺς μεγάλους, "the small and the great," is in the accusative case, it is in apposition with the preceding datives, προφήταις, ἁγίοις, φοβουμένοις, "prophets, saints, those that fear." The wicked are those who "destroy the earth," since it is on their account that the world is destroyed; they "destroy the earth" also by *corrupting* it, which is the force of διαφθεῖραι. In what way this destruction of the wicked is accomplished we are not told.

Ver. 19.—And the temple of God was opened in heaven; *and there was opened the temple of God that is in heaven* (Revised Version). "The temple" (ναός), the dwelling-place of God (cf. ver. 1; ch. iii. 12; vii. 15). Again, but a glimpse is afforded; and yet more is revealed than at the conclusion of the former series of visions; while the chief description is reserved to a later part of the Revelation. And there was seen in his temple the ark of his testament; or, *ark of his covenant.* This seems to be introduced in order to render more emphatic the steadfastness and unchangeableness of God. As in the case of the witnesses, the figure is taken from the Old Testament, and the symbol would be pregnant with meaning to Jewish Christians and others who had learnt to think of the ark as the sacrament of

God's abiding presence and continual help. He who now promises aid to his people, and threatens judgment upon the wicked, is the same God who formerly had displayed his power on behalf of his people Israel. And there were lightnings, and voices, and thunderings, and an earthquake, and great hail; *there followed* (Revised Version). The usual token of any special manifestation of God's presence, or direct dealing with men (see on ch. vi. 1).

This, then, forms the conclusion to the series of trumpet-visions. These visions, evoked by the cry for vengeance in ch. vi. 10, have demonstrated the need for patience and endurance on the part of Christians, by indicating the punishments meted out to the wicked on this earth and at the final judgment, together with the final triumph of the faithful. The seer next proceeds to elaborate a fact alluded to in the measuring of the temple in ch. x. 2, and to point the moral that it is possible for Christians within the Church to lose their final reward by their apostasy.

HOMILETICS.

Vers. 1—14.—"*My two witnesses.*" Following on the reception of the little book from the angel's hand, the seer is directed to measure the temple of God, the altar, and the worshippers. The outer court is not to be measured; for it, with the holy city, is to be trampled underfoot forty-two months. During this period (or a like period) there are to be two witnesses for God, clothed in sackcloth, who, though they have power with God, are slighted by men; against them a great onrush is to be made. They are silenced, and that effectually, by being put to death. The honour of burial is not to be theirs. This the world refuses. Rejoicing that it has stilled their disturbing voices, their bodies are to lie exposed, and the helplessness of their cause is to be the subject of merriment and ridicule. But lo! after a period of three days and a half, they again come to life, to the terror of their persecutors. Their ascension follows on their resurrection. As they have been made partakers of the sufferings of Christ, so also are they of the glory that should follow. What does all this signify? Dean Alford declares that no solution has as yet been given of it. The late Bishop of Manchester (Dr. Fraser) says, "I have no interpretation of this vision, nor any but the most vague and general key to its meaning." [1] Those who regard the tenth chapter as indicative of the Reformation look at this one as pointing out the main features of the epoch which should follow it. We readily, as we have often done in previous homilies, recognize the correspondence between prophecy and event. This is what we might expect. But the correspondence is not such as to warrant us in saying that this or that event is *the* fulfilment of the Word, although it may be a partial one. Nor is it in any one's power to decide when the twelve hundred and sixty days begin. If they represent as many years, and are, according to the prophecy, to follow on from the events in the preceding chapter, and if those events signify the Reformation, then there are twelve hundred and sixty years to follow on the Reformation. In other words, we are at least seven hundred or nine hundred years from the end. But we have long ago given up this sort of attempt to assign dates, as at once impracticable and unprofitable. We see in the chapter before us a symbolic setting-forth of that which is ever, ever fulfilling itself again and again before our eye.[2] It is a stay to our faith to study the principles here disclosed.

I. THE EXTENT AND LIMIT OF THE TRUE CHURCH OF GOD ARE CLEARLY DEFINED. (Vers. 1, 2.) At the time of this prophecy the literal temple was no more. The once-holy city was defiled by the "abomination of desolation." Then the true temple, the true holy city, existed in "the Church of the living God." The outer enclosure is not to be reckoned as a part of the temple in this divinely appointed remeasurement. All this most impressively sets forth the fact that Zion's external buildings cover a much wider space than the real heart-worshippers whom God will own. There may be, and there are, large masses of people at the outer fringe of our Christian services. But if

[1] Supplement to the *Cambridge Review*, October 22, 1884.
[2] "The gospel has elevated the history and places of the past into a grand allegory, and breathed into their dead names the life of an ever-applicable symbolism" (Bishop Carpenter, *in loc.*).

now a heavenly messenger were to come among us who was appointed to measure the real living temple of God, would it not turn out that, of a very large part of our surroundings, the order would be, " *Measure it not* " ? This measurement from on high is ever going on. And if the great Lord of the Church saw fit to show us in a vision who are in his Church and who are not, many would be without whom we thought were in, and many within whom we thought were out. But not by any human hands can the true temple of God be built; nor yet by any human eye can its limits be discerned.

II. The space without the temple and city of God is left for a while in hostile hands. "It hath been given unto the nations : and the holy city shall they tread under foot forty and two months." We know not what period of time is thus indicated; nor from what moment it begins. We know only three things concerning this matter : 1. That the worldly power will act in opposition to and preponderate over the Church. 2. That this will be for a limited time. 3. That this permissive limit is fixed by our God.[1] Thus far all is clear. The world in its facts answers to the Word in its statements. If we attempt to go beyond this, we shall be in confusion.

III. During the whole of this period our Lord will preserve his faithful witnesses. "My two witnesses." Why two ? "Is it not written in your Law that the testimony of two men is true ?" Although the number should be small, there should always be enough to preserve in the world a testimony for God. Further, the symbolism is based on the vision of Zechariah (iv.). Therein we have two olive trees conveying oil, and two lamp-stands holding light. Just as in the times following the Captivity there were anointed ones to stand by the Lord of the whole earth, so throughout the times of the Christian Church there will be men anointed by him to maintain on his behalf a faithful testimony ; whose witness-bearing would be at once " means of grace and centres of light " (Vaughan). We have several details here given respecting them. 1. *They are to prophesy in sackcloth.* So much of their witness has to be a protest against sin in the world and against corruption in the nominal Church, that their work often bears upon it an impress of sadness which cannot be removed till the corruption ceases. 2. *They are to have power with God and for him.* As Moses and Elijah had power to smite the earth or to shut up heaven, so with those who should come " in the spirit and power of Elias." They would make men feel that God is among them still. 3. *Their work is also to give out a testimony to man.* Even under the Old Testament, when a priestly order was in accordance with Divine appointment, God set it aside because of its corruption and inutility, and brought on the scene prophets to declare his will. Much more now, under the New Testament economy, where every human priesthood is but a pretence and a sham, will he carry on his work by the voice of the prophet, that men may learn through the ear that which they will fail to see by a histrionic parade. 4. *Around these witnesses there should be a special guard.* (Ver. 5.) No one can willingly wound or plot against any witness for God without suffering for it, either in his reputation or in his peace. Nor can any one seek to injure a Church that is true to its Lord, without bringing on himself, sooner or later, the judgments of God. God surrounds his witnesses as with a wall of fire. 5. *This guard will be around them till they have finished their testimony.* (Ver. 7.) "Man is immortal till his work is done." There are forces of ill, concealed, pent-up, restrained, which, if they were but let loose, would soon make havoc of the Church ; but an all-controlling Power keeps them in check, and as long as God has anything for a witness to say, that witness will be spared and empowered to say it. 6. *At some time or other there will be such an onrush of the great world-power as to seem, for a while, to silence this witness-bearing.* Just as our Lord was hedged round with an impenetrable guard until his hour was come, so shall it be with his witnesses. Just as there came a time when his voice was stilled in death and the enemy triumphed, so shall it be with them. There is yet to be permitted such an onrush of the powers of darkness as shall seem for a while to carry all before it, and the voices of the witnesses shall be stilled. 7. *The silencing of the witnesses will cause their foes to triumph.* (Vers. 8—10.) These pro-

---

[1] " The period of forty and two months is the symbol of a period limited in length, and under the control of him who holds the seven stars, and lives through the ages. It is the pilgrimage-period of the Church, the period of the world's power, during which it seems to triumph " (Bishop Carpenter, *in loc.*). Professor Milligan has a thoughtful paragraph on this point, which is worthy of attention, although we cannot regard it as satisfactory.

phets were the torment of the ungodly (ver. 10). Hence the world's hatred. In proportion to its hatred of the message and the messengers will be its gladness when the messengers can trouble it no more. Ill will run riot. The wickedness of a Sodom will be renewed. The Holy Ghost has forewarned us what to expect. Tares will ripen; evil men will grow worse and worse. Perilous times will come. "When the Son of man cometh, will he find the faith on the earth?" 8. *The triumph of the foe is but for a season.* (Vers. 11, 12.) Just as the Master put to shame all his foes by rising again on the third day, and afterwards ascending to heaven, so, after a like period, will that power, which the enemy thought was at an end, revive again. The world shall yet see that those whom it vilified are those whom God has glorified. 9. *The Divine glorification of his witnesses will be accompanied with a mighty visitation of judgment on the world.* (Ver. 13.) They who think to stop the mouths of God's witnesses will have to meet a Power before which they will melt away in terror, and the very earth on which they were committing these crimes will be made to reel beneath their feet. Providence will affright those who sneered at the voice of the prophet. "He that sitteth in the heavens shall laugh, and the Lord shall have them in derision" (Ps. ii.). "And the rest were affrighted, and gave glory to the God of heaven." In all these nine points of detail the chapter gives us not only that which is true now and then, but that which is continuously true in one part or other throughout the Christian age; and instead of the chapter seeming to be shrouded in unintelligible mystery, it is actually radiant with a light that makes all things clear. For note, in conclusion: (1) It behoves us to ask the question—Are we in the real Church of God as well as in the nominal one of Christendom? (2) Should we not be ambitious to join the band of holy witnesses for God? (3) If we are testifying for God, let us not expect all ease or comfort. Every part of our message runs counter to the prepossessions of the ungodly. If we do not meet, again and again, with direct opposition, we have reason to suspect that we do not with sufficient clearness and boldness testify against sin. (4) Let us take comfort from the thought that not one of God's witnesses can possibly be swept away until his testimony is finished. (5) Let none be deterred from loyalty to the Lord Jesus because of the repeated onsets which may be made upon them, nor on account of the scorn which will ever and anon be cast upon the witness-bearers. For furious as the wrath of the enemy may be, it is curbed.

Vers. 15—18.—*The seventh trumpet and the song which is to follow.* Although we have found manifold reasons why we cannot fix dates in interpreting the Apocalypse, we find equally manifest reasons for doing that which is of far more importance—even for indicating the principles which it discloses. The previous section taught us that the extent and limit of the Church of God are perfectly measured; that God will preserve for himself a succession of witnesses during the mysterious and protracted period of the Church's witness-bearing; that at some time or other there would be such an onrush of evil as if a beast were let loose from the deep abyss; that, for a while, the witnesses would be silenced; but that God would interpose, and cause providence to work where prophecy had failed, until the last obstruction to the final triumph of the Church should be taken out of the way. Then the seventh trumpet shall sound; under that seventh trumpet the end should come; and following on the end there shall be heard heaven's triumphant song. We therefore regard the words from the fifteenth to the eighteenth verses inclusive as overleaping the rest of the book; as, in fact, retrospective, giving us a hint of the sublime satisfaction which all holy souls will feel, in the review of God's dealings, when all those events are accomplished which the remaining chapters are about to specify. Here we propose to indicate these only in briefest outline, as the several details will be hereafter dealt with one by one.

I. HOWEVER GLOOMY AND PROTRACTED THE PERIOD MAY BE THROUGH WHICH GOD'S WITNESSES MAY HAVE TO PROPHESY, LIGHT WILL BREAK AT LAST. From ch. vi. 9, 10, and viii. 3, 4, we see that a great burden of prayer has been for long, long years spread out before God, the cry of which is, "Thy kingdom come. In the verses before us we catch a glimpse of the time when this prayer shall have been fulfilled, and when the fulf;ment will call forth a shout of praise (vers. 15—18). And in the words of this song, which is sent up in praise to God on account of the conflict being at an end, we get an indication of what had happened ere the strife ceased, *as they look upon the struggle from its further side;* cf. ver. 18, "The nations were angry"—the spirit of revolt against God rose to its height (Ps. ii.)—"and thy wrath came;" *i.e.* its manifestation. In the kingdoms of olden time, when the cup of iniquity was full, the judgments of God came and swept them away. So it will be again. We nowhere get any warrant from Scripture for supposing that God will govern in a future age on any different principles from those on which he has governed in the past, or on which he governs now. But those principles will be manifested more clearly than they have been. "And the time of the dead, that they should be judged." This is spoken of as belonging to a bygone time. So that the passage brings us, by anticipation, to the other side of the judgment of the dead, actually past the dread scene in ch. xx. 11—13. "And to give their reward to thy servants the prophets"—those who bore faithful testimony for God for the twelve hundred and sixty years, clad in sackcloth—"and to the saints"— to the holy ones who were in covenant relation to God by sacrifice—"and them that fear thy Name," "in every nation under heaven" (cf. Acts x. 35), "both small and great." All life's "poor distinctions" will vanish most utterly away in the light of the great white throne. "And to destroy them that destroy the earth." Those who destroy the earth by corrupting it with their sin, God will destroy by desolating with his judgments. This expression again overleaps the scenes of ch. xii.—xxii., and includes all those wild and weird forms of ill which are referred to in the remaining eleven chapters of this book. These are: (1) The dragon (ch. xii. 3, 9). (2) The first beast (ch. xiii. 1). (3) The second beast (ch. xiii. 11). (4) Three unclean spirits (ch. xvi. 13). (5) Babylon the Great (ch. xvii.). (6) The ungodly (ch. xx. 12—15). (7) Death and Hades (ch. xx. 14). (See the homilies under these several passages.) When the decisive judgment on all these is over, then does Jehovah take to himself his great power, and reign. And then the four and twenty elders, seated on their thrones, as if associated with their Lord in regal state, and sharers in his triumphs, rejoice over the grand issue, when every enemy is still as a stone.

II. THE PARAGRAPH BEFORE US INDICATES NOT ONLY WHAT THE ISSUE WILL BE, BUT ALSO THE MAIN EVENTS WHICH WILL PRECEDE IT. (Ver. 18.) (These will be found to be dealt with in the homilies on the passages indicated above. The order of those events will be found to be indicated in the homily on ch. xxii. 20.) These verses are, in fact, as stated above, an anticipatory summary of the whole.

III. WHEN THE RIGHTEOUS SEE THE ISSUE OF THE GREAT CONFLICT, THEY WILL BE FILLED WITH JOY, AND WILL GIVE VENT THERETO IN ADORING PRAISE. The results of the resurrection, of the judgment, and of the sentence, will perfectly satisfy all *righteous* souls (ver. 7). Let us note here that only righteous souls will be satisfied. No unrighteous man ever will be satisfied with what God does. Such will be speechless, because they know that God does only what is right, and the fact that a righteous administration condemns them can never bring them rest. So that it is not the fault of the administration if it brings torment to the ungodly, but of the ungodliness. But as for the righteous, even here they gave thanks at the remembrance of God's holiness; how much more will they do this when it

"... shall break thro' every cloud
That veils and darkens his designs"!

Then, with the clearer vision with which they will be endowed in their glorified natures, with the views of the manifold wisdom of God which the unfoldings of providence shall yield, with the glory of the Son of God unveiled before them without a cloud, when redemption's work is completed, when all the chosen are gathered, when the righteousness and love of God are perfectly vindicated, when all the ransomed ones are found as an unbroken unity at the feet of him who died for them,—then will the hallelujahs of the glorified rise up in holy song! All conflicts will be past, believers will be ushered into that rest which remaineth, and the "joy of their Lord" will be complete.

In conclusion: 1. Let us not be astonished at any violent outbreaks of evil which may perplex and bewilder many. The Holy Ghost hath said, "perilous times shall come." 2. Let us not judge of the progress of the work of God by the aspect of the world at any one moment. As reasonably might one think, when he watched the ebbing tide, that the sea was disappearing! 3. Let us not forget, that however dark the avenues through which the Church of God may have to pass, yet (1) this book has sketched them in all their darkness, and (2) has shown us also the brightness that lies beyond them. **4.** However fierce the conflicts of our age may be, never let us falter in the witness which we bear for God and the right. Ours is a good fight. " In your patience possess ye your souls." The light will break at last. **5.** Finally, if we would be kept in perfect peace, let our minds ever be stayed on him who " rides upon the storm." In his own time he will say, " Peace, be still," and the tossing billows shall subside to an eternal calm.

HOMILIES BY VARIOUS AUTHORS.

Vers. **1, 2.**—*The measuring of the temple.* Whether this chapter be the history of events that had already taken place when it was written or were then happening ; or whether it consists of predictions inspired of God of events then future, though near at hand in the history of Judaism and of the Church ; or of events yet future in the experience of the whole Church, as many affirm ; or whether, yet again, the whole chapter be an inspired allegory which, under the likeness of actual historical events, or of incidents recorded in the ancient Scriptures, were intended to convey to us spiritual teachings applicable to all times ;—who can positively and certainly say ? And like doubt hangs over the interpretation of the forty and two months told of here and elsewhere, whether they are to be taken literally, symbolically, or according to the reckoning of those who count each day to mean a year. We stay not, however, to discuss these questions, but prefer to take these verses which tell of the measuring of the temple as echoes of those earlier teachings of this book, and of many other Scriptures beside, which tell us of the Lord's perpetual presence in his Church, his strict investigation and his perfect knowledge of all who constitute her membership, and of all that occurs therein. " The Lord is in his holy temple ; his eyes behold, his eyelids try the children of men : " of such words does this command to " Arise, and measure the temple" remind us, and in the sense they suggest we desire to consider them now. Let us observe, therefore—

I. The measuring. We have a similar command in Ezek. xl., when in like inspired vision that prophet beholds the glorious restored temple of God. And so in ch. xxi. of this book we read of the angel who had the golden reed to measure the holy city. But as in those other representations we cannot think that material earthly buildings are meant, or any literal measurements whether of city or temple, so here we regard the temple as telling of that glorious spiritual fabric of which we so often read under like imagery in the Epistles of St. Paul ; and the measuring is a metaphor to signify that careful investigation and scrutiny whereby true knowledge is gained as to the nearness or otherwise of that which is measured to its proper standard and ideal. For it is to be noted : 1. *God has an ideal for everything,* a standard to which he would have it conform. He had in the creation of the world, and we are told how he saw all that which he had made, and declared that it answered to his ideal, and that it was "very good." And he looks down from heaven—so we are told—to see what is done upon the earth ; he taketh account of all that men do. All other creatures fulfil their ideal,—there is no need to take account of them ; but man, endowed with the terrible power of contradicting and refusing his Maker's will, as well as of assenting to it—and he could not have the one without the other—it is needful that the Lord should " behold " and " try " *his* actions by an unerring standard in order that he may be the more readily led to try them in like manner himself, and so conform them thereto the more nearly. 2. *Christ is the ideal Man,* and therefore called " the Son of man." He did in all things so answer to his Father's intent that he was the " beloved Son in whom " God was " well pleased." That is the standard to which we are to look, and by which we are to regulate our lives. Happy they who follow him closely " whithersoever he goeth." 3. *And this " measuring " is continually going on.* There is an inward monitor as well as an outward one. Conscience affirms, consents to, and confirms what the Word of God declares, and is perpetually holding up both the standard and ourselves, and making us inwardly if not outwardly blush when we see the contrast between the two. 4. *How grateful we should be for this !* " Lord with what care thou hast begirt us round !"—so sings holy George Herbert ; and one evidence of this care is in the constant bringing before our consciences the rigid rule of right. But note next—

II. The measured that are spoken of here. The temple, the altar, and the people. 1. *The temple of God.* No doubt St. John, as a devout Jew, and one who had often frequented with joy the courts of the Lord's house at Jerusalem, had that temple—for it was still standing, though soon to fall—before his mind. And it was to him a symbol and type of all Israel, if not of the whole Church of God (cf. St. Paul, "In whom the whole building fitly framed together groweth into a holy temple unto the Lord"). He is telling of the Church of God throughout the whole world and in all ages of time. Therefore we may take "the temple of God" as representing the Church in its outward form. Now, God has his ideal for this. What is it? The Catholic declares the true Church to be the great body of the baptized, organized into one organic whole. The individualist asserts that there is no such body that man can know of, but that the Church consists of "living stones," that is, of individual souls who have been quickened into the life of God by personal faith in Christ. And there are multitudes of subdivisions under each of these two ruling beliefs. But all such outward forms will be measured, tested, tried. And what will the standard be to which conformity will be demanded? Christ's herald said, "Now also the axe is laid at the root of the trees : every tree therefore which bringeth not forth *good fruit* is hewn down, and cast into the fire" (Matt. iii. 10). By this supreme test will all our Church organizations be tried. What fruit have they borne in that which is the end of all religion— the making of bad men good, and good men better? Have souls in such Churches been quickened, converted, cheered, built up, and helped heavenward? If so, well. If not, then not well. No antiquity, orthodoxy, catholicity, popularity, beauty, wealth, or any other such plea will stand if God's standard be not answered to, and his demand for "good fruit" be not met. The axe will fall, and the tree will go down. 2. *The altar.* This also was to be measured. We may take "the altar" as the symbol of the worship of the Church. Around it Israel gathered ; on it the fire was perpetually burning ; from it was taken the fire which enkindled the incense that went up in the immediate presence of God. It was the centre of Israel's worship : there was but one altar for them all. It therefore does set forth the worship of the Church according to the Divine ideal, and the altar was to be measured, that that worship might be compared with that ideal. Is our worship *fervent?* On that altar was an ever-burning fire. Upon the heads of the disciples at Pentecost descended fire, telling that Christ's people were to be known by their ardour. And the altar fire tells that worship is to be *fervent.* Is it *spiritual?* Does it ascend up to God as the smoke of the sacrifice mounted up and up into the heavens,—symbol, beautiful, striking, appropriate, of that uplifting of the heart, that real outgoing of the soul after God, which belongs to all true worship? And, above all, is it *sacrificial?* The altar was for *sacrifice.* Worship that has not this element in it will be rejected when that measurement of the altar told of here takes place. And let no one think that having correct views as to the atonement of Christ, and making mental reference thereto, or verbal, by adding on, as we should, to all our prayers, "through Jesus Christ our Lord"—let no one think that that fulfils the ideal of altar worship. No ; our worship may ring with the mention of that ever-blessed Name, and our views may be of the most unexceptional sort, and there be not one atom of "sacrifice" in our worship. And often and often, as in the Lord's prayer, that Name may not be heard at all, and ideas about the atonement may be very crude, and yet the worship be full of sacrifice, and will bear well the measuring which is to be applied to all our worship. Sacrifice means giving up something which we should like to keep. Was not Christ's sacrifice such? Is not all sacrifice such? If, then, worship do not carry with it the giving up of anything, save the little time that it occupies to get through with it ; if sin be not given up, nor self, nor that which we have and could spare, and our brother needs ;—if there be naught of this, where is the sacrifice? how will our worship bear God's test? 3. *The people.* "Them that worship therein"—so we read. Now, the Divine ideal for these may be learnt by noting what was *not* to be measured. And we are told in ver. 2 that "the court which is without the temple . . . measure it not." It was to be cast out, left out of the reckoning altogether. Now, the outer court of the temple was the addition of Herod ; he was given to erecting magnificent buildings, and the addition of this outer court did undoubtedly add much to the splendour of the whole fabric. But such court had no place in the tabernacle nor in the temple of Solomon or that of Zerubbabel. But Herod had made this outer court in the temple at Jerusalem. It was thronged by all manner of people. There it was the money-changers had their tables, and they who bought and sold doves. The Gentiles might come there, though they might not pass into what was especially the temple, and which was sacred to Israelites only. And so it represented all those outer-court worshippers, those mixed multitudes which are found associated with God's true people everywhere—of them, but not truly belonging to them. The courts of the temple were separated literally. No Gentile durst pass the boundaries which parted the outer court from the rest of the temple on pain of death. But there is no such visible, material, separation in the throng of worshippers in the professing Church of God. We cannot draw the line nor apply the measure. But all the same there is such a line drawn, and it is clearly visible to the eye of God. He can discriminate, though we cannot, between those who profess and those who possess true religion, and one day he will make this difference plain. Tares get in amongst the wheat, bad fish amid the good, the foolish virgins were associated with the wise; and the worshippers in the true temple of God to-day are mingled with those whose place is in the outer court. But as in the parables referred to separation did come at last, so will it be for the Church of to-day, when the Son of man sends forth his angels, and they "gather out of his kingdom all that do offend, and they that work iniquity." The question, therefore, for us all is—Where do *we* belong! In that outer court were many who were well disposed towards Israel's God, and professed more or less of attachment to his worship; but they were not true Israelites. And the like is true still. "Let a man examine himself, and so let him" take his place in the Church of God.

III. THE MEANING OF ALL THIS. It was because a time of sore trial was imminent, close at hand. For "forty and two months" the court and the city were to be trodden underfoot by the nations. The invasion and overthrow of Jerusalem by the Romans, and the escape of the Christian Church to Pella, supply illustrative historical incidents of the treading underfoot told of here, and of the measuring, like the sealing of ch. vii., for the purpose of separating and preserving God's faithful ones. God ever has, even in the worst of times, a remnant of such; like the "seven thousand" who had not bowed the knee to Baal. And he takes notice of them, and will keep them securely, whilst those who are not as they are subjected to his sore judgments. The measuring means preservation for the faithful, judgment for all else. "As the mountains are round about Jerusalem, so the Lord is round about his people." The measuring is ever going on. Let us each ask—On which side of that unerring line am I?—S. C.

Vers. 3—13.—*The two witnesses.* In the absolute impossibility of certainly ascertaining what definite historical events were in the mind of St. John when he penned these mysterious chapters of his Apocalypse, we are driven, as perhaps it was designed we should be driven, to take them as an inspired parable or allegory, and so gather from them lessons for our own times. We have done so in regard to the "little book" told of in ch. x.; and in regard to the measuring of temple, altar, and worshippers, told of in the first ten verses of this chapter; and we purpose dealing with this record of the two witnesses in a similar way; for we know of no other in which our consideration of them can be of any service to us. This entire episode, stretching from ch. x. 1 to ch. xi. 13, has to do with these witnesses; ch. x. showing their preparation by means of the book; ch. xi. 1, 2 showing the people before whom they would witness; and now the vers. 3—13 tell more especially of the witnesses themselves and their witness for God, and then that of God for them. It might seem as if in ver. 4 we had an authoritative explanation of these two witnesses, as it points us back to the prophecy of Zech. iv. 1—3, and tells us that what he saw was now fulfilled. But Zechariah's symbol merely tells of the characteristics of these witnesses; that they were to be as the olive trees were—supporters and sustainers of the life to which they ministered. The olive trees so ministered to the lamps, and these witnesses so ministered to the people of God. They were also to be as lamps, letting their light shine in such wise as should glorify God. St. John's word, "These *are*," etc., therefore means no more than that these are represented by, and correspond to, the two olive trees, etc. But we may, we believe, find the antitypes of those ancient symbols and types of St. John's allegory in our Lord Jesus Christ and his Church. They are the two witnesses, and are one to the other as the trees and the lamp; but before the world, both witness. Look at the life of our Lord and the history of his Church; all that is told of here may be read therein. Christ himself is called in this book, "The faithful and true Witness;" and he himself said of his Church in her ministry, "This gospel shall be preached for a witness in all nations;"

and it is written of old, "Ye are my witnesses, saith the Lord." Hence in Christ and his Church we may find these witnesses, and in what is here recorded of them we may see the mutual fellowship that exists between them. See this—

I. IN MINISTRY. For both that of Christ and his Church was a ministry: 1. *Of prophecy.* Not in the sense of predicting the future, but in uttering forth the will of God—preaching and proclaiming God's message to mankind. In both there were works of Divine power, signs and wonders; but these were of but subordinate importance as compared to their ministry of the Word. Our Lord was the great Teacher, and he bade his disciples "preach the gospel." 2. *Of brief duration.* Who knows what precisely is meant by these mysterious twelve hundred and sixty days? It is the same period of three years and a half whether told of as days here or as months in ver. 2. It is the half of seven, the number denoting completeness and perfection. There may be allusion to the time of our Lord's ministry on earth, or to that of the investment of Jerusalem by the Romans, or, taking the year-day theory, to some twelve hundred and sixty years during which this ministry is to be carried on. We prefer to take the numbers as telling of a time limited and brief. Such was our Lord's ministry; such the duration of the Church in Jerusalem ere it fled away to Pella; such, in comparison with the eternal ages in which the blessed results of their ministry shall be realized, is the ministry of the Church of to-day and all past and future days. 3. Characterized by *much of sternness and sorrow.* "Clothed in sackcloth"—so is it described. Was it not so with our Lord? He was "the Man of sorrows." And has it not been so with his Church oftentimes, just in proportion as they have been faithful to their Lord? See the life of Paul, of Peter, of the martyr Church in many generations, under both pagan and papal Rome. How can it be otherwise when we think of the ends that are to be secured—so momentous—and of the tremendous hindrances in the way of securing these? Such ministry is no holiday pastime, no decorous profession merely, but one that for our Lord and his apostles, for his martyrs and for all his faithful, seems oftentimes to be "clothed in sackcloth." 4. *But it is of resistless force.* Like as was the ministry of Elijah and Moses. Elijah literally called down fire from heaven, and Moses did that which is here said of these witnesses. And in a real, though not literal sense, vers. 5 and 6 are true. Was not our Lord's word as a fire to his enemies? How it scathed and tormented them! And were not his words fulfilled when Jerusalem was overthrown? And so of the other witness, the Church. What has become of her persecutors—Rome, Spain, and many more? Has it been well with those who have hurt the Church of God? "He that toucheth you toucheth the apple of mine eye"—so hath God said, and historic fact vindicates that word. And so of the withholding of the rain. Elijah did this literally; but was not the righteous and universal judgment on the hardened ones whereby, as our Lord said, "seeing they may see and not perceive, and hearing they may hear and not understand"—was not this a yet more real and terrible withholding of the rain and shutting of heaven against them? Christ was "set for the fall" as well as "the rise" of many in Israel; they would have it so. And the words of the other witness have had like effects. "Whose sins ye retain, they are retained," said the Lord to his Church. "What thou shalt bind on earth shall be bound in heaven," he also said. And was not this word fulfilled when such as Paul turned from the Jews who had rejected him and went unto the heathen? What would become of a nation, a community, if the good all went away? What became of Sodom when Lot left it; of Jerusalem, when the Church of Christ left it? Parodies of this power of the Church were seen in the interdicts which proud popes and prelates would at times lay on the lands that believed in them. The threat of such interdict seemed like shutting heaven against them, and they dreaded it with a great dread. And the plagues Moses inflicted on Egypt have their counterpart in the sorrows that have come on men in all ages who have sought to hurt the Lord's anointed ones, and to do his witnesses harm. Yes; this ministry of the witnesses has had resistless force accompanying it, before which its foes have fallen again and again. Let none of us be found fighting against God.

II. IN SUFFERING. We seem in vers. 7—13 to have a piece of the gospel history, of the life of our Lord, given to us. For he was met with the hostile rage of hell. The "beast that ascendeth out of the bottomless pit" did make war against him. And for a time hell seemed to have vanquished the Christ. For he was betrayed condemned, and crucified. And with contempt like to that of refusing burial was our Lord treated. "He was despised and rejected of men." It was their "hour, and the power of darkness." And the Church, his co-witness, has had fellowship in his sufferings, and been once and again "made conformable unto his death." The same foe, the same rage, the same suffering, the same seeming vanquishment, the same scorn,—these have been her lot as well as her Lord's. And over both have been the like short-lived exultation. Herod and Pontius Pilate became friends over the condemned Christ. His enemies breathed more freely when they knew he was dead. How they mocked him as he hung on the cross! Their joy, as well as their hatred and scorn, are clearly audible in those hideous insults which they heaped upon him. And again and again have the persecutors of the Church exulted in imagined success. Pagan and papal, still worse than pagan Rome, have alike flattered themselves, once and again, that heresy—as they deemed it—was completely put down. They have been "drunk with the blood of saints," and in their wild orgies have rejoiced and made merry as the manner of such is to do. Let us, whose lot has fallen in these quiet days, learn lessons of thankfulness that no such suffering as the Church has had to endure falls to our share, and that, when such suffering had to be borne, grace sufficient for the day was given. What an implied promise of ever-present help there is in that! And let us be ashamed to shrink from any suffering allotted to us, seeing how incomparably less it is, which, in witnessing for God, we may be called upon to bear. And let us remember, and be comforted by the remembrance, whence and when such sufferings come. *Whence?* From hell, and such as were the men of Sodom and Egypt, and the murderers of the Lord. If friendship with such would save us from suffering, would we be their friends? God forbid! And *when?* It was when the evil they could do could do no harm (see ver. 7). The witnesses had *finished* their testimony. What a shutting of the door after the horse has been stolen! God's witnesses had done their work; it did not matter now what their foes might do against or with them. God's servants are immortal, yea more, are left unhindered, until their work is done.

III. IN TRIUMPH. (Ver. 11.) Our Lord's resurrection, the fear which fell on his foes, his ascension, Pentecost and its marvels, are all referred to here as patterns of the triumph of the witnesses. In these great events are found the archetype and model, and not merely the mere illustration, of what St. John tells of. It is easy to see what answers in the history of our Lord to what is here said. He was glorified, declared to be the Son of God with power, by means of them. And in his triumph his people share, so that, in a very real sense, what is said of him can be, and is, said of them. Church revivals, of which there have been many, are instances of fellowship in Christ's triumph. Often have hell and Satan, and all that are theirs, thought that Christianity and the Church were crushed. Voltaire vowed that it should be his *écraser l'infame*, and he thought that by his writings it should surely be done, and in the awful days of the revolutionary terror it seemed as if his vaunt were not vain, but valid. But revival came. In the blessed Reformation times, what a resurrection unto life for the faith and the Church there was! In the Diocletian persecutions it seemed as if all were lost, but in brief while, Constantine avowed himself a Christian, and the faith which was once persecuted was now praised and preferred everywhere. And to-day in many quarters, it is feared that faith is dead. Perhaps some fear it for themselves. But behold this parable of the witnesses. Over the grave of all such "Resurgam" may, should be, written. "Failure" is a word unknown in the vocabulary of God, but ultimate and complete triumph is absolutely sure.

CONCLUSION. Witnesses for Christ, does not this bid us be of good cheer? Enemies of Christ, does not the word of his witnesses "torment" you? Does it not rankle within you, driving away your peace, refusing to let you alone in your sins, however much you might wish it would? It scorches and burns inwardly, as if the fire unquenchable were already kindled. Blessed be God that the witness of the Word doth torment, pricking you to the heart, and causing perpetual pain. Yield to it, as did Saul the persecutor, who, by yielding, became Paul the apostle. "The Word is quick and powerful;" it goes straight to the conscience, making many a Felix "tremble" and many an Agrippa resolve "almost to be a Christian." But remember, it may do all this and not save your soul. Oh for that one little step which yet remains to be taken! that actual "arising and going to your Father"! that real coming to Christ that you may have life! If the Word torments, it is only that it may arouse you to listen; it is only that you may take it to you as your guide, your light, and your comforter. Trifle not with that Word which must one day judge you. May Christ give it entrance while it is still light and not fire—"a light to cheer and to enlighten, not a fire to burn and to consume"! (Vaughan).—S. C.

Ver. 19.—*The rent veil.* In the foregoing part of this chapter, which tells of the two witnesses, we have seen how the path along which they were led resembled that of the Lord Jesus Christ himself. They had fellowship with him in ministry, in suffering, and in triumph. It is ever so with the servants of Christ. And now in this verse our thoughts are sent back to those miracles which were attendant upon his death. In Matt. xxvii. 50, 51, etc., we are told of the veil that was rent from the top to the bottom, and of the earthquake, and of the opened graves. And so in this chapter, which tells of the winding up of the Jewish dispensation, we see the innermost recesses of the temple thrown open, and all that it contained laid bare to men's sight and approach, as it had never been before. So was it when on the cross Christ said, "It is finished!" so is it now in this vision in which the end of all that old order of things is portrayed. But what meant that rent veil there, and this opened temple and ark of the covenant disclosed to all eyes? They have a meaning. "To the few eyes that witnessed that rending of the temple veil it must have been a most mysterious spectacle. Our Lord died at the third hour after midday, the very hour when eager crowds of worshippers would be thronging into the courts of the temple, and all would be preparing for the evening sacrifice. Within the holy place, kindling, perhaps, the many lights of the golden candlestick, some priests would be busy before the inner veil which hung between them and the holy of holies—the dark secluded chamber within which once lay the ark of the covenant, with the cherubim above it shadowing the mercy-seat, which no mortal footstep was permitted to invade, save that of the high priest once only every year. How strange, how awful, to the ministering priests, standing before that veil, to feel the earth tremble beneath their feet, and to see the strong veil grasped, as if by two unseen hands of superhuman strength, and torn down in its centre from top to bottom ; the glaring light of day, that never for long centuries gone by had entered there, flung into that sacred tenement, and all its mysteries laid open to vulgar gaze!" Now, that which this disclosure of the most holy place meant when our Lord was crucified, is meant also by what St. John tells us here in his vision. But more than this is meant. For when the veil of the temple was rent no ark of the covenant was seen. That had long ago disappeared, having been either burnt or carried off when Jerusalem and the temple were overthrown by Nebuchadnezzar. Hence neither in the second temple, nor in that of Herod, in the days of our Lord, was there any ark of the covenant. It seems never to have been replaced (cf. Esdras, Josephus, Tacitus). But here, in St. John's vision, the ark of the covenant is seen again. Fuller meaning, therefore, is to be found in the vision than in the rent veil. Much is common to both; something, however, belongs peculiarly to each. Let us, therefore, note—

I. WHAT IS SPECIAL TO EACH. And : 1. *As to the veil rent in twain.* "It is not fanciful," says one, "to regard it as *a solemn act of mourning* on the part of the house of the Lord. In the East men express their sorrow by rending their garments, and the temple, when it beheld its Master die, seemed struck with horror, and rent its veil. Shocked at the sin of man, indignant at the murder of its Lord, in its sympathy with him who is the true Temple of God, the outward symbol tore its holy vestment from the top to the bottom" (Spurgeon). But, with far more certainty, we may see in it the symbol of *our Lord's sacred humanity.* The Epistle to the Hebrews expressly tells us this in x. 19, 20, where we read, "Having therefore, brethren, boldness to enter into the holiest by the blood of Jesus, by a new and living way, which he hath consecrated for us, through the veil, that is to say, his flesh." "The weak, human, mortal flesh was the state through which he had to pass before he could enter into the holiest in the heavens for us, and when he put off that flesh the actual veil in the temple was rent in twain." That perfect human life, this life in our suffering humanity, opened to our sight and to our feet the way to God. Recall the ancient type. Ere ever the high priest could enter into the holiest of all, he must push aside or lift up the separating veil which hung before it. Now, that veil symbolized Christ's flesh, that is, his life in the flesh—his earthly, human life. And, ere he could enter into the holiest for us, he must live that life, must pass through it as through the veil. And this is what he did. And now, relying on that blood of Jesus which atones for us with God, because it evermore makes our flesh, that is, makes our life, pure, trustful, consecrated, as was his life—so, by this "new and living way" we must draw near, keep drawing near, to our Father and our God. His way into the holiest is our way, only the way for him was far more severe than ours. For he had to be perfectly holy, "as a lamb without blemish and without spot," and to suffer as none other ever did or could. But our marred and imperfect holiness is accepted for the sake of his, which was all perfect, and so, even through the coarse and tattered veil of our flesh, we shall enter, by his grace, into the presence of God. 2. *The vision of the ark of the covenant.* We may take this as telling (1) of the unchangeableness of God. When St. John wrote, the very foundations of the earth seemed to be shaken and in course of being moved. That Judaism of which the temple was the centre was dying, dying hard. Jerusalem and her people were in the last throes of their national existence, and the old order was changing every hour and, amid sore travail, giving place to new. To many eyes it seemed as if all was lost, and the end of all things was at hand. Now, what a reassuring vision this would be! The ark of the covenant that enshrined God's holy Law; the ark that was covered with the mercy-seat, that told of the eternal grace of God; that ark of the covenant, now seen in beatific vision, said to the beholder, "The Lord liveth, the Lord holy and full of compassion, just, yet delighting in mercy, *he* liveth." Moreover it told (2) of the certainty of victory over all foes. It was the ark of God's strength, God's resting-place, where he dwelt between the cherubim. Under its shadow Israel had dwelt, as under the shadow of the Almighty. At its presence the rushing river rolled back its flowing flood, and piled up its awestruck waters, and held them bound until all the people of God had passed by. At its presence the walls of Jericho had fallen flat, and under its leadership Israel had gone on from victory unto victory. It had made them invincible a thousand times. And now the persecuted people of God beheld this ark of the covenant once again. "When the enemy came in like a flood, the Spirit of the Lord lifted up the standard against him." It was an omen of victory, a prophecy of good, a lifter-up of all hearts that were cast down. It meant all that.

II. WHAT IS COMMON TO BOTH—to the veil of the temple rent and this vision of the ark of the covenant. One chief meaning belongs to both—that meaning which our Lord declared when on the cross at the moment of his death he cried, "*It is finished!*" The veil and the shrine wherein the ark was seen represent the whole of the Mosaic ceremonial, the system of types, the Levitical Law, the whole body of Jewish ordinances. And the rent veil, and the vision of the ark alike show that all that is done with and for ever. Freedom of access is given to all, and we are bidden therefore to come boldly to the throne of grace. "The veil is not rolled up, but rent, so that it cannot be put up again;" and in this vision there is no sign of it at all. Now, this means that all that separates the soul of the believer from God is clean gone for ever. 1. *All legal ordinances.* And yet how slow men are to believe this—to believe that the worshippers whom God seeks are those who worship him in spirit and in truth! It is not papists alone, but so-called Protestants also, all too many of them, who have not yet realized what the rent veil, and the ark of the covenant visible to all, mean. Hence the often hurried sending for ministers of religion to pray by the sick and dying. Hence, too, those many evidences which we meet with that men's minds are not yet emancipated from reliance on certain persons, ordinances, and the like; and that they yet know not that none can make them more acceptable to God, or as acceptable, as when they themselves come through the blood of Christ. 2. *All guilt.* This separates indeed, and would for ever do so, had not the veil been rent and the way opened. 3. *All depravity.* The evil bias of our nature—that in us which makes us do the things we would not, and forbids our doing those we would. And: 4. *The flesh itself;* for this veil, too, will one day be rent, and then our soul, escaped as a bird out of the hand of the fowler, shall go into the presence of God for ever. *Conclusion.* Then if all that separates, every veil, be done away, let me draw near, as I am bidden to do—in prayer, in praise, in communion; asking or giving thanks for blessings on my soul, in pardon, peace, purity, consolation, strength; blessings on others, those whom I love, those who love me, and for all for whom I am bound to pray. We may, we should, we must.—S. C.

REVELATION.

X

Vers. 3—13.—*The continuous witness.* The Lord calls forth his faithful witnesses, and makes promise that their voice and testimony shall not be silenced, even though the holy city be trodden underfoot. Mark—

I. THE UNFAILING TESTIMONY. Throughout the entire period during which the usurping worldly power shall oppress and tread down the adherents to the truth, the voice of testimony is heard. It cannot be silenced. Forty and two months is the holy city trodden underfoot; a thousand two hundred and three score days do the witnesses prophesy. Not any particular two; but the confirmatory two. The number may be minished; but the voice is clear. One herald is sufficient to make a proclamation.

II. THE PAINFULNESS OF WITNESSING AGAINST EVIL AND THREATENING JUDGMENT IS BUT TOO OBVIOUS. The witnesses prophesy, "clothed in sackcloth." So must all who stand in opposition to evil find the painful bitterness of their sad duty.

III. THE DIVINE DEFENCE OF THE WITNESSES. " If any man desireth to hurt them, fire proceedeth out of their mouth." The Lord defends his witnesses; his anointed must not be touched. The word of their mouth is itself a penetrating sword of flame; nor can the adversaries of the truth escape those external judgments which fire always represents, and which the God of truth uses for the punishment of evil-doers. This is further seen in—

IV. THEIR PUNITIVE POWER. But it is of a nature correspondent to the entire character of the gospel. "They shut up heaven." Sad indeed is it for them who stay the holy work of the heavenly witnesses. For if their work be hindered, it is as the shutting up of the heavens—no spiritual rain, no teaching. The world is the sufferer. The loss is unspeakable. By the removal of the earth-preserving salt—the Word—a plague is brought upon the earth. Alas! though the testimony is continuous through all the time of the worldly oppression, yet the witnesses are finally slain! Here the vision may be for the comfort of the witnesss to the truth themselves. And we reflect—

V. Upon THEIR TEMPORARY DESTRUCTION AND FINAL TRIUMPH. They are slain, and so far the world triumphs. So it did with the one faithful and true Witness. Or we may see here a temporary triumph of the evil worldly spirit, and the final supremacy of the truth. Probably the former. But in either case the faithful witnesses to the truth are assured in this, as in many other ways, of the final reward to their fidelity and the final triumph over them who make them their foes.—R. G.

Vers. 15—19.—*The final victory.* Again, as frequently in the course of the writing, the assurance of the final triumph of the truth over all opposers is clearly, definitely, and unequivocally given—given to the comfort and joy of the toiling, patient, enduring followers of the Lamb. Great voices in heaven are heard, and they proclaim one all-sufficient and grand truth: " The kingdom of the world is become the kingdom of our Lord, and of his Christ." This word runs through the ages. It is the word of prophecy. It has ever and ever will comfort the hearts and stimulate the faith of the Christian warrior. It is the song of assurance with which the hosts of the contending forces of " him that sitteth on the white horse " are cheered and urged to unflagging zeal. Always before the eye of faith this assurance of victory floats. It is the summing up of all the prophetic words in one. It needs no exposition. The figure is too plain. It borders on the realistic.

> " Jesus shall reign where'er the sun
> Doth his successive journeys run,
> His kingdom stretch from shore to shore,
> Till suns shall rise and set no more."

Universal, complete, and final, shall that conquest of the nations be. It is a complete rout. The long-continued struggle is at an end. The truth has triumphed over error; righteousness over sin. The King long " set " upon the " holy hill of Zion " is now acknowledged as the lawful Heir, the rightful Sovereign. The holy oracles themselves define this complete reign over the individual, national, and universal life.

I. THE SUPREMACY OF THE DIVINE RULE SHALL BE UNIVERSALLY ESTABLISHED AND ACKNOWLEDGED. " The kingdom of this world is become the kingdom of our Lord, and of his Christ."

II. THE DIFFUSION OF DIVINE TRUTH SHALL BE UNIVERSAL. " The knowledge of the Lord shall cover the earth as the waters cover the sea."

III. THE PRINCIPLES OF THAT GOVERNMENT SHALL PERMEATE NATIONAL LIFE, LITERATURE, AND INSTITUTIONS. "The little leaven shall leaven the whole lump."

IV. UNDER THIS GRACIOUS RULE NATIONAL ANIMOSITIES SHALL BE AMELIORATED. "The swords shall be beaten," etc.

V. CONFLICTING AND ANTAGONISTIC FORCES SHALL BE HARMONIZED. "The wolf shall dwell with the lamb, the leopard lie down with the kid," etc.

VI. HUMAN LIFE SHALL BE BEAUTIFIED, ADORNED, AND BRIGHTENED. "The wilderness and the solitary place shall be glad, and the desert blossom as the rose."

VII. TO THE MILD AND BENEF.CENT SWAY OF THE REDEEMER SHALL BE HANDED OVER THE OUTLYING AND OUTCAST NATIONS OF THE EARTH. "He shall have the heathen for his inheritance, and the uttermost parts of the earth for his possession."

VIII. THIS REIGN SHALL BE CHARACTERIZED BY THE MOST BLESSED CONDITIONS. "In his day shall righteousness prevail, and abundance of peace, so long." etc.—R. G.

Vers. 1—19.—*The cause of right on earth.* "And there was given me a reed like unto a rod: and the angel stood, saying, Rise, and measure the temple of God, and the altar, and them that worship therein. But the court which is without the temple leave out, and measure it not; for it is given unto the Gentiles: and the holy city shall they tread underfoot forty and two months," etc. What does this chapter mean? Has it any intelligible meaning? Is it to be taken literally or ideally? One of our most modern, able, and distinguished biblical critics—Archdeacon Farrar—has said concerning it, "There neither is, nor ever has been, in Christendom, in any age, or among any school of interpreters, the smallest agreement, or even approach to an agreement, as to the events which the seer had in view. . . . There are no two writers of any importance who even approximately agree in their interpretation." Shrinking, as I do, from contributing anything to the unsightly pile of interpretations which have been given to this chapter, I shall merely use it as the heavenly Teacher used the lilies of the field and the birds of the air—to *illustrate truth.* The subject which it serves in some extent to set forth is *the cause of right on earth.* It illustrates the fact—

I. THAT THE CAUSE OF RIGHT ON THIS EARTH HAS ITS MEASURING RULE. "And there was given me a reed like unto a rod: and the angel stood, saying [one said], Rise, and measure the temple of God, and the altar, and them that worship therein." Two things are suggested. 1. *That in the human world there is right and wrong.* There is the temple of God, the altar, and "them that worship therein." At the same time, there is the court that is outside—the "court which is without the temple "—a sphere discarded by the right and trampling on the holy. This, however, is only for a time. 2. *That right here has its measuring-line.* Take the "temple" here as the emblem of right on the earth, and the "reed" as that of the moral Law of God—the Law that measures moral character. Such a Law we have here, here in the conscience, here in the Decalogue, here in the life of Christ. This measuring-line concerns qualities rather than quantities; it analyzes all the elements of character and decides their qualities. It is a plummet that sounds the deepest depths of being; it is a moral analyst to test the quality of every thought, affection, and deed; a moral gauge to measure the height, breadth, depth, of all. *Supreme sympathy with the supremely good is the Law.* "Thou shalt love the Lord thy God," etc. "Though I bestow all my goods to feed the poor, and though I give my body to be burned, and have not charity [love], it profiteth me nothing." This is the "reed" to measure the moral temple of the soul and all its worshippers. Right here requires testing; so much passes for right that is wrong that a measuring-line is necessary for testing.

II. THAT THE CAUSE OF RIGHT ON THIS EARTH HAS ITS MIGHTY DEFENDERS. "I will give power unto my two witnesses, and they shall prophesy." Who are the two witnesses? Moses and Elijah? Caleb and Joshua? John the Baptist and Christ? Enoch and Elijah? Peter and John? No one knows, although hundreds pretend to say. Did I believe that the chapter had a literal or historic meaning, I would accept the theory that they were the collective representatives of the Jewish and Gentile converts in preference to any other. I take them here to illustrate the *mighty defenders of the cause of right in this world.* The cause of right has ever required defenders, for in every age it has countless hosts of antagonists. It has had its Elijahs, and its Johns, and its Pauls, its Luthers, its Cromwells, its Garibaldis, etc., men who have stood up, spoken in thunder, and shed their blood for the right. The vision here suggests three things concerning these defenders of the right. 1. *They do their work in sadness.* "Clothed in sackcloth." To fight for the right has never been an easy work, and perhaps never will be. They fight not in radiant robes, but in sackcloth. It is not a light work to stand up against a corrupt world and struggle against an age grinning with selfishness, sensuality, and cupidity. 2. *They contribute Divine light.* "These are the two olive trees, and the two candlesticks." Language borrowed from the Book of Ezekiel. The olive trees fed the lamp, and the candlesticks diffused the light. Were it not for the Divine defenders of the right, grand heroes in moral history, all the lamps of truth would go out, and the whole race would be mantled in midnight. They are the lights of the world. 3. *They exert tremendous power.* "If any man will [desire to] hurt them, fire proceedeth out of their mouth, and devoureth their enemies: and if any man will hurt [shall desire to hurt] them, he must in this manner be killed," etc. (see vers. 5, 6). The true defenders of the right are invested with a terrible power. Their words flash devouring flames, so shake the corrupt moral firmament under which their contemporaries are living, that the very heavens seem shut up and the rolling streams of life seem turned into blood. It is said that Moses turned the Nile into blood, that Elijah prevented rain descending on the earth for the space of three years. The true defenders of the cause of right are the *organs* of Omnipotence; their words are mighty through God. To them is committed the work of causing the moral heavens to melt with fervent heat, and spreading out " a new heaven and a new earth wherein dwelleth righteousness."

III. THAT THE CAUSE OF RIGHT ON THE EARTH HAS ITS TERRIBLE ANTAGONISTS. "When they shall have finished their testimony, the beast that ascendeth out of the bottomless pit shall make war against them, and shall overcome them, and kill them," etc. (vers. 7—10). 1. *The antagonists of the right are malignant.* They not only murder, but they exult in their cruelty. They are "wild beasts" that fight and kill; they arise from the abyss of depravity. The spirit of persecution is an infernal virus that gallops through the veins of the intolerant persecutor, and physical violence is the weapon. Not only did their malignity destroy, but revelled in the cruelty and destruction: " shall rejoice over them, and make merry." Their feet are "swift to shed blood;" like savage beasts of prey, they revel in the tortures of their victims. Who can study martyrology without being astounded at the ruthless cruelty that runs in the blood of those that hate the right? They rent the heavens with the cry, "Away with him! away with him!" 2. *These antagonists of the right are ever frustrated.* It is said, "After three days and a half the Spirit of life from God entered into them, and they stood upon their feet," etc. (ver. 11). Observe: (1) Their victims were divinely reanimated. If the bodies of the two which lay crushed upon the "street" were not reanimated, their spirit, which was Divine, appeared in others. The bodies of good men fall to the dust, but the spirit that animated them lives in others. The spirit of Elijah enters John the Baptist in the wilderness. The spirit of truth and goodness is a *resurrection*-spirit; it enters those who are in the graves of sin, and they start to life and stand forth a mighty army to defend the right. Such a resurrection may well alarm the persecutors. "A great fear fell upon them which saw them." (2) Their victims ascended to heaven. "And they ascended up to heaven in a cloud" (ver. 12). Heaven is ever open to welcome and receive the faithful defenders of the right. With their ascension terrible calamities befall the earth. "And the same [that] hour was there a great earthquake" (ver. 13). The eternal hour of retribution towards their persecutors moves on; the earth quakes, and thousands are engulfed in ruin. "Be sure your sin will find you out."

IV. THAT THE CAUSE OF RIGHT ON THE EARTH IS DESTINED TO TRIUMPH. After the passing of the first two woes there is yet another to come, and after the close of the sixth trumpet the blast of the seventh is heard. "And the seventh angel sounded; and there were [followed] great voices in heaven, saying, The kingdoms [kingdom] of this [the] world are [is] become the kingdoms [kingdom] of our Lord, and of his Christ; and he shall reign for ever and ever" (ver. 15). Two things seem now to occur. 1. *The rapture and adoration of the good.* Sainted men and angels are represented as rising from their seats, falling on their faces and worshipping, and the reason of their worship is that the kingdoms of this world have passed into the actual possession of

Christ. "The kingdoms of this world." What have they been? What are they now? Hellish mimicries of eternal right and power. Like muddy bubbles on the great stream of life, they have broken into the clear and fathomless river of rectitude, and will appear no more, and this will continue "for ever and ever"—"unto the ages of the ages." Well, then, might the righteous worship and thank God. "We give thee thanks, O Lord God Almighty, which art, and wast, and art to come," etc. (ver. 17). 2. *The increased accessibility of heaven.* "And the temple of God was opened in heaven" (ver. 19). When right shall become universally triumphant, heaven will come near to man. The holy Jerusalem will come down from heaven; heaven and earth will become one.

CONCLUSION. Suspect not the failure of right; have faith in its winning power. It has life in it, indestructible life, life that will germinate in every land, which will multiply and cover all parts of this globe. "The kingdoms of this world shall become the kingdoms of our Lord." "There shall be a handful of corn in the earth upon the top of the mountains; the fruit thereof shall shake like Lebanon: and they of the city shall flourish like grass of the earth."—D. T.

EXPOSITION.

CHAPTER XII.

This chapter commences another series of revelations. Again St. John returns to the beginning, and traces the spiritual history of the Church and the Christian in their warfare with Satan. But the visions which now follow are somewhat different in character from those already related, inasmuch as the conflict is now described rather as between the powers of heaven and hell than between the individual Christian and his oppressors. As with the other visions, so here, the recital seems calculated to support the suffering Christian in his trials, since the overthrow of the powers of darkness is foretold; and the whole series culminates in an account of the final abasement of the devil, and the exaltation of the Church and the bliss of heaven.

The following analysis will help to make clear the relation of the several parts of the vision.

I. THE ORIGIN OF THE ENMITY BETWEEN CHRIST AND THE WORLD. (Ch. xii. 7—13.)

II. THE PROGRESS OF THE WARFARE.

1. *The assaults of the devil.* (1) The *dragon's* direct attacks on Christ (ch. xii. 1—7 and 13—17). (2) On the Church by means of the *wild beast* (ch. xiii. 1—10). (3) On the Church by means of the two-horned *beast* (ch. xiii. 11—18).

2. *The overthrow and punishment of the devil.* (Ch. xx. 1—10.) (1) The fate of the *dragon* (ch. xiv. 7). (2) The fate of the *wild beast* (Babylon) (ch. xiv. 8; xvii.; xviii.;

xix. 19, *et seq.*). (3) The fate of the two-horned *beast* (ch. xiv. 9; xix. 19, *et seq.*).

3. *The victory of the faithful.* (Ch. xiv. 13; xix. 1—10; xxi.; xxii.)

Ver. 1.—And there appeared a great wonder; *and a great sign was seen* (Revised Version). This *sign* consists of the whole of the appearances, the account of which is contained in this verse and the following one. The vision is thus plainly declared to be figurative (cf. the use of the corresponding verb in ch. i. 1). In heaven. Though the scene of the vision opens in *heaven*, it is immediately afterwards transferred to the earth. It is doubtful whether any particular signification is to be attached to the expression, though Wordsworth notes concerning the Church, "For her origin is from above; hers is the kingdom of heaven." And Bengel, "The woman, the Church, though on earth, is nevertheless, by virtue of her union with Christ, in heaven." A woman. The *woman* is undoubtedly the Church of God; not necessarily limited to the Christian Church, but the whole company of all who acknowledge God, including the heavenly beings in existence before the creation, as well as creation itself. The figure is found both in the Old Testament and in the New. Thus Isa. liv. 5, 6, "For thy Maker is thine Husband. . . . For the Lord hath called thee as a woman forsaken and grieved" (cf. also John iii. 29; 2 Cor. xi. 2; Eph. v. 25—32). Clothed with the sun. The whole description is intended to portray the glory and beauty of the Church. Most of the ancient commentators give particular interpretations of the symbols employed. Thus the *sun* is believed to represent Christ, the Sun of Righteousness. Primasius quotes Gal. iii. 27, "For as many of you as have been baptized into Christ have put on Christ." And the moon under her feet. This is interpreted as showing the permanent nature of the Church; she treads underfoot the *moon*, the symbol of changing times and seasons. It is thought that a reference is thus intended to the futility of the endeavours made to subvert the Church (cf. Cant. vi. 10). Others variously interpret the *moon* of (1) the Mosaic Law; (2) the irreligion of the world; (3) the Mohammedan power. But the figure is probably intended simply to enhance the beauty of the vision, and to portray the exceeding glory of the Church. We may also imagine the symbol to denote stability of existence in the midst of change of outward appearance, as the *moon* is ever-existent and ever reappearing, though obscured for a time. And upon her head a crown of twelve stars. This image immediately suggests a reference to the twelve apostles of the Christian Church, and the twelve tribes of the Jewish Church. Wordsworth observes, " *Twelve* is the *apostolic* number, and *stars* are emblems of Christian teachers." In like manner the Jews were accustomed to speak of the minor prophets as " the twelve." The *crown* is στέφανος— the crown of victory—the idea of which is prominent throughout the vision.

Ver. 2.—And she being with child cried, travailing in birth, and pained to be delivered. The present, " crieth," κράζει, is found in א, A, P, Coptic, Andreas in *a* et *bav.*, etc.; the imperfect, ἐκράζεν, is read in C, Vulgate, 7, 8, 31, etc., Andreas in *c* et *p*, Primasius; the aorist, ἐκράζεν, in B, twelve cursives (cf. the words of our Lord in John xvi. 21, 22). A similar image occurs in Isa. xxvi. 17; lxvi. 7, 8; Micah iv. 10. The trouble which afflicted the Jewish Church, and the longing of the patriarchs for the advent of the Saviour, are here depicted. So also St. Paul, encouraging the Romans to bear patiently their sufferings, says, " The whole creation groaneth and travaileth in pain together until now" (Rom. viii. 22).

Ver. 3.—And there appeared another wonder in heaven; *and there was seen another sign in heaven* (Revised Version). (See on ver. 1.) The appearance seen is not a representation of the devil as he actually is, but the sign—the dragon—is figurative and descriptive of the particular characteristics now about to be exhibited. *In heaven*—most likely merely *in the space above*, where he could be easily seen. Wordsworth, however, says, " Because the power here represented assails the Church, the kingdom of *heaven*." And behold a great red dragon. His identity is established by ver. 9, where he is called " the great dragon,

the old serpent, the devil, Satan, the deceiver." *Red;* no doubt to enhance his terrible appearance; suggestive of his murderous, destructive character. " Dragon" (δράκων) in the New Testament occurs only in this book. In the Old Testament the word is of frequent occurrence. In the LXX. δράκων is used seventeen times to express the Hebrew *tannin* (a sea or land monster, especially a crocodile or serpent); five times it stands for *leviathan*; twice it represents *kephir* (young lion); twice *nachash* (serpent); once '*attud* (he-goat); and once *pethen* (python). *Tannin* (singular) is always rendered by δράκων except in Gen. i. 21, where we find κῆτος; but twice it is corrupted into *tannim* (viz. Ezek. xxix. 3; xxxii. 2). The latter word, *tannim*, is the plural of *tan* (a jackal), and is found only in the plural; but once it is found corrupted into *tannin* (Lam. iv. 3). There is no doubt as to the signification of the appearance. The *dragon* is, in the Old Testament, invariably a symbol of what is harmful, tyrannous, murderous. It is a hideous, sanguinary monster, sometimes inhabiting the sea, sometimes the desolate places of the earth, always " seeking whom it may devour." In some passages it refers to Pharaoh (Ps. lxxiv. 13; cf. Ezek. xxix. 3; xxxii. 2); in others it is a type of what is noxious or desolate (Job vii. 12; Isa. xiii. 22; xxxiv. 13; Ps. xliv. 19; Jer. ix. 11, etc.). In Isa. xxvii. 1 we have the combination, " leviathan the piercing serpent, even leviathan that crooked serpent; . . . the dragon that is in the sea." Having seven heads and ten horns. The description of the beasts in ch. xii.—xvii. is evidently derived from the vision of Daniel (vii.), although the details differ. It seems reasonable to conclude, therefore, that the interpretation generally should follow the same lines as that applied to the Old Testament symbols, with which the writer was so familiar. The appearances described in Daniel are universally considered to typify various worldly powers which oppressed the Church and nation of the Jews. Similarly here the symbolism seems intended to portray the opposition of the devil to the Church of God, working through the power of the world. The heads and horns are both declared in ch. xvii. 10, 12 to typify kingdoms—in what way we shall presently see (ch. xvii. 10). The numbers *seven* and *ten* are both symbolical of completeness (see ch. i. 4; v. 1; xiii. 1; xvii. 3). We have, therefore, in this picture of the dragon, the idea of the full and complete power of the world arrayed on earth against God and his Church. This power, connected with and derived from the devil, the prince of this world (John xii. 31), is often alluded to by St. John as being opposed to, or in contrast with, the godly (see John vii. 7; xiv. 17; xv.; xvi.; xvii.; 1 John ii. 15; iii. 13; v. 4, etc.). **And seven crowns upon his heads;** *seven diadems* (Revised Version). That is, the kingly crown, the symbol of sovereignty, worn by the dragon to denote his power as "prince of this world." The word διαδήματα is found in the New Testament only here and ch. xiii. 1 and xix. 12. It is not the στέφανος, the crown of victory worn by the saints (see ch. ii. 10; iii. 11; vi. 2, etc.). No account is given of the disposition and arrangement of the heads, horns, and diadems; nor is it necessary. The seven crowned heads signify universal sovereignty; the ten horns, absolute power. Probably those to whom St. John wrote understood the symbol as referring specially to the power of heathen Rome, which was at that time oppressing the Church; but the meaning extends to the power of the world in all ages (see on ch. xiii. 1).

Ver. 4.—**And his tail drew the third part of the stars of heaven, and did cast them to the earth;** *draweth* (Revised Version). Not the *stars* with which the woman is crowned (see ver. 1), but other *stars*. In describing the vast power of the devil, St. John seems to allude to the tremendous result of his rebellious conduct in heaven, in effecting the fall of other angels with himself (Jude 6). The seer does not here interrupt his narrative to explain the point, but returns to it after ver. 6, and there describes briefly the origin and cause of the enmity of the devil towards God. **The third part** (as in ch. viii. 7, *et seq.*) signifies a considerable number, but not the larger part. **And the dragon stood before the woman which was ready to be delivered, for to devour her child as soon as it was born;** *which was about to be delivered, that when she was delivered, he might devour her child* (Revised Version). A graphic picture of what is true of Christ himself, of the Church, both Jewish and Christian, and of every individual member of the Church. This is another example of the personal history of Christ being repeated in the history of his Church. The devil, in the person of Herod, attempts to prevent the salvation of the world; through Pharaoh he endeavours to crush the chosen people of God, through whom the Messiah was to bless all the earth; by means of the power of Rome he labours to exterminate the infant Church of Christ.

Ver. 5.—**And she brought forth a manchild, who was to rule all nations with a rod of iron;** *a son, a male*—the Greek υἱόν, ἄρσεν, renders it emphatic—*who is to rule,* as in the Revised Version; *to rule,* or *to govern as a shepherd* (cf. the verb in Matt.

ii. 6). This reference and Ps. ii. 9 leave no doubt as to the identification of the manchild. It is Christ who is intended. The same expression is used of him in ch. xix., where he is definitely called the "Word of God." And her child was caught up unto God, and to his throne. The sentence seems plainly to refer to the ascension of Christ and his subsequent abiding in heaven, from whence he rules all nations. The seer, perhaps, wishes to indicate at once the absolute immunity of Christ from any harm proceeding from the power of the devil, whose efforts are henceforth directly aimed only at the Church of Christ. Satan still hopes to injure Christ through his members. As remarked above (see on ver. 4), what is true of the personal history of Christ is often true of his Church and of his true members. And thus some have seen in this passage a picture of the woman, the Church, bringing forth members, to devour whom is Satan's constant purpose, but who in God's good time are taken to his throne to be near himself.

Ver. 6.—**And the woman fled into the wilderness.** As with Christ, so with his Church. His great trial took place in the wilderness; so the trial of the Church occurs in the wilderness, by which figure the world is typified. It is generally pointed out that this verse is here inserted in anticipation of ver. 14. We prefer rather to look upon it as occurring in its natural place, the narrative being interrupted by vers. 7—13 in order to account for the implacable hostility of the devil. **Where she hath a place prepared of God.** ℵ, A, B, P, and others insert ἐκεῖ as well as ὅπου, "where she there hath," etc.—a redundancy which is an ordinary Hebraism. Though the Church is "in the world," she is not "of the world" (John xvii. 14, 15); though the woman is in the "wilderness," her place is "prepared of God." The harlot's abode (ch. xvii.) is in the wilderness, and it is also of the wilderness; it is not in a place specially prepared of God. **That they should feed her there a thousand two hundred and three score days.** The sense is the same as in ver. 14, "that she should be sustained there." The interpretation of the 1260 days, or 3½ years, coincides here with that adopted in ch. xi. 2. It describes the period of this world's existence, during the whole of which the devil persecutes the Church of God. As Auberlen points out, this is, in ch. xiii. 5, declared to be "the period of the power of the beast, that is, the world-power." (For a discussion of the whole subject of this period, see on ch. xi. 2.)

Vers. 7, 8.—**And there was war in heaven.** The passage vers. 7—13 is an interruption of the narrative of the persecution of the woman by Satan. It is caused, apparently, by a desire to account in some degree for the relentless hostility of the devil towards God and his Church. Two explanations of the passage may be referred to. (1) Vers. 7—13 relate to the period anterior to the Creation, concerning which we have a slight hint in Jude 6. This, on the whole, seems to agree best with the general sense of the chapter, and to present fewest difficulties. Thus : (a) It accounts for the insertion of the passage (see above). (b) The war is directly between the devil and Michael, not between the devil and Christ, as at the Incarnation and Resurrection. (c) Vers. 8 and 9 seem to require a more literal interpretation than that which makes them refer to the effects of Christ's resurrection. (d) It was not at the period of the Incarnation that the scene of Satan's opposition was transferred to the earth, as described in ver. 12. (e) The song of the heavenly voice may be intended to end with the word "Christ" (ver. 10), and the following passages may be the words of the writer of the Apocalypse, and may refer to the earthly martyrs (see on ver. 10). (f) This attempt of the devil in heaven may be alluded to in John i. 5, "The darkness overcame it not" (see also John xii. 35). (2) The passage may refer to the incarnation and resurrection of Christ, and the victory then won over the devil. This interpretation renders the whole passage much more figurative. (a) Michael is the type of mankind, which in the Person of Jesus Christ vanquishes the devil. (b) Subsequent to the Resurrection Satan is no more allowed to accuse men before God in heaven, as he has done previously (see Job i.; ii.; Zech. iii. 1; 1 Kings xxii. 19—22); he is thus the accuser cast down (ver. 10), and his place is no more found in heaven (ver. 8). (c) The earth and sea represent the worldly and tumultuous nations. Perhaps the strongest argument in favour of the second view is found in Luke x. 18 and John xii. 31. Michael and his angels fought against the dragon; *Michael and his angels [going forth] to war with the dragon* (Revised Version). Alford explains the infinitive phrase as compounded of the genitive τοῦ and depending upon ἐγένετο. *Michael* (מִי־כָאֵל) signifies, "Who is like to God?" We may compare this with the cry of the worldly in ch. xiii. 4, "Who is like unto the beast?" In Daniel, *Michael* is the prince who stands up for the people of Israel (Dan. xii. 1; x. 13, 21). *Michael*, "the archangel," is alluded to in Jude 9 as the great opposer of Satan. St. John, perhaps borrowing the name from Daniel, puts forward *Michael* as the chief of those who remained faithful to the cause of God in the rebellion of Satan and his angels. The

angels of the dragon are the stars of ver. 4, which he drew with him to the earth, and possibly the reference to this event in ver. 4 gives rise to the account in vers. 7—13. Some commentators interpret the war here described as that between the Church and the world. *Michael* is thus made to be symbolical of Christ, and some have no difficulty in indicating a particular man (such as Licinius) as the antitype of the dragon. And the dragon fought and his angels, and prevailed not; neither was their place found any more in heaven. The Greek is stronger, *not even their place*, etc. Οὐδέ is read in א, A, B, C, Andreas, Arethas; οὔτε is found in P, 1, 17, and others. So complete was the defeat of Satan that he was no longer permitted to remain in heaven in any capacity.

Ver. 9.—And the great dragon was cast out, that old serpent, called the Devil, and Satan, which deceiveth the whole world; *cast down* (Revised Version); *the whole inhabited earth* (Revised Version, margin). " The dragon :" so called, because he is the destroyer (see on ver. 3). "The ancient serpent," as he was revealed in Gen iii. So in John viii. 44 he is "the destroyer from the beginning." "The devil" (Διάβολος) is the Greek rendering of the Hebrew *Satan*, שָׂטָן, "the accuser, the adversary;" reference is made in ver. 10 to the signification of the name, " The Deceiver." Wordsworth says, " The deceits by which Satan cheated the world in oracles, sorcery, soothsaying, magic, and other frauds, are here specially noticed. These were put to flight by the power of Christ and of the Holy Ghost, in the preaching of the gospel by the apostles and others in the first ages of Christianity. Our Lord himself, speaking of the consequence of the preaching of the seventy disciples, reveals the spiritual struggle and the victory: 'I was beholding Satan as lightning fall from heaven' (Luke x. 17, 18)." He was cast out into the earth, and his angels were cast out with him; *cast down to the earth*, etc. (Revised Version). " To the earth " in a twofold sense : (1) the phrase is a description of the loss of dignity and power on the part of Satan, in being cast to *earth* as opposed to heaven; (2) *earth* is the scene of his future operations, where he may still in some degree sustain the struggle against God.

Ver. 10.—And I heard a loud voice saying in heaven. The " great voice " is characteristic of all the heavenly utterances (cf. ch. v. 2; vi. 1, 10; xvi. 17, etc.). The personality of the speaker is not indicated. From the following chorus the *voice* would seem to proceed from many inhabitants of heaven. Now is come salvation, and strength, and the kingdom of our God, and the power of his Christ; *the salvation and the power, and the kingdom of our God, and the authority of his Christ* (Revised Version). The Revised Version marginal reading may also be noticed, *Now is the salvation . . . become our God's, and the authority [is become] his Christ's.* The heavenly inhabitants celebrate the triumphant confirmation of God's supremacy, which has been vindicated by the defeat and expulsion of the rebellious hosts. "The salvation of God" (σωτηρία) is that which proceeds from him; "that salvation which belongs to God as its Author" (Alford); cf. ch. vii. 10; xix. 1. "The authority of his Christ" is first manifested in heaven; Satan is cast down to the earth, and here again at a subsequent epoch the *authority of Christ* is displayed, and another victory won over the devil. This seems to be the conclusion of the heavenly song. As before stated (see on ver. 7), the three and a half verses now concluded seem to relate to a period previous to the creation of the world. It seems equally probable that the following two and a half verses refer to those earthly martyrs and suffering Christians for whom this book is specially written. These two views can be reconciled by supposing the song of the heavenly *voice* to cease at the word "Christ" (ver. 10); and then the writer adds words of his own, as if he would say, "The cause of the victorious song which I have just recited was the fact that the devil was cast down, the same who is constantly accusing (ὁ κατηγορῶν) our brethren. But they (our brethren) overcame him, and valued not their lives, etc. Well may ye heavens rejoice over your happy lot, though it means woe to the earth for a short time." For the accuser of our brethren is cast down, which accused them before our God day and night. *The one accusing them* (ὁ κατηγορῶν); not the past tense. Satan does not cease to accuse, though he may not do so with effect, since he may be overcome by the "blood of the Lamb." The heavenly beings are henceforth beyond his reach. He can yet accuse men—our brethren —says St. John; but even here his power is limited by the victory of the death and resurrection of Christ referred to in ver. 5. "Accuser" (κατήγορος) is found in א, B, C, P, Andreas, Arethas. The form κατήγωρ, found in A, is rather the Targumic and rabbinic corruption of the word קטיגור, than the Greek word itself. "Of our brethren," the saints and martyrs (see above); "is cast down" (or, "was cast down") from heaven.

Ver. 11.—And they overcame him (cf. the frequent references to those who overcome, and the promises made to them, ch. ii.; iii.; xxi. 7, etc.). The reference "they" is to "our brethren," the accused ones of

ver. 10. By the blood of the Lamb; *because of the blood,* etc. (Revised Version). That is, "the blood of the Lamb" is the ground or reason of their victory, not the instrument. So in ch. i. 9, "I John . . . was in the island called Patmos, *because of* the Word of God (διὰ τὸν λόγον)" (cf. ch. vi. 9). Winer agrees with this view of the present passage, against Ewald and De Wette (p. 498 of Moulton's translation). "The Lamb," who was seen "as it had been slain" (ch. v. 6)— Christ. And by the word of their testimony; *and on account of the word,* etc. The one phrase is the natural complement of the other. "The blood of the Lamb" would have been shed in vain without the *testimony,* the outcome of the faith of his followers; that *testimony* would have been impossible without the shedding of the blood. And they loved not their lives unto the death; *their life even unto death.* That is, they valued not their life in this world, even to the extent of meeting death for the sake of giving their testimony. There is no article in the Greek, merely ἄχρι θανάτον; so also in the same phrase in Acts xxii. 4. The article of the Authorized Version in Acts xxii. 4 is probably derived from Wickliffe's Bible; that in the present passage, from Tyndale's.

Ver. 12.—Therefore rejoice, ye heavens, and ye that dwell in them; *O heavens* (Revised Version). Κατοικοῦντες, "that dwell," is read in א, 26, 29, 30, 31, 98, Andreas, Vulgate, Primasius, Memphitic, Armenian. The Revisers have followed the common reading of σκηνοῦντες, "tabernacled," which is found in the majority of manuscripts. Alford observes, "There is no sense of transitoriness in St. John's use of σκηνόω, rather one of repose and tranquillity (cf. ch. vii. 15)." Κατασκηνοῦντες is found in C. So in ch. xiii. 6 the abiding-place of God is called his *tabernacle.* These are the words of the writer (see on ver. 10). The cause for this rejoicing has been given in ver. 9; the devil having been cast out, those in heaven enjoy absolute immunity from all harm which he can work. Woe to the inhabiters of the earth and of the sea! *Woe for the earth and for the sea!* (Revised Version). A few cursives give τοῖς κατοίκουσιν, "to the dwellers." The influence of the devil works woe to the whole world—to the human inhabitants, to the animal and vegetable life of the earth which was cursed for man's sake (cf. Gen. iii. 17). For the devil is come down unto you, having great wrath, because he knoweth that he hath but a short time; or, *came down* (aorist). "A short season" (καιρός) in which to exist in the world. His *wrath,* kindled by his ejectment from heaven, is the greater because of the comparative shortness of his reign on earth. This "short season" is the period of the world's existence from the advent of Satan till the final judgment. It is *short* in comparison with eternity, and it is frequently thus described in the New Testament (Rom. ix. 28; 1 Cor. vii. 29; ch. iii. 11, etc.). It is the "little time" of ch. vi. 11; the "little season" of ch. xx. 3, during which Satan must be loosed. Here ends the digression descriptive of the struggle in heaven before the creation of the world, and the following verses take up and continue the narrative which was interrupted after ver. 6.

Ver. 13.—And when the dragon saw that he was cast unto the earth, he persecuted the woman which brought forth the man-child. (For an explanation of the characters here alluded to, see on the previous verses.) The devil, defeated in his attempts against God in heaven, and foiled in his attack upon the *man-child*—Christ Jesus (see ver. 5), now directs his efforts against the *woman* —the Church. The interpretation must not be confined to one peculiar form of evil which assails the Church, but must include all—the bodily persecutions with which those to whom St. John wrote were afflicted, the heresies which arose in the Church, the lukewarmness of her members (ch. iii. 16), and all others.

Ver. 14.—And to the woman were given two wings of a great eagle. "The two wings of the great eagle" is found in most authorities, though ℵ omits both the articles. The symbol of the eagle is a common one in the Old Testament, and this may account for the presence of the article. The escape of the Jewish Church from the power of Pharaoh, and her preservation in the wilderness, are referred to under a like figure (see Exod. xix. 4; Deut. xxxii. 11, "Ye have seen what I did unto the Egyptians, and how I bare you on eagles' wings, and brought you unto myself"). The natural enmity between the eagle and the serpent is alluded to by Wordsworth (Wordsworth, *in loc.*, where see a full exposition of the symbolism here employed). "The two wings" may typify the Old and New Testaments, by the authority of which the Church convicts her adversaries, and by which she is supported during her period of conflict with the devil. That she might fly into the wilderness, into her place. The reference to the flight of Israel from Egypt is still carried on. "Her place" is the "place prepared of God" (ver. 6). The Church, though in the world, is not of the world (see on ver. 6). Where she is nourished for a time, and times, and half a time, from the face of the serpent. Still the history of Israel is borne in mind. As the chosen people were nourished in the wilderness, so the Church of God is sustained

in her pilgrimage on earth. The redundant ὅπου ἐκεῖ, "where there," follows the analogy of the Hebrew (see on ver. 6). "The time, times, and half a time," is the period elsewhere described as 42 months, 1260 days, 3½ years. It denotes the period of the existence of this world (see on ch. xi. 2). The expression is taken from Dan. vii. 25; xii. 7. By this verse and ver. 6 is established the identity of the two expressions—1260 days, and the time, times, and half a time (*i.e.* one year + two years + half a year). The plural καιροί is used for "two times," as no dual occurs in the Greek of the New Testament (see Winer, p. 221, Moulton's translation). The construction, "nourished from the face" (τρέφεται ἀπὸ προσώπου τοῦ ὄφεως), is built upon the analogy of the Hebrew. The "serpent" is the "dragon" of ver. 13 (cf. ver. 9, "the great dragon, that old serpent, called the Devil, and Satan"). The two words are used as convertible terms (cf. ver. 17, where he is again called "the dragon").

Ver. 15.—And the serpent cast out of his mouth water as a flood after the woman, that he might cause her to be carried away of the flood; *cast out of his mouth after the woman water as a river . . . carried away by the river.* A *flood*, in the Old Testament, has several significations. It frequently expresses overwhelming misfortune. Thus Ps. lxix. 15, "Let not the waterflood overflow me;" xc. 5, "Thou carriest them away as with a flood" (cf. also Dan. ix. 26; xi. 22, Isa. lix. 19; Jer. xlvi. 7; Amos ix. 5, etc.). The *flood* is typical of every form of destruction with which the devil seeks to overwhelm the Church of God. At the period of the writing of the Apocalypse, it plainly symbolized the bitter persecutions to which Christians were subjected; but its meaning need not be limited to this one form of destruction. Thus all those writers are correct, so far as they go, who interpret the *flood* of the Mohammedan power, of heresy, of the Gothic invasion, etc.

Ver. 16.—And the earth helped the woman, and the earth opened her mouth, and swallowed up the flood which the dragon cast out of his mouth; *swallowed up the river* (Revised Version). "The earth" frequently, but not invariably, in the Revelation signifies "the wicked." It is doubtful, therefore, how far the figure here employed should be pressed. What is certain is that the writer intends to express the idea that the Church is preserved in a wonderful and even miraculous way from the efforts of the devil. Further than this we cannot proceed safely. Possibly we may see in the passage an allusion to the world embracing Christianity, by which the instrument of Satan's ill will became a defence to the Church: though an earlier period and earlier deliverances seem more likely to be intended (such as the conversion of St. Paul); for after endeavouring to destroy the woman at one stroke, the dragon proceeds to war with her seed. The words recall another incident in the history of the Israelitish flight from Egypt and sojourn in the wilderness, viz. that of the destruction of Korah and his company; though, of course, the nature of the incidents is not the same in both cases.

Ver. 17.—And the dragon was wroth with the woman, and went to make war with the remnant of her seed; *waxed wroth . . . went away to make*, etc. (Revised Version). Having failed to prevent the mission of the man child—Christ Jesus—and having been foiled in his attempts to overwhelm the Church of God, Satan proceeds to attack the individual members of the Church—the seed of the woman. The method by which he endeavours to do this is related in the following chapters. Wordsworth points out an analogy between the means which Satan employs to destroy the Church as described here, and those described in the seals. The "rest of her seed" (Revised Version) signifies all the children of the woman, excluding the man-child of ver. 5. All members of the Church of God are thus referred to, those who are brethren of Christ (cf. Heb. ii. 11, "For which cause he is not ashamed to call them brethren"). Which keep the commandments of God, and have the testi-

mony of Jesus Christ (nearly all manuscripts omit "Christ"); *hold the testimony* (Revised Version). This plainly points out who are the "rest of the seed"—they are those who are God's faithful servants. We may see in the description a reference to the Church of God, both Jewish and Christian. The members of the Jewish Church were they to whom "the commandments of God" were specially revealed, and Christians are they who specially "hold the testimony of Jesus." (For an explanation of the latter phrase, see on ch. i. 2.)

We have now reached another stage in the history of the warfare carried on by the devil against God. Vers. 7—12 of this chapter describe the origin of the hostility of Satan towards God; vers. 4 and 5 relate the attempts of the devil to destroy Christ and to thwart his mission; vers. 13—16 refer to the attacks of Satan upon the Church of God, by which he hoped to destroy it as a whole, before there was time for the "seed" to spring up. Having failed in every attempt, the dragon now sends other agents by whom he hopes to destroy the individual members of the Church—the other seed of the woman—the brethren of Christ.

HOMILETICS.

Vers. 1—17.—*The foes of God and of his Church.* "*That old serpent.*" In previous chapters of this book there have been hints of sundry evil forces which would at divers times harass the Church of God. Who they would be, or what, or how they would work, has not yet been shown to us. This is done, however, in chapters which we have yet to consider. Of them there are *several*. Of each one we have a representation in the form of allegory or parable. In this chapter the first of them is shown us. We can be in no doubt as to who it is that is intended; nor is there any very great difficulty about the main features of the sketch, however obscure some of the minor details may be. The enemy is the devil. The object of his rage is the faithful Church, represented under the symbol of "a woman, clothed with the sun," etc. When we find, too, that this woman brought forth a man-child, who is sought to be devoured as soon as born; who is, in spite of all, caught up to God and to his throne, from which seat of power he is to rule the nations as with a rod of iron;—we have very distinctive marks pointing unmistakably to our Lord. The enemy, failing to devour him, persecutes the woman, and failing in his designs against her, he goes on to war with the remnant of her seed. But, as the chapter shows, in every instance the evil one rushes on only to his own defeat. So that this chapter contains a parable of glorious meaning, as it sets forth the working of Satan against the Church of God. His present work is to make war against those who keep the commandments of God and the faith of Jesus. Why should he select these as the objects of his attack? Why? Because others are doing his work for him! He disturbs himself only about his disturbers. He has little need to look after others. Let us, then, try, in the light of this chapter, to look our foe full in the face, and to find out what he is, what he can do, and what he cannot. Our subject, then, is—*our foe, as sketched by a Divine hand.*

I. OUR FOE IS A PERSONAL ONE. (Ver. 9.) It would be of little avail to say that the personality of the evil one cannot be decided from such a chapter as this; for the allusions to Satan elsewhere are so numerous and so varied that they shut us up to the conviction of his personality; *i.e.* that he is a distinct being, with a will, plan, and purpose of his own, moving in "the heavenly places," *i.e.* in the realm of spirit. We often find the personal pronouns used concerning him (John viii. 44). The names and epithets applied to him indicate the same. The name "the devil" means "the slanderer." He is represented in Scripture as slandering God before men, and as slandering men before God. The apostle speaks of him as "going about seeking whom he may devour." Nor can there be a doubt that we are taught by our Lord and his apostles that to Satan's pernicious agency much of the evil in the world must be traced. Let us remember our Lord's conflict with him.

II. HE IS AN OLD ONE. "The devil sinneth from the beginning" (1 John iii. 8; John viii. 44). He first sinned in heaven, and was cast out from thence ere he came to deceive the whole world. Then he tempted Adam in Eden. He came into conflict with our Lord. He hindered apostles in their work (1 Thess. ii. 18). He has been counterplotting the sowings of the Son of man for eighteen hundred years (Matt. xiii. 39). And he is at work still. We well know, indeed, that there is one difficulty which often presses upon thoughtful minds. It is this: Can it be that God should let one being have such tremendous power for evil? Now, although the devil's power is not so great as some people seem to think it to be, we confess that it would be a very great relief to us if we felt warranted in saying, No. But there are three remarks which have to be set over against this question. 1. Whatever evil is in the world is here, whether there be a devil or no. And if evil is only a spontaneous product of man himself, then human nature is much worse than the Bible declares it to be. 2. But if we grant that some of it comes from outside, it is then merely a question whether the outside evil is led on by one single force, or by an indefinite number of agents, organized or unorganized. 3. If we accept the doctrine of the unity of leadership in the forces of ill *outside* earth, the difficulty is merely one of degree, not of kind; *e.g.* if one pope can by his will move his organized forces at any part of the world, why may not a like power be, for aught we know, outside the limits of this globe?

III. HE IS A DARING ONE. The flashes of light which we get on this point in Scripture are many. Michael and his angels. Our Lord. Peter. Judas. In heaven. In Eden. In the desert. At the last Supper. In Gethsemane. He carefully selects those on whom he will try his temptations. The greater the object, the fiercer the onset. If a man stands up for Jesus, Satan will desire to have him, that he may sift him as wheat. It is a far greater thing to bring an eagle to the ground than a sparrow. It is a vaster achievement to batter a fortress than a hut. And the greater our influence, and the higher our standing in the Church, the more fiercely will the evil one assail us.

IV. HIS ATTEMPTS ARE OFTEN FAILURES. (Ver. 8, "The dragon warred and his angels, *and they prevailed not.*") It is a relief to find that it is so; and that the evil one's most daring attempts have been the signal for most humiliating failures. The supreme illustration of this is his onset upon our Lord in the desert (Matt. iv. 1—11). From heaven he was cast out, and even on this earth he is an outcast still (vers. 9—11). His power in far-off realms is at an end. His pride was his condemnation. He was overpowered by a Greater, when Jesus died. "Now is the prince of this world cast out" (John xii. 31). And already, in prospect of his complete, utter, and final defeat, is the heavenly song begun, "Now is come the salvation," etc. (vers. 10, 11). It is no wonder that we go on to read that—

V. HE IS AN ANGRY FOE. (Ver. 12, "He has great wrath, knowing that he hath but a short time.") In what way this has been revealed to the evil one, we do not know; but we shall do both ourselves and Scripture a wrong if we refuse to let this thought bring us its appropriate inspiration and comfort. Truly it is good to know that the end of his power is foreseen.

VI. HE IS A MALICIOUS ONE. (Ver. 13.) If defeated in one scheme, he tries another. If cast out of heaven, he will plague the earth. "He worries whom he can't devour." And as he prevailed not against the Lord of the Church, he persecutes the Church of the Lord. He has long been engaged in plotting schemes against the people of God, desiring to have them, that he may sift them as wheat.

VII. He is a watchful and crafty one (vers. 4, 13, 15), varying his methods according to the case in hand. "We are not ignorant of his devices" (2 Cor. ii. 11). We have to contend against "the wiles of the devil" (Eph. vi. 11). He is active, too, in executing his plans. The whole of this chapter is one lengthened sketch, in symbol, of the manifold forms of his activity. And perhaps we are hardly prepared to see how varied are his methods of work, until we collect the several hints scattered throughout the Word of God. In the world at large he counterplots the sowing of the Son of man (Matt. xiii. 38, 39); he deceives by powers, and signs, and lying wonders (2 Thess. ii. 9, 10); in a city like Pergamos he sets up his throne (ch. ii. 12, 13); he collects his followers in a synagogue of his own (ch. ii. 9); he preys on the body, inflicting dumbness on one (Mark ix. 17), and binding another for eighteen years (Luke xiii. 16); he casts some of the saints into prison (ch. ii. 10), and hinders apostles in their work (1 Thess. ii. 18); he inflicts on Paul a thorn in the flesh (2 Cor. xii. 7, 8), and goes about in search of prey (1 Pet. v. 8), in a constant state of unrest (Matt. xii. 43); he lays snares for the ungodly (2 Tim. ii. 26); causes many to turn aside after him (1 Tim. v. 15); he puts it into the heart of Judas to betray his Master (John xiii. 2), and leads Ananias and Sapphira to lie to the Holy Ghost (Acts v. 3); if men are just coming to Jesus, he throws them down and tears them (Luke ix. 42); and while the Word is being heard, he stealthily takes it out of the heart, lest they should believe and be saved (Luke viii. 12). So terrible is the tale of his deceit that we are ready to give up heart, till we note—

VIII. He is a circumscribed foe. This chapter tells us of three limits put to him and to his power. 1. One, of *space*. He is cast down to earth. He is "the god of this world" (2 Cor. iv. 4). 2. A second, of *time*. "A time, and times, and half a time." The same mysterious period of twelve hundred and sixty days, during which the witness-bearing is to go on, and the beast (ch. xiii.) is to continue. 3. There is yet a third limit, that of *force* (ver. 16, "The earth helped the woman," etc.). Nothing can be plainer than that in this chapter we are shown the cheering fact that the evil one cannot have it all his own way. If his work counterplots the good, none the less surely does the good counteract him. He is mighty; but there is a Stronger than he. We are taught in Scripture that there are five ways by which his power is restricted and his intention foiled. (1) There is providential dispensation (vers. 6, 14, 16; 1 Cor. x. 13). (2) There is angelic ministry (ver. 7). (3) There is the direct exertion of Christ's commanding word (Matt. xvii. 18). (4) There is the counteracting power of Divine grace (2 Cor. xii. 9). (5) There is the intercession of our Redeemer (Luke xxii. 31, 32).

IX. He is a foe with whose devices we have to reckon in fighting the battle of life. (Ver. 17.) Note: 1. He is one at whom we cannot afford to laugh, and whose existence we cannot afford to deny. Nothing gives the enemy such leverage as the denial of his existence. It is the very lie he loves to put into our mouths. The only "father," surely, who loves his children to disown his existence. 2. He is a foe before whom we need not quail. While we may not laugh in careless indifference, we need not cower in fear. Life is not so easy as if there were no devil to fight; it is not so hard but that we may ensure his defeat. 3. He is a foe to whom not an inch of room should be given (Eph. iv. 27). Let us ever be wary lest he get advantage over us; and let us swear eternal enmity to him and all his works. 4. He is a foe for whose onsets we should prepare, by a survey and appropriation of heavenly forces. We stand between two opposing agencies—the Spirit of God on one side, and the devil on the other. Let us not grieve the Spirit by toying with the devil. 5. He is a foe on whose ultimate defeat and complete discomfiture we may surely and confidently reckon if we look to Jesus. "Greater is he that is for us," etc. Our Lord hath overcome him for us, and in his strength we shall overcome too. And we shall be better and stronger Christians for having had such a foe to fight. Not only is it the battle that *tries* the soldier, but that *makes* him. We have, however, not just one skirmish, and then peace. Oh no! "Patient continuance in well-doing." Daily fighting, daily praying, daily victory, till the end.

> "The land of triumph lies on high;
> There are no foes t' encounter there!"

HOMILIES BY VARIOUS AUTHORS.

Ver. 6.—*The Church in the wilderness.* This ver. 6 is repeated in **ver. 14**, as if calling special attention to the facts which it declares. But it cannot be understood, nor its lessons learnt, until sundry questions are asked and answered. 1. *Who is the woman told of?* She is the same as we read of in ver. 1, where she appears, not in distress, humiliation, and fear, fleeing with all speed from her dreaded foe, as is the case in this ver. 6; but in all august splendour, with radiant vestments and starry crown, with the moon as her footstool, and the glory of the sun shining upon her. But who is she? "The blessed Virgin Mary," answers the whole Catholic world without a moment's hesitation; and in innumerable paintings and sculptures, sermons and songs, they have so set her forth as she is represented here. And that there is no reference to the nativity and incarnation of our Lord Jesus Christ in this chapter, he would be a bold man who would affirm; but that the mother of our Lord is mainly, and, much more, exclusively meant, we cannot think. What is further said concerning her is impossible as applied to the virgin-mother. But, without question, Mary, "the handmaid of the Lord," was a true and beautiful type of that queenly woman who is portrayed in the opening verses of this chapter. And that woman is none other than the Church of God, she of whom it was so often said, "Thy Maker is thy Husband;" "Behold, I am married unto thee." And in this very book how often we read of "the Bride, the Lamb's wife"! Of that faithful Church of God under the ancient dispensation, Christ, according to the flesh, came. "Born of a woman, made under the Law." 2. *What is meant by the "travail" of the woman* at the hour of her child's birth? The sweet story of Christmas is indeed pointed at here; but much more than that. Are we not reminded of those words of Isaiah, "As soon as Zion travailed, she brought forth children;" and of St. Paul's words to the Galatians, "My little children, of whom I travail in birth again until Christ be formed in you"? And so did the ancient Church, with much spiritual travail, in earnest trust and fervent prayer, in patient hope, "waiting for the consolation of Israel," give birth to the Christian Church, of which Christ himself was the Head and Type and Lord. And then: 3. *Who is, or what is, the great red dragon*—that portentous monster whose hideous portrait and purpose are here revealed? Who is that who is as Pharaoh, watching for the birth of Israel's babes, in the far-off evil days of their bondage in Egypt, that he might destroy them; or as Herod, inquiring diligently concerning the birth of the holy Child Jesus, that he might murderously rid himself of the possible rival "King of the Jews,"— who is meant here? And surely not Herod, nor, exclusively, Nero or Rome, but the prince of this world, Satan, the old serpent, the devil—he and none other—is the "great red dragon." "Red, as the colour of fire and as the colour of blood. Red, as the emblem of the waster and destroyer, as the emblem of him who ' was a murderer from the beginning.'" The dragon is that fabulous monster of whom ancient poets told as "huge in size, coiled like a snake, blood-red in colour, or shot with changing tints," insatiable in voracity and ever athirst for human blood. In Ps. xci. it is linked with "the lion and adder, and the young lion"—all which, together with the dragon, God's servant should "trample underfoot." Fit emblem, therefore, for that cruel, bloodthirsty, and persecuting power with which Christ's Church has so often had to contend. Its variety of assault is told of by the "seven heads;" its huge strength, by the "ten horns;" its exalted authority amidst men, by the "seven diadems;" and its arrogant and audacious dominance, by "the tail which drew the third part of the stars of heaven, and cast them down to the earth." Such is the Church's adversary, the devil, who, in St. John's day, assumed a form which justified this horrid portraiture, but who, in whatever form he may assume, from whichever of his "seven heads" his attack may spring, is ever, in spirit, purpose, and aim, one and the same, always and everywhere. We need not linger on the next question : 4. *Who is the child that was born?* That the Lord Jesus Christ is meant is, we think, incontestable; but as it is not of his life and ministry that this vision mainly tells, but of that Church in which and for which he was born, his sojourn and sufferings here are passed over. Only his entrance into and departure from this world are spoken of, and we are bidden contemplate him not here, but at the right hand of God, whither he ascended after his work on earth was done. But "the woman," and not her child, lingers here, exposed to the cruel assaults of her dread foe until the twelve hundred and sixty days, the period of time which we find so perpetually mentioned in this book, and which equals the three years and a half, the half of the complete number seven, and therefore type of a period not complete, but brief and broken,—until this time be done, the woman—the Church—must remain in the wilderness to which she has fled, or, rather, has been borne of God (ver. 14), and where she is sheltered from the power of her dread foe, and nourished by the ministers of God. It now only remains to ask : 4. *What is this wilderness which is spoken of here?* And the reply is that it is a type of the condition of the Church until the twelve hundred and sixty days, the time allotted for the Church's trial, be accomplished. And concerning that condition we would now speak—of its privations and perils, but, most of all, of its privileges.

I. ITS PRIVATIONS. No doubt there are these; the very name of "wilderness" indicates that there would be. We cannot have the good things of the world—"the flesh-pots of Egypt"—and the good things of Christ too. We have to make choice between them. Making the best of *both* worlds is generally, if not always, a very doubtful procedure, though not a few professed Christians are for ever attempting it. "How hardly shall they that have riches"—the specially good thing of this world—"enter into the kingdom of heaven !" So said our Saviour, and all experience confirms his word. For such things are but hindrances and *impedimenta,* that do but render our way through the wilderness yet more difficult, where it was difficult enough before. It is told of a great cardinal how, when in his last illness, he had himself wheeled into his sumptuous picture-gallery, and as he wistfully looked at one art treasure after another, he said to a friend who was with him, "Ah, these are the things that make it hard to die ! " No doubt it is so; and hence we are bidden go by the way of the wilderness, so that we may escape the besetments that would otherwise delay our progress. *Nor may we look for rest here.* The pilgrim may never here say to his soul, "Soul, take thine ease." Here we have no continuing city, but we seek one to come. There were Elims and other "quiet resting-places" where, once and again, Israel was permitted to relieve the stress and strain of their long pilgrimage ; but the common characteristics of their life was that of pilgrims, and their forty years' sojourn in the wilderness are spoken of, not as rest, but as their "wanderings." And, indeed, the providence of God is ever busy to prevent his people from settling down here as if it were their rest. Hence the disquiet and trouble, the "black care" which enters every abode—the palatial as well as the poorest; the loss and bereavement, all that which the Bible calls the "stirring up the nest,"—all is for the purpose of reminding us that this is *not* our rest, and to induce us—so slow, generally, to be induced—to seek the better country, even the heavenly one. Oh that men would remember this, and reckon on all these things as the necessary, indispensable, and salutary, if severe, conditions of our present lot ! They would then be far less hard to bear, and would more readily fulfil their mission, and serve as a spur to urge us forward in the heavenly road. And there are also—

II. PERILS BELONGING TO THIS PILGRIMAGE. One we have now glanced at—the persistent temptation to make the wilderness a home; to so bring the world into the Church, as that the Church itself should become a world ; so to mingle the worldly with the religious life, that the latter should partake more of the former than the former of the latter. This is no imaginary peril, but one actual and visible, and yielded to in cases not a few. And another is *the failure of faith.* Ah, what trouble came to Israel of old from this one fatal fountain ! Their miserable record of sinning and repenting, which went on almost from the day they left Egypt till the day they entered Canaan, caused that all that time should be branded with the reproachful name of "the day of provocation in the wilderness." And it was all owing to their persistent unbelief. And the like peril exists still. Without doubt the difficulties of unbelief are greater than those of faith ; but these latter are so great and pressing, oftentimes, that faith well-nigh suffers shipwreck. It is easy, comparatively, for the comfortable and well-to-do, in whose even tenor of life little occurs to ruffle or disturb, much less distress—it is easy for such to say fine things about faith, and to censure and condemn those for not believing whose whole life is one long trial of faith ; but let those who thus condemn be themselves likewise tried, and then it is probable that their condemnations will gradually change into comprehension, and that into sympathy with, and that into actual sharing of, their brothers' unbelief. Yes, this is a real peril of our wilderness-condition, and it is one which, if we do not conquer, it will conquer us. It is this which gives force to another peril—the temptation *to go back to Egypt*, to return to the world which we have avowedly forsaken. Israel was on the point of doing this, and often looked longingly back to the lives they had left. And some yield to it. How many are there who apostatize—leave the Church of Christ, and become, to all intents and purposes, what they were before they entered it, if not worse! Such are some of the perils of the wilderness, from all which may God in his great mercy deliver us! But—

III. The privileges and blessings of the wilderness-condition are far more than either its privations or perils. Look back to that ancient record which tells of God's favour to Israel when they were in the wilderness, for the types of the like favour which he shows towards his people now. 1. Think of *their security*. The free air of the wilderness played upon them instead of the stifling heat of the valley of the Nile. They were on the high mountain plateau of Sinai, wandering over its grassy Alps, on which their flocks and herds freely fed, and over which the mountain breezes played. And they had seen their enemies dead on the sea-shore; they had no longer any fear of them. Their bondage was over, and they were free. And if *we* be the Lord's redeemed people, and have trusted in Christ our Passover, who was sacrificed for us, if we be of that blood-besprinkled band, then we, too, are free. The guilt of sin, the tyranny and torture of sin, torment us no more. Ours is " the glorious liberty of the children of God," and we stand fast in " that liberty wherewith Christ has made his people free." 2. *Unfailing sustenance*, too, was theirs, and is ours. He fed them with angels' food; he gave them bread from heaven to eat. The manna fell morning by morning, and they all drank of the water from the smitten rock, which, for its perpetual, free, full-flowing streams, was so fit a type of Christ, that St. Paul says of it, " which rock *was* Christ." The antitype of all this in the spiritual sustenance—the bread of life, the water of life, the communion of his body and blood, and the manifold means of grace— are manifest, and his people know them, and rejoice in them day by day. 3. *Guidance*, too, was theirs. The pillar of cloud by day, and the pillar of fire by night,—" so it was always." And he guides *us* by his counsel. His Word is " a lamp unto our feet, and a light unto our path." By the promptings of his Holy Spirit, by the indication of his providence, he causes us to "know the way wherein we should walk," and makes "plain our path before our feet." None who seek that miss it; for those who "commit " their " way unto the Lord," he does " bring it to pass." 4. *Instruction*, more- over, was given Israel. God gave them his holy Law. To them were committed " the oracles of God." And so likewise to us, in his Word, the Holy Scriptures, which are able to make us " wise unto salvation." 5. Nor must we forget that great privilege—*the presence of God with them*. God " tabernacled amongst them." In that sacred tent, hovering over the ark of the covenant, rested the cloud of glory, the visible sign of him who " dwelt between the cherubim." St. John teaches us that this was the type of the yet more blessed fact, the incarnation of him who was " made flesh and tabernacled amongst us," and who now, by his Spirit, is with us evermore. In our hallowed moments of communion do we not know that he is with us? Cannot we see his face, hear his voice, feel the touch of his hand, behold the radiance of his countenance? It is so, and we know it. 6. Finally, they had *a bright, sure, and ever-nearing hope* of the rest God had promised them. Every day brought them " a day's march nearer home." More surely is this true of us than it was of Israel. For they were made, for their unbelief, to turn back and go over the way again, which can hardly be said of us. And ours is no earthly Canaan, but the heavenly rest, the "inheritance of the saints in light."

Conclusion. Shall, then, the privations or perils of the wilderness make us think lightly of these wondrous privileges; much less shall they make us abandon them? Ah no! Gladly will we bear all that now may pain or distress, comforted—as surely we ought to be—by the presence, the promise, and the power of God.—S. C.

Ver. 11.—*The holy war.* " They overcame him by the blood of the Lamb," etc. Without attempting to identify " Michael and his angels," or " the dragon and his angels," or the "heaven" where no longer "place" was "found any more" for them; nor attempting to explain exactly what is meant by the dragon being "cast out into the earth," or how he "accused" the "brethren . . . before our God day and night "—what all this means none know; but we may take the text as telling of that holy war which all Christians have to wage, and of the weapons whereby they overcome. Note—I. THE PEOPLE WHO OVERCAME. Those spoken of: 1. *Stand for the whole Church of God*, the whole company of the redeemed. " There is no discharge in this war." Not one will be in glory by-and-by who has not waged, who has not won, this holy war. We, as they, must take our part. And: 2. *They did as we must.* We paint fancy pictures of the saints in glory, as if they were beings different from ourselves, and had never known the strain and stress of life as we know them. But they did know it all. Christ, our Lord, was "in all things made like unto his brethren," and therefore all of them have the common characteristics of this warfare upon them. Only: 3. *The lot of those specially referred to here was harder than ours.* Had St. John lived in our days of quiet ease, when persecution, much less death, for Christ's sake is a thing unknown or most rare, he would hardly have used imagery of so tremendous a kind as he has here. But it was because the trial was so terrible for all those "who would live godly in Christ Jesus," the foe so fierce and cruel and strong in those dreadful days during which St. John wrote, that imagery so vivid, startling, and terrific is made use of. But it would be affectation if we were to say our lot to-day is as theirs was in St. John's day. How much more, then, may God require from us than from them! Will he obtain it? 4. In this holy war *they all fought.* It was not merely appointed for all, but accepted by all of them. They did not refuse or retreat from it. That was not their way. Like as the brave little drummer-boy, when captured by the French army, was bidden sound the "retreat," he replied that he did not know how to, for the British army never retreated; so may it be said of every true soldier of Christ's army—they never retreat. 5. *And they overcame.* "Oh, remember the slaves of sin are not the children of God. If Satan has dominion over you, you are not in Christ Jesus. Where the ark of the Lord is, Dagon must fall upon his face and be broken. 'That which is born of God overcometh the world.' Are we, then, resisting? are we conquering? Do not let us deceive ourselves. If sin is our master, we perish. Grace *must reign* in us, or we are wretched indeed. Holiness is not a luxury for the few, it is a necessity for all."

II. THE POWER IN VIRTUE OF WHICH THEY OVERCAME. It is said that this was: 1. *By the blood of the Lamb,* i.e. in virtue of, on account of, on the ground of, that blood. Now this is so because the blood of the Lamb is: (1) *The basis of our peace.* There must be steady standing-ground if a man is to fight. The engineer is very careful to have firm foundation for his work. And if we are to contend in this warfare, our souls must be at peace in regard to our acceptance with God. The torture of doubt and the torment of fear will be fatal to our accomplishing aught worthy of the name. We *must* have peace with God; and we have this only in virtue of Christ's atoning sacrifice. (2) *The antidote of our sin.* Many think the doctrine of full, free forgiveness through the blood of Christ a doctrine that encourages men in sin. They argue that what is so freely forgiven will be freely incurred. The elder son in the parable thought it was scandalous that his young ne'er-do-well of a brother should be so freely forgiven by his father, and so " he was angry, and would not go in." And there have ever been people who have thought this. But we appeal to the records of the Church. Who have been the most faithful, the most pure, the most Christ-like? Has it not been they who have clung, like Paul did, to this blessed truth with all their hearts? And we appeal to experience. Is it not the memory of our crucified Lord that is mighty to the purification of the heart? Can the recollection of his love and the love of sin abide together? It is impossible. So does the blood of Christ cleanse us from all sin. (3) *Worketh in us patience.* How this is needed, in such a warfare as that which the much-tried believer has to wage, is evident. Blessed is he that endureth. But what an aid to such patient enduring is found in the example of our Lord! We think of him in all his holy meekness; how "as a sheep before her shearers is dumb," etc. And as we contemplate that perfect pattern of patient enduring of wrong, how our own trials and sorrows become little, and less and less in comparison with his! (4) *The inspiration of our love.* " Alexander, Cæsar, Charlemagne, and myself," said Napoleon,

REVELATION.

12

"founded great empires; but upon what did the creations of our genius depend? Upon force. Jesus alone founded his empire upon love, and to this very day millions would die for him." Thus does the blood of the Lamb become to us a power indeed, in virtue of which we overcome. 2. *The word of their testimony.* This is joined on to that which we have but now spoken of. For the blood of the Lamb, unseen, unbelieved, unaccepted, will do no one any good, will aid no one to overcome; but it is when that blood is seen, believed, accepted, and *confessed* by the word of their testimony, the open avowal, the good confession—then, in virtue of this, the Father confesses them. In response to the word of their testimony goes forth the word of his power, and they become mighty through God. Committing ourselves to any course, breaking down the bridges, burning the ships that would help us to retreat—such conduct greatly strengthens purpose and resolve. And so, when by spoken word of testimony for Christ we have committed ourselves to follow and serve him, the very fact that we have done this strengthens us and gives us fresh force for his service. Both by way of Divine reward, and by way of natural consequence such word of testimony would help to overcome.

III. THE PROOF OF THE OVERCOMING. "They loved not their lives unto the death." They went on resisting, when not only it involved much suffering and distress, but even when it involved death itself. That is the meaning. And what proof of overcoming is there comparable to this? As at Waterloo, when the English forces endured, all that long summer Sunday, the fierce and incessant cannonading of the French, together with their repeated charges, led as they were by the most famous of the marshals of France, what did such endurance show but that they were *not* to be conquered? And so the resistance told of in Christ's holy war—the loving "not our lives unto," etc.—this shows that *we* are not to be conquered, but will conquer, will overcome. If we see a man swerve, and edge back, and shift his ground, and retreat, that is not a proof of victory, but vanquishment. But he who is steadfast, immovable, even though death threaten, neither sin nor Satan will ever conquer him. Are we giving this proof of our really belonging to the number of the overcoming ones? When the adversary assails us, as we know he does, do we or does he gain the victory—which? Let us not think that there is any other proof of our being victors at last beside this one of our being, in the main, victors now. It will not do to rely on anything else, however specious, however plausible, however popular. It is in the overcoming *now* that we have the evidence that we shall be victors at the end. And that we may now overcome, let us draw near unto our crucified Lord, and come under the influence of his unspeakable love. And confess him. So shall our text then become true of us, as God grant it may be of us all!—S. C.

Ver. 12.—*Satan's rage so great because his time so short.* "The devil is come down unto you, having great wrath," etc. The text—

I. ASSUMES THE EXISTENCE OF SATAN. Many question the reality of any such being, but: 1. *We may ask—Why should it not be?* (1) We ascribe all effects to given causes. Instinctively we do this. A child hears a noise, and at once looks round to find out the cause. (2) And we see many evil effects, sad, dreadful ones, and we are therefore led to look for *their* cause. (3) The same argument that tells against the existence of the evil one tells equally against the existence of One who is the All-good, that is, God. If there be no prince of evil, there is no "Author and Giver of all good." If it be said our own nature is sufficient to account for all the evil we find, then it may be said our own nature is sufficient to account for all the good we find. (4) It is not sufficient to say that evil is the mere absence of good—a negative, not a positive quality. That only pushes the question further back, and leads us to ask—Why should the absence of one quality cause such wretchedness in those surroundings which it has left? If the earth had not been made incapable of light apart from the sun, there would be no darkness. Darkness, therefore, and evil also, require a cause, are a distinct creation. 2. *The Bible affirms such existence.* Take but one instance out of the many affirmations of this truth. Our Lord taught us to pray, "Lead us not into temptation, but deliver us from *the evil one.*" He had just come away from fearful conflict with that evil one, and therefore bids us thus pray. If our Lord's words, and those of his apostles, do not teach the personality and real existence of Satan, then no language could be devised that would teach it. **3. *And it is good news—a gospel.*** For evil being summed up in a person, in one head, destroy that, as it shall be destroyed, and evil ceases to be (cf. story of the Roman emperor, who wished that all Rome had but one neck, that he might destroy it at a blow; in a very real sense it is thus with the kingdom of evil). Satan broke as a wolf into the fold—he has no rightful inherent place therein—and he can be driven forth, or destroyed by the good Shepherd, and will be.

II. TEACHES US THAT THE POWER OF SATAN IS LIMITED. It would be dreadful to think otherwise. In dark moments men are tempted so to think. Pessimism so thinks. And it may be asked—Why should not evil be eternal as well as good? The whole doctrine of evolution is against it. We see perpetually the lower forms of life giving place to the higher, the less good to the better. It is thus in all departments of life. The fittest survives. The unfit disappears. Therefore we believe in the limit taught by the text. The whole Bible asserts it. To teach it is almost the Bible's *raison d'être.* And whilst on the most reasonable hypothesis—that our life here is but a school, an education—we can explain, at least to a large extent, the presence of evil in its varied forms, notwithstanding, and even because, infinite wisdom and power and goodness are at the head of all things; but if the devil be head of all, then there is no accounting for the much and manifold good that we know exists and increases day by day. Believing, therefore, that beneficence reigns, evil must have an end.

III. EXPLAINS THE VIRULENCE OF EVIL EXISTENT AMONGST MEN. It says it is because Satan is in "great wrath, knowing that," etc. Such representation is in keeping with the malignant character which the Bible ever attributes to, and which must belong to, Satan. See in the Gospel narratives, when commanded to go forth from those he had taken possession of, with what violence he maltreats them, throwing them down, tearing them, casting them into convulsions, etc. It is that which Satan would and does do. And in Christian experience there is the counterpart of this (cf. Bunyan's ' Pilgrim's Progress ').

IV. LEADS US TO ASK—WHEREFORE ARE WE TOLD ALL THIS? It was and is : 1. *To prevent dismay, bewilderment, and despair.* One can understand how not a few would be, for many yet are, fastened upon by these foes of faith. 2. *To inspire hope and courage, patience and trust.* How calculated to render us this high service these teachings are! 3. *That we may tell them to others.* Many yet are sitting in the land of darkness and the shadow of death, not knowing that *he* hath come who shall destroy " death, and him that hath the power of death, that is, the devil." " Go, preach my gospel, saith the Lord." 4. *To set us on our guard,* and to make us more heedful of the commands of Christ, the Captain of our salvation, in whom abiding, neither death nor hell can work us harm.—S. C.

Vers. 1—6.—*Signs.* It has been wisely said, " The Revelation of St. John gives no regularly progressive disclosure of the future, advancing in unbroken series from beginning to end; but it falls into a number of groups, which, indeed, supplement each other, every successive vision giving some other aspect of the future, but which are still formally complete in themselves, each proceeding from a beginning to an end." We have but just heard the accents of the shout of final triumph. Now we are thrown back again to scenes of strife and conflict—the prevailing condition until the end cometh. This section is preparative. The agents in the great strife are set before us in symbolical form—" signs." The things signified it behoves us to seek to know.

I. THE FIRST IS THE SIGN OF " A WOMAN ARRAYED WITH THE SUN, AND THE MOON UNDER HER FEET, AND UPON HER HEAD A CROWN OF TWELVE STARS." In this we are to see a symbolical representation of the Zion of God—the Church; not the Christian in contradiction to the Jewish; but the true Israel of God—under the Old and perpetuated in New Testament times. Not an unfamiliar figure of both Old and New Testaments to represent the Church as a woman, whether a bride or a mother (Isa. liv. 5, 6; ch. xxi. 2, 9). Is the sun that glory of God which now lightens the holy city ; and the moon the previous, the lesser light which ruled the comparative night before the morning star appeared ? The crown of the Church is ever the twelve tribes supplanted by the twelve apostles of the Lamb.

II. THE SECOND SIGN IS THE MAN-CHILD BORN OF THE WOMAN. Christ in his human nature, born of that Church which for so long before his coming endured the pangs of travail. From the bosom of the people of God, Christ according to the flesh came. This is he of whom it is declared, " Thou art my Son; this day have I begotten thee. Ask of me . . . thou shalt rule them with a rod of iron."

III. THE THIRD SYMBOL OR SIGN IS "A GREAT RED DRAGON, HAVING SEVEN HEADS AND TEN HORNS, AND ON HIS HEADS SEVEN DIADEMS." The interpretation of this is given explicitly in ver. 9. The seven heads may fitly represent the multiplied worldly powers which the evil one brings against Christ and his Church, and in the ten horns may be hidden a reference to that great world-power which, in the days of St. John, sought, as the agent of Satan, to destroy the Church of Christ. The whole scene is expressive of the great powers which from the beginning wage war with the Lamb.

IV. A FOURTH SIGN IS FOUND IN THE ATTITUDE OF THE RED DRAGON BEFORE THE WOMAN, SEEKING TO DESTROY HER CHILD. But the Divine care defends him, and the woman flees into the wilderness—" a place prepared," and that " they may nourish her."

Let the whole for our instruction resolve itself into a teaching concerning: 1. *The habitual antagonism of the great powers of evil to him who is the Church's Lord and Son.* The whole book portrays the strife between the great antagonistic powers—light and darkness, sin and holiness, Christ and Satan—" the proper factors of history." This vision is, for us, one of warning and admonition. We learn the conditions on which we hold life. Our hearts are the battle-ground, and for dominion over them the two forces contend. Our duty is plain. 2. *The Divine care for the Church.* The " wilderness " is not a place of danger, but of safety. The city, with its corruption, is the deadly place. True, the wilderness affords not luxury; but luxury is danger. In the wilderness the Church is fed and nourished. God has prepared the conditions of safety for his Church during the times of the great strife which is afterwards to be detailed. Then let the lowly disciple have both faith and hope. The Lord will defend him in the day of battle, and will nourish him unto eternal life.—R. G.

Vers. 7—12.—*War and triumph.* The heavenly things ("in heaven ") are again represented by a battle—a war. There is ever contention on the earth between those forces that are evil and those that are Divine. The history of the human race is the history of an undying struggle—a struggle between the heavenly and the earthly elements; the good and the bad; the flesh and the spirit. Here the whole contending forces are leagued under *two great captains,* " Michael " and " the dragon." " Michael and his angels going forth to war with the dragon; " and " the dragon warred and his angels." There is no difficulty in deciphering their names. " Michael " is the angel of the Lord—" *Who is like God.*" It is he who enters " the strong man's house, and spoils his goods; " he that " brings to nought him that hath the power of death, that is, the devil; " he who " was manifested for this purpose, that he might destroy the works of the devil." Yea, it is he, the " King of kings and Lord of lords." And the dragon is expressly affirmed (ver. 9) to be " the old serpent, he that is called the Devil and Satan." This scene is the central scene of the entire book, and represents the ceaseless strife. *The issue* is not doubtful. For the comfort of the Church, in all ages of her strife, " the great voice in heaven " proclaims " the salvation, and the power, and the kingdom of our God, and the authority of his Christ." The struggle is elsewhere depicted. Here is the simple word of triumph. 1. " They [the dragon and his angels] prevailed not." 2. They were cast out: " Neither was their place found any more in heaven." 3. They were utterly routed : " The great dragon was cast down," " and his angels were cast down with him." 4. The triumphant reign of the Redeemer follows : " Now is come the salvation, and the power, and the kingdom of our God, and the authority of his Christ." The words of the great chorus rise to our lips, " And he shall reign for ever and ever." 5. The accuser is silenced : " Who is he that condemeth ? " 6. The triumph is traced to its true source. (1) " They overcame him because of the blood of the Lamb, and (2) because of the word of their testimony; " and (3) because of their entire self-devotion : " And they loved not their life even unto death." 7. The consequent heavenly jubilation : "Therefore rejoice, O heavens, and ye that dwell in them." Truly he is blessed who reads and understands these words. Herein the final triumph of the heavenly over the earthly, the sensual, the devilish, is distinctly depicted and undeniably affirmed.—R. G.

Vers. 13—17.—*Safety in Satanic persecution.* The anticipated defeat—a defeat already effected in the Divine counsels—excites the wrath of the dragon, who reads assuredly his own condemnation and subjugation in that "blood of the Lamb" which the hands of his own "cruel and wicked" ones shed. The time of his power is limited; it is "a short time." Satan will rage his hour, and persecute the woman. Thus we are brought back to the earlier part of the vision, and we behold—

I. THE SATANIC PERSECUTION OF THE CHURCH OF GOD. John is speaking out of the depths to the Church in all ages, during which the same virulent spirit shall vent itself. How often has the little flock had to look upon these words, when the ravenous wolf has scattered and devoured and torn! It must needs be that persecutions come. The heavenly spirit meets with so great an opposition in the earthly, that there can be no concord. The great promise made to the demand, "What shall we have therefore?" closes with the dread announcement—"with persecutions." It is ever so; but not only so.

II. THE DIVINE PROTECTION OF THE PERSECUTED CHURCH. The Lord provides for his own: "Not a hair of your head shall perish." The safety of the Church is represented by her dwelling and nourishment in the wilderness. The persecuted Church flies unto her place. God has prepared for her a place of safety. She flies with wings he too has given. Ah! he "bears on eagles' wings" as of old. He has provided a place—rather a condition, or state—on earth, for his own. It is one of endurance. It could not be one of luxurious self-indulgence, which the city-life would represent "They loved not their lives." It is a condition of suffering, of denial, and privation. They take up the cross. The words are so interwoven with our common speech, that the figure is become familiar to us all. But God "nourishes" his people in their wilderness-life. He feeds them with manna—bread from heaven. He leaves not, neither does he forsake them. The old words come to our thoughts: "They shall dwell safely in the wilderness;" "I will allure her, and bring her into the wilderness, and speak comfortably unto her;" "Who is this that cometh up from the wilderness, leaning upon her Beloved?" It is the place of discipline and training and hardship, of testing and putting to the proof. But it is the place of blessing. Through it he leadeth his people like a flock. He goeth before them, and is their Rearward—their Defence and Salvation. He will safely and gently lead them even to the land of promise. The wilderness-days shall end. There is a limit. It is but for "a time, and times, and half a time."—R. G.

Vers. 1—6.—*Social Christhood and social fiendhood.* "And there appeared a great wonder in heaven," etc. What strange objects the human imagination can create, or in a passive state receive! What a remarkable dream or vision this is of the apostolic hermit on Patmos! "A woman arrayed with the sun, with the moon beneath her feet, and a crown of twelve stars around her head, brings forth a man-child. A huge scarlet dragon with ten horns and seven diademed heads, whose tail sweeps after it the third part of the stars to the earth, stands before her to devour the child the moment it is born, since the child is to rule the nations with a rod of iron. But the child is snatched up to the throne of God, and the woman flies into the wilderness, where she is nourished for twelve hundred and sixty days." I shall take this strange creature of the imagination as I have taken the other visions—not to represent things of which we know nothing, but to *illustrate some important realities* with which we are more or less acquainted. There are two subjects here—(1) social *Christhood,* and (2) social *fiendhood.*

I. SOCIAL CHRISTHOOD. By "social Christhood" I mean the existence of Christ in a human society, or in a community of men. I use this language in preference to the term "Church," for that term now, alas! seldom represents Christhood, but often the reverse. The expressions in the Episcopal community, "our Church," and, in the Nonconformist domain, "our Churches," are, alas! far enough from representing Christ, either in his doctrines, ethics, or spirit. *Self-sacrificing love* is the essence of Christhood; but where do we find that, either in "our Church" or "our Churches"? Christhood is peace, eternal antipathy to all anger, resentment, ambition, war. But "our Church" gives war a sanction, a licence, a blessing. The word "Church," therefore, in its conventional sense, I repudiate as a calumny on Christ. Using this vision, therefore, to illustrate *social Christhood*, two remarks are suggested concerning the society or community in which Christ lives and works. 1. *It is glorious.* "A woman clothed [arrayed] with the sun, and the moon under her feet, and upon her head a crown of twelve stars" (ver. 1). It is encircled with the solar beams of Divine truth. Beneath the feet is the world. It treads down all worldliness in its spirit and aims. Around its brow, as a peerless diadem, are twelve stars. The *true* Church as a community of Christly men—Christly in idea, spirit, and pursuit—is the most glorious object under the grand heavens. It reveals more of God than all the globes that roll through immensity. It is a *glorious* Church. The conventional Church is a crawling sycophant; the true Church is a crowned sovereign. 2. *It is multiplying.* "She being with child cried, travailing in birth, and pained to be delivered" (ver. 2). The true Church is not sterile or barren, but otherwise; it is fecundant and multiplying. Three remarks are suggested concerning its offspring : (1) It is brought forth in pain. "In pain to be delivered." "All life," it has been said, "dawns in anguish, according to the fiat (Gen. iii. 16)." There is an anguish of the Church which Christ laid upon her; it is the law of her life that she must bring forth Christ to the world, but she cannot work deliverance without knowing suffering. Paul speaks of himself as "travailing in birth." Who knows the anguish of those earnestly engaged in endeavouring to form Christ in men, and to bring him forth? What is genuine, personal religion but Christ in men, working within them to "will and to do his own good pleasure"? (2) It is brought forth to govern. "And she brought forth a man-child who was to rule all nations with a rod of iron" (ver. 5). Every Christly convert is a ruler—is born to rule. Servility and flunkeyism in all its forms are foreign to its instincts and spirit. His instincts and bearing are imperial. All the offspring of the true Church are kings as well as "priests unto God." (3) It is destined for Divine fellowship. "And her child was caught up unto God, and to his throne" (ver. 5). Whatever might be the trials of the truly Christly, here is the end. Sublime destiny this. "God hath raised us up together, and made us sit together in heavenly places in Christ Jesus." Though the mother had in her trials and persecutions to flee unto the "wilderness," even there she was secure. "She had a place prepared of God."

II. SOCIAL FIENDHOOD. Not only is there a society on earth in which Christ is, but there is a society in which the devil is. "And there appeared another wonder in heaven; and behold a great red dragon, having seven heads," etc. There is as truly a social fiendhood as there is a social Christhood. The "great red dragon," the old serpent, the "prince of the power of the air," works in the children of disobedience everywhere. Two facts are suggested by the highly symbolic and probably uninterpretable description here given of this fiend in human society. 1. *His possession of enormous power.* (1) Enormous power of *intellect.* "Seven heads." The devil has a larger amount of human intellect at his command than Christ; sevenfold, peradventure, more. (2) Enormous power of *execution.* "Ten horns." Horns are the emblems of force. How mighty is the devil amongst men! He works in all the navies and armies of the world. (3) Enormous power of *empire.* "Seven crowns [diadems] upon his heads." The human world abounds with chiefs and princelets, and kings and queens; but in how many is there Christhood? The "great red dragon" seems to master most, if not all; the "kingdom of Satan" is all but world-wide. (4) Enormous power of *mischief.* "And his tail drew [draweth] the third part of the stars of heaven, and did cast them to the earth." There are stars in the moral firmament of the human soul, stars of social love, of reverent piety, of moral intuition, of spiritual insight, of infinite worship. These stars Satan sweeps away, and leaves us to grope our way in nocturnal gloom. Where are these stars seen in the political management of England to-day? Truly we are walking in darkness and have no light.[1] 2. *His determined antagonism to Christhood.* It is said, "The dragon stood before the woman which was ready to be delivered, for to devour her child as soon as it was born." It is against Christ in his true Church, Christ in his few but multiplying progeny, that this "great red dragon" stood.

CONCLUSION. This determined and active antagonism between social Christhood and social fiendhood is a commentary on the old text, "I will put enmity between thee and

[1] Read in the journals of the time the conduct of our army amongst the Soudanese; also a little work entitled, 'Spoiling the Egyptians.'

the woman, and between thy seed and her seed." It explains, moreover, all domestic conflicts, all political battlings, and national wars. Evil and good are at war on this earth. This is the grand campaign, inspiring and explaining all other feuds.—D. T.

Vers. 7—11.—*The great campaign.* "And there was war in heaven," etc. There is undoubtedly "war in heaven"—in the *heaven of our being.* War in the soul individually, war in the soul collectively, war within and war without. We "wrestle not against flesh and blood, but against principalities and powers of this world; against wickedness in high places." The vision brings to our notice the contending *armies* and the contending *issues.*

I. THE ARMIES IN THE CONTEST. Who are the armies? "Michael and his angels fought [going forth to war] against the dragon; and the dragon fought [warred] and his angels" (ver. 7). Many expositors will tell us all about Michael and the dragon and their angels, but I cannot. I take them as the ever-acting *representatives of good and evil.* Both have their leaders, their Michaels, and their dragons with their respective followers or angels. Christ and his disciples represent the one. He is the "Captain of salvation;" all his disciples are enlisted as his soldiers, they are inspired with his purpose and fight under his banner. The "dragon," called the devil and Satan, and his votaries, represent the other. There is not a man who breathes who is not actively engaged in one or other of those armies. The grand question to determine is, "Who is on the Lord's side?"—the side of moral reality, right, and benevolence. "He that is not with me is against me."

II. THE ISSUES OF THE CONTEST. 1. *The one army was utterly discomfited.* What became of them? "And prevailed not; neither was their place found any more in heaven" (ver. 8). The prince of this world is cast out. A Stronger than he has entered the palace, and he is overcome, and "hath taken from him all his armour wherein he trusted, and divided his spoils."

> "Him, the Almighty power
> Hurl'd headlong flaming from the ethereal sky,
> With hideous ruin and combustion, down
> To bottomless perdition; there to dwell
> In adamantine chains and penal fire
> Who durst defy the Omnipotent to arms."
> (Milton.)

2. *The other army was sublimely triumphant.* Observe: (1) The triumphant song. "And I heard a loud [great] voice saying in heaven, Now is come salvation, and strength [power], and the kingdom of our God" (ver. 10). The celestial pæan proclaims the deliverance of man, the reign of God, and the adoration of Christ, and portrays in graphic delineation the miserable victim as the "accuser of our brethren before God day and night" (ver. 10). (2) The triumphant weapons. How was the victory won? (*a*) By the life of Christ. "The blood of the Lamb." What meaneth this? (*b*) By the Word of truth. "By the word of their testimony" (ver. 11). The Divine Word is the all-conquering sword. (*c*) By self-sacrificing love. "They loved not their lives unto the death" (ver. 11). Self-sacrificing love is the inspiring spirit in this warfare. "The God of peace shall bruise Satan under your feet shortly" (Rom. xvi. 20).

CONCLUSION. Evil on this earth, though it is strong, has the multitude and the empire on its side. Although it has lived long, won victories, and is active and vigorous to this hour, it will not live for ever. Its doom is sealed, its head is bruised, its limbs are withering, and its death approaches. What Christ himself saw will one day be witnessed by an adoring universe. "I saw Satan fall like lightning," etc.—D. T.

Ver. 11.—*Moral conquest won through Christ.* "They overcame him by the blood of the Lamb." It is trite, but ever solemnly true, to say that life is a combat. Moral antagonists of the soul meet us everywhere in all departments of life, circles of society, spheres of action. Nay, they rise up within us. These can be only overcome by the "blood of the Lamb," that is, by the self-sacrificing life of Christ.

I. IT IS THROUGH HIS BLOOD (OR LIFE) THAT WE GET OUR ANTAGONISM TO MORAL EVIL ROUSED. Where do we learn the turpitude, the enormity, the ruinousness of sin, as we learn it in the cross? There, indeed, "sin appears exceeding sinful." When we are enabled to look upon it in the light of that cross, the whole soul rises in determined opposition to it.

II. IT IS THROUGH HIS BLOOD (OR LIFE) THAT WE GET OUR WEAPONS SUPPLIED. What are the weapons with which evil is to be restored? 1. *A clear knowledge of the right.* It is by right alone that wrong can be put down. His life was the intelligible embodiment, and the all-convincing demonstration of moral right. 2. *An inflexible love for the right.* Right as an idea is no weapon. But right as a love becomes a triumphant implement in this warfare.

III. IT IS THROUGH HIS BLOOD (OR LIFE) THAT WE GET OUR COURAGE INSPIRED. In this warfare we require a courage unflagging and invincible—a courage impelling us to fight, even to the death. Whence cometh this? Only from Christ. His self-sacrificing spirit is the soul of all true courage.—D. T.

Vers. 12—17.—*The defeatability of the devil.* "Therefore rejoice, ye heavens, and ye that dwell in them. Woe to the inhabiters of the earth and of the sea!" etc. This portion of John's vision *illustrates* four facts of great importance and of vital interest to all men.

I. THAT MIGHTY AS IS THE MASTER-FIEND OF EVIL, HE IS NOT PROOF AGAINST DEFEATS. "Therefore rejoice, ye [O] heavens, and ye that dwell in them" (ver. 12). 1. *Here is a defeat implied.* The efforts of this matchless fiend, however wisely directed and mightily wrought, are evermore exposed to failure. There is nothing *permanent in error,* there is *no stability in wrong.* All systems untrue to fact and unrighteous in principle are but houses on the sand of time. The laws of the universe flow in ever-increasing volume against wrong. The devil is truly a defeatable agent; he has no power over those who are prepossessed with goodness. "The prince of this world cometh, and findeth nothing in *me.*" The command is, "Resist the devil, and he will flee from you." As light extends and virtue grows, all schemes of wrong, political, social, and religious, crack to pieces and tumble to ruin. 2. *Here is a defeat righteously exultable.* "Rejoice, ye heavens." In whatever heaven this defeat is witnessed, whether in the *individual soul* or in the *social circle,* it is a reason for rejoicing. In every error corrected, in every prejudice crushed, in every unholy purpose broken, in every impure impulse conquered, there comes to the soul the command, "Rejoice, ye heavens." It is the *joy of the prisoner quitting his cell, of the patient returning to health.*

II. THAT GREAT AS HIS DEFEATS MAY BE, THEY DO NOT QUENCH HIS ANIMOSITY. "Woe to the inhabiters of the earth and of the sea! for the devil is come down unto you, having great wrath, because he knoweth that he hath but a short time." Hunted from one arena, he enters another, flaming with indignation, and the more so as he feels that his time for work is shortening. "He hath but a short time." "When the unclean spirit is gone out of a man, he walketh through dry places, seeking rest, and finding none." He is "a roaring lion, going about seeking whom he may devour." As every defeat enfeebles his power, contracts his reign, and decreases his opportunities, his malign nature becomes more intense in hatred. Like the ravenous beast of the desert, his failure to fasten his tusks in one victim whets his appetite for another. Evil is insatiable.

III. THAT HIS ANIMOSITY IS ESPECIALLY DIRECTED AGAINST THE TRUE CHURCH. "And when the dragon saw that he was cast unto the earth, he persecuted the woman which brought forth the man-child" (ver. 13). Let the woman stand as an emblem of the true Church, or *Christly men collectively,* and we have before us a picture of the mighty fiend tormenting it and its progeny. We read that "the serpent cast out of his mouth water as a flood [river] after the woman" (ver. 15). And again, "The dragon was [waxed] wroth with the woman, and went [away] to make war with the remnant [rest] of her seed" (ver. 17). What on this earth doth he hate most and yearn to crush? Not politics, learning, commerce, science, literature, art. None of these as such, but the Christly in men. Wherever the Spirit of Christ is, the spirit of tenderness, humility, self-sacrificing love, this he hates and seeks to destroy. On such he "pours out water as a flood," that he may "cause them to be carried away of the flood [stream]." Who shall say what he pours forth from his mouth? *False accusations, pernicious errors, social persecutions.* etc.

IV. THAT THE TRUE CHURCH, EVEN IN TRYING CIRCUMSTANCES, IS UNDER THE SPECIAL PROTECTION OF HEAVEN. "And to the woman were given two wings of a great eagle, that she might fly into the wilderness, into her place, where she is nourished for a time, and times, and half a time, from the face of the serpent" (ver. 14). Notice: 1. *The Church is in the wilderness.* "That she might fly into the wilderness." The home of Christly men on this earth has always been more of a wilderness than a Canaan—intricate, dangerous, gloomy. 2. *Though in the wilderness, it has enormous privileges.* (1) It is endowed with *heaven-soaring power.* "To the woman were given two wings of a great eagle." It is endowed with soaring instincts and faculties. Like the eagle, the Church has the power to rise from the earth, penetrate the clouds, and bask in azure. "It can mount up on wings as eagles." (2) It has the *whole earth to serve it.* "And the earth helped the woman, and the earth opened her mouth," etc. (ver. 16). —D. T.

Ver. 16.—*Nature serving Christliness.* "The earth helped the woman." By common consent "the woman" here means redeemed humanity, or the children of God collectively, or, in other words, what is called the Church. 1. Her *appearance* is wonderful. "Clothed with the sun." 2. Her *progeny* is wonderful. "She brought forth a manchild." 3. Her *antagonist* is wonderful. The devil is the great enemy of redeemed humanity, and the description given of him indicates that he is a being of stupendous force and malice. 4. Her *influence* is wonderful. Supernatural beings engage in fierce conflict on her account. There was war in heaven. The subject here is *Nature serving Christliness.* The earth—nature—"helped the woman"—embodied Christianity. Nature helps Christliness in various ways.

I. BY ITS GRAND REVELATIONS. Nature reveals all the grand subjects that constitute the very foundation of Bible-discoveries. 1. *There is God.* All nature proclaims, not only his existence, but his personality, unity, spirituality, wisdom, goodness, power. 2. *There is law.* Every part is under the rigorous reign of law. Any infraction of nature's laws carries penalties. 3. *There is mediation.* The principle of mediation runs through all nature. One element, one agent, one being, everywhere serving another. 4. *There is responsibility.* In the human world men are everywhere recognized as responsible, men everywhere feel their responsibility. 5. *There is mystery.* There is a haze over all nature. Every part has arenas which no intellect can penetrate. The whole universe seems to float on the dark sea of mystery. Now, all these subjects which we find in nature we find also in the Bible. Hence nature comes, also, to illustrate the meaning of the Bible and confirm its truth. It is a grand parable. Hence "the earth helps the woman."

II. BY ITS MORAL IMPRESSIONS. Nature is suited to make impressions upon the earth corresponding exactly with those which Christianity essays to produce. 1. *The sense of dependence.* How infinitesimally little man feels beside the great hills, confronting the ocean billow, and under the awful stars! Amidst the majesty of Nature's appearances he feels himself to be nothing, and less than nothing. He feels borne along as a straw upon the resistless flood of destiny. 2. *Reverence.* How great does God appear in nature, in the minute as well as the vast! "An undevout astronomer is mad." There is a spirit in nature that seems to say to every thoughtful soul, "Take thy shoes from off thy feet," etc. 3. *Contrition.* The streams of Divine goodness seem to well up from every blade, flow down on every ray, beat in every wave of air, and are vocal with reproof to guilty man for his ingratitude and disobedience towards his Maker. 4. *Worship.* In reason's ear a thousand voices speak to man. "Make a joyful noise unto the Lord, sing forth the honour of his Name." Now, these are just the impressions that the gospel aims to produce; and thus nature serves Christianity by endeavouring to produce the same spiritual results; and in this way, again, "the earth helps the woman"

III. BY ITS MULTIPLIED INVENTIONS. Men, by studying nature and employing its laws, elements, and forces for their intellectual and temporal uses, have attained those arts which are highly conducive to the advancement of Christianity. 1. *There is merchandise.* Trade brings the remotest nations together in a common interest. The means for exporting commodities are available for exporting the Word of God. 2. *There is the press.* The press is an invention of nature, and an invention which is admirably suited to advance Christianity. It has already borne the gospel to the most distant part of the earth. 3. *There is painting.* The art by which man transfers the forms of nature, and embodies his own conception of beauty on the canvas. By this noble art the scenes and characters of the Bible, and even our blessed Lord himself, are brought with a vivid reality under the notice of men. 4. *There is music.* The magic art which catches the floating sounds of nature and weaves them into strains of melody that stir the deepest feelings. Never does truth come with such strange majesty to the heart as when it comes floating on the wave of melody. 5. *There is government.* Government is of the earth, earthy; but it helps Christianity. The Roman government, in the first ages, did it good service, and all civil governments that keep to their true province serve it now.—D. T.

EXPOSITION.

CHAPTER XIII.

Ver. 1.—And I stood upon the sand of the sea. The Revised Version, agreeing with ℵ, A, C, Vulgate, Syriac, Æthiopic, Armenian, Victorinus, reads ἐστάθη, "he stood." The Authorized Version follows the reading ἐστάθην, "I stood," which is found in B, P, Coptic, Andreas, Arethas. Fortunately, the point is not important. Whether St. John or the dragon stood on the edge of the sea is not material, since we are distinctly told that the ten-horned beast rose from the sea. Wordsworth aptly contrasts this station on the unstable sand in proximity to the sea, the element of commotion, with the vision of the Lamb on Mount Zion (ch. xiv. 1—5). The imagery which follows is founded upon the vision of Dan. vii. The phrase should probably be joined on to the preceding passage, as in the Revised Version. The new vision then opens in the customary manner with εἶδον, "I saw," as in ch. iv., v., vi., vii., etc. And saw a beast rise up out of the sea. Supply "I," and make this the beginning of the fresh paragraph (see above). The one beast here takes the place of the four beasts of Dan. vii., and is distinguished by the characteristics of the first three (see on ver. 2). This beast arises from the *sea*, the second beast from the *earth* (see ver. 11). They are the instruments of the woe which is denounced against the *earth* and the *sea* in ch. xii. 12. The *sea*, again, is the type of instability, confusion, and commotion, frequently signifying the ungovernable nations of the earth in opposition to the Church of God (cf. ch. xvii. 15; xxi. 1). Probably this is the beast referred to in ch. xi. 7, and (more fully) in ch. xvii. It is the power of the world which is directed towards the persecution of Christians. Having seven heads and ten horns. Nearly every manuscript has, *having ten horns and seven heads.* The order is reversed in ch. xii. 3 and xvii. 3; possibly the horns are mentioned first in this passage, because they are first seen as the beast rises from the sea.

The essential identity of this beast with the dragon of ch. xii. 3 is plainly shown. There Satan is described in his personal character; here he is described under the aspect of the persecuting power of the world. The symbolism is analogous to that found in Dan. vii., where we may find the key to the interpretation. First, the *heads* signify dominion. The head is naturally looked upon as the chief, the controlling and guiding part of the body; that part to which all the members of the body are subject. This is the idea conveyed in Dan. vii. 6. The third beast there is distinguished by the possession of four heads, and (we are immediately told) "dominion was given to it." *Seven*, as we have repeatedly seen, is the number typical of universality (cf. ch. i. 4; v. 1, etc.). The *seven heads*, therefore, are symbolical of universal dominion. In the second place, *horns* are the type of power. Thus, in Dan. vii. 7, the beast which is distinguished by the possession of the horns is described as being "diverse from all the beasts that were before it." It was "dreadful and terrible, and strong exceedingly; and it had great iron teeth: it devoured and brake in pieces, and stamped the residue with the feet of it" (cf. Deut. xxxiii. 17; Ps. cxxxii. 17; Jer. xlviii. 25, etc.) The number *ten* is the sign of completeness; not of universality or totality, but of sufficiency and abundancy for the purpose in view (cf. Gen. xviii. 32, the ten righteous wanting at Sodom; Exod. xxvii. 12, the ten pillars of the tabernacle; the ten commandments; the tithe; Ps. xxxiii. 2, etc.). The *ten horns*, therefore, denote plenitude of power. The words of this passage thus signify that the beast should possess world-wide dominion and ample power. These are the qualities ascribed to the power which Satan now directs against the "seed of the woman." At the time of the writing of the Apocalypse, this power was evidently heathen Rome; but the meaning may be extended to embrace all the forms which this world-opposition has assumed whether Roman,

Mohammedan, or Gothic, etc. It is consequently unnecessary, as it certainly seems fruitless, to attempt to interpret the *heads* and *horns* of individual nations and kings. In endeavouring to do so, many writers have imported into the description here given other details from Daniel, or deduced by themselves, for which there is no warrant in the narrative here supplied. For the same reason, it is useless to inquire into the disposition of the *ten horns* and *seven heads;* since the whole is a figure intended to convey certain ideas, and is not a description of an actual bodily form. And upon his horns ten crowns. "Ten crowns;" διαδήματα, crowns denoting sovereignty; not στέφανος, the victor's wreath. The *crowns* upon the *horns* denote the sovereign nature of the power with which the beast is invested. The nations of the world who have persecuted the Church of God have the chief rule in this world. And upon his heads the name of blasphemy. The plural ὀνόματα, "names," adopted by the Revised Version, is found in A, B, Vulgate, Coptic, Andreas, Primasius. Alford reads the singular ὄνομα, with א, C, P, Coptic, Andreas, Primasius. There is no article. Possibly each head bore a name, which was the same in each case, and which might therefore with equal propriety be described as *name* or *names.* "Upon his heads" (ἐπὶ κεφαλάς); the accusative being used (as Alford suggests) because the action of inscription carries with it a tinge of motion. In the preceding clause we have the genitive ἐπὶ κεράτων, where the preposition denotes rest. We have no hint given as to what the *name* was; the nature only is indicated. St. John very possibly had in his mind the mitre of the high priest, upon the plate of which was inscribed, "Holiness to the Lord" (Exod. xxviii. 36). It is a "name of blasphemy;" that is, the worldly power, typified by this beast, denies the Divinity and might of the true God, and exalts itself above him. Bede, Hengstenberg, etc., see the fulfilment in the assumption by the Roman emperors of titles which belong rightly only to Christ—King of kings, Divus, etc. But the application is wider. As partial fulfilments of that which will never be completely fulfilled until the end of the world, we may mention Pharaoh, when he said, "Who is the Lord, that I should obey his voice?" (Exod. v. 2); Sennacherib (2 Kings xviii.); Herod Agrippa (Acts xii. 22); as well as those since St. John's time who have blasphemed by denying the existence or omnipotence of Christ.

Ver. 2.—And the beast which I saw was like unto a leopard, and his feet were as the feet of a bear, and his mouth as the mouth of a lion. The similarity to the vision of Dan. vii. is very evident; the resemblance extending even to the language, which is here very like the LXX. version of Daniel. Cf. especially the form ἄρκος (found in all the best manuscripts) with that of the LXX. of Dan. vii. 5. In the vision of Daniel four beasts are seen rising from the sea. The first was like a *lion,* the second like a *bear,* the third like a *leopard,* the fourth was distinguished by the *ten horns.* Here the four are combined in the one appearance of the beast. The qualities which are indicated by the animals named are very generally agreed upon. The *lion* denotes lordly dominion and rule; the *bear* suggests crushing force and tenacity of purpose; the *leopard* is distinguished for its swiftness and cruel blood-thirstiness. These characteristics marked the Roman empire at the time of this vision, and this probably was the first fulfilment of the vision. The same qualities have, however, been exhibited at all times by the persecutors of the Church of God, and thus the application may be extended, and the vision represents (as Alford says) "not the Roman empire merely, but the aggregate of the empires of this world as opposed to Christ and his kingdom." And the dragon gave him his power, and his seat, and great authority; *and his throne.* The dragon and this beast are essentially one, since the latter wields all the influence of the former. The devil lost his throne in heaven; through the power of the world he temporarily regains a throne as the "prince of this world." Christ, by his incarnation, destroyed much of the personal nature of the devil's influence over men. By that the devil was completely bound as regards the righteous (cf. the interpretation of ch. xx. 2); but his power to work mischief he transfers to the nations of the world, who become his instrument for that purpose.

Ver. 3.—And I saw one of his heads as it were wounded to death; and his deadly wound was healed; *and one of his heads as though it had been slain unto death; and his death-stroke was healed.* The writer wishes to express the coexistence of two mutually antagonistic qualities. The head had received a fatal wound, and yet the beast continued to exist and exert his power. There may be a contrast and a comparison intended between the Lamb, as it had been slain, worshipped by his adoring followers, and the beast, usurping the honour due to Christ, imitating him even in the respect of having been slain, and exacting homage from those who "wondered after the beast." But the "head smitten unto death" must still possess some special significance of its own. What that is we are not plainly told; but it seems reasonable to refer it to the blow dealt to the power of Satan by the death and resurrection of Christ. It almost seemed at first as though the power of the world must succumb to the influence of the life and death of our Lord, and for a time great progress was made in the increase of the number of believers (cf. Acts ii. 41, 47). But the power of the world was not yet destroyed; it continued to exist in spite of the seemingly fatal wound. Some see in this account a reference to the destruction of the Roman pagan empire, and the establishment of the Christian empire. Others believe the blow to be that administered by Michael, when Satan was ejected from heaven. Others refer the wounded head to different individuals; *e.g.* Nero. That *one head* is wounded out of the seven probably denotes the partial nature of the wound as visible to an observer. And all the world wondered after the beast; *the whole earth wondered after the beast.* The pregnant construction. That *earth.* for which the advent of the dragon meant *woe* (ch. xii. 12), *wondered* 'at, and followed *after* the beast. The sense of *earth* must here be restricted to the followers of the world, as opposed to the followers of God.

Ver. 4.—And they worshipped the dragon which gave power unto the beast; *because he gave his authority* (Revised Version) is found in all the best manuscripts. The devil had sought to beguile Christ by offering to him all the kingdoms of the world. His efforts with men are more successful. They worship him on account of the worldly wealth and influence which he bestows. And they worshipped the beast, saying, Who is like unto the beast? who is able to make war with him? Insert "and" with Revised Version: *and who is able,* etc.? The beast usurps the homage due to God alone (cf. the song of those who had triumphed in ch. xv. 4, "Who shall not fear thee, O Lord, and glorify thy Name?" cf. also Exod. xv. 11; Micah vii. 18, etc.). The adherents of the beast thus intimate their belief in his superior prowess and his ability to succeed in his war against those who "keep the commandments of God, and hold the testimony of Jesus."

Ver. 5.—And there was given unto him a mouth speaking great things and blasphemies. So the horn which sprang from the fourth beast of Dan. vii. 8 had given to it "a mouth speaking great things." The power of the beast is, after all, only held by the consent of God, who for his own good purpose permits him to exercise it for a time. The "great things" are the promises of superior power and good, with which the devil seeks to allure men, as he did Adam and Eve at the first. All attempts to decry God's omnipotence and the power of Christ are *blasphemies.* And power was given unto

him to continue forty and two months; *or, to work forty and two months.* Again note the power is given to him; that is, he holds it only subject to the will of God. The "forty and two months," or three years and a half, signify the period of the world's existence. (For a full discussion of the subject, see on ch. xi. 2.) It is the "little time" of ch. vi. 10, 11, during which will be fulfilled the number of the saints. It is the "little season" of ch. xx. 3, during which Satan is "loosed," that is, during which he has this power to work given to him (cf. ch. xi. 2, 3; xii. 14). The different readings in this passage, though resting on insufficient authority, serve to amplify the meaning. ℵ reads ποιῆσαι ὅ θέλει, "to do what he willeth." Ποιῆσαι with πόλεμον, "to wage war," is found in B and others, and is the marginal reading of the Authorized Version, but is rightly omitted in the Revised Version.

Ver. 6.—And he opened his mouth in blasphemy against God, to blaspheme his Name, and his tabernacle, and them that dwell in heaven; *for blasphemies against God.* The balance of authority is in favour of omitting "and" (before "them"), thus making (as in the Revised Version) the last clause in apposition with the preceding: *his Name and his tabernacle, those tabernacled in heaven.* The punishment for this sin among the Jews was death by stoning (see Lev. xxiv. 16). God's servants fear his Name (ch. xi. 18). God's *tabernacle,* or temple, is the Church, in the midst of which he dwells (cf. ch. xi. 2), and which exists in the wilderness of the world for the forty and two months, and which yet exists also in heaven, honoured of God (cf. Phil. iii. 20, "For our citizenship is in heaven," Revised Version).

Ver. 7.—And it was given unto him to make war with the saints, and to overcome them. This clause is omitted in A, C, P, and some others. So in Dan. vii. 21, "The same horn made war with the saints, and prevailed against them; until the Ancient of days came, and judgment was given to the saints of the Most High." And in ch. xi. 7, "The beast that ascendeth out of the bottomless pit shall make war against them [the two witnesses], and shall overcome them, and kill them." *Overcome;* that is, apparently; so far as is seen by the world. In the same way the world overcame Christ; but by his death came victory. So in ch. ii. 10 the Church at Smyrna is encouraged by the words, "Fear none of those things which thou shalt suffer . . . be thou faithful unto death and I will give thee a crown of life." And power was given him over all kindreds, and tongues, and nations; *over every tribe, and people, and tongue, and nation.* Λαόν, "people," is inserted in every manuscript except a few cursives. The fourfold enumeration, applied to the earth, denotes the universal character of the description (cf. the four living beings, ch. iv. 6. Also ch. v. 9; vii. 9; xi. 9; xiv. 6). The same classification is adopted in the song of the redeemed (ch. v. 9), which may be contrasted with this passage. Although the power of Satan extends to every section of the nations of the earth, yet men are not irrevocably delivered into his hand. From every part of mankind men are also redeemed.

Ver. 8.—**And all that dwell upon the earth shall worship him, whose names are not written in the book of life of the Lamb;** [*every one*] *whose name hath not been written,* as in the Revised Version. "Him," αὐτόν, masculine, although referring to the neuter, θηρίον, because the personality of Satan under the figure of the beast is borne in mind. "Whose name," singular, referring to the individuals of whom the πάντες, "all," are composed. This verse states in another form what has been related in the latter part of the preceding verse. Those over whom the beast has authority are those who worship him, and whose names have not "been written in the book of life." The expression, "book of life," is found only in this book and Phil. iv. 3. In all the places where it occurs it seems to refer primarily to Christians (cf. Phil. iv. 3; ch. iii. 5; xx. 12, 15; xxi. 27; xxii. 19). At baptism the Christian's name is written in the "book of life," from which there is always a possibility of it being blotted out (ch. iii. 5). Those who are not Christians have not their name in the "book of life," but *worship* the beast, that is, pay allegiance to him. It is "the book of life of the Lamb," because it is through "the Lamb" that there exists a "book of life" for men. Slain from the foundation of the world; or, *that hath been slain.* It is natural to connect the words, "from the foundation of the world," with "slain," and not with "written." The latter course has been followed by Bengel, Düsterdieck, De Wette, Ewald, Hengstenberg, and others, and in the margin of the Revised Version, and is in accordance with ch. xvii. 8, "Whose names were not written in the book of life from the foundation of the world" (see also Matt. xxv. 34; Eph. i. 4). "The Lamb hath been slain from the foundation of the world," because from "the foundation of the world" (cf. Heb. ix. 26) his death has been efficacious for the salvation of men; and because his death "was foreordained before the foundation of the world," although manifest only in the last times (1 Pet. i. 20). What was foreknown to and ordained by God is

spoken of as having taken place. This latter sense must be the meaning if we adopt the alternative reading.

Ver. 9.—**If any man have an ear, let him hear.** This verse draws attention to the solemn declaration which follows in the succeeding verse (cf. ch. ii. 7; iii. 6; also Matt. xi. 15, etc.).

Ver. 10.—**He that leadeth into captivity shall go into captivity: he that killeth with the sword must be killed with the sword. Here is the patience and the faith of the saints.** There is a twofold difficulty in this verse: first, as to the correct text; secondly, as to the meaning. There are two chief readings. Codex A has Εἴ τις εἰς αἰχμαλωσίαν εἰς αἰχμαλωσίον ὑπάγει; literally, *if any one into captivity, into captivity he goeth;* which probably means, "If any one is ordained unto captivity, into captivity he goeth." The reading of the Textus Receptus looks like an attempt to amplify and make clear the above reading: Εἴ τις αἰχμαλωσίαν συνάγει εἰς αἰχμαλωσίαν ὑπάγει. א, B, C, have the reading of A, omitting the repetition of εἰς αἰχμαλωσίαν. This omission is easily explained by homœoteleuton, and accordingly the majority of critical editors follow Codex A. There are two passages in Jeremiah which are suggested by these words. Jer. xv. 2 reads, "Such as are for death, to death; and such as are for the sword, to the sword; and such as are for the famine, to the famine; and such as are for the captivity, to the captivity;" Jer. xliii. 11, "And deliver such as are for death, to death; and such as are for captivity, to captivity; and such as are for the sword, to the sword." Matt. xxvi. 52 may also be referred to: "All they that take the sword shall perish with the sword." The verse in the text appears to contain both the meanings of the passages referred to. The first half seems to point out that there are woes foreordained for Christians which they must undergo: "He for whom captivity is appointed must be content to suffer captivity." The next part extends the meaning, adding a warning: "You Christians must suffer these things; not only not relinquishing your faith, but also not meeting force with force; remembering always your Master's saying, 'They that take the sword shall perish with the sword.'" Then the verse concludes, "Here is [the proof of] the patience and the faith of the saints." St. John has just described to his hearers the extensive nature of the power of the world (vers. 3, 7, 8); the obvious conclusion was that captivity, etc., was the lot appointed for some of them. He has also told them of the war waged by the world against Christians, and now he adds the necessary caution against any attempt to defend themselves by the use of the sword. And thus not only their patience but their faith was to be tested. They were not only to bear patiently evils which they could not avoid, but they must have sufficient faith to enable them voluntarily to forego any opportunities which might occur to prevent their sufferings by force of arms.

Ver. 11.—And I beheld another beast. Compare the wording of this introduction with that of ver. 1. We shall find reason to interpret this *beast* as self-deceit—that form of plausibility by which men persuaded themselves into a belief that they might without harm worship the former beast. (see on following verses). It has been remarked that mention is often made of the first beast without the second (cf. ch. xi. 7; xiii. 1; xvii. 3, etc.), but never of the second without the first. This fact supports the interpretation given above. Coming up out of the earth. Perhaps in contrast with the former beast, which arose from the sea (ver. 1). In the vision of Dan. vii. the four beasts, which rise from the sea (ver. 3), are declared in ver. 17 to typify four kings which arise from the earth. It is doubtful, therefore, whether we are justified in attaching special significance to this phrase. Some writers understand thereby, "rising up from amongst settled, ordered society of men." More likely, the writer wishes to show the universal character of the temptations with which Christians are assailed; and thus one beast seems to pertain to the sea, and the other to the earth, thus dividing the whole world between them. And he had two horns like a lamb, and he spake as a dragon. That is, while simulating an appearance of Christ, his words betrayed his devilish nature. The aim of this beast throughout is to assume a plausible exterior, that men may be beguiled by him (cf. vers. 13—17). Such is the nature of that self-deceit which we believe this beast to typify. Many men, who were not to be tempted into a renunciation of Christ by the bitter persecution of the first beast, because coming in such a form they recognized easily its true nature, were nevertheless beguiled into such acts by specious reasoning and the deceit of their own hearts. Christians at all times are only too ready to be deceived by those who "by good words and fair speeches deceive the hearts of the simple" (Rom. xvi. 18). Whether as in ancient times it be merely to throw a few grains of incense upon the altar of some heathen deity, or as in modern times to conform to some common but unworthy requirement of society, men are apt to be led astray by arguments which look fair, but which as surely accomplish the devil's object as if it had been attained by direct

persecution. (On the form of the word "lamb," ἀρνίον, see on ch. v. 6.)

Ver. 12.—And he exerciseth all the power of the first beast before him; all the authority . . . in his sight (Revised Version). That is, his influence over men, though less directly asserted, is equal to that of the first beast. And he exercises this influence "in his sight," that is, by his permission and contemporaneously with the exercise of power by the first beast. So Christians both of St. John's and of our own time seek to escape direct persecution by justifying to themselves their unworthy compliance with the unrighteous requirements of the world. And causeth the earth and them which dwell therein to worship the first beast, whose deadly wound was healed. Here we have an explanation of the two preceding clauses. Though like a lamb in appearance, his words denote his deadly nature, which is shown by causing men to worship the first beast; and thus he exercises the authority of the first beast, and accomplishes his work. Those who dwell in the earth are the worldly, not faithful Christians, but those "whose names are not written in the book of life of the Lamb" (see on ver. 8). This beast causes men to worship the first beast by persuading them into a compliance with his will, and making them pay homage to him. For this reason he is called in ch. xvi. 13 the "false prophet." (For "whose deadly wound was healed," see on ver. 3.)

Ver. 13.—And he doeth great wonders. Men are apt to deceive themselves by attributing to other agencies the power to work wonders which belongs only to God himself. In St. John's time the arts of magic were used; in modern times the marvels of science often lead men to a disbelief in God. Archdeacon Lee, in his commentary, says, "We cannot doubt that there is also a reference to the wonderful power over nature which the spirit of man has attained to, and which has too often been abused to the deification of Nature and her laws, and to the disparagement of the Divine action which is ever present in creation." So that he maketh fire come down from heaven on the earth in the sight of men; that he should even make fire, etc., as in the Revised Version. We are not to understand this literally. It is given as a kind of sample of the power possessed by the beast, being a form of miracle which would be well known to St. John's readers (cf. Elijah on Carmel, 1 Kings xviii.; Korah's company, Numb. xvi. 35, etc.; also the request of SS. James and John, Luke ix. 54). The descent of fire is also frequently a sign of God's approval (cf. Gen. xv. 17; Lev. ix. 24; Judg. xiii. 19, 20; 2 Chron. vii.

1). The two witnesses possessed the power of sending forth fire (see ch. xi. 5). In this respect, therefore—in the very nature of his signs—the beast still seems to counterfeit the power of God.

Ver. 14.—And deceiveth them that dwell on the earth by the means of those miracles which he had power to do in the sight of the beast. He deceives by employing false signs, and he deceives by inducing men to believe that the worship of the first beast is allowable. Those "that dwell on the earth" are the worldly minded, as in ver. 12. "Which he had power to do" should rather be "which it was given him to do," as in the Revised Version. The power possessed by the beast does not originate with himself; he possesses it only subject to the will of God (cf. vers. 5 and 7). Thus the second beast—self-deceit—beguiles men. They accept exhibitions of power external to God as evidences of an independence and self-sufficiency which do not exist apart from God, forgetful of the fact that this power is derived from God: *it is given* by him. (For "in the sight of the beast," see on ver. 12.) Saying to them that dwell on the earth. Λέγων, "saying," masculine, agrees with the neuter θηρίον. The writer uses the masculine, as in ver. 8, because of the personified nature of the beast. It is not fair to press the word (as some writers do) into the signification that a man must be intended. "Them that dwell on the earth"—the worldly minded (*vide supra*). That they should make an image to the beast, which had the wound by a sword, and did live; *who hath the stroke of a sword, and lived,* as in the Revised Version. The masculine as before (*vide supra*). This beast suggested that men should set up an image of the first beast, not in order to pay greater honour to the first beast, but that an apparent alternative might be offered to men, so that those who hesitated to pay direct allegiance to the first beast might overcome their scruples and worship something which resembled him, while allowing them to, as it were, cheat their own consciences by persuading themselves that they were not worshipping the beast himself. These two classes of men are, of course, essentially one; they are, in reality, all followers of the beast; but still there is a difference in the manner in which they become worshippers of the beast. The distinction of the two classes seems to be kept in mind in ch. xix. 20 and xx. 4, where, however, all are included in the same condemnation. Thus the apostle teaches us that those who, by specious and plausible reasoning, who, in short, by self-deceit, allow themselves to cast in their lot with the worldly—the avowed followers of the first

beast—are equally guilty with those who openly proclaim themselves followers of the world. (On the last part of the verse, the nature of the sword-stroke, see on ver. 3.)

Ver. 15.—And he had power to give life unto the image of the beast, that the image of the beast should both speak, and cause that as many as would not worship the image of the beast should be killed; *and it was given to him to give breath,* etc. א and a number of cursives read the indicative future, ποιήσει, that is, "he [the beast] shall cause," etc. The symbolism is most probably derived from the heathen oracles. This beast is permitted *to give life,* to impart spirit to the *image;* that is, he gives it an appearance of reality which a mere image could not possess. This is the dangerous power of self-deceit. If men would face the naked truth, stripped of plausible arguments and specious resemblances, they would see that there was no reality in the ideal which they place before their minds, and their worship of which is prompted by love of the world, and the denial of God's power. Together with the attempt to deceive men into worshipping the image, is offered the alternative of death, or, should we not say, apparent death? It is only self-deceit which makes men imagine that the alternative to an acceptance of the sovereignty of Satan and the world is death. No doubt many Christians in St. John's time were thus beguiled. They deceived themselves by imagining that they must either conform to the heathen practices required of them, or suffer death; those with clearer mental vision saw that the threatened death was in reality life.

Ver. 16.—And he causeth all, both small and great, rich and poor, free and bond, to receive a mark in their right hand, or in their foreheads; *that there be given them a mark on their right hand, or upon their forehead.* Δώσῃ, "he may give," found in the Textus Receptus, is unsupported by any uncial; δῶσιν, "they may give," is read in א, A, B, C, P; and most cursives have either δῶσιν or δώσωσιν. Wordsworth translates, "give to themselves," and adds, "a remarkable sentence, intimating *compulsion* under the semblance of *choice.*" But it does not seem fair to press the meaning so far. The third plural is often used in a perfectly general way in the Apocalypse (cf. ch. xii. 6, and Moulton's Winer, p. 655), and the Revised Version is probably correct in translating by the passive (*vide supra*). Certainly the other passages in the Apocalypse, where the *mark* is mentioned, seem to show that men have absolute freedom of choice (see especially ch. xiv. 9 and xx.

4). Again the beast seeks to imitate God

(cf. ch. iii. 12, "I will write upon him my new name;" ch. xxii. 4, "His name shall be in their foreheads;" ch. vii. 3; ix. 4; xiv. 1). The idea is taken from the Mosaic customs (cf. Deut. vi. 8, "And thou shalt bind them for a sign upon thine hand, and they shall be as frontlets between thine eyes"). Some writers see also an allusion to the heathen custom of branding slaves and others who were devoted to the service of temples; and recall the fact that χαράγματα, or "cuttings," such as are here mentioned, were forbidden to the Jews (Lev. xix. 28).

Ver. 17.—And that no man might buy or sell, save he that had the mark, or the name of the beast, or the number of his name. "And" is omitted in ℵ, C, some cursives and versions and Fathers: *no man should be able to buy,* etc. A, B, C, P, and most cursives also omit ἤ, "or," before "the name," thus reading, as in the Revised Version: *save he that hath the mark, even the name of the beast, or the number of his name.* This expressly asserts what we might have gathered from the analogy of the mark of the true Christian (see on ver. 16), viz. that "the mark" was "the name" or "the number of his name." The manner in which this was fulfilled in the early ages of the Church is sufficiently notorious. Then faithfulness to the cause of Christ frequently meant banishment from friends, kindred, and home. St. John himself was feeling the effect of this at the time when he wrote these words in exile at Patmos. So, at the present day, the Jews regard as an utter alien any one of their number who embraces Christianity. So also, at the present day, the faithful Christian is often interdicted the society of the world, is declared a social nuisance, and is shunned by the worldly minded, who pay allegiance to the beast. (On the "number," see on ver. 18.)

Ver. 18.—Here is wisdom. Let him that hath understanding count the number of the beast: for it is the number of a man. The last clause has no article, ἀριθμὸς γὰρ ἀνθρώπου ἐστί. Compare the expression, "Here is the patience," etc. in ver. 10, where it relates to what precedes. Here it evidently refers to what follows. The form of expression is frequent in St. John's writings (cf. 1 John ii. 6; iii. 16, 19; iv. 10, etc.). The plain meaning seems to be that men may display their wisdom and understanding in discovering the meaning of the number of the beast. But the interpretation which Auberlen gives may be correct; viz. that as the first beast is met and vanquished by patience and faith, so this second beast is to be met by *wisdom.* This agrees with our interpretation of this second beast as

symbolizing self-deceit. St. John evidently intends that the meaning of the number should be known: "Let him that hath understanding count the number;" that is, "Let him that hath understanding discern in what sense the symbol is used." It is the "number of man;" that is, it describes symbolically something which is peculiarly a characteristic of mankind. Some writers have understood the words to mean, "the number refers to an individual man;" but the absence of the article militates against this view. Others explain, "It is a number which is to be reckoned according to man's mode of reckoning," just as in ch. xxi. 17, "a measure of a man." If this be the meaning, it leaves open the question as to what St. John meant by "the usual mode of man's reckoning." His own use of numerals throughout the Apocalypse is, as we have repeatedly seen, symbolical of general qualities, and does not indicate either individuals or exact numbers. We are justified, therefore, according to this view, in interpreting the number symbolically (*vide supra*). And his number is Six hundred three score and six. The Revised Version is better, *Six hundred and sixty and six;* it preserves the similarity of form which is found in the Greek words, ἑξακόσιοι ἑξήκοντα ἕξ, as found in A. In ℵ we have ἑξακόσιαι, etc.; in P, Andreas, ἑξακόσια. The shortened form χξϛ´ is found in B and most cursives. C, 11, and some manuscripts known to Irenæus and Tichonius differ by reading ἑξακόσιαι δέκα ἕξ, "six hundred and sixteen," but this is probably incorrect. Commentators have universally attempted to discover the name denoted by this number, by attaching to each letter of the name (generally the Greek letters) its numerical value, the total of which should equal the number 666. To this method there are several objections. In the first place, St. John nowhere else makes such use of a number, though numbers form a prominent feature of the book. In the second place, the adoption of this method seems to have been a consequence upon the interpretation of the words, "number of a man," as meaning "a number to be calculated according to man's methods." But this may not be the meaning at all (*vide supra*); and, if it is, "man's method" would surely signify the symbolical method which St. John adopts all through the rest of the book, as being a language perfectly well understood by himself and his readers. And thirdly, this numerical method has proved entirely unsatisfactory in the hands of those who have hitherto adopted it. For a complete *exposé* of the fallaciousness of such attempts, we may refer the reader to Dr. Salmon's 'Introduction to the New Testament,' p

291, *et seq.* A commonly received interpretation makes the name of the beast to be Nero Cæsar, written in the Hebrew characters נרון קסר; and as the name may be written *Nerôn* or *Nero*, the difference of the final *n* (= 50) is thought to account for the discrepancy in the manuscript authorities. Dr. Salmon shows that Nero could not have been intended, because (1) the prophecy in that case would have been immediately falsified ; (2) the solution would have been known to the early Christians; but it was *not* known, according to Irenæus. Dr. Salmon then adds (p. 300), "Pages might be filled with a list of persons whose names have been proposed as solutions of the problem. Among the persons supposed to be indicated are the emperors Caligula, Trajan, and Julian the Apostate, Genseric the Vandal, Popes Benedict IX. and Paul V., Mahomet, Martin Luther, John Calvin, Beza, and Napoleon Bonaparte. There are three rules by the help of which I believe an ingenious man could find the required sum in any given name.[1] First, if the proper name by itself will not yield it, add a title; secondly, if the sum cannot be found in Greek, try Hebrew, or even Latin; thirdly, do not be too particular about the spelling." The above objections also hold good very generally with regard to the suggestion of λατεινος, by which may be indicated the Roman or Latin power, either pagan or papal. But if we attempt to interpret this number in the same way as we have dealt with all other numbers in the Apocalypse, viz. by regarding them as symbolical of qualities, we shall be on surer ground. In the first place, the number *six* is typical of what is earthly as opposed to what is heavenly. As seven is the number of perfection, and is descriptive of universality, and is therefore the symbol pertaining to God, so six is a type of what falls short of the heavenly ideal. Cf. the *six* days of the creation; the *six* years of servitude (Exod. xxi. 2, etc.) and of work (Exod. xxiii. 10). Again, the threefold employment of the number *six*, while emphasizing the fact of the number referring to what is essentially earthly, has a fulness, importance, and seeming completeness which makes it a type of that which appears to be perfect, but in reality falls short of perfection. It is, in short, symbolical of a deceit, a sham. It is therefore descriptive of the nature of the second beast; of that self-deceit which causes men to accept the world as a substitute for God, or, at least, as not antagonistic to him; which enables men to thus quiet their consciences, while in reality becoming followers of the worldly power and subjects of Satan. That this is the meaning of the number *six* is recognized by some writers, though they do not here so apply it. In the 'Speaker's Commentary,' Introduction, § 11 (*a*), we find, "Six is the 'signature' of non-perfection;" and, "This number is also a symbol of *human rule and power.*" Wordsworth says, "The numerical symbol of the beast, 666, indicates that he aims at and aspires to the attributes of Christ, and puts forth a semblance of Christian truth, but falls away from it in a triple decline and degeneracy."

[1] One example which he gives elsewhere, not, of course, seriously, is amusing, particularly if vers. 16, 17 be borne in mind. It is παρρνέλλος ($\pi = 80 + a = 1 + \rho = 100 + \rho = 100 + \nu = 50 + \epsilon = 5 + \lambda = 30 + \lambda = 30 + o = 70 + s = 200$; total = 666).

HOMILETICS.

Vers. 1—18.—*The foes of God and of his Church: the two beasts.* The evil one is responsible for much of the mischief in the world, but his responsibility for it is not an unshared one. Two other enemies are here portrayed as the emissaries and agents of the first (ver. 2). The thought underlying the chapter is that of the predominance of brute force over moral power; or, in other words, of might over right. Here are two beasts. *The first,* described in vers. 1—10, is seen "coming up from the sea," as if it were the product of the surging restlessness of the troubled sea of godless strife; "having seven heads"—these are so many phases of a corrupt, ungodly world-power. The expression cannot refer to any one distinctive power as such, for none has ever yet been seen, nor can be, having power over "*all* kindreds, and tongues, and nations." As the dragon has seven heads and ten horns, so likewise has this first beast; whatever power the devil wields, he wields through it. And as wide as is the devil's sway, so wide is the sway of this hostile force. Thus, in this symbolic form we get precisely the same truth which meets us elsewhere—that Satan is "the prince of the power of the air," "the spirit that now worketh in the children of disobedience." Again, this beast has "upon his heads the names of blasphemy" (ver. 1). A supremacy is assumed which belongs to God alone. "The beast was like unto a leopard," etc. (ver. 2). All three figures denote the terribly savage and devouring energy put forth by the powers of evil. "The dragon gave him," etc. (ver. 2). The ungodly power of earth is backed up by the evil one. "One of his heads . . . wounded," etc. (ver. 3). This worldly power was smitten, and yet rose again in all its dominance and pride, so that "all the world wondered after the beast" (ver. 4). "Authority was given to him to continue forty-two months" (ver. 5).[1] This is the fourth time this mysterious period is named. It is the time during which the witnesses are to prophesy, the time during which the woman is to be hidden in the wilderness, the time for the serpent to rage and wound, and the time for the beast to continue. His sway is to be so great that all, save the very elect, shall go after him. "Here is the patience and the faith of the saints" (ver. 10). *The second beast* is also from the earth (ver. 11). It is a low, carnal, worldly power. "It has horns like a lamb," etc. (ver. 11). It puts on a pretence of meekness, and seems lamb-like in its gentleness, albeit it speaks like a dragon, and is fiendish in its ferocity. He panders, too, to the first beast (vers. 12—15). He doeth great signs, deceiving men by prodigies of various kinds (ver. 13; cf. Matt. xxiv. 24; 2 Thess. ii. 9). On all he causes a mark to be affixed (ver. 16), and no one who had not that mark might buy or sell or have any social standing. Evidently, here is described some power or other, meek and sleek in appearance, yet fierce in spirit, prompted by the dragon, and doing his work, yet pretending to have a commission from Heaven, doing such wonders as to carry multitudes away, and withal so intolerant that none except its followers should be allowed to take their proper place in the social ranks, while it appeals to the love of thaumaturgy, yet cares not about the true or the right so long as men pay homage to the first beast to whom he yields obedience. *Can we mistake the meaning of all this?* It is certainly some mighty antichristian force, putting on the pretence of being in communion with Heaven, while it is a sycophant and abject minion of earthly power. Lamb-like in its mien, it is intolerant in its speech. *This* power is not dead yet, any more than the former. On the perplexing verse which concludes the chapter, we have no opinion to offer. The various attempts at explanations may be seen in the 'Speaker's Commentary,' *in loc.*[2] We only quote from thence the opinion of Bellarmine, "Verissima igitur sententia est eorum qui ignorantiam suam confitentur."[3] If, however, we set in order the points of similarity and of difference between the two beasts, and their relation to one another, the meaning of the description may be more clearly seen. *Seven points of difference:* The first beast has his power from the dragon; the second beast has his power from the first. The first daringly blasphemes; the second deceives. The first makes war; the second practises thaumaturgy. The first succeeds by force; the second, by persuasion. The first rules through fear; the second, by craft. The first teaches his followers to worship the dragon; the second persuades his to worship the first. The first openly slays; the second puts men under a social ban. *Six points of similarity:* They are both opposed, in spirit, to God, to his Church, and to heaven. They are both arrogant, haughty, and imperious. They both involve in much suffering those who will not yield to them. They both try the patience and faith of the saints. They both have a power equally wide. They are both deplorably successful. *Six points of relation between them and their workings:* The second causes all the earth to worship the first; causes an image of the first to be made; commands men to worship the image of the beast; pretends to make the image speak; causes that as many as would not worship the image should be killed; will allow no one any social status, nor even a stand in the market

---

[1] On this chapter, and especially on the period of forty and two months, see P. W. Grant's Exposition, pp. 352, *et seq.*

[2] On the number of the beast the work of Dr. Warren should be consulted, as well as on the thousand years' reign.

[3] "We know from Irenæus that this number was expressed in Greek letters ($\chi\xi\varsigma$). He speaks of a different reading ($\chi\iota\varsigma$) [616] (which is found in C), and he rests for the true reading 666 on the authority of 'correct and old copies,' and the information of those who had known the apostle, 'Qui facie ad faciem Joannem viderunt'" (Tregelles). See also Archdeacon Farrar, Bishop Boyd Carpenter, Professor Milligan. A thoughtful and wise article on the "Apocalyptic Beast," by Mr. Proctor, will be found in the *Clergyman's Magazine* for October, 1887

unless they acknowledge and worship the first. Now, when we thus carefully set in order the two descriptions, who can help seeing symbolic sketches of precisely the two great adverse forces which have been the plague of the world and of the Church— even an ungodly world-power, and a false religious teaching in alliance with it, supporting it and supported by it? And who that knows the general history of the world but must be aware that these two forces, leagued together, have been the foes of the Church of God? Not any one power only, nor any one form of false religion only, is indicated here; the description is broad enough to embrace them all, and indeed demands that all be embraced, for their sway is alike over *all* nations and tongues. Well do we know how exactly the state of things corresponded, at the time of the founding of the Christian faith, to the descriptions in this chapter. *Religion had long been regarded as a piece of statecraft.* "The rulers took counsel together," etc. (Ps. ii.; Acts iv. 25, *et seq.*). During the early struggles of the Christians the force of a false religion in alliance with a heathen state strove to compel men to act in subservience to a heathen emperor, in spite of conscience and of God. Then, disorders, droughts, famines, pestilences, were ascribed to the Christians; men were debarred the ordinary rights of citizens except they acknowledged the supremacy of the state in religious affairs. Far later, in our own land, when the temporal sovereignty of this realm was in alliance with popery, what pains and penalties were endured for conscience' sake! And in many countries, what harrowing tales of worry, persecution, and suffering are left on record; and even at this day there is often furnished a new contingent of those who will not worship the beast nor his image, and who will risk their all for the truth and for God! For even now these two beasts are living; the first beast gets wounded now and then, but still survives, having wondrous tenacity of life. At divers times and places, with oft-recurring onsets, do these two foes of the Church seek to ravage, to spoil, and to devour. And although at this moment, in our peaceful land, the wild savagery of their coalition is toned down, yet every one knows that the stigma of a social inferiority is still set on many who will not acknowledge state authority in religion. By the social ban referred to in ver. 17 Dean Alford understands "the commercial and spiritual interdicts which have, both by pagan and by papal persecutors, been laid on Nonconformity . . . down to the last remaining civil disabilities imposed on Nonconformity in modern papal or Protestant countries."[1] "Here is the patience and the faith of the saints." This chapter may serve two purposes.

I. IT SHOULD YIELD US UNSPEAKABLE COMFORT. In four respects: 1. Here we find sketched for us beforehand the checkered course of truth and right in the world; sketched, too, in precise accordance with the facts of history. The great Lord has foreseen the struggle. 2. He who foresees, and has thus sketched for us the forms of evil, has also assigned a limit to their duration. 3. In the worst of times, a faithful few shall be preserved. 4. The people of God will overcome at last by the two weapons of faith and patience.

II. IT SUGGESTS MANY A LESSON FOR THE PRACTICAL RULING OF LIFE. It says to us: 1. Do not be caught by appearances. There may be more show in might than in right. God approves only the latter. 2. Do not expect the immediate triumph of God's work. The end is not yet. The twelve hundred and sixty days are not yet closed; perchance they are not even near to their end. 3. Do not let us be in a state of agitation and of perpetual fear, as if something might happen to undo God's work. Never! 4. Do not let us mistake our own proper work. Never let us swerve a hair's breadth from right to gain a momentary end. All the right is essentially—success. All the wrong is essentially—failure. 5. Let us rest in the knowledge that one eye discerns all, and one hand infallibly overrules all, to bring about the right end at the right time. 6. However long the time may be ere the salvation is brought in, it cannot be very long that any of us will have to maintain an attitude of vigilance and of war. A few short years at most, and the struggle between us and this coalition of evil will be over. We are nearing the river. We shall soon cease to hear the clang of arms and the rush of the troops; and shall exchange the noise of a militant for the harmonies of the triumphant Church. Then, brothers, on—even unto death!

---

[1] Quoted in 'Speaker's Commentary,' *in loc.*

HOMILIES BY VARIOUS AUTHORS.

Ver. 1.—*Seaside lessons.* " I stood upon the sand of the sea." (See homily on Jer. xlix. 23: vol. ii. ' Pulpit Commentary,' p. 261.)—S. C.

Vers. 1—18.—*The two wild beasts; or, the world and its wisdom.* There are few chapters in the Bible which have been entirely passed over by Christian preachers as containing nothing that would edify and instruct men living in circumstances like our own. But this chapter seems to have been so dealt with. We have searched the lists of thousands of printed sermons, and not one, or rather but one, have we found which seeks to show that this portion of God's Word has anything to do with us to-day. The vast majority of Protestant commentators have rolled it up, as they have the Apocalypse generally, into as hard a missile as they could manufacture, and then have hurled it with all their might against unhappy Romanists and the Church to which they belong. And no doubt there has been reciprocity. But this chapter has a meaning, and a momentous one, for the men of to-day, although, as we think, for the men of St. John's day it pointed to that awful persecuting power, summed up in the monster Nero, then Emperor of Rome, and who, like the foul, fierce beast that he was, had been making dire havoc in the Church of Christ. This man, or monster rather, was the dragon's, that is the devil's, chief agent, and had to aid and abet him the second beast, lamb-like in look, but fierce in heart, of which we read in ver. 11. By this second beast was meant, we think, that whole system of heathen imposture and manifold superstition which ever played into the hands of the mere brute force wielded by the state. Simon Magus, and vast numbers more such as he, were its ministers. (For detailed proof, see Farrar, *in loc.*) And this entire chapter was to the persecuted Church of that day a solemn announcement of suffering appointed for them which they could not hope to escape (vers. 9, 10), which demanded patience and faith, but which, however (ch. xvii. 14), should issue in glorious victory through the might of their Lord, whose "called and chosen and faithful" they were. Such then were the preparations for martyrdom with which the Church was supplied in those awful days of testing and of trial. How do the poor petty persecutions—scarce worthy of the name—which now and again some of us have to put up with, dwindle into insignificance by side of the fiery trials appointed for them for whom St. John wrote! And how should we be ashamed to shrink from ours when we know they never shrank from theirs, but endured and overcame, and wore the martyr's crown! But Rome and pagan persecutions have passed away. They answered to these symbols of the beasts then: what answer to them now? And we reply—

I. THE ANTICHRISTIAN WORLD answers to the first of the wild beasts of which we here read. See the resemblance. Rome and Nero's were not more exact. 1. *It has assumed successive forms.* " Seven heads" we read of, and they denote the multiplication and succession of hostile powers arrayed against the Church of God. Egypt and Assyria, Babylon and Persia, Greece and Rome, and by-and-by the final antichrist,—these may be the seven heads. But they are all but successive forms of the same God-defying world. 2. *And it has ever had immense strength.* " Ten horns," and these encircled with diadems, telling how the world-spirit has ever made use of the princes and potentates of earth to work its will. 3. And it has ever raged against the Church *as a wild beast.* Under all its forms it has hated the people of God. From Pharaoh even to the last of the persecutors it has been the same. And in modern days, though in different ways, it has continued unchanged in spirit and aim. Voltaire's wild cry, " Écrasez l'infame! " and the hatred with which he and his fellow-atheists toiled to overthrow the Christian Church, were but modern manifestations of the same mind. And if it be difficult, as it is—and we are thankful that it is—to point in our day to any one party or person in whom this God-defying antichristian spirit is specially embodied, none the less does it exist. " The prince of this world "—he who inspired the whole succession of these monsters—he still " worketh in the children of disobedience." Experience and observation alike attest this. What relentless opposition to God we often see and feel! How good is crushed and trampled on, and every attempt to assert Christ's will is ruthlessly put down! 4. *And its deadly wounds heal.* (Ver. 3.) Whether the death and supposed return of Nero, or the overthrow of paganism by the conversion of Constantine, and the revival of its worst features afterwards, be St. John's meaning, there can be no doubt that the world's seemingly deadly wounds do heal. If its dominion be overthrown in a given locality, or in your heart and mine, do we not know how the evil spirit; who has left for a while, comes back; and unless he be driven forth again, he will come back stronger than before, and the last state of that place, that heart, that character, be worse than the first? 5. *It is popular.* It has the *vox populi.* "All the world wondered after" and "worshipped." Openly and avowedly in St. John's day, but as really, though more reverently, now. 6. *And it blasphemes still.* It claims Divine power. "All these things will I give thee, if," etc.—this still it says, and the most of men believe it. 7. *And it wages war and wins.* (Ver. 7.) Let families, Churches, congregations, tell how this war has been waged in their midst, and how some, often many, of their most hopeful members have fallen. What decimating of the ranks of the Church goes on continually through the might of this great adversary! 8. *And none but those who are really Christ's withstand.* (Ver. 6.) Yes, we are sent forth as sheep amid wolves. It seems as strange as it is sad. But so it is. For our comfort remember that it is the sheep who have ever made short work with the wolves. We should surely have thought it would have been the other way. See, literally, in lands where wolves once ran wild, as in our own, the pastures are covered over with flocks; but the wolves, where are they? As the anvil, though smitten hard, and year in and year out, yet it wears out many a hammer (Spurgeon); so the smitten Church wears out the persecutor's hammer. But let us not go ransacking ancient history for the lessons of this chapter; our own times, our own circumstances, and very likely our own hearts' experience, will supply them in plentiful way.

II. THE WISDOM OF THIS WORLD answers to the second "beast." St. James tells us that "this wisdom descendeth not from above, but is earthly, sensual, devilish." This monster (ver. 11) is seen to ascend from "the earth," as St. James tells. In ch. xix. 20 it is called "the false prophet." 1. *It is said to have "deceived."* True type of the wisdom of this world, that godless, antichristian wisdom which encounters us to-day just as it did them of old. It deceives: (1) By its innocent appearance, its lamb-like look. True, it had ten horns, but they meant nothing, so small, so slight, so incapable of injury. So this wisdom. No one would ever suspect it of being a fierce beast. It is known as modern thought, science, philosophy, liberal culture—lamb-like words whom none would suspect to harbour ill. (2) By its words, so subtle and serpentine. "He spake as a dragon," that is, as a serpent, as did the "old serpent," the devil, who over-persuaded and beguiled our first mother. So this wisdom of the world is plausible, popular, prevalent. It seems so untrammelled in its researches, so broad in its conclusions, so courageous, so unprejudiced, so candid, so fair. But it further deceives (3) by its "lying wonders" (ver. 14). The juggleries and tricks of heathenism, its magic and sorcery, explain St. John's words. But for us they point to the glamour and witchery which the wisdom of this world casts over us when it points to the marvellous results it has achieved. Have not most eminent names, most wonderful discoveries, most famous reputations, been amongst the rewards it has given? And thus speculation and scepticism, doubt and denial, the rejection of old faith and the discontinuance of old habit, have been permitted and invited, and we come to believe in nothing but ourselves and this wonderful century in which we live. But: 2. *Its falsity may be detected.* There is an Ithuriel spear which shall compel it to self-revelation. By its fruits it shall be known. See, then: (1) *It is in alliance with the God-defying world.* (Cf. vers. 12—15.) Mere brute force could not get on without the tricks and frauds which this lamb-like, lying thing concocts and displays. The first beast would be powerless without the cunning of the second. And here is a test for us. Do we find that any set of opinions, any new beliefs and maxims we may have adopted, are such as the godless and the antichristian world choose and cherish as of great advantage to them? Can they claim them as on their side? If so, that is a very suspicious fact. (2) *It transforms you into the world's likeness.* (See ver. 16.) On the forehead or on the right hand the mark of this beast was to be. That is to say, the stamp of the world was to be visibly and confessedly on us. All the transactions of life would reveal this. We could do nothing that did not betray it. The wisdom of this world will thus claim for the world those whom it has first beguiled. Thus by the effect of it may we know its real character. Does the stamp of the God-despising world become visible in our daily conduct, bearing, and words? Do these things show the "mark of the beast"? If so, what loud call comes to us to have done with all such so-called wisdom, and to give heed to our Saviour's words, "Beware of false prophets, which come to you in sheep's clothing, but inwardly," etc. 1—S. C.

Vers. 1—10.—*Safety in times of worldly oppression.* The twelfth chapter, with which the thirteenth is to be connected, closes with an assertion of the wrath of "the dragon" towards "the woman." The Church of God is ever the object of Satanic wrath. In these two chapters the enmity that the Church has to contend with is represented by three beasts. Much ingenuity has been expended already on the exposition of these dark words, and much more will be until in the light of history we see clearly what, in the words of prophecy, is but imperfectly seen. The first beast was distinctly declared to be "the old serpent, he that is called the Devil and Satan, the deceiver of the whole world." The beast now spoken of, the second, receives "his power, and his throne, and great authority" from the dragon. It is a power animated by the one spirit of evil—the adversary, the devil. It is the many powers so animated. It is an active brute force, and may specially refer to the antichristian pagan power (certainly to this as one of many). It arises from "the sea," the invariable symbol of the many peoples of earth—the restless world, the agitated state of human affairs. We cannot limit the application to any one power, or any seven, or any ten. We are dealing with symbol, not realism.

I. HEREIN WE SEE THE BELIEVING CHURCH OPPOSED AND OPPRESSED BY GREAT EXTERNAL POWERS. We must not interpret these of mere kings of the earth, but of those many forms of worldly power which dominate over the life of man. Special prominence is given in this figure to the speaking of blasphemies against God, his Name, his tabernacle, and them that dwell therein. The utmost blasphemy of the Divine Name is in repudiating and opposing it. Every name by which the creature assumes the place of God is a name of blasphemy. Alas! how many such are around the humble believer! And he who stands in opposition to Christ and his faithful ones, usurping power over them by savage, beast-like persecution, surely he is branded with the name "blasphemy."

II. THE EXTENT OF THE POWERFUL WORKING OF THESE EVILS is (1) *very great:* "over every tribe, and people, and tongue, and nation;" but (2) *it is limited in time:* "forty and two months." It is not "for ever."

III. SAFETY IS ASSURED TO HIM ONLY WHOSE NAME IS WRITTEN IN THE BOOK OF LIFE OF THE LAMB. The Lord defends his own even here. "What shall separate us from the love of Christ? shall tribulation, or anguish, or persecution, or famine, or nakedness, or peril, or sword? . . . Nay, in all these things we are more than conquerors through him that loved us." Thus is the Church to gather comfort in all times of exposure, temptation, persecution, or suffering from mighty worldly powers. Here is—here must be—the call for "the patience and the faith of the saints."—R. G.

Vers. 11—17.—*Subtle dangers.* The Book of Revelation presents us with a view of the conflict between the varied kingdoms of this world and the undivided kingdom of our God and of his Christ, and it uniformly declares to us this one consolatory truth, that these kingdoms shall become submissive to his kingdom. These kingdoms present themselves in the great world-drama as various powers standing more or less in active opposition to the dominion of Christ over the life of men—in opposition to truth, to righteousness, and to God. "Another beast" arises, not from the sea, but "coming up out of the earth;" not from the world, in its heaving, disordered, tumultuous state, but from the solid earth—from the world in its settled order. It is not the power of rude violence, but as it were of meekness. "He had two horns like unto a lamb"—a smaller measure of power than pertains to the true Lamb, and smaller than is found on the seven-headed beast. But the character is complex. The speech is "as a dragon." It is foul, hellish, Satanic. He doeth great signs. "He deceiveth them that dwell on the earth by reason of the signs." The beast is distinguished by speech. This may indicate a connection with the intellectual and moral, not the physical or even the political, world. Is it a representation of the vast intellectual powers of the world if, and when, inspired by the evil spirit? Is it "wisdom"—the wisdom of this world in its opposition to the wisdom that cometh down from above? It has elements of the world, for it is of the beast; it has elements of the fiend, for it partakes of the quality of the dragon; it is a spirit of error, for it is a false prophet. But it is not merely error, for it is animated by an evil spirit. It is worldly wisdom, the tongue set on fire of hell—the human mind in its opposition to God. " Intellectual weapons which have united with external violence to attack the new principle which had begun to manifest itself in the life of mankind " (Neander). " He doeth great wonders " (see Matt. xxiv. 24). Here are all " signs and lying wonders," by which men are deceived who cleave not to the truth. Perhaps visible signs, prestiges, prodigies, wonders, soothsayers, witchcraft, and fraud of a barbarous age; and then, as times change, the pretended wonders of the intellect. " It would seem like a new heathendom sinking down again to the deification of nature and humanity." It maketh an image. Often in heathen Roman times was the image of the beast set up, and the alternative lay between martyrdom and apostasy. But not only in imperial Roman times, or papal or Protestant persecuting times, but in times of proud philosophical, materialistic, atheistic, earthly wisdom that stands in opposition to God; and that is none the less exclusive towards men that accept it not. Proud, anti-Godlike, anti-Christlike wisdom persecutes to the death. The profession of the simple Christian faith is a sign for exclusion and proscription. Intellectual pride laughs in its sleeve at the simplicity of Christ. Here the Church is to learn—

I. THE EXCEEDINGLY VARIED CHARACTER OF THE ENEMIES OF THE TRUTH. Every spirit not of God will oppose the true.

II. THE NECESSITY FOR WATCHFULNESS AGAINST THE MOST SPECIOUS OPPONENTS.

III. THE EXTREMELY DANGEROUS CHARACTER OF EVERY SPIRIT THAT IS OF THE EARTH, OR THAT PARTAKES OF THE NATURE OF THE BEAST.

IV. THE NECESSITY FOR PURITY, FIDELITY, AND PATIENCE. Purity (1) of doctrine, and (2) of life. Fidelity (1) to the Word, and (2) to convictions, and (3) to the indications of Divine providence. Patience (1) in maintaining the reproach and profession of Christ, and (2) in enduring the severities of rude persecution or the proud rejection of a self-wise world.—R. G.

Vers. 1—18.— *The domain of antichrist.* " And I stood upon the sand of the sea, and saw a beast rise up out of the sea, having seven heads and ten horns, and upon his horns ten crowns, and upon his heads the name of blasphemy," etc.[1] Fanciful interpretations of this chapter, as well as other portions of this book, are abundant. The last (see ' The Early Days of Christianity,' p. 452, by Archdeacon Farrar) seems to us not less unfounded and absurd than those that have gone before. Most of such interpretations assume that the comparatively few people who lived in Rome centuries ago were of such immense importance as to absorb the mind of the Infinite; that " papal Rome," as it is called, was the one great moral foe of creation, unmatched and matchless. But our method of treating this Book of Revelation, whether right or wrong, philosophic or foolish, *ignores all fanciful interpretations,* and seeks to turn even the dreams of old dreamers, like the prisoner on Patmos, and the prisoner in Bedford Gaol, to such a practical account as to serve the *ethical interests* of the men that are, and the men that are yet to be. Hence we use this chapter to throw light upon the *domain of antichrist.* But what do we mean by " antichrist "? Not an institution, ecclesiastical, political, or social, connected with any geographical spot or chronological period, but a moral state of mind pervading all places, and running through all times. Whatever state of mind is opposed to that moral state of mind which Christ incarnated, exemplified, and inculcated, *I call antichrist.* His state of mind was one of *truth,* reality; hence all falsehoods, shams, hypocrisies, are antichrist. His state of mind was one of *supreme worship.* He realized and reverenced the Eternal Father in all; hence all irreverence and idolatries are antichrist. His state of mind was a state of *self-sacrificing philanthropy.* He loved men, and gave himself for their benefit. He did not please himself. Hence all selfishness, worldliness, self-seeking, is antichrist. St. John says, " Even now are there many antichrists." There are anti-christs in Protestant churches and chapels, and in thousands of those who call themselves Christians. Some of the fiercest denouncers of popery as antichrist are those who have the most of popery and antichrist in their hearts. This chapter serves to illustrate some facts in connection with the domain of antichrist on this earth.

[1] See Excursus at end of ch. xxii.

I. IT HAS A MANIFOLD DEVELOPMENT. The huge and monstrous forms that seem to pass before the imagination of the lonely prisoner on Patmos, as here recorded, are full of forms, grotesque, huge, and hideous. Here is a huge beast rising out of the sea, the scene of tumults. His power is great—he has " ten horns ; " his intelligence is great—he has " seven heads ; " his influence is great—he has " ten crowns [diadems]." In form " he was like unto a leopard, and his feet were as the feet of a bear, and his mouth as the mouth of a lion " (ver. 2). Then there is another beast " coming up out of the earth ; and he had two horns like a lamb, and he spake as a dragon " (ver. 11). He, like the former, is endowed with tremendous power, invested with extraordinary attributes, and is one in spirit and aim with the former, the beast that rises out of the realm of tumult, the sea. So that from the sea and from the land, the whole terraqueous globe, monstrous forms of evil appear in the domain of antichrist. What imagination can depict and what arithmetic could compute the hideous and monstrous forms in which antichrist appears in the world to-day ? In the commerce of the world, in the governments of the world, in the campaigns of the world, in the literature of the world, in the religions of the world, in fact, in the social, industrial, and professional life of the world, antichrist appears in aspects as hideous and in a spirit as savage and blasphemous as the monsters depicted in this vision. Where in any part of the world do we not find antichrist in some form or another ? Whatever the form it assumes, it is hideous and monstrous. What can be more monstrous than to find a human being rising and acting in opposition to him who is the all-loving and all-blessed, the Christ of God and the Saviour of the world ? Concerning this domain of antichrist it is suggested that—

II. IT HAS ONE MASTER-SPIRIT. The dragon is here represented as the presiding genius over all. " The dragon gave him his power, and his seat [throne], and great authority " (ver. 2). The presiding genius in this chapter and in the preceding one is called the dragon. Reason and analogy concur with the Bible in teaching that there is on this earth a great master-spirit of evil, one that leads the world " captive at his will." He is, in spirit, character, and aim, against Christ. He is, in a pre-eminent sense, antichrist. There is nothing Christly about him, but otherwise. Satan is the enemy of Christ, the old serpent, the " prince of the power of the air," that " worketh in the children of disobedience." The record of this vision serves to illustrate several things concerning this master-spirit of evil. 1. *He is endowed with tremendous power.* It is said of this dragon that " he doeth great wonders [signs], so that he maketh [should even make] fire come down from [out of] heaven ; " that he works " by the means of miracles [signs] " (vers. 13, 14). The Jewish Scriptures speak of him as a being of tremendous energy, leading the world captive at his will, and even Christ who knew him seems to speak with deference concerning his extraordinary power. 2. *His grand pursuit is moral mischief.* (1) He promotes blasphemy. " He opened his mouth in [for] blasphemy [blasphemies] against God, to blaspheme his Name, and his tabernacle, and them that dwelt in heaven " (ver. 6). His grand aim seems to be to bring the Infinite himself into contempt. (2) He promotes deception. " And deceived them that dwell on the earth " (ver. 14). He is a liar and the father of lies. The first stone of his empire in the world was a lie, and by lies he has built it up and supports it. A life of wickedness is a life of delusion. All his followers walk in " a vain show." (3) He promotes destruction. " It was given unto him to make war with the saints, and to overcome them " (ver. 7). Malignity is his inspiration. His battle is with the saints. He works to destroy goodness, and to destroy goodness is to destroy souls. He has no fight with fiends, but with saints. 3. *His sphere is coextensive with the world.* " He causeth all, both small and great, rich and poor," etc. (vers. 15—17). One of his prime ministers, or rather chief generals, came out of " the sea," and the other came up from " the earth." The whole terraqueous globe is the arena of this arch-enemy of souls. He is the god of this world. Wherever falsehood, dishonesty, impurity, revenge are, there he is. And where are they not ? 4. *However great his influence, he is under a restraining law.* An old writer has said, " He is limited in point of time ; his reign is to continue forty and two months. He is also limited as to the persons and people that he shall entirely subject to his will and power ; it will be only those whose ' names are not written in the book of life of the Lamb slain from the foundation of the world.' Though the devil and antichrist might overcome their bodily strength and take away their natural life, they could never conquer their souls, nor prevail with them to forsake their Saviour and revolt to his enemies." 5. *His mission will ultimately prove self-ruinous.* "He that leadeth into [if any man is for] captivity shall go into captivity [into captivity he goeth]" (ver. 10). Here is the principle of retribution attested by all human experience and philosophy, and felt to be just. "He that killeth [if any man shall kill] with the sword must be killed" (ver. 10). This applies to Satan; he brings men into captivity, and into captivity shall he one day go. Sin is suicide, wrong is self-destructive. In every act the devil performs, he is forming a link in that adamantine chain that shall bind him, not merely for a thousand years, but for ever.—D. T.

Ver. 8.—*Christ sacrificed in eternity.* "The Lamb slain from the foundation of the world." From this wonderful declaration we conclude—

I. THAT THE THINGS THAT ARE TO HAPPEN IN THE UNIVERSE IN THE MOST DISTANT FUTURE ARE TO GOD AS FACTS ALREADY ACCOMPLISHED. As a fact in this world's history the crucifixion of Christ was enacted about eighteen centuries ago, and yet here it is declared to have occurred before all time, before any creature existed, when he lived alone in the solitudes of eternity. Two things are here disclosed: 1. *That God's intelligence is infinite.* He knows not only all that has been, and all that is, but all that ever will be. All the generations that are yet to appear on this earth, with their commerce, politics, literature, religions, are facts to him. All the worlds and systems which are yet to be launched into immensity are to him realities. The slaying of Christ on Calvary was a fact to him ages before his purpose became realized to men.

> "Eternity, with all its years,
> Stands open to thy view:
> To thee, great God, there's nothing old appears;
> To thee there's nothing new."

2. *That God's purposes are unfrustratable.* Christ's death was according to God's eternal decree. It was his "determinate counsel," and after millions of ages it was accomplished. What God has purposed must come to pass—the conversion of the world, the resurrection of the dead, the transactions of the judgment-day, etc., all are inevitable things. "Heaven and earth shall pass away."

II. THAT SELF-SACRIFICING LOVE IS AN ETERNAL PRINCIPLE IN THE CREATION. Here it is in the mind of God before all worlds. Christ was slain before the "foundation of the world." Self-sacrificing love is a new and a rare thing to us, the men of this little planet, because we have fallen from the eternal order of things; but it is an old and common principle in God's creation. 1. *It is the root of the universe.* What is the creation but love going forth in infinite gifts? Every life that breathes, every plant that blooms, every star that shines, is a gift of love. 2. *It is typified in all material existences.* Where is there a thing to be found throughout the vast domain of nature that is made for itself? All existences work, live, and die for the good of others. "The several kingdoms of nature depend on and, therefore, help each other. The mineral is the solid basis on which is spread out the vegetable—the body that its vesture clothes. The vegetable directly nourishes the animal. The tree does not grow for itself; it cradles the birds, and feeds animated races, and shades the traveller until he blesses it. Of all the thousand and ninety species of plants that botany has classified, not one, from the vast oak to the weed that springs out of its mould, and the moss that clings to its bark, but takes its appointed place in a related family. The atmosphere would lose its salubrity but for the salt and bitter sea. The ground would catch no fertilizing streams if the clouds did not kindly drop them from the sky. The flowers wait for the falling light before they unveil their beauty. All growing things are buttressed up by the vast ribs of everlasting granite that sleep in sunless caverns. Heat, electricity, magnetism, attraction, send their subtle powers through nature, and play through all its works, as unseen and silent as the Eternal Spirit they bear witness of. Everything helps, and everything is helped." 3. *It agrees with the moral constitution of the soul.* The soul is so formed: (1) That it can recognize nothing morally praiseworthy that does not spring from it. Disinterestedness must be the soul of any conduct it can heartily commend. (2) Its conscience can approve of no act of its own that is not inspired by it. Our consciences have not a single smile for the avaricious and self-seeking. (3) Its happiness can only be realized as it is controlled by it. "He that seeketh his life shall lose it, and he that loseth it shall find it." Self-oblivious benevolence is the fountain of human joy. This eternal principle of self-sacrificing love we must have in us before we can be saved; it is, in fact, salvation. " Except ye eat the flesh of the Son of God and drink his blood, ye have no life in you." The flesh and the blood here stand for the *vitality* of Christ. And what was this moral life, the moral essence of Christ, the soul of his soul, the moral blood? *Self-sacrificing love.* And this we must get into us or die.

III. That redemption is no after-thought in the arrangements of the universe. It is true that the slain Lamb of Calvary came to meet and master an evil—the world's depravity. He came to "put away sin by the sacrifice of himself." But it was all according to the eternal order of things. Miserably narrow and God-degrading ideas of Christ's work are popular in the pulpits of some of the sects. Sometimes it is spoken of as an expedient which the Almighty took a long time to contrive in order to overcome a state of things that had sprung up in his kingdom. Like some human king, he had a great deal to do in order to hit upon the best plan to harmonize his attributes, to reconcile mercy to justice, to maintain the order of his government, and, at the same time, save and forgive repentant rebels. And sometimes it is so spoken of as if the original system which God established with humanity was defective, did not work well, broke down, and thus not only disappointed the Creator, but taxed his wisdom greatly in order to invent an expedient that should meet the difficulty. Away with such notions! They are repugnant to reason, they are an insult to Omniscience, they are a libel on the gospel, they are obstructive to Christianity. 1. *God foresaw the fall from eternity.* This is an undeniable fact. Why did he not prevent it? Ah! why? 2. *God ordained the remedy from eternity.* Redemption was no after-thought; it is an essential part, and, perhaps, a primary part of the *original scheme of the universe.* All that are redeemed to moral order, rectitude, and peace by Christ, are so redeemed " according to his own purpose and grace, which was given us in Christ Jesus before the world began."

IV. That our planet was probably formed for the special purpose of becoming the theatre of God's redemptive love to man. This is saying more than that Christ came into the world. There are men who argue from the littleness of this planet the absurdity of this. But material magnitude is nothing to God; spiritual existences and moral facts are *vitally* interesting to him. But the text leads us beyond —leads us to believe that this world was made for the express purpose. As God had the idea of redemption before the " foundation of the world," and as the idea is being worked out here, is it not probable that this idea guided him in its formation? Small in bulk as our planet is when compared with that of other orbs that roll in splendour under the eye of God, it has a grand moral distinction. Its dust formed the fruits that fed the body of the Son of God. Here he lived, laboured, suffered, and was buried, and here his grand work is being carried on. If it be moral facts that give importance to places, is there a more important spot than this earth?—D. T.

EXPOSITION.

CHAPTER XIV.

Ver. 1.—And I looked; *and I saw*, indicating a fresh phase of the vision (cf. ch. iv. 1, etc.). Having described (ch. xii. and xiii.) the trinity of enemies with which Christ and his people contend, the vision now passes on to depict the blessedness in store for the faithful Christian, and, on the other hand, the final fate of the dragon and his adherents. We are thus once more led to the final judgment. And just as in the former vision, after the assurance of the salvation of the faithful (ch. vii.), came the denunciation of woe for the ungodly

(ch. viii.—xi. 14), leading once more to a picture of the saved (ch. xi. 15—19), so here we have the assured blessedness of the faithful portrayed (ch. xiv. 1—13), followed by the judgments upon the ungodly (ch. xiv. 14—xviii. 24), and leading on once more to a picture of the saints in glory (ch. xix.). And, lo, a Lamb stood on the Mount Zion; *and behold, the Lamb standing on the Mount Zion*, as in the Revised Version. " The Lamb," with the article, referring to " the Lamb" described in ch. v., whom the second beast had attempted to personate. He stands on Mount Zion (cf. Heb. xii. 22, " Mount Zion, the city of the living God, the heavenly Jerusalem"). The appropriateness of the position is seen (1) in its strength (cf. the position of the beast, rising from the sea, perhaps standing on the sand, ch. xiii. 1; and cf. Ps. lxxxvii. 1, 2, "His foundation is in the holy mountains. The Lord loveth the gates of Zion more than all the dwellings of Jacob"). (2) Because there is the temple of God, in the midst of which is *the Lamb*, and there is the new Jerusalem (ch. xxi. 2). (3) Zion is the new Jerusalem, the opposite extreme to Babylon (ver. 8). And with him an hundred forty and four thousand, having his Father's Name written in their foreheads. The reading, τὸ ὄνομα αὐτοῦ καὶ τὸ ὄνομα τοῦ Πατρὸς αὐτοῦ, *his Name and his Father's Name,* adopted in the Revised Version, is supported by אֵ, A, B, C, with most cursives, versions, and Fathers. Note the similarity to the description in ch. vii. Here, as there, the hundred and forty-four thousand are those "redeemed from the earth" (ver. 3). The number denotes a large and perfect number; a multitude of which the total is complete (see on ch. vii. 4). In ch. vii. the sealing in the forehead is described. This sign marks out the redeemed in contradistinction to those who have received the mark of the beast (ch. xiii. 16).

Ver. 2.—And I heard a voice from heaven, as the voice of many waters, and as the voice of a great thunder. Evidently the song of the heavenly inhabitants, as described also in ch. vii. 9—11, where we are told they "cried with a loud voice." The greatness of the voice is evidence of the vastness of the number. "Heaven," from which the sounds come, includes the "Mount Zion" of ver. 1, on which the Lamb and his followers stand. And I heard the voice of harpers harping with their harps. The Revised Version is better, *and the voice which I heard* [*was*] *as* [*the voice*] *of harpers harping with their harps.* This reading is supported by אֵ, A, B, C, and other good authorities. *As the voice;* that is, in regard to its pleasantness; reminding the hearer of the temple-worship. (On the word "harp," see on ch. v. 8.)

Ver. 3.—And they sung as it were a new song before the throne, and before the four beasts, and the elders. *They sing;* that is to say, the heavenly inhabitants. *The four living beings;* viz. those of ch. iv. 9, where see an explanation of the positions occupied, and of the nature and signification of the "living beings and the elders." The "new song," which can only be understood by the hundred and forty-four thousand, is (as explained by ver. 4) a song of victory won by those who have been tried in the world and subjected to temptations. And no man could learn that song but the hundred and

forty and four thousand, which were redeemed from the earth; *even they that had been purchased out of the earth* (Revised Version). These only can know the song for the reason given above. The joys of heaven and the song of victory are not for those who have succumbed to the world.

Ver. 4.—These are they which were not defiled with women; for they are virgins. There is little doubt that these words are intended in a spiritual sense. In the Old Testament the employment of the figure of adultery and fornication to denote spiritual unfaithfulness is common (cf. 2 Chron. xxi. 11; Jer. iii. 9, etc.). St. John elsewhere in the Apocalypse makes use of the same symbolism (cf. ch. ii. 20, "That woman Jezebel, which calleth herself a prophetess, to teach and to seduce my servants to commit fornication, and to eat things sacrificed unto idols;" also ch. xvii. 5, 6). Similarly, also, St. John pictures the faithful Church as the bride adorned for her Husband the Lamb (ch. xix. 7, 8). So also St. Paul (2 Cor. xi. 2), "I espoused you as a chaste virgin to one Husband, Christ." Παρθένοι, "virgins," is a word equally applicable to men or women. This verse, therefore, seems to describe those who are free from spiritual impurity and unfaithfulness; those who have not worshipped the beast and his image. Alford, however, thinks the words should be understood literally. These are they which follow the Lamb whithersoever he goeth. These words describe the great source of the bliss of the redeemed, viz. that they are continually in the presence of Christ. This is their reward for following him on earth; but the words must not be taken as referring to the earthly course of the saints (as Bengel, De Wette, Hengstenberg, and others). These were redeemed from among men, being the firstfruits unto God and to the Lamb; *these were purchased from among men, the firstfruits unto God and unto the Lamb.* Some have erroneously concluded that a reference is made to a portion of the redeemed to whom special honour is conceded; or to some who attain to glory before the rest. *The firstfruits* were the best of their kind (Numb. xviii. 12), selected from the rest, and consecrated to the service of God. So the redeemed are the best of their kind; they who have proved themselves faithful to God, who voluntarily separated themselves from the world, and consecrated themselves to the service of God while in the world, and who are thus afterwards separated by him and consecrated to his service for ever.

Ver. 5.—And in their mouth was found no guile; *no lie* (Revised Version). They had not suffered themselves by self-deceit (the second beast) to be beguiled into worship of the first beast—the world. Alford very appropriately refers to Ps. xv. 1, 2, "Lord, who shall abide in thy tabernacle? who shall dwell in thy holy hill? He that walketh uprightly, and worketh righteousness, and speaketh the truth in his heart." For they are without fault before the throne of God; *they are without blemish.* The following phrase is omitted by nearly every authority. The word ἀμώμος, "without blemish," reminds us of the "Lamb without blemish" (cf. 1 Pet. i. 19; Heb. ix. 14). Thus again they receive appropriate reward. While on earth they kept themselves undefiled; now they are, like the Lamb, free from blemish (see on ver. 4).

Ver. 6.—And I saw another angel fly in the midst of heaven. "Another" is omitted in some manuscripts, but should probably be inserted. "In mid-heaven," as in ch. viii. 13, etc. Having the everlasting gospel to preach unto them that dwell on the earth, and to every nation, and kindred, and tongue, and people; *having an eternal gospel . . . every nation and tribe and tongue and people.* Probably (though not certainly) "the gospel" in the ordinary sense, which is the signification of the expression throughout the New Testament, though the word is not found elsewhere in St. John's writings. The idea of this and the following verses is to portray the certainty of coming judgment. As a preliminary to this, the gospel is proclaimed to the whole world, in accordance with our Lord's words in Matt. xxiv. 14. The *gospel* is *eternal* in its unalterable nature (cf. Gal. i. 9), and in contrast to the power of the beast, which is set for destruction (cf. ch. xiii. 7). The fourfold enumeration shows the universal nature of the proclamation of the gospel (cf. ch. v. 9, etc.) in reference to the world.

Ver. 7.—Saying with a loud voice. Λέγων, "saying," in nominative, though agreeing with the accusative ἄγγελον, "angel." The "great voice" is characteristic of all the heavenly utterances (ver. 2; ch. xi. 12, 15, etc.). Fear God, and give glory to him. Thus the angel proclaims the gospel in opposition to the second beast, who bids those that dwell on the earth to make an image to the first beast (cf. ch. xiii. 14). Compare the effect of the coming judgment, described in ch. xi. 13. For the hour of his judgment is come. This is the reason given for the *fear* mentioned. That it has effect is seen by ch. xi. 13. *Is come;* that is to say, is at hand. And worship him that made heaven, and earth, and the sea, and the fountains of waters. As remarked above, the angel thus directly opposes the invitation of the second beast to pay homage to the first beast. Again we have the fourfold enumeration of objects of creation, de-

noting the universal nature of the assertion (cf. on ver. 6).

Ver. 8.—And there followed another angel, saying; *and another, a second angel, followed.* That is, of course, the second of the three who here make their appearance in close connection. Each new scene is unfolded by its own special messenger. Babylon is fallen, is fallen, that great city, because she made all nations drink of the wine of the wrath of her fornication; *fallen, fallen is Babylon the great, which made,* etc. The second "is fallen" is omitted in א³ᵃ, C, etc., but is inserted in A, P, some cursives, versions, and Fathers. Omit "city." *Babylon* is the type of the world-power. Like so much of the Apocalypse, the image is supplied by the Book of Daniel. There the kingdom is spoken of as *great* (Dan. iv. 30; cf. also Isa. xiv.). In its oppression of the Jewish nation, Babylon is a type of the world-power which persecutes the Church of God. At the time when St. John wrote, this power was preeminently possessed and wielded by Rome, and that empire may thus be intended as the immediate antitype of Babylon. But the description is also applicable to the persecuting power of the world in all ages, and its denial of and opposition to God. Babylon is representative of the world, as Jerusalem is of the true Church of God. Alford observes, "Two things are mingled: (1) the wine of her fornication, of which all nations have drunk (ch. xvii. 2); and (2) the wine of the wrath of God, which he shall give her to drink (ver. 10 and ch. xvi. 19). The latter is the retribution for the former; the former turns into the latter; they are treated as one and the same." The description seems taken from Jer. li. 7, 8, "Babylon hath been a golden cup in the Lord's hand, that made all the earth drunken: the nations have drunken of her wine; therefore the nations are mad. Babylon is suddenly fallen and destroyed." Again is the figure of *fornication* used to depict idolatry and general unfaithfulness towards God (see on ver. 4).

Ver. 9.—And the third angel followed them, saying with a loud voice; *and another, a third angel,* etc. (see on ver. 8). (On "loud voice," see on ver. 7.) If any man worship the beast and his image. Here those who worship the beast and those who worship his image are regarded as one class, which they practically are (but see on ch. xiii. 14). This is the *fornication* referred to in ver. 8, the retribution for which follows in ver. 10. And receive his mark in his forehead, or in his hand; *a mark;* but doubtless the mark of the beast alluded to in ch. xiii. 16 (which see). *In his forehead,* etc. (see on ch. xiii. 16).

Ver. 10. — The **same** shall drink of the wine of the wrath of God, which is poured out without mixture into the cup of his indignation ; *he also . . . which is mingled unmixed* (i.e. undiluted) *in the cup of his anger* (Revised Version). The warning is given to men while there is yet time ; the fall of Babylon, which is prophetically spoken of as having taken place (ver. 8), being yet in the future ; that is to say, at the end of the world. The language in which the retribution is couched corresponds to that in which the sin is described (see on ver. 8). The verb κεράννυμι, which originally signified "to mix," gradually came to signify "to pour," from the ancient custom of mixing spices, etc., as well as water, with the wine. The Authorized Version "poured out," therefore, is a correct translation. The *pouring* is in this case not accompanied by dilution with water ; that is, God's wrath will not be tempered, but the wicked will feel the full force of his anger. And he shall be tormented with fire and brimstone in the presence of the holy angels, and in the presence of the Lamb. The figure which is here used to portray the punishment of the wicked is common in the Bible. Isa. xxxiv. 9, 10, cf. with Gen. xix. 28, may supply the origin of the simile. The punishment is in *the presence* of the angels and of the Lamb ; that is, probably, the purity and bliss of heaven is visible to the wicked, and the sight of it, combined with the knowledge of its inaccessibility to themselves, is part of their torment (cf. Luke xvi. 23). It is part of the wrath of God described in the first part of the verse.

Ver. 11.—And the smoke of their torment ascendeth up for ever and ever. Compare the wording of the passages quoted above on ver. 10, especially Isa. xxxiv. 9, 10, "The smoke thereof shall go up for ever." This statement of the eternity of punishment is also in agreement with Luke xvi. 26 and Mark ix. 44. And they have no rest day nor night, who worship the beast and his image, and whosoever receiveth the mark of his name. "No rest," in contrast with the blessed rest of the saints (ver. 13). Wordsworth says, "Οἱ προσκυνοῦντες τὸ θηρίον is a stronger expression than 'those who worship the beast ;' it means those whose distinguishing characteristic is that they *are worshipping* the beast, and persist in worshipping him, even to the end. This characteristic is so strongly marked that they are here represented as keeping it even after their death." (On the "mark," see on ch. xiii. 16—18.)

Ver. 12.—Here is the patience of the saints : here are they that keep the commandments of God, and the faith of Jesus ;

here is the patience of the saints, they that keep, etc. The patience of the saints is exhibited in believing in, and waiting for, the due retribution which will overtake the wicked at the last, and in maintaining the conflict against the dragon who goes to war with those "who keep the commandments of God, and have the testimony of Jesus" (ch. xii. 17), the testimony which is the outcome of *faith* (see also on ch. xiii. 10).

Ver. 13.—And I heard a voice from heaven saying unto me. It seems most natural to suppose that the voice is that of the angel who directs the visions of St. John (cf. ch. i. 1; iv. 1; xix. 9, 10), but there is no certainty in the matter. Omit "unto me," with א, A, B, C, P, and others. Write, Blessed are the dead which die in the Lord from henceforth. "Henceforth" should probably stand thus, and not in connection with the following sentence. We have just had mentioned the necessity for patience on the part of the saints ; here we have an encouragement and incentive to that patience, inasmuch as they who die in the Lord are henceforward blessed. In what their blessedness consists, the next sentence states. The full consummation of their bliss may not occur until after the judgment, but the faithful have not to wait until then for peace ; their conflict is, after all, only for this life, and thus they may well be content to suffer for so short a period (comp. ch. vi. 11). Yea, saith the Spirit, that they may rest from their labours ; and their works do follow them ; *that they shall rest . . . for their works,* etc. The first part explains the "blessedness" of the previous passage ; in this *rest* consists their blessedness. The last clause, "for their works," etc., explains why the blessedness consists in rest ; they have henceforth no need of labours, for the effects of their former works accompany them and permit them now complete rest. Contrast the opposite fate of the wicked, described in ver. 11. St. Paul urges upon Christians the same duty, and proffers the same encouragement : "Therefore, my beloved brethren, be ye steadfast, unmovable, always abounding in the work of the Lord, forasmuch as ye know that your labour is not in vain in the Lord" (1 Cor. xv. 58).

Ver. 14.—And I looked, and behold a white cloud ; *and I saw,* introducing a fresh phase of the vision (see on ver. 1, etc.). *White ;* the heavenly colour (see on ch. iii. 18, etc.). *Cloud* is the symbol of Christ's glory (Acts i. 9, 11 ; cf. Matt. xxiv. 30, "And they shall see the Son of man coming on the clouds of heaven ;" also ch. i. 7, "Behold, he cometh with the clouds"). And upon the cloud one sat like unto the Son of man ; *one sitting.* That Christ is here intended is shown by (1) the cloud (cf.

Luke xxi. 27, "They shall see the Son of man coming in a cloud "); (2) the expression, "Son of man" (cf. John v. 22, "For the Father judgeth no man, but hath committed all judgment unto the Son ; " and John v. 27, "And hath given him authority to execute judgment also, because he is the Son of man ; " and Acts xvii. 31, "He will judge the world in righteousness by that Man whom he hath ordained "); (3) the white colour (cf. ch. vi. 2); (4) the golden crown, which distinguishes him from the other appearances. He who, as Man, redeemed the world, comes as Man to judge the world. He *sits*, because he comes in judgment. Having on his head **a golden crown**. The *crown* of victory, στέφανος, which he gained as Man (cf. also ch. vi. 2, where the description is similar). And in his hand **a sharp sickle**. With which the "Lord of the harvest" (Matt. ix. 38) reaps the harvest of the world. The figure is found in Joel iii. 12, 13, "Then will I sit to judge all the heathen round about. Put ye in the sickle, for the harvest is ripe " (cf. also John iv. 35—38).

Ver. 15.—**And another angel came out of the temple, crying with a loud voice to him that sat on the cloud**; *another angel;* in addition to those already mentioned, not implying that he who sat on the cloud was an angel. *Out of the temple*, or *shrine* (ναός); the inner sanctuary of God (cf. ch. vii. 15). The angel acts as the messenger of the will of God to Christ in his capacity of Son of man, because the command is one concerning the times and seasons which the Father hath kept in his own power (Alford). The characteristic "loud voice" (see on vers. 7, 9, etc.). **Thrust in thy sickle, and reap**: for the time is come for thee to reap ; **for the harvest of the earth is ripe**; *send forth thy sickle and reap : for the hour to reap is come ; for the harvest of the earth is over-ripe* (Revised Version). *Over-ripe,* or *dried ;* that is, as Alford explains, perfectly ripe, so that the stalk is dry, the moisture having been lost.

Ver. 16.—**And he that sat on the cloud thrust in his sickle on the earth ; and the earth was reaped**. "Cast his sickle ; " not the same verb as that in ver. 15, but which, nevertheless, has the same signification (cf. the use of this verb in John xx. 25, 27). There are two gatherings described in this place : (1) the harvest of the earth by the Son of man ; (2) the gathering of the vintage by the angel. On the whole, it seems probable that the first refers to the selection by Christ of the faithful at the end of the world, while the second describes the ingathering of the wicked for punishment immediately afterwards. This agrees with the general tenor of the whole chapter, viz. a portrayal of the

opposite fates in store for the faithful and the wicked. The description thus corresponds with the account of the end of the world given in ch. vii., with which chapter this one has so much in common (see on the first verses of the present chapter). In ch. vii. the saints are first selected and sealed, before the wicked meet their doom. Thus, also, the judgment is described by our Lord in his parables of the wheat and the tares, and the sheep and the goats. This accounts also for the first gathering being presided over by the Son of man, while the second is conducted by an angel. The punishment in connection with the vintage seems to distinguish it from the first harvest. This also corresponds with the announcements of the former angels, who first preach the everlasting gospel, and afterwards denounce those who serve the beast (vers. 6—11).

Ver. 17.—**And another angel came out of the temple which is in heaven, he also having a sharp sickle**; *from the shrine*, or *sanctuary* (as before, see on ver. 15), the dwelling-place of the undivided Trinity, from whence come God's judgments (Alford; cf. ch. xi. 19).

Ver. 18.—**And another angel came out from the altar, which had power over fire.** Both in ch. vi. 9 and viii. 3 the *altar* is connected with judgment. The angel here described is he who is referred to in those places, the *fire* being the fire of the altar, the fire of judgment (ch. viii. 3), or, less probably, the angel who has power over fire generally (as ch. vii. 1 ; xvi. 5). **And cried with a loud cry to him that had the sharp sickle, saying. Again the "loud voice," characteristic of the heavenly utterances (cf. ver. 15, etc.). Thrust in thy sharp sickle, and gather the clusters of the vine of the earth ; for her grapes are fully ripe ;** *send forth thy sharp*, etc. (see on ver. 16). The sickle is figurative of the instrument by which the career of those on earth is terminated. The "sickle" and the "winepress" are both alluded to in the passage quoted above (on ver. 14) from Joel iii. 13. (For the meaning of this gathering of the vintage, as representing the punishment of the wicked, see on ver. 16.)

Ver. 19.—**And the angel thrust in his sickle into the earth, and gathered the vine of the earth.** This angel is described in quite a different manner from "him who sat on the cloud" (ver. 16). **And cast it into the great wine-press of the wrath of God**; *into the wine-press, the great* [wine-press], etc. The feminine substantive has agreeing with it a masculine adjective. It is doubtful whether we ought to see in this anything more than a mere slip of grammar. Possibly the word is of either gender. It is connected with the festival of Bacchus.

Wordsworth, however, accounts for the masculine form of the adjective by supposing that the writer wishes to give a stronger force to the word, and to emphasize the terrible nature of the wrath of God. We have the same image in ch. xix. 15, and it seems derived from Isa. lxiii. and Lam. i. 15. Destruction by an enemy is alluded to as the gathering of grapes in Isa. xvii. 6 and Jer. xlix. 9. The text itself explains the signification of the figure. There seems also some reference in the language to those who "drink of the wine of the wrath of her [Babylon's] fornication" (ver. 8).

Ver. 20.—And the wine-press was trodden without the city. "The city" is Jerusalem (cf. ver. 1), that is, the Church of God; the idea thus being either (1) that the wicked are punished in a place apart from the just (cf. ch. xxii. 15); or (2) that no unclean thing (e.g. the blood) can enter the city of the saints (cf. ch. xxi. 27). And blood came out of the wine-press, even unto the horse bridles, by the space of a thousand and six hundred furlongs; as far as sixteen hundred stadia. The Greek stadium is rather less than an English furlong, being about six hundred and six English feet; it was the length of the race-course at Olympia, and the eighth part of the Roman mile. The "blood," of which the juice of the grape is a type, depicts the punishment inflicted. Horses seem to be mentioned by proleipsis, in anticipation of ch. xix. 14. The description, of course, implies the terrific nature of the punishment—probably nothing more. In the same way the distance mentioned is no doubt intended to denote the extensive nature of the punishment, though why that particular number is chosen is not absolutely clear. Possibly it is derived from the square of 4 multiplied by the square of 10; four being significant of the created world (see on ch. iv. 6), and ten being the sign of completeness (see on ch. xiii. 1); the number thus portraying completeness as regards the created world, and the inability of any one to escape God's judgment.

HOMILETICS.

Vers. 1—5.—*Light-gleams in the darkness.* "*Without fault!*" The apostle in this book never keeps us too long in the shade without a break. Just as, after the terrible convulsions depicted in the sixth chapter, we had the glorious vision of the blest in heaven in that which followed, so it is here. We have watched the working of three of the foes of God and of his Church. Now we are bidden to turn our eye upward, and behold again the hundred and forty-four thousand whose blessedness had been already portrayed. "*And I saw*"—the formula which introduces a separate vision. "*Behold!*" —indicating abruptness and surprise. The raging of the dragon and of the two wild beasts is exchanged for the sight of purity and calm. "A Lamb." The Lamb. The Lamb of God. "*Standing on Mount Zion.*" Mount Zion was where the temple stood. The old Jewish figure sets forth new Christian realities. "Ye are come unto Mount Zion," etc. (Heb. xii.). "*The* hundred and forty-four thousand." We have seen them before; we recognize them again. They are not only seen, but heard (vers. 2, 3). "*They sing*," etc.—are singing. Their melody and harmony ring in the apostle's ear. "*As it were a new song.*" Not actually new. It is the old, old song of redemption which is their theme. But their circumstances are so changed that it is sung with new joy, and through endless ages it will be ever new. Only those can learn this song who are redeemed from the earth. It befits only the Church of God; and not only is their position clearly defined, but their character is definitely given (ver. 4). There are "more to follow." For these whom the apostle saw are but the "firstfruits." In the fifth verse, however, there is one expression concerning them—a very short one, it is true—so significant, that it attracts us more than all the rest; it is one on which we love to linger. It is this: "They are without fault."

I. LET US STUDY THIS CHARACTERISTIC OF THE SAINTS IN HEAVEN. We say, "in heaven," for there need be no fear as to whether we are right in doing so. They are "redeemed from the earth" (ver. 3): this points to what they *were*. They are with the Lamb on Mount Zion: this tells us where they are. They are the "redeemed:" this tells us how they came to be where and what they are. The assertion that they are "without fault" is much more striking than if it had been made by man. It is a phrase inbreathed by the Spirit of God, telling us that in the sight and light of heaven itself they are "faultless." Shall we try and see what a character without flaw would be? The expression must mean: 1. *That there is nothing wrong in them.* Not a single sin do they commit. Every word, deed, and thought is pure. Nor is there even any sinfulness of nature out of which aught that is corrupt can arise. Not one inferior motive mars their actions; not one waste by-thought intrudes into their devotion. Nor is there the least wish or thought but such as is perfectly in harmony with the will of him who sits upon the throne.   2. *There are no infirmities of nature.* Those frailties which, though not sinful, yet may be the inlets of sin into a disordered constitution, and may make it more difficult to resist evil, are done away. Here the physiological accidents of our birth are perpetually telling on us, causing each of us to be surrounded by an easily besetting sin, and making it hard to withstand temptation. The eye, the ear, the hand, the foot, yea, any member of the body, may be an occasion or a vehicle of wrong. But in the redeemed on high, all this is for ever done away. True, this is only the *negative* side of their character. *Only* the negative! Blessed would it be if we could present such a negation! In consequence of this, however—because there is nothing to repress the growth or manifestation of what is Divine—the image of God in them must needs be seen in its perfection. Not that each one will be equally developed. There will be many a flower whose opening has been retarded by chilly winds and adverse weather, and that has been waiting for eternity's sun to shine upon it ere it opened its petals at all. Besides, there must be different stages of growth, etc. "One star differeth," etc. Remembering this, let us glance also at the *positive* side of their character. Their judgment is sound. Their perceptions are clear. They see light in God's light. Every perception of truth is attended with corresponding emotion, and every recognition of duty is followed by corresponding action. Every determination of the will is "holiness unto the Lord." Their work for God is as perfect as their wills are pure. Their social life is all that it should be. Intense sympathy with each other's joys marks them all. Benevolence moves the heart to kindly willing, and beneficence prompts the hand to kindly action; while the sense of a common obligation to a redeeming Lord causes them to unite in the "new song" with rapturous and transcendent joy. But, ah! what pen can sketch the life of beings so perfectly Divine? All that we can say is poor. We can conceive more than we can say. But the one touch of our text suggests that which surpasses alike word and thought—they are *without fault!*

II. THE PASSAGE SHOWS THE CONNECTION BETWEEN THEIR PRESENT FAULTLESSNESS AND THEIR EARTHLY LIFE. This it does in two ways. It shows us: 1. *God's work for and on them.* (1) They were purchased (ver. 3; cf. ch. v. 9, 10; Titus iii. 5; 1 Pet. i. 18, 19; ch. vii. 14). (2) They were begotten (ver. 3); "purchased *to be* the first-fruits," etc. (cf. Jas. i. 18). (3) They were sealed (ver. 1, "his name . . . written," etc.). This is the triple order of the Divine work in every case (Eph. i. 13, 14). The sealing marks them (*a*) as God's own, (*b*) as the object of God's care, (*c*) as having forthwith on their forefront the badge of service. Their constant motto is, "Whose I am, and whom I serve." There is also indicated: 2. *Their work for God.* (1) Acknowledged devotion to God and his cause. The seal on their foreheads, while graven by God, is also a visible and constant pledge of loyalty and fidelity to him. Secret discipleship is not the law of Christian life. Men are to *say*, "I am the Lord's." (2) Avoidance of sin. They stand in contrast from those named in vers. 9—11; and are those specified in ch. xv. 2. They have gained the victory over (*a*) Satan; (*b*) the first beast, or worldly pomp; (*c*) the second beast, or ecclesiastical show; (*d*) all filthiness of the flesh and spirit (ver. 4). (3) "Following the Lamb whithersoever he goeth." These are the men. There is no mistaking them; their marks are plain enough. They stand out from the crowd while on earth, and in the midst of a crooked and perverse generation shine as lights in the world. The Word of God abideth in them, and they overcome the wicked one. Surely it is natural to expect for such a continuity of life. Theirs is just the life which may well give promise of emerging out of the great tribulation to the calmer scenes above. It is by no "sudden strange transition," by no leap from complacent impurity to spotlessness, that they find them-selves there. Ah! no. Their being without fault is but the completion of a work which was going on here; it is a receiving the last finishing touch and impress of the Spirit's seal. That last impress stamped out the marks of the last sin.

III. SUCH SCENES AS THESE SHOULD HAVE OVER US AN ELEVATING POWER. 1. The very fact of such an issue being set before us as the rightful goal of the individual life is of itself an ennobling of human existence. There is, it may freely be confessed, something to inspire one in the thought of the race rising to any such greatness after evolution has had time enough to work out to such an issue. But when the deduction has to be made of the extinction of individuals in the race-process, the heart is taken out of us the moment our hope sets to work. The redeeming grace of God rescues the individual, and gives him a living hope. And one of the most painful features of the day is to find many, trained and nurtured in, and even saturated with, the beautiful and consoling truths of the glorious gospel of the blessed God, casting away from them the only props on which such a hope can rest. The hope survives a while, but cannot long continue when its support is gone. The only alternative is supernaturalism or despair. " Blessed be the God and Father of our Lord Jesus Christ, which according to his abundant mercy hath begotten us again unto a living hope by the resurrection of Jesus Christ from the dead." 2. We may well admire the high standard of gospel morality. Some there are who accuse us of a low-toned morality in preaching, " Believe, and be saved." One would think that we stopped with the word " believe," and went no further. But the fact is, no sinful man can start fairly for holiness until he has a firm standing and a new power. Faith in a living Saviour ensures both these, and faith in him alone. 3. Let us be filled with thankfulness that we are permitted such a fore-glance of those who once

> " Wrestled hard, as we do now,
> With sins, and doubts, and fears."

What they *were*, we are. What they are, by the grace of God we too may be. 4. Be it ours to imitate those who have gone before. The victory they now enjoy was not won without many a hard struggle. Supposing we had before us now two men : one, a model of faultless social propriety, yet steeped in self-complacency ; the other, the worst of publicans and sinners. We would gather from the scenes reviewed in this chapter a word of equal appropriateness to both. To the open sinner we would say, " You may be separated from your sins, if you will. Christ will kill them and save you ! " To the other we would say, " You *must* be separated from your pride ; for you can no more enter heaven in your spirit of self-righteousness than the most openly abandoned sinner." Mercy is free to all. The best need it. The worst may have it. Without it, we must all likewise perish. 5. Let no Christian struggler despair. God is able to keep him from falling, and to present him faultless before the presence of his glory with exceeding joy.

Vers. 6—11.— *The three angels.* The varied scenes in this book are, to us, not so much pictures of events which, when once occurring, exhaust the meaning of the prophecy, but rather representations of what is continuously going on and repeatedly renewing itself—of present-day realities, and not merely of passing incident. The passage before us, looked at in this light, is full of most stimulating teaching ; full of comfort to those whose faces are set in the right direction, and full of terrific warning to others. We can bear a great deal if we know what the worst will be, and that sooner or later it will be over. To see through a trouble is a great relief in it, and, *à fortiori*, if at the end there is glory. In these sentences will be found the key to a great deal in the book, and, in fact, an indication of its aim. The believer is shown that there is much tribulation awaiting the Church ere the end shall come ; but there *will* be an end to it, and brightness beyond it. It is otherwise with the scene set before the ungodly. In their horizon there is no discernible ray of light. And all the visions of this book thus alternate between the light and the shade. In the paragraph before us for present study we have a vision of three angels flying in the midst of heaven. Their messages are precisely those which are being given throughout the Christian age ; they belong as much to this century as to any other ; to any other as much as to this. They give three messages which are perpetually true. We will study their messages *seriatim.*

I. The first angel. (Vers. 6, 7.) 1. *He has something.* (1) What is it ? " A gospel "—good tidings.[1] We know what these are. Free salvation for every penitent. (2) For whom is it ? For " every nation," etc. No nation so civilized that it is not needed. No nation so degraded that it will not suffice. (3) For how long ? " An eternal gospel." One that will be suitable, true, and adequate throughout the whole

[1] Professor Milligan's remarks on these verses are very singular, but deserve attention.

age for which it is intended. To the end of the age there will be no other. No advance in natural knowledge can ever put men beyond the need of it, and no philosophy of man can ever be any substitute for it. (4) For what purpose? To proclaim it. It is to be heralded far and wide. Not merely as a witness, to condemn the rejectors of it; but mainly as " the power of God unto salvation to every one that believeth." This gospel is the rod of God's strength. 2. *He says something.* To this gospel (in itself a message) there is also attached a message: " Fear God . . . the hour of his judgment is come." Κρίσις, not κρίμα—the judging process ever going on; not the issue, or sentence. The way in which man receives the gospel is in itself a test or proof of what he is. " For judgment I am come into this world." This is not the hour of God's final sentence. That is in reserve. But it is a judging hour. Whenever and wherever the gospel is preached—and *only* there—is the actual trial going on, whether men will turn to the light or turn from it. Men are called on to give glory to him, acknowledging his majesty, confessing their sin, and receiving God's pardon.

II. THE SECOND ANGEL. (Ver. 8.) He has to make the proclamation, "Babylon the great," etc. It seems as if this were inserted by anticipation. The fuller detail of this is given later on. "Nothing," says Dr. Lee,[1] "is more marked than the contrast which is maintained between Babylon as the type of the world, and Jerusalem as the type of the Church. The one is introduced by the foundation of Babel soon after the Deluge; the other by the establishment of the house of David in the city of Zion. Babylon is a scene of confusion. Jerusalem is as a city that is compact together." Babylon breaks up. Jerusalem is the city that emerges out of the ruins. Thus the second angel is a co-worker with the first. One is God's messenger to draw men out of the world. The second is one who proclaims the certain downfall of the great world-agency which has set up its false attractions and lured men by its harlotry to forsake the Lord. And from the very first the sentence hath gone forth against this great Babylon, that she must fall. The false in life, in religion, in commerce, must go. All wickedness is decaying, and will utterly perish before the Lord. The heathen were wont to say, "The feet of the gods are shod with wool, but their hands are hands of iron."

III. THE THIRD ANGEL. (Vers. 9—11, "If any one," etc.) This is a proclamation to the individual. " *If (τις) any one.*" The judgment on great world-powers may be national; that on the individual is personal. The former in this life only; the latter in the next also. "Worshippeth;" present tense, "is worshipping." If any is so found when the Lord cometh to judgment, if he is then drinking of "the wine of the wrath of Babylon's fornication," another cup shall be given him ("*him*" emphatic). "He also shall drink," etc. Of what? Of the wine of the unmixed wrath of God. *Unmixed wrath?* What *can* that be? God grant that we may never know! But may we not say thus much? It will be pure and holy wrath, unmixed with any foreign ingredients. It will not be marred by weakness, nor by excess, nor by defect. It will be a pure and perfect equity dealing with sin. The figurative expressions here— "fire," "brimstone," "smoke"—are terrible ones, drawn from the destruction of Sodom and Gomorrah; and only such figures will avail to set forth the destructive and devouring effect of holy wrath upon a guilty soul. What is the effect? "No rest;" "torment." There never can be any rest for a guilty conscience under the sway of Infinite Holiness. To those ill at ease with God there must be torment. The structure of mind and conscience necessitates this. For how long? "For ever and ever" (Authorized Version); in the margin of the Revised Version, "for ages of ages." This is the more nearly exact translation of the original. It does not affirm the absolute endlessness of the punishment. Since the word "age" has a plural, it plainly is not necessarily infinite. For no such word could have a plural. Infinity cannot even be doubled, much less be multiplied indefinitely. Further, no finite multiple of a finite term can possibly reach infinity. So that to affirm the absolute unendingness of this punishment would be to go beyond the text. At the same time, it is equally clear that the words are so terrible that they do not bring in sight any end of it. Nor is there the slightest gleam of light in the horizon for the finally impenitent. More at length, elsewhere, has the present writer developed this dread theme.[2] The

---

[1] 'Speaker's Commentary,' *in loc.*

[2] 'Future Punishment,' published by J. Snow and Co.

position to which we are shut up in Scripture is this : *God has not shown us an end to future punishment. We dare not affirm that it never will end ; but if any one does that, he does it entirely at his own risk. Objection :* " But this phrase is the very strongest which is employed in the Word of God to denote absolute unendingness." We reply, No. It is a fearfully strong expression for an indefinitely prolonged period ; but there are stronger expressions ; *e.g.* " Thy kingdom is a kingdom of *all* the ages " (Ps. cxlv. 13) ; " To him be glory . . . through *all* the generations of the age of the ages " (Eph. iii. 21) ; " My salvation shall be for ever, and my righteousness shall *not* be abolished " (Isa. li. 6) ; " Not after the law of a carnal commandment, but after the power of an indissoluble life," etc. (Heb. vii. 16). The strongest expressions, which declare absolute unendingness, are reserved in Scripture for the good alone. Even when we grant all this, however, the outlook for the wicked is one of unspeakable gloom ; of a night with no revealed morn beyond it. There is, however, one more feature of this penalty. It will be inflicted " in the presence of the holy angels, and in the presence of the Lamb." There is a profound interest taken in the destinies of man in the distant places of creation. The angels are supremely concerned for the honour of the Son of God. And they will acknowledge that God's judgments are right. The Son of God, too, who died for us, will himself be the Judge. All things are put into his hand. " God so loved the world that he gave his Son ; " but he does not love less that Son whom he gave. And while he will not dishonour that Son by letting any sinner who repents remain unforgiven, so neither will he dishonour him by letting any one who rejects such a Saviour remain unpunished. Finally, we deem it of infinite moment, when a preacher has to handle these awful themes (and handle them he must if he would declare " the whole counsel of God "), that he should show with vivid clearness that *it is sin which is to be mainly dreaded, rather than its penalty.* Sin is the infraction of law. The punishment is God's defence of law. Could we wish for a time to come when existing sin would not be punished ? Could we wish that the punishment of sin should be in any other hands than those of a pure and holy God ? Could we wish that God should give a law, and never guard its honour ? Could we wish that he should give us a gospel, and then let it be rejected with impunity ? Could we wish that he should surrender the Son of his love, and then let him be trampled underfoot, and remain unvindicated ? " But," it may be said, " while I fully confirm that, still I do long for the time to come when sin will cease altogether." Be it so. If God wills it, so it will be sooner or later ; but we cannot find any clear disclosure of that. Three things only remain for us to see to : (1) To hate sin as God hates it. (2) To seek his grace to slay it in us. (3) And then to co-operate with him in putting it down everywhere.

Ver. 13.—*A voice from heaven : the blessed dead.* However deep the gloom in which the description of the future struggles of the Church may plunge us, the Holy Ghost never suffers it to be indefinitely prolonged. We have stood with wondering awe amid the deep recesses of a glacier, and, as if lest the chill should be too severe and the gloom too intense, many a chink overhead let in a light and a glow that revealed wondrous glory above. Even so, as we stand in the midst of the threatening conflicts of the Church, we see light let in from above—a glory shining in the gloom. Thus it is here. We have witnessed the rise and power of the dragon, of the first beast, and of the second beast. We have looked upward and caught a glimpse of the heavenly state. We have heard the voices of the three angels, proclaiming (1) the everlasting gospel, (2) the fall of Babylon the great, (3) the punishment of the ungodly ; and again there is a gleam of heavenly brightness shining in upon us. A voice is heard—whose, we are not told—but it is a commanding voice, under the direction of the Holy Ghost, and that is enough for us. Moreover, it is from heaven, from the realm of light, from the region whence the shadows have fled away. From that higher region the changing scenes of life and death, of struggle and of victory, are beheld ; and from the clearer light in which these earthly incidents are viewed, there is an emphatic testimony given to us which is of priceless value. As so much of the book deals with the struggles of earth, it is restful indeed to be permitted to hear something as to how they fare who have passed beyond them.

I. IN THIS DYING WORLD THERE IS A FEATURE WHICH DISTINCTIVELY MARKS SOME

DEATHS. "The dead which die in the Lord." The dead which *are dying*. The believers in Christ under the present dispensation, who are, one by one, passing away, are evidently intended. "Dying in the Lord" is no vague expression. It defines. It includes. It limits. Otherwise were there no meaning in the phrase. It indicates, indeed, nothing special as to the physical mode of decease; nor as to age; nor as to the accidents of death. The expression, "from henceforth," is ambiguous. (For various interpretations, see expositors.) We incline to the opinion that the "henceforth" here referred to is the time of weariness, in which the faith and patience of the saints will be severely tried by the raging of the powers of evil; that it will be blessed to die in Jesus, and pass away to the realm where the weariness (cf. ἐκ τῶν κόπων αὐτῶν) will be known no more. The significance of the expression, "die in the Lord," should be carefully studied. Deaths are not alike any more than lives are. The deaths of Lazarus and Dives were as widely different as their lives. To die "*in* the Lord" is the natural sequence of living *to* the Lord. No change of state can affect the relation of believers to their Saviour (1 Thess. v. 10; ch. i. 18). Such a dying as is here referred to must include (1) trust, (2) union, (3) communion, (4) surrender, (5) rest—in Christ—all going on in the act of dying, as really as in the act of living. Whether we live or die, we continue to be the Lord's. Once his, we are ever his.

II. THERE ARE MANIFOLD GROUNDS ON WHICH WE KNOW THOSE TO BE BLESSED WHO THUS DIE IN THE LORD. Each phrase in the text is full of meaning. 1. Their blessedness is declared by the Holy Ghost. "Yea, saith the Spirit." 2. It is proclaimed to the apostle by a voice from heaven. 3. There is a command to place it on record for all time. Each of these three lines of thought is indicated by the *words* of the verse. Much more is indicated, however, by the *doctrine* underlying the expression, "in the Lord." This phrase is used to express the unique relation between Christ and the believer. It is constantly recurring. "*In* Christ." From this the blessedness of those dying in him may be confidently affirmed; *e.g.*: 1. Our Lord, in his work for men, contemplated the whole duration of their existence. 2. He is the Saviour of man's whole nature—body, soul, and spirit. 3. Our Saviour's work for believers touched every point of their need. 4. He is himself the Lord of life. 5. Being *in him* is enough for time and eternity. We know whom we have believed. 6. He is guardian of believers as much after death as before it. Hence it must be the case, "Blessed," etc.

III. WE ARE DISTINCTLY TOLD IN WHAT THE BLESSEDNESS CONSISTS. There is no ground in Scripture for asserting the sleep of the soul between death and the resurrection. It is, indeed, only "the body" which "is dead because of sin; the spirit is life because of righteousness." And Jesus expressly declared that whoso keepeth his sayings should never taste of death. "Absent from the body," they are "at home with the Lord." Not, indeed, that the fully glorified state is theirs as yet, nor will be till the resurrection. Not till Christ, our Life, is manifested, shall we be manifested with him in glory. The heavenly life has three stages. The first beginning at regeneration, and closing with the dissolution of the body. The second beginning at death, and ending at the resurrection. The third beginning with the resurrection, and *never* ending. It is this intermediate stage which is pronounced "blessed." They are blessed *in* death, and blessed *after* it. "The having died is gain" (τὸ ἀποθανεῖν). How? 1. *Negatively.* "They rest from their labours." (1) From struggles with sin. (2) From wearying conflict. (3) From every fault and flaw. (4) From all the frailties incident to a disordered frame. 2. *Positively.* Their works follow with them. They not only leave behind them blessed impulses which will follow *after* their earthly works have ceased, but they take *with* them their works into another life; *i.e.* the works of faith and patience and holy activity which were the outwork of their devotion and zeal were a part of themselves; they not only expressed what they were, but they played their part in the growth and perfecting of their characters. And not only so, but the Lord, into whose presence they are ushered at death, sees both them and their works too, as one. As Ewald, "Their works are so far from being lost through their death, that they follow them into eternity" (quoted in 'Speaker's Commentary,' *in loc.*). The same law works in the case of the righteous as in the case of the wicked. "Some men's sins are open beforehand, going before them to judgment;" *i.e.* a man goes into eternity, *plus* his works, whether they be good or bad. Blessed, indeed, is it when the works have been those of faith and love, which, though in many cases forgotten by the worker, shall be remembered by the great Saviour-Judge.

IV. A COMMAND IS GIVEN TO PUT THIS ON RECORD. The truth contained in this verse is too precious a one to be left to the uncertainty of a merely verbal tradition. We know not to what shreds and patches our glorious gospel might by this time have been reduced, had it been thus left at the mercy of floating reports handed down by word of mouth. It was "safe" to write this. The value of this truth is simply unspeakable. 1. *It shows us that death is not a terminus of life, but an incident in living.* It is a change of states under the guardian care of a Divine Redeemer, who loves his own too much to let them perish. 2. *In the light of such a truth, we should dread death less.* Nay, more; we ought not to dread it at all. Our Saviour has passed through the gates of the grave himself, that he might deliver them who through fear of death have been all their lifetime subject to bondage. 3. *A right use of this truth will prepare us for enduring with more calmness and bravery the trials and hardships of this life.* Persecution. Insult. Martyrdom. What fretfulness under sorrow is often shown by those who abandon the evangelical faith! Life of Carlyle; a man who, though a prodigy of intellectual acquirement, lived a life which was one continuous whine. 4. *Let us not grieve unduly over those who are gone.* If they have died in the Lord, and if we are living in the Lord, we shall go to them, but they shall not return to us. We can rejoice in the thought of the increasing wealth of our treasure in the heavenly state, as saint after saint is caught upward into light. 5. *Let us look forward hopefully and cheerfully to our own future.* What work the Master may have appointed for us we cannot foresee, nor do we at all know when we shall be called up to join the "men who are made perfect." But we need not wish to know. It is enough for us that they and we are one.

> "The saints on earth and all the dead
> But one communion make;
> All join in Christ, their living Head,
> And of his grace partake."

6. *Knowing how well we are cared for in life and in death by our blessed Lord, let us concentrate all our energies on glorifying our Lord.* This is the conclusion to which the Apostle Paul himself arrived. Knowing that when we are absent from the body we shall be at home with the Lord, we should make it the object of our supreme ambition to be well-pleasing to him. This, indeed, is our one concern. To work, and love, and obey, and wait. And in time our Master will come and fetch us home, and we shall be for ever with him.

Vers. 14—20.—*Harvest-time.* Any attempt to interpret the visions of this book as if they followed each other chronologically only, will inevitably fail. Sometimes, at any rate, the visions are such that they overleap the near future and glance forward to one far more remote. In fact, speaking generally, the order of them is far more moral than it is temporal, following not so much the order of years as the evolution of principles and the growth of souls. It certainly is so in the paragraph before us, in which we are carried forward in thought and symbol to Heaven's great harvest-day—a day of which our Lord had himself spoken, not only in a parable, but in an exposition of that parable (Matt. xiii.), in which terms that were figurative and symbolic are exchanged for such as are plain. It will be a study of no small interest to see how our Lord, in his communication to his apostle from heaven, sets forth the same truth which he had taught to his disciples when on earth. Ver. 14, "I saw, and behold, a white cloud." This is the symbol of the Divine presence, so that we are not surprised when we read further, "On the cloud I saw one sitting like unto the Son of man"—emblem of the Lord appearing in his glory—" having on his head a golden crown "—in token of royalty—" and in his hand a sharp sickle "—setting forth the work for which he will come in his glory, viz. to reap "the harvest of the earth." Ver. 15, "Another angel . . . crying . . . Send forth," etc. That this angel came forth out of the temple speaks his authority as from thence. Nor should it seem strange that thence should come the commission to the Son of man to reap. For *as* the Son of man, our Lord has his authority and appointment from the Father (John v. 22, 26, 27). Ver. 16,

"He . . . cast his sickle upon the earth." The final reaping is under the superintend-
ence of the Son of man. Ver. 17, " Another angel . . . he also having a sharp sickle."
The ministry of angels will be employed by our Lord in gathering in the harvest
(Matt. xiii.). Ver. 18, " Another . . . he that hath power over fire." Each of our
Lord's host has his own department of service. "Her grapes are fully ripe "—
have reached the *acme* of ripeness,—their full growth. Ver. 19, " The angel . . .
gathered the vintage of the earth." As believers are branches in Christ, the living Vine,
bringing forth good fruit, and only good, so there shall be an earthly product, a mimicry
of the heavenly, bringing forth bad fruit, and only bad. " And cast it into the wine-press
. . . of the wrath of God." A striking figure drawn from the Old Testament (see Isa.
lxiii. 1—6). As there, so here, the treading of grapes in the wine-press represents the
defeat of the foes of God and of his Church. Ver. 20, " Without the city." The Church
is the city of God. All the wicked are outside of it. " There came out blood from the
wine-press " (cf. Gen. xlix. 11; Deut. xxxii. 14). The sap of the grape is called the
blood of the grape, as being the element of its life. In an actual material conflict
actual blood would be shed. Here the whole of the reality is in the spiritual realm,
though the figures are drawn from the material. The main, yea, the sole thought is
the defeat of the enemies of God. " Blood . . . even unto the bridles of the horses."
It is said in ch. xix. 14, " The armies which were in heaven followed upon white horses,"
etc. The hosts of God ever have, ever do, ever will, join him in trampling down the
foes of righteousness. And it is but the carrying out the figure when the chapter
speaks of the blood coming up to the bridles of the horses. " As far as sixteen hundred
furlongs." Hengstenberg understands this as equivalent to "a judgment encircling
the whole earth." [1] What can we learn in so obscure a vision? We reply—The vision
is not an obscure one, if we let Scripture be its own interpreter. There are at least
six lines of high and holy thought, which, on the basis of it, may be profitably
followed up.

I. LONG, LONG BEFORE THE END COMETH, THE SPIRIT OF GOD HAS TOLD US WHAT IT
WILL BE. We gather not only from other Scriptures, but from the fact that our Lord
spoke in parables when on earth. and thus set forth truth in parable when he spake
from heaven, that there is an analogue between the earthly and the spiritual kingdoms.
As in the natural world there are tendencies ever at work which move forwards towards
development and completion, so is it in the spiritual. "First the blade, then the ear,
after that the full corn in the ear." So is the kingdom of God. And because the great
Creator perfectly understands the tendencies of to-day, he can with entire certainty
forecast the issues of the last day. In fact, *the foreknowledge of God is an infinite
power of the calculation of chances.* As he knows perfectly the meaning of what is
to-day, he clearly sees what will be on any given day. And in his fellowship with
men, he has taught them to write the main feature of the end, viz. the harvest-time of
seed already in the ground, whether good or bad.

II. IT IS A MANIFEST FACT THAT THERE ARE ON EARTH AT THIS MOMENT MEN IN
THE TWO WIDELY DIFFERENT CLASSES OF GOOD AND EVIL. No one can deny this unless
he ignores plain facts before every one's eyes. There are men who are stainless in their
sanctity. There are others who are fiendish in their vileness. And it is not in reference to such widely contrasted lives that men find so much difficulty. Many years
ago, an Oxford professor remarked that there were some who had never known anything
about repentance towards God or faith towards our Lord Jesus Christ, and who yet
therefore could not be classed among the wheat, yet they were externally so moral
and irreproachable they could not be classed among the tares! What was his conclusion?
That there must be an intermediate class! There is another and a sounder conclusion
Our Lord declares there are two, and but two. But even if there are some that *seem to
us* to come between, we dare not impeach the verdict of him who searcheth the hearts.
The fact is, we can understand only issues. Christ can discern tendencies. He knows
them *now,* and by their fruits *we* shall know them. Germs. Growth. Development.
Manifestation.

III. FOR WISE REASONS, NOT ALL OF WHICH ARE KNOWN TO US, BOTH GOOD AND EVIL

[1] So also Bishop Boyd Carpenter, Dr. Currey (quoted by him), Professor Milligan, Dr
Warren, Dr. Craven, Rev. W. Robinson, Rev. P. W. Grant, and the ' Speaker's Commen
tary ' (*in loc.*) for different interpretations of the sixteen hundred furlongs.

ARE TO GROW TOGETHER SIDE BY SIDE. The good have to confront the evil and keep it in check. The evil is permitted to counterplot the good and to retard its spread. But we must not speak only in the abstract. Rather let us say, good *men*, evil *men*. For when we bring human nature, with all its powers of willing and combating, into the question, then we can at once see that at least one purpose is gained by this temporary co-mingling together. Good men are made better, sturdier, and braver for having a conflict to endure. And much of the evil is turned into good through the grace of God. Note: Do not let us fall into the millennarian heresy of supposing that the tares are going to increase prodigiously and the wheat to diminish, until the Lord comes. There is not one Scripture text for that. Scripture only says, both are to get riper—the good, better; the bad, worse.

IV. AT THE TIME FORESEEN BY GOD THIS PROCESS WILL, ON BOTH SIDES, BE CONSUMMATED. Do we understand by this that in the spiritual world there comes a time when character cannot possibly advance further either in goodness or in wickedness? We do not so understand it. Analogy is not identity, but only resemblance with some difference. And because there is all the difference between natural growth and spiritual, we must not expect a resemblance on every point. But two points are certainly clear, and a third is possible. 1. A time will come in the development of character when all doubt ceases as to what a man is. 2. Then there can be no question whether his destiny is the garner or the fire. 3. It *may* be that then no such thing as a change of character is possible. Eternal punishment will only be in the case of eternal sin (Mark iii. 29, Revised Version).

V. AT THIS STAGE THE GREAT REAPING-TIME WILL COME. Then the commission to consummate all will be fulfilled by the Lord Jesus Christ (Matt. xiii. 41). The angels will be the reaper-band. The result will be the complete manifestation—the final division—the great decision. The gathering in of the righteous into the kingdom. The trampling down the grapes in earth's vineyard in the wine-press of the wrath of God! Dread words! whose detail no pen of man can sketch; but that towards one end or the other every one is at this moment tending, is one of the most certain of the laws of human nature.

VI. THIS DREAD VISION IS GIVEN US FOR HIGH AND HOLY PURPOSES. 1. It should relieve those whose faith and patience are now being so sorely tried by the growth of error and sin. Both *are* putting on riper forms than ever. Well, the end will come. " The fire will try every man's work." 2. It should lead us all to estimate the value of this life. The end towards which we all are tending is one of ripeness, either in righteousness or sin. 3. It should lead each one to look solemnly at the fact that, however long it may be before the universal consummation will be, (1) God will act *then* on the very same principles on which he worketh *now*. (2) *Now* there are working in us tendencies which shall be developed *then*. The law of continuity holds in the Divine procedure. The law of growth in human character. Note : There m y be in grace, what can never be in nature, the conversion of tares into wheat. I' is is to be, it must be before the harvest-day. (3) The sickle may cut down individuals long before its final thrust.

HOMILIES BY VARIOUS AUTHORS.

Vers. 1—5.—*The perfect Church.* How well it is for us, in forming our estimates and in regulating our conduct, to have set before us a true ideal and a faultless standard ! To compare ourselves with ourselves, that is, with men like ourselves, is, so St. Paul tells us, not wise. And all experience proves the truth of his word. The low levels of ordinary religious life in the present day all result from our practically, not professedly, putting before ourselves standards which are faulty and inferior, instead of those which would be constantly summoning us to higher and holier attainment. Now, the Word of God is ever furnishing us with such perfect standards. Our Lord again and again bids us turn our gaze heavenward, that we may see there how we ought to judge and what we ought to be. How frequently he speaks of our Father in heaven, that we may behold in God the true ideal of all fatherhood ! And that we may the better understand and act towards our children, he tells us that " in heaven their angels do always behold," etc.   And when his opponents murmured, as was their wont, at his receiving sinners and eating with them, he rebuked them by the reminder that in heaven there is not murmuring, but *joy*, even over " one sinner that repenteth." And here in these verses we who belong to the Church on earth have given to us a vision of the perfect Church—the Church in heaven.   And the contemplation of it cannot but be well for us, that we may judge thereby our beliefs, our worship, our selves, and seek more and more to conform them to the heavenly pattern.   Observe, then—

I. THAT WE CANNOT LIMIT THE CHURCH TO ANY ONE VISIBLE CORPORATE BODY.   The claims of any such Church body here on earth to be exclusively *the* Church, and the denial of membership therein to all outside that body, are shown to be false by the fact that the notes and characteristics of the true Church are found in many Churches, but exclusively in none.   There are, thank God, few Churches, if any, that have not some of them.   Out of all of them the Church is gathered, but to no one of them is it confined.   The members of the Church are described here as having the name of the Father of our Lord Jesus Christ " written upon their foreheads."   Now, this is a figure of speech to tell of the *character* of those who form the Church ; that that character is : 1. *God-like.*   It is the Father's name which is written ; hence they who bear it are holy and without blemish, perfect even as the Father in heaven is perfect.   2. *Visible.*   It is written on their foreheads.   The light shines before men ; it cannot be hid.   That godliness is much to be questioned which no one can see, or which is hidden away and kept for only certain seasons, places, and surroundings.   That which is here said teaches the reverse of such a doubtful thing.   3. And it is *permanent.*   It is " written." " Litera scripta manet."   It abides, not being a thing assumed for a time, and like the goodness told of by Hosea, which as the " morning cloud " and " early dew goeth away." It is the habit of the life, the continual characteristic of the man.   Such, in general terms, is the distinguishing mark of membership in Christ's true Church.   And again we gratefully own that in all Churches it is to be found.   Would that it were on all as in all !

II. THE CENTRE OF THE WORSHIP OF THE PERFECT CHURCH IS " THE LAMB."   St. John says, " I beheld *the* Lamb ; " not " *a* Lamb," as the Authorized Version reads.   He does not stop to explain.   He has so often spoken of the Lord Jesus Christ as the Lamb, that there can be no room for doubt as to his meaning.   It is the Lord Jesus Christ, not so much in his more majestic attributes—his might, majesty, and dominion—that we are bidden behold, but in his sacrificial character as " the Lamb of God who taketh away the sin of the world."   As such he is the Centre of the Church's adoration.   He is seen on Mount Zion, that site of Israel's temple being taken continually in Scripture as the symbol of the home of God's redeemed and the scene of their eternal worship. He is surrounded by the Church of the Firstborn—" the firstfruits " unto God, whom he has redeemed by his blood.   The number named here, twelve and the multiples of twelve, is ever associated with the Church.   And the twelve times twelve tells of the Church's completion, the " accomplishment of the number of the elect."   Now, in the midst of that perfect assembly, that Church of which these are the representatives, stands " the Lamb " as the Object of the adoration, the love, and the worship of all. That Church on earth must, then, lack this distinct note of the heavenly Church if in it Christ the Son of God, as the Redeemer, the Saviour, the Sacrifice for the world's sins, be not lifted up as the Object of all trust, love, and obedience, and if he be not so regarded by the members of such Church.   Let us ask—What is he to ourselves ?   How do we look upon him who is thus looked upon by the Church in heaven ?   In the midst of our Zions, do we see, as the chief, the central, the pre-eminent figure, the Lamb of God ?   And in the inner temple of our own hearts, is he there enshrined and enthroned as he hath right and ought to be ?   What is our hope and what our trust ? How can we ever hope to be numbered with " the Church of the Firstborn," if the name of him, to which every heart there responds, awakes no echo, no answering thrill, in us ?   Our lips utter that name often enough, and in all manner of ways ; but what do our hearts say ?   That is the question to which this vision of the Lamb on Mount Zion, surrounded by the adoring Church, should give rise in every one of us.   And may God grant that it may meet with a satisfactory answer !

III. THE WORSHIP OF THE PERFECT CHURCH IS A JOYFUL WORSHIP.   We are told that " they sung a new *song.*"   Joy finds utterance in song ; it is its natural expression ;

and when, therefore, we read of the songs of heaven, it is proof of the joys of that blessed place. The worship of heaven takes this form. Here, prayer and preaching form, and properly form, part of our worship; but there, praise alone is heard. Here, we wail our litanies and pour forth our supplications; but there worship is all song—the voice of glad thanksgiving and joyful praise. How much is told us of the blessed future in that one fact! And of this song we are told many precious things. 1. *How full-voiced it is!* St. John likens it to that "of many waters"—that loud, resonant sound as when the floods lift up their voice, or the sea roars, or where some vast volume of water pours itself from over a great height to some far-down depth. What a sound comes up from that boiling caldron of tossing waves! The magnitude of the sound of that song is what St. John seeks to set forth by his similitude of "many waters." 2. *And its majesty also* is indicated by its comparison to "a great thunder"—the voice of the Lord as they of old regarded it. It is no mean, trivial theme that has inspired that song, but one that wakes up every heart, and opens the lips of all the redeemed, to show forth the praise of him who hath redeemed them. It is a noble song, grand, glorious. How could it be otherwise, telling as it does of deeds of such Divine heroism, of conquests of such moment, and of sacrifice so vast? 3. *And how sweet a song is it also!* For St. John supplies yet another similitude: its sound was like that "of harpers harping with their harps." So sweet, so soul-subduing, so full of heavenly delight, that it brought smiles to the saddest countenance, and wiped away all tears. And is not the song of redemption just such a song as that? Even we know of songs of Zion so unspeakably beautiful, and set to music such as, it seems to us, even angelic choirs might rejoice in. But if earthly song can be so sweet, though coming from lips and hearts so little pure, what must that song have been which is told of here, and which St. John can only compare, for its unutterable beauty, to the strains of the most perfect instruments that the ancient world knew of—the harp, Judah's national symbol, and best-beloved accompaniment of praise? But not alone the mingled magnitude, majesty, and sweetness of the sound of this song is set forth here, but also its substance. 4. *It was "a new song."* There had never been anything like it before. They who sang it had never joined in, or even heard of, such song till they sang it in the presence of the Lamb on Mount Zion. It could not but be new, for it was inspired by new and glorious revelations of God; sung amid conditions and surroundings that were all new, and by hearts and lips made new by the renewing grace of the Holy Spirit of God. Much there had been in days past for which they had been constrained to praise and give thanks, but till now the half had not been told them, and hence none of their old songs would serve. They *must* sing a new song; it could not but be new. 5. And it was *known by none but those who sang it.* "No man could learn that song but," etc. How can he who has never even been to sea know the joy of him who has been saved from shipwreck? Who but the child knows the mother's love? The song told of here is but the result of the experiences through which they who sing it have been led. How, then, can they sing it who have known none of these things? But those represented by the hundred and forty-four thousand know the depths of sin and sorrow from which, and the heights of holiness and joy to which, and the love by which, and the purpose for which, they have have been uplifted. They know the conviction of sin, and the joy of pardon, and the Holy Spirit's grace, and the love of Christ. But what does the unbeliever know of these things? and how, therefore, can he learn this song? The question comes—If such be the worship of the heavenly Church, are our Churches on earth preparing their members to join therein? Churches here should be vestibules for the heavenly Church. Is the Church with which we are associated so to you and me? No one can learn that song unless they be redeemed. Have we the qualification? Have we come to Christ? Are we trusting in him? "We must begin heaven's song here below, or else we shall never sing it above. The choristers of heaven have all rehearsed their song here ere they took their places in the choir of heaven." But only Christ can touch the soul's sin-darkened eye, and cause it to see that truth which will make redemption precious, and hence he who is our Saviour must be also our Teacher. So only can we learn the new song of his redeemed.

IV. Its MEMBERS ARE WITHOUT FAULT. After that the blessed condition of the redeemed has been set forth, we are next shown their character. The general and symbolic expression which tells how they all have the "Father's name written on their foreheads " is expanded and explained by the more definite declarations which we must now notice. It is said " they are without fault," or " blameless," as the Revised Version reads ; and the apostle specifies four of the chief temptations to which they had been exposed, and which they had resisted and overcome. 1. And the first he names is that of *impurity*. In the unusual expression in which this sin is referred to, there is no countenance of any teachings which would give higher place to the single over the married life. If the unmarried alone are amongst the redeemed, it is questionable if one of the apostles of our Lord would be found there. But that which is pointed at is those sins of which it is best not to speak, but which we know full well have their roots in the very centre of our nature, and which it is a lifelong struggle to repress and subdue. But this *must* be done, and—blessed be he who saves not only from the guilt, but the might of sin!—it may be done, and is being done, even as it was with " these" of whom our text tells. 2. *Half-heartedness*. Great was, and great is, the temptation to follow Christ only along paths not difficult. But to follow him " whithersoever " he went—ah ! how many would be and are sore tempted to shrink from that ! They would follow their Lord for some way—even at times a long way; but to follow where difficulty, danger, disgrace, death, waited for them—from that how many would shrink ! But " these" did not. 3. *Conformity to the world*. " These " had the holy courage to be singular, to come out " from among men," to go against the stream, to be other than the rest of men. How difficult this is those only know who have tried to do as " these" did. The assimilating power of the society in which we mingle is almost resistless, and often it is full of spiritual peril. It was so to those for whom St. John wrote, and not seldom it is so still. Hence we have to go unto Christ " without the camp, bearing his reproach." " These " did this, and so won the high honour and rich reward told of here. 4. *Insincerity*. When to confess Christ meant, perhaps, the loss of all things, yea, their very lives; when martyrdom was the guerdon of faithful acknowledgment of their Lord, how tremendous must have been the temptation to tamper with truth, to conceal, to compromise, to evade, to equivocate! But of " these" it is said, " in their mouth was found no guile." He who is the God of truth, yea, who is the Truth, ever lays great stress on this virtue of guilelessness, whilst deceit and lies are declared abominable in his sight.

CONCLUSION. Such was the character of that perfect Church—" the firstfruits unto God and to the Lamb." Doubtless there were all other forms of Christ-likeness—love, patience, meekness, and the rest—for the varied forms of Christ's grace as seen in character are generally found in clusters. Where you find some you generally find others, yea, in some measure, all of them. But as we read of only what is said here, our heart well-nigh despairs, and would altogether were it not that the same source of all goodness is open to us as to them of whom we here read.

> " Oh, how can feeble flesh and blood
> Burst through the bonds of sin ?
> The holy kingdom of our God,
> What man can enter in ? "

And the sad reply would be, " None," were it not that he who summons us to such high attainment ministers all needed grace. Therefore we may and we must be " holy as he is holy."—S. C.

Ver. 4.—*The greater salvation*. " Firstfruits unto God and to the Lamb." From this and the many like expressions which are scattered over the New Testament, we gather that there is a salvation greater and less. For here it is said that these hundred and forty-four thousand are " firstfruits." Therefore we learn—

I. WHAT THESE ARE NOT. 1. *They are not all the saved*. The very word indicates that there is much more to follow. They are but the beginning. Nor: 2. Are these firstfruits *the mass of the saved*. True, a large number is named, but what is that compared with the " great multitude that no man can number, out of every," etc. ?

II. WHAT THEY ARE. The word " firstfruits " teaches us that these thus named are: 1. *The pledge of all the rest*. Thus Christ has " become the Firstfruits of them that slept " (1 Cor. xv. 20). He is the pledge and guarantee that in him " all shall be made alive." And so the natural firstfruits of corn guaranteed the rest of the harvest.

For the same sun, and all other nurturing forces which had ripened the firstfruits, were there ready to do the same kindly office for all the rest. And so we are told, "The Spirit of him that raised up Jesus from the dead shall also quicken your mortal bodies." The same power is present for both the first and after fruits. 2. *The pattern and representative of all the rest.* Compare the first and after fruits. In *the main* they were alike; and so in the spiritual world also. But : 3. The firstfruits *were pre-eminent over the rest.* They were specially presented to God, and held in honour; so was it with the natural grain. But, without question, there is pre-eminence implied in being the firstfruits of the heavenly harvest. (1) *In time.* Theirs is "the first resurrection," of which we read in ch. xx.—that resurrection of the dead which St. Paul calls "*the* resurrection," and "the mark" towards which he pressed, if by any means he might attain unto it (Phil. iii.). "The rest of the dead lived not again until the thousand years," etc. (cf. ch. xx.). (2) *In honour.* St. Paul called it "the prize of our high calling of God in Christ Jesus." Now, a prize implies special honour. And our Lord tells us that there is a "first" and "last" in the kingdom of heaven; "a least" and "a greatest." "One star differeth from another star in glory." There is "an entrance administered abundantly," and there is a "being saved so as by fire." As here there is no dead level of reward, so we might believe, and we are taught, that there is none such in heaven. Infinite mischief is done by the belief that all will be equally blessed, equally honoured, equally like God. It is as if we had adopted the creed of Ecclesiastes, where we are told, "One end cometh alike to all," instead of St. Paul's, who tells us, "What a man soweth *that*"—not something else—"shall he also reap," in quantity and quality too. (3) *In service.* That they were pre-eminent here, who that knows their history on earth, or reads even this book, will question? (4) *In character.* See how they are described as to their spiritual purity, their unreserved consecration, their separateness from the world, their guilelessness and freedom from all deceit. (5) *In the approval of God.* Of them it is written, "Blessed and holy is he that hath part in the first resurrection" (ch. xx.). How could it be otherwise than that such as they should stand highest upon the steps of the everlasting throne, and nearest God and the Lamb? 4. *They are the elect of God.* In another part of this book they are spoken of as "the called, and chosen, and faithful." They answer to the description of God's chosen, and so we learn that "whilst all the elect are saved, all the saved are not elect" (Alford). All are not firstfruits, greatest, first, in the kingdom of heaven. The very words imply order, gradation, rank. But it is for us to take heed as to—

III. WHAT WE SHOULD STRIVE TO BE. There are some who say that they will be content if they can only "get just inside the door of heaven"—such is the phrase. This sounds very humble-minded, and if it be so, then those who thus speak are just those who would not be content with any such place. For, and to their credit be it said, they are such as desire to be like their Lord—to resemble him, to possess his Spirit, and to please him in all things. But if they desire, or will be content with, the lowest place in heaven, they must get rid of all these beautiful and blessed qualities. But rather than this they would die. Too often, however, the phrase is but a substitute for diligence and faithful following of Christ. They are content to be but little like their Lord; they do not follow after holiness in the fear of God; they are the worldly hearted, those the least worthy of the Christian name. But who would be content to be as these? Who would not be in full sympathy with St. Paul, who said, "I labour . . . to be accepted of him" (2 Cor. v. 9)? Ours, then, is to be not contented with any lowest place—if we be, there is grave doubt whether we ever attain to that—but to "press toward the mark for *the prize* of our high calling of God in Christ Jesus."
—S. C.

Vers. 6, 7.— *The gospel of judgment.* St. John beholds "another angel flying in mid-heaven, having an eternal gospel to proclaim." Concerning this gospel note—

I. IT IS NOT *THE* GOSPEL. The gospel is that which tells to sinful man that there is eternal life for him in Christ; "that Christ Jesus came into the world to save sinners." This is a very different gospel. It is one of judgment. Its message is, "The hour of God's judgment is come." And the message of the second angel (ver. 8) points to one scene where that judgment has already fallen; and the message of the third angel (ver. 9) is one of awful threatening against the sin which would bring the judgment upon "any man." Very far removed, then, is this gospel from that which we commonly understand by the word "gospel."

II. BUT IT IS A GOSPEL. Any message that announces the destruction of a power that is cursing the human race, and spreading misery and despair on all sides, must be a gospel. Like the news that a ferocious wild beast that has slain many is at last itself slain. There have been men who, from their crimes, their ambition, their unscrupulous cruelty, and the devastations that they have caused, have won for themselves the name of "enemies of the human race." When, then, these cruel oppressors have met their fate and been overthrown, the tidings have justly filled men's hearts with joy. In view of similar facts, the psalms bid us "Sing unto the Lord a new song: sing unto the Lord, all the earth . . . for he cometh to judge the earth." Judgment and joy are joined together as cause and effect. And so here this message from God, that "the hour of his judgment has come," is a joyful message, a gospel. In the New Testament Christ's destructive work, his overthrow of Satan and all the power of hell, is, as is right, gratefully and constantly commemorated. And to the persecuted Church, groaning beneath the oppression of the tiger in human shape, who then ruled the world, and whose thirst for blood no amount of slaughter could slake, must it not have been a gospel for them that this angel proclaimed?

III. AND IT IS AN "ETERNAL" GOSPEL. For not once alone, but throughout all the ages of the world, its message has been sooner or later embodied in deed. The tyrants and oppressors of God's people have been hurled from their place of power which they had so abused, and have had to meet and endure the awful judgment of God. The records are in the Bible, and in all the world beside. It is a fearful fact for him to face who, Pharaoh-like, is hardening himself against God, but a blessed fact for those who groan beneath his cruelty. It is the conviction of this eternal gospel which gives patience to men who witness cruelty and outrage inflicted on those who cannot defend themselves. They know that the God of this gospel lives, and in due time will reveal and vindicate himself as the Refuge of the distressed, and the Helper of the helpless.

IV. AND IT IS FOR ALL NATIONS—FOR HUMANITY AT LARGE. As in ch. xiii. 7 "the beast" had power given him by the devil "over all kindreds, and tongues, and nations," so now this gospel was to be proclaimed from the mid-heavens, where the angel was seen swiftly flying "over [the word, ἐπὶ, is the same] every nation, and tribe, and tongue, and people." God forgetteth none; he knows and is touched with the sorrows of all; he is the all-Father, the "our Father, which art in heaven." His "chariot-wheels" do doubtless oftentime seem "long in coming;" but he will come. Man anxiously scans the heavens, and frequently fails to see the angel that St. John saw; but the rush of his pinions shall one day be heard, and the brightness of his countenance shall one day be seen, and the "great voice" with which he shall give forth his message shall fall upon our listening ears. Let all who hope in God rejoice; let all his foes and ours be in great fear.

V. GOD IS CONCERNED TO MAKE IT KNOWN. The gospel is entrusted to men. "We have this treasure in earthen vessels," said St. Paul, "and he hath committed unto us the word of reconciliation." But this gospel of judgment is committed to an angel, who is seen flying swiftly to make proclamation of it far and wide. These facts, that it is an angel to whom it is entrusted, that the angel flies swiftly, that he proclaims his message with "a great voice,"—all seem to point to the Divine urgency and concern that it should be made known. Nor is the reason far to seek. There is nothing so hinders man's belief in the goodness of God as the experience of the cruelty of his fellow-man. The children of Israel would "not listen" to Moses, who came to them with the good news of deliverance, "by reason of their bondage." Their fellow-man was the highest placed of any being they knew, and he was hard and cruel, and shut out sight and thought and faith of that far other Being, who was their fathers' God—the God of Abraham, Isaac, and Jacob. And how many there are who through fear "are all their lifetime subject to bondage"! It is of no use to proclaim to such a scheme of mercy; they ask for justice—justice upon their oppressors, justice for themselves and those who suffer with them. Men can believe in and respect justice without mercy, but they can neither respect nor believe in mercy without justice. Therefore, to the great company of the oppressed, the proclamation of judgment is a gospel, and must precede the message which we specially call *the* gospel. And therefore the angel is sent, and on speedy wing and with loud voice the gospel of judgment is proclaimed. VI. WHAT SHOULD BE ITS EFFECTS. 1. *The fear of God.* (Ver. 7.) What other could result from such a message? And a blessed result it would be. 2. *The giving of glory to God.* From the delivered people, and from those who were filled with salutary fear, there would be this giving of glory. And this for God's revelation of his righteousness; for his deliverance of them from oppression. And on the part of the wicked who had heard and believed God's warning, they would give glory for that they had been spared, and not cut off in their sins, as they well might have been. 3. *Worship.* This, with fear and the giving of glory, had been demanded for "the beast" by himself, and the demand had been complied with. But it is now demanded for God, who, as the Creator of all things and the Judge of all the earth, alone has right to worship. Oh that wherever there be a hardened heart, the message of judgment may come with such power as that there shall be real repentance, revealing itself in holy fear of God, in giving him glory, and in the worship of his Name!—S. C.

Ver. 8.—*The voice of the second angel: the judgment of Babylon.* I. WHAT IS MEANT BY "BABYLON"? There can be scarce any doubt that the name points to: 1. *Persecuting Rome.* She is spoken of under this pseudonym because it was not safe to write, or in any way openly utter, words which might be construed as treasonable to the empire. There were laws sharp and stern, and accusers only too willing to bring those laws into action, which would involve in ruin and death those who spoke or wrote such open word. Therefore under this disguise, penetrable enough by the Christian Church, the name of Rome, her cruel and relentless persecutor, was concealed. Because also she stood in the like hateful relation to the Church of God as in ages gone by Babylon had stood to the Church of her day. Babylon had been of old, as Rome was now, the ruthless ravager and the bloodthirsty destroyer of God's people. And as the judgment of God was denounced and came upon Babylon because of her crimes against God's Church, so now like judgment had been denounced, and was about to come upon Rome for her crimes against the Church of the Lord Jesus Christ. And as Babylon had been one of the world-wide empires, so now Rome occupied the same pre-eminence. None could compare with Babylon, in the days of her greatness, for wealth or power or glory; and so, when St. John wrote this book, none could compare, in any of these respects, with Rome. And there is yet, perhaps, another purpose in this name here given to Rome—the purpose to recall to the mind of the suffering Church the certainty of the coming judgment on Rome, by the fact that such judgment had come on Babylon. 2. *All persecutors.* The mind of God to such is shown by what he did to Babylon of old. He would have us learn that he will ever do the like to those who sin in like manner. Did ever any persecuting power find that it had done wisely and well? Let the records of history reply from Egypt down to Spain. 3. *And all idolaters.* Idol-worship was not a merely intellectual preference for one form of religion rather than another; had it been only that it would not have brought down upon it so many awful judgments, nor have been branded with so foul a name. But it was a system of abominations; it was "earthly, sensual, devilish." It was a religion that laid no constraint on the passions, no bridle upon the will; that left man to his likings so only as the ceremonial of idolatry was observed. And every religion that leaves man thus has an idol. A creation of the mind, if not of the hands, instead of God, is idolatry in substance, whatever it may be in name. II. IN WHAT SENSE COULD BABYLON BE SAID TO HAVE FALLEN? 1. Rome had fallen in a very real way when St. John thus wrote. For there had been *a great moral fall.* Rome had a noble past. God had raised her up to great power, had endowed her with magnificent qualities, and made her the mother of many noble sons. In the unfolding of the great drama of Divine providence, she had a high and honourable part to fill, and none who know her history can deny that for a long time she fulfilled the will of God. But an evil spirit took possession of her, and then she became what is here said. Cruelty and lust, pride and oppression, and whatever was unclean and abominable, found welcome and home in her. "Fallen" was the absolutely true and righteous verdict that could alone be given concerning her. But there was to be an outward fall corresponding to this inward one. And it is spoken of as already come, because: 2.

It was already decreed. The sentence had gone forth, and was but awaiting execution. 3. *It had begun.* An empire that had become the prey and prize of one successful general after another; that might be won and lost any day at the caprice of bribed bands of soldiers, had lost all stability, and was already "as a bowing wall and a tottering fence." 4. But chiefly because *it was so soon to be accomplished.* To the quickened vision of the seer, the barbarian nations were already plunging over her borders, and wasting and destroying on every hand. Rome was to him as if already in the deadly grip of those fierce hordes who should one day crush out her life. The vision was so vivid to him that he speaks of it as actual, real, and present. And in all these senses the judgment of God is gone out against ungodly men. "Condemned already" is our Lord's word for such; and "is fallen, is fallen," is St. John's. Oh for the quickened vision to make all this real to godly men, that they might labour and pray more in order to "snatch brands from the burning;" and to ungodly men, that they might "flee from the wrath to come"!

III. THE GROUNDS OF THIS AWFUL JUDGMENT. It was no arbitrary sentence, nor one that had been hastily or without righteous reason pronounced. Yea, there had come to be imperative necessity for it, and it would have been unrighteous had it been withheld. 1. Rome had come to be *one mass of corruption.* St. John adopts the prophetic style, and speaks of the "wine of her fornication," by which he means that she had come to "work," not "all uncleanness" alone, but all manner of godless abomination besides, "with greediness;" as with greedy grip the drunkard grasps the wine-cup. Rome had become a "putrefying sore." Let Tacitus tell. 2. And she was *the seducer of others.* Holding the position she did, she could not but be a fountain of influence for all cities and lands that came under her wide-reaching rule. And she had corrupted them all; she had "made all nations drink of the wine," etc. And he who branded for ever the name of Jeroboam the son of Nebat because he "made Israel to sin," has here again declared his wrath against all, whether nations or individuals, who do the like. And: 3. *The cup of sin becomes the cup of wrath.* Such is the Divine law. This is the meaning of the condensed sentence, "the wine of the wrath," etc. The wine of her sin, and the wine of God's wrath upon it, are drunk out of the same cup. "In the hand of the Lord there is a cup, and the wine is red . . . but the dregs thereof, all the wicked of the earth shall wring them out, and drink them" (Ps. lxxv. 8). "Our pleasant vices," Shakespeare tells us, become our scourge; and life is full of proof that so it is. At the bottom of every cup of sin there is "wrath." Ah! what need have we all to offer continually the prayer, "Give us a heart to love *and dread thee,* and diligently to live after thy commandments"!—S. C.

Vers. 9—12.—"*The most awful threatening the Bible contains*" (Bengel). Undoubtedly it is so. It makes our flesh creep and our heart shudder as we read it. It is to be noted that these three angels (vers. 6, 8, 9), who "excel in strength," bear messages of increasing severity. The first bids us "fear." The second tells of the dread judgment upon Babylon. This third threatens all men everywhere with like and yet more awful doom, if they "worship the beast" or "receive his mark." Now—

I. WHAT DOES ALL THIS MEAN? 1. *It seems to mean that the ungodly shall be punished with incessant and unspeakable torments in hell-fire, and that for ever and ever.* This is the doctrine that has been deduced from this passage again and again. It is one of the buttresses of the popular theology. It is always quoted in support of this doctrine, and is regarded as one of the chief of the proof-texts. But if it do teach this, we ask: (1) Would not the language be more clear? Who certainly knows what the two beasts, the first and second, stand for? Who can do more than guess, with more or less of probability, what St. John meant by them; much less what it was intended we, in our day, should understand by them? And what is "the mark of the beast"? and how do men receive it "in their forehead," or their "hand"? We may think we understand all this. But can any one be sure? But consequences so awful as are threatened here would not be told of in language so ambiguous. If we to-day be threatened with such doom, the offences that incur it will surely be set forth in words unmistakably plain, and not such as we find here. (2) May not temporal judgments be so described? May not the same language be used for something quite different from what it is said this means? Yes, for Isaiah thus speaks of Edom (xxxiv.

8—14): "The smoke thereof shall go up for ever." The temporal judgments that came upon Edom are thus described. And so, in ch. xviii., we have word for word *the fulfilment on earth*, not in Gehenna, of the threatenings we are now considering (cf. vers. 9, 15, 18). Why, then, may not temporal judgments be what are meant here? (3) Why, in the closing vision of this book, are death, hell, and the lake of fire, pain, sorrow, death, and all such things, declared to have "passed away" and to be "no more" (cf. ch. xxi.)? All these things have not been transferred to some other planet, to defile its surface and darken its heavens. They have "passed away," he alone abiding who "doeth the will of God." (4) Why is the language of the Bible so constantly of such a kind as to lend the strongest colour to the belief that death, destruction, perishing—not a never-ending existence in suffering—is the doom of the finally impenitent? That this is so can hardly be denied. The passage before us is, probably, the only one which seems to teach everlasting suffering. (5) And, if it were a Divine doctrine, would it not, like all other Divine doctrines, "commend itself to every man's conscience in the sight of God"? The truth that St. Paul preached did so commend itself. If this be part of it, why does it not also so commend itself? It is notorious that it does not. Conscience revolts against it, and insistence upon it has generated more unbelief and atheism than, perhaps, any other cause whatsoever. We, therefore, cannot believe that what this passage seems to many minds to mean, it actually does mean. But: 2. *We note the following facts.* (1) The occasion of this threatening. Terrible persecution, when it was absolutely necessary to fortify and strengthen the minds of Christians with every consideration that would help them to be faithful under the dreadful trials that beset them. (2) And in this way this threatening, and others like it (cf. Matt. **x.**), were used, and were no small help to the steadying of the wavering will and the strengthening of the feeble heart. "The ancient Cyprian often strengthened his exhortations to steadfastness under bloody persecutions with this word." (3) The fulfilment of this word (cf. ch. xviii. and parallels). Therefore, whilst not limiting it to temporal punishments: 3. *We regard it as telling of that "everlasting destruction from the presence of the Lord,"* which shall be the doom of all apostates and all who persist in rebellion against the Lord.

II. WHAT DOES IT TEACH? Amongst other lessons these: 1. The retribution of God upon unfaithful and wicked men is an awful reality. 2. That in the midst of temptation the remembrance of this will be a great help. 3. That it is the love of God which tells us the truth. 4. That they are fools and self-destroyed who will not "come unto" Christ that they "might have life."—S. C.

Ver. 13.—*The blessed dead.* "And I heard a voice from heaven saying unto me, Write, Blessed are the dead which die in the Lord from henceforth." By such word as this it is that Christ "hath abolished death." True, it is at the side of the open grave and over our dead that we read them, so that the stern, hard fact of death is still with us, and often well-nigh crushing our hearts with its load of sorrow. Death yet reigns. But his sovereignty is shorn of its worst power, since words like these fell upon the ears and hearts of men. The *Vale, vale, in æternum vale!* of broken-hearted paganism is gone, never to return. The broken pillar and the extinguished torch are no longer fit emblems to place over the grave of our loved ones. The pillar rears its fair shaft and lacks not its beautiful coronal, and on the eternal shore the torch burns more brightly than ever, and is by no means gone out, though our dim eyes for a while see it not. And this unspeakably precious gospel, which brings us such glad tidings of great joy, it is which some men want to silence as effete and incredible, that they may substitute for it their own dismal speculations, the only outcome and clear utterance of which is that, in regard to religious faith, there is nothing solid under our feet, nor clear over our heads; all is one great "perhaps;" nothing certain—nothing; neither soul, nor God, nor eternal life. To all such we say, "If we be dreaming, as you affirm, then for God's sake let us dream on, unless you have some better, surer belief to which we may awake." But let us now think awhile of the unspeakably precious truth our text contains. And we note—

I. WHOM IT CONCERNS. 1. *Those "in the Lord."* "It is obviously of the utmost moment that we rightly understand who are spoken of. Alas! the context has warned us that the blessing here pronounced is not for all. The blessed dead are placed in marked contrast with those who in this life have borne the mark of the beast, which is the world, in their forehead and upon their hand. How glad are we, for ourselves and for those dear to us, when it comes to the last solemn moment, to forget that there is any distinction between the death of the righteous and of the wicked; between the death of one who has loved and served Christ, and of one who has lived 'without him in the world'? It seems so hard to preserve that distinction" (Vaughan, *in loc.*). But there it is, and may *not* be overlooked, though, to the unspeakable hurt of men's souls, it too often is. Now, "to die in the Lord," we must first have been "in the Lord." And can any be said to be "in the Lord" if they never think of him, never call upon him, never look to him, and never seek to live to him? "In the Lord" is the constant phrase which tells of a living trust and hope and love towards the Lord; and how can the description be applied where none of these things are? God help us all to remember this! 2. *And these when they are dead.* Just then, when we want to know something of them; when with streaming tears we yearn

"For the touch of a vanished hand,
And the sound of a voice that is still."

II. WHAT IT SAYS OF THEM. 1. *That they are "blessed."* What unspeakable comfort there is in this assurance for those who are left behind! Not unconscious, for such high epithet as "blessed" belongs not to mere unconsciousness. Not in purgatorial pains, for neither could that be called blessed. Doubtless Christ's transforming, assimilating power, through the energy of the Spirit of God, goes on in the departed believer, as it is necessary that it should. For St. Paul teaches us that "he who began a good work in us will perfect it until the day of Jesus Christ" (Phil. i. 6). Therefore that good work is going on still; death does not hinder, but accelerate, it. But the process is not by those hideous means which mediæval monks imagined, and which the very word "purgatory" suggests. But they are blessed; that is enough to know, enough to uplift the mourner's heart. 2. *And immediately that they quit this life.* Such is the meaning of the word "henceforth." "It means substantially *even now;* not merely in the new Jerusalem which is one day to be set up on the renovated earth, but from the very moment of their departure to heaven" (Hengstenberg, *in loc.*). 3. *They die to rest.* "Yea, saith the Spirit, in order that (*ινα*) they may rest [or,'that they shall rest'] from their labours." Death, therefore, is for them but the Divine signal that the day's work is done, that the evening hour has come, and that they are now to go home and rest. The wearisome work and toilsome trying task, which has often well-nigh worn them out—such is the significance of the word "labours"—all that is over, and death is the Lord's call to them to now lie down and rest. 4. *Their works follow with them.* Not their labours, the element of distress and pain in their work, but their works. How do they follow? Perhaps: (1) *In that they are carried on still.* They were works for the honour of their Lord, for the good of their fellow-men—prayers and endeavours to draw others to Christ, intercessions for the Church of God, all manner of beneficent deeds. Are all these to cease? Is there no room for them where the blessed dead now are? Shall the sainted mother who here besought the Lord for her children that they too may be saved—shall she cease that "work"? The Lord forbid that she should; and our text seems to tell us that she, and all they like her, will not, for their works follow them. (2) *For reward.* There is the scene, there the day, of recompense. Not here or now. "Let thine eyes look right on, and thine eyelids straight before thee." "Oh how great is thy goodness which thou hast *laid up* for them that fear thee!" (3) *In their effects upon their character.* We cannot see the soul, we saw only the man, and faulty enough he was, we well knew; but all the while, as the days of his life went on, and this or that work was put upon him to discharge, the soul was, by means thereof, as the marble by the sculptor's chisel, being wrought into a condition of beauty and faultlessness such as from the first had been in the Creator's mind. (4) *As ministers to their joy.* The joy of gratitude that they were enabled to undertake and accomplish them. The joy of knowing that as seed they will yield blessed harvest, and, perhaps, of witnessing that harvest. St. Paul spoke always of his converts as his "joy and crown of rejoicing in the day of the Lord Jesus." Such "works" will be a joy to remember, to look upon in their results and to continue in. They cannot but be, every way, ministers to our joy.

III. THE EMPHASIS THAT IS LAID UPON IT. 1. *It is declared by* "*a voice from heaven.*" This voice "may well be conceived to be that of one of 'the just made perfect,' testifying from his own experience what the true members of the militant Church on earth have to expect in heaven" (Hengstenberg, *in loc.*). When we remember that the attestations to our Lord's Divine Sonship were made in similar manner by a voice from heaven, this declaration is thereby lifted up to a like high level of authority and importance. 2. *It was commanded to be written.* "This command to 'write' is repeated twelve times in the Revelation, to indicate that all the things it refers to are matters of importance, which must not be forgotten by the Church of Christ." 3. *It is confirmed solemnly by the Holy Spirit.* "Yea, saith the Spirit." With such solemn sanctions are these words so inestimably precious to the Church, introduced to our notice and commended to our reverent heed.

IV. THE PURPOSE OF ITS PROCLAMATION. 1. It was a truth *most necessary for the time when it was given.* See the circumstances of the faithful Church, how fearful their trial, how dire their need of all and everything that would fortify their minds amid such awful temptations to be unfaithful to their Lord. And what truth could be more helpful than such as this? 2. *And it is needed still.* (1) To comfort us concerning our departed brethren in Christ. (2) To strengthen us in view of our own departure. (3) To cheer us amid work that often seems thankless and unfruitful, although it be the "work of the Lord." With *our* hope we ought never to be weary in such work. Noble work has often been done by men who had no such hope. Think of the three hundred at Thermopylæ. Think of the holy men of old to whom the grave seemed to end all, to be the place where they should be "no more," and yet who became heroes of the faith (cf. Heb. xi.). (4) To every way ennoble and elevate our lives. (5) To draw forth our love and devotion to him "who having overcome the sharpness of death, hath opened the kingdom of heaven to all believers." Are these purposes fulfilled in us?—S. C.

Vers. 14—20.—*The harvest and the vintage.* It is held by many that both these refer to the same fact of God's judgment against sin and sinners. And no doubt, at times, the "harvest," does mean such judgment (cf. Joel iii. 13; Jer. li. 33). In Matt. xiii. both harvests—that of good and evil alike—are told of. "Let both grow together until," etc. Still more commonly the figure stands for the people of God and their ingathering into his blessed presence. And we think that here, whilst there can be no doubt as to what the vintage means, the "harvest" does not mean the same, but that gathering of "the wheat into his garner" which shall one day most surely be accomplished. For see the preface (ver. 13) to this vision. It speaks of the blessed dead and their rest. And but for the plain pointing out that the vintage did not refer to them, *that* also would have been so understood. And the Lord Jesus Christ—for he is meant—is himself the Reaper (ver. 14), himself thrusts in the sickle (ver. 16), whilst the vintage of judgment is assigned to an angel (ver. 17), indicating that it is a different work from the other. And the figure itself, the harvest, the precious corn fully ripe, belongs generally and appropriately to that which is also precious and an object of delight, as is the company of his people to the Lord whose they are. It is not the *time* of the harvest, but the *corn* of the harvest, which is spoken of here, and this is ever the type of good, and not evil. Thus understood, let us note—

I. THE HARVEST. "The harvest of the earth." This tells of: 1. *The multitude of God's people.* Who can count the ears of corn even in one harvest-field? how much less in the harvest of the whole earth? 2. *The preciousness of them.* What do we not owe to, what could we do without, the literal harvest of the earth? Our all, humanly speaking, depends upon it. 3. *The joy of God in them.* Cf. "They shall joy before thee with the joy of harvest." 4. *The care that has been needed and given.* 5. *The "long patience" that has been exercised.* Who but God could be so patient? We often cry, "How long, O Lord, how long?" But he waits—and we must learn the like lesson—for the harvest of the earth, for that which is being ripened in our own soul. Harvest comes only so. 6. *The evidence of ripeness.* We know of the natural harvest that it is ripe by the grain assuming its golden hue. "Knowest thou what it is that gives that bright yellow tinge of maturity to that which erst was green and growing? What imparts that golden hue to the wheat? How do you suppose the husbandman judges when it is time to thrust in the sickle? I will tell you. All the time the corn was growing, those hollow stems served as ducts that drew up nourishment from the soil. At length the process of vegetation is fulfilled. The fibres of the plant become rigid; they cease their office; down below there has been a failure of the vital power, which is the precursor of death. Henceforth the heavenly powers work quick and marvellous changes: the sun paints his superscription on the ears of grain. They have reached the last stage; having fed on the riches of the soil long enough, they are now only influenced from above" (Spurgeon). And when it is thus with the people of God, when the golden light of the Sun of Righteousness shines on them and they are transformed thereby, then the evidence of ripeness is seen, and the season for the sickle has come. 7. *God will certainly gather in his people.* "Harvest shall not fail"—such was the primeval promise, and it has never failed; nor shall *this* harvest either. "Look up, lift up your heads; for your redemption draweth nigh."

II. THE VINTAGE. Under the altar on which was "the fire," over which the angel told of in ver. 18 "had power," were the souls of them that had been slain for the testimony of Jesus (ch. vi. 9). They had asked, "How long, O Lord, . . . dost thou not judge and avenge our blood on them that dwell on the earth?" And now the answer is given. The vintage of vengeance has begun. For the "grapes" of the "vine of the earth" are fully ripe. It is the judgment of the whole earth, when "all nations" shall be gathered (Matt. xxv.) before the Son of man. The square of four—four ever the symbol of the earth—amplified by hundreds, the "one thousand and six hundred furlongs" of ver. 20, likewise point to the universality of this awful judgment. Minor fulfilments—presages, predictions, and patterns of the final judgment—of these there have been many and will be many; but in this vintage of vengeance upon the world's sin all are summed up and fulfilled. *But will there be any such event at all?* Will Christ "come again to judge the quick and the dead," as the Creed declares? or is it all a myth and imagination, a nightmare, which the sooner the world shakes off and awakes from the better? Many affirm that it is this; many more would like to think so. But what is the truth? 1. *Men have ever felt that there ought to be such judgment.* See in the Old Testament, in the Psalms, Job, in the prophets, what distress of soul God's people were in, because they feared for the faith of a just God. So many wrongs were perpetrated, and no one called to account. Wicked men in great prosperity, "flourishing like a green bay tree," and all the while godly, innocent men trampled in the very dust by these wicked, well-off ones. And many saints of God were heart-broken under the pressure of indubitable facts like these, asking for, and not finding any, redress. Men who were not saints, as they could not find any law of judgment, took the law into their own hands. And hence they added torture to death. For merely to kill a man was no punishment at all. Who would care for that? Death rids a man of all trouble. Make him suffer, therefore, whilst he is alive. So they thought and acted, and hence the whole system of tortures, from the imagery of which some of the most dread emblems of this book are drawn. But the tears of good men, in view of this problem of righteousness unrewarded and persecuted, whilst unrighteousness went not only unpunished, but held high festival; and the tortures inflicted by cruel men when they got a criminal into their hands;—both are testimonies to the conviction that a Divine and perfect judgment ought to be. 2. *And now it is declared that such judgment shall be. Conscience assents to it.* What endorsements of God's Word the guilty conscience gives. Read 'Macbeth' for one illustration out of thousands more. 3. *Human law and justice strive after right judgment.* What consternation there is when some great criminal escapes and baffles all means of discovery, and what joy when such are caught and tried and condemned! It is all confirmation of the truth taught by this "vintage." 4. *And the judgments that come now* on ungodly nations, communities, and individuals are all in proof. History rightly read reveals the truth in luminous light: "Verily there is a God that judgeth in the earth." This harvest for God's holy ones, and this vintage of those for whom his holy vengeance awaits, are both to be. When the sharp sickles that gather the one and the other are put in, *where shall we be found?* That is the question of questions for us all to answer. God, of his mercy, give us no rest until we can answer it aright!—S. C.

Vers. 1—5.—*The triumphant host.* Again amidst the threatenings of danger and trial, words of consolation and assurance mingle. And out of the midst of the contemplation of the most virulent opposition to the truth, the holy seer is called to lift up his eyes on high, and behold the Mount Zion and the host of the pure and faithful surrounding the Lamb. The hundred and forty-four thousand—the Church's symbol of twelve reproduced and multiplied. It is the Church in her triumph. "The elect" whom Satan has not been able to "deceive" are now in presence of the Redeemer—ever "the Lamb" in this book. Their "tribulation" is over; their enemies subdued. They have "kept the faith." Thus is fidelity through trial predicted; thus is it encouraged. There are who will "endure to the end" and "be saved." In viewing this triumphant host we must take notice of—

THE DISTINGUISHING FEATURES OF THEIR CHARACTER AND THE DETAILED ELEMENTS OF THEIR REWARD. 1. *These are the pure, the undefiled.* They are distinguished as free from the prevalent sinfulness of the hour. Nor could symbolism more strikingly stand allied to realism than by describing the saintly hosts as " virgins." 2. *They are the obedient.* "They follow the Lamb whithersoever he goeth." Holiness of life is the invariable adjunct of sanctity of spirit. These "take up the cross and follow him" whom they love, through evil report and good report. 3. *They are the truthful.* No lie is found in their mouth—neither the lie of error nor of untrue profession; nor are they given to falsity and deceitfulness of life. 4. *They are blameless.* "Without blemish." These are the redeemed : "the firstfruits unto God and unto the Lamb." The great harvest lies beyond in the unnumbered host. Their reward is thus detailed : (1) They are purchased : the Lamb's own property, "whose own" these sheep are. (2) They are admitted and received within the heavenly courts : they stand on "Mount Zion." (3) They bear the symbols of their confession and of their recognition : the holy name is on their foreheads—signifying their devotion to Christ; as they who were the servants of the beast bore his name. (4) In eternal joyfulness they sing ever-new songs of praise to God, their Creator and Redeemer. A song unknown and unlearned by any but the faithful in Christ Jesus. Truly may we hear an undertone of exhortation : (*a*) "Wherefore comfort yourselves with these words;" and (*b*) "Be thou faithful unto death."—R. G.

Vers. 6, 7.—" *The everlasting gospel.*" The hearts of the faithful have been strengthened and comforted by the vision of the pure heavenly community whose united voice was as that of "harpers harping with their harps." Now another vision brightens the eye of the holy seer. At present the idea of a gospel universally diffused has not been specially represented. Incidentally we have heard the voices of the elders proclaiming praise to him who had redeemed them from "every tribe, and tongue, and people, and nation." And we have heard the word of the angel concerning the little book : "Thou must prophesy again before many peoples, and nations, and tongues, and kings." Now, in harmony with the prevalent habit of the book, the vision or teaching is repeated, but in another form. It is a definite assurance to the little Church, in its dispersion, and apparent conquest,' when its voice is silenced by the severities of persecuting violence. Fear not ; the gospel shall be proclaimed, and proclaimed to all; nor shall it be crushed; it is an everlasting gospel. Inasmuch as he who partakes of the gospel partakes of the spirit of the gospel, it would be his most fervent desire that all should participate in the blessedness and peace of that gospel. To him, therefore, the cheering news of its universal diffusion must bring—what the whole book is designed to bring—the utmost consolation. Of the gospel we learn—

I. THAT IT IS A GOSPEL OF PERPETUAL ENDURANCE. "An eternal gospel." It is ever to be proclaimed as good news. It never ceases to be good news. It may be hindered, and for a time even apparently destroyed; but it still lives. It is eternal.

II. IT IS FOR ALL. The good news is not to be confined to a few, or to favoured races only. It is for "them [*i.e.* all them] that dwell on the earth," even for "every nation, and tribe, and tongue, and people." The universal diffusion of the gospel is a pledge that persecution shall not "stamp it out."

III. IN ITS TEACHING IT URGES: 1. *The fear of the Lord*—"Fear God"—which is the beginning of all wisdom; and to heathen and idolatrous nations the first truth. 2. *The paying to him due honour.* "Give him glory." 3. *It declares the approach of his judicial rule.* "The hour of his judgment is come." 4. *It calls to his worship* as the true Lord, who "made the heaven, and the earth, and sea, and fountains of waters."—R. G.

Ver. 8.—*A further vision of triumph.* Again "another angel"—a second—follows the first, and with a separate message. It is brief, but pregnant. The earnest desire of the good is satisfied. That which shall sustain the "patience of the saints, they that keep the commandments of God, and the faith of Jesus," is here. It is an authoritative declaration of the final fall of the antagonistic kingdom, is that whatever it may. "Babylon" ever symbolizes the oppressor of Jerusalem—the antagonistic kingdom that opposes and oppresses the true Israel of God. Babylon is "great;" Babylon has power over "all nations," for she compels their aceptance of her corruption ; Babylon makes all nations to join her in her degradation and impurity and unfaithfulness. But she is "fallen"—"fallen is Babylon the great." From this prophetic word the Church, struggling against the oppression of a Babylonish yoke—struggling to free the nations from Babylonish corruption, deceit, and wrath, which is ruin—cannot but derive the deepest consolation.

I. IT IS A PLEDGE OF DIVINE CO-OPERATION. For the puny arm of the feeble flock cannot grapple with the great and mighty nation that can compel obedience. But God is above all.

II. IT IS THE SATISFACTION OF THE CHURCH'S UTMOST DESIRE CONCERNING EVIL. For it is its uttermost destruction. The Church is ever to be comforted by the assured hope of the conquest of all evil.

III. IT IS THE ASSURANCE OF THE CHURCH'S FINAL DELIVERANCE FROM ALL OPPOSING AND OPPRESSING POWER. And as such—

IV. IT IS THE TRUEST ENCOURAGEMENT OF THE CHURCH TO "PATIENCE"—to "keep the commandments of God," and to the maintenance of "the faith of Jesus."—R. G.

Vers. 9—12.—*Punishment.* The punishment threatened upon the worshippers of "the beast and his image" is represented by imagery of the most truly awful character. What that "beast" is, what is "his image," and what his "worship," are points not to be left in uncertainty; while the terrible denunciations of wrath must stand as an effectual warning against any such homage. "The beast" here must represent the utmost spirit of evil—foul, filthy sin. It stands in opposition to the Lamb, the embodiment of all purity. It is the antagonist, the opposer of all good, whether ideally considered, or as found embodied in Satan—the devil. It is the antithesis of holiness ; it is an active opposition also to all holiness ; it is an active opposition to God. The "image" may be any form which this essential evil, this anti-righteous spirit, may assume. The "worship" of such a spirit implies submission to it; an affirmation of its supremacy and worthiness and power ; a giving honour to the beast— the honour due to God. What a signal of unfaithfulness, of corruption, of sin! As such it is punishable with the utmost punishment. The figures in which this awful punishment is represented indicate the keenest severity of suffering. As the worship of the beast indicates the utmost devotion to sinfulness, so the punishment threatened denotes the utmost suffering. It includes—

I. THE DIREST EXPRESSION OF THE DIVINE DISPLEASURE. The worshipper shall "drink of the wine of the wrath of God."

II. THE INFLICTION OF DIRECT PERSONAL SUFFERING. "He shall be tormented with fire and brimstone."

III. AN ESPECIAL AGGRAVATION OF THE SUFFERING. It is endured in the presence of the holy angels, and in the presence of the Lamb.

IV. IT IS A STATE OF CEASELESS DISTURBANCE. "They have no rest day nor night."

V. IT IS UNENDING. "For ever and ever." Let any read this, and say if the consequences of devotion to evil are not in the highest degree dreadful.—R. G.

Ver. 13.—*The blessedness of the departed faithful.* If the threatenings of judgment upon the worshippers of the false are motives to patience and fidelity, how much more is the promise of a blessed reward ! Between these two the tried and persecuted Christian disciple is hedged in. This blessedness is (1) assured by the heavenly proclamation: "a voice from heaven." It is (2) confirmed by the Spirit's testimony:

" *Yea*, saith the Spirit." It is (3) promised to them who are spiritual : "in the Lord." It is (4) the reward of fidelity maintained to the end of life : they " *die* in the Lord." The reward is (1) *a state of felicity :* " blessed " are they. (2) It consists in a *state of repose after toil, danger, and exposure:* " They *rest* from their labours." (3) It is exhibited as *the consequence of and acknowledgment of their diligent, obedient labour:* " Their works follow with them." Here is the encouragement to (1) self-denial; (2) patient labour ; (3) undying devotion.—R. G.

Vers. 14—20.—*Judgment again represented.* In the spirit of the former words, and as a further confirmation of them, the process of judgment is again set forth under fresh images. So is consolation borne to the suffering and afflicted Church, and warning and admonition dealt out to the ungodly. Under the imagery of a harvest and of the gathering of the vintage, the certainties of the threatened judgment and the promised blessedness are set forth. The afflicted, down-trodden, despised Church must here see mighty motives urged upon it to maintain a steadfast faith and hope and patience. This vision declares—

I. THE FINAL CESSATION OF THE CHURCH'S SUFFERING. Her warfare may be long continued. Generation after generation of believers may be called upon to suffer, but an end is appointed. It will be proclaimed : " The hour to reap is come." The life of " earth "—ever the symbol of that which stands in opposition to the heavenlies—has been patiently borne through much long-suffering. But this is at an end—" the harvest of the earth is over-ripe." The command is issued, " Send forth thy sickle, and reap."

II. THE GATHERING OF A HARVEST HAS THE PREVAILING CHARACTER OF GRACIOUS-NESS. It is the ingathering of that which sprang from " the seed " which " is the Word ; " and, in our view, indicates *the gathering for the heavenly garner.*

III. THE FIGURE OF THE VINTAGE IS RESERVED FOR THE EXPRESSION OF THE WRATH OF GOD. " Wherefore art thou red in thine apparel ? ... I have trodden the wine-press alone." Here it is distinguished as " the great wine-press of the wrath of God." No such designation is given to the wheat-harvest. In this, then, we are to see *the final judgment upon the wicked.* Thus are set before us both the ingathering of the holy—the harvest waiting for which " the husbandman " has had " long patience," and the ingathering or crushing of the wicked. " Terrible," indeed, " is he in his doings to the children of men."—R. G.

Vers. 1—5.—*The supersensuous heaven of humanity.* " And I looked, and, lo, a Lamb stood on the Mount Zion, and with him an hundred forty and four thousand, having his Father's name written in their foreheads. And I heard a voice from heaven," etc. May we not regard these verses as a pictorial representation of the *supersensuous heaven of humanity ?* If so, the following facts are suggested concerning the unseen realm of the good or the Christly.

I. IT IS A SCENE IN WHICH CHRIST IS THE CENTRAL FIGURE. " And I looked [saw], and lo [behold], a [the] Lamb stood [standing] on the Mount Zion " (ver. 1). No one acquainted with the Scriptures needs to ask who the Lamb is. Christ is the " Lamb of God." Why is Christ called " the Lamb " ? Is it because of his innocence, or because of his moral and sacrificial character, or both ? Morally he was innocent as a lamb, " holy, undefiled." " He did no sin, neither was guile found in his mouth." Or is it on account of his sacrifice ? He was, indeed, a sacrifice ; his whole being was a sacrifice. There have been those who have answered these questions to their own satisfaction, and there are now those who render replies without hesitation or doubt. I cannot. My eyes are too dim to penetrate into the *rationale* of Divine operations. What seems clear is that Christ is the central Figure in man's heaven. He stands on the citadel on which all eyes are fastened, and to which all hearts point and all sympathies flow.

II. IT IS A SCENE INTERESTINGLY POPULATED. 1. *The population is very numerous.* " An hundred forty and four thousand " (ver. 1). This I take to be a definite number used to represent an indefinite multitude—a " multitude which no man could number." The dreamer being a Jew, his visions are, of course. full of Jewish facts and sentiments. Hence he thinks of the Jewish scene of worship, Zion, and the Jewish tribes, incalculably numerous. To us, however, all these are mere illustrations of things higher, more important, and lasting. The human tenants in heaven were in number beyond calculation in the days of John, and they have been multiplying ever since. 2. *The population is divinely distinguished.* " His Father's name written in their foreheads " (ver. 1). Me glory in things that are supposed to distinguish them advantageously from their fellow-men—the attractions of physical beauty, the glitter of wealth, the pomp of power; but the greatest of all distinctions, the grandest and highest, is to have the *name of the great Father manifest in our lives*—written on our very " foreheads." (1) It is the most *beautiful* distinction. The face is the beauty of man; there the soul reveals itself sometimes in sunshine and sometimes in clouds. The beauty of the face is not in features, but in expressions, and the more it expresses of purity, intelligence, generosity, tenderness, the more beautiful it is. How beautiful, then, to have God's name radiating in it! God's name is the beauty of the universe. (2) It is the most *conpicuous* distinction. " In their foreheads." It is seen wherever you go, fronting every object you look at. Godliness cannot conceal itself. Divine goodness is evermore self-revealing. As the face of Moses shone with a mystic radiance when he came down from the mount after holding fellowship with God, so the lives of all godly men are encircled with a Divine halo. (3) It is the most *honourable* distinction. A man sometimes feels proud when he is told he is like some great statesman, ruler, thinker, reformer. But how transcendently honourable is it to bear in our face the very image of God! Let us all seek this distinction. With the Father's " name in our foreheads " we shall throw the pageantry of the shahs, the emperors, and all the kings of the earth into contempt. 3. *The population is rapturously happy.* " And I heard a voice from heaven, as the voice of many waters, and as the voice of a great thunder : and I heard the voice of [the voice which I heard was the voice of] harpers harping with their harps : and they sang [sing] as it were a new song " (vers. 2, 3). All souls yonder run into music! Here is music loud as booming billows, pealing thunders, and melodious as the enrapturing strains of the harp. How mean and unworthy are men's views of religious music. " Let us sing to the glory and praise of God," says the leader of public worship. And forthwith a whole congregation breaks into sound. And if the sound is regulated by the harmonious blending of notes, the production is called a " Service of Song ; " and more, alas! is made an article of trade. Large incomes are made by the sale of such music. Can such be the music of heaven? Nay. *True music is the harmony of soul*—souls moving ever in accord with the Supreme Will. True music consists not in blending of sounds, whether vocal or instrumental, however charming to the senses, but in sentiments unuttered, perhaps unutterable, yet entrancing to conscience and pleasing to God. 4. *The population is redemptively trained.* " No man could learn that song but the hundred and forty and four thousand, which were redeemed [purchased] from the earth " (ver. 3). Heaven, it has been said by men of old, is a prepared place for a prepared people. It is verily so. Observe : (1) Man requires training for heaven. (2) Redemption is the method of training for heaven. (3) Earth is the scene of this redemptive training. 5. *The population is spotlessly pure.* " These are they which were not defiled with women; for they are virgins " (ver. 4). There are those of our race who have never fallen, who have retained their virgin innocence, who required no pardon for their sins, nor regeneration. What millions of the human population die in their infancy, and go on unfolding their faculties and invigorating their strength through indefinite ages, in scenes of absolute holiness and infallible intelligence! They were not " redeemed from the earth ; " such redemption they required not. From the dawn of their being they were ushered into the realms of immaculate purity and perfect bliss. 6. *The population is absolutely loyal.* " These are they which follow the Lamb whithersoever he goeth " (ver. 4). All follow the Lamb, the Christ of God. " Two words, " Follow me," embody at once the whole duty and perfect Paradise of souls. " Whithersoever he goeth." He is always moving. " The Father worketh hitherto, and I work." We cannot do exactly what he does, but we can imbibe that spirit which inspires him in all he does. Would I become a great painter? then how shall I proceed? If I copy the exact style and method of one of the greatest masters of the art, I shall only become a mere mechanic in the profession, never an artist. But if I catch the *genius* of the great master, I may, peradventure, leave him behind, and win a place and a distinction all my own. Let us catch the moral genius of Christ 7. *The population is incorruptibly truthful.* " In their mouth was found no guile [lie]: for they are without fault before the throne of God [they are without blemish]" (ver. 5). No lie! How unlike us! The social atmosphere of our world teems with lies as with microbes. Lies in parliaments, in markets, in Churches. The whole world teems with impostors. What a blessed world must that be where all is truth and reality!—D. T.

Ver. 3.—*Man training for the supersensuous heaven.* "No man could learn that song but the hundred and forty and four thousand, which were redeemed from the earth." The subject of these words is *man training for the supersensuous heaven.* Notice—

I. HEAVEN REQUIRES HIS TRAINING. "No man could learn that song." Man cannot blend in the happy harmony of the celestial state without previous training. Analogy would suggest this. In the physical system every being is fitted to his position, his organism is suited to his locality. These bodies of ours, as now constituted, could probably live in no other planet than this. In the social system the same principle of fitness is required. The stolid clown could not occupy the professor's chair, nor could he who is reckless concerning law, right, and order occupy the bench of justice. It is just so in relation to heaven. To feel at home in the society of the holy, cheerfully to serve the Creator and his universe, and to be in harmony with all the laws, operations, and beings in the holy empire, we must manifestly be invested with the same character. But what is the training necessary? 1. *Not mechanical.* Ceremonial religion enjoins this. 2. *Not intellectual.* Theological training may be conducive, but it is not sufficient. 3. It is *moral*—the training of the spiritual sympathies, the heart being brought to say, "Thy will be done." No one can "sing the song," blend in the harmonious action of heaven, without this. A man with corrupt sympathies could never sing in heaven; he would shriek. In the midst of happy myriads he would be alone. His darkness would conceal from him the outward sun; his inner flashes of guilt would change for him the God of love into a "consuming fire."

II. REDEMPTION IS THE CONDITION OF HIS TRAINING. "Those who were redeemed from the earth." The redemption here referred to is evidently that procured by the love of Christ. The training requires something more than education; it needs *emancipation*, the deliverance of the soul from certain feelings and forces incompatible with holiness—a deliverance from the *guilt* and *power* of evil. The grand characteristic of Christianity is that it is a power to redeem from all evil. No other system on earth can do this.

III. THE EARTH IS THE SCENE OF HIS TRAINING. "Redeemed from the earth." The brightest fact in the history of the dark world is that it is a redemptive scene. Amidst all the clouds and storms of depravity and sorrow that sweep over our path, this fact rises up before us a bright orb that shall one day dispel all gloom and hush all tumult. Thank God, this is not a retributive, but a *redemptive* scene. But it should be remembered that it is not only a redemptive scene, but the *only* redemptive scene. There is no redemptive influence in heaven—it is not required. A wonderful world is this! True, it is but a spark amidst the suns of the universe—a tiny leaf in the mighty forests! Let the light be quenched and the leaf be destroyed, their absence would not be felt. Still it has a moral history the most momentous. Here Christ lived, laboured, died. Here millions of spirits are trained for heaven. What Marathon was to Greece, and Waterloo to Europe, this little earth is to the creation. Here the great battles of the spiritual universe are fought. It is the Thermopylæ of the creation.—D. T.

Vers. 6—8.—*The dissemination of good, and the destruction of evil.* "And I saw another angel fly in the midst of heaven, having the everlasting gospel to preach unto them that dwell on the earth, and to every nation," etc. In these verses two subjects are suggested—

I. THE DISSEMINATION OF GOOD. The good here is called "the everlasting [eternal] gospel" (ver. 6). 1. *The gospel in itself is good.* It is at once the mirror and the medium of eternal good. It contains and communicates to man that which reflects the Divine character and constitutes the heaven of souls. "Everlasting"—eternal. Good is eternal. Unlike evil, it never had a commencement, and will never have an end; it is as old as God himself. 2. *The gospel in its ministry is good.* "And I saw another angel fly [flying] in the midst of [mid]-heaven" (ver. 6). It comes from heaven and is conveyed by heavenly messengers to men. Angels are so interested in this gospel that they speed their flight through mid-heaven bearing its blessed message. 3. *The gospel in its universality is good.* "Having the everlasting [eternal] gospel to preach [proclaim] unto them that dwell on the earth, and to every nation, and kindred [tribe], and tongue, and people" (ver. 6). It overleaps all geographical boundaries, all tribal, national, linguistic distinctions, and addresses *man as man.* 4. *The gospel in its purpose is good.* "Saying with a loud voice [he saith with a great voice], Fear God, and give glory to him; for the hour of his judgment is come: and worship him that made heaven, and earth, and the sea, and the fountains of waters" (ver. 7). The supreme aim of the gospel is to induce all men to worship him who made heaven, earth, and sea. Man is made for worship. There is no *instinct* in the soul deeper, stronger, more operative; there is no *service* for the soul more worthy, nay, so worthy and so blest, as that of worship. Worship is the Paradise of souls.

II. THE DESTRUCTION OF EVIL. "And there followed another angel [another, a second angel, followed], saying, Babylon is fallen, is fallen [fallen, fallen is Babylon], that great city [the great], because she [which hath] made all nations drink of the wine of the wrath of her fornication" (ver. 8). I take Babylon here as standing, not for the capital of Syria, not for Rome, either pagan or papal, nor for the site, the masonry, the institutions, or the populations of any city that ever has been or ever will be, but as representing the *spirit of evil* that moulded and mastered the old metropolis of Assyria. Babylon to me stands as the *mighty aggregation of all the moral evils* at work throughout all society in all the metropolises of the universe. This aggregation of evil is what Paul calls "the world." Two remarks are suggested. 1. *This aggregation of evil must fall.* Babylon must tumble into dust. The colossal image will not only be smashed into atoms by the "little stone" of truth, but every particle will be borne away by the winds of Divine influence, so that "no place will be found for it." Faith is to overcome the world. 2. *This aggregation of evil falls as the good advances.* The gospel having been proclaimed to every "nation," and "tongue," and "people," and all brought to worship him that made heaven and earth, Babylon totters, crumbles, and rots. The gospel destroys the *spirit* of evil, and its forms fall to pieces. You may destroy the forms of evil in the habits and institutions of the world, but unless the spirit is extinguished you have done no good. Burn up Rome, but if its *spirit* remains it will grow and work, and produce, perchance, forms more hideous and oppressive. No pontiff that ever occupied the papal chair has ever had more popery in his nature than can be found in many a Protestant clergyman, ay, and in many a Nonconformist minister too.

CONCLUSION. Would you have Babylon to fall? Then speed on the gospel; not the gospel of *sects* or of *creeds*, but the gospel of the evangelists.—D. T.

Ver. 6.—*An ideal preacher.* "And I saw another angel," etc. It is legitimate, and it may be useful, to look at these words as symbolizing the *ideal preacher.* Looking at them in this light, we observe concerning the ideal preacher—

I. HIS THEME IS GLORIOUS. "The everlasting gospel." Observe: 1. *It is a gospel.* That is "good news," or "glad tidings." It is a message, not of Divine partiality or Divine wrath to the world, but of Divine love—the love of the great Father for his fallen children. 2. *It is an ever-enduring gospel.* Everlasting: (1) Because its elementary truths are absolute. These truths are the existence of God as Maker and Manager of the universe; the obligation of all moral beings to love him supremely because of his supreme goodness, etc. These are mere specimens of the truths that abound in the gospel, and as such they cannot die out, they must continue as the laws of nature. Continue, not only amidst all the revolutions of time, the discoveries of true science, but amidst all the cycles of eternity. (2) Because its redemptive provisions are complete. Its special mission is to effect man's restoration to the knowledge, image, and enjoyment of his Maker. It has all the elements and the powers for the purpose. Nothing is lacking, nothing can be added to it. It is complete. It is everlasting in the sense that the sun is everlasting, because it contains all that the centre of the planetary system requires to fulfil its purpose. Thus it contains the things that cannot be moved. 3. *It is a world-wide gospel.* "To preach unto them that dwell on the earth, and to every nation, and kindred, and tongue, and people." This means that it is not for a sect or a class, but for humanity. It is for man as man, irrespective of his colour, his country, his character. (1) It is a *necessity* to all mankind. It is the supreme necessity of unregenerate mankind the world over and the ages through. If a man is to be happy, he must have it. It is not merely adapted to him, it is *essential* to him. (2) It is *equal* to all mankind. It is not like a feast, prepared for so many and no more; it is more like a perfect piece of music, having in it an exhaustless power—a power as capable of charming all souls as one, pouring its thrilling and inspiring influence over all lands, down through all times with unabated power Such, then, is the theme which the ideal preacher has to propound; not the speculations of the theologists or the crotchets of the sect, not the crudities of his own brain, but the "everlasting gospel." What a sublime mission !

II. THAT HIS MOVEMENTS ARE EXPEDITIOUS. "Fly in the midst of heaven." He is to move, not like the ordinary terrestrial beings on the earth, but rather like the swift fowls of the air—impulses excited, eyes dilated, pinions expanded, darting on their ethereal way. It is characteristic of an ideal preacher that he is expeditious. He is not a drone; he is on fire. He is "instant in season and out of season," like his great Original; he worketh while it is "called to-day," knowing "the night cometh when no man can work." Why thus expeditious? 1. *The message is urgent.* The world is guilty; it bears pardon. The world is diseased, about dying; it bears elements of life. The world is enthralled a captive of the arch-enemy of the universe; it bears liberty. 2. *The time is short.* Short, when compared not merely with a future life, but with the work necessary to be done. There is not a moment to spare. "To-day, saith the Spirit." The Spirit knows the urgency of the work, and the time necessary for its fulfilment. 3. *Life is uncertain.* Uncertain both for the preacher and for his hearers. "Boast not thyself of to-morrow; for thou knowest not what a day may bring forth." Hence the necessity of this expeditious movement.

III. THAT HIS SPHERE IS ELEVATED. "Fly in the midst of heaven," or "in mid-heaven." It is the characteristic of all truly regenerated men that they are not of the flesh, but of the Spirit; that they set their "affections on things above;" that though "*in* the world," they are "not *of* the world;" that they live in heavenly places. All these representations mean that they live and move on a level high up and distinct from the level on which worldly men live and work. Like Christ, they have "meat to eat" that the world knows nothing of. They are "separate from sinners." This is preeminently the case with the ideal preacher. He moves above the highest; he does not mind earthly things; uninfluenced by worldly motives, despising worldly aims and fashions, towering like an angel above them all. Ah me! how different this ideal to the actual conventional preachers! Do they move through mid-heaven? Do they not rather crawl on the earth, trade even in the gospel, and make gain of godliness? The great reason why preaching is so ineffective now is because we preachers move not in this elevated sphere, but are down with the common herd in spirit.

CONCLUSION. Such, then, is the ideal preacher, and all Church history shows that the men who have approached nearest to this ideal have achieved the greatest victories for souls—Paul, Augustine, Savonarola, Tanner, Whitefield, Wesley, etc.—D. T.

Vers. 9—12.—*Soul-prostitution and soul-loyalty.* "And the third angel followed them, saying with a loud voice, If any man worship the beast and his image, and receive his mark in his forehead, or in his hand, the same shall drink of the wine of the wrath of God," etc. In this part of John's wonderful mental vision, or dream, on the island of Patmos, we can find illustrations of two great subjects.

I. SOUL-PROSTITUTION. "And the third angel followed them, saying with a loud [great] voice, If any man worship the beast and his image, and receive [receiveth] his mark in his forehead, and in his hand," etc. (ver. 9). The "beast and his image." What meaneth this? Does it mean some king or pope? Or some great wrong institution, civil or religious? No one knows, and it matters not. I take the expression as a symbol of *wrong* in its spirit and forms. Two things are suggested in connection with this. 1. That the prostitution of the soul to wrong *is an alarming crime.* Here is a warning. "The angel followed, saying with a loud voice." Amongst the teeming populations of this earth there is nothing more terrible and alarming than to see human souls made in the image of God, rendering a practical devotion of all its spiritual powers to the morally unworthy, "the world, the flesh, and the devil;" because, according to a law of mind, the object of the soul's devotion transfigures it into its own character. Hence the human spirit gets buried in the fleshly, absorbed in the selfish and the worldly. Thus everywhere we find minds that should expand into seraphs sinking into grubs, worshipping the " beast ; " sordid sycophants, not soaring saints ; the miserable creatures, not the mighty masters of circumstances. 2. That the prostitution of the soul to wrong *always incurs lamentable suffering.* It is said, " The same [he also] shall drink of the wine of the wrath of God, which is poured out without mixture [prepared unmixed] into the cup of his indignation [anger] ; and he shall be tormented with fire and brimstone in the presence of the holy angels, and in the presence of the Lamb " (ver. 10). The metaphors here are borrowed from the sacred books of the Hebrew people, and they convey the idea of suffering of an alarming kind, suggesting : (1) A consciousness of Divine antagonism. " Wine of the wrath of God." In the sense of malignant passion there is no wrath in him who is *Love.* But it is a psychological fact that the man who suffers because he has done another an injury, has a consciousness that the one he has offended is angry with him, and this consciousness is the chief element in his suffering. (2) A sense of intense agony. " Shall be tormented with fire and brimstone." Brimstone adds intensity to the heat and fury to the flames of fire. " My punishment is greater than I can bear," said Cain. A guilty conscience has its Tartarus or Gehenna within itself. (3) A state of constant restlessness. " They have no rest day nor [and] night " (ver. 11). There is no rest in sin. " The wicked are like the troubled sea." A guilty soul under a sense of sin is like Noah's dove fluttering over tumultuous billows.

II. SOUL-LOYALTY. " Here is the patience of the saints " (ver. 12). " The meaning here," says Moses Stuart, " is either thus : here then in the dreadful punishment of the wicked every Christian may see of what avail his patience and obedient spirit and faith in Christ are ; or here is a disclosure respecting the wicked which is adapted to encourage a patient endurance of the evils of persecution, and a constancy in obedience to the Divine commands and to the Christian faith." What is patience ? It is not insensibility. Some people are lauded for their patience who should be denounced for their stoicism and indifference. Patience implies at least two things. 1. *The existence of trials.* Where the path of life is all smooth, flowery, and pleasant, where all the winds of life are temperate, bright, and balmy, where all the echoes of life are free from discordant notes, and beating the sweetest melodies, where, in fact, life is entirely free from trial, there is no room for patience. Patience lives only in difficulty and danger, in storms and tempests. 2. *The highest mental power.* Man's highest power of mind is seen, not in unsurpassed mechanical inventions, or the sublimest productions of art, not in the most baffling and confounding strategies of bloody war, hell's own creation, but in the successful effort to govern all the impulses and master all the boisterous passions of the human soul. " The Lord is slow to anger, and great in power." This is a remarkable expression. It seems as if the Prophet Nahum meant that God is slow to anger *because* he is great in power ; if he had less power he would be less patient. A man may be slow to anger and slow to deal out vengeance because he lacks power to do so. But God is slow to anger because he has abundance of power. His power of self-control is infinite. Truly does Solomon say, " He that is slow to anger is better than the mighty ; and he that ruleth his spirit than he that taketh a city." [1] The greater the sinner and the greater the sneak, the better able to take cities ; but it requires the greatest man to govern his own soul.

" Be patient, oh be patient ! Put your ear against the earth,
    Listen there how noiselessly the germ of the seed has birth ;
    How noiselessly and gently it upheaves its little way,
    Till it parts the scarcely broken ground, and the blade stands up in day !

" Be patient, oh be patient ! The germs of mighty thought
    Must have their silent undergrowth, must underground be wrought.
    But as sure as there's a power that makes the grass appear,
    Our land shall be green with liberty, the blade-time shall be here.

---

[1] See ' Practical Philosopher,' p. 331.

" Be patient, oh be patient! Go and watch the wheat-ears grow,
So imperceptibly that ye can mark nor change nor throe,
Day after day, day after day, till the ear is fully grown,
And then again, day after day, till the ripened field is brown.

" Be patient, oh be patient! Though yet your hopes are green,
The harvest-fields of freedom shall be crowned with sunny sheen ;
Be ripening, be ripening, mature your silent way,
Till the whole broad land is tongued with fire on freedom's harvest-day."

(R. C. Trench.)

D. F.

Ver. 13.—*Heaven's description of the sainted dead.* "And I heard a voice from heaven saying unto me, Write, Blessed are the dead which die in the Lord from henceforth : Yea, saith the Spirit, that they may rest from their labours; and their works do follow them." Here is a voice from heaven. Voices from earth are plentiful—they load our air and din our ears. We have voices from the markets and voices from the Parliament, voices from the Church and voices from the college, voices on every subject and in every key. They are contradictory and unsatisfactory ; they solve not the deepest problems of the soul. Thank God, there is a voice from heaven—let us listen to it. It comes from infallibility itself; and teaches the most momentous questions of interest and destiny. Notice—

I. HEAVEN'S DESCRIPTION OF THE CHARACTER OF THE SAINTED DEAD. "Blessed are the dead which die in the Lord." Their character was that of vital union with Christ. The Scriptures represent this union by a great variety of figure. It is compared to the union of a *building* with its *foundation-stone*—its existence depends upon it; to that of the *branch* and the *vine*—its strength, foliage, fruit, life, of the one depend upon the sap it derives from the other; to that of the *spirit* and the *body*—the former being the source of animation, the impulse of activity, and the guide of the movements of the latter. These figures confessedly indicate a union the most close and the most vital. This union may include two things. 1. *Their existence in his affections.* We live in the hearts of those who love us. Children do thoroughly live in the affections of their loving parents, that they control their plans and inspire their efforts. Because the child lives in the heart of the affectionate parent, the parent lives and labours for his child. In this sense Christ's disciples live in him; they are in his heart; he thinks upon them, he plans for them, he works for them, he causes "all things to work together for good." 2. *Their existence in his character.* Without figure, we live in the character of those we admire and love. Arnold's most loyal pupils live in his character now. They see their old master in their books, and hear him in their sermons. Christ is the grand Object of their love, and the chief subject of their thought, and to please him is the grand purpose of their life. As loving children identify themselves with all that pertains to their parents, so they feel a vital interest in all that relates to the cause of Christ. This Paul felt. " I live; yet not I, but Christ liveth in me." This character implies two things. (1) A *moral* change. Men are not born in this state. " If any man be in Christ, he is a new creature." The change is so great that the man must be conscious of it. (2) A *judicial* change. " There is therefore now no condemnation to them which are in Christ Jesus." Their sins are pardoned, their iniquities are forgiven; they " have peace with God through our Lord Jesus Christ." Such is the character of the sainted dead as here described. " They die in the Lord."

II. HEAVEN'S DESCRIPTION OF THE CONDITION OF THE SAINTED DEAD. " *Blessed* are the dead." 1. *Their blessedness is in rest from all trying labour.* Not rest from work, for work is the condition of blessedness ; but from all *trying* labour, all anxious toil, all wearying, annoying, irritating, fruitless toil. (1) Rest from all trying labour pertaining to our *physical subsistence.* By the sweat of our brow here we have to eat bread. Not so yonder. (2) Rest from all trying labour pertaining to *intellectual culture.* How much trying labour is there here to train our faculties and to get knowledge! "Much study is a weariness of the flesh." Not so yonder. (3) Rest from all trying labour pertaining to our *spiritual cultivation.* Here we have to wrestle hard against our spiritual foes, and often have to cry out in the struggle, " O wretched man that I am! who shall deliver me from the body of this death?" Not so yonder. (4) Rest from all trying labour to *benefit our fellow-men.* To do good here is a trying work. The ignorance, the callousness, the ingratitude of men whom we seek to help, often distract and pain the heart. Not so yonder. *Rest!* What a cheering word! It is the couch of the weary traveller; it is the haven for the storm-tossed mariner; it is home for the veteran who, after many a battle, has won the victory. 2. *Their blessedness is in the influence of their works.* "Their works do follow them." No one act truly done for Christ and in his spirit will be lost. All good works springing from faith in Christ shall follow the worker into the eternal world—follow him in their blessed influence upon himself, in the happy results they have produced in others, and in the gracious acknowledgment of God. The moment we appear on the other side, we shall hear the voice addressing us, "Call the labourers, and give them their hire." We shall then find that the smallest effort is not lost. 3. *Their blessedness began immediately after death.* "From henceforth, saith the Spirit." From the moment of death the blessedness begins. This stands opposed to two errors. (1) That there is an obliviousness of soul until the resurrection; and (2) that there are purgatorial fires which must follow death. "From henceforth." "Not from the waking of the soul into consciousness after the sleep of centuries; not from the extinction of purgatorial fires; but from death. "To-day shalt thou be with me;" "Absent from the body, present with the Lord." 4. *Their blessedness is vouched by the Spirit of God.* "From henceforth, saith the Spirit." Who declares this blessedness? An erring Church? Not even the highest angel. It is the Spirit. He who knows the present and the future; he who hears the last sigh of every saint on earth, and his first note of triumph. The Spirit saith it. Let us believe it with an unquestioning faith. The Spirit saith it. Let us adore him for his revelation.

This subject speaks: 1. *Comfort to the bereaved.* Weep not inordinately for the good that are gone. "Sorrow not as those who are without hope." Your loved ones still live: they "rest from their labours; and their works do follow them." 2. *Courage to the faint.* You disciples of the Lord, who feel the journey of life to be trying, the battle to be severe, and feel at all times depressed—take heart; yet a little while all your trials will be over. You shall "rest from your labours; and your works shall follow you." "Go thou thy way until the end be: for thou shalt rest, and stand in thy lot at the end of the days."

> "I would die my death *in Christo;*
> Breathing in his love, I'm blest;
> When this frame to dust returneth,
> I shall enter into rest.
> In that rest I shall adore him,
> In the strains of sacred love,
> With the ransomed of all races
> Gathered in the heavens above.
> Aid me, Lord, to die *in Christo* ·
> Oh, *in Christo* let me die!"
>
> (See the 'Biblical Liturgy.')
>
> D. T.

Vers. 14—20.—*The moral seasons of humanity.* "And I looked, and behold a white cloud, and upon the cloud One sat like unto the Son of man, having on his head a golden crown, and in his hand a sharp sickle," etc. There are three *moral seasons* implied in this section of the Apocalyptic vision.

I. THE RIPENING SEASON. "And I looked [saw], and behold a white cloud, and upon the cloud One sat like unto the [a] Son of man, having on his head a golden crown, and in his hand a sharp sickle" (ver. 14). This language may be taken as an illustration of that supreme Divinity that presides over all the moral seasons of mankind. He is *glorious.* He is encircled with a "cloud," dazzling and splendid. He is *human.* He is "like unto the Son of man." Supreme Divinity is full of humanity, and humanity is full of God. He is *royal.* He has "upon his head a golden crown." He is "the King of kings, and Lord of lords." He is *absolute.* He has "in his hand a sharp sickle." He has the power to put an end to the whole system whenever he pleases; he kills and he makes alive. Such is the Being that presides over our histories, our lives, and destinies. Our world is not left to chance or fate, blind force or arbitrary despotism. There is an intelligent Being over it, all-glorious, yet human, royal and absolute. He presides over the ripening season. Months before the sickle is thrust in the ripening has been going on. There are two classes of principles, good and evil, which are seeds growing in all human souls. Both are *implanted*. Neither of them is *inbred*. The seed of evil is not constitutional; the seeds of good are almost exterminated by the seeds of sin. "A man sowed good seed in his field; but while men slept, his enemy came and sowed tares among the wheat." The spirit of evil implants the one. "An enemy came and sowed tares." The Son of man implants the other. Both, in all souls, are constantly growing and advancing to ripeness. Although human nature is made for truth and right, it can grow error and wrong. It can develop a false impression or an erroneous sentiment into a upas that shall spread its baneful branches over empires, and poison the heart of ages.

II. THE HARVEST SEASON. "Thrust in [send forth] thy sickle, and reap: for the time is come" (ver. 15). All life culminates in maturity. " First the blade, then the ear, then the full corn in the ear." Growth is but life running into ripeness, as the river runs to the ocean. "The harvest of the earth is ripe, the grapes are fully ripe." In connection with this it is suggested that the harvest is under the direction of a supreme intelligence. "And another angel came out of the temple, crying with a loud voice to him that sat on the cloud" (ver. 15). The angel had no power to snatch the sickle from the Divine hand and employ it. The Divine permission is absolutely necessary; life and death are with him. "There is an appointed time for man upon the earth." No creature or combination of creatures, however mighty, can abbreviate or prolong the appointed period. There are no premature deaths in human history. Angels, it may be, in countless numbers await his behest. They are ready to strike down when he permits. Death is ever on the wing; silently and stealthily he approaches every human being, and strikes the moment he has permission.

III. THE VINTAGE SEASON. "Thrust in [send forth] thy sharp sickle, and gather the clusters of the vine of the earth; for her grapes are fully ripe" (ver. 18). The vintage is a section of the harvest. The vine reaches its maturity and has its harvest as well as the ears of corn, and the pressing of these grapes is the vintage. Three things are suggested in connection with this vintage. 1. *Divine severity.* "The great wine-press of the wrath of God. And the wine-press was trodden without the city, and blood came out of the wine-press" (vers. 19, 20). Grapes in the press were usually trodden by the feet of men (see Isa. lxiii. 2, 3; Lam. i. 15). The idea of severity could scarcely fail to be conveyed to the spectator whose feet trampled on the soft, blooming, beautiful grape, so that the juice like its very blood streamed forth. "The wrath of God." There is no wrath in God but the wrath of love. Divine law is but love speaking in the imperative mood; Divine retribution is but Divine love chastising the child to bring him back to the right and the true. 2. *Great abundance.* "Blood came out of the wine-press, even unto the horse bridles" (ver. 20). That is, the juice flowing like a deep river, rising to the very bridles of the horses. Who shall measure the final issues of the moral seasons of humanity? 3. *Extensive range.* "A thousand and six hundred furlongs" (ver. 20)—a hundred and fifty miles. A definite number of miles for an indefinite space. The final issue of souls will be as wide as immensity. —D. T.

EXPOSITION.

CHAPTER XV.

Ver. 1.—And I saw another sign in heaven. The last time we had this expression was in ch. xii., where the history of the war between Satan and the Church was begun. Once more we have a new departure, the seer again, as it were, returning to the beginning, in order to trace the course of the punishments inflicted on men for their worship of the devil. Ch. xv. gives a short summary of this, which is expanded in ch. xvi.; and it is introduced, as usual, by a vision of the saints in glory, in order to comfort and support the Christian in his warfare (cf. ch. vi. 1, 2; vii. 3; xiv. 1—5, 13). The "sign" is what is described in the following account. "In heaven" probably merely means in a conspicuous position (cf. ch. xii. 1). Great and marvellous. On account of the terrible nature of the events depicted. Seven angels having the seven last plagues; for in them is filled up the wrath of God; *seven angels having seven plagues, the last [ones], because in them is finished the wrath of God.* The seer describes what he sees subsequently, as if all the actors were present at one moment. In reality, he sees the actions of the "seven angels" in succession. The number *seven* denotes the universal, all-extending nature of the plagues (see on ch. i. 4; v. 1, etc.). They are the *last* plagues, because they lead on to the description of the final fall of the power of the devil in its various forms, and to the account of the last judgment of God and the eternal bliss of the saints in glory.

Ver. 2.—And I saw as it were a sea of glass mingled with fire. "And I saw" indicates a new phase of the vision (cf. ch. xiv. 6, 14, etc.). The *sea* was like *glass*, either because of its pure transparent appearance, or on account of its consistency; the saints being subsequently described as standing on it. (For a full discussion of the meaning, see on ch. iv. 6.) The sea, the elders, and the triumphal hymns of praise are all characteristic of the vision in ch. iv. *Mingled with fire.* In ch. iv. it was described as "like unto crystal." The fire is an emblem of purity; the same idea is also conveyed by the "crystal." Fire is also a symbol of judgment, which is the theme of the song of the saints (ver. 4). And them that had gotten the victory over the beast, and over his image, and over his mark, and over the number of his name, stand on the sea of glass, having the harps of God; *and them that come victorious from the beast and from his image, and from the number,* etc. Omit "and over his mark," according to all the best authorities. *Standing by* (or, *on*), *having harps.* (On "the beast" and "his image," etc., see on ch. xiii.) These victorious ones stand *by* (such, probably, is the force of ἐπί) the sea (see above and on ch. iv. 6). The "harps" are characteristic of the heavenly melodies (ch. v. 8; xiv. 2). This multitude has been before described in ch. vii. 9. *From his image;* that is, from the temptation to worship the *image.*

Ver. 3.—And they sing the song of Moses the servant of God, and the song of the Lamb. Most probably the song of deliverance after the passage of the Red Sea (Exod. xv.), to which this bears a general resemblance. Moses is called the "servant of God" in Exod. xiv. 31 and elsewhere. The song of Moses is also the song of the Lamb; the Old Testament and the New

Testament Churches are one. Saying, Great and marvellous are thy works, Lord God Almighty (cf. Exod. xv. 7, "And in the greatness of thine excellency thou hast overthrown them;" also Ps. cxi. 2; cxxxix. 14). This song, like that in ch. iv. 8, is addressed to the "Lord God Almighty." Just and true are thy ways, thou King of saints. The reading of the Textus Receptus, ἁγίων, "of saints," is certainly incorrect. It does not appear in any Greek manuscripts, but was inserted by Erasmus to represent the *sanctorum* of his Vulgate, which word, however, is itself a corruption of *sæculorum*, the true Vulgate reading representing αἰώνων. Ἐθνῶν, "of nations," is read in ℵᶜ, A, B, P, 1, 7, 8, 14, etc., Andreas, Primasius; while αἰῶνον, "of ages," is the reading of ℵ*, C, 95, Vulgate, etc. It has been conjectured that ΑΙΘΝΩΝ (by itacism for ἐθνῶν) has been confused with ΑΙΩΝΩΝ. A parallel to the reading, "King of nations" is found in Jer. x. 7, Hebrew text and Theodotion, but not LXX.: "Who would not fear thee, O King of nations?" which is very like the succeeding clause in ver. 5, especially in connection with the "nations" there mentioned. The title "King of the ages," or "eternal King," is applied to God in 1 Tim. i. 17, and in the Book of Tobit twice (xiii. 6 and 10), but seems unknown to the Old Testament.

Ver. 4.—Who shall not fear thee, O Lord, and glorify thy Name? Omit "thee." The latter part is from Jer. x. 7 (see on ver. 3). The former part contains the same idea as Jer. x. 6, "Thy Name is great in might." Compare the similar ascription of praise to the beast in ch. xiii. 4. The following three clauses supply the reasons for thus fearing and glorifying God. For thou only art holy: for all nations shall come and worship before thee; for thy judgments are made manifest; *for thy righteous acts have been made manifest* (Revised Version). "Holy" is ὅσιος, not ἅγιος. It is a word which is applied more particularly to human acts. Perhaps it is used here in connection with the manifest justice of God's acts before all nations; cf. the song of Moses (Exod. xv. 11), "Who is like thee, glorious in holiness," etc.? The three clauses supply the reason for fearing and glorifying God, as mentioned in the first part of the verse. (1) He himself is in his nature holy; (2) his sway extends over all nations; (3) the righteousness of his acts is now visible to all. Alford adds, "Thy deeds of righteousness acted out towards the nations, both in the publication of the gospel and in the destruction of thine enemies."

Ver. 5.—And after that I looked, and, behold; *and after these things I saw.* The characteristic commencement of a new vision or portion of a vision (see on ch. iv. 1, etc.). The temple of the tabernacle of the testimony in heaven was opened. The *tabernacle* had its counterpart in heaven (Heb. viii. 5). In Exod. xxv. 16, 21 we have the reason of the title " tabernacle of the testimony "—a name which is common in the Bible (see Exod. xxxviii. 21 ; Numb. i. 50, 53 ; ix. 15 ; x. 11). The " temple " is the *vaós*, the inner shrine, the holy of holies which contained the ark of the testimony, which in ch. xi. 19 is seen in connection with the judgments of God. Thence now proceed the angels bearing the plagues for men.

Ver. 6.—And the seven angels came out of the temple, having the seven plagues ; *there came out the seven angels that had*, etc. These angels are distinguished from the other angels only by the fact that they bore the seven plagues. These they have not yet, but they receive them directly after. The phrase is added here to distinguish the angels meant. These angels have once before (ver. 1) been described in the same manner. Clothed in pure and white linen, and having their breasts girded with golden girdles. Λίνον, " linen," is found in א, B, P, 7, 14, 97, Andreas, Primasius. Λίθον, [precious] " stone," is read in A, C, 38 (margin), 48, 90, Vulgate. It seems more probable that λίθον is the correct word ; for in no other place in the New Testament is λίνον found except in Matt. xii. 20, where it signifies " flax ; " while the ordinary word for linen, viz. βύσσος or βύσσινος, is found in ch. xviii. 12, 16, and xix. 8, 14, as well as in Luke xvi. 19. If λίνον be the correct reading, the image is perhaps suggested by the priestly garments (cf. Exod. xxviii. 42, and *vide infra*). For the idea of " clothed in precious stone," the LXX. reading of Ezek. xxviii. 13 is usually quoted. We may refer also to the stones of the high priest's breastplate, and to the description in ch. xvii 4. *And having their breasts girded with golden girdles* (cf. the vision of our Lord in ch. i. 13, and the priestly attire described in Exod. xxviii. 8).

Ver. 7.—And one of the four beasts gave

unto the seven angels ; *four living beings.* These, as representing life on the earth (see on ch. iv. 6 ; v. 9), are appropriately chosen as the medium for conveying to the angels the plagues about to be inflicted on men. This description is very like what is related of the cherubim—from which the idea of the living beings is evolved (see on ch. iv. 6)—in Ezek. x. 7, " And one cherub stretched forth his hand from between the cherubims unto the fire that was between the cherubims, and took thereof, and put it into the hands of him that was clothed with linen : who took it, and went out." (On the " seven angels," see on ver. 1.) Seven golden vials full of the wrath of God, who liveth for ever and ever. *Seven ;* as showing the complete nature of the wrath of God (cf. ver. 1, " In them is fulfilled," etc.). *Golden ;* the characteristic of the heavenly things and places (cf. ch. iv. 4 ; xxi. 18, etc.), and which is also sometimes used of other things to indicate gorgeousness and unusual splendour (cf. ch. xviii. 16). (On " vials," see on ch. v. 8, and compare with ch. xiv 10, " the cup of his indignation.") Compare the expression, " who liveth for ever and ever," with the possible reading of ver. 3, " thou King of the ages."

Ver. 8.—And the temple was filled with smoke from the glory of God, and from his power. The " smoke " suggests (1) the cloud, or Shechinah, the symbol of God's presence and glory (cf. Exod. xvi. 10 ; xxiv. 16); (2) the sign of God's active operation (Exod. xix. 18) ; (3) the token of judgment and calamity (Isa. xiv. 31 ; Ps. xviii. 8; ch. xiv. 11). All three significations receive their fulfilment in this place. And no man was able to enter into the temple, till the seven plagues of the seven angels were fulfilled ; *should be finished* (Revised Version). Just as when God manifested his presence on Sinai the people were not allowed to approach, so here no one is allowed to approach the *vaós*, the dwelling-place of God, while he is manifesting his judgments. The description is intended to convey an impression of the awful sacredness of God's presence. (For the explanation of the parts of this verse, see on previous verses.)

HOMILETICS.

Vers. 1—8.—*The victors' song.* The visions of this book are drawing to a close. Those immediately before us are meant to indicate the *last* judgments which must fall on the world, ere out of the ruin and from it there shall emerge the new heavens and the new earth. But another break in the gloom is permitted to us here. The apostle casts his eyes, not downward, but upward. He beholds two groups of beings in the upper realm. The first is composed of seven angels who have seven plagues, which are the last. The second is composed of great multitudes—of those who, while the struggle was going on below, soared out of it, and were victorious. The work of the first group will be noted in subsequent homilies. The song of the second is before us now. If we ask and answer four questions, we shall know as much about the song and the singers as it is possible to do in this state. The four queries are : (1) Who are singing the song? (2) At what time? (3) What are the contents of it? (4) Where is it being sung?

I. Who are singing the song? They "that come victorious from (ἐκ) the beast," etc. (ver. 2). Then it is evident that they are those who once were in the scene of conflict here below; who had to maintain a fight, hard and stern, against a godless world and a corrupt Church ; in fact, against all the forces which, led on by "the dragon," are used by the first and the second beasts. We cannot mistake them, any more than we can the glorious company mentioned in the seventh and fourteenth chapters. They once were strugglers and wrestlers here. But their toils are over, and they have gained the victory. They it is who now are singing the song.

II. When? To what time does the apostle point us? It may be remarked by some, that inasmuch as the visions of the conflict indicate future troubles, so the brighter visions indicate future glories. True. But we must remember that we are already more than eighteen hundred years onward, and therefore that the struggles of this present time are "future" from the Patmos standpoint. Besides, the song is being sung simultaneously with the raging of the conflict. They sing in one realm who have sped out of (ἐκ) the other. The dragon, the first beast, the second beast, war still. Some have already escaped out of the confusion, have gained the victory, and are singing (ᾄδουσι) the song. A further indication of time is given in ver. 4, " All nations shall come and worship "—future—προσκυνήσουσιν. So that it is evidently before the great work of the world's conversion is completed. Thus we are brought by the time-marks in the paragraph to the conclusion to which we have previously come, viz. that the Church of God exists in two realms. One part of it is in the struggle; another has risen beyond it. Their gladness and song have already begun.

III. What of the song itself? 1. It has a remarkable name. "The song of Moses . . . and . . . the Lamb." By the former the deliverance out of Egypt was effected. By the latter a redemption infinitely greater, of which the earlier one was but a faint and feeble type ; i.e. the song is a celebration of redeeming love, and reviews the great redemptive work in all its phases, stages, and ages.[1] 2. It has joyous accompaniments. " Having the harps of God." Under the Jewish worship, as far back as David's time, the harp was used to aid in sacred song. In a higher realm, where the joy is complete, the " harp " will never be hung on the willows, and will never be out of tune. 3. Its contents are manifold. (1) It celebrates Divine attributes. " Thou only art holy." (2) It magnifies the rectitude of the Divine government. " Righteous and true are thy ways." (3) In it the Divine greatness is extolled. " King of the ages ; " " The Almighty." (4) It finds inspiration in the manifestation of the righteous acts of God. To saints above, from their loftier standpoint, the glory of the Divine dealings is far more clear than it can possibly be to us. We "dwell in clouds below." (5) The certainty of the coming triumph gladdens their hearts. "All nations shall come," etc. (cf. Ps. lxxxvi. 9; Isa. ii. 2—4; lxvi. 23; Zech. viii. 22; Mal. i. 11). Our Saviour's words intimate to us that the progress of the kingdom of God on earth is witnessed by the saints from their blissful seat in Paradise (cf. John viii. 56, Greek).

IV. Where is the song being sung? " I saw . . . them . . . standing by the glassy sea." Here, as indeed throughout the chapter, there is an allusion to the ransomed host of Israel when they stood by the shores of the Red Sea and sang, "Sing ye to the Lord," etc. That sight furnishes the material for the imagery here. And the underlying thought which that imagery conveys is this—they stand now in the realm of victory, like as Israel of old when they saw their enemies dead upon the seashore. They are in " the land of triumph." "There are no foes to encounter there." Here is the fighting ; there, is the rest. Here, the cross ; there, the crown. Here, the sigh ; there, the song. Here, the foreboding fear ; there, all fear is for ever done away.

In view of all this, let us note : 1. It is not for nought that we are asked to main-

---

[1] " The song includes everything that God had done for his people alike in Old and New Testament times. How clearly does it appear that the beast cannot be Nero ! Only one generation, not the whole Church, could sing of deliverance from him " (Milligan).

tain the conflict with evil, in the Name and on behalf of our Lord. " If we suffer, we shall also reign with him." In the day of victory, his triumph will be ours. " Be thou faithful unto death, and I will give thee a crown of life." 2. However much perplexity and distress the mystery of the Divine ways may occasion us now, we may rest assured that when God's judgments are made manifest, they will be the theme of adoring praise. There will be seen to be a unity about them which as yet we can scarcely discern; a steadfast advance through age after age which in the present brief span of our earthly life we cannot trace; and we cannot doubt that the ultimate issue will reveal a grandeur, a vastness, and a completeness in redemption's plan, which only the Infinite Eye can now discern. Therefore observe: 3. Meanwhile it is an infinite comfort and stay to our souls amid this troubled scene, to have had sketched beforehand for us the tribulations through which we must enter the kingdom, and the glories of the kingdom in which we shall triumph when the tribulation is over.

HOMILIES BY VARIOUS AUTHORS.

Vers. 1—8.—" *The wrath of God.*" Such is the subject of this and the following chapters.

I. WHAT IS IT? "The wrath of God" is simply that will of God which for ever has linked together sin and suffering; that will by which woe follows wickedness everywhere and always. It is calm, not passionate; inexorable, not capricious; ever just, as man's wrath too often is not; and never selfish, as ours too often is.

II. Is TERRIBLE TO EVIL-DOERS. See the several symbols of it as they are given one by one in the account of the outpouring of the seven vials. And, separate from all symbol, see how everywhere and always and evermore, suffering, like a sleuth-hound, tracks the steps of sin, and sooner or later fastens its fangs in the sinful man or sinful people. So sure is this, that that shrewd, wise, observant man who wrote the Book of Proverbs declared it as the testimony of all experience that they are "fools" who "make a mock at sin."

III. WILL HAVE AN END. Not that the will of God, without which he could neither be the God of holiness nor the God of love; that ordains the everlasting union of sin with suffering—not that that will can ever end or change, but that, the purpose of his will being accomplished by the extirpation of sin, there shall no longer be occasion for suffering. Hence we say the wrath of God will have an end. And accordingly these very plagues are called "the seven *last* plagues." It would be dreadful to think that the moral condition of men should ever be as it is, and has been during all the past. But it will not. The day will dawn when there will no longer be need for any more plagues, and when the last of them, they all having done their work, shall pass away for evermore (ver. 1).

IV. Is CONSENTED TO BY ALL THE COMPANY OF HEAVEN. The saints, they celebrate its manifestation by their song. The living ones (ver. 7) consign to the charge of the seven angels the seven vials of the wrath of God. Angels, who come forth from the inmost shrine of the temple of God, and are vested as his priests, undertake this awful work; the holy, the blessed, the glorified, the redeemed, those saved by the mercy of God, all alike consent. It is a fearful, but a most solemn and salutary fact, to remember that there will not be found a solitary individual amongst the holy and the good who will intercede against or do aught but consent to God's judgments against sin. Even he who is the Lamb of God, the Friend and Saviour of sinners, consents; yea, more than this, for it is his song that his saints sing in celebration of these judgments of God. Left utterly alone with his sin—without one friend—will he be who now refuses to give up his sin and submit to Christ.

V. EVIDENCES THE HOLINESS OF GOD. (Vers. 3, 4.) The conviction constrains the confession, "Thou only art holy;" "Righteous and true are thy ways"—so sing they who sing the song of Moses and of the Lamb. What worth is any government, what worth especially would be the government of God, if it were as the sceptic cynic in Ecclesiastes says it is, that "there is one end to the righteous and to the wicked"? There would be no need of a hell by-and-by, for earth would be hell already. Blessed for ever be his Name, who makes "the way of transgressors hard."

VI. WILL BE FOLLOWED BY THE COMING "OF ALL NATIONS TO WORSHIP BEFORE" GOD. (Ver. 4.) This most precious truth explains the song that the saints sing. How could they sing if sin and suffering were to go on for ever; if evil were to be eternal, or if the woes of the world meant the destruction of the world? But knowing and seeing clearly, as they do, how all these judgments of God conduce to the glory of God; and that as the cloud of his majesty filled the temple (ver. 8), so shall that glory fill all the earth; therefore they can, not merely with calmness, but with joy, contemplate the pouring out of the vials, even of the wrath of God. But for the faith of this how could thoughtful men endure to live?

VII. WARNS US TO FLEE FROM THE WICKEDNESS THAT AROUSES IT TO THE LORD JESUS CHRIST. For he it is in whom we are sheltered from the wrath due to sin of the past, and from the power of sin present and future.—S. C.

Vers. 3, 4.—*The prelude of the plagues—the beginning of the end.* It seemed as if all was ended with the harvest and the vintage, of which we are told in the close of the previous chapter. What can come after the ingathering of the saints and the final judgment? And, indeed, nothing can. But what is here given in the chapters that follow is the more detailed setting forth of the Divine judgments upon the Church's three great enemies—the dragon and the two beasts; or, in other words, the dragon, the beast, and the false prophet. The overthrow of Satan is, however, related last of all. Ere the Divine judgments on these enemies of the people of God begin, we have the song of the redeemed—the song, as it is termed, "of Moses the servant of God and of the Lamb." An objection may be felt by some that the saints of God should be represented, as they are here, as exulting over the awful woes which had come upon their enemies. Is such triumph over a fallen foe in harmony with the Spirit of Christ, and with the perfectly sanctified nature of the inhabitants of heaven? In reply, we may say that what is right anywhere is right everywhere; and if it were right for Israel to exult over the dead Egyptians and the utter destruction of Pharaoh and his hosts—as surely it was—then like exultation over far worse foes cannot be wrong. We are scarcely able to comprehend either Israel's or St. John's condition of mind. We have so long dwelt at ease, in the enjoyment of full liberty, none daring to make us afraid, that the intense feeling aroused by hideous murder, bloody cruelty, monstrous injustice, and relentless oppression, threatening, not one or two, but a whole people, and enacted under our own eyes, and felt in our own persons—what all this would arouse in men's minds we do not know, and can scarce imagine. One present amid the Sepoy massacres in the Indian Mutiny tells with what fresh understanding he and his fellow-worshippers listened in church to the lessons which fell then to be read out of the Book of Joshua. Burning indignation against wrong can never be wrong. It was in Christ, and should be in us. Exultation, therefore, over its downfall is not only natural, but right. The coupling together of the song of Moses and of the Lamb teaches that in the first we are to find the pattern of the second. Note, therefore—

I. THE SCENE. Our thoughts are sent back to the thrilling story of Israel in Egypt. The pouring out of the vials is called by the same name—"plagues"—as were God's judgments in Egypt. And the scene of this song alludes plainly to Israel at the Red Sea. We are standing before a sea of glass, as we read in ch. iv. But that sea now seems "mingled with fire." On its margin stand the throngs of the redeemed. That sea so lustrous, so still, so smooth, so firm, like as the Red Sea seemed in comparison with the fearful storm of the night of the Exodus. But it had been a sea of judgment to their foes. In its depths lay horse and rider, chariot and horseman, Pharaoh and his army. Fitly did the sea mingled with this sea of glass, tell of that. And the rejoicing Israelites were the type of which the redeemed Church of Christ, safe in glory, is the antitype. This scene is another reminder, out of many more, that in the story of Israel may be read, as symbol, the story of the Christian Church. The comfort, the counsel, and the warning—for all are there—of the one are for the other also.

II. THE SONG. 1. *It is a song, not a speech.* Sung, not said. Music, the vehicle of song, is the language of thoughts that lie too deep for words. Words are not adequate to tell of the heart's feelings. The flush of shame; the flash of the angry eye—as his, whose "eyes were as a flame of fire;" the tears of sorrow; the sigh of distress. More than words is wanted, and music is one of the many means, more expressive far than words, whereby the deeper feelings and thoughts of the heart are uttered. Music is especially animated with joy, and the fact that the heavenly company "sing," tells of their "joy of heart." 2. *It is a song wherein all the glory is given to God.* Moses does not say one word of himself, but bids the people "sing unto the Lord." So was it, so will it be. 3. *It lingers on the terribleness of their enemies.* It tells of their proud boast, their cruel intent, their formidable power. Thus the "wrath of man" praised God. And in the future review, when we think of our adversaries, the seemingly insuperable difficulties—these will be, as the like were, part of our song. 4. *It tells of the enemies' complete overthrow.* 5. *The future consequences of this victory.* Moses celebrates that. How "the dukes of Edom, the people of Palestina," will be moved with fear. And so in the song of the Lamb, "Who shall not fear," etc. ? (ver. 4). The redeemed distinctly contemplate further triumphs for the Lord over those as yet not yielded to him. The "firstfruits," "the Church of the Firstborn," "the elect of God"—and it is these, and their glorious salvation, which is portrayed here—are, as their prototypes were, for the blessing of others, many others; "all the nations of the earth" are to be blessed in Christ and in his seed. And the elect are to be the instruments. And the mighty lever that shall overturn the mass of error and sin shall be God's marvellous mercy to them. Oh to be numbered amongst "the sacramental host of God's elect"! For they are—

III. THE SINGERS OF THIS SONG. They were and are such as: 1. *Once were bondmen.* 2. *Had been in sore peril of being re-enslaved.* 3. *Their preservation due to the fact that they had been "kept by the power of God."* It was his restraining hand had held back the waves, that but for this would have overwhelmed them. 4. *They are a "blood-besprinkled band."* On the lintel and doorposts of every house of Israel the blood of the Paschal lamb had been sprinkled, and so had they and theirs been saved alive. Never were they to think that it was for their own worthiness they were saved. To crush such thought the Passover sacrifice was ordained. And the singers of *this* song owe their all to the fact that for them Christ's blood was shed. In virtue of that they are what and where they are. Do any ask—How is this? We answer—

> "I cannot tell the woe
> Which thou wast pleased to bear,
> O Lamb of God: but this I know—
> That all my sins were there."

S. C.

Vers. 1—4.—*The song of the redeemed.* A further vision is permitted—"another sign"—with which the faithful but tried ones are to be cheered. The vision, as a whole, is "great and marvellous." It reaches to the end of the eighteenth chapter. "Seven angels" have "seven plagues"—"the last, for in them is finished the wrath of God." With these solemn words the announcement of the coming judgments—the final ones—is prefaced. As before, the hearts of the faithful are comforted and assured by a vision of their glorious lot, before the revelation of the judgments upon the earth is made. So are they encouraged to fidelity, and prepared for the terrible scenes which are about to be presented. It is needless to search for an explanation of every detail of the symbol. The vision is of the holy ones, who sing a psalm of praise to God for his manifested judgments. "Thy righteous acts have been made manifest." It has its hidden assertion. Thy judgments hitherto, thy judgments ever, those which have been, those which are, and those which shall be, are true and righteous altogether. This ascription is thrown into the form of a song, which is—

I. A SONG OF PRAISE. Praise to God for the greatness and marvellous character of his works, and for the righteousness and truthfulness of his ways.

II. A SONG OF TRIUMPH. Like the several songs of the Revelation, it anticipates the final issue of the struggle between good and evil. "All the nations shall come and worship before thee."

III. A SONG FROM A FAITHFUL AND REDEEMED HOST. "Them that come victorious from the beast, and from his image, and from the number of his name." Only the redeemed who have been faithful in their struggle against evil can rejoice in the final overthrow of that evil.

IV. A JUBILANT SONG. They who sing stand "by the glassy sea, having the harps of God." It is a song of salvation and deliverance: "the song of Moses "—the triumphant exultation of the redeemed host when they, having crossed the flood, saw their enemies engulfed. "The song of the Lamb," when the whole work of the Lamb has been effected, when the redemption from sin is complete, and the overthrow of whatever opposes the Name of the Lamb is utterly crushed and destroyed. Then truly shall it be said, "Who shall not fear, O Lord, and glorify thy Name? for thou only art holy; for all the nations shall come and worship before thee." Thus is anticipated in song what is about to be portrayed.—R. G.

Ver. 3.—*The praise of the Divine works.* It is most meet that all should praise the works of God—those works which themselves do praise him. But the Church of God is especially called upon to view the works of God in the world. There the Almighty Ruler displays his power and wisdom and goodness. There the thoughtful may learn of him; for the righteousness and the truthfulness of his ways are a revelation of the righteousness and truth of his Name.

I. Praise is the creature's becoming ascription to Almighty God. His supremacy and government, his wisdom and power, his goodness and beneficence—every attribute which the human mind may be able, even dimly, to trace, it is the duty of the human heart to praise. It is little that can be offered by a creature to the Creator. His best service is his true, lowly, reverent, sincere praise. "He that offereth praise glorifieth God;" "Praise waiteth for thee, O God, in Zion."

II. Praise appropriately assumes the form of an inspiriting song of faith. Faith has its one foundation in God. Whatever lifts man upward to God stimulates to faith in the Divine Name. Without the knowledge of God there can be no faith in him; but as the glory of the Divine Name shines upon the human soul, that soul grows up into filial, obedient confidence in God. The song of praise stirs the sleepy spirit as the battle-cry the warrior. To praise God for the goodness and greatness of his works is sure to inspirit the faith that is in him.

III. Praise recognizing the might and majesty of God assures the heart of a final conquest over the feebleness of evil. This is the subject of the song in these words : "Who shall not fear, O Lord, and glorify thy Name? for thou only art holy."

IV. Praise calmly anticipates the ultimate happy and peaceful submission of all to the righteousness of "the Lord God, the Almighty." "All the nations shall come and worship before thee."

V. This praise has for its subject the holy Name and righteous way of God.—R. G.

Vers. 5—8.—*Final judgments proclaimed.* From this point commences the final delineation of the overthrow of the kingdom of evil. It may be difficult, if not impossible, to interpret the symbolical language in detail into realistic descriptions. Probably such interpretation is misleading. But the great ideas stand out prominently, and afford matter for contemplation, and, without puzzling the lowly reader, will help him to a knowledge of the "ways" and "judgments" of God. The complete vision of the destruction of "Babylon" reaches to the end of the eighteenth chapter. The portion named above is preliminary. A glance through the whole is sufficient to assure us that it represents a widespread struggle—a struggle of the utmost intensity and severity, and a final one. Within it occur the significant, prophetic words, "It is done!" Let this first glance, starting at the first words and reaching to the last, embrace the whole in a preliminary view, and we shall be instantly arrested—

I. By the severity of the judgment threatened. The vision is one of judgment, not of warfare. It is only incidentally that the idea of war is introduced (ch. xvi. 14, 16; xvii. 14). Judgment is the burden of the vision. The severity of the judgments is seen in the terms used. There are seven vials, or bowls. The first becomes "a noisome and grievous sore," etc. (ver. 2); the second a cause of death—"every living soul died;" the third turns "the rivers and fountains of the waters" into "blood;" the fourth, "men were scorched with great heat;" the fifth, "they gnawed their tongues for pain;" the sixth prepares the way for the coming of (antagonistic) kings (this requires a subsequent interpretation); the seventh brings "lightnings and voices and thunders" and "a great earthquake, such as was not since there were men upon the earth." Thus is set forth ideally the utmost painfulness and severity of judgments. Much of the imagery carries us back to Egypt's plagues.

II. We are further arrested by the UNIVERSALITY OF THE JUDGMENT. There is no reference to portions of the earth, as earlier (ch. viii. 7—11).

III. By THE FINALITY OF THE JUDGMENTS, "In them is finished the wrath of God." It is the judgment of "Babylon the great," "the great harlot that sitteth upon many waters." "Babylon the great, the mother of the harlots, and of the abominations of the earth," whose flesh they shall eat, and "shall burn her utterly with fire." Thus by outward materialistic judgments are we to see a spiritual conquest and destruction and judgment ideally represented. Blessed are they who are not included in "the judgment of the great harlot"!—R. G.

Vers. 1—4.—*Divine severity and human heroism.* "And I saw another sign in heaven, great and marvellous, seven angels having the seven last plagues; for in them is filled up the wrath of God. And I saw as it were a sea of glass mingled with fire: and them that had gotten the victory over the beast," etc. This fragment of John's vision, or dream, brings under our attention and serves to illustrate two subjects: (1) *Divine severity;* and (2) *human heroism.*

I. DIVINE SEVERITY. "And I saw another sign in heaven, great and marvellous, seven angels having the seven last plagues; for in them is filled up [finished] the wrath of God" (ver. 1). Undoubtedly in the government of this world there is the stormy as well as the mild, the gloomy as well as the pleasant. The government under which we live on this earth often assumes aspects of terrible severity. Its manifold ministers or angels bear to us manifold "plagues"—afflictions, which our sin-stricken consciences refer to Divine indignation or wrath. 1. *The principle of severity is seen in material nature.* In the inorganic realms all things do not seem mild and pleasant. We have tornadoes sweeping destruction over sea and land, we have earthquakes that engulf cities, sounds are heard and sights are witnessed that overwhelm with terror and alarm. 2. *This principle of severity is seen in the plantal realm.* In gardens and orchards, as well as in the fields and woods, the open commons and the wild prairies, there is heard the moaning groan and felt the blasting breath of severity shivering the fruit, scattering the blossoms like hoar-frost, freezing the very roots of life. 3. *This principle of severity is seen in the sentient domain.* From the behemoths that prowl in the forests, and the leviathans that sport in oceans, to the tiniest microbes in the microscopic world, there are aspects of severity, pains of birth and death, of hunger and thirst, and of predatorial ravages and tortures. There is an undertone of sadness heard throughout. "The whole creation groaneth," etc. 4. *This principle of severity is seen in human history.* Bodily diseases, secular indigence, social annoyances, heart-bereavements, physical dissolution,—in all these there is often the ghastly appearance of Divine severity. The "seven angels," with their "seven plagues," appear in all directions. I am far enough from averring that the ministry of pain is a malignant ministry, but, otherwise, it is benign. Will the ministry of pain ever continue? Will the "seven angels" be ever on the wing, bearing the "plagues"? Cowper says—

> "The groans of nature in this nether world,
> Which Heaven has heard for ages, have an end."

Will they have an end? Heaven grant they may!

II. HUMAN HEROISM. "And I saw as it were a sea of glass [a glassy sea] mingled with fire: and them that had gotten the victory over [that come victorious from] the beast, and over [from] his image, and over his mark, and over [from] the number of his name, stand on the sea of glass [standing by the glassy sea], having the harps of God. And they sing the song of Moses," etc. (vers. 2, 3). The heroes here suggested are: 1. *Those who have conquered the wrong.* They are those "who have gotten the victory over the beast." And what is the beast? *Moral wrong* in all its elements and forms. Sin is a hideous, ravenous, iniquitous "beast," served and worshipped by unredeemed men the world over. The foe against which the true hero fights is sin, and sin only. He who destroys life and tramples on human rights is no hero, but a mercenary murderer. From no character do I recoil with such horror as from him who sells his time, his body, his all, to slaughter his fellow-men. Nor do I feel scarcely a greater abhorrence for such a character than for those who, professing to be the ministers of Christ, rhetorically extol such as heroes, and subscribe to monuments to perpetuate their infamous history. I wonder greatly that the reports of the horrors of that war lately going on in the Soudan, inaugurated and supported, alas! by what has been rightly denominated the shuffling, starving, slaughtering Parliament of the time, do not rouse all England to arms against the Governments and the Churches that can tolerate for an instant such stupendous crimes. 2. *Those who ascribe their victory to God.* Observe: (1) Their *posture.* "They stand on the sea of glass, having the harps of God" (ver. 2). It is suggested that their position is one of *safety.* The sea does not surge about them; it is beneath them, hard as ice. It is a position of *splendour.* The crystal sea on which they stand is made brilliant by fire. There is no posture of soul so sublime and safe as the true posture of worship. The Shechinah beams around them as their glory and defence. (2) Their *anthem.* "They sing the song of Moses the servant of God, and the song of the Lamb" (ver. 3). (a) Their anthem breathes *triumphant praise.* They recognize in their triumphs the "great and marvellous works" of God, and the truth and rectitude of his ways. God is righteous. "Just [righteous] and true are thy ways, thou King of saints [the ages]" (ver. 3). Notice: (a) *The demands of his Law attest the truth of this testimony.* The heavenly Teacher has reduced all the demands which the eternal Governor makes upon us to a twofold command. (i.) "Thou shalt love the Lord thy God with all thy heart." His demand is our supreme love. Is this demand just? This depends upon three things: (a) Whether we have the power of loving any one supremely. (b) Whether God has attributes adapted to awaken this love within us. (c) Whether these attributes are revealed with sufficient clearness to our minds. The affirmative to these things must be admitted by all. All men do love some object supremely. The Eternal has attributes in every variety of aspect and attraction. The heavenly Teacher has reduced the demands to another command. (ii.) "Whatsoever ye would that men should do unto you, do ye even so unto them." Not "whatsoever men *do* unto you"—that might be sinful; but "whatsoever ye *would* that men should do unto you." Would you have them false, dishonest, unkind, tyrannic, towards you? Whatsoever ye would that they should *be,* be so to them. Can anything be more just? (β) *The intuitions of his moral creatures attest the truth of this testimony.* In all moral intelligences there is: (i.) An intuitive *sense of the right.* All have an inbred sentiment of right and wrong. This sentiment implies a moral standard; and what is this standard but God? (ii.) An intuitive *love of right.* All moral souls love the right in the abstract; they are bound to do it. "I delight in the Law of God after the inward man." All consciences go with God. (iii.) An intuitive *remorse.* Misery springs up in the soul from a conscious departure from the right. Cain, Belshazzar, Judas, are examples. (iv.) An intuitive *appeal to God under the wrong as the Friend of the right.* Oppressed humanity involuntarily looks to God as Judge of all the earth. Deep in the soul of the moral creation is the feeling that God's ways are just and right. No argument can destroy this consciousness. (γ) *The mediation of his Son attests the truth of this testimony.* Christ came to establish judgment—rectitude in the earth. "What the Law could not do in that it was weak through the flesh, and for sin condemned sin in the flesh." (i.) His life was the development of Divine righteousness. He was incarnate judgment. "He did no sin, neither was guile found in his mouth." (ii.) His death was the highest homage to Divine rectitude. He could have escaped death. It was the inner sense of right that urged him on. (iii.) His system is the promoter of Divine righteousness. His truth inculcates it. His Spirit promotes it. His Spirit comes to convince the world of sin, of righteousness, etc. (δ) *The retributions of his government attest the truth of this testimony.* Look at the expulsion of Adam, the Deluge, the burning of Sodom, the extermination of the Canaanites, the destruction of Jerusalem, and the dispersion of the Jews. (b) Their anthem breathes *philanthropic devotion.* "Who shall not fear thee, O Lord, and glorify thy Name? for thou only art holy: for all nations shall come and worship before thee; for thy judgments [righteous acts] are made manifest" (ver. 4). The words may be regarded as expressing a desire that all men, all the nations, should worship God. Genuine piety is always philanthropic. He who loves the Father will love his children, and will desire all the brethren to worship the Father "in spirit and in truth." Genuine piety and genuine philanthropy are convertible expressions, modifications of the same sovereign principle—love.—D. T.

Vers. 5—8.—*Genuine discipline of soul.* "And after that I looked, and, behold, the temple of the tabernacle of the testimony in heaven was opened : and the seven angels came out of the temple, having the seven plagues, clothed in pure and white linen," etc. I do not know that I can turn these words to a more legitimate and practical use than by using them as an illustration of *genuine soul-discipline.* In this light they suggest to us the *source,* the *ministers,* and the *indispensability* of genuine soul-discipline.

I. THE SOURCE OF GENUINE SOUL-DISCIPLINE. "After that [these things] I looked [saw], and, behold, the temple of the tabernacle of the testimony in heaven was opened" (ver. 5). The discipline, as we have seen, was of a *painful* character. It involved "seven angels" with "seven plagues." Whence did it proceed ? Not from secondary instrumentalities, fortuitous circumstances, or a heartless, rigorous fatality, but *direct* from the presence of the Infinite. The language here points to the inner compartment of the old Jewish tabernacle, known as the "holy of holies." There the Jew regarded Jehovah as especially revealing himself to them, and as communicating to them his ideas and plans. To a genuinely disciplined soul all influences from heaven tending to purify and ennoble are regarded as coming direct from the presence of the great Father. Its inner eye, so to speak, is so opened and quickened that it glances into the very shrine of the Almighty. It feels that "every good and perfect gift cometh down from the Father of lights," etc. It is a characteristic, or rather a law, of true religiousness that it bears the soul away through nature, churches, and chapels, right up into the very presence of God, to the very fontal Source of all good, the mighty Mainspring that works the universe. God is its all in all. It can truly say, "I looked, and, behold, the temple of the tabernacle of the testimony in heaven was opened" (ver. 5). The grand difference between a spurious and a genuine religiousness of soul is this—the one busies itself about the fussy doings and foggy dogmas of little sects, and the other is so absorbed with the Supreme Good, that it feels with the old Hebrew, "Whom have I in heaven but thee? and whom on earth do I desire but thee?"

II. THE MINISTERS OF GENUINE SOUL-DISCIPLINE. "And the seven angels came out of the temple, having [that had] the seven plagues" (ver. 6). The great Father who makes his children "meet for the inheritance of the saints in light," carries on his sublime educational work by angels or ministers. Concerning those ministers, observe: 1. *They are complete in number and qualification.* "Seven angels" and "seven plagues." 2. *They go forth direct from his presence.* "Came out of the temple," etc. 3. *They are divinely marked and attired as God's priests.* "Clothed [arrayed] in pure and white linen [precious stones pure and bright], and having their breasts girded [girt about the breasts] with golden girdles" (ver. 6). 4. *They have a commission of severity.* "And one of the four beasts [living creatures] gave unto the seven angels seven golden vials [bowls] full of the wrath of God, who liveth for ever and ever" (ver. 7). (The wrath of God is his antagonism to sin.) In the great moral school of humanity there has always been, as in all schools, not a little *severity.* True soul-education involves pain. The very severity is a blessing. "What son is he whom the father chasteneth not?" "Our light afflictions, which are but for a moment," etc. Whilst the majority of men regard this life as a market, or a banquet, or a playground, he who regards it as a great moral school has the only true idea—as a school in which every object is a lesson, every agent a teacher, and every teacher coming forth directly from God.

III. THE INDISPENSABILITY OF GENUINE SOUL-DISCIPLINE. "No man [no one] was able to enter into the temple, till the seven plagues of the seven angels were fulfilled [should be finished]" (ver. 8). The idea suggested is that no man could enter into the shrine or into the immediate presence of God until the discipline had been fully accomplished. Here is a commentary on this : "Who shall ascend into the hill of the Lord ? or who shall stand in his holy place ? He that hath clean hands and a pure heart, who hath not lifted up his soul unto vanity." Cleanness in hands and heart means having conduct void of offence towards God and man. Freedom from vanity means moral reality. These two things, moral *cleanness* and moral *reality,* are the qualifications for ascending to the "holy hill," or fellowship with God. "It is not," says Luther, "he who sings so well or so many psalms, nor he who fasts or watches so many days, nor he who divides his own among the poor, nor he who preaches to others, nor he who lives quietly, kindly, and friendly, nor, in fine, is it he who knows all sciences and languages, nor he who works all virtuous and all good works that ever any man spoke or read of; but it is he alone who is *pure within and without*."—D. T.

EXPOSITION.

CHAPTER XVI.

In the judgments of the *vials*, or *bowls*, we have undoubtedly a recapitulation of what has been already foretold in the trumpet and seal visions. This recapitulation is not a mere repetition; but the idea contained in the first visions is strengthened and set forth more forcibly, in conformity with ch. xv. 1, where we are told the wrath of God is finished in these plagues of the vials. The following comparison will illustrate the points of resemblance and contrast between the visions of the trumpets and of the vials.

Trumpets.	*Vials.*
1. Hail, fire, and blood cast UPON THE EARTH; *one-third* trees, etc., burnt.	1. Vial poured ON THE EARTH; sore upon *the followers* of the beast.
2. *One-third* of SEA made blood; one-third of creatures therein and of ships destroyed.	2. The SEA made blood *as of a dead man; every soul* therein destroyed.
3. *One-third* of the RIVERS made bitter; *many* men destroyed.	3. RIVERS made blood; declared to be God's vengeance upon [ALL] men.
4. *One-third* of the SUN, etc. smitten; one-third of the day darkened.	4. SUN smitten; *men* scorched; men blaspheme, men *repent not.*
5. Star from heaven falls into the ABYSS; he sends forth locusts; men *seek death; Hebrew* name of their king is Abaddon.	5. The THRONE and kingdom of the beast smitten; men, in pain, *blaspheme* God; men *repent not.*
6. Armies from the EUPHRATES destroy *one-third* part of men; men *repent not.*	6. The way prepared for kings beyond the EUPHRATES.
Episode :— The two witnesses of *God* WITNESS for him and work MIRACLES; WAR against them by the beast.	Episode :— Three unclean spirits of the *dragon* WITNESS for him and work MIRACLES; WAR by the world at (the *Hebrew*) Armageddon.

7. VOICES in heaven; the JUDGMENT; earthquake, etc., and HAIL.	7. VOICES in heaven; the FALL of Babylon; EARTHQUAKE, etc., and HAIL.

We may from this comparison notice—

(1) The vials form a series of visions denouncing God's judgments against the wicked.

(2) The number seven as well as their character indicates the universal and complete nature of these judgments.

(3) The events portrayed occupy the same period in time as the seals and trumpets; that is to say, the period of the world's history terminating with the last judgment-day.

(4) As in the cases of the seals and trumpets, they are general indications of God's judgments; and though particular events may be partial fulfilments, the complete fulfilment is in all time.

(5) In comparison with the seals and trumpets, we may observe some points in common and some in which the visions differ. (*a*) Like the former visions, these may be divided into two groups of four and three (see on the trumpets). (*b*) The structure of the vial-visions is almost exactly parallel to that of the seals. (*c*) The visions all terminate with the same events portrayed in similar language, though, as the three sets of visions proceed, more stress is laid upon the judgment of the wicked, and less on the victory of the redeemed. (*d*) An episode occurs after the sixth vial of almost identical nature with, though much shorter than, that after the sixth trumpet. (*e*) The severity of the nature of the vial-judgments is conspicuous. Whereas under the seals one-fourth was afflicted, and under the trumpets one-third, there is nothing to indicate any exemption in the vial-visions.

(6) The reason of the employment of the term "vial," or "bowl," is most likely to be found in the expression, "cup of God's anger," in ch. xiv. 10. It indicates the pouring out of God's wrath in an overwhelming and

irresistible flood. It is, therefore, significant of retribution more dire than that symbolized by the trumpet, just as the trumpet indicated greater severity than the seal.

Ver 1.—And I heard a great voice. Characteristic of all the heavenly utterances (cf. ch. xiv. 7, 9, etc.). We have now the narration in full of the events of which ch. xv. has given us a summary. Out of the temple. The *vaós*, shrine of God, mentioned in ch. xv. 8, and which no one could enter; the *voice* must, therefore, be the voice of God himself. Saying to the seven angels (see on ch. xv. 1). Go your ways, and pour out the vials of the wrath of God upon the earth ; *go ye and pour*, etc. *The seven vials* is read in ℵ, A, B, C, Andreas, Arethas, Primasius, and others. So, in ch. viii. 5, the angel casts fire on the earth.

Ver. 2.—And the first went, and poured out his vial upon the earth; *his bowl into*, etc. (Revised Version). (On "vial," see on ch v. 8.) The preposition *eis*, "into," distinguishes the first three vials from the last four, which have *epi*, "upon," and some writers make this the basis for classifying the vials into groups of three and four ; but it seems better to divide into groups of four and three (see on ver. 1, and preliminary remarks on the trumpet-visions). And there fell ; *and it became* (Revised Version). Compare the phraseology of Exod. ix. 10. A noisome and grievous sore upon the men which had the mark of the beast, and upon them which worshipped his image. The counterpart of the sixth plague of Egypt. The word *ἕλκος*, "sore," used here, is the same used in LXX., Exod. ix. It is impossible to say with certainty what (if any) particular judgment upon the ungodly is intended to be signified by St. John in this plague. From amongst the numerous interpretations which have been given to illustrate this passage, we may mention that of Andreas, who sees in it a reference to the "ulcer" (*ἕλκος*) of conscience. Or it may be that the writer has in contemplation that bodily disease which is the inevitable outcome of sin, and which often afflicts men in this world as the direct result of their misdoings ; though, of course, it cannot always be asserted to be a consequence of a man's own personal misdoings. (On the latter part of the verse, see on ch. xiii.)

Ver. 3.—And the second angel poured out his vial upon the sea. Omit "angel," which is not found in the best manuscripts, though it is understood. "Into the sea," as in ver. 2. The *sea* is also the object of the second trumpet-plague (see on ver. 1). And it became as the blood of a dead man ; *became blood as of a dead man.* Almost an exact reproduction of the second trumpet, and of

the first of the Egyptian plagues. The last clause intensifies the horrible nature of the judgment, and thus in some degree increases the severity of this plague over that of the trumpets. And every living soul died in the sea ; *and every soul of life died, [even] the things in the sea*, though *living soul (ζῶσα)* is found in ℵ, B, P, some cursives, versions, and Fathers. Not merely human lives. *The things, τὰ,* is omitted in ℵ, B, P, and others. In ch. viii. 9 we have, "Even the creatures that were in the sea." The interpretations are as numerous as in the case of the second trumpet (see on ch. viii. 9). It is most probable that the sea is here mentioned as part of creation (another part of which is mentioned in the following verse), the whole of which suffers for the sin of man, and the whole of which, intended for his benefit, becomes a source of affliction and woe to him through sin.

Ver. 4.—And the third angel poured out his vial upon the rivers and fountains of waters; and they became blood. Omit "angel" (see on ver. 3). "Into the rivers," etc., as in the previous cases. The singular *ἐγένετο,* probably on account of the neuter *ὕδατα* being understood. The idea of the second vial is carried on here (cf. on ver. 3) Note the corresponding judgment of the third trumpet. In addition to the interpretation of the second vial given above, it is probable that the blood signifies the slaughter and death which is part of God's vengeance on the wicked (cf. ver. 6). The divisions adopted in the first four vials correspond to those in ch. xiv., which designate the whole of God's created world, "heaven, and earth, and the sea, and the fountains of waters."

Ver. 5.—And I heard the angel of the waters say. The angels, throughout this book, are represented as having individual offices to fulfil. Here we have a reference to the angel whose duty it is to control the rivers, just as, in ch. xiv. 18, another angel is represented as having authority over fire. This verse and the following one are anticipations of ch. xix. 2, which is a commentary on ch. xviii., which latter is an elaboration of the judgments here described. Thou art righteous, O Lord, which art, and wast, and shalt be, because thou hast judged thus; *righteous art thou, which art and which wast, thou Holy One, because thou didst thus judge* (Revised Version). There is scarcely any authority for inserting "O Lord," or "and shalt be" (cf. ch. xi. 17). The angel, as having authority over the waters, and, as it were, a commission to see that they do their duty for men, acknowledges the justice of the sentence which makes them into an instrument for, and type of, man's destruction. Though there is no authority for inserting "and shalt be," the idea is, no doubt, to express the eternal nature of God. The same expression occurs in ch. xv. 3 (Revised Version) in almost exactly parallel connection; so also in ch. xi. 17, 18. *Thou hast judged thus* refers to the judgment of the third vial, possibly to all the first three. Note the marginal reading of the Revised Version (supported by Alford), which disconnects this verse from the succeeding one.

Ver. 6.—For they have shed the blood of saints and prophets, and thou hast given them blood to drink; for they are worthy. This supplies the key to the interpretation of the previous visions. The ungodly have shed the blood of saints, therefore God deals out death to them. This is the meaning signified by the "blood" of the previous verses (cf. the doom of Babylon, described in ch. xvii., especially ver. 6.; and ch. xviii. 6, 24. Cf. the words, "they are worthy," with ch. iii. 4). It is correct to consider that this prophecy received its first fulfilment in the violent deaths of so many of those who were the earliest Christian persecutors. On this subject see Lactantius, 'De Morte Persecutorum.'

Ver. 7.—And I heard another out of the altar say. Omit "another out of." The *altar* is connected (1) with the martyred saints (ch. vi. 9, 10; viii. 3); (2) with the judgments that fall on the earth in vengeance for the blood of the saints (ch. viii. 5; ix. 13; xiv. 18); hence the appropriateness of this voice from the altar, which acquiesces in the judgments inflicted. The altar is here personified, and speaks concurring in the justice of those judgments sent on account of the saints who are represented by it. Some writers, however, understand "the angel of the altar," which is similar to the reading of the Authorized Version. **Even so, Lord God Almighty, true and righteous are thy judgments;** *Yea, O Lord God, the Almighty* (Revised Version). Reaffirming what has been declared by the angel of the waters (ver. 5), and expressing concurrence therein. (On "true" (ἀληθιναί), see on ch. iii. 17.) Compare the expression in ver. 5. There God is declared *righteous* because he has thus judged; here the judgments are *righteous* because they are his. Both phrases are equally true, giving the same truth from different standpoints. The same verdict is endorsed by the heavenly multitude in ch. xix. 2, when they celebrate the downfall of Babylon; another proof of the identity of the world which is here the object of the vial-judgments and the Babylon, which is afterwards described, and whose doom is pronounced.

Ver. 8.—And the fourth angel poured out his vial upon the sun. Ἄγγελος, "angel," is omitted in nearly all manuscripts, though,

of course, it is understood. For the first time we have ἐπί, "upon," instead of εἰς, "into" (see on ver. 2). Another part of creation is visited, thus completing the visitation of the fourfold division of the universe—the earth, the sea, the rivers, the heavens—as foretold in ch. xiv. 7. And power was given unto him to scorch men with fire. "And it was given to it" is more probable than "to him;" the angels do not directly punish, but indirectly by pouring out the vials. This form of words expresses the permissory nature of the evil which is wrought; nothing can be done but by the will of God (cf. ch. xiii. 5, 7, 14). Bengel, Hengstenberg, and others consider that the permission to scorch men is given to the angel. *The men* (with the article); perhaps referring to those mentioned in ver. 2. who had the mark of the beast, and those who worshipped his image, and who are the object of all the vial-plagues. Though differing in form from the fourth trumpet, where the sun was darkened, yet the judgment is similar, though here of a more intense nature. In both cases, those objects which are given to men for their good are converted into instruments of punishment. We may, perhaps, see here an allusion to the heat of men's passions and vices, by which physically as well as morally they are destroyed; and which are also an emblem of the pains of hell as pictured in Luke xvi. It has been noticed as a coincidence that the objects of creation which are the subjects of the judgments of the fourth trumpet and fourth vial, were created on the fourth day.

Ver. 9.—And men were scorched with great heat, and blasphemed the Name of God. *The men* (see on ver. 8). (On the meaning of the first clause, see on ver. 8.) This is the first mention in the vials of men blaspheming. As with Pharaoh and the Egyptians, the judgments of God, instead of awakening them to repentance, only serve to harden their hearts. This again occurs under the fifth and seventh vials. So also in the sixth trumpet, we are told, men repented not—a statement also made in the subsequent part of this verse. As before pointed out (ch. xiii. 1), the two things are identical; non-repentance, continuance in the service of the dragon, is blasphemy against God; though we generally reserve the name "blasphemy" for the open avowal of infidelity to God. Which hath power over these plagues. This is what is implied in the words of ver 8, "it was given to it." In this visitation men distinctly recognize the hand of God. And they repented not to give him glory. *Vide supra*, on the "blasphemy;" and contrast with ch. xi. 13 —another example of the sense in which these **vials are the "last plagues"** (ch. xv. 1).

Ver. 10.—And the fifth angel poured out his vial upon the seat of the beast. Omit "angel" as before (see on ver. 8). The *throne of the beast.* That throne which had been given to him by the dragon (ch. xiii. 2), and which here typifies the centre and source of his power. While this *throne* may aptly refer to the Roman empire in St. John's time, its position varies at different times; wherever the world-power is worshipped, there the beast has his throne. And his kingdom was full of darkness; *was darkened.* Another allusion to the plagues of Egypt. The darkness is a type of the spiritual darkness which prevails among the subjects of the beast, and which they themselves frequently realize in the course of their career. The fear of the future sometimes arouses their misgivings, and then there is no light or hope in their hearts. And they gnawed their tongues for pain. The pain arising from the darkness of their minds; the misgivings as to their future (*vide supra*); or perhaps also on account of their sufferings under the former plagues, to which this is an addition.

Ver. 11.—And blasphemed the God of heaven because of their pains and their sores. The expression, "God of heaven," seems to enhance the exaltation of God, and to place in more terrible contrast the sin of those who ventured to blaspheme One so high, so far above them. This title is only mentioned here and in ch. xi. 13, where, however, some repented. (On the word "blaspheme," see on ver. 9.) In spite, therefore, of their plagues, and perhaps as a consequence of their spiritual darkness, they still own the supremacy of the beast and deny God ; just as Pharaoh hardened his heart. Compare the previous verses for an account of their *pains and their sores;* the allusion to which shows plainly that these plagues are not necessarily consecutive in time. And repented not of their deeds (see on ver. 9).

Ver. 12.—And the sixth angel poured out his vial upon the great river Euphrates. Omit "angel" (see on previous verses). (On the *Euphrates,* see on ch. ix. 14.) This river also figures in the sixth trumpet-vision, and possesses the same signification in both places. It is the natural direction from which enemies arise ; and it derives this signification from the fact that the enemies of the Jews often came from that direction. The next sentence leaves no doubt that this is the meaning, and supports the view taken of ch. ix. 14. It is to be noticed that, though the vial is poured out upon the Euphrates, it is not with the purpose of inflicting injury on the river, but upon the men who are thus laid open to the attacks of their

enemies. And the water thereof was dried up, that the way of the kings of the east might be prepared. The Revised Version gives the sense more plainly, *That the way might be made ready for the kings that* [come] *from the sunrising.* The meaning is that a barrier that wards off hostile hosts is removed. The "kings of the east" represent God's judgments; those who are laid open to attack are the adherents of the beast. The imagery may be derived : (1) From the fact (as explained in ch. ix. 14, which see) that the enemies of the Jews generally came from beyond the Euphrates. This accounts for the employment of this figure in ch. **ix.,** and may reasonably be considered to contain the same allusion here. In this case the minor details do not agree; the idea is merely to convey the central fact of an advance of enemies. (2) From the historical fact of the taking of Babylon by Cyrus, by means of a diversion of the waters of the Euphrates—a circumstance referred to in Jer. li. 31, 32, etc.; Isa. xiii.; xliv. 27, 28. In this case the details are more in accordance with the general symbolism of the Apocalypse. Babylon would signify the kingdom of the beast (as in ver. 19). The *kings of the east* would still represent God's judgments, which now assail the kingdom of Satan. Satan attempts to meet this assault by the three spirits, which gather kings from the whole world (ver. 14) to battle against the Almighty. The "kings of the east" are certainly the forces ranged on the side of God. Many writers see an allusion to Christ and the saints. The sun is a frequent figure of Christ in Scripture (cf. Mal. iv. 4 ; Zech. iii. 8 and vi. 12, LXX.; Luke i. 78 ; also ch. vii. 2; xii. 1; xxii. 16). "The kings of the east" may thus be identified with the armies of ch. xix. 11—16.

Ver. 13.—And I saw; introduces a new phase of the vision (see on ch. iv. 1). The mention of the punishment of the ungodly by the kings of the east causes the seer to look forward to the conflict, the end of which is described in ch. xix. 19—21. He therefore now digresses somewhat, in order to describe the means by which the dragon endeavours to enlist the hosts of the world on his side. Three unclean spirits like frogs. These *three spirits* represent the influences of the dragon, the first beast and the second beast, which we have interpreted as the devil, the love of the world and worldly power, and self-deceit ; in other words, the devil, the world, the flesh These influences are spiritually *unclean,* and suggest the loathsome Egyptian plague of the *frogs;* that is to say, their likeness to frogs consists in their common quality of uncleanness. Perhaps also there is a reference to their devilish origin, in which they resembled the *unclean* spirits so frequently cast out by our Lord while on earth. Burger very aptly refers to the contrast afforded by the dove-like form of the Holy Spirit of God. Come out of the mouth of the dragon, and out of the mouth of the beast, and out of the mouth of the false prophet. Omit "come." The seer does not behold the three spirits proceeding from the mouths of the evil trinity, but he sees those that are out of their mouths; he sees them in their works exhibited in the world. The second beast is here called the "false prophet," since he deludes men, and persuades them against their better judgment to worship the first beast (see on ch. xiii. 11).

Ver 14.—For they are the spirits of devils, working miracles. This explains the account given in ver. 13. In the plague of the frogs, the Egyptian magicians imitated the plague of Moses; the second beast (the false prophet) is represented as leading men astray by his miracles (ch. xiii. 13). After the sixth trumpet came the digression, in which an account was given of the two witnesses of God, who worked miracles (ch. xii.); here, after the sixth vial, we have a short digression, in which an account is given of the three witnesses of Satan, who endeavour to work on his behalf, by exhibiting miracles. (For the meaning of this working of miracles, see on ch. xiii. 13.) Which go forth unto the kings of the earth and of the whole world; *the kings of the whole world*—omitting " of the earth " (Revised Version). *The kings of the world* are those whose aim and delight is the possession of the pleasures of this world; those who have their treasure in this world, and whose hearts are therefore also there; those who exercise their influence and power in regard only to the things of this world; in short, the worldly. To gather them to the battle of that great day of God Almighty; *God, the Almighty*. This battle is described in ch. xix. 11—21, which see. *The great day* is the last great judgment-day. The battle referred to here, and described in ch. xix., and again in ch. xx. 1—10, is apparently the battle which is being waged against God by the forces of evil all through the history of the world, from the fall of Adam until the last judgment-day. This seems certain from the description given in ch. xix. and xx. How, then, can it be described as the "battle of the great day "? Probably because on that day will occur the crisis, as it were, of the conflict; on that day will the issue be plainly determined, and the struggle terminated. Though the battle is proceeding daily, there is little to remind us of it; the very existence of, and necessity for, such warfare is sometimes forgotten in the daily round of life: at the last day will be plainly exhibited the

nature of the incessant hostility between God and the devil, and the power of the latter will be manifested only to be visibly shattered and finally destroyed.

Ver. 15.—Behold, I come as a thief. The very words addressed to the Church at Sardis (ch. iii. 3), and similar to those connected by our blessed Lord with the great day (see ver. 14). The mention of that day, and perhaps the knowledge that the battle is a daily one (see on ver. 14), naturally leads to the solemn warning given here. It is worth notice how St. John adopts this idea; and this of itself should suffice to demonstrate the incorrectness of endeavouring to compute the times and seasons, as has been done by so many Apocalyptic writers (cf. also Matt. xxiv. 43; Luke xii. 39; 1 Thess. v. 2, 4; 2 Pet. iii. 10). Blessed is he that watcheth, and keepeth his garments, lest he walk naked, and they see his shame. The same figure again as in ch. iii. 17. Isaac Williams correctly points out that these words seem to indicate that the battle of ver. 14 is a daily one, in which Christians are themselves engaged (see on ver. 14). The garment is the garment of righteousness, the fervent love of God (see on ch. iii. 17).

Ver. 16.—And he gathered them together into a place called in the Hebrew tongue Armageddon; or, as in the Revised Version, *they gathered;* that is, the " spirits " of ver. 14, of which this is a continuation, the same verb συνάγω being repeated. By the employment of the Hebrew term, attention is called to the symbolical nature of the name. Similar cases occur in ch. ix. 11 and elsewhere in St. John's writings (see on ch. ix. 11). The correct reading, 'Αρμαγεδών, *Har-Magedon*, signifies " Mountain of Megiddo;" the Authorized Version, 'Αρμαγεδών, *Armageddon*, " City of Megiddo." *Mount Megiddo* possibly refers to Carmel, at the foot of which lay the Plain of Megiddo, which was well known to every Jew as a gathering-place for hostile hosts and as the scene of many battles. It is referred to in Zech. xii. 11 as a type of woe, on account of the overthrow and death of Josiah having taken place there (2 Kings xxiii. 29). Ahaziah also died there (2 Kings ix. 27); and there also the Canaanitish kings were overthrown (Judg. v. 19). The name is, therefore, indicative of battle and slaughter, and intimates the complete overthrow in store for the dragon and the kings of the earth, which is described later on (ch. xix.).

Ver. 17.—And the seventh angel poured out his vial into the air. Omit " angel " as before. *Upon the air;* perhaps as the typical abode of the spirits of evil (cf. Eph. ii. 2, " the prince of the power of the air "); the seat also, so to speak, of the thunders and lightnings which follow. And there came a great voice out of the temple of heaven, from the throne, saying, It is done. There are slight variations in the text here. The best authorities omit "of heaven." One manuscript, ℵ, instead of "throne" inserts τοῦ Θεοῦ. "of God." (On the characteristic *great voice*, see on ch. vi. 1, etc.) The same voice as in ver. 1, probably that of God himself, as the words, "from the throne," seem also to show. It is noticeable that here, as in the seal-visions and trumpet-visions, we are not explicitly informed of the nature of the last vision. We have the accompanying circumstances described in ver. 18, which are always attendant on the last great manifestation, but the end itself is left unrecorded. In the seals, the last vision is described by the silence in heaven; in the trumpets, the nature of the last judgment is only vaguely alluded to in the triumphant heavenly song. So here, only a brief summary is given (vers. 18, 19) of what actually falls as the last extremity of God's wrath; a fuller account is reserved for ch. xix.

Ver. 18.—And there were voices, and thunders, and lightnings; and there was a great earthquake, such as was not since men were upon the earth, so mighty an earthquake, and so great. The usual accompaniments of any special manifestation of God's power or presence (see on ch. iv. 5 and vi. 12—17). A similar description is given of the close of the seal and the trumpet visions.

Ver. 19.—And the great city. The words which follow, as well as ch. xi. 8; xiv. 8; xvii. 18; xviii. 10, 16, etc., leave scarcely any doubt that the "great city" here is Babylon. These are the only passages in the Apocalypse where this title is found; for in ch. xxi. 10, "great" is not the true reading. Was divided into three parts. The signification of this clause is somewhat uncertain. The idea is probably that of total destruction, as in Ezek. v. 2, where a similar description is applied to Jerusalem. Possibly there is a reference to the trinity of evil mentioned in ver. 13. And the cities of the nations fell. *The nations* signifies the ungodly, who stand in the same relation to the godly as the Gentiles to God's chosen people (cf. ch. xi. 18, etc.). This sentence declares the fall of every lesser form of evil, together with the greater typical form symbolized by "the great city." And great Babylon came in remembrance

before God; *and Babylon the great was remembered in the sight of God* (Revised Vertion). Cf. the title of "great city" (*vide supra*). Cf. also the similar expression in Acts x. 31. This clause, together with the following one, taken in conjunction with the preceding and succeeding verses, must be referred to the great judgment-day. To give unto her the cup of the wine of the fierceness of his wrath. This is the beginning of the fulfilment of the doom predicted by the angel in ch. xiv. 10. The judgment is more elaborately described in ch. xviii.

Ver. 20.—And every island fled away, and the mountains were not found. This continues the description of the earthquake in ver. 18, the parenthesis concerning Babylon occurring owing to the mention of the destruction of the city (cf. the account given under the sixth seal). Such convulsions of nature generally, in biblical descriptions, accompany the near approach of the last judgment. Some writers interpret the islands and mountains of kingdoms (cf. ch. xvii. 9, 10).

Ver. 21.—And there fell upon men a great hail out of heaven, every stone about the weight of a talent; *cometh down upon,* the present tense, rendering the description more graphic. Commentators usually quote ' Diodorus Siculus ' (xix. 45), who mentions, as something marvellous, hailstones of a mina in weight; the mina being one-sixtieth of a talent; and also the account of Josephus, who speaks of stones a talent in weight being thrown by machines at the siege of Jerusalem (see Wetstein, *ad loc.*). "The men," though not pointing to any particular group of men who have been definitely mentioned, nevertheless necessarily refers to the wicked, who are the object of this punishment. "Hail" is frequently mentioned as a judgment of God, and is added here to heighten the general effect of the description (cf. Exod. ix.; Josh. x. 11; Ps. lxxviii. 47; cv. 32; Isa. xxviii. 2; xxx. 30; Ezek. xiii. 11; xxxviii. 22; Hag. ii. 17; also ch. viii. 7; xi. 19). And men blasphemed God because of the plague of the hail; for the plague thereof was exceeding great; *is exceeding great* (*vide supra*). As in ver. 9, men repent not. Like Pharaoh, their hearts are hardened. These words end the general description of the vial-judgments, but the events alluded to under the seventh vial are elaborated and particularized in the chapters which follow; the whole concluding at the end of ch. xix.

HOMILETICS.

Vers. 1—11.— *The first five bowls.* While we by no means follow the historical interpreters of this book in the attempt to identify any chronological sequence of actual events with the seven seals, trumpets, and bowls, respectively, yet (as is well pointed out by Professor Godet[1]) there is undoubtedly a moral progression indicated. The *seal* points out an event concealed as yet, but foreseen by God. The *trumpet* points out an event announced as forthcoming. The *bowl* points out the event in actual execution. We have studied the ground-plan of the Apocalypse with reference to the seals and trumpets; we now witness the pouring out of the bowls, *i.e.* the carrying out of the great judgments on the foes of God and of his Church, which in anticipation had been forecast already. The seven seals set before us the kind of events which were to be looked for—victory, war, famine, pestilence, martyrdom, convulsion; then the end. The seven trumpets have pointed out the sphere over which the several judgments shall fall which are to bring about the end. These correspond almost precisely with the seven bowls; thus confirming the impression that between trumpets and bowls there is the distinction between announcement and effect.

	1	2	3	4	5	6	7
The trumpets follow thus in order:	Earth, viii. 7	Sea, viii. 8	Waters, viii. 10, 11	Sun, viii. 12	Smoke out of the abyss, ix. 1—11	The great river, ix. 13—21	The issue, xi. 15—18
The bowls follow thus:	Earth, xvi. 2	Sea, xvi. 3	Waters, xvi. 4—7	Sun, xvi. 8, 9	Throne of the beast, xvi. 10, 11	The great river, xvi. 12—16	"It is done!" xvi. 17—21

There is one feature common to all the bowls—they are "the bowls of the wrath of God." By "the wrath of God" we understand nothing like revenge, malice, or vindictiveness; but that pure and holy indignation against sin, which is a necessity of nature in a Being of perfect love. As, however, we have so frequently found the scenes of the Old Testament furnishing material for the gorgeous imagery of this book, so it is here. The student can scarcely help noticing the similarity in the effect of the bowls with that of the plagues of Egypt. Thus they one and all seem to say, as the Lord once "put a difference between the Egyptians and Israel," so it will be again. The first deliverance was from the hosts of Egypt. The second was from the hosts of hell, when Jesus died. The third shall be the final one—from the hosts of earth *and* hell, when the Lord shall appear in his glory![2] While we reverently refrain from attempting an interpretation in detail of the effects of the pouring out of the several bowls, we can as little refrain from pointing out the manifold distinctive features of them, as illustrating permanent truths concerning the government of God.

I. Ere the end cometh, God's judgments of wrath will be poured out upon the world. Our Lord, in his sermon on the mount, as well as in his parables, teaches us that up to the time of the end there will be impenitent men; and that the clashing of good with evil will go on to the time of the great harvest-day. The Old Testament prophets indicate the same, and they repeatedly declare that on the wicked the wrath of God will fall. The Lord did of old "put a difference between the Egyptians and Israel;" and he will, in his own time and way, show the difference between the Church and the world. The wicked shall be "broken to shivers."

II. God hath his "bowls" in which are the contents of his wrath waiting to be outpoured. "The 'vials' point to the metaphor in ch. xiv. 10, 'the cup of God's anger.' The 'vial' (cf. Amos vi. 6) was the shallow 'bowl' in which they drew from the larger goblet."[3] There are many weapons hidden in God's armoury,

---

[1] "Essai sur l'Apocalypse," 'Études Biblique,' deuxième série, p. 296.

[2] "The statement that these are the last plagues seems to show that the set of visions now commencing carry us down to the end of the age . . . they are strokes upon the wilful and hardened; they are directed against those who are deliberately hostile" (Bishop Boyd Carpenter).

[3] 'Speaker's Commentary,' *in loc.*

many arrows in his quiver, many forces stored-up ready to be brought forth; as yet he holdeth them back. He waiteth. He is long-suffering. He hath forgotten neither his promises nor his threatenings. "He waiteth to be gracious." But he will not wait always. The Lord is a jealous God, and will not suffer his people always to be discomfited.

III. THE BRINGING OUT OF THESE HIDDEN FORCES IS FORESEEN AND DETERMINED. Three truths are taught us here. 1. That the authority to pour out the bowls comes from "the temple" (ch. xvi. 1). From the sanctuary. "Heaven itself." 2. That there is an angelic ministry ready to be employed on this service (ch. xv. 6). "There is nothing in prophetic imagery more striking than this picture of the seven angels issuing, in solemn procession, from the sanctuary."[1] 3. The angel-bands wait the word of command, "Go ye," etc. The angels of God are all ministering spirits, ascending and descending upon the Son of man.

IV. WHEN THE ANGELS OF JUDGMENT POUR OUT THE "BOWLS," ALL NATURE MAY BE FULL OF WHIPS AND STINGS. (Cf. vers. 1—4, 8—11.) Here the elements of nature, which are the conditions and media of man's comfort, are all turned into so many instruments of torture, when used in wrath. When will men learn that nature brings us joy only through the mercy of God? that it is "of the Lord's mercies we are not consumed"? How little might suffice to make life intolerable! One equivalent less of oxygen in the air, or one equivalent more, and life would be unendurable. Sooner or later God will convict ungodly men of their "hard speeches," by sore judgments.

V. THE EFFECT OF THESE JUDGMENTS ON UNGODLY MEN WILL BE TO EXCITE TO ANGER, AND NOT TO BRING TO REPENTANCE. (Vers. 9, 11, "They repented not;" "They blasphemed.") Men, in their disloyalty to high Heaven, seem to think that the function of a Divine Being is just to make his creatures as comfortable as possible; as if there were no principles of righteousness for which a holy Governor should contend, and as if there were no claims on our obedience on which the great Governor ought to insist. And if *he* whom they have offended makes them smart, they "blaspheme"! "The foolishness of man perverteth his way, and his heart fretteth against the Lord." Note: Here is a refutation of the error that *all* suffering is disciplinary, and tends to improve. The vile heart of man perverts it, and makes it a means of his own hardening in sin.

VI. THE HOLY ONES SEE IN THE DIVINE RETRIBUTION A MANIFESTATION OF RIGHTEOUSNESS. In ver. 5 "the angel of the waters" celebrates the righteousness of God, and in ver. 7 "the altar" is said to do it; so the Revised Version reads; meaning, probably, the souls of the martyrs beneath it[2] (ch. vi. 9). Only those beings who are in full sympathy with the Divine righteousness and love are in a position to judge rightly of the Divine procedure. And these, whether they be the ministering angels or the once-suffering saints, see in the recompenses of a holy Governor new manifestations of that rectitude which presides over all. "It is a righteous thing with God to recompense affliction to them that afflict you, and to you that are afflicted, rest" (2 Thess. i. 6, 7). There are times even now when the righteous find the sight of deeds of atrocity and wickedness more than they can bear, and they cry aloud in the language of the ninety-fourth psalm (cf. Ps. xciv. 1—4). That cry will be answered. But although in the cry there may be traces of human passion, in the answer there will be nothing contrary to perfect equity. Note: 1. Although all Scripture points to trouble on a vastly greater scale than we as yet see it, ere the end shall come, yet on a smaller scale God's judgments are ever at work. "Though hand join in hand, the wicked shall not be unpunished." That which is a bulwark to the good is a detective to the evil. 2. Let us not forget that the wondrous way in which the balance of nature's forces is preserved, so as to bring us life and peace and comfort, is owing, not to nature, but to God. His attempering care and constant remembrance alone preserve our souls from death, our eyes from tears, and our feet from falling. Let us, then, not look too much at, nor lean too much on, earthly comforts. If they are comforts, it is God that makes them so, and we hold them at his disposal. 3. In our daily life we can sing of both mercy and judgment. No cup is *all* sweetness. A dash of bitter mingles with all. Not all bitter, lest we should pine away; not all sweet, lest we should become insensible to life's peril and responsibilities. We need the

---

[1] 'Speaker's Commentary,' *in loc.*

[2] See Dean Alford's and Webster and Wilkinson's notes on this verse

chastening reminders of our own faults and sins. 4. We are indebted to Divine mercy even for the sanctifying effect of our trials. It is not the natural influence of trouble to improve the soul. By itself it wears, worries, vexes. We chafe against it. It galls. Only when the sanctifying grace of God works with it and by it will it mature the spirit in meekness, submission, and love. Of all things to be dreaded, the very worst evil is that of being abandoned by God to that hardness of heart which will turn even the just penalty for our sin into an occasion for fiercer revolt of the heart, and viler words on the tongue!

Vers. 12—16.—*The sixth bowl.* In the prophetic parables of this book there is, as we have before remarked, a manifest moral progression, although the varied attempts to indicate in detail an exact historic progression, with dates assigned, has resulted, and *must* result, in repeated and disappointing failure. We should also note that at about this part of the book many of the historical interpreters stop short, and give considerable scope to conjecture. But while on their method we always find ourselves "at sea," if we adhere to the plan of exposition we have thus far adopted, no extreme difficulty will present itself, since all falls in with the general tenor of the Word of God. In this paragraph there are two distinct parts, in each of which the imagery is drawn from Old Testament history. We have here indicated : 1. A great providential preparation for the overthrow of huge and mighty forms of evil. We see in this paragraph that the sixth angel poured out his bowl upon the great river, the river Euphrates; and the water thereof was dried up, that the way might be made ready for the kings that come from the sunrising, *i.e.* from the east.[1] In olden time there had been a great city, Babylon. It was doomed. It was to fall by means of " the man from the east" (Isa. xli. 2, 25 ; xlvi. 11). There was a river that ran through Babylon— the river Euphrates. Long outside the city gates the invader waited. The bed of the river was dried up, through the river itself being turned into another channel. Thus the way of the man from the east was prepared, and he entered in and took the city. While in this paragraph we have a prophetic parable, in those events we have the historic parable on which the prophetic one is based. " Babylon the great " (what that is we have yet to see) is doomed. And as of old the way was prepared for the destruction of "great Babylon," so will there be preparations (perhaps prolonged ones) for the downfall of this mystic Babylon. We have here: 2. A great onrush of the hosts of evil for a mighty conflict, which will be to their own downfall. The seer further descries a new outbreak, and apparently a simultaneous one, on the part of the three enemies of the Church already named—the dragon, the first beast, the second beast (the latter here named "the false prophet"). Out of their mouth go forth "three unclean spirits, as it were frogs," *i.e.* loathsome and detestable; these, we are told, are the spirits of demons, doing wonders (cf. Matt. xxiv.; 2 Thess. ii.). The effect of these seducing agencies will be to gather together to their culmination the forces hostile to the Most High. This daring, aggregate attempt will be the final one, for it will be one that shall end in most utter defeat. Again we are thrown back for illustration on ancient incident and on familiar name. This final struggle is at Har-Magedon, or the mountain of Megiddo, "which more, perhaps, than any other spot, is celebrated in the history of Israel as a scene of judicial and decisive conflict."[2] Here was there a decisive conflict between Deborah and Sisera. Here Josiah was slain (2 Kings xxiii. 29; also cf. Zech. xii. 11). Here Ahaziah died of his wounds. But mainly, on the mountain of Megiddo, *i.e.* Mount Carmel, took place that decisive contrast between Jehovah and Baal, which forced conviction on the people, and ended in the destruction of the spurious prophets and priests. A notable name, indeed, for suggesting disaster and overthrow. And by no more significant symbolism could the truth be suggested—*evil is hastening to its own defeat.* We are not to think simply of literal warfare. The sacred seer gives us only " the outward sign, the corporeal type. Under Christianity we can only see the broad line which

[1] See both Dr. Milligan and Dr. Carpenter concerning the phrase, "the kings from the sunrising." Their views thereon are widely divergent. The meaning of it, surely, can only be—"the instrumental agents by whom, under God, great Babylon must fall."

[2] Porter, 'Christian Prophecy,' p. 311.

will finally separate the righteous and the wicked."[1] Here, however, we meet (shall we say unexpectedly?) with a gracious word of monition, in ver. 15. As a writer[2] strikingly says, "Suddenly the Spirit takes the reader aside, and whispers, 'Behold, I come quickly,'" etc. Thus we gather that this final struggle is to precede the coming of our Lord Jesus Christ; and so we are taught (1) that the issue of that struggle is clearly seen; and (2) that, let it come when it may, our life-work is perfectly clear. In anticipation of his coming we are to watch; we are not to take off our garments as if preparing for repose, but we are to stand " with our loins girded about, and our lights burning." We are to be ready at a moment's notice for any duty that may be required. Hence we have a theme as plain and practical as any other part of the Word of God supplies.

I. WHATEVER MAY HAVE BEEN THE TROUBLES AND CONFLICTS OF THE CHURCH OF GOD IN THE PAST, SEVERER ONES ARE YET IN THE DISTANCE. Even if this were not indicated here, it would be clear from other parts of Scripture. The parable of the wheat and the tares would, indeed, involve all this. For if both are growing, that means that the good will get better, and the bad worse; thus antagonisms will become sharper, and conflicts fiercer and more daring.

II. ALREADY TO CHRISTIAN FAITH AND HOPE THIS FINAL CONFLICT OF EVIL IS REPRESENTED as "that great day of God Almighty." It will be a day in which the old word concerning human agency shall again be accomplished, "Howbeit he meaneth not so" (Isa. x. 7). Man means one thing; God intends and fulfils another. The outcome of the whole will be as the prophet declares, " Then shall ye return, and discern between the righteous and the wicked, between him that serveth God and him that serveth him not."

III. THE CRISIS HERE INDICATED WILL PRECEDE THE COMING OF THE SON OF GOD. (Ver. 15.) We cannot doubt who the speaker is that says, "Behold, I come as a thief." "He is coming" is, indeed, the thesis of the entire Apocalypse. He will come: 1. To consume evil. 2. To complete his reign of righteousness, by consummating the kingdom of grace and ushering in the kingdom of glory. 3. To make his people glad in him. "When Christ, who is our Life, shall be manifested, then shall ye also be manifested with him in glory."

IV. CERTAIN EVENTS MAY HERALD HIS APPROACH, BUT YET HIS ACTUAL COMING WILL BE "AS A THIEF." This is the repeated teaching of the Word of God. It will be at the last moment sudden. "As it was in the days of Noah, so also shall the coming of the Son of man be." There are obvious reasons for this. Did we know precisely the moment, such knowledge would instantly paralyze society. Our Lord intends that the break-up of things should be instantaneous. A sudden stop will be put to the world's machinery.

V. IN VIEW OF THIS ISSUE—CERTAIN IN FACT, THOUGH UNCERTAIN AS TO TIME— WE ARE TO KEEP ON THE WATCH. We are to be ready for the last moment by being ready at every moment. It is not in perpetually rushing to the door and peeping out to see if the master is near, that a servant's readiness for him consists; but in so attending to every duty that, let him come when he may, he finds the house in perfect order, awaiting his return.

VI. CONSEQUENTLY, BEING ON THE WATCH MEANS STANDING READY TO DO ANY DUTY WHATEVER, THE MOMENT IT IS REQUIRED. When a soldier enlisted in the Roman army, he had, before the tribune, to take a triple oath, viz.: (1) That he would do whatever he was called on to do. (2) That he would be ready at any moment. (3) That he would never leave the army without the commander's consent. This triple oath was called sacramentum. Hence our word "sacrament"[3]—the believer's military oath of obedience to the great Commander.

> "Think not of rest; though dreams be sweet,
> Start up, and ply your heavenward feet.
> Is not God's oath upon your head,
> Ne'er to sink back on slothful bed,

---

[1] 'Speaker's Commentary,' in loc.; so also Dr. Carpenter.
[2] I. Williams, quoted in 'Speaker's Commentary.'
[3] A different account of this word is given by some; but the one given above most commends itself to us.

> Never again your loins untie,
> Nor let your torches waste and die,
> Till, when the shadows thickest fall,
> Ye hear your Master's midnight call?"

VII. ON WHOMSOEVER IS STANDING IN THIS ATTITUDE OF SERVICE, THE MASTER'S BLESSING IS PRONOUNCED. "Blessed is he," etc. 1. He has the Lord's approval now. 2. The "signs of the times," so portentous to the ungodly, are for him full of hope. 3. The coming of the Lord will usher him in to the blessedness and glory of a new and renovated state of being.

Then let each one inquire—How am I standing at this moment in the sight of my Saviour-Judge? Am I so living that, if he were to come now, he could truthfully say, " Well done, good and faithful servant "?

Vers. 17—21.— *The seventh bowl.* The precise identification of " Babylon the great " must be reserved for our study of the next chapter; the paragraph before us shows us what a downfall is awaiting her. For the present it is enough to remember that it is some vast power of the earth, earthy, whose influence and action have been against righteousness and peace. Under the sixth bowl we witnessed the gathering together of great hosts for a final conflict. Now that last conflict is decided. Man has summoned his forces. God brings his also to bear. With man it is the clash of arms. With God the forces are silent as light, potent as lightning, terrible as the earthquake, and, as if to set forth the exhaustless force stored up in heaven's armoury, we are told that "hailstones" fell, of the weight of a talent. And then, then it is that "Babylon the great" comes up into remembrance before God. Some great, yea, gigantic form of evil, proud as Babylon, lustful as Sodom, cruel as Egypt, which has thriven for long unpunished, comes up for remembrance at last. How far physical convulsions are here intended we do not venture to say, though such may precede the final stroke. It is very clear that judgment in some form or other is intended. And the strong probability is that, as in the cases of the Deluge, Sodom, Canaan, Tyre, Egypt, etc., both physical and moral crises will synchronize. The expression, that " Babylon the great was remembered in the sight of God," is full of deep meaning in its moral bearing, though its temporal and local application it may be, as yet, impossible to decide.

I. How MUCH OF EARTH'S SIN MUST THERE BE FOR GOD TO WITNESS! In the storehouse of his eternal and infinite mind, all the wrong of which earth has been the theatre and witness is "treasured up." How soon even we can summon up more than we can bear to reflect upon! The Amorites; Sodom; Egypt; Canaan; Babylon; pagan Rome; papal Rome; Mohammedanism; the Bartholomew Massacre; papal England; Madagascar martyrs; the Indian Mutiny; and an indefinite number more of nameless horrors. Together with a measureless amount of sin, and an innumerable multitude of sins that, in every village, town, and city are being committed in the light of day and in the shades of night. All seen, known, infinitely.

II. MEN OFTEN ASK—WHY IS GOD SILENT SO LONG? There are few trials of faith more severe than this. Why do millions have to endure so much of unnamed suffering without redress? And all this when so many prayers are being offered up to heaven. Why is it? "Our God," cried one in anguish, "is a God that does nothing!" Again and again the cry of the ninety-fourth psalm comes unbidden to the lips.

III. WHATEVER MAY BE THE TRIAL OF FAITH THUS CAUSED, WE ARE CERTAIN THAT GOD FORGETS NOTHING. He is neither indifferent, forgetful, nor weak. Not one unrepented sin is forgotten. Not one cry of the humble is unheard. The widow's moan, the orphan's tears, the miseries of the slave, and all the horrors connected with that "open sore of the world," are remembered by him.

IV. GOD HAS GREAT PURPOSES TO ANSWER IN PERMITTING EVIL TO GO SO LONG UNPUNISHED. We know not all of them. We know none of them fully. But we can, though with fear and trembling, suggest: 1. By suffering sin to come to its uttermost ripeness, he reveals to men what an evil it is. "By their fruits ye shall know them." He knows tendencies; we see issues. 2. When the blackness of evil is seen, the righteousness of God's judgments will also be manifest. Is it not in this direction that light comes on the text, "The Lord hath made all things for himself; yea, even the wicked for the day of evil "? 3. Meanwhile, God is "long-suffering, . . . not willing that any should perish, but that all should come to repentance."

V. AT THE APPOINTED HOUR THE "LONG-SUFFERING" WILL CEASE. By this it is not meant that patience, as a Divine attribute, will be exhausted, but that there will come a time when the Divine Being will no longer refrain from inflicting his judgments on sin and sinners. Even now, "because sentence against an evil work is not executed speedily, therefore the heart of the sons of men is fully set in them to do evil." Soon will the Divine will be manifested, and the punishment of sin will be the vindication of the right and the condemnation of the wrong.

VI. THEN "BABYLON THE GREAT," WITH ALL HER SINS, SHALL COME UP FOR FINAL RECKONING AND RECOMPENSE. God will "render unto her even as she rendered." "Whatsoever a man soweth," etc.; "We must all be made manifest at the tribunal of Christ;" "God shall bring every work into judgment," etc.; "There is nothing covered, that shall not be revealed;" "With what measure ye mete, it shall be measured to you again;" "Vengeance is mine; I will repay, saith the Lord."

VII. THE FACT THAT ALL IS IN THE HANDS OF GOD IS A GUARANTEE OF PERFECT EQUITY. "He will render to every man according to his deeds." In the future retribution there will be no flaw in time or degree; no defect, no excess. The Judge of all the earth will do right; it is "in the sight of God" that great Babylon will be remembered.

VIII. WITH OUR GOD THE EXECUTION IS AS CERTAIN AS THE PURPOSE. The seer heard "a great voice from the temple, out of the throne, saying, It is done!" The fulfilment is perceived as well as decreed. Not a word shall fail of all that the Lord hath spoken. His plans can never be frustrated. Our Lord Jesus Christ has all authority in heaven and on earth.

Note: 1. Amid the perplexity caused by the prevalence and power of evil, let us stay ourselves on God. We know what he *is*, though we often fail to read what he *does*. 2. Let us do right, and wait God's time. We are not to shape our course according to expediency, but according to right principle. 3. Revenge is never to be any part of *our* policy. We are incompetent judges, and we ourselves are too often swayed by passion. God reserves vengeance to himself. Let us, therefore, not take the law into our own hands, but "leave room for the wrath of God." [1] 4. Let us be glad and grateful that believers in God are not left in the dark as to the meaning, aims, and issue of the Divine government of the world. This Book of the Apocalypse is written in parable, doubtless for the same reason that our Lord spake in parables when on earth (cf. Matt. xiii.). They are so couched that unbelief cannot read them, but that faith can. And is there not infinite wisdom in this? Who would entrust his secrets to one who was known neither to trust nor to be trusty? Jesus did not commit himself to men, because he knew all men. The faith was delivered "once for all to the saints." They only are expected to keep it who love it. Hence to them only is it committed. Those who trust God are trusted by him. His secret is with them. And the contents of that secret are twofold—grace in saving, and equity in ruling. These are the pivots on which the Divine government turns. Grace reigns through righteousness; and where grace is refused and heaven is defied, there will yet be pure and unswerving equity. 5. Hence it behoves the righteous to walk this earth with a sense of their dignity, as those who are entrusted with the mysteries of the Divine plans: not, indeed, so minutely as to be inconsistent with the calm and steadfast fulfilment of duty, but yet in broad outline so clearly that for them there is no such thing as "the burden and mystery of an unintelligible world." That helpless and hopeless perplexity is removed from all those who know that "the Father loveth the Son, and hath given all things into his hand." 6. But, whether in the portentous imagery of the Apocalypse or in the clearer language of the Epistles, it is revealed with an impressive clearness that the man who is trifling with the Divine loving-kindness, not knowing that the goodness of God is drawing him with a view to repentance, is but treasuring up to himself wrath against the day of wrath, and of the revelation of the righteous judgment of God! All that is involved in the words, "He must reign till he hath put all enemies beneath his feet." 7. Is it "in the sight of God" that there will be remembrance of peoples hereafter? Then "in the sight of God" the

[1] See Tyndale's version of Rom. xii. 19

people must fulfil their obligations now. It has been asked if faith in God is essential to the discharge of moral obligation. We answer—Loyalty to God is the first of all moral obligations, and none are rightly fulfilled where this is lacking. A striking commentary on all this is that most painful life of George Eliot, who, though living in outrageous defiance of the first duties of social life after she had given up faith in God, sneered at the words—

> "Talk they of morals? O thou bleeding Love!
> Thou Maker of new morals to mankind!
> The grand morality is love of thee."

Finally, that which is the law for the individual is the law for the nation and for its rulers, viz. to learn the mind and will of the King of kings and Lord of lords, and then to carry that out irrespectively of human praise or blame. Woe to that nation which applauds a policy that will come in remembrance before God only to be everlastingly disgraced! Woe to the people whose trust is in chariots and horses, in armies and in fleets, in guns and in swords! Ever are we surrounded by men who clamour for glory, for conquest, for annexation, for empire! And this cry must be resisted by all who have learnt the Divine secret that "righteousness alone exalteth a nation," that "sin is a reproach to any people." Every great Babylon is doomed.

HOMILIES BY VARIOUS AUTHORS.

Ver. 6.—*Be done by as you did.* "They have shed the blood . . . thou hast given them blood to drink." Grateful, indeed, ought men to be not alone for the golden rule which commands us to do unto others as we would be done by, but also for the converse of that rule, the eternal law—that as we have done so shall we be done by. It is the *lex talionis*—the law that ordains "an eye for an eye, and a tooth for a tooth;" that "with what measure ye mete, it shall be meted to you." And here in the text we have a vivid and awful illustration of it. And there have been a vast number more. They, everywhere and always, who have shed the blood of God's servants, have had given to them, sooner or later, "blood to drink." Their turn has come, and it has been the more terrible because of what they have done to bring it upon themselves.

I. CONSIDER SOME ILLUSTRATIONS OF THIS LAW. *Egypt.* The memory of how she shed the blood of God's servants, and how blood was given her to drink, not merely in symbol by the water of her river being turned into blood, so that her people loathed to drink of it, but actually by the destruction that came upon her—the memory of all this is evidently fresh in the writer's mind. The atmosphere of Egypt, the bondage, and the Exodus, is all around this record of the seven vials. *Israel under Ahab and other idolatrous kings.* He and they shed the blood of God's prophets. But sure revenges came. At Carmel; in Assyria, where Israel was carried away captive, and where as a nation she perished. *Assyria.* Cf. the Book of Jonah for its sins and its predicted doom. Fate of Sennacherib. Destruction of Nineveh about B.C. 606, when Sardanapalus the king, in despair, burnt himself, with his concubines, eunuchs, and treasures. *Persia.* Cf. the Book of Esther, and the king's edict for the destruction of the Jews, and how averted and avenged. *Greece.* Cf. the Books of Maccabees, as to persecutions under Antiochus Epiphanes; his miserable death. *Jerusalem.* Cf. our Lord's words, "It cannot be that a prophet should perish out of Jerusalem," etc. (Luke xiii. 33, 34). Her siege and fall. *Rome,* both pagan and papal (cf. Gibbon, for fall of pagan Rome; Alison, for calamities that came on Rome and Italy during the wars of the Revolution). *France.* Her persecutions of the Huguenots led on to the horrors of her revolution. *Spain,* once the greatest of European powers, became infamous for her bigotry and cruelties on all outside the Romish Church; she was the home of the Inquisition, and the *auto-da-fé.* But the persecutor's doom came upon her. Her glory has departed. *The Stuart* dynasty in England, who harried and drove tens of thousands of godly men out of the Church and out of the land; and then their turn came, and their race and name passed away in ignominy. And had *England's* loss of her American colonies nothing to do with her maintenance of the accursed slave-trade? And did not *America's* civil war spring from that same bad cause? Such are some fulfilments of this law, some more, some less, evident. Doubtless Jerusalem, at the hour when St. John wrote in the very throes of her mortal agony, when blood was indeed given her to drink; and Rome, racked with civil war and the fierce factions fomented by this chieftain and that, and for whom yet more fearful fate waited—these were uppermost in St. John's mind. But the law lives yet, and lived before St. John's day; not one jot or one tittle of it has failed or can ever fail. And the Bible and the facts of life supply illustrations not a few of the fulfilment of this law in individuals as well as nations. And where the eye cannot trace the fulfilment, it is not to be thought that the law has failed. In his moral life—that which is within and unseen—the law can lay hold on the transgressor, and does so. Every man's sin finds *him* out, even if he be not found out.

II. ITS MODE OF ACTION. It is, like as most of God's laws are, self-acting. There is no need for God to interfere to see that the law is vindicated. Power, perverted to persecution and oppression, and pampered by such means, becomes hideous and hateful to mankind, who after a while will turn upon the tyrant and hurl him from the place of power which he has prostituted to such vile uses. And so because he or they have "shed blood," blood is given, etc. Man may as well think to put in motion any given cause and to hinder the due effect from following, as to hinder the fulfilment of the law we are considering. Sow the seed, and *its* harvest will follow, not some other; there will be no need of miracle to secure this. And the seed of blood shed will infallibly secure a like harvest. Men may deny the existence of God, but they cannot deny the existence of laws, self-acting, and which have an awful power of ensuring their own vindication, let men's opinions be what they will.

III. ITS LESSONS TO US ALL. 1. *" Be not deceived; God is not mocked: for whatsoever a man soweth, that,"* etc. 2. The *inveteracy, violence, and virulence of sin.* Notwithstanding all that God has done, and does, to deter men from it, they will cling to it still. 3. *" Precious in the sight of the Lord is the death of his saints."* " When he maketh inquisition for blood, he remembereth them."—S. C.

Ver. 9.—*The hardened heart.* " They repented not to give him glory." This impenitence is told of in ch. ix. 20, and in this chapter again at vers. 11 and 21. This repeated reference is designed to, as it well may, impress our minds with a fact at once so sinful, so solemn, and so sad. For such impenitence is—

I. A VERY CERTAIN FACT. The late Mr. Kingsley, in his book, ' The Roman and the Teuton,' draws out at length the evidence both of the horrible sufferings and the yet more horrible impenitence of the Roman people in the days of their empire's fall. He refers to these very verses as accurately describing the condition of things in those awful days, when the people of Rome " gnawed their tongues for pain, and blasphemed," etc. (ver. 11). And it is to Rome and her fall that St. John is here alluding. There can hardly be doubt of that. But the sinners at Rome were not the only ones who, in spite of the judgments of God resting upon them, have, nevertheless, hardened their hearts. Who has not known of such things?

II. AND VERY WONDERFUL. We say a burnt child dreads the fire, but it is evident that they who have been " scorched with great heat " (ver. 9) by the righteous wrath of God are yet not afraid to incur that wrath again. Nothing strikes us more than the persistent way in which, in the " day of provocation in the wilderness," the Israelites went on sinning, notwithstanding all that it brought upon them in the way of punishment. There was every reason and motive for them to obey God, and yet they did scarce anything but provoke him. And it is so still.

III. AND VERY AWFUL. "Ephraim is joined to idols: let him alone." " Why should ye be stricken any more?"—no good comes of it, punishment does not make any difference. Such are the despairing words of the prophets of God. There are few surer signs of perdition than when a man is hardened in sin and more set in enmity against God by reason of his righteous judgments. What can even God do then? If what is designed to lead us to repentance only drive us into more sin, what hope is there? See those told of here; what a description of unspeakable distress—" gnawing their tongues for pain," but blaspheming God the while and repenting not! " From hardness of heart, . . . good Lord, deliver us."

IV. BUT YET NOT INEXPLICABLE. For: 1. *Times of such distress* as are told of here are just the *most unfavourable times* of all others for that serious, earnest thought which would lead to repentance. Distress distracts the mind, drags it hither and thither, so that it cannot stay itself upon God. To trust to the hour of death to turn unto God is, indeed, to build upon the sand. 2. *Resentment against their ill treatment* holds their mind more than aught else. Thrice are we told how the men who "gnawed their tongues for pain" blasphemed God. Burning rage against *him* enwrapped their souls. As if he were to blame, and not they! They explain that difficult verse in the ninetieth psalm, "Who regardeth the power of thy wrath? even according to thy fear, so is thy wrath." It is only they who have a holy fear of God who will regard his wrath; according to the measure of that fear will be the measure of right regard of the wrath of God. Where that fear is not, God's wrath will exasperate, enrage, and harden, but there will be no repentance. 3. *They attribute their sufferings to every cause but the true one.* How easy it is to do this! how commonly it is done! How men snatch at every suggestion that will help them to lay the blame upon other men or things! It is part of "the deceitfulness of sin" to make men do this. But until a man is led to cry, with him of old, "God be merciful to me, the sinner!" (Luke xviii. 13), he may groan in agony of body or mind, but he will never turn in heart to God. 4. *Sin has such hold on them that they cannot give it up.* Yes, deeper than the dread of its punishment is the love of the sin. Once it might have been broken through as easily as the cobweb that stretches across the garden path; but, indulged and indulged, it has become a cable that holds the man in spite of all the storm of God's judgments and the tempest of his wrath. Cries and tears, protestations and prayers, may be extorted from the man through his terror and pain; but they are but surface-sounds, and touch not the depth or reality of the man's soul. 5. "*Because sentence against an evil work is not executed speedily*, therefore the hearts of the sons of men is fully set in them to do evil" (Eccles. viii. 11). The interval between the sentence and its being carried out is given for *repentance;* but men have made it a means of greater sin. Such are some of the reasons that explain the seemingly wonderful fact we are considering.

V. AND IT IS FULL OF WARNING. Even torture does not turn a man, nor suffering save. That old and awful puritanic cry to sinners, "Turn or burn!"—a cry which, we believe, never yet turned one heart to God, for it is not the nature of terror to do that— has a yet more dread sequel; that if a man will not now, in "the day of salvation," turn to God, he may burn and yet not turn. Such is the teaching, not of our text alone, but of all experience too. O God, fill our hearts with the fear and love of thee!—S. C.

Vers. 12—16.—*Armageddon.* It is the name of a place. It lies to the north-west of the Plain of Esdraelon, on the southern slopes of Carmel. It is mentioned on various occasions in the Bible (cf. *infra*). But these verses tell of *a great event connected with it.*

1. WHAT WAS THIS? It is called "the battle of that great day of God Almighty" (ver. 14). Whether St. John had some *literal battle taking place in his day* present in his mind, we cannot certainly say. Not improbably he had. Most of the symbols of this book refer, we think, to events with which he was familiar. Thus is it with all prophecies, not least with this one. Such events form the basis of those wider facts which alone can fill up the prophet's words. In this case it is *the last great conflict with evil* to which his words point, and of which we have not a few premonitions in the Scriptures. How far we are to understand what we read, here and elsewhere, literally, and how far figuratively, it is impossible to say, as the prediction is for the future, and is yet unfulfilled. But *why it is called Armageddon* may be because the Plain of Esdraelon was the battle-field of Palestine. And at Megiddo—and Armageddon means the hill of Megiddo—it was that King Josiah was defeated, and great sorrow had come upon God's people. And it was the hope of the adversary of God that what had been done to Josiah should be done to Jesus (Hengstenberg). Also it was, like Marathon, Waterloo, etc., a name for a *decisive* conflict, and this last one should be such. But this Scripture will be of little avail to us if we think only of the past or of the unknown future. *The conflict of good and evil is ever proceeding.* And, in this soul and that, Armageddons—decisive conflicts—are continually being fought. See, in the conversion of Saul at Damascus, how the forces of evil were overthrown. There comes in most men's lives a crisis in which the question—Whose shall I be—the Lord's

servant, or the servant of selfishness and sin?—has to be settled. When all the clamour of passion and the might of temptation are resisted, and the heart goes over to the Lord's side, *that* has been the spiritual fulfilment of this mysterious vision.

II. WHAT CAME OF IT? This is given not here, but in ch. xix. 17—21, where the *utter discomfiture of Christ's enemies* is told of in the vivid, graphic way common in this book. Yes, the last great conflict shall be a triumphant one for Christ's Church. Oftentimes now the Church, in this or that part of the battle-field, seems to be worsted; but, at the last, victory "all along the line" shall be the Lord's, and, through him, hers also. And in those spiritual Armageddons *which to-day are fought*, and every day, there, too, victory is the Lord's. Let the noble army of martyrs tell. Let all who have witnessed faithfully for him say, "If he who will be with his people in the last decisive battle be with us now, then all the unclean spirits of hell, all the devil's might and power, bearing down against us shall leave us the victor still."

III. WHAT LED TO IT? Two facts, and very suggestive ones, are named. 1. *The drying up of Euphrates.* (Ver. 12.) That was an apparent providential preparation and prospering of the devil's purpose. Such things do happen. Some have thought that the drying up of Euphrates means the conversion of the East, the coming to the Lord's help against the mighty, of those remote lands. But what is told of here is part of the sixth vial of judgment; it is not a manifestation of grace, but of wrath. Therefore we understand by this symbol a seeming furtherance of evil designs by providential means. When Jonah went to flee from the presence of the Lord, there was a ship at Joppa ready for him. When men determine they will follow evil ways, how smooth the path becomes! *Facilis descensus*, etc. How many aids and abettors they meet with! A way being easy, a Euphrates dried up, a barrier removed, is no proof that God approves that way. Israel murmured for quails, and they had them, and died. These "kings of the east," who were part of the great aggregate of kings told of in ver. 14, like the rest, had been persuaded to this awful war by the "unclean spirits" (ver. 13). And lo, it seemed as if it were certainly the right and wise thing to do; for here was the great hindrance taken out of the way—Euphrates was dried up. What a Euphrates against evil a Christian home, or religious surroundings, or God-fearing friends, or wholesome public opinion, may be! But God's providence may take these away from you, and so that barrier against sin be put out of the way. But God does not mean you to sin on that account, nor will he excuse you if you do. 2. *The power of the unclean spirits.* They are said to have been "like frogs." (1) *Whom do they represent?* See whence they issued. (a) From the dragon; that is, the devil. Therefore the unclean spirit that thence came forth represents the malignant, wicked spirit that ever opposes itself against God. (b) From "the beast;" that is, the world in its hostile manifestations against Christ's Church. It was represented chiefly by Jerusalem and Rome in St. John's day. (c) From the false prophet, or the beast from the sea (ch. xiii. 11); that is, the superstitions, lies, and manifold deceits of heathenism, whereby the people were beguiled and bound to the will of the godless world, which is emphatically called "the beast." Malignant hate, worldly power and policy, deceit,—these are the three frog-like, unclean spirits. (2) *What do they do?* They persuade the nations to war against Christ. They are a sort of hellish trinity: the spirit of the dragon as opposed to the Father; of the beast, as opposed to the Son; of the false prophet, as opposed to the Holy Ghost (Hengstenberg). (3) And they are *likened to "frogs,"* partly because of the Egyptian symbols which are prevalent in this chapter, and this was one of their plagues. Also because of their loathsomeness—mud and mire their habitation, hideous in appearance, repulsive and abhorrent everywhere. Thus would St. John excite detestation of these spiritual evils, which he likens to these loathsome creatures. (4) And these spirits *are at work still*, and do yet the same deadly work in leading human hearts to fight against God. Does not that old serpent, the devil, still stir up hard thoughts of God, and make God's "Law" the very "strength of sin"? And the spirit of "the beast," the world, its manifold opposition to Christ, how conscious we all are of its working day by day! And that of the false prophet, that second beast, which gave his strength to the first—how, in the subtle sophistries, the plausible philosophies of the day, the deceitful handling of Divine truths, the pandering to our lower likings, which so many of the popular teachings are chargeable with, do they not beguile and seduce many hearts into opposition to God and to his Christ? Without doubt they do.   And, therefore, *the lesson of the whole*, which in ver. 6 the Lord himself solemnly interposes to teach his Church, is for us to-day as for them of old. "Behold," he says, "I come as a thief." Many there were, many now are, in open association with his people who are not really of his people. To such especially he addresses his warning word.   The time of trial, of his judgment, will come thief-like— suddenly, unexpectedly, stealthily, surprisingly, with hostile intent—to those who do not watch.   For these will be as a man who has laid himself down to sleep, and has put off his clothes.   And so the sudden coming of the thief finds him unclothed.   All which means that we are never to allow ourselves to be separated from Christ.   We are to abide in him whom we profess to have "put on," never to put off.   The love, faith, and fear of him are to be our garments, the Christian state and condition, in which we are always to be.   Now, he who does not watch puts off, if, indeed, he ever really put on, that state.   And hence, when trial comes, he will be detected, exposed, and scorned, for the pretended, but not real, Christian, which he really is.   *Abide in Christ*, then, is the word to us all, and we need fear no conflict, not even the fiercest, which our foe may wage.—S. C.

Vers. 5—7.—*The Divine righteous judgments.*   The spiritual aspects of these judgments must be especially kept in view.   For under the veil of outward things the invisible and spiritual things are represented.   The entire symbolism of these verses, and, indeed, of the whole section, plainly shows—

I. THAT JUDGMENT PROCEEDS FROM GOD.   They are the judgments of the "Lord God, the Almighty."   "Righteous art thou, which art and which wast, thou Holy One, because thou didst thus judge."

II. THAT THE JUDGMENTS ASSUME THE FORM OF WRATHFUL INDIGNATION.   "In them is finished the wrath of God."   "Seven golden bowls full of the wrath of God, who liveth for ever and ever."   The terribleness of that "wrath" must be gathered from the character of the symbols of its expression.   The *nature* of that "wrath" must be ascertained from the teachings on the nature of him whose "wrath" it is.

III. THAT THE JUDGMENTS ARE CHARACTERIZED BY GREAT SUFFERINGS ON THE PART OF THEM ON WHOM THEY ARE INFLICTED.   Here, doubtless, the spiritual is represented by the visible and material.

IV. THAT THESE JUDGMENTS ARE JUSTLY AND RIGHTEOUSLY INFLICTED.   "Righteous art thou, which art and which wast, thou Holy One, because thou didst thus judge;" "Righteous and true are thy ways, thou King of the ages;" "Yea, O Lord God, the Almighty, true and righteous are thy judgments."   From these direful words we must exclaim truly, "It is a fearful thing to fall into the hands of the living God," when he ariseth to judgment.   How definite is the call to men: 1. To guard against that devotion to evil which is "worshipping the beast and his image." 2. To the faithful to await with awe the final judgments of God upon the enemies of the truth, when he will "separate the just from the unjust," when "the tares shall be cast into the fire"!—R. G.

Ver. 12.—"*The great river, the Euphrates.*"   The details of the wonderful symbolism of this book must find their interpretation, if it be needful, at the hands of the expositor.   For the purposes of homiletic teaching, selections only can be treated.   Of the parts of this chapter which serve our purpose we select the pouring forth of the "sixth vial," or "bowl."   The whole book has but one burden—the conflict of the two kingdoms, light and darkness, Christ and Belial, good and evil in the world.   It embraces the painfulness of the struggle to all men; the safety of the faithful under the Divine keeping; the judgment of God upon the evil ones, and the crushing of the kingdom of evil; and finally the perfect triumph of the Lamb, and of all who are in him or with him, and their perfect, undimmed, and eternal blessedness.   These principles run, like a golden thread, through all the book.   They belong to all time, and to all the varying conditions of the Church.   To affix them to one period only is a grievous limitation that overlooks the world-wide use of the book, and turns into a mere temporary history what is an embodiment of ever-active principles.   We can see no individual and no particular cluster of individuals represented to whom the words of the book must be limited in their application.   There is a sequence in the order of events, but we can see no history and no chronology in any true or precise sense ; but the reiteration of the same truth so deeply needed by the early Church, and so applicable to the Church in all ages and in all its varying conditions. With these views we proceed to interpret the present symbol—the drying up of the river, the great river "Euphrates"—and the coming forth of "three unclean spirits, as it were frogs." What the latter are is told in language that approaches to the literal and realistic. "They are spirits of devils, working signs; which go forth unto the kings of the whole world, to gather them together unto the war of the great day of God, the Almighty." Our interpretation of these symbols leads us to see *the final removal of all hindrances to the perfect development of the antagonistic spirit of evil and error.* That the symbols have a cumulative, an increasing force, seems most obvious; this sign is "great and marvellous;" this is the preparation for "the war of the great day of God." The effectual conquest can only be made when all let and hindrance shall have been taken off the enemy. Error must fully develop itself. The utmost malignity of evil must be revealed. "The way" must be "made ready for the kings that come from the sunrising." Doubtless in the great human history all forms of error and evil shall present themselves to "the truth," and the truth shall vindicate itself in presence of all. Foul sin shall put forth its utmost vileness; but righteousness shall hold its own, and be finally triumphant. Thus is "revealed the lawless one, whom the Lord Jesus shall slay with the breath of his mouth, and bring to nought by the manifestation of his coming" (2 Thess. ii. 8). The enemies of "the Church of the living God"—that is, and must be, *the living Church* of God—shall be crushed. That they may be so crushed, let the way for their coming be opened. Comforting is this word of assuring, confident faith. The "little flock" need not fear, even though their enemies be let loose. The practical lessons are simple. The scene urges—

I. To FIDELITY TO THE RIGHT, EVEN THOUGH EVIL GAIN POWER.

II. To FEARLESSNESS IN PRESENCE OF THE GREAT FORCES OF EVIL.

III. To A PATIENT ENDURANCE OF THE OPPRESSION OF EVIL.

IV. To ASSURANCE OF ULTIMATE VICTORY, FREEDOM, AND PEACE.—R. G.

Vers. 13, 14.—*The unclean spirits.* Following the steps hitherto taken, we come to a symbol of great repulsiveness—a symbol doubtless intended to represent evil in its repulsive form. Again we premise we see no individual persons or individual systems in this figure. "The descriptions here, as well as in the parallel passage, point to the last, the most reckless antichristian and blasphemous manifestations of the beast and the false prophet, when impregnated to the full with the spirit of Satan, and acting as his agents in the final effort he makes against the kingdom of God" (Fairbairn, 'Prophecy,' p. 423). "By likening the spirits to *frogs* some respect is had, according to the just remark of Bossuet, to one of the plagues of Egypt. The point of comparison is the uncleanness, the loathsomeness, which is expressly noticed." Our attention is called to spirits and powers of evil who are directly under the control of the evil one, and subject to his inspiration ("the devil having already put it into the heart of Judas, . . . then entered Satan unto him")—"the spirits of devils." These "go forth unto the kings of the whole world, to gather them together unto the war of the great day of God, the Almighty." The servant of sin obeys the behests of sin. He whose heart is open to Satan will find Satan walking in sooner or later. With the great battle we have not now to do. We see how the Church has to maintain her wrestling against "the principalities, against the powers, against the world-rulers of this darkness, against the spiritual hosts of wickedness in the heavenly places." This vision seems to represent an especial malignity and effort of evil in this "war of the great day of God." We can hardly forbear seeing some final intensifying of the Satanic power, some temporary prevalence of evil. But the admonition of the Lord sounds with especial force upon our ear, and must be removed from its merely parenthetical position. "Behold, I come as a thief. Blessed is he that watcheth, and keepeth his garments." In order to this let the Church be roused to behold the evilness of the enemy and the greatness of the danger.

I. THE UNCLEAN SPIRITS ARE "SPIRITS OF DEVILS." The devil stands as the representative and head of all that is unlike God, and that is antagonistic to his Name and kingdom—"the adversary."

II. THE SPIRITS ARE SPECIALLY DISTINGUISHED AS "UNCLEAN SPIRITS." All unholiness is uncleanness. They prompt to all disobedience and worldly lust and foulness of life, all unbelief and evilness of conduct.

III. THEY STIMULATE AND INSPIRE "THE KINGS OF THE EARTH"—the subtle ruling powers, passions, habits, and other forms of evil which hold sway and dominion over men. The king is the symbol, not of weakness, but of power and authority and government; fit emblem of whatever domineers over the life of man.

IV. THEY STAND IN DIRECT ANTAGONISM TO GOD. This is the utmost evilness conceivable. To be led astray by temptation, to fall by unwatchfulness, to yield to evil, is bad enough, and entails just and merited punishment; but the utmost vileness is that which places itself in direct and active opposition to the Holy One. "He that opposeth God and exalteth himself against all that is called God."

V. THEREFORE LET THE LOWLY BELIEVERS (1) take heed : watching; (2) keep free from the contamination of sin in every guise: "keepeth his garments." (3) For the danger is great; (4) and the great Master cometh at an hour when we think not: "Behold, I come as a thief in the night." (5) He that so watcheth is verily "blessed."
—R. G.

Vers. 1—21.—"*The seven vials:*" *predestined suffering in the government of the world.* "And I heard a great voice out of the temple saying to the seven angels, Go your ways, and pour out the vials of the wrath of God upon the earth. And the first went," etc. "It is incredible," says Bishop Horsley, "to any one who has not made the experiment, what proficiency may be made by studying the Scriptures without any other commentary or exposition than what the different parts of the sacred volume naturally furnish for each other." Whoever has, with honesty of purpose and persevering endeavour studied the Bible for himself, will readily endorse this statement of the bishop. I would add to this, and say that it is incredible to any one who has not made the experiment, what an amount of priceless, vital, and practical truth can be got out of the Bible by studying its utterances in connection with the unbiassed reason and common sense of the human mind. Using these Apocalyptic visions of John as an *illustration of the great truths dictated by reason and confirmed by the consciousness of every man, they come to us as a priceless revelation.* The great truth which this chapter suggests to us, and strikingly illustrates, is that there is *predestined suffering in the government of the world.* There are "seven plagues," sufferings, that have been developing, still are being developed, and will be to the end. The abyss of agony contained in these seven plagues is immeasurable to all but the Infinite. The old dogma fabricated by the old makers of our theology, viz. that the physical suffering in the world is caused by sin, is an exploded fallacy, which all geological museums ridicule in mute laughter. Suffering is an element in the government of this world. Taking the whole of this chapter, we shall find it illustrative of three subjects, viz. (1) *that all the dispensations of this suffering are under the direction of God ;* (2) *that they have all a great moral purpose ; and* (3) *that they have all an influence coextensive with the universe.* Observe—

I. ALL THE DISPENSATIONS OF THIS SUFFERING ARE UNDER THE DIRECTION OF GOD. "And I heard a great voice out of the temple saying to the seven angels, Go you ways [Go ye], and pour out the vials [seven bowls] of the wrath of God upon the earth " (ver. 1). From the very shrine of the Almighty, the holy of holies, he deals out and regulates every item of the sevenfold plagues. 1. *He orders their agents.* Each of the "seven angels" or messengers are sent forth by him. "Go your ways." The supreme Governor of the universe conducts his affairs through the agencies of others—a vast system of secondary instrumentalities. Thus, through all nature, he gives life, supports life, and takes away life. Albeit he sits at the head and is the absolute Author of all. There is not a pain that quivers in the nerve of any sentient being that comes not from him. He says, "Go your ways," and nothing moves but by his behests. He kills and he makes alive. Is not this a soothing and a strengthening thought under all the dispensations of sorrow? 2. *He appoints their seasons.* The "seven angels" do not all come together; each has its period. Every impulse that moves throughout the creation, whether it be to shake a leaf in the forest or to wheel systems throughout immensity, goes forth at his own time. All times and seasons are with him. When Shakespeare says, " Troubles come not singly, but in battalions," he is not right. Mercifully they do come singly to individuals and communities, some in one period of life and some in another. To man, collectively, they are ages apart—from the groans of Abel to the throes of the last judgment. There is not a drop of sorrow in any cup that comes not from Heaven. 3. *He fixes their places.* Each of the seven angels who, under God, are to dispense the plagues, has his place assigned him. Each had his " vial," or bowl, and each bowl had a place on which it was to be poured. The first came upon " the earth," the second on " the sea," the third upon " the rivers and fountains," the fourth upon " the sun," the fifth upon " the seat [throne] of the beast," the sixth upon " the great river Euphrates," and the seventh " into the air " (vers. 2—12). Whether there is a reference here to plagues in Egypt, or suffering else-where, I know not; no one does know, nor does it matter. They were phantoms that rolled like clouds in the vision of John, and as such they *illustrate the grand truth that even the very scenes and seasons of all our sorrows come from him who is, and was, and is to be, the Everlasting Father.* 4. *He determines their character.* The sufferings that came forth from the bowls were not of exactly the same kind or amount ; some seemed more terrible and tremendous than others. It appeared as a painful " sore " upon the men of the earth ; it was as " death " to those on the sea ; it appeared as " blood " upon the fountains and the rivers; it appeared as scorching " fire " in the sun ; it appeared as " darkness " and " torture " upon the throne of the beast; it appeared as a terrible " drought," and as the spirits of devils like " frogs," on the rolling Euphrates; and it appeared as terrible convulsions of nature in the air. How different in kind and amount are the sufferings dealt out to men! The sufferings of some are distinguished by physical diseases, some by social bereavements, some by secular losses and disap-pointments, some by mental perplexities, some by moral anguish, etc. " Every heart knoweth its own bitterness." So much, then, for the fact that all the dispensations of *predestined* sufferings are under the direction of God.

II. ALL THE DISPENSATIONS OF THIS SUFFERING HAVE A GREAT MORAL PURPOSE. The suffering of the sevenfold plagues is settled in the government of God for *moral* ends. These ends are not malignant, but merciful. They are not to *ruin* souls, but to *save* them. They are curative elements in the painful cup of life ; they are storms to purify the moral atmosphere of the world. Disrobing these verses of all metaphorical incongruities, they suggest the grand purpose of God in all the dispensations of suffer-ing. They appear to involve three things. 1. *The righteous punishment of cruel per-secution.* " And I heard the angel of the waters say, Thou art righteous, O Lord [Righteous art thou], which art, and wast, and shalt be [thou Holy One], because thou hast judged thus. For they have shed the blood of saints and prophets, and thou hast given them blood to drink; for they are worthy " (vers. 5, 6). To " shed blood " any-how is one of the foulest crimes man can commit; it is an impious infraction of a fundamental law of Heaven, " Thou shalt not kill." Words which apply to man in every conceivable capacity and relation—to the hangman and the warrior as well as to the assassin. They speak as truly to Wolseley amidst his murdering exploits in the Soudan as to any other man on the face of the earth. Blood-guiltiness is the chief of crimes. But to murder " prophets," good men and true teachers, is the chief of murders. For this Heaven would be avenged, and the whole intelligent universe will so recognize this as to break into the anthem, " Even so [yea], Lord God Almighty, true and righteous are thy judgments " (ver. 7).

" Avenge, O Lord, thy slaughtered saints," etc.

(Milton.)

2. *The righteous punishment of supreme worldliness.* " And the fifth angel poured out his vial [bowl] upon the seat [throne] of the beast; and his kingdom was full of dark-ness; and they gnawed their tongues for pain " (ver. 10). Worldliness in the ascendant is indeed like this beast portrayed in the Apocalypse. It sits supreme; it has a throne, a crown, a sceptre that extends over all. Supreme worldliness, whether in the individual or the society, is a " beast " coarse and hideous ; and this beast, with all its votaries, is to be crushed. The whole government of God moves in that direction. Truly " blessed is he that overcometh the world "—this " beast." 3. *The overwhelming ruin of organized wrong.* " And the great city was divided into three parts, and the

cities of the nations fell : and great Babylon came in remembrance before God, to give unto her the cup of the wine of the fierceness of his wrath " (ver. 19). Great Babylon, what is it? *The moral evils of the world organized into its metropolis.* Falsehood, sensuality, pride, ambition, impiety, fraud, tyranny, embodied in a mighty city. This is the Babylon, and all unredeemed men are citizens in it. The Divine purpose is to destroy it. All his dispensations are against it, and will one day shiver it to pieces. " The kingdoms of this world shall become the kingdoms of our God, and of his Christ ; and he shall reign for ever and ever." Wrong will not stand for ever before right. Though mountains of ice may stand before the glowing sunbeams of a thousand summers, wrong is bound to fall ultimately before the right. Take courage ; be of good cheer !

III. ALL THE DISPENSATIONS OF THIS SUFFERING HAVE AN INFLUENCE COEXTENSIVE WITH THE UNIVERSE. There was not a drop from the bowl in either of the angels' hands that terminated where it fell. The contents of these bowls are not like showers falling on the rocks in summer, which having touched them are then exhaled for ever. No, they continue to operate. The bowl that fell on the earth became an evil and painful sore ; that which fell on the sea became blood and death ; that which fell upon the sun scorched mankind ; that which fell on the beast spread darkness and agony in all directions ; that which fell upon the Euphrates produced a drought, and drew out of the mouth of the dragon wild beasts and strange dragons ; the bowl that poured out its contents on the air produced lightnings and thunders and earthquakes, causing Babylon to be riven asunder, and every mountain and valley to flee away (vers. 2—13, 19, 20). Observe : 1. *Nothing in the world of mind terminates with itself.* One thought leads to another, one impression produces another elsewhere, and so on. In matter the roll of an infant's marble shakes the massive globes of space. " No man liveth unto himself." Each step we give will touch chords that will vibrate through all the arches of immensity. 2. *Whatever goes forth from mind exerts an influence on the domain of matter.* These angels, unseen messengers of the Eternal, go forth from that shrine into which no eye has ever pierced—the secret place of him " who dwelleth in the light, whom no man hath seen or can see." Who are they? What eye has ever seen them ? what ear has ever heard the rustle of their mystic wings ? the " vials " or bowls they bear in their mystic hands, what eye has seen them, and what hand has touched them ? And yet these invisibilities from the invisible world produce an influence upon the material. Not only do sentient creatures from the earth and the waters and the air writhe and bleed and die, but inanimate matter also. The earth quakes, the mountains tremble at their influence. Human science seems to be reaching a point when we shall find that human minds in all directions exert an influence upon the forces and the operations of material nature. Mind is the primordial and presiding force of all forces. Morally, like Jacob on his stony pillow at Bethel, we are all dreaming, unconscious of the presence of the great Spirit. Ere long, however, we shall be wakened and exclaim, " Surely God is in this place, and I knew it not." [1]—D. T.

EXPOSITION.

CHAPTER XVII.

Ver. 1.—**And there came one of the seven angels which had the seven vials, and talked with me, saying unto me ;** *and spake with me, saying.* Omit " unto me." This and the following chapters (to xix. 21) consist of visions which are really included under the seventh vial, but which, on account of their length and elaboration, may be considered apart from the other judgments of that vial. In the preceding chapters we have had placed before us a conspectus of

three classes of ungodly people, and the three principles of evil in their abstract form, as represented by the world (the first beast), the flesh (the second beast), and the devil (the dragon). The personal final overthrow of the devil is described in ch. xx. 10 ; ch. xvii. and xviii. are devoted to the description of the judgments of the two former—the world, in its character of the openly hostile persecutor of the Church of God ; and the other portion of the ungodly who, while still professing Christianity, find excuses for conforming to the worship

[1] It will be seen that each division of this homily contains brief suggestive homilies.

of the image of the beast. The first beast is, therefore, identical with Babylon, and represents, as we have seen, the openly hostile and persecuting world-power of all ages, of which, in St. John's time, Rome was the foremost embodiment. The second beast is identical with the harlot, and represents faithless Christians, the apostate portion of the Church. The very *raison d'être* of the Apocalypse is to deal with these two forms of evil; to declare the overthrow of the one, and to warn and, if possible, reclaim those under the influence of the other. In the latter case, the warning consists in setting forth the judgment in store for faithless Christians; and as this is the course pursued with the former also, the two merge into one, and indeed are declared to be one. The apostle in substance declares that, though there is a *primâ facie* difference between the two forms of ungodliness, there is in reality no distinction to be made, but both are involved in one common final judgment. He thus twice solemnly asserts that the harlot is, Babylon (vers. 5 and 18). The comments upon the following chapters will be based upon this hypothesis, the reasons for which will be brought out more clearly as we proceed. The opening words of this chapter leave no doubt that the visions which follow are connected with the vial judgments. The "one of the seven angels" may be the seventh angel, to whom it pertained to unfold the circumstances connected with the last judgment. Come hither; I will show unto thee the judgment. *Hither*, δεῦρο, without the verb, as in ch. xxi. 9 and John xi. 43. Though this particular narration necessarily takes place after the account of the vials, yet we are not to understand that the events here related are subsequent to those related in the concluding verses of the previous chapter. Note the remarkable similarity between these words and those of ch. xxi. 9, and the contrast between the bride, the wife of the Lamb, and the harlot who is connected with the beast. Wordsworth carries the comparison even to the form of words, thus—

The harlot and the beast.
'Η πόρνη καὶ τὸ θηρίον.

'Η νύμφη καὶ τὸ ἀρνίον.
The bride and the Lamb.

Of the great whore; *harlot* (Revised Version) There seems no doubt that this figure describes the degenerate portion of the Church of God. (1) As we have already seen, this symbolism is made use of by St. John to portray the faithlessness of those who are professedly servants of God (see ch. ii. 20; xiv. 4), and in this sense it is applied in the great majority of passages of Scripture

where it occurs (cf. Isa. i. 21; Jer. ii. 20; iii.; Ezek. xvi.; xxiii.; Hos. ii. 5; iii. 3; iv. 15; Micah i. 7). In Isa. xxiii. and Nah. iii. 14 the term refers to Tyre and Nineveh respectively. (2) There is an intended contrast between the bride and the Lamb, and the harlot who allies herself with the beast (*vide supra*). (3) A contrast is also probably intended between the woman clothed with the sun (ch. xii.), bringing forth the man-child, Christ Jesus the Saviour—the representation of the pure Church—and the harlot clothed in scarlet, the mother of harlots and abominations—the representation of the faithless part of the Church. (4) Both the woman of ch. xii. and the harlot of this chapter reside in the wilderness, that is, this world (see on ch. xii. 14); indeed, they are to men sometimes indistinguishable (cf. the parable of the wheat and tares). (5) The faithful Church, the bride, is called a city (ch. xxi. 2, 9, 10); so the faithless portion of the Church, the harlot, is identified with the city Babylon (ch. xi. 8; xvii. 4, 5). Other coincidences will be noted as we proceed. But it seems equally impossible to accept the view that this faithless portion of the Church refers to papal Rome, *and none other*. We must include all the faithless of God's Church in all time. If the fulfilment is to be limited at all, it seems more reasonable to suppose that the first reference of St. John was to the faithless members of the seven Churches to which he addresses the Apocalypse. But we are, no doubt, intended to see here a picture of the position of the unfaithful part of the Church wherever it exists, at any time, and which men are certainly not able always to specify and judge. On this point see Professor Milligan's 'Baird Lectures' for 1885, on "The Revelation of St. John." In lect. v. he says, "But Babylon is not the Church of Rome in particular. Deeply, no doubt, that Church has sinned. . . . Yet the interpretation is false. . . . Babylon cannot be Christian Rome; and nothing has been more injurious to the Protestant Churches than the impression that the two were identical, and that, by withdrawing from communion with the pope, they wholly freed themselves from alliance with the spiritual harlot. Babylon embraces much more than Rome, and illustrations of what she is lie nearer our own door. Wherever professedly Christian men have thought the world's favour better than its reproach; wherever they have esteemed its honours a more desirable possession than its shame; wherever they have courted ease rather than welcomed suffering, have loved self-indulgence rather than self-sacrifice, and have substituted covetousness in grasping for generosity in distributing what they had,—there the spirit of Babylon has been manifested. In short, we have in the great harlot-city neither the Christian Church as a whole, nor the Romish Church in particular, but all who anywhere within the Church profess to be Christ's 'little flock' and are not, denying in their lives the main characteristic by which they ought to be distinguished—that they 'follow' Christ." (For the distinction between the harlot and Babylon, see above.) That **sitteth upon many waters.** "The" is inserted in B and other manuscripts, probably on account of the reference in ver. 15, but is omitted in ℵ, A, P, and others. This is the description of Babylon in Jer. li. 13, whence, doubtless, the expression is derived. In the place quoted, the sentence refers to the many canals of Babylon; but the interpretation of this passage is given in ver. 15, where the *waters* are stated to be "peoples." This fact sufficiently demonstrates that, though the imagery of the Apocalypse be taken from the Old Testament, it is not always safe to insist on an exactly similar interpretation; the symbols employed may be applied in an independent manner. That the harlot sits on many waters therefore shows us that the faithless portion of the Church is to be found distributed amongst "peoples, and multitudes, and nations, and tongues."

Ver. 2.—**With whom the kings of the earth have committed fornication, and the inhabitants of the earth have been made drunk with the wine of her fornication.** "Of the earth" is used here (as it frequently is) for the worldly as distinguished from the righteous; and the two classes mentioned indicate the universality of this faithlessness—it is not confined to any one grade of society. As we have seen (see on ver. 1 and ch. xiv. 8), the figure of *fornication* is repeatedly used to describe faithlessness towards God. The verse, therefore, declares that this faithless portion of the Church has chosen rather to render to the world that love which is due to God, and to be connected rather with the powers of this world than to have its treasure in heaven. The expression, "wine of her fornication," is a repetition of that in ch. xiv. 8, and is derived from Jer. li. 7 (cf. also ch. xvi. 19 and xviii. 3).

Ver. 3.—**So he carried me away in the spirit; and he carried,** etc. (cf. ch. i. 10 and xxi. 10). In the latter reference the analogy is sufficiently close to lead us to believe that it is intended. **Into the wilderness;** *a wilderness,* according to the Revised Version, which is the rendering of Wordsworth and others; but Alford strongly supports the Authorized Version rendering, notwithstanding the absence of the Greek

article (see Alford, *in loc.*). Some commentators have thought that the "wilderness" signifies the desolation which is the lot of the harlot (see ver. 16; ch. xviii. 2, 19; also Jer. li. 26). But we can hardly avoid the conclusion that the "wilderness" here is that spoken of in ch. xii. 6, 14, which is symbolical of this world, particularly when we remember that the "wilderness" in both cases is the abode of a woman, who moreover is representative of the Church; though in ch. xii. she represents the Church of God as a whole, persecuted by Satan, and in this place the woman is representative of the faithless part of the Church (see also below on "beast"). Vitringa, referring to Isa. xxi. 1, and ch. xvii. 1, 15, and Ezek. xx. 35, arrives at a similar conclusion; it is a "wilderness of the people." **And I saw a woman.** There is no article, but this vision, occurring immediately after the words of ver. 1, "I will show thee ... the great harlot," identifies this *woman* with the harlot of ver. 1. This woman represents the faithless portion of the Church (see on ver. 1); that part which, following after worldly things, has thereby rendered to the beast the love and honour due to God alone. This *woman* is not identical with the woman of ch. xii. The latter represents the faithful, the former the faithless, part of the Church. **Sit upon a scarlet coloured beast, full of names of blasphemy, having seven heads and ten horns.** Here again, as in "wilderness" (*vide supra*), we have θηρίον, a "beast," without the article; but the identity of this "beast" with that of ch. xiii. 1 is established by (1) the same outward characteristics of names of blasphemy, seven heads and ten horns; (2) its connection with "kings," etc. (vers. 12—14 and ch. xix. 19, 20); (3) its connection with the "false prophet" (ch. xiii. and xix. 20); (4) its connection with the harlot—the one representing the world-power, the other the faithless, worldly portion of the Church. That the *woman sits upon the beast* denotes, not that she exercises control and guidance over it (as Alford), for comp. ver. 16, but rather that the *woman* relies upon the *beast* for support and safety; thus presenting an accurate description of those who prefer to trust to the power and influence of the world rather than to God. *Scarlet* (whether the colour of the beast itself or of its trappings is immaterial) may signify either (1) the worldly pre-eminence and power of which it is the sign, and for which the woman allies herself with the beast; or (2) the blood-stained persecution of which the beast is the author. The first interpretation coincides best with the words which immediately follow; the second one agrees with the description in ver. 6 and

ch. xiii. 7. (On the "names of blasphemy,"
as signifying opposition to and rivalry with
God, see on ch. xiii. 1.) The *seven heads*
denote universality of (earthly) dominion,
and the *ten horns* denote plenitude of power
(see on ch. xiii. 1).

Ver. 4.—And the woman was arrayed in
purple and scarlet colour. These words,
taken in connection with those that follow,
seem to signify the worldly magnificence
which may be the portion of the faithless
Christian. Some writers see an allusion to
the *purple* robe of Christ. (On the meaning of "scarlet," see on ver. 3.) And decked
with gold and precious stones and pearls;
gilded with, etc. Similar descriptions are
given in Ezek. xvi. 13 and xxviii. 13.
Compare the description in ch. xxi. 11.
This account is sufficiently characteristic of
the world's attractions to need no comment.
Having a golden cup in her hand full of
abominations and filthiness of her fornication; *full of abominations, even the unclean
things of*, etc. (Revised Version), the Authorized Version reading being placed in the
margin. Another reference to Jer. li. 7
(cf. also ch. xiv. 10). *Abominations* are
all things that are displeasing to God.
(On "fornication," see on ch. xiv. 8 and
ch. xvii. 1, 2; it signifies unfaithfulness
towards God.)

Ver. 5.—And upon her forehead was
a name written. Omit "was." Ὄνομα,
"name," is dependent upon ἔχουσα,
"having," in ver. 4. This practice was
customary with harlots (Juv., 'Sat.,' vi.
123; Seneca, 'Controv.,' i. 2). In ch. xiv.
1 and vii. 3 the faithful members of God's
Church have his Name in their foreheads;
here the faithless ones, represented by the
harlot, exhibit a spurious imitation. As
God's Name marked the former as his, so
the name Babylon, etc., marks the latter as
belonging to the world (see on ch. xvi 19;
xvii. 5; xviii. 2). The *name* consists of
the words following, to the end of the verse.
MYSTERY, BABYLON THE GREAT, THE
MOTHER OF HARLOTS AND ABOMINA-
TIONS OF THE EARTH. The word
"MYSTERY" may be (1) part of the name,
standing co-ordinately with "BABYLON"
(Alford, Bleek, Hengstenberg, Vitringa,
Wordsworth); (2) a description of the following title, being thus in apposition with
ὄνομα, "name" (Auberlin, De Wette, Düsterdieck, Ebrard); (3) an adverb used in
the same sense as in the last case (Stuart).
Whichever view be taken, there can be no
doubt that the purpose is to draw attention
to the fact which is contained in the following words—a fact which might otherwise be
exceedingly difficult to receive. For the
rest of the verse asserts that the harlot is
Babylon; that is, that the worldly portion

of the Church, though nominally Christian,
is in reality identical with the world, which
is openly antagonistic to God. Indeed, the
latter portion of the verse goes even further
than this. This faithless (though outwardly
Christian) portion of Christ's Church is the
mother, that is, the cause of the existence of
unfaithfulness to God. So true is it that
the professing Christian who is worldly
minded does more to cause in others disobedience and unfaithfulness to God, than
he who openly declares himself in opposition
to God, and even persecutes the faithful;
cf. the words to the Church in Laodicea,
"I would thou wert cold or hot" (ch. iii.
15). (On "ABOMINATIONS OF THE EARTH,"
see on ver. 4.)

Ver. 6.—And I saw the woman drunken
with the blood of the saints, and with the
blood of the martyrs of Jesus; *of the witnesses* (cf. ch. xi. 7). Another point of contrast between this *woman* and the woman
of ch. xii.; the former persecutes, the latter
is persecuted. It may be asked—How can
these words be applied to professing Christians, as they must be, if such be the interpretation of the "harlot"? The answer
may be found in Jeremiah. In Jer. ii. 33,
34 and iii. 1—11 we find the origin of this
passage. Judah is a harlot (Jer. ii. 20;
iii. 1, 8) with a sign upon her forehead
(Jer. iii. 3), who causes transgression in
others (Jer. iii. 33; and compare above,
"Mother of harlots"), and in whose "skirts
is found the blood of the souls of the poor
innocents" (Jer. ii. 34). She is clothed in
crimson (Jer. iv. 30) and golden ornaments
(cf. ch. xvii. 4); her lovers will despise her
(Jer. iv. 30) and seek her life (cf. ch. xvii.
16). Just as it was declared that in Judah
was found the blood of the innocent poor,
so here we are told that the faithless part
of the Church is guilty of the blood of the
saints. The reason is found in the inscription. The harlot is absolutely identified
with Babylon. No distinction in guilt can
be allowed between the openly hostile world
and the faithless Christian. "He that is
not with me," God declares, "is against
me" (Matt. xii. 20). The description
"drunken with," etc., is similar to that of
Babylon in ch. xviii. 2; and also in Jer. li.
7. And when I saw her, I wondered with
great admiration; *with a great wonder*
(Revised Version). Probably because the
seer can scarcely realize that some who are
professing Christians must be held guilty of
such enormities; that the harlot, representing a portion of the Church, faithless even
though it be, should be classed with the
world, as represented by Babylon and the
beast. Perhaps the *wonder* is caused by
the fact that such a thing should ever be
permitted to be; this leading to the follow-

ing explanation, which shows how the unfaithfulness is avenged.

Ver. 7.—And the angel said unto me, Wherefore didst thou marvel ? *did thou wonder?*—the same word as in ver. 6. Though the seer cannot fully comprehend the terrible significance of the sign he sees, viz. that a portion of the Church is one with the hostile world (see on ver. 6), yet there are sufficient marks wherewith to identify it. The woman, the wilderness, the reliance upon the world-power, the inscription, the similar description of Judah in Jer. ii. and iii. (see on ver. 6), might have made the interpretation plain. I will tell thee the mystery of the woman, and of the beast that carrieth her, which hath the seven heads and ten horns ; *the ten horns* (cf. ver. 5, which declares that this essential unity is a *mystery*). Observe, too, that the "mystery of the woman and of the beast" is all one. (On the "beast," the seven heads," and "the ten horns," see on previous verses, especially ch. xiii. 1.) In ver. 1 the harlot is said to sit on the waters; here the beast carries her. The two statements are really identical; both the beast and the waters represent the worldly power found among "peoples, multitudes, nations, and tongues" (ver. 14).

Ver. 8.—The beast that thou sawest was, and is not; and shall ascend out of the bottomless pit, and go into perdition ; *and is about to come up out of the abyss* (Revised Version). "And to go" (*ὑπάγειν*) is read in א, B, P, Vulgate, and almost all cursives; while *ὑπάγει*, "he goeth," is found in A, 12, Arethas, Irenæus. The latter part of this passage is related again in ch. xix. 20. *The beast*, as we have seen, is the world-power—Satan in his character of "prince of this world." Three stages are marked out in the existence of this world-power : first, it *was;* second, it *is not* now ; thirdly, it reappears, to be cast into perdition. The first period describes the condition of things before the sacrifice of Christ. Then it was that Satan ruled supreme in the world ; that the power of the world—*the beast—was.* But Christ overcame the world (John xvi. 33); henceforth to all true believers there is "peace," although they may "have tribulation" in the world (John xvi. 33); for the faithful Christian the power of the world—*the beast—is not.* Yet, though for the true servant of God there is a sense in which it may be said that this power has no existence, it nevertheless exists in the abyss, that is, in its natural abiding-place in the world, among the worldly minded, and thus may cause "tribulation" to the faithful. A further downfall is, therefore, prepared for it—that which will take place at the last day, when it "will ascend from

the abyss to go into perdition." This non-existence, contemporaneously with existence, and subsequent reappearance, is exactly what is described in the wound healed (ch. xiii. 3; see also the remainder of this verse). The period, therefore, embraced in these words is that of the whole existence of this world. It coincides with the period referred to in ch. xii. 14 and 17, and in ch. xx. 3. Throughout the Apocalypse the word ἄβυσσος, translated "bottomless pit" (Authorized Version) and "abyss" (Revised Version), is used to describe the dwelling-place of Satan (see ch. ix. 1, 2, 11 ; xi. 7; xx. 1, 3) while working in the world. "Perdition" is described in ch. xix. 20 as the "lake of fire burning with brimstone." And they that dwell on the earth shall wonder, whose names were not written in the book of life from the foundation of the world, when they behold the beast that was, and is not, and yet is ; *whose name hath not been written upon the book . . . beast, how that he was, and is not, and shall be present.* The last words show exactly what is meant in the first part of the verse (which see). The first words are a repetition of words in ch. xiii. 8 (which see).

Ver. 9.—And here is the mind which hath wisdom. Omit "and." Read, *Here is the mind* (or, *meaning*), etc. These words (as in ch. xiii. 18) draw attention to the explanation which follows—or else that which precedes (cf. ch. xiii. 18). They also make it appear that the explanation which the angel offers of the "mystery" is not one to be understood without some difficulty. The seven heads are seven mountains, on which the woman sitteth. The diversity of opinions on the interpretation of this passage is mainly owing to the fact that writers are not consistent in their application of symbols and numbers; in one place interpreting figuratively, in another literally. We have repeatedly seen that the language of the Apocalypse and its numbers are symbolical. The seals are not literal seals, the Lamb is not a literal Lamb, the beast is not a literal beast, etc. So here, the *mountains* are not literal mountains. A mountain is a symbol of power (see on ch. viii. 8); *seven* is the number significant of universality (see on ch. i. 4 ; v. 1, etc.). The plain meaning of the passage, therefore, is that the woman relies upon a visibly universal power. This is precisely the idea contained in ver. 3, which describes the faithless part of the Church (the harlot) trusting to the power of the world (the beast). Of course, the most prominent form of this world-power in St. John's time was heathen Rome, hence some writers believe that "the seven-hilled city," Rome, is referred to here—either pagan or papal Rome. And, indeed, this may be a partial fulfilment of the vision; but it is not the whole signification. To understand *seven mountains* literally in this place renders it necessary to interpret forty-two weeks, etc., literally in another.

Ver. 10.—And there are seven kings; *and they are*. Here we have the same idea (cf. ver. 9), with a somewhat different aspect. The phrase in ver. 9, "seven mountains," regarded the world-power as one universal indivisible whole, without respect to particular times or modes in which it might be exhibited. In this phrase, "seven kings," we have the same world-power viewed in its successive exhibitions by different nations; though here again we must be on our guard not to interpret the number *seven* literally of seven nations. The *kings* represent worldly states or kingdoms; *seven*, again, betokens universality. We are thus told that this world-power on which the woman relies is exhibited in the manifestation of power by successive nations, *e.g.* Egyptian, Assyrian, Roman, etc., as many as have ever existed or shall exist; for this is the meaning of *seven*. Five are fallen, and one is, and the other is not yet come; *the five; the one; the other*. Omit "and." Here, again, not literally *five*. The seer divides the whole series of anti-theistic world-powers into three groups, and he would say, some, probably the majority, of these are passed away; the second group embraces the world-power as it is exhibited now, whether Roman, Jewish, or any other; in the third group are included those yet to come. Thus those writers who enumerate Egypt, Nineveh, Babylon, Persia, Greece, Syria, etc., in the first group, are partially correct, and only wrong in so far as they attempt to limit and define the kingdoms; and similarly also those who in the third group place the Roman empire after the barbarian invasions, or imperial Germany, etc. And when he cometh, he must continue a short space; *a little while* (Revised Version). This "short space" describes the remainder of the time of the world's existence. Such is its meaning in ch. vi. 11 and xii. 12, and again in xx. 3. In a similar manner, also, "shortly come to pass," etc. (ch. i. 1, 3; ii. 5, 16, etc.; cf. also John xvi. 17, 28).

Ver. 11.—And the beast that was, and is not, even he is the eighth, and is of the seven, and goeth into perdition; *and the beast* (neuter, θηρίον) *that was and is not, he himself is also an eighth* (masculine), *and is of* (ἐκ, out of) *the seven*, etc. We may note (1) that "eighth" refers to "king" in ver. 10, being masculine gender; (2) the absence of the article before ὄγδοος, "eighth," shows that this is not the eighth in a successive series, in which the kings already mentioned

form the first seven. The Revised Version probably gives the correct meaning, "is of the seven;" that is, the beast himself consists of, and is formed by, what has been denoted by the seven kings. We have already interpreted the beast as the worldly power—Satan in his capacity of "prince of this world." We have also shown that the "seven kings" describes this worldly power as it exists throughout all ages. This verse, therefore, sums up and reasserts briefly what has been already virtually intimated in the symbolism employed, viz. that the beast is the sum total of what has been described under the form of five kings, then one king, and then one king again (ver. 10). His final doom is also reasserted, "he goeth into perdition" (cf. ver. 8 and ch. xix. 20)

Ver. 12.—And the ten horns which thou sawest are ten kings, which have received no kingdom as yet. The *horns*, as we have seen, are symbolical of power (see on ch. xiii. 1), and *ten* signifies completeness and sufficiency (ch. xiii. 1). By the *ten horns*, therefore, is expressed widespread, complete power. But this power, says the seer, has not come into existence *as yet*. He thus points to a coming power, hostile to God, such as is described in that part of the account of the seven kings which states "the other is not yet come" (ver. 10). It seems probable, therefore, that in describing the forces opposed to God—those past, those present, and those yet to come—St. John foresees that the hostile world-power will not be always pre-eminently wielded by one nation, as in his own time; but will be divided into many parts, here represented by the number *ten*, though not necessarily exactly ten in number. This, indeed, exactly describes what has really been the case since St. John's time, and what, humanly speaking, seems likely to continue to the end of the world. These *ten horns* seem thus to be identical with the seventh king of ver. 10. Compare the account given of the *horns* in Dan. vii. But receive power as kings one hour with the beast; *authority* (Revised Version). *One hour* denotes "a short time," in which way the Bible constantly describes the period of the world's existence, and especially that period which intervenes between the time of the writer and the judgment-day (cf. Rom. xvi. 20; 1 Cor. vii. 29; ch. vi. 11; xii, 12; xxii. 20, etc.). This sentence thus declares that, though in the future divided into many parts, and thus not being visibly as potential as former single united kingdoms, nevertheless this hostile world-power will be still formidable, having ranged itself on the side of the beast, acting for and with him, and receiving power from him.

Ver 13.—These have one mind, and shall

give their power and strength unto the beast; *they give* (present tense) *their power and authority*, etc. That is, though apparently split up into many sections, they form practically one, acting by and for the beast on whose side they range themselves (see on ver. 12).

Ver. 14.—These shall make war with the Lamb, and the Lamb shall overcome them; *shall war against.* This connects the description with ch. xvi. 14 and with ch. xix. 11—21. This war between the Lamb and the powers of evil is that which extends throughout the history of the world (*vide infra*); it occupies the "one hour" of ver. 12, which is equivalent to the period of the world's existence. But the seer in this verse looks forward also to the termination of the conflict, the result of which, here briefly indicated, is soon to be narrated more fully. For he is Lord of lords, and King of kings. This is the reason given to the Israelites (Deut. x. 17) for obedience to God (cf. also Dan. ii. 47; 1 Tim. vi. 15; and ch. xix. 16). Though the beast may exercise in this world dominion and power as "prince of this world," yet the Lamb is King still greater, to whom the beast must finally succumb. He is thus *King* above the kings of ch. xvii. 2, 10. And they that are with him are called, and chosen, and faithful. The Revised Version is more correct, *And they that are with him, called and chosen and faithful [shall also overcome]*. Another evidence of the lifelong nature of this war. Not only Christ wars and overcomes, but those associated with him are permitted to share in the battle and the victory. Christ's saints are *called* here to battle; in ch. xix. 9 they are *called* to the marriage-supper of the Lamb (cf. also the exhortation to *faithfulness* in ch. ii. 10). The three epithets describe the progressive life of those who share Christ's victory. They are *called*—as all men are—to serve him; having heard the call, they dedicate their lives to his service, and become his *chosen* servants; finally, having remained *faithful* to him, they share in his victory.

Ver. 15.—And he saith unto me. As in ver. 7, these words form the preface to a particular description. Having explained the mystery of the beast, to whom the woman looks for support, the angel now proceeds to unfold the mystery of the harlot herself. The waters which thou sawest, where the whore sitteth; viz. those mentioned in ver. 1. In ver. 7 we are told that the beast carries the woman. Both statements are correct. The beast is the world-power, which is found among the "peoples, multitudes, nations, and tongues." Are peoples, and multitudes, and nations, and tongues. The fourfold description of the human race (cf. ch. v. 9, etc.). which, as a

whole, serves the beast (cf. ch. xiii. 3, **8, 12,** 16), and out of which are selected the redeemed (ch. v. 9; ix. 9).

Ver. 16.—And the ten horns which thou sawest upon the beast; *and the ten horns which thou sawest, and the beast.* There is no authority for the ἐπὶ τὸ θηρίον of Erasmus except the Vulgate, *in bestia,* and, of course, the description given of the beast (ch. xiii. 1, etc.). The two are spoken of separately, on account of the separate jurisdiction wielded according to vers. **12, 13.** These shall hate the whore, and shall make her desolate and naked, and shall eat her flesh, and burn her with fire; *and shall burn her utterly with fire* (Revised Version). These words describe the fate in store for the faithless portion of the Church. That world, to which she trusts, shall turn and rend her—a fitting sequel to her want of faith in the power of Christ. This is exactly the description given of the harlot in Ezek. xvi. 37 (cf. also Ezek. xxiii. 22). "Eat her flesh" and "burn with fire" both describe similar results; possibly the one is thought of in connection with the symbol of "harlot," the other with the symbol of "city," with which the harlot is identical (see on ver. 5; but see Gen. xxxviii. 24; Lev. xxi. 9; cf. also the judgment upon the wicked rich in Jas. **v. 3,** "shall eat your flesh as it were fire").

Ver. 17.—For God hath put in their hearts to fulfil his will, and to agree, and give their kingdom unto the beast, until the words of God shall be fulfilled; *God did put . . . to do his mind. and to come to one mind* (Revised Version). "His mind" is thought by Bengel, De Wette, and Düsterdieck to signify the beast's mind. Others understand God's mind. In either case the general sense is plain. While the world-power is apparently performing the will of the beast, God is working above all; only by his permission can anything be done (cf. the "it was given" of ch. xiii.). The "words of God" are his denunciations against those who trust to the world (cf. Ezek. xvi. 37, quoted on ver. 16).

Ver. 18.—And the woman which thou sawest is that great city, which reigneth over the kings of the earth. A repetition of the assertion made in ver. 5, viz. that the harlot and Babylon are identical (see on ver. 5). Many writers have been led by this verse to believe that Rome, either pagan or papal, is thus pointed out as the antitype of the harlot. That this is one fulfilment of the vision need hardly be doubted. Rome was in St. John's time the foremost embodiment of the hostile forces of the world. But this is not the whole fulfilment, which is in all time (see above, especially on ver. 1 of this chapter).

HOMILETICS.

Vers. 1—18.—" *Babylon the great.*" Our aim in this homily will be to show to what form of evil the name "Babylon the great" specially seems to point. The complexity and difficulty which have gathered round this chapter seem to the writer to arise rather from the enormous incubus of human interpretation which has pressed it down. In this passage we are shown rather a twisted rope than a tangled web. If we untwist the threads and lay them side by side, we shall not have much difficulty, specially if we exercise all that reverent and painstaking care which is due to the examination of every part of the Word of God. *The main figure in the symbolism of the chapter is an infamous woman.* Those who are familiar with Old Testament prophecy will know how often the terms "fornication," "adultery," etc., are used. As in Isa. i. 21; Jer. ii. 20; iii. 1, 6, 8, and in many other places, such terms are used of an apostate Church. In Isa. xxiii. 15—17 the like terms are used of Tyre; in Nah. iii. 4, of Nineveh. So that, so far as the use of such terms in Scripture is concerned, they may mean apostasy from God under the form either of secular rule or of religious corruption (cf. Porter, p. 292). Nor can we have any difficulty in seeing the propriety of such figures. As fornication and adultery are forms of false affection, and are the prostitution of the most sacred part of our nature to alien purposes, so the alienation of the heart from God, and the departure of a Church from fidelity to him, is a violation of the most sacred ties, and is the leaguing of the heart in a false alliance, which is odious to our God. *Where is* THIS *harlot seen ?* There is a triple combination of expressions here. (1) She is seen seated on the beast with seven heads and ten horns; (2) seated on seven hills; (3) seated on many waters, which are peoples, nations, and tongues. Her being seated on the beast, or resting on the civil world-power, is one form of expressing her alliance with state authority. The seven heads of the beast are so many forms of worldly dominion—five of which had passed away, viz. Egypt, Assyria, Babylon, Persia, and Greece. The sixth existed at the time of the apostle. This was Rome. The seventh was another which, when Rome was no more Rome, would rise up, and would be manifest in ten forms. The number ten may be a definite expression for an indefinite number, or it may be that the world-powers may yet be resolvable into ten before Babylon's fall. And the beast himself—being an eighth—is also doomed to perdition. That the woman is also spoken of as seated on seven hills, and (in ver. 18) as " that great city," again indicates a very precise reference to Rome.[1] That she was seated on many waters indicates her sway being as wide as that of the great world-power with which she was in base alliance. Seated on this earthly power, and yet controlling it, as a rider is seated on a horse and yet controls the beast. This is the harlot, Babylon the great, which made all nations to drink of the wine of her fornication. *Nor must we fail to notice the several descriptive features of the harlot.* She is: (1) Clad in gorgeous aray (ch. xvii. 4). (2) Holding out an enticing cup (ver. 4). (3) Mother of harlots and abominations (ver. 5). (4) Drunk with the blood of the holy (ver. 6). (5) Poisoning the inhabitants of the earth (ch. xviii. 3). (6) Bearing names of blasphemy (ver. 3). (7) Yet in a wilderness (ver. 3). (8) Ruling over the kings of the earth (ver. 18). (9) One by whom the merchants grow rich (ch. xviii. 3). (10) Presumptuous in her self-security (ch. xviii. 7). (11) Hated by the very powers whom she has ruled (ver. 16). Hence we are bidden, by the very terms of the symbolism, to look out for some form of evil, which manifests a glaring alienation and apostasy from God—while yet putting on a form like that of the faithful Church; which at once relies on worldly power, and yet assumes its direction; which invests itself in gorgeous array, assumes pompous titles, even such as are names of blasphemy against our Lord and against his Christ; which should exert a most baneful influence on the inhabitants of the earth, and fill the air with the miasma of her pollutions and her crimes; which should be at ease in her self-security, as if no power could disturb her; which should shed the blood of the saints without measure; and which should be in itself the very filth and scum of wickedness. The apostle is astonished with a great astonishment at the symbols of such an incarnation of evil. And a voice is heard crying

---

[1] Some (*vide* Russell, *et al.*) regard Jerusalem as the seven-hilled city. But Dr. Geikie knows of four hills only (see 'The Holy Land and the Bible," vol. i. p. 468).

aloud, "Come out of her, my people . . . that ye receive not of her plagues." *Can we now point to any form or forms of evil that answer to this symbolism?* We have no hesitation in saying—*Yes.* In so doing, let us observe that there really is not room for any great diversity in applying *such* symbolism as we have here, for surely there are few forms of evil so gigantic as to suit the words, "She hath made *all nations* drink," etc. It is, however, clear that whatever form of evil there may be, known or unknown to us, which presents all the features named here, or even the greater part of them, there is *a* great Babylon which is doomed to a fall that will be utter and irretrievable. Therefore observe—

I. One form of Babylon the great is seen in that terrible, awful, universal departure from God which has corrupted all nations, perverted politics, poisoned commerce, and marred social life; by which, as manifested in the iniquitous pursuit of gain, many have grown rich; which has manifested itself in "the lust of the flesh, the lust of the eye, and the pride of life;" which has assumed a domineering air, commanding men to bow down to it, under pain of social ostracism or petty persecution. This spirit of exaltation against God has often puffed men up in false security. It hath been the curse of mankind; for when men are unfaithful to God, they are untrue to themselves. The cup of iniquity becomes fuller and fuller. Often the land mourneth because there is no truth nor justice, nor knowledge of God, therein. Yea, in legion forms this world-wide poison of sin, which works out in blasphemy towards God and ruin towards man, is a great Babylon, which will be smitten, and reel, and fall. And in so far as any so-called Church puts itself between man and God, and usurps his rights, it is akin to Babylon the great.[1]

II. At the same time, we cannot fail to see that there is one special form of evil which more than anything else in the world is pointed out in the symbolism of this chapter, and that is THE APOSTASY OF THE CHURCH OF ROME. Not that we can agree with those who think papal Rome the *sole* enemy of God here referred to. For we shall find in the lamentation over Babylon's fall much that leads us to think not only of a huge ecclesiastical Babylon, but also of a huge commercial one. But that papal Rome is one form of this mystic Babylon we can entertain no doubt whatever. The student of history can follow out at leisure thirteen or fourteen lines of inquiry, on which we can but give a few illustrative remarks. 1. The woman was seated on the beast as if supported by it (ver. 3). Rome has relied on the worldly power to put her decrees into execution by brute force; both in using temporal powers, and in herself claiming temporal power as well as spiritual. 2. She yet rides the beast as if to govern it (ver. 3). We know but too well how Rome has aimed at, and does still aim at, controlling the power on which she relies; claiming even to regulate allegiance to earthly princes. 3. She is seated on many waters (ver. 1). In every quarter of the world her emissaries are sent. And in many a land where the pure gospel of Christ has been preached, she sends her emissaries to undo the holy work by sowing tares among the wheat. 4. She rules over the kings of the earth (ver. 18). Kings are but the "sons of the Church," to do the bidding of their "holy" (?) mother; otherwise she may absolve subjects from allegiance to their sovereign. 5. She holds out a golden cup full of abominations (ver. 4). Papal Rome makes large offers of indulgences and absolutions, and positively lures men into sin. 6. The merchants grow rich by her (ch. xviii. 3). Many are enriched by the ungodly traffic to which she consents in making the house of prayer a den of thieves; for her indulgences and absolutions will cover any kind and degree of sin, whether in the getting of wealth or otherwise. 7. She is presumptuous in her self-security (ch. xviii. 7). Papal Rome acknowledges no other Church, and looks for the time when all will be absorbed in her, while she is to be "a lady for ever." 8. She is adorned with pompous array—in gold (ver. 4), purple, scarlet, and precious stones. Any

---

[1] "Babylon embraces much more than Rome, and illustrations of what she is lie nearer our own door. Wherever professedly Christian men have thought the world's favour better than its reproach; wherever they have esteemed its honours a more desirable possession than its shame; wherever they have courted ease rather than welcomed suffering, have loved self-indulgence rather than self-sacrifice, and have substituted covetousness in grasping, for generosity in distributing what they had,—there has been a part of the spirit of Babylon" (Milligan's 'Commentary,' *in loc.*). (The whole of the professor's able and weighty note on Babylon should be studied.)

one who has watched the working of papal Rome *at* Rome will need no words to convince him of her gorgeous display and dazzling sheen. 9. She is drunk with the blood of the holy (ver. 6). What tales does history unfold! A hundred and fifty thousand persons perished under the Inquisition in thirty years; and from the beginning of the Order of Jesuits, in 1540, it is supposed that nine hundred thousand persons perished through papal cruelty. While, although it is impossible to estimate the exact number, yet it is supposed that during the papal persecutions of the Waldenses, Albigenses, Bohemian Brethren, Wickliffites, and other Protestants, those who perished are counted by the million. The same spirit exists still. In Ireland the priests keep the people in terror, and if Rome does not persecute us, it is because she *dare not*. 10. She is the mother of abominations (ver. 5). Students of history and tourists in papal districts know that this is literally true. Indulgences for an indefinite number of years may be purchased with money. No viler-looking set of faces could ever be beheld than the present writer has seen surrounding the confessional-boxes in St. Peter's at Rome. 11. The beast she rides is full of names of blasphemy (ver. 3). The proclamation of infallibility is the one fulfilment of this that surpasses all others. 12. The inhabitants of the earth are led by her into sin (ch. xviii. 3). The papal Church notoriously leads people into the sin of idolatry. The worship of Rome is largely the adoration of a great goddess.[1] Papists pronounce accursed those who do not "honour, worship, and adore the adorable images." 13. The several kings or kingdoms into which the civil power of the beast is to be divided shall "hate the whore, and make her desolate," etc. (ver. 16). How true! If there is an object of imperial hatred, it is papal Rome, which is hated most of all. She is regarded as the disturber of states everywhere. 14. Yet within this great Babylon there will be to the last some saints of God, who will be called on to come out of her (ch. xviii. 4). Even so. Fearfully apostate and adulterous as is papal Rome, there are in her pale many holy ones who are profoundly ignorant of the abominations, done by her in religion's name. The Lord will know his own in the day when he maketh up his jewels. But this great Babylon of harlotry, pomp, pride, and all abominations, is doomed to fall terribly, suddenly, completely, and for ever![2] Earnestly do we press on the student carefully to follow up each of these fourteen lines on which history will be found to confirm the prophecy here couched in symbolic form. The identification is such that not one point seems lacking. How this great mystery of iniquity is to fall we have yet to consider.

Vers. 16, 17; ch. xviii. 4—8.—*Means and methods of the fall of Babylon the great.* Every great Babylon must fall; whether by such a term it be intended to denote a huge commercial or a huge ecclesiastical Babylon. A corrupt world and an unfaithful Church must both come to ruin. The *name* "Church" will give no security against destruction if the salt have lost its savour. If *any* Church allies itself with an ungodly world-power, leaning on it for support, and gathering its prestige from thence, it is, so far, committing spiritual fornication. "The wine of her fornication" intoxicates men. Precisely so. It is the glamour, the glitter, the pomp, and prestige that attend a Church in her connection with the state, that lead men away into a deceptive admiration, and even intoxicate them with thoughts of her magnificence and power. In the Church of Rome, however, all the evils of spiritual whoredom are at their topmost height. In no other Church in the world is there so much pomp and yet so much carnality. And the Holy Ghost has in these chapters not only given us a sketch beforehand of what she would be, but (though with less of detail) has indicated the means and methods by which she would be destroyed, and has also pointed out the guarantees of the fulfilment of this.

I. A CONSTANT OVERRULING POWER, GOVERNING BY MEANS OF THE LAWS OF MENTAL SUGGESTION, IS AT WORK WITH THAT END IN VIEW. The impulses in human spirits

[1] See Dean Alford's ' Letters from Abroad,' No. iv., "From Rome;" in *Good Words*, 1864, p. 469.

[2] See Bishop Wordsworth's pamphlet on this subject; Rev. Grattan Guinness's book, 'Romanism and the Reformation,' 1887; and for a different view of the expression, "the seven-hilled city," see the Introduction to the second edition of the Rev. Dr. Russell's 'Parousia,' 1887. (The homilies of the present writer which follow, on ch. xviii. and xix. 1—10 are a continuation of the same theme.)

are so directed as to serve God's purposes and not man's (vers. 16, 17). "The king's heart is in the hand of the Lord, and he turneth it whithersoever he will;" "The lot is cast into the lap, but the whole disposal thereof is of the Lord;" "A man's heart deviseth his way, but the Lord directeth his steps." God says to Cyrus, "I girded thee, though thou hast not known me." So of another we read, "Howbeit he meaneth not so; it is in his heart to destroy nations not a few." "God hath put it into their hearts to fulfil his will, till the words of God shall be fulfilled." The right or the wrong of the willing is man's own. The issues thereof are overruled by God for *his* ends. Scripture abounds in illustrations of this. Joseph is cast into the pit. Man meant one thing; God accomplished another. God meant it for good, to save much people alive. Paul is thrown into prison; his bonds turn out rather unto the further-ance of the gospel. Luther is imprisoned, and his castle becomes a Bethel. Bunyan is thrown into prison, and it becomes a second Patmos. Every diligent student of God's providence must have observed the like again and again. Even so, that which is made use of by man to prop up a system may be employed by God to overthrow it. Thus it is to be with Babylon the great. In spite of all that man can say and do, however imposing the names and pretensions of this harlot, however widely spread and deeply rooted may be the ramifications of the evil, however much the worldly interests of men may be bound up therein, there is a sure process of undermining going on at every hour—that undermining being none the less speedy at the moment men are taking the pains to prop it up. It was so with slavery in America. It is so with popery at Rome. The plans of men for upholding both the one and the other have issued, and will issue, in results the very opposite of those which man intended. The world is not in man's hands, after all, but in God's. He puts it in men's hearts to fulfil his will.

II. The very powers on which Babylon relied will turn round against her to hate and harm her. (Ver 16, "The ten horns . . . shall hate the harlot," etc.) How truly is this being fulfilled! Not one of the European powers that has not in some period or other been relied upon by Rome. And now there is not one of the main kingdoms of the world that is not "hating" her. They are working in their own defence against papal intrigue.[1] Historical incidents of the last twenty years are a startling fulfilment of the Apocalyptic word. Thus "the Word of prophecy is made more sure" (2 Pet. i. 19, Revised Version).

III. There will be judgments and plagues that will consummate her ruin. (Ch. xviii. 8, 10; xvi. 18—21.) Regularity and continuity combine with catastrophe to advance the world. There is a long period of orderly, even, and regular sequents. Then there comes an upheaving, and effects in one hour that for which ages have been preparing the way. In the blasting of rocks we see the slow boring and undermining; then the laying of the train of powder. So far all is done deliberately. Then a match is applied; a spark is fired: there is a moment of suspense; then a small curling wreath of smoke, followed in an instant by a mighty blast, and lo! the rock is rent, and reels and falls. So there are wondrous works going on unobserved in the bowels of the earth—that storehouse of molten flame. For years the crust is undisturbed; then comes one mighty heaving, and lo! in one awful moment cities and palaces, temples and towers, are overthrown. So shall it be at last with Babylon the great. The issue alone can explain the detail. But some six or seven words are sufficiently significant—"A great earthquake" (ch. xvi. 18); "a great hail" (ch. xvi. 21); "death, and mourning, and famine," "plagues" (ch. xviii. 4—8); "burned with fire" (ch. xviii. 8); and at the last her judgment shall come "in one hour" (ch. xviii. 10).

IV. The attendants of her ruin will be retribution and desolation. *Retri-bution;* for she is to be rewarded as she rewarded others. She trifled with and even trampled on the temporal powers in time past, and now of her temporal power she herself is shorn. *Desolation:* the description of this is taken from the corresponding passages in Isaiah and Jeremiah concerning Babylon of old (Isa. xiii. 19—22; Jer. li. 37). Those words have come to be literally fulfilled.[2] Like words are on record con-cerning papal Rome. They too will be fulfilled. The time will come when no priests

---

[1] See Mr. Gladstone's striking pamphlets on the Vatican; also Bishop Wordsworth's, entitled, 'Is not the Church of Rome Babylon the Great?' 9th edit., p. 97, *et seq.*

[2] See Keith's 'Evidence of Prophecy.'

shall minister at her altars. The walls of her mighty temples will be shattered, and the shrieks of many an unclean bird shall reverberate from column to column of her dilapidated pile.

"Thus terribly shall Babel fall,
Thus—and no more be found at all!"

Note: 1. *The amazing extent of the dominion of papal Rome may well fill us with wonder.* It is terrible indeed to see this harlot committing fornication with the kings of the earth, seated upon many waters, intoxicating the nations with her greatness, and carrying her corruptions and abominations to the ends of the earth. But all is forewritten, that we might not be alarmed, however we may be distressed. Therefore: 2. *We ought not to be dismayed, as if some calamity had unawares befallen the world* It has not come otherwise than was foretold to the apostle in Patmos. The fourteen outlines of the ground-plan described in the preceding homily show an exact correspondence between the Word of God and the events of history. 3. *Nor should we fear for the final issue.* The word which forecast Babylon's rise has foretold its fall. 4. *Meanwhile, be it ours not to be caught by appearances.* To this day the harlot is bedecked and bedizened in gold and silver and precious stones. Her pomp and pride and the prestige of her ancient date charm many into a blind compliance with her amours. Many wish to drink of the golden cup which is in her hand. But ah! even apostasy may be covered with pearls, and the beast may be clad in scarlet. *What is beneath?* 5. *Even when, however, the fall of Babylon the great shall come,* that will not be the end; one more conflict will await the Church. The ten horns that have turned round on the harlot will make war with the Lamb. There will remain the war between the beast and the King of kings and Lord of lords. 6. Therefore, finally, *be it ours to be among those who are with Christ,* and to whom the three epithets may be fitly applied—"called," "chosen," and "faithful." All tawdry show and carnal blaze are doomed. Only what is true and real will live on unharmed for ever. *Laus Deo!*

HOMILIES BY VARIOUS AUTHORS.

Ver. 14.—*The war with the Lamb.* This chapter and the next are mainly occupied with the description of the combatants—the city, the court, and the provinces of Rome—who waged war against the Church of Christ, and therefore are said to "make war with the Lamb;" and with (ch. xviii.) the fall of the city, which was the centre and head of the whole war against Christ. We hold to the belief that St. John was telling, not of something in the far future, which could be but of little avail to the persecuted Church of his day, but of events which were near at hand, imminent, and should "shortly come to pass." Therefore, concerning the interpretation which makes Daniel explain St. John, and understands the seven kings as the seven world-empires from Egypt to Rome, and the ten horns as the future dismemberment of the Roman empire—how, we ask, could the knowledge of this then far-future event help the suffering saints, to cheer and strengthen whom was the one chief purpose of this book? To say nothing of the incongruity of speaking of Rome in St. John's day as a power that "was, and is not" (ver. 11); or that in his day it had received a "deadly wound" (ch. xiii. 3); or that the dismembered Roman empire, of which we and most of modern Europe have for nigh a thousand years formed parts, should continue only "a short space." We should feel pressed with the difficulties of this interpretation were there none other which avoided them. But as there is such other, we feel compelled to adopt it. We do not say that this one has no difficulties, but they are small in comparison with those belonging to the one we have refused. And now let us consider—

I. "THESE" WHO MAKE WAR WITH THE LAMB. Who are they? We believe St. John to refer: 1. *To the court of Rome,* especially to the monster Nero, the emperor. (1) He is described: (*a*) As "the beast." Sometimes this name stands for the God-and-Christ opposing world-power in general, the secular antichrist of the several ages; and sometimes for the embodiment of that power in one person, as in Nero. How he deserved the name by reason of his ferocity, cruelty, and bestiality, let Tacitus tell, and many others who knew (cf. Renan's 'L'Antichrist'). (*b*) As soon to be no more. So soon, so certain, was his removal, that he is spoken of in ver. 8 as "the beast that was, and is not, and yet is;" and again (ver. 11), as "was, and is not;" though, from ver. 10 and many other sources, we know that when St. John wrote Nero was yet living, and furiously persecuting the Church of God. This is an inspired prediction of what was soon to come, and is clothed, after the frequent manner of prophecy, in the language of an event already past, though indeed it was future. (c) As one day to reappear (ver. 8, "He shall ascend out," etc.). The belief that Nero should return was notorious (cf. Stuart and Farrar, *in loc.*). (2) He is identified: (*a*) By the city over which he rules (ver. 9). Seven-hilled Rome, "the city of the seven hills," was as frequent and well-understood a name for Rome as would be "the city on the banks of the Thames" for London. (*b*) By his place in the succession of kings. He stands sixth in the list of the Roman emperors. "Five" had passed away of the twelve Cæsars. He was the sixth—the "one is" (ver. 10). (*c*) His successor's short reign. Galba reigned but three months: "He must continue a short space." (*d*) By the universal belief that he would return (cf. *supra*). (3) He is doomed to go "into perdition" (ver. 11). Such was the man or monster—beast, rather—who led the war against the Church of Christ in his day. 2. *To the city of Rome.* She is branded with the name of "Babylon . . . mother of harlots" (ver. 5), and is described as an utterly abandoned woman, revelling in wealth and splendour, exercising her deadly seductive influences over all the empire, flaunting forth her shame with unblushing effrontery, and cruel with a ferocity that the beast she sat upon, and who sustained her, could hardly rival or satisfy. "Drunk with the blood of the saints." Such was the seven-hilled Rome when St. John knew it. Even a monster like Nero would hardly have dared to rage as he did had he not been encouraged by the brutal populace that swarmed in Rome. 3. *To the consuls and proconsuls.* The ten provincial governors who aided and abetted "the beast" in his war against Christ. There were ten of these: Italy, Achaia, Asia, Syria, Egypt, Africa, Spain, Gaul, Britain, Germany (Farrar). And in all these the will of Nero was law. His persecution was by no means confined to Rome—this entire book shows that, though it began there. It was, as ver. 13 says, they gave "their power . . . unto the beast."

II. THE METHODS OF THEIR WARFARE. 1. *Then, when St. John wrote,* it was by cruel, horrible, widespread, and bloody persecution. So that Rome is represented as "drunk with blood," and the description is confirmed by historic fact. But: 2. *Now, in our day,* the secular, antichristian spirit manifests itself in quite another form. The beast-spirit "yet is," though clothed in other garb. The world is the world yet, and still makes "war with the Lamb." It aims now not so much to hurt the body as the soul. The former it may not touch, but the latter it can and does. It kills holy habits, wounds conscience, defiles the thoughts, stuns religious sensibilities, mocks at religious earnestness, exiles her language, her literature, and her laws. All this the world-spirit does by its customs, maxims, and its administration of its rewards and punishments. It has corrupted public opinion, poisoned the atmosphere which daily the believer has to breathe; its influence is often, generally, unseen, intangible, indescribable, but nevertheless as real and deadly to the souls of men as were the bloody laws of Rome to the bodies of the believers in the Church of the first century. But consider—

III. THE LAMB AGAINST WHOM "THESE" WAR. A Lamb, and yet "Lord of lords, and King of kings." The ideas seem incongruous. How, then, is "the Lamb" this? 1. *By rightful authority.* Though Son of man, he is also Son of God (cf. Ps. ii.). 2. *By virtue of his sacrifice.* It is this great fact that he keeps prominently through his chosen name—"the Lamb." In heaven he is thus seen as "a Lamb who had been slain" (ch. iv.; cf. Phil. iii., "Therefore hath God also highly exalted him, and," etc.). 3. *By the might of meekness.* See how at his nativity the shepherds were told they should see the "Saviour, Christ the Lord." And what was it that they did see? A babe, "wrapped in swaddling-clothes, and lying in a manger." But in that utter humiliation and self-abnegation of the Son of God lay the might that should make him, as it has made him, "King of kings, and Lord of lords." Meekness is might, sacrifice is sovereignty, losing life is gaining it; the cross creates the crown. It is no arbitrary arrangement; it lies in the constitution of our nature, to which his meekness and love appeal with such resistless force. "O Galilæan, thou hast conquered!" said the

Emperor Julian. And Constantine confessed the same, and Rome bowed to Christ. 4. *By the consent of conscience.* Blessed be God, there is a better self in the worst of men, and the appeal to that better self in men, though drowned by many a vile clamour for a long time, will yet be heard and obeyed. And Christ by his gospel made such appeal. 5. *By the grace he imparted to his people.* "Their patient continuance in well-doing put to silence" all their foes. Rome looked on at these Christians and wondered, and, after a while, gave way and worshipped with them. For not alone in and by himself does the Lamb overcome, but: 6. *In his people.* "They that are with him." The Revised Version rightly renders St. John's words, "They also shall overcome that are with him, called, chosen, faithful." St. John does not teach that the Lamb was indebted to them for this victory, as a general is indebted to his army. That, though the Authorized Version seems to lend countenance to such idea, is very far from the truth. But what is meant is that, *like* their Lord, "they that are with him" overcome. "The noble army of martyrs praise thee." In them he repeats and reproduces his victory. It is, therefore, of great interest and importance to know who they are that are "with him." For the conditions of victory are the same to-day as they were of old. The enemy has not changed in reality, though he has in form. And would we overcome, we must be as they of old who overcame. Well, then, see how they are described. They are: (1) *Called.* We answer to that description. So far so good. We, the avowed Christian people of our day, have been called by God's providence, by his Spirit, through his Word, his ministers, and by his manifold means of grace, and we are in his Church because of it. (2) *Chosen.* Are we this? It does not at all follow that we are so because we are called. All the chosen are called, but not all the called are chosen. "Many are called, and few," etc. How, then, may we know if we are elect, chosen? Not by frames and feelings, fitful emotions of the mind, which come and go like the clouds. Not by position and office. We may be recognized communicants and pastors, teachers, or aught else of the kind. God forbid that we should say all this counts for nothing as evidence of our Christian standing! It does count for something, but in itself is by no means sufficient evidence as to whether we be God's chosen or not. And not by Church or creed. We may prefer our own and feel persuaded that we are in the right. But Churches and creeds other than our own have furnished many of Christ's elect, and not all ours are certainly chosen. But thus we may know if we be chosen: (3) If we be of those who are *faithful.* Called we are; chosen we may be. If faithful, then we are of the chosen too; and this, and this only, is the proof. They of old through the Lamb overcame. It is they who to-day through him alone overcome. May we not, then, hear the apostolic word addressed to us, "My brethren, give all diligence to make *your* calling and election sure"?—S. C.

Ver. 1—ch. xviii. 24.—*Babylon.* We read her name, "BABYLON THE GREAT, THE MOTHER OF THE HARLOTS AND OF THE ABOMINATIONS OF THE EARTH." Now, the whole idea of the sinful opposition to God is gathered together in a unit. It is a city; it is a woman. We must forsake all guides, and declare our conviction that Babylon means neither Christian nor heathen Rome, nor any other city, kingdom, or state *in particular ;* but the one kingdom of evil manifesting itself in many kingdoms and systems, both political and ecclesiastical, and equally independent of either. The essential idea is the Babylon of evil as it stands in antithesis to the holy Jerusalem—the pure, the bride, the Lamb's wife. Two chief divisions will comprehend the teaching concerning "Babylon:" (1) *Its description ;* (2) *its destruction.*

I. THE DESCRIPTION OF BABYLON. 1. Its corrupt character. As before the prophets were "false" and the spirits were "unclean," and stood opposed to God; so now harlotry, fornication, drunkenness, blasphemy, abominations, luxury, persecuting violence, sorcery, submission to the beast, warring against the Lamb, are the terms employed to describe or indicate the excessive foulness and corruption of the faithless city. This is "the woman," having in her hand "a golden cup full of abominations even the unclean things of her fornication." This the "Babylon the great," which is become "a habitation of devils, a hold of every unclean spirit, and a hold of every unclean and hateful bird." 2. Virulent antagonism to the good, even to the loftiest ideals of goodness. "War against the Lamb;" "blasphemed the God of heaven;" "gather together unto the war of the great day of God;" "poured out the blood of saints and prophets;"—in such terms is the antipathy to all righteousness declared. 3. Occasion of all evil, seen in the corruption of life, the deceitfulness of iniquity, the loss of the blessings of righteousness, degradation in sin, to which the "peoples, and multitudes, and nations, and tongues" are reduced "where the harlot sitteth;" and the judgments and consequent sufferings in which they are involved. 4. The widespread, universal character of the desolation caused. In every aspect this vision is "great and marvellous." It is "Babylon the great." The harlot "sitteth upon many waters," which waters are "peoples, and multitudes, and nations, and tongues." "And the woman is the great city which reigneth over the kings of the earth;" "by the wine of the wrath of her fornication all the nations are fallen." "What city is like the great city," with whose "sorcery were all the nations deceived"? "In her was found the blood of all that have been slain upon the earth." This is the universal kingdom of evil, whose "sins reached unto heaven." Again and again has it seemed as though these words of widespread import found their fulfilment; but no complete idea can be formed that shuts out any part of the one all-pervasive kingdom of wickedness. This great kingdom shall come to an end. Such is the ever-recurring promise of this book.

II. ITS DESTRUCTION IS COMPLETE. The "harlot" is made "desolate and naked;" hated by all over whom she sat as a queen; they shall "eat her flesh, and burn her utterly with fire." "Woe, woe!" is pronounced against the great city, Babylon; "for in one hour is thy judgment come." "Fallen, fallen is Babylon the great." "In one day shall her plagues come, death, and mourning, and famine: and she shall be utterly burned with fire; for strong is the Lord God which judgeth her." "The Lamb shall overcome," and thus shall they also overcome that are with him. "And a strong angel took up a stone as it were a great millstone, and cast it into the sea, saying. Thus with a mighty fall shall Babylon, the great city, be cast down, and shall be found no more at all." Then shall the kings of the earth that committed fornication with her, and the merchants of the earth who were made rich by her, and every shipmaster and mariner, and all that were made rich by her, weep and mourn and lament; while to heaven a sweet song of joy and thankfulness shall rise from them who with the Lamb have overcome—who are "called, and chosen, and faithful."—R. G.

Vers. 1—6.—"*The great whore:*" *a corrupt Christianity.* "And there came one of the seven angels which had the seven vials, and talked with me, saying unto me, Come hither; I will show unto thee the judgment of the great whore that sitteth upon many waters," etc. What a strange woman loomed in John's vision here! He calls her "the great whore [harlot]." He saw her seated upon a "scarlet-coloured beast, . . . decked with gold and precious stones and pearls, having a golden cup full of abominations: . . . and upon her forehead was a name written, Mystery, Babylon the Great, the Mother of Harlots and Abominations of the Earth. And she was drunken with the blood of the saints, and with the blood of the martyrs of Jesus" (vers. 3—6). A strange creation this, truly, but scarcely stranger or more grotesque than many of the objects that have entered and still do enter into human dreams. We must ask Protestant interpreters to say who this woman is, for they know all about her. They, forsooth, are certain that she is *pagan* or *papal Rome.* I cannot say who she is; nor does it matter. I shall make use of her to illustrate *corrupt Christianity;* and this includes Protestantism as well as popery. Conventional Christianity is as truly corrupt as papal, and, in some respects, it is even worse.[1] The description here given of this harlot suggests and illustrates three great evils ever conspicuous in corrupt Christianity Here is—

I. POLITICAL SUBSERVIENCY. "Come hither; I will show unto thee the judgment of the great whore [harlot] that sitteth upon many waters [or, 'many nations']" (ver. 1). This woman, clothed in "purple and scarlet," and gorgeously adorned, yielded herself up to the desires and lusts of worldly authorities; empty voluptuaries "drest in a little brief authority." "With whom the kings of the earth have committed fornication" (ver. 2). The *essence* of genuine Christianity is *spiritual supremacy and invincible sovereignty over the princelets, kinglets, and emperors of the world, in all the little, as well as great, temporalities of life.* Essentially Christianity is the absolute queen of

[1] See "Conventional Christianity, the Great Hindrance to the Extension of the Christianity of Christ," in 'Septem in Uno,' p. 337.

life. Although her kingdom is "not of this world," her demand is that the world should bow to her. In yielding to worldly influence she lost her pristine purity and primitive power; she got corrupted, and became more and more the servant of rulers and the instrument of states. This she has been from before the days of Constantine down to this hour. What is conventional Christianity, not only throughout England but throughout Christendom, to-day? Verily, she is rather a *serf* than a *sovereign*. Worldly rulers employ her to consecrate their coronations and to give the aspect of sanctity to their tawdry pageantries, their sensual indulgences, their unrighteous exactions, and their bloody wars. Truly, the purest virgin from heaven has become a harlot, the mere creature of worldly power. I am wearied of the cant of making this harlot the symbol of papal or pagan Rome; she is as truly a symbol of Protestant Christendom as of papal Rome. The Reformation, in which Wickliffe, Melancthon, and Luther so heartily engaged, is, for many reasons, more urgently required now in the realm of conventional Christianity. And the reiterated cry of Voltaire against popery in his day, "Crush the monster! crush the monster!" all thoughtful men should raise now in relation to *conventional Christianity*. Until conventional Christianity is banished from the land, and the Christianity of the sermon on the mount is restored, the moral condition of the human race will sink lower and lower into devildom and corruption.

II. WORLDLY PROCLIVITY. "And the woman was arrayed in purple and scarlet colour, and decked with gold and precious stones and pearls, having a golden cup in her hand" (ver. 4). Here is worldliness, worldly vanity, and worldly greed. Genuine Christianity is essentially *unworldly*. Its Founder was born in a stable and cradled in a manger; he had nowhere to lay his head. At night the green sod was his pillow, and the sable heavens his covering. His disciples he despatched on their mission without "purse or scrip," and none of his apostles preached the gospel as *a means of livelihood*. "I have coveted no man's silver, or gold, or apparel," says Paul. "Yea, ye yourselves know, that these hands have ministered unto my necessities." But what of *conventional Christianity*? It is an instrument for *worldly gain and aggrandizement*. Everywhere men *trade* in the gospel, and the trade is carried on with all the passionate avarice, foul fallacies, and flatulent puffings that characterize the market. Pulpits are regarded as means of livelihood, chapels and churches are become shops, ecclesiastics are the grandees of the world, robed in costly attire and rolling in chariots of opulence. Institutions abound and multiply, baptized with the name of Christian, where men of feeble talent but crawling craftiness creep into offices of salary and show. I protest that conventional Christianity is not the Christianity of Christ—a Divine entity that "seeketh *not* her own." The Christ exhibited in the creeds and institutions is as unlike the Christ of the Gospels, as the mechanical force of the manufacturing machine, throwing off commodities for trade, is unlike that vital energy in nature that clothes the landscape with verdure and fills the earth and the water with countless tribes of life.

III. RELIGIOUS INTOLERANCE. "And I saw the woman drunken with the blood of the saints, and with the blood of the martyrs of Jesus" (ver. 6). "The phraseology," says Moses Stuart, "is derived from the barbarous custom, still extant among many pagan nations, of drinking the blood of enemies slain in the way of revenge. Here, then, the fury of the persecutors is depicted in a most graphic manner." *Genuine Christianity is essentially tolerant.* "Charity suffereth long, and is kind; charity vaunteth not itself, is not puffed up; charity believeth all things," etc. But Christianity corrupted has always been cruelly intolerant, and this, whether it is called Protestant or papal! True, it does not shed blood as much as of yore, but if it does not take away life it may inflict life annoyances and disabilities in many respects more painful than bloodshedding. This harlot is a "mother;" her progeny is numerous and ever multiplying. "The mother of harlots." The religious sects which crowd Christendom are all her daughters, and each sect has the intolerant spirit of its mother, each according to its measure is a persecutor, and, as a rule, the smaller the more virulent the spirit. Curs snarl and bark more as a rule than mastiffs. Large and affluent congregations can afford to overlook denominational circumstances, that irritate the smaller and the poorer to wrath and rage.

CONCLUSION. Such is corrupt Christianity, which is, alas! the *current* Christianity.

It is very like the "harlot" on account of its political subserviency, worldly proclivity, and religious intolerance. What are we to do with this abomination? Flee from this Sodom; come out of this Babylon. "Crush the monster!"—D. T.

Vers. 7—13.—*A picture of moral error.* "And the angel said unto me, Wherefore didst thou marvel? I will tell thee the mystery of the woman, and of the beast that carrieth her, which hath the seven heads and ten horns," etc. Whilst to the eye of the Infinite the greatest cities of the world, the mightiest empires, the most stupendous productions of human art are as nothing, and less than nothing, vanity," those great *moral principles* which are the expressions of his own nature, the laws that control the destinies of moral mind, are of transcendent import. What are Egypt, Babylon, Rome, Paris, St. Petersburg, New York, London, etc., to him? Shifting clouds, melting into infinite space; little bubbles, rising from and breaking into the ever-changing, ever-rolling stream of time. *But justice, truth, love,—what are these?* As real, as changeless, as lasting, as God himself. Hence it is that in going through this Apocalypse I all but ignore the fanciful and conflicting interpretations presented by what are called Evangelical expositors, and concern myself with those *two principles, good and evil, that touch the spring of all human activities.* Looking at these verses as an illustration of moral error, three things are observable.

I. ITS HISTORY IS MARVELLOUS. John, in his vision, seems to have wondered at this vision of the "mother of harlots," riding on the beast with "seven heads and ten horns." "The angel said unto me, Wherefore didst thou marvel [wonder]?" (ver. 7). Evil is indeed a "marvel," a wonder. It is mysterious on several accounts. 1. *On account of the darkness that enfolds its introduction.* When thinking of the introduction of moral evil, there are four questions which we ask with intense anxiety, but to which we seek a satisfactory solution in vain. (1) *When* did it arise? A commencement it must have had. Evil is not eternal; there is but one Eternal Being in the universe, and he is "glorious in holiness." Evil, then, had a beginning; but when? Who shall tell the morning when the first dark cloud rose upon the bright firmament of moral mind? Who shall tell when the first breath of sin ruffled the peaceful atmosphere of God's creation? The events of that morning are not chronicled in the annals of our world. (2) *How* did it rise? There are two principles on which we can account for the prevalence of sin amongst men now—*internal tendencies* and *external circumstances.* Man now has a strong disposition to sin, so that as soon as he begins to act he begins to sin, and then the outward circumstances under which he is brought up tempt him to wrong. To the latter we refer the introduction of sin into our world. Adam had no unholy tendencies, but an external force was brought to bear upon his holy nature, which turned him from rectitude. But the first sinner, whoever he might be, had neither this *internal tendency* nor the *external circumstances.* All within and without, above, beneath, and around, was in favour of holiness. The whole current of inner feeling and the mighty tide of outward events were all flowing in favour of perfect purity. How could a being sin in such circumstances? How could he strike a discordant note amongst such harmonies? How could he rise up against and conquer all the mighty influences which were in favour of holiness? How could he lift his nature against the Eternal and "defy the Omnipotent to arms"? All is mystery. (3) *Where* did it arise? In what province of the universe? Amidst what order of intelligences? (4) And then, *why* did it arise? Omniscience must have foreseen it, and all the evil consequences that must start out from it. Almightiness could have prevented it. Why did he allow it to enter? Oh, why? 2. *On account of the mask under which it works.* Evil never appears in its own true character. Dishonesty wears the aspect of rectitude; falsehood speaks the language of truth; selfishness has the voice of benevolence; profanity robes itself in the garb of sanctity; the "prince of darkness" appears like an angel of light. The most monstrous deeds that have been perpetrated under these heavens have been done in the name of religion. The Alexanders and the Cæsars of this world have fought their sanguinary battles, and reared their empires upon slaughtered nations in the name of religion. The popes of the world have erected their iron throne upon the soul of Christendom in the name of religion. The persecutors of the world have invented their Inquisitions, built their dungeons, and kindled their fires in the name of religion. Ah me! the Son of God himself was put to death in the name of religion. Wrong is *necessarily* hypocritical. 3. *On account of the wonderful issues that will result from it.* Results will spring from evil which the originators and agents never designed, nay, which they would dread. The introduction of sin became the occasion of a new and brighter manifestation of God. All the glorious developments of Divine justice and love and power which we have in Christ owe their existence to evil. Evil has done an immense injury to the universe, but I believe that in the long run of ages it will be found to have been overruled for a greater good.

II. ITS COURSE IS LAMENTABLE. "The beast that thou sawest was, and is not; and shall ascend out of the bottomless pit [is about to come out of the abyss], and go into perdition" (ver. 8). What meaneth this? The Roman emperors, especially Nero, is the answer of some. My answer is deeper, broader, more practical. It is *moral error;* that which originated all that was bad in Rome, in Babylon, ay, and in the world and ages throughout. Moral error is the *beastifying* force in human nature; it makes men beasts everywhere. Its beginning and end are lamentable; it rises from the "bottomless pit," from the fathomless abysses of impure lusts, ravenous greed, burning ambition, sensual yearnings, impious irreverences, and blasphemous assumptions, etc. Its *end* is lamentable. It leads to "perdition," to ruin. The course of moral error is like the course of the meteor, which, rising from the abysses of the sulphurous cloud, flashes across the concave heavens, and then falls into darkness and forgetfulness. "Lust, when it conceiveth, bringeth forth sin; sin, when it is finished, bringeth forth death." "The wages of sin is death"—the death of everything that gives value to life; the death of an approving conscience, pure friendships, bright hopes, etc. What a glorious contrast is the course of *moral truth* to this! "The path of the just is as the shining light, that shineth more and more unto the perfect day." Light is the emblem of intelligence, purity, and blessedness. The march of the good is like the march of the sun. 1. *Glorious.* How glorious is the sun as it rises in the morning, tinging the distant hills with beauty, at noon flooding the earth with splendour, in evening fringing the clouds with rich purple, crimson, and gold! 2. *Commanding.* The sun is the ruler of the day; at his appearance the world wakens from its slumbers; the winds and waves obey him; as he moves, all nature moves. 3. *Useful.* The sun enlightens the system and maintains harmony throughout every part. It renews the earth, quickens the seeds into life, covers the landscape with beauty, ripens the harvest for man and beast. 4. *Independent.* Troops of black clouds may roll over the earth, but they touch not the sun; furious storms may shake the globe, but the sun is beyond their reach. It is always behind the darkest clouds, and looks calmly down upon the ocean in fury and the earth in a tempest. 5. *Certain.* The sun is never out of time; it is ever in its place at the right hour. In all this it is the emblem of the good.

III. ITS SUPPORTS ARE UNSTABLE. "And the beast that was, and is not, even he is the [is himself also an] eighth, and is of the seven, and goeth into perdition" (ver. 11). This "mother of harlots" (the emblem of corrupt Christianity) is here represented as sitting "on the beast with seven heads and ten horns." The seven heads are "seven mountains" (vers. 9, 10). What mountains? The seven hills on which Rome was built, is the answer of popular expositors. There are "seven kings." Who are these kings, five of whom are gone, one remaining and waiting for another—who are they? One expositor suggests that "the reference is rather to seven great monarchies, five of which, viz. Assyria, Egypt, Babylon, Persia, and Macedon, had fallen before the time of St. John. The pagan empire of the Roman Cæsars then existing would be the sixth, the papal power might be the seventh, and the last form of antichrist the eighth." I confess my utter inability to give any verbal interpretation agreeable to the dictates of common sense or the conditions of spiritual culture. The *one* idea which it suggests to me and serves to illustrate is that the *supports of moral evil are unstable.* Moral evil in our world has its supports. Many seem strong as "seven mountains," mighty as "seven kings," and more, but all are shifting and transitory. Many have been and are not, some have risen and have passed away, others in their course have come and will disappear. This has been the history of moral evil in our world. Many of the arguments that have sustained it from time to time have appeared as settled and imposing as mountains, as gorgeous and majestic as kings; but "mountains have fallen and come to nought," and even imperial bulwarks have disappeared as visions of the night. So it has been, so it is, and so it must be to the end. *Moral error has no lasting foundation.* Its superstructures are **not** houses **on** the rocks, but **on** shifting sands. Whether it appears in the form of thrones, governments, churches, colleges, markets, it stands nowhere but on volcanic hills. They may be clad in loveliest verdure and enriched with the choicest fruit, but fires lie beneath them which will rive them to pieces and engulf in ruin all that have stood and flourished above.—D. T.

Vers. 14—18.—*The great moral campaign.* "These shall make war with the Lamb, and the Lamb shall overcome them: for he is Lord of lords, and King of kings: and they that are with him are called, and chosen, and faithful," etc. To our mind these verses seem to adumbrate the greatest of all the campaigns this world has ever witnessed or ever will. In every department of sentient being there seems to be an arena of conflict, and physical wars in human life have been rife in every part of the world, from the first periods to the present hour. But the great *moral campaign* is the most universal, unremitting, and momentous. The words serve to bring to our notice two subjects in relation to this campaign—

I. THE CONTENDING FORCES. "These shall make war," etc. (ver. 14). What are these? Truth and falsehood, selfishness and benevolence, right and wrong,—these are the battling powers. "We wrestle not against flesh and blood, but against principalities, against powers, against the rulers of the darkness of this world, against spiritual wickedness in high places." Each of these contending forces has its own leader or general. 1. *The one is represented as a "beast."* The beast is the emblem of the mighty aggregate of wrong in all its elements and operations; wrong in theories and in institutions; wrong in sentiments, ideas, and habits; wrong as imposing as seven mountains, as majestic as kings and empires; wrong sitting as empress over all "nations, and peoples, and tongues." Wrong is the greatest thing in this world at present; it is the mighty Colossus with the "head of gold, breast and arms of silver, his thighs of brass, his legs of iron, his feet part of iron and part of clay."[1] 2. *The other is represented as a "Lamb."* "These shall make war with [shall war against] the Lamb" (ver. 14). The Lamb is the emblem of innocence, mildness, and purity. In Daniel's vision *wrong* was a colossal figure, and *right* a little stone. Here wrong is a terrible "beast," and right a tender "Lamb." Here are the two great generals in this mighty campaign.

II. THE MARVELLOUS CONQUEST. Observe: 1. *The Conqueror.* "The Lamb shall overcome them" (ver. 14). The Lamb, not the beast, is the Conqueror. Power is not to be estimated by size or form. The little stone shivered the image; the Lamb strikes the beast into the dust. The Lamb, though not a bellicose existence, is: (1) Invested with the highest authority. "He is Lord of lords, and King of kings" (ver. 14). The greatest sovereignty that man wields over his fellows is lamb-like rather than leonine. It is not that of physical force and gorgeous form, but of lowliness and silence. (2) Followed by a noble army. "They that are with him are called, and chosen, and faithful" (ver. 14). Who are his followers? Whom does he lead into the battle? "The called, and chosen, and faithful." Soldiers in the physical battles of nations are men who have embarked in the campaign, not from disinterested love of their country or admiration for their generals, but from motives sordid and sinister; they have *sold themselves to the execrable work.* Not so with the armies under the command of the Lamb, who is "Lord of lords, and King of kings." They are "called, and chosen, and faithful." Love to him and his grand cause fills and fires their souls. 2. *The conquered.* "These shall hate the whore," etc. (vers. 16—18). (1) The conquered turn with indignation on themselves. The "beast" with the "ten horns," all his mighty armies, "hate the whore," the harlot whom they fondled and adored, strip her of her grandeur, devour her, and "burn her with fire" (ver. 16). Thus it has ever been. Those whom Christ conquers in his love and truth turn in devouring indignation against their old comrades. Thus Paul turned against the Hebrews, in whom at one time he gloried as a Hebrew of the Hebrews. (2) This wonderful change in them is the result of the spiritual influences of God. "He hath [did] put in their hearts to fulfil his will [to do his mind], and to agree [to come to one mind]" (ver. 17). The moral conquest of wrong is ever ascribable to him who is the Fountain of truth and right. "Now thanks be unto God, which always causeth us to triumph," etc.—D. T.

[1] On Daniel's vision, see *Homilist* vol. x. p. 277.

EXPOSITION

CHAPTER XVIII.

Ver. 1.—And after these things I saw another angel come down from heaven; after [omitting "and"] . . . coming down, etc. The usual form of introduction to a new vision (cf. ch. iv. 1; vii. 1, etc.). The "mystery" of the beast and the harlot having been declared, the angel now describes the doom in store for them. The angel is from heaven, as carrying the news of the judgment which is sent from heaven (cf. ch. x. 1; xix. 6, 15, 17; xv. 1, etc.). Having great power; and the earth was lightened with his glory. The great "authority" refers to the judgment which follows, which, however, is not acted out before the seer, but only described. The last clause records the visible manifestion of the great power (cf. the description in Ezek. xliii. 2).

Ver. 2.—And he cried mightily with a strong voice, saying; and he cried with a strong voice, saying. This "strong voice" is characteristic of the heavenly utterances (cf. ch. vii. 2; xiv. 7, etc.). Babylon the great is fallen, is fallen. The event, though future, is described as past, being predetermined in the counsels of God. The words here are a reproduction of Isa. xxi. 9. And is become the habitation of devils, and the hold of every foul spirit, and a cage of every unclean and hateful bird; a habitation . . . a hold of every unclean spirit, and a hold of every unclean and hated bird. "Devils" (Greek, δαιμόνια), inferior evil spirits. The three phrases express the same idea, viz. the loathsome and hateful state to which Babylon is reduced. The language is derived from the prophets (cf. Isa. xiii. 21, 22; xxxiv. 11—15; Jer. l. 39; li. 37). A hold (Greek, φυλακή, "a strong place"); the natural and fitting stronghold of the devils, rather than a place to which they are involuntarily confined.

Ver. 3.—For all nations have drunk of the wine of the wrath of her fornication. "The wine" is omitted in A, C, but it is inserted in ℵ, B, and retained in the Revised Version. "The wrath" is omitted (cf. the expression in ch. xiv. 8 and xvii. 2). And the kings of the earth have committed fornication with her. (On the figure employed, as well as the identical language, see ch. xvii. 2.) And the merchants of the earth are waxed rich through the abundance of her delicacies. The "abundance" (Greek, δύναμις, which Vitringa renders by copia, referring to Job xxxi. 25; Ezek. xxviii. 4, LXX.). "Delicacies." (Greek, στρῆνος, occurs in the New Testament only here, and as a verb in vers. 7, 9, and (compounded) in 1

Tim. v. 11. It signifies overweening pride and insolence and wantonness, arising from superfluity of wealth and gifts. Cf. the warning to the Church of Laodicea (ch. iii. 17).

Ver. 4.—And I heard another voice from heaven, saying. Probably the voice of another angel in succession to the one mentioned in ver. 1. Another angel takes up the theme, because the message is now directly addressed to Christians. Come out of her, my people, that ye be not partakers of her sins, and that ye receive not of her plagues. The angel says, "my people," because he is representing God. These words, resembling Isa. xlviii. 20; lii. 11; Jer. l. 8; and especially Jer. li. 6 (cf. also ver. 8), 45, recall also the warning of our Lord in Matt. xxiv. 16 (cf. also Gen. xix. 22, "I cannot do anything till thou be come thither"). Since the harlot, who is identical with Babylon, is representative of the faithless part of the Church of God, these words form a direct warning to Christians. The departure which is commanded is not necessarily a literal, visible one; but the command implies a dissociation from, and condemnation of, the works of Babylon. Lot's wife literally departed from Sodom, but was overtaken with punishment, because her heart was not dissevered from the wickedness of the city.

Ver. 5.—For her sins have reached unto heaven, and God hath remembered her iniquities. That is, the accumulation of sin is so great as to reach up to the heaven. Exactly the description of the judgment of Babylon given in Jer. li. 9, "Forsake her, and let us go every one into his own country: for her judgment reacheth unto heaven, and is lifted up even to the skies." The last part of the verse is a repetition of ch. xvi. 19.

Ver. 6.—Reward her even as she rewarded you, and double unto her double according to her works: in the cup which she hath filled fill to her double. "You" is omitted in all the best manuscripts. The second "unto her," though supported by P, Syriac, Coptic, is omitted in ℵ, A, B, C, etc.: Render to her as she also rendered, and double the doubled things according to her works, etc. The description of God's judgment is still founded on the denunciations against Babylon in Jeremiah (see Jer. l. 15—29; li. 24; xvi. 18; cf. also Isa. lxi. 7; Zech. ix. 12; and the legal retribution ordered in Exod. xxii. 4—7). The cup which she hath filled is that containing "the wine of her fornication" (cf. ver. 3); she is now to receive a double measure of the cup of God's wrath (cf. ver. 3).

Ver. 7.—How much she hath glorified herself, and lived deliciously, so much torment and sorrow give her. (For "lived deliciously," see on "delicacies," ver. 3.) The words are a re-echo and expansion of those in ver. 6 (cf. Luke xvi. 25). For she saith in her heart, I sit a queen, and am no widow, and shall see no sorrow; *because she saith,* etc.; and connect with the succeeding verse. The prophetical writers still supply the imagery (cf. Isa. xlvii. 8, "I shall not sit as a widow;" see also Lam. i. 1).

Ver. 8.—Therefore shall her plagues come in one day, death, and mourning, and famine. This is the retribution for her boasting in ver. 7 (cf. Isa. xlvii. 9, "These two things shall come to thee in a moment in one day," etc.). Alford says, " *death,* for her scorn of the prospect of widowhood; *mourning,* for her inordinate revelling; *famine,* for her abundance" (cf. ver. 3). The description is not to be taken literally, but is typical of a sudden and overwhelming reverse, viz. that which will occur at the last judgment-day (cf. the words of our Lord in Matt. xxiv. 37—42). Some writers see here an allusion to the second, third, and fourth seals (see ch. vi.). And she shall be utterly burned with fire: for strong is the Lord God who judgeth her. *Who judged her; κρίνας* is found in א¹, A, B, C, P, and others. This is the fulfilment of the predicted punishment of the harlot (ch. xvii. 16). The last clause replies, as it were, to the boast in ver. 7, "I sit as a queen," etc.

Ver. 9.—And the kings of the earth, who have committed fornication and lived deliciously with her, shall bewail her, and lament for her, when they shall see the smoke of her burning; *and the kings of the earth, who committed fornication and revelled with her, shall weep and wail over her, when they see,* etc. It is noteworthy that this sentence is in the future tense; that in ver. 11 in the present; that in vers. 17, 18 in the past. (On "committed fornication," see ver. 3; ch. xiv. 4, 8; xvi. 14; xvii. 2. On "lived deliciously," see vers. 3, 7.) "Lament" is the same word used in ch. i. 7, "All kindreds of the earth shall wail because of him." Cf. the description of the fall of Tyre (Ezek. xxvi. 16). (On "smoke," see on ch. ix. 2.)

Ver. 10.—Standing afar off for the fear of her torment, saying. Unconsciously acting upon the command in ver. 4, "Come out of her, . . . that ye receive not of her plagues." Alas, alas that great city Babylon, that mighty city! for in one hour is thy judgment come; *Woe, woe, the great city* (cf. the previous declaration of *woe* in ch. viii. 13). *In one hour* (cf. ver. 8). Some writers understand the "one hour" to refer to the

space of time during which the kings rule (see ch. xvii. 12); but a comparison with ver. 8 leads to the conclusion that the meaning is "suddenly;" the contrast in a short time between the two positions of Babylon enhancing the fearfulness of the visitation.

Ver. 11.—And the merchants of the earth shall weep and mourn over her. *Weep and mourn;* the historical present (see on ver. 9). The *kings* have been mentioned; the *merchants* and next the *seamen* are referred to, showing the wide distribution of "Babylon," and forbidding the application to a single state or city. The description which follows is analogous to that in Ezek. xxvii.; Isa. xxiii. For no man buyeth their merchandise any more; *their cargo.* We are naturally reminded of the action of the second beast in forbidding to buy and sell (ch. xiii. 17). Alford here recognizes the difficulty in applying the prophecy to Rome, either pagan or papal, and adds, "I leave this difficulty unsolved. . . . The details of this mercantile lamentation far more nearly suit London than Rome." (See the interpretation given of the harlot and Babylon on ch. xvii. 1.)

Ver. 12.—The merchandise of gold, and silver, and precious stones, and of pearls, and fine linen, and purple, and silk, and scarlet. (On "precious stone" and "linen," see on ch. xv. 6.) Such was the attire of the harlot (ch. xvii. 4). Writers have endeavoured to classify in various ways the articles mentioned, in order to obtain some signification from the numbers used. Thus Hengstenberg sees four hard and then four soft articles mentioned, and he reminds us that the number four is symbolical of the world: but this does not carry him beyond ver. 12. The articles enumerated seem naturally to fall into six classes (from which we can gather no information, unless we look upon six as typifying the world, as in ch. xiii. 18). First, articles of personal adornment; second, articles used for furniture, etc.; third, objects of sensual gratification—smell, etc.; fourth, articles of food; fifth, animate possessions; sixth, souls of men. These certainly seem to be arranged in a kind of progressive order of importance. All the articles mentioned in the text above were of the highest value. *Purple* and *scarlet* (see ch. xvii. 3) were the prerogative of kings; *silk* was so scarce, that its use was forbidden in the reign of Tiberius. And all thyine wood, and all manner vessels of ivory, and all manner vessels of most precious wood, and of brass, and iron, and marble; *and every ivory vessel, and every vessel,* etc. *Thyine wood* is "that of the *Thuya articulata,* Desfont., the *Callitris quadrivalvis* of present botanists. This tree was much prized by the ancient Greeks and Romans, on account of the beauty of its wood for various ornamental purposes. By the Romans the tree was called citrus, the wood citrum. It is a native of Barbary, and grows to the height of fifteen to twenty-five feet" (Smith's 'Dictionary of the Bible'). In this passage the accusative case is used; the preceding nouns are in the genitive.

Ver. 13.—And cinnamon, and odours, and ointments, and frankincense; *and cinnamon, and amomon, and incense, and ointment, and frankincense.* These constitute the third class (see on ver. 12). *Cinnamon,* an Indian tree, was in use in the Levitical ritual (Exod. xxx. 23). It is referred to as a perfume in Prov. vii. 17. *Amomon,* which is omitted in the Textus Receptus, is found in א¹, A, C, P, etc. It is rendered in the Revised Version by "spice." Its use was similar to that of *cinnamon.* Its seeds are used under the name "cardamoms." **And wine, and oil, and fine flour, and wheat.** These form the fourth class (see on ver. 12; cf. Lev. ii. 1, 2). **And beasts, and sheep, and horses, and chariots, and slaves;** *and cattle,* etc. The word rendered "slaves" is σωμάτων, "bodies," *i.e. slaves.* At the word "horses" the nouns are again placed in the genitive (see on ver. 12). These form the fifth class (see on ver. 12). "Chariots," ῥέδη, is not the word used in ch. ix. 9. It is a word probably of Gaulish origin. **And souls of men.** The accusative again. Not in the ordinary acceptation of the word "souls," but rather "lives of men," as the Revised Version margin; that is, "living men." It is probable that the two expressions, "bodies" (*vide supra*) and "souls of men," refer to two classes of slaves.

Ver. 14.—And the fruits that thy soul lusted after are departed from thee, and all things which were dainty and goodly are departed from thee, and thou shalt find them no more at all; *all things that were dainty and splendid are perished from thee, and* [*men*] *shall find,* etc. The Textus Receptus reads ἀπῆλθεν, "are gone," as in 1; ἀπώλοντο is found in א, 7, and about twelve other cursives; ἀπώλετο is supported by A, B, C, P, and others, besides many versions and Fathers. This verse, containing a direct address to Babylon, has been thought by Vitringa and others to be misplaced; but this is unnecessary (cf. the similar circumstance in vers. 21—24).

Ver. 15.—The merchants of these things, which were made rich by her (cf. ver. 11), shall stand afar off for the fear of her torment. The future tense is now used (see on ver. 9); cf. ver. 10, where the same thing is related of the kings. Weeping and wailing (cf. ver. 9, where, however, we have κόψονται, "wail," instead of, as here, πενθοῦντες, "mourn;" cf. also ver. 11).

Ver. 16.—And saying, Alas, alas that great city! Most authorities omit "and." *Woe, woe, the great city!* (nominative case); exactly as in ver. 10. That was clothed in fine linen, and purple, and scarlet, and decked with gold, and precious stones, and pearls. *She that was clothed,* etc. *Decked;* "gilded," as in the Revised Version margin, as in ch. xvii. 4. The identity of description of the woman and Babylon is another proof of the essentially identical nature of the two (see on ch. xvii. 1; cf. also ver. 12).

Ver. 17.—For in one hour so great riches is come to nought; *because* (ὅτι) *in one hour was made desolate that so great wealth.* This is given as the reason of the "Woe, woe!" of ver. 16, and is to be connected with the preceding clauses. (On "one hour," see ver. 10, where the same reason is given as in this verse.) And every shipmaster; *pilot;* found only here and in Acts xxvii. 11. And all the company in ships; *and every one who saileth to a place.* Such is probably the correct text, though there are several small variations. The Authorized Version has little support. The Revised Version renders, *And every one that saileth anywhither.* And sailors, and as many as trade by sea; *as many as work the sea;* i.e. gain their living by means of the sea. Thus are enumerated all who are connected with the sea in any capacity (cf. Ezek. xxvii. 27). Stood afar off. Like the kings (ver. 10) and the merchants (ver. 15), and doubtless for the same reason; viz. to avoid being overwhelmed in the destruction of the city.

Ver. 18.—And cried when they saw the smoke of her burning, saying. The same description as in ver. 9 (which see). What city is like unto this great city! (cf. Ezek. xxvii. 32, "And lament over thee, saying, What city is like Tyrus, like the destroyed in the midst of the sea?").

Ver. 19.—And they cast dust on their heads. This continues the description as given in Ezek. xxvii. 30, "Shall cast up dust upon their heads." And cried, weeping and wailing, saying, Alas, alas that great city! *Weeping and mourning, saying, Woe, woe!* etc.; an exact repetition of vers. 15, 16. Wherein were made rich all that had ships in the sea by reason of her costliness. Like the merchants, the men here described regret the loss of their wealth (cf. vers. 11, 15, 16). So in Ezek. xxvii. 33, "When thy wares went forth out of the seas, thou filledst many people; thou didst enrich the kings of the earth with the multitude of thy riches and of thy merchandise." For in one hour is she made desolate. Exactly as in ver. 17; and similarly to ver. 10.

Ver. 20.—Rejoice over her, thou heaven. These words are best understood as being uttered by the writer, as in ch. xii. 12 (see on ch. xii. 10). And ye holy apostles and prophets ; *and ye saints, and ye apostles, and ye prophets,* is read in א, A, B, P, etc., and adopted by the Revisers. The Authorized Version reading is found in C, 1, 17. Not only the heavenly inhabitants are to rejoice, but also those on earth who have been persecuted by her, as mentioned in ver. 24. The time is again described which has been already referred to in former parts of the book, and especially in ch. xi. 18. Some authors have held this verse to prove that the writer of the Apocalypse was not the *Apostle* John ; either because (1) he speaks as if he were not an *apostle*, or (2) because they assume that all the *apostles* are here referred to, and that they are in heaven. There is no ground for either presumption : (1) A rhapsodical utterance of this nature cannot be interpreted literally ; (2) the word "apostles" cannot be limited to the twelve ; (3) as Düsterdieck justly observes, one might as well argue that the writer was not a *prophet*. By the " prophets " are primarily intended, perhaps, the Christian prophets (cf. Eph. iii. 5) ; but if Babylon is typical of the hostile world-power, and the harlot of the faithless, worldly portion of God's Church, as we have seen them to be, the words are applicable to the Church of God in all ages. For God hath avenged you on her ; *for God hath judged your judgment on her.* The answer to the prayer of the martyrs in ch. vi. 10. The words, "your judgment," probably mean " that judgment which is her due for her treatment of you," as in the Authorized Version. Hengstenberg gives " the doom which she pronounced upon you." Wordsworth, laying stress upon ἐξ, " out of," makes the words mean, " He has taken your cause out of her hands into his own."

Ver. 21.—And a mighty angel took up a stone like a great millstone, and cast it into the sea, saying ; *and one strong angel* (cf. the "mighty voice" in ver. 2 ; also ch. x. 1, and elsewhere). The adjective, of course, refers to the mightiness of the deed wrought (cf. Jer. li. 61—64, " Thou shalt bind a stone to it, and cast it into the midst of Euphrates ; and thou shalt say, Thus shall Babylon sink, and shall not rise," etc.). The *sea* may be typical of the nations of the earth (see ch. xiii. 1). Thus with violence shall that great city Babylon be thrown down, and shall be found no more at all ; *Thus with a mighty fall shall Babylon, the great city, be cast down,* etc. (Revised Version). Alford translates " with a rush ; " ὅρμημα is peculiar to this passage. The complete nature of this extinction is indicated by the frequency of the words, "no more at all," in vers. 21—23.

Ver. 22.—And the voice of harpers, and musicians, and of pipers, and trumpeters,

shall be heard no more at all in thee ; *harpers and minstrels and flute-players*, etc. (Revised Version). Cf. the description of the desolation of Tyre in Ezek. xxvi. 13 and Isa. xxiv. 8. And no craftsman, of whatsoever craft he be, shall be found any more in thee. "Every craft" is omitted in א, A. (On the last phrase, see on ver. 21.) And the sound of a millstone shall be heard no more at all in thee. This passage, together with the following verse, is founded on Jer. xxv. 10.

Ver. 23.—And the light of a candle shall shine no more at all in thee ; and the voice of the bridegroom and of the bride shall be heard no more at all in thee ; *of a lamp* (cf. Jer. xxv. 10, " I will take from them the voice of mirth, and the voice of gladness, the voice of the bridegroom, and the voice of the bride, the sound of the millstones, and the light of the candle "). For thy merchants were the great men of the earth ; *were the princes.* The cause of this overthrow is thus again stated. It is a repetition of the idea in vers. 7, 15, 19, " I sit a queen ; " " The merchants which were made rich by her ; " " That great city, wherein were made rich all that had ships in the sea " (cf. Isa. xxiii. 8, " Whose merchants were princes ; " also Ezek. xxvii. 20—22). For by thy sorceries were all nations deceived. The judgment is the result of the non-repentance of ch. ix. 21.

Ver. 24.—And in her was found the blood of prophets, and of saints, and of all that were slain upon the earth. At first sight it seems difficult to understand that these words are spoken not only of Babylon, but of the faithless portion of the Church, symbolized by the harlot. But we must remember (1) that he who is guilty in respect of one commandment, is guilty of the whole Law ; (2) similar words are addressed by Jeremiah to Judah (ii. 34) : " Also in thy skirts is found the blood of the souls of the poor innocents " (see on ch. xvii. 1). Auberlen remarks, " Wherever true, faithful Christians are neglected and oppressed by the rulers of the Church, from avowed or secret antipathy to God's truth ; where a false theology and science robs youth of its faith ; where a pastor neglects, and keeps at a distance, the true living Christians in his flock, on account of the *signum crucis* which they bear ; wherever we refuse or are ashamed to bear the reproach of Jesus Christ, our heavenly Master, even as he bore it, there we commit murder against the saints of God."

Here is concluded the pronouncement of the judgment of Babylon ; which may be said to answer the prayer in ch. vi. 10 ; and which forms the conclusion of the revelation commencing at ch. xvii.

HOMILETICS.

Vers. 9—24.—*Lamentations over the fall of Babylon.* In our previous study of "Babylon the great," we had occasion to remark that there were three forms under which a great Babylon might be recognized. 1. In that world-wide spirit of alienation from God which has corrupted every form of human life everywhere. 2. In any Church which, allying itself with the world-power, fornicates therewith, and puts itself on the throne instead of God. 3. Most manifestly of all in the papal Church, where every form of spiritual harlotry is seen at its very worst. Mr. Porter remarks,[1] "Zion is the place where God dwells with men; great Babylon, the place where the priest sits in the seat of God." We would rather say, "Zion is where God dwells with men; Babylon the great is where any *x*, any unclean spirit, commercial or religious, sets aside the will of God, and so comes between men and their Maker." This harlot is seated on seven mountains—which are seven kings or kingdoms—which are seven heads of the beast. The world's might and energy are "beheld concentrated under this mystic number seven—in the one symbol of the beast; and this, it is important to bear in mind, is not merely Rome, nor the Roman empire, but a general symbol of secular anti-Christian power." If we thus see *spirit* rather than *form* referred to under this varied symbolism, we shall perceive at once the reason why some parts of these chapters apply rather to a huge commercial power and other parts to a huge ecclesiastical one; and hence the difficulty which is so frankly and clearly stated by Dean Alford[2] will no longer be felt. As the writer in the 'Speaker's Commentary' remarks, "The whole passage points not to any single city, at any one single period, but to the world-city throughout all time;" and, we would add, not only to a religious but to a commercial harlotry; to any and every attraction by which the spirit of man is seduced from allegiance to God.

I. The same spirit of alienation from God, which assumes a religious form, also presents itself in a commercial aspect, all the world over. It is just as possible to put "business" between man and God as it is to put a priest between man and God. So far as we can read this Apocalyptic word, the commercial will survive the downfall of the papal Babylon. For (ch. xvii. 17) we are told that when the kings of the earth have ceased their amours with the papacy, they will "give their kingdom to the beast, until the words of God should be fulfilled;" as if there would be even a more determined manifestation of carnal world-force after the death or, at any rate, during the decline of the papacy. Certain it is that these are the two lines along which history is moving at this hour. The papacy as a whole is on the decline. The world is opening up more and more to commercial interchange; and it is just as clear that the commerce of the world, in the godlessness which so largely pervades it, is Babylon the great on the secular side, as that papal Rome is Babylon the great on its ecclesiastical side. And just as easily as we could draw out a ground-plan in outline of a papal Babylon from the details in ch. xvii., so can we draw out a ground-plan of the commercial Babylon from the details supplied in ch. xviii.[3] Ten features. 1. Seated on many waters. 2. A dominant power: "ruling over the kings of the earth." 3. Proud and boastful: "I sit as a queen." 4. Serenely secure: "I shall see no mourning." 5. Self-sufficient: "I am no widow." 6. Luxurious living in "wantonness." 7. Intoxicated, and intoxicating others, with her splendour. 8. Carrying on an international merchandise. 9. Engaged in shipping. 10. Exporting or importing in sevenfold variety: (1) precious metals; (2) costly attire; (3) materials for furniture; (4) spices; (5) food; (6) cattle, sheep, etc.; (7) bodies and souls of men. Could there be a more precise description of the commercial world-spirit, which is at work among all nations, and kindreds, and people, and tongues—a spirit of which this

---

[1] 'Expositions of the Book of Revelation,' p. 314.　　[2] 'Commentary,' *in loc.*

[3] How largely the symbolism is drawn from the prophecies which announced the fall of Babylon and of Tyre, the student will ascertain from comparing ch. xviii. 2 with Isa. xiii. 20—22, xxxiv. 10—16, and Jer. ix. 11 and li. 37; ver. 4 with Jer. li. 6, 45, 48 and Zech. ii. 10; ver. 5 with Jer. li. 9; ver. 7 with Isa. xlvii. 7; ver. 8 with Isa. xlvii. 10, 11; vers. 11—19 with Ezek. xxvi. 1—36; ver. 21 with Jer. li. 63, 64; ver. 22 with Jer. vii. 34 and xxv. 10.

England of ours in her world-wide transactions is the chief manifestation at this moment? So that, as Dean Alford ominously remarks, some parts of the description rather suit London than Rome. Commercially, indeed, we have done with any *avowed* traffic in the bodies of men. But that in the sight of God many of the accepted maxims of some men of business involve a fearful trifling with consciences and souls, is not open to question. It is well known that almost every variety of export and import named here is ours. Our shipping interests are far larger than those of any other nation on the face of the earth. Our gross tonnage through the Suez Canal alone shows this. Our merchandise touches every shore. The splendour and renown of our name and fame intoxicates many and many a merchant. Luxury, self-sufficiency, pride, godlessness,—these are to a grievous extent our bane and our poison. And who would venture to dispute the fact that, from sheer love of greed and gold, thousands on thousands will play fast and loose with truth and principle, and the right and God, and will say, "Let us break their bands asunder, and cast away their cords from us"? And the fearful fact ought to be recognized and acknowledged, that even the hatred which some entertain of the priestly yoke arises from a refusal to wear any yoke at all. "Our tongues are our own; who is Lord over us?" So men speak. This evil is certainly so huge that it is nothing less than a "Babylon the great."

II. THIS BABYLON IS DOOMED. The means and methods of Babylon's fall have been indicated in the preceding homily (*q.v.*). They are fourfold. 1. Divine overruling. 2. Human desertion. 3. Heavy judgments. 4. Retribution and desolation.

III. THE FALL OF BABYLON WILL CALL FROM MANY A BITTER LAMENTATION. There are three sources from which the lament will come. 1. *From kings*, as they see the great city which was the glory of their empire reduced and brought low. 2. From merchants, whose sources of wealth are dried up, so that "no one buyeth their merchandise any more."[1] 3. From men of the sea, who gained their living by trading from port to port, because there is no longer any principal mart with which to trade. And clearly this is such a lamentation as godless men would make. We read in ch. xvi. 21 that when the destruction came men blasphemed God because of the hail. In strict accordance therewith is the spirit of the wail over Babylon's fall. It is not that God has not been glorified. It is not that her busy life has been used for purposes most utterly selfish and often vile, for the lamentation over the ruin is just as selfish as their commerce itself has been (ver. 11). *Their cargoes no one buys any more!* Surely, nothing could bespeak the degradation of man when in apostasy from God, more than such a lamentation as this. It all centres in self. They have made their commerce their god. Ah! earthly souls will be earthly still, even under the ruin of all they hold most dear. Here we see sketched before us men —men made for God, to enjoy him, to love him, and to obey him—clad in sackcloth; and why? Because they have not honoured their God? Ah, no! But because *no one buys their cargo!* It is as if an orphan child should centre all his grief on a lost farthing, and think nothing of his disobedience to his lost parents. Nor can we fail to detect in this lament a note of bitterness against God. They see that the great Power they have been ignoring is working against them, and that they are bankrupt for eternity Terrible beyond expression must it be for a man who has lived for earth, to find the world for which he lived departing for ever. How bare and forlorn and desolate must he feel! The harpers, and singers, and pipers, and trumpeters are for ever still; the sound of hammer and anvil is heard no more; the whirl of the mill has ceased; the sheen of the silver, the glitter of the gold, the light of the lamp, have vanished away; the voice of gladness, and of the bridegroom and the bride, are hushed; and the man is left alone. His gods are gone, and he is confronted with the God whom he neglected, to find—alas! too late—that his whole life has been a mistake. He has loved and served the creature more than the Creator, and now, instead of finding his joy in God when every earthly joy is gone, his only look-out is a vista of bankruptcy and of irreparable woe. All his dignity has disappeared, and is reduced to a moan and groan *that no one buys his cargo!*

IV. THIS PICTURE OF GODLESS AND HOPELESS LAMENTATION OUGHT NOT TO BE

[1] See a valuable note on the "Lament of the Merchants" in Bishop Carpenter's 'Commentary.'

STUDIED IN VAIN. 1. We should first of all learn that *the hold of God on all that we have and are is absolute.* We are but tenants-at-will. The proud and conceited talk as if the world were ours—" My river is my own, and I have made it for myself "— is an abomination to the Lord. God has never waived his rights in entrusting to us his loans. Let merchants, stockbrokers, bankers, bondholders, traders, learn this lesson. In our great city it is too often forgotten. At any moment God may bring all our possessions to nought; and he will do that at his own time, not waiting for ours. 2. It may well yield us matter for lamentation that *the use of so much earthly capital is a perverted one.* Many of God's gifts are put in alliance with overreaching, corruption, and fraud. In themselves they are not to be despised. " Every creature of God is good," etc. But when things of wealth and beauty become the instruments of apostasy, it is sad indeed. And the more so when we add to all this the thought that Divine gifts misused do, in so being misused, deceive and ruin the souls of men, and in proportion to the joy which their right and proper use would have brought is the treasured-up woe which their abuse will certainly ensure. 3. Let us learn to look at whatever is beautiful and costly and artistic as precious in the truest sense, only as it is allied to or in harmony with righteousness. Beauty and wealth are only of genuine value when employed in accordance with God's will and Word. 4. Let us take care that, so far as we are concerned, we have no share in this heart-apostasy of Babylon the great, even in the commercial world. The voice cries now, " Come out of her, my people" (cf. Isa. xlviii. 20; lii. 11; Jer. l. 8; li. 6, 45; 2 Cor. vi. 14—17). If we would not share her plagues, we must not share her sins. "Come ye out from," etc. For in this London of ours Babylon the great and the New Jerusalem are side by side. There are those who are in Babylon the great, the slaves of godless gain or godless pleasure. There are those who belong to the new and eternal city, the New Jerusalem, who grave on the bells of the horses, " Holiness to the Lord," and whose daily toil is being sanctified for him. And oh! it is worth a struggle to be living even now in that city of God, into which no foe can enter and which no convulsion can for a moment disturb. It may cost something to renounce all fellowship with Babylon. But it is worth infinitely more than it costs. Yea, to be *right* is so transcendently great, that the question of cost should scarce be deemed worth a thought. Better die with Christ than reign with Cæsar. Let us dare to be singular. By the gewgaws of this Babylonian harlotry many are attracted. So be it not with us. A nobler aim be ours, even to " seek the things which are above, where Christ sitteth on the right hand of God;" and when our communion with this earth is sundered, we shall find our home in the New Jerusalem. Hence we may " go forth of Babylon . . . with a voice of singing," and may " utter it even to the ends of the earth. . . . The Lord hath redeemed his servant Jacob."

HOMILIES BY VARIOUS AUTHORS.

Vers. 1—24.—*The overthrow of wickedness.* This, in symbolic form, is the real subject of this chapter. Wickedness shall be utterly and for ever destroyed.

I. A GLORIOUS ANGEL PROCLAIMS THIS. (Cf. ver. 1 as to this angel.) Then such overthrow must be: 1. *Righteous.* 2. *Blessed.* 3. *Divine.* Had it been possible for men to affect this, it would have been done long since.

II. GOD'S PEOPLE RECEIVE COMMAND. 1. *To separate themselves from sin.* From which we learn: (1) That God's people may have to dwell in the midst of sin. (2) That though where wickedness is, they are not to be partakers of it. (3) That they shall one day be effectually separated from it. 2. *To avenge themselves upon it.* Resentment and wrath are passions given us by God. Our peril and propensity is lest we turn them in a wrong direction. We do so when we use them for private revenge. This is what our Lord forbids. But against the forces of sin they may, they should, be used. This the command here.

III. THE FRIENDS OF WICKEDNESS LAMENT. 1. *Wickedness has friends.* Those who find delight in it, who "live deliciously " in it (ver. 9). Those who make profit out of it. The merchants, etc. (ver. 11). And: 2. *Their lament is loud and long.* They weep, mourn, wail; say, " Alas, alas!" cast dust on their heads, etc. (vers. 11, 15.

16, 19). 3. *But the lament is utterly selfish.* They mourn not because of the wickedness; that does not trouble them. Nor even for Babylon's sufferings. But because the hope of their gain is gone (ver. 19). 4. *And they do not go to her help* (ver. 15). They stand afar off for the fear of her torment. Look well at these friends, for such are they that sin and sinners call friends. "There is a Friend that sticketh closer than a brother," but such Babylon never gets.

IV. ALL HEAVEN, ANGELS AND SAINTS, REJOICE. When we read over the subject of their joy, we find that: 1. *It is not because in this Babylon there was nothing innocent or good.* There was much. Vers. 22, 23 tell of what was lawful and right in any community. In the worst of men there is good. None are utterly bad. But: 2. *That the main characteristic of her life was evil.* And, therefore, her destruction was a matter of joy. She deceived all nations. She slew God's saints. Thus: 3. *Justice was done.* And: 4. *It was completely done.* See the symbol of the angel with the millstone (ver. 21). Nothing like this has ever been accomplished yet, but this prophecy is a sure promise that it will be. "Who shall live when the Lord doeth this?" Amongst whom shall we be found? Let us now "come out of her, that we be not," etc. (ver. 4).—S. C.

Ver. 4.—*The fall of Babylon.* "Come out of her, my people." This is not the sole similar warning which Scripture contains. Cf. the warning to Lot to come out of Sodom; the warning to Israel to come away from the tents of Korah, Dathan, etc.; the warning to God's people (Jer. li. 45) to come away from Babylon, the old literal Babylon: "My people, go ye out of her, and deliver ye every man his soul." And now we have the same warning concerning the Babylon told of in this chapter. Inquire, therefore—

I. WHAT CITY OR COMMUNITY IS MEANT? And we reply: 1. *Not ancient Babylon.* For we have here not history, but prophecy. Nor did the ancient Babylon answer in all respects to the description here given. It was never a mercantile city. 2. *Nor, exclusively, the Rome of St. John's day.* For, again, the resemblance is lacking in many important particulars, though unquestionably present in others. And although there was a destruction of Rome, more than one such, during the awful days of Nero and the wild anarchy of his immediate successors—and, no doubt, these facts formed the groundwork of the description here given—still, what happened then does by no means fill up the language used here. And the large space given to the mercantile and maritime greatness of this city has never been applicable to Rome. 3. *Nor the Rome destroyed by the Goths.* When she fell she had long ceased to be "drunk with the blood of God's saints." Nor was she then the great city of the world. Constantinople had taken that place. 4. *Nor papal Rome.* She oftentimes in her history presents a hideous resemblance to the city told of here. This feature and that are frightfully like. But nothing but the blindest bigotry can assert that St. John would have drawn the picture he has if papal Rome had been in his mind. 5. *Nor is it London;* though, if there be any city in the world that answers to the Babylon of St. John, London is, far and away, that city. For where, more than in London, will you find a city that doth more glorify itself (ver. 7); or spends more in wanton luxury; or that is more self-confident, thinking, if not saying, "I am a queen, and am no widow, and shall see no sorrow"? Or where is there a city that has wider connections with the whole world, so that all the merchants of the earth look to her; for she it is who more than any other is the buyer of their goods? And what city has a vaster multitude of bodies and souls (ver. 13) given up and enslaved to minister to her luxury, her lust, her wealth? Is she not "clothed in fine linen, and purple, and scarlet, and decked with gold, and precious stones, and pearls," because she is possessed of " so great riches"? And see the forest of masts in her river and docks; and the throng of shipmasters and sailors and them that trade by sea. And if "the beast" meant, as it did, the ungodly world-spirit, embodied now here, now there, but which always and everywhere, though in varied form, "makes war with the Lamb," and is essentially antichristian,—if such beast sustained the Babylon of this chapter, what else sustains the metropolis of our land? But though all this may well cause much searching of heart to ourselves, we do not for a moment think that Babylon is London. No: that Babylon is: 6. *Every nation, city, community, or person who shall become in God's sight what Babylon was.* Be like Babylon, and you are Babylon. Her doom is yours, and her final fate yours also. For the law of God is, " Wheresoever the carcase is, there will be the vultures," etc. (Matt. xxiv. 28). For this is—

II. THE LAW THAT THEY EXEMPLIFY. Our Lord had been telling of Divine judgments coming, and his disciples had wanted to know to whom he referred, and when. and where. And our Lord's answer is the declaration of this law. And, like so many of our Lord's sayings, it is vividly symbolic in form. It appeals to the imagination and uses it that the mind may be more impressed. Often had his hearers seen such incident as that told of in this law. " For in the lands of the East, when a wild beast falls in the desert, or a beast of burden on the highway, there is for a time no stir in the heavens. But far above human ken the vulture is floating, poised on his wings and looking downward. His eye soon detects the motionless thing, for he hunts by an eyesight unequalled in power among all living things, and like a stone he drops through miles of air. Others floating in the same upper region see their brother's descent, and know its meaning. One dark speck after another grows swiftly upon the horizon, and in a few moments fifty vultures are around the carrion. Now, this illustrates, and with astonishing point and sharpness, the suddenness, the usefulness, and the necessity, of judgment. There is no delay if utter corruption has set in. Inevitable, swift, unerring, as the vultures' descent on the carcase, is the judgment-coming of the Son of man to corrupt communities and to corrupt men " (S. Brooke). Given the body, the bird will not be far off. The city told of here was such a carcase, and the vulture-swoop is what the chapter describes. *And there have been, are, and will be, many fulfilments of this law.* Sodom and Gomorrah; the Canaanites; the first fall of Jerusalem; Babylon; Persia; Jerusalem's second and last fall; Rome by the Goths; papal Rome at the Reformation; the French Revolution; etc.;—all these and many others reveal the working of the same law. But no doubt Rome was most of all in St. John's mind, and of her fall his thoughts were full.

> " Rome shall perish—write that word
> In the blood that she hath spilt;
> Perish, hopeless and abhorred,
> Deep in ruin as in guilt."

And it is as true of individuals as of communities. See that blear-eyed, ragged, shivering, and every way disreputable-looking wretch, that is reeling out of the ginshop, and as he staggers along poisoning the air with his foul breath and yet fouler words— what a wreck the man is! Health gone and character; home, and friends, and livelihood, and all that made life worth having; and life itself going likewise. The vultures of judgment have plucked him well-nigh bare, and they are at their deadly work still. Go into the wards of hospitals, the cells of prisons, the asylums for lunatics, in convict-yards, or mounting the steps of the scaffold on which they are to die,—in all such places you may see wretched men and women in whom is fulfilled the law, of the operation of which this chapter tells. Note, therefore—

III. THE NATURE AND NECESSITY OF THE " COMING OUT " HERE COMMANDED. And: 1. *As to the first of these:* how may we come out, etc.? (1) Sometimes we must literally do this. As Lot from Sodom; as the Christians from Jerusalem; as Paul did from the synagogues. But very often we cannot leave where we are. Then we must obey this word by seeing to it (2) " that we be not partakers of her sins." Come out professedly and avowedly in confession of Christ. Come out from the company, the pleasures, the habits, of the ungodly place in which your lot may be cast. And especially (3) come out unto Christ (cf. Heb. xiii. 13, " Let us go forth therefore *unto him* "). Consecration to him will be a real obedience to this word. 2. *And this is needful.* How little we fear the judgments of God on sin! We do not see the vultures, and therefore think the carcase will be let alone. If it be some present, seen, peril that threatens the lives of men, how eager then are we to warn and save! A short while ago the Marjelen See, that is formed by the melting of one part of the great Aletsch Glacier, suddenly burst through its icy barriers. The whole volume of waters began pouring down beneath the glacier, along the rapid descent of its sloping floor, towards the edge of the gorge over which they would plunge in leap after leap down to the Rhone valley far beneath. A village lies at the foot of the gorge where the glacier stream pours itself into the Rhone. That village was now in awful peril. The people who lived near the See telegraphed instantly—for the hotel hard by had a telegraph station—to the village the tidings of what had occurred, that they might, if possible, escape. Happily the Rhone was very low and shallow at the time, and so the immense rush of waters that suddenly poured in was able to get away without much damage accruing to the people on its banks. *That* peril was believed in, and endeavour made to save those exposed to it. But the judgment of God against sinful nations and people—who realizes or fully believes that? Who *flees* from the wrath to come? And yet, if there be one atom of truth in God's Word, and in all history, that wrath will come on every sinful soul. God give us to really believe this!—S. C.

Ver. 21.—"*No more.*" Six times over does this word recur, and always concerning the same fact. That fact, therefore, must be notable, and is intended to be noticed by us. Of what, then, is it thus repeatedly said, it is "no more"? A glance at this chapter shows that "the great city Babylon" is spoken of, and that accursed city meant heathen Rome to the mind of St. John. But full well we know that even when Rome pagan gave way to Rome papal, evil and sin, bloody persecution and cruel wrong, did not disappear. Therefore we take Babylon to mean far more than any Rome, or any city that is or has been on the face of the earth; we take it as telling of *the whole kingdom of evil*—that mighty empire, that hoary sinner against God and man. Though St. John meant Rome, his words tell of far more than Rome. And we, coming so far further down in the world's history, are able and glad to read in them this fuller meaning which we believe to have been in the Divine mind, though not in that of his servant. Let Babylon stand, then, for the city where Satan's seat is—the whole kingdom and dominion of the devil, and let us listen to the six times repeated stroke of the word "no more," which in our text and two following verses may be heard. The city is to be "no more," and her music "no more," and her trade "no more," and her food-supplies "no more," and her lamp-lit feasts "no more," and her marriage festivals "no more." Thus, by the utter desolation of a great city, such as that which came on Babylon, is set forth the fact of the final and complete overthrow of that kingdom of evil of which Babylon was the ancient type, and Rome, in St. John's day, the embodiment. Such utter overthrow is—

I. SIGNIFIED BY SYMBOL. See the mighty angel lifting aloft the huge and ponderous millstone and then hurling it, with all his force, into the depths of the sea. There, buried out of sight, sunk down into the bed of ocean, it shall never more be seen. Such is the symbol. One that seemed little likely of fulfilment when it was given, and even now, oftentimes, seems as if it never would be fulfilled.

II. VERIFIED BY FACT. Babylon had fallen, in spite of all its greatness, and heathen Rome was hastening to her fall. And other such Babylons have risen, and wrought their evil, and rioted in their sin, and, like her, have fallen. Therefore we may be assured that the last and greatest of them all will also one day be "no more."

III. LONGED FOR BY THE OPPRESSED. "How long, O Lord, how long, dost thou not avenge?"—such has been the cry of the oppressed for weary ages. "Thy kingdom come," is the cry we put up day by day.

IV. PROMISED IN THE GOSPEL. "The Spirit of the Lord is upon me," said Jesus, "because he hath anointed me to preach glad tidings to the poor," etc. (Luke iv.). And this is the gospel, that the kingdom of evil shall be "no more." It is present with us now, we know, in all its forms. But it is not always so to be. Ere the glad tidings were proclaimed, good men, sore perplexed and troubled, pondered much and sadly over the mystery of evil. They could not understand how God could let it be. Nor do we fully understand even now. But this much we know, that it is but for a time. And faith is able to grasp the promise of the gospel, and to "rest in the Lord, and wait patiently for him."

V. REJOICED IN BY SAINTS. The joy of all heaven because of this overthrow of evil is told of in the next chapter. Their Alleluias ascend unceasingly, for that God hath judged the accursed city and established his own reign.

VI. CREDIBLE TO REASON. The evidence for the Divine existence and the Divine character—as holy, just, wise, and good—becomes more convincing the more it is considered, notwithstanding the existence of a kingdom of evil. Doubtless that kingdom is a great stumbling-block to both reason and faith, but it is not an insurmountable one. But were it not for the truth we are considering now, that all this accursed rule of evil shall one day be "no more," we do not see how faith in God could live. For that faith necessitates as its corollary that evil should terminate and be "no more." Reason reiterates her conviction that if God be, evil must one day be "no more."

VII. Accomplished by Christ. "For this purpose the Son of God was manifested." "I saw," he says, "Satan as lightning fall from heaven." "The prince of this world is judged." There was that, however imperfectly we may understand it, in the life, death, and resurrection of our Lord Jesus Christ, which effected the virtual overthrow of evil. Satan received his death-stroke ; he is no longer what he was. We know and confess that in some aspects of life it seems very hard to believe this. But when we consider what the power of our blessed Lord and Master has already done; how the might of his meekness, the love of his sacrifice, the attraction of his cross, have already subdued so many hearts and triumphed over so many foes,—then faith revives, and we can believe that, as he said, " the prince of this world *is* judged." Lord, we believe ; but help our unbelief.—S. C.

Vers. 1—8.—*The fall of corrupt society.* " And after these things I saw another angel come down from heaven," etc. Regarding, as I do, this book as a record of *visions* which its author had in Patmos, at a period when the most stupendous events were occurring around him, the only practical use that can be made of them is *to illustrate and impress those moral principles that are true to man as man, the world over and the ages through.* It appears absurd and useless, and an utter waste of labour, to attempt (which most expositors have done and are doing) an interpretation of a dream containing, as it generally does, objects that are grotesque, unnatural, and monstrous. Albeit it is most rational and practically valuable to employ it to set forth and impress the *eternal realities of the spirit-world.* Our subject is the *final fall of corrupt society.* "Babylon is fallen, is fallen " (ver. 2). Babylon here represents *society.* It is a city. It is not the private residence of an individual, isolated from all others, but congeries of houses for the dwelling of a community. Because man is a gregarious animal and sympathetic, he lives, for the most part, in communities. A community may be as small as a family, as vast as a city, or as wide as an empire. It may be barbaric or civilized, civil or religious, or a combination of both. But Babylon not only represents society, but *corrupt* society. The moral character of the population was an outrage on all the laws of true morality and genuine religion. Human society was not only corrupt in Babylon, but it is corrupt in all its sections throughout the world. What an old Hebrew writer says of the Jewish nation, is true, more or less, of all society " From the sole of the foot to the crown of the head there is no soundness, ... but wounds and bruises, and putrefying sores." *Morally,* all society is Babylonianized. In this Babylon—this corrupt society even as it exists here in Christendom—we have all the evils and the vices that were found in pagan Rome. The distinction between pagan Rome and papal Rome is purely fictitious. What cardinal sins find you in the former that were not embodied in the history of the latter? "Is fallen, is fallen : " what in the history of Divine truth will be in fact and form millions of ages hence *is* now in spirit and reality. Hence "Babylon *is* fallen." The following remarks are suggested concerning the fall of Babylon, this fall of corrupt society.

I. It is divinely proclaimed. Who proclaims it? A Divine angel, a minister from the Eternal. "After these things I saw another angel come [coming] down from [out of] heaven, having great power [authority]; and the earth was lightened with his glory" (ver. 1). " After these things." After the stupendous events recorded in former visions, this mighty angel, clad with authority and corruscating in splendour, comes down from the eternal heavens of reality, and proclaims with a loud voice this fall of moral Babylon. The ultimate fall of all that is *morally corrupt* in human communities is not a matter of speculation and mere probability ; it is absolutely *inevitable.* Wrong cannot stand for ever; though, like the colossal image in Daniel, it may be constructed of gold, and silver, and brass, and iron, and be associated with the splendours of empire, yet its "feet are of clay," and it must sooner or later tumble to pieces. Head of gold, but feet of clay ! It is not a fixed star in the immeasurable expanse of space, but a mere meteor, brilliant and swift for a moment, then black and still for ever. As there is a law of disintegration in the material universe, that so separates the hugest mountains that they ultimately disappear, so there is in the moral a law of retribution, which will ultimately break into pieces the world of corrupt society. Babylon must fall.

II. IT IS MANIFESTLY DESERVED. The description here given reveals such a condition of moral foulness and wickedness as not only to merit but to demand this doom. " Is become the [a] habitation of devils, and the [a] hold of every foul [unclean] spirit, and a cage [a hold] of every unclean and hateful bird " (ver. 2). As in the ruins of old cities, the cormorant, the screech-owl, the vulture, and other hideous creatures are found, so in this *moral* Babylon are found the most horrible and detestable of all existences. The utter extermination, or rather extinction, of such objects is urgently required. But this is not all. Mark its appalling wickedness. " For all nations have drunk of the wine of the wrath of her fornication [For by the wine of the wrath of her fornication all the nations are fallen], and the kings of the earth have committed fornication with her, and the merchants of the earth are waxed rich through [by] the abundance [power] of her delicacies [wantonness] " (ver. 3). " Reference here is not," says an expositor, " made to earthly but to spiritual wares—indulgences, idolatries, superstitions, and worldly compromises." Does not such a corrupt society, such a moral Babylon, justly deserve this miserable ending ? "Sin, when it is finished, bringeth forth death." The seeds of ruin lie in every evil principle, and are found in the moral heart of men. These seeds must break into fruits of rankling poison sooner or later.

III. IT IS A REASON FOR QUITTING IT. " And I heard another voice from heaven, saying, Come out of her, my people [Come forth, my people, out of her], that ye be not partakers [have no fellowship] of [with] her sins, and that ye receive not of her plagues " (ver. 4). As the house is falling, let the tenants quit and save their lives; the city is about breaking into flames, therefore escape to the mountains. This voice from heaven suggests : 1. *The possibility of good men living in this corrupt society—* this moral Babylon. " Come out of her, my people." Good men are found living and working in the midst of a " wicked and perverse generation." There were a few men in corrupt Sardis who " walked with God." The depravities of our contemporaries and neighbours are no justification for our defects. They should rather warn us against the wrong, and stimulate us to the right. 2. *That good men, unless they quit this corrupt society, will be involved in its guilt and fate.* " That ye be not partakers of her sins." The exodus here demanded is not, of course, bodily, but spiritual; not from places, but from principles; not from persons, but from characters; from the corrupt spirit of places and persons. " Come out from among them, and be ye separate, saith the Lord, and touch not the unclean thing; and I will receive you." Unless you do so you will be tainted with their impurity and afflicted with their plagues.

IV. IT IS A DEVELOPMENT OF RETRIBUTION. " For her sins have reached unto heaven, and God hath remembered her iniquities. Reward her [render unto her] even as she rewarded you [rendered], and double unto her double [the double] according to her works " (vers. 5, 6). " The idea is of a great heap firmly fastened, and towering, like another Babel, as far as heaven (comp. 2 Chron. xxviii. 9 ; Ezra ix. 6). The idea is more than that of the cry of sin reaching heaven, as in the case of Sodom (Gen. xviii. 20, 21); the sins themselves, many and imperial, have touched the face of heaven. God hath remembered her. Sometimes the oppressed have thought that God hath forgotten the voice of the enemy; but the long-suffering of the Lord is salvation. The same voice which bids the people of God come forth summons the agents of vengeance. Many Old Testament parallels will suggest themselves (Jer. li. 18; Ps. lxxix. 12 ; cxxxvii. 8; Isa. xl. 2). The ' double' must not be taken to mean ' double her sins.' Her sins are themselves called double, and her judgment is according to her sins. She is double-stained in wickedness, and the law of retribution fiercely works in her. The cup of her luxuriousness becomes the cup of vengeance. The flowery path has led to the broad gate and the great fire " (Bishop of Ripon). The ruin comes, then, not as a casual event, nor as a positive infliction, but as the result of the *eternal law of retribution :* a law silent in its operations, resistless in its force, and inevitable in its issues. " Be not deceived ; God is not mocked : for whatsoever a man soweth, that shall he also reap." This law of moral causation links sin to misery as indissolubly as attraction links planets to the sun. "As you stood some stormy day upon a sea-cliff, and marked the giant billow rise from the deep to rush on with foaming crest, and throw itself thundering on the trembling shore, did you ever fancy that you could stay its course, and hurl it back to the depths of ocean? Did you ever stand beneath the leaden, lowering cloud, and mark the lightning's leap as it shot and flashed, dazzling athwart the gloom, and think that you could grasp the bolt, and change its path? Still more foolish and vain his thought, who fancies that he can arrest or turn aside the purpose of God, saying, 'What is the Almighty, that we should serve him?' 'Let us break his bands asunder, and cast away his cords from us.' Break his bands asunder! How he that sitteth in the heavens shall laugh!"

V. IT INVOLVES AN OVERWHELMING CATASTROPHE. "Therefore shall her plagues come in one day [in one day shall her plagues], death, and mourning, and famine; and she shall be utterly burned with fire: for strong is the Lord God who judgeth [which judged] her" (ver 8). "She thought herself strong," says a modern expositor. "She forgot the strength of the Almighty. Her plagues were fourfold, as though from every quarter her trouble came. Death, for her scorn of the prospect of widowhood; mourning, for her inordinate revelling; famine, for her abundance; and fire, the punishment of her fornication." When full judgment comes upon a corrupt community, the horrors involved not only transcend description, but even imagination. What is lost? Friendship gives way to fiendish battlings; peace gives way to furious storms; hope gives way to black despair and terrible apprehensions; liberty gives way to a crushing thraldom, in which every faculty of the soul is bound in chains of darkness. All the lights of the soul are quenched, and the whole heavens are mantled in a starless midnight.

CONCLUSION. Mark well, brother, and study deeply the final fall of corrupt society. Every corrupt soul is in truth a moral Babylon that "is fallen, is fallen." "Fallen" from whither? From some *local* height? From some Himalayan apex to a fathomless dungeon, or from some *worldly* pinnacle? From a mansion to a cot, from a princeling to a pauper? Such falls are not vital. Change of *place* does not necessarily affect the highest *interests of the soul.* "The mind is its own place." Nor change of *circumstances.* In truth, a descension from the highest affluence to the lowest indigence may conduce to its true elevation. The fall is from *virtue* to *vice*, from *truth* to *error*, from *liberty* to *thraldom*, from *sunshine* to *midnight*, from the *Divine* to the *devilish.* What more terrible sentence can be pronounced on a soul than "It is fallen, it is fallen"? Will it continue to fall for ever? Is there no hand to arrest the descent, and to lift it to the heights from whence it has fallen? "The hand of mercy is not shortened, that it cannot save." On the pages of ecclesiastical history, of sacred biography, and of our own memory, we read of souls that have fallen low, but have been raised again. They have been able to appropriate the language of an old Hebrew writer, and say, "He brought me up also out of an horrible pit, out of the miry clay, and set my feet upon a rock, and established my goings."

> "Thy mercy, Lord, is like the morning sun,
>   Whose beams undo what sable night hath done;
> Or, like a stream, the current of whose course,
>   Restrained awhile, runs with a swifter force.
> Oh! let me glow beneath those sacred beams,
>   And bathe me in those silver streams.
> To thee alone my sorrows shall appeal—
>   Hath earth a wound too hard for Heaven to heal?
>   (Quarles.)

                                                                D. T.

Ver. 7.—*The rule of retribution.* "How much . . . so much," etc. The subject here suggested is *man's future retribution ruled by his present condition.* "How much she hath glorified herself, and lived deliciously, *so* much . . . sorrow give her." This, stripped of all historical and metaphorical allusions, means the present circumstances of the sinner shall rule his future suffering. I offer three remarks on this subject.

I. THIS RULE COMMENDS ITSELF TO OUR SENSE OF JUSTICE. That those of the wicked who in this world live in affluence, and have more than heart can wish, possess abundant opportunities for intellectual and moral improvement and means of doing good, should in future retribution fare alike with those who have none of these blessings or advantages, would be an outrage on our sense of right. Justice requires a balancing of human affairs—a kind of compensation for existing discrepancies, and this mankind will have in the great retributive future.

II. THIS RULE ANSWERS TO BIBLICAL TEACHING. Throughout the whole Scripture record it is taught that sinners, after they have passed through their probationary period, will be dealt with according to the mercies they have abused, the opportunities they have neglected, and the advantages they have wasted. "He that knoweth his master's will, and doeth it not," etc.; "Son, remember thou in thy lifetime didst receive," etc.

III. THIS RULE AGREES WITH UNIVERSAL EXPERIENCE. *Conscious contrast* between a propitious past and a distressing present is, and must ever be, an element in mental suffering. There are two paupers equal, 1 will suppose, in age, capacity, sensibility, and character. The hovels they live in and the means of their sustenance are also equal; but the one is intensely wretched, and the other is comparatively happy. Why this? The wretched man has come down into that hovel from the home of opulence and luxury, and the other has never had a better home. Thus the contrast gives a misery to the one which the other cannot experience. So it must be in the future; the sinner who goes into retribution from mansions, colleges, and churches will, by the law of contrast, find a more terrible hell than the poor creature who has fallen into it from ignorance and pauperism. Far more terrible, methinks, will be the hell of the aristocracy than the hell of the struggling and starving millions. " How much she hath glorified herself, and lived deliciously, *so* much torment and sorrow give her." Worldly advantages are not always transitory, but often permanently injurious. "Though the sinner's excellency mount up to the heavens, and his head reach unto the clouds, yet he shall perish for ever."—D. T.

Vers. 9—24.—*The fall of the corrupt in human life.* "And the kings of the earth, who have committed fornication and lived deliciously with her," etc. All along through my remarks on the Apocalyptic visions of this book I have not only discarded any attempt at a *literal* interpretation, but have affirmed that, as a rule, such interpretations of dreams or visions can seldom, if ever, from the nature of the case, be correct; and more especially so with the visions and dreams recorded in this book. The objects seen, the voices heard, the acts performed, are so incongruous with the course of nature and the concurrent experience of mankind, that the attempt at a literal exposition would seem to be the height of absurdity. Anyhow, though it has been tried a thousand times, and is still being tried, all the results are utterly unsatisfactory to the unprejudiced and unsophisticated intellect and conscience of mankind. Common sense repudiates all such interpretations. Using, however, such visions and dreams as the great redeeming Teacher of mankind used the blooming lily, the fruitful vine, the toiling fishermen, the flowing river, the booming sea, and the beaming heavens—viz. to suggest and illustrate the eternal realities of the supersensuous realm—is to use them not only legitimately, but usefully in the highest degree. Still proceeding on this principle, we may perhaps get out of the strange scenes here recorded some things that may quicken our intellect, encourage our conscience, and inspire our hope The subject here is—*The fall of the corrupt in human life.* The corrupt thing is here symbolized by Babylon. "Babylon is fallen." If Babylon here be understood to mean the old city of whose infamous history we have all read, the language used is historically true, for it had fallen to ruins five hundred years before this, and had become "the habitation of devils, and every foul thing." If, as some say, it means pagan Rome, it is not true, for that is as strong and numerically influential—if not more so —now as it ever has been. Take Babylon as standing for *wrong* everywhere throughout society, and the expression is not true. Moral Babylon in the aggregate still lives and works on this planet. Albeit, regarding it as an event perpetually occurring, it is true enough. Wrong, including all that is morally evil in human thought, feeling, and action, is constantly falling. It has been falling from Adam to Christ, and from Christ to this hour. Such stupendous events were occurring in connection with it in the days of John, that he might well have dreamt that he heard some angel say,

"Babylon is fallen." The false and the wrong everywhere are constantly falling, and must continue to do so. Do not, then, understand that the whole of corrupt society on this earth will in some distant day in the mighty aggregate be at once clearly swept from the face of the earth. There is no reason to believe this. The idea is contrary to the analogy of nature, where all things move gradually. Wrong has a very slow death. If we use the word "falling" for "is fallen," it will give us a universal truth—viz. that *moral* Babylon, the corrupt in society, is falling. I stand upon the brow of some firm and lofty mountain, and I say, "This mountain is falling;" and I say truly, for there is not a moment in its existence when it is not crumbling into the atoms that made it up, for the great physical law of disintegration will never cease operating upon it, until it shall "become a plain." "The mountains falling cometh to nought," etc. Or I stand by the trunk of some huge tree, and I say, "This tree is falling." And I speak truth, for the great law of vegetable decay is working in it, and will one day bring it down into the dust. So with the wrong thing in human life. Though it stand as a huge mountain filling the horizon of humanity, it will, by the eternal law of moral disintegration, be one day brought down. Or though it stand as some huge tree whose branches spread over the race, and under whose shadows mighty populations live, the invincible and unalterable law of moral retribution will rot it clean away. The record here given of this highly symbolic vision suggests its influence upon two classes of mind. It excites—

I. THE LAMENTATION OF THE BAD. Who are the men who feel distressed at the fall of the wrong thing—the moral Babylon? We find at least two classes in these verses. 1. The *ruling* class. "And the kings of the earth, who have committed fornication and lived deliciously [wantonly] with her, shall bewail her, and lament for her [weep and wail over her], when they shall see [look upon] the smoke of her burning" (ver. 9). Throughout the human race the world over, we find a class of men who are the chiefs, the masters, the kings, who control and determine the destinies of others. 2. The *mercantile* class. " And the merchants of the earth shall weep and mourn," etc. (vers. 11—17). The mercantile principle is an instinct Divine and beneficent. Its operations are not limited to shops, storerooms, markets, exchanges, or land; it extends to the ocean. "And every shipmaster, and all the company in ships, and sailors [every one that saileth anywhither, and mariners]," etc. (ver. 17). The ships of commerce are found ploughing every sea and lying in every port. The principle is found working among savage hordes as well as amongst civilized men. But whilst the principle is right enough, and transcendently beneficent when rightly directed, it has, like all other instincts of our nature, been sadly perverted. It is perverted when it is directed not to the good of the commonwealth, but to the gratification and aggrandizement of self. Hence the enormous private fortunes on the one hand, and the starving destitution of millions on the other. Now, this morally wrong thing, this *every man for himself*, is a principle that has been so much criticized, not only by political and moral philosophers, but by the thinking men in all conditions of life, that it is getting weak, beginning to fall, and must ultimately be destroyed. When the grand altruistic truth of Christly socialism becomes realized by the masses, "Let no man seek his own, but every man another's wealth," then this *every-man-for-himself principle* will fall, and with its fall what will become of the enormous possessions which they have obtained merely by working for themselves? No wonder they are distressed at the prospect. Every day this wrong thing is gradually falling, and the best men everywhere are becoming altruistic. "Go to now, ye rich men, weep and howl for your miseries that shall come upon you." How they struggle to arrest this wrong principle in its fall, to buttress it up; but it is the fiat of eternal justice that it should fall and rise no more.

II. THE JUBILATION OF THE GOOD. "Rejoice over her, thou heaven, and ye holy apostles and prophets," etc. (ver. 20). Whilst those who have a vested interest in the maintenance of the wrong thing—whose pomp, and wealth, and luxurious sensualities, and gilded pageantries would have never existed but for the Babylonian spirit that permeates social life—howl in anguish at the fall of wrong, there are others transported with rapture as they see it giving way. Who are these? Unfallen angels, saints, and holy intelligences throughout the empire of God. "Thou heaven, and ye holy apostles [ye saints] and prophets." Heaven knows what is going on on earth, and is thrilled with delight at the sight of even "one sinner that repenteth." The change of governments, the fluctuation of markets, the revolution of empires—such things as these awaken the deepest concern of the ignorant and erring sons of men. But they wake no ripple on the deep translucent river of celestial minds. Whereas every fraction of wrong which they see falling into ruin from this huge Babylon gives them a new thrill of delight. Why should these peers in the spiritual universe thus exult at the fall of wrong? 1. *Because the fall is just.* Evil has no right to exist; it is an abnormal thing. The father of lies is a usurper in the universe. All the wrong systems, theoretical and practical, in every department of human life, political, commercial, ecclesiastic, he has built up on falsehood and deception; and their destruction is an act of eternal justice. God speed the right! This is the instinctive prayer of all consciences. 2. *Because the fall is beneficent.* The giving way of the wrong thing in society is as the breaking up of the dense cloud that darkens the whole heavens of man, the bringing down of fertilizing showers on the earth, and brightening the sky into sunny azure. It is the uprooting of those thorns and thistles and noxious weeds that have turned the paradise of our being into a howling wilderness. What benevolent nature could fail to exult in such an event as this? "Rejoice over her, thou heaven, and ye holy apostles and prophets." 3. *Because the fall is complete.* "And a mighty [strong] angel took up a stone like a [as it were a] great millstone, and cast it into the sea, saying, Thus with violence [a mighty fall] shall that great city Babylon [Babylon the great city] be thrown [cast] down, and shall be found no more at all," etc. (vers. 21—23). All this imposing symbolical description suggests the enormous curses associated with moral Babylonianism, and the strong reason for jubilation at its final fall. The fall of moral evil, even in part or whole, in the individual soul, in small or large communities, is not a temporary event. Destroyed once, it is destroyed for ever. "It shall be thrown down, and shall be found no more at all." It is "cast into the sea." What does the mighty "millstone" suggest? What was the "little stone" in Daniel's vision cut out of the rock without hands, and which became a great mountain? This, I trow—the gospel, which is the "power of God,"—this is the only instrument that can hurl Babylon into the depths of the sea.—D. T.

Ver. 21.—*Moral evil symbolized.* "And a mighty angel took up a stone like a great millstone, and cast it into the sea," etc. In these words we have a *symbolization of moral evil.*

I. A SYMBOLIZATION OF ITS NATURE. Babylon is a symbol. Not unfrequently is moral evil in the aggregate represented by some one object. Sometimes by the "old man," that is, the unrenewed, depraved man; he is the embodiment of all the elements of sin. Sometimes by the "world," that is, the moral evil embodied in the world. "He that loveth the world," etc., that is, the moral evil embodied in the world. In Nebuchadnezzar's dream it is represented as a colossal image, representing the wealth and power of empire, the pride of the idolatry, the wickedness of all kingdoms. Here in these words it is represented by the great city Babylon. Babylon stands here as the grand symbol of moral evil. If you want to see sin, or moral evil, in all its hideous aspects, in all its infernal operations, in all its damning consequences, study the great city of Babylon. In this city you will find not only the evils of the Roman Catholic Church, but of all Churches, of all institutions, of all countries and climes, ay, of all human hearts. The great city Babylon is in every unreserved soul. Here is—

II. A SYMBOLIZATION OF ITS OVERTHROW. "And a mighty angel took up a stone like a great millstone, and cast it into the sea, saying, Thus with violence shall that great city Babylon be thrown down, and shall be found no more at all." The moral evil of the world is to be destroyed; it is not to exist for ever. The various figures used to symbolize it are set forth as objects for utter destruction. The world is to be "overcome," as Christ overcame it. The old man, which is corrupt, is to be "crucified with his affections and lusts." The great image is to be shivered to pieces by the "stone," the symbol of Divine truth; and here the great city Babylon is represented as being thrown like a great millstone "into the sea." Two remarks are suggested concerning its overthrow. 1. It is to be overthrown by *superhuman agency.* "A mighty angel," a messenger from heaven. Was not Christ a mighty Messenger sent from heaven for this purpose? Yes; he came to "destroy the works of the devil." It is said that good alone can overcome evil. True, but it must be good in a supernatural form; and in this form the gospel brings us the good. 2. It is to be overthrown in such a way as *never to appear again.* Babylon is thrown like a great millstone into the sea. "And shall be found no more at all." As Pharaoh sank like lead in the mighty waters, and rose no more to life, so shall moral evil like a mighty millstone fall into the fathomless abysses of eternal ruin. "Shall be found no more at all." No less than six times are these words repeated. Some one has said that they toll like a funeral knell. I would rather say that they chime like a triumphant peal. Thank God, mighty and wide as is the dominion of evil in the world, I am prone to believe that it will not endure for ever. All the holy prayers in the universe cry for its ruin. All holy agencies work for it, and omnipotence is pledged to its overthrow.—D. T.

EXPOSITION.

CHAPTER XIX.

Ver. 1.—**And after these things I heard a great voice of much people in heaven, saying**; *after these things I heard, as it were, a great voice of a great multitude,* etc. The usual introduction to a new phase of a vision (see ch. iv. 1, etc.). The "great voice," as usual, characteristic of the heavenly utterances (see ch. v. 2, etc.). Again, we are not told whose the utterance is. It may well be that of all the heavenly inhabitants and saints in glory (cf. ch. vii. 9). As usual in the Apocalypse, at the termination of a description of the last judgment comes the triumphant song of the heavenly host (cf. ch. vii. 9—17; xi. 17). Thus the account of the conflict between God and the devil, which was begun at ch. xii., is here concluded at ver. 8; after which the narrative takes a fresh departure, once more returning, as it were, to the beginning, and tracing anew this warfare. The remaining portion of the book is analogous to the latter part of Ezekiel. **Alleluia; Salvation, and glory, and honour, and power, unto the Lord our God**; *Hallelujah; the salvation and the glory and the power belong to our God.* Ἡ τιμή, "the honour," found in several cursives, is omitted in ℵ, A, B, C, P, etc. So also with the word "Lord." *Hallelujah*—"Praise ye Jehovah"—is found in Ps. cxxxv. 1 and elsewhere. It is translated in ver. 5 of this chapter, as is St. John's custom (see on ch. ix. 11). It has been remarked that the word "Hallelujah" is chiefly used in connection with the punishment of the wicked; in which manner it is also used here. (For a similar ascription of praise, see ch. iv. 11, etc.)

Ver. 2.—**For true and righteous are his judgments.** This reason for the worship of ver. 1 is similar to that in ch. xvi. 7 and xv. 3. For he hath judged the great whore, which did corrupt the earth with her fornication, and hath avenged the blood of his servants at her hand. A second reason

for the worship of ver. 1. *Corrupt the earth;* as in ch. xi. 18, where a form of the same verb is used (cf. also Jer. li. 25). *Her fornication;* her unfaithfulness and deceit (see on ch. xiv. 4, 8). The prayer of ch. vi. 10 has now been heard (cf. also ch. xviii. 20).

Ver. 3.—**And again they said, Alleluia. And her smoke rose up for ever and ever;** *goeth up.* The "smoke" is that of the burning of Babylon, mentioned in ch. xviii. 9, 18. The final nature of this judgment is indicated by the closing words.

Ver. 4.—**And the four and twenty elders and the four beasts fell down and worshipped God that sat on the throne, saying, Amen; Alleluia.** (On "the twenty-four elders" as representing the Church of God, and "the four living beings" as typical of creation, see on ch. iv. 4, 6.) *God that sitteth* (present tense, as in ver. 3) *on the throne;* as he is described in ch. iv 2 and **v. 13.** *Amen; Hallelujah* (see Ps. cvi. 48).

Ver. 5.—**And a voice came out of the throne, saying.** Ἐκ, "out of," is found in ℵ, P, 1, 34, etc.; ἀπό, "forth from," is supported by A, B, C, etc.; while B reads οὐρανοῦ, "heaven," instead of θρόνου, "throne." Alford suggests that the direction rather than the source of the voice is intended. It is impossible to say to whom the voice should be attributed (cf. ch. x. 4, 8, etc.). As an invitation to the Church to praise God, we might expect the voice to be that of one of the elders. Praise our God, all ye his servants, and ye that fear him, both small and great. ℵ, C, P, omit the first "and," thus reading : "ye his servants, ye that fear him," etc. The first words are a repetition of the "Hallelujah" of ver. 1. The following phrases are found in Ps. cxxxiv. 1; cxv. 13.

Ver. 6.—**And I heard as it were the voice of a great multitude.** This is the response to the invitation just uttered in ver. 5. Again "the voice of a multitude," as in ver. 1. **And as the voice of many waters.** That is, in its suggestiveness of great power and magnitude (cf. ch. i. 15; xiv. 2; Ps. xciii. 3; Jer. li. 16). And as the voice of mighty thunderings, saying. A repetition of the idea contained in the preceding clause. The case of the participle is doubtful ; A, P, and others have λεγόντων ; many cursives λεγόντας; ℵ has λεγούσων ; the nominative λέγοντες is found in B and others. Alleluia : for the Lord God omnipotent reigneth. (On "Hallelujah," see ver. 1.) These words connect the present passage with ch. xvii. 14. They exhibit, as it were, the culminating reason for this adoration of God. He has exhibited his almighty power in the overthrow of Babylon, who said, " I sit a queen ; " and in the overthrow (which has yet to be narrated more fully) of the kings of the earth.

Ver. 7.—Let us be glad and rejoice, and give honour to him ; *let us rejoice and be exceeding glad, and let us give the glory unto him.* Alford reads δώσομεν, " we will give," with ℵ²ᵃ, A. P, 36 ; but the T.R. δῶμεν, " let us give," which is found in ℵ¹, B, 1, 7, 38, Vulgate, Cyprian, Primasius, is to be preferred. For the marriage of the Lamb is come, and his wife hath made herself ready. This is somewhat anticipatory ; the full vision of the bride of the Lamb is reserved until ch. xxi. But the rejoicing over Babylon and the harlot naturally suggests the allusion to Christ's faithful Church, just as the vision of ch. vii. is suggested by the concluding words of ch. vi. " The marriage of the Lamb " is the figure under which is depicted that complete union between Christ and his faithful Church, which will be consummated at the last day, when Satan has been overcome and sin destroyed. It stands in contrast with the fornication of the harlot—the union of the spiritually unfaithful portion of Christ's Church with the powers of the world (see on ch. xvii. 1, 2). Alford remarks, " This figure, of a marriage between the Lord and his people, is too frequent and familiar to need explanation (cf. in the Old Testament, Isa. liv. 1— 8; Ezek. xvi. 7, etc. ; Hos. ii. 19, etc. ; and in the New Testament, Matt. ix. 15; xxv. 1, etc. ; John iii. 29; Eph. v. 25, etc.)." This symbol of the *wife* or *bride* indicates the redeemed, who have already in several places been alluded to in this book (ch. vii. 9; xii. 1; xiv. 1; xvii. 14, "they that are with him "). The saints have made themselves *ready* by enduing themselves with the robe of righteousness (ver. 8).

Ver. 8.—And to her was granted that she should be arrayed in fine linen, clean and white ; *and it was given unto her that she should array herself in fine linen, bright [and] pure.* The double nature of the process is here set forth. " It was given

her," the power comes from God (cf. ch. xiii. 5, etc.), and yet " she arrays herself ; " the action is still voluntary. (On " white linen," see on ch. iv. 4; vii. 9 ; xv. 6.) The following words are a sufficient commentary. This verse appears to contain the words of the writer, the heavenly song having ceased at the end of ver. 7. For the fine linen is the righteousness of saints ; *the righteous acts of the saints.* That is, their former righteousness, exhibited in fidelity to God and hostility to the world, obtained and retained by the grace of God, now forms their chief glory. So " their works do follow them " (ch. xiv. 13).

Ver. 9.—And he saith unto me, Write, Blessed are they which are called unto the marriage supper of the Lamb ; *which are bidden* (Revised Version). Cf. the command in ch. i. 11 and xxi. 5, and the prohibition in x. 4 ; cf. also the expression in ch. xiv. 13, " Blessed are the dead," etc. It almost seems as if the writer has in his mind the connection of ideas indicated by the words quoted above on ver. 8, " Their works do follow them." The figure of the " marriage supper " is rather a new symbol than the continuation of the symbol of the bride ; though very probably suggested by it. For those who partake of the " marriage supper " are those who constitute the bride, viz. the faithful Church of God. Cf. ch. iii. 20, the words which are spoken by the " Amen, the faithful and true Witness " (ch. iii. 14): " If any man hear my voice, and open the door, I will come in to him, and will sup with him, and he with me." It is impossible to say who the speaker is that thus addresses St. John, except in so far as may be gathered from ver. 10. And he saith unto me, These are the true sayings of God. Cf. the words of ch. iii. 14, quoted above, and ch. xxi. 5 ; also the " Yea, saith the Spirit " of ch. xiv. 13. (On the word " true," see ch. iii. 7.) These words have been restricted to different portions of the Apocalypse by different commentators ; but it seems best, on the whole, to understand them as referring to the whole series of visions connected with the harlot and Babylon and the faithful bride of Christ.

Ver. 10.—And I fell at his feet to worship him. The same thing happens again in ch. xx. 7, 8, and this makes it improbable that St. John imagined the angel to be Christ himself, as some think. More probably (as Alford, Bengel, Vitringa, Wordsworth, and others) St. John was so overwhelmed with the tremendous character of the revelation just made to him, that in his humility he pays undue reverence to the angel who had communicated it to him. This reverence may not have been exactly of the nature of that which he would render to God ; but it is evident, from the reproof of the angel, that it was more than could be becomingly and safely paid to a created being. And he said unto me, See thou do it not: I am thy fellow-servant, and of thy brethren that have the testimony of Jesus; *saith . . . I am a fellow-servant with thee and with thy brethren,* etc. So the apostles styled themselves (Rom. i. 1; 2 Pet. i. 1, etc.). (On "hold the testimony of Jesus," see ch. i. 2, 9; xii. 17.) Worship God. Such also is the command of our Lord (Matt. iv. 10). For the testimony of Jesus is the spirit of prophecy. Like the words of ver. 8, these words are probably an explanation added by St. John. To prophesy is to understand and proclaim the truth concerning God, especially in the face of prevalent ignorance or opposition; this is also what is meant by holding "the testimony of Jesus." The angel in revealing these visions, the martyrs in openly professing Christ, St. John in receiving and handing on the Apocalypse, were prophesying. Thus it was that the angel announces himself to be the fellow-servant of St. John, and a fellow-servant with the prophets, and with those "who keep the sayings of this book" (ch. xxii. 9).

Ver. 11.—And I saw heaven opened, and behold a white horse. A new vision now opens, which is, however, part of the preceding series, commencing at ch. xiii. 1. The destruction of certain forms of evil—typified by Babylon and the harlot—has been declared; the final overthrow of the dragon has yet to be related, though there may be no such separation in the actual infliction of these punishments as there necessarily is in the relation of them. The warfare now to be described must be understood to be that which is taking place between the hosts of Christ and Satan throughout the period of the world's existence. *The heaven opened* (cf. ch. iv. 1). A similar figure has been already employed in the first seal-vision (ch. vi. 2). It has been pointed out that the same image is employed at the beginning and at the end of the description of the warfare between Christ and the devil. He who is the First and the Last, the Alpha and Omega (ch. i. 8), rides forth conquering and to conquer (ch. vi. 2). And he that sat upon him was called Faithful and True, and in righteousness he doth judge and make war. Even the participial construction here employed connects this account with ch. vi. 2. "Faithful and True" are the titles applied to our Lord in ch. iii. 14, which see. *In righteousness he doth judge;* cf. Isaiah's prophecy of Christ: "But with righteousness shall he judge the poor" (Isa. xi. 4); cf. ver. 2 of this chapter. The purposes of this expedition are "to judge and make war."

REVELATION.

Ver. 12.—His eyes were as a flame of fire; *and his eyes [are] a flame of fire.* Again as in ch. i. 13. "Fire" is the type of purity and judgment (see Ps. xcvii. 3; Isa. xlvii. 14; lxvi. 15; Amos v. 6; 1 Cor. iii. 13, etc.; ch. iii. 18). And on his head were many crowns; *and upon his head [are] many diadems.* Διαδήματα, "kingly crowns" (cf. ch. xii. 3; xiii. 1), because he now comes as a King to judgment. The plurality of "crowns" points to his character as King of kings (see ch. xvii. 14; cf. ch. xiii. 1). And he had a name written, that no man knew, but he himself; *hath a name . . . no one knoweth.* Evidently the "new name" of ch. iii. 12, the significance of which St. John is unable to comprehend (see on ch. ii. 7; iii. 12). From the connection with the preceding clause, we naturally infer that this *name* was written upon his forehead (cf. ch. vii. 3); xvi. 1); but the writer does not explicitly state this. In B, twenty-five cursives, and Syriac, the words, "names written and," are inserted before "name."

Ver. 13.—And he was clothed with a vesture dipped in blood; *and he [is] arrayed in a garment,* etc. The idea here is evidently derived from Isa. lxiii. 3, "I have trodden the wine-press alone; and of the people there was none with me: for I will tread them in mine anger, and trample them in my fury; and their blood shall be sprinkled upon my garments, and I will stain all my raiment" (cf. ver. 15). Probably the similarity of this passage has caused the reading, "sprinkled with blood," which is found in a few manuscripts. In the original passage in Isaiah, the *blood* is doubtless the *blood* of his enemies; but it is possible that there is here a reference to the blood of Christ himself, which he shed in his warfare with Satan. And his Name is called The Word of God. Only in St. John's writings does this title appear—a strong argument in favour of his authorship of the Apocalypse (cf. John i. 1; 1 John i. 1). This cannot be the "name" of ver. 12, which, as there explained, is unknown. This *Name,* the *Word of God,* is appropriately used when he is going forth to judgment.

Ver. 14.—And the armies which were in heaven followed him upon white horses, clothed in fine linen, white and clean; *which are . . . white, pure.* These *armies* are not merely the angels, but the "called, chosen, and faithful" of ch. xvii. 14, "the bride" of ver. 8, who are described as being arrayed in white in ch. vi. 11, and ver. 8 of this chapter. Those commentators who consider that the angels only are intended, and not the saints, forget the double nature of the vision; it is not only a description of judgment meted out, but also of a war

16

waged. (On "white" and "fine linen," see previous chapters.)

Ver. 15.—And out of his mouth goeth a sharp sword, that with it he should smite the nations : and he shall rule them with a rod of iron. The description is still similar to that given in ch. i. (see ch. i. 16; ii. 12, 16). (For the last clause, see ch. ii. 27 ; xii. 5 ; and cf. Isa. lxiii. 3.) The symbolism is descriptive of warfare, victory, and judgment. "He" is emphatic : "he shall rule "—no longer the kings of the earth. *The nations;* in the sense of the ungodly (cf. ch. xvi. 19, etc.). And he treadeth the wine-press of the fierceness and wrath of Almighty God ; *the wine-press of the wine of the fierceness of the wrath*, etc. In ch. xiv. 10 we have the figure of "the wine of the wrath" of God, and in ch. xiv. 19 that of the "wine-press of the wrath;" here the two are combined (cf. also Isa. lxiii. 3, quoted on ver. 13).

Ver. 16.—And he hath on his vesture and on his thigh a name written. What this means is doubtful. The following suggestions have been made : (1) The name, written at length, is written partly upon the vesture and partly upon the thigh itself, where the garment would (in an equestrian figure) fall away from the thigh (Alford). (2) The name is written on the vesture, even (καί) on that part of it which covers the thigh (De Wette, Düsterdieck, Hengstenberg). (3) On the thigh, as the place where the sword usually hangs. (4) A reference to the custom of engraving the name of the artist upon the thigh of a statue (Cic., 'Verr.,' iv. 43; see Wetstein). KING OF KINGS, AND LORD OF LORDS. As in ch. xvii. 14 (but inverted), where, as here, it portrays the victorious career of Christ over the " kings of the earth."

Ver. 17.—And I saw an angel standing in the sun. That is, in mid-heaven (as in ch. viii. 13, etc.); in a place befitting his glory, and also whence he can appropriately issue his summons. And he cried with a loud voice. As is usual in all the heavenly utterances (see ch. v. 2, etc.). Saying to all the fowls that fly in the midst of heaven; *the birds that fly in mid-heaven* (Revised Version) (*vide supra*); see Ezek. xxix. 17, *et seq.*, for the origin of the imagery here employed. Come and gather yourselves together unto the supper of the great God; *come, be gathered together unto the great supper of God* (Revised Version). Not, of course, the " supper " of ver. 9, but rather a contrast to it ; that *supper* which is reserved for the ungodly, at which they form the prey. The language is employed in filling in the accessory details of the central image, and must not be pressed too far in particular directions ; *e.g.* Andreas considers the birds o be good angels.

Ver. 18.—That ye may eat the flesh of kings, and the flesh of captains, and the flesh of mighty men, and the flesh of horses, and of them that sit on them, and the flesh of all men, both free and bond, both small and great (cf. the description in Ezek. xxxix. 17). *All men;* that is, all the ungodly. Cf. the description of the same event at the conclusion of the seal-judgments (ch. vi. 15). The whole account indicates the widespread and complete nature of God's judgments, which none shall be able to escape.

Ver. 19.—And I saw the beast ; viz. that described in ch. xiii. 1, typical of the hostile world-power. And the kings of the earth, and their armies. The *kings* summoned by the unclean spirits of ch. xvi. 13, 14, typical of the forces which the beast employs in his spiritual warfare with God. The armies are the adherents of the beast, described in ch. xiii.—the ungodly, those who follow the world rather than God. Gathered together to make war against him that sat on the horse, and against his army. Gathered as described in ch. xvi. 14 and ver. 17 of this chapter. Again (as in ver. 7) a double operation. The gathering is voluntary on the part of the wicked (ch. xvi. 14). and yet it is overruled by God, and made to serve his ends (ch. xix. 17). *Him that sat on the horse;* Christ (see ver. 11). " His army" consists of the faithful followers of Christ. They are here pictured as a heavenly army (ver. 14), because the victory which they achieved is the leading feature here depicted, but their warfare took place while they were on earth (cf. ch. xiv. 13). *The war* (with the article); viz. that war which is perpetually waged between the powers of light and darkness, and which will not be terminated until the great judgment.

Ver. 20.—And the beast was taken, and with him the false prophet that wrought miracles before him, with which he deceived them that had received the mark of the beast, and them that worshipped his image *that wrought the signs in his sight* (Revised Version). Here we have described the destruction of the earthly manifestations of Satan's power; the means by which he seeks to achieve his purposes, and which we have interpreted as the hostile world-power and self-deception (see on ch. xiii.). The whole account contained in vers. 11—21 is a brief recapitulation of the whole period of warfare between Christ and Satan, with special attention given to the final overthrow of the powers of evil. It, therefore, covers the same ground as the vision of seals, and then that of the trumpets, then that of the vials, and afterwards that of the beasts, each occupies. The chief difference is that in all those visions the everyday conflict is more particularly described; whereas in this passage the termination of the conflict is specially brought before us. The same ground is covered in the next chapter, advancing, however, one step further, and showing us the final punishment of Satan himself, as well as of his instruments (ch. xx. 10). These both were cast alive into a lake of fire burning with brimstone; *they twain were cast alive into the lake,* etc. (On "brimstone," etc., see on ch. ix. 17, 18. Cf. ch. xx. 10, 14, 15; xxi. 8.) This " lake of fire " is the place of punishment for Satan and his hosts; not the place in which he at present works and reigns—

which is described as the abyss (ch. ix. 1; xi. 7; xvii. 8; xx. 1, 3).

Ver. 21.—And the remnant were slain with the sword of him that sat upon the horse, which sword proceeded out of his mouth: and all the fowls were filled with their flesh. *The remnant;* that is, the adherents of the beast, the " armies " of ver. 19. (For this description of Christ, see vers. 11, 15.) Spiritual death is inflicted upon those who have proved themselves hostile to God. The last sentence emphasizes the nature of the punishment by the reference to the indignity offered to their bodies after death.

HOMILETICS.

Vers. 1—9 (coupled with ch. xviii. 20).—*Rejoicings over the fall of Babylon.* When we put side by side the lament of the kings, merchants, and seamen, with the rejoicings of the great multitude in heaven over Babylon's fall, the effect is very strange. At first sight there seems an incongruity between them. We are taught in the Word that there is such deep sympathy between heaven and earth, and that there are emotions of tenderest pity felt in heaven towards man below. And yet in this series of symbolic visions we have the representation that heaven is made glad by that which brings wailing on earth. How is this to be accounted for? Observe: (1) It is not the wailing itself at which there is rejoicing, nor yet at its immediate cause. (2) It is not from any vindictive feeling. All such feelings are, we are sure, dead in the completely sanctified character. But (3) there are matters of immensely greater importance than the happiness or misery of individuals. It may be a grievous thing to see a human being with a tear in his eye; it is much more so to see him in rebellion against God. And if there are those who need to be taught this, it is better to see them weeping over the bitter fruits of rebellion than to see them at ease in the revolt itself. (4) That may be joyous in one aspect which is sad in another. It may be a sad thing to see so many precious things perishing. It is good to find that when aught is poisoned by sin it is not allowed to continue. (5) As the great multitude in heaven often grieved over the burden of sin which the earth was carrying, how can they but rejoice that from it the earth is freed? (6) While angels in heaven have sympathy with man, they have no sympathy with his sin, but much, very much, with God. (7) Hence they see that while man's sin is the blight of earth, God's righteous judgments against sin are the guard of righteousness. Especially when (8) the Divine vengeance is a perfectly righteous one, never erring by excess or defect. At the same time, it may be thought that not even these considerations entirely remove the difficulty. One may say, " Think of all the souls who are lamenting over Babylon's fall! I for one do not feel as if I could be happy, or take up such a song of praise as the passage contains, so long as there is a single being in the universe who is not rejoicing in God. I would not have the slightest speck or flaw anywhere—no, not one unhappy soul in all creation!" There is a great deal to admire in such philanthropic feeling, and yet even such a state of mind may bring its own perils. For even such feelings have to be regulated by the disclosures of God's Word, and ever to be kept in curb by an absolute faith in God himself. To such a one we would therefore put queries like these: Would you be satisfied with the dealings of God if God himself is satisfied with them? Would you be satisfied if those in heaven are so? Would you be content if our blessed Saviour were satisfied with the joy set before him? Would you not be vastly more than content if you could see that the fall of Babylon was but preliminary to the ushering in of a brighter glory? Would you not even be transported with delight if God should show you that he means from the present chaos of sin to gather up things anew, and to bring about an issue more glorious than if sin had never been permitted to intrude? because, if such should be the case, even this fall of Babylon may be but one event in a process in which God is going to do exceeding abundantly for us above all we can ask or think. Let us, then, watch for the sequel. And meanwhile let us, in the light of the paragraph before us, ask and answer three inquiries—

I. WHO ARE THE REJOICING ONES? "A heavenly hallelujah celebrates the first act of the final sentence upon the antichristian powers which served as Satan's instruments. At each crisis in the Apocalypse we find a similar hymn of praise (ch. iv. 8; v. 9; vii. 10; xi. 15; xv. 3; xvi. 5)."[1] An unknown voice—possibly from "him that sitteth upon the throne;" this would seem to be the more appropriate conclusion, as the word is in the form of a mandate. The song itself comes: (1) From the four living creatures—representatives of the higher orders of creation. (2) From the four and twenty elders—the representatives of the Old and New Testaments. (3) From the great multitude in heaven, whose voices rise up as the voice of many waters. From the point of view at which the blessed in heaven study the works of God, they see ground for adoring praise and for rapturous song. It is only here among ourselves, who dwell in clouds below, that the song is checked by our misapprehension and partial sight.

II. WHAT IS IT THAT FURNISHES MATERIAL FOR SONG? 1. "*He hath avenged the blood of his servants,*" etc. (Ver. 2.) This one expression, "the blood of his servants," carries with it a tale of fearful import. It would include: (1) The blood of the millions slaughtered under the sanction of papal Rome. (2) The blood of those put to death under paganism. (3) The blood of those who have perished under the iniquities of the slave-trade. (4) The blood of those whose consciences and souls have been trampled on by mammon's greed. There are two sorts of feelings which may be cherished under these crying ills—that of angry revenge; that of a burning indignation at a moral outrage. The first is wrong, and has no place in this song; the second is right—yea, and not only right, but one which it would be wicked not to have. And when God arises in his strength to avenge the cause of the helpless, he would be unworthy the name of a man who would not rejoice over this. 2. "*He hath judged the great harlot.*" This great harlot, Babylon, corrupted the earth. Whether the iniquity thus specified assumed the commercial or the ecclesiastical form, in either case it was a huge system of iniquity, of apostasy, whereby either "the priest" or "mammon" sat in the seat of God. The seventeenth chapter points to the former; the eighteenth chapter, to the latter. And surely when apostasy from God is exposed in all its ugliness, and branded with everlasting shame, that is enough to cause a mighty shout of joy to peal forth from the mighty host above. What has so often made pleasure a forbidden thing? Apostasy! What has befouled commerce? Apostasy! What has dragged the banner of science in the mud and the mire? Apostasy! What has made even religious forms a stumbling-block and a shame? Apostasy! And surely it will be a festive day alike for earth and heaven when this gilded and bedizened demon shall be stripped, exposed, and slain. 3. *The downfall of so much evil is the prelude to the salvation.* (Ver. 1, "The salvation . . . unto the Lord our God.") By this is meant not so much that aspect of salvation which belongs to the forgiveness of sins—that had been long ago enjoyed; but that which pertains to deliverance from the burden of evil in many and every form. After long and weary conflicts with iniquity, after seeming to be almost smothered with the weight of outside ungodliness, after the voice of the righteous was all but drowned in the confusion and roar of Babylon—*then* comes *the deliverance!* Their great foe is for ever dead. "Alleluia!" 4. *The Lord God hath taken the kingdom.* (Ver. 6.) Hath showed himself to be King indeed, as he was before King by right of his enthronement in heaven; *i.e.* the Lord Jesus Christ, who now is exalted "a Prince and Saviour," shall then be acknowledged as King. And certainly the universal acknowledgment of Jesus as Lord may well call forth a shout of praise from all the blest in heaven! 5. *The Church is prepared for her Lord.* (Vers. 7, 8.) The Lord God will not only crush sin in the world, but will also purge it out of the Church; and all unclean rags of Babylon the great, some of which may be found in the purest Church on earth, shall be burnt up. "In fine linen, clean and white," the bride of Christ shall shine. In the seventh verse this is looked at from one point of view, and in the next verse from another. In the former, as an act of personal preparation for the appearing of the Bridegroom; and in the latter, as a grant from the grace of God. These are the two aspects of

[1] 'Speaker's Commentary,' *in loc*

Divine truth which always coalesce—human effort and the grace of God.   6. *The Lord cometh to claim his Church.* " The marriage of the Lamb is come." These words, like many others with which we have met in the course of our expositions, overleap the intervening distance and events, and glance onwards to the outcome. The fall of Babylon will be one of the preliminaries to heaven's great bridal-day ! And then, then the mutual rejoicing ! " Blessed are they which are called unto the marriage supper of the Lamb." This is the festive scene which is descried in the distance, as that to which the evolution of things is pointing. It is sketched in ch. xxii. Between now and then are the binding and loosing of Satan, the victory over Gog and Magog—and after these things the New Jerusalem appears. And each incident as it occurs is a new pledge of the nearing of heaven's great triumphal feast. But we have not gone far enough yet in interpreting the spirit of this chapter. We have seen what we may call the *momenta* of the joy—the items which furnish the material of it. We have yet to ask—

III. ON WHAT GROUNDS DOES THAT JOY REST WHICH THUS EXPRESSES ITSELF IN SONG ? All these events which prompt the joy do so because they are, to the eye of renewed creatures, the expression and development of the infinite perfections of God. Here they see our God unveiling his purposes of grace. It is in him and in his holy will that all these events have their unity and their continuity. " The salvation, and the glory, and the honour . . . unto the Lord our God." Glancing over the paragraph, we find that there are no fewer than five different manifestations of the Divine perfections. 1. *There is a manifestation of power.* (Ver. 1.) The power belongs to God. In him is the origin of force; its eternal and exhaustless fount. Even when Babylon is at the height of its pride, he can hurl it down and cast it for ever away. Is it not matter for infinite joy to know that evil is not strong enough to perpetuate itself ? " Though thou make thy nest among the stars, from thence will I bring thee down, saith the Lord." 2. *There is a manifestation of equity.* " He hath judged . . . he hath avenged " (ver. 2). " He will render to every man according to his deeds." 3. *There is a manifestation of grace.* (Ver. 8.) " To her was *granted*"—as a free gift. It is the glory of the Divine sovereignty to enrich out of the aboundings of grace, and thus to do exceeding abundantly for us above all that we ask or think. 4. *There is a manifestation of the Divine mercy.* For he hath conferred salvation on those who were ready to perish ; and hath, of his own pity to the unworthy, made them fair, though he found them foul. 5. *There is a manifestation of faithfulness.* Of faithful adhesion to all the promises; of perpetual continuation in faithful love to the bride whom he will come to claim as his own. This union is for ever ! The tie between the Redeemer and his redeemed shall never be dissolved, but shall outlive the "wreck of matter, and the crash of worlds."

Note: The one lesson which the unrolling ages teach us is—*God.* There is a profound truth hidden in pantheism, albeit it perverts the truth which alone gives it its plausibility. All events—in the town, the city, the empire, the world—are hastening on the unfolding of God, and writing new pages of that unfinished and unfinishable Name ! Hence the deep meaning in the prophecy so oft repeated, " The glory of the Lord shall be revealed, and all flesh shall see it together : for the mouth of the Lord hath spoken it." It is not in heaven that we shall find God; it is in the eternally unfolding manifestation of God that the righteous will find their heaven, and the theme for a song that will be ever new.

Vers. 11—21.—" *King of kings, and Lord of lords.*" In this paragraph we have a marvellously vivid sketch of a mighty conflict, in which the most high God, in the Person of his Son, goes forth to war and victory. Strange as it may seem to speak of God being engaged in a struggle, it is clear that what we call " good " is in the world with its legion forces, and that what is evil is also here. Both are at work. They are necessarily opposed. God *must* be on the side of good. Hence the war. Probably we have reason to believe that God could, if he pleased, terminate in a moment all that is opposed to his infinitely holy nature. But he does not see fit to do this. We do not know why, except as he tells us. It may be that in and by the conflict lessons are to be taught which otherwise could not be learnt. Any way, while this strife lasts, it is the Lord's controversy, which will be brought to an issue in " the battle of the great day of God Almighty." Not that we are to look for the literal fulfilment of such words in a material contest headed by the Messiah in person leading an army! No, no! nothing so sensuous. God's battle is a silent one. Its weapons are not carnal. Though we walk in the flesh, we do not war after the flesh. The forces which have to be subdued are spiritual. Hence the war must be spiritual too. The forces which have to be subdued are: (1) Worldly power and policy in every unrighteous form. (2) False religious systems of every kind. (3) Varied false and corrupt forms of Christianity itself. (4) Sin and crime, whether open or secret. These are the adverse forces which are sketched in this book. These are the evils which are manifest in the world. And it is against them that the mighty conflict is going on. But by whom it is to be headed, and to be so conducted that the victory is sure—what human intellect can solve the problem? what human foresight peer into the future? what human strength grapple with the foes? Woe be to us if the whole were left in human hands! But it is not so. The apostle sees heaven opened, and lo! he sees above, the Lord and Leader in this mighty conflict. Concerning him and it the paragraph gives us replies to five questions.

I. WHO IS THE LEADER, AND WHAT IS HIS NAME? This question receives here a threefold answer. Surely no student of Scripture can fail to see that here is a vision of the Lord Jesus Christ, although neither the personal nor the official name is given. But we are told: 1. *He has a name which no one knoweth but he himself.* There are aspects of his nature which are known to us, or it would be impossible to reverence and love him. But there are other aspects which to us are unknown. There are fathomless depths in his own infinite nature. "No one knoweth the Son but the Father." 2. *He has a name which is known.* A name which expresses at once his relation to God and to man. "His name is called The Word of God." This is the name in which the beloved apostle so much delights (John i. 1—5). The "Word;" the expression of thought. The Lord Jesus as "the Word" is the revealed expression of the mind of the invisible Father. 3. *He hath also a title* expressive of kingly authority, of supremacy over all earthly names—"King of kings, and Lord of lords." "All kings shall fall down before him." His monarchy shall put all else into the shade.

> "The might of the Gentile, unsmote by the sword,
> Hath melted like snow in the glance of the Lord!"

II. WHAT ARE THE ATTRIBUTES OF THIS LEADER? They are such as absolutely to qualify him for the work here assigned to him. 1. *His eyes are as a flame of fire.* Here his omniscience is set forth as that which no sin, no sinner, can escape. 2. *He is called Faithful.* The Faithful One, in whom fidelity is embodied as its archetype, its source. 3. *He is True.* The Truth. The Substance. These attributes bespeak the almightiness and essential Godhead of the Son. Creatures have them partially and derivatively; he, infinitely and independently. 4. *Equity, too, is his.* "In righteousness he doth judge and make war." In the integrity of his sway there is no flaw. In the rectitude of his decisions there is no defect. These are the names and titles; these are the attributes by which he is distinguished. "Gird thy sword upon thy thigh, O most mighty, and in thy majesty ride prosperously, because of truth, and meekness, and righteousness."

III. HOW DOTH HE APPEAR IN GOING FORTH TO WAR? The characteristics here specified are three. 1. *He is seen on "a white horse."* So at the opening of the first seal. The *white* horse being the emblem of dignity, and of the peaceful triumphs he was about to win. *There*, however, he went forth at the beginning of his triumphs. *Here* he is seen going forth to a decisive and final conflict. 2. *He is "arrayed in a garment sprinkled with blood."* The question has been asked—Is the blood his own, or that of his foes? We reply—The symbolism is drawn from the responsive song in Isa. lxiii., and we cannot question that here the blood intended is that of his foes. Not, of course, to be taken as otherwise than symbolic of the completeness of the victory he has achieved, having put all enemies beneath his feet. 3. *On his head are many diadems.* In allusion, perhaps, to the ancient custom of a conqueror wearing the diadems of the vanquished kings. If so, the figure is one of immense suggestiveness and power. The beast, or the ungodly world-power, had seven heads—seven kings or kingdoms. Of these, at the time of the writing of the Apocalypse, five had fallen—

Egypt, Assyria, Chaldea, Persia, Greece. Rome hath gone also since then. And as earthly crowns one by one are falling from kingly brows, he to whom the globe belongs shall bear the glory. The glory of Egypt is gone; but the men of Egypt shall rise again, and crown him Lord of all. So with other realms, empires, nations. All worldly glory must depart, to reappear no more, save as all honour gathers round his majestic brow. The world's crown is waiting for Jesus! From every nation, kindred, tribe, and tongue, men shall exclaim—

> " Take the kingdom, it is thine,
> King of kings, and Lord of lords! "

IV. By what methods doth Christ bring this about? Andrew Fuller remarks, " Christ's war is of a twofold kind—spiritual . . . and providential." This is true. And though we need not regard the symbolism of this passage as a complete indication of the methods of Christ, yet there are three methods specified here. 1. *By the sword,* which may signify (1) judgment, and also (2) the Word which goeth forth out of his mouth. In fact, both (1) and (2) may blend as one, as the Word of his mouth is living and mighty, and sharper than any two-bladed sword; this is the rod of his strength. The " sword of the Spirit is the Word of God." 2. *By the armies of heaven.* Some take these to be the glorified saints; others, the angels. But seeing this is a vision of a conflict which is to take place on earth, it would seem to be more in accordance with the analogy of Scripture and with the nature of the case, to regard these armies as the friends of the Saviour, who, first redeemed by him, afterwards co-operate with him, going forth under his direction to pursue the holy war. Thus they may include (1) believers on earth; (2) departed saints; (3) angels, who minister to the heirs of salvation. These, these make up the glorious armies of heaven. All who are working and warring for God are now enrolled therein, " clothed in fine linen, white and clean." 3. *By stern and terrible judgments.* Surely nothing less than this can be intended by the expression (ver. 15), " He treadeth the wine-press of the fierceness of the wrath of Almighty God." Judgment is God's strange work. But when it comes, it will be terrible. " That great and terrible day of the Lord."

V. What are the issues of this mighty conflict? (Vers. 17—21.) These may be grouped around four of the figures employed in the text—the sword, the wine-press, the rod of iron, the lake of fire. All images of terror, because the theme in hand is the Divine triumph over sin; and righteousness must often—perhaps always—have an aspect of terror with reference to sin. Hence the apparent severity of the symbolism. Infinitely pure love must be severe upon sin. Sinners may be renewed; sin must be expelled. Enemies may be reconciled; enmity cannot. And it is sin itself, as the foe alike of God and man, that is ultimately to be put to shame; and so must all who strive against God, and in final impenitence reject his grace. By the sword of judgment they will be smitten down. As grapes are crushed in the wine-press, so will the enemies of God and the right be crushed. With a rod of iron shall they be ruled and be utterly powerless to resist when he riseth up in his day of final conflict. " The God of peace will bruise Satan under our feet shortly; " " He must reign till he hath put all enemies under his feet." Babylon hath already fallen. Next, the first beast is captured and thrown into the lake of fire; the second beast likewise, and they that worship his image. And thus one by one the foes are falling, till all things shall be subdued unto him. The whole creation will acknowledge the equity of the Great Supreme, and whether in joy or terror will own that Jesus Christ is Lord. Then, then the enemy shall be still as a stone. Temptation shall have sped for ever. " Alleluia! Alleluia! the Lord God Omnipotent reigneth."

Thus have we traced in outline the sketch which the Holy Ghost by the apostle's pen hath given us, of the great Destroyer of evil as he is now enthroned in glory, preparing to overturn, and overturn, and overturn, till he shall come, in the glory of his majesty and might, and claim the kingdom as his own. " What shall we then say to these things? " Note: 1. *How great is the mercy that heaven hath been " opened " for us to have such visions!* We are not left to the adventurous flights of human speculation, nor to the curious varieties of human guessing, nor even to the devout aspirations of philanthropic zeal. However decidedly any or all of these might tend in one direction, they could not—even if they all coincided—give us solid ground on which to rest

But here, here we have a firm rock on which we stand; here we fix our hopes; here we cast anchor; nor can our vessel ever be drifted from her mooring. "The glory of the Lord shall be revealed, and all flesh shall see it together: *for the mouth of the Lord hath spoken it.*" And however we may have been disheartened by the tangled maze and troubled aspect of this world's affairs, when we ponder over such visions as these, our hope revives. In him who is the Word of God, whose eyes are as a flame of fire, we see an amplitude of wisdom and a plenitude of power. In the blood-stained robes we see marks of a conflict already encountered, and pledges of a victory already secured. For such a Leader no mazes of evil can be too complex, no massing of power too strong. "Alleluia!" 2. *The vision shows us the grandeur of the strife between good and evil.* When the everlasting Son of the Father takes it up as his own cause, it assumes new dignity. In an ancient battle it inspired God's people when they were told, "The battle is not yours, but God's;" and since that which was true in a material conflict cannot be less so in a spiritual one, we may well draw a holy inspiration for our contest with sin, in the thought that the King of kings, and Lord of lords, is the sole Leader in the fight. *His* honour is engaged. He hath it in trust from the Father to put down evil, and to gather home the redeemed. "In righteousness doth *he* make war!" Never was there such a holy war, never one on which such stupendous issues hung, as that one with which we are asked to identify ourselves. 3. *It is an act of great condescension that, in going forth with his armies, our Saviour deigns to make use of human instrumentality.* He would use us. He commands us to enter his army. (1) Some *are* engaged on his side. And they find it their noblest joy and their highest honour to co-operate with their redeeming Lord. Let them not forget the garb in which the Saviour's hosts go forth—"*clothed in fine linen, white and clean.*" (2) Some there are who have not yet openly espoused the Saviour's cause. Let such remember that there are *only* two sides. "He that is not against us is for us;" here is what Vinet called "the tolerance of the gospel." "He that is not with me is against me;" here is what the same writer called "the intolerance of the gospel." Christ allows no neutrality. We are either siding with the armies of heaven or with the worshippers of the beast and his image. But let us remember that just in proportion to the severity of the defeat which awaits us if we are on the wrong side, is the greatness of the joy which will attend us if, through the Holy Spirit's grace, we are won over to the side of Jesus. We go not a warfare at our own charges. We shall be well equipped for the most perilous expedition and the longest marches, and also furnished with wisdom and strength for the severest fight. And if we could but cause men to see the glory of the conflict, instead of having to plead with them to side with Jesus, the pleading would be heard from their side that they might have the privilege of fighting in the holy war!

HOMILIES BY VARIOUS AUTHORS.

Vers. 1—10.—*The triumph of the redeemed.* When Handel wrote the "Hallelujah Chorus" he endeavoured, so he said, to picture to himself what the great gladness of the glorified must be. He rightly and reverently sought—and, it seems to us, sought not in vain—to imagine the whole scene as it is recorded here. And it is good for us to muse much on a scene like this. It is a veritable *sursum corda* for poor sin and sorrow laden men such as we are. It helps us to obey the word, "Be not weary nor faint in your minds." Let us, then, observe—

I. TO WHOM THIS TRIUMPH IS ASCRIBED. The "Alleluia" and all the resonant rejoicing praise is "unto the Lord our God." When we consider who join in this praise, we shall see amongst them many who were eminent in service, who did heroic work for Christ and his cause—prophets, apostles, martyrs, and ministers of God of all degrees. They had not stinted their toil, nor grudged aught they could do and be for their Lord; but not to them, not even to the greatest, is the praise of heaven ascribed, but all "unto the Lord our God." There and then will it be seen, as it is not now, how insignificant in comparison with his work was that of any of his servants, and how even that was only in his strength. This vision, therefore, endorses our Saviour's words, "When ye have done all, say, We are unprofitable servants."

II. By whom. A goodly company is presented to our view. For: 1. "*Much people in heaven*" *were seen* by St. John, and he heard the "great voice" of their united praise. And as they beheld the proof of their ancient adversary's utter overthrow, in that "the smoke" of the fire by which his city was consumed "rose up for ever and ever," then their praise burst forth again: "and again they said, Alleluia" (ver. 3). 2. And next, *the representatives of the whole Church of God,* "the twenty-four elders," and the representatives of the creation of God, "the four living creatures"—join in this praise, and prostrating themselves worship him, saying, "Amen; Alleluia." 3. Then is heard "*the voice of a great multitude*" (ver. 6), and the sound of their praise was as vast in volume and force as that of the many waters of the much-resounding sea, or the deep reverberating thunders which roll amidst the clouds of heaven. Blessed it is to see the great throng of those who render this praise; let us be thankful for the multitude of the saved, but mindful, too, that not one was there, whether small or great, but were "servants" of God, and feared him.

III. How. The words which express their gratitude and joy are worthy of our careful heed. 1. *Alleluia.* Here alone in the New Testament is this word found, where it is repeated four times. It is borrowed from the Psalms, of which fifteen either begin or end with "Hallelujah." In Ps. civ. 35 it is first found, and allusion seems to be made here to that passage. "The sinners shall be consumed from the earth, and the wicked shall be no more. Praise the Lord, O my soul. Hallelujah." Thus in the dark times of old the Church sustained her faith by these holy songs, and now the redeemed in heaven, having realized what then was but hoped for, lift again their "Hallelujah." The praises of earth are prophetic of and preparatory to the praises of heaven. 2. Then comes the ascription to the Lord of *salvation.* It is meant to affirm that salvation *is* of the Lord. There had been times when their faith faltered and well-nigh failed amid the darkness and distress of their earthly lot. But now they know and they acknowledge that salvation is of the Lord. And of him only. It is all due to him. 3. *Glory.* Of this, too, there had at one time been sad misgiving. For the cause of God seemed to be everywhere suffering defeat. The world seemed everywhere to win, and the Name of God to be held in contempt. The glory did not seem to belong to God, but to some other. But now all doubt was gone. The glory was the Lord's. His foes had made war with him, but had suffered complete overthrow at his hands. 4. *Power.* This also was now evidently the Lord's. Sometimes it had seemed as if the might and malice of the devil were too strong to be overcome. But now it was certain. "Salvation, and glory, and power belong to our God." And all this they repeat, and with them the elders and the living creatures unite. Thus in innumerable throng, with loud acclaim and with deepest, holiest love, they render praise to the Lord, to whom they owe their all, and to whom, therefore, all praise is due. Let us listen to this glorious praise, this heavenly hallelujah, and learn to doubt our doubts and deny our denials; learn that salvation *is* of the Lord, and glory and power likewise, however much our unbelieving hearts may question and fear and faint.

IV. Wherefore. A threefold cause is given. 1. *The judgment of the harlot-city.* For (1) she had made others sin; she had corrupted the earth with her abomination. She had, by her emissaries, spread her deadly influence far and wide, poisoning the springs of life, making them fountains of evil and sin. Ah, how differently we judge here on earth! If a bad, depraved, vicious man—a corrupter of youth, a poisoner of men's moral life—live amongst us, and he be but wealthy as this harlot was, and has, like her, pleasing and attractive manners, we condone his wickedness and make all manner of excuse for his sins. But not so with the saints of God. And (2) she had shed the blood of God's saints. Those who were the salt of the earth she had put out of the way; those who were the light of the world she had ruthlessly extinguished as far as she could. They who would have been as breakwaters, buffeting back the inrushing floods of sin, she put to death. All her power had gone to make earth like hell. That such a one should be judged was indeed good cause for heaven's hallelujahs. Have we sympathy with such joy? Would the like reason excite in us like delight? Do we hate such as Heaven hates, such as this harlot was and is evermore? 2. *The marriage of the Lamb.* (Ver. 7.) Marriage festivals are ever, and rightly, regarded as joyous seasons if the marriage be worthy of the name. How much more, then, the marriage, the consummation of the union betwixt Christ and his Church! *There is joy on account of the Bridegroom.* The bride he has so long and truly loved he possesses at last. " He that hath the bride is the Bridegroom." But, long ere this, this Bridegroom had sought his bride, had loved her from the first, had shed his blood to save her. But he had a formidable rival. Another suitor sought his bride, and endeavoured by every beguilement to win her for himself. The world wooed her, and sometimes it seemed as if it had really won her. But at length the Bridegroom told of here won her heart. That was at length fully, freely given, so that when he asked, "Lovest thou me?" the answer came back, "Lord, thou knowest that I love thee." But with all this love she was not yet ready for her Lord. And the preparation was a long process. But her Lord waited for her patiently; visiting her often in her earthly home, loading her with tokens of his love; and at length, dearer to him than ever, she stands at his side, for the marriage-day is come. May not the friends of the Bridegroom rejoice on his account? And *there is joy because of the bride.* That she should have been led to give her heart to One so worthy; that she should have been chosen by him who was so worthy, when she herself was so unworthy; oh, what wondrous happiness was that for such as she was! And now that she should be deemed worthy, and through his grace *be* worthy. And that at last, made ready, she should stand by his side to whom her heart has been so long given, and know now that they can never be separated any more. No wonder, then, when we remember who the bride is, and who the Bridegroom, that at this marriage there is great joy. The union of Christ and his Church, which has of necessity been so imperfect and interrupted here, now perfected for ever. Well may the bride put on the lustrous linen raiment, white and glistering in the sheen of its exquisite beauty, and the symbol of the purity and righteousness with which she had been spiritually endowed! For: 3. *The preparation of the bride* is named as another spring of the heavenly joy. "His wife hath made herself ready." But never could she have done this had it not been "granted to her" to array herself in the bright and pure spiritual raiment which became her marriage dress. So that it is both true that the Church makes herself ready for Christ, and that it is Christ who makes her ready. But for him she could not make herself ready, and without her consenting heart he will not make her so. She works out her own salvation, because he worketh in her both to will and to do. But no matter how the blessed work has been accomplished, there is the unspeakably joyful fact that it is accomplished. His wife is "ready." The vision is yet future. The robing of the redeemed, the making ready of the bride, is yet going on. This is the meaning of all our disciplines and trials, of all the pleadings of God's Spirit, of all the means of grace which we are bidden employ, of all the strain and toil of heart which we often have to bear; it is all the making "ready" of the bride. But when it is all complete for all the redeemed, all done that had to be done, all borne that had to be borne, and God shall have wiped away all tears from off all faces—that, too, may well call forth, as it assuredly will, another of the hallelujahs of heaven. See to it that we are present at that marriage; for "blessed are they which are bidden to the marriage supper of the Lamb."—S. C.

Ver. 8.—*The "linen" of Scripture.* "For the fine linen is the righteousness of saints." There are highways and byways of the Bible. Many think they have exhausted the Scriptures when they have traversed the King's highway. But there are, as many a delighted traveller has found, byways less known, and far less frequented paths, which yield up to the explorer knowledge and beauty and good which they were ignorant of before. The land of Scripture is a glorious land. There is no region upon earth, however endowed with well-nigh all forms and possibilities of the beautiful, that can compare, for variety and sublimity, for loveliness and richness, to the Word of God. But whilst we may be familiar with its main features, if we will be at the pains to search out its less-trodden paths and its hidden nooks and corners—if we may so speak,—it is wonderful what fresh interest and instruction may be often gained. Now, one of those more diligent searchers of the Bible (B. W. Newton) has noted the fact that there are three different kinds of linen spoken of in Scripture, and that the vestments made from them were worn on specific and appointed occasions; so that each kind of linen had its religious significance. Let us try and see what that was. Now, of this familiar fabric there were three different kinds. 1. *The ordinary material,* which gives the name to all varieties of it. The Greeks translated the Hebrew word and called it λίνον, as we also call it. Now, in four books of the Bible this common and inferior variety of linen is referred to. In *Leviticus*, twice. (1) When the priest is renewing the fire upon the altar, that it may not go out (Lev. vi. 10). He comes in the early morning, gathers up the ashes, etc. In doing this he was to wear a particular dress made of this linen. (2) On the great Day of Atonement (Lev. xvi.), Aaron and his sons are not to be arrayed in their "garments of glory and beauty," but in their plainest attire. Hence they were to put on vestments of this linen. In *Ezekiel* (ix. 2, 3, 11 ; x. 2, 6, 7), where the vision of Jerusalem's coming desolation is given. Ezekiel sees a man with an ink-horn by his side, who is in company with five others. Their mission is to execute God's vengeance; his, to report of it. Now, this man is dressed in this linen. Six times (see verses given) attention is called to this fact. In *Daniel* (x. 5), where a similar vision is recorded, the Divine messenger is dressed in like manner, and foretells the judgments of God. Then, in ch. xv. 6, "the seven angels, having the seven last plagues," are arrayed in this linen. 2. *Then there is a second and superior kind of this fabric,* and of this we have a twofold mention. It is distinguished from the former by being called "fine linen," or "fine twisted linen." It was made not merely of a finer thread, but was composed of six threads twisted, and therefore called "fine twined linen." Now, this fabric formed the vestments of the chief and other priests when arrayed in their "garments of glory and beauty " (Exod. xxxix. 27). Then it was used also (Exod. xxvi. 1) for the hangings of the tabernacle, in the most holy place. There were ten of these, all made of this fine twined linen. 3. *And there is a third and choicest kind of all,* and to this we have several references. It was a most costly fabric, and of such fine and skilful manufacture that its whiteness came to have a "glistering," a bright and dazzling, appearance. It was of great value, and used only by monarchs and the very wealthy, or upon great occasions. As (1) when David brought up the ark to Jerusalem from the house of Obed-edom, he was clothed, so we read (1 Chron. xv. 27), in a robe of this magnificent texture. There was a splendid procession, and all the tokens of the gladness and triumph which filled the hearts of king, people, and priests. David "danced before the Lord," thus vested in royal and priestly array. (2) At the dedication of the temple by Solomon (2 Chron. v. 12) the priests were similarly arrayed. (3) So in Mordecai's triumph (Esth. viii. 15), there were put upon him royal apparel of blue and white, a great crown of gold, and a garment of fine linen. Now, our version, neither in the Old Testament nor in the New, ever distinguishes this most beautiful fabric from the others named above; but both in the Hebrew and Greek Scriptures it is clearly defined by the use of an entirely different word. (4) In our Lord's transfiguration, he was seen by the three disciples in raiment "white and glistering." This is probably an allusion to the known appearance of that rare and costly fabric of which we are now speaking. (5) Finally, in our text, it is again named as the raiment of the redeemed. Now, on all these observe : (*a*) That in each case *there is an essential oneness.* That which was worn was in substance the same in all. It was "linen, white and clean," which was on the priest when tending the altar fire, and on the Day of Atonement, as truly as when arrayed in their pontificals, their garments of glory and beauty, or as in the hangings of the most holy place. And so, too, in the raiment of the redeemed. It is essentially the same in all. Different in texture, but one in substance. (*b*) *When any particular form of this fabric is spoken of, it is always connected with one class of circumstances.* The first is always associated with the ideas of sorrow, sin, judgment (cf. *supra*). The second, with the idea of God's gracious acceptance. The priest is arrayed in garments of glory and beauty, to symbolize the honour and joy which are his as God's accepted priest. And in the tabernacle hangings the same idea is set forth. The third, with glad triumph and glory won (cf. instances). Therefore inquire—

I. WHAT IS TAUGHT BY THE ESSENTIAL ONENESS OF THE FABRIC IN ALL ITS FORMS? In all there is the "linen, white and clean." This, therefore, tells of the common and essential qualification of all believers—to be clothed with righteousness. And as it is "put on," something not inherent, but external, it shadows forth the righteousness which is ours in Christ, "who is made unto us Righteousness," who is "the Lord our Righteousness." Every one of us, in whatever stage of the Christian career—at its beginning or at its consummation has his acceptance not in himself, but in Christ. He is "all and in all." "Him first, him midst, him last, and without end." That is the declaration of Scripture, of conscience, of right reason, of Christ's people always and everywhere, and of this symbol of the "linen, white and clean."

II. WHAT BY ITS VARIETIES? They tell of the different circumstances in which the believer is found. 1. The first tells of him *as conscious of sin.* He is a believer, a saved soul—his raiment proves that; but when conscious of sin, garments of glory and beauty would be out of place. (1) Thus, when conscious of sin's magnitude and amount, as on the annual Day of Atonement, when Israel was commanded "to afflict their souls," the priests were to wear these vestments. And so before the altar, as the believer before the cross. (2) Or of sin's awful consequences. See Ezekiel; Daniel; seven angels (cf. *supra*). There, again, this raiment. Yes, if we be Christ's, we shall often, daily, in our hours of confession and penitential prayer, be thus vested spiritually. But this not "the sorrow of the world," but that "godly sorrow" which worketh eternal life. 2. The second, *as conscious of Christ.* He is not only accepted, but conscious of it. Hence he wears the "garments of glory and beauty." It was fitting the priest should; it is fitting that we, when realizing that we are Christ's and he ours, should in heart be vested thus. The symbolic "fine linen" clothed his limbs, the seat of his strength; was in the most holy place; was worn as a fair mitre upon his head; all this telling how his daily life, his approaches to God, his intercessions for others, were accepted of God. May not a man's heart sing for joy, may he not spiritually put on this "fine linen," when he knows that he and all he does is accepted of the Lord? 3. *As possessed of eternal glory.* The source of his blessedness still the same, but now he realizes all he had anticipated. And, moreover, the righteousness which it was given him to put on has become a righteousness in him, and has developed in "righteous acts;" for so the Revised Version renders our text: "The fine linen is the righteous acts of the saints." It would be false to Scripture, to conscience, and to fact, to teach that all the righteousness needed for the bride of the Lamb is one that is put on as a vestment. No; it is one formed within also, and expressed in "righteous acts"—in that "holiness without which no man shall see the Lord."

Would we wear that splendid vestment at the last? Then see to it that we wear the plain one now.—S. C.

Vers. 11—21.—*The four names of Christ.* There were three great enemies of Christ and his Church, each of which have been told of in the previous chapters of this book—the dragon, the first beast, and the second beast, or the false prophet. In the immediately foregoing chapters we have had told the destruction that came upon them that worshipped the beast. Generally upon them all by the outpouring of the seven vials; and then, more particularly, upon the city Babylon, which was the seat and centre of the authority of the beast. Then there came the vision of the blessed in heaven—a vision once and again given in this book, to reassure those on earth that, amid all the awful judgments of God upon their enemies, they, his faithful witnessing people here upon earth, should not be, were not, forgotten. Their bright, blessed condition in the presence of God is what is shown them for their comfort, their hope, their strength. That cheering vision having been given, the awful judgments upon the beast and the false prophet are next shown. We see the Lord summoning his armies, his eyes flashing in anger, the diadems on his head, the crimson vesture, the sharp sword, and the four names emblazoned thereon. Probably St. John had in view some near catastrophe on the enemies of the Church of his day, which supplies the groundwork of this vision. Or, as some affirm, the heathen nations who were slain, not so much by awful war as by the sword of the Spirit, and ceased to be heathen, and became Christian. For the kings—these say—are the heathen Goths, Vandals, and the rest who invaded the empire everywhere and destroyed Rome, but who soon became Christian and were received into the Church. Or, it may be, that the vision is all for the future. Who can tell? But the names of Christ, as here given, are for all time, and are full of instruction and help.

I. THE "FAITHFUL AND TRUE." (Ver. 11.) So was he: 1. *In avenging his people.* This is the thought suggested to those for whom St. John wrote. And so will he ever be. 2. *In carrying out his purposes.* It mattered not who or what withstood. 3. *The past proves the righteousness of this name.* His prophecies have been fulfilled.

His promises made good. His precepts owned as just. Whoever disputes a verdict he has given? Who does not feel that, when he has spoken, the last word, be the subject what it may, has been said, and that there is nothing more to be said?

II. THE UNKNOWN NAME. (Ver. 12, "And he had a name written, that no man knew, but he himself.") It was a written name, but illegible, incomprehensible, to all but himself. The names advance in majesty. "Faithful and True"—that is an august name, but it cannot be said to be incomprehensible, and known to none but himself. Glory be to him that we do know him by that name, and that the name is rightly his. But now the ineffable nature of the Son of God seems to be suggested. "Who by searching can find out God?" Christ is more than all our thought, than all we have understood or have imagined. In him are "unsearchable riches." Who knows what is the relation between him and the Father, and what the nature of the union in him of humanity and God? Who can understand the profound philosophy of the atonement, the Incarnation, the Resurrection? "No man knoweth the Son but the Father"—so said our Lord; and this unknown name, written, though not read, endorses that sublime saying. And do we wonder that we cannot understand? Why, this we fail to do even with our fellow-men if they be of higher nature than our own. Let us be glad and grateful that, whatever riches of grace and glory we have already known, there is an inexhaustible fountain and an unsearchable store yet remaining. And now a name more majestic still is given.

III. "THE WORD OF GOD." (Ver. 13.) This name refers to that "Word of God which is . . . sharper than," etc. (Heb. iv. 12). Also it points back to his name as given in John i. 1, "The Word, which in the beginning was with God, and was God." For the Word is the expression of the inner thought. And so Christ declares the mind of God; he is "the heart of God revealed." Hence "he who hath seen the Son hath seen the Father." Now, all this is true, or else he is what we would not even say. *Si non Deus, non bonus*—so of old was it argued, and so it must be still. The doctrine declared by this name is, therefore, of infinite importance. All our conceptions of Christ, all our hope, all our salvation, depend on it. If he be not the very Word of God, then we have no Saviour and no hope. The last of these names is—

IV. "KING OF KINGS, AND LORD OF LORDS." (Ver. 16.) It is the battle of the ten kings against him to which he is on his way when St. John beholds him (vers. 18, 19). And now on his vesture and on the scabbard of his sword—"on his thigh"—are emblazoned these majestic words, this title prophetic of victory for himself and those with him, but of utter defeat to those who dared to oppose him. But how blessed to humanity at large is this name and the fact that it declares! Vast is the power that monarchs wield, and—alas, that it should be so!—bad is the use that most of them have made of it. And so the days of kingship are—it is said—numbered. But there may be worse depositaries of power even than kings, seeing that others called by lowlier names have used it not much better. But it is blessed to know that, let kings and rulers do and be what they may, our Lord is "King of kings, and," etc. Meanwhile (1) see that he rules in *us;* (2) take the rich comfort there is in these names. —S. C.

Ver. 12.—*The coronation of the Saviour.* "On his head were many crowns." We know whose head is meant. It was "the head that once was crowned with thorns;" the head that was once pillowed on a human mother's breast; the head that "had not where," during the days of his earthly ministry, "to lay" itself down to rest; the head that once and again was a fountain of tears because of man's sorrow and man's sin; the head that was beaten and spit upon by his enemies; the head that was bound about by the linen wrappings of the tomb; the head that was "bowed" when on the cross "he gave up the ghost;"—on that head St. John saw in vision "many crowns." To see desert rewarded, especially when the deserving has been conspicuous, marked by great toil, great self-sacrifice, great suffering, great purity, great love, and great good gained for those for whom all this was borne—to see such deserving duly recompensed is ever a real joy. What, then, must be the believer's joy to see on his Lord's head the many crowns which tell of his reward! The figure is taken from the ancient diadem, which consisted of many circlets, or bands, the whole forming one crown, though consisting of many diadems. Now, it is given to us not only to rejoice in, but to add to, these many crowns; and that we may be roused to a holy ambition thus to minister to our Saviour's glory, let us consider these "many crowns." And—

I. THOSE THAT ARE NOT OF EARTH. 1. *The heavenly crown.* What glorious scenes does this book present to us of the palace and court of heaven, and of him who is the Centre and Sovereign of it, "Lord of lords, and King of kings"! Have we not had shown to us the adoration of the Lamb? All these, love, worship, and obey. 2. *He is Sovereign of death.* "I," said he, "have the keys of hell and of death." By this is meant that all that unseen world where the departed are owns him as its King. He "openeth, and no man shutteth; he shutteth, and no man openeth." Blessed thought! they who have left us went only at his bidding, and they have gone where he is Lord. 3. *Hell is beneath his feet.* It did its best and worst to defeat and to destroy him, but in vain. When he was but a Babe, hell put it into the heart of Herod to seek to kill him. When he went forth to his ministry, he was forty days and forty nights tempted of the devil. During that ministry hell assailed him, now with blandishments, now with terror. At last the powers of hell had their way, and Jesus was hung up and crucified. And he entered the shades of death. But it was "not possible that he should be holden" of the grave. He broke through its power, and overcame its sharpness, and opened the kingdom of heaven, which hell would have shut, to all believers. And by virtue of his great atonement Satan has received a "deadly wound," is fallen, is doomed, is "reserved unto the judgment of the great day." And the lion, the hold, that hell had on humanity, Christ has destroyed by his death, which, though not a ransom paid to Satan—as the ancient Church long thought—was, nevertheless, effectual as a ransom, opening the prison doors and setting at liberty them that were bound. Yes, Christ has this crown also—iron crown though it be—amid his many crowns.

II. THOSE OF HEAVEN AND EARTH COMBINED. By these we mean his mediatorial crown, by which he becomes the King of grace. For he united heaven and earth. He was the true Ladder set upon earth, but whose top reached to the heaven, and upon which the angels of God ascend and descend. So he himself explained the vision of Jacob at Bethel. And in his nature he was Son of man and Son of God; born of Mary, and yet "in the beginning was with God, and was God." "The Word was made flesh." Thus has he become the "one Mediator between God and man." In his hand, therefore, is the bestowal of all grace. Whatever I need I can turn to him to give to me. Pardon, peace, holiness, heaven—all are in him for his people. He is my very Brother as well as my Lord, Friend as well as Sovereign. His is the mediatorial crown.

III. THOSE OF EARTH. 1. The material earth owns him her Sovereign. By him "the worlds were made." He sustains them in all their orderly course. "By him all things consist." He directs and governs by his unerring laws all their movements. His miracles showed his sovereignty over nature. "What manner of Man is this, that even the winds and the sea obey him!" 2. But especially does he wear the crown of sovereignty in *regard to man.* (1) Even those who say, "We will not have this Man to reign over us," though they may be suffered for a while to slight his authority, yet will one day own that "his are all their ways;" that it is "in him they live, and move, and have their being." "To him every knee shall bow, and every tongue confess." God has placed that crown upon his head. (2) But especially is he the crowned King of his Church. Redeemed, saved, men delight to "crown him Lord of all." All they who know his love—and what an ever-growing multitude they are!— "old men and maidens, young men and children," all ages, ranks, and conditions of men, for that they each and all have some special knowledge of his grace, are eager to crown him with their love. Myriads of children transplanted in infancy from this drear, desert-world to the fair garden of heaven; sufferers so sustained that they could rejoice even in tribulation; great workers for him who could do all things, and did all they did, through his strength; hoary age, to whom he gave light at eventide;—but what a throng is there of those whose love would add yet another to the many crowns of their Lord! Have *we* none to lay at his feet, to place on his head? None, though forgiven; none, though his Spirit dwells within us; none, though his home waits for us? Enthrone him in thy heart, crown him there, for that is his desire.—S. C.

Vers. 1—10.—*The bride of Christ.* "After these things"—the overpoweringly impressive vision just granted to the holy seer—a song as "of a great multitude in heaven" breaks upon the ear. It is a song of praise to God, ascribing to him the "salvation" wrought out for his people, and the "glory" of that salvation, and the "power" by which it has been accomplished—a song of praise for his "true and righteous judgments" upon "the great harlot," and the avenging of "the blood of his servants at her hand." And again and again loud "Hallelujahs" follow. The song is from the heavenly multitude rejoicing over the destruction of the kingdom and power of evil, and in its chorus is heard the voice of the universal Church represented by "the elders," and of the whole creature-life by "the four living creatures." Now a voice is heard "from the throne" calling upon all the "servants" of the Lord, "the small and the great," to "give praise to our God." Then is heard the voice—a mighty voice—as "of a great multitude, as the voice of many waters, as the voice of mighty thunders." It is still a song of triumph and a song of praise—"Hallelujah: for the Lord our God, the Almighty, reigneth." He has laid low his adversaries. He has taken to himself his mighty power. Babylon licks the dust. As a consummation, the song bursts into a marriage-song. The undying relation of Christ to his Church is herein anticipated; and our thought rests on *the final blessedness of the Church as the bride of Christ.* This condition is coincident with the destruction of the kingdom of evil. The harlotry of evil is at an end. The pure love of the pure and faithful bride, and her joyful union with the Lamb, form the antithetical idea.

I. THE CHURCH'S FINAL BLESSEDNESS IS FOUND IN AN INDISSOLUBLE UNION WITH CHRIST. It is a union that never loses sight of the redemption that is by Christ Jesus. He is ever, in the Church's view, "the Lamb." Hitherto the union has been by faith, and subject to all the fluctuations of the frail heart. Now the bond is indissoluble. It is eternal. It is a marriage which no death occurs to dissolve.

II. FOR THIS THE CHURCH IS PREPARED BY SANCTITY AND FIDELITY. The sanctity is seen in that she "hath made herself ready." She is arrayed in "fine linen, bright and pure," which symbolizes at once the pure spirit and faithful service: "the righteous acts of the saints."

III. THE ULTIMATE BLESSEDNESS OF THE SAINTS IS THE OCCASION OF JOY TO ALL. "Blessed are they that are bidden to the marriage supper of the Lamb." They who sang loud "Hallelujahs" because the harlot was judged now find a spring of new blessedness in the purity, triumph, and felicity of the faithful saints—the bride, the Lamb's wife.—R. G.

Vers. 11—21.—*The holy war.* There now opens to our view another scene of warfare. It is brief, comprehensive, and decisive. It is a view of the heavenlies. The conflict is between the heavenly and the earthly powers. It is a "representation of the conquest of the kingdoms to Christ, which, like all his conquests, is accomplished by the power of the truth, wielded by a faithful Church, and rendered efficacious by the power of his Spirit."

I. THE COMBATANTS ARE DISTINCTLY BROUGHT TO VIEW. These are: 1. One called "Faithful and True"—"the Word of God." He is distinguished by symbols which indicate his Divine power and authority. He is "KING OF KINGS, AND LORD OF LORDS." His visage corresponds to earlier descriptions: "his eyes are a flame of fire;" "on his head are many diadems;" his name is unknown but to himself; his garment is sprinkled with blood; from his mouth proceeds a sharp sword; his feet tread the wine-press of the Divine wrath; he is seated on a white horse. 2. He leads forth an army also upon white horses, and clothed in "fine linen, white and pure." Thus is represented the Divine Captain, the Lord Jesus, leading forth his faithful ones to do battle against sin in its various guises. 3. On the other hand is represented the contending foes: "the beast, and the kings of the earth, and their armies." Against these Christ and his faithful Church wage war: war against sin—foul, filthy sin— "the beast;" and against all the spirit of error and untruth, "the false prophet;" and against all the powers of evil which by them inspired domineer over the life of men, and they wage war against whatever stands in opposition to the idea of "the Christ"—the King set upon the holy hill, of whom the psalmist sings. They are the enemies, the "foes" of David's Son and Lord, which shall be made his "footstool."

II. THE CONFLICT IS NOT DELINEATED. It has been already, and abundantly. We are to see in it all the contention long continued between the diverse elements, light and darkness, truth and error, righteousness and sin, Christ and Belial, the judgment of human conduct by the true standard of right, the life of Christ. This is the struggle now going forward.

III. THE ISSUE IS A VICTORIOUS CONQUEST GAINED BY CHRIST AND HIS ARMY OVER ALL THE POWER OF THE ENEMY. "The beast was taken, and with him the false prophet." Their destruction is complete and final. They are cast alive, as in their activity, into a "lake of fire that burneth with brimstone."

IV. THE INSTRUMENT OF WARFARE SUFFICIENTLY INDICATES THE NATURE OF THE STRIFE. In a few words is indicated the nature of the weapons (weapon), and so the nature of the strife. He smites the nations with the sword which proceeded out of his mouth: "The sword of the Spirit, which is the Word of God." With this only weapon the "rest are killed."

V. THE FINAL JOY OF ALL in the ascendency of the truth is indicated in the gathering of the fowls of the air to the supper of the great God, called by an angel standing where all can see—in the sun.—R. G.

Vers. 1—21.—*The Eternal in the universe, and his Representative to man.* "And after these things I heard a great voice of much people," etc. "Babylon" in this book I take as the *symbol of moral evil* on this earth, or, in other words, of all that is corrupt in human life. From its establishment on this globe, it has been "falling." It is "falling" now, and will continue to fall until its mighty mountain shall become a plain, and there will be found "no place" for it. In the preceding chapter the effect of its fall was seen. How the bad howled lamentations! and how the good shouted its *jubilations!* Looking at this chapter, not as a verbal critic, a prophetic interpreter, or as a sensuous pietist, but as a practical man, it suggests and portrays to me the *Eternal in the universe, and his Representative to man.* We have here—

I. A SYMBOLIC ASPECT OF THE ETERNAL IN THE UNIVERSE. How does he appear here? As receiving the highest worship. "After these things I heard [as it were] a great voice of much people [a great multitude] in heaven, saying, Alleluia," etc. 1. *The worship was widely extensive*—"much people," "elders" (vers. 1—3), "beasts," "small and great," "a great multitude." In this worship, the "four and twenty elders," the representatives of the sainted dead who have reached the heavenly state, and the "four beasts" [living creatures], unfallen spirits through all ages and worlds, all these unite in the one grand "Alleluia," "Praise our God [give praise to our God]." Worship is the vital breath and inspiration of all holy intelligences. On the Eternal their eyes are fixed with supreme adoration, and their hearts with intensest love turned in impressive devotion. 2. *The worship was supremely deserved.* "True and righteous are his judgments" (ver. 2). He is true and righteous, absolutely so in himself is he. "He is light, and in him is no darkness at all." Not one dark thought has ever passed through his infinite intellect, not one sentiment of evil has ever ruffled the immeasurable sea of his emotionality. The Father of lights is he; all the beams of holy thoughts and ideas stream from him, as rays from the central sun of immensity.

> "O holy Sire, O holy Sire,
> Sole Fount of life and light!
> Thou art the uncreated Fire,
> Burning in every pure desire
> Of all who love the right."

Not only is he absolutely "true and righteous" in himself, but it is suggested that he is so in his procedure against the wrong. "He hath judged the great whore [harlot], which did corrupt the earth with her fornication, and hath [he hath] avenged the blood of his servants at her hand" (ver. 2). This "great whore" stands, I think, the same as Babylon, for the moral evil in the world. Her description is given in ch. xvii. It suggests and illustrates three great evils in the world: (1) Political subserviency; (2) worldly tendency; and (3) religious intolerance. Is he not "true and righteous" in crushing such a moral monster, such a curse to the earth, so that her "smoke rose [goeth] up for ever and ever" (ver. 3), which means utter destruction? Now, were he not "true and righteous," both in himself and in his procedure, who could worship him? Moral mind is so constituted, that to worship the false and the wrong would be an impossibility. You may urge me to do so with the threat of eternal damnation, but I could not bow my knee to such; nor ought I, if I could. But the worship of an immaculate God meets the moral cravings of my soul, and brings out all the faculties of my nature in harmonious play and rapturous delight. 3. *The worship was intensely enthusiastic.* "Alleluia," "Praise our God," etc. "In the present episode," says Moses Stuart, "trichotomy as usual is plainly discernible. In the first division, all the inhabitants of the heavenly world are represented as uniting in a song of triumph and of thanksgiving on account of the righteous judgments of God which are about to be inflicted (vers. 1—4). In the second, a voice from the throne in heaven speaks, and requires of all his servants everywhere, renewed praise, which accordingly is shouted (vers. 5—8). In the third, a glorious prospect of suffering martyrs is disclosed. They will be guests at the marriage supper of the Lamb; the Church is indeed the Lamb's bride, and the exaltation of the Messiah is vividly sketched in the declaration of the angel-interpreter, at whose feet John, in a state of astonishment, falls. Jesus, the angel declares, is the Object of worship by him; and therefore he (the angel) cannot claim the worship of his fellow-servants, who, like him, are merely instruments in making known the prophecies respecting the triumph of redeeming grace (vers. 9, 10)." The "Alleluias" seem to wax louder and louder as they are repeated, until they become as "the voice of many waters, and as the voice of mighty thunderings [thunders]" (ver. 6). The voice seems as loud as the vociferous noise of a mighty army when victory has been won, or as the boom of old ocean when lashed into fierce storm.

II. A SYMBOLIC ASPECT OF THE ETERNAL IN HIS REPRESENTATIVE TO MAN. "Let us be glad and rejoice [rejoice and be exceeding glad], and give honour to him [let us give the glory unto him]: for the marriage of the Lamb is come," etc. (ver. 7). As Christ is in other places of the Bible represented as the "Lamb of God," and also as being wedded to his genuine disciples, the symbolic language here suggests him to our minds in some of his grand relations to mankind. He appears here: 1. *As the loving Husband of the true.* "The marriage of the Lamb is come, and his wife hath made herself ready" (ver. 7). By the true, I mean his genuine disciples, those of Christly character. In various places elsewhere, his relation to such is represented as the foundation to a building, as the root to a branch, as the head to a body. But his relationship here represented varies from these in at least three respects. (1) *There is mutual choice.* There is no mutual choice of the superstructure to the foundation, of the branch to the root, of the limb to the head. But there is a *mutual choice* in the connection between husband and wife, bridegroom and bride. In true marriage, which, I trow, is somewhat rare amongst what are called the marriages of the race, the true are brought together, not by coercion, or accident, or blind passion, but by mutual selection; the one offers, the other accepts, freely and fully. Christ says to all of us, "Will you accept me as your Husband, your Guardian, Protector, and Friend?" Whilst the millions say, No, there are some who say, Yes, and the two become one; there is a vital identification. (2) *There is mutual sympathy.* Not convenience or passion, but pure, disinterested love—the love of admiration on the one side, and the love of condescending pity on the other. (3) *There is a mutual aim.* Christ's aim is to promote the glory of his Father, in advancing his benevolent plans and the best interests of the human race. This is also the grand purpose of those who in very soul wed themselves to him. They accept him as their Bridegroom, not from selfish motives, not from the dread of hell, nor for the hope of heaven; not to escape Gehenna, and reach a Paradise; but in order to promote the true well-being of humanity, and the glory of their Maker. The scene here suggested is that of a bridal feast, a banquet to celebrate the sublime union of souls. "Let us be glad and rejoice, and give honour to him: for the marriage of the Lamb is come." Observe: (1) The bridal costume on this occasion. "And to her was granted [it was given to her] that she should be arrayed [array herself] in fine linen, clean and white [bright and pure]: for the fine linen is the righteousness of saints [righteous acts of the saints]" (ver. 8). The bridal garment here described agrees with that worn by the bride at the Jewish nuptials. And here it must be regarded as a symbolic representation of the soul's attire. The pure, refined, righteous character, which covers and adorns the spirit of the bride—"the ornament that covers a meek and quiet spirit, which is in the sight of God of great price." Moral character is evermore the garment in which the soul is clad. If the character is impure, its apparel is but filthy rags; if holy, it is clad in the "robes of righteousness." There is no bridal union with Christ when souls are not thus enrobed. (2) The happy guests on this occasion. "Write, Blessed are they which are called [bidden] unto the marriage supper of the Lamb" (ver. 9). All the guests themselves are brides; all of them have on the wedding garment; with hearts of joyous gratitude, they have come to welcome one or more of those who have just entered into the blessed community. "These are the true sayings [words] of God." They are not fictions, not poetic rhapsodies; they are attested by the dictates of nature and the facts of experience. "There is joy in the presence of the angels of God over one sinner that repenteth." (3) The suggestive talk on this occasion. "And I fell at [down before] his feet to worship him. And he said unto me, See thou do it not : I am thy fellow-servant [with thee], and of thy brethren that have [hold] the testimony of Jesus : worship God," etc. (ver. 10). John, in this vision or dream of his, seems so enraptured, so transported with ecstasy at the scene, that his devout emotions overcome him, and he falls down at the feet of the angel-interpreter, the man who bade him "write" the words, "Blessed are they," etc. The words which this interpreting spirit addressed to John as he prostrated himself before him are very beautiful and suggestive. "He saith unto me," says John, as I lay overwhelmed with emotion at his feet, "See thou do it not ; " my relationship to thee forbids it : "I am thy fellow-servant, and of thy brethren." We are engaged in the same work and members of the same family. "See thou do it not." It is the characteristic of small men that they require their fellow-servants to worship them, to render them homage. Hence their assumptions, their glitter, their pomposity, and parade. The greatest man is ever the most humble. "That have [hold] the testimony of Jesus : worship God." His testimony is the spirit of all true teaching and "prophecy." John and his coadjutors are both sent on the same errand, engaged in the same work, partakers of the same prophetic spirit; the one must not, therefore, worship the other.

> "The more thy glories strike my eyes,
> The lower I shall lie ;
> Thus while I fall my joys shall rise
> Immeasurably high."

How sublimely blessed the condition of all genuine disciples of Christ! They are wedded to him; he is their spiritual Husband, and each can say, "I am his, and he is mine." 2. *As the triumphant Conqueror of the wrong.* Earth is the arena of a tremendous campaign, the battle of the right against the wrong, of the true against the false, of the benevolent against the selfish. As a Chieftain in this grand moral campaign against wrong, the following points are suggested as worthy of note. Observe : (1) The *instrumentality* he employs, and the *titles* he inherits. "And I saw heaven opened, and behold a white horse; and he that sat upon him was called Faithful and True, and in righteousness he doth judge and make war" (ver. 11). A portion of the machinery (perhaps the greatest) which this great Hero uses is represented as a "white horse." In the sixth chapter of this book, which we have already noticed, there is a similar picture of the implements employed. "And I saw, and behold a white horse : and he that sat on him had a bow; and a crown was given unto him : and he went forth conquering, and to conquer." A "horse," strong, swift, daring, manageable, like the war-horse in the Book of Job. "White," emblem of the pure and the right. The campaign in which Christ is engaged and the methods he employs are all right and pure. "He that sat on him"—the triumphant General—"had a bow : and . . . went forth conquering, and to conquer." The bow projects the arrow, and the arrow penetrates the heart of the foe. See what titles this Hero inherits. He is called "the Faithful ; " he never breaks a promise. "True"—true in his conceptions of realities, and true in his representation of those realities; ever in lip and life in strict conformity to eternal facts. "In righteousness he doth judge and make war." All his campaigns are right; he fights not against existence, but against its evils. He never strikes a blow but to crush a wrong, and to save a soul. "His name is called The Word of God" (ver. 13). The Revealer of the Absolute, and his Representative to man. Here are titles how unlike those which ignorant men confer on their fellows—titles which disgrace alike the donors and the donees! (2) The *aspect* he wears, and the *followers* he commands. (*a*) "His eyes were [are] as a flame of fire" (ver. 12). The eye is the best mirror of the soul; one glance reveals more of the inner self than the strongest words in the most affluent vocabulary. The eyes of this conquering Hero, riding forth victoriously on his white horse, are like a "flame of fire"—all-pure, all-searching, ablaze with an unquenchable fire. (*b*) "On his head were [are] many crowns [diadems]" (ver. 12). These crowns were the emblems of that empire of his, which is coextensive with the universe, and as lasting as eternity. They had names or titles written on them. "He had [hath] a name written, that [which] no man knew [no one knoweth], but he himself" (ver. 12). They had a significance surpassing the interpretation of all minds but his. He is "the fulness of him that filleth all in all." (*c*) "He was clothed [arrayed] with a vesture [garment] dipped [sprinkled] in blood" (ver. 13). This is true of a worldly conqueror; he comes up from Edom, the scene of the campaign, with garments "dipped in blood." Of the spiritual warrior, it only expresses the vital expenditure of the struggle. The very life has been sacrificed to it. As to the followers he commands, who are they? Who are his battalions in this grand campaign? Who does this majestic Chieftain lead forth to battle? "The armies which were [are] in heaven followed him upon white horses, clothed in fine linen, white and clean" (ver. 14). Who knows the numbers of his armies? They may baffle all arithmetic to calculate; but their moral character is known. "They are clothed in fine linen, white and clean," exquisitely refined and spotlessly pure—sainted men and holy angels. (3) The *course* he pursues, and the *greatness* of his supremacy. "Out of his mouth goeth [proceedeth] a sharp sword, that with it he should smite the nations" etc. (ver. 15). His force is moral. "Out of his mouth goeth forth a sharp sword." It is not by physical force, such as bayonets, cannons, swords, that he wins his victories; but moral words. His words are as a "sharp sword;" they cut down the errors, the wrongs, the miseries, of the race. Mind alone can conquer mind. His force is mighty. "With it he should smite the nations: and he shall rule them with a rod of iron" (ver. 15). How mighty is his word! It creates, sustains, and destroys universes every day. How independent is his course! "He treadeth the wine-press of the fierceness and wrath of Almighty God" (ver. 15). In the corresponding expression in Isa. lxiii. 3 it is said, "I have trodden the wine-press *alone*." The "wrath" or the anger of God! What is this "wrath"? Not passion, but principle; not indignation against existence, but antagonism to all the *wrongs* of existence. Against these wrongs Christ fought alone. "I have trodden the wine-press alone: and of the people there was none with me." Mark also the greatness of his supremacy. "He hath on his vesture [garment] and on his thigh a name written, King of kings, and Lord of lords" (ver. 16). There are degrees of authority in the empire of God, one ruling power over another, rising up to the highest heights of being; but Christ is over all, the King of all kings, and the Lord of all lords. He is "exalted far above all heavens." There are heavens rising above heavens. No astronomy can measure the height of the lowest, the highest transcends all imagination; Christ is far above the highest. All authorities, worlds, systems, laws, events, are under his vast and absolute control. What a benediction to know that he is love, and that he "knoweth our frames, and remembereth that we are dust"! He knows man, for manhood belongs to his wonderful personality. (4) The *war* he wages, and the *victories* he achieves. It is suggested that this *war* he wages deserves the attention of all. "And I saw an angel standing in the sun; and he cried with a loud voice, saying to all the fowls [birds] that fly in the midst of [in mid] heaven, Come and gather yourselves [be gathered] together unto the supper [great supper] of the great God [of God]" (ver. 17). Mark the *author* of this address. How grand his position! "Standing in the sun." Mrs. Browning, perhaps struck with its sublimity, sings of "God's archangel standing in the sun," wrapped in luminous splendour and exposed to all eyes. How earnest his effort! "He cried with a loud voice." How vast his audience! "Saying to all the fowls that fly in the midst of heaven" (ver. 17). The birds are personifications of men—men, perhaps, of genius, ambition, and celerity in movement. But the men, perhaps, especially of martial passion and purpose are meant here; hence the imperial bird. The cruel, ravenous eagle is the symbol of war. How strange and startling his summons! "Come and gather yourselves together unto the supper." "Wheresoever the carcase is, there shall the eagles be gathered together" for feasting. The ravenous vultures devour the flesh of thousands. The carrion on the battle-field is a rich feast for those armies, who, like the rapacious birds of prey, not only kill, but devour. These are the men engaged in this tremendous battle, in destroying all that makes human existence worth having—purity, freedom, kindness, friendship, worship. "Unto the supper of the great God." What is the feast of God? It is the utter ruin of all that is opposed to the interests of the soul. Does not Heaven call on all to rejoice in the fall of wrong? This feast is here represented in striking symbol as the "flesh of kings, and the flesh of captains, and the flesh of mighty men, and the flesh of horses, and of them that sit on them, and the flesh of all men, both free and bond, both [and] small and great" (ver. 18). The utter ruin of all those mighty forces, who fought for moral wrong, portrayed as a "beast," the "great whore," etc. Such a ruin is in truth a rich feast of God to all regenerate souls. Mark the *victories* he achieves. "And I saw the beast, and the kings of the earth, and their armies," etc. (ver. 19). All the abettors and promoters of wrong. The great truth suggested by these verses on to the end of the chapter is that moral evil shall one day be utterly destroyed from off the earth; even its last remnant shall be consumed. The great Chieftain came to "destroy the works of the devil," to "put away sin by the sacrifice of himself," to sweep the world of it.—D. T.

Ver. 10.—*Servility and humility.* "And I fell at his feet to worship him. And he said unto me, See thou do it not: I am thy fellow-servant, and of thy brethren." These words may be taken as a representation of one bad thing and one good thing.

I. SERVILITY THE BAD THING. John fell down before some one whom he regarded as greater than himself; not to one true God. This state of mind: 1. *Bad in itself.* The crawling, sycophantic, cringing spirit is one of the most detestable things in human life. It is opposed to true manhood; it spanielizes the human soul. 2. *Bad in its influence.* It is just that element in human life that makes heroes of the base, saints of hypocrites, lords of money-grubs, and divinities of rulers. It builds up and sustains in society all manner of impostures in Church and state. It is that which has stolen nearly all true manhood from England.

II. HUMILITY THE GOOD THING. He to whom this homage was rendered refused it. "See thou do it not." Worship belongs only to God. "I am thy fellow-servant, and of thy brethren." How unlike is this man to the millions who are hungering for the cheers, the plaudits, the flatteries, the "praise of men"! Authors, artists, preachers, premiers, prelates—most of them also love the "praise of men." A truly great man, however, despises it; he shrinks with disgust from the courtiers, and kicks with indignation the canting spaniels.—D. T.

Ver. 12.—*The dignities of Christ.* "On his head were many crowns." It is suggested—

I. THAT THESE DIGNITIES ARE OF PRICELESS VALUE. What on earth does man regard as more valuable than a "crown"? Poor fool! He has waded through seas of blood, wrecked thrones, ruined empires, risked all he possessed, even life itself, in order to win a "crown." But what are all the crowns of the world compared to the diadems that encircled the Being of Christ?

II. THAT THESE DIGNITIES ARE MANIFOLD. "Many crowns." There is the dignity of an all-knowing intellect, the dignity of an immaculate conscience, the dignity of an absolutely unselfish love, the dignity of a will free from all the warping influences of sin, error, and prejudice. These diadems of priceless worth, though manifold, are as yet undiscovered by the multitude.

III. THAT THESE DIGNITIES ARE SELF-PRODUCED. The honours which unregenerate men possess, such as they are, are conferred by others, and the giver and the receiver of them are alike morally dishonoured in their acts of bestowment and acceptance. But the dignities of Christ, like the majestic branches of a tree, or the splendid pinions of a bird, grow out of himself. All his dignities are but the brilliant evolutions of his own great soul.

IV. THAT THESE DIGNITIES ARE IMPENETRABLE. How soon the "crowns" worn by men grow dim and rot into dust! But Christ's diadems are incorruptible; they will sparkle on for ever, and fill all the heavens of immensity with their brilliant lustre. —D. T.

Ver. 12.—*The manifoldness of Christ's dominion.* "On his head were many crowns." Crowns are man's emblems of the highest dignities and powers; and, in accommodation of our poor thoughts, Christ is here spoken of as having "many crowns." And truly he has many dominions.

I. THE DOMINION OF MATTER IS HIS. 1. *Inorganic matter* is under his control. Atoms, mountains, rivers, oceans, planets, suns, and systems. He controls the atoms; he heaves the ocean; he rolls the heavenly orbs along; he is the Master of all chemical and mechanical forces. 2. *Organic matter* is under his control. (1) All *vegetable* life. The tiniest blade, up to the hugest monarchs of the forest, are under him. He quickens, sustains, and develops them. (2) All *animal* life. All that teem in earth and air and sea; he is the Master of all life-forces.

II. THE DOMINION OF MIND IS HIS. 1. All *mind in heaven.* He inspires and directs all the hierarchies of celestial worlds. 2. All *mind on earth.* The thoughts, impulses, passions, and purposes of mankind are under his masterhood. He originates the good and controls the bad. How impious, how futile, how monstrously foolish, is it for man to oppose the great Redeemer! He does reign, he must reign, and will reign for ever. He will reign over you, with your will or against your will.—D. T.

Ver. 13.—*Intense earnestness of being.* "Clothed in a vesture dipped in blood." What was the "blood" that dyed the robes of the illustrious Chieftain? Not that crimson fluid that streams from the veins of slaughtered men. It may be regarded—

I. AS A SYMBOL OF HIS OWN AGONIZING EARNESTNESS. In Gethsemane it is said that he "sweated great drops of blood." It was earnestness. The man who wrote the Epistle to the Hebrews speaks of those who have not resisted unto blood, "striving against sin." There is *moral* blood—the blood of *intense earnestness.*

II. AS A SYMBOL OF THE MORTAL ENMITY OF HIS FOES. During the three years of his public ministry they thirsted for his blood. "His blood be upon us." It is characteristic of the enemies of the Church in all ages that they seek his destruction— the destruction of his character, his influence, himself.

Our great Leader does not prosecute his grand campaign against evil in a cold, mechanical, professional manner, but with the earnestness of "blood."—D. T.

Ver. 13.—*The Word of God.* "The Word of God." The infinite Father has spoken two great words to his intelligent family. One word is *nature.* "The heavens declare his glory," etc. The other word is *Christ.* He is the Logos. The latter word is specially addressed to fallen humanity, and is a soul-redeeming word. In relation to this Word the following things may be predicated. He is—

I. THE WORD OF ABSOLUTE INFALLIBILITY. Conventionally, men call the Scriptures the Word of God. Mere traditional believers assert their infallibility. The best, however, that can be said concerning that book is that it *contains* the Word of God. It is not the Divine jewel, but the human chest. Christ is *the Word itself,* absolutely true, the Bible. He is *the* Word. By him every word, whether oral or written, written in whatever form, language, style, or book, is to be tested, whether true or false. "No man hath seen the Father at any time:" nor Moses, or the prophets, or the evangelists, but "the only begotten Son, who is in the bosom of the Father, he hath revealed him." Let us, therefore, reject all words, wherever we find them, if they agree not with the spirit, character, and aim of Christ.

II. THE WORD OF EXHAUSTLESS SIGNIFICANCE. There are faculties and possibilities in him, ideas, purposes, and susceptibilities in him that will take ages upon ages without end fully to develop. "In him dwells all the fulness of God." In this he meets the law of mind, which bids it ever to search after the new and the fresh.

III. THE WORD OF ALMIGHTY POWER. The character of a word is determined by the character of the mind that utters it. Weak minds utter weak words; strong minds, vigorous words. The words of some are as empty as the wind; others are as vigorous as electricity; they shatter the mountains and shake the globe. Christ, as the Word, is Almighty. He has not only created Christendom, but by him were "all things created."

IV. The Word of universal interpretability. Even the written words that make up what we call the Bible are frequently uninterpretable. Hence their renderings and meanings are constantly fluctuating, and often contradictive. But here is a word that stands for ever—" the same yesterday, and to-day, and for ever." This Word is a life. A life a child can interpret; and the greater the life of a man, the more generous, truthful, loving he is, the more readily a child can read and understand him. Hence no life is so interpretable as Christ's life.—D. T.

Ver. 14.—*Armies invisible and distant on the side of good.* "The armies which were in heaven followed him upon white horses, clothed in fine linen, white and clean." Heaven, it would seem, is populated with numerous intelligent beings, existing in various types of condition, influence, power, etc. It is suggested—

1. The hosts of heaven are interested in the moral campaign which Christ is prosecuting on this earth. They not only know what is going on on this little planet, but throb with earnest interest in its history. They desire to look into its great moral concerns. No wonder some in heaven are related to some on earth; they participate in the same nature, sustain the same relation, and are subject to the same laws. Here, too, stupendous events have occurred in connection with him who is the Head of all principalities, powers, and that must ever thrill the universe.

II. The hosts of heaven lend their aid to Christ in his tremendous battles. " The armies which were in heaven followed him upon white horses." If you ask me in what way they can render him aid, I can suggest many probable methods. We know that one great thought struck into the soul of an exhausted and despairing man can revive and reinvigorate him. May it not be possible for departed souls and unfallen spirits to breathe such thoughts into the breasts of feeble men on earth? If you ask me why Christ should accept such aid as theirs, or the aid of any creature in his mighty struggles, I answer, not because he requires their services—for he could do his work alone—but for their own good. By it he gratifies their noblest instincts, engages their highest faculties, and gains for them their highest honours and sublimest joys.

III. The hosts of heaven are fully equipped for service in this martial undertaking on earth. "Upon white horses, clothed in fine linen, white and clean." It was customary in Oriental lands for soldiers of the highest rank to go forth to battle on steeds. It is a law of Christ's kingdom that those only who are holy and pure can enter therein; hence these heavenly soldiers are furnished with " white horses," the emblem of purity, and "white linen" also. No one in heaven or on earth will Christ allow to fight under his banner who are not qualified, both in capacity and character, for the work they undertake.

Encouraging subject this! Small as this little planet of ours is, it is not isolated from the family of worlds. As materially this globe, by the law of gravitation, is linked to the most distant planet, so the meanest human spirit here is linked to the highest hierarchies in the great realm of mind. They are all at the bidding of the great Leader in the battle of life. "Thinkest thou that I could not pray to my Father, and he will send me twelve legions of angels?" etc. "More are they that are for us than those that are against us."—D. T.

EXPOSITION.

CHAPTER XX.

Ver. 1.—And I saw an angel come down from heaven; *coming down out of heaven.* The usual mode of introducing a new vision (cf. ch. iv. 1, etc.). On account of ch. i. 18, some have considered this angel to be Christ himself; but this is incorrect. As in ch. xii. 7—9, an angel is the immediate agent in this expulsion of Satan (*vide infra*).

Having the key of the bottomless pit; *the abyss;* as in ch. ix. 1, 2, 11; xi. 7; xvii. 8. In all these places the word signifies the present abode of Satan and his angels, whence they direct their operations in hostility to God, not the place of their final punishment (see ver. 10). In Luke viii. 31 the word has exactly the same meaning; while in the only remaining place where it is used in the New Testament, viz. Rom. x. 7, it stands for the place of abode of the souls of the dead. *Having the key of the abyss* therefore informs us that power is given to this angel over Satan during the time of this world's existence. And a great chain in his hand ; literally, *upon his hand*, as if lying on it and hanging from it ; the chain evidently symbolizing the power of the angel over the inhabitants of the abyss, and the purpose with which he now comes, viz. to restrain the power of Satan.

Vers. 2, 3.—And he laid hold on the dragon, that old serpent, which is the Devil, and Satan. These titles are an exact repetition of ch. xii. 9 (which see). And bound him a thousand years, and cast him into the bottomless pit. *The abyss*, as we have seen (on ver. 1), is the present abode of Satan ; the act of binding, therefore, is now over. This fact opposes the interpretation which makes "the thousand years" yet in the future. When, then, did this binding take place ? Only one answer can be given. It was when Christ bruised the serpent's head by his act of redemption. Thus, "Christ was manifested that he might destroy the works of the devil" (1 John iii. 8); "Now shall the prince of this world be cast out" (John xii. 31); "The prince of this world hath been judged" (John xvi. 11). Satan is the strong man bound (Matt. xii. 26, 29). Next, what is meant by "for a thousand years"? The best interpretation seems to be that this phrase expresses a quality, and does not express a period of time. That such a method of employing numbers is usual in the Apocalypse we have frequently seen (see on ch. i. 4, "seven ;" ch. xiii. 1, "ten," etc.). Here, therefore, as in ch. vii. 4, "one thousand" signifies "completeness." Satan is bound "for a thousand years ;" that is, Satan is completely bound. In Ezekiel (from which the following part of the vision is certainly derived) a similar use is made of the terms "seven years" (Ezek. xxxix. 9) and "seven months" (Ezek. xxxix. 12). But, again, in what sense can Satan be said to have been "completely" bound by our Lord's work of redemption? The answer is—In relation to the godly. The purpose of this sentence is that which is one great purpose of the whole book, viz. to encourage the struggling Christian. Thus this sentence assures Christians that, for them, Satan has been completely bound, and they need not despair nor fear his might [1] (cf. "loosed," *infra*). The chapter thus describes, not a

---

[1] The interpretation given here and in the following verses follows closely the exposition of Professor Milligan, in the 'Baird Lectures' for 1885, where the reader may find the whole question of the millennium more fully treated.

millennium of the saints, but the overthrow of Satan. Before the picture of the war and the overthrow, the saints are invited to behold the complete security of those who have not worshipped the beast nor his image; just as the vision of Christ victorious introduced the seal-visions. And shut him up, and set a seal upon him, that he should deceive the nations no more, till the thousand years should be fulfilled; *and shut* [it] *and sealed* [it] *over him*, etc. It is possible that there is here a reference to the death and burial of Christ (Matt. xxvii. 66). Satan "met in reality that fate which he was able, in a shadowy and temporary form, to inflict on Jesus—he was bound and shut up in the abyss, and the abyss was sealed over him" (Milligan. Cf. also the word "abyss," *supra*). Satan was thus bound "that he might deceive the nations no more," etc.; that is, Satan, in his character of the deceiver (cf. ch. xii. 9) of the world, is thus limited in his power by the binding which has been described. *The nations ;* in the sense of the world, not the ungodly world. And after that he must be loosed a little season. Omit "and." "A little time" (μικρὸν χρόνον) is the exact phrase used in ch. vi. 11, where it certainly means the period of this world's existence. Such also is its meaning here. "He must be loosed" signifies that Satan is, in regard to the ungodly, allowed to work his will during this period. The thousand years' binding, and the loosing for a little time, describe two events which occur contemporaneously. While the godly need have no fear, because even in this world Satan's power as regards them is completely limited by Christ's act of redemption, yet in another sense, as regards the ungodly, Satan is loosed and obtains power over them. The chief difficulty in this interpretation lies in the words, "after this." But it must be remembered that the "thousand years" do not express a period of time, but the quality of completeness. Therefore the loosing of Satan must not be supposed to take place in a period subsequent to the period of the binding. The seer wishes to describe the devil in a twofold character, subordinating the second to the first. He thus says, "By Christ's redeeming work Satan is bound and fettered in regard to you faithful Christians; but there is also a second subordinate fact to remember, that at the same time he is powerful in his natural sphere, among his own adherents." The binding of Satan in one direction being immediately followed by a display of power in another, and the former fact being expressed by the chronological symbolism of being bound for a thousand years, it is part of this chronological symbolism to express the second fact as taking place *after* the first, though a subordination of the secondary to the primary effect is really what is intended to be conveyed (see Milligan, quoted above).

Ver. 4.—And I saw thrones, and they sat upon them, and judgment was given unto them. This describes the position of Christians in this life. They sit upon thrones; that is, they reign with Christ. Judgment is given unto them; that is, by their conduct in the world the world is judged and condemned. St. John continually thus describes the Christian's position; and such a picture is specially applicable for his purpose here, which is to portray the glory of the Christian calling, and the certainty of the Christian's hope. The redeemed have been made kings, and reign (ch. v. 10). So also St. Paul says we are " blessed with all spiritual blessings in heavenly places in Christ " (Eph. i. 3). And I saw the souls of them that were beheaded for the witness of Jesus, and for the Word of God, and which had not worshipped the beast, neither his image, neither had received his mark upon their foreheads, or in their hands. This is a special reference to the martyrs made with the object mentioned above, viz. that of encouraging Christians in their warfare. The class here described forms part of the whole body of Christians alluded to in the first part of the verse (cf. ch. vi. 10; i. 9; xii. 17; xix. 10; also ch. xiii.; xv. 2). In the same way the *souls* referred to in ch. vi. 9 are those existing during the period of this world, which we have here understood to be denoted indirectly by the "thousand years." And they lived and reigned with Christ a thousand years. "The thousand years" adopted in the Textus Receptus, is found in B and others, but omitted in ℵ, A, and others. "They lived and reigned with Christ" in complete and perfect assurance, as in ver. 2, and for the reason given in ver. 2, viz. that Satan was bound completely. This living and reigning must not be limited to the period after the death of the martyrs (though it is doubtless true in this sense also), notwithstanding the fact that St. John sees them here after their death. It is as though he would say, " You Christians sit upon thrones and reign with Christ; yea, even those who suffered shameful deaths shared this perfect safety and exaltation, though to the eyes of the world they were so afflicted and degraded." *They lived* is described in ver. 5 as the "first resurrection." This can only be referred to that first awakening from sin to the glorious life of the gospel, which St. John elsewhere describes in a similar manner. " He that heareth my Word . . . hath everlasting life, and shall not come into condemnation; but s passed from death unto life " (John v.

24); " We have passed from death unto life " (1 John iii. 14).

Ver. 5.—But the rest of the dead lived not again until the thousand years were finished; *should be finished.* Omit " but; " omit " again." It is important to notice the omission of " again; " *the rest of the dead lived not until,* etc. The best explanation of these words seems to be that the " rest of the dead " refers to those Old Testament saints and others (such as godly heathens) who were in the world before Christ's act of atonement—" the thousand years " (see on ver. 2, above)—had been accomplished. They could not be said to have *lived,* in the high sense in which St. John uses the word, not having known Christ; for "in him was life" (John i. 4; v. 40, etc.). But by Christ's redeeming work, these were placed on a level with Christians (cf. Luke vii. 28, "John the Baptist: but he that is least in the kingdom of God is greater than he;" also Heb. xi. 39, 40, " And these all, having obtained a good report through faith, received not the promise: God having provided some better thing for us, that they without us should not be made perfect "). This is the first resurrection. These words refer both to the reigning of those mentioned in ver. 4, and to the living of those in ver. 5 (*vide supra*). This " first resurrection " is the spiritual rising with Christ, which is a consequence of his redeeming work. It is to be noticed that St. John nowhere makes use of the phrase, " second resurrection," though he does use the words, "second death." Both the " first resurrection " and the " second death " are spiritual operations.

Ver. 6.—Blessed and holy is he that hath part in the first resurrection: on such the second death hath no power, but they shall be priests of God and of Christ, and shall reign with him a thousand years; *over these the second death hath no authority.* The first words describe the state of those who have part in the spiritual resurrection with Christ (see on ver. 5). The second clause gives to the oppressed Christian the culminating reason for patience and perseverance. The " second death " is the spiritual death of the lake of fire (ver. 14). *Priests of God,* etc. (cf. ch. i. 6; v. 10). *A thousand years;* in complete and everlasting security (see on ver. 2, *et seq.*). We may in this place briefly indicate some of the other interpretations which have been given to this reign of the saints for a thousand years, or, as it is generally styled, the millennium. (1) The literal interpretation of a future reign on earth of Christ with his saints for a thousand years. According to this view, there is to be a first resurrection of the dead (either of the holy dead or of all the dead), then the period of a thousand years, during which

Satan will be bound, and the saints will reign; then finally the ultimate punishment of Satan—the casting into the lake of fire. Some limit the locality of this reign to a particular spot on the earth (e.g. Jerusalem), beyond which live the ungodly. The objections to this theory are : (a) Amongst its advocates almost every detail is a matter of dispute. Some place the millennium in the future, others in the past. Of these latter some specify the first thousand years of the Christian age, others the thousand years from the time of Constantine. " The length of the period, the number and class of the believers who shall be partakers of its glory, the condition in which they are to live, the work in which they are to be engaged, the relation in which the exalted Redeemer is to stand to them," are all subjects for disagreement. (b) The carnal nature of such a resurrection is at variance with the general teaching of the Bible, and unlike the spiritual nature which our Lord himself assumed after his resurrection. (c) If the saints receive a glorified body for that period, it is impossible to conceive of them as living in the world in its present state, and a large part of which is inhabited by the ungodly. (d) It is impossible satisfactorily to conceive what relations could exist between the saints in such a case and the ungodly. If Satan is bound during this period so that he can deceive the nations no more, whence comes the evil which exists among the ungodly portion of the world ? (e) There is no other example of a literal use of numbers in the whole of the Apocalypse. (f) The teaching of the Bible elsewhere not only negatively fails to support this view, but is in positive opposition to it, in such points as a continuance of evil after Christ's second coming; the existence of an interval between his coming and the judgment instead of a sudden coming to judgment (comp. John vi. 40, "I will raise him up at the last day "). (2) The spiritual interpretation, which makes the thousand years expressive of the whole Christian age. This seems to a certain extent true, since what the thousand years signifies does have its effect during this time in the reign of the saints. But it seems inexact, since it makes the thousand years symbolical of a length of time, instead of a quality attached to an action. What is meant is not that Christ bound Satan during the period of the Christian age (though, as we have seen, there is a sense in which he is so bound as regards believers), for, on the contrary, he goes about like a roaring lion ; but that he bound and overthrew him completely for all Christians by his redeeming work.

Ver. 7.—And when the thousand years are expired, Satan shall be loosed out of his prison ; are finished; that is, the power of the devil having been in principle completely overthrown by our Lord (see on preceding verses), Satan is still permitted to wage war and exercise sway on the earth. " His prison " is the "abyss" of vers. 1, 3 (cf. also ver. 3).

Ver. 8.—And shall go out to deceive the nations which are in the four quarters of the earth, Gog and Magog; four corners. The signification of "Gog and Magog" (vide infra) shows in what sense "the nations" is used. It is in the limited sense of the ungodly of the world, not in the wider sense in which the expression is used (without any qualifying clause) in ver. 3. Magog in Gen. x. 2 is mentioned among the sons of Japheth who were the ancestors of the northern nations (cf. Ezek. xxxviii. 15 and xxxix. 2). Hence the name Magog is used to denote the northern tribes, whose invasion of Palestine and adjoining parts took place about B.C. 630—600. From Ezek. xxxix. it seems that Gog was originally a leader among these tribes ; and from Ezek. xxxviii. 17 it seems that Ezekiel took these names to be symbolical of all the foes of the people of God. Jewish tradition makes use of these names to indicate those nations who were expected to war against Jerusalem in the last days, and to be overthrown by the Messiah. Hence the employment of the terms here by St. John as denoting the ungodly people of the world, amongst whom Satan still exercises his power, though that power is limited to these, and he is completely bound as regards true believers. To gather them together to battle : the number of whom is as the sand of the sea ; to the war; the article points definitely to the war of ch. xix. 19 and xvi. 14. It is a prolonged war, not a battle, because lasting throughout life. The vastness of the hosts of Gog and Magog is alluded to in Ezek. xxxviii. 9, 16. This is in conformity with our Lord's teaching: "Many are called, but few are chosen" (Matt. xxii. 14; cf. also vii. 14).

Ver. 9.—And they went up on the breadth of the earth, and compassed the camp of the saints about, and the beloved city; over the breadth. "They went up " as an army to attack the enemy (cf. Judg. i. 1). Either we must render the camp . . . even the beloved city, or else we must understand the camp as a defensive outpost placed around or near the city. In Acts xxi. 34 the same word is rendered "castle." " The beloved city " is evidently Jerusalem (cf. Ps. lxxviii. 68), that is, the Church of God, of which it is always a type in the Apocalypse (cf. ch. iii. 12 ; xxi. 2, 10). The description plainly portrays the Church militant here on earth. And fire came down from God out of heaven.

and devoured them. "From God" is omitted in A, a few cursives, and Primasius, but appears in א, B, P, 1, 7, and most cursives and versions; but these authorities vary in the position of the added clause. So in ch. xi. fire devours the enemies of the two witnesses. This sentence is introduced in connection with the description of Gog and Magog, following the account of Ezekiel, where the same punishment is foretold (see Ezek. xxxviii. 22; xxxix. 6). It is probable, therefore, that nothing more definite is intended than to convey the general idea that God aids and protects his Church even while on earth. He, as it were, gives the enemies of his people a foretaste, while here on earth, of their future punishment of the lake of fire (see also on the seal-visions).

Ver. 10.—And the devil that deceived them was cast into the lake of fire and brimstone, where the beast and the false prophet are, and shall be tormented day and night for ever and ever; and they shall be tormented. The last clause shows that this is the final judgment and punishment of the devil. Thus at this verse is completed the whole series of visions commencing at ch. xii., in which are set forth the origin and progress of the influence of evil, and the final termination of the conflict between God and his Church on the one hand, and the devil and his adherents on the other. It remains now only to shadow forth the surpassing glory of the saints in their everlasting home, and thus to bring the book to a conclusion. This, therefore, is the theme of the remaining chapters. (On "the devil that deceiveth them," see on ver. 3; and on "the lake of fire and brimstone," see on ch. xix. 20.) Shall be tormented (cf. Matt. viii. 29, "Art thou come hither to torment us before the time?").

Ver. 11.—And I saw a great white throne. And I saw; introducing a new phase of the vision (cf. ver. 1, etc.). A throne is seen as in ch. iv.2; it is great, perhaps, by comparison with those mentioned in ver. 4; white, because this is the colour of purity and all heavenly virtues (cf. ch. i. 14; ii. 17; iii. 4, etc.). And him that sat on it, from whose face the earth and the heaven fled away; and there was found no place for them. The true reading, "before the throne," in the following verse makes it clear that God the Judge is here intended. Perhaps from Matt. xxv. 31 and John v. 22 we must infer that God the Son is meant. The destruction of the world is complete—"no place is found for them;" they are annihilated. Such an event is nearly always portrayed in the description of the last judgment in the Apocalypse and in the New Testament generally (cf. ch. xvi. 20).

Ver. 12.—And I saw (see on ver. 11) the dead, small and great, stand before God; the dead, the great and the small, standing before the throne. All the dead, good and bad, as in Matt. xxv. 31—33. This is the general resurrection; what St. John might have called the second resurrection, with regard to the godly, who have once before risen to a life with Christ (see on ver. 5). Now, those who would not voluntarily share in the first resurrection are compelled to share in the second. And the books were opened. Omit the article (cf. the description in Dan. vii. 10). And another book was opened, which is the book of life. This book has been frequently referred to (ch. iii. 5; xiii. 8; xvii. 8). The idea is not uncommon throughout the Bible (cf. Ps. lxix. 28; Dan. xii. 1; Luke x. 20). And the dead were judged out of those things which were written in the books, according to their works. Both the godly and the ungodly. "The books" show fully why certain names are selected and inscribed in the "book of life." Here is enforced again the lesson with which the Apocalypse opens in the epistles to the seven Churches, viz. that the reward will follow according to the works (cf. ch. ii. 5; iii. 15, etc.).

Ver. 13.—And the sea gave up the dead which were in it. It is difficult to decide upon the exact signification of this clause. (1) It may be inserted in order to show the universal nature of this resurrection, although it may not, in conjunction with the next part of the verse, constitute a strictly logical classification of the dead. (2) The sea being a type of the ungodly nations, the sentence may mean those spiritually dead, but living on the earth at the time of the judgment. The next clause seems to support this view. And death and hell delivered up the dead which were in them; death and Hades (see ch. i. 18; vi. 8). As in ch. vi. 8, the two—really one—are mentioned separately, the latter being looked upon as the guard-house of those whom the former has seized. This clause, taken in conjunction with the preceding one, may mean—From the ungodly nations, those physically living but spiritually dead were called up for judgment, and also those who were actually dead, having been seized by death and Hades. And they were judged every man according to their works. A solemn repetition of ver. 12 (which see).

Ver. 14.—And death and hell were cast into the lake of fire; death and Hades (see on ver. 13). Lake of fire (see on ver. 10). This is described in accordance with St. Paul's teaching. "The last enemy that shall be abolished is death" (1 Cor. xv. 26, Revised Version). Death and Hades, though in reality abstractions, are here personified. This is the second death. Add [even] the *lake of fire.* St. John has not used the phrase, "the first death," but he has alluded to the fact. The first death is the actual death of the body, and which is the natural result of that spiritually dead state into which, since the Fall, man is born, and which is therefore, as it were, his normal state. In a similar manner, the first resurrection is the risen spiritual life of conversion; while the second resurrection is the resurrection of all men, and the bestowal of eternal life upon the just.

Ver. 15.—And whosoever was not found written in the book of life was cast into the lake of fire; *and if any was not,* etc. This is practically a reiteration of what has been twice before solemnly asserted (see vers. 12, 13).

HOMILETICS.

Vers. 1—3.—*Satan bound for a thousand years.* God sees the end from the beginning. If he pleases, he can disclose the future to others, although even then, by reason of the limitation of creature-faculties, the unfolding of the future must be limited too. There is, moreover, one feature of that limit which cannot be too clearly recognized, viz. that inasmuch as man has no strictly creative power, and can only weave new patterns by putting together in different forms the materials ready to his hand, so also he can conceive of the new life of the ages to come only by means of some varied setting of the scenes of the ages that are past. Hence our God graciously stoops to our capacity, and puts his revealings of the forthcoming years under the form of the facts which have marked those that are past. Thus the events which are to mark the consummation of this age are set forth in two forms, viz. (1) by a representation of the good we already enjoy as wrought up to a higher degree of perfection; and (2) by setting forth the evil over which we mourn as brought to extinction, or as restricted within narrower bounds. Now, under this last-mentioned form, a prolonged period is here set forth, spoken of as a thousand years, as one during which the evil one shall be bound and pent up within his own place. Many questions naturally start up as we study this passage—a passage which is not specially easy, under any circumstances, but which we cannot help thinking has been made to appear vastly more difficult than it is in itself, by reason of the enormous incubus of fanciful theories by which it has been all but smothered. We venture to think that even although, owing to lack of *data,* there are some queries the full answer to which must yet be left in abeyance, yet there is quite enough in the verses before us that is sufficiently clear to make the heart leap with delight, to stimulate our hopes, and to excite our prayers Who is the angel? What is the period of a thousand years? What is the binding " When does it begin? These are the queries which seem to need a reply before we can appreciate and appropriate the disclosures which the paragraph contains. 1. *Who is the angel?* Some say the Lord Jesus Christ, because he alone controls Satan's power. It is quite true that Jesus alone controls the evil one, but it is also true that he does so at times by the instrumentality of others. So far as the symbolism of the text goes, there is no reason for thinking the angel to be other than a created one. Still, if any see reason for thinking otherwise, even then the main sense of the passage is the same. Our Lord Jesus may bind the evil one directly or mediately. 2. *What is the period specified?* There are four hypotheses respecting the thousand years. One that it is to be taken literally; a second, that on the "day for a year" principle it is equivalent to 365,000 years; a third, that it is an indication of completeness, but not of time; a fourth, that it is a definite expression for a period indefinitely prolonged. The first of these is the one most commonly adopted; although why, if twelve hundred and sixty days mean twelve hundred and sixty years, the "thousand years" should be less than that by two hundred and sixty days is to the writer extremely puzzling. The second and third views have few defenders. It seems to us to be much safer to look at the expression as indicating an indefinite period of time, of immense duration—a time of peace and freedom from ill, which will vastly exceed the period of trial and sorrow during which the Church's wilderness-life will have lasted. 3. *What is the binding?* At present it may suffice to say that it certainly denotes such a restriction upon Satan, his doings and rovings, that during this period he will not be able to "go about seeking whom he may devour" to the extent he would desire. 4. *When does the binding begin?*

According to some, it is past. (1) According to Hengstenberg, the thousand years began on the Christmas Eve of the year 800, when the pope placed the crown on the head of Charlemagne. But surely there was not at that time, nor during the thousand years after, such a state of things as would seem to be represented by a binding of Satan for the whole time. Hengstenberg takes the thousand years literally, and thinks that even now Satan is loosed from his prison, and that depravity has reached its utmost height. (2) According to many, and among them the most thoughtful and devout expositors, the binding of Satan began when Jesus came. Our Lord's casting out devils proved that a check was put on Satan's power; this restraint was increased when Jesus died, and is continued in the perpetual advance of the kingdom of Christ. They refer to such passages as Matt. xii. 29; Heb. ii. 14, 15; 1 John iii. 8; Col. ii. 15; Luke x. 18. But (a) the symbolism of the text seems to indicate a more effectual restraint on evil than the earth as yet has known; and (b) since the binding of Satan is placed so nearly to the consummation of all things, since the kingdom of Christ had actually been in progress for some thirty years when the book was written, and since the prophecies were declared to be of " things which should be hereafter," it seems much more consonant with the date, the aim, and the plan of the book to think of the binding of Satan as that which was yet to come in the revolutions of the ages. At the same time, it is quite possible to combine this second view with another, (3) according to which, even if the binding of Satan did commence with the establishment of the kingdom of Christ, the results of that binding would take ages to work out, and would, in the long run, bring about more of calm and of rest than earth has yet been permitted to see. Even the expositors who adopt the second view do in many cases combine it with the third, and regard the binding here specified as something so much more effective than any hitherto known, as to be virtually new. It is to this conclusion that we find ourselves shut up: that this period which is spoken of as a thousand years is one of a blessed calm yet to be realized, surpassing all that earth has known; that though the causes are already at work to bring it about, and though the train of events is laid which is to usher it in, yet that the passage refers to the blessed issue in days to come, when evil shall be kept under more effective restraint than before. This period is what is generally thought of as " the millennium." From the passage before us it is perfectly clear that the millennium is not a period of the extinction of evil, but only of its restraint. Neither sin nor death nor the curse will cease till the new heavens and the new earth are brought in, and they are not yet. While, however, the righteous on earth will enjoy a period of delightful calm, the faithful ones who shall have gone hence will be living and reigning with Christ all that while. They will be enjoying " the first resurrection " (see next homily). Let us now, after these few preliminary explanations, look at our present theme, " the binding of Satan," in the light of the entire Scripture teaching, that we may learn what is to be the state of the world during this period of halcyon calm, and how it is to be brought about by forces and agencies already in operation. We shall approach our subject cautiously and gradually. May we in God's light see light!

I. THERE IS IN THE WORLD A MIGHTY FORCE OF EVIL. As set forth in these Apocalyptic visions, we have seen: 1. That old serpent, called the devil. 2. The first beast, or worldly power opposed to God, having its power from the dragon. 3. The second beast, or false prophet, having his power from the first. 4. The harlot, Babylon the great, or apostasy, whether in the ecclesiastical or commercial sphere. We have seen No. 4 destroyed; Nos. 3 and 2 cast into the lake of fire; still No. 1 remains. We are to watch what becomes of him. His power in the world is too well known.

II. MIGHTIER FORCES OF GOOD, ALTHOUGH UNSEEN, ARE IN THE BACKGROUND. As we read this book, we can but note that evil is surveyed from above; held in check by God; allowed to work for a time—known to the year, the month, the day, and the hour. And as we have seen the downfall of three of the forms of evil, we here watch with deepest interest a new check upon the first.

III. THE EMPLOYMENT OF THE MIGHTIER AGAINST THE MIGHTY HAS BEEN MATTER OF ANCIENT PROMISE. No sooner had the tempter marred Eden's bowers than the promise was given (Gen. iii. 15). The serpent might bruise the seed of the woman, but he would do so at a fatal cost to himself. Dim promise! needing the evolution of ages to interpret it, but yet containing that which is the basis of our hope when in agony over the tempter's power.

IV. THE STRONGER FORCE OF GOOD HAS EVER BEEN AT WORK. This world has never been given up to the evil one. He has never roamed unchecked. He has gone about only so far as the Lord of souls has permitted. When Jesus hung on the cross, his power was grappled with ; when he died, "the prince of this world" was "cast out." Through death our Lord means to destroy him that has the power of death, even the devil, and to deliver them who through fear of death are all their lifetime subject to bondage. "For this purpose the Son of God was manifested, that he might destroy the works of the devil." And when the Prince of life resigned his breath, crying, "It is finished ! " then did the empire of darkness receive a fatal blow, and the death-knell of sin was sounded in the hearing of heaven, earth, and hell (cf. Gen. iii. 15 ; John xii. 31 ; Heb. ii. 14, 15 ; Col. ii. 15 ; Matt. xii. 29 ; Acts xxvi. 18).

V. WHEREVER THE GOSPEL HAS BEEN PREACHED THERE A BINDING OF SATAN HAS BEEN AND IS BEING EFFECTED. Probably no one supposes that the phrase " binding " is to be taken literally. One way in which an effect would be wrought which would most naturally and impressively be described as a binding of Satan, would be that of transferring his subjects to another power, and so despoiling his kingdom. When Satan is rendered powerless to retain his prey, and more powerless still when he has lost them, surely he is bound. Now, we know not only that in and on the cross our Lord spoiled principalities and powers, and made a show of them openly, but also that Paul and others were sent forth to turn men from the power of Satan unto God, and that the great apostle praised God that the Colossians were snatched from the power of darkness and transferred to the kingdom of the Son of God. Even so. Satan is no match for the Saviour's cross and the Spirit's sword. He has ever moved in chains, but never were his chains so heavy or so fast as since Jesus died.

VI. NEVERTHELESS, THE PASSAGE BEFORE US LEADS US TO EXPECT A MUCH GREATER RESTRAINT ON SATAN'S ACTIVITY THAN HAS AS YET BEEN KNOWN. Peter refers to him as "going about," etc. Paul said, "The God of peace shall bruise Satan under your feet shortly." So that we are already prepared to expect a time when Satan's power on the earth shall be curtailed more and more. The verb here used ($\dot{\epsilon}\kappa\rho\acute{a}\tau\eta\sigma\epsilon$) gives the impression of some very strong, decided, and perhaps sudden arrest. *What will be the means by which this will be carried out* we are not here told. In the absence of aught to the contrary, we have a right to expect that the "Word of truth and the power of God " will suffice to bring about the whole, when the Spirit of God " convicts the world of sin " (John xvi. 8). No one can show that these "weapons of the holy war " are inadequate, nor that the power of the Holy Ghost is to be supplanted by aught more effective for the subjugation of evil. Let but the Divine power which has subdued *our* hearts be universally diffused, and it is enough. For surely Satan will be effectually bound when hearts refuse to give him room.

VII. WHEN THE BINDING OF SATAN IS COMPLETELY EFFECTED, THERE MUST NEEDS BE A PERIOD OF REST, SUCH AS NEITHER THE WORLD NOR THE CHURCH HAS ENJOYED SINCE "SIN ENTERED INTO THE WORLD, AND DEATH BY SIN." We are more and more drawn towards the conviction that our Lord himself commenced this binding of the evil when he began his public ministry ; and that as the power of the gospel advances, the binding becomes more and more stringent. The duration of time intended by a thousand years we cannot define. Some, as Professor Milligan,[1] regard it as giving no temporal indication at all, but as expressive of completeness. But if the binding of Satan has been going on ever since our Lord was on earth, the thousand years begun then are going on now, and are moving forward to their completion. Well may we pray,

[1] See both his work and his ' Commentary ' on the Revelation. For a history of various views on the millennium, see ' Theories concerning the Millennium,' by Dr. Craven, American editor, in Lange's ' Commentary,' p. 345 ; art. "Chiliasm," in Dr. Bomberger's edition of Herzog ; and art. "Millennarianism," in Dr. Schaff's edition of the same. The Rev. E. Storrow, in his ' Coming Reign of Christ,' has some valuable notes on ch. xx. 1—6, in Appendix D ; his fifth chapter, on " The Great Features of the Millennium," is admirable. Dr. David Brown's and Dr. Urwick's books on the second advent, Bishop Waldegrave's ' Bampton Lectures,' Dean Vaughan's ' Lectures on the Revelation,' and Mr. Lyon's ' Millennial Studies,' are books of which students should not lose sight. Webster and Wilkinson's ' Introduction to the Apocalypse ' and their notes on this chapter will be found extremely helpful.

" O Lord, hasten that day when Satan shall be so completely bound that he will be unable to retain a single captive in his hold!" How will an emancipated world rejoice! The rebuke of God's people will be taken away from off all the earth. The reign of peace and righteousness shall set in, and the time be come when on the bells of the horses shall be graven, " Holiness to the Lord." Why it should be that after this effectual binding there should be allowed another onrush of evil, we cannot tell; but the holy seer bids us look to the end even of that, and to luxuriate in the blessed vision of complete and endless rest.

Note : 1. Let our faith embrace all that is in the Word, and we shall then find nothing in the fiercest conflicts of the age to shock or disturb it. 2. Let us thank God for the restraint which we know is even now put upon Satan. He worries, but he cannot devour. Christ prays for us, that Satan may not sift us as wheat. 3. Let us be stimulated by the fact that, through the energy of the Spirit of God, the power of evil is being subdued within us and around us. 4. Let us, with renewed faith, energy, prayer, and hope, be found doing our part towards bringing about earth's time of rest. Let no disbelief, either in the efficacy of the gospel or in the power of the Spirit, be allowed to paralyze our movements by lessening our hope. The grace which has conquered millions on millions of hearts is adequate still to go forth conquering and to conquer.

Ver. 4.—*The blessed dead living and reigning with Christ during the thousand years.* We are compelled to differ more widely from the great bulk of expositors in regard to this than in regard to almost any other passage in the entire Apocalypse. It seems to us that, in order to piece out a tolerably complete theory, many interpreters do very frequently assume some matters of great magnitude for which there is no warrant either in the text or the context. It is well known that this passage is the one which is supposed, above all others, to teach the doctrine of the personal reign of Christ upon the earth during the millennium. It is supposed that Jerusalem will be his central seat of authority and power; that the righteous dead will then be raised in such bodies as are to be immortal; that the saints will be Christ's attendants, and will participate with Jesus in the government of the world; that this will last through a period of a thousand years; that during this period the world will be subdued and converted, not by such means as are now used, but by those peculiar to the new dispensation to be ushered in by Christ's personal reign; that at the close of this period all the dead will be judged, and the affairs of this earth consummated. Some who do not fully adopt this view regard the first resurrection as one taking place on earth. According to some, it is a resurrection of bodies; according to others, it is a resurrection of principles; according to a third group, it is a resurrection of the Christian party; according to a fourth, it is one of memories and names. Others, again, regard it as a resurrection *from* earth, not *on* it; and here also we have to divide expositors into two groups— some looking at this first resurrection as a resurrection to heaven of the martyrs only; and others, as of all the blessed dead. Amid such a confused Babel, let us, as Ridley used to say, " give ourselves up to the text, and let it lead us by the hand." We see that the statement before us stands in connection with that period of a thousand years during which Satan is said to be bound. During this period in which the earth is released to a great extent from the power of the evil one, the apostle sees a vision of some who *during that thousand years were living and reigning with Christ.* On this statement let us ask—When? who? where? how? May be, on comparing Scripture with Scripture, we shall find more light thrown on this theme than we are prepared to expect. 1. *When?* " They lived and reigned with Christ a thousand years." Whoever and wherever they were, it was apparently during the thousand years in which Satan was bound that they were living and reigning. 2. *Who are they?* Our text speaks of two classes. First, of the martyrs; second, of those who had refused to succumb to the spirit of evil. These two put together make up all the faithful ones. So that we may call them the blessed dead, whether they quietly fell on sleep after serving their generation, or whether they were hurried off to their home in a chariot of fire. 3. *Where are they seen?* On earth, say the great bulk of interpreters. " *With Christ,*" says the text. It does not indeed specify whether in heaven or on earth, but simply that they are " *with Christ.*" Is not that clear enough? The text indicates not that Christ came down to earth to live with them, but that they had soared upward to live and reign with Christ.

The expression is akin to many more in the New Testament. "To-day thou shalt be with me;" "Absent from the body, at home with the Lord." Thus much, and this is all that is said. Oh! the refreshing invigoration which we get when we drink pure water from this crystal spring! "With Christ!" Enough![1] And this blessedness is theirs during a thousand years. Probably, though not necessarily, the same thousand years as those during which Satan was bound. 4. *In what state are they seen?* Εἶδον . . . τὰς ψυχὰς—"*the souls.*" Not in their bodily forms, as if on earth, but in the disembodied state. In this state they are with Christ, realizing more fully than they could do here their priesthood and kingship with God. For they are seated on thrones, sharing with their Lord the government of the world. Here they resisted even unto blood (when needed), striving against sin; they would neither worship the beast nor his image, and now, far from this world, they are living with Christ. *This is the first resurrection.*[2] Having attempted to clear the way by offering these preliminary remarks, we may now pass on to expound more fully the doctrine thus taught, in its bearing on and harmony with the rest of the Word of God.

I. HERE IS A VISION OF MEN FROM EARTH—not of men *on* it. "The souls." So in ch. vi. 11. That the expression refers here to men in what is called the disembodied state, scarcely admits of question. Not that we are taught in Scripture that the blessed dead are altogether "unclothed." For the Apostle Paul, in 2 Cor. v., seems to teach that immediately following on death the soul puts on another vestiture, awaiting the resurrection, when it will put on over that the house which is from heaven. Whatever may be, however, their "clothing," it is enough for us here to note that they are "*with Christ.*" This is just what we are taught in repeated Scriptures. Our Lord Jesus "died for us, that, whether we wake or sleep, we should live together with him." Thus are we taught that during that long interval which must elapse ere "the sea shall give up its dead," those who are "absent from the body" are "at home with the Lord." As one has well put it, "Here is no reference whatever to a visible manifestation of Christ, nor to a new kingdom on earth; nor is there any separation between one class of Christians and another, nor of the rising of the saints from their graves, nor of their living upon earth." Letting the words of the text speak for themselves, we find them far removed from the amazing obscurity with which the incubus of interpreters has invested them. They are clear and distinct words, fitting in with other statements o God's Word, teaching us that the souls of the blessed dead have already passed into a higher life: that there is no lapse in their blessed relationship to Jesus.

II. THE BLESSED SAINTS ARE SEEN IN A MORE ELEVATED SPHERE OF HOLY SERVICE. They are "living and reigning with Christ." They share with him the government of the world. Here they were "kings and priests" unto God. But in the higher state of being the meaning of these names, and the glorious dignity they include, become far more manifest than when here below. They were priests even here, in leading men to God and in pleading with God for men. They were kings too, ruling men for Jesus;

[1] Cf. an article by Dr. Owen, New York, in the *Bibliotheca Sacra*, April, 1861, "Exposition of Zech. xiv." Dr. Warren, of America, annotating this passage, and comparing it with Matt. xix. 28, says, "That is, while Christ shall reign in his Church over his enemies on earth, his faithful martyrs and confessors shall reign with him in glory on thrones above. It shall be a special reward for special fidelity" ('The Book of the Revelation,' p. 249).

[2] In order not to interrupt the direct line of statement, and in order to meet a query which at once arises, we put the following in a foot-note:—

It may be asked—What does the expression in ver. 5 mean: "The rest of the dead," etc.? "The rest of the dead" seems to mean the ungodly dead. "Lived not again" cannot mean that they were out of existence. The word is not ἔζησαν, but ἀνέζησαν; not "lived not until," etc., but *lived not anew*, i.e. the life to which they were destined. What that is appears from what follows. During the thousand years believers lived and reigned with Christ, and at the end go into perfect bliss. But during that time there was no re-living for the ungodly; they were in ᾅδης and in torment, and at the end of their provisional state they pass into the final one. And it should never be forgotten that their main point in the resurrection is not the local rising out of the grave, but the transition to another stage of being; and in the case of the blessed dead, this first transition is to a state of blessedness and honour with Christ. This is the first resurrection: not one in which Christ comes down to reign with the saints, but one in which they rise to reign with him; and such blessed resurrection is not and cannot be enjoyed by "the rest of the dead."

influencing the world's thought by the presentation of truth; swaying men's conscience by insisting on righteousness; and winning men's hearts by the philanthropies of love. It was no merely empty title with which they were honoured. They had the dignity of a royal priesthood below. But they know more fully now its deep meaning. The Syriac Version significantly and suggestively reads, "They shall be, [nay] are, priests of God and of his Messiah, and they will reign with him the thousand years."

III. THEIR PASSING UPWARD, IN DEATH, TO THIS HIGHER STATE IS CALLED THE FIRST RESURRECTION. And most intelligibly so. "Surely," says the Rev. F. D. Maurice, "if one takes the words as they stand, they do not describe a descent of Christ to earth, but an ascent of 'the saints' to reign with him." The thought of a real resurrection without a bodily rising from the grave ought to be no difficulty to those accustomed to scriptural phraseology. If, when a man passes from death to life, the phrase, "risen with Christ," is not inappropriate, neither can it be so when he makes the transition from earth to heaven to be "at home" with Jesus. And when we find the apostle saying, "I saw the souls . . . *this* is the first resurrection," we do not feel at liberty to maintain that it is a resurrection of the body which is referred to. The first resurrection is the rising of the saint at death to a higher life in Christ, which will be consummated at the general resurrection when the thousand years have expired. To quit the body—to be with Jesus? Is it hard to see why this is called the first resurrection? Nay, verily. You saw that friend of yours, breathing his last. He passed away. Your heart said, "He is not here; he is risen." He is a priest and king to God, and he is gone upward to reign with Jesus.

IV. BLESSED EVEN IN THIS FIRST RESURRECTION, THE SAINTS AWAIT IN HOPE THE CONSUMMATION OF THEIR BLISS. The blessedness indicated here extends over the thousand years. While the Church on earth is enjoying its millennial calm, believers above are reigning in life with Jesus Christ. Knowing the blessedness of their first resurrection, they can look forward with joyful hope to their second. There is no reason to doubt that from their heavenly rest they watch the progress of the kingdom of Christ on earth (cf. John viii. 56, Greek). They see Satan restrained, the saints possessing the kingdom, the wicked subdued, and righteousness advancing. They await with calm delight the revolutions of ages, for on them the second death will have no power; cycles on cycles of years can only bring new blessedness to them. "Blessed and holy is he that hath part in this first resurrection."

V. THEIR GLORY WILL BE CONSUMMATED AT THE RESURRECTION OF THE BODY. For this, as the ultimate outlook, the apostle says, believers are waiting (Rom. viii. 23). The first resurrection is that to a higher state of spiritual being. The second will be to the completed state of glorified life of both body and spirit. Then "all that are in their graves shall hear his voice, and shall come forth." Then there shall be a resurrection of the dead, both of the just and of the unjust. "Then, when the Son of God shall be manifested, will his saints also be manifested with him in glory." This will be the fulness of their bliss.

VI. FOR THE WICKED THERE IS NO SUCH FIRST RESURRECTION. "The rest of the dead lived not again (ἀνέζησαν) till the thousand years were expired." For the wicked, death brings nothing which can be called a resurrection at all. "The wicked is driven away in his wickedness." After death they are not extinct. They exist. They are in Hades. But their life in the invisible realm is no "resurrection." No such reward is theirs. They chose the paths of sin and selfishness, and they can but reap as they have sown. The statement of the text is, however, only negative. "They lived not again till," etc. What their state is, positively, we are not told. And where Scripture is silent, so must we be. But at the far end of the thousand years the outlook is gloomy enough. When we are told that on those who know the first resurrection "the second death hath no power," we see at a glance that just in proportion to the brightness of the light on one side is the depth of the shade on the other. They who are the Lord's rise twice, and die but once. They who are not the Lord's rise but once, and die twice.

Note : 1. We have reason for abundant joy over those friends in Christ who have passed onward and upward to be with the Saviour. What glorious accumulations of life are being garnered for us ready for the great harvest-day! The true continuity of spiritual being is only manifested to us in revelation. 2. How loud should our praise be to the great Son of God, that through his resurrection we have ours! If it had not been for his, then "those who have fallen asleep in Christ would have perished." But those who know him, and share his life, know also "the power of his resurrection." 3. How immeasurably does the issue of a godly life repay any amount of suffering that fidelity has incurred! Those whom the apostle saw had, in some cases, been "beheaded for the Word of God." But when the beheaded ones passed away "to reign with Christ," what a change! Though "counted as sheep for the slaughter," they were "more than conquerors." 4. How awful the penalty of ungodliness, even if reckoned only by its loss! "They lived not," etc. No. There is and can be in the unseen state nothing like "life" or "resurrection" to those who are godless. Being "without God," they are also "without hope." How completely the symbolism of the Apostle John accords with all the rest of Scripture as to the state of the dead!

Vers. 7—10.—*Satan loosed from his prison after the thousand years.* During the millennial period on earth, while the departed saints are living and reigning with Christ, evil will be subdued and restrained, but by no means will it be extinct. Had it been extinct it could not have broken out again, nor would there be any need for the παρεμβολή of the saints. The godless ones dispersed abroad, who will at the close of the thousand years break out afresh, are mentioned here under the peculiar names "Gog and Magog." [1] If any one will examine the account of the dispersion of the nations in Gen. x., he will find that one of Japheth's sons was named Magog. "Magog," says Josephus, "founded those that are after him called Magogites, but the Greeks call them Scythians." There is little or nothing more to call attention to these people till we come to the Book of Ezekiel, where the name Magog is again used, but not in the sense of a people so much as of a land, the syllable *Ma-* being equivalent to land or district. Since, then, Magog is the land of Gog, Gog is the name of a prince supposed to rule over that territory; obviously, ideally so, since he is commander over a group of peoples covering a much greater space of ground than the Scythians, and also peoples who were at a great distance from each other, viz. the Scythian hordes, the Persians, the Ethiopians and Libyans of Africa, Gomer or the Cimmerians; Togarmah or the Armenians, and the multitude that peopled the regions beyond them. Now, in Ezekiel we have a prophecy that, after the restoration of Israel, this Gog, with all his bands, shall come against that people, and that his onset shall only issue in his own destruction. We have so often seen and observed how largely the symbolism of the Apocalypse is based on the facts and symbols of the Old Testament, that it can be no surprise to us to find that it is so when we are approaching the theme of the Divine treatment of sin in its final onset on God's people. Even the names Gog and Magog turn up again, not, however, as the names of a prince and his land, but as "the nations which are in the four corners of the earth," who, after the millennium, will emerge from their retreat, and come in full force against "the camp of the saints." The new uprising of evil after the thousand years' rest is certainly not what we should expect or desire. But doubtless there is a Divine reason for permitting it so to be, or it would not be. Let us look at this matter closely in the light of God's Word, and maybe we shall find more to instruct us on this theme than at first sight appears probable.

I. WE GATHER FROM THIS PASSAGE SOME HINTS AS TO THE STATE OF THE CHURCH ON EARTH DURING THE MILLENNIAL PERIOD. 1. There is no reason to doubt that the millennium, owing to the effective restraint then put upon evil through the Word of truth and the power of God, will be a period of very great blessedness. Seeing that Satan is the active agent in so much evil, it is almost impossible to avoid the conclusion that, when he is bound, a large proportion of evil will cease to exist, and a far more rapid diffusion of good will be the blessed result. During, or possibly even before this period, we may expect the restoration of the Jews, and, consequent upon that, the bringing in of the fulness of the Gentiles, and the fulfilment of the glowing vision of the sixtieth chapter of Isaiah. 2. There is no reason whatever to suppose, from any of the teaching of Scripture, that our Lord Jesus Christ will then be present on the earth in any other way than in the power of his Spirit. The chapter before us, which is supposed to teach the reign of Christ with his risen saints on earth, teaches only, as we have already seen, that the departed saints are seen living and reigning

[1] *Vide* Fairbairn's 'Commentary on Ezekiel.' Also some useful references in Barnes's notes on this chapter.

with Christ. 3. It is equally clear that the millennium will not be a period of unmixed good, nor will it be a time when the saints can dispense with the παρεμβολή. Compared with things as they are now, the earth will be still and at rest; there will be a sabbatic calm, but it will not be heaven. Evil will be subdued, but far from extinct. The possibility of an outbreak will exist still. 4. There will also still be death in the world. The deathless state enters not in till the new heavens and the new earth appear, and Paradise is regained. Not till then will there be "no more curse." 5. The Church will still have to be prepared for war. Obviously, if the state of things on earth during the millennium were one of universal righteousness, there would be no nations to be deceived. Still less can we suppose that, after the resurrection from the dead, the glorified saints are to go about, sword in hand, to the holy war. It is a trial to our faith to read of an inrush of evil after a prolonged period of comparative calm. Scripture puts no such strain upon us, however, as that which is involved in the pre-millennial theory, viz. that, even after Paradise is regained, Satan will rush in and lead on *in person* the hosts of evil to a final attack.[1]

II. What do we gather from Scripture concerning this onset of ill after the millennium? 1. It is necessary. There is a little word in the third verse of this chapter of which we are too apt to lose sight. It is the word "must." "After that, he *must* be loosed a little season." Must! Why? We are not told. But we ought to take note of the word "must" for all that. What this hidden necessity in the government of God may be for the permission of such a disaster, is all dark to us. But we believe it, because the mouth of the Lord hath spoken it. 2. It will be a fierce onset. It will be after the old kind, by "deception" (ver. 8). What will be the special form of deceit he will use we are not told, and conjecture is useless. But it will be so successful that, with a strange unanimity, a great host will band together, and attack the saints of God. We do not dream of a material struggle, but one resembling that which we are waging every day with principalities, with powers, with the world-rulers of this darkness. 3. It will be a restricted struggle. Satan will be bound by time even when loosed as to space. The same Hand that bound retains its power even when the evil one is loosed. Not even at the worst of times is the world given over to the devil. No! nor ever will be. Even when the water-floods are at their height, and the billows are angry, Jehovah rides upon the storm. 4. It will be for a *little* season. Not only restricted, but within very narrow limits. The conflict may be sharp, but it will be short. 5. It will be suicidal. Satan will overshoot the mark, and fall into his own snare. He aims at deceiving the nations, and succeeds in leading them on to a guilty war; and lo! when engaged therein, we read that "fire came down out of heaven, and devoured them." 6. The struggle will be even serviceable to the Church; for not only will it reveal more and more the majesty of God in defending his own cause, but it will end in the hurling of Satan to a lower depth than before. In ch. xii. 9 we read that the devil was cast down to earth. In ch. xx. 3 he is cast into the abyss. But in ver. 10 he is cast into the lake of fire. This would seem to mean extinction, if such a conclusion were not forbidden by the closing phrase of the tenth verse. What it means we dare not presume to say, except that it certainly conveys the impression that his power for evil over mankind is brought to an end. Hence: 7. The struggle will be—the last. If the reader has followed the plan of the book and our exposition of it, he will have noted how one after another of the foes of God and man are destroyed. There were four. (1) The dragon—Satan. (2) The beast. (3) The false prophet. (4) Babylon the great. We have noted the fall of the fourth, the third, the second. Only the first was left, and now he is thrown into the lake of fire. After this, no foe is seen outside of man. Only men have now to be dealt with, and these have, whether they be good or bad. "So let all thine enemies perish, O Lord; but let them that love thee be as the sun when he cometh forth in his might!"

III. What are the related truths to which this passage points us? 1. In the light of the views of the millennium and of what is to follow, *two sets of apparently conflicting passages fall into place.* There is one set which indicates that, as the result of the first coming of Christ, all the earth shall be full of the knowledge of the Lord;

[1] See some of the extraordinary phases of pre-millennial theories in Jameson's 'Commentary'

there is another set which indicates that there will be a fierce outbreak of evil before our Lord shall come. It is no small confirmation of the correctness of an interpretation of this passage if thereby apparently conflicting statements fall in place. The binding of Satan, which was and is effected through our Lord Jesus Christ, has become more and more stringent as souls are plucked from his grasp; and we are to see a time of peace and calm when he will be even more completely bound than he is now. But after that there is to be the new onrush of evil, so that before our Lord shall come a fiercer conflict than has ever been known will be fought, ere the great struggle shall be completely at an end, and then the Lord shall come. So that we can at once look forward to the fulfilment of the seventy-second psalm as the result of the forces already at work; and yet see the harmony of that with words that declare that " that day shall not come, except there be a falling away first; . . . and then shall that wicked one be revealed, whom the Lord shall consume with the spirit of his mouth, and destroy with the brightness of his coming." 2. We see that there are two ways in which evil is being dealt with. That of removal, when souls are being renewed; and that of restraint, when evil beings are kept within prescribed limits. And both these ways of working are going on now, and will do during this millennial age. If it were not for these renewals of souls, no such time of calm could ever come in; and if it were not that there is much evil slumbering, as it were, that is *only* restrained, obviously it could not rush forth again. However much we may wonder at evil breaking out once more, even on the post-millennial view of our Lord's coming, yet on the pre-millennial view it would be impossible, since there would be none. And so severe is the pressure of this upon pre-millennialists, that one of them ventures on the supposition that God will create some wicked men for the purpose out of the slime and the mire! 3. Be it ours to take heart as we get a fresh glimpse of the Divine plan, viz. that however oft the conflict with evil and the evil one may be renewed, yet in every case the issue is that of the defeat of evil, and its banishment to a lower depth of disgrace than before. "Who hath ever hardened himself against God and prospered?" "Woe unto him that striveth with his Maker!" 4. Finally, what God will ultimately do with evil and the evil one, no one can positively say. We do not find the possibility of extinction shut out. At the same time, it is by no means so clear that such will be the issue that we feel warranted in saying it will be so. In our homily on the after-state of the ungodly, we deal with this question as concerns man. Here we have to do with it as regards Satan. We think that no one can help seeing that his fate is here set forth as that of utter, hopeless, final defeat. But we demur to the phrase, "eternal torment," as so applied—yea, more, we eschew it, on two grounds: (1) That our English word "eternal," as now understood, goes far ahead of the expression, "to ages of ages." The English word means an infinite duration; the Scripture phrase points to indefinite duration. In the former case *an ending is negatived;* in the latter *no end is disclosed.* (2) The word "torment" has a gross, material, carnal significance. It is used in the narrative of Dives and Lazarus, and in the symbolism of this book. It is a material figure to indicate spiritual issues. Where there is rebellion and final impenitence, there must be defeat; and where there is defeat, there must be "weeping, wailing, and gnashing of teeth." There will be nothing contrary to perfect equity in the fate of the evil one; we may be quite sure of that. And we are such inadequate judges of the guilt of any—yea, even of our own—and of what a righteous penalty requires, that it is far better for us that we should leave the matter in the hands of God, knowing that he will do only what is right, than that we should know beforehand what the precise issue will be. Surely it is not without reason that we say—We can rest more completely in uncertainty than in a certainty, *when we rest absolutely in God.* He will do what is right.

Vers. 11—15 (compared with ch. xxii. 12).—" *The day of the Lord.*" The several enemies of the Church—Satan, the first beast, the second beast, and the harlot— have one by one passed away from view. Now only men remain to be dealt with, both good and bad. It is necessary for us to avoid a confused blending of themes, as well as too frequent reiteration. We shall, therefore, pursue the following plan (which, indeed, is that required by the Apocalypse itself): We shall first deal with three themes common to all : the day of the Lord; the resurrection; the judgment. Then we shall see what light Scripture throws on the destiny of each; studying first the doom of the ungodly, and then the glory of the new heaven and the new earth. The topic of our present homily is—*The day of the Lord.* Inasmuch as our exposition of this and kindred themes can be valid only as it accords with the general tenor of the Word of God, we must ensure a wider basis on which to rest our unfolding of this stupendous theme than can possibly be found in this symbolic passage alone. If we group three other passages with it, our course will be clearer. The first is one which follows very shortly on our present one, and is in the twelfth verse of the last chapter of the Apocalypse. The second is that declaration of the Apostle Peter in Acts ii. 17—21. The third is the passage of the Prophet Joel, on which the apostle based his declarations concerning the "great and terrible day of the Lord." In combining the three we shall therefore be locating the second advent just where it is set in this book, and indicating its purposes in harmony with the whole tenor of Scripture.

I. ALL PARTS OF SCRIPTURE CARRY FORWARD OUR THOUGHTS TO A GREAT DAY. The Apocalyptic word, in ch. xxii. 12, is but the final setting of a truth which pervades the whole of Scripture. "That day," "the great day," "the day of the Lord," "the great and terrible day of the Lord," "the day when the Lord Jesus shall be revealed from heaven," "the last day," "the harvest,"—these and many other such phrases are found. Enoch prophesied, "Behold, the Lord cometh," etc. Job declared, "He shall stand at the latter day upon the earth." Asaph sang "Our God shall come, and shall not keep silence." The preacher said, "God shall bring every work into judgment." The prophets cast their glances forward far beyond the first appearing of our Lord. Isaiah, Hosea, Joel, and the rest. Our Lord, in the three several stages of his teaching, declares the same. When in the flesh, he spake of the time when he should come in his glory. He inspired Peter, Paul, and John to write of his reappearing. And all but his last word in the Apocalyptic unfoldings is, as it were, the final seal upon all this: "Behold, I come quickly; and my reward is with me, to give every man according as his work shall be."

II. THE TIME IS FIXED FOR THE COMMENCEMENT OF THAT DAY. "I come quickly." This was said eighteen hundred years ago, and our Lord is not come yet. But "one day is with the Lord as a thousand years," etc. Time is not counted only by the ticks of a dial, but by the growth of men. The second coming is, according to the Apostle Peter, the event which is at once to consummate and close this æon. Paul tells us, "Now is the day of salvation;" and "He hath appointed a day in which he will judge the world," etc. The Prophet Joel tells us, "In those days, and in that time, when I shall bring again the captivity of Judah and Jerusalem, I will also gather all nations." So we find in the New Testament that the receiving of Israel once more shall be followed by the bringing in of the fulness of the Gentiles. These two great issues are to be witnessed before the end cometh. As the world is not moving on blindly without any definite end at all, so neither is it moving on without a Divine foresight and purpose as to when or how the end shall come. "The spirit of the living creature is in the wheels;" "The wheels are full of eyes." Towards this momentous point all things are tending. To the last the world will seem indifferent thereto. "As it was in the days of Noah . . . so shall it be in the day when the Son of man is revealed."

III. STARTLING SIGNS WILL HERALD THE APPROACH OF THAT DAY. Our Lord and his apostles were very clear on this matter (Matt. xxiv.; Acts ii.). Nor was the Prophet Joel, among others, less so (ii. 31; iii. 15; comp. also Hag. ii. with Heb. xii.). There is room for wide differences of opinion here as to whether all these expressions signify extraordinary and marvellous natural phenomena, or rather great convulsions in the ecclesiastical and political spheres. Possibly both are intended. Moral and physical crises and epochs have often coincided, and may again. In Humboldt's 'Kosmos'[1] no fewer than seventeen instances are given of remarkable natural phenomena similar to those described in Scripture, some of which occurred at great crises in national life or in the world's history.

IV. A VAST ASSEMBLAGE WILL BE GATHERED ON THAT DAY. What a vision before the mind's eye when we look at the Apocalyptic words! "To give every man;" "Every eye shall see him;" "We must all stand before the judgment-seat of Christ." See also the Prophet Joel's words, "Multitudes, multitudes in the valley of decision;"

· Vol. iii. pp. 282, 283, and in Note 481 (Sabine's translation).

where the term "decision" is from a word that denotes a threshing-instrument, by which the wheat is separated from the chaff; and the word "multitudes" is from one that signifies " a hum," and brings vividly before the mind the confused noise of a vast crowd. Crowds on crowds! One living, surging sea of human souls. A threshing process is being carried on, and " *He* shall separate them one from another ! "

V. THE LIFE-WORK OF MEN WILL BE FINISHED ON THAT DAY. "To give every man according as his *work* shall be." Not his works, as if they were isolated details; but *work*, as if it were a definite whole. Even so. *The work is as the man is.* On the side of good or of evil, as he has taken his stand, there will his work be ranged. "Ye did it unto me," "Ye did it not unto me," are phrases so comprehensive as to include and to classify all moral acts whatsoever. And however doubtful it may have seemed at life's earlier stages, on which side any one might be ranged, no doubt will be possible when wheat and tares alike are ripe at the great harvest-day. As we have shown in an earlier homily, we can know men by their fruits. God knows them by their tendencies. And when tendencies have developed to issues, the righteousness of God in judging accordingly will be made manifest. For—

VI. A RIGHTEOUS RECOMPENSE WILL BE AWARDED ON THAT DAY. " To give every man *according* as his work shall be." Here we have the distinct statement of the meaning and object of our Lord's second advent—a meaning and an object so momentous, that we cannot dislocate this reappearing without seriously affecting our conception of the whole plan of redemption. If we look at our Lord as coming to bring in a regeneration which the gospel has—designedly—failed to achieve, our views of our duty and of the glorious gospel will be very seriously lowered. But it is not thus that Scripture locates the great day. It is the decisive day, the day of ripeness, the day of separation, the day of final award (cf. ch. xxii. 12). Then God will judge the secrets of men. We shall all be made manifest before the tribunal of Christ.

VII. RESULTS WILL CONTRAST AS WIDELY AS CHARACTERS ON THAT DAY. "Whatsoever a man soweth, that shall he also reap." Every man will receive in his body the things done, whether good or bad. "The heavens and the earth shall shake, but the Lord shall be the Hope of his people, and the Strength of the children of Israel." On one side we read that the wicked "shall be punished with everlasting destruction," etc. On the other, "He shall come to be glorified in his saints, and to be admired in all them that believe." So that it is easy to see the reason why, on the one hand, the second coming of our Lord is "the blessed hope," while on the other it is "the great and terrible day." It will be to a man glorious or terrible according to the attitude of the man towards his God and Saviour. There is a day coming that shall burn as an oven, when men will "return, and discern between the righteous and the wicked, between him that serveth God and him that serveth him not."

VIII. THESE RESULTS ARE FINAL. So far as the disclosures of the Word of God are made,[1] the horizon is bounded by these two issues—glory to the righteous, condemnation to the wicked. On the question—What do these severally mean? we treat afterwards.[2] But the dread aspect of finality which characterizes the varied passages of the Word of God which speak of the doom of the wicked, precludes us from asking— What lies beyond these disclosures? Where Scripture bounds its testimony, we must end our thinkings, for the one and sufficient reason that thought has no further basis on which to act. For our part, we can affirm neither the endlessness of future punishment, nor annihilation, nor restoration. "But," it may be demurred, "the ultimate issue *must* be one *or* the other." Possibly so. But even if it be so, it does not follow that we can tell any individual soul *how it will be with him.* If we be asked again, " Why can you not *affirm* either? " we reply—We cannot affirm restoration, because many passages seem to us to preclude it. We cannot affirm annihilation, because it loses sight of the fact that, according to the *usus loquendi* of Scripture, there may be existence in a state of death. We cannot affirm the endlessness of punishment, because: (1) That would be affirming the tremendous doctrine that sin will last as long as God lasts. (2) The assertion would go beyond the necessary meaning of the phrases used to imply duration, which only—so far as evil is concerned—indicate indefinite rather than endless duration. (3) It would also ignore the fact that the

---

[1] Cf. the writer's 'Future Punishment,' ch. vii.
[2] Cf. homily on 'The Second Death : the Lake of Fire.'

strongest phrases in the Word of God for duration, and those which involve endlessness, *are all on the side of good.*[1] But while we refrain from asserting the absolute endlessness of future punishment, we do affirm: (1) That God has not shown us an end to it. (2) That every moment a sinner continues to harden his heart against God, he is doing what he can to make repentance an impossibility. (3) That if a man resists Divine love here, no one can show what is to make him more yielding hereafter. (4) That every man will be dealt with by God in absolute and unswerving equity. Whatever may be any individual theory, all these four last-named positions are absolutely certain. Objection: But how about the heathen world? What will be the condition of the men who have lived in pagan darkness? Will they necessarily be lost because they have had less light than others? We reply: (1) No; not necessarily. The Scripture again and again teaches that men's salvation does not depend on the measure of light God saw fit to send them, but on the use which they shall have made of the light they had. (2) We have no doubt whatever that before this great decisive day comes, every child of man will have been brought into direct contact with the claims of the Lord Jesus Christ, for acceptance or rejection; and that no soul ever reaches the crucial point of its probation till such is the case (cf. 1 Pet. iv. 6). How could there be a common basis of judgment if some had never heard of Jesus? Our Lord will not come till he has all things in readiness to judge the living and the dead.

IX. Finally, IT BEHOVES EVERY MAN TO PREPARE FOR THAT DAY. Whatever may be obscure as to the time or place in which these tremendous scenes will be enacted, there is quite enough of clearly revealed truth respecting it to give men urgent reasons for preparing to meet their God; and to make pastors and teachers passionately earnest in setting before their hearers the solemnity of the destinies which loom before every man. Just as each atom of matter is related to every other, so has each moment of our time a bearing upon the last, the supreme, the decisive day. Every day we are piling up thoughts, words, deeds, which take their place for good or evil in the fabric of character; and as is character at last, so will be the award.

> " Oh, to be ready, ready for that day,
> Who would not fling earth's fairest toys away? "

Vers. 11—15.—*The resurrection from the dead.* This paragraph is an amazingly compressed eschatology. We have already studied the Scripture teaching on "the day of the Lord" which it opens up to us. We have now to look at the dread incidents which will mark that day. One of these is indicated by the words, "I saw the dead, the great and the small, standing before the throne. . . . And the sea gave up the dead which were in it; and death and Hades gave up the dead that were in them." We will, with these words as our centre-point, survey the doctrine in the light of the general tenor of Scripture.

I. AT THE COMING OF OUR LORD JESUS CHRIST THERE WILL BE A GENERAL RESURRECTION FROM THE DEAD. There is nothing in Scripture to lead to the conclusion that there will be two bodily resurrections. Those which are mainly supposed to teach it do not. Others teach precisely the contrary. 1. There are two passages which are among the principal ones that are adduced for the doctrine of two bodily resurrections, one of the saints, and afterwards of the wicked. (1) The first is ch. xx. 3. This we have dealt with in the homily on ver. 4. (2) The other is 1 Thess. iv. 16, which is looked at by some as if it taught that the dead in Christ should rise first, and the dead out of Christ afterwards. But the antithesis is not between the dead *in Christ* and other dead, but between the *dead* in Christ and those who are living at the coming of the Lord. First, the dead; then we who are alive. 2. Other passages leave distinctly on the mind the impression of one resurrection, not of two; *e.g.* John v. 28; Matt. xxv. 41; Acts xxiv. 15; Dan. xii. 2. We are pointed to one day or time, whether Scripture speaks of the righteous, or of the wicked, or of both. (1) Of the righteous (2 Thess. i. 10; Heb. ix. 28; 1 John ii. 28, 29; iv. 17; Phil. i. 10; iii. 20, 21). (2) Of the wicked (Rom. ii. 6; 2 Pet. iii. 7, 13). (3) Of both (Matt. vii. 21—23; x. 32,

---

[1] Let the student study carefully (in the origina.) Isa. li. 6; Ps. cxlv. 13; Eph. iii. 21; Heb. vii. 16

33; xiii. 30, 42, 43; xvi. 27; xxv.; Acts xvii. 31; Rom. ii. 6, 16; xiv. 10; 1 Cor. iii. 12—15; 2 Thess. i. 7—10). It is scarcely too much to say that it is impossible to explain all these passages except on the supposition that there is to be *a* resurrection of the dead, both of the just and of the unjust. There is, however, another passage, which, if possible, is more decisive still, viz. John vi. 39, 40, 44, 54. Here it is four times stated that the resurrection of the believers shall take place at the last day, which could not be if that of the wicked were separated from it and appointed for a later period. There will be one resurrection from the dead.

II. WHAT WILL THE RESURRECTION BE? Granted that it will be of all the dead (John v. 28): what is meant by it? We reply—*It will be a resurrection of bodies.* 1. The bodies of the righteous will rise (Phil. iii. 21; 1 Cor. xv. 43; Rom. viii. 11, 23). 2. The bodies of the wicked will rise (John v. 29; Acts xxiv. 15; Matt. v. 29, 30; Mark ix. 43—47; Matt. x. 28; 2 Cor. v. 10, Greek). The dead will rise with bodies which will be according to character, and which will contain within themselves provision for joy or woe. Query: Have we any clue in Scripture as to the relation which exists between the body that is laid in the grave and that which will rise from it? We reply—Not any direct clue; but we have a very clear statement of an apostle in 1 Cor. xv. 36—38, concerning four well-known principles and methods of God in the natural world; and if we apply these, as he would have us do, to the doctrine in hand, we shall find many difficulties cleared out of the way. The four facts are these. (1) There can be no rising without a previous sowing and decay. (2) The body that is sown is *not* the body that shall be. (3) Yet to every seed there is its own body. (4) The relation between the two is a secret in the mind of God. "God giveth it a body as it hath pleased him." If these are borne in mind and carried out to their legitimate issue, they will leave us no difficulty in the matter save the one, *that we do not know the whole of anything.*

III. HOW WILL THE RESURRECTION BE EFFECTED? 1. By the power of God (Matt. xxii. 29). 2. By the authority of the Lord Jesus Christ (John v. 28, 29; Phil. iii. 21). 3. By the energy of the Holy Ghost (Rom. viii. 11). 4. Angels will be the attendants and instruments (Matt. xiii. 39—41; 1 Thess. iv. 16). If we here do little more than quote Scripture, it is because that is all that we can do. We know nothing more about the resurrection than we are told by our Lord and his apostles. We cannot forget that the Redeemer, in his memorable reply to the Sadducees, in which he showed them that their blundering over the doctrine arose from ignorance of Scripture, also pointed out in what the real glory of the resurrection consists, viz. not in the reproducing of like flesh and blood, nor in the repetition of an earthly life, but in the raising of the entire man to a life of nobler energy, in which it would be possible for him to realize the full meaning of the words, "I am the God of Abraham, of Isaac, and of Jacob." He who was their God would be to them all that a God could be, and would raise them up and present them to himself in all the perfection of a complete and glorified manhood.

IV. ON WHAT GROUND MAY OUR BELIEF IN THE RESURRECTION SECURELY REST? There is one ground which is sufficient in itself, viz. *the testimony of Jesus Christ and his apostles.* Well aware are we that this is an age of revolt from authority. Or, rather, it is supposed to be so. And men think that they require clear proof from actual experiment before they believe. But a little close examination will dispose of this self-laudatory theory. For first, if the proof of *x* be direct and personal, based on his own trial, to him the issue is knowledge, not faith. And second, unless his own proof can be repeated or actually is repeated by others, they must accept another's finding on faith in him. And so it is in the entire scientific realm. There is no man of science that does not owe to the experiments of others ninety-nine hundredths of all his knowledge. In other words, the great bulk of scientific knowledge rests on the authority of others. There are three kinds of authority which will stand as long as the race lasts. (1) That of personal proprietorship. (2) That of adequate knowledge. (3) That of intrinsic and self-evident truth or worth. With regard to the resurrection. The Lord Jesus Christ, as Lord of all, has authority of the first-named order. His apostles, as taught by the Holy Ghost, have authority of the second order. Hence the question between faith and unbelief regarding the resurrection ceases to be one of the surrender of authority as a ground of faith, and becomes merely one of the transfer of authority. Are men prepared to accept as authorities on this matter men who ask them to disbelieve the resurrection, because science can give them no information respecting it? We, for our part, challenge men to produce more trustworthy testimony on any matter, than that of our Lord and his apostles concerning the resurrection. If asked, then, for the ground on which we believe it, we would reply: 1. The Lord has assured us of it (John xi. 23)   2. He regards it as a part of the trust committed to him (John vi. 39, 40). 3. He has led the way by his own resurrection (1 Cor. xv. 17). 4. He has declared his will that his people shall follow him to glory (John xvii. 24). 5. The completion of his own mediatorial work demands it (1 Cor. xv. 29—32; 1 Thess. ii. 19; Col. i. 28; Jude 24).

V. WHAT WILL FOLLOW FROM THE RESURRECTION? (Ver. 14, "Death and Hades were cast into the lake of fire.") The bodies of men before the resurrection were, so to speak, held in the grasp of death. The spirits of men were in Hades, *i.e.* in the invisible realm—those of the blessed in a state of happy rest and honour in and with Christ; those of the ungodly and unbelieving under the guard of Christ, with a view to the great, the decisive day, ushered in by the resurrection. When the mighty voice of the Son of God shall wake the dead, then Death shall resign his hold of the bodies, and the invisible world must open its gates for all its occupants to quit those mysterious realms. Thus Death will be dead. And the invisible realm will be vacant. Both will have served a purpose in the development of the Divine plans, but they will be no longer. They will be "cast into the lake of fire."

VI. WHAT USES HAVE BEEN MADE OF THE DOCTRINE OF THE RESURRECTION? Perhaps few doctrines have suffered so much as this from the meddling and muddling of man. And in part, at any rate, it is owing to this that it has been so misused. Yet not altogether to this cause must we attribute such abuse. For the doctrine is confessedly so mysterious, that the proud heart scorns it. It is so fraught with terrors to the ungodly that the wicked tremble at it. (See Sir Samuel Baker's conversation with an African youth on the resurrection; Dr. Moffat's with an African chief upon it.) It is very remarkable that we have in Scripture illustrations of no fewer than seven ways of treating this doctrine. 1. Some denied it altogether (1 Cor. xv. 12). 2. Some declared that it was past already (2 Tim. ii. 18). 3. Some made it a plea for putting forth curious questions (Matt. xxii. 28). 4. Some mocked (Acts xvii. 32). 5. Some postponed the consideration of the matter (Acts xvii. 32). 6. Some believed (1 Pet. i. 3—5). 7. One, at least, with a touching blending of faith, fear, and common sense, was unable to formulate the doctrine, but reposed implicitly in the Lord Jesus Christ (cf. John xi. 26, 27, "Believest thou *this*?" etc.). We admire the answer of Martha, in which she seems to say, "Yea, Lord, I believe *it*, because I believe *thee*, though I scarcely understand what it means!" Happy they who, with extreme difficulty in formulating the doctrine in detail, can fall back in loving faith in him in whom it centres, and who "will make it plain." As that excellent man, Dr. Clerk Maxwell, said, shortly before death, "It is but a very little of pure truth that we can reach; but what a mercy to be able to say, 'We know whom we have believed!'"

VII. BELIEVING THE DOCTRINE, WHAT OUGHT TO BE ITS PRACTICAL POWER? 1. *It has a gladsome side.* Herein: (1) Let the believer rejoice (Col. iii. 3, 4). (2) Let the Christian worker gather from it a holy stimulus, and keep it in view in all his teaching of Jesus Christ (Col. i. 28, 29; 1 Thess. ii. 19, 20; 1 Cor. xv. 58). (3) With this great crisis in view, let the hearer of the gospel remember his responsibilities (Heb. xiii. 17). (4) Let all Christian people see to it that they abound in the work of holy living (1 John ii. 28; 2 Pet. iii. 14). 2. *It has, moreover, an aspect of unspeakable solemnity.* (Ch. i. 7; John v. 28, 29.) To rise from the dead to confront the Judge of all, in an unprepared and unpardoned state, how terrible! The Lord grant that we may find mercy of the Lord in that day!

Vers. 11—15.—*Judgment; or, the opening of the books.*[1] Following on the resurrection is the judgment. In connection with this, we read that before the face of him that sat upon the throne the heavens and the earth fled away. This may include the final conflagration. But what the phrase actually means, no man is in a position adequately

[1] The student will find very many valuable hints in a small work entitled, 'The Judgment Books,' by Alex. Macleod, D.D., Birkenhead. Elliot, Edinburgh: 1865.

to judge. Such passages as Ps. cii. 26, 27; Matt. xxiv. 35; xix. 28; Heb. i. 12—14; 2 Pet. iii. 7, 10—12; 1 John ii. 17, prepare us to expect vast changes. "If there is any analogy between what has been and what is to be, there may yet be another catastrophe on the surface of the earth by virtue of which present forms of life will cease to be, and give place to others of a higher order than ever earth has known." Now, the Bible presents to us a moral development. Science shows us physical development. And we are led, by comparing both together, to the conclusion which we have before expressed, that as in the past so in the future, moral and physical events will synchronize, and that when the earth is ripe for geologic change it will also be ripe for a moral one. Planting our feet firmly on the words which the Holy Ghost teacheth, we say—There cometh a great decisive day, as tremendous in its moral and spiritual revelations and issues as it will be august in its physical changes. We recognize Divine disclosures concerning the latter as well as concerning the former. There are Divine disclosures to reason in the stone-book of nature, and Divine declarations to faith in the written revelation. Where science ends revelation carries us forward, and while the former forecasts the re-preparation of the stage for further action, the other reveals the action which is to take place on that stage. Science brings to view natural law; revelation, a series of laws equally firm and sure; even those of a moral government superadded to physical control, and of a redemptive work inserted into a moral administration. There is a day coming when the working of these varied sets of laws will culminate. In the "economy of the filling up of the seasons" things are kept in store against that day. It is very remarkable to find such vast events indicated in so few words as we find here. But the fact is that all physical charges are but subordinate to the supreme moral and spiritual issues which are pending. On these we at once proceed to dwell.

I. "THE GREAT DAY" WILL PROVE AT ONCE A CLIMAX OF HISTORY AND A REVELATION OF CHARACTER. Its bearing on the human race is indicated by the words, "day of judgment;" in which term there are included: 1. The appearing of mankind before God. 2. The manifestation of character. 3. Approval or disapproval. 4. Recompense or penalty. "It has for a long time been disputed whether the judgment of the world will be an *external, visible, formal* transaction, or whether *the mere decision respecting the destiny of man*; the actual taking effect of retribution is represented under the image of a judicial proceeding, like what is common among men."[1] The latter opinion would have more on its side if it were *only* in such a symbolic book as this that the latter is suggested. But the Scriptures of the Old and New Testaments combine in presenting the judgment as a vast solemn last assize.

II. THE ENTIRE ADMINISTRATION OF JUDGMENT IS IN THE HANDS OF THE LORD JESUS CHRIST. (John v. 22, 27; Acts x. 42; xvii. 31; Rom. xiv. 10; 2 Cor. v. 10; Phil. ii. 11.) He is the Head of the human race, both by his original position as Son of God, and by his assumed position as Son of man. He "both died, and rose, and re-lived, that he might be Lord both of the dead and of the living."

III. SCRIPTURE TELLS US WHO WILL BE CONCERNED IN THE TRANSACTIONS OF THE JUDGMENT-DAY. Devils (Jude 6; 2 Pet. ii. 4; Matt. viii. 28). Men (Rom. ii. 4—11), including pagans, Jews, Christians, nominal and real. All (Rom. xiv. 10). None will elude the judgment of God (Rom. ii. 3). "Every one shall give account of himself" (Rom. xiv. 12).

IV. WE ARE ALSO TOLD WHAT WILL BE JUDGED. 1. Deeds (2 Cor. v. 10). 2. Words (Matt. xii. 36, 37). 3. Thoughts (1 Cor. iv. 3—5). 4. Secret things (Rom. ii. 16). 5. "*Every* secret thing" (Eccles. xii. 14). "There is nothing covered, that shall not be revealed; and hid, that shall not be known."

V. MEN WILL BE JUDGED ACCORDING TO THE LIGHT THEY HAD; *i.e.* according to the use they made of the light God had granted them (Rom. ii. 11—15; Matt. x. 15; xi. 21—24; Luke xi. 31, 32; xii. 47, 48; Acts x. 34, 35). The principles here laid down are those of most manifest equity, and we are quite sure that there will be nothing contrary thereto in the sentence of God. The late Dr. Lawson, of Selkirk, was once asked by a flippant young man how he could think that any, such as Plato and Socrates, would be lost because they had not heard of Jesus Christ. He replied, "If it please God in his mercy, and through faith in his Son, to take you and me to heaven,

[1] Knapp, 'Christian Theology,' sec. clv., note.

and that we shall find there Socrates and Plato, I am sure we shall be glad indeed to meet them ; but if we shall not find them in heaven, I am also sure that the Judge of all the earth will be able to assign a good reason for their absence, and that none in heaven will be either able or willing to dispute either the justice or the wisdom of his sovereign arrangements." [1] We may also add that Scripture not obscurely intimates that every soul will, before the dread day comes, be brought into contact with the Lord Jesus for acceptance or rejection ; and those who followed conscientiously the dimmer light will surely accept joyfully the clearer.   Certainly the Judge of all the earth will do right.

VI. WHERE IS THE RECORD OF THE ACTS, WORDS, AND THOUGHTS WHICH WILL BE DISCLOSED AT JUDGMENT?   In " the books." What are these ?   Who can tell ?   We would reverently suggest : 1. *There is that unerring record—the memory of God.*   To the Divine mind everything is present (Ps. cxxxix.).   By him nothing is forgotten. All the manifold and complicated currents of human thought, the varied fluctuations of human wills and impulses, the maze of human design and plan, past, present, and future, are all laid open to his searching glance.   Not one passing thought eludes his notice or escapes from his memory.   In his mind is a complete and permanent photograph of every soul.   2. *Then there is our own memory.*   Judging from the collection of facts from which Science essays to draw her conclusions, nothing ever drops completely from man's memory.   A word, a look, a sound, a song, a feature, a locket, a hair, may recall deeds and thoughts of a generation past.   Let but the barriers which imprison memory be removed, as they seem to have been in the case of many persons near death, and the whole of one's life may rush back in an instant, and reveal the man to himself in a way that shall either make him dumb with horror or inspire him with joy.   3. *If this be so, then the memory of others must be a permanent record of a large part of our lives.*   For if our memory records the impulses we *give*, it would seem also, by parity of reasoning, to be a record of the impulses we receive. Thus the power exerted by us over others, and by others over us, creates indelible impressions on their minds and ours, so that their "books" and ours mutually supplement and confirm each other.   " You cannot meet a stranger in the streets, nor utter a word in your remotest solitude, nor think a thought in your inmost heart, but lo ! this recording angel has noted it down upon the tablets of your soul for ever " (Macleod). 4. *Science itself suggests wondrous disclosures in this direction.*   The great mathematician Babbage, in his Bridgewater Treatise, remarks, " The whole atmosphere is one vast library, on whose pages are recorded all that man has ever said or woman whispered." The air, the light, are ever the bearers of our deeds and words.   " It is probable," says Coleridge, " judging from the facts presented in medical records, that all thoughts are in themselves imperishable ; and that if the intelligent faculty should be rendered more comprehensive, *it would require only a different and apportioned organization—the body celestial instead of the body terrestrial—to bring before every human soul the collective experience of its whole past existence.   And this—this, perchance, is the dread book of judgment, in the mysterious hieroglyphics of which every idle word is recorded.*" [2] 5. And then there will be another record—*in the countenance of the man.* The spirit forms the face.   Even here, " it is not in words explicable with what Divine lines and lights the exercise of godliness and charity will mould and gild the hardest and coldest countenances, neither to what darkness their departure will consign even the loveliest. For there is not any virtue the exercise of which even momentarily will not impress a new fairness upon the features ; neither on them only, but on the whole body." [3] The work of grace reforms the countenance.   The work of sin deforms it.   To a sufficiently keen observer, a man's face is a living book in which his character may be read.   Yea, it is even so.   " Books " in abundance are every moment having entries made therein from which the character and desert of each can be clearly read at last.   So much so is this the case, that it is far easier to see how ruin impends than how salvation is possible, with such a long catalogue of sins as must attach to every man's life. Knowing as we do that in the physical world there is no forgiveness of sins, it is impossible, without Bible teaching, to see how salvation ever can be inserted into the condition of a sinful man.   This naturally leads us to another inquiry—

[1] 'Life,' by Dr. Macfarlane.
[2] Coleridge, ' Biographia Literaria,' quoted by Macleod.
[3] Ruskin. See also Joseph Cook's lecture on ' The Solar Light.'

VII. WHAT WILL BE THE ISSUES OF THE JUDGMENT? These will be twofold. 1. *Eternal life.* (Comp. Matt. xxv. 31—40; Rom. viii. 33, 34; 1 John iv. 17; 2 Tim. iv. 8; ch. ii. 10; iii. 5.) Scripture is very clear as to the issues of the judgment in the case of the blessed. There is, in fact, one sentence in the paragraph before us which indicates the joyous aspect of the judgment to them. " Another book was opened, which is the book of life" (cf. Isa. iv. 3; Luke x. 20; Phil. iv. 3; Heb. xii. 23; Phil. iii. 20). This book of life includes all the saved. Every one of them is written there. The Father's name is written on their foreheads. Their names are written in the Father's book. And this is emphatically a book of grace. Without the redemptive scheme of Divine love, there never would have been any such book at all. Nor should it be left unnoticed that it is called in ch. xiii. 8 and xxi. 27 *the Lamb's* book of life. The names recorded there are of those who have been redeemed by his blood, and who are his purchased possession. These shall be welcomed by him to the everlasting kingdom "prepared from the foundation of the world." *Difficulty* (1) : Difficulties may here occur to the minds of many; such as these: If it be a matter of revealed truth that acts, words, and thoughts shall be brought forth to light, and if the sins of the believer in Christ are thus brought to view and exposed before all, will not that interfere very materially with the joy of the saved? *Reply :* (*a*) It is not surprising if, when we attempt detail, we soon get beyond our reach in dealing with themes so vast. (*b*) In this case, however, whatever sin comes out to light, does so as that which is repented of on the one side, and forgiven on the other. So that (*c*) even thus the testimony would be borne more vividly to the renewing and forgiving grace of God. *Difficulty* (2) : We read in John v. 24 that he that believeth shall not come into judgment; and yet we read elsewhere, "We must *all* stand before the judgment-seat of Christ : " how is this? *Reply :* Believers, with others, will *be made manifest* before the judgment-seat of Christ; but their manifestation will be that of pardoned and of sanctified men, whose guilt is cancelled and whose sin is removed. Surely, when this is taken into account, the difficulty ceases. There will be no such judgment as involves condemnation. 2. *On the other side, the issue will be condemnation.* The terrible word "Depart ! " sums up all hell (cf. ch. ii. 6—16; 2 Thess. i. 10—17; 2 Pet. iii. 7; Mark ix. 43—48). What further remarks we have to offer on the after-state of the ungodly we reserve for the next homily, observing here only that κατακρίμα cannot mean anything less than "an adverse verdict ; " and what that may involve, as a final sentence from the lips of the King of kings, we pray God we may never know !

Note : That scenes so solemn as the one put before us in this paragraph are meant to tell mightily upon us, and that they ought to do so, we cannot question, however incapable we may be of realizing all the details thereof. Any one or more of the following applications may well be earnestly pressed on the conscience by pastors and teachers. 1. Let every believer keep in view the judgment-day, with anxious desire then to be approved of the Judge (1 John ii. 28). 2. Let us endeavour more fully to realize the fact that we are perpetually under the scrutinizing gaze of him "with whom we have to do." 3. Let us regard every action as a laying up of treasure or of wrath against the great revealing day (Rom. ii. 5; 1 Tim. vi. 19). 4. How intensely momentous does a pastor's or a teacher's work appear in view of that day (Heb. xiii. 17) ! It is not to be wondered at if at times the weight of responsibility is more than he knows how to bear. 5. The responsibility of those who hear the Word is obviously correspondingly great. It also is implied in Heb. xiii. 17. 6. None should forget that there is a Divine, a gracious meaning, in the prolonging of the " day of salvation." The promise and the menace are not forgotten. God is not weak. Neither is he indifferent. He is " long-suffering towards us, not willing that any should perish, but that all should come to repentance." With a view to this his goodness is drawing men now. He waits to be gracious. But we have no reason for thinking that he will wait always.

Vers. 11—15.—*The second death : the lake of fire.* "This is the second death, the lake of fire." Few of our readers, if any, are likely here to lose sight of the symbolic style of the Apocalypse—a style which, indeed, so largely pervades it, that if there were not other passages bearing on like themes and couched in different phraseology, its interpretation would be impossible. And even with the aid of the plainer words, the theme before us is so vast, so dread, so fraught with terror, that for our part we scarcely know how to write upon it or even to approach it. Nor even now can we pretend to do more within the space at our command than to lay down some seven distinctly revealed lines of Divine teaching concerning the future state of the ungodly. When these seven lines are put together they will be found to include all the main teachings of the Word containing so dread a theme. We regard it as needless to do more at this stage of the exposition than to remind the reader of the point we have reached in the grand unfoldings of this book. The resurrection is past, the judgment has been set, men have been adjudged each one according to his works. And it is from this revealed point of time that we now start. May the writer's pen be guided, and his heart inspired in a holy and a trembling awe, as he now essays to point out the results of the Judge's solemn word, "Depart!"

I. AT THIS POINT THE REVEALED PERIOD OF PROBATION FOR THE RACE CLOSES. It is very clear, from the apostolic explanation in 2 Cor. vi. 2 of the phrase, "a day of salvation," that the present gospel day is thereby intended. This is the day of salvation, in which mercy may be obtained. To this day there is a limit. "After that thou shalt cut it down." The vine-dresser could not ask for any further postponement of the act when fruitlessness was decisive and final. We are not in a position to look at the meaning of the great decisive day in relation to the government of God until we understand the Scripture doctrine of human probation. We know that nations, empires, and cities have a day of probation. So have Churches. So have individuals. Their probation may close even before their natural life ends. It was so with Judas. The line, however, which marks the close of probation is not a temporal one, but a moral one. *The close of probation is reached when the state of fixedness in sin is reached* (cf. Mark iii. 29, 30, Revised Version). Hence we have but to expand the conception of that of individuality to that of universality to see how completely this accords with the frequent reference in Scripture of "the harvest-day." Whoever lives in the habit of resisting God is hardening himself into a state of fixed unfruitfulness. And the last day will be the decisive day of treatment, because it is the consummation-day of character.

II. "THE DAY OF SALVATION" WILL BE FOLLOWED BY "THE DAY OF JUDGMENT." The latter may be a period as prolonged as the former. During "the day of salvation" grace reigns. In "the day of judgment" absolute and unswerving equity will mark the Divine procedure in every case (Rom. ii. 6—16). And, as we understand the meaning of that, in its bearing on our present theme, we would express it thus: *Whosoever refused grace, when it was freely offered him in the day of salvation, will be dealt with according to equity when that day is over.* There will be nothing of vindictiveness, harshness, or excess. Nothing in degree or duration which will not be known by the individual conscience, to be absolutely right.

III. AT THIS DAY OF JUDGMENT THE RIGHTEOUS WILL NO MORE BE MINGLED WITH THE WICKED. The two solemn words, "Come!" "Depart!" will mark a difference in lot corresponding to difference of character, and also a separation of the one from the other. And it may well be made a theme of prolonged study to inquire into the meaning of the several words which express the character of those "without." There are no fewer than thirteen terms by which they are indicated. "Dogs," "sorcerers," "whoremongers," "liars," "the fearful," "unbelieving," "idolaters," "murderers," "fornicators," "abominable," "those who worship the beast," "those who worshipped the dragon," "those who are not in the Lamb's book of life." Such is the terrible list. On earth they met with the righteous, but were never confounded with them; in the next they shall neither mix nor meet (cf. Matt. vii. 23; Heb. xii. 14). We know that such characters may be met with on earth now; what they will be is but the continuation of what they are (see ch. xxii. 11).

IV. FOR SUCH THE JUDGMENT-DAY WILL INVOLVE A LOT WHICH IS THE TENFOLD ANTITHESIS OF LIFE. Let the student reverently compare the several terms which are set over against the word "life": 1. Life and punishment (Matt. xxv. 46). 2. Life and judgment (John v. 29). 3. Life and wrath (John iii. 36). 4. Life and the second death (ch. xx. 14, 15). 5. Life and destruction (Matt. vii. 13, 14). 6. Life and the lake of fire (ch. xx. 15). 7. Life and hell-fire (Matt. xviii. 9). 8. Life and everlasting fire (Matt. xxv. 41). 9. Life and the unquenchable fire (Mark ix. 48). 10. Life and everlasting contempt (Dan. xii. 2). What a burden for men to unfold to their fellow-men—" the terrors of the Lord "! Yet this must be done. Who can gauge the contents of these phrases?

V. THIS RENDERING TO EVERY MAN ACCORDING TO HIS DEEDS WILL BRING APPALLING SUFFERING. It is very common for those who wish to prejudice their hearers or readers against the doctrine of future punishment, to use more frequently than any other phrase the words "eternal torment." This is exceedingly unwise—and worse, as an examination of the use of the word in the New Testament will show. Twice is this word, however, used in the symbolic language of this book. What was its intention? It is used to denote the tormenting process inflicted on accused ones, to extort from them the confession of the truth. May there not be herein a deep truth indicated, that even the perishing ones will clearly see, yea, and confess, that God is righteous? But if we are asked the question—In what will the sufferings of the lost consist? we reply: 1. We earnestly trust we may never know. 2. So far as Scripture teachings guide us, we cannot avoid seeing that six features will mark them. (1) There will be the unrest of spirit under the just wrath of God. (2) There will be a sense of defeat. (3) Of loss. (4) Of exclusion. (5) Of remorse. (6) Of hopeless and unavailing regret at the thought of what might have been (cf. John iii. 36; 1 Cor. xv. 25; Matt. xxv. 28; Luke xiii. 28; Matt. xxvii. 4; xxv. 10; Luke xiii. 24; 2 Thess. i. 8, 9; Matt. vii. 23; Heb. x. 26, 27).

VI. THERE IS A DREAD CONSENSUS OF CONVICTION AMONG EVANGELICAL PREACHERS AND TEACHERS ON THESE STUPENDOUS THEMES. Startling as such an assertion may be, when the controversies on future punishment are borne in mind, it is one which we venture to make, and one which we deem of infinite importance. We are well aware of the different theories on this subject.[1] There is what is called the "orthodox" theory—that the punishment of the wicked will be endless. There is the annihilation theory. There is the future restoration theory. There is the theory of the relativeness of revelation with regard to time. It is no part of our purpose here to defend or to criticize either. Our space will not permit of it. The books mentioned in the footnote will furnish the needed material for this. Our aim is rather to indicate how much common ground there is for evangelical preachers and teachers to occupy in proclaiming "the terrors of the Lord." The following statements will show how far earnest representative men in the several leading divisions of eschatological thought travel together on similar lines. They teach: 1. That when the Son of God comes as the Judge of all mankind, the time of probation for the human race will have closed. 2. That then every eye shall see him, and that all things will be in readiness for a righteous administration of judgment. 3. That all men will then appear before the tribunal of the Lord

[1] Note: For accounts of the various theories, see 'First Lines of Christian Theology,' by the late Dr. J. Pye Smith, bk. iv. ch. iv. " On the Consequences of Sin; " ' Future Punishment: an Inquiry into Scripture Teaching,' by Joseph Angus, D.D. Hodder and Stoughton: 1871; 'Life in Christ,' by Edward White, 3rd edit., 1878. Elliot Stock; 'The Second Death and the Restitution of all Things,' by Andrew Jukes, 5th edit. Longman: 1876; 'Future Punishment: Some Current Theories concerning it stated and estimated,' by Clement Clemance, B.A, D.D., 2nd edit. Snow: 1880.

The student will find much suggestive material in Dr. Farrar's 'Eternal Hope,' and 'Mercy and Judgment' (although in both works the style is too feverish and rhetorical for such a theme); also in 'Facts and Theories as to a Future State,' by F. W. Grant. Cathcart, New York: 1879. See articles in British Quarterly Review, July, 1878; in the Church Quarterly Review, January, 1881; also 'The Spirits in Prison," by Dean Plumptre, Isbister: 1884. The following words clearly indicate the crucial difficulty in the way of the acceptance of the doctrine of final restoration: " Maurice says he cannot see the doctrine of the restoration of all fallen beings, and thinks that, if it be so, we need a revelation to declare it. He seems to think (if I understand him rightly) that it may be possible for a being to exercise his own free will in resisting God, till it becomes impossible for him to be influenced by any good " (letter of Mr. Strachey to Lady Louis, in ' Life of Rev. F. D. Maurice,' vol. i. p. 208). This is the thought which holds in check many writers whose yearnings are all in the direction of restitution. For illustration, cf. ' The Harvest Past; or, the Dying Universalist,' in Spencer's 'Pastor's Sketches' (Nelson); another edition, edited by Rev. J. A. James (Hamilton); also ' Anecdotes Illustrative of New Testament Texts,' cxli. " Repentance." Clerical Library. Hodder: 1884.

Jesus Christ. 4. That every man will, ere then, know of his own personal relation to the Lord Jesus, and that *he* is to be the Judge of all mankind. 5. That the final state of every soul will depend on its attitude to the Lord Jesus Christ. 6. That men will be sentenced, not according to the light God saw fit to send them, but according to the use they have made of the light granted to them. 7. That the Lord Jesus Christ, as an omniscient and unerring Judge, will sentence every man ; that this sentence will be according to truth ; and that it will be the outworking of moral laws that are in operation now, which are like their Author, " the same yesterday, and to-day, and for ever." 8. That the measure of punishment will be according to the measure of guilt. 9. That for the righteous there will be joy and honour unspeakable, which will never end. 10. That for the wicked there will be irremediable loss, unutterable woe, for a duration of which no man can gauge the extent, accompanied with a depth of remorse that no tongue nor pen can describe. 11. That for those who reject Jesus Christ in this life there will be no such thing as making up lost time, and that they will *never* attain to the blessedness they would have reached if they had received Christ in this, the accepted time. Their time once lost is lost for ever, and the corresponding loss of blessedness will never be retrieved.

Surely here is enough, and more than enough, for focussed power in the pulpit in the presentation of the revealed truth of God on the future destiny of the ungodly. And when we see what a dread aspect of finality there is in such words as " The door was shut ; " when we remember how repeatedly the trumpet-call *Now* is sounded ; when we know that these are spoken of as the *last* days, and that the day of judgment is " the *last* day ; " when there is no hint of an offer of mercy in the next life *to those who have rejected Jesus Christ in this* ; when we know that, by continued sin, men are getting into a state of hardness in which no means known to us can possibly reach their consciences ;—to shrink from the presentation to them of their risks would be gross unfaithfulness. There is no need to indulge in the excessive statement that sin will last as long as God lasts; there is no need to indulge in flaming descriptions of material fire and of bodily torture ; there is no reason for so setting things as to make one's moral nature and conscience revolt therefrom ; in fact, there is every reason for *not* doing anything of the kind. For, within the lines indicated of a widely spread agreement among men of diverse conclusions as to the *ultimate* issue, the facts of life are so real, the drift of evil is so manifest, the penalties on sin are so stern, the Word of God is so clear, the commission to the Christian teacher is so direct, and the importance of commending ourselves to every man's conscience is so vast, that with the most careful accuracy, measured statement, calm reasoning, pungent appeal, impassioned fervour, we are bound—even weeping—to plead with men in Christ's stead, to " be reconciled to God," reminding them that

> " 'Tis not the whole of life to live,
> Nor all of death to die."

There is—there is—*the second death, even the lake of fire.*

HOMILIES BY VARIOUS AUTHORS.

Ver. 6.—" *The first resurrection.*" " Blessed and holy is he that hath part in the first resurrection." It is a common remark that we are to learn much concerning the Divine administration in the kingdom of heaven by observing the laws of his administration amongst men now, in this present life. And there can be no question that God deals with men here by a system of special rewards. He holds before us, as we enter life, prizes of greater or less value, that we may be stimulated to diligence in the road along which these prizes lie. But it has been too commonly thought that in the kingdom of heaven there is nothing of this kind. That there one reward awaits all alike, and one penalty all to whom penalty is appointed. And the effect has been to make imperfect, unspiritual, and self-indulgent Christians all too content with themselves and their condition before God. They have what they are pleased to call faith, which in them is only a lazy reliance upon what the Lord Jesus Christ has done ; and as they believe, certainly, in justification by faith, they deem themselves justified, and on the way to be glorified ; and what can any one need more ? But the subject which our text brings before us, and the whole teaching of God's Word, is utterly subversive of this popular and plausible but pernicious belief. It teaches that there is a "prize" of our high calling of God in Christ Jesus; a being, if faithful, first in the kingdom of heaven, or, if unfaithful, last; a being greatest or least; a crown of life; a recompense of ten cities as well as of five; and much also of the same kind. Especially is this doctrine of special reward to the faithful confirmed by this truth of the first resurrection. Let us inquire—

I. WHAT DOES IT MEAN? Surely that which it seems to say—that the faithful servants of Christ, of whom those who had been beheaded for his sake are named as representing all the rest, shall rise from the dead, and live and reign with Christ for a vast period, here called a thousand years, whilst all the rest of the dead shall have no resurrection until this period be past. Therefore there is a first resurrection for the saints of God, and another, inferior and later one, for all the rest of the dead. So this Scripture seems to teach. But many have affirmed that, however much it may seem to teach this, in reality it does not. For, it is affirmed: 1. *That there is nothing else like it in all the rest of Scripture.* It stands all alone. But if it be really taught here, our failing to find it elsewhere will not excuse us from accepting it. We accept other doctrines even if declared but once. Take 1 Cor. xv. Where but there shall we find not a few of the truths it teaches? And there are other instances beside. But we do not admit that it stands alone, not by any means (cf. *infra*). 2. *That it is all metaphor,* like the rest of the book. But all is not metaphor, and what is and what is not can be readily distinguished. The resurrection is not a metaphor. 3. *That it means baptism.* We read that Christians have "risen with Christ in baptism" (Rom. vi. 4; Col. ii. 12). Here, then, it is said, is the first resurrection. But St. John, in our text and its context, is speaking of men who have died, have been beheaded for Christ; the death is a literal one, so therefore must the resurrection be. If it were a spiritual death that were told of, then the resurrection might be spiritual also. And the living with Christ comes after death. How, then, can it be baptism? 4. Others, many, say that it tells of *the thousand years or more which stretch from the fourth century to the fourteenth.* At the beginning of the fourth, persecution by heathen Rome ceased, Rome herself adopting the Christian faith. For a thousand years after, her ministers and Churches, it might be said, lived and reigned. But then came the capture of Constantinople, and the establishment of the Turkish empire, and the dominance over so large a portion of the once Christian world of the Mohammedan imposture. Well, if Satan was "bound" during all that period whenever—so one would ask—was there a time when he seemed more free? If that thousand years were the millennium, or like it, then may we be delivered from such another one! 5. *The entire present dispensation.* Reference is made to our Lord's word as to the "fall" of Satan "from heaven;" as to his being "judged" and "cast out;" and it is said that this is Satan's condition now—fallen, judged, cast out, bound, shut up in the abyss, reserved for condemnation—and has been so ever since our Lord was here on earth; and that during all this period the faithful have lived and reigned with Christ. Again, we say, such interpretation makes a mockery of the millennium, and empties St. John's words of well-nigh all their meaning. Therefore, on the sound principle of interpretation that, when a literal meaning will stand in any Scripture, the meaning furthest from that is generally the worst, we accept that literal meaning, and the more so that the question—

II. WHERE IS THE PROOF OF IT? is one that can be satisfactorily answered. 1. *In the Old Testament* there were many Scriptures which had led the Jews to the belief that for faithful Israel there was to be a special resurrection. Such texts were Isa. xxv. 8; xxvi. 1; Ezek. xxxvii.; Dan. xii. And this belief of their resurrection when Messiah came was what St. Paul called "the hope of Israel." And this general belief our Lord never contradicted, which he who said, "If it were not so I would have told you," would assuredly have done. But: 2. *The New Testament* must, of course, furnish the larger proof. Our Lord perpetually speaks of the resurrection of the good and of the evil as of separate things. He tells (John v. 29) of "the resurrection of life" and of "the resurrection of judgment;" and in ver. 24 he has said that believers "shall not come into judgment." Here, then, is a resurrection with which believers can have nothing to do, and another which is specially theirs. Then cf. John. vi. 39, 40, "I will raise him up at the last day." This is several times repeated. But why, if every one is to be raised up at the last day—if that be the general resurrection, why is there this mark of distinction for "him" if there be none? We conclude there is a distinction. Another and a more glorious resurrection awaits "him" than awaits others. Then (Luke xiv. 14) the Lord speaks of "the resurrection of the just." Why does he not speak of the general resurrection if there be nothing special for "the just"? He teaches us that there is. Again (Luke xx. 35), he speaks of a resurrection for the children of God, who shall be equal to the angels, which is a resurrection "from among the dead" (ἐκ), and for which they who shared in it needed to be "counted worthy." But this is not the case with the general resurrection; therefore we gather that this is a special one. Then 1 Cor. xv. 22—24, where the order of the resurrection is given—"every man in his own order: Christ . . . afterward they that are Christ's at his coming;" and then, after the great work of subjugating all things is accomplished—"then cometh the end." But with this we know is associated that resurrection of "the rest of the dead" of which we read in this chapter (ver. 12). See, too, in Matt. xxiv. 31. The gathering together of the elect is told of, and then afterwards—we know not how long—the judgment of the heathen, the nations, of which we are told at the close of Matt. xxv. See, too, Phil. iii. 14. Now, "the resurrection from the dead" which St. Paul there speaks of as "the prize of his high calling," and after which he strove, if "by any means he might attain unto it"—for as yet he had not attained to it, and therefore he still pressed, as an eager racer, towards the goal—this resurrection could not be the general one, for he knew that he would rise again; nor either does it mean simply being saved, for he knew that he was saved already. It must mean, therefore, a special resurrection—this of which our text tells; a prize—the prize, indeed. And we read of "a better resurrection" after which the saints of old strove. And Christians are called "firstfruits," and "the Church of the Firstborn"—expressions which denote priority and privilege such as the first resurrection declares. We hold it, therefore, to be no vain and unauthorized imagination which believes that in these remarkable verses St. John does teach what his words so evidently seem to affirm.

III. WHAT IS THE INFLUENCE IT SHOULD HAVE UPON US? *St. John's purpose*, or rather the *Holy Spirit's purpose* through him, was by this glorious revelation to do in an especial manner that which was the great design of the whole book—to comfort, strengthen, and inspire with holy courage the persecuted Church. And we can hardly imagine that it failed to do this. The imagery is taken from facts within their own experience—the constitution of the empire, in which the varied kings who ruled over the provinces each contributed to the power and glory of the whole; and the priestly service in the temple with which they had long been familiar. The book is full of Jewish imagery throughout. The vision, therefore, assured to them that the lot of their faithful brethren the martyrs, and all of like mind with them, should speedily and wondrously be changed. Poor, persecuted, down-trodden, the offscouring of all things now, they should be as kings; their dungeons they should exchange for thrones; their dreadful death for life—life eternal, life with Christ. Vast capacity for ministering to the glory of the reign of Christ should be theirs, for they should be kings under him, their Lord. Constant access to his presence and the ministry of intercession for their brethren—these, too, should be theirs, for they were also to be his priests. 'Twas worth living for, worth suffering for, worth dying for, let the death come in what dreadful form it might. So would they feel and speak and act, and this was what was intended. "Strong consolation" they needed, and "strong consolation they had," as God's people ever have had and will have when placed in like circumstances. *And for ourselves*—for the vision is for all Christ's faithful ones as well as for the martyrs—what should be the influence of this doctrine of the first resurrection upon us? Surely we should "have respect unto the recompense of the reward." If Christ have put this reward before us, we should have respect to it. Is it fitting, some may ask, that Christ's servants should serve him with their eyes on the reward? Was it fitting that any reward which Christ promised to bestow should be without appreciation? Think what this promise is. It is not merely blessedness—it could not but be that—but it means kingship and priesthood. That is to say, dropping the metaphors, it means infinitely increased capacity for serving Christ and furthering his glory; it means, as his priest, constant access to his presence, and the duty and privilege of intercession for his people.

Yes, the faithful now with Christ are serving him as they never could before. It is no indolent ease in which they abide, but one of service as well as honour, in forms which as yet we cannot know. The kingdom of Christ is the better for what they do. "Are they not all ministering spirits, sent forth to minister?" Nor can we doubt that the great functions which are involved in the idea of priesthood are theirs also—to draw near to God and to intercede for the people. They who on earth were so fervent in prayer are they all at once stricken dumb there? No; they are priests of Christ, and by virtue of that office they are intercessors. Is this a recompense of reward for which we need have no respect? Should it not rouse our energies and call forth our most strenuous endeavours? Holiness, conformity to the mind and will of God, is the condition of this blessedness. The rewards of Christ are not mere external things, but inward and spiritual possessions. Therefore to say that we shall be content with the lowest place in heaven, as many do say, may sound like humility and Christian meekness; but it means being content with less of likeness to Christ, less of his spirit, less of his love. Priority and privilege in heaven, the share in this first resurrection, are according to these things; and how can we be content with but little of them? It is not humility, it is not self-denial, it is wrong to Christ himself, to be indifferent to this reward. Whilst low in the dust as regards yourself, have a lofty ambition in regard to this. Oh, then, seek, strive, pray, for this holiness of heart and life, that you may be of those blessed ones who have part in the first resurrection!—S. C.

Vers. 11—15.—*The final judgment.* Stripped of its imagery, this most solemn Scripture declares to us the truth which is found in records manifold. *Those of the Bible.* The confirmatory passages are everywhere throughout its pages, and especially in those which record the very words of Christ. The most dreadful things in the Bible fell from his lips. *Those of the traditions of ancient and heathen peoples.* Everywhere we find, as especially in Egypt, creeds which declare a final and awful judgment. *Those of conscience.* They tell of "a fearful looking for of judgment." Read 'Macbeth,' and wherever any great writers have drawn true portraitures of men, the witness of conscience may be heard in them all. The imagery here is taken from the tribunals, and the procedure in them, with which the age of St. John was familiar—the august and awe-inspiring paraphernalia of justice, the magnificent and elevated throne of the judge, the giving of the evidence, and the sentence. But underlying all this metaphor are such truths as these—

I. THAT DEATH DOES NOT END ALL. This great transaction takes place when life is over, when this world is done with. Men, therefore, live on after death, or else they could not appear at this judgment-bar. And that men do thus continue to live in their true real self, there is much evidence, beside that of Scripture, to show. The ancient Greeks disputed whether the relation of the soul to the body was that of harmony to the harp, or that of the rower to the boat. *If the former,* then, if you destroy the harp, you destroy the harmony it gave forth; and so, if you destroy the body, you destroy the soul too, and death does end all. *But if the second,* then the boat may sink or go to pieces, but the rower lives on still. And so is it with the soul. The body —its boat—may sink into the depths of the grave, but the soul sinks not with it. Professor Huxley has affirmed that "life is the cause of organization, and not organization the cause of life;" and Tyndall has shown that dead matter cannot produce life. Life, therefore, must exist prior to and independent of matter, and therefore can exist after the material organization which it for a while animated has decayed. We are the same self-conscious beings in old age as we were when in childhood, though our bodies have changed over and over again meanwhile. Death, then, does not end all; we live on, and so one demand of the doctrine of final judgment is met.

II. THAT THERE SHOULD BE RECORDS UPON WHICH THE JUDGMENT SHALL PROCEED. They are spoken of in this Scripture (ver. 12) as "books." "And another book, which is the book of life." The books contain biographies, and therefore are voluminous. The "other book" contains but names, and therefore is but one. No biography is needed; nought but the fact that they believed in Jesus. But what is meant by the "books"? Simply that there are records of the soul's life, which will be opened and read in the great judgment-day. They are found: 1. *In the souls of others.* In the character we have helped to impress upon them. There is no one but what has written down evidence about himself on the souls of others. If we have helped them heavenward, that is there; if we have urged them hellward, that is there. 2. But chiefly *in our own souls.* We are always writing such record, and it may be read even now in the body, in the countenance, in the very way we bear ourselves before our fellow-men. Character can be read now. It comes out at the eyes, in the look, the aspect, is heard in the tone of voice. But much more helps to conceal it. The restraints of society, the regard to the opinion of others, make men reticent and reserved and full of concealment of their real selves. But in the spiritual body it is altogether probable that the essence of the man will be far more visible—may, in fact, be, as many have thought, the creator of its body, so that "every seed" shall have "its own body." But on the soul itself its record will be read. Many a man can trace yet the scar of a wound, and that not a severe one, which he received thirty, forty, fifty, years and more ago. The ever-changing body will so hold its record. And there are *scars of the soul.* Wounds inflicted on it will abide and be visible so long as the soul lasts. Like the undeveloped plate of the photographer, a mere blurred surface until he plunges it into the bath, and then the image comes out clearly ; so our souls are now illegible and their record indistinct, but when plunged into the bath of eternity, then what has been impressed thereon will be distinct and clear. Then the image of "the deeds done in the body" will come out with startling but unerring accuracy. If man can find out means, as he has found, so to register the words and tones of a speaker that they can be reproduced years after, and whenever it is desired, is there not in that discovery of science a solemn suggestion that all our "idle" and worse "words" may be recorded somewhere, and be heard again when we thought they were forgotten for ever ? Yes, there are records. And—

III. A JUDGMENT. "It is appointed unto men once to die, and after death the judgment." "And they were judged every man," etc. (ver. 13). What do these Scriptures mean ? Now, the Greek word for "judgment" is "crisis ;" that is the Greek word, simply, in English letters. But what is more is that our word "crisis" does more accurately set forth the meaning of "judgment" than what is commonly understood thereby. When we speak of a "crisis," we mean a turning-point, a decisive settling as to the course which affairs will take. That is a crisis. But when we speak of "judgment," the imagery of these verses rise up before our minds, and we think of an external judge, and a sentence that he passes upon us. Judgment, however, often takes place. How common it is to hear it said of a man who has passed through some great experience, "He has never been the same man since"! Great trials, disappointments, distresses of any kind, and great successes and wealth also, act as crises, turning-points, judgments, to a man. They act like the water-shed of a district, which determines which way the streams shall flow ; so these great crises of a man's life turn this way or that the moral and spiritual dispositions which dwell in him. . They do much to settle him in a fixed habit of character, for good or ill, as the case may be. How much more, then, after "death" must there be "judgment"! Then, freed from all the restraints of life, from all that hindered the manifestation of what he really was, his nature now gravitates towards that side of spiritual character to which it has long been leaning, but from which it has hitherto been held back. It takes up its position according to its nature. If evil, with the evil ; if good, with the good—for in this case his name is found "written in the book of life." It is ill for us to put off the idea of judgment until some far-distant day, amid some unwonted scenes. God's judgments are continually taking place, and every thought, act, and word is helping to determine to which side, whether to the right hand or to the left, our souls shall go.

IV. THE SENTENCE. It has been said that this judgment told of here is of the ungodly only, and that the book of life is mentioned only for the sake of showing "that their names are not there." We cannot think this. Nothing is said about the sentence of any, only the final fate of the ungodly. "The lake of fire," the "oven of fire" (Matt. xiii.), and similar expressions, are metaphors taken from the barbarous punishments of that age. To cast men alive into fire was a fearful but not unusual punishment. Hence it is taken because of its fearfulness as a figure of the final fate of the ungodly. Evil character such as that into which they have settled is like a raging fire, and the blindness of heart and mind which attends such character is like "the blackness of darkness" itself. We may see men in hell to-day when filled with the fury of rage and passion; and, blessed be God, we may see others in heaven because filled with the peace of God. Heaven or hell is, in great degree, in a man ere ever he enters either the one or the other. They are in us before we are in them, and the judgment is but each man's going to his own place. What solemn confirmation, then, do such Scriptures as that before us receive from observed facts and experiences of men in this life! What urgency, therefore, do they lend to the exhortation, "Commit thy way unto the Lord"! And how prompt should be our resolve to entrust the keeping of our souls unto Christ, so that in the great judgment after death they may go with Christ and his saints into eternal life! "Jesus, by thy wounds we pray, help now that our names may be written in the book of life" (Hengstenberg).—S. C.

Vers. 1—10.—*The restraint upon evil.* Following most appropriately upon the foregoing description of a conflict, and the conquest by the truth and the power of righteousness, is a representation, in most significant imagery, of the restraint that is put upon evil by the prevalence of righteousness—the chaining back the clouds of night by the rising sun. The spirit of evil, "the dragon, the old serpent," "the devil and Satan," is "laid hold" by "an angel coming down out of heaven," and bound with "a great chain," and cast "into the abyss," which is shut and sealed. This is to be for "a thousand years;" after that "he must be loosed for a little season." With as great distinctness as could well be employed herein is set forth—

I. THE EFFECTUAL RESTRAINT OF THE POWER OF EVIL. It is here pictured as a single act. But we must read the history of the strife which is ever proceeding—the gradual leavening of the entire life of humanity by the principles and the power of the holy gospel. Whatever may be the oscillations between the probabilities of success and the danger of defeat, this picture must be held to declare the ultimate happy triumph of the true and good over the false and the evil. Satan is held in chains; his power is restricted. The heavenly holds back the earthly and the hellish. It is the comfortable encouragement to the patient, suffering toiler that the agency employed of God is effective. That binding and restraining every faithful servant must see to be now going on.

II. THE DURATION OF THIS RESTRAINT. The millennium—"a thousand years"—a long but definite period, now reigns; yet must we not forget the symbolical character even of the definite words of this book. *No time* must be affixed. It is a period of blessing, of rest, of rejoicing. The toils of the Church, and the patience of the suffering faithful ones, have, by Divine grace, become fruitful. Now in the world, permeated by the pure and lofty principles of Christianity, peace, truth, righteousness, reign; and by how much they prevail, by so much evil is restrained. In their supremacy is to be seen the complete chaining of the evil agents of an evil kingdom.

III. THIS PERIOD IS MARKED AS ONE OF TRIUMPH AND REJOICING on behalf of the faithful Church of Christ. Thrones are set, the faithful reign with Christ, and judgment over human conduct is given to them—a significant indication that principles of righteousness are predominant, and that by them human life is adjudged. These are "blessed and holy;" they have priestly functions, they approach, they mediate, they are channels of blessing, they live to reign; they escape that second death which is the penalty of sin, from which they have been raised—they partake in a first resurrection which presages another.

IV. To this happy period of the universal prevalence of Christian truth there succeeds A TEMPORARY RELAPSE. Like all human blessedness, even this has the signature of imperfectness upon it. It is historical, not imposed. But this is only temporary, "for a little time," and issues in a final destruction of all tempting and evil power—even "for ever and ever."

In this the Church is to find (1) *encouragement to faith;* (2) *motive for diligent labour;* (3) *the most cheering assurances in times of discouragement and fear.* The truth shall ultimately prevail; the false, the foul, the vile, shall be restrained.—R. G.

Vers. 11—15.— *The final judgment upon evil conduct.* The scenes of the Book of Revelation are now approaching completion, and they present more definitely the characteristics of "the end." Judgment proceeds on human conduct daily, but there is a final judgment, "the judgment of the great day," when "we shall all stand before the judgment-seat of God." That dread day is now present to the mind of the seer, and before that inner eye, by a spiritual illumination, the solemn scene is depicted. It is pictorial, and, like the Lord's own picture of the separating of the sheep from the goats, though it lacks the completeness of this teaching, it has aspects of the most awful grandeur. In the symbolical presentation the following dreadful features are prominent—

I. The AUTHORITY, SANCTITY, AND DREAD TERRIBLENESS OF THE DIVINE JUDGMENT. The symbol of the authoritative character of the judgment is represented in "a great throne;" its sanctity in the ever-present symbol of purity—it is a "white" throne, "we know that his judgment is according to truth;" while the terribleness of the holy judgment is indicated in the assertion that the very "earth and the heaven fled away" from "the face" of him that sat on the throne.

II. The UNIVERSALITY OF THE JUDGMENT. The symbol here approaches a terrible realism. The seer beheld "the dead, the great and the small, stand before the throne," and "the sea" and "death and Hades gave up the dead which were in them, and they were judged." The judgment is upon the "dead," and it transplants our thoughts to the final issues of human history.

III. The judgment which is universal is also MINUTE AND INDIVIDUAL. "They were judged every man." None escape or pass by. Every servant to whom the Lord has entrusted goods must give account of the same.

IV. The judgment proceeds UPON THE CONDUCT OF THE EARTHLY LIFE. "They were judged every man *according to their works*." Then shall be brought to pass the saying that is written, "Every idle word that men shall speak they shall give account thereof in the day of judgment."

V. The FINAL, TERRIBLE AWARD OF EVIL-DOING. "If any was not found written in the book of life, he was cast into the lake of fire." That this represents the termination of the present order of things is indicated by the destruction of death and Hades; the present, the temporary, is swallowed up in the final. One side only of the judgment is represented—that of the wicked.

Truly these awful scenes are not for the eye, but for the heart. No picture is permissible of any part of these unspeakable things. Men must take the terrible intimations, and ponder them in their hearts; and "blessed" is the man that so "reads" and so "understands the words of the prophecy of this book," that he turns in lowly meekness to him who is the one and only Saviour of men, and seeks by his grace to walk "in all the commandments and ordinances of the Lord blameless."—R. G.

Vers. 1, 2.—*The first scene in the moral history of redeemed humanity : the scene of moral struggle.* "And I saw an angel come down from heaven," etc. No inspired book presents a greater scope for visionary and idle speculation than this Apocalypse. Here every imagination has the widest sweep for its wildest evolutions. Hence we have almost as many interpretations of its contents as we have expositors. One can scarcely pursue a more easy or certain path to popularity than by propounding some ingenious exegesis of this book. I intend going through the whole of this chapter and the first four verses of the succeeding one, in *five analyses of homilies ;* because I think I discover there what seems admirably adapted for deep and practical moral impression. The nineteen verses may be fairly taken as an illustration of *the moral history of humanity*. They disclose no less than *five* moral scenes through which the redeemed portion of our race is to pass; namely : (1) *The scene of moral struggle ;* (2) *the scene of moral triumph ;* (3) *the scene of moral reaction ;* (4) *the scene of an awful retribution ;* and (5) *the scene of the final destiny of the good.* The first—*the scene of moral struggle* —is the one unfolded in these verses. This scene shows us two things.

I. That REDEEMED HUMANITY HAS A FEARFUL ANTAGONIST TO CONTEND WITH. This enemy is called "dragon," "serpent," "devil," "Satan." This highly symbolic language, applied to the great antagonist of the good, implies three things. 1. *The actual existence of such an enemy.* The names "dragon," "serpent," etc., must stand for *something.* They are the names of *real* beings, and cannot be supposed as used to designate the mere phantoms of the imagination. Most conclusive arguments for the existence of some mighty agent of evil, whose influence is world-wide, may be drawn from three considerations. (1) The universal belief of humanity. (2) The opposite classes of moral phenomena. In the world we have error, selfishness, infidelity, and misery; and truth, benevolence, religion, and happiness. Can these be branches from the same root? or streams from the same fount? (3) The general teaching of the Bible. 2. *The personality of such an enemy.* These are names of creatures having *individual* existence and attributes. The Bible always speaks of this *evil existent* as a *person.* It is far too great a demand upon our credulity to believe that the various inspired writers, from Moses to John, extending over a period of more than two thousand years, possessing various idiosyncrasies and attainments, and living under different economies, governments, and circumstances, could all fall into the common habit of speaking of evil as a person if it were only a principle. This, I say, is too much for our faith. Moreover, *an evil principle implies an evil person.* Sin is not some mysterious entity, separate from moral existence. Is sin an *act?* Then it must have an agent. Is it a *motive?* Motive implies thought, and thought implies a thinker. 3. *The characteristics of such an enemy.* "Dragon" stands as the emblem of *power.* Probably the leviathan described in Job xli. is of the same class: "Shall not one be cast down, even at the sight of him?" "Serpent" stands as the emblem of *cunning* and venom. "Devil" means accuser. "Satan" signifies opposer. This adversary of redeemed humanity, then, is *mighty, crafty,* and *virulent.* The New Testament is full of the doctrine that this being is the determined foe of humanity (Matt. iv. 10; xii. 26; Mark iv. 15; Luke x. 18; xxii. 3, 31; Acts xxvi. 18; Rom. xvi. 20; 2 Cor. xi. 14; ch. ii. 13; xii. 9).

II. THAT HEAVEN HAS VOUCHSAFED AN AGENCY WHICH IS DESTINED TO MASTER THE ADVERSARY. "And I saw an angel come down from heaven, having the key of the bottomless pit [abyss]." Who is this angel that descends from heaven? The word "angel" both in Hebrew and Greek, means *messenger.* It is applied to impersonal as well as personal agents; and it is applied to evil, as well as good, personal agents. It is evidently used here to designate some *good* personal agent, for he descends from heaven, and descends from heaven to do battle with evil. The language applies *pre-eminently* to Christ, but refers also to every *true religious teacher.* Let the word "angel," here, then, stand for every true religious teacher—including Christ and all his true servants; and we shall get a most clear and practical meaning from the passage. We have here two things about this *true teacher*—this angel. 1. *His authority.* He has the "key" of the bottomless pit. A key is the emblem of authority. Christ is said to have the keys of death and hell (Hades) at his girdle; and to his servant Peter he gave the "keys" of the kingdom—the authority to open the kingdom of truth, by true preaching, to Jew and Gentile. Every man who has the true *spirit* and *power* of a teacher, has the "key" or the authority to teach. He has a right to do battle with the enemy wherever he is found; whether in literature or commerce, Churches or governments, theories or practices. A true man has Heaven's key in his hand for this work. 2. *His instrumentality.* What is the instrument employed? "A chain." What is the chain? Iron, brass, adamant? No, no! These cannot fetter intellect—these cannot manacle soul. Nothing can curb or restrain the influence of Satan but *Christian truth.* What is meant by binding Satan? It does not mean the binding of his *being* or *faculties,* but the binding of his *influence.* He is to be bound, in the sense of limiting his sway, by closing up human hearts against him. As liberty binds the influence of slavery, intelligence the influence of ignorance, and religion the influence of infidelity, so Christian truth is to bind the influence of Satan. Every truth is a link in that mighty chain. The chain of Christian teaching is far too weak and short at present to restrain the force or measure the dimensions of Satanic influence.

This is the scene through which we are passing. All is battle *now.* For the subjugation of the common foe, let each forge some holy thought-link for the all-enfettering chain.—D. T.

Vers. 3—6.—*The second scene in the history of redeemed humanity: the age of moral triumph.* "And cast him into the bottomless pit, and shut him up, and set a seal upon him," etc. The *first* scene in the history of redeemed humanity—namely, the scene of moral struggle—occupied our attention in the last homily. The passage before us is a very glorious, though highly symbolic, view of the scene which will succeed it—

the scene of moral triumph. This scene is, probably, many long centuries in the future; for as yet the great enemy of souls is the "prince of this world." But prophecy, the tendency of Christianity, the victories which the gospel has already achieved, and the unequivocal assurances of God's Word in general, *all* show that, however **far off**, the bright era will dawn on the world when the "will of God shall be done **on earth as it is** in heaven." Stripping the words before us of their highly figurative **garb**, I discover four great features which will distinguish this glorious age.

I. THE ENTIRE OVERTHROW OF MORAL EVIL. Satan, the great adversary, is said to be cast into "the bottomless pit." This figurative language suggests two thoughts. 1. *That the great enemy will have lost his stand-place in the world.* His throne will have lost its foundation; he will not have a resting-place for his foot in this period. What *had* been his stand-place in the world? Error, prejudice, selfishness, evil passions, etc.; but these will have gone. He will have no fulcrum for his lever. 2. *That the fall of the great enemy will be complete for a time.* "Bottomless pit." He will be sinking for ages. The more humanity progresses in intelligence, rectitude, and holiness, the more hopeless his condition becomes. As humanity rises, he must sink.

II. THE UNIVERSAL SOVEREIGNTY OF CHRIST. Christ is here spoken of as reigning for a "thousand years" (ver. 2). There are many who judge this passage "after the flesh," give it a carnal and Judaic interpretation. They infer from it a *personal* manifestation of Christ, with all the appendages of a temporal dominion. I disclaim this, for two reasons. 1. *The only true sovereignty is spiritual.* Who have been the greatest sovereigns of the world? The men who have sat on thrones of gold, and ruled with the sceptre of force? No! it is not your Pharaoh, Cæsar, Alexander; but your Aristotle, Bacon, Milton, and Bunyan. Men who direct the *thoughts* of humanity are the *real* rulers. Christ is the greatest spiritual Sovereign, and his sovereignty is destined to increase. 2. *A religious spiritual sovereignty over man is the great want of the race.* He who rules the human mind, directs its faculties, energies, and feelings rightly, is man's greatest benefactor. This Christ does in the highest and most perfect manner. Let every philanthropist, therefore, pray that his kingdom may come—that he may become the moral Monarch of all souls.

III. THE GENERAL ASCENDANCY OF GREAT SOULS. The world, hitherto, has been under the dominion of weak and wicked men. Its kings and heroes have generally been as small as their hearts have been corrupt. In this scene the *great* soul will be "on thrones," and reign with Christ. The words suggest three things about the men who will then be in power. 1. *They will be men who have passed through a spiritual resurrection.* They had a part in the "first resurrection" (ver. 6). That a *spiritual* resurrection is here referred to is obvious, from three considerations. (1) The idea harmonizes with the symbolical character of the whole book. (2) The passage specially mentions "souls," and not bodies. (3) The New Testament represents the awakening of a new spiritual life in man as a resurrection (John v. 24—29; Col. iii. 1, etc.). Indeed, the resurrection of the body is but a type of the resurrection of the soul; the resurrection of the soul is the *true* resurrection. That of the body is but figurative. Two ideas are implied in the resurrection : (1) *The resuscitation of an old moral life in man—Divine love.* (2) *The resuscitation of an old moral life by God himself.* It is God's work alone to raise the dead. 2. *They will be men of martyr-mould.* "The souls of them that were beheaded for the witness of Jesus, and for the Word of God, and which had not worshipped the beast, neither his image, neither had received his mark upon their foreheads or in their hands" (ver. 4). The idea unquestionably is, not that the "souls" of the old martyrs who have long since departed will be brought back to this earth, but souls like theirs will exist in this age. Souls marked by invincible attachment to truth, by the most generous sentiments, Divine aspirations, and noble daring; feeling truth to be ever more precious than existence itself. This interpretation agrees with the interpretation which one is bound to give such scriptural language as that which speaks of the ministry of John, the ministry of Elijah, and the conversion of the Jews, as a "life from the dead." 3 *They will be men possessing exclusive ascendancy.* "But the rest of the dead lived not again" (ver. 5). In this glorious age there is no reproduction of those *little* and *corrupt* men who, in every age, have played the despot, both in Church and state. Your Herods and Caiaphases, your Henrys and your Lauds, will have no representatives in this glorious age. "The rest of the dead lived not again." 4. *They will be men raised for ever beyond the reach of all future evil.* "Blessed and holy is he that hath part in the first resurrection : on such the second death hath no power " (ver. 6). Such men are delivered for ever from all the influences and all the fears of Hades. What an age is this! Would it had dawned!

IV. THE EXTENSIVE DURATION OF THE WHOLE. "And shall reign with him a thousand years" (ver. 6). If you suppose that this is literal, that ten centuries are meant, it is a long period for the continuation of *one* moral scene in man's history. How short was the scene of primeval innocence! The scene of wickedness, too, is never long without being broken. Conscience is everlastingly breaking in upon, and disturbing, wickedness here. Ten centuries of unbroken holiness and peace for the world are a long period! But I am disposed to regard the period referred to here as *much longer* than ten centuries. A little interpretation would not agree either with the general structure of the book or with this passage. Nor would it fully meet the nature of the case. I therefore regard the period either as meaning three hundred and sixty-five thousand years, or some vast indefinite period of time. The Jews and other nations were in the habit of using the expression, "a thousand years," to denote a period of *immense duration.* 1. *This long period of holiness is a glorious set-off against all the preceding ages of depravity and sin.* When we think of the past ages of corruption, the millions who, from period to period, have passed away without a knowledge of the gospel, we are sometimes confounded. But all this may appear but as a few vibrations of a pendulum, when compared with the long ages of universal purity and peace. The lost, perhaps, will be as units to millions, compared with the saved. 2. *This long period of holiness serves wonderfully to heighten our ideas of the grandeur of Christ's work.* Although the influence of Christianity as yet is confessedly limited compared with the widespread districts lying on all hands beyond its present reach, still no one who honestly looks at its past history will be disposed to deny that its conquests over the minds, systems, and institutions of humanity are unparalleled in the history of religions, and far out-measure the appreciative faculty of the world's greatest intellects. But, in the view of the effulgent ages before us, its past most brilliant achievements pale their fires. Hitherto its rays have only fallen in twilight dimness upon the summit of an isolated mountain here and there; but in the glorious time coming it shall flood the world in warm, cloudless, and life-imparting light. Oh! let me learn, then, to estimate the greatness of Christ's work, not by what he has done or is doing, but by those glorious achievements of his which prophecy has foretold. Let me not judge in this respect before the time. Shall I judge the husbandman just as he commences the cultivation of one of the hundred acres committed to his care? or the architect just as the scaffolding is reared and a few stones are brought together? Still less will I dare pronounce upon the work of Christ until in the great eternity I shall behold *redemption finished.*—D. T.

Ver. 4.—*Martyrdom a testimony.* "I saw the souls of them that were beheaded for the witness of Jesus, and for the Word of God." Martyrdom is the subject of these words. The words suggest four facts.

I. MARTYRS ARE SOMETIMES MURDERED MEN. John saw the souls of those who were "beheaded." All murders are not martyrdoms; all martyrdoms are murders. There has often been martyrdom, and still is, where there is no killing. There are sufferings inflicted on men on account of their conscientious convictions that are often as bad, if not worse, than death itself. There is slander, contumely, the loss of freedom, the destruction of rights. For a man to spend his life amidst social scorn, civil disabilities, and religious intolerance on account of his conscientious beliefs, is a martyrdom; his life is a protracted and painful dying. But thousands have been murdered, and that by every variety of method which Satanic cruelty could invent. Paul summarizes some of the tortures of ancient martyrdom. "Some had trials of cruel mocking," etc.

II. MARTYRS ARE ALWAYS WITNESSING MEN. "Beheaded for the witness." Indeed, the word means a witness. All witnesses are not martyrs, but all martyrs are witnesses. The man who dies on account of conscientious beliefs, whether they are right or wrong, bears witness to several things. 1. *To the invincibility of the human will.* The ablest metaphysical works cannot give you anything like the impression of the freedom and the force of that power in man which we call will, as one martyrdom. The martyr rises up against the powers of the world, and dares it to do the utmost. 2. *To the force of the religious element.* When religious convictions get hold of a man's soul, whether the convictions be right or wrong, they invest him with an unconquerable power. The stake, the faggot, the fire, have no power to crush or to subdue him. 3. *To the power of the soul over the body.* Men who have had their souls filled with religious feeling become physically insensible to all the tortures and fires of martyrdom; they have sung in the flames. I say that a martyr, whether his religious convictions are right or not, is a mighty witness to these things.

III. MARTYRS ARE OFTEN CHRISTLY MEN. Those whom John saw were those who were "witnesses of Jesus, and for the Word of God." I say *often* Christly men, for false religions as well as the true have had their martyrs. Who but God can tell the number of men that have been put to death on account of their fidelity to Jesus and the Word of God? In the first ages under Nero, Domitian, and Trajan, Christians were slain by thousands, and who but God knows the number of those whose blood in Christian Europe has been shed on account of their attachment to Christianity? These *Christian* martyrs were witnesses of something more than the invincibility of the human will, the force of the religious element, and the power of the soul over the body. 1. *They bore witness to the sustaining grace of Christ.* In the midst of their torturing agonies they gloried in their attachment to him. Their grim persecutors, when endeavouring to extort from them recantation of their faith, were answered in the same spirit as that expressed by the ancient martyr, "Sanctus Christianus sum." They all "gloried in tribulation," etc. They endured "joyfully the spoiling of their goods," etc. 2. *They bore witness against the lukewarmness of living Christians.* The martyrs were earnest men.

IV. MARTYRS WHO ARE CHRISTIANS ENTER HEAVEN. John now saw the souls of "those who were beheaded" raised to immortality, and invested with imperishable dignities. Men whom the world considered unworthy to live, but of whom the world is not worthy, are welcomed into the Paradise of God. This fact should act: 1. As an *encouragement to the persecuted Christian.* 2. As a *warning to persecutors.* How much greater was Stephen than all the members of the persecuting Sanhedrin! How angelic his countenance, how calm his spirit, how peacefully he passed away into the serene heavens of love!—D. T.

Vers. 7—10.—*The third scene in the history of redeemed humanity: the age of moral reaction.* "And when the thousand years are expired, Satan shall be loosed out of his prison," etc. The long ages of earth's millennial glory described are run out. The harmony which had reigned through indefinite centuries is broken into tumult; the sun of absolute truth and blessedness, under whose genial and unclouded beams unnumbered generations had come and gone, getting new vigour and catching new inspiration in every successive step of their mortal life, is veiled in clouds again; the arch foe of humanity has burst his moral chains—is "loosed out of his prison," and is once more *deceiving* the nations "which are in the four quarters of the earth." There is a tremendous reaction. This age is here presented under a veil of imagery, if possible, more variously coloured and thickly folded than either of the preceding epochs already noticed. My work is not to *describe* the veil, but gently to draw it aside, in order to discover the great facts which lie beneath. Disrobing this passage of its highly symbolic garb, I discover three facts which mark this age of *moral reaction.*

I. THE REACTION IS BROUGHT ABOUT IN THE MANNER IN WHICH MANKIND HAVE EVER DEGENERATED. Let us mark the process. 1. *Here is deception.* "The nations" are *deceived* (ver. 8). Certain ideas, directly opposed to the eternal principle of truth, the settled conditions of virtue, and means of true blessedness, but at the same time most plausible to the reason, prompting to the lusts, and gratifying to the selfhood of the human heart, are put into circulation; men receive, follow them, and fall. Sin came first into the world through *deception,* and it has been propagated and nourished by it ever since. Men fall by error, and rise by truth. Hence the seducer and the Saviour alike deal with the judgments of men. Hell and heaven are acting on our world through thoughts; the one through the false and the other through the true. 2. *Here is deception employed by Satan.* "Satan shall be loosed out of his prison, and shall go out [come forth] to deceive the nations " (vers. 7, 8). Christ, who knows his entire history, has declared that he " abode not in the truth, because there is no truth in him; " and that " he is a liar, and the father of lies." He has filled the world with lies—charged our atmosphere with lies—political, social, moral, and religious. " Every man walketh in a vain show." Who can " fathom the depths of Satan "? He " beguiled " our first parents; he prompted Ananias " to lie to the Holy Ghost." He " hath blinded the minds " of men. 3. *Here is deception employed by Satan, first, upon those who are most assailable, and afterwards through them upon others.* " He goes out to deceive the nations which are in the four quarters [corners | of the earth, Gog and Magog," etc. (vers. 8, 9). No one has been able to determine with certainty who Gog and Magog are. I am inclined to believe, with Bloomfield, " that no particular nations are meant, but that these are only names designating bodies of men inimical to the gospel." Probably, through all the ages of the millennial period, there had always continued some disaffected towards Christ, some who loved darkness rather than light, some " Gog and Magog." Upon these Satan now acted. By his suggestions he evoked their latent depravity, kindled into a flame the long-smouldering fires of their rebellion against heaven. The more evil there is in a man, the more accessible that man is to Satan, and the more susceptible to his influence. The more virtue in the heart, the stronger its safeguard. Hence he ever begins his work with the most assailable—with those who are *morally* the most remote from Christianity, who dwell " in the four quarters of the earth." And through them he goes on to propagate his cause. From Eve he proceeds to Adam; from Gog and Magog he proceeds to the very " camp of the saints " (ver. 9).

II. THE REACTION IS OF A CHARACTER THE MOST THREATENING. There are two things in the passage which suggest this. 1. *The vast number of its agents.* Those whom Satan enlists in his cause from the " four quarters of the earth "—these moral tribes, called Gog and Magog, constitute a great multitude, " the number of whom is as the sand of the sea " (ver. 8)—a figurative expression indicating their *numerousness.* It is not necessary to suppose that these unbelievers had been numerous through all the centuries of the millennial times. Nor is it necessary to suppose that any *genuine Christians* had really and finally been tempted to renounce their principles. It seems to me highly improbable that a man whose nature has been *thoroughly* Christianized will ever finally degenerate into a *life* of sin. We may suppose that for many ages there were but few whose spirits did not flow with the clear and majestic stream of Christian truth and practice. If, however, at one time there were only a dozen, or even fewer, sinners among the teeming millions of saints, it is easy to see how they could multiply in the course of time, without causing any of the *really* good to apostatize. These twelve, we will suppose, become parents; their children, on the principle of filial love and dependence, will catch their spirit and be moulded by their example; they, in their turn, become parents; and thus, according to the common law of generation, in a few years these few may multiply to thousands. Amongst the angels, who do not probably derive their existence from each other, between whom there is not this relation of parent and child, there is not this character—propagating power. 2. *The anti-Christian aim of its agents.* " And they went up on the breadth of the earth, and compassed the camp of the saints about, and the beloved city " (ver. 9). The idea, symbolized, I take to be this—they made efforts to assault the most *central* and *vital* part of religion. They sought, perhaps, to argue away the being of God, the doctrine of human responsibility, the necessity of mediation, and the existence of a future life of rewards and punishments. There are minor attacks which unbelievers make upon Christianity, but the attempt to disprove these fundamentals is a blow aimed at the most vital part—it is to compass " the camp of the saints about, and the beloved city."

III. THE REACTION TERMINATES IN THE EVERLASTING DESTRUCTION OF ALL ITS AGENTS. " And fire came down from God out of heaven, and devoured them. And the devil that deceived them was cast into the lake of fire," etc. (vers. 9, 10). From this language we learn the following truths: 1. *That there is in the universe of God a distinct local scene, where the wicked of all classes are to receive their righteous retribution.* This is implied in the expression, " lake of fire." There are other scriptural expressions which imply it; such as " Gehenna," " furnace of fire," etc. Reason would also suggest this. (1) *All existence implies place.* You may think of space apart from being, but you cannot think of being apart from space. You think of an infinite being in connection with infinite space, and finite being in connection with limited locality. (2) *A wicked existence implies a miserable scene.* Antecedently, we should infer that the outer scene of a moral being's existence would resemble his moral character and mood. This world was made for innocence, and it is beautiful, etc. It seems fitting that a dark, inharmonious, deformed spirit should have a sunless, tumultuous, and horrid world as its residence. (3) *Moral beings, of directly opposite sympathies, habits, and aims, as are sinners and saints, imply separate local homes.* There is a mutual repugnance to each other's society here, and it is natural to suppose that, when retribution comes, they shall have their "own place." We know not where this place is, whether in the depths of the earth or in regions far beyond this planet. There may be, perhaps, in some district of the creation, a scene without a streak of beauty, a gleam of light, or a drop of goodness, on which justice frowns and thunders. 2. *That the retribution which the wicked will endure in this scene will be of a most terrible description.* "Fire and brimstone" (ver. 10). The allusion here is most likely to the fate of Sodom and Gomorrah (Gen. xix. 24—28); *fire* is the emblem of *suffering* (Zech. xiii. 9; 1 Cor. iii. 13—15; 1 Pet. i. 7); *brimstone* is the emblem of *desolation* (Job xviii. 15). Nothing will grow on any soil that is covered with sulphur. The Bible employs other figures equally terrible, such as "outer darkness," "blackness of darkness," "prison," etc. Here, then, is the end of the enemies of Christ. Redeemed humanity, henceforth, will be freed from "Gog and Magog," from the beast and the false prophet, and from the devil, the prince of darkness, for ever and ever. Glorious day! Though countless ages in the future, this faint glimpse of thee adds energy to our faith and brightness to our hope! But how long will this reaction continue? We have an answer to this in the third verse of the chapter, "And after that he must be loosed for a little season." Its duration will be short compared with either of the two following periods: (1) *Compared with the preceding period of almost universal holiness.* The period of millennial holiness continued for a thousand years—*i.e.* either three hundred and sixty-five thousand years, or some immense period of duration. This period of reaction is called a "little season" in relation to that. (2) *Compared with the succeeding period of perfect holiness to be enjoyed by the redeemed in the heavenly world.* In the twenty-second chapter of this book it is said of the state and residence of the redeemed that "there shall be no night there; and they need no candle, neither light of the sun; for the Lord God giveth them light: and they shall reign for ever and ever." "For ever and ever." What arithmetic can compute the ages contained in this "ever and ever"? All the preceding periods in the world's history are but as a "little season" compared with this "ever and ever;" less than an hour to the geological cycles that are gone; less than a spark to the central fires that light and warm the unnumbered worlds of space.—D. T.

Vers. 11—15.—*The fourth scene in the history of humanity : the age of retribution.* "And I saw a great white throne," etc. There was one fact common to all the preceding epochs through which redeemed humanity had passed—they were all *probationary*, all connected with the overtures of mercy to the guilty, and the means of spiritual purity, blessedness, and elevation for the polluted, unhappy, and degraded. But the probationary element, which had run on through all dispensations from Adam to Christ, and through all revolutions from Christ to the consummation of the world, is now closed; its last ray has fallen, its sun has gone down to rise no more. Henceon, every man shall be treated according to his past works, and shall reap the fruit of his own doings. The morning of *retribution* has broken. The magnificent passage before us points to the period designated in Scripture "the day of God," "the judgment of the great day," "the revelation of the righteous judgment of God," "the eternal judgment." It may be well to premise at the outset, in order to guard against the tendency of associating too much of what is merely material and human with the circumstances and transactions of this period, that this retribution will literally involve the judiciary circumstances here portrayed. I have heard and read discourses on this subject, which impress the mind more with a kind of *Old Bailey* scene, than with the great moral facts which distinguish that period from all preceding times. It is true that we have here the mention of the "throne" and "books" common to human courts;

but it should be remembered that inspired writers, in accommodation to our ordinary habits—ay, and laws of thought—reveal to us the unknown through the medium of the known. What mind, in sooth, can receive any new idea without comparing it with the old? We judge of the unseen by the seen; we learn what the testimony of others unfolds to us through the medium of what we have already beheld. Thus "the day of judgment" is set forth under the figure of ancient courts of judicature, which in general features agree with all the modern courts in the civilized world. There is the judge on his seat or throne; there is the prisoner arraigned; there is the investigation carried on through "books" or documents; and there is justice administered. Now, there is quite sufficient resemblance between these courts of human justice and the judicial transactions of God at the last day, to warrant the former being employed as illustrations of the latter, without supposing a "throne" or a "book" whatever. For example: 1. *There is the bringing of the Judge and the accused into conscious contact.* 2. *There is the final settling of the question of guiltiness or non-guiltiness, according to recognized law.* 3. *There is the administration of an award to which the accused is bound to submit.* Let us now proceed to notice a few facts in relation to this retributive period.

I. THIS RETRIBUTIVE PERIOD WILL DAWN WITH OVERPOWERING SPLENDOUR UPON THE WORLD. Observe: 1. *The character of this manifestation.* He comes on a throne. A "throne" is an emblem of glory. It is generally valuable in itself. That of Solomon consisted wholly of gold and ivory; but its glory mainly consists of its being the seat of supremacy. Hence ambition points to nothing higher. The people have ever looked up with a species of adoration to the throne. But what a throne is this! "His throne was like the fiery flame, and his wheels as burning fire." It is a "white throne." Human thrones have often, perhaps generally, been stained by sensuality, injustice, and tyranny. The throne has sometimes become so loathsome that the people, roused into indignation, have seized and burnt it in the streets. But this is a "white throne." There is not a single stain upon it. He who has ever occupied it "is light, and in him is no darkness at all." It is a *great* "white throne." Great in its occupant: "He filleth all in all." Great in its influence. Toward it the eyes of all intelligences are directed; to it all beings are amenable; from it all laws that determine the character and regulate the destiny of all creatures proceed. 2. *The effect of this manifestation.* Before its refulgence this material universe could not stand; it melted—it vanished away. "No more place was found for them" (ver. 11). It will pass away, perhaps, as the orbs of night pass away in the high noontide of the sun: they are still in being, still in their orbits, and still move on as ever; but they are lost to us by reason of a "glory that excelleth." What a contrast between Christ now as the Judge, and Christ of old as the despised Nazarene!

II. THIS RETRIBUTIVE PERIOD WILL WITNESS THE RESURRECTION OF THE DEAD, AND THE CONSEQUENT DESTRUCTION OF HADES AND THE GRAVE. "And the sea gave up the dead which were in it; and death and hell [Hades] delivered up the dead which were in them" (ver. 13). The words suggest two thoughts on this subject. 1. *That in the resurrection there will be a connection between man's raised and man's mortal body.* A resurrection of the material relics is a traditional dogma of the stupid, not a conviction of the studious. It is evidently implied that the resurrection-body is a something that has come out of the body, deposited either in the grave or the sea. What is the connection? Is it meant that men will come up with exactly the same bodies as they had during their probationary state? This, probably, is the vulgar idea, and this is the idea against which infidels level their objections. The question is now, as of old, "With what body do they come?" And assuming that they come in the same body, they commence their antagonistic reasonings and their sneers. But this is *not* the Scripture doctrine. "That which thou sowest, thou sowest *not* that body that shall be." If it be said—Is there no identity, no sameness? I ask—What do you mean by "sameness"? If you say sameness, in the sense of *particles, bulk,* or *capacity,* I answer—*No!* The *sameness* between the old body and the resurrection-body is not the sameness between the seed you deposit in the soil and the wheat which in autumn is produced by it. The one grows out of the other, has the form of the other; the resurrection-body is not the *same* as the old probationary body, in the same sense as the body of any given individual is the same in its *man*-state as it was in its *child*-state.

Take the case of a man in two different periods of life—say, ten years of age and sixty. In the intervening periods his body has passed through several *radical* changes; yet at sixty he *feels* that he has the same body which he had at ten. It is not until your *science* comes that he questions it; and where the science has been the most convincing, it has never destroyed this underlying *consciousness of physical identity.* How can you account for this *consciousness* of sameness? (1) *Not because he knows the particles to be the same.* He cannot know that, for it is contrary to fact ; the particles of his body, when a child, having gone off long ago, and mixed themselves, perhaps, with a hundred different bodies. (2) *Not because he knows the amount is the same.* He may know that there are ten times the quantity in the one body-state as in the other. (3) *Not because he knows the capability is the same.* In its childish stage it was weak, incapable of much labour or endurance; but in its man-state it is vigorous—its physical powers have increased manifold. How, then, can you account for this consciousness? Consciousness must have some truth as a foundation. (*a*) *Because he knows the one has risen out of the other.* It has been an evolution. The casual connection has been preserved. The one was the outcome of the other. (*b*) *Because he knows the one has retained the same plan, or outline as the other.* If the body, in the man-state, had taken a form different to that of its child-state, the consciousness of identity might have been lost. If it passed, for instance, from the human form to the lion, eagle, or any other form, though the particles might have been all retained, and bulk and capacity continued as ever, the sense of identity would have been lost. (*c*) *Because he knows the one fulfils the same functions as the other.* The body, in the child-state, was the inlet and outlet of himself. Through it, in all cases, he derived and imparted his feelings and ideas. It was the great medium between his spirit and the material universe. Now, for these *three reasons,* man may *feel* that his resurrection-body is the same as the one in which he spent his probationary life. *It grows out of the buried.* There is in the body that went down to the grave a something, I know not what, which the man, the spiritual self, takes into his immortal frame. *The resurrection-body may retain its present form or outline;* it may be moulded after the same archetype. *It may also fulfil many of the same functions.* Ever will it be the medium between the material and the spiritual. I know, then, of no objection that you can urge against the fact of a man having a resurrection-body which he may feel to be identical with his probationary body, that could not antecedently be urged against a fact in the present experience of every adult—the fact of an individual having a man-body which he *feels* to be the same as his child-body. 2. *That the resurrection will be coextensive with the mortality of mankind.* "The sea gave up its dead." What a vast cemetery is the sea ! Here mighty navies slumber; millions of the industrious, the enterprising, and the brave, lie beneath its restless waves. But all must now come forth. All that have perished—whether in the barques of scientific expedition, or the ships of commerce, or the fleets of conquered nations, must come forth in this dread day. "Death and hell delivered up the dead which were in them" (ver. 13). This is the grave. "All that are in their graves shall hear the voice of the Son of man, and shall come forth." What a voice is that ! It would reverberate over sea and land, from island to island, from continent to continent; roll its thunders through the deepest vaults and catacombs; and soon the mouldering skeletons and the scattered dust would feel the stir of life, and spring to immortality. Martyrs, who had no grave to shelter them from the storm of ages, whose dust was consumed in the flames, and left at the mercy of the wild elements, would appear again; as the field of battle, where mighty armies struggled in demon fury, would start to life on the plains where, in hellish rage, they fell. "And hell gave up its dead." Hell here means, not the place of punishment, but the universe of disembodied spirits, both good and bad. This *Hades* of the Greeks, and *Sheol* of the Hebrews, sends forth all the myriads of human souls that it has ever received, from Abel to the last man that grappled with the "king of terrors." "The small and great." Not an infant too young, not a patriarch too old. Tyrants and their slaves, sages and their pupils, ministers and their people—all will appear.

III. This retributive period will bring humanity into conscious contact with God. "And I saw the dead, small and great, stand before God" (ver. 12). They *stand* before God; they confront him, as it were, eye to eye, being to being. Each *feels* God to be the All to him now. The idea of God fills every soul as a burning flame. They *stand* before him, *feeling* his presence, and *awaiting* his doom-fixing word. This is a distinguishing feature of the retributive period. In every preceding period of human history, with the exception of the millennial ages, the vast majorities of all generations had no *conscious contact with God.* Some denied his very being, whilst others desired not a knowledge of his ways. But hence-on, for ever and ever, all the good and the bad will " stand before God "—will be in *conscious* contact with him. His *felt* presence will be the heaven of the good, and his *felt* presence will be the hell of the evil. 1. *There will be no atheism after this.* How will the atheist teachers of the past ages feel now? Lucretius, Democritus, and Strabo among the ancients; Diderot, Lagrange, D'Alembert, Mirabeau, and Hobbes amongst the moderns, will *feel* now, and *evermore,* that the greatest reality in the universe was the Being whose existence they impiously ignored or denied. 2. *There will be no deism after this.* The men who taught, through preceding ages, the doctrine that God had no immediate connection with his creatures; that he governed the universe through an inflexible system of laws; that he took no cognizance of individuals, and felt no interest in them, will *know* now that no being in the universe had been in such *close* contact with every particle and period of their existence as God. All the objects that intervened between God and the soul will be withdrawn now; the veil of sense and matter will be rent asunder, to unite no more. 3. *There will be no indifferentism after this.* God's Being, presence, and claims will no longer be subjects of no importance. They will be every-thing to all. God's presence will fill the conscious life of all, as midday sun without a cloud the day.

IV. THIS RETRIBUTIVE PERIOD WILL SETTLE FOR EVER THE QUESTION OF EVERY MAN'S CHARACTER AND DESTINY. "And the dead were judged out of those things which were written in the books, according to their works," etc. (vers. 12, 13). Here observe three things. 1. *That the worth of a man's character will be determined by his works.* " According to their works." Not by religious position, or creed, or profession, or office ; but by " works." " What has a man done? " will be the question. 2. *That a man's works will be determined by recognized authorities.* " Books" will be opened. God's *moral* and *remedial* laws are books, and these books will now be opened—opened to memory, to conscience, and the universe. This will be a day of *moral conviction.* 3. *That according to the correspondence, or non-correspondence, of man's works with these recognized authorities will be his final destiny.* " Whosoever was not found written in the book of life was cast into the lake of fire " (ver. 15). " The book of life "—the *remedial* law or scheme of salvation—the gospel. Whoever was not found *vitally* interested in this was cast into the lake of fire.

What a scene is this that has passed under review! In *its* light how mean do man's highest dignities and honours appear! How ineffably paltry the pageantry of courts! how empty the pretensions of sovereigns! How solemn is life, in all its stages, rela-tions, and aspects! God help us to live in the light of "*that day*"! —D. T.

EXPOSITION.

CHAPTER XXI.

Ver. 1.—**And I saw.** The usual introduc-tion to a new vision (cf. ch. xx. 11, etc.). Having described the origin and progress of evil in the world, the final overthrow of Satan and his adherents, and the judgment when every man is rewarded according to his works, the seer now completes the whole by portraying the eternal bliss of the re-deemed in heaven (cf. on ch. xx. 10). The description is based upon Isa. lx. and Ezek. xl., *et seq.*; especially the latter, which follows the account of Gog and Magog, as does this. **A new heaven and a new earth.** The dispute as to whether a new creation is intended, or a revivified earth, seems to be founded on the false assumption that the dwellers in heaven must be localized in space (cf. Isa. lxv. 17, "I create new heavens and a new earth;" also Isa. lxvi. 22; 2 Pet. iii. 13). For the first heaven and the first earth were passed away. The Revisers follow B and others in reading ἀπῆλθον, and render it by the English per-fect tense. In ℵ, A, is read ἀπῆλθαν, while other manuscripts give ἀπῆλθεν and πα-ρῆλθε. *The first heaven and earth;* that is, those now existing pass away as described in ch. xx. 11. **And there was no more sea;** *and the sea no longer exists.* The threefold division of heaven, earth, and sea represents the whole of this world (cf. ch. x. 6). Some interpret the *sea* symbolically of the restless, unstable, wicked nations of the earth, which now exist no longer; others understand the absence of *sea* to typify the absence of instability and wickedness in the New Jerusalem.

Ver. 2.—**And I John saw the holy city, new Jerusalem.** "John" must be omitted, according to all the best manuscripts. "The holy city" is the Church of God (see on ch. xi. 2), now glorified and prepared for perfect communion with her Redeemer (cf. the promise in ch. iii. 12, which is now fulfilled; cf. also Gal. iv. 26; Heb. xi. 10, 16). Contrast this figure of the *holy city* with that of Babylon (see on ch. xviii.). **Coming down from God out of heaven.** Connect "out of heaven" with "coming down." The same words occur in ch. iii. 12 (which see). **Prepared as a bride adorned for her husband.** Here is the contrast to the "harlot" (see on ch. xvii. 1). Though many of those forming the *bride* are rewarded according to their works (see ch. xx. 13), yet their own works are insufficient to fit them for their future life; they are *prepared* by God. This appearance is anticipated in ch. xix. 7 (which see).

Ver. 3.—**And I heard a great voice out of heaven saying.** *Out of the throne* is read in ℵ, A, and others; *out of heaven* is the reading of B, P, etc. As usual, the *voice* is described as a *great* voice (cf. ch. xix. 17, etc.). It is not stated from whom the voice proceeds, but comp. ch. xx. 11. **Behold, the tabernacle of God is with men, and he will dwell with them;** literally, *he shall tabernacle with them.* Still the seer is influenced by the language of Ezekiel: "And the heathen shall know that I the Lord do sanctify Israel, when my sanctuary shall be in the midst of them for evermore" (xxxvii. 28). Thus God makes his abode in his glorified Church—the New Jerusalem, among his spiritual Israel (cf. ch. vii. 15, where this vision has been already anticipated). **And they shall be his people, and God himself shall be with them, and be their God;** *and they shall be his peoples, and himself shall be God with them, their God.* The balance of authority is in favour of retaining the two last words, though they are omitted in ℵ, B, and others. Evidently the same words as Ezek. xxxvii. 27 (see above), "My tabernacle also shall be with them: yea, I will be their God, and they shall be my people." Cf. "God with them" with "Emmanuel" (Matt. i. 23; Isa. vii. 14). Now, the promise is redeemed in all its fulness. The plural "peoples" seems to point to the catholic nature of the New Jerusalem, which embraces many nations (cf. ver. 24; also ch. vii. 9).

Ver. 4.—**And God shall wipe away all tears from their eyes; and there shall be no more death, neither sorrow, nor crying, neither shall there be any more pain;** *and death shall be no more, neither shall there be mourning, nor crying, nor pain, any more* (Revised Version). *All tears;* just as in ch. vii. 17 (cf. Isa. xxv. 8, "He will swallow up death in victory; and the Lord God will wipe away tears from off all faces;" cf. also Isa. lxv. 19). There is "no more death" because sin is no more (cf. Isa. li. 11, "Sorrow and mourning shall flee away"). **For the former things are passed away.** Ὅτι, "for," should probably be omitted, as in A and P, and ℵ as first written. *The former* state of things is the state now existing, which will then have passed away as described in ver. 1.

Ver. 5.—**And he that sat upon the throne said;** *that sitteth* (cf. ch. xx. 11 and Matt. xxv. 31). **Behold, I make all things new.** As in ver. 1. So in Matt. xix. 28, "Ye which have followed me, in the regeneration when the Son of man shall sit in the throne of his glory," etc. **And he said unto me, Write;** *and he saith, Write.* Probably the angel (cf. ch. xix. 9; xiv. 13). The change from εἶπεν to λέγει, and the immediate return to εἶπεν, appear to indicate a change of speaker. **For these words are true and faithful;** *faithful and true.* So also in ch. xix. 9; iii. 14, etc.

Ver. 6.—**And he said unto me, It is done;** *and he said unto me, They are come to pass* (Revised Version). It is uncertain what is the nominative intended. It may be the "words" just mentioned; or the incidents described in vers. 1—5; or the Divine promises and judgments in general. The analogy of ch. xvi. 17 supports the last, but it is not conclusive. **I am Alpha and Omega, the Beginning and the End;** *the Alpha and the Omega.* As the book opens, so it closes, with the solemn assurance of the certainty and unchangeableness of God's eternal promises (cf. ch. i. 8; xxii. 13). The second clause interprets the first; a third form of expressing the same idea occurs in ch. xxii. 13, "the First and the Last." **I will give unto him that is athirst of the fountain of the water of life freely.** The same ideas are repeated in ch. xxii. 13—17. Again the symbolism of the prophet (cf. ver. 3). There is also another reminiscence of ch. vii. 17 (cf. also ver. 4 of this chapter). In exactly the same sense the words, "living water," are used in John iv. 10 (cf. also Matt. v. 6, "thirst after righteousness").

Ver. 7.—**He that overcometh shall inherit all things.** The correct reading makes the sense plain: *He that overcometh shall inherit these things,* i.e. the promises just enumerated. These words show the reason for the words of ver. 6; and may be called the text on which the Apocalypse is based (cf. ch. ii.); for, though the words themselves do not often recur, yet the spirit of them is constantly appearing (cf. ch. xii. 11; see also John xvi. 33). And I will be his God, and he shall be my son (cf. Lev. xxvi. 12, "And I will walk among you, and will be your God, and ye shall be my people"). Some have thought that these words prove the Speaker to be God the Father; but it is impossible to separate the Persons of the Blessed Trinity in these chapters. This promise, first made to David concerning Solomon (2 Sam. vii. 14), received its mystical fulfilment in Christ (Heb. i. 5), and is now fulfilled in the members of Christ (Alford).

Ver. 8.—But the fearful, and unbelieving, and the abominable, and murderers, and whoremongers, and sorcerers, and idolaters, and all liars, shall have their part in the lake which burneth with fire and brimstone: which is the second death; *but for the fearful*, etc. The construction is changed in the middle of the verse. The *fearful* are those who, through cowardice, have not overcome (cf. ver. 7). *Abominable;* those defiled with abominations (cf. ch. xvii. 4). *And murderers, and fornicators* (cf. ch. xiv. 4; xvii. 1, 2). *And sorcerers* (cf. ch. ix. 21; xviii. 23); those who deceived the heathen. *And idolaters;* the heathen who were deceived by them. *All liars;* all who are false in any way. *Their part* is *in the lake*, etc. (see on ch. xx. 10). These took no part in the first, spiritual, resurrection (ch. xx. 6); they now, therefore, inherit "the second death."

Ver. 9.—And there came unto me one of the seven angels which had the seven vials full of the seven last plagues. Omit "unto me." "Full of" must be connected with "angels." Just as these angels had carried out God's judgments upon the ungodly, and one of them had exhibited the judgment of the harlot (ch. xvii. 1), so now one of them shows the picture of the bliss of the faithful—the bride of the Lamb. And talked with me, saying, Come hither, I will show thee the bride, the Lamb's wife ; *hither* (omitting " come "). The wording of this verse (except the last phrase) is almost identical with ch. xvii. 1. The last phrase is the great contrast to the former chapter. In ch. xvii. 1 was seen a picture of a harlot, the unfaithful part of Christ's Church; here we have a description of those who have been "faithful unto death" (ch. ii. 10), and whose purity and faithfulness are symbolized under the figure of the "wife of the Lamb" (see on ch. xvii. 1).

Ver. 10.—And he carried me away in the Spirit (so also in ch. xvii. 3; cf. ch. i. 10) to a great and high mountain. From which a clear view of "the city" might be obtained (cf. Ezek. xl. 2). The preposition ἐπί implies "on to." And showed me that great city, the holy Jerusalem, descending out of heaven from God ; *showed me the holy city Jerusalem;* not *great*, which is the title of Babylon (cf. ch. xvi. 19). Just as the harlot, signifying faithless Christians, was identified with Babylon, the world-city (see on ch. xviii.), so the bride, the faithful portion of Christ's flock, is merged in Jerusalem, the heavenly city. *Coming down*, etc. (cf. ver. 2).

Ver. 11.—Having the glory of God. That is, the abiding presence of God, as the Shechinah (cf. Exod. xl. 34; 1 Kings viii. 11. Cf. also ver. 3, *supra*). And her light was like unto a stone most precious, even like a jasper stone, clear as crystal; *as it were a jasper stone* (Revised Version). This *light* is again alluded to in ver. 23. The *jasper* probably represents the modern diamond (see on ch. iv. 3). The brilliant light which illumines the city is the characteristic of "him that sat on the throne" (ch. iv. 3).

Ver. 12.—And had a wall great and high ; *having a wall*. Omit each introductory "and." The wall is a type of the absolute security of the heavenly city; not that any further assault is expected. In Ezek. xxxviii. 11 Gog and Magog prey upon the unwalled villages. And had twelve gates, and at the gates twelve angels, and names written thereon, which are the names of the twelve tribes of the children of Israel (cf. the description in Ezek. xlviii.). *Twelve;* as signifying completeness (cf. ch. iv. 9; vii. 4—8), and as being the number of the tribes of Israel, which are the type of the spiritual Israel of God. *Gates;* rather, *portals*. The picture of the angels placed at the portals, still fulfilling their mission as guardians of men, shows the absolute security of the city. *The names are written thereon;* as on the stones of the ephod (Exod. xxviii. 9) and breastplate (Exod. xxix. 14). Contrast the names of blasphemy (ch. xviii. 3).

Ver. 13.—On the east three gates; on the north three gates; on the south three gates; and on the west three gates. The following are the dispositions of the tribes in the Old Testament :—

Order in Numb. ii.	Order in Ezek. xlviii. 30.
East—	*East—*
Judah.	Joseph.
Issachar.	Benjamin.
Zebulun.	Dan.
North—	*North—*
Dan.	Reuben.
Asher.	Judah.
Naphtali.	Levi

South—	*South—*
Reuben.	Simeon.
Simeon.	Issachar.
Gad.	Zebulon.
West—	*West—*
Ephraim.	Gad.
Manasseh.	Asher.
Benjamin.	Naphtali.

Ver. 14.—And the wall of the city had twelve foundations, and in them the names of the twelve apostles of the Lamb; *and on them twelve names*, etc. (cf. Eph. ii. 20). The imagery is, of course, symbolical, and there can, therefore, be no question as to individual names of apostles, *e.g.* whether St. Matthias or St. Paul is the twelfth. Some writers have, without sufficient reason, brought forward this verse as indicating that the writer of the Apocalypse was not an apostle.

Ver. 15.—And he that talked with me had a golden reed to measure the city, and the gates thereof, and the wall thereof; *had for a measure a golden reed to measure*, etc. " He that spake " is the angel of ver. 9 (cf. the action of ch. xi. 1; and Ezek. xl. 3, 5; xlii. 15, *et seq.*). Here the measuring is evidently to indicate the large extent of the city (see on ch. xi. 1). The *reed* is *golden*, as being the typical heavenly material.

Ver. 16.—And the city lieth foursquare, and the length is as large as the breadth. The shape is doubtless typical of that which is complete and symmetrical, to which nothing is wanting to render the shape perfect. The word τετράγωνος, " foursquare," is thus used by Greek philosophic writers. And he measured the city with the reed, twelve thousand furlongs. That is, in each direction. (On στάδιον, " furlong," see ch. xiv. 20.) The number twelve thousand, which is the number of the sealed in each tribe (ch. vii.), is typical of (1) a large number, (2) a complete number (see on ver. 12). There seems to be in this description a designed reference to the literal Babylon (see Smith's ' Dictionary of the Bible,' art. " Babylon "). The length and the breadth and the height of it are equal. The plain meaning seems to be that the city forms a vast cube, and this is typical of its perfect nature. The account given is that of a vision, and not of a reality, and therefore there is no need to attempt to reduce the enormous dimensions given here, as is done by some writers. The holy of holies was thus cubical in shape (1 Kings vi. 20).

Ver. 17.—And he measured the wall thereof, an hundred and forty and four cubits. (For the signification of the number, see on ch. vii. 4.) The parallel between the shape of the city as just related and the holy of holies (*vide supra*) almost seems to have insensibly suggested the transition from *stadia* to *cubits*. The discrepancy between the height of the city, which is twelve thousand furlongs (ver. 16), and the height of the *wall*, which is a hundred and forty-four cubits, has led to the suggestion that in the height of the city is included the hill on which it stands (Alford). Others understand that the wall is purposely described as of small height, because the writer wishes to indicate that " the most inconsiderable wall is sufficient to exclude all that is impure " (Düsterdieck). According to the measure of a man, that is, of the angel; *of an angel*. That is, the measure here used by the angel is that used by men (cf. " the number of a man," ch. xiii. 18).

Ver. 18.—And the building of the wall of it was of jasper: and the city was pure gold, like unto clear glass; *pure glass*. The exceeding brightness and purity is the idea contained in both expressions—the light of ver. 11, which is there associated with jasper and crystal. (On " jasper," see on ver. 11 and ch. iv. 3.) The whole description is, of course, typical, not literal.

Ver. 19.—And the foundations of the wall of the city were garnished with all manner of precious stones. Omit " and " (cf. Isa. liv. 12, " All thy borders of pleasant stones "). *Foundations* (cf. ver. 14). The first foundation was jasper. Probably the diamond (see on ch. iv. 3). The second, sapphire. Thought to be the modern lapis-lazuli. It was of a clear blue colour (Exod. xxiv. 10), and very precious (Job xxviii. 16). The third, a chalcedony. Not the modern stone of that name, but a green carbonate of copper, found in the mines of Chalcedon. It was, therefore, a kind of inferior emerald. The fourth, an emerald. The same as the modern stone (cf. ch. iv. 3).

Ver. 20.—The fifth, sardonyx. A variety of agate—a kind of *onyx*, valued for its use in engraving into cameos. The name *onyx* appears to be owing to the resemblance in colour to the finger-nails. The sixth, sardius. Probably the modern *carnelian* (see on ch. iv. 3). The seventh, chrysolyte. A variety of the gem of which that called topaz (the ninth stone) is another kind. This species contained a considerable amount of yellow colour, whence the name " golden stone." It has been suggested that it is identical with the modern jacinth or amber. The eighth, beryl. A variety of emerald, of less decided green shade than the pure emerald. The ninth, a topaz. Not the modern *topaz*, but a variety of chrysolite (see the seventh stone, *supra*), of a yellowish-green colour, the latter predominating. The tenth, a chrysoprasus,

The name "golden leek-green" appears to point to a species of beryl, and the modern aqua-marine. It is thus probably a variety of emerald, being of a yellowish pale-green hue. The eleventh, a jacinth. "A red variety of zircon, which is found in square prisms, of a white, grey, red, reddish-brown, yellow, or pale-green colour" (Smith's 'Dictionary of the Bible'). "The sapphire of the moderns" (King). The twelfth, an amethyst. A purple stone, possibly the common amethyst.

Ver. 21.—And the twelve gates were twelve pearls; every several gate was of one pearl. The *pearl* was known to the ancients from the earliest times, and was always held in high honour by them (cf. ch. xvii. 4). And the street of the city was pure gold, as it were transparent glass (cf. ver. 18). The brilliancy was so far beyond ordinary gold as to make it apparently transparent like glass. "The street" is not merely one street, but the whole collective material of which the streets are composed.

Ver. 22.—And I saw no temple therein: for the Lord God Almighty and the Lamb are the temple of it. No ναός, "inner shrine," or "sanctuary" (cf. ch. vii. 15). The whole city is now the ναός (cf. on vers. 16, 17, where the shape of the city is that of the holy of holies). The presence of God pervades all the city (cf. ver. 11); all the redeemed are within the sanctuary, and are now priests (cf. ch. xx. 6). There is, therefore, no ναός, or "temple," within the city, for the whole city itself is the temple. The Object of all worship and the great Sacrifice are there (Alford).

Ver. 23.—And the city had no need of the sun, neither of the moon, to shine in it; *hath no need.* So Isa. lx. 19, 20, "The sun shall be no more thy light by day; neither for brightness shall the moon give light unto thee: but the Lord shall be unto thee an everlasting Light, and thy God thy Glory." For the glory of God did lighten it, and the Lamb is the Light thereof. *The glory of God* (cf. ver. 11). No distinction is to be made between God and the Lamb; both are the Light (cf. John i. 5).

Ver. 24.—And the nations of them which are saved shall walk in the light of it; *and the nations shall walk by means of her light.* Omit "of them which are saved." The description, following that of Isaiah, makes use of earthly symbolism; but it is not, therefore, to be supposed (as Alford) that

there will be hereafter a real earth with inhabitants. "The nations" are the redeemed, described in this way on account of their selection from every "kindred, and nation, and tribe, and tongue" (ch. vii. 9); not the wicked nations of ch. xvi. 19. Though the Authorized Version is probably incorrect in inserting "of them which are saved," yet these words appear to give the correct sense of the passage. The description is evidently still founded on the prophetical writings, "And the Gentiles shall come to thy light, and kings to the brightness of thy rising" (Isa. lx. 3). And the kings of the earth do bring their glory and honour into it. Omit "and honour," according to ℵ, A, P, and others. Not that there are literal kings and earth. The language is intended to convey an idea of God's supreme glory and unquestioned authority. There are now no kings to dispute his sway. Instead, all join in promoting his glory.

Ver. 25.—And the gates of it shall not be shut at all by day: for there shall be no night there. The Revised Version correctly places the last clause in parentheses. The meaning is: The gates shall never be shut, either by day or night; but it is superfluous to say, "by night," for there is no night there. Some commentators think the open gates are a sign of perfect security; others, that they are open to admit the nations, as described in the following verse. Both ideas may well be understood.

Ver. 26.—And they shall bring the glory and honour of the nations into it; that is, *the glory and the honour of the nations shall be brought into it.* The verb is used impersonally, as in ch. x. 11 and many other places. A repetition of ver. 24 (*vide supra*).

Ver. 27.—And there shall in no wise enter into it any thing that defileth, neither whatsoever worketh abomination, or maketh a lie; *anything unclean, or he that doeth an abomination, and a lie.* It is thus evident that "the nations" of ver. 24 are among the redeemed (cf. Isa. lii. 1, "O Jerusalem, the holy city: for henceforth there shall no more come into thee the uncircumcised and the unclean"). The lot of such as are here described is the lake of fire (ver. 8); cf. the "abomination" of the harlot (ch. xvii. 4, 5). (On "lie," cf. ch. ii. 2; iii. 9. "Unclean," cf. ch. iii. 4; xiv. 4.) But they which are written in the Lamb's book of life; *but only they,* etc. (cf. ch. iii. 5; xiii. 8; xvii. 8; xx. 12, 15).

HOMILETICS.

Ver. 1—ch. xxii. 5.—*The holy city; or, the Church triumphant.* Whether by intuition or otherwise, we know not, but certain it is that Plato seized hold of and expressed a profound truth when, in his 'Phædo,' he maintains that "things are the passage to their opposites." The seven angels with the seven last plagues having set before the vision of the apostle scenes of awe and terror, he is now carried forward to the vision that lies beyond them all—even to the glory that is yet to be revealed. When the warrior hath done with fighting, it must be pleasant for him to lay aside his armour; when the mariner has been often tempest-tossed, he must be glad to reach the desired haven. So it is here. In going through the homiletic exposition of the plan of this book, we have found ourselves, as it were, in incessant conflict; and if one struggle passed, it was but followed by another and another still. But now "the war is over." The harlot is judged. The dragon is defeated. The first and second beasts are cast into the lake of fire. Hades and death are no more. The resurrection is past. The judgment is ended. The award is made. And now a voice is heard from the throne, "Behold, I make all things new." In the twenty-first chapter, and in the first five verses of the twenty-second, we have a glowing picture of the new state of purity and bliss which awaits the redeemed from among men. We will try and indicate in outline—for this is all we can do—the features of the new state and the new place. Let us "look" in by faith now, and, by-and-by, the Lord grant that we may go in! We have set before us—a new sphere of life, a new abode of life, and new conditions of life. Undoubtedly there is a very large amount of symbolism in the three sketches; but the symbolism is such as to indicate an unspeakable measure of glory.

I. THERE WILL BE FOR THE GLORIFIED CHURCH A NEW SPHERE OF LIFE. "A new heaven and a new earth" is a phrase which certainly conveys the idea of locality; of a place for the righteous, in which and on which their inheritance finds its ground. To the meaning of the phrase, "a new heaven," we have scarcely any clue. Often heaven means the surrounding atmosphere. The rabbis taught that there were three heavens—the first, where the birds fly; the second, where the stars are; the third, where God is. Here it signifies apparently the surrounding atmosphere of the new earth on which the righteous dwell; or, it may mean, that there shall be new spiritual environments to correspond with changed physical conditions. This latter phrase, "the new earth," seems to mean *this* earth renovated and purified by the fires of the last day; retouched and beautified by the hand that built it first. It is not unreasonable to suppose that the same earth, which was the theatre on which the Saviour suffered, should be also the scene of his final triumph. How far the expression, "the sea shall no longer be," is to be taken literally, we cannot tell. As the definite article is used, the phrase may be equivalent to "that sea," *i.e.* the tossing, restless sea of former days. Even then it may also be symbolical, and may thus mean that the restless tossing to and fro of this world's surging strife shall be no more. Certainly the more we let the literal and material sink into the background, and the more that which is spiritual comes into fuller prominence, the more power and glory will this vision have for us. For whatever interest—and it is not slight—the question of *place* has for us in reference to the next life, the question of *state* is so immeasurably greater, that, compared with it, the other is of no consequence at all. If men are but free from sin, and for ever with the Lord, what matters it *where* God appoints their abode? All space is his; and in any section of it he can prepare a heaven for the glorified.

II. IN THESE REALMS THERE IS A NEW ABODE OF LIFE. Within the new heaven and on the new earth there is "the holy city." Let us gather up one by one the features which mark it. 1. *Its name.* It is called "New Jerusalem." Before the apostle was prisoner under Domitian, the Jerusalem of olden time had fallen. And many a devout Jew would be almost heart-broken to think that the sacred walls, and the still holier fane enclosed therein, for him existed no more. And, with a wondrous touch of tenderness, the apostle points them far ahead to a new Jerusalem, in which all that was precious in the past shall be reproduced and exceeded—a Jerusalem which should indeed be "holy," which should be free from an alien's tread, and which should endure for ever. For whatever the olden city might have of the glory of the Lord, the new Jerusalem shall have the Lord in his glory. 2. *Its wall.* (Ver. 12, "great and high;" ver. 17, "a hundred and forty-four cubits" = 240 feet, indicating stupendous height and complete security; cf. 1 Sam. xxv. 16; Zech. ii. 5; Isa. xxvi. 1.) The city of the saints is safe against all assault. 3. *Its entrance gates.* Here there are remarkable features. Where the protection of the walls ceases—at the gates—there is another guard, even "at the gates twelve angels," so that none can enter with hostile aims. And not only so, but on the several gates the name of a tribe of Israel is found. None but Israelites enter there. 4. *Its foundations.* (Ver. 14.) (1) There are inscribed the names of the twelve apostles of *the Lamb.* In the Apocalypse, the song is the song of *the Lamb;* praise is to *the Lamb;* in the midst of the throne is *the Lamb;* the book of life belongs to *the Lamb;* the seals are opened by *the Lamb;* the apostles are the apostles of *the Lamb.* Even so. The whole of this glory is based on the sacrifice of the atoning Lamb. (2) The foundations are lustrous in their splendour (ver. 18). The most exquisite and costly things are lavished here. The pearl, with glistering radiance; the amethyst, with its red or violet hue; the jacinth; the translucent chrysoprasus, with its golden gleams; the topaz and emerald; the beryl, sardius, and chrysolite; the chalcedony, shining as a lamp; the sapphire, in its azure blue; the jasper, so resplendent that it is a fit image of the glory of God. All such precious stones, flashing and gleaming, are there; so precious is the foundation work of this city of the Lamb! 5. *Its citizens.* These are from "the nations," but not as of earthly nationality. This is past. They are the *nations of the saved* (ver. 24, Authorized Version). We have brief hints as to their character (ch. xxi. 6, 7; xxii. 14, Revised Version). Brief as these expressions are, they are enough; specially when we read the list of the excluded ones (vers. 8, 27). Only holy ones are in the holy city. The separation from the unholy is complete and final. 6. *Its magnitude.* It is measured. The measuring-reed was a golden one, and showed its size—12,000 stadia in length. Alexandria, according to Josephus, was 30 stadia by 10; Jerusalem was, in circuit, 33 stadia; Thebes, 43; Nineveh, 400; Babylon, 480; the holy city, 48,000! How puny are the measurements of earth's great cities compared with those of the great city of God! (Such is the case with this symbolic description, even if we take 12,000 stadia to be the compass of the city, rather than a side thereof.) There will be room in the holy city for men from every nation, and kindred, and people, and tongue. None of the artificial divisions or nomenclatures of ecclesiastical boundaries will count for anything there. Only love and life will enter there. 7. *Its glory.* Ver. 11, "Her light is like unto a stone most precious;" "The glory of God doth lighten it, and the Lamb is the light thereof." We could almost say, with Payson, "Lord, withhold thy hand, and show us no more, or we shall be overpowered by the splendour of the vision!"

III. IN THIS HOLY CITY THERE ARE NEW CONDITIONS OF LIFE. Here, too, we can but analyze and arrange the description before us, dropping a hint or two as we advance. 1. *There is one comprehensive, all-embracing condition which covers the whole ground.* Ver. 3, "Behold, the tabernacle of God is with [the] men," etc., *i.e.* with the sanctified men who are in this holy city. The home of God is there. Their spirits are at home in God. The work of redemption is perfected. The communion is entire and complete; never to be interrupted for a moment, nor to be marred by one sin. The revelations of the past secured an approximation to this. The earthly worship was an earnest of it (cf. Exod. xxv. 8; xxix. 45; Numb. xxxv. 34; 2 Kings xix. 15; 1 Chron. xxiii. 25, margin; Ps. lxviii. 16, 18; cxxxii. 14; Isa. lvii. 15; Ezek. xliii. 7; 1 Cor. vi. 19; iii. 16; 2 Cor. xii. 9 (Greek); Eph. ii. 22). These passages are but specimens of many more which show that the whole drift and aim of the gospel redemption has been to bring together God and man in sublimest fellowship. The perfection of this is realized in "the holy city;" and it is the one condition of blessedness which includes all else. 2. *There is a double set of detailed conditions of life,* which follow on the complete realization of this full redemption. (1) The first set includes *the cessation of what used to be.* (*a*) No more death. When the redemption in Christ has done its work on the body at the resurrection, there can be no more dying. No element of perishableness will exist in the "spiritual body." It is "incorruptible." Death will have been swallowed up in victory. (*b*) No mourning nor crying. No physical distress nor spiritual ill shall grieve. Joy shall have no shade. The day of eternity will know no cloud. (*c*) No pain; no tension from excessive exertion; no aching from disease; no disappointment at the failure to realize our ideal; no cutting-off of work ere it can be completed. (*d*) No more curse. No condemnation will press on the conscience, nor will any sin pollute the soul. (*e*) No alien. "There shall enter nothing that defileth." There will be no intrusion of aught that is evil within or without. (f) No night there. No pause in the activities of life, because no weariness will ever be felt. There will be constant work and constant worship. (g) No temple. Not only will hindrances which existed here be banished there, but helps which were precious here will not be needed there. If, as one has said, the most exquisitely tender text in the Bible is, "God shall wipe away all tears from their eyes," surely the most far-reaching text given through an inspired pen is, "I saw no temple therein." No forms will be wanted when the ideal of worship is perfect and permanent. No place for worship, when every spot is holy ground. No day for worship, when every moment is sanctified. No external acts of worship, when every act is "holiness to the Lord." Many a thinker is yearning for *the pure thing in itself without form*. Here it is. Their yearnings were anticipated eighteen hundred years ago. And to it we are pressing on by stages. (h) No light of the sun. No lamp. No artificial light kindled by man, nor even the present forms of light created by God. "The city hath no need of the sun, neither of the moon, to shine in it: for the Lord God giveth them light," etc. What meaneth this? Surely nothing less than that created media will not be needed to intervene between us and God. We shall need no borrowed light when we see face to face *the* Light! We shall see him *as he is!* What life is this! No moon, no sun, no night, no temple, no curse, no pain, no tears, no sorrows, no death! All these things will have passed away. Happy state, even if known only by such negatives as these! (2) The second set of details includes—*the inbringing of what is new*. The heavenly state is pictured here not only as one in which we shall miss much that we now experience, but also as one in which all that is true and precious here will be reproduced, exceeded, and perfected. Here, too, as in every other part of the Apocalypse, the scenery is based on Old Testament representations. Six features : (a) The river (ch. xxii. 1). In Eden was a fertilizing stream. Israel drank of the river which followed them. "There is a river, the streams of which make glad the city of God." The good Shepherd now leads his flock beside still waters. And in the heavenly world he leads them still by the fountains of the water of life. The water of life shall no more have its purity marred by coming through earthen channels. There we shall be at the fountain-head. (b) The tree (or trees) of life (see Revised Version, margin). In Eden the tree of life would have counteracted the tendency to decay and death. But from this man was debarred when he fell. Christ has restored it to us. And he will himself give it to the victor. Full supplies of heavenly food ensuring immortality will be given by Christ's own hand. (c) The throne of God is there. Another symbol to indicate the *immediateness* of relations to God in the heavenly state. No intervening authority of priest or king; but close and absolute allegiance to the Eternal. (d) The service (ch. xxii. 3). Service in the sense of worship. "They serve him day and night in his temple." (e) The sight (ch. xxii. 4). "They shall see his face" (cf. 1 John iii. 1, 2; 2 Cor. iii. 18). This sight will have transforming power. (f) The royalty. "They shall reign for ever and ever" (ch. xxii. 5). This "reigning" is not the preliminary and limited one referred to in ch. xx. 4; but the final, the complete one, to which no ending is assigned (cf. ch. iii. 21). Well may we say with one, "I am content that I have seen the city, and without weariness will I go nearer to it; not all my life long will I suffer its bright golden gates to disappear from my sight" (Hengstenberg).

IV. THE GLORY OF THIS CITY LIGHTS UP WITH ITS BRIGHTNESS THE LIFE THAT NOW IS. At any rate, it ought to have this effect, for most assuredly this is the intent of the disclosures. We shall do our God a wrong, and ourselves too, if we pursue our course here as if it were meant to end in gloom, or as if we were left in uncertainty as to what lies beyond it, or whether there is anything at all. Note : 1. Let us recognize the glory of life's goal, if properly spent, as the working out of Divine grace, love, and faithfulness. 2. If we are indeed the children of God, we have even now the earnest of the Spirit, and are being wrought for that selfsame thing. 3. Let us bless God for the progressiveness of revelation and of redemption. The whole of the sacred Word is threaded by one infallible clue. It opens by showing us "Paradise lost." It closes by showing us "Paradise regained." And the intervening stages, taken chronologically, show us the Divine advance on the first, and the Divine preparation for the last. 4. If even now we have a vision so glorious of the holy city, let us go in the strength of it to work, to toil, to suffer, and to die, pressing forward to the glory yet to be revealed.

5. Seeing that in that future home nothing can enter that defileth, let us ever swear eternal enmity to sin, cultivating all the graces of the Spirit, perfecting holiness in the fear of God, for only so can we have any reasonable hope of finding our place at last in the inheritance of the saints in light.

HOMILIES BY VARIOUS AUTHORS.

Vers. 1—4.—*The new heavens and earth.* The retribution of God has fallen on the enemies of Christ and his Church. Death and hell, Satan, the beast, and the false prophet, have been cast into the lake of fire. The thunders of God's vengeance are hushed; the manifestations of his love to his redeemed now only remain to be told. And here their ultimate and eternal blessedness is shown to us. Their abode and condition are described as "new heavens and a new earth." Let us inquire—

I. WHEREFORE ARE THEY CALLED "NEW"? The heaven, the earth, the holy city, are each called "new." Now, this may be because, in part, they are: 1. *Physically new.* We do not think this earth will be "burnt up," nor the elements "melt with fervent heat," nor that there shall be, literally, "a new heaven and a new earth;" all such representations we regard as metaphorical, and as telling only of great moral and spiritual changes that shall take place. But in so far as this earth has been marred and defiled, injured and degraded, by man's sin—as it has been—in that respect and degree will it be made new. The thorns and briars, the poisonous and hurtful herbs, and all else that is significant, and the result of sin, will disappear; the pestilence will no longer walk in darkness, nor destruction waste at noonday. So far will it be new. There will be: 2. *A new manner of dealing with us on the part of God.* This may be intended by the expression on which we are commenting. For "heaven and earth" is an expression used in Scripture to denote the dispensations of God. "Thus saith the Lord of hosts; Yet once, it is a little while, and I will shake the heavens and the earth" (Hag. ii. 6). The prophet is telling of the whole Jewish economy, which was to disappear and to give place to another and better. So it had been in the past; the patriarchal gave way to the Mosaic, and that was to give way to the Christian; and that, in its turn, will give way to the new heavens and new earth—a new order of things between God and man. 3. *And, assuredly, it will seem new.* For "no truth is more clear than this, that the world is to a man according to the state of his mind." To the voluptuary, it is a scene of animal gratification; to the worldling, it is a scene for barter; to the poet, it is beauty; to the philosopher, it is science; to the saint, it is a temple. Change a sinner's mind, and you change the world to him. He feels, and sometimes says, "The world is a new thing to me"—"a new heaven and a new earth." And may we not, therefore, be sure that, to the new, regenerated, and perfect nature, all things will wear another aspect, the heaven and the earth will be as new?

II. WHEREIN WILL THE NEWNESS APPEAR? There will be, according to these verses: 1. *A newness of absence.* Much that we have known here we shall not know there, for they will no longer be. See the things of which it is here said they shall be no more. (1) *The sea.* It is the emblem of all unrest. Here there is, indeed, much of this, and its causes are manifold. But there, "no more sea." (2) *Death.* (Ver. 4.) Here it may be said, "death reigns." His might, past, present, or near at hand, is scarce ever unfelt. What a change, for there to be "no more death"! (3) *Pain.* "Neither sorrow nor crying." That will indeed be a new world where these are not. Here, where are they not? (4) *Night.* Twice is it told "there is no night there" (ver. 25 and ch. xxii. 5). As to the meaning of this, cf. homily on ver. 25. (5) *Sin.* (Ver. 27.) Here sin rushes as a raging river down our streets; but there, "there shall in no wise enter," etc. (6) *The curse.* (Ch. xxii. 3.) Here it is everywhere. On health and wealth, home and friends, business and pleasure; for there is no one of them that may not be a source of sore sorrow to us, and a very fountain of tears. Paradises are still turned into thorn-beds as of old. The curse does it. "I will curse your blessings." But there, no more. 2. *And there will be newness in what is present.* Take only these opening verses as proof. They assure us of: (1) *A new revelation of God.* The holy city, the new Jerusalem—the place where of old God revealed himself— "having the glory of God." (2) *A new revelation of the Church.* "As a bride adorned," etc. Fair and comely, rich and honoured, blessed because perfectly satisfied. Never has it been possible to describe the Church in such way before. (3) *A new realization of God.* In intimate fellowship; as a tent shall he shelter and enclose them, tabernacling over them. This abiding, "He shall dwell with them." As to the depth of his love to them, "They shall be his people, and he . . . their God."—S. C.

Ver. 1.—"*No more sea.*" We must remember that, to the ancient Jews, the sea was an object of almost unmixed terror. Nearly all the allusions to it in the Bible tell of its destructive power and of its peril. The Jews were never a seafaring people. They dreaded the sea. An added element of terror is given to the solemn warning addressed to them (Deut. xxviii. 68), when it is said, in case of their sin, that not only should they be taken back to Egypt to their old bondage, but that they should go there in "ships." They had no seaport worth mentioning. Their histories of the sea were all associated with its terribleness: the Deluge; the Exodus; Jonah. The epithets they apply to the sea are none of them of a pleasing character, but all more or less forbidding and fearful. They tell of its being "troubled," of its "raging," "roaring," breaking ships, filling men with utter terror, making them "reel to and fro," "stagger like a drunken man," and be "at their wits' end" (Ps. cvii.). They noticed only its "noise," and they likened its waves to the wild, cruel, fierce "tumults of the people." It was "great and wide," vast and lonely. To be "far off upon the sea" was the summing up of all separateness and isolation. And besides what was the common feeling of the Jew, there was, in St. John's special circumstances, sufficient to account for the peculiar dislike of the sea which our text expresses. He was in exile, at Patmos, a lonely barren island, amid a proverbially tempestuous sea, and cut off by its waves from all he loved best. It is told how he was wont daily to ascend the hills, and wistfully look towards Ephesus and his own beloved land of Palestine. What wonder, then, that, in telling of the final, blessed, condition of the Church, in its new and eternal home, he should say, "And there was no more sea"? But we *need not take his words literally.* The surrounding Scriptures do not require it. How much of manifest metaphor there is in this chapter! Moreover, such expressions as "the sea," "heaven," "earth," "sun," etc., are figures for great moral and spiritual facts, and their being removed or changed tell only of what shall be done in regard to these facts of which they are the figures (cf. St. Peter's quotation, on the Day of Pentecost, of the prophecy of Joel as to the "sun" being "darkened," and the "moon turned into blood,"— all which, he said, was fulfilled then). But, literally, this did not happen; only great moral changes typified by them. And so here, "the new heavens and the new earth" refer, not to literal facts, to the physical geography of the future world, but to a blessed new order of things in the moral and spiritual world. For this earth is to continue. How else shall the meek inherit it, and shall God dwell here with men? And the sea likewise, though it be typical of moral conditions which shall then cease to be. Moreover, in reality, though not in Jewish conception, *the sea is one of God's most blessed gifts to man.* Life would be impossible without it. It has been justly called "the life-blood of the land," as the blood is the life of the body. "It is the vital fluid that animates our earth; and, should it disappear altogether, our fair green planet would become a heap of brown, volcanic rocks and deserts, lifeless and worthless as the slag cast out from a furnace." We remember, too, how God said of the sea that it was "very good;" and no mistaken Jewish ideas must be allowed to reverse that verdict. Think of: 1. *Its vapours.* The corn-harvest is really the harvest of the sea. For the sea yields up her strength in the form of vapour. These create the clouds, which, touched and tinged by the sun, are so exquisite in their loveliness. And these discharge themselves upon the earth in varied form, and so come the rivers which water the earth and make it bring forth abundantly. 2. *Its currents,* bearing along the sun-heated waters of sub-tropical climes, far away northward and southward, and giving to regions like our own that mildness of climate which we enjoy; whereas, but for the warm waters of the sea, our shores would be bleak, inhospitable, barren, all but uninhabitable, like the shores of Labrador. 3. *Its breezes,* so health-giving, imparting fresh life to the feeble and the sick. 4. *Its beauty,* ever presenting some fresh form of loveliness in colour, movement, outline, sound, fragrance. Oh, how beautiful is the bright, bounding sea! 5. *Its tides,* sweeping up the mouths of our great rivers and estuaries, and all along our shores, washing clean what else would be foul, stagnant, poisonous. 6. *Its saltness,* ministering to the life of its inhabitants; by its weight aiding in the transmission of those warm currents of which we have spoken ; preventing corruption; and much more. But what we have said is sufficient to show that the sea is indeed a gift of God, "very good" and precious; and therefore, as the future shall preserve all that is good, we believe, notwithstanding our text, that there shall be still the blessed, beautiful sea. But we are glad and grateful to know that those facts, of which to the Jewish mind it was the emblem, will not be hereafter. Of those facts were—

I. Unrest. The sea tells of that. Cf. "The wicked are like the troubled sea, when it cannot rest" (Isa. lvii. 20). "There is sorrow on the sea; it cannot be quiet" (Jer. xlix. 23).

> "Thou troubled sea,
> Oh, troubled, fretful sea!
> What can the causes be
> That thy soft, silvery breast
> So rarely is at rest?
>
> "E'en when there wind is none,
> And thou art let alone,
> Thy heart, self-troubled, will
> Keep palpitating still.
>
> "Ah, well may thy unrest
> Emblem the human breast;
> Yea, the great world around,
> Where troubles so abound!"

Yes; such is our life now. "Man is born to trouble;" and were it not that there is One who is able to hush the waves and say, "Peace, be still!" our hearts would know no rest. But yonder we shall rest. *Quies in cœlo.*

> "There shall I bathe my weary soul
> In seas of heavenly rest,
> And not a wave of trouble roll
> Across my peaceful breast."

II. Painful mystery. So was the sea to the Jew, though it be not so to us. Scripture so speaks of it. "Thy way, O Lord, is in the sea;" "Thy judgments are a great deep;" "Thy path is in the great waters, and thy footsteps are not known." The "depths of the sea" tell of that which can never be discovered; hidden from all knowledge. Now, that there is much of such mystery here, we all know. It is part of our trial and discipline, designed to educate us in the blessed lessons of trust in God. So that, in view and in spite of such mysteries, we may be able to say, "I will trust, and not be afraid." But yonder we shall know even as we are known. Here "we see as through a glass, darkly; but then face to face." Therefore let us "rest in the Lord, and wait," etc.

III. Separation. The sea of old was a complete barrier to intercourse. It was to St. John, and, even now, it so separates that many shrink from emigration to lands where life would be far brighter for them. But of old, to be "far off upon the sea," to "dwell in the uttermost parts of the sea," was indeed to be cut off almost from the land of the living. Only God could make his "way in the sea, and his path in great waters." It was possible only to Christ to walk upon the sea that he might go and succour his disciples. But to men the sea was an impassable barrier, a separating wall. Therefore a fit emblem of separation. How many such barriers there are to our intercourse with Christ and with our fellow-men! The power of this present world, the things seen and temporal, this body of flesh,—these, and yet others, separate between us and our Lord. And between man and man. Distance, time, diversity of language, habits of thought, position in life, uncongeniality, ignorance, and many more. But in Christ and with Christ we all shall be one. Drawn to him, we shall be drawn to one another also; and as nothing shall separate us from him, so nothing shall separate us from each other. "There shall be no more sea."

IV. Rebellion against God. "The noise of their waves, the tumult of the people"

(Ps. lxv.). **The one stands for the other.** The same thought lies in the words in Ps. xciii., "The floods have lifted up, O Lord, the floods have lifted up their voice; the floods lift up their waves. The Lord on high is mightier than the noise of many waters, yea, than the mighty waves of the sea." The rebellious heart of man, therefore, is that which under this imagery is set forth. And here in this Book of Revelation: "The waters . . . are peoples," etc. (ch. xvii. 15). The multitude of the ungodly and rebellious—these are likened to the sea. Now, in this sense, there shall be no more sea. No more ungodly people, no more rebellious hearts. And my heart, O my God, shall, then and there, rebel no more.—S. C.

Ver. 4.—"*Neither shall there be any more pain:*" *a Hospital Sunday sermon.* If the wards of our hospitals could declare what words of Holy Scripture, what gracious promises out of God's book, are, more often than almost any other, spoken, read, or thought of, and most beloved, by the suffering inmates of those wards, it would be found that they are such as our text. For pain is indeed a terrible thing. No language can adequately describe what it is when, in its intenser forms, it fastens upon us. Even from great saints of God it has wrung words which have shown that the burden of it was almost greater than they could bear. The holy Job, under the stress of it, could scarce resist the temptation to "curse the day wherein he was born," and in his anguish he declared, "My soul chooseth strangling and death rather than life." "Why am I thus afflicted more than others?" he passionately asks. "Why hast thou set me as a mark for thy arrows? why dost thou not let loose thy hand and cut me off from the earth?" And not such utterances as these only attest the severity and strain which pain puts upon the soul, but, also, the glad thanksgivings which rise up to God when deliverance from such pain has been given. Take Ps. cxvi., for example. And though many of you may scarce know what real pain is, never having experienced it or anything like it, yet you are able, we trust, both to feel very grateful for your happy exemption hitherto, and also to sympathize, deeply and tenderly, with those to whom a harder lot is assigned. You have had some vision of the anguished face, and of the deadly chill and faint, that are associated with extreme pain; and your heart has been touched, as it well may, with compassion. Therefore, though you know not pain by experience yet, along with those who do, you also can rejoice in this promise, as to an eternal home, that there "there shall be no more pain." And meanwhile let us gratefully remember *how much our Lord Jesus Christ has done to turn this curse of pain into a blessing.* It will not make us less ready to sympathize with or succour those who now are suffering, but will qualify us to do both better than before. For—

I. CHRIST HAS DONE THIS. First of all: 1. *By taking it upon himself.* "He himself bare our infirmities, and carried our diseases." So was it predicted concerning him; and when he came here he fulfilled Isaiah's word by the intensity of his holy sympathy, whereby the sorrows, pains, and distresses of those whom he healed were felt by him as if they were his own. And yet more, by himself submitting to pain so terrible that he could say to all suffering ones in all ages, "Come, see if there ever was sorrow like unto my sorrow." Then he took the lot of pain upon himself. He has entered into it not only by Divinest sympathy but by actual experience. So that now the sufferers tread no solitary path; One is with them in the roughest, sternest of its ways, and that One is "like unto the Son of man." They may have the fellowship of his sufferings, because he certainly has the fellowship of theirs. Have we not seen or heard oftentimes how, in the paroxysms of agony with which poor pain-stricken ones are now and again seized, they love, when the dread dark hour comes upon them, to have by them some one dear to them, the dearest they possess, and to clasp his or her hand and to feel the clasp of theirs; to pour out to them their cries and tears, and to be soothed and strengthened by the loving sympathy on which they lean? Maybe some of us have taken part in scenes like that. But such blessed aid, and more than that, our Lord wills that every sufferer should have by reason of his sympathy, his presence, and his own dear love. The present writer well remembers how a poor young girl, dying in much pain, told him that she loved to look at a picture, which hung by her bedside, of the Saviour bearing his cross; for, she said, "it helps me to bear my pain better." Yes, every sufferer may grasp his hand, and be assured that, though unseen and unfelt by the bodily senses, he grasps theirs. For just as he went down amongst the "multitude of impotent folk" that lay in the porches of Bethesda, so still he comes down amongst our poor suffering humanity, himself a "Man of sorrows, and acquainted with grief." And now the Marah-like waters—the bitter wells of human life—he has for ever made sweet and wholesome by the healing influence of that cross—that tree so accursed for him, so precious for us—upon which, for us all, he suffered and died. Yes, as it has been beautifully said, "he has done all this. It was for this that he came—for this, among many other reasons. His was pre-eminently, as we know, a painful life. He was acquainted with grief, and a Man of sorrows; and this acquaintanceship was sought and formed for our sakes, because no man knew what to do with grief. Our Lord came hither, and, being made man, entered upon a brief pilgrimage in the earth—brief, yet sufficient to find out what was here, and what had need to be done. And scarcely had he commenced his journey before he met with that ancient form of Grief. She had been walking up and down the earth for thousands of years. She first appeared in the garden of Eden. She stood forth from behind the fatal tree, and emerged from those bounds which, before the first offence, she had never dared to cross; and ever since she had been going about and haunting men. When Christ began his pilgrimage, he met her and she met him, and they looked one another in the face; and she never left him. 'He was acquainted with grief.' And through this acquaintance-ship it would seem, as happens when a lower nature feels the influence of a higher, that she became changed. She had been hard and cold, she became tender and gentle; she had been tyrannical and imperious, but under the influence of that Divine Companion she lost her old harshness and severity, and seemed to do her work with a half-reluctance, and without the old readiness to add torment to the unhappy. We cannot tell how it happened, but Grief, through her acquaintance and familiarity with the Son of man, became like a new creature. In her were seen a certain softness and pensiveness which she never had before; her form became altered and her footsteps light; until she seemed to take the air of a sister of mercy, and to breathe forth a wondrous benediction while she walked with him. Doubtless it was his influence that worked the change. It was he who turned that scourge of small cords, which she had carried from time immemorial, into a cross, and gave to her eyes that tender look which seems to say, 'I do not willingly afflict nor grieve you, O children of men.' Thus they went through the world hand-in-hand, until he went out of it by the gate of the grave, tasting death for every man. And Grief has been acting ever since as one of his ministers, and representing him, and doing the work of mercy in his kingdom. She has given to men in these latter days more than she ever took away. She is a dispenser, not a spoiler; her hands are full of goodly gifts, and though her discipline be painful, yet it is ever merciful; and, as a gentle almoner, she offers and bestows, wherever faith and love dispose the heart to receive them, new and perfect pledges of eternal blessing and glory." Thus has Christ transformed Grief and Pain, who is one of her chief ministers. Pain is still like the rough ore dug out of the heart of the earth; but it need no longer be used, as it so long has been, to forge harsh chains of bondage, but it may, it shall be, if only we be willing, fashioned into crowns of glory, yea, diadems for the blessed themselves. And: 2. *By his acceptance of our pain as an offering we may present to him.* We often feel and say that all *we do* may and should be consecrated to him, and, without doubt, he accepts it. But this is not all that he is willing to accept. All that we have *to bear* he will also, and as willingly, accept. Was not his own offering unto God one in which he suffered? His submission rather than his activity constituted the very essence of his sacrifice. Not alone were the gold—symbol of all man's wealth—and the frankincense—symbol of worship—presented to him; but the myrrh—symbol of suffering, of sorrow, of pain, of death. For it was used in the embalming of the dead and for ministering relief to sufferers in their agony, and hence it was offered to our Lord upon the cross. And so, from its constant association with scenes of sadness and distress, it came to represent and symbolize all pain. And this was offered to the Lord, and may be and should be still. In our moments of most terrible pain there is nothing better to do than to offer it all to him, for his glory, and so to lay it at the feet of the King of sorrows. 3. *And by the revelations he makes to us concerning it.* (1) He has told us whence it came. Hence we know that it is not an inherent, a constituent, part of our nature, as joy is; but it is a stranger, a foreigner, an alien, and an intruder. It came in with sin and shall go out therewith. (2) That it is rendering high and holy service. Cf. St. Paul, "Our light affliction which is," etc. (2 Cor. iv. 17). "In these verses it is not merely asserted that one day we shall be rid of pain, but also that meanwhile it is working out for us 'glory.' It not merely precedes, but produces, is the mother, the progenitor, of glory." Does the mariner grieve over the rushing wind which fills his sails, and bears him swiftly on to the haven where he would be? No more should we over pain, since it is our helper forward, homeward, heavenward. (3) That it will one day certainly and for ever cease.

II. CHRIST ALONE DOES THIS. "Human wisdom has from the first been helpless before what may be called the problem of pain. It has no explanation of suffering; it cannot give it a satisfactory position in the scheme of life. To philosophy sorrow is an anomaly and an offence. Philosophy hath builded her house, she hath hewn out her seven pillars, and she hath acquainted her heart with all wisdom; and yet there is a skeleton in her house, a spectre glides through her pillars, and a presage of hollow, final failure is in every effort to keep up appearances. She cannot contrive what to do with that problem of sorrow, suffering, and pain. She has but two things to which to trust, and she can trust in neither. The first is stoicism, the second anodynes. With stoicism she tries to meet the question on the spiritual side; with anodynes, on the physical. In each direction she encounters defeat. She tells the sufferer to harden his heart and set his teeth, and bear it if he can, not in faith and love, not in hope and trust, but in stern, stiff defiance. And when she finds it useless to try and help him that way, and hears his shrieks repeated, and meets his reproachful and despairing eyes, she has but one expedient more, in the anodyne and anæsthetic. She exhibits the drug or the subtle vapour, and thereby stills the pain. In this she admits defeat, and flies before the foe. She has relieved the body indeed, but it is at the expense of the spirit. The sense of pain is gone, but the light of the soul is also extinguished. The dying flesh feels no more its own agony because the heaven-born flame of reason is quenched, and the man is drugged and crazed into stupefaction and unconsciousness. Thus does Philosophy deal with the terrible problem of this painful life. She has no spiritual medicine for it; while physical remedies amount at last to the suspension and temporary destruction of conscious existence." But we have seen our Lord's more excellent way—a way so blessed that it is an insult to compare the one with the other. Glory be to his Name for ever for that which he hath done!

III. WHAT WE ARE TO DO. See to it: 1. That when suffering comes on you, you have Christ near you to turn your pain into blessing. Come to him now, that he may come to you then. 2. Think of, sympathize with, pray for and succour those who now are suffering. Ask him to be near them, and go you near them yourselves with loving help. So join with him in his merciful work, and there shall come on you the blessing, "Inasmuch as ye have done it unto my brethren, ye have done it unto me."—S. C.

Ver. 5.—"*All things new:*" *a spring sermon.* What a vivid and glorious illustration of these words we witness in the beautiful spring-tide season! For in the natural world God is, indeed, making all things new. The bare brown stretches of land have become verdant with the springing corn; the skeleton-like branches of the trees, which a few weeks ago tossed their gaunt arms and moaned sadly beneath the pitiless tempest and cold, are now covered with rich foliage, and many are bright with beautiful blossoms, lovely for the eye to look upon. The glades of the wood and the hedgerows which were mute but a while ago, because their feathered songsters were away in warmer climes, are now once more resonant with song; for "the winter is over and gone, and the time of the singing of birds is come." The aspect of universal nature is completely changed—transfigured and transformed from that which it wore in the weary wintry time. God has made "all things new." We never could have believed it possible had we been less familiar with many a previous spring. Were we able to think of ourselves as utterly ignorant of the resurrection and regeneration of spring, did we know nothing of what God is wont to do in this season of the year, we could never have believed such a change possible. As we looked upon all the rich beauty of the earth, we should be ever asking, "Who are these, and whence came they?" We could never have imagined that those bare seeds, which were cast into the ground, would have become the blade and the springing corn as we now see them. We should gaze with admiration, but with wonder, at the glorious garment of forest and of field. Apart from our knowledge, all this new creation which the returning spring presents would have been as incredible to us as the resurrection of the dead was to the Athenians. And that which, but for long experience, we could not have believed of the natural world, we, for want of such experience, are slow to believe in regard to the spiritual world, to which the words of our text do, of course, refer. We read of the new heavens and the new earth, of the freedom from the manifold evils and distresses with which we are so sadly familiar here; but because we know not these things by experience they are not real to us, they do not affect us as they would were we as sure of them as we are of the new creation of spring. For here and now, in this poor present life of ours, we are for the most part in a spiritual winter. "It doth not yet appear what we shall be," any more than it appears in the winter-time, to the uninstructed eye, what the earth shall be. Life, looked at in the mass, is so sombre, so drear, so cheerless and cold, notwithstanding a bright gleam here and there, irradiating now this home circle and now that; yet for the most part life is one long winter, and its spring-time is not yet. And hence all discourse about the other and better life has, more or less, the semblance of unreality and vagueness about it. We smile sadly as we hear or read what men have thought on the subject, and we say, "How does he know? It is but a perhaps; we cannot really know." The best we can say is, "It may be, and we hope it is so." And none realize so clearly, or grasp so firmly, as they should, the promise of the blessed future spiritual spring which is affirmed in our text. But may we not do something to reanimate and strengthen our faith? May we not listen to the Lord God saying to us in this spring-tide, "Behold, I do make all things new; believe, O my children, that even yet, in far fuller and more glorious way, I will, as I have said in my Word, again and perfectly make all things new"? And let us answer back, "Lord, we believe; help thou our unbelief. Lord, increase our faith." Now, help may come to us through letting our thoughts dwell a while on some of the characteristics of the new creation told of here.

I. OUR CONCEPTIONS OF GOD WILL BE NEW. Frequently does our Lord speak in this book of his "new name"—"a name which no man knoweth saving he that receiveth it." And from this we gather that none of us here, not even the saintliest and most devout, knows God as he is to be known.

II. AND THERE SHALL BE A NEW BODY. In that great Scripture, 1 Cor. xv., St. Paul enlarges on this theme—the spiritual body, the corruptible exchanged for the incorruptible. And if any doubt, he points them to the new body which God is ever fashioning out of the "bare grain, it may chance of wheat, or of some other grain." In the blade, the ear, the full corn in the ear, he bids us behold the pattern, type, and analogy of our resurrection-life.

III. AND A NEW CHARACTER. The impartation of new moral dispositions and habits; or, if not new, so intensified and exalted in their force as to be practically new —in degree, if not in kind.

IV. AND A NEW SOCIAL CONDITION. Probably nothing will be more marked in the kingdom of God than the total reversals of the judgments of the world. That which the world highly esteems will be as naught, that which it despises honoured (cf. Luke xvi. 15).

V. AND THERE WILL BE A NEW DWELLING-PLACE. Not literally do we understand the words about the new heavens and new earth; for there is no need that we should, and much reason why we should not. But we take them as telling of the great moral changes that shall take place, and the physical changes that will result therefrom. For during all the past man's material habitation has been largely dependent upon, and the result of, his moral character. Ps. cvii., "The fruitful field becomes a wilderness because of the wickedness," etc. And then again, "He turneth the wilderness into a standing water, and the dry grounds into water-springs." So is it for the righteous. So many are the aids to the faith, that, given a new moral character, there will be a new dwelling-place. Look at Palestine, the Holy Land. Once her fields flowed with milk and honey; but now, and for long centuries, through the cursed misrule of Mohammedanism, vast regions of that land are but desert. Again, go over the Campagna of Rome, once thronged with human life and wealth, but now for the most part a deadly plain in which men cannot live. And, on the other hand, where men have obeyed the laws of God, there the reverse has been everywhere seen. In the great missionary ages of the Church companies of God-fearing men would go to some desolate district, often wild, bare, and miserable in the extreme. In the heart of forests, in the midst of fens, on rugged cliffs, or in lonely islands; and there they would alternate their prayers and psalms, their sacraments and other sacred services, with hard labour and diligent toil, until they had made the wilderness to rejoice and blossom as the rose. And now, rabid Protestantism sneers at those old monks because, it is said, they always knew how to choose the best and fairest of earth's dwelling-places. But it was their fear of God that led to the regeneration of the earth on which they dwelt. And when Ps. lxvii. is fulfilled, and "all the people praise thee, O God; then shall the earth yield her increase; God shall bless us, and all the ends of the world shall fear him." Now, of all this, and much more this blessed spring-tide tells to those who have ears to hear its prophecies. But, remember, *spring-tide can do nothing for things that are dead*. Have we, then, the seed of the life of God within us? "I am come," said the Lord, "that they might have life, and that they might have it more abundantly."—S. C.

Ver. 6.—*The free salvation.* "I will give . . . freely." "What! free?" says one, "When I have to watch and pray, to struggle and strive, if I am to obtain the crown of life? How can it be free when I have thus to strain every energy in order to make it mine?" But, the very fact that you do thus strive shows that you have already drunk of this water of life. It is the energy of that grace working in you. If you had never drunk at all you would not be thus "striving against sin." It is from life, because of it, that you are thus aroused. If you were dead you would make no effort at all. So that the conflict you endure is no proof against the freeness of the water of life, but rather for it. And the conflict would not be so severe if you obeyed the laws of the conflict. If you come to it but partly equipped, no wonder you are at a disadvantage. Matthew Henry says, "If a beast have to draw a load, a yoke will help him." But if the yoke be only half on, he will find the work much harder. And so with us. Christ says, 'Take my yoke upon you, and learn of me.' But if we will only half wear his yoke, if we are seeking to compromise with the world, no wonder that our Christian life is hard." Still, that we struggle at all proves that Christ's grace has been given, and is not withdrawn. Now, our text says that this grace which bringeth salvation, and which is here called "the water of life," is *freely given*. Now note—

I. MEN ARE SLOW TO BELIEVE THIS. Of course, those who are not "athirst" don't think anything at all about the matter. They don't care for salvation, and, therefore, the conditions of its bestowal are no concern to them. But there are those—many, thank God—who "thirst," but who are slow to believe in this "freeness" of the gift of the water of life. Now, why is this? Perhaps it is: 1. *They cannot feel that God is good.* They know he has a right to be "hard" with them, and they think he is so. Earthly fathers would be hard with children who have behaved as they have done, and so it is concluded the heavenly Father will be likewise. They are slow to forgive: will not he be? 2. *Their pride.* They would like to bring something in return—character, conduct, gifts, prayers. 3. *The laws of their common life tell against this belief.* Nothing for nothing is the law of life. In the sweat of their brow they must eat bread. They must pay the price for whatsoever they want. And they think so is it with this blessing that they desire. 4. *The mass of mankind everywhere and always have disbelieved.* Certainly there is no religion, and never has been anywhere, whose terms are like those in the text. And the mass of those who profess this one explain these terms away. The opinion of mankind is, and ever has been, against this freeness. Such are some of the reasons why many who "thirst" are yet slow to believe.

II. BUT YET THERE IS GREAT REASON WHY THEY SHOULD BELIEVE. All God's best and greatest gifts are free. 1. *Life itself.* We certainly paid nothing for that, but is it not precious to us? How we struggle to preserve, adorn, and prolong it! 2. *And all the essentials of life.* The air we breathe, the water we drink, the light and warmth of the sun, the land which produces our food,—these were all freely given, though, indeed, man, in his selfishness, has hindered that freeness so far as he can, and, doubtless, would far more were it but in his power. 3. *And all that makes life blessed.* The mind, with all its powers; the affections, which are the solace and sweeteners of life; the sense and love of the beautiful, in art, in nature; conscience, the guide of life;—all these are given freely, and they are God's best earthly gifts, and are free. Therefore this gift—the " water of life," which is more precious than all—may well be free likewise. Furthermore: 4. *It is the Lord who giveth.* Shall he descend to bargain with man, to let man transact with him his salvation? For him there can be but one relationship in which he stands to us in this matter. He must, because he is what he is, freely give. 5. *And the gift itself, how could it be purchased?* If it were but of slender worth man might, perhaps, find a price; but being what it is, what can purchase it? 6. *And we being what we are,* altogether without righteousness, merit, or claim, whence have we that which we could bring as compensation for this gift? Therefore, if there be that which may make us question the freeness of this gift, there is far more to make us believe therein.

III. AND HOW BLESSED THE BELIEF! For: 1. *There are none to whom we may not go with the gospel message.* Were there limitations, terms, and conditions, we could not invite all. 2. *It kills the power of sin.* To grieve One who has shown such mercy and grace is felt to be impossible. What he hates we must hate, and what he loves we must love. 3. *It inspires us with holy purpose.* It is a continual spur to all Christian endeavour. It is ever prompting the question, " Lord, what wilt thou have me to do?" 4. *It imparts a blessed satisfaction.* "He that drinketh of the water that I shall give him," said our Lord, "shall never thirst." He will thirst for more of that water, but never for aught beside. 5. *It fosters humility,* and frowns upon and forbids all pride. " Where is boasting? It is excluded." So said St. Paul, and reason and experience prove his saying true.

IV. BUT THE QUESTION IS—DO WE BELIEVE? Believing, according to a good theological, if not etymological, definition, is what a man " lives by." Therefore a mere mental assent is not believing. But if we believe, if we live by this faith, then we shall be joyful, holy, strong, beneficent. These will be the natural outcome of a life sustained by this belief. What shall a man say if at the last he be found unsaved when he might have freely partaken of this living water had he chosen so to do? Let us go at once and take thereof. If never before, then now; if before, then again and yet again.—S. C.

Ver. 7.—*The predominant practical purpose of the Apocalypse.* " He that overcometh," etc. At the beginning of this book—in the epistles to the seven Churches— we had this repeated promise, " to him that overcometh." And its reiteration there as well as here alike proves that the purpose of this book was an intensely practical one. It was not given to furnish food for mere mental or sentimental musings, or to be only a treasure-house of poetical imagery. Far other and higher than these were the ends contemplated. Think of some of them.

I. THAT ONE HERE NAMED—to encourage the persecuted, much-tried Church, into whose hands the book first came, to continue patient, to increase courage, to endure still the trials of their lot. For this were all its awful warnings, its vivid pictures of judgment, its entrancingly beautiful promises—so exceedingly great and precious. They all aimed to deepen in the mind of each member of the Church the conviction of Rom. viii. 18, " I reckon that the sufferings of this present time are not worthy," etc.; and to convince of the truth of the Lord's words (Matt. xix. 29), " Every one that hath forsaken," etc. Such was the primary purpose of the book. But there are others.

II. To VINDICATE THE CHARACTER OF GOD. It has ever been the trial of the thoughtful in all ages how the present condition of the world could be consistent with the conviction of the character of God as holy, just, and good. This Apocalypse of the end and issue of all things does not a little to reassure and re-establish the tottering faith. When we know we are being conducted to a glorious and beautiful city where we would fain be, we do not heed overmuch the discomforts of the way.

III. To ENNOBLE LIFE. It does this: 1. *By revealing a noble destiny.* The elevating power of such a revelation cannot but be, for it always is, great. 2. *By inspiring scorn for what is inconsistent therewith.* **3.** *By uplifting our desires and aims.*

IV. To IMPART PATIENCE IN SUFFERING. If I believe in the issue of suffering, and know the good it is to " work out," must not this minister patience ?

V. To MAKE US "ALWAYS ABOUNDING IN THE WORK OF THE LORD," because here we have shown to us "that our labour is not in vain in the Lord." No faithful effort is thrown away, or can be.

VI. To FURNISH US WITH A GOSPEL FOR THE POOR. Because, when here we have done what we can for those who need our help, ministering to them to the best of our power, if we have nothing else to say to them, our all is but little. But this Apocalypse gives us much else—much indeed.

VII. To MEET AND MINISTER TO THE NATURAL DESIRE FOR BLESSEDNESS. Man is made to be blessed. His constitution demonstrates that, and his incessant desire for happiness is that which lends greatest force to the lies of the world, the flesh, and the devil. Now, in such revelation of the future of God's redeemed as these chapters give, there is the response to that hunger of the soul which others falsely promise, but which this alone can give.

VIII. To MAKE THE LORD JESUS CHRIST PRECIOUS TO US. For he it is who, having " overcome the sharpness of death," has opened " the kingdom of heaven to all believers." We owe it all to him, and by him alone can we keep in that "patient continuance in well-doing," which by his grace lands us at last on that blessed shore. Such are some of the ends contemplated by this book. Are they being fulfilled in us ?—S. C.

Ver. 9—ch. xxii. 5.—*The holy Jerusalem.* Not "the heavenly Jerusalem," the "Jerusalem that is above," of which we read in Heb. xii. 22 ; xi. 10, 16 ; xiii. 14; Gal. iv. 26—the heavenly community of the righteous. Nor the Jerusalem here below, in the present life—the Church in her militant state. But the New Jerusalem on the glorified earth, with the introduction of which the others vanish. Now, in the ample and beautiful description of that which as yet is not, we have not merely what may well uplift and make glad our hearts by way of holy anticipation, but also we have portrayed, in beautiful symbol, the pattern of what the true Church of Christ, even now and here, should ever aspire to be. St. John was blessed with the beatific vision of "the holy Jerusalem ; " and to this end—as when we would well see a great mountain we need to be ourselves on a similar elevation—St. John was carried away to a great and high mountain ; as Moses on Mount Pisgah, that he might the better see the promised land. But whilst this Word of God tells of the chosen Church in her consummated and perfect condition before God, it is also a glorious picture, not merely to be looked at and longed for, but, to the uttermost of our power, to be embodied in our own Church-life here on earth. Bunyan, in his treatise on the New Jerusalem, has worked out this idea at length ; he holding that these chapters tell of not the final condition of mankind, the end of all things—for then there will be no longer heathen to be healed, and living yet outside the city—but of the perfected Church, perfectly redeemed and restored, and "without spot, or wrinkle, or any such thing." But what we have here is the description of *the true New Testament Church.* "As there were three states of Jerusalem, so there are of the Church. The first, for the city, was that under Solomon, and answers to the Church in the days of our Lord and his apostles ; the second was Jerusalem's degraded and captured state, and answers to the Church ever since the apostolic age ; the third, of which Nehemiah and Isaiah so largely tell, is her recovered state when the exiles returned and rebuilt their city and walls again." The foundation chapter is Isa. lx., which was written for the comfort of the captives in Babylon, as is this for the comfort of the Church of to-day. Rapidly reviewing this glorious promise for Christ's Church, we are told—

I. OF HER GLORY. (Vers. 11, 23.) This is named first in order, as it is first in importance. It means that the grace of God which is ever in his Church shall appear, be manifest, conspicuous. It is likened to the most precious of stones—not the jasper which we know, for that was never most precious nor otherwise such as is here described ; but probably the diamond, which does answer to what is here said. Now, this " glory " is the all-important thing (cf. Isa. lx. 19). In the ideal Church, which comes down from God and is according to his mind, *its gracious character*, **the** Christ within her, will be the all-conspicuous thing.

II. HER SECURITY. (Vers. 12—14; cf. Isa. liv. 14.) The Church is likened to a city for its strength. Isa. xxvi. 1, "We have a strong city," etc. The perfect Church shall be impregnable. "No weapon formed against her shall prosper." The Church of to-day is exposed to all manner of attack, and here and there succumbs. But it is because she lacks this wall. The holy city has many gates, but all are angel-guarded. There is freedom of entrance for those who should enter, but none for those who should not. The angel-guards keep watch and ward. Believers—the seed of believing Abraham, the true Israel of God—these, whose names are written on the gates, have right of entrance. But they shall come from no one nation. On either side are three gates. They may, they will, come from every quarter of the earth (cf. Luke xiii. 29). And this Church is the "city which hath foundations" (Heb. xi. 10), and it is "built upon the foundation of the apostles and prophets" (ver. 14). The blessed doctrine which they taught will be the basis of the Church's security—the Christ they preached, the gospel they proclaimed (Eph. ii. 20; Matt. xix. 28).

III. HER FAULTLESSNESS. As in ch. xi. 1 the measuring meant inspection and test, so here (vers. 15—17). This city will bear Divine scrutiny; in regard to her people, "the city;" her conditions of entrance, "the gates;" her confident security, "the wall." The whole corresponds to the Divine ideal. What contrast to the Church of to-day! And this city is built in perfect symmetry. The square was regarded as the symbol of completeness and all-perfect proportion (cf. Eph. iii. 4, "comprehend . . . the breadth, and length, and depth, and height," by which St. Paul meant the symmetry and fair proportion of the Christian Church and character). And not perfect only in proportion, but *vast in extent*. "In my Father's house are many mansions." The heart of Christ shall "be satisfied," not alone with the beautiful form of his Church, but with its greatness. Such seems to be the meaning of the fifteen hundred miles square which is said to be the measurement of this city. There never was or could be a literal city so vast. It surpasses all human conception—as shall the reality, the Church. The height of it is named only to intensify the ideas of proportion and extent. The wall, compared with the height of the city, is but low. Sufficient for security, but not for obscurity. It would not hide the magnificence of the city as it stood on the sides of the vast eminence on which it was built, but yet the wall would well defend it. "Beautiful for situation, the joy of the whole earth," etc. (Ps. xlviii.). Translated out of metaphor, the meaning is that the Church which fulfils the Divine ideal will commend itself by its moral and spiritual symmetry, its correspondence to the plan of the great Architect—its "Maker and Builder," God.

IV. ITS ADORNMENTS. (Vers. 18—21.) The symbolism of these verses is taken from Isa. liv. 11, 12. The walls and city flashed with light, as the diamond, and like to burnished gold. So that the vision of it would attract, fix, and delight the mind of the beholder (cf. "Let your light so shine before men," etc.). If the jasper or diamond tell of Christ, he being the Corner-stone, elect, "precious," then the Church's glory (ver. 11), her defence (ver. 18), and her adornment (ver. 19), are alike Christ. And this is so. And the city is like pure gold, for all spiritual riches and treasure are in her. To bring her to this condition involved much refining work. But now no fire can harm her, for her dross is all gone. But *the foundations also* have their adornment. The apostles were adorned, as are all true ministers of Christ's Church, with the gifts and graces he bestows upon them—many, varied, and all precious; and with the converts to Christ whom they have won. "Ye are our glory and joy," said St. Paul to the Thessalonians (cf. Dan. xii. 3, Revised Version). These converts also are all "living stones," but all precious, though varied in every way in which human souls can be varied. The Church of Christ has her bride-like adornments (ver. 2), in the grace of spiritual character, the goodly gifts, and in the power to bless others, with which he endows her. Nor must we forget *the glory of her gates* (ver. 21). "I am the way," said our Lord. He is the Gate of entrance, and he is as a Pearl of great price. Bunyan notes that whilst we are told the measurements of the city and the wall, we are told nothing of the gates. And, he says, "it is because Christ, the Way, is beyond all measurement." And the "unsearchable riches" of his grace are also set forth by the figure of the gates of "one pearl." Who could compute the price of such a pearl? It will be the glory of the perfect Church that "one pearl," and that "the Pearl of great price," even Christ himself, is presented to every man at every entrance to the Church, so that none can come save by him. And even "the street" was of "pure gold." The street, the places of concourse, the ways in which the people of the city walk, are golden. That is, they are ways of holiness, godly ways, ways good and precious, ways of pleasantness and paths of peace. The spiritual glory, beauty, and riches of this way are what is meant, and what each heart knows to be true.

V. ITS MATURITY OF SPIRITUAL CHARACTER. As the ordinances of the tabernacle and temple gave way to the ordinances of Christ, so these ordinances will themselves give way to the worship "in spirit and in truth," which shall be the most perfect worship of all. "When that which is perfect is come, then that which is imperfect shall be done away" (1 Cor. xiii. 10). The temple was to the Jews the means of access to a revelation of, and a place of instruction concerning, God. But in Christ's very presence no medium is needed, for access is direct to God. And in a Church that aspires after this model there will be not a discarding and rejection of all ordinances and forms, but there will be a growing independence of them. Whilst prized and used, they will not be indispensable. Being what we are, we may be thankful that still the ordinances of religion—sacred seasons, sanctuaries, and services—are continued to us still. But there, in the holy Jerusalem, they will not be needed. And like as the shrine, the most holy place in the tabernacle and temple, was lit up with no earthly light, but with the Shechinah-cloud, the visible glory of God, so shall it be in the city of God. Translated, this means that in the perfect Church the glory of the grace of Christ in her shall render unnecessary all lesser glory, though in the eyes of men such glory should be as the sun and moon for greatness.

VI. HER ATTRACTIVENESS. Nations outside the city are clearly supposed. "Nations," not "nations of the saved," is the true reading (see Revised Version). The heathen are meant. Then will be the true missionary age. Then shall be fulfilled, as cannot be now, the promises of the universal spread of the knowledge of the Lord (cf. Isa. lx. 11). The heathen shall come and their kings, and they shall consecrate their all to Christ. And this shall continually be going on. For (ver. 27) the gates shall never be shut, but kept ever open for this blessed inflow of all to Christ. She is likened to a city, for cities are centres of influence, and affect for good or ill all around. Think of what London and like cities do in this way. And "the holy Jerusalem" shall thus influence and attract "the nations," who shall gladly walk in her "light." The blessing of God, the absence of which is the meaning of "night" in St. John's language, shall be ever present (cf. John xiii. 30, "And it was night"). Hence the blessed power of this city over the heathen around.

VII. HER HOLINESS. (Ver. 27.) Note this frequent form of expression. Denying one thing and asserting its extreme contrast. "There shall not enter any," etc., but there shall enter those in the book of life (cf. ch. iii. 5, "I will not blot out . . . but I will confess," etc.; ch. xx. 6, "the second death . . . but they shall be priests," etc.). The darkness of an evil condition is named to be denied, in order to serve as a foil to the glory of the blessed condition which is affirmed. And so it is here. The perfect holiness of the city is rendered more conspicuous by the denial of entrance to all abomination. Let us remember, therefore, "Without holiness no man shall see the Lord."

VIII. HER PROVISION AND BLESSEDNESS. (Ch. xxii. 1—5.) 1. As to the first, this consists of the river (ver. 1) and of the tree of life (ver. 2). The provision is plenteous, as is a river for they that would drink, and as are the trees bearing its twelve harvests year by year, and standing on either side the river. Accessible, also; for the river flows through the street of the city, and the trees are on either side. No flaming sword now bars access thereto, but it is in view and in reach of and for the enjoyment of all. By these symbols of the river and the tree are meant—as when we read (Isa. xxxiii. 16) of bread and water being sure—all necessary food. But as all here refers to spiritual things, we take our Lord's own interpretation, and read in the river the fulness of the Holy Spirit's blessing. Here we receive that blessing as a refreshing dew or as drops of rain, but there it shall flow forth as a river from the throne of God and the Lamb. For the Holy Ghost proceedeth from the Father and the Son; and when Christ spoke of tne water that he would give, St. John adds, "This spake he of the Spirit." And as to the tree of life, Jesus said, "I am the Way, the Truth, and *the Life;*" "I am the Resurrection and *the Life;*" and repeatedly, "I am the Bread of life." Himself, then, in his sustaining, strengthening grace; and the Holy Spirit in his sanctifying, refreshing, reviving power;—all this in abundance shall be the spiritual portion of the inhabitants of the holy city. And though none there ever have to say, "I am sick," yet there are those outside the city who are, and the leaves of this blessed tree are for their healing. So that it not only blesses those who eat of it, but makes them a blessing to others also. 2. And now, finally, *the exceeding blessedness* of the people of the holy Jerusalem, God's servants, is set forth in a series of striking statements. (1) "There shall be no more curse." Here, again, note the form of expression—naming the evil, whilst denying it, to set off more vividly the exceeding good which is affirmed. The "curse" is everywhere here—on man, and on the earth, his dwelling-place, alike. Death, the most awful form of the curse, "reigns." "But there," etc. (2) "The throne of God and the Lamb shall be in it." The will of God, his holy Law, his righteous authority, shall be confessed and rejoiced in. (3) "His servants shall serve him "—with ease, alacrity, delight, and effect. Not, as here, with a poor, maimed, marred service, and even that too often rendered reluctantly, or from impure motive. (4) "And they shall see his face." The joy of intimate fellowship shall be theirs. (5) "And his name ... foreheads." They shall be confessed before all, sealed and owned, manifested, as the sons of God. (6) "And there shall be no night." When the Lord was betrayed, St. John tells that "it was night." Here, in the city and scene of his triumph, he tells us repeatedly that "there is no night." The light of God's love shall never be lacking. (7) "And they shall reign for ever and ever." What sentences these are! how full, how inexhaustible in their meaning! "Reign "— so also our Lord said. Yes, the chosen Church shall be the aristocracy, the ruling class, exercising wise, holy, and beneficent rule over the masses of mankind in the kingdom of God. Such rule is ever the greatest blessing to men—their real need and right. Wise rule—that is what is wanted, and that shall be. It shall be no selfish blessedness which the elect of God shall enjoy, but one that shall flow forth in beneficence for which they will have both the will and the power.

> "Come, kingdom of our God,
> And raise thy glorious throne,
> In worlds by the undying trod,
> Where God shall bless his own."

S. C.

Ver. 23.—*The glory-light: a sermon for Midsummer Day.* "And the city had no need of the sun," etc. To-day is the longest day of the year—the day in which the light of the sun lasts longer than on any other day. It may be allowed, therefore, to suggest thoughts concerning that place and time when the sun shall no longer be needed, its light being superseded by the light of the glory of God. Now, it may be that our text is to be taken literally. What is here said is clearly not impossible, for there has been the resemblance of it already in the most holy place of the taber-nacle. But if the sun be really no longer needed, then we may believe that there will be—

I. BETTER MEANS THAN THE PRESENT OF REVEALING WHAT IS TO BE KNOWN. The sun is our revealer here. Its light is that which makes all things manifest. All light, artificial as well as natural, comes from one central sun. Either from the sun's direct rays, as in daylight, or from those rays stored up in primeval forest products, and now liberated again for our use. But when we see things in the light of God's glory, we shall see far more than we do now. Our judgments of what is seen will, after such vision, be changed not a little.

II. BETTER MEANS OF GROWTH. The sun is such a means. Harvests spring and ripen beneath its beams. And because "growth" will belong to the better world—for we cannot conceive of an everlasting halt and standstill—even more than to this, there must be means of growth. The sun here represents all such means, whether in things

REVELATION.

2 M

material, mental, or moral. But if these means are superseded, then the glory of God must be—and in things spiritual we can well understand this—a better means.

III. AND OF ADORNMENT. It is the sun which, touching, tinges with all loveliest hues even the dullest and dreariest things. Out of the dreary rain it calls forth the gorgeous " bow in the cloud," the seven-hued arch that spans the heavens, so unspeakably lovely that St. John makes it again and again the symbol of the glory that overarches the throne of God. But in the light of Christ and God, told of here, *we* shall become spiritually beautiful. Here we may see all manner of beauty, and remain foul at heart—

> " Where every prospect pleases,
> And only man is vile."

But that light likens those on whom it falls to him from whom it comes. What, then, is the adornment of the natural sun compared to that ?

IV. AND OF SERVICE. " Work . . . while it is day : the night cometh, when no man can work." So, and truly, spoke our Lord. Sunlight and strength alike fail us, though service needs to be rendered and work waits to be done. So is it here. But there the essentials of service will be present in degree and kind such as here we have not known.

CONCLUSION. 1. In order to our possession of all these, we must use the means we have. They that cannot bear a weak light, will yet less bear a strong one. 2. As there are better things provided for us, we may be sure that we shall be made better likewise, so as to be fit for them. Our future home is a prepared place for a prepared people.—S. C.

Ver. 25.—" *No night there.*" I. THE NIGHT A COMMON EMBLEM OF THINGS EVIL. The Bible notices of it are, like this of our text, almost always of a disparaging and deprecatory tone. It is represented as undesirable, and as telling of things that are evil. *Sorrow* (Isa. xxi., " Watchman, what of the night ? "—speaking of Edom's affliction). " Songs in the night " mean songs in sorrowful seasons. *Ignorance.* " Darkness shall cover the land, and gross darkness the people." And concerning this land it was said that " it sat in darkness," so dense was the ignorance of the people. *Sin.* " Men love darkness rather than light, because their deeds are evil ; " " We are not the children of the darkness, but of the light." *Death.* " Work . . . while it is day : the night cometh, when no man can work." *The power of Satan.* " This is your hour, and the power of darkness." And there are many more of a like sort. And yet—

II. THE NIGHT IS ONE OF GOD'S GOOD GIFTS. In *plant-life* it is essential to their growth. Night—so naturalists tell—is the time that the root of the plant feeds. During the day the light acts as a force upon the lining of the bark of the plant or tree, by which the nutriment is drawn up from the root. Now, at night that action ceases, and the root is able to thrust itself downward, deeper and deeper into the soil, wherever it can gain the nourishment it needs, and which it will have to supply when again the light comes, and yet more when the spring comes. The night is needed for this. And it is the time when the plant rids itself of that which would be hurtful to its life. The sap that the light and warmth of day have drawn up from the roots returns thither at night, but changed because charged with elements that the root will reject. It is these rejections of the root that render necessary the rotation of crops. The soil is poisoned for the same plant, but is ready for others. Now, for this, and much more in vegetable life, the night is needed. And for *animal life.* Ps. civ. sings, " Thou makest darkness, and it is night : wherein all the beasts of the forest do creep forth. The young lions roar after their prey, and seek their meat from God." Night is their feeding-time, the sleeping-time of most of their victims. Thus much suffering is avoided, and yet ' the young lions " are fed. And for *human life.* The body is compelled to rest if its powers are to continue in vigour, and the night-time is plainly given for that end. They who turn night into day and defraud the body of its due rest, frustrating the purpose for which night was given, violate the Creator's laws, and must pay the certain and severe penalty which such violation involves. And *the mind* owes much to the night season, for it gains enlargement and instruction by the spectacle of the starry heavens ; they, then, declare the glory of God. And *the soul* is uplifted by the contemplation of that glory. Thus, and for yet other reasons, is night to be regarded as one of God's good gifts to men. Nevertheless, in the new heavens and the new earth it is said, "There is no night there."

III. HOWEVER UNDERSTOOD, THE TEXT IS A BLESSED PROMISE. 1. Suppose we understand it *figuratively*. Then the promise is that all those varied ills of the mind and the soul which night hath been the symbol of—as in the declaration that there shall be "no more sea"—shall be absent from the saints' eternal home. 2. Or if we take the words *literally*—and it is possible that this may be meant—then they involve other glorious elements of the future which God's Word leads us to look for; *e.g.* a new *physical nature*. For if there be no night, then no need of rest. Indeed, we are told "they cease not" in their high employ "day nor night." But for such unresting and yet untiring occupation a body not limited, frail, and easily fatigued, like our present body, must be given; a physical nature altogether different from the present. And that which we should have inferred is clearly stated in other Scriptures. "There is a natural body," such as we now have, "and there is a spiritual body," which is what we shall have. But if there be a new and a more glorious body, that is the index of a *new and more glorious spiritual nature*. The external is the fit clothing of the internal. There is congruity between them, so that we argue, and for the most part rightly, from the outward to the inward, and we gather much as to the character of any creature from its external form. If, then, there shall be a new and glorious body, what shall be the spirit within, which is furnished with so glorious an instrument for the carrying out of its purposes? But if a new physical and spiritual nature, then there must be a *new mind towards God*. For it is plain that the embargo laid upon our present nature, by which it is "made subject to vanity," has been taken off. That limitation was because we were not to be trusted with larger powers. "And now," said God, "lest he put forth his hand and take also of the tree of life, and eat, and live for ever" (Gen. iii. 22); "so he drove out the man." Man was, because of sin, made as he is, because if more had been given him he could not be trusted to use it aright. That is the teaching of the verse in Genesis. But the possession of the new physical and spiritual nature proves that that restriction has been removed. But that proves that a new mind is in man towards God. No longer a rebellious disobedient mind, but "the mind of Christ," of "a dear child." But if this, then there must be a *new social state*; no longer discord and strife, because there is one mind towards God, and hence all are one. But this is the Paradise of God, the kingdom of heaven itself. That we may have ever-growing surety that we shall come to that blessed home of God's saints, let us look within the region of our own hearts, and see if there be no night *there*—no darkness of sin and unbelief. If there be, then at once let us turn to him, who giveth to all who seek, that he may "shine into our hearts, to give us the light of the knowledge of the glory of God in the face of Jesus Christ."—S. C.

Ver. 27.—*The heavenly Church-book.* "The Lamb's book of life." So has one named this book. Some pastors are very familiar with "Church-books," containing, as they do, the roll of the names of those under their pastoral charge. With what gladness have they entered names there, when those who bore those names have avowed themselves the servants of the Lord! With what sorrow have they removed names from that book when death or, far worse, evil conduct, has compelled such removal! How often they have prayed over that book, remembering one by one those whose names are there written, and supplicating God's grace for them! And in the text we read of a like book. Note—

I. THE WRITING—the book itself. "The Lamb's book of life." It is the heart of Christ.

> "The names of all his saints he bears
> Deep graven on his heart."

As the high priest of Israel bore on his jewelled breastplate the names of the twelve tribes, so the record of Christ's people is Christ's heart. He forgets no name and no "work of faith and labour of love" done for him; not even the "cup of cold water" given for his sake. Is it hard to believe? Why, do we not know how he *is* remembering us every day?—our wants, our weaknesses, our sorrows? And he supplies all our need. These facts of experience may well make us trust this record more than any book—the heart of Christ, the true book of life.

II. THE WRITER OF THIS BOOK. It is Christ himself. Ministers cannot enter your name there. Sacraments and sacred services, though often observed, have not this power. Birth and parentage, creed and profession, likewise fail.

III. THE WRITTEN THEREIN. We have spoken of the record and the Recorder; we speak now of the recorded ones—those written in the book. And who are these? We reply—All save those whose names have been blotted out of that book. When any child of man is born into this world, at once his name goes into this book; and because it is there, Christ's representative, his Church, through her ministers, lays claim to the child at the very beginning of its life. Children are baptized in the name of the Triune God, because they belong to him, are his by creation, redemption, and the gift of his blessed Spirit. So have we "learned Christ." But will the name stay in the book? We are clearly taught that a process of erasure as well as entry goes on in regard to that book. "Lord, blot not out my name!" should be the prayer of each of us. And what will ensure its permanence in the record? Faith, love, obedience,—these three. And where one is, the others are never far off.—S. C.

Vers. 1—8.—*The spiritual kingdom.* Now, to the eye of the weary seer—and in him to the eye of the weary, suffering Church—there appear new scenes. The darkness is past. The judgments of the Lord upon the evil powers, and upon all who take part with them as antagonists of the good, the pure, and the true, are passed away. And to the comfort of the waiting, faithful ones, who endure "as seeing him who is invisible," the vision of the blessedness of the righteous in the kingdom of their Father is granted. The judgment which has just been represented, and in which the punishment of the wicked is brought especially into view, needs the supplement of the present vision. It commences an entirely new series; it is set over against that which has just closed. To the end of the book now the brighter scenes of the Church's triumph, sanctity and joy are given. Here seems to be represented the bright and happy condition of the Church—the glory of the kingdom of truth—in its contrast to the power and evil-working of the kingdom of evil. These may be contemporaneous. If so, the eye of the seer is lifted from the struggle of evil to the rest of the gospel salvation. This is certainly the brighter side of human history. It is the Divine and heavenly side. But it appears to run on into the great future—the final conditions. To them, however, it must not be confined. It is "the kingdom of *heaven*" upon *earth;* which as a seed becomes, in its fruit and harvest, the everlasting kingdom *in heaven.*

I. THE SPIRITUAL KINGDOM IS REPRESENTED AS HAVING ITS BASIS IN AN ENTIRELY NEW CONDITION OF THINGS. "I saw a new heaven and a new earth;" "the sea"—the wild tumultuous sea of the raging peoples—"is no more" (ver. 1).

II. THIS KINGDOM HAS ITS SPECIALLY DISTINGUISHING CHARACTERISTIC OF SANCTITY. It is "the holy city;" it comes "down out of heaven from God." It is "made ready as a bride adorned for her husband" (ver. 2).

III. ITS MOST PROMINENT FEATURE IS FOUND IN THE INTIMATE COMMUNION OF GOD WITH MAN. His "tabernacle is with men." He dwells with them; they are his people, and he is with them, and is their God (ver. 3). This is the supreme blessedness.

IV. THE CONSEQUENCE OF THE SWAY OF THE SPIRITUAL KINGDOM IS THE REMOVAL OF HUMAN SORROW. "Every tear" is wiped from the eyes of men. Death, mourning, crying and pain are no more (ver. 4).

V. ALL IS ACCOMPLISHED BY DIVINE AGENCY. "Behold, *I* make all things new" (ver. 5).

VI. THE WHOLE PROMISE IS SUPPORTED BY SPECIAL PLEDGES relating: 1. To the Divine Name (nature) of the Church's Head. "I am the Alpha and the Omega, the Beginning and the End." 2. To the promise of eternal life and blessing. "I will give unto him that is athirst of the fountain of the water of life freely." 3. To the final inheritance of the utmost possible blessedness in a Divine relationship. "I will be his God, and he shall be my son." Thus "he that overcometh shall inherit all things;" for he shall be the son of the great King. 4. To the inevitable conditions of punishment which fall upon the subjects of the evil kingdom. This stands in contrast to the former, and is a word of warning and admonition.—R. G.

Vers. 9—27.—*The New Jerusalem.* We must see in this a portrayal of that holy community which is "the bride, the wife of the Lamb." It is the ideal representation of vital Christianity—Christianity as a system, but as a system embodied in the lives of men. The descriptions are of a glorious character. What can exceed the essential glory of the true Christendom, the true Church, the true bride, the veritable "wife of the Lamb"? It must not be separated from the heavenly, the final Jerusalem, the happy home of every weary pilgrim, the final abode of every spiritual citizen, the final resting-place whither the feet of all humble, holy souls tend. But the heavenly begins on earth. And in this vision we must see *the heavenly on the earth.* The ornate language suits its heavenly character and its heavenly prototype. Babylon was the seat of the beast; this is the city of the great King. It may be practically impossible to decipher the symbolical writing, especially in its details, and it may be as unwise to attempt it as it is impracticable to accomplish it; but the main features of the symbolical teaching, considered in the light of our previous interpretations, may doubtless be traced. Not without fear that our prepossessions may mislead us, we will attempt to find in the words of this section a setting forth of the essential glories of the true and actual Christianity, however ideally considered.

I. ITS FIRST CHARACTERISTIC IS HOLINESS. It is set up in the midst of evil and in opposition to it. It is holy, for it is "from God;" it is holy, for it promotes holiness in its subjects; all who pertain to it are called to be saints. Whatever is not in harmony with true ideas of holiness can have no part in the holy city.

II. ITS ORIGIN IS DIVINE. "It cometh down out of heaven from God." The true Church has its fount in him. He calls the first band out of the surrounding darkness. All is of his grace. He gives the Word which is the seed of the kingdom. He is the Father of all. The Church's grandest idea is that it is of God.

III. IT HAS ITS HIGHEST ADORNMENT IN THE MANIFESTATION OF THE DIVINE GLORY. But "the glory of God" is the symbol of God himself. We approach the true Shechinah. The glory of the Church is the presence of God. How near is that manifested glory brought to us in the Incarnation! how near in the abiding Spirit's presence! This is the true light that shineth over the city.

IV. ITS STABILITY, HARMONY, AND ORGANIC UNITY ARE REPRESENTED IN THE FIGURE OF THE CITY. Here are taught the intercourse, the fellowship, the safety, the mutual interest, of the holy ones. What is here ideally presented may not always be actually found. We deal with the patterns of the heavenly things.

V. THE FREEDOM OF ITS ACCESS TO ALL NATIONS is here declared. The gates of the city, ever open, stand to the east, the west, the north, the south. But one city; but all may enter.

VI. THE CHURCH IS BUILT UPON THE FOUNDATION OF THE APOSTLES AND PROPHETS. All the living Christianity has its basis here.

VII. THE SPLENDOUR, BEAUTY, PERFECTNESS, STRENGTH, AND GREATNESS OF THE CHURCH OF GOD—the living Christianity of ours and of every day, and the whole idea of the same—are set forth in the utmost wealth of symbolical extravagance.

VIII. THE INTIMATE ALLIANCE OF THE DIVINE SETS ASIDE THE EARTHLY AND IMPERFECT ELEMENTS. There is no visible temple. "The Lord God the Almighty, and the Lamb, are the temple of it." The illumination of the whole city is found in the life and grace of Christ.

IX. THE UNIVERSALLY DIFFUSED BENEFICENT INFLUENCE OF CHRISTIANITY is declared. The nations walk in the light of it, and—

X. THEIR RECIPROCAL ACKNOWLEDGMENT is found in that they "bring their glory and honour into it."

XI. ITS IMMUNITY FROM THE CONTAMINATION AND DEFILEMENT OF EVIL is indicated. Nothing unclean, nothing untrue, nothing of evil nature, enters it. It is ideal. True. Yet no evil elements shall ultimately be found in the Church of Christ; and, as at first we stated, the earthly is lost in the heavenly, of which it is at once the beginning, the type, and the pledge.—R. G.

Vers. 1—4.—*The fifth scene in the history of redeemed humanity : the unending age of blessedness.* "And I saw a new heaven and a new earth," etc. The retributive process is over; the characters of all have been tried, and the doom of all pronounced.

The wicked are driven away into punishment, but the righteous have entered into life eternal. These words suggest two thoughts in relation to this final state—

I. THAT IT WILL BE IN A SENSE A NEW STATE. "A new heaven and a new earth," and a "new Jerusalem" (vers. 1, 2). In what sense will it be "new"? I can conceive of three senses in which it will be new. 1. *It may be physically new*. There is reason to believe that a great change will take place in the material creation. Indeed, there are forces which are constantly changing the earth, and the heavens, and the atmosphere in which our clouds swim and stars shine. The inorganic, the vegetable, and the animal worlds are constantly changing. The belief of the ancients, the doctrine of geology, and the testimony of the Scriptures, favour the opinion that the fires which burn in the centre of the globe will one day burst into a universal volcano, mantle the earth in flames, and reduce its fairest forms to ashes. Out of this ruin may rise "a new heaven and a new earth." 2. *It may be dispensationally new*. Heaven and earth are sometimes used in Scripture to designate the dispensations under which men have lived. "Thus saith the Lord of hosts; Yet once, it is a little while, and I will shake the heavens and the earth." The reference is, undoubtedly, to the Jewish economy. The patriarchal gave way to the Mosaic, the Mosaic to the Christian, and now the Christian will give way to something else. Christ will deliver up the kingdom to God the Father. 3. *It may be relatively new*. New in the estimation and feeling of the occupants. No truth is more clear than this, that the world is to a man according to the state of his mind. To the voluptuary it is a scene of animal gratification; to the worldling it is a scene for barter; to the poet it is beauty; to the philosopher it is a school; to the saint it is a temple. Change a sinner's mind, and you change the world to him. He feels, and sometimes says, "The world is a new thing to me—a new heaven and a new earth." Let the men who now people this world come back to it in a perfect state, possessing a thorough sympathy with each other, the universe, and God. Will not the heavens and the earth be *new* to them? Will not all nature appear entirely different to what it was when they lived here, the creatures of imperfection and sin? Give the soul new moral senses, and you will give the material universe new attributes.

II. THAT IT WILL BE A STATE WIDELY DIFFERING FROM ALL PRECEDING ONES. 1. *The difference will arise from the absence of some things which were identified with all the preceding states*. There are three things mentioned here as being absent from this state. (1) *Agitation*. "No more sea" (ver. 1). The sea is here, undoubtedly, used as an emblem of commotion and distress. It is never at rest. The atmosphere may sink into passivity; no breeze may stir its heart; the clouds may rest on its quiet bosom, and the trees may sleep in its calm embrace. Night outspreads her sable mantle over the world, and all the busy tribes of earth and air sink to repose. But for the sea there is no rest; wave succeeds wave; a restless pulse throbs through all its particles. This is a true emblem of what the human world has been ever since the introduction of sin. Billow after billow of painful thought and feeling has been surging in rapid succession over the spirits of men through all preceding times. But now there is no "*sea*." The Church, agitated by the storms of ages, is at rest. All the elements of mental agitation will be excluded from heaven. What are they? *Pride, ambition, avarice, revenge, doubt, fear, envy, guilt*. These lash the soul into stormy billows now. But in the final state these will not be—there will be "no more sea." Another thing mentioned as being absent is: (2) *Death*. "And there shall be no more death" (ver. 4). Death has been the terror of all preceding periods; it has reigned through all. But there is no death in this final state. Death-beds, funeral processions, cemeteries, are not known there. (3) *Suffering*. "Neither sorrow, nor crying, neither shall there be any more pain" (ver. 4). All these are excluded for ever from this final state. 2. *This difference will arise from the presence of some things which have not been in connection with any preceding states*. What are they? (1) *A full manifestation of God*. "And I John saw the holy city," etc. (ver. 2). Jerusalem was the special residence of God, and the scene where his glory was displayed. The language, therefore, implies a *full* manifestation of God. (2) *A perfect fellowship with God*. The fellowship will be: *Direct*. God *himself* with them; not through mediums. *Permanent*. He will "dwell with them" (ver. 3).

I have, with great brevity, endeavoured to portray the epochs which are disclosed in the preceding chapter and verses before us—the epochs through which redeemed humanity has to pass. I believe that this is a correct interpretation of this passage. But were it not so, the sketch is still true. The ages I have mentioned are ages that belong to redeemed humanity. The first we are passing through now; and the others, though the nearest be immeasurably distant, are approaching with the march of time. Indeed, these epochs dawn in every redeemed soul. Our first stage in the Divine life is conflict; then a partial triumph; then, perhaps, a reaction; then the retribution, and then the unending blessedness. May this unending blessedness be thine, my friend!—D. T.

Ver. 1.—*The world without a sea.* "There was no more sea." A world without a physical sea, we confess, does not strike us as attractive. The sea is one of the grandest and most beneficent parts of this world. It is to the earth what the blood is to the body; it circulates through its every part, animates and beautifies the whole. The negation is to be understood in a *spiritual* sense. Division, mutation, agitation, are ideas we associate with the sea. In heaven these things will not be.

I. THERE IS NO DIVISION THERE. The sea is the great separator. It divides the great family of man into separate sections. The sea forms the boundary of kingdoms, continents, and races. The more fallen the world is the more necessary for such divisions. Let the race advance in intelligence and purity, and a commingling will become more possible and desirable. Indeed, as the world advances, the sea becomes less and less a divider. Ship-building and navigation are making old ocean the highway of nations, and the mighty channel of intercourse between the most distant peoples of the earth. Meanwhile, however, it is a separator. "And there was no more sea." To John these words would have a special significance. He was a prisoner in Patmos, a small desolate island in the Ægean. A treacherous and tempestuous sea divided him from the great world of men and from all the objects of his affection. "A touching tradition pictures the aged apostle going day after day to an elevated spot on the ocean rock, to which, Prometheus-like, he was chained, and casting a long look over the wide waste of waters, with his face like that of the captive Daniel in Babylon, steadfastly fixed towards Jerusalem; as if, by thus gazing with all his soul in his eyes on the open sea, he could bring nearer to his heart, if not to his sight, the beloved land and the cherished friends for whom he pined." How much there is in this world that divides men! There are: (1) Social caste; (2) national prejudices; (3) religious sectarianism; (4) selfish interests; (5) mutual misunderstandings. None of these will exist in heaven.

II. THERE IS NO MUTATION THERE. What so changeable as the sea? A pulse of restlessness throbs through every part. It knows no repose. Sometimes it moves in silence, at other times its march is as the roll of terrible thunders. It is not only ever changing in scene and sound, but it is ever *producing* change in the world. It levels the mountains, it fills up valleys, it creates new land. It is in all the changes of the face of the sky; all the organic and inorganic departments of the world it transfigures. Human life on this planet is, like the sea, in constant mutation. Not only does one generation come and another go, but the life of the individual man is a continual change—sorrow and joy, friendship and bereavement, prosperity and adversity. In heaven there is no such change. The only change is that of progress. Progress in (1) higher intelligence; (2) loftier services; (3) nobler fellowship. No change in the way of loss. The crown, the kingdom, the inheritance, all imperishable.

III. THERE IS NO AGITATION THERE. The sea is a tumultuous world. What human agony has its furious billows created! Human life here has many storms. Most men here are driven up and down like Paul in the Adrian, under starless skies, by contrary winds, and through treacherous and unknown seas. In how many hearts does deep call upon deep, and billows of sorrow roll over the soul! In heaven there are no spiritual storms.—D. T.

Ver. 4.—*The painless world.* "Neither shall there be any more pain." The greatest realities of life need no explanation. Pain in this world is an undoubted reality. It visits all, and though in its advent it bears greater anguish to some than to others, all feel its torturing touch. Pain meets man as he enters the world, follows him through all the stages of life, and leaves him not until his heart grows still in death. It attends us as a dark angel wherever we go, through all seasons of the year, and through every period of our mortal life. Its ghostly form makes our limbs tremble at its touch, and our nerves quiver with anguish before it. Now, the text directs our attention to a world where there is no pain. The negation suggests several things.

I. Pain is not needed there to STIMULATE SCIENTIFIC RESEARCH. Who shall tell how much the cause of science is indebted to pain? As a rule, men's love for truth is not strong enough to urge them in the search of it for its own sake. Natural history, botany, anatomy, physiology, chemistry, owe to a great extent their existence and advancement to pain. The proverb says, "Necessity is the mother of invention," and no necessity does man feel more than to deliver himself from pain. Pain is the power that whips all the faculties of the soul into strenuous exercise. Without it would there be any intellectual action? Would there be any development of our mental powers? When we are told, therefore, that there will be no pain in heaven, we infer that men will not require such a strong stimulus to inquire after truth and so search after knowledge. Supreme love for the Creator will give all these such a delightful interest in all his works as will make inquiry the highest delight of their natures.

II. Pain is not needed there to test the REALITY OF MORAL PRINCIPLE. Were there not pain in the world, by what means could we ascertain the reality and the strength of our love, our integrity, our faithfulness? Pain is the fire that tries those metals and removes the dross, the fan that winnows those grains and bears away the chaff. Pain tried Abraham and Moses. Pain tried Job. It came to him in its most torturing character; but his principles stood firm before it, and he said, "Though he slay me, yet will I trust in him." Pain tried Paul. Hear his description of his sufferings: "In labours more abundant, in deaths oft; of the Jews five times received I forty stripes save one," etc. (2 Cor. xi. 26). Now, in heaven there will be no need for such a trying test of principles; the character will be perfected. The gold will be purified from all alloy.

III. Pain is not needed there to PROMOTE THE DEVELOPMENT OF CHARACTER. Pain is needed here. First, in ourselves, to *promote patience, resignation, forgiveness.* "Our light affliction." Pain is needed here, secondly, in others, in order to *awaken our charities.* Were there no suffering about us, generous virtues, which are essential to the Christian character, would have neither scope nor stimulus. The naked, the hungry, the imprisoned, the afflicted,—these furnish a field for the exercise of our benevolences. In heaven the character being perfected, no such discipline will be required. We shall be made like Christ, "changed into his image from glory to glory."

IV. Pain is not needed there to aid us in APPRECIATING THE SUFFERINGS OF CHRIST. Christ proved his love by suffering. He suffered poverty, contumely, persecution, ignominy, crucifixion. He "made himself of no reputation." He took on him the "form of a servant," became "obedient unto death, even the death of the cross." Now, to estimate suffering, we must know what suffering is, know it experimentally. Every man must bear a cross in order to know what the cross of Christ really was. In heaven we shall not require this. We shall have learnt it in our measure, and be qualified to sing, "Worthy is the Lamb that was slain!"

V. Pain is not needed there to IMPRESS US WITH THE ENORMITY OF SIN. The first thing for a sinner to feel in order to renounce sin is a conviction of its terrible consequences. It is the cause of all sorrow, suffering, and death. But in heaven, sin having been done away, the consequences and effects will be done away also; sin being pardoned, it will be unnecessary to impress us with its enormity.

What a blessed place is heaven! A world without pain of any sort—physical, social, intellectual, moral.—D. T.

Ver. 5.—*The new creation.* "And he that sat upon the throne said, Behold, I make all things new." Two facts suggested in these words are worthy of notice. 1. *Christ is invested with the government of our world.* "He that sat [sitteth] upon the throne." "He is exalted far above all principalities," etc. Glorious fact this. It explains the continuation of sinners in such a world as this, and encourages us to take a deep interest in all the operations of Providence. 2. The other fact suggested is, *Christ in the exercise of his authority is engaged in the work of moral creation.* " He that sitteth upon the throne said, Behold, I make all things new." The spiritual renovation of our world is here represented as a creation. Notice two things: the *resemblance* and the *dissimilarity* between the *spiritual reformation* of man and the *natural creation.*

I. THE RESEMBLANCE. There must be a resemblance, or else the figure would not be employed as it is here and elsewhere (see Isa. lxv. 17—19; 2 Cor. v. 17). What are the points of resemblance? 1. In both there is the production of a new *order of things.* From chaos of old, God, by his creative fiat, brought life, beauty, light, etc.; and from the corrupt soul of man, by his redemptive power, he evolves high spiritual virtues. 2. In both there is the production of something new by the *Divine agency.* Who created the heavens and the earth, etc.? God, and he only. Who creates a soul? The same glorious Being. 3. In both there is a production of the new according to a *Divine plan.* Every part of the universe is created on a plan. Science discovers this. In conversion it is so (Eph. ii. 10). 4. In both there is the production of the new for *his own glory.* "The heavens declare his glory." The conversion of men reveals the glory of God. 5. In both there is the production of the new *in a gradual way.* Geology and the Bible show that the work of creation is a very gradual work. It is so with the work of spiritual reformation—very gradual.

II. THE DISSIMILARITY. 1. The one was produced out of *nothing*; the other from *pre-existing materials.* In conversion no new power is given to the soul, but the old ones are renovated and wrought into right action. 2. The one was effected without any *obstructing force*; the other is not. In creation God had only to speak, and it was done. Not so with conversion. There is the principle of free agency and depravity to contend with. 3. The one was produced by mere *fiat*; the other requires the intervention of *moral means.* Nothing in the creation came between the work and the Divine will. In spiritual reformation it does; hence God had to bow the heavens and come down and become flesh. 4. The one placed man in a position *material* and *insecure*; the other placed him in a *spiritual* and *safe abode.* Adam was placed in a material paradise, and from his original position he fell. Conversion places men in a spiritual paradise, from which they will fall no more. They are "kept by the power of God." 5. The one develops and displays God as the *absolute Spirit*; the other as the *Divine Man.* In spiritual manifestation he is " God manifest in the flesh," full of condescension, tenderness, love.

CONCLUSION. The subject presents: 1. *A solemn question for us all.* Are we "new creatures in Christ Jesus"? Have we been brought out of the moral chaos? 2. *A bright prospect for the world.* Christ is on his throne, and the work of moral creation is carried on, and will one day be completed.—D. T.

Vers. 5—8.—*The new moral creation.* " And he said unto me, Write, for these words are true and faithful," etc. Some remarks on the new moral creation were offered in our last homily, and were suggested by the last clause of the fifth verse. The subject now is *the one matchless Creator.* Who is he that brings into existence on our planet a new order of spiritual things, that creates a new moral heavens and earth? The representation here gives us to understand that he is One who is all-truthful, everlasting, infinitely beneficent, surpassingly condescending, and essentially sin-resisting.

I. HE IS IMMUTABLY TRUTHFUL. " For these words are true and faithful " (ver. 5). What words? The words that had reference to the things that had already come to pass. What he had promised and what he had threatened had come to pass. What he has spoken not only has been done, but is being done, and must be done. He is the Truth, the unalterable Reality, the one Rock that stands immovable amidst all the fluctuations of creature thought and speculation. Whatever in creature-opinion is conformable to him is relatively true and beneficent, and whatever disagrees is false and pernicious.

II. HE IS EVERLASTING. "I am Alpha and Omega [the Alpha and the Omega], the Beginning and the End " (ver. 6). He is without a beginning, without a succession, without an end; the Cause, the Means, the End of all things but sin. All that exist throughout immensity are but evolutions of him; ever multiplying and growing branches from him, the eternal Root. The capability of forming such a thought is the glory of our nature; the power of properly entertaining it is the only means of possessing true mental life and progress.

III. HE IS INFINITELY BENEFICENT. " I will give unto him that is athirst of the fountain of the water of life freely " (ver. 6). Souls are ever thirsting. Of all animal sensations, none is more agonizing than a burning, unquenched thirst. But soul-thirst unquenched is far more agonizing and destructive. And soul-thirst seems to be almost the mainspring of all human actions. " Who will show us any good ? " This seems to be the cry of all. This thirst there is One and only One who can quench, and for this he is ever working. He pours forth in all directions the refreshing and crystal streams. And all this "*freely,*" without any coercion, limitation, partiality, or pause; freely as he gives the beams of day and the waves of vital air. From the heavens above, and the earth beneath, and the waters under the earth, there goes forth from him, as from an ever-acting, fathomless, and inexhaustible fountain, that which can quench the thirst of all human souls.

IV. HE IS SURPASSINGLY CONDESCENDING. "He that overcometh shall inherit all [these] things; and I will be his God, and he shall be my son" (ver. 7). Two things are here stated which suggest this amazing condescension. 1. *This recognition of every individual man who does his duty.* "He that overcometh shall inherit all things." That he should notice man in the mighty aggregate may well impress us with his condescension, but that he should notice individual man, how much more! Here we have the universe won by *self-conquest.* Notice: (1) Self-conquest as the grand work of man. What is it overcomes self? A man may overcome others by violence, overcome difficulties in his secular pursuits, overcome the forces of nature so as to make them subserve his will, and yet not overcome himself. Self-conquest includes at least two things—the subordination of the *body to the soul,* and the subordination of the *soul to sympathy with God.* The soul may rule the body, but it may rule it for selfish, or sceptical, or ambitious ends. Such a rule would not be self-conquest. The soul should be ruled by sympathy with God, sympathy with his character, his operation, his plans. In these two things self-conquest consists, and such conquests require battling—resolute, brave, persistent, invincible battling. (2) Self-conquest as *winning the universe.* "He that overcometh shall inherit all things." The millions of men who live in the universe do not inherit it; it inherits, possesses them, uses them, plays with them, absorbs them. But the man who has conquered himself comes under the control of sympathy with the great God—inherits all things—gets the universe. He gets the whole of it; he penetrates its meaning, appropriates its truths, admires its beauties, drinks in its poetry, revels in its spirit, exults in its God, and says, " The Lord is my Portion." He gets the whole of it to enjoy for ever. 2. *The affiliation of every individual man that does his duty.* "And he shall be my son " (ver. 7). The conquering of sin and the rendering of the external universe into subservience of the higher interests of his nature is the grand duty of every man, and every man that does this God will make his son. Are not all men his children ? By no means. They are all his creatures, his offspring, but not his *sons.* A man may have a dozen or more offspring, but not one *son.* He only is a son who has the true filial instinct, involving trust, love, obedience, acquiescence. The great mission of Christ into our world was to generate in humanity this true filial disposition, enabling them to address the Infinite as " our Father." This is the true adoption. He, then, who conquers evil becomes a son of God. He does not receive " the spirit of bondage again to fear, but . . . the Spirit of adoption," etc.

V. HE IS ESSENTIALLY SIN-RESISTING. " But the [for the] fearful, and unbelieving, and the abominable, and murderers, and fornicators, and sorcerers, and idolaters, and all liars, shall have their part [their part shall be] in the lake which [that] burneth with fire and brimstone, which is the second death " (ver. 8). All these hideous characters are but the creatures of sin. Sin is cowardice, sin is faithless, sin is abhorrent, sin is murderous, sin is lascivious, sin is deceptive and idolatrous. All these productions of sin are abhorrent to the Divine nature. "It is the abominable thing " which he hates, and he consigns sin to irretrievable destruction, and it is destined to have its part in " the lake which burneth with fire."

CONCLUSION. Such, then, is that ever-blessed One who is engaged in the *new moral creation of our world.* The creative work has begun; its progress seems to us slow, but its consummation is inevitable.—D. T.

Vers. 9—21.—*The spiritual commonwealth of the good.* "And there came unto me one of the seven angels," etc. There is a spirit-world. This is a fact, established by conclusive reasoning and accordant with the concurrent beliefs of mankind. This spirit-world is a *commonwealth.* It has a social order. The existence of spirits destitute of gregarious instincts and social affinities is conceivable, and may be perhaps somewhere in existence in the great spirit-world—the world of which the material universe is the offspring, mirror, and servant. But of such non-social beings we have no proof or information. The great spirit-world in which we believe, and of which we read, is a community that has its laws of intercourse, sympathy, and co-operation. Hence in Scripture it is frequently figurated as the Jerusalem from above, the heavenly Jerusalem, etc. Jerusalem is its metropolis, the centre of its authority and influence. Now, the magnificent capital of this great commonwealth of the good is the grand picture in this dream, for a dream or vision it manifestly is. Literally, a city like the one here represented has never existed, and, according to the laws of architecture, proportion, and gravitation, perhaps never could exist; and hence prosaic interpreters, however learned, incapable of distinguishing between fact and figure, have, in their expositions of this and other visions, produced such a jumblement of incongruities which disgraces their own common sense and discredits the Scriptures. Taking the vision before us as a parable, or a pictorial illustration, of the *social state or order of the good*, we may attach to it the following characteristics.

1. HEAVENLINESS. Heaven *reveals* it to man. "And there came unto me one of the seven angels which [who] had the seven vials [bowls] full of the [who were laden with] seven last plagues, and talked with me [he spake unto me], saying, Come hither, I will show thee the bride, the Lamb's wife [the wife of the Lamb]" (ver. 9). Ministers from the celestial world are represented not only as talking to the author about it, but as inviting him to look at it. All the ideas of men concerning a perfect social state have come to us, not as the deductions of our own reasoning, but as communications from heaven. Heaven *enables* man to see it. "And he carried me away in the Spirit to a great and high mountain, and showed me that great city, the holy Jerusalem [showed me the holy city Jerusalem], descending [coming down] out of heaven from God" (ver. 10). It is not until we are elevated into the higher modes of thought and feeling that we have reached a standpoint from which we can command a view of this supernal state. Down in the valley of worldliness, under the shadow of the hills, and amid the exhalations and fogs of sensualities, it would be impossible to catch a glimpse of the King in his beauty, in the land that is afar off. We must climb the mental Pisgah, and reach the Mount of Transfiguration. Heaven *brings it down* to man. "Descending [coming down] out of heaven from God." This perfect social state must come down to us from heaven, if we are ever to realize and possess it. Men from ages of false religious teaching have come to regard heaven as something at a distance, as something yonder, not here; something in a certain locality in the universe, not something in a certain *state of mind and character.* Hence the cry, "Oh that I had wings like a dove! for then would I flee away, and be at rest!" But he who would have heaven in the soul, its perfect state, must bring it down, its sympathies, purposes, down *into his own heart.* His prayer should be, "Thy kingdom come: thy will be done on earth as it is in heaven."

> "In sacred silence of my mind,
> My heaven, and there my God, I find."

II. DIVINITY. "Having the glory of God: and her light was like unto a stone most precious, even like [as it were] a jasper stone, clear as crystal" (ver. 11). As the Shechinah lit up the holy of holies in the temple, God's presence radiates through every part of this spiritual communism of the good. He is its Essence and its Inspiration. He is its Light, transparent as the crystal and beautiful as the gleaming shot from the precious jasper. A poet has spoken of "looking through nature up to nature's God." He should have said look *down on nature through God.* God is in his great social system of order what the cloudless midday sun is to our globe. All other lights are buried in the brightness of its rays, and from it all life, and beauty, and motion, and order proceed. Human systems of government, what are they? Black, battling, boundless chaos. But the perfect social order is Divinity itself, all filled with God;

he is All in all—the Centre, the Circumference, the Beginning, and the End of all. God is the Light of it.

III. SECURITY. "And had [having] a wall great and high, and had [having] twelve gates, and at the gates twelve angels," etc. (vers. 12—14). The metropolis of this spiritual commonwealth is abundantly protected. It had a wall "great and high," impregnable and unscaleable. It had "twelve gates," three for each point of the compass—"north," "south," "east," "west." "Twelve foundations" also it had, and all the twelve gates guarded by "angels," that excel in strength. The systems of government and social order that men construct, how frail and transient they are! They are constantly changing, breaking up in confusion, and themselves sinking into ruin.

> "Here a vain man his sceptre breaks,
> The next a broken sceptre takes,
>   And warriors win and lose;
> This rolling world can never stand,
> Plundered and plucked from hand to hand,
>   As power decays and grows."

But here is a kingdom that cannot be moved, a "city that hath foundations, whose Builder and Maker is God."

IV. SYMMETRY. "And he that talked [spake] with me had a golden reed [had for a measure a golden reed] to measure the city, and the gates thereof, and the wall thereof" (ver. 15). The metropolis of this commonwealth is not reared capriciously and without plan. Every material is properly measured and put in its right position. The Architect is of unerring skill. Is there any symmetry in our schemes of government, whether political, social, or ecclesiastic? What one generation has constructed, and admired as just and wise, the next, blessed with a higher education, pronounces both unrighteous and unwise. The Architect of this city measured the whole by "the golden rule." "Thou shalt love the Lord thy God with all thy heart, and thy neighbour as thyself."

V. AMPLITUDE. "The city lieth foursquare, and the length is as large [great] as the breadth" (ver. 16). The city is of vast dimensions. The walls that enclose it stretch over about fifteen hundred miles. "The length and the breadth and the height of it are equal." There is nothing limited or narrow in the scheme of social order which God has established for the government of communities; it embraces all, of whatsoever tribe or land, secular condition, or grade of intellect or culture. Look at the *political* schemes that men formulate! As a rule, they are ever in favour of the rich and the powerful—the few, to the disadvantage of the multitudes. Look at the *religious* schemes! As a rule, how miserably narrow! Officialdom has turned temples into shops, preachers into traders, and the God of infinite love into an object whose approbation is to be obtained by fulsome flattery, whining cajolery, and cringing servility, expressed in prayers and hymns that shock the common sense and conscience of the unsophisticated amongst mankind. Oh that we could "comprehend with all the saints what is the height, the depth, the length, the breadth, of God's love"!

VI. COSTLINESS. Things that men regard as the most precious and costly are here mentioned as belonging to this wonderful social edifice. "And the building of the wall of it was of jasper: and the city was pure gold," etc. (vers. 18—21). In the description we have "jasper," "gold." "precious stones," "sapphire," "chalcedony," "emerald," "pearls," etc. The pearl was regarded by the ancients as of all things the most precious. Elsewhere God's truth, his Word, his moral system, is represented as "more precious than gold, yea, than even fine gold." It is the transcendent good. 1. The greatest thing in the *universe* is *mind*. Mind is the maker and manager, the owner and lord, of all material systems. 2. The greatest thing in *mind* is *love*. Pure, disinterested, self-sacrificing, Christ-like love, this identifies us with God, makes us one with him. "There abideth," says Paul, "faith, hope, charity; . . . the greatest of these is charity." This love is the essence of that social order which God has established in his moral creation. All the precious stones, the gold, the pearls, etc., of the creation, are puerilities compared to this.—D. T.

Vers. 22—27.—*The negative glory of heaven* (*No.* 1). "And I saw no temple therein:

for the Lord God Almighty," etc. There are *three ways* of describing to others scenes unlike those with which they are acquainted. 1. A statement of those things which e not there, but which are found elsewhere within their sphere of observation. 2. A statement of those things which are found in them in common with those scenes wi h which they are familiar. 3. A statement of those things which are *peculiar* to them, and which are found in no other scene within their knowledge. These three methods are employed by the sacred writers in order to present to us the heavenly Jeiusalem—the eternal inheritance of the good. The verses before us are a specimen of the first method. Certain things are here mentioned which belong to our earthly sphere, but which have no existence there, and this very *negative* description has a power to make on us a deep impression that heaven is a scene of transcendent essedness. Looking a little closely into the negative record in the text, we may infer—

I. THAT IN THAT STATE THERE IS NO SPECIALITY IN THE FORMS OF RELIGIOUS WORSHIP. "And I saw no temple therein: for the Lord God Almighty and the Lamb are the temple of it" (ver. 22). A city without a temple would strike the common notions of men as atheistic. To the Jewish mind especially it would give the idea of a city to be avoided and denounced. The glory of the metropolis of their country was its temple. When the Prophet Ezekiel would cheer and animate them in their Babylonian bondage, he presents to them a graphic description of the temple that was to be reared in their city, with its ornaments and ordinances, its chambers for the priests, its altars for the sacrifices. Still, whatever might be the popular notions of men about temples, with their methods of worship: 1. Their existence implies spiritual blindness and imperfection; they are remedies for evils. 2. Their history shows that men, in many instances, have turned them to a most injurious account. They have nourished *superstition.* Men have confined the idea of sacredness and worship and God to these buildings. They have nourished *sectarianism*, the devilism of Christendom. Different classes have had their different temples and modes of worship, and often regard with sectarian jealousy and loathing those who kneel not at their altar and adopt not their theory of doctrine and ritual of worship. When it is said, therefore, that there is "no temple in heaven," it does not mean that there will be no worship in heaven, but that there will be no temple like that on earth, always implying imperfections and often used to foster the superstitious and sectarian. The reason assigned for the non-existence of a temple in heaven is a very wonderful one: "The Lord God Almighty and the Lamb are the temple of it." God and his holy Son are not only the Objects of heavenly worship, but the very temple of devotion. All there feel not only that they have to render to God and his Son worship, but they are *in* them in the worship. All there feel that "in him they live, and move, and have their being;" that he is the very breath of their existence. Where he is—and he is everywhere—there is their temple, there is their worship. The doctrine of worship propounded by Christ to the woman of Samaria is there felt in all its intensity and developed in all its perfection. "God is a Spirit: and they that worship him must worship him in spirit and in truth." The "no temple" in heaven really means "all temple"—worship everywhere, under all circumstances, and for ever. Brethren, are we learning a worship here to prepare us for the worship yonder? Is our worship a thing of buildings, liturgies, ritualisms, and sects? Such worship will not do for heaven. Our conventional worship, in the light of the worship of eternity, is as contemptible as a rushlight in the beams of the noonday sun.

II. THAT IN THAT WORLD THERE IS NO NECESSITY FOR SECONDHAND KNOWLEDGE. "And the city had no need of the sun, neither of the moon, to shine in it: for the glory of God did lighten it, and the Lamb is the light thereof" (ver. 23). Moons and suns are but secondary organs of light. The moon borrows from the sun; the sun, perhaps, from another orb; and that from another. The Fountain of all light is God himself. He is "the Father of lights." The grand central orb in the material universe catches his radiance, and flings it abroad on the million globes of space. When we are told, therefore, that the city will have no need of the moon and the sun, it figuratively expresses the idea that the holy tenants of that blessed state will have no need for any *secondary* means of knowledge. Here a secondhand knowledge is indispensable to us. Most of the knowledge we have is derived from others—parents, teachers, ministers, books. Knowledge about our own being and relations, about Christ and God and worship, come to us, not directly from God, the great Fountain of light, but through a variety of secondary agencies. Even the higher light of the Bible comes to us in this way. "Holy men of God spake as they were moved." It is moon and sun light; the light of secondary orbs we have here, and we cannot do without it. Not so in the celestial world. That spiritual intelligence in that blessed state will be derived from communion with spirit can scarcely admit a doubt. In that society, as here, there will be the teacher and the learner. But the idea symbolized by the verse is that that secondhand knowledge will not be *needed*, will not be indispensable as here. Here, like Job, we hear of God by the hearing of the ear; there we shall see him as he is, and be like him. He will be the Light, the clear, direct, unbounded medium, through which we shall see ourselves, and our fellow-worshippers, and the universe. "Now we see through a glass, darkly; but then face to face." This light will be enjoyed by all the saved. "And the nations of them which are saved shall walk in the light of it, and the kings of the earth do bring their glory and honour into it" (ver. 24). Observe: 1. The saved will be *numerous*. "Nations." "The Gentiles shall come to thy light, and kings to the brightness of thy rising," etc. (Isa. lx. 3—5). 2. The saved will be *progressive*. "They shall walk in the light," ever onward. 3. The saved are *self-surrendering*. "The kings of the earth do bring their glory." All the honours, even of kings, shall be laid in reverence at his feet. "The kings of Tarshish and of the isles shall bring presents: the kings of Sheba and Seba shall offer gifts. Yea, all kings shall fall down before him: all nations shall serve him."

III. THAT IN THAT WORLD THERE WILL BE NO APPREHENSION OF DANGER FROM ANY PART. "And the gates of it shall not be shut at all by day: for there shall be no night there" (ver. 25). Never shut by day, then never shut at all, for the day there is eternal. Fear, which hath torment, and which often shakes our spirits here, as the wind shakes the leaf in the forest, will find no place in any breast in heaven. An unshaken consciousness of safety will reign universally. No fear of *temptation*; here we are bound to watch and pray lest we fall into temptation; we are surrounded by tempters on every hand. No seductive serpent will ever find his way into that Paradise restored by Christ. Why should we say so? Has there not been a fall in heaven? Did not a host of bright angels leave their first estate? And may not such a rebellion again break forth? Never! Why? Because of the great amount of motive that now exists in heaven to bind the virtuous to virtue, the Christian to Christ, the godly to God. 1. There is a motive from a contrast between the present and the past. 2. There is the motive from the appearance of the Lamb in the midst of the throne. The memory of Calvary is a golden chain, linking all to the eternal throne of purity and love. There is no fear of *affliction*. We are told in the fourth verse that there shall be no sorrow, nor crying, neither shall there be any more pain. The countless ills to which flesh is heir will never find their way thither. There is no fear of *death*. Death here is the king of terrors. Through fear of death we are all our lifetime subject to bondage; but death will never enter there. The gates, then, might well be left open, for there is no fear.

IV. THAT IN THAT WORLD THERE WILL BE NONE OF THE INCONVENIENCES OF DARK- NESS. "There shall be no night there." 1. Night interrupts our vision. It hides the world from our view, and is the symbol of ignorance. The world is full of existence and beauty, but night hides all. 2. Night interrupts our labour. We "go forth unto our labour until the evening."

V. THAT IN THAT WORLD THERE WILL BE NO ADMISSION OF IMPURITY OF ANY KIND. "And there shall in no wise enter into it anything that defileth, neither whatsoever worketh abomination, or maketh a lie: but they which are written in the Lamb's book of life" (ver. 27). Observe: 1. The *excluded*. All impurities of all kinds and degrees. 2. The *included*. All who are "written," etc. All who are registered on the grand roll of redemption. What a roll is this!—D. T.

Ver. 25.—*The negative glory of heaven* (No. 2). "For there shall be no night there." In our observations on the preceding verses we pointed to the spiritual commonwealth of the good and the negative glory of heaven. Of the latter point the text at the head is not the least suggestive. The commonwealth of the good in its perfect state will be nightless, and the vision suggests (1) *constant luminosity*; (2) *unclouded beauty*; and (3) *uninterrupted favours.*

I. CONSTANT LUMINOSITY. Night draws her veil over nature, and hides from mortals the world in which they live, and it is therefore the symbol of ignorance. Never, of course, shall we see all things in heaven. There will always be universes lying beyond the ken of the most penetrating eye. The elevation that lies to-day at the utmost boundary of an angel's horizon he may perhaps reach in the course of time, and one day stand upon its lofty brow. But even from this towering apex he may find other elevations concealing the infinite beyond. The finite intellect will never grasp the Infinite. Nor do I believe that different minds will ever have exactly the same view of things, see things exactly in the same light. This seems to me impossible, from the fact that no two spirits are exactly alike, nor can any two occupy exactly the same *points of observation.* Our views will necessarily be relative. They will be true to us, but not necessarily true to others. God alone can see the whole of a thing. We only see sections and sides. Not only does it appear impossible, but also undesirable. Diversity of view gives a freshness and charm to society. A city where all the citizens had precisely the same views on the same subjects would be characterized by a drowsy monotony. A loving comparison of views, a generous debate, a magnanimous controversy, are amongst the blessings and charms of social life. Still, our range of vision, though relative, and our views though relative, will be *clear* and *accurate.* Here, in a world of nights, our most correct conceptions of things are clouded more or less with error. We see now through a "glass, darkly," says Paul. The glass he refers to was not like our window-glass, offering no obstruction to light, but a semi-transparent horn. How different the landscape looked through such a thick medium, as looked at directly with a clear, strong eye! Notwithstanding this, all will be light enough to make the path of duty clear. The depravities of our nature, the carnal and selfish inclinations of our hearts, often throw the darkness of night upon that course of life which is true and just. But in that world without a night, eternal sunshine will settle on the path of duty; it will lie straight before us, and we shall move on with the steps of certitude. God's will will radiate on everything without, and will express itself in every impulse within. In that nightless sphere all will be morally pure. Moral impurity reigns in the night. It is the season in which great sins are generally committed. The thief and the assassin go forth with stealthy tread on their mission of wickedness in the night. The gambler, the debauchee, and the serfs of carnal appetites meet and hold their revelries in the night. "They that be drunken are drunken in the night." The prince of darkness and all his ghostly legions win their most terrible victories in the gloom and the silence of nocturnal hours. The day is the emblem and the minister of purity. How pure is the light! In heaven all is pure. There are the holy angels whose natures, through the ages of their being, have never been clouded by one impure thought or touched by the thrill of one unholy passion. The redeemed of all ages are there.

II. UNCLOUDED BEAUTY. The negation implies that it is a realm ever *beautiful in aspect.* Darkness hides the beauty of the world, but light is the creator and minister of beauty. All the variegated colours of the summer's landscape we owe to the sun; and all the exquisite forms of life owe their existence to his renewing power. The sun is nature's great painter. All the pictures of loveliness that charm us as we walk the galleries of life have been photographed by his smiles and tinged by his hues. What, then, will be the beauty of a world where there is "no night"—a world of perpetual sunshine? All the beauties of *nature* will be clear. The very distant shores and the seas, the meads and the mountains, the rivers and the ravines—all, in fact, beneath, around, above—will be one grand universe of beauty. All the beauties of *artists* will be clear. The very instinct of genius is to invent, imitate, and create, and there genius will flourish in perfection. May it not be that numbers will there be employed in copying the forms of loveliness around them with pencils more delicate, lines more life-like, hands more skilful, than our Raphaels and Rubenses, our Da Vincis and Correggios? May it not be that we shall see numbers there employed in weaving the sounds of nature into melodies more soul-stirring and Divine than ever struck the lyre of our Handels and Mozarts? May it not be that numbers will be there hymning their praises in strains of seraphic poetry, compared with which the epics of Milton and the lyrics of Cowper are but the vapid fancies of childhood? Genius there will undoubtedly be active, and all her productions will be distinguished by the highest perfection of beauty. All the *moral* beauties will be clear. The beauty of holiness, the beauty of the Lord, will adorn every spirit. All will be endowed with those attributes of moral loveliness that will command the admiration of each and all. Thus all will rejoice in each other, and all rejoice in the Lord, whence all their beauty came.

III. UNINTERRUPTED FAVOURS. Night checks the progress of life. The processes of life, it is true, go on in the night, but they are slow and feeble. Life cannot bear the darkness long ; pulse grows feeble under its ebon reign. Its tide ebbs under its cold breath. Take a vigorous, blooming plant, and shut it up in the dark. How soon will it lose its vitality, become delicate, colourless, and die! Were our sun to shine on without setting from year to year on this earth, who could tell how high the tide of life would rise in every living thing? Where there is "no night," there will be no check to the *advance of life*. The vital energies will always be increasing. Sinew and soul, character and conscience, will be ever growing in force. "From strength to strength" all these proceed. No blight to wither, no shadow to chill, there. But all the influences that play around existence there inspire, invigorate, and uplift. Night checks the progress of *labour*. We "go forth unto our labour until the evening;" then night shuts us in. We retire to unconsciousness and inaction. "Are there not twelve hours in the day? If any man walk in the day, he stumbleth not, because he seeth the light of this world. But if a man walk in the night, he stumbleth, because there is no light in him." "The night cometh, when no man can work." But in a world where there is "no night," there is no checking of labour. Our range of action would be unrestrained. We shall be always abounding in the work of the Lord. Night checks the progress of *happiness*. Darkness is depressing. Hence it is often used as the emblem of misery ; the scene where the wicked one is is spoken of as "outer darkness." Even the irrational creatures around us feel the depressing influence of a gloomy day. Under the dark clouds and murky sky, the cattle cease to gambol on the hills, and the fowls of heaven cease their music in the groves. All feel the pressure of darkness. Light is the condition and emblem of joy. A bright day sets the world to music. What happiness, then, must there be in a world where there is no night! In what does its happiness consist? The context answers the question—the absence of all evil. No pain, no sorrow, no death, no hunger, no thirst, no temple, no night. The presence of all the good: the river of life, the tree of life, companionship with the holy, fellow ship with God, oneness with Christ. This is heaven.

Such are the ideas suggested by this nightless condition. It is a scene where the vision is ever clear, where the character is ever pure, the aspect is ever beautiful, life is ever advancing, joy is ever rising. The sun never sinks beneath the hills, nor does a cloud ever intercept his rays.—D. T.

EXPOSITION.

CHAPTER XXII.

Ver. 1.—And he showed me a pure river. Omit "pure." "And" connects this part of the vision with what precedes (ch. xxi. 9—27). It would have been better, perhaps, if the twenty-first chapter had included the first five verses of the twenty-second, so as to take in the whole of the description of the heavenly Jerusalem. But there is a break at this point, as is indicated by the repetition of "And he showed me," which points to a new phase or section of the vision. In the previous section (ch. xxi. 9—27) the angel had showed St. John the city and its walls with their gates and foundations ; in this section he shows him the river of the water of life, and the tree of life. The latter part of each section is occupied with the evangelist's own observations (ch. xxi. 22—27; xxii. 3—5), for we cannot suppose that the phrase, "these words," in ver. 6, is intended to apply specially to anything in these particular sections. *He* is the angel mentioned in ver. 9, and again referred to in vers. 10, 15, 16, 17. Most probably the pronoun "he" in ver. 6 does not refer to the same angel as this one. *River*. The source of this stream, its course or channel, and its fertile banks, are mentioned or implied in what follows; but there is no reference to any estuary or mouth: eternity is the ocean in which this river is lost. Of water of life. Ὕδωρ ζωῆς is perhaps identical in meaning with "living water," ὕδωρ ζῶν, but is properly distinguished from it in translation. The two expressions are peculiar to St. John's writings in the New Testament; the genitival form, which is the more Hebraizing, only occurs in this book in ch. vii. 17; xxi. 6; xxii. 1, 17; whereas the participial and more classical form is confined to the Gospel (John iv. 10; vii. 38). "Living water," in its simplest literalness, means such water as is pure, flowing, clear, fresh, and wholesome; not stagnant, or turbid, or salt. Hence it is a proper term for the water of a beautiful and fertilizing river. Here, however, the genitival form reminds us of the familiar expression, similarly moulded, "the tree of life," which inclines us to think that "water of life" signifies water possessing life-giving powers, water which restores, refreshes, supports life, and is therefore to be compared with "living water" taken in its spiritual sense. Of this whosoever drinketh shall never thirst again; when it has been once received within the soul, it becomes a well of water springing up into everlasting life (John iv. 14). Clear as crystal, proceeding out of the throne of God and of the Lamb; *clear*, or *transparent*. We seldom use the rendering of the Revised Version, *bright*, as an epithet of water. *As crystal* (see note on ch. iv. 6, the only other place in the New Testament where the word occurs). The source of the river was in the Divine throne, the seat of the Triune God and the crucified Saviour. All eternal life is derived from our heavenly Father by the Holy Spirit for the sake of the Redeemer.

Ver. 2.—In the midst of the street of it. This sentence appears to belong to the preceding verse, as in the Revised Version. For (1) the καί, "and," which follows, seems the beginning of the fresh feature of the description (cf. ver. 1); and (2) the account here given is evidently derived from Ezek. xlvii., where the river is connected with trees, but no such mention is made of *streets*. And on either side of the river, was there the tree of life; *and on this side of the river and on that was the tree of life*. The beginning of the new sentence (*vide supra*). The singular "tree" seems intended to be understood generically of the whole of that class of trees. For this reason probably the LXX. renders the Hebrew of Ezek. xlvii. 7 by the plural "trees." We may see in this bountiful supply of the trees of life an image of the abundance of grace and life in store for the redeemed (cf. the description in Ezek. xlvii.). Which bare twelve manner of fruits, and yielded her fruit every month; rather, *twelve crops of fruit, yielding its fruit every month*; i.e. one crop in each month. The number *twelve* signifies completeness (see on ch. iv. 9; vii. 4—9, etc.). This fruit

is yielded twelve times as often as ordinary fruit. The signification, therefore, is that there is an ever-present supply. The *fruit* is not of twelve different kinds; the tree of life bears but one kind (cf. Ezek. xlvii. 12, "And by the river upon the bank thereof, on this side and on that side, shall grow all trees for meat, whose leaf shall not fade, neither shall the fruit thereof be consumed: it shall bring forth new fruit according to his months"). And the leaves of the tree were for the healing of the nations (cf. Ezek. xlvii. 12, quoted above, "And the fruit thereof shall be for meat, and the leaf thereof for medicine"). "The nations" are not the heatnen, but the multitude of the redeemed, gathered out of every nation (see on ch. xxi. 24). It is, of course, not implied that there is, in the new Jerusalem, any disease which needs healing, but the tree of life is put forward as the means by which the perpetual health and life and general well-being of the inhabitants are sustained.

Ver. 3.—And there shall be no more curse; *and there shall be no accursed thing any more*. Nothing accursed exists in that city, because there is no sin there. The narrative here passes into the future tense (cf. ch. xx. 7). But the throne of God and of the Lamb shall be in it; and his servants shall serve him; *and the throne*, etc. This is the consequence of there being no accursed thing (cf. Josh. vii. 12, 13, "Neither will I be with you any more. . . . There is an accursed thing in the midst of thee, O Israel"). God dwells in the city because all is holy. The throne of God and of the Lamb is one—God and the Lamb are one. Again, *his servants*, the servants of God and the Lamb (cf. John x. 30). They "serve him," as described in ch. xix. 1—7 and elsewhere.

Ver. 4.—And they shall see his face; and his name shall be in their foreheads. Another consequence of there being no accursed thing —no sin (see on ver. 3). All are pure in heart, and therefore they see God. The same promise is made in 1 John iii. 2. The last clause connects this chapter with ch. iii. 12, and shows that these who are here described are those who have overcome (cf. also ch. vii.; xiv. 1).

Ver. 5.—And there shall be no night there; and they need no candle, neither light of the sun; for the Lord God giveth them light; *and there shall be night no more; and they need no light of lamp, neither light of sun; for the Lord God shall shine upon them*. A repetition of ch. xxi. 23, 25 (which see). In xxi. 23 we are told "the Lamb is the Light thereof;" here, "the Lord God shineth upon them." Again an assertion of the Divinity of the Son (cf. ver. 3). And they shall reign for ever and ever. This prediction and promise ends the Revelation, as such. It is the reward placed before those who strive, in order to induce them to "overcome" (see on ver. 5 above, and ch. iii. 12).

Ver. 6.—And he said unto me. Probably the angel who has exhibited the vision of the holy city (ch. xxi. 9); perhaps the angel of ch. i. 1. The concluding portion of the book is now entered upon; it contains a brief summary of (or rather reference to) the chief events which have been narrated, and enforces the lesson which is intended to be taught, viz. that Christians should persevere in well-doing amid all persecutions, for their reward is certain, and that the punishment due to the wicked will surely overtake them at last. The angel asserts the veracity of what is contained in the book (ver. 6; cf. ch. i. 1, 2; iii. 14); the time in which to prepare is brief (vers. 6, 7, 12; cf. ch. i. 3, 7); the prophecy is to be communicated to others (ver. 10; cf. ch. i. 1—3); God is eternal (ver. 13; cf. ch. i. 8); the just are rewarded (vers. 14, 17; cf. ch. i. 3); the wicked are punished (ver. 15; cf. ch. i. 7); the prophecy is to be faithfully handed on (vers. 18, 19; cf. ch. i. 2). These sayings are faithful and true. That is, all that has been conveyed to the seer (cf. the following verses). This is a repetition of ch. xxi. 5; xix. 9; iii. 14; so also Dan. viii. 26. And the Lord God of the holy prophets sent his angel to show unto his servants the things which must shortly be done; *and the Lord, the God of the spirits of the prophets. . . . the things which must shortly come to pass.* That spiritual part of the nature of the prophets, by which they are made to discern and to communicate God's will. The expression is used here in connection with the "prophecy" mentioned in the following verse. The greater part of this verse is worded exactly as ch. i. 1. *His servants;* cf. the address to the seven Churches (ch. i.—iii., especially ch. i. 11).

Ver. 7.—Behold, I come quickly (cf. vers. 12, 20; ch. iii. 11). The narration passes into the words of Christ himself, just as in ver. 12 and ch. xi. 3. Blessed is he that keepeth the sayings of the prophecy of this book. Because they are "faithful and true" (ver. 6). The command given in ch. i. 11, 19 is now supposed to have been carried out (cf. the same words in ch. i. 3).

Ver. 8.—And I John saw these things, and heard them; literally, *and I John [am] the [one] hearing and seeing these things.* The absence of the verb (the present participle being used alone) indicates the person to whom the revelation is made, without assigning any specific period as the particular time when the revelation took place. The same statement is made in ch. i. 1 (which see). "These things" are all that have been related in the book. And when I

had heard and seen, I fell down to worship before the feet of the angel which showed me these things; *and when I heard and saw,* etc. The tense here becomes aorist (*vide supra*). St. John has once before fallen into the same error, viz. that of paying undue homage to the angel (see on ch. xix. 10). The beatific vision overwhelms him with awe, and he is bowed down with his own humility.

Ver. 9.—Then saith he unto me, See thou do it not: for I am thy fellow-servant, and of thy brethren the prophets, and of them which keep the sayings of this book: worship God; *and he saith,* etc. (cf. the words of ch. xix. 10). Here we have "the prophets;" in the former passage we have the "spirit of prophecy," in much the same sense; here, again, we have "them which keep the sayings of this book," in place of "that have the testimony of Jesus," in ch. xix. 10. In the latter case, also, there is little difference of meaning, since the "sayings of this book" are exhortations to a faithful bearing of "the testimony of Jesus;" those, therefore, "who keep" (that is, carry out) "the sayings" are those who "hold the testimony of Jesus." "The prophets" need not be restricted in meaning to either Old or New Testament prophets, but may include both. The direct inspiration of the message which St. John has to deliver is here asserted. In unison with the teaching of the Mosaic covenant, the angel commands to *worship God* alone (cf. Exod. xxxiv. 14, etc.).

Ver. 10.—And he saith unto me, Seal not the sayings of the prophecy of this book: for the time is at hand. The visions being now complete, St. John is commanded to communicate them to the world (cf. ch. x. 4, where a contrary direction is given). The last sentence is again a repetition of the assertion of the shortness of this our time of preparation (cf. on ver. 7). The revelation deals not with events far distant in the future, but with those immediately present; for this reason the message is to be communicated (cf. Dan. viii. 26, where the reason given for "shutting up the vision" is that the visions "belong to many days to come," Revised Version).

Ver. 11.—He that is unjust, let him be unjust still: and he which is filthy, let him be filthy still: and he that is righteous, let him be righteous still: and he that is holy, let him be holy still; *he that is unrighteous, let him do unrighteousness still,* etc. (Revised Version). These words seem to be used ironically, as was sometimes the case with the prophets (cf. Ezek. iii. 27; xx. 39). The intention seems to be to stir men up to a realization of the nature of their conduct in continuing to reject the warnings of God. Note that the words immediately succeeding, as well as those immediately preceding, are connected with the judgment.

Ver. 12.—And, behold, I come quickly. Omit "and" (cf. vers. 7, 10, etc.; see also on ver. 11). Note also that once more the words are spoken as by Christ himself (cf. ver. 7). And my reward is with me, to give every man according as his work shall be; *as his work is*, according to the best authorities. This is one of the fundamental truths enforced throughout the book; cf. the epistles to the seven Churches (ch. ii. 5, 10, 16, 17, 22, 26, etc.). Similar language is found in Isa. xl. 10; lxii. 11. The infinitive phrase seems to be explanatory of the idea contained in the word μισθός, "reward;" the double nature of the *reward* being thus indicated.

Ver. 13.—I am Alpha and Omega, the Beginning and the End, the First and the Last; *the Alpha*, etc. Reverse the position of the two last phrases. These words, which appropriately open and close the book (cf. ch. i. 8), occur (like those in ver. 11 above) continually in Isaiah (see Isa. xli. 4; xliii. 10; xliv. 6; xlviii. 12). All three titles are here combined, as if to finally gather up into one impressive assertion the titles hitherto used separately (cf. ch. i. 8, 17; ii. 8; xxi. 6). "The first title is symbolical; the second is borrowed from the Old Testament; the third is philosophical" ('Speaker's Commentary').

Ver. 14.—Blessed are they that do his commandments. The Revised Version adopts the reading, οἱ πλύνοντες τὰς στολὰς αὐτῶν, "they that wash their robes," which is found in א, A, 1, 33, Vulgate, Æthiopic, Armenian, Primasius, and which is probably correct. The reading of the Textus Receptus, ποιοῦντες τὰς ἐντολὰς αὐτοῦ, "they that do his commandments," is found in B, Syriac, Coptic, etc. The Vulgate adds, "in the blood of the Lamb," as in ch. vii. 14, which is, of course, the full meaning. The free-will of man is implied in the active form of the participle. That they may have right to the tree of life; *in order that they may have authority over the tree of life*; i.e. the right to partake of it. Ebrard makes this clause dependent (as a consequence) upon "do:" "They do them in order that they may have," etc. Others attach this clause to "blessed:" "They are blessed because they may have the right," etc. Both significations may well be implied. "The tree of life" is that described in ver. 2, and promised "to him that overcometh" in ch. ii. 7. And may enter in through the gates into the city; *by the portals;* that is, in the natural way of people who have a right to enter.

Ver. 15.—For without are dogs, and **sorcerers, and whoremongers, and murderers, and idolaters, and whosoever loveth**

and maketh a lie; *without* (omit "for") *are the dogs, and the sorcerers, and the fornicators*, etc. The article renders each term general in its signification (see on ch. iv. 11). "The dogs" are those who are described in ver. 11 as "the filthy;" the term is proverbial amongst Eastern nations as an expression for what is most degraded. The epithets in this verse occur (with others) in ch. xxi. 8. A contrast is forcibly presented between these wicked ones here indicated, and those who have (in the preceding verse) the right to enter the city, owing to their purity obtained by washing their robes.

Ver. 16.—I Jesus have sent mine angel. Here our Lord himself asserts what was at the very beginning set forth (ch. i. 1). The revelation proper being now ended, the epistolary form in which the book opens is now resumed. Either our Lord himself is here the speaker, or the angel speaks in his name (cf. vers. 9, 10, 12, etc.). To testify unto you these things in the Churches (ἐπὶ ταῖς ἐκκλησίαις). The Revised Version translates, *for* [margin, or *over*] *the Churches* (cf. the expression in Matt. xxiv. 33). Probably this preposition is used as expressing the idea of motion towards, especially from above, which is contained in the fact that the message is from heaven to the Churches. Düsterdieck, Hengstenberg, and others would translate, "concerning the Churches." Ἐν, "in," is found in A and some other manuscripts. Some cursives omit the preposition entirely. This gives another possible reading: "to testify these things unto you, the Churches." I am the Root and the Offspring of David, and the Bright and Morning Star. Omit the second "and." (On "Root," see on ch. v. 5; for "Morning Star," cf. ch. ii. 28.) At the word "David," the manuscript 1, from which Erasmus compiled the Textus Receptus, ends. In order to supply the remainder, which is deficient, Erasmus retranslated the Vulgate Version into Greek. The Greek, therefore, of the Textus Receptus from this point onwards is the Greek of Erasmus.

Ver. 17.—And the Spirit and the bride say, Come. These words are best understood as uttered by the writer. The Holy Spirit working in the Church, through whom she is bound to Christ as his bride, and the Church herself, eagerly welcome the fulfilment of Christ's promise made in ver. 12. (On "come," cf. ch. vi. 1.) And let him that heareth say, Come. The Church in her corporate capacity welcomes her Lord; so, also, let each member in his individual capacity, who hears this "testimony" (ver. 16), be desirous of the advent of his Master. And let him that is athirst come; *athirst* for the water of life (cf. ch. xxi. 6). And whosoever will, let him take the water of life freely. Omit "and." Again the active participle indicates the voluntary nature of the action; though the living water be freely given without money and without price, it is not enforced upon any.

Ver. 18.—For I testify unto every man that heareth the words of the prophecy of this book. Omit "for." The pronoun "I" is emphatic. Here is the solemn appendix or seal of the veracity of the book, somewhat similar to the prefatory words in ch. i. 1—3. This is the fulfilment of the duty laid upon St. John in ch. i. 1, not an announcement of our Lord himself (cf. the wording of ch. i. 3). If any man shall add unto these things, God shall add unto him the plagues that are written in this book; cf. the command in Deut. iv. 2, " Ye shall not add unto the word which I command you, neither shall ye diminish from it " (Revised Version). " The plagues that are written in this book " are those of the seals, the trumpets, the vials, the doom of Babylon, etc.; cf. the command of St. Paul to Timothy (2 Tim. i. 13), and cf. also what is said in 2 Tim. ii. 16—18 concerning the heretical teaching of Hymenæus and Philetus.

Ver. 19.—And if any man shall take away from the words of the book of this prophecy, God shall take away his part out of the book of life, and out of the holy city, and from the things which are written in this book; *from the tree of life;* i.e. that mentioned in ver. 2 and in ver. 14, where also the *city* is mentioned. *Even from the things written in this book* seems to be the real meaning of the last clause; not merely the *tree* and *city* which are written, etc. Just as the evils set forth in the Apocalypse are declared in ver. 18 to be the portion of those who *add to* the book, so those who *take from* the book are deprived of those blessings which have been constantly referred to in the book.

Ver. 20.—He which testifieth these things saith—viz. the Lord Jesus, as in ver. 16— Surely I come quickly; *yea, I come quickly.* As the book opens, so it closes with this promise. This is the anchor and stay of the faithful, the sound of an alarm and a warning cry to the wicked. Amen. Even so, come, Lord Jesus. Omit "even so." Thus in calm and patient hope the apostle answers his Lord. So the writer who delivers the message is the first to proclaim his belief in what is herein contained.

Ver. 21.—The grace of our Lord Jesus Christ be with you all. Amen; *the grace of the Lord Jesus be with the saints. Amen.* So the delivery of the message was commenced (cf. ch. i. 4; cf. the form in 1 Thess. v. 28). Bearing in mind that the theme of the book is the conflict between good and evil, we may well conclude our study of it by joining in the prayer of the author, that the help of the Lord Jesus may be on the side of his saints to enable them to overcome, and then receive their reward.

HOMILETICS.

Vers. 1—5.—(See preceding homily.)

Vers. 6, 7, 16.—(See homily on ch. i. 1—3.)

Vers. 10, 11.—(See homily on ch. xx. 11—15.)

Ver. 12.—(See homily on ch. i. 7.)

Ver. 13.—(See homily on ch. i. 8.)

Ver. 14 (Revised Version).—(See homily on ch. vii. 14—17.)

Ver. 15.—(See homily on ch. xx. 11—15.)

Ver. 17.—*Closing words of invitation : " Come."* We have closed our exposition of the plan of the book, so far as its Apocalyptic unfoldings of scenes yet to come are concerned. But we should deem our work incomplete if we did not, ere we lay down our pen, indicate in outline four homiletic studies suggested by the last six verses of this chapter, giving us as they do, a closing invitation, a closing warning, a closing aspiration, and a final benediction. First in order of these four comes the invitation. So far as the first " Come " is concerned, the word might be supposed to be the call of the Church to our Lord, entreating him to come and rule in righteousness. And so, in fact, some do regard it. But the wording of the second phrase seems to us to put such an interpretation on one side. For to him that heareth, it is said, " Catch up the sound and pass it on—'Come'!" So that it is evident that the first "Come" is addressed to the individual who is here exhorted to pass on the sound. For this reason we deem ourselves shut up to the specific interpretation we have here adopted. We therefore, regard the verse as an invitation to every one to come and partake of those joys which are made over by Christ to all who will take them.

I. THERE ARE JOYS IN THE HOLY CITY WHICH ARE INFINITELY WORTHY OF ACCEPTANCE. The word "Come" naturally suggests the question, "To what?" or "To whom?" And if the clause stood alone, the answer would not unnaturally be, "To the Saviour," for he is the one Object to whom men are expected to come. But if we look at the close of this verse, we find it said, "Whosoever will, let him take the water of life freely;" and when we read, "Let him that is athirst come," we find additional reason for supposing that the meaning of the word is, "Come to the water of life." And, so far, there is no reason for doubting the correctness of this. But, then, the next query is, "Where is this water of life?" And if we turn to ch. vii. 17; xxi. 6, 7; xxii. 1, we find that in heaven the blessed are seen beside the fountains of the water of life; so that, although it is true that even here Christ gives us the living water, that even here there is a river, the streams of which make glad the city of God, yet no one can study this book without seeing that there is in it a "tendency forward;" that there is a finger beckoning and a voice urging us onward to a holy city, "the New Jerusalem," of which it is said "the throne of God" is there, from which the living water is seen to flow, a pure, a crystal stream. All those who reach that city will drink thereof. And it is unquestionably with all this in view that the invitation is given. Yonder, at the end of the pilgrimage of the saints, is a land no foe can enter; there is this refreshing stream. Thousands have already reached that land, and thousands more are on the way; and the Holy Ghost, having thus set the land Beulah before our vision, will not let the apostolic seer close the book until, in the name of the Lord of the land, he has summoned our attention to it, and until, through him, "the Spirit and the bride" have said, "Come to that heavenly land, drink its living stream, and thus share its eternal joy."

II. THE JOYS OF THE HOLY CITY ARE FOR THOSE WHO WILL COME TO THEM. No one will get to heaven by chance. Nor is it by merely idling life away that we shall find ourselves there. For although the act of coming is all that is required, there must be *that*. This truth is one which, if analyzed into its several parts, may be put thus: 1. *The eye of the soul must be fixed on this as the true goal of life.* It will not do to have an aimless life. Life without aim is life without power. But what aim can be compared to this, of knowing God and enjoying him for ever? 2. *We must learn the rules by which life is to be regulated.* These are two: (1) Repentance towards God. (2) Faith towards our Lord Jesus Christ. These are to be, not occasional acts, but the habits of a life. It is not by a rush and a leap, uncalculating and blind, that this heavenly home is to be attained, but by humbly and lovingly accepting all that Jesus says, and in his strength setting the face towards Zion. 3. *This involves, evidently, coming to Jesus,* who is the Lord and Leader of every pilgrim. This is imperative. The last step implies the first, and all that intervene. And whosoever comes to Jesus will at that moment take his first sip of the living water.

> "*Rivers* of endless joys above,
> And *rills* of comfort here below."

III. TO THESE HEAVENLY JOYS IN CHRIST WE ARE INVITED. The whole verse is an invitation. It is, indeed, a royal command. But whereas the commands of an earthly sovereign may be obeyed literally, yet with reluctance, here there are no unwilling responses. "Whosoever will, let him come." The form of invitation, however, takes for granted two things. 1. That the object to be ensured is one that is sufficiently attractive to make an invitation appropriate. And who can call this in question? Not even the stoutest unbelievers deny the attraction of the heavenly city and of the privileges of its citizens. The invitation assumes: 2. That, manifold as are the charms of the place, with its fountains of living water, God is willing to make over to the invited ones all its blessedness, wealth, and glory; *provided always* that men will come penitently, believingly, and lovingly, and accept all as a free gift from the heart of Infinite Love, out of the storehouse of his exhaustless wealth.

IV. THIS INVITATION IS THROWN INTO VARIED FORMS. These are four. 1. *The Spirit saith,* "*Come.*" In three ways. (1) In the visions of glory which are designed to attract. (2) In the clear statements of those for whom the glory is designed. (3) In the fact of his inspiring the apostle to pen these words, the Holy Ghost has recorded for all time an imperishable invitation to the thirsty ones to come to the waters of life. 2. *The bride saith,* "*Come.*" The bride is the Church. (1) The Church on earth, in all her services, her ordinances, her teaching, is saying, "Come." If she indulges in terrorism rather than in invitation, she mistakes her mission. (2) The Church of the redeemed above—the great cloud of witnesses—beckons to us to come. 3. *Every one who heareth is to say,* "*Come.*" Not one voice is to be mute. From the earliest to the latest, all who have responded to the call are to hand it on to others: "Come! come! come!" The student of the original will see an untranslated force in the verb "say"—even—"The Spirit and the bride *are saying.*" The air is ringing with their voice, and every one who hears the sound is to add his voice to theirs. Then: 4. *Jesus is the Leader of the mighty choir.* This is seen when vers. 16, 17 are put together. "I Jesus have sent mine angel," etc. Yea, it is as if a grandly perfect peal of bells were hung aloft, and as if our Saviour would have their chimes ever filling the air with the music, "Come! come! come!"

V. THE INVITATION IS SPECIFIC IN ITS FORM. "Let him that is athirst come" (cf. Isa. lv. 1). Thirsting spirits may be divided into two classes. 1. *There are those who thirst, but know not for what.* This was long the experience of Augustine. So it is of many now. 2. *Some thirst, and do know for what.* Even as David (Ps. xlii. 1). (1) Some are just convinced of sin, and are thirsting for pardon and purity. (2) Some who have tasted of the river of the water of life thirst for more of it. We never want more *than* Christ; we often want more *of* Christ. (3) Some are aged Christians; they find that the older they get, the more they want of God and of his love. And truly blessed is it for them, though their ears may be getting dull for earthly sounds, to hear the cheery chimes ringing in the Father's house, "Come! come! come!" They will not have to listen from afar much longer. They will soon be by the banks of the river, rejoicing in the fulness of joy. They have gloried in the invitation for, perhaps, fifty years; and blessed are these old disciples, for they shall hear the chime-bells of heaven more distinctly till they are rung in to the better land.

VI. THE INVITATION IS AS WIDE AS IT IS SPECIFIC. "Whosoever will." These words should put the vast breadth of the invitation beyond all cavil or dispute. "*Whosoever!*" However great may have been his former thirst after sinful pleasures, if now he is thirsting for Jesus, let him come! The great tempter tries to frighten men away. He tells some, "You are too old;" others, "You are too young;" others, "You are too bad;" others, "You are too late." But surely here is a sword which, if it be vigorously plied, will make the evil one retire in defeat and shame: "*Whosoever will!*" Coming one, Satan is fond of hurling his fiery darts at thee. Hurl this at him: "*Whosoever will!*" He will soon tire of his attacks, if thou wilt renew thine. Why, brother, have you not more faith in this one cheery word of thy Saviour's, pealing out from millions of voices, than in the chill, the dark, the deadly suggestions of unbelief? Heaven: "*Whosoever will!*" The water of life: "*Whosoever will!*" None are shut out but those that keep out. And whosoever misses the fountains of the water of life will do so only because he refused to accept the largest invitation that ever came to mortal ears!

VII. THE INVITATION IS ON TERMS OF GOD-LIKE FREENESS. "Freely." The only terms on which we can buy the gifts of God are these—"without money and without price."

"Nothing in my hands I bring,"

are words which are suited for us. For we live on free gifts from a bounteous God. We have nothing but what is from above. It must be so, it is so, in spiritual blessings. 1. *The first drop of the living water* for which the thirsty soul applies is given freely (John iv. 10). 2. *Every day* the believer has to come afresh, to receive new life, freely; new strength, freely; more of God, freely. How great is the blessedness of thus living on "the water of life" day by day, getting it fresh every hour from One whose fulness no giving can diminish, whose giving no receiving can tire. 3. *Thus living on free mercy while on earth, the like living on free mercy above will be heaven.* The next state will be the continuity of this. Ah! we might live with music—the music of heaven—in our ears, if we were not so dulled with the sounds of earth. Every morning when we wake there is the Father ready to give us new blessing, freely. Every day, for the demands which new toil will make upon us, we may have new strength, freely. And so on till the last. And then—heaven, freely! Having lived on free grace below, we shall be well content and pleased, living on free grace, to take our place in heaven.

In conclusion? who would not respond at once to an invitation so rich, so large, and so divinely free? Would that, in our urging this, we could adequately represent the tenderness and love of our God! Let not our coldness repel thee, O thirsty one! Come now, and taste for yourself the sweetness of the living stream! What will your response be? We have given the invitation in Heaven's Name; and to him in whose Name we have spoken, you must reply.

Vers. 18, 19.—*Closing words of warning.* It would be deemed an unpardonable offence for an ambassador to add words to, or to subtract them from, any royal mandate which he was commissioned to deliver. And if any one in dispensing a physician's prescription, when the life or death of a patient trembled in the balance, were wantonly to tamper with it, what condemnation could be too severe? Yet we fear that the tendency of many in our day is to treat a message in this book far more lightly than they would any important official human document; and instead of sympathizing with the words before us, and adding their reverent "Amen," they would in all probability either condemn the severity of these words, or else pass them by as out of date and altogether effete. On this account we deem it needful, in approaching the close of our expositions, to look into these verses with special care. We will first inquire what additions to the book or subtractions from it we may suppose men to make, from what we know of human treatment of the Word of God. We propose then to see what is the threatening here denounced against such. Having done this, we will endeavour to ascertain reasons for a sentence so severe. Then we shall be prepared to see how this passage may help us in the formation of religious thought, and how it may bear practically on the life.

I. JUDGING FROM WHAT WE KNOW OF THE FACTS OF HISTORY, IN WHAT WAY MAY MEN BE SUPPOSED TO ADD TO OR TO SUBTRACT FROM THIS BOOK? The words of the text evidently embrace any kind of treatment of this Book of the Apocalypse which seemed to assume that a man was at liberty to take the book into his own hands, and to deal with it as he thought fit. Men do this: 1. If they put any merely human production alongside of it as if it were on a level therewith. 2. If they distort the book at pleasure to make it fit in with a preconceived theory about it; *e.g.* a preconceived and extreme theory of evolution is even now (1889) leading some to treat the old book most unfairly. 3. If they summarily reject the account which the book gives of itself, out of dislike to the supernatural, or from hostility to the principle of authority in religion. 4. If they make a human interpretation of the book of equal dignity or authority with the book itself. 5. If they deny and disown any of those great doctrines which are inwrought into the very texture of the book; *e.g.* the glory of Christ's Person; the meaning of his work; the reality of his administration; the freeness of his grace; the certainty of his victory. These and cognate doctrines pervade the entire Apocalypse, and to omit, ignore, deny, or condemn them, from wilful refusal to submit to Divine authority, would be to commit the sin which is here exposed to view. The words of the Apocalypse as a whole, and of these two verses in particular, are not human; they are Divine. We should hear a voice saying, "Take thy shoes from off thy feet; for the place whereon thou standest is holy ground."

II. WHAT IS THE THREATENING HERE UTTERED AGAINST THOSE WHO TAMPER WITH THE BOOK? The threatening assumes a positive or negative form according to the positive or negative form of the sin. In the one case it affirms that any actual and wilful ill treatment of, or adding to this book, will bring down the curse of God upon the guilty one's head. In the other case, it declares that any rebellious rejection of the divinely revealed doctrines of this book will incur rejection from God.

III. CAN WE DISCOVER REASONS FOR A SENTENCE SO SEVERE? Certainly we can: seven. 1. *The book is Divine in its origin; it is, therefore, too sacred for human hands to mar.* (For treatment of the question of the origin of this book, see our first homily in this section.) In ver. 16 we have the explicit statement, "I Jesus have **set** mine angel," etc. In ver. 18 we have the emphatic Μαρτυρῶ ἐγὼ [1] beginning the verse. It is not absolutely clear whether the speaker in the second case is Jesus himself or his angel. If the latter, the angel testifies for Jesus. If the former, Jesus speaks for himself. Either way the testimony is divinely authorized, and therefore must ever be too sacred for the trifler's touch. 2. *The book is a Divine manifesto to the Churches;* therefore no others can have any right to touch it. It was given at first to those who loved our Lord, that they might keep and shield it. And any one professing to be an ambassador for God, who wilfully tampers with it, is false to his commission from the throne. What nation would bear with its sovereign's legate, if he were known to add, alter, or delete a word issued from the throne? He would be visited, and rightly, with penalties of terrible severity. Is God's sanction to be less stern? 3. *The book is a disclosure of the future;* and no one can possibly be competent to alter a single word of his who sees the end from the beginning. To disclose in a succession of parabolic or symbolic settings the future scenes which are to appear, and that in their order, is a task to which none but God himself can possibly be equal. Therefore the visions must remain untouched. 4. *The book is a declaration of doctrine*— of doctrines on which souls live and grow and thrive; and therefore it is a very serious thing to meddle therewith. By contrary teaching, men may be led astray and ruined for time and for eternity. If there be a reservoir which supplies a town with water, or a well springing up in a barren land, the only one from which a traveller could drink, what curses would be—yea, ought to be—pronounced against him who should poison either the one or the other? Is it a less serious thing to poison the wells from whence the living water is drawn? 5. *The book abounds in words of consolation;* of the supports of which men may not be deprived. Few books in the Word of God are richer in consolation than this closing one; and who can estimate the guilt of depriving millions of souls of the words of solace uttered from the eternal throne? To strike a thousand men at once with paralysis would be nothing to such a crime as this! 6. *The attempt to substitute human words for the Divine is unspeakably rash.* For our part, we have ever felt that it would be a sheer impertinence if we were to take it upon ourselves to guide men through this life to the life to come, if we had not a "Thus saith the Lord" for every direction we gave. But if, when the Lord has spoken, any man deliberately substitutes words of his own, this is an action which no words of ours can adequately characterize. 7. *There is desperate wickedness in that disloyalty and rebellion which would play fast and loose with the words of this book.* We may not lose sight of the fact that this censure is here pronounced, not *merely* because of an evil *act*, but on account of the wickedness of heart which can consent to an act so evil. Any one who can deliberately handle the Word of God deceitfully commits a crime in sacred things, which society would absolutely refuse to tolerate in the common affairs of life. What place could such a one possibly find in the holy city? So far, then, from thinking the sentence even seemingly severe, we deem it one of the clearest proofs of Divine kindness and care that he has thrown the guard of so solemn a sanction around words which are meant for our guidance through this life to that which is to come. For the fact is that God's severity to the trifler is the outcome of his care for us all.

IV. LET US SEE WHAT BEARING THIS PASSAGE HAS ON THE FORMATION OF THOUGHT AND ON THE DIRECTION OF LIFE. 1. It should lead us to admire the wonderful concern of God for our guidance and safety in thus guarding for us his own message of love. We ought not for a moment to forget that for our sakes these words were written; for our sakes they have been preserved till now through fire and flood, and all the vicissitudes of earth. We can quite imagine a man under the influence of unbelief or hostility, taking fire at such a passage as this, deeming it a flash of fiery wrath directed against himself. But in so doing he would totally misapprehend the words. They are fraught with terror only to those who wilfully pervert them. And we have no hesitation in saying that menace to such is mercy to the rest. Is it no safeguard to the people to be told that the enemy shall not be permitted with impunity to poison the wells of living water? Whoever robs a people of their dearest treasure will have to smart for it. God's goodness to us ensures that. 2. The words should lead us to admire

[1] See the Revisers' text, and that of Westcott and Hort.

and adore the far-seeingness of the great Inspirer in inditing such words as these. For who does not know that one "Church," at any rate, has heaped words on words, and added them to the faith, to be accepted under pain and penalty of "*anathema sit*"? And not content with this, but as if in order to prevent the discovery of her own fraud, she debars the people at large from free access to the book which would expose it, which is at once the charter of the people's freedom from man, and defines the extent and the limits of the "true sayings of God." 3. The words which are so stern a guard around the Book of the Apocalypse do also apply with equal force to whatsoever writings stand on an equal footing of Divine authority (cf. Deut. iv. 1—24; Jer. xviii. 16, *ad fin.*; Gal. i. 6—9; Matt. xv. 9). Hence we should learn (1) to deal with most conscientious care with whatever comes to us with the weight and sanction of Divine authority; (2) to remember that there is not anything *outside the pages of the Word of God* that does or can present such binding authority; (3) to deal with all that is so outside the book as the word of man, and not as the Word of God (see Acts xvii. 11; 2 Cor. i. 21; 1 Cor. ii. 5). Our faith must not stand "in the wisdom of men, but in the power of God." 4. The words before us show how an expositor of the holy book is to treat it in his teachings to the people. His task is at once grand in its simplicity, yet awful in its responsibility. He has, by every possible means, (1) to find out exactly what the Spirit of God says; and (2) to impress that, *and that only*, on the heart and conscience of the people. 5. We here see also how the people are to regard an expositor of God's Word, viz. as one whose work is to teach them, not his own thoughts, but the thoughts of God; and they are ever at liberty to appeal from the human speaker to the book. They must not be pulpit Christians, but Bible Christians. 6. Finally, we learn with what state of mind we ought to study the book in which is contained what the Lord hath spoken. There should be humility, readiness of mind to hear what God the Lord will speak, and also unswerving loyalty to the God of truth in every point in which we see the truth of God (1 Pet. ii. 1, 2). And in practical obedience to what the Lord teaches us in his Word, we shall come to know its glory as our truest guide, and our glory in having such a guide.

Ver. 20.—*The closing aspiration :* "*Come, Lord Jesus.*" In the homilies on ch. i. 7 and xx. 11—15, compared with xxii. 12, we have touched on the second coming of Christ. But in each case we have done so in direct pursuance of our aim of giving a homiletic exposition of the plan of the Apocalypse. Hence in one case we dealt with it as the one clue threading the entire Scripture; in another case we looked at it as bringing about the consummation of all things. In the passage before us now there is presented to us yet a third point of view from which it is to be regarded, even as the object of the believer's hope, longing, and prayer. "Come, Lord Jesus." Three inquiries will come up before us, replies to which may throw light on a most important aspect of the Christian faith and expectation.

I. What is included in this one hope of the Church? The glorious appearing of the great God, even our Saviour Jesus Christ, is, without doubt, the "blessed hope." The Church is longing for the personal presence of her Saviour. Love cannot be fully satisfied while its fondest Object remains unseen. Still, the expectation of the coming of the Lord is one which includes a great deal more than the hope of his personal presence. For that of itself, without very much more, would not by any means secure all that believers desire. In fact, even as it is, we are better off than the disciples were when Jesus was on earth. "It is expedient for you that I go away," etc. It is not, then, as if we were here weeping and mourning, without a Christ, that we long to see him, but because of the glory which shall be ushered in at his coming. It may be well for us, at this stage of exposition, to locate the personal advent of Christ according to New Testament eschatology.[1] Increasing, repeated studies of the Word drive us further and further away from the pre-millennial hypothesis (although, for the sake of students, we have indicated in a foot-note below where they may turn for the clearest arrangement of it which has come before us). We do not look for the personal reappearing of Jesus as near at hand, in point of time, as yet (1889). It is not at the commencement of an era of blessedness that Scripture warrants us in placing it, but at the consumma-

[1] The Rev. E. H. Elliott, in his 'Horæ Apocalypticæ,' 5th edit., vol. iv. pp. 196—223, indicates the pre-millennial order of incident

tion thereof. Looking, however, at his coming as taking place at the restitution of all things, we must needs include in our aspirations after that glorious goal of human progress *every step on the way thither.* These steps towards the final blessedness are shown in the New Testament in the following order: 1. The advance of truth and the proclamation of the gospel among all nations must take place before the end. 2. The promise of the outpouring of the Holy Ghost is very far from complete fulfilment. Our Lord lives and reigns to bestow this gracious baptism. The Holy Ghost will both train the Church and convict the world. 3. Through the pouring out of the Holy Spirit Israel is to be restored (Ezek. xxxv.—xxxvii.). 4. The effect of Israel's restoration will be " as life from the dead," and will be followed by the inbringing of the fulness of the Gentiles (Rom. ix.—xi.). 5. Then will follow a long period of millennial rest, during which righteousness, though not absolutely universal, will be in the ascendant; while at the same time the tares as well as the wheat will be ripening for harvest (Isa. lx.; Matt. xiii.). 6. After this, for reasons known only to the great Disposer, the evil one, having long been bound, will be " loosed again," but only for a season. He will go forth to deceive. This will be his last effort, which will issue in his destruction. The enemies of God and of his Church will one by one be overthrown. 7. Then will come the appearing of our Lord; the general resurrection;[1] the gathering of the nations; the judgment; the award—for the wicked, the second death; for the righteous— 8. The inbringing of the new heavens and the new earth, wherein righteousness will dwell. It is for this we long. For this believers are waiting, anxiously watching every step in the process which is to bring about that halcyon calm. Yea, in our eagerness for it, we sometimes wish to push forward the wheels of time. We ask impatiently, "Why is his chariot so long in coming?" We cannot rest while wickedness rides high, nor while tares so much abound. Hence our prayer, " Come, Lord Jesus, come quickly. Come and complete thy reign. Overturn, and overturn, and overturn. Throw down the wrong; bring in the right, and let the groaning and travailing of the creation cease because of the manifestation of the sons of God ! "

II. WHY IS THIS IN SUCH AN ABSORBING DEGREE THE HOPE OF THE CHURCH? We are not careful to disguise the fact that in this respect the Church's outlook is very different from that of some who devote themselves to science, philosophy, and literature. There are, indeed, men of highest literary and scientific standing who join heartily in the prayer, " Even so, come, Lord Jesus." At the same time, there is no doubt that while men generally deem it wise and right to seek and to expect human progress, there is a great divergence among them in their opinions as to what such progress means, and how it is to be secured. The hope of some is that, through the advance of science, the race will reach its goal; that as law comes to be more definitely understood, nature will be brought more thoroughly under control, etc. In distinction from any or all of these, stands out the Christian hope. If we be asked a reason for it, we are prepared to give it in a series of considerations which, we cannot but think, are too frequently overlooked. Accordingly, we now give in outline the reasons which Christians have for the conviction that nothing less than the inbringing of the Christian hope will meet the cravings of our hearts. These reasons are so given as to be taken cumulatively. 1. We cannot but recognize the superiority of moral considerations to those which are merely physical. Doubtless, neglect of sanitary laws may prove a serious obstruction to men. But that neglect is itself a wrong moral act. And the immorality of the neglect must be done away ere the physical ill can be cut off. In a word, the moral and mental rule the physical. 2. We recognize also the immense importance of *men* over *things,* or over any combination of things. There is more worth in one human spirit than in all the material atoms in the universe of God. Nothing can content us that fails to renovate spirit. 3. The true moral and spiritual advance of men depends on what they are, rather than on what they know. Loyalty of heart is more than the furniture of the intellect. And when men talk about science being the regenerator, we ask—Which science? We ask—How is it, then, that the most accomplished men are sometimes the greatest rogues, and that some who are masters in knowledge are slaves to sin? Man is made for God, and only as he becomes God-like is his weal secured. 4. It is impossible to secure the world's peace while sin reigns in man's nature. Sin is the great mar-plot of the world. But: 5. With all sin put away, what a change would

[1] For the meaning of the phrase, " the first resurrection," see our homily thereon.

be brought about! If men were all righteous, if they were like him who went about doing good, our race would forthwith have Paradise again! 6. Now, as a matter of fact, no founder of a religion has ever set on foot a scheme of truth or an apparatus of power with the express purpose of putting down wrong and of bringing in righteousness, but the Lord Jesus Christ. He only has recognized fully the needs of our spiritual nature. But he has. And he is "mighty to save." He has saved millions, and is doing so now. But he alone. 7. This being so, we look to him who is the Author of our faith to be its Finisher too. And he who by his Spirit now quickens men so that they are alive unto God, is effecting a work which is bringing in the issue for which we long. Of this, evolution gives no account, and can give none. 8. The Lord Jesus Christ has left us the direct and positive assurance that "he will make all things new." And if it be said to us, "Do not the terrible disorders of earth shake your faith?" we reply—Not for a moment. Why should they? Nothing worse has happened yet than the seven seals, trumpets, and vials have indicated. And the end is *beyond* all these! How far beyond in point of time none can say. 9. Already, in the millions of souls ingathered, we have had many an earnest and pledge of the glorious harvest-day. History *is* opening up strictly according to the lines of the holy book, and it *will!* "He who hath begun the good work will perform it unto the day of Jesus Christ." 10. And the riper we get in grace, the more intense our love for our Lord, the more eagerly and passionately do we long for him to "complete the number of his elect," and to manifest her power and glory. And this desire, which by Christ has been created, by Christ himself shall be ultimately fulfilled. Surely these ten reasons, separately and fairly estimated, and then put together in cumulative force, do furnish an ample reason why believers in Jesus should regard the progress of their race and the glory of their Lord as leagued together in an everlasting bond. Reason enough is there here for the cry, "Come, Lord Jesus: come quickly!"

III. IN WHAT LIGHT DO ALL THESE CONSIDERATIONS SET THE ASPIRATION OF THE TEXT? 1. They account for the text being the prayer of the Church, for they show that it expresses the longing that the redemption already enjoyed by believers may be manifested in our race. 2. This petition, "Come, Lord Jesus: come quickly!" is a constant revealer of the unity of the true Church. The words go up from *all* Christian hearts. Romanist, Anglican, Protestant, Conformist and Nonconformist, all unite here. 3. The acceptance of the hope indicated in the prayer of the text is a test of the accuracy of a man's mental science and philosophic insight. That is no true science, that is no true philosophy, in which there is no room for this blessed hope. Its value can be denied only where plain and palpable facts of human nature, which ought to be taken into account, are ignored. 4. The text becomes a test of character. "As a man thinketh in his heart, so is he." Similarly, as a man *longeth* in his heart, so is he. Let a man tell us for what he most wishes, and we will tell him what he is. He will thereby show us: (1) The direction of his life. Every man hopes most for that to which his soul is most akin. And (2) the intensity with which he is moving in that direction. Hence: 5. The text becomes a criterion of safety. If a man is among those who are looking for Christ, he is among those to whom Christ's coming will bring in the salvation yet to be revealed. If a man is among those who care not for these things, he is one to whom the second coming will bring weeping and wailing and gnashing of teeth. "Wherefore, beloved, seeing that ye look for such things, be diligent, that ye may be found of him in peace, without spot, and blameless." And should any urge that "he prophesieth of the times afar off," let such remember that, however distant the consummation may be, the previous preparation is in all cases a continuous process, which *is going on now.* "Seek ye the Lord *while he may be found.*" "Now is the accepted time; now is the day of salvation."

Ver. 21.—*The closing benediction.* The Revised Version reads, "The grace of the Lord Jesus be with the saints." Pleasant is it to find the seer of Patmos, ere he lays down his pen, breathing out to the saints this pious and holy wish. No conclusion to the holy volume could be more suitable in itself or more grateful to the feelings of the believer. It will form an appropriate close to our homiletic expositions if we look at this final benediction from a triple point of view—the historic, the dogmatic, the practical.

I. THE BENEDICTION HAS A RICH HISTORIC INTEREST. We may regard it either as being an apostolic wish in his own name, or in the name of all believers. Supposing it to be the former (and, anyway, it is certainly *that*), it has all the weight and worth that an apostolic utterance can carry with it. Supposing it to be also the latter, then it is a new, a Christian form of brotherly well-wishing, which within about sixty years before the time that the apostle wrote, had been newly created. It was, in fact, a totally new expression of sacred friendship; it was a new birth; it was an indication of a new love uniting believers in one Being, whom before his advent earth had never known. The old formula, " Peace be with you," is now supplemented by " The grace of the Lord Jesus be with you." This is an historic fact of no small interest and importance. It is one of those " evidences of Christianity " which can never be questioned by those who understand the matter, showing us that a new tidal wave of love swept over mankind when Jesus came. It is well known that Christian tourists in Rome can discern in the differences between the epitaphs and epithets on pagan and Christian tombstones, the evidences of a new life and love in the latter marking them off from the former. So here, in the indication which these words furnish of a newly living friendship and brother-hood in Christ, is a proof of the new fraternity in himself which he alone created, and which, apart from him, had never been. Historically, the benediction before us serves another purpose. It was written by the Apostle John. Even unbelief allows this, albeit it makes the allowance with a questionable purpose.[1] Still, it *is* allowed, and we have no need to argue it. The Apostle John wrote these words when he was an exile in Patmos, under Domitian, about the year A.D. 96. This brings the writing of the text well within the lines of the first century, and also as written by one who had held and taught the same faith about Jesus Christ for more than half a century. What that faith was we have yet to see. It is enough just now to observe only how far we get histori-cally in the survey of this parting blessing. Even thus far—that we know, as a matter of historic fact, that within the first century, faith in Jesus Christ was so far rooted, established, and ramified, as to have produced a brotherhood welded together in him, on which the invocation of his grace and blessing was felt to be a suitable and adequate outpouring of the wishes of the Christian heart. Now, it is of some moment to remember this, and to inform others of it. For there are not wanting those—albeit they are not found in the circles of the ripest and devoutest scholars—who have main-tained, and do maintain, that nothing certain can be laid hold of about Jesus Christ till from sixty, seventy, or even a hundred and twenty years after his death.[2] This bene-diction alone refutes that assertion; and whoever makes it is either dishonest or incompetent—which, we do not care to decide.

II. THE BENEDICTION HAS AN EQUAL DOCTRINAL VALUE. If we come closely to examine it, we shall perhaps be surprised to find how much can be gathered from it. It is said that if a bone be put into the hands of a skilled anatomist, he can judge therefrom what was the form of the entire bodily framework of which it was a part. So, give this text to a Christian theologian, and he can construct therefrom the outlines of a fairly complete theology. Let us, then, see what the words involve. 1. Certainly they assume the actual existence of the Lord Jesus Christ, although at the time they were written, some sixty years had passed since his ascension. The Lord Jesus is evidently regarded as still living, as having overcome " the sharpness of death." For surely the " grace " of a dead Christ is altogether inconceivable. 2. The words assume the existence of " grace " in Jesus Christ; *i.e.* of mercy, favour, and of the fulness thereof in him. It is the same term as is applied to God. " The grace of God that bringeth salvation hath appeared," etc. So the like term is applied to Christ in a sense in which it never can be applied to any mere creature. Our Lord said to Paul, " My grace is sufficient for thee." As " grace " resides in him, it is virtue, power; as it comes to us it is blessing, various as the need; coming to us as sinful beings it is mercy, pity. And, as such, the words assume its exist-ence in our Lord Jesus Christ. 3. They also imply the close relationship between

---

[1] See 'Supernatural Religion.'

[2] So much out of date is such an assertion that we feel as if an apology were due to our readers for even referring to it. But, in fact, we had, during our own pastorate, to engage in battle with unbelievers on this very point. So that we deem it best not to omit it.

the Lord Jesus in heaven and his saints on earth, and the communicableness of the grace which is in him to them. Otherwise the words are unintelligible. If he could not communicate his grace, it could not be *with* us. 4. They involve also the truth that the disposal of this grace is according to the will of the Saviour. They assume that he will be as ready to grant it, as believers are to wish it for each other. 5. The words are such as would be uttered by one who felt it to be appropriate to breathe out a pious wish, mentioning only the Lord Jesus Christ, without specifying either the Father or the Spirit.[1] As if it were felt that his grace is from the Father, and that he gives it by the bestowment of the Spirit. It is even so. Thus invoking the grace of the Lord Jesus Christ is to invoke that of the Holy and Blessed Three in One. It is no fragmentary or broken wish, it is no half-prayer that is breathed, when we say, "The grace of Christ be with you." It is equivalent to saying, "May you be filled up to all the fulness of God." 6. Yea, more, we gather also that for an apostle or for a Church to wish for believers that the grace of Christ might be with them was deemed an adequate expression of their feelings of yearning desire. For consider the wide range over which the expression, "the saints," extends; think of the diversity of condition and requirement which it comprehends; think of the long vista of time into which it peers; and when we fairly weigh *each one of these three* considerations, we shall begin to feel what a conviction of infinite variety and adaptedness in the Saviour's grace these words imply. Yet more: 7. They involve the truth of the omnipresence of the Saviour. Surely the words did not contemplate the grace of Christ being now here and now there, filling some while others were pining, enriching the saints at Ephesus and leaving those at Smyrna to starve! We may be quite sure of this. But, then, this benediction involves a faith in and conviction of the glory of an omniscient, an omnipresent, an ever-living Saviour, who can supply *all* saints with *all* grace, through *all* time, even to the end of the age. Thus we can gather, from this holy breathing of Christian love, what was the believer's faith in our Lord Jesus within the first century; yea, from the time of his ascension to heaven. The Church had a book before it had a human creed; it had a faith even before it had the New Testament. Just as millions enjoy the light by the action of life, who have never defined it by an intellectual formula, so the believers of old rejoiced in and lived on their living Lord from the first. Their formulation of the faith was not till long afterwards. We see, moreover, that it is only the evangelical faith in the Divine glory of our Lord that harmonizes with this first faith of the Church. Yea, here, in this faith in him, Catholic, Anglican, Protestant, are one. We know that our Lord has grace enough for rich and poor; for the prisoners in the dungeon and the martyrs at the stake. When we are weary, we have rest; when hungry, food; when thirsty, living water; when in darkness, light; when in weakness, strength; when dying, life;—and all in him! Such a Saviour is to us no less than the true God and eternal life.

III. THIS BENEDICTION SHOULD HAVE GREAT PRACTICAL POWER. For it indicates lines of life equally with those of doctrine. It shows us: 1. *That Christian love has its root in Christian faith.* The wishes and prayers of the saints for each other have their peculiar direction and intensity because of their living faith in that Saviour in whom they are one. Many can admire a true and pure Christian love. Few would wish it weakened in its firmness or fervour. But it may be, sometimes is, forgotten, that true Christian love is nothing less than one of the fruits of the Spirit. It is a growth from life in Christ. That life is through faith in him. Weaken the faith, and you cool the love. Let the one cease, the other will pine away from the lack of nutriment. But this benediction shows us also: 2. *That Christian faith is a living growth which blossoms into love.* As there can be no love without faith as its root, so there is no genuine faith without love as its fruit. When men are "in Christ," they have a bond of undying attachment for each other, in a fellowship which can never be destroyed, but which is destined to ripen until in the Father's house it shall be perfected. 3. What an unspeakable comfort it is that Christians can express their most fervid longings for each other's weal in one petition that covers all possible ground of every need of every believer for all time! We know very little of each other's wants. Owing to distance, differences of clime, of custom, of modes of thought and life, variations in

---

[1] The history of the Church's views on the baptismal formula may well be studied in this connection.

constitution and circumstances, no one can even approximately guess the wants of the rest. But when we say, "The grace of the Lord Jesus be with them"—that meets every case. It is, indeed, a prayer sent up for them to heaven—a prayer which will be answered, not according to our imperfect knowledge and thinking, but according "to the riches of his grace." 4. Hence it is an infinite privilege to be numbered among "the saints," so as to have a perpetual interest in their prayers. For let us consider over what a vast extent the prayer of our text now doth spread. It goes up from millions on millions of hearts the wide world over; from private and family altars, from many a Church and congregation. Surely it is a privilege of no mean order to have a share in petitions which span the globe, speed to heaven, and find their way to the heart of Jesus. 5. For, although it may be and is impossible for us to say along what lines such and such an answer may come to such and such a prayer, yet we are perfectly sure that he who has taught his own thus to pray for each other, has done so in fulfilment of his own law and in the working out of his own plan; and that, however eagerly any believers may send up the prayer, with far more eagerness does Jesus send down the answer. Certainly, believers owe much of their now advancing unity to the fulfilment of each other's prayers. Finally, this fervent wish with which the apostle closes the canon of inspiration is surely not an unsuitable one for believers at any moment. Nor can the writer refrain, in writing his last words for this commentary, from saying, "Grace be with all the saints!" not forgetting those into whose hand this book may fall. May his grace be with those who shall study this book in private devotion, and with those who shall read it to gain help in speaking to others! May his grace be with all the saints, of every name, of every land, under every circumstance of life, through every age, until we all meet in the Father's house, having washed our robes, and having entered in through the gates into the city!

"Now unto him that is able to keep us from falling, and to present us faultless before the presence of his glory with exceeding joy, to the only wise God our Saviour, be glory and majesty, dominion and power, both now and ever. Amen."

HOMILIES BY VARIOUS AUTHORS.

Ver. 2.—" *The tree of life.*" There was, there is, there shall be, this life-giving tree. Consider—

I. THE PRIMEVAL TREE. What was it? 1. *Not a mere symbol.* This has been affirmed by many, from Origen downwards. It has been compared to the visions of the Apocalypse. But those are said to be visions; the early chapters of Genesis are not. This tree, therefore, is as real as any other of the trees of the garden. 2. *It perpetuated not bodily life,* for the life of the body was sustained by other food. The body lived when access to this tree was denied. Moreover, on such earth as ours bodily life could not be perpetual. 3. *Nor spiritual life.* For spiritual life is far more than immortality; it is life holy and like God, and had this tree been capable of imparting such life, access to it would not have been forbidden. 4. *But for soul-life.* There is a distinction between body, soul, and spirit. St. Paul prays that "the whole body, soul, and spirit may be preserved blameless," etc. In the Epistle to the Hebrews we read of the "Word of God . . . dividing asunder the soul and spirit." Cf. also 1 Cor. ii. 15; also 1 Cor. xv., where the contrast between the nature which belongs to the soul and that which is of the spirit is drawn out at length. "Sown a natural body," *i.e.* a body whose chief principle is the soul; "raised a spiritual body," *i.e.* a body whose chief principle is the spirit. We have no one English word which exactly answers to the Greek word, which is rendered sometimes "natural," sometimes, as in St. James and St. Jude, "sensual." But it is in nearly all cases spoken of as in sharp contrast to the spirit. But though the Scripture draws so clear a distinction, we, in our common speech, scarce make any. Now, the soul seems to include the animal life. Gen. i. 30, "wherein there is life," is really, "wherein there is a living soul." So, again, Gen. i. 24, "Let the earth bring forth the living soul." So in Lev. xvii. 11, "The soul of the flesh is in the blood." And it is the basis both of the reason and conscience; for men who have not had spirit (cf. St. Jude) have yet had these. And it is "born of the flesh;" souls are said to be begotten by or born to parents. But it outlives the flesh; for mental existence, which is independent of the body, belongs to the soul. Reason as well as Scripture seem to teach this. And, unlike the spirit, it is not immortal. With the body, it can be destroyed. But the spirit is heaven-born; is superior to the soul; is immortal, and supersedes the soul as the basis of all other life, and is nurtured only by what is akin to itself. No "tree," therefore, could furnish food for the spirit. But for the soul-life it might; and hence man was forbidden access to the tree, lest he should "eat, and live for ever." For the soul, as distinct from the body and the spirit, the first tree of life ministered.

II. THE PRESENT. For still there is a tree of life. Christ is such; for faith in him gives eternal life—the life in the spirit. Life is in Christ, who is "the Life." Thus the soul, which otherwise would have perished, has what in itself it cannot have—eternal life. Apart from Christ there is no eternal life; but because in him there is this life, he is for us to-day "the Tree of Life."

III. THE PROMISED. That told of in the text. It may be literal, or at least as much so as was the primeval tree, and may minister to the life of the spiritual body. But "our knowledge of that life is small;" all that we do know is, that whatever will further our life, our joy, our every good, will be forthcoming. Wrapped up in this promise is all that we can desire. The lost tree of life is more than restored; "where sin did abound, grace does much more abound." That is all we can say, and, thank God, we can say this.—S. C.

Ver. 2.—*Faith's foliage.* "The leaves of the tree were for the healing of the nations." In ancient times the leaves of certain trees were used for medicinal purposes (see the old herbalists, etc.). And increasingly it is being discovered how God has placed healing power in the varied forms of plant-life. The proportion of the physician's pharmacopœia occupied by leaves and such-like plant products is no slight one. The old story of Marah, and the healing of the bitter waters there by the tree cast into them, has its antitype in the cross of the Lord Jesus Christ, and its repetition in the healing properties which the leaves and other parts of many trees possess. Now, concerning the tree of life told of in our text, and its leaves, and the nations that are healed by them, many questions may be asked which it is not easy to answer. But, nevertheless, it is neither improper nor unprofitable to follow out the suggestions which the words of our text supply. Taking, then, the tree of life as telling of Christ, whether seen in his gospel, or in his Church, or in the lives of individual believers, the leaves of the tree mean much. Take them as representing—

I. SCATTERED MEMBERS OF CHRIST'S CHURCH. Missionaries, Christian emigrants, soldiers, merchants, sailors. All these are like the leaves which are scattered hither and thither as they are torn off by the wind. What do not heathen lands owe to such scattered ones as these leaves tell of? Any of us may, by the wind of God's providence, be carried far away into heathen lands. If so, God grant that we may be as one of these leaves of the tree of life.

II. THE HUMBLEST AND MOST ORDINARY MEMBERS OF CHRIST'S CHURCH. As the leaves are individually but insignificant parts of the tree, they seem to represent those members of Christ who are like them. And yet what force and efficacy are attributed to them! In every leaf the whole tree—so botanists say—is discernible; its image can be clearly traced. And this is why each leaf can do so much. God often chooses things that are foolish and least and despised (cf. 1 Cor. i., etc.) for the accomplishment of his ends.

III. THE HOLY SCRIPTURES. We speak of the leaves of a book. Whether that common phrase refer to the leaves of a tree or no, it is certain that the leaves of the Bible may be called leaves of the tree of life. For where those leaves have gone, what have they not done? The indebtedness of the world to the Bible has long been a favourite theme of Christian advocates. They have been for the healing of the nations, and are so still. And they who circulate religious tracts and leaflets, as they term them, do so in the belief that the truth of Christ which is in them will have, as it often has had, healing power.

IV. CHRISTIAN CONDUCT. The leaves are the portion of the tree which is visible, prominent, and seen by all. They may, therefore, stand as the symbol of all that outward life of the Christian which appears before men. All the characteristics of the leaves suggest similar ones in conduct. The leaves are the conspicuous parts of the tree; by their elevation, their colour, their number, their sound, their movements, their beauty, their shadow, and much else. So that everybody notices the leaves. For the most part it is all they can see, and always the most marked feature of the tree. Now, such is the outward life, the conduct, the ten thousand common actions, the innumerable everyday doings and sayings, multitudinous as leaves and as visible, of Christian men. And such leaves have healing power. It was so at the first. Rome was converted from paganism to Christ by the silent but mighty force of the pure, beautiful, blameless, and spiritually elevated lives of the Christians. The heathen gazed with wonder, and an ever-increasing number of them came to desire such life for themselves. And there is no healing force anywhere like such leaves. But though, in the blessed future condition of the Church, the lives of all her members will be of so salutary a sort, it is very far otherwise now. Too many Christians are upas trees rather than trees of life, and their leaves are deadly rather than healing. Who does not know this? And such sad fact should lead to the question—What is the influence of my life? are its leaves healing leaves or the reverse? And no more fervent prayer should we pray than that we, each one, may become ourselves trees of life.

V. The secondary results of Christianity. Leaves are not the purpose of a tree. To have nothing but leaves is condemnation, not praise. Fruit is the end of a tree. "I have ordained you," said our Lord, "that ye should go and bring forth *much fruit*" (cf. John xv. 2, "Every branch that beareth not fruit," etc.). Leaves, therefore, are but the accidents, the subordinate purpose, the secondary results, of the tree. And our Lord came that we might bring forth fruit unto God. Still, along with this, the tree has borne precious leaves. See the influence of Christianity upon art, law, society, commerce—indeed, on all departments of life. What does not art—music, painting, sculpture, architecture—owe to the faith of Christ? This was not the main purpose of Christ. That was to create holy souls; to redeem men from all iniquity. But in the accomplishment of this, in bringing forth this most precious fruit, the tree has yielded leaves also, such as these, and yet others. Shall we, then, listen to speculations and arguments, the aim and too frequent effect of which is to destroy the faith of Christ in men's minds? Shall we knowingly cut down a tree the very leaves of which have healing power?—S. C.

Ver. 4.—*The beatific vision.* "They shall see his face." We often think, and think truly, that it must have been a great joy to see our Lord as he was here on earth. What would we not give could we now see him as his apostles did? Everything associated with him has gained sacredness and sanctity by that association. The land where he lived—

> "Those holy fields,
> Over whose acres walked those blessed feet
> Which, many hundred years ago, were nailed,
> For our redemption, to the cruel cross,"

—that land we call the Holy Land. The particular places most closely connected with his life on earth we call the holy places. The men whom he chose to minister to and for him we call holy ones, or saints. The day on which he rose from the dead we observe as a holy day. All this is but the result of that mighty influence which he exercised over those who came under the spell of his wondrous personality. Hence one would like to have known him as he was—in his childhood, as he "grew in wisdom and in stature, and in favour with God and man;" in the midst of his ministry, as he toiled and taught for thankless men; as he hung upon the cross; as he rose from the dead. But such vision is impossible to us now. All the more, therefore, do we hail with joy the promise of our text. Let us try and tell a little of what is contained in it.

I. That we shall see the Lord Jesus Christ himself. No doubt that in that blessed future world: 1. *There is very much besides that is blessed.* The scene, how glorious! See St. John's descriptions. The inhabitants, how illustrious, how glorious, how holy, how blessed! And some of them beloved ones of our own; how blessed will be the sight of them! But, after all: 2. *The chief joy will be our seeing him.* For think what seeing Jesus, even in our present poor and imperfect way, has done for men. At the beginning of their life as his disciples, when filled with fear because they had seen somewhat of the iniquity of their sin, the seeing of Jesus allayed that fear and gave them peace. During the progress of that life, when sin has reasserted its cruel power, and they have been heart-crushed in consequence; when the cares of this world have well-nigh overwhelmed them; when sorrow has saddened their very souls; when temptation has drawn near in its most deadly, because in its most enticing, form;—at all such times the seeing of Jesus, by the quickened eye of faith, has given hope and help, strength and deliverance, according as the need has been. And in the hour of death the seeing him has soothed the sufferings of that last time, and snatched victory from the last enemy, death, and given it to the dying saint whose succour and salvation the sight of Jesus has then secured. If, then, our poor vision here has been so full of blessing, what shall not our perfect vision yonder be?

II. AND IT WILL BE A SEEING HIM. Not a mere hearing concerning him. 1. *Hearing is a great blessing.* What do we not owe to the gospel story that we have heard read or preached, so many times? "Faith"—the faith that saves—"cometh by hearing." 2. *But seeing is far better.* Word-pictures describing some fair landscape are often interesting, and sometimes so well done that they help us much to realize what the scene described must be. But how the best of such descriptions fails before the seeing of the landscape itself! And even the gospel story of Jesus will be as nothing to the *seeing* him—seeing his face.

III. AND HIS GLORIFICATION WILL BE NO BAR TO OUR JOY. For we have not to say of him now that he is a spirit. If he were that, if his glorification had transformed him into an entirely spiritual being, then our Lord would be lost to us, for we could form no idea, no clear conception, of him. But it is not so. He wears his humanity; he has glorified that, and still he is the Son of man. The pierced hands and feet, the brow that was crowned with thorns, the side that was riven by the spear, he has taken with him into heaven. Therefore we shall see his *face*—the very face that sweat great drops of blood, and that was marred more than any man's. Literally our text is true.

IV. AND WE SHALL KNOW HIM. Not merely recognize him, but know him as here we have never done. His people will read his heart, will understand him as now they cannot. Much there is here which hinders our understanding, our true knowledge of him. Sin, sorrow, worldly pursuits, earthly mindedness of all kinds, serve to hide him from our hearts, and so hinder our knowledge of him. But there these things shall not be.

V. AND IT WILL BE "A LASTING SIGHT." It will not be a mere glimpse—a fitful, fleeting vision, which is all that we now enjoy. But our "joy shall remain."

VI. AND IT IMPLIES MUCH THAT IS VERY BLESSED. For example: 1. *That we are really his.* Were we not, the sight of that face would be unendurable. The wicked cannot bear it. And yet they *must* behold it. Ah! would that all such would think of this, and now be reconciled to God! But the fact that we rejoice to see his face is "an evident token of salvation." 2. *That we shall not see our sins.* Whether or no we shall remember our sins in heaven, and if so, whether that memory will sadden heaven for us, is a question that has often been asked. That we can actually and entirely forget them is impossible; but that the "remembrance of them" will be "grievous to us, and the burden of them intolerable," as here we confess they are, we cannot think. For, on a bright starry night, what is it that we notice, that arrests our attention, as we delightedly gaze and gaze upon the magnificent scene? Is it the black stretches of cloud through which the stars shine down upon us? Certainly not, but the stars themselves. And so "his face," as compared to our sins, will be as those stars to the clouds. In that beatific vision the darker memories will be swallowed up and, as it were, unseen. 3. *That we shall be like him.* For seeing assimilates. "We shall be like him," says St. John; "for we shall see him as he is."

CONCLUSION. Are we of the number who shall enjoy this beatific vision? How can we tell? St. John supplies the answer. "He that hath this hope in him purifieth himself"—that is the test. Are we thus striving after Christ-like purity?—S. C.

Ver. 11.—*Permanency of character: a sermon for the closing year.* These very solemn words have been used again and again to illustrate and enforce the lessons of this great truth of permanency of character—the fact that after a while character becomes fixed, stereotyped as it were, and therefore unalterable; so that he that is unrighteous remains unrighteous still, and, thank God, he that is holy remains holy still. But this is not their true meaning, though by their form and sound they seem to teach this. But their purport is to exhort and encourage the faithful, by bidding them yet hold on, yet persevere; for the time of recompense, the Lord's coming, is at hand. Let the unrighteous, since they are so determined, be unrighteous still; and let the foul, since they love to be so, be foul still; let them, if they will have it so, if men will be wicked they must; but let you righteous and holy ones be righteous and holy still; your trial will soon be over, and your day of reward have come. The parallel passage in Dan. xii. 9 confirms this interpretation, and seems to have been in St. John's mind when he wrote our text (cf. also Ezek. iii. 27). But because what a man wills to be he eventually and increasingly comes permanently to be, therefore we may yet use our text as teaching that tendency of character to become permanent, let the character be what it may. He that is righteous will go on doing righteousness; whilst he that is filthy will go on making himself yet more foul. Both will have it so, and it comes to be so, blessed as is the fact for the righteous, terrible as it is for the unrighteous. Now, this is a subject appropriate to the closing year. For at such times we are wont to look back along the way we have come, and to ascertain where we stand. We do so in regard to our business, our health, our position in society, our attainments in knowledge, etc. And such review is right. Look back, then, on the paths along which we have gone during the past year. There have been *some in which we have made too little progress*, in which we have halted too often, and at times turned back—the paths of prayer, of trust, of obedience, of love to God and man, of service, of charity, and the like. And there have been *others in which it would have been well if we had not gone at all*, or had halted in them, and come away from them—paths sinful, foolish, injurious to ourselves and others. Halt now, if any be in such paths, and forsake them at once. *But there are others in which we cannot halt.* This dying year tells of one such—the path that leads to death and eternity.

> "Our hearts, like muffled drums, keep beating
> Funeral marches to the grave."

Along that path, whether we will or no, we *must* go, without halt or pause: and here we are, a long stretch of that way left behind us in this past year. And another of these paths along which we are ever proceeding is that one which *leads to fixity of character*, the permanent bent and bias of the will. It is to this that our text specially summons our thought. We are ever engaged in gathering together the materials which go to the formation and fixing of character, no matter whether it be good or ill. All our pursuits, pleasures, companionships, books, work; all our thoughts, words, and deeds are busy, like a very colony of ants, all at work, and all tending to that ultimate result in character which binds us down to be ever still the same. Each day finds that work nearer done, and a year must make, does make, a great difference. The walls of the building may have risen hardly above the foundation a year ago, but now, at the year's end, they are a good way up; and a year hence, if we be spared so long, the whole structure will be much nearer completion. What inquiry, then, can be more important than this, as to the direction which our character is taking? It would not matter so much, though even then it would be serious enough, if our varied, separate acts were isolated and independent, without linking on the one to the other; and not, as they are, all tending to fix and stereotype character in one direction or the other, for good or for evil. It would not matter if at any time we could, as we say, "turn over a new leaf;" if it were "never too late to mend." But there comes a time when that new leaf will not be turned over, and it *is* too late to mend. A time when, like Esau, we find no place of repentance, though we seek it carefully with tears, as he did (cf. Prov. i. 24—32). When the great suspension bridge over the Niagara Falls was built, first of all a slender wire was carried over by a kite to the other side; that drew over a stronger one; that a chain; and that, one heavier; and so by degrees the bridge was put together and completed. So is it with our characters. Some slight, insignificant action, as we deem it, draws after it some others which are not so insignificant; and these draw others more important still; and so at length the whole structure of our completed character, whatever it be, is brought together and remains permanently fixed. There are harbours round our coast within whose shelter large and numerous ships were wont to gather, so that important towns grew up on their banks, and much trade was done. But rivers that flowed into those harbours brought down with them, year after year, such amount of sandy deposit, though only a very little each year, that after a while the accumulation became so great that a huge bar began to stretch across the harbour mouth; and this increased until at length the port was blocked and all its prosperity at an end. That result was brought about by the sum of small and trifling additions, each one but little in itself, but together accomplishing so much. And so with the myriad minute acts that go to make habits, and habits form character. Well, then, *looking back over the year, what does the retrospect declare?* How is it with our souls? The year cannot but have done much in regard to them. Is it leaving us nearer God, more in sympathy with his will, more desiring to be, and more actually, what he would have us be? With some, no doubt, it is so, and let such give thanks; for, indeed, they have cause so to do. Others may have mournfully to confess that they are further off, that they have gone back, have lost much of their religion, its joy, strength, and peace. Let such cry unto the Lord and turn unto him with all their hearts; for they have need so to do, lest they fall further away still. "I remember, some time ago, hearing a remarkable circumstance related by a public speaker to whom I was listening. It happened that a ship was being towed across the Niagara river, in America, some little distance above the well-known falls. Just as she got into the middle of the stream the hawser parted, and the unfortunate ship began to drift down the river, stern foremost. Efforts were made to save her from impending ruin, but every effort failed, and the unfortunate ship kept drifting further and further down the stream towards the terrible abyss below. The news of the disaster spread along the banks of the river, and in a very short time there were hundreds of people, and they soon swelled to thousands, looking on in breathless anxiety to see what was to become of this unfortunate crew. There is a point that stretches into the river, which bears the name of 'Past Redemption Point,' and it is believed in the neighbourhood that nothing that passes that point can escape destruction. The current there becomes so strong, the influence so fatal, that whatever goes by Past Redemption Point is inevitably lost. The excited multitude upon the banks of the river watched the helpless ship drifting down further and further, till she was within a few hundred yards of the fatal point. One after another were efforts made, but of no avail; still she drifted on. Only a few moments, and she passed the point. There was a kind of sigh of horror from the vast multitude as they saw that she had passed, for they knew she was lost. But just as they rounded the point the captain felt a strong breeze smite upon his cheek. Quick as thought, he shouted at the top of his voice, 'All sails set!' and in almost less time than it takes to tell, every stitch of canvas on board the ship was stretched to catch the favouring gale. A cheer broke from the multitude on shore as they witnessed this last effort for salvation. But would it succeed? The ship was still drifting, though the wind was blowing against it, and she was still moving downwards, stern foremost, though the wind was bulging out all her sails. It was a battle between the wind and the current. With breathless anxiety they watched the result. She slacks! Another moment—they scarcely dare whisper it—she stands! Yes, that terrible, downward course was actually stopped. There she was, still as a log upon the water. Another moment, and inch by inch she began to forge her way up the stream, until the motion was perceptible to those on shore, and one great shout of victory burst forth from a thousand voices, 'Thank God, she is saved! Thank God, she is saved!' In a few moments more, with considerable headway upon her, she swept right up the stream, by Past Redemption Point, right into the still water, saved from what appeared to be inevitable destruction, just because in the very moment of moments she caught the favouring breeze" (Aitken). Now, if any have, like this all-but-lost ship, drifted ruinwards and away from God during this past year—and, doubtless, some have—and if conscience be now rebuking and the Holy Spirit pleading with you by quickening in you desires after a truer, better life, do not delay, but at once take advantage of the favouring breath of the Spirit of God, and let him waft you away from where you are to where you fain would be. "On your knees fall down and pray," lest you be hardened by the deceitfulness of sin.—S. C.

Ver. 12.—*The day of recompense.* "My reward is with me, to give every man according as his work shall be." It is related of Daniel Webster, the regality of whose moral endowment no one disputes, that when once asked what was the greatest thought that had ever occupied his mind, he replied, "The fact of my personal accountability to God." And yet this thought is one not frequently present in men's minds, because it is one that is but little welcome. The very phraseology of the text, its several words, seem to point at one and another of the hindrances to the reception of this thought. As, for example—

I. INDIFFERENCE. How many minds are wrapped up in this! They feel no concern; they are spiritually asleep, as was Jonah literally, though the ship and all in it were nigh to perishing; and though the great day of Christ's award is hastening on. Now, to arouse such as these, the text begins with the startling word, "Behold!" Thus does it "cry aloud."

II. PROCRASTINATION. Many, Felix-like, put off to "a more convenient season" the consideration of a fact like this. It was this very fact that Paul reasoned about and at which Felix trembled; but, nevertheless, the consideration of which he, as thousands are ever doing, put off. Now, as if to protest against and to prevent such conduct, Christ says, "Behold, I come *quickly*." There is no time for delay; "now is the day of salvation."

III. NOTIONS AND IDEAS OF PRIVILEGE. There were, there are, those who counted themselves God's favourites. The Jews did, and, in a very real sense, so they were; but not in such sense as would suffer them to be indifferent to the moral demands of God. They, however, flattered themselves that God would not judge them as he did others. And there are those who have persuaded themselves that they are God's elect, but who pervert the doctrine of God's election to allowance of themselves in evil. Now, as if to meet these, the Lord here makes no difference, but says, "I will give *every man* according," etc.

IV. ABUSE OF DOCTRINE OF FAITH. The doctrine of justification by faith has come in many minds to mean little more than a mere mental reference to the atonement of Christ. They think that a passport to eternal life. Such people say, "Oh, we believe, we trust in Jesus," and with this their faith ends. But Christ here declares, not only the rewardableness of works, but also that his reward will be according to each man's work. No profession of faith only, or talking of "casting deadly doing down"—see the well-known but mischievous mission hymn—will avail where the question of what our "work" is will be the all-important, all-decisive one.

V. RELIANCE ON PAST EXPERIENCES. It is said of Cromwell that on his death-bed he asked one of his chaplains, "If a man were once in grace, would he be always so?" And his chaplain answered, "Yes, certainly." "Well, then," said Cromwell, "it is well with me, for I know I was once in grace." We presume not to judge him or any man, but these words of the Lord do not countenance any such reliance on the past. For his reward is "according as his work *shall be*." Not according as it once was, but as it is when the Lord comes. Thus does he beat down these "refuges of lies," and take away "these battlements which are not the Lord's." But our real refuge is to awake now and turn unto the Lord as they who have no hope but in him, and at once to manifest the reality of our repentance and faith by doing those works which he has commanded.—S. C.

Ver. 13.—"*The First and the Last.*" So is Christ. The text is one of those clear, strong statements which compel the mind of him who accepts the authority of Scripture to assign to the Lord Jesus Christ that position of Divine dignity and rank which the Church has ever ascribed to him. He is the First and the Last. Like as some vast mountain, towering aloft into the clouds, is the first object that catches the eye of the voyager on board a ship approaching the land, and, when again she sails, is the last that lingers in his view; so the Lord Jesus Christ, when we approach the study of God's revelations of himself, is the first Object that arrests our view, as he will be the last when we look back from the ocean of eternity. And as in our illustration, so in him to whom we have ventured to apply the illustration. Not only first and last, but in all the interval between. As the mountain dominates the whole landscape, and is seen from all points, go where we will, so the Lord Jesus Christ occupies and fills up the chief place in our study, no matter from what side we contemplate the ways and works of God. We behold "him first, him midst, him last, him without end." So is it—

I. IN THE UNIVERSE OF GOD. For: 1. He is first *in time*. "In the beginning was the Word." Ere ever aught was he was. 2. *In position and rank*. None so great as he. "Let all the angels of God worship him." 3. *As being the Object of all*. Creation is to show forth his glory. Man, to subserve his will. Events, to further his purpose. 4. *And he is the Last also*. Omega as well as Alpha. When man and the universe, as we now know them, shall have passed away, "his years shall have no end." "They shall perish, but thou remainest."

II. IN THE HOLY SCRIPTURES. In their opening statement we read, "In the beginning Elohim created," etc.—the plural form suggesting, if it does not declare, the then existence of the Son of God. He is "the Seed of the woman," the promise of whom lights up the first prophecy. The first sacrifice, the first death, speak of him. And from these earliest teachings concerning him right down to the last utterance of the Word of God, in what book, chapter, or page is he absent? Patriarchs saw his day; types told of him; laws led to him; psalmists sung of him; prophets prophesied of him; princes and rulers, and the events which the sacred history records, prepared the way for him; and the New Testament is all of him. He it is who gives unity to the Scriptures, which otherwise would be a mere collection of ancient writings, having no point, or aim, or plan. He is the Keystone of the arch, without which it would have neither symmetry nor strength.

III. IN THE LIFE OF THE BELIEVER. He is "the Author and Perfecter of our faith." He begins the work, having made it possible by his death, his resurrection, and the gift of his Spirit. "All things" thus being "ready," he gives regenerating grace, whereby we are grafted into him as our second Adam; then converting grace, leading us to believe; then sanctifying grace; and, finally, grace for the hour of death, grace to meeten us for the Divine presence; and at last glorifying grace. Think, then, all these things being so, what: 1. Must he not be in himself? 2. Ought he not to be to us? 3. Will he be to us if "we will not have him to reign over us"?—S. C.

Ver. 14.—*The blessed ones*. In the Revised Version and the Authorized Version there is a notable difference of reading. In the former the text reads, "Blessed are they that wash their robes;" in the latter it is, "Blessed are they that do his commandments." But there is no real contradiction; for they that wash are they that will therefore obey, and they that obey are those who by their obedience show that they "wash their robes." For note—

I. WHAT IS IT TO THUS "WASH"? What does the expression mean? Some copies add on what is found in ch. vii., "in the blood of the Lamb," and no doubt such washing is meant. But what does it all mean? Let it be remembered that by "Christ's blood is meant the spirit of his whole life—his love poured forth in sacrifice for men, his self-devotion unto death for truth and righteousness' sake, all concentrated, fulfilled, and brought to the point when, on the cross, he bowed his head and died. Drink in that spirit, and you possess, not only hereafter, but now, eternal life. It is life, and it alone. Bathe your heart and intelligence, imagination and spirit, in the spirit of that life and death, till all it was and means flows through your whole nature and life as blood through your veins; wash all your outward life, your habits, your manners, your doings at home and abroad, all the robes of your life, in the spirit which made Jesus pour forth his blood upon the cross, and make them white and pure thereby. Then you will understand—no, not understand, but know—for ever, and live for ever by the truth that 'the blood of Jesus Christ cleanseth from all sin.'" In short, the possession of, and yet more the being possessed by, the mind and spirit of the Lord Jesus Christ when he shed his blood for us, is to be washed in his blood, and to have our robes made white therein. This, surely, is the meaning of this much misunderstood but precious word. Then note—

II. WHO THEY ARE THAT THUS WASH. 1. *They were such as needed cleansing*. The blessed were not always holy, but sin-defiled as are we all. 2. *They sought this cleansing*. It does not come unsought. If we have no love for the cleansing it brings, we shall not have it. It cannot be hurried up in a moment at the last extremity of life, as too many think it can, and so leave seeking it till then. 3. *And have obtained it.* For it is said "they wash," that is, they come to him whose it is to impart this cleansing, and they gain it. 4. *And this they continue to do.* It is not an act done once for all. It is not true that "there is life for a look at the Crucified One;" there is the beginning of life in such look if it be genuine and real, but if the life is to continue and grow and develop, and become eternal life, we must be ever "looking unto Jesus;" it must be the habitual posture of the soul. Such are the blessed.

III. WHEREIN THEIR BLESSEDNESS CONSISTS. 1. *"They have right to the tree of life."* (1) To its fruit, which in some mysterious way nurtures and preserves the life of the spiritual body as did the original tree of life, told of in Genesis, the life of the natural body. After man had sinned the perpetuation for ever of that life would have been a fearful calamity, and therefore man was driven forth from the place where that tree stood, for the express purpose, so we are told, "lest he should put forth his hand, and take of the fruit, and eat, and live for ever." But now that man, as seen in our text, is restored, because washed in the blood of Christ, perpetuated life may be given him, and it is given him. All that he lost by the first Adam is given back to him through the second. Paradise is more than regained. How can he, then, be otherwise than blessed? (2) And to the leaves; those leaves which are said to be "for the healing of the heathen." They are without the city; for it is they who are told of, by their common characteristics, in the next verse. Without the city is not the same as the lake of fire, but within reach of the light that radiates and streams forth from the city. They yet need healing, and to minister to that shall, it is probable, be part of the blessed employ of the blessed in the holy city. 2. *Their entry "through the gates into the city."* As in triumphal procession, not in any concealed or forbidden way. But through the gates of pearl—the new and living way, which is Christ. Theirs is the greater salvation—salvation in fulness; an entrance "administered abundantly" into the kingdom of the Lord. For others there may be, there seems to be, a lesser salvation, a place without the city; a walking in its light, though not admitted within as its citizens. Thus is the living God in Christ the "Saviour of all men, but *especially* of them that believe." In other parts of this book, and of this and the foregoing chapter, many of the elements of the joy that belongs to the citizens of the holy Jerusalem are set forth; the ills that are here, but are not there; the blessings that are not here, but are there. Shall we be of these blessed ones? Have we come to Christ, and do we keep coming? *That* is to wash our robes, as is here said. God help us so to do!—S. C.

Ver. 16.—*The Root, the Branch, and the Star.* We are perpetually bidden in God's Word to look to Christ. All manner of means are employed to lead us so to do. Amongst others, the vast variety of names that are given to our Lord serve this purpose. There are some two hundred of these, and they cannot but arrest attention, excite inquiry, and impress the mind, of any thoughtful reader. Here we have three of them.

1. THE ROOT OF DAVID. So is Christ named here, or rather so does he name himself. What is the meaning of this name? The reference is to Isa. xi., where we read, "Behold, there shall come forth a shoot from the stock of Jesse, and a scion shall spring forth from his roots; . . . and in that day there shall be a root of Jesse." Hence the meaning is: 1. *Not that our Lord was the Author, the Source of the family of David,* as well as its Offspring. It does not mean that before David was, Christ was, as he said concerning Abraham. Many, however, have so understood these words as if they were equivalent to what we mean when we call our Lord "the second Adam," as St. Paul does. No doubt Christ is, in this sense, the Root of David, as he is of us all. Unless we believe matter to be eternal, man must have sprung from some spiritual root. We are told that God by Christ "created the heavens and the earth," and that "the things which are made were not made of things which do appear." We and all men and things are the product of his Divine essence. No doubt these words are beyond our comprehension. It is "by faith" we accept them. Therefore, in this sense, Christ was the Root of David. But it is not the truth taught here. That truth is: 2. *Christ is as a stem springing from the root of David.* Oftentimes there may be seen springing up from the roots of a tree which has been cut down or broken off, and which has disappeared all but its roots, a vigorous but slender stem, which may grow up to be itself a stalwart tree. Now it was when the house of David had fallen low,

its glory all gone, that as a stem out of the ancient root Christ appeared. True, he was of the house and lineage of David, but the fortunes of that house were at their lowest when Jesus was born. The crown of Judah had left the line of David, and had passed into the Asmonean, and then into the Maccabean, and then into the Herodian dynasties. And now when the noble tree had fallen, and nothing but the roots were left, and these hidden, buried, altogether unnoticed by men, lo! there springs up a stem, a shoot, out of that ancient root, small and insignificant to the eye, but destined to be great indeed. *And in a spiritual sense* Christ is the Root, not only of David, but of many others also. How often, when all men's earthly pride and greatness have been taken away, the tender plant of grace springs up, and Christ becomes in and to them "the Hope of glory"! What an encouragement this fact is! Nothing seemed less likely than that the house of David should flourish once more. But in Christ it does so still. Yes, out of the roots, when all else is gone, this new, blessed, and Divine growth may spring.

II. The Offspring of David. That Christ was so is shown : 1. *By many Scriptures.* Continually is he called the "Son of David." 2. *By the silence of his enemies.* Could they have shown that he was not descended from David, they would have gained a great advantage against him. But they tacitly admitted it because they could not disprove it. 3. *By the genealogies* given in Matt. i. and in Luke. The former gives our Lord's *legal* descent, the latter his *natural* descent. Jesus being adopted by Joseph, whose descent St. Matthew gives, took the place of his son, and was reckoned legally as such. But St. Luke gives the descent of Mary from the elder branch of the house of David. God had promised that it should be so, that Christ should be born of his house, and when it seemed as if the promise had failed, lo! it was abundantly fulfilled. Learn : "He is faithful that promised."

III. The Bright and Morning Star. This august name declares our Lord to be : 1. *The Brightness of the Father's glory.* Stars have been chosen by all nations as fit symbols of majesty, and especially by the nations of the East, where the stars shine out with a glory of which we in our cloudy climates little know. Hence they were regarded as symbols of kingly rule (cf. Numb. xxiv., "A star shall rise, and a sceptre," etc.). And their majestic appearance led to their worship (cf. the Magi). The kingly glory of Christ, the brightness of the Father's glory, is there meant. "Thou art the King of glory, O Christ." 2. *The Pledge and Bringer-in of the perfect day.* Not only is he the Star, but the Bright and *Morning Star.* The Star which foretold the day-dawn ; the "Day Star," as he is elsewhere called. And Christ is this. The shadows of night rest on man and his dwelling-place ; but Christ has come, and what treasure-store of hope is there not in him for us all?—S. C.

Ver. 17.—*The good will of God to man.* It is all-important, would we win men's hearts for God, that we represent him as having good will towards them. If we let men think of him as hard, unloving, indifferent, or unjust, not all the threatenings in the world will win them. Man can only love that which he conceives as lovable. Now, this well-known and most precious verse renders great service in this direction. Were a man to pick it up from off the streets, he would gather this much at any rate, even supposing he knew nothing of its writer or meaning, that whoever wrote it was in earnest for the good of those for whom it was written. And studying it attentively, with the added light of other Scriptures, the evidence of this good will becomes full and clear indeed. For note—

I. The gift offered. "The water of life." It is the constant symbol of the grace of the Lord Jesus Christ. That grace which : 1. *As water, cleanses.* It is a river of water of life ; no mere circumscribed shallow pool or tiny rill, but a river, full, flowing, in which a man may "wash and be clean." Now, the putting away of our sin, our spiritual defilement, is through the grace of our Lord Jesus Christ. "We have redemption through his blood, even the forgiveness of our sins." 2. *As water, revives and strengthens.* In hot Eastern lands, where water was so much more precious than with us, because they had so little whilst we have so much, this emblem of water had more force of meaning than it has to us. The wearied traveller, faint and ready to perish, "drank of the brook by the way," and "lifted up his head" (cf. Hagar and Ishmael). And the meaning, therefore, of this word is that Christ's grace, as water revives, strengthens the soul. 3. *And, as a river of living water, abides.* A pool, a shallow stream, dries up, but a river goes on for ever. The permanence, therefore, of the grace of Christ is thus set forth. 4. *And this gift is the very one man needs.* A gift may be ever so valuable, but if I do not want it I do not feel the love which offers it. But if I do need it, if it be the very gift of all others which I need, then he who comes to me with just that does show his good will. And thus is it with this gift. It is no mere temporary and temporal gift, but one eternal and spiritual, suited to me as an immortal being destined to dwell in the presence of God. Seeing what a shred of my entire existence is my life here, would it have been a token of real love for me if, instead of that which is given, I had been granted all manner of mere earthly good? But "God commendeth his love towards us," not only in the gift he offers, but in—

II. THE MANNER OF THE OFFERING. For: 1. *The invitation is repeatedly given.* The Spirit, the bride, and every one who hears, is to say, "Come." An immense significance lies in the manner of an invitation. One can learn much as to the sincerity of him who gives it by noting how he gives it. If, then, he repeat it again and again, as this invitation is repeated, I cannot doubt as to the real desire that it should be accepted. And this is seen: 2. *In the messengers who are entrusted to give this invitation.* They are *so well qualified* to give it effectually. (1) *The Spirit.* He is in *full sympathy* with the Giver of it. He is the Holy Spirit of God. A messenger may nullify the effect of a message if he have no sympathy with him who sends it; but if he have such sympathy, is, as the giver, deeply desirous that it should be accepted, then with what force will he urge it! And so it is here. Does he not urge it on us, plead with us to accept it? We know he does. And he *has skill and tact* to urge it wisely and effectually. Ah! what clumsy messengers we often are who have to give this message! What mistakes we make! How faultily and imperfectly we do our work! But he, the blessed Spirit of God, makes no such mistake. He knows when, where, and how to best urge on us this message of God's great love. And he has, too, *knowledge of our character* and circumstances. He will not address one character in a way suited only to another, as we often do. He will not come at a most unfit time, but will choose the best time. And *he has constant access* to us. When the doors of the church are closed, the Sunday over, and the sacred services have come to an end; when the preacher and those to whom he speaks have separated—he shut off from them and they from him; then the Spirit of God can come to us, does come oftentimes, in the silence of the night, in the intervals of business, in lonely, quiet hours when none but he can come. Thus qualified is one of these messengers who are sent. Does not the sending of such a messenger prove the sincerity of him who sends the message? Then: (2) *The bride.* She also is to say, "Come." And who is the bride, but the company of Christ's redeemed, they who know *by actual experience* the preciousness and the power of this "water of life"? He who hath taken of this water knows its life-giving power. They can tell what Christ has done for them. It was the healed ones who, when our Lord was here on earth, sent multitudes more to him. And they are bidden do the like now. They are to say to the yet unhealed, "Come." And they are prompted to do this by mighty motives—gratitude, compassion, desire for Christ's approval, which depends upon their fidelity to this commission. (3) And *him that heareth* is to repeat the message. If this direction had but been obeyed, heathendom would not now be so vast as it is, nor will it long continue so if we now will but obey this word. What more could he, whose message it is, have done to secure its promulgation and its acceptance? 3. *The form of the message.* It is "Come," not "Go." It means that they who deliver it are first to go themselves, and then bid others come likewise. Many are perpetually saying to others, "Go;" but if they do not come themselves, those others are not likely to heed their word. The Scotch mother, in the well-known engraving, wanting her child to cross the brawling stream, goes first herself, and shows her where to put her trembling feet, now on this stone and now on that and that, and so the timid little one, seeing her mother go first, comes after her. Parents, so must it be with you and your children if you want them to be brought to Christ. *You* must go first, and say, "Come," and then they will follow.

III. THE WAY IN WHICH HINDRANCES TO ITS BEING ACCEPTED ARE MET AND PROVIDED AGAINST. Such hindrances are: 1. *Doubts as to who are invited.* But such doubts are met by " Whosoever will." None can shut themselves out of that " whosoever." But it is added, "and let him that is athirst." Such are very often the last to believe that the water of life is for them. Their very need and longing make them think such an offer as this is "too good to be true." And by this special reference to them this doubt is met; cf. the angel's word on Easter Day, "Go tell his disciples *and Peter*." He was the one who most of all needed and longed to know that he had not lost utterly his Lord's love; and the Lord knew that, and so sent a special message to him. And so it is here; the "athirst" are specially called. 2. *Requirement of qualifications.* Were such demanded, many could not come, but everybody can take a gift. Hence it is said, let him take "freely." 3. *Doubt as to motives.* How many distress themselves by scrutinizing the motives which lead them to desire the Lord's grace! "Have I repented enough, prayed enough, felt the evil of sin enough," etc.? But no question will be asked as to motives. It is "whosoever *will*." No matter how you came to will, to desire, the water of life, whether it were hope or fear, or you know not what, all that is needed is that you should desire it, and there it is for you.

CONCLUSION. 1. Does not God by all this commend his love to us? 2. Shall we not come at once? 3. If we never come, whose fault will it be?—S. C.

Ver. 20.—*Longing for Christ's advent.* As to the expression "quickly," it is to be understood either on the principle (1) that one day is with the Lord as a thousand years; or (2) that there are many advents of Christ besides that last glorious one of which the New Testament says so much. In support of this it is to be noted that the prophecies of this book, as other prophecies, refer to classes of events, and not exclusively to any one event. Hence, wherever there is like conduct, whether good or evil, there will be like recompense. Persecuting governments, and religions upholding them, will bring down on themselves Divine judgments. Such conditions of things were present when St. John wrote, and the punishment of them was speeding on to its fulfilment. So we prefer to understand the words of our text. Now, of the comings of Christ there are four, though not to all of them can the "quickly" of the text be applied, except on the principle first named above, and which St. Peter teaches us.

I. To PUNISH NOTORIOUS WRONG. The destruction of Jerusalem was then, when St. John wrote, nigh at hand. The overthrow of the persecuting, pagan Roman empire was not far off; and, again and again, in the judgments that have befallen nations and wicked rulers and Churches, of which the records of history tell so much, may be seen fulfilments of this word. And without any vindictive spirit, from pure love of truth and righteousness, and from concern for human well-being, the faithful Church has responded, and will respond, to the announcement of Christ's advent for this end: "Amen. Even so," etc. What a solemn reminder does this give to those who, in daring, presumptuous way, sin against God! In the midst of their proud defiance of the Lord, he may—it is likely that he will—come and judge them for their sins.

II. To REIGN ON EARTH. That he will thus come the Scripture statements plainly declare. And these statements are very numerous. This coming of the Lord is perpetually referred to in the New Testament, and is predicted likewise in the Old Testament. No doubt the apostles believed it would be in their time. The Lord had not said it would not, and hoping that it might—their wish becoming father to their thought—they spoke and wrote as if it would. We are distinctly forbidden to look to them for information as to the date of this advent, for the Lord said to them, "It is *not* for you to know." Therefore any words of theirs that seem to imply, as they do, the speedy coming of Christ, are to be read with this remembrance, that it was not given to them to speak authoritatively on this matter. And in the later Epistles it is evident that their earlier thoughts had become modified, and they had learnt to contemplate as probable the fact that the Lord's advent would not be in their time; and hence they give directions for the ordering of the Church after they are gone (cf. Second Epistle to Timothy, etc.). And the declarations concerning our Lord's advent to reign on earth *are to be understood literally.* Many, no doubt, affirm that they are to be all interpreted of a spiritual reign, and to be explained as figures, metaphors, and the like. But we have a principle of interpretation laid down for us in the predictions concerning our Lord's first advent. What was there said of him *literally* came to pass. A large part of the gospel history may be compiled from those ancient prophecies which told of what literally came true in the life and death of our Lord. The Scriptures were fulfilled in him in no figurative, but in a literal sense. So was it, and, therefore, we believe, so will it be. And when we think of what is involved in the coming of our Lord to reign—of glory to God, of good to man—how can the Church do otherwise than say, "Amen. Even so," etc.?

III. To RECEIVE US UNTO HIMSELF. For death is for us practically a coming of the Lord. We go to be with him; he comes to receive us. And this, at the furthest, will be "quickly." "Brief life is here our portion." Few and evil are the days of our pilgrimage. And to this coming the believer assents. Not from any fretful longing to have done with this life—such longing is always more or less morbid, though explicable and excusable under the distressing circumstances in which it is felt and uttered— but to Christians, as to others, life is and should be sweet, precious, clung to. But his "Amen" here is that of submission, of cheerful assent and acquiescence to the Lord's will. For him death has no terrors, but is the entrance on eternal joy. Nevertheless, the ties of earth, the claims and needs of those we love, are many and strong, and therefore for their sake life is precious. Otherwise death has no sting.

IV. To JUDGE THE WORLD. This is not the same as his coming to reign. Then he shall come for his saints, but in this last advent he shall come with them. Then shall the great white throne be set up, then shall be gathered all nations, and then the final judgment take place. And this, too, for each one of us, comes "quickly." For after death it virtually takes place. We each go to our "own place." But can we each one say concerning this coming of the Lord, "Amen. Even so," etc.?—S. C.

Ver. 21.—"*The grace of our Lord Jesus Christ.*" The Lord's ministry on earth ended with benediction. It is fitting that this revelation, which he gave by his servant St. John, should end in like manner.

I. THE MEANING OF THESE WORDS. 1. *To the careless* they are but as the playground bell to the schoolboy, which tells him that he may cease from his drudgery and go to his games again. So, because these words generally form part of the sacred formula with which our Christian worship is wont to end, they are to the careless who may be present scarce any more than the welcome signal that at last the dreary service is all done, and they may go back to the world again. 2. *To the many amongst Christian worshippers.* These have no precise, definite meaning attached to the constantly heard words, but they know they mean blessing, and blessing from the Lord Jesus Christ, and therefore they delight in them and their heart answers "Amen" to them. 3. *Their real meaning.* No doubt they have primary reference to that "grace of God which," through the Lord Jesus Christ, "bringeth salvation" to us and to all men. But this is not their exclusive meaning. Yet they tell of blessing in which all can share, which may be asked for and pronounced upon all. Hence, blessings which only some need, such as temporal relief from poverty, perplexity, persecution, and the like; or even spiritual good, such as conversion, or deliverance from some special temptation, or the bestowment of some particular form of Christian excellence and character,—not even these, or any one good of any kind, are what is comprised in this much-meaning word "grace." But if we go back to the root-meaning of the word, we find it denotes *that which causes joy ; that* is grace. All the uses and forms of the word spring from this root. Therefore "the grace of our Lord Jesus Christ" is that gift from him, whatever it be, that will minister joy to us. Hence it may be one thing to one person, and another to another, and something still different to yet others. Therefore note—

II. ITS APPLICATION. Consider this: 1. *In reference to those to whom St. John wrote,* the Churches of Christ in Asia. Amongst them there were those who needed temporal relief because of their poverty; others, to be thoroughly converted to Christ; others, to be endued with a holy courage; all, a higher degree of Christian life. Now, according to the need of each would be the grace of the Lord Jesus Christ to them. 2. *To ourselves.* Varied are our wants, none needing exactly the same gift, none finding *the* grace of the Lord Jesus Christ in what is so to another. Whether it be Christ's ministry to our present temporal need, or to our spiritual condition. One needs one thing, another another. And this benediction is for each according to the want of each. That from Christ which will truly gladden and give joy to each one is the grace of the Lord Jesus Christ to that one.

III. ITS APPARENT CONTRADICTIONS. For though "grace" means that which brings joy, it does not always appear so. At the time it may seem not at all "joyous, but grievous." It is often disguised so that we do not know it. Christ's grace in the form of earthly good comes to us frequently by strange ways, and in strange and often repelling aspect. And yet more in regard to spiritual good. Newton, in one of his hymns, says—

> "I asked the Lord that I might grow
> In faith and love and every grace;
> Might more of his salvation know,
> And seek *more earnestly* his face.
>
> *   *   *   *   *
>
> "I hoped that in some favoured hour,
> At once he'd answer my request.
>
> *   *   *   *   *
>
> "Instead of this, he made me feel
> The hidden evils of my heart;
> And let the angry powers of hell
> Assault my soul in every part.
>
> *   *   *   *   *
>
> "'Lord, why is this?' I trembling cried.
>
> *   *   *   *   *
>
> "'Tis in this way,' the Lord replied,
> 'I answer prayer for grace and faith.'"

As from the miry, foul soil the fairest flowers spring; as the mother's travail precedes her joy; as our Lord's own bitter sorrows and death went before, and were needful to, "the joy set before him,"—so is it that grace must often come out of, pass through, and for a time assume the form of, grief.

IV. ITS BENEDICTION. The blessed Scriptures, and the holy apostle who wrote this closing book, bid us farewell with this blessing pronounced upon us. Are we willing to receive it? Do we not need it: you, yet unsaved; you, weak, feeble, halting in the Christian way; you, tempted and sore beset; you, drawing near to death; you, weighed down with sorrow and care? Yes, you do need it; nothing can compensate for it, though the world and sin and the wicked one are busy with their suggestions that you can do without it. And it waits for you. The apostles who first uttered it invoke it on us now. Let our hearts respond, "Amen."—S. C.

Vers. 1—6.—*The conditions of blessedness.* These must be thought of as first on earth, afterwards in heaven. The river of the water of life must be the life-giving and sustaining power of the Holy Spirit. It is life—life indeed and of a truth. But man has no life apart from God, and most truly no spiritual and blessed life. "The fountain of life is with thee." It would not be improper to include here the idea of "the Word of life;" for by the Word only are the seeds of life sown in the heart, and by the Word the ever-present Spirit refreshes and revives the weary and dying. This life-giving Word, made powerful by the heavenly life-giving Spirit, spreads healing and joy, loveliness and verdure, wherever it comes. But we cannot separate these elements; they are one. And beautiful is the figure of the life-giving river, "bright as crystal, proceeding out of the throne of God and the Lamb." But the issue of the above is presented to us in the following verses.

I. IN THE UTTER DESTRUCTION OF THE CURSE AND CONSEQUENCE OF SIN. The first and last, the complete idea of the evil results of sin, is to be found in "the curse." It is now removed. Blessing prevails. Happy they over whom the shadow of a curse falls not! So far of the negative results. The positive follow; and the blessedness of the righteous is set forth—

II. IN THE SUPREME AUTHORITY OF THE MOST HIGH. In obedience is life and blessedness. His laws are holy, just, and good. The perfectness of life is reached when God reigns perfectly in the hearts of his people; when there his throne is set.

III. IN THE UNVARYING OBEDIENCE OF THE HOLY PEOPLE. "His servants shall do him service."

IV. IN A GRACIOUSLY PERMITTED APPROACH TO GOD. "They shall see his face;" they know him. It is the approach of love. It is the child before the face of the Father.

V. IN THE SIMILARITY OF NATURE. The Divine Name is on the forehead. This is at once an attainment and a reward.

VI. IN THE DISPERSION OF IGNORANCE AND THE DECEPTIONS OF ERROR. No night. No mere earthly illumination. The Lord God himself, by his own direct illumination, giveth them light. They who follow the light of life walk not in darkness.

VII. IN EVERLASTING EXALTATION AND HONOUR. "They shall reign for ever and ever."—R. G.

Vers. 7, 12—15.—*The final word of blessing.* The holy book opens with a vision of paradisaical blessedness. Alas! soon the feet of men tread the sands of the wilderness. But the purposes of the Ever-Blessed are to lead men back to a regained Paradise. This is the mission of the Redeemer. In his great sermon on the mount he opens his mouth and pronounces as a first word, "Blessed." It was his programme to restore men to blessedness. His last word corresponds with his first, and is in harmony with the spirit of his whole life-work. For the comfort of his Church in all ages of her struggle with the powers of evil that from the first have brought only cursing upon men, he has pictured to the eye of faith and hope the visions of his own conquest over evil, and has appended the promise of the highest estate of blessedness. With these words cometh the end. In the keeping of the words of this book that blessedness is gained (ver. 7). And so the righteous one is urged to continue in his righteousness, and the holy to seek a perennial holiness, even though the filthy and the unrighteous remain in their filth and uncleanness (ver. 11). "The Alpha and the Omega" who spake the alpha of blessing now utters the omega. It is a final word—the last till "he cometh." This blessedness is to the pure—they who "wash their robes." He has opened the fountain where all sinful stains may be cleansed away. The blessedness consists—

I. IN THE ATTAINMENT OF TRUE LIFE. The tree of life is no longer unapproachable. Now they may "eat and live for ever." The tree is "in the midst of the Paradise of God." It is the sacramental pledge of a life of eternal blessedness. "Neither can they die any more" is fulfilled in them. The pure only truly live. For the true life of man is only to be had in fellowship with God—the Pure. The unholy cannot see God; they cannot walk with God; they cannot share the blessedness of the holy communion. Separate from him, they die as a branch broken from a tree. Now the pure live, "I in them, and thou in me."

II. IN THE FELLOWSHIP OF THE HOLY COMMUNITY, AMIDST THE SANCTITIES AND SECURITY OF THE HOLY CITY. They are separated from the impure and the vile. These are "without." The love of God has issued in the eternal life with God; the love of man in the everlasting communion of the holy. Personal and individual life in its utmost blessedness, and the communal life restored—peace, truth, and love reigning. Blessed, blessed lot of them who are wise enough to hear and to keep the sayings of this book! Wherefore let us bend our heads lowlily over its sacred page, and read, mark, learn, and inwardly digest, that by patience and comfort of the Scriptures we may embrace and ever hold fast the blessed hope of everlasting life which we have in our Saviour Jesus Christ. Now unto him who hath begotten us to this hope be paid the praise of eternity. Amen.—R. G.

Ver. 1.—*Christianity a transcendental system.* "And he showed me," etc. Philosophers have their transcendental theories, but Christianity transcends their highest speculations. Taking these words as a symbolic representation of it, we make two remarks.

I. IT IS TRANSCENDENTAL IN ITS VALUE. It is "water." What on earth, what throughout the whole material universe, so far as we know, is of such worth as water? So impressed were some of the greatest sages of antiquity with its value, that they regarded it as the first principle, the fontal source of all things. But what is the character of this water? 1. It is a "*river*." It is not a stagnant pool, a sleeping lake, or a purling brook; but a river, profound in depth, majestic in volume, resistless in movement. **2.** It is a "*pure*" river. No impurities have been drained into it. Its channels are clean; it is fresh and pure from the holy heavens. How pure is Christianity! How holy its morals, how morally perfect its leading character, Christ! **3.** It is a "pure" river of *life.* It not only diffuses life through all the regions through which it rolls its waters, but goes up into the air, forms clouds, sails through the heavens, and discharges itself upon the barren hills, thus giving life to the world. Christianity is a quickening system; it quickens intellect, conscience, heart. **4.** It is a "pure" river of life that is *transparent.* "Clear as crystal." This river, like a perfect looking-glass, mirrors the bright heavens above, and all the objects around it. How transparent is Christianity! It can be seen through and through. What character was ever so transparent as the character of Christ? You see with a glance the one ruling principle that worked all his faculties and explained his life—love. Here there is a transcendental system that rolls in the moral domain of earth like some mighty Amazon in the material. What would man's moral world be without it? Ah, what?

II. IT IS TRANSCENDENTAL IN ITS ORIGIN. Whence does this river take its rise? Where is the fountain-head? Not on earth, not from any particular province of the universe, but from the "throne of God and of the Lamb." **1.** It proceeds from the "*throne.*" It comes from the centre of universal authority. Christianity is a system of authority. It is a code rather than a creed; it is more regulative than speculative. **2.** It proceeds from the throne of "*God.*" There are many thrones. We read of thrones and principalities, etc. But this is the throne from which all other thrones derive their authority, to which all are amenable—the throne of God. Christianity is a Divine system; its congruity with all collateral history, with our moral intuitions, with all our *a priori* notions of a God, proves its Divinity. **3.** It proceeds from the throne of God *and of the Lamb.* Christ has to do with it. It contains his life, it mirrors his character, it bears on its majestic bosom his provision for the world.

Such is the gospel. Value this river. What are other books compared to the gospel? Mere puddled pools to the Mississippi. Kind Heaven, speed the course of this river! May it penetrate every region of the world, and roll its waves of life through every heart!—D. T.

Ver. 1.—*Divine love a river.* "He showed me a river." "There is a river," says the psalmist, "the streams whereof shall make glad the city of God." Divine love is indeed a river.

I. EXHAUSTLESS. It rises from the infinitude of the Divine nature—a source unfathomed and unfathomable.

II. UNIVERSAL. This river rolls everywhere. It rolls under the universe, and all things float on its waves. It refreshes and beautifies all. The ancient sages considered water ἡ ἀρχή. We scarcely wonder at this when they saw water everywhere in the material world. But water is but the symbol of love. Love is indeed ἡ ἀρχή.

III. EVER-FLOWING. The inexhaustible fountain is always acting—outpouring itself. Creation is a work never finished, for the river of Divine love is overflowing.

IV. RESTORATIVE. This river to human souls is restorative. It at once resuscitates and cleanses; it quenches thirst and removes defilement. Christ is the channel through which flows this soul-restorative love.

> " Flow down, thou stream of life Divine,
>   Thy quickening streams deliver;
> Oh, flow throughout this soul of mine
>   For ever and for ever!

> " Flow down, and cause this heart to glow
>   With love to God the Giver—
> That love in which all virtues grow
>   For ever and for ever.

> " Flow down, as flow the ray and rain,
>   In vital work together,
> Refreshing roots and quickening grain
>   For ever and for ever.

> " Flow down, as flows the living sun
> Upon the sparkling river,
> Which, chanting to the boundless, run
> For ever and for ever.
>
> " Flow down, revive this famished soul,
> And bear away all error;
> And I will praise thee, God of all,
> For ever and for ever."

D. T.

Ver. 1.—*Subjective Christianity:* 1. *A river.* "And he showed me a pure river of water of life, clear [bright] as crystal, proceeding out of the throne of God and of the Lamb." All along this book of gorgeous imagery and symbol we have been looking at Christianity as a *subjective reality. Objective* Christianity is simply a speculation; a thing of criticism, imagination, and logic; a thing for men to quarrel about, and even to fight about at times. It is a creed—nothing more. But *subjective* Christianity is a life; it is the creed eaten, digested, and transmitted into the blood and fibre of the soul. In this verse this *life* appears in three aspects.

I. As FLOWING. It is a "river," not a stagnant lake, confined within certain banks, without any progressive motion, but a river flowing on, winding its way through every faculty of the soul, and giving to all new freshness and vigour.

II. As TRANSLUCENT. "Pure river of water of life, clear as crystal." What object in nature is more sublimely beautiful than a deep-flowing river, so pure as to mirror all the pearls and shells and living creatures that lie fathomed below, and all the shifting clouds and brilliant orbs that circle above? Vital Christianity is essentially clear and cleansing; it flows through the soul, and leaves no "spot" or "wrinkle," or any such thing.

III. As IMPERIAL. "Proceeding out of the throne of God and of the Lamb." It does not spring from any human fountain. It is from the primal force of all life—God and the Lamb. It is a river, "the streams whereof make glad the city of God." "The water that I shall give him shall be in him a well of water springing up into everlasting life."—D. T.

Ver. 2.—*Subjective Christianity:* 2. *A tree.* "In the midst of the street of it, and on either side of the river, was there the tree of life, which bare twelve manner of fruits, and yielded her fruit every month: and the leaves of the tree were for the healing of the nations." Here is *organized* life—"a tree." Here are the various elements and gases brought into an organic whole—a tree; the product and provision of vital force. Look at this tree in three aspects.

I. As CENTRALLY ROOTED. "In the midst of the street of it." Between the street and the river on each side there grows this majestic tree, well fed and well protected, in the very midst of the holy metropolis. Between the water and the street the whole side is lined with the tree of life. Christianity is a life well rooted and well guarded. It is an incorruptible seed, that "liveth and abideth for ever." "The sun will not smite it by day, nor the moon by night."

II. IT IS ESSENTIALLY VITAL. It is the "tree of life." It is not the mere form of life, or the product of life; it is life itself. Life of all kinds, even vegetable and animal, is, say men of science, inextinguishable. It is a spark that can never be put out, that will burn through the ages. This is true of this spiritual life, this life of Christianity in the soul. There is no indivisible atom nor any *unquenchable life.*

III. IT IS MARVELLOUSLY FRUITFUL. "Which bare twelve manner of fruits." It has twelve fruit seasons; that is, it yields twelve crops instead of one. How abundantly fertile is living Christianity in the soul! What new thoughts, affections, resolves, are constantly evolved, one growing out of the other in rapid succession and endless variety, grain coming out of grain, and boundless harvests sleeping in their shells!

IV. IT IS ALWAYS SEASONABLE. "Yielding her fruit every month." All life everywhere has its seasons, and in all seasons its particular fruits—spring, summer, autumn, winter. The fruits of living Christianity in the soul are *always seasonable.* "Be not weary in well-doing: for in due season ye shall reap, if ye faint not."

V. It is universally healing. "The leaves of the tree were for the healing of the nations." Even the leaves of this tree are salutary to all. All the nations of the earth are morally diseased. Their disease is a leprosy—the leprosy of sin. Living Christianity in the soul is the antidote.—D. T.

Vers. 3—5.—*Subjective Christianity:* 3. *An empire.* "There shall be no more curse: but the throne of God and of the Lamb shall be in it; and his servants shall serve him," etc. Here is a *state,* not a mere life, but a state in which that life is found—an empire. "The kingdom of God is within you." The words lead us to look at this inner kingdom in three aspects.

I. As entire freedom from malediction. "There shall be no more curse." The soul that comes under the living reign of Christianity is freed entirely from the curse— the curse of *guilt, corruption,* and *bondage.* "Being justified by faith, we have peace with God."

II. As conscious realization of the Divine. In this blessed state God is all in all. It is all God. He is: 1. Their *Sovereign.* "The throne of God and of the Lamb." His authority everywhere recognized and his servants rendering him homage. He fills the horizon of their being. All is seen *through* him, and all is done *for* him. 2. Their *Image.* "They shall see his face." Everywhere he is mirrored before their eyes. As to his Name, his character, it is engraved on their foreheads. "Beholding as in a glass the glory of God," etc.; "Changed into the same image," etc. 3. Their *Light.* "There shall be no night there," etc. Their state is a bright one; no clouds roll over their sky; no secondary orbs convey to them the light. Neither the radiance of the sun nor the beams of candle are there required; "for the Lord God giveth them light.".

Conclusion. Thus I have given three phases of *subjective Christianity;* a Christianity which, being a matter of *consciousness* and *experience,* is intelligible, and which gives to us a somewhat rational view of all these gorgeous symbols, of which some of our most distinguished expositors and pulpiteers make arrant nonsense, and sometimes impious blasphemy. Perhaps some may think I have spoken of *objective* Christianity as utterly worthless and unnecessary; but this I would not do. Christ himself is the pure Bread of life, and this must be eaten and rightly digested, in order to get and sustain this *subjective* Christianity. When, indeed, the loaf of objective Christianity is corrupted, as is, alas! generally the case, the eating of it, and the digesting of it, if indeed it can be digested, only generates a *subjective* life, that is full of evil passions and wickedness; it makes men fiends rather than angels, and fits them more for Pandemoniums than for Paradises.—D. T.

Ver. 6.—*Glimpses through the barrier: God's communications to humanity.* "And he said unto me, These words are faithful and true," etc.

I. God speaks to individual man. "He said unto me [John]." Jehovah, the "God of the spirits of the prophets," is not a Being that sits mute in his universe. He speaks, and speaks to individual men. He speaks in nature. His voice is gone out through all the earth, and he speaks to human souls through nature and also through the written Word. "God, who at sundry times and in divers manners spake . . . by the prophets," etc. To every *individual* man he communicates his eternal ideas.

II. God speaks of the absolutely credible. "These words are faithful and true." His words agree with unalterable facts and unchangeable principles. They are the revelations of things that have been, things that are, and things that might be. Heaven and earth shall pass away, but not one "jot or tittle" of his Word shall perish.

III. God speaks the things that must be shortly realized. "The things which must shortly come to pass." His ideas are practical, and must ever take their actual embodiment and form in human life.—D. T.

Ver. 7.—*Glimpses through the barrier: the moral advent and mission of Christ.* "Behold, I come quickly," etc.

I. The moral advent of Christ. "I come quickly," or, "I am coming quickly." There are four advents of Christ. 1. *His incarnation.* God was manifest in the flesh. 2. *His dispensation in human history.* The destruction of Jerusalem, as well as the death of individual man, are spoken of as the coming of Christ. In fact, every event in human life is a Divine advent. 3. *To his spiritual influence on the human mind.* He says, "I will not leave you comfortless: I will come to you," etc. He comes to convince the world of "sin, righteousness, and judgment;" comes to establish his reign over human souls. 4. *The final day of retribution.* There is every reason to believe there is to be a grand crisis in human history—a crisis that shall usher in the ultimate, the permanent reign of universal retribution. All these advents are going on in every department of human life, and going on quickly. There is no suspense, no delay.

II. HIS MORAL MISSION. "Blessed is he that keepeth the words of the prophecy of this book." "Prophecy" does not, of course, mean prognostications or idle fables, the inventions of imposture, but didactic truth, veritable facts and principles. The testimony of Christ is to eternal facts and absolute principles. Hence he himself is the Truth. He himself is the *Word* of God.

CONCLUSION. Brothers, let us profoundly ponder the constant comings of Christ to us. Indeed, his constant visitation preserves our existence every moment. Let us mark well that in all, in each event, he has a moral mission, some mighty testimony to the immutable realities of human life, duty, and destiny.—D. T.

Vers. 8—10.—*Glimpses through the barrier: revelation.* "And I John am he that heard and saw these things. And when I heard and saw, I fell down to worship," etc. These verses bring under our notice two or three very suggestive circumstances, which we shall merely state in the briefest manner.

I. ETERNAL REALITIES BROUGHT TO THE CONSCIENCE OF INDIVIDUAL MAN. "And I John am he that heard and saw these things," etc. "I John," the beloved disciple of Christ. "I myself heard and saw these things." How did he hear them? And how did he see them? Was it with the outward ear or with the outward eye? I trow not; for have we not read, the whole was a vision, a kind of dream—a long, grotesque, terribly suggestive dream? In truth, all outward vision and sight are but emblems of the mental faculties of sight and sound which are within us, and which are ever active, voluntarily and involuntarily. What are the creations of poetry, the inventions of romance, and the revellings and riotings of our visions in the night, but sights and sounds? In visions John saw this, as I have elsewhere indicated.

II. THE INSTINCT OF WORSHIP WRONGLY DIRECTED. Psychology, as well as the history of our race, show that deep in the centre of our nature is the hunger for worship. Man must have a God, whatever else he may lack. He has been called a worshipping animal. The wonderful things which came within the mind of John seem to have aroused this religious instinct to a passion. "He fell down to worship before the feet of the messenger." Superstition has ever been, and still is, one of the regnant curses of the race.

III. THE RECOIL OF GENUINE SAINTS FROM FLATTERY. "See thou do it not," etc. This angel, or messenger, a man, was superior to that vanity which will do everything, almost, to attract attention, to win a cheer or receive an empty compliment. What does he say? "See thou do it not: I am a fellow-servant with thee and with thy brethren the prophets, and with them which keep the words of this book: worship God." This genuine saint, whilst he repudiated the idea of being a God, humbly identified himself with truly good men of every order, sphere, and time.

IV. THE PRACTICAL ALLEGIANCE OF CHRISTLY MEN TO ONE GOD. "Worship God." What a name! The Cause, Means, and End of all things in the universe—but sin. God! The Supreme, not only in might and wisdom, but in all goodness and truth; the one Being in the universe around whom all thoughts and sympathies should revolve in all reverence and devotion.

CONCLUSION. Here, then, are subjects for thought most quickening, elevating, and devout.—D. T.

Ver. 11.—*Moral character becoming unalterable.* "He which is filthy, let him be filthy still." Detaching these words from the context, they suggest the dawning of a crisis in human history when *moral character becomes unalterable.* Notice—

I. THAT THE MORAL CHARACTER OF MAN SOMETIMES BECOMES UNALTERABLE BEFORE DEATH. There is reason to believe that this crisis occurs in this world. We find in the Bible, for example, such expressions as, "My Spirit shall not always strive with man;" "Ephraim is joined to idols: let him alone;" "If thou hadst known . . . the things that belonged to thy peace! but now they are hid from thine eyes;" of men having their conscience "seared with a hot iron;" of souls being "twice dead, and plucked up by the roots." If these passages mean anything, they mean that in this life a corrupt character may become unalterable. The alteration of character requires deep thought and earnest resolve. It requires effort of the most strenuous and determined kind.

II. THAT IF IT IS NOT ALTERED BEFORE DEATH, IT IS NOT LIKELY TO BE ALTERED AT DEATH. There is no opportunity afforded at death for such a work as this. The character that has been built up by a lifetime cannot be altered in a few hours or days at most, and that in most cases amidst physical agony and moral forebodings. True, death does effect great changes in men. The greatest change is the breaking up of the bodily organization, reducing it to its primitive elements; but there is no power in this to alter character. There is no tendency in bodily changes to effect a positive reformation. Such changes in the body are constantly going on here. Once in every seven years every man receives a new body, and yet the moral character remains unaltered. Wrong moral principles and habits do not pass away from us as the particles of our body depart day after day, and year after year. Death, therefore, seems to us powerless to effect any change in moral character.

III. THAT IF IT IS NOT ALTERED BEFORE DEATH, IT IS NOT LIKELY TO BE ALTERED AFTER DEATH. 1. *A change in moral character can only be effected by the force of moral truth.* Truth alone can expel errors, and generate true motives and impulses of action. 2. *We cannot conceive of moral truth in a mightier form than we have it here.* Truth in example is truth in its mightiest form, and the gospel is truth in the highest example; hence it is "the power of God unto salvation." Christ says, "If they hear not Moses and the prophets," etc. 3. *The longer the force of truth is resisted, the less likely is it to succeed.* If truth does not succeed with souls who come into the world free from all prejudices and tenderly susceptible of impressions, its probability of success in this life, we know, weakens as habits are formed and the heart grows harder. Supposing that a soul who has passed unrenovated through all the influences of moral truth in this life enters eternity, and comes under a system of truth even as powerful as the one that has worked on him here, its chances of failure on him are perhaps greater there than here. Now is the time for moral reformation. Earth is the scene for regenerating corrupt souls.—D. T.

Vers. 12—15.—*Three facts in the moral empire of God.* "Behold, I come quickly; and my reward is with me, to render to each man according as his work is," etc. These words suggest to our notice three supreme facts in the moral condition of mankind—the *requital*, the *beatified*, and the *execrable*.

I. THE REQUITAL. "Behold, I come quickly; and my reward is with me, to render to each man according as his work is." "When the light of the world shines fully forth, then will each man be found to have the thing for which he has toiled. 'The wages of sin,' 'the gift of God'—each will be received in its fulness. We are continually fancying there will be some reversal of that law—that somehow we shall not reap what we have sown" (Maurice). But the fact is, the law of a *requital* goes on inviolably from the dawn of our moral life through all the years and ages of our existence; the sowing and the reaping are settled facts in our biographies. "With what measure we mete, it is measured to us again." Every voluntary action vibrates and reverberates through all the hills and valleys of our conscious life. Three remarks are here suggested concerning this law of requital. 1. *Its action is prompt.* "I come quickly." No sooner do you discharge the act than the retribution is at hand. There is not a moment's delay. "Sin lieth at the door." No sooner is the blow struck than its vibration is felt. 2. *Its action is just.* "Each man according as his work is." It is with every man individually; not man in the mass, but man in the unit. 3. *Its action is immutable.* "Alpha and Omega." He who originated and who every instant administered this law, is the "same yesterday, to-day, and for ever." The Beginning, the Means, and End of all things but sin. Thus, brothers, none of us can extricate ourselves from our deeds, or break our shackles of responsibilities. Nemesis is always at our heels. Though it walks with woollen feet unheard, it approaches "quickly," without a pause.

II. THE BEATIFIED. "Blessed are they that wash their robes, that they may have the right to come to the tree of life, and may enter in by the gates into the city." Wherein does the true blessedness of man consist ? Not in his professions, or theories, or ceremonies, but in his "deeds." "Show me thy faith by thy works." Who are the men that are going constantly into eternal life ? Those that do the works of the Father. " Inasmuch as ye have done it unto the least of these," etc. The "deeds" of a man are not formal or occasional accidents, but the *fruit* of his life—the exudation and fruition of his whole life. Herein, then, is the beatification of our whole nature—keeping the commandments. Mark this beatifying—keeping the commandments. Working out the will of God involves our moral cleansing ("was their robes "); the high, moral right to the highest life as a right to come to the tree of life and to enter into the gates. "Blessed are they who do his commandments "—the commandments of Christ—that the authority may hereafter be continuously over the " tree of life, that they may have the right given them to eat for ever the tree of life, and that they who have entered in may, once for all, enter in by means of the gate-towers ; that is, openly and without challenge, not surreptitiously or by climbing up some other way into the city. Not all shall possess this knowledge " (Vaughan).

III. THE EXECRABLE. "Without are the dogs, and the sorcerers, and the fornicators, and the murderers, and the idolaters, and every one that loveth and maketh a lie." All souls who are outside this truly beatified state—this state of practical obedience to the Divine will—are truly *execrable*. For outside that blessed realm of experience are "dogs "—the unclean and ravenous appendages of Eastern cities, types of all that is rapacious in human nature. And " sorcerers "—those who practise imposture in arts and religions, and trade on the credulity of ignorant men. And "fornicators "—the dissolute and immoral. And "murderers "—private assassins, hireling soldiers, and malignant spirits. And " idolaters "—those who bow down before the empty fashions of vanity, the parade of wealth, and all the pomp and glitter of titled fools. Whatsoever in the human mind rules the soul is idolatry. There is but one true God and one true worship. The true God is the one supreme Object of worship. Oh, the awful world that lies outside the realm of the good !—D. T.

Ver. 16.— *The self-declared titles of our Lord Jesus.* " I Jesus have sent mine angel to testify unto you these things for the Churches. I am the Root and the Offspring of David, the Bright, the Morning Star." Homiletically, we employ these words in fastening attention upon two subjects of thought.

I. HE CALLS HIMSELF THE " ROOT AND OFFSPRING OF DAVID." What does this mean ? Is it to be taken in a *lineal* sense ? We are told that he came from the line of David. He was the " Son of David." He came from the same ancestral line (Luke ii. 4 ; iii. 31). He was the " Son of David." Or is it to be taken in an *official* sense ? David by the permission of Jehovah became a king. We are told that he was a " man after God's own heart." A misunderstood passage, I trow, meaning only that he was so from Divine permission. In kingly office Christ may be said to have sprung from David. But whilst *lineally* and *officially* Christ may be represented as the " Root and Offspring of David," the supposition that he sprang from him *morally*, or in respect to character, is an idea that must be repudiated with abhorrence. *Morally*, David was confessedly a very corrupt man. Christ was holy and Divine, and "separate from sinners."

II. HE CALLS HIMSELF THE " BRIGHT AND MORNING STAR." This is the "light that lighteth every man that cometh into the world," reflecting all the rays of him who is the Light, and in whom is no darkness at all. This is a Star whose orbit encircles the moral universe, whose revolutions are without pause or cessation, and whose beams no clouds can obscure, no time can quench. " Christ was the Brightness of his Father's glory."—D. T.

Ver. 17.—*God's mercy towards a soul-thirsting world.* " And the Spirit and the bride say, Come," etc. Men's souls everywhere burn with a thirst for a good they have not. " Who will show us any good ? " God has attended to the cry, and in doing so we discover his wonderful mercy—

I. IN THE PROVISION HE HAS MADE FOR IT. "The water of life." 1. *The pro-*

vision is exquisitely suitable. What can quench the thirst like water? What water is to the thirsty body, the gospel is to the ever-craving soul, exquisitely fitted to meet the case. 2. *The provision is absolutely free.* It is free to us all. " Whosoever will." All tribes and classes of men are included in this " whosoever." It is free, without payment, "without money and without price." The provision is as free as the air we breathe.

II. In the pressing invitation to the provision. 1. *The Divine Spirit says,* " *Come.*" He is constantly wooing souls to this water of life. 2. *The Christian Church says, " Come.*" The Church takes up the invitation of the Spirit, repeats, and spreads it. 3. *The mere hearer is commanded to say, " Come.*" He on whose ear the distant echo of the word "Come" may fall, should take it up and voice it on. Thus infinite mercy has not only made such a provision, but sounds the invitation through the Spirit, through the Church, through all that hear. Come! come! come! He speaks to the world through a thousand voices.—D. T.

Vers. 18, 19.—*The possibility and penalty of a great crime.* "I testify unto every man that heareth the words of the prophecy of this book, If any man," etc. In these very remarkable words we have two things—the *possibility* and the *penalty* of a great crime. The great crime is adding to and taking from the Word.

I. The possibility of a great crime. What is the possible crime so solemnly addressed to all who peruse this Apocalypse—this Apocalypse of unseen and eternal truths? 1. There is a sense in which things *can* be added to this book. By giving interpretation which misrepresent it. 2. There is a sense in which things *cannot* be added to or taken from this book. What are those things? The absolute truth, the immutable love, the eternal rectitude, and the moral excellence of God. You cannot add to these. They are the spirit, the essence of all—the all-pervading and indestructible element of the whole book. Who can destroy or add to the rudimental elements of the *material* universe—the elements that build up and remove mountains, that create rivers and oceans, that spread out the landscapes, plant the forest, and cause the atmosphere, the waters, and the earth itself to teem with untold millions of living things, the forms of all we see in the heavens above, and around, and beneath us? Were they all to vanish away, the rudimental element that produced all will remain indestructible—remain to produce all these objects, and ten thousand more. So in the *moral* domain of truth, rectitude, and love. You cannot add anything to them, nor can you take anything from them—"not one jot or tittle."

II. The penalty of a great crime. "If any man shall add unto them, God shall add unto him the plagues that are written in this book," etc. What does he put upon this book? Vain and fanciful glosses; makes it speak of things trifling, or, still worse, makes it speak things untrue to fact; or yet worse still, makes it curse those whom God has not cursed, those whom prejudice and party spirit alone have wilfully and uncharitably set up as foes. Does he not add to the words of the prophecy? And what, again, does he who closes his Bible at the Epistle of St. Jude, and never studies or ponders the solemn or momentous pages which follow? Does he not practically take away from the words of the prophecy, and forget, at least, the blessing of those who keep and love it? From these, and all such errors, on the right hand and on the left, may God of his great mercy preserve us all! (Dr. Vaughan).—D. T.

Ver. 20.—*Man hailing the judgment.* "Amen. Even so, come, Lord Jesus." There are four states of mind amongst men in relation to the last day. Some are indifferent to it, as were the antediluvians in relation to the Deluge; some scornfully deny it, as did the infidels in the days of Peter; some are horror-stricken at it, as were the demoniacs in the time of Christ; and some welcome it, as John did now. Three things are implied in this last state of mind.

I. A conviction that such a day will dawn.

II. A conviction of a preparedness to enter on the trial.

III. A conviction that the results of that day will be fraught with personal good.—D. T.

Ver. 21.—*Supreme benediction.* "The grace of our Lord Jesus be with the saints.

Amen." What an inexpressible blessing is here anxiously desired for all mankind! A higher wish for the whole human race cannot be imagined.

I. The chief good. It is "grace." Maurice takes the expression to mean "gracefulness of character—gracefulness of Jesus Christ." This means, I think, something more than favour. Even the favour of God conferred on one who lacks a graceful disposition is not likely to be rightly received or appreciated. However valuable in itself, the gift bestowed, if it is not bestowed freely and unrestrained, can never be appreciated. But a graciousness of nature or character is in itself a boon. Great favours are often bestowed in an ungracious manner; therefore, if received at all, it is with reluctance and pain. The grace of a Christly character is delicately and tenderly alive to all that is beautiful in form, and tender and courteous in our intercourse with men. Indeed, all nature is graceful. How graceful are the movements of every form of life, etc.! And all art struggles to shape itself into the gracious.

II. The chief good from the Highest. From all beings that have ever entered this circle of humanity, Christ in goodness transcends them all. "He is our Lord"—our Master, "King of kings, and Lord of lords," exalted above all principalities and powers, etc. He is Jesus, "Lord Jesus," Saviour of mankind, Christ anointed of the Father, consecrated to the highest functions under God, having in all things the pre-eminence.

III. The chief good from the Highest to all. "Be with you all." Not only all the Churches in Asia Minor, but all mankind everywhere. He is good to all, and "his tender mercies are over all the works of his hand." St. Paul told the savages of Lycaonia that God was sending the rain from heaven for a fruitful season. Real gracefulness is not artificial, but *natural*. Take trees of the same order—let it be the oak, the elm, or any other. From the one the vital sap has departed and life is extinct. It is cut into artistic forms, stained with beautiful hues; to the eye it has a charm of special beauty. The other tree, of precisely the same order, grows on the same soil from which its young roots sprang up at first. It has reached maturity; the vital sap streams through all its veins, its green and leafy branches bow down in circling forms to the mother-soil. It shivers in the strong breeze, but gently moves in the zephyr. It is perpetually changing in shade, shape, and size. And then a delicious aroma pervades the whole, and scents the air with fragrance. Which of these trees, say you, is the more graceful? Not the *former*, however exquisitely artistic. From year to year it stands, bearing the same aspect. It wakens within you no fresh inspiration. But the *latter* is all gracefulness; it is graceful in all its lines, curves, and shades; graceful in all its motions, whether it bends violently to the hurricane or poses peacefully on the silent air. It is somewhat thus with men. This is the *made* gentleman, shaped according to all the niceties of conventional etiquette, like the æsthetic timber, without heart; and there is the *true* gentleman, born of all that is truly graceful in sentiment and sympathy. The snobs and flunkeys are at best but highly ornamental furniture, utterly destitute of that inner graciousness which touches all unsophisticated natures into a blessed kindredship of heart.

Conclusion. What can we desire more than this gracefulness of Christ? This gracefulness of Christly character pervades his whole history, character, life, and death. His spirit is the quintessence of the gospel.—D. T.

In conclusion, I would heartily recommend readers carefully to peruse the Bishop of Ripon's Excursus on the whole of this book as given below.

Excursus A.—*The angels of the Churches.* The most usual interpretation regards the angels of the Churches as the chief ministers or presiding elders of the congregation. This interpretation is so very widely adopted that it has been mentioned in the notes; but the reader will have perceived that it is not a view which can be considered altogether satisfactory. In the first place, whatever date we accept for the Apocalypse, it is at least strange to find the titles "elders" or "bishops," which were in common use, exchanged for the doubtful one of "angel." A common explanation is that the term is derived from the synagogue staff, where the messenger, or "angel of the synagogue," was a recognized officer; but the transference of such a title to any office in the Christian Church is at least doubtful, and as the officer so styled was only a subordinate in the synagogue, a " clerk " or " precentor " to conduct the devotions of the worshippers, it becomes very improbable that such a term or title would have been employed to describe the presiding elder of a Christian Church. Turning to the Old Testament, it is true that the word " angel " is used in a higher sense (Hag. i. 13; Mal. ii. 7), being employed to describe the messengers of God; but the usage here is different. " It is conceivable, indeed, that a bishop or chief pastor should be called an angel, or messenger of God, or of Christ, but he would hardly be styled an angel of the Church over which he presides " (Lightfoot, 'Epistle to the Philippians,' p. 197). Thus the interpretation under consideration appears scarcely satisfactory. Others have thought the word "angel" is not to be applied to the individual presiding elder, but to the whole ministry of the Church treated as one. This view, though in some senses approaching nearer to the truth, can hardly be sustained without considerable modification. Others, again, fall back upon Jewish authorities, and see in the angels the guardian angels of the Churches. " In Daniel every nation has its ruling angel; and, according to the rabbins, an angel is placed over every people." The angel, then, would be a literal real angel, who has the guardianship of the Church in question. In popular thought, then, the angel would be one of the good angelic beings whose special duty it was to bear up the Church under its trials, by such providential ministries as were needed and ordered. There are some difficulties in accepting this interpretation. In particular, the language of rebuke which is addressed directly to the angel himself— the threatening to remove his candlestick, for example—sounds meaningless. But here it is that we may inquire whether the angel of a particular community, nation, or people is to be understood always of a good and powerful being sent forth by the Almighty to love and watch over it. It is believed that this view does not satisfy the case. It is certain that Daniel represents the guardian angels of nations as opposed to each other, and not co-operating always for the same great and good end. "The prince [guardian angel] of the kingdom of Persia withstood me," is the language addressed to Daniel by him whose face was like lightning (Dan. x. 13). Such passages seem to suggest that the " angels " are the powers in the spiritual sphere corresponding to the peoples or communities in the earthly. If the Church at Ephesus has left its first love, the angel is spoken of as sharing the same fault. The influences seen on the spiritual side correspond with those at work in the actual earthly community. The angel of the Church or of the individual thus becomes their manifestation in the heavenly sphere. For all our life is thus double; our actions have an earthly meaning, and also a heavenly; what they touch of worldly interests gives them their earthly meaning, what they touch of spiritual welfare is their heavenly meaning. Like the planets, we lie half in shadow and half in light. From the earthly side the world meaning of our actions lies in the light, and their spiritual value or force is only dimly seen as it lies in at least partial shadow; but, seen from the heavenly side, the position is reversed, the worldly significance of human action is cast into comparative shade, the actual spiritual influences of them are brought into clear light, and it is the spiritual significance of our actions which reveals what we are; in this is concentrated the true force which we are exerting. Seen from the heavenly side, the angel of our life mingles in the great spiritual war, and takes its part as a combatant there; while on the earthly side we are seen carrying on our daily occupations. Measured on the earthly side, the balance is not struck; there is inconsistency in us; we are partly good and partly bad, sometimes helping, sometimes hindering the work of God on earth, as we judge; but the actual resultant of these inconsistent powers is seen in the heavenly sphere, either helping or thwarting the cause of good. Thus we are double combatants—in the world, for our livelihood, for our ease, for our advancement; in the heavenly, for good or for evil. And it is on the spiritual side that we lie open to spiritual influences; here, where our true self is seen more clearly than anywhere else, are the appeals to our better nature, as we say, most powerful; here he who holds the stars in his right hand makes his voice to be heard when he addresses, not merely the Church or the individual, but the angel of the Church; here he calls them to see that there is a war in heaven, in which all are combatants, but in which he is the Captain of our salvation. Here too, on the heavenly side, are the wounds of the spiritual and better nature more plainly seen; the offence or blow given to the little one of Christ is not noticed on the earthly side, but the inner nature is wounded, and the wound is seen in its real dimensions in the presence of

God, for the angel-nature beholds God's face. It is this thought which gives force and solemnity to our Lord's warning (Matt. xviii. 10). The angel of the Church, then, would be the spiritual personification of the Church; but it must not be concluded from this, as Lillig does, that these angels are in " the mind of the poet himself nothing more than imaginary existences," or reduce the angel "to be just the community or Church itself." It is no more the Church itself than the "star" is the same as the candlestick. "The star is the supra-sensual counterpart, the heavenly representative; the lamp, the earthly realization, the outward embodiment." The angel is the Church seen in its heavenly representative, and seen, therefore, in the light of those splendid possibilities which are hers if she holds fast by him who holds fast the seven stars. Space forbids any treatment of the wider questions on the ministry of angels, or the nature of angelic beings. That such are recognized in Scripture there can be no doubt, and nothing written above is designed to militate against such a belief; but it seems well to remember that where we are dealing with a symbolical book it is more in harmony with its character to treat symbols as symbols. The forces of nature are God's messengers, and we may regard them as truly such, and feel that the expressions, "the angel of the waters," "the angel of fire," "the angel of the abyss," and so forth, are designed to remind us that all things serve him, and are the ministers of him, to do his pleasure; we may even believe that the various forces of nature, so little really understood by us, are under the guardianship of special personal messengers of God; but there is nothing in the imagery of the book which necessarily demands such a belief. It is, moreover, surely not inappropriate in our own day to reassert with some pertinacity the lofty thoughts of ancient belief, that winds and storms, ocean and fire, do in truth belong to him round whom are the clouds and darkness, whose is the sea, and whose hands prepared the dry land.

On the literature of this subject, see Godet's 'Studies on the New Testament;' Schaff, 'History of the Apostolic Church;' Lightfoot's article on "The Christian Ministry," in the 'Epistle to the Philippians,' pp. 193—199; Hengstenberg's lengthy note on ch. i. 20; Professor Milligan's article, "The Candlestick and the Star," in the *Expositor* of September, 1878; Gebhardt, 'Der Lehrbegriff der Apokalypse,' article "Die Engel," p. 37, or p. 36 in the English translation ('The Doctrine of the Apocalypse'), published by Messrs. Clark, in the Foreign Theological Library. Also "Excursus on Angelology" in the 'Speaker's Commentary' on Daniel, p. 348; article "Angel," in Smith's 'Bible Dictionary.'

EXCURSUS B.— *The wild beast.* It is to be noticed that the interpretation of the whole Apocalypse is coloured by the interpretation given to the wild beast. The book, as we have seen (see 'Introduction'), is one of hope, but it is also one of warning; not without a struggle would the foe be driven from the earth where he had usurped power for so long. The devil is cast down; in the higher, the heavenly sphere, he is regarded as a fallen and defeated enemy; but this conflict has its counterpart on the arena of the world. The Apocalypse gives us in symbol some features of this conflict. It shows four powers of evil—the dragon, the first and second wild beasts, and Babylon the harlot. It is with the beast that we are now concerned, but one or two remarks on this family of evil will not be out of place.

I. THE FAMILY OF EVIL. 1. The four antagonists of good are *related to one another.* The resemblance between the dragon and the wild beast (comp. ch. xii. 3; xiii. 1; xvii. 3, 7, 10) is too obvious to be passed over; it seems designed to show us that the same principle and spirit of evil is at work in both. Again, the way in which the first wild beast gives place to the second wild beast, or false prophet (comp. ch. xiii. 11, 12; xvi. 13; xix. 20; xx. 10), and yet retains its ascendency (comp. ch. xiii. 14—17), makes plain the close connection between them; and lastly, the appearance of the harlot, riding on the scarlet-coloured beast (ch. xvii. 3), completes the chain of association between them. The same principles and spirit of evil make themselves manifest in different spheres. 2. The four antagonists of good are *arrayed to meet the four corresponding manifestations of good.* For every power of good we have the three Persons of the blessed Trinity—the Throned One, the Lamb, and the Holy Spirit—besides the Church, the bride, the Lamb's wife, the heavenly Jerusalem; we have on the side of evil, the dragon, the beast, the false prophet, as a sort of trinity of evil, besides the harlot

Babylon. The dragon being a kind of anti-God, the wild beast an anti-Christ, the false prophet an anti-Spirit, the Babylon an anti-Church. The minor features in the same way correspond; the true Christ died and rose again; the anti-Christ, the wild beast, was wounded unto death, but his deadly wound was healed. The crucified Christ was exalted to be Prince and Saviour, and the outpoured Spirit upon the Church glorified him by taking of the things of Christ and showing them to the disciples, and by convincing the world of sin because Christ went to the Father; the second beast, or false prophet, works wonders, causes an image of the first wild beast to be made and worshipped. The followers of the Lamb are sealed with the Holy Spirit of promise; the worshippers of the wild beast receive from the false prophet the mark of the beast (see ch. xiii. throughout). It is desirable to keep those lines of parody and correspondent antagonism in mind.

II. The wild beast, or anti-Christ. It is with the wild beast that we are concerned in this Excursus; but we cannot altogether dissociate the first beast from the second, though their work is diverse. 1. *The first wild beast is clearly to be connected with the vision of* Dan. vii. 2—7. The identification of the beast described by Daniel with four great empires is unquestionable; it is hardly our purpose to inquire whether the four empires are Babylonia, Medo-Persia, Macedonia, and Rome; or Babylonia, Media, Persia, and Greece. The former, which is the more ancient opinion, appears the more probable; but it is enough to remember that these four beasts represent four great world-powers. St. John saw rising out of the sea (comp. Dan. vii. 2) not seven diverse beasts, but one seven-headed beast. Now, it is perfectly true that to the early Christians pagan and imperial Rome was the one great world-power whose shadow darkened the earth, and that a seven-headed monster might well depict this pagan Rome, as a four-headed beast had represented to Daniel an earlier empire (Greece or Persia); and the wild beast of ch. xiii. from one aspect undoubtedly represents this great tyrant power; but it seems to the present writer that the genius of the Apocalypse is concentration —that which to earlier prophets was seen in detail is to the Christian seer grouped. Daniel saw four beasts rising one after another; St. John saw one wild beast uniting in himself all the early, present, and future manifestations of that world-empire which has ever been hostile to the spiritual kingdom. Two reasons may be noticed—one from the Book of Daniel, and the other from Revelation. This concentration of different world-powers into one representative body was not foreign to the thought of the earlier prophet. Daniel relates the vision in which the diverse monarchies of the world were represented as one huge human figure cast out of gold, silver, brass, and iron (Dan. ii. 31—49); the diverse powers were thus seen as one, and the little stone, which represented the true spiritual kingdom, in smiting upon one, caused the whole image to fall. The world-kingdoms were thus seen in prophetic vision as one great age-long world-power, which must be smitten by Christ's kingdom. The Book of Revelation also gives us a hint that the sevenfold aspect of the wild beast must not be given too limited or too local an interpretation. The wild beast, with seven heads and ten crowns, is in these features reproducing the appearance of the red dragon, who is also represented as having seven heads and ten crowns (comp. ch. xii. 3; xiii. 1). Now, the dragon is surely the type of the great arch-enemy, the devil, the anti-God; the seven heads and ten crowns denote that he is the prince of this world, who has more or less animated the successive great world-powers by hostility to righteousness; the empires of the world have been his in so far as they have been founded on force or fraud, oppression or unholiness. When, then, the seven-headed wild beast rises from the sea, must we not see in the seven heads the counterpart of those which the dragon bore? The dragon carries those seven heads, as he is the great spiritual prince of this world, the one who is practically worshipped in all mere world-made empires. The wild beast carries these seven heads because he is the great representative of all these world-powers themselves; and what may give almost certainty to this interpretation is the fact that the wild beast unites in himself the appearances of leopard, bear, and lion, which were the emblems employed by Daniel to represent earlier monarchies. Actually at the moment St. John saw the vision, the wild beast was to him Rome, because through Rome the great world-empire was then working. The seven heads might also look like types of successive emperors; but the more important, because age-long, reading of the vision sets before us the concentration in one great monstrous wild beast of all these powers

Powers which were diverse and even politically hostile were yet ethically *one* power opposed to the fundamental principles of righteousness and peace, of purity and true godliness. The first wild beast, then, becomes the symbol of confederated and age-long world-powers. 2. *The second wild beast as allied with the first.* His origin is not of God; he is of the earth. He is more peaceable in his appearance than the first beast, but his speech bewrays him; the dragon-voice is his, and he revives the worship of the first wild beast. In him, therefore, are combined the powers of the dragon and the first wild beast. Yet he yields homage to existing order; unlike the first wild beast, which rises out of our ocean of disorder and tumult, he springs out of the earth. He assumes in part, also, a Christian appearance; he is as a lamb. These features would lead us to expect a power not wholly irreligious—indeed, in some features Christian, yet practically pagan; observing order, yet arrogant; a second power resembling the first, yet possessing a more specious appearance to mankind. It is on this second wild beast that the seer bids us fasten our marked attention. It is this second wild beast who deceives by false wonders and false worship, and introduces a great and grinding tyranny. It is this second wild beast to whom is attributed the mysterious number 666. It is well now to turn back to earlier writings. In Dan. vii. we read of a "little horn," and in the description there we find much that is parallel with the description here (comp. Dan. vii. 8 with ch. xiii. 5; Dan. vii. 21 with ch. xiii. 7). This "little horn" of Daniel has been identified (comp. 'Excursus on Interpretation of 2 Thess. ii. 3—12') with the "man of sin" spoken of by St. Paul (2 Thess. ii. 3). Some think that the little horn of Dan. vii. is identical with the horn of ch. viii. Into this question we not have space to enter; it will be enough here to keep in mind that St. Paul looked for the manifestation of an antichrist, a man of sin, whose type in all likelihood he found in the little horn of Dan. vii.; and that the picture of the antichrist painted by St. Paul is that of a power not professedly irreligious, but yet claiming from mankind the homage due to God (2 Thess. ii. 4). This seems quite in harmony with the characteristics of the second wild beast, who, it is to be remembered, is described (ch. xvi. 13; xix. 20; xx. 10) as the "false prophet." We may, then, take the second wild beast as the picture of a power, cultured, quasi-religious, borrowing much from Christianity, yet built upon anti-Christian principles, and animated by an anti-Christian spirit. 3. *The identification of the wild beast, false prophet, or antichrist.* "Ye have heard that antichrist shall come" (1 John ii. 18). This is St. John's acknowledgment of the widespread belief that a great falling away shall precede the second coming of Christ. Here he is at one with St. Paul, but it is consistent with the spirit of St. John's thought that he should remind his hearers that the spirit of antichrist was abroad already, and that in a present antagonism to this spirit lay true Christian duty; accordingly he indicates in more than one place what were some features of the antichristian spirit (1 John ii. 22; iv. 1—3). It is also significant that he uses the phrase, "false prophet," reminding us of the Apocalypse, which identifies, as we have seen, the wild beast, or antichrist, with the false prophet. St. John thus appears to regard the spirits and false prophets abroad in his day as at least anticipations of the great future antichrist and false prophet. Actually there were antichrists then in the world; but the prophetic ideal of all these was as one great antichrist. In the Apocalyptic vision the scattered spirits grew into one great representative opponent—the wild beast, the false prophet. Is there, then, no personal antichrist? It has been ably argued (see 'Excursus on Prophecy of 2 Thess. ii.') that the man of sin must be an individual. There are certain expressions which seem to point to a single person, notably the remarkable use of the masculine gender when the wild beast is referred to (see ch. xiii. 5); but it seems more consonant with the symbolism of the Apocalypse to regard the wild beast as the figurative embodiment of the false, seductive, anti-Christian principle and spirit, which belongs to more ages than one, which reveals itself in diverse aspects, and yet always manifests the same hostility to the Divine Spirit. It must not, however, be supposed that this view denies a personal antichrist. On the contrary, it is perfectly in harmony with this view to note that the wild-beast spirit has often culminated in an individual; the typical forecasts of antichrist have often been individuals. Antiochus Epiphanes, Herod, Nero, might fairly be regarded as the incarnation of the ungodly spirit. Similarly, in later ages, it is not to be wondered at that holy, Christ-taught men, groaning for the sorrows of the world and the corruptions of Christianity, saw in many who occupied the papal chair the very representatives of the false prophet, the antichrist. Not more need it surprise us to find the same thought passing through men's minds when pretensions which would be ridiculous if they were not blasphemous have been advanced on behalf of the Roman pontiff, till the Church becomes a parody rather than a witness of Divine truths. It follows that the view here maintained does not exclude the possibility of a future personal antichrist, in whom the typical features shall yet find clearer and fuller manifestation than in any previous age. But though all this may be, and though godly men tell us that all these things must be, it appears to the writer infinitely more important to notice the principles which may constitute the antichrist in every age—the denial of the Father and the Son (1 John ii. 22); the denial of the Mediator and incarnate God (1 John iv. 2, 3); the arrogant claim of Divine honours, the specious resemblance to him who is the Lamb of God, the disregard of sacred ties (2 Thess. ii. 10; 1 Tim. iv. 3); the possession of wonderful power and culture (ch. xiii. 11—14). The spirit which is depicted is one which might well develop one of the elements around us. It would not be impossible to imagine the rankest materialism allying itself with a gorgeous ritual, to see the high priests of science acquiescing in the most elaborate of ecclesiasticisms, and the agnostic in creed becoming so ceremonialist in worship, till the satire should be only too sadly true, "I found plenty of worshippers, but no God." We should then have every element in human nature allowed its nutriment—for the mind, science; for the emotions, worship; for the conduct, direction. The tripartite nature of man would be thus provided for; but the unity of his manhood would be at an end, for the worship would be unintelligent, the moral tone lifeless, because deprived of the vital sense of personal responsibility, and the intellect uninspired, because godless. Such an age would be the reign of that climax of antichristian spirit which is the perfection of man's powers without God, foreshadowed by the mysterious number 666, which is seeming exaltation of all human powers, but which is, in truth, their degradation and their discord.

III. THE NUMBER OF THE BEAST. It would serve but little purpose to recapitulate the various solutions of the number of the beast. An account of them will be found in Elliott (vol. iii.). The most ancient, and perhaps most general, solution sees in the number the equivalent of Latenios. Others see in it the numerical equivalent of one of the Roman emperors. Nero, advocated by Renan; Otho, advocated by an Italian writer, who accounts for the reading "616" instead of "666" by the alteration made by the copyist to suit the name of another emperor, Caligula; Γάιος Καισάρ, 616. None of these numerical solutions appears to the writer adequate to the whole depth of the seer's meaning, though they may be included in the significance of the work.
—D. T.

HOMILETICAL INDEX

TO

THE REVELATION OF ST. JOHN THE DIVINE.

is unauthentic in many details of words and phrases, most (but not all) of which are of comparatively little importance; but the authenticity of the book, considered as a whole, is not open to doubt. No one has ever hinted that our 'Revelation of St. John the Divine' is a totally different work from the original book similarly entitled; no chapter is supposed to be a later interpolation; no copyist or redactor is accused of having, to any large or serious extent, wilfully corrupted the text by mutilating or altering it in any way whatever. All references to the book by name, and all express quotations from it, correspond with our present book so exactly as to furnish no ground for the least suspicion that a different book was at any time in circulation under the same title.

The authenticity of the statements contained in the Revelation is peculiarly difficult to establish, owing to the character of its contents. A description of visions, written by the only person who beheld them; a record of words penned by the only human being who heard them; a series of prophecies that belong, at least in part, to the future; these statements are, from their very nature, incapable of being tested and attested, confirmed and verified, supported and illustrated, in the same way as ordinary historical statements of matters of fact. But so far as the narrative can be tested, it stands the tests well. The "isle called Patmos" was suited for a place of banishment; and banishment was a practice common in those times. The epistles to the seven Churches of Asia are singularly in harmony with what is known from other sources concerning the respective communities to which they are addressed. The diction of the whole book remarkably corresponds with the period and the authorship to which it is generally ascribed.

So far, therefore, as the authenticity of the book called, 'The Revelation of St. John the Divine,' and of the statements therein contained, forms a separate subject for consideration, we hold that it is satisfactorily established.

§ 11. ANALYTICAL CONSPECTUS.

BOOK OF THE REVELATION.

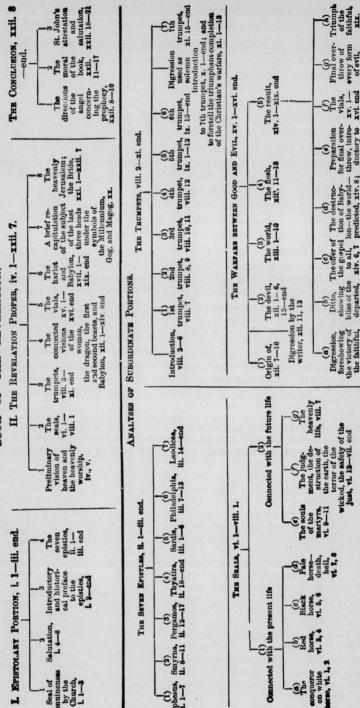

I. EPISTOLARY PORTION, i. 1—iii. end.

1. Seal of genuineness by the Church, i. 1—3.
2. Salutation, i. 4—8.
3. Introductory and historical preface to the epistles, i. 9—end.
4. The seven epistles, ii. 1—iii. end.

II. THE REVELATION PROPER, iv. 1—xxii. 7.

1. Preliminary vision of heaven and the heavenly worship, iv., v.
2. The seals, vi. 1—viii. 1
3. The trumpets, viii. 2—xi. end.
4. The connected visions of the dragon, the first and second beasts, and the woman, xii. 1—xiv. end.
5. The vials, xv. 1—xvi. end.
6. The harlot and Babylon, xvii. 1—xix. end.
7. A brief recapitulation of the subject of the last three heads under the symbols of the Millennium, Gog, and Magog, xx.
8. The heavenly Jerusalem; the Bride, xxi. 1—xxii. 7.

THE CONCLUSION, xxii. 8—end.

1. The directions of the angel concerning the prophecy, xxii. 8—10.
2. The moral of the book, xxii. 11—17.
3. St. John's attestation and salutation, xxii. 18—21.

ANALYSES OF SUBORDINATE PORTIONS.

THE SEVEN EPISTLES, ii. 1—iii. end.

(1) Ephesus, ii. 1—7.
(2) Smyrna, ii. 8—11.
(3) Pergamos, ii. 12—17.
(4) Thyatira, ii. 18—end.
(5) Sardis, iii. 1—6.
(6) Philadelphia, iii. 7—13.
(7) Laodicea, iii. 14—end.

THE SEALS, vi. 1—viii. 1.

Connected with the present life —
(a) The conqueror on white horse, vi. 1, 2.
(b) Red horse, vi. 3, 4.
(c) Black horse, vi. 5, 6.
(d) Pale horse, death, hell, vi. 7, 8.

Connected with the future life —
(e) The souls of the martyrs, vi. 9—11.
(f) The judgment, the destruction of the earth, the terror of the wicked, the safety of the just, vi. 12—vii. end.
(g) The heavenly life, viii. ?

THE TRUMPETS, viii. 2—xi. end.

Introduction, viii. 2—6.
(1) 1st trumpet, viii. 7.
(2) 2nd trumpet, viii. 8, 9.
(3) 3rd trumpet, viii. 10, 11.
(4) 4th trumpet, viii. 12.
(5) 5th trumpet, ix. 1—12.
(6) 6th trumpet, ix. 13—end.

Digression, used as solemn introduction to 7th trumpet, x. 1—end; and to foretell the triumphant completion of the Christian's warfare, xi. 1—13.

(7) 7th trumpet, xi. 15—end.

THE WARFARE BETWEEN GOOD AND EVIL, xv. 1—xvi. end.

(1) Origin of, xii. 7—10.
Digression by the writer, xii. 11, 12.
(2) The devil, xiii. 1—6, 13—end.
(3) The world, xiii. 1—10.
(4) The flesh, xiii. 11—18.
(5) The result, xiv. 1—xix. end.

(a) Digression, foreshowing the victory of the faithful, xiv. 1—5.
(b) Ditto, showing bliss of the departed, xiv. 13.
(c) The offer of the gospel to all, xiv. 6, 7.
(d) The destruction of Babylon—the world—predicted, xiv. 8; of the flesh, 9—12.
(e) Preparation for final overthrow, introductory to the vials, xiv. 14—20.
(f) The vials, xv. 1—xvi. end.
(g) Final overthrow of every form of evil, xvii., xviii.
(h) Triumph of the faithful, xix.

THE

REVELATION OF ST. JOHN THE DIVINE.

—◦◦◦—

EXPOSITION.

CHAPTER I.

THE TITLE. The simplest form of this, as of other books of the New Testament, is the oldest: 'The Revelation of John' ('Αποκά-λυψις 'Ιωάννου). Other forms worth noting are: 'The Revelation of John the Apostle and Evangelist;' 'The Revelation of the holy and most glorious Apostle and Evangelist, the virgin, the beloved, that leaned on the breast, John the Divine.' 'The divine' as a title for St. John, which is retained here in both the Authorized Version and the Revised Version, is certainly as old as Eusebius ('Præp. Evan.,' xi. 18). Recent discoveries at Ephesus have shown that "divines" (θεολόγοι) was a title of the chief priests in the temple of Artemis at Ephesus. It is possible, but hardly probable, that this suggested the title for St. John. It probably points to his witness to the Divinity of the Logos or Word. Eusebius ('Hist. Eccl.,' III. xxiv. 13) remarks that John omitted the human genealogy of the Saviour, and began with his Divinity (τῆς δὲ θεολογίας ἀπάρξασθαι).

Ver. 1—ch. iii. 22.—THE INTRODUCTION. Most writers agree that the first three chapters are introductory. They may be thus subdivided: ch. i. 1—3, *the superscription;* vers. 4—8, *the address and greeting;* vers. 9—20, *the introductory vision;* ch. ii., iii., *the epistles to the seven Churches of Asia.*

The earliest systematic commentator on the Apocalypse in the Greek Church, Andreas of Cæsarea, in Cappadocia (A.D. 450—500), divides it into twenty-four λόγοι, or

REVELATION.

narratives, to correspond with the twenty-four elders; and each of these into three κεφάλαια, or chapters, to correspond with body, soul, and spirit, making seventy-two chapters in all.

Vers. 1—3.—*The superscription.* This consists of a brief description of the contents and origin of the book, and a commendation of it to the reader and hearer.

Ver. 1.—The Revelation of Jesus Christ. This phrase occurs elsewhere in the New Testament only in 1 Pet. i. 7, 13 (comp. 1 Pet. iv. 13; 1 Cor. i. 7; 2 Thess. i. 7; Gal. i. 12). It means the revelation which Jesus Christ makes, not that which reveals him. John is the *writer.* Jesus Christ the *Author,* of the book. Revelation (ἀποκά-λυψις) is a word reserved for the gospel; no Old Testament prophecy is called a revelation (contrast 1 Sam. xx. 30). It means the *unveiling* of Divine mysteries (Eph. iii. 3), and from this it easily slips into meaning the mystery unveiled. Christ is both the Mystery and the Revealer of it. He comes to reveal himself, and in himself the Father, whose Image he is. Thus in its opening words the book takes us beyond itself. What is revealed is not secrets about the future, but a Person. And the Revealer is not man, but God; not John, but the Divine Son, commissioned by the Father. For even the unincarnate Word receives from the Father that which he reveals. Which God gave unto him. This is remarkably in harmony with the Christology of the Fourth Gospel (v. 20; vii. 16; xii. 49; xiv. 10; xvii. 7, 8: comp. Mark xiii. 32; Acts i. 7). The simple infinitive to express a purpose after "give" is common to Gospel and Apocalypse (iii. 21; vii. 2; xiii. 14; John iv. 7, 10; vi. 52). His servants All Chri-

2

tians, not exclusively seers like St. John. "*Even* the things which" (Revised Version) makes "things which" in apposition with "the Revelation," which is probably right. **Must** (δεῖ); because God has so decreed. This Divine "must" is frequent in the Gospel (iii. 14, 30; ix. 4; x. 16; xii. 34; xx. 9). Shortly. The meaning of ἐν τάχει is much disputed. But, like "firstborn" in the question about the brethren of the Lord, "shortly" ought not to be pressed in determining the scope of the Apocalypse. Calling Jesus the *firstborn* Son of Mary tells us nothing as to her having other children. Saying that the Apocalypse shows things which must *shortly* come to pass tells us nothing as to its referring to events near St. John's own day. Probably it refers to them *and* to much else in the Christian dispensation. In the language of the seer, past, present, and future are interwoven together as seen by God, and more truth is contained than the seer himself knows. "The whole book ought to be received as a single word uttered in a single moment" (Bengel) It does not follow, because St. John had events near to his own day in his mind, that his words are limited to those events for us (comp. Luke xviii. 7, 8; Matt. xxiv. 29; 2 Pet. iii. 4, 8; Hab. ii. 3; see Westcott, 'Historic Faith,' pp. 74, 75, and note on 1 John ii. 18 in the 'Cambridge Bible for Schools'). **Signified.** Jesus Christ signified, i e. made known by symbol and figure, the things which must come to pass. "Signify" (σημαίνειν) is characteristic of St. John, to whom wonders are "signs" (σημεῖα) of Divine truths. "This he said, *signifying* [by means of an allegory] by what manner of death he should die" (John xii. 33; comp. xviii. 32; xxi. 19). By his angel; literally, *by means of his angel* (διὰ τοῦ ἀγγέλου). "Angel" here probably has its common meaning of a spiritual messenger from the unseen world; but it is the fact of his being Christ's messenger, rather than his heavenly character, that is specially indicated. Whether one and the same angel is employed throughout the Revelation is not clear. He does not come into the foreground of the narrative until ch. xvii. 1, 7, 15 (comp. ch. xix. 9; xxi. 9; xxii. 1, 6, 9). The Revelation is begun (vers. 17—20) and ended (ch. xxii. 16) by Christ himself; but the main portion is conducted "by means of his angel." Thus St. Paul says of the Law that it was "administered by means of angels in the hand of a mediator," *i.e.* Moses (Gal. iii. 19). In this case the mediator is John, a "servant" specially selected for this work (Isa. xlix. 5; Amos iii. 7). Thus we have four gradations—the primary Agent, the Father; the secondary Agent, Jesus Christ; the instrument, his angel; the recipient, John.

Ver. 2.—Who bare record. "To bear witness" (μαρτυρεῖν) and "witness," or "testimony" (μαρτυρία), are characteristic of St. John's writings, and serve to connect together his Gospel, the First Epistle, and the Apocalypse. Such words should be carefully noted, and, so far as possible, uniformly translated, in order to mark their frequency in the English Version. The Authorized Version rings the changes on "bear witness," "bear record," "give record," and "testify," for μαρτυρεῖν; and on "witness," "record," and "testimony," for μαρτυρία. The Revised Version has here made great improvements. To bear witness to the truth and the Word of God was St. John's special function throughout his long life, and to this fact he calls attention in all his chief writings (see Haupt on 1 John v. 6). The testimony of Jesus Christ, like "the Revelation of Jesus Christ" (ver. 1), means that which he gave, not that which tells about him. **And of all things that he saw**; better, as in the Revised Version, *even of all things that he saw*, taking ὅσα εἶδεν in apposition with what precedes. The seer is here speaking of the visions of the Apocalypse, not of the events in Christ's life. The aorists, ἐμαρτύρησεν and εἶδεν, are rightly compared to the συνέγραψε of Thucydides (i. 1; vi. 7, 93).

Ver. 3.—He that readeth this book publicly in the church, and **they that hear** the book read, are equally blessed. There is grace promised to both minister and congregation who live up to the spirit of the Scriptures. St. John here suggests that a usage common in the Jewish Church (Luke iv. 16; Acts xv. 21; 2 Cor. iii. 15) may be adopted in the Christian Church. Probably this verse is the earliest authority for the public reading of the New Testament Scripture. It is very precarious to argue that "the Apocalypse, which points to this custom, cannot have been composed in the year 68," because this Christian custom is of later origin than 68. The official communications of apostles were sure to be read publicly in the churches (see Lightfoot on Col. iv. 16). Until the new lectionary came into use, the blessing here promised to the liturgical use of the Apocalypse was sadly neglected in the English Church. One might almost have supposed that a blessing had been pronounced on those who do *not* read and do *not* hear the prophecy. The words of this prophecy; literally, *of the prophecy*; i.e. "the prophecy of this book" (ch. xxii. 7, 18). That which is a revelation in reference to Christ is a prophecy in reference to John. "Prophecy" must not be narrowed down to the vulgar meaning of *fore*telling future events; it is the *forth*telling of the mind of God. Prophecy, in the narrow sense of prediction, cannot well be *kept*. It is God's call to